T4-ACV-707

The Abraham Lincoln Encyclopedia

The Abraham Lincoln Encyclopedia

Mark E. Neely, Jr.

McGraw-Hill Book Company
New York St. Louis San Francisco Auckland
Bogotá Hamburg Johannesburg London
Madrid Mexico Montreal New Delhi
Panama São Paulo Singapore
Sydney Tokyo Toronto

Library of Congress Cataloging in Publication Data

Neely, Mark E., date.
   The Abraham Lincoln encyclopedia.

   Includes index.
   1. Lincoln, Abraham, 1809–1865—Dictionaries,
indexes, etc. 2. United States—History—1815–
1861—Dictionaries. 3. Presidents—United States—
Biography. I. Title.
E457.N48   973.7′092′4 [B]   81-7296
                                        AACR2

*To the memory of Lottie Wright Neely (1909–1979) and
Mark Edward (Ned) Neely (1899–1980)*

Copyright © 1982 by McGraw-Hill, Inc. All rights reserved.
Printed in the United States of America. Except as permitted
under the Copyright Act of 1976, no part of this publication
may be reproduced or distributed in any form or by any means,
or stored in a data base or retrieval system, without the
prior written permission of the publisher.

1234567890 HDHD 8987654321

ISBN 0-07-046145-7

*The editors for this book were Robert A. Rosenbaum, Thomas H. Quinn, and
Tobia L. Worth, the designer was Naomi Auerbach, and the
production supervisor was Teresa F. Leaden. It was set in
Renaissance by The Kingsport Press.*
Printed and bound by Halliday Lithograph, Inc.

Preface

When I became the director of the Louis A. Warren Lincoln Library and Museum, I was pleasantly surprised by the abundant evidence of continuing curiosity about our sixteenth President. I had been told that interest in Abraham Lincoln had peaked with the centennial of the Lincoln-Douglas Debates in 1958, the sesquicentennial of his birth in 1959, and the long celebration of the Civil War centennial which followed, from 1961 through 1965. Yet I was faced with a steady stream of inquiries about Lincoln. They came to my office every day by mail and by telephone. Puzzled scholars, students, buffs, and collectors walked into my office holding questionnaires, fragments of term papers, old letters, newspaper clippings with curious allegations about Lincoln, or odd artifacts. I had a vast library at my disposal from which to respond to them, but I was less pleasantly surprised by the difficulties encountered in finding answers. In which of the six or seven thousand books and pamphlets on Lincoln was I to look? Some of the answers I simply could not find. Others I found after much searching, only to have my sense of triumph diminished by seeing the questioner's curiosity quelled by the lapse of time.

I was starving in the midst of plenty. In time, I gained some proficiency at using the vast literature. Roy P. Basler's *Collected Works of Abraham Lincoln* puts Lincoln's own writings at my fingertips. Archer H. Shaw's *The Lincoln Encyclopedia* provided important Lincoln quotations keyed to terms such as "slavery," "law," and "Republican party." Earl Schenck Miers's *Lincoln Day by Day* gave an astonishingly complete summary of Lincoln's activities for many dates in his 56 years of life. Yet Lincoln's *Collected Works* fill nine substantial volumes, and though I read them straight through twice and consulted them until the edges of the pages turned brown, his views on many subjects still elude me. *The Lincoln Encyclopedia* provided information more accessibly, but it included only a chaos of snippets quoted out of context. It used occasionally spurious quotations and presented no coherent rendering of Lincoln's changing views on slavery, race, Reconstruction, or the Whig and Republican parties. Some important subjects were missing. For example, Lincoln scholars have argued for decades about his relationship with the Radical Republicans, but there is no entry for that subject in Shaw's

Preface

book. *Lincoln Day by Day* offered a tantalizing three-volume menu of the daily meetings, travels, and events in Lincoln's life, but no taste of Lincoln's views of the events or the personalities of the men and women with whom he dealt. Most important of all, given the many controversial aspects of Lincoln's life, no single book briefed me on the "state of the art" on these questions.

Experience proved to be the best aid: only by reading as many of the books as possible could I learn the answers. Even familiarity with the literature failed in the case of questions such as these: Are there any living direct descendants of Lincoln? What happened to the "Big Five" Lincoln collections? How do I write the Abraham Lincoln Association? What happened to the letter Lincoln wrote Grace Bedell, the 11-year-old girl who suggested that he grow a beard? Is there anything to see at the site of Lincoln's boyhood home in Indiana? Here only newspaper-clipping files and discussions with other Lincoln curators, collectors, dealers, and scholars proved fruitful.

I have attempted to write the book I needed when I began to answer the public's questions about Lincoln 9 years ago. The titles of the articles were suggested by examination of the indexes to important Lincoln books and—I think this may be important—by experience. Tradition played as large a role as "science" in determining the entries. Benjamin F. Wade, for example, appeared in the index of almost every biography I consulted, yet many other senators did not. I respected this tradition on the grounds that this was surely a sign of his importance. In other cases, where I was less certain of the importance thereby connoted, I usually accepted it on the grounds that discussion of the subject by so many of the Lincoln scholars of the past was itself worthy of consideration and comment. I kept in mind the questions I had heard over the years, and they dictated other main headings. Granted that the headings chosen are infinitely arguable, I still have confidence that the index will remedy most of the problems of inclusion and exclusion.

In writing the biographical sketches of Lincoln's contemporaries and associates, I attempted at first to base the portraits on biographies (where they existed). This soon proved unsatisfactory. The resulting articles rarely conveyed any personal flavor of the subject. Therefore, I sought wherever possible to read some of the letters or speeches of these figures, to flesh out what otherwise appeared to be anemic, even skeletal portraits. It was impossible to go to the far-flung manuscript sources for the people who appear as primary entries, but the Abraham Lincoln Papers in the Library of Congress, readily available on 97 reels of microfilm, provided a happy solution. This collection contains the bulk of President Lincoln's incoming mail. Naturally, those figures closest to him were well represented in the collection, and their letters were wonderfully revealing of their relationships to Lincoln. The candor of nineteenth-century political letters, which readily discussed those sensitive matters which twentieth-century politicians deal with on the telephone, was a major asset. Moreover, the collection, because it is immense in size and has been available to scholars for only 34 years, has not been mined as Lincoln's own letters and the more famous diaries of the period

Preface

have been. This added an element of originality to many of the sketches. Letters from that collection and from other manuscript collections, including the newly acquired letterbooks of Robert Todd Lincoln at the Illinois State Historical Library, are cited by date and correspondents in the sources section following each entry. Other quotations in the entries, not so noted, come from *The Collected Works of Abraham Lincoln*, edited by Roy P. Basler et al. (New Brunswick: Rutgers University Press, 1953–1955), the *Supplement, 1832–1865*, edited by Basler (Westport, Conn.: Greenwood Press, 1974), or from the books and articles cited in the sources for the particular article. This section is intended for those readers who wish to pursue the subject further. The citations to printed sources constitute a bibliography of the most up-to-date and important sources for the subjects.

Of course, there are entries for persons other than Lincoln's contemporaries: biographers, collectors, and even some famous latter-day Lincoln-haters are included, but only dead ones. I have not sought, for obvious reasons, to appraise living Lincolnians.

Though hundreds of other people appear in this encyclopedia, it remains essentially a Lincoln book. In dealing with other figures, the focus is primarily on their relationship with Lincoln. In the cases of figures like George Washington, Thomas Jefferson, and Henry Clay, the entries discuss only Lincoln's views of these great men; their own lives receive no direct attention. Other contemporaries of Lincoln who were famous in their own right demanded biographical sketches that focused on their relationship to Lincoln with little attention to the other aspects of their careers. In the case of Charles Francis Adams, for example, the great work of his life, handling diplomatic relations with England during the Civil War, was important, but it was a matter mostly between Secretary of State William H. Seward and Adams; it receives only brief coverage. At the opposite end of the spectrum are those figures briefly glimpsed in history only because of their relationship with Lincoln—those who plotted with John Wilkes Booth to assassinate him, for example. It seemed more important, though it was also much more difficult, to describe their otherwise unknown careers in general.

This is not a Civil War encyclopedia. No battle earned a primary entry because Lincoln was not a field commander, and only those field commanders with whom Lincoln had extensive contact—usually as much political as military in nature—are included (e.g., McClellan, Grant, Banks, and Frémont). Of course, Lincoln's conduct as commander in chief is assessed at length in an article under that title.

New questions and new themes emerged as I did the research for this book. Letters in the Abraham Lincoln Papers frequently caused me to change my mind about various figures' relationships with Lincoln. Moreover, in writing biographies from the presidential period, I attempted to inject an element of system, to give a sense of unity to a multitude of portraits based on the works of many biographers, by seeking always to answer certain questions. I sought each subject's views on secession, General Frémont's proclamation to free the slaves of Missouri rebels, Lincoln's own Emancipation Proclamation, the black race, the extent of disloyalty in the North and South, and the means of dealing with those two problems by curtailing Northern civil liberties during the war and by reconstructing the South after the war. This was not possible in every case, but I saw enough variety in the views to learn that simple formulas placing figures in the Radical or conservative wings of the Republican party were inadequate to explain behavior throughout the war years, not to mention the prewar period of political conflict between the sections. I did not force these figures into traditional molds. I became increasingly convinced, for example, that a politician's view of the extent of disloyalty to the Union in the South was an excellent indicator of his view of Reconstruction. In other words, I came to see Reconstruction, a question on all thoughtful politicians' minds from 1861 on, more as a problem of loyalty than of vindictiveness toward traitors or of humanitarian concern for the Negroes or of racial hatred of them. It is perilous to relate views held early in the war with those held at its end, as the sketch of Orville Hickman Browning shows, but views of secession and of Reconstruction were often related. If one thought of secession as a coup by a small Southern elite, one often saw Reconstruction as a simple problem of getting the great, essentially loyal Southern majority into control of their government. If one saw secession as a genuine mass movement, Reconstruction would necessarily require more time and more political control of the South by the only large group of indigenous loyalists, the Negroes, and by Northern politicians and soldiers. True, people's estimates of the extent of Southern rebelliousness changed over time, but Reconstruction policies often changed with them. Abraham Lincoln's own views are a good case in point, as the article "Reconstruction" shows.

The picture of Lincoln that emerges from an encyclopedia is necessarily fragmented but not necessarily self-contradictory or conventional. I was surprised to find that the discipline and focus imposed by writing encyclopedia articles on special topics gave me better answers to some of the perennial questions about Lincoln than I had ever come up with by attempting to look at the whole of his political life and thought. This was true of even the largest questions. The central question for the history of Lincoln's administration was well posed in 1948 by British historian K. C. Wheare (objectivity and perception in the observations of British historians on America are traditions that extend back to Lincoln biographer Lord Charnwood). Wheare claimed that Lincoln "was prepared to go much farther to prevent the breakup of the Union than ever he proposed to go to prevent the extension of slavery." Rephrased as a question, the problem becomes: was Lincoln more a nationalist than a humanitarian? An answer emerged from a number of different articles in this book.

In examining the sources for the article "Constitution," I found that the generally apologetic tone of most writers on Lincoln's rather rough handling of the Constitution during the Civil War was somewhat off the mark. True, the President was apologetic for curtailing civil liberties, but, in what his private secretaries regarded as one of his most effective state papers, he speculated that he might well be criticized by posterity for not making enough arbitrary arrests instead of too many. He proved wrong about the direction historical writing would take after his death, but the statement is significant. Lincoln as President moved rapidly away from the Constitution worship of his early forties, when he clung to the document as the only bulwark against what he saw as President Polk's tyrannical war-mongering. In suspending the privilege of the writ of habeas corpus and abandoning his old constitutional conservatism, Lincoln acted to save the Union. But he moved almost as rapidly and radically away from his old constitutional ideas to free more than 3 million human beings from bondage. After Frémont's proclamation in 1861, Lincoln rather hotly told Orville Hickman Browning that no general or President could determine the laws of property for all time without entering the realm of despotism; perhaps Congress might legislate on such a point, but he and his generals could do nothing. In less than a year, Lincoln was ready to do what Frémont had done, only for all slaves in most of the country, and he was firmly convinced that Congress could not touch slave property constitutionally, a conviction he carried to his grave. Lincoln, who did not experience an amendment to the Constitution in his lifetime and who had warned against so meddling with the document in his forties, made endorsement of the Thirteenth Amendment abolishing slavery in the United States a criterion of Republicanism in 1864.

The gloomy summer of 1864 provided another test of Lincoln's humanitarian conviction. Convinced in August that he would lose the autumn election, Lincoln wrote a proposal for peace with reunion as the only condition to be met by the South; he did not mention his customary insistence on its recognition of emancipation. True, he never finished the letter, but in this desperate moment he seemed to reach for what was most important to him—the Union—and to let the slaves fend for themselves. When I studied his famous "Blind Memorandum" of August 23, 1864, however, I discovered a different meaning. That document, usually cited as proof only of Lincoln's feeling that he would lose in 1864, also shows clearly what he thought he would lose—the Union itself. He was as convinced as any Republican that the Democrats would write a platform that would threaten to surrender the Union. He thought the Union itself was lost unless it could be saved before a Democrat assumed the Presidency in March 1865. Therefore, he had no reason to think he could demand the freedom of the slaves as a condition for peace. The slaves could be freed only in this Union, as the secessionists had known only too well. Humanitarianism was impossible without national reunification.

Confirmation of this interpretation came from an unexpected direction. As I read Frederick Douglass's only letter to Lincoln in the Abraham Lincoln Papers, by way of preparing my sketch of Douglass, I learned that Lincoln had proposed to him—significantly, in August 1864—a plan to spread word of the Emancipation Proclamation to Negroes in the Confederacy so that as many as possible could make their way to freedom before the Democrats assumed the Presidency. Clearly, the Union was sacred for Lincoln—after 1861 if not before—*because* it embodied for him the greatest humanitarian experiment in freedom in the world.

Events soon obscured this wonderfully revelatory moment for Lincoln.

Preface

General Sherman's victory at Atlanta in September assured Lincoln's reelection. The desperate Douglass scheme was no longer necessary, and it was dropped and forgotten. After his November victory at the polls the President bolstered Union sentiment by saying that no politician had dared run against the Union itself—proof, Lincoln argued, of the people's deepest desire for military victory. This statement ignored his own feeling two months earlier that the Democratic party threatened to give up the Union and caused us to lose the import of the Blind Memorandum.

Focus on particular aspects of Lincoln's life repeatedly led to new views. Throughout the modern literature on Lincoln there has been much emphasis on his growth in the Presidency, by which is meant primarily that he changed his views on race in a more humanitarian direction. I found evidence of "growth"—I greatly prefer the less loaded word "change"—in many other areas of Lincoln's life. Immediately upon attempting to write on Lincoln and the Constitution or some similar subject, one realizes that Lincoln's views were different at different times, and one is driven immediately to a chronological approach to the subject—always the best approach for a historian. Lincoln often did not have *a* view of something; he had different views of it at different times.

For example, from the earliest years of this century, if not before, Lincoln's abilities as a politician—indeed, his total absorption in politics—have been accepted as a given. He seems always to have been political. Albert J. Beveridge, writing in the 1920s, saw Lincoln's early career as too political by far, and Beveridge was a politician himself. James G. Randall, the greatest of modern Lincoln biographers, even came to think of Lincoln's growth in the Presidency as his becoming much less the narrow partisan he had been in his youth. I was astonished to find change in this area, as I prepared "Patronage," and change in quite the opposite direction from what Randall had prepared me to expect. In his early Whig years, Lincoln had taken to heart enough of that party's revulsion at the disciplined political methods of the Democrats to state—even while he recommended names for government appointments—that he was opposed to removing men from office simply because they were of the other party. President Zachary Taylor's failure to give Lincoln the appointment he wanted for himself—a cataclysmic event in Lincoln's political life which also led him to doubt the Whig belief in the virtues of weak Presidents—caused Lincoln to see the importance of the spoils system to party health. By the time he was President himself, Lincoln boasted that his administration had given to its party friends in almost as many offices as any in American history.

In most respects, of course, I did not change my view of Lincoln, but in many cases I became more convinced that what I had learned heretofore was correct. I have always been convinced of the importance of Lincoln's Whiggery. I first became aware of this when I studied his opposition to the Mexican War, which all Whigs hated. I concluded in 1978 that this was above all else an aspect of his thoroughgoing Whiggery. In writing this encyclopedia, I discovered—by using Illinois poll books as an infallible guide to partisanship (they show precisely, by name, how each person voted in

Illinois before 1848)—that Lincoln's earliest environment was more Whiggish than anyone has heretofore suspected. His father, Thomas, was a staunch Whig; his cousin Dennis Hanks even ran for a minor office as a Whig. The intensity of Lincoln's attachment to the Whig party lay in forces stronger than the charisma of Henry Clay or the abstract programmatic virtues of Clay's platform of economic development, which predicted America's commercial future while Democrats reveled in its agrarian past. Research for the articles "Economics," "Whig Party," and "Indiana" revealed that Lincoln's earliest political platform—with its Whiggish emphasis on government-sponsored transportation improvements and education—was not so much a convenient package borrowed from Henry Clay as a deeply longed-for solution to the problems of Lincoln's own wretched agrarian past: too much wilderness and too little education. Whiggery offered the program that would have righted the wrongs of Lincoln's economically blighted youth, lived in isolation without economic opportunity in hardscrabble Indiana. Lincoln's love of the Whig party was bound up with the deepest springs of his personality.

In every article I attempted to render the information according to the state of the art today. The articles and their sources, then, are intended at the least to give the reader the most up-to-date scholarship on the subjects. I have also attempted on occasion to offer information that is available nowhere else in the Lincoln literature. I chose the illustrations with two objects in mind. The portraits, I think, help us to remember and distinguish the many characters in the Lincoln story. The cartoons, prints, and photographs help illustrate points made in the relevant articles. They were chosen not only for appropriateness but also for originality, and several are published here for the first time. Unless otherwise noted, all art is from the collection of the Louis A. Warren Lincoln Library and Museum.

Writing this encyclopedia renewed my enthusiasm for the cooperative spirit within the Lincoln fraternity. I am grateful to Professor Richard N. Current for suggesting my name as a possible author of the book. R. Gerald McMurtry, director emeritus of the Louis A. Warren Lincoln Library and Museum, read every article in draft and made numerous suggestions for improvement, catching, I'll admit, many outright errors. Frank J. Williams, president of the Lincoln Group of Boston, also read and criticized most of the articles and made many particularly helpful suggestions in regard to subjects to be covered or ignored. Professor William Hanchett, of San Diego State University, whose forthcoming book on the Lincoln assassination promises to fill a big gap in the literature, read all the assassination-related articles and made many improvements and corrections. Winfred Harbison, the distinguished historian of the American Constitution, read the articles that deal with constitutional questions and steered me clear of many technical hazards. Professor G. S. Boritt, of Memphis State University, read the articles on economic subjects and on biographers. His suggestions were always helpful, as were those of Professor John David Smith, of Southeast Missouri State University, who also read the articles on biographers. Harold Holzer, of New York City, an expert on Lincoln iconography, read the articles on art with a keen, critical eye. Professor Robert Sutton, of the University of Illinois, read some of the articles on Illinois figures, and the late Holman Hamilton read the article on Zachary Taylor. James T. Hickey, the helpful Lincoln curator at the Illinois State Historical Library, introduced me to the wonders of the letterbooks of Robert Todd Lincoln, which he procured for that society in the most important single Lincoln acquisition in the last 50 years. The errors that remain after the labors of these good and generous men are entirely attributable to my incorrigible self.

I owe a special debt to the editors at McGraw-Hill. Robert A. Rosenbaum, then the editor of General Reference Books, suggested the book to me in 1977. His original conception of the nature of the encyclopedia was very near the end result. Tobia L. Worth, senior editing supervisor, was immensely helpful in matters of style and consistency. Thomas H. Quinn, editor in chief, Social Sciences, patiently saw the book through production and answered every question clearly and accurately.

Vera Goebel typed the manuscript and bolstered my will at the same time. Sylvia Neely welcomed the characters that I brought home at night, on weekends, and for all holidays as though Lincoln and his associates were her old friends too.

Mark E. Neely, Jr.

A

Abe Lincoln in Illinois A popular play by Robert Emmet Sherwood that opened on Broadway on October 15, 1938. The play ran for 472 performances and won a Pulitzer Prize (1939). Its success made Sherwood, actor Raymond Massey (who played Lincoln), and a number of questionable Lincoln anecdotes famous and led to an RKO film, *Abe Lincoln in Illinois*, in 1940. Influenced by Carl Sandburg's *Abraham Lincoln: The Prairie Years*, Sherwood dealt with Lincoln only up to the time of Lincoln's departure from Springfield for Washington in 1861.

The play pictures a self-doubting hero. In the first act, Lincoln's character is forged by the tragic death of Ann Rutledge. In the second, Lincoln somewhat unwillingly accepts his destiny, personified in the difficult and ambitious character of Mary Todd. In the third and most popular act, he emerges as a character of destiny embracing difficult tasks with compassion and stern political independence. This last act used Lincoln's own words to a much greater extent than the first two acts.

Part of the play's appeal was its timely quality: Sherwood's Lincoln was a Lincoln in the image of a New Deal liberal. In a 10-minute speech to the audience in Act III, Lincoln says, "As an American, I can say—thank God we live under a system by which men have the *right* to strike!" He attacks the Supreme Court as an institution "composed of mortal men, most of whom . . . come from the privileged class in the South." Raymond Massey, in a *New York Times* interview, said that "The Civil War President . . . was definitely a New Dealer, broadly speaking."

Despite a lengthy appendix on historical sources, the book version of *Abe Lincoln in Illinois* perpetuated many myths about Lincoln, some of which had been discredited by scholars for a decade. It suggested that Lincoln's father was a shiftless ne'er-do-well, that Ann Rutledge's death was a major turning point in Lincoln's life, that Lincoln broke his engagement to Mary Todd the day the wedding was to be held, and that his wife's ambition and superficial concern for appearances were a trial for him.

SOURCES: For the contemporary political context of *Abe Lincoln in Illinois* see Alfred Haworth Jones, *Roosevelt's Image Brokers: Poets, Playwrights, and the Use of the Lincoln Symbol* (Port Washington, N.Y.: Kennikat Press, 1974).

Abolitionism Although Lincoln "always hated slavery, . . . as much as any Abolitionist," he was always critical of abolitionists in his prepresidential career. His earliest pronouncement against slavery (in the Illinois House of Representatives on March 3, 1837) also denounced "the promulgation of abolition doctrines" for tending "rather to increase than to abate its evils." He developed his first appreciation of the political power of abolitionism in the 1840s. He blamed the Whig loss in the national election of 1844 on the abolitionist Whigs of New York who, by refusing to vote for Henry Clay, guaranteed Democrat James K. Polk's victory. He claimed that "it was extremely probable, beforehand, that such would be the result." In 1848 he admitted that the Whigs had gained their only national victory,

William Henry Harrison's election in 1840, by "falling in company with" abolitionists. "Not that we fell into abolition doctrines," Lincoln hastened to add, "but that we took up a man whose position induced them to join us in his election." That his own opposition to the Mexican War and support of the Wilmot Proviso put him in agreement with abolitionist views never bothered Lincoln.

Lincoln carried his attitude into the Republican party. In 1854, when he was still a Whig but vehemently opposed to the Kansas-Nebraska Act on antislavery grounds, he advised other Whigs to "Stand with anybody that stands RIGHT. . . . Stand WITH the abolitionist in restoring the Missouri Compromise; and stand AGAINST him when he attempts to repeal the fugitive slave law." He regarded early Illinois converts to Republicanism as extremists and did not attend a Republican State Central Committee meeting in November 1854, though Illinois abolitionists like Ichabod Codding had put his name on the list of Committee members. Even when Lincoln became a Republican and embraced a platform not simply for restoring the Missouri Compromise line but also for preventing any expansion of slave territory, his disinclination to criticize the Fugitive Slave Law still distinguished him from abolitionists and from the more radical members of the Republican party.

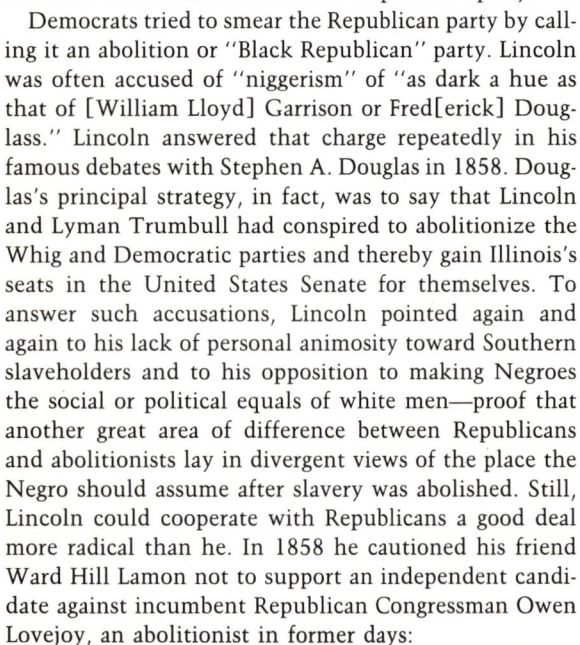

Democrats tried to smear the Republican party by calling it an abolition or "Black Republican" party. Lincoln was often accused of "niggerism" of "as dark a hue as that of [William Lloyd] Garrison or Fred[erick] Douglass." Lincoln answered that charge repeatedly in his famous debates with Stephen A. Douglas in 1858. Douglas's principal strategy, in fact, was to say that Lincoln and Lyman Trumbull had conspired to abolitionize the Whig and Democratic parties and thereby gain Illinois's seats in the United States Senate for themselves. To answer such accusations, Lincoln pointed again and again to his lack of personal animosity toward Southern slaveholders and to his opposition to making Negroes the social or political equals of white men—proof that another great area of difference between Republicans and abolitionists lay in divergent views of the place the Negro should assume after slavery was abolished. Still, Lincoln could cooperate with Republicans a good deal more radical than he. In 1858 he cautioned his friend Ward Hill Lamon not to support an independent candidate against incumbent Republican Congressman Owen Lovejoy, an abolitionist in former days:

> There is no safe way but a convention; and if, in that convention upon a common platform, . . . one who has been known as an abolitionist, but who is now occupying none but common ground, can get the majority of votes to which *all* look for an election, there is no safe way but to submit.

For their part, abolitionists knew a nonabolitionist when they saw one. Eastern abolitionists, like most others from their region, knew nothing about Lincoln when he gained the Republican presidential nomination in 1860. "Who is this huckster in politics?" Wendell Phillips asked. "The Republican party means to do nothing . . . for the abolition of slavery in the slave states," Garrison declared. "The Republican party stands on a level with the Fugitive Slave Law." Indeed, as Lincoln had explained 5 years before, he (and the Republicans in 1860) "do no more than oppose the *extension* of slavery." Many abolitionists considered both parties too conservative and refused to vote. Those who did vote, however, voted for Lincoln. And a few abolitionists campaigned actively for Lincoln, among them Theodore Tilton of New York and Moncure D. Conway, a Virginia-born abolitionist residing in Cincinnati. Garrison softened before the election and gave the Republican party his "sympathies and best wishes."

When war broke out, Garrison and Phillips led other abolitionists in support of the war effort, the latter renouncing his own former willingness to see the Union dissolved. The honeymoon between the administration and the abolitionists ended in September 1861, when Lincoln revoked General John C. Frémont's emancipation proclamation for Missouri out of fear that it would drive Kentucky out of the Union. Conway said in disgust, "there is no President of the United States—only a President of Kentucky." The steps that Lincoln took toward emancipation in 1862 generally made the abolitionists hopeful. When Lincoln announced his March plan for federal compensation to states with plans for gradual abolition, Phillips said: "If the President has not entered Canaan, he has turned his face Zionward." But Phillips lost patience by August and gave a scorchingly critical speech calling Lincoln "a first-rate *second-rate* man."

At the same time, other abolitionists took hope from Lincoln's reply to Horace Greeley's "Prayer of Twenty Millions." Though in it Lincoln said he would save the Union, if he could, by freeing no slaves, he also said that he would save it, if he had to, by freeing the slaves. For some this was a sign that, having tried the first policy, presently he would try the second. The preliminary Emancipation Proclamation delighted the abolitionists; only a few dwelled on the reservations in the document exempting Federal-occupied areas from its effect. They took heart, too, from promises in Lincoln's letter to James C. Conkling of August 26, 1863, and his Proclamation of Amnesty and Reconstruction of December 8, 1863, that he would not renege on the Proclamation. They cheered his acceptance of Negro soldiers in the Union army.

Abolitionists disagreed with Lincoln's Reconstruction policies, particularly as those policies developed in Louisiana in the winter of 1863–1864. They objected to Lincoln's failure to promise the Negro more than apprenticeship status after freedom. The approaching presidential election brought about a great split among the abolitionists. Phillips aided the movement to nominate a more radical candidate and the movement to replace Lincoln as the candidate once he was nominated. On the other hand, Garrison was impressed with Lincoln's capacity for growth and supported his renomination. Phillips allied himself closely with Frémont's "Radical Democratic" candidacy; Garrison, symbolically, attended the Baltimore convention which renominated Lincoln. Garrison visited Lincoln in June—the abolitionist's first time in the National Capital—and Lincoln thanked him for his support and told him that the plank for an antislavery amendment was in the Republican platform at the President's request. Numerous abolitionists campaigned for his reelection.

When Lincoln acknowledged by letter a painting Garrison had sent him, the Boston abolitionist in turn thanked the President for "putting me in possession of what I shall value very highly—namely, your autograph." Garrison delivered a eulogy of Lincoln in ceremonies for the Union League of Rhode Island in June.

SOURCES: James M. McPherson traces the abolitionists' views of President Lincoln in his fine book, *The Struggle for Equality: Abolitionists and the Negro in the Civil War and Reconstruction* (Princeton, N.J.: Princeton University Press, 1964). Garrison's letter to Lincoln (February 13, 1865) is in the Abraham Lincoln Papers, Library of Congress.

See also FUGITIVE SLAVE LAW; LOVEJOY, OWEN; RADICAL REPUBLICANS; REPUBLICAN PARTY.

Abraham Lincoln Association A private organization widely credited with bringing high standards of professional scholarship to the study of Lincoln's life. The organization originated as the Lincoln Centennial Association in 1908 to prepare for the celebration of the hundredth anniversary of Lincoln's birth. Its purpose was at first strictly celebratory: organizing annual banquets at which (among others) William Jennings Bryan, William Howard Taft, Booker T. Washington, and Henry Cabot Lodge spoke.

In 1924 Yale graduate and Springfield lawyer Logan Hay (the grandson of Stephen T. Logan, the cousin of John Hay, and the son of Milton Hay, who had studied law in Lincoln's office) became the Association's president and began to alter its purpose in the direction of collecting documents and sponsoring serious historical research. He wanted the Association "to contribute something solid and lasting to the understanding and appreciation of Lincoln's life." In the same year the first volume of the *Lincoln Centennial Association Papers* appeared. A year later the Association sought a secretary "trained in the special requirements of research work," and it chose Paul M. Angle. He initiated a *Bulletin*, began research on a history of Lincoln's Springfield, and started work on a compilation of a day-by-day record of Lincoln's life. Several secretaries and decades later, the compilation became an essential reference work: *Lincoln Day by Day: A Chronology, 1809–1865.*

The appearance of Wilma Frances Minor's forged Lincoln–Ann Rutledge love letters in the *Atlantic Monthly* of December 1928 made Angle and the Lincoln Centennial Association famous. Angle immediately denounced the letters, his only problem in credibility being the misleading name of the organization he represented. The organization recognized the problem, and in 1929 it chose the name The Abraham Lincoln Association. *The Abraham Lincoln Association Papers* continued publication through 1939. In 1940 the Association began publication of the *Abraham Lincoln Quarterly*, which was issued through 1952.

Logan Hay was unable to see even the initiation of a project he wanted the Association to undertake: the editing and publication of a definitive edition of Lincoln's works. The Great Depression not only ended any hope of it but also sent Angle, who feared the fledgling organization would never make it through the economic crisis, to the Illinois State Historical Library in 1932. Benjamin P. Thomas was his able successor. After writing *Lincoln's New Salem* (1934) and continuing work on the day-by-day project, Thomas left in 1936. Harry E. Pratt succeeded him and wrote the definitive *Personal Finances of Abraham Lincoln* (1943). William E. Baringer followed Pratt.

Roy P. Basler, the Association secretary from 1947 to 1952, edited *The Collected Works of Abraham Lincoln*, the organization's greatest contribution to Lincoln scholarship. In publishing *The Collected Works*, however, the Association exhausted its resources, and it dissolved in 1952. It was later revived to raise money for restoration of the Old State Capitol in Springfield. Clyde C. Walton was the first secretary of the revived Association; he was followed by William K. Alderfer. (The secretary was now also the Illinois State Historian, head of the Illinois State Historical Library.) In 1974 the Association established an annual Lincoln Symposium to be held in Springfield on Lincoln's birthday. In 1979 it began to publish the *Papers of the Abraham Lincoln Association.*

Memberships, which bring a subscription to the *Papers* and other benefits, are available from the Secretary, Abraham Lincoln Association, Old State Capitol, Springfield, IL 62706.

SOURCES: See Mark E. Neely, Jr., "The Abraham Lincoln Association," *Lincoln Lore*, Number 1697 (July 1979), pp. 1–3; Paul M. Angle, *On a Variety of Subjects* (Chicago: Chicago Historical Society and The Caxton Club, 1974); and Don E. Fehrenbacher, *The Minor Affair: An Adventure in Forgery and Detection* (Fort Wayne, Ind.: Louis A. Warren Lincoln Library and Museum, 1979).

See also ANGLE, PAUL MCCLELLAND; RUTLEDGE, ANN.

Abraham Lincoln Quarterly See ABRAHAM LINCOLN ASSOCIATION.

Adams, Charles Francis (1807–1886) Minister to England during the Lincoln administration. Charles Francis Adams was the son of President John Quincy Adams and grandson of President John Adams. A Massachusetts Republican member of Congress in 1860, he hoped for William H. Seward's nomination for the Presidency and was "much cast down" by Lincoln's nomination. Some Republicans suggested Adams as a Cabinet appointee, especially those who did not want to see Seward in the Cabinet, but Lincoln decided to nominate Seward for Secretary of State and to give New England's spot in the Cabinet to Gideon Weller of Connecticut. The President's first choice for the London mission was William

Charles Francis Adams

L. Dayton of New Jersey, but Secretary of State Seward insisted on Adams, stressing the importance of New England to the Republicans. "New Jersey," he said pointedly, "gives us little, and that grudgingly."

Adams met Lincoln only twice, but the second meeting left him with a low opinion of the President. On March 28, 1861, as Adams remembered it, the Secretary of State took him to Lincoln's office to introduce him to the President. When Adams graciously thanked Lincoln for the appointment, Lincoln brushed it off by saying that he should thank Seward, for he was Seward's man and not Lincoln's. Without any comment on the mission to England, Lincoln then turned to Seward to inform him that the appointment for the Chicago post office had been settled!

Adams was forever mortified by the equation of his distinguished foreign mission with the lowly patronage plum in Chicago, but there was more to the meeting than the Adams family's accounts of it admitted. Seward's call on Lincoln was unannounced. Moreover, before they visited the President, Seward had told Adams that he would be stuck with Charles L. Wilson as Secretary of Legation. Wilson was Seward's man too, but Seward had wanted him to be the appointee for the Chicago post office. Because Lincoln owed a debt to John Locke Scripps of Chicago, he gave Scripps the post office and mollified Seward by sending Wilson to London. When Adams and the Secretary of State entered Lincoln's office, Isaac N. Arnold, the Representative of the Chicago district in the House, was already in the office. In truth, the Chicago post office was the only subject that Arnold, Adams, Seward, and Lincoln had in common.

Adams's mission in London was successful, but he had very little contact with American politics for the period of the war. He corresponded principally with the Secretary of State. Adams softened as best he could Seward's immoderate dispatch of May 21, 1861, when he read it to Lord John Russell. He advised apologizing to England for the *Trent* affair and was much relieved when Seward did apologize. He handled the prevention of the purchase of the Laird rams for Confederate sea raiders with skill and daring by assuring Russell that the departure of these ships from port would mean war.

In 1873 Adams delivered a memorial address on Seward before the New York state legislature. In it he characterized Lincoln as "a person selected [to run for the Presidency] partly on account of the absence of positive qualities, so far as was known to the public, and absolutely without the advantage of any experience in national affairs." Lincoln considered only "geographical relations and party services" in choosing his Cabinet. Seward was Lincoln's superior "in native intellectual power, in the extent of acquirement, in breadth of philosophical experience, and in the force of moral discipline." Yet the Secretary of State nobly sacrificed his hopes for the Presidency to serve the nation for another who would "reap the honors due chiefly to his labors." This view of Lincoln as a figurehead President provoked Gideon Welles to write three long articles, published as a book in 1874. The book, entitled *Lincoln and Seward*, constituted one of the earliest informed works to present the case for Lincoln's greatness as the true guiding spirit in the Civil War government.

In 1880 Adams wrote O. H. Oldroyd, a Lincoln collector, that his initial meeting with the President had made him "a very lukewarm admirer of his," though he "became . . . one of the most appreciative of his high qualities." In his address on Seward, he had listed these as purity, bravery, honesty, and faithfulness to his arduous task.

SOURCES: Martin Duberman's *Charles Francis Adams, 1807–1886* (Cambridge: Houghton, Mifflin, 1961) is a solid biography, but it repeats Adams's view of the meeting in Lincoln's office. Mark E. Neely, Jr.'s "Abraham Lincoln and the Adams Family Myth," *Lincoln Lore*, Number 1667 (January 1977) questions the anecdote. *A Cycle of Adams Letters, 1861–1865*, 2 vols., ed. by Worthington C. Ford (Boston: Houghton, Mifflin, 1920) shows how isolated Adams was from American politics by his residence in England. Seward's letter to Lincoln about Adams's appointment (March 11, 1861) is in the Abraham Lincoln Papers, Library of Congress. Adams's letter to Oldroyd (August 10, 1880) was listed in the *Americana Mail Auction* catalog of July 18, 1979.

See also HAMLIN, HANNIBAL; *TRENT* AFFAIR.

Agriculture   *See* ECONOMICS.

Alcohol   *See* TEMPERANCE.

"Almanac Trial"   *See* ARMSTRONG, WILLIAM ("DUFF").

Alton, Illinois   Site of the seventh and last Lincoln-Douglas Debate, October 15, 1858. Located 25 miles north of St. Louis, in Madison County, Alton was not firmly in either political camp.

The day of the debate was cloudy, but numerous visitors paid a $1 round-trip fare to come from St. Louis by steamboat. The Chicago and Alton Railroad brought people at half fare from as far away as Springfield. Still, only 5000 people, one of the smaller crowds for the debates, stood at the public square in the afternoon to hear Lincoln and Douglas.

Douglas, now hoarse from the many speeches in the long campaign, opened by attacking Lincoln's "House Divided" speech as a radical threat to the Union. Only "popular sovereignty" could keep the country together, he claimed. Reacting, perhaps, to his careless remark at Quincy two days before that the country could remain forever half slave and half free, Douglas gave popular sovereignty a more Northern flavor than in any previous debate: "How has the South lost her power as the majority section of this Union, and how have the free States gained it, except under the operation of that principle which declares the right of the people of each State and each territory to form and regulate their domestic institutions in their own way." He repeated his customary charge that Lincoln refused to say whether he would vote to admit a new state which had chosen to allow slavery. Douglas was at some pains to show that he had stood with Henry Clay in fighting for the Compromise of 1850. He also spent more than a third of his time attacking President James Buchanan, who, he claimed, was urging his faction of the Democratic party to support Lincoln. As usual, Douglas insisted that Negroes were not included in the assertion of the equality of all men in the Declaration of Independence.

Old Whigs were numerous in Madison County; the local newspaper was still called the Alton *Daily Whig.* Therefore, Lincoln was quick to point out that Douglas's Kansas-Nebraska Act had repealed Henry Clay's Missouri Compromise. Lincoln denied that his principal disagreement with the Dred Scott decision lay in the decision's prohibiting Negroes from American citizenship. He said that he had never "complained *especially*" on that point; rather, he had seen the decision as "a portion of a system or scheme to make slavery national in this country." Lincoln knew that he must place himself before this "audience, having strong sympathies southward," in a position that showed he was no abolitionist. The way to do so was to put himself, "in connection with Mr. Clay, as nearly right before this people as may be." By excluding the Negro from the promises of the Declaration of Independence, Douglas showed "a tendency to dehumanize the negro—to take away from him the right of ever striving to be a man." Moreover, Douglas thus clearly violated Henry Clay's legacy. Lincoln skillfully quoted Clay to the effect that slavery was "a great evil": "If a state of nature existed, [Clay had said] . . . no man would be more strongly opposed . . . to incorporate the institution of slavery among its elements." The territories presented just such a state, Lincoln suggested; there America was "laying the foundations of societies." Lincoln added that, "irrespective of the moral aspect of this question," he was "still in favor of our new Territories being in such a condition that white men may find a home . . . where they can settle upon new soil and better their condition." He continued to emphasize Douglas's careless remark at Quincy *"that he looks to no end of the institution of slavery."*

Douglas's rebuttal included an attack on Lincoln's taking "sides with the common enemy" in the Mexican War. Douglas belittled Lincoln's claims to being an "old line Clay Whig" by insisting that Lincoln had thrown Clay "overboard" in 1848 for Zachary Taylor. "The Little Giant" professed to care "more for the great principle of self-government . . . than . . . for all the negroes in Christendom," and he would fight to preserve that principle even if a state should "choose to keep slavery forever." Douglas repeated a new argument he had developed at Quincy that the Republican doctrine of "surrounding" and "hemming in" slavery would eliminate the institution only by "starvation" of the black race.

The moderate size of the crowd was an index of the somewhat anticlimactic nature of the debate. As a consequence of the substantial press coverage of the preceding six debates, the people were not as curious to hear what the candidates had to say. In truth, the candidates themselves did not have much to say that was new.

SOURCES: See Edwin Erle Sparks, ed., *The Lincoln-Douglas Debates of 1858* (Springfield: Illinois State Historical Library, 1908).

Altoona Conference A meeting of Northern governors in Altoona, Pennsylvania, on September 24, 1862, to discuss war policy. The conference had its origins in discontent with the Lincoln administration. There had been much to disturb the state executives in the weeks preceding the call for the conference. President Lincoln had answered Horace Greeley's "Prayer of Twenty Millions" by saying that his policy on slavery was subordinate to saving the Union (August 22); the North had lost the Second Battle of Bull Run (August 30); Lincoln had restored George B. McClellan to the command of the Army of the Potomac (September 2); and Robert E. Lee had invaded Maryland (September 4). Pennsylvania Governor Andrew G. Curtin and Massachusetts Governor John A. Andrew organized a conference of loyal governors to meet on September 24. Andrew wanted "to save the Prest. from the infamy of ruining his country." Some governors wanted William H. Seward out of the Cabinet; others disliked McClellan; still others wanted slavery abolished.

Seven days before the governors met, McClellan stopped Lee at Antietam, and just two days before, Lincoln issued the preliminary Emancipation Proclamation, which newspapers reported the day before the conference met. Twelve governors came to the meeting. New York's Edwin D. Morgan refused to attend, and of the four Border States, only Maryland was represented. Governor Augustus W. Bradford of Maryland was made chairman to assure an image of moderation at the meeting.

Andrew apparently criticized McClellan but later repeatedly denied that he had urged the governors to request his removal from command. Curtin and Ohio's David Tod defended McClellan. All except Bradford praised the Emancipation Proclamation. The final address issued by the governors commended the Proclamation and suggested the organization of a reserve of 100,000 men to repel invasions like the recent one of Maryland. Only Bradford refused to sign the address. A meeting begun in criticism ended in praise.

Lincoln invited the governors to Washington, where, on September 26, he heard their address and blunted criticism of McClellan. Andrew secured the signatures of the governors who could not attend, except New York's Morgan, Charles Smith Olden of conservative New Jersey, and those from the Border States.

Democrats charged that the meeting was "a Second Hartford Convention" aimed at treason; they alleged that the conference forced Lincoln to issue the preliminary Emancipation Proclamation. Lincoln, in a statement to George Boutwell reported in James G. Blaine's memoirs, denied that the conference had anything to do with the Proclamation:

Amnesty Proclamation

The truth is, I never thought of the meeting of the governors at all. When Lee came over the Potomac I made a resolve that if McClellan drove him back I would send the proclamation after him. The battle of Antietam was fought Wednesday, but I could not find out until Saturday whether we had won a victory or lost a battle. It was then too late to issue it that day, and on Sunday I fixed it up a little, and on Monday I let them have it.

SOURCES: William B. Hesseltine's *Lincoln and the War Governors* (New York: Alfred A. Knopf, 1948) has the fullest treatment of the conference. The author exaggerates the importance of the conference and is suspicious of Lincoln's claim that the conference did not force the Proclamation. Lincoln's side of the story is in James G. Blaine's *Twenty Years of Congress*, 2 vols. (Norwich, Connecticut: Henry Bill, 1884), I, 439.

Amnesty Proclamation *See* PROCLAMATION OF AMNESTY AND RECONSTRUCTION.

Ancestry *See* GENEALOGY.

Andrew, John Albion (1818–1867) Governor of Massachusetts during the Civil War. Andrew was born in Windham, Maine. A graduate of Bowdoin College, he became an antislavery advocate in his teens. He practiced law in Boston and helped organize the Free Soil party in 1848. He had little sympathy for the Know-Nothing movement, which swept Massachusetts in the mid-1850s. In 1857 he was elected to the General Court, where he was a factional enemy of Nathaniel P. Banks. Two years later Andrew praised John Brown when most Republicans were denying any sympathy with that revolutionary and wrote a letter to his friend Montgomery Blair urging him to defend Brown in court. He was chairman of the Massachusetts delegation to the Republican convention which nominated Lincoln for President in 1860. He met Lincoln as a member of the committee sent to Springfield to notify him of his nomination, and he reported never having seen "a human face, in which more transparent honesty and more benignant kindness were combined with more of the intellect and firmness which belong to masculine humanity."

Andrew was, "down to the very depths," opposed to Simon Cameron's appointment to the Cabinet. He claimed to be a "Seward Man," but he distrusted Seward's manager, Thurlow Weed. He recommended Charles Francis Adams, if "any man is taken from Mass.," but he found Gideon Welles an acceptable representative of New England's interests. He thought the administration must absorb "the best part of the true Barnburner Element," former Democrats in the Republican party, for they were "of the bravest of our men & they mean the most." He was a fast friend of Montgomery Blair (and his father) throughout the war, despite their ideological differences.

Andrew ran for governor in 1860 and won easily; he garnered only 1000 votes fewer than Lincoln, who had not praised John Brown. Having prepared for war since January, Andrew dispatched troops to Washington quickly when war came. He appointed his previous Breckinridge Democrat opponent for governor, Benjamin F. Butler, to head the first Massachusetts brigade. Andrew came to regret that attempt to demonstrate the Bay State's solidarity in upholding the Union. While preparing a May message for the legislature, he sought guidance from Washington as to what he should say. "Drop the nigger," Blair told him. Andrew did; he maintained silence on the slavery question for a year. He admired John C. Frémont's emancipation proclamation for Missouri, but he did not oppose Frémont's removal from command later.

In the autumn of 1861, Governor Andrew began to quarrel with Butler over the general's right to recruit regiments in Massachusetts personally. Lincoln, apparently impressed with Butler's idea that he could recruit Democrats who would otherwise stay home and vote against the Republicans, gave the general permission to raise an army despite War Department orders that state governors should control such regiments. Andrew refused to accept Democratic politician Jonas C. French as an officer in Butler's command because French had led an antiabolition mob in Boston—precisely the reason Butler thought him a suitable appointee. The administration in Washington regarded the dispute as a factional squabble in which it wished not to take sides and asked Andrew to compromise. The dispute lasted into February 1862, when the new Secretary of War, Edwin M. Stanton, finally resolved it. Andrew, who had doubted in December whether Lincoln was "quite sure that we were in a war at all," was increasingly distrustful of the President.

In the fall of 1861 Andrew secretly proposed a naval campaign to capture Texas. We "virtually bought" Texas anyhow, he said, and "her rebellion makes her a dependency for treatment under the War power and through Congress." The invaders should "proclaim martial law, when the proper times arrives, to free all the slaves, compensating loyal owners if necessary." Thereby, the United States would "open a way out for Cotton," cut off "future annexations in the interest of the rebels," and show "foreign powers . . . this war is to stop the spread of slavery." It would also establish a beachhead for a "European emigration which will demonstrate, as the Germans of Texas are now doing, that Cotton can be raised without slaves, though hired negroes may be also used." Connecting Texas by railroad with Kansas and Missouri would ensure the freedom of the West. The letter was eventually referred to Lincoln, but nothing came of the proposal.

Though the Governor's private letters denounced as "twaddle" the notion that the war's purpose was only to "restore the Union," he held his peace on slavery until May 19, 1862, when he warned in a public letter against revoking General David Hunter's emancipation proclamation for South Carolina, Florida, and Georgia. If Northerners must fight rebels who use "all the means known to savages" but "must *never 'fire at an enemy's magazine,'*" Andrew chided, "the draft is heavy on their patriotism." In August he made a speech in which he said that "from the day our government turned its back on the proclamation of General Hunter, the blessing of God has been withdrawn from our arms."

Andrew interpreted Lincoln's reply to Horace Greeley's "Prayer of Twenty Millions" hopefully as a sign that slavery policy would soon change. When Lincoln issued the preliminary Emancipation Proclamation, the governor hailed it as "a poor *document*, but a mighty *act;* slow, somewhat halting, wrong in its delay till January, but grand and sublime after all."

After the final Emancipation Proclamation of January 1, 1863, Andrew quickly gained permission to raise a Massachusetts Negro regiment. The black population in his state was too sparse for the purpose, and Andrew was soon employing agents to recruit Negroes in other states. The other governors objected when they learned the men would not be counted toward their own quotas.

Even that effort to further administration policies brought Andrew into conflict with Lincoln. On February 12, 1864, he complained to the President "that persons of color, both freemen and refugees from slavery, desiring to pass northward from Washington, seeking to better their fortunes and support their families by reaching Massachusetts, are forcibly . . . detained." Lincoln was not fooled by the Governor's plea that the "industry of Massachusetts imperatively demands every laborer now on her soil or willing to come." "If I were to judge from the letter," the President responded, "without any external knowledge, I should suppose that all the colored people South of Washington were struggling to get to Massachusetts; and that Massachusetts was anxious to receive and retain the whole of them as permanent citizens." In fact, "you are engaged in trying to raise colored troops for the U.S. and wish to take recruits from Virginia, through Washington, . . . for that object." Lincoln added a stinging conclusion: "If, however, it be really true that Massachusetts wishes to afford a permanent home within her borders, for all, or even a large number of colored persons who will come to her, I shall be only too glad to know it. It would give relief in a very difficult point." Eventually, Andrew did recruit in Virginia, but he fared less well in his long and abrasive campaign to procure equality in pay for Negro soldiers. He chose the case of a Negro chaplain of the 54th Massachusetts who was paid a $10 laborer's wage (minus clothing allowance) rather than the customary $100 and double rations. Lincoln asked for an opinion from Attorney General Edward Bates, who thought the chaplain should certainly be paid what every chaplain was and that Negro soldiers probably should be paid as white ones were. Lincoln ignored the opinion and Andrew's repeated complaints and let Congress settle the matter of pay for black soldiers.

By 1864 Andrew had seen enough of Lincoln to be convinced that he lacked magnetism and the "quality of leadership." The party needed "a positive man, of clear purpose and more prophetic instinct" as its standard-bearer in November. He was involved as late as September in movements to get both Lincoln and Radical nominee John C. Frémont to withdraw in favor of someone else. He particularly feared any entrance into peace negotiations with the Confederacy. Nevertheless, after Lincoln's reelection, he hoped for a Cabinet post.

Andrew ran for reelection every year and won handily. He chose not to run again in 1865. Despite his reputation as a Radical, Andrew took a surprisingly moderate approach to Reconstruction, which he saw as "not so much of a political, as of an economical character." In the fall of 1865 he turned his interest to the American Land Company to bring Northern capital and Southern planters together. He showed little interest in the political device of the suffrage, and he felt that the leaders who took the South out of the Union would have to be relied upon to bring it back. A successful free-labor economy would lead soon enough to free political institutions.

SOURCES: Henry Greenleaf Pearson's *Life of John Andrew, Governor of Massachusetts, 1861–1865*, 2 vols. (Boston: Houghton, Mifflin, 1904) is old but solid. William B. Hesseltine's *Lincoln and the War Governors* (New York: Alfred A. Knopf, 1948) adds only a little, but Lawrence N. Powell's "The American Land Company and Agency: John A. Andrew and the Northernization of the South," *Civil War History*, XXI (December 1975), 293–308, is essential for his postwar views. Andrew's letters about the Cabinet (to Charles H. Ray, January 8, 1861), about Welles (to Lincoln, January 20, 1861), and about Texas (to Gustavus V. Fox, November 27, 1861) are in the Abraham Lincoln Papers, Library of Congress.

Angle, Paul McClelland (1900–1975) Author and administrator. Angle was born in Mansfield, Ohio. He attended Oberlin College for one year and graduated from Miami University (Ohio) in 1922. He earned a master's degree at the University of Illinois in "a wasted year." In 1925 he became the Executive Secretary of the Lincoln Centennial Association. At the time he "knew nothing about Abraham Lincoln, but . . . did manage to read most of Lord Charnwood's biography" on the train ride to the job interview.

Angle became famous when he denounced as forgeries the documents which Wilma Frances Minor published in the *Atlantic Monthly* as proof of Lincoln's love for Ann Rutledge. He, together with Lincoln collector Oliver R. Barrett and Worthington C. Ford of the Massachusetts Historical Society, "bombarded" the press with denunciations of the Minor forgeries. Eventually the *Atlantic Monthly* allowed him to write "The Minor Lincoln Collection: A Criticism" for its April 1929 issue.

Angle began "to think of books that might add something to the existing knowledge of Abraham Lincoln." For the most part, the books proved to be compilations: of useful dates, useful quotations, and previously unpublished letters. The most important by far was the *New Letters and Papers of Lincoln* (Boston: Houghton, Mifflin, 1930), which included hundreds of newly found letters and which printed the seemingly unimportant "scraps" ignored by heavier-handed editors. In 1935 Angle published *"Here I Have Lived": A History of Lincoln's Springfield, 1821–1865* (Springfield, Ill.: Abraham Lincoln Association), still the only modern history of Lincoln's home town. In 1946 he published *A Shelf of Lincoln Books: A Critical, Selective Bibliog-*

Paul McClelland Angle. (Courtesy of the Illinois State Historical Library)

Arbitrary Arrests

raphy of Lincolniana (New Brunswick, N.J.: Rutgers University Press), which remains the best general guide to what is worthwhile in the vast Lincoln literature. A year later *The Lincoln Reader* (New Brunswick, N.J.: Rutgers University Press) appeared; it was a biography of Lincoln cleverly woven together by selecting from 65 different authors the best treatment of each phase of Lincoln's life.

Angle's principal contribution to the Lincoln field consisted of capable administration of institutions with important Lincoln collections. In 1932 he became the head of the Illinois State Historical Library, a post he held until 1945. Under his administration, the Illinois State Historical Library became the holder of one of the best Lincoln collections in the country. In 1945 he became the Director of the Chicago Historical Society, a position he held for 20 years.

SOURCES: See Paul M. Angle's delightful *On a Variety of Subjects* (Chicago: Chicago Historical Society and The Caxton Club, 1974).

Arbitrary Arrests See HABEAS CORPUS.

"Abraham Lincoln Defending Young Armstrong," published by H. Cassens and lithographed by Theodore Schrader of St. Louis, is the only contemporary print showing Lincoln in a courtroom scene. It erroneously shows him with a beard, which he wore only after his legal career was over. The print is very rare.

Armstrong, John ("Jack") (?–1857?) Leader of the Clary's Grove boys, who lived near New Salem. Armstrong challenged Lincoln to a wrestling match soon after Lincoln arrived in New Salem in 1831. Though details vary, accounts agree that the match ended in a draw and in friendship between Lincoln, Armstrong, and the Clary's Grove boys. In 1832 Armstrong was sergeant in the militia unit which elected Lincoln captain in the Black Hawk War. His wife, Hannah, also became Lincoln's friend; she sewed for Lincoln while he rocked the Armstrong baby, William ("Duff"). In 1837 Lincoln named Armstrong as one of two commissioners in a bill to survey and locate a state road from Jacksonville to Syracuse and Bloomington.

Jack Armstrong died "about 1857," Hannah recalled later, but Lincoln served as defense counsel for "Duff" in a famous murder trial a year later.

SOURCES: See Benjamin P. Thomas, *Lincoln's New Salem* (Springfield, Ill.: Abraham Lincoln Association, 1934) and Geoffrey C. Ward, *Lincoln and the Right to Rise* (Springfield, Ill.: Sangamon State University, 1978).

See also ARMSTRONG, WILLIAM ("DUFF").

John "Jack" Armstrong. (Courtesy of the Illinois State Historical Library)

Armstrong, William ("Duff") (1833–1899) The son of Lincoln's New Salem friends John and Hannah Armstrong. On the periphery of a camp meeting revival in Mason County, Illinois, on August 29, 1857, Duff Armstrong, James H. Norris, and James Preston Metzker got into a drunken brawl. Norris struck Metzker with a piece of wood resembling a wagon yoke, and Armstrong struck him with a metal object called a slungshot, a sort of blackjack. Metzker mounted his horse and rode away, though he fell from the horse several times. Metzker later died, and Norris and Armstrong were indicted in October. Norris, who had previously killed another man, was tried quickly, convicted of manslaughter, and sentenced to 8 years in prison.

William "Duff" Armstrong

Hannah Armstrong appealed to Lincoln to defend her son. In a trial in Beardstown which began on May 7, 1858 (*People* v. *Armstrong*), Lincoln disputed the testimony of the prosecution's star witness, Charles Allen, who testified that he saw the fatal blow struck at about 11 p.m. He was 150 feet away, but the scene was lighted by the moon overhead. Lincoln produced an almanac for the year which showed that the moon was near the horizon at that time of night. Lincoln also produced a witness who testified that the slungshot was his property and in his possession the night of the brawl. A doctor testified that Metzker could have died from injuries received by falling off his horse. The jury's verdict was "not guilty." Lincoln charged no fee for his services. The story that Lincoln used a bogus almanac in the trial is strictly a piece of Western folklore.

Duff Armstrong enlisted in the 85th Illinois Volunteers in the Civil War. In 1863 Lincoln again answered an appeal from Hannah Armstrong and obtained Duff's discharge, as he was ill in a hospital in Louisville. She nursed him back to health, and Armstrong died in Cass County, Illinois, in 1899.

SOURCES: See John J. Duff, *A. Lincoln: Prairie Lawyer* (New York: Rinehart, 1960). J. N. Gridley's "Abraham Lincoln's Defense of Duff Armstrong: The Story of the Trial and the Use of the Almanac," *Journal of the Illinois State Historical Society*, III (April 1910), 24–44, contains an astronomer's computation of the height of the moon and other interesting details.

Arnold, Isaac Newton (1815–1885) Congressional supporter of President Lincoln and one of Lincoln's earliest biographers. Arnold was born in Hartwick, New York, but moved to Chicago in 1836. There he became a successful lawyer. A Van Buren Democrat, he was elected to the state legislature in 1842. He supported James K. Polk for President reluctantly in 1844, and in 1848 he became a member of the Free Soil party.

In 1856 Lincoln termed Arnold, then a Free Soil member of the state legislature, "talented, a practiced debater." Two years later Arnold failed in his bid for nomination as a Republican candidate for Congress, but in 1860 he was elected. In March 1861 he was among the many Republicans embroiled in disputes over the administration's patronage; he was miffed at not being allowed to dictate the appointment to head the local post office, a job that went to his enemy, Lincoln campaign biographer John Locke Scripps. The Scripps-Arnold feud would cause many headaches for President Lincoln.

As a Congressman, Arnold sought a naval depot for Chicago and an enlargement of the Illinois-Michigan Canal into a ship canal to connect the Mississippi with the Great Lakes. He felt that previous pro-Southern Democratic administrations had neglected what was due to the Midwestern granary, now even more important because of the war. Arnold managed to get Lincoln to support the project to make the old canal a great ship canal in his annual message to Congress, December 8, 1863. Arnold was also an antislavery man. In May 1862 he spoke for confiscation of the property and slaves of rebels. He interpreted his reelection by a 2000 majority in 1862 as Cook County's endorsement of Lincoln's Emancipation Proclamation.

When General Ambrose E. Burnside suppressed the antiadministration Chicago *Times* on June 1, 1863, Congressman Arnold and Senator Lyman Trumbull forwarded a petition of prominent Chicago citizens to suspend the order. The next day Arnold sent a telegram saying that he did not endorse the petition himself, but the Trumbull-Arnold dispatch had, Lincoln said, "turned the scale in favor of my revoking the order." Thereafter Arnold sent Lincoln a set of bitter resolutions by Chicago Germans satirizing the revocation, and he admitted that the revocation "has caused much excitement of which I am the special object."

Arnold had urged Lincoln to dismiss General Henry W. Halleck, but Lincoln ignored the advice of his "good friend" in this case. Arnold was instrumental in getting Lincoln to donate the original manuscript of the Emancipation Proclamation for auction at the Northwestern Sanitary Fair in Chicago in 1863.

In 1864 Arnold's past came to haunt him. Scripps sought the nomination for Arnold's congressional seat, and the two men became embroiled in a fight over Scripps's use of the 100-man post office patronage against Arnold. When Arnold complained that the power of the government should not be so used against its friend, Lincoln rebuked Scripps, who "was not pleased" with the President's note. Arnold's enemies also used against him the story that he was responsible for the revocation of the suspension of the *Times*, and Arnold got Lincoln to write a letter playing down his role in the affair. He also asked Lincoln not to renew the administration's advertising in the *Illinois Staatszeitung* unless the paper promised to support the Republican nominee for Congress. The split between Scripps and Arnold threatened Republican control of the district, and on August 29, 1864, Arnold withdrew from the race for the nomination. John Wentworth became the compromise candidate.

Arnold was active in the canvass for Lincoln's reelection that fall. The printed version of his speech *Reconstruction: Liberty the Corner-stone, and Lincoln the Architect* (delivered in Congress, March 19, 1864) was, according to Arnold, "in greater demand than any other document published by" the Union Congressional Committee for the campaign. Earlier in the year, he had written an influential letter opposing postponement of the Republican nominating convention, a postponement sought by enemies of Lincoln's renomination. After the election, Arnold reminded Lincoln that there had been less unanimity in Congress for his renomination than among the people at large and pressed his claim for a patronage reward. He mentioned the mission to Spain but soon expressed a desire for a job—any job—in Washington, where he could observe the great events of the day and work on a history of the administration. On March 13, 1865, Lincoln agreed, and President Andrew Johnson honored the pledge by appointing him Auditor of the Treasury for the Post Office Department.

Arnold's *History of Abraham Lincoln and the Overthrow of Slavery* (Chicago: Clarke & Co., 1866) praised Lincoln as a gentleman but also as "the most democratic of all the Presidents" and as the most prolific source (next to the Bible and Shakespeare) of "household words" for Americans. "His Emancipation Proclamation

Far left: Isaac Newton Arnold photographed in front of Leonard W. Volk's bust of Lincoln. (Courtesy of the Lloyd Ostendorf Collection)

is the most important historical event of the nineteenth century," Arnold said, and, "If he did not act more promptly, it was because he knew he must not go faster than the people." As a Congressman, in truth, Arnold had thought Lincoln should move more quickly against slavery, should include all the rebel states in the Emancipation Proclamation, was tardy in removing incompetent men, and was somewhat rude and rough. But he proved to be a diamond in the rough, and Arnold summed up his views succinctly to William H. Herndon: Lincoln was "the greatest, take him all in all, [and] best man, our country has produced."

By 1885 Arnold had rewritten his book, which was now entitled *The Life of Abraham Lincoln* (Chicago: Jansen, McClurg, 1885). Herndon and later scholars thought Arnold made Lincoln too conventionally pious. And Arnold now emphasized that Lincoln "had more *faith* in mankind, the masses than any other man I ever knew" because Lincoln had seen man on the frontier and not "in the great corrupt cities." The book is still valuable for Arnold's first-hand views of the Lincoln administration.

Among the best of the early biographies of Lincoln, Arnold's work nevertheless contained few clues that Lincoln was not an abolitionist. Arnold saw Lincoln's life as the fulfillment of a youthful vow to abolish slavery. Characteristically, in dealing with the First Inaugural Address, Arnold quoted most of the document but omitted the President's promise to uphold the Fugitive Slave Law and his mention of a constitutional amendment to guarantee slavery in the states where it already existed. Much of the work of twentieth-century biographers would be aimed at qualifying this influential but over-simple interpretation.

SOURCES: Arnold's career is described in *Biographical Sketches of the Leading Men of Chicago* (Chicago: Wilson & St. Clair, 1868). For an appraisal of his biography of Lincoln, see Benjamin P. Thomas, *Portrait for Posterity: Lincoln and His Biographers* (New Brunswick, N.J.: Rutgers University Press, 1947). David M. Potter's *The Lincoln Theme and American National Historiography* (Oxford: Clarendon Press, 1948) contains a brief but penetrating assessment of Arnold's place among Lincoln biographers. Arnold's letters to Lincoln about the excitement after the suppression of the *Times* (June 9, 1863), about Scripps's displeasure (July 16, 1864), about the *Illinois Staatszeitung* (August 23, 1864) and about the popularity of his "Reconstruction" speech (December 12, 1864) are in the Abraham Lincoln Papers, Library of Congress.

See also, ADAMS, CHARLES FRANCIS; BIOGRAPHERS; CHICAGO *TIMES*, SUPPRESSION OF THE.

Arnold, Samuel Bland (1834–1906) One of John Wilkes Booth's coconspirators in the plot to kidnap President Lincoln. Arnold had known Booth from his boyhood years in Baltimore: he and Booth were schoolmates at St. Timothy's Hall, an Episcopal military academy at Catonsville, Maryland. Arnold served briefly as a soldier in the Confederate army but was discharged on account of bad health. Later he served as a civilian clerk. In 1864 he returned to Baltimore with his younger brother because his mother was seriously ill. When Booth recruited him in the late summer of 1864, he was unemployed and bored. He and Booth thought it would be easy to kidnap the President as he rode without military escort to the Soldiers' Home.

The conspirators spent most of their time in Washington "in drinking and amusements." By his own admission, Arnold was as zealous to kidnap the President and exchange him for Confederate prisoners as Booth, but in mid-March 1865 he and Booth had a sharp disagreement. Booth outlined a plot to kidnap Lincoln from Ford's Theatre. Arnold objected, mainly on tactical grounds. He mentioned the fact that the government had resumed prisoner exchanges (Lincoln was thus no longer needed for that purpose). He argued that security had tightened in Washington, and he protested the plan's "utter impracticability." "I wanted a shadow of a chance for my life," he recalled. Booth threatened to shoot Arnold; Arnold made counterthreats; but the conflict ended in compromise. Arnold agreed to stay with the scheme one more week. Under that pressure, Booth gathered the group on March 17 to kidnap the President on his way to a theatrical performance near the Soldiers' Home. Booth was misinformed; Lincoln did not appear on the road.

On March 20 Arnold returned to Baltimore. Booth wanted to try again, but on March 27 Arnold wrote him a letter explaining his fear "that the G[overnmen]t suspicions something" and suggesting that Booth, "for the present, desist." Arnold had told his parents he was finished with Booth, and he had applied for a clerk's job. Arnold was badly "in need." He did not like being "in rags" like "a beggar" when he "ought to be well clothed." He felt his "dependence" on Booth but wanted to wait for a "Time more propitious." They should find out how the plan would be taken in Richmond.

Arnold got his job and was employed as a clerk at Old Point Comfort, Virginia, from April 2d until his arrest on the 17th. Officers searching Booth's trunk had found his incriminating March 27 letter to Booth (signed "SAM"), but fellow workers provided Arnold's solid alibi for the time of the assassination: he was steadily employed as a clerk at Old Point Comfort. The military commission which tried the conspirators made no distinction between the kidnap and assassination plots and sentenced him to life imprisonment at hard labor. He served time at Fort Jefferson until President Andrew Johnson pardoned him in 1869.

Arnold's confession of 1867, made for a commissioner investigating the assassination for Congress, as well as his March 27 letter and a later apologia, are important evidence that the plot was not a Confederate scheme. They are also important sources for the origins of the kidnap conspiracy and for its changes in strategy over time.

SOURCES: Samuel Bland Arnold's *Defence and Prison Experiences of a Lincoln Conspirator* (Hattiesburg, Miss.: The Book Farm, 1943) is the principal source, but only 199 copies were printed. *See also* Benn Pitman, ed., *The Assassination of President Lincoln and the Trial of the Conspirators* (Cincinnati, Ohio: Moore, Wilstach & Baldwin, 1865).

Ashmun, George (1804–1870) Massachusetts politician and lawyer. George Ashmun became acquainted

Samuel Bland Arnold

with Abraham Lincoln when both served as Whigs in the Thirtieth Congress. Ashmun was one of the "immortal fourteen" who voted against the army supply bill of May 14, 1846, which embodied the Democratic rationale for war as well as a declaration of war on Mexico. Lincoln's opposition did not go so far, but he did vote for Ashmun's amendment, to a resolution of thanks to General Zachary Taylor, declaring the war "unconstitutionally and unnecessarily begun by the President" (January 3, 1848).

An ardent champion of Daniel Webster, Ashmun lost favor when his idol did, after his "Seventh of March Speech" in support of the Compromise of 1850. He did not return to Congress after 1851. Later he became a Republican, was permanent chairman of the Republican National Convention in 1860, and was a member of the committee which called on Lincoln in Springfield to give him formal notification of his presidential nomination. On April 14, 1861, after the fall of Fort Sumter, Ashmun visited Senator Stephen A. Douglas and persuaded him to go to the White House and pledge his support for the war effort. He also persuaded Douglas to issue a public statement of his purpose the next day— a most important act in giving direction to the loyal opposition to Lincoln's administration.

Ashmun saw the President on numerous occasions during the war years. In late 1861 he was intermediary for an important visit to the President by Canadian Finance Minister Alexander Galt to discuss the strained relations between the two North American powers. Ashmun seems to have benefited from his closeness to the administration, being involved in at least one contract for arms and apparently representing clients involved in the trade in contraband Southern cotton. Massachusetts Radicals like John A. Andrew and Charles Sumner opposed any political appointment for him. The conservative Ashmun became a foe of Salmon P. Chase's bid for the Republican nomination in 1864 and supported Nathaniel P. Banks's conservative regime in occupied Louisiana.

On Lincoln's last day in office, April 14, 1865, Ashmun called on the President in regard to the cotton trade. Lincoln, according to Francis B. Carpenter, exploded, and said he was "done with" cotton commissions. But then he apologized to Ashmun and wrote his last note: "Allow Mr. Ashmun & friend to come in at 9 a.m. tomorrow."

SOURCES: See F. Lauriston Bullard, "Abraham Lincoln and George Ashmun," *New England Quarterly*, XIX (June 1946), 184–211.

Assassination On April 14, 1865, Abraham Lincoln became the first American President to be assassinated. Indeed, there had been only one previous assassination attempt against a President. In 1835 Samuel Lawrence, a house painter born in England, tried to shoot Andrew Jackson because he believed that Jackson had denied him the crown of England. Even after the Baltimore Plot (and perhaps because the precautions taken then proved so embarrassing to Lincoln), the administration showed little outward fear of assassination. Secretary of State William H. Seward assured John Bigelow in a letter written July 15, 1862, that

> Assassination is not an American practice or habit, and one so vicious and so desperate cannot be engrafted into our political system. This conviction of mine has steadily gained strength since the Civil War began. . . . The President, during the heated season, occupies a country house near the Soldiers' Home, two or three miles from the city. He goes to and fro from that place on horseback, night and morning, unguarded.

Lincoln himself tended to be fatalistic; he felt that no security system could exclude assassins who would very likely be Southerners, one's own countrymen. Security precautions were minimal, therefore, and there was opportunity aplenty to assassinate President Lincoln.

John Wilkes Booth first revealed his plot to kidnap President Lincoln to his boyhood friends Samuel B. Arnold and Michael O'Laughlin in Barnum's Hotel in Baltimore in late August or early September 1864. In a sense, it was a second "Baltimore Plot," for Booth and his two original coconspirators were from the Baltimore area. Like the first plot, too, it was hatched at a time of great political excitement; the Democratic nominating convention was held in late August 1864. Maryland was fertile ground for opposition to Lincoln. A slave state in a country fighting slavery, it had been the scene of the first violence of the Civil War. On April 19, 1861, Massachusetts soldiers on their way to protect Washington were involved in a melee in Baltimore which saw 12 Marylanders and 4 Federal soldiers killed. Maryland Governor Thomas H. Hicks had written a letter to Con-

The simplest interpretation of Booth's crime is portrayed in this print published in Philadelphia in 1865. It suggests that Booth was simply the devil's tool.

gressman Edwin H. Webster, an officer in the Maryland militia, at about the time of Lincoln's election in 1860:

> [I have] no arms at hand to distribute, at earliest possible moment you shall have arms. . . . Will they [your militia company] be good men to send out to kill Lincoln and his men. If not, I suppose the arms would be better sent South.

The letter is controversial and must have been facetious, but it shows how easily such an idea came to mind in Maryland's fevered politics.

James Ryder Randall's famous poem "Maryland, My Maryland," written soon after the Baltimore riot, warned that "The despot's heel is on thy shore, Maryland." The Maryland House of Delegates debated the "gross usurpation, unjust, oppressive tyrannical acts of the President of the United States"—and Booth's cry after he assassinated Lincoln would be *"Sic semper tyrannis."*

There was nothing unique about the political thought of John Wilkes Booth. In a long letter left with his sister in Philadelphia in 1864, Booth said that he had "ever held the South were right," and added: "People of the North, to hate tyranny, to love liberty and justice, to strike at wrong and oppression, was the teaching of our fathers. The study of our early history will not let me forget it, and may it never."

Like many others in the North, Booth denounced Lincoln's racial policies, claiming that "This country was formed for the *white*, not for the black man." He considered slavery "one of the greatest blessings (both for themselves and us) that God ever bestowed upon a favored nation." He claimed that Lincoln's policy toward blacks was "only preparing a way for their total annihilation." Maryland Congressman John W. Crisfield told the House of Representatives the same thing, that Negroes must be kept in slavery, for otherwise "degradation, poverty . . . and ultimate extinction" would befall them.

Since April 1864 General Ulysses S. Grant had refused to exchange Confederate prisoners. Booth planned to kidnap Lincoln on his way to the Soldiers' Home, take him to Richmond, and exchange him for Confederate prisoners. Arnold and O'Laughlin agreed, and over the next few months Booth calculated his plot rationally. He tidied up his personal affairs by going to Montreal, Canada, where he consigned his $15,000 theatrical wardrobe to an agent who would try to run it through the blockade to the Confederacy. He obviously thought he would resume his career in the South after the successful kidnapping. On returning to Washington, Booth explored southern Maryland in November and December, claiming to be in the market for land, but actually looking for escape routes and recruits. He picked up a valuable accomplice on December 23 in John H. Surratt, who, as runner for the Confederate "mail" between Baltimore and Richmond, knew the likely escape routes in Maryland and shared Booth's Confederate sympathies. Surratt provided entree to the network of disloyalists in Washington and southern Maryland, among them David E. Herold and George A. Atzerodt. Herold hunted partridges in southern Maryland and claimed to know the area of escape; Atzerodt ferried Confederate spies across the Potomac and was knowledgeable about the route as well. Finally, on March 1, 1865, Booth added the dangerous, strong, and violent Lewis Thornton Powell (better known by the alias Lewis Payne, or Paine), an escaped Confederate prisoner from Florida.

The motivation of the conspirators was clear. Arnold, O'Laughlin, and Powell had been Confederate soldiers. Surratt and Atzerodt had served the Confederacy in surreptitious roles. All but Powell were Marylanders, and Powell had found a congenial board in Baltimore. Only Herold came from Washington, and he spent considerable time hunting in southern Maryland. Each had more than reasons of political sympathy to join Booth. Arnold was unemployed, as was Herold; Powell was broke and desperate in a strange land. Surratt loved adventure and had learned not to fear Federal detectives. Atzerodt and all the others probably enjoyed the notoriety of associating with the famous Booth; Louis J. Weichmann, a key government witness at the trial of the assassins, claimed most of them were in it for the money. Booth was a wealthy man and supported members of the group in Washington and provided them with horses. The conspirators also expected to become Southern heroes.

By the time Booth had enough men to kidnap the President, his opportunity was gone, for the season of hot weather in Washington was gone, and the President no longer traveled regularly to the Soldiers' Home. Therefore, Booth changed his plans—still kidnapping, but now from Ford's Theatre while Lincoln watched a play. Booth's coconspirators did not like the idea; in the words of Samuel Arnold, they "wanted a shadow of a chance for" their lives. When Booth revealed the plan in March, serious disagreement followed, and Arnold swore to leave the plot in a week.

Under the pressure of Arnold's ultimatum, Booth tried to capture the President on March 17 when he was supposed to go out of Washington to a theatrical performance. Booth's information proved erroneous, and the conspirators rode out in vain. After the attempt, Arnold and O'Laughlin left Washington and the plot, and Surratt resumed his activities for the Confederacy. Booth now had too few men to kidnap even so loosely guarded a President as Lincoln.

This rare print interpreted Booth's crime as inspired by disloyal political movements in the North, epitomized here by the Knights of the Golden Circle.

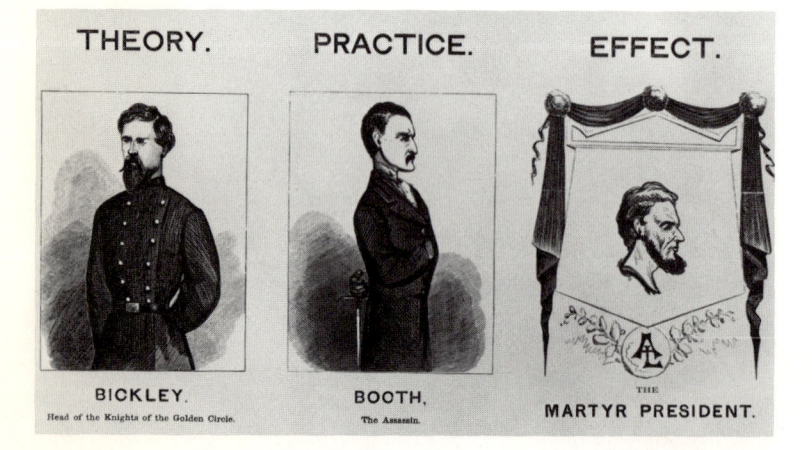

THEORY. PRACTICE. EFFECT.

BICKLEY. BOOTH. THE MARTYR PRESIDENT.
Head of the Knights of the Golden Circle. The Assassin.

By April 3 there was no Richmond government to which to take a kidnapped Lincoln. By noon of April 14, Booth decided to kill the President while he watched *Our American Cousin* at Ford's Theatre; the performance starred Laura Keene, famed comedienne who first produced the play in New York in 1858. Booth had free run of the theater and even picked up his mail there. That afternoon, apparently, Booth bored a peephole in the door of the President's box and prepared a pole to jam the door so it could not be opened behind him once he entered the box.

Booth decided to kill Vice President Andrew Johnson and Secretary of State Seward too, probably because, as he later related to a woman who helped him escape, he thought it might lead to a political revolution in the North that would benefit the South. He did not assign his coconspirators their roles until 2 hours before the crime. In an 8:00 p.m. meeting at the Herndon House, he instructed Atzerodt to kill Johnson, Powell to kill Seward, and Herold to lead the Floridian Powell out of Washington. Atzerodt failed even to try to kill Johnson. Herold, too, failed: he fled without helping Powell, and Powell's inability to leave the city led to his capture.

Booth asked Edman Spangler, a scene changer, to hold his horse behind the theater. Spangler gave the job to "Peanut John" Burroughs. Booth encountered no obstacle from Lincoln's guard, John F. Parker, who apparently left the door to Lincoln's box unguarded to watch the play. In any case, such a famous actor as Booth would have had no trouble getting in to see a President notoriously fond of theater. Armed with a dagger and a single-shot Deringer pistol, Booth committed a crime that bore the idiosyncratic marks of his own personality. He guaranteed its theatricality by committing it in a theater. Lincoln was shot from behind while sitting in his private box overlooking the stage. The assassin, famous for his athletic acting, then leaped some 12 feet to the stage. Most accounts agree that he shouted *"Sic semper tyrannis!"* Thus the political motive was on his mind at the moment of the crime.

Powell came very near killing Seward as well. Pretending to deliver medicine, Powell forced his way into Seward's home. He injured the Secretary's son Frederick, stabbed Seward's cheek and neck, and might well have killed the Secretary but for the heavy brace the bedridden man wore on his neck as the result of a recent carriage accident. Seward's nurse, George Robinson, also helped save the Secretary, but not without serious injury to himself. On his way out, the dangerous Powell wounded another of Seward's sons, Augustus, and a State Department messenger who happened to be on the first floor.

Thus ended America's first successful presidential assassination. The shabbily run trial wreaked considerable hysterical vengeance on the perpetrators (and perhaps on some of their innocent acquaintances as well), but it failed to clear up all the circumstances of the assassination because it focused primarily on the idea that the crime was a Confederate plot.

Over the years, the motives of the conspirators were obscured in popular writings. The great effort to bring the nation back together was not aided by memories that Lincoln was killed by a group of Confederate sympathizers, disloyal spies, and ex-Confederate soldiers. To ease sectional tensions, the real political motive tended to be forgotten. Moreover, few were concerned enough about racism to remember or care that the crime had been motivated by racist hatred for Lincoln's policies toward the Negro. The real reasons for the crime receded so far from popular memory that Booth came to be seen as a madman, the perpetrator of an irrational crime.

Sensationalists and misguided zealots supplied reasons for the crime that made Booth's group the mere tools of persons with larger motives; Jefferson Davis, Catholics, and even a member of Lincoln's Cabinet have been accused of being the true perpetrators. But the conspirators' motive and opportunity are entirely explained by their Confederate sympathies and race hatred and by the loose security measures of the Lincoln administration.

SOURCES: The best book on the assassination is George S. Bryan's *The Great American Myth* (New York: Carrick & Evans, 1940). On Maryland's fevered politics see Jean H. Baker, *The Politics of Continuity: Maryland Political Parties from 1858 to 1870* (Baltimore: Johns Hopkins University Press, 1973), and Charles L. Wagandt, *The Mighty Revolution: Negro Emancipation in Maryland, 1862–1864* (Baltimore: Johns Hopkins University Press, 1964).

See also ARNOLD, SAMUEL BLAND; ATZERODT, GEORGE A.; BALTIMORE PLOT; BOOTH, JOHN WILKES; CHINIQUY, CHARLES PASCHAL TELESPHORE; CORBETT, THOMAS P. ("BOSTON"); CROOK, WILLIAM HENRY; EISENSCHIML, OTTO; FORD'S THEATRE; FORT JEFFERSON; HEROLD, DAVID EDGAR; HOLT, JOSEPH; JONES, THOMAS A.; LAMON, WARD HILL; LINCOLN, ROBERT TODD; LLOYD, JOHN MINCHIN; MUDD, SAMUEL ALEXANDER; O'LAUGHLIN, MICHAEL; OUR AMERICAN COUSIN; PARKER, JOHN FREDERICK; PETERSEN HOUSE; POWELL, LEWIS THORNTON; RATHBONE, HENRY RIGGS; STANTON, EDWIN MCMASTERS; SURRATT, JOHN HARRISON, JR.; SURRATT, MARY EUGENIA; TRIAL OF THE ASSASSINS; WEICHMANN, LOUIS J.

Atzerodt, George A. (1835–1865) A wagon painter who conspired with John Wilkes Booth to kidnap Abraham Lincoln and, later, to kill Andrew Johnson. Atzerodt, a native of Germany, was the oldest man involved in the conspiracy to kidnap President Lincoln. Reporter Ben: Perley Poore described him as a "short, thick-set, round-shouldered, brawny-armed man with a stupid expression, high cheek-bones, a sallow complexion, small grayish-blue eyes, tangled light-brown hair, and straggling sandy whiskers and mustache." He spoke with a German accent, and his Teutonic name gave rural Marylanders so much trouble that they frequently called him "Port Tobacco," the name of the village where he lived. Atzerodt apparently ferried spies across the Potomac during the war and thus knew Confederate spy John H. Surratt, who probably introduced him to Booth. Atzerodt joined the plot and agreed to furnish a boat for the escape. He was almost broke at the time and apparently

George A. Atzerodt

dreamed of enough gold to keep him a lifetime. He enjoyed being supported by and associating with the famous actor.

As the assassination was planned in a meeting at the Herndon House at 8 p.m. on April 14, 1865, Atzerodt was assigned to kill Vice President Andrew Johnson. He had already taken a room at the Kirkwood House, where Johnson was staying, Booth having earlier suggested that Atzerodt could get a pass from the Vice President so they could open a theater in Richmond. He began drinking at various taverns, lost his courage, and took flight to western Maryland on horseback. On April 20, 1865, Sergeant L. W. Gemmill arrested him, moping over a neighbor girl's rejection of his advances. He was staying at the house of a cousin named Hartman Richter in Germantown, Maryland. Nine men split a $25,000 reward for his capture.

Atzerodt's attorney was W. E. Doster, whose principal defense was that his client was a constitutional coward whom Booth would never have trusted to kill Johnson. Atzerodt's confession to participating in the kidnap plot was not admitted as evidence but was read to the commission in Doster's final argument. On June 30 Atzerodt was sentenced, and on July 7 he was hanged with three other alleged accomplices of Booth and buried at the penitentiary where the execution took place. In 1867 part of the prison was razed, and Atzerodt's body was moved to "Warehouse 1" on the grounds of the prison.

SOURCES: See George S. Bryan, *The Great American Myth* (New York: Carrick & Evans, 1940); Benn Pitman, ed., *The Assassination of President Lincoln and the Trial of the Conspirators* (Cincinnati, Ohio: Moore, Wilstach & Baldwin, 1965); and Ben: Perley Poore, *The Conspiracy Trial for the Murder of the President*, 3 vols. (Boston: J. E. Tilton, 1865).

See also ASSASSINATION; TRIAL OF THE ASSASSINS.

Autobiography A modest man, Lincoln never wrote his memoirs or kept a diary. When he became a national political figure, his reticence in that respect posed a problem for party leaders anxious to publish campaign biographies to promote his candidacy.

Lincoln's autobiographical statements were always solicited by others. His first was elicited by Charles Lanman in 1858. While preparing a *Dictionary of Congress*, which was to include all the men who had ever served in Congress, Lanman wrote Lincoln for an autobiography. His standard letter made no suggestion about length of reply, and some Congressmen sent 20-page answers. Lincoln's answer follows:

> Born, February 12, 1809, in Hardin County, Kentucky.
> Education defective.
> Profession, a lawyer.
> Have been a captain of volunteers in Black Hawk war.
> Postmaster at a very small office.
> Four times a member of the Illinois legislature, and was a member of the lower house of Congress.

Jesse W. Fell requested a biographical sketch for Joseph J. Lewis, editor of Pennsylvania's *Chester County Times*, in December 1859. Lincoln replied with a longer answer than he had given Lanman, but still "There is not much of it," he said, "for the reason, I suppose, that there is not much of me." He cautioned that any use of it should "be modest, and not . . . go beyond the material." The sketch described his parents as descendants "of undistinguished families—second families, perhaps I should say." He disparaged the "so called" schools he attended in southern Indiana and admitted, "when I came of age I did not know much." He called his election as captain in the Black Hawk War "a success which gave me more pleasure than any I have had since." Losing the race for the Illinois House the same year was "the only time I have been beaten by the people." He said he "was losing interest in politics" when the Kansas-Nebraska Act aroused him. He concluded with a physical description. Lewis published the letter in 1860, and it was widely reprinted in the Republican press.

John Locke Scripps of the Chicago *Press and Tribune* requested the third, longest, and last autobiography in order to write a campaign biography for Lincoln's presidential race. The resulting document, written in the third person, is a substantial one and constitutes the principal source of information about Lincoln's early life. Lincoln described his father somewhat uncharitably as "a wandering laboring boy" who "grew up litterally without education" and "never did more in the way of writing than to bunglingly sign his own name." He gave no description of his mother but said his stepmother "proved a good and kind mother." His knowledge of grammar was acquired after he was 23; he "studied and nearly mastered the Six-books of Euclid" after he had been to Congress (1849). Lincoln gave details of his two flatboat trips to New Orleans, including "the ludicrous incident of sewing up the hogs eyes" to get them on the boat. He spoke kindly of his New Salem neighbors and stated that he thought for a time of becoming a blacksmith. "He studied with nobody" when he prepared for the bar.

Lincoln was careful to mention his first antislavery protest (1837) and that he voted supplies for soldiers even though he opposed the Mexican War. He explained the reason for his opposition at considerable length and stressed that it "was determined upon, and declared before he went to Washington" that he would not run for reelection. He concluded by saying he had "no recollection" that his speech in Galena in 1856 had stated that the Supreme Court was the proper tribunal to determine the constitutionality of laws restricting the expansion of slavery.

B

Baker, Edward Dickinson (1811–1861) Friend and political associate of Lincoln. Baker was born in London, England, but came to the United States with his parents in 1816. He briefly attended his father's Lancastrian school in Philadelphia, then worked in a cotton mill. In 1825 the Bakers moved to British socialist Robert Owen's utopian community, New Harmony, Indiana. After a few months they moved to Belleville, then on to Carrollton, Illinois, where Edward studied law with A. W. Caverly. He also married a local widow, Mary Ann Lee, and became a member of the Disciples of Christ (Campbellite) Church. In 1832 Baker served in the Black Hawk War. His men elected him second and, later, first lieutenant. In 1835 he moved to Springfield, where he opened a law office.

Two years later Baker was elected to the state legislature on the Whig ticket, and Whig politics brought him into close association with Abraham Lincoln. Baker was reelected in 1838 and served in the Illinois Senate from 1840 to 1844.

Vying for still higher office brought the two friendly Whigs into rivalry. In 1843 both Lincoln and Baker desired to run for the United States House of Representatives from Illinois's eleven-county Seventh Congressional District. Sangamon County Whigs chose Baker over Lincoln. Lincoln, appointed a delegate to the district nominating convention, had to work for his rival's nomination—"a good deal like a fellow who is made groomsman to a man what has cut him out, and is marrying his own dear 'gal.'" Lincoln's quest for the nomination was hurt by a reputation "as the candidate of pride, wealth, and aristocratic family distinction" and by "the strangest combination of church influence." Baker got the Campbellites. Mrs. Lincoln's relatives were Presbyterians and Episcopalians, and each religious group was told that Lincoln belonged to the other. Some even said that he was a deist. "With all these things Baker, of course had nothing to do," Lincoln explained. Baker then failed to gain the district nomination, which went to John J. Hardin. To prevent future factional strife the Whigs endorsed Baker "as a suitable" nominee for the next convention. In 1844 Baker won nomination and election (over Democrat John Calhoun); he would assume his seat in Congress in December 1845. With only a little reluctance Baker agreed to honor the spirit of the Whig agreement and let Lincoln take his turn running for Congress. Hardin tried to contest Lincoln's candidacy, and no love was lost between them thereafter. By contrast Lincoln named a son after Baker just after the succession was settled.

Congressman Baker spoke vehemently for America's "manifest destiny" to acquire Oregon up to 54°40' latitude. When war broke out with Mexico in 1846, Baker dutifully asked Daniel Webster, on May 18, whether he approved of his intention to enter military service. Webster assured him that it was all right for Whig young men to fight in this Democratic war. Baker organized the Fourth Illinois Volunteers and became their colonel. He was wounded near the Rio Grande putting down a rioting Georgia regiment. He returned to Washington

Edward Dickinson Baker. (Library of Congress)

and on December 28, 1846, delivered a speech in uniform urging that Congress cease squabbling and support the volunteers in the field. On December 30 Baker resigned his seat; some members of the House had questioned the constitutionality and propriety of his being an officer and a member of Congress at the same time. He fought at the Battle of Cerro Gordo in April 1847. Visiting Congressman Lincoln in Washington early the next year, Baker assured Lincoln that he agreed with the Whig position on the unjust origin of the war and would say so in public.

Baker returned to Springfield but moved to Galena in the spring of 1848. He campaigned for Zachary Taylor for President and was himself nominated for the United States House of Representatives from the Sixth Congressional District. He won election again in this previously Democratic district. In Congress he supported the Wilmot Proviso, which would have excluded slavery from territory acquired from Mexico, and declared the dissolution of the Union to be simply "impossible." He neglected congressional duties near the end of his term to build a railroad across the Isthmus of Panama. He contracted a fever (probably malaria) there and returned to the United States.

Baker moved to San Francisco in 1852 and made an unsuccessful bid for the United States Senate on the Free Soil ticket three years later. In 1856 he became a Republican. Having incurred the disfavor of the powerful Vigilance Committee in San Francisco, he moved to Sacramento in 1856 but returned to San Francisco the next year. In 1859 he ran for Congress as a Republican and lost.

Late in 1859 Baker moved to Oregon to run for the United States Senate. The Democratic party was extremely powerful in the West; victory depended on wooing antislavery Douglas Democrats, and Baker's official position, unlike Lincoln's, was "the doctrine of non-intervention by Congress, or anybody else, with the people of the territories." He would "permit them to govern themselves as to slavery." In 1860 Baker won election to the Senate with the support of the Douglas Democrats in the legislature. He was the first Republican to be elected to high office on the Pacific Coast.

After war broke out, Baker was authorized to raise "a military command to be known as the California Regiment." In truth, Baker's law partner, Isaac Wistar, recruited the regiment in Philadelphia after bestowing on them numerous drinks of "bad whiskey." Lincoln appointed Baker brigadier general, but he declined the commission in order to retain his Senate seat. With extreme fervor Senator Baker defended Lincoln's actions in mobilizing for war, on July 10, 1861:

> I propose to ratify whatever needs ratification. I propose to render my clear and distinct approval not only of the measure but of the motive which prompted it. I propose to lend the whole power of the country, arms, men, money, and place them in his hands with authority almost unlimited, until the conclusion of this struggle. . . . I want sudden, bold, forward, determined war; and I do not think anybody can conduct war of that kind as well as a dictator.

In June he had urged a forward movement by the Union armies, in part "to cooperate with what I suppose to be a northern movement in Richmond."

Colonel Baker had joked about becoming a "venerable martyr" in June, but he did write his will. At the Battle of Ball's Bluff on October 22, 1861, he was killed in action. His body lay in state in Washington and later at Independence Hall in Philadelphia and City Hall in New York. On December 11 he was buried in San Francisco. On the same day President Lincoln attended services in the Senate.

Lincoln and Baker had risen to prominence together in the Whig party in large part because both were superior stump speakers always much in demand at election time. Prominence led to some political rivalry for the limited honors available to Whigs in Democratic Illinois, but it never led to a personal rivalry like that which developed between Lincoln and Hardin. In personal habits Baker was like Lincoln only in being a rather disorderly lawyer who kept important documents in his hat. Stephen T. Logan had been willing to take Lincoln on as a law partner in 1841, in part because Logan felt that Baker could not be trusted with money. Lincoln, by contrast, was fanatically honest in money matters. Joshua Speed told Lincoln in 1849, when Baker was hoping for a Cabinet post from the Taylor administration, that Senator John J. Crittenden considered Baker lacking in "those patient, plodding, business qualifications so necessary to make a first rate Cabinet officer." Nor did Lincoln share his friend's fondness for champagne and gambling at cards. After their long separation caused by Baker's move to the West Coast, the two quickly got back together again, and Baker rode in Lincoln's carriage in the inaugural parade and introduced him before his First Inaugural Address. Nevertheless, Baker, though he considered Lincoln still "my very good friend," had been disappointed in the President's distribution of the patronage on the West Coast, and it is possible that Baker's dalliance with Stephen A. Douglas's doctrine of popular sovereignty was not entirely forgotten.

SOURCES: See *Colonel Edward D. Baker: Lincoln's Constant Ally* by Harry C. Blair and Rebecca Tarshis ([Portland]: Oregon Historical Society, 1960). Baker's letter to Lincoln about cooperating with "a northern movement in Richmond" (June 16, 1861) is in the Abraham Lincoln Papers, Library of Congress. His letter about martyrdom (to Mrs. Georgiana S. Peters, June 17, 1861) is in the Louis A. Warren Lincoln Library and Museum, Fort Wayne, Indiana.

Baltimore Convention, 1864 *See* ELECTION OF 1864.

Baltimore Plot An alleged conspiracy to assassinate Lincoln while he was en route to his inauguration. As the President-elect prepared to make his journey to Washington, S. M. Felton, president of the Philadelphia, Wilmington and Baltimore Railroad, hired Allan Pinkerton of Pinkerton's National Detective Agency to investigate rumored plots to sabotage the railroad in Maryland over which Lincoln was to travel. Pinkerton received a tip that there was a plan to kill Lincoln when he changed trains in Baltimore for Washington. On Felton's orders, Pinkerton contacted Norman B. Judd, a Chicago politician traveling with the presidential party, and Judd met Pinkerton and Felton in Philadelphia on February 21, 1861. That night Judd warned Lincoln of Pinkerton's discovery. Pinkerton suggested that Lincoln go straight to Washington from Philadelphia the same night, but Lincoln refused because he had scheduled speaking appearances in Philadelphia and Harrisburg the next day.

Independently of Pinkerton's investigation, New York policemen detailed to Washington to work for Colonel Charles P. Stone of General Winfield Scott's staff also discovered a plot in Baltimore. Scott reported the plot to William H. Seward, the Secretary of State–designate. Seward's son Frederick reported the plot to Lincoln in Philadelphia just after the President-elect had learned of Pinkerton's investigation. In his speech at Independence Hall the next morning, Lincoln showed the effects of the ominous news of the previous night. Declaring his allegiance to the promise of equality in the Declaration of Independence, Lincoln remarked, "I was about to say I would rather be assassinated on this spot than surrender it."

On the train to Harrisburg, Judd revealed Pinkerton's plan to travel to Washington that night. After returning from Harrisburg, Lincoln would take the 10:50 p.m. train from Philadelphia to Washington and would ride in the rear of a sleeping car closed off by a curtain. He would pose as the invalid brother of one of Pinkerton's female agents, Mrs. Kate Warne, who would engage the car.

That night Lincoln wore an overcoat and carried a soft felt hat and a shawl. Accompanied by Ward Hill Lamon, an old Illinois friend armed to the teeth, Lincoln passed quietly through Baltimore and arrived in Washington at about 6:00 a.m. on the 23d.

The secret passage to Washington aroused controversy at the time and has continued to arouse it ever since. Joseph J. Howard, Jr., a New York *Times* correspondent, wrote a widely copied story claiming that Lincoln had sneaked through Baltimore disguised in "a Scotch plaid cap and a very long military cloak." It was untrue, of course, but journalists and political cartoonists had a field day with the story. In 1872 Lamon, who had been called "a brainless egotistical fool" by Pinkerton, took revenge on the detective by asserting that Pinkerton invented the rumor of the assassination plot as publicity for his business. Since Pinkerton had proved in the meantime to be a very unreliable spy for the Army of the Potomac during the Civil War—he was constantly sending wildly erroneous reports of the size of Confederate armies—Lamon's allegation gained some credence.

In truth, however, Baltimore *was* a dangerous city with a long heritage of political violence and secret societies. The city was so pro-Southern in sentiment that it had extended no official invitation or welcome to the Republican President-elect. Baltimore's police force was controlled by a Southern sympathizer who spent the war years behind Confederate lines. The change for the Washington train required a carriage ride through the city to another station, and Lincoln was definitely vulnerable. On April 19, 1861, when Massachusetts soldiers passed through Baltimore to relieve Washington, a mob attacked them and several were killed. Moreover, Lamon's allegation failed to account for the independent corroboration of the plot by the detectives working for Winfield Scott. There certainly would have been danger in making the well-publicized trip through Baltimore as planned. Indeed, a plot hatched in Baltimore by Maryland men four years later led to Lincoln's assassination.

SOURCES: George S. Bryan's *The Great American Myth* (New York: Carrick & Evans, 1940) defends Lincoln's decision to avoid Baltimore. However, the author lacked documents now available in Norma B. Cuthbert's *Lincoln and the Baltimore Plot* (San Marino, Calif.: Henry E. Huntington Library, 1949). Cuthbert explains carefully the circumstances of the Lamon-Pinkerton feud and publishes Pinkerton's evidence.

See also PINKERTON, ALLAN.

Banking Abraham Lincoln's first published political platform included a plea for laws against usurious interest rates. A debtor himself for much of his early career, Lincoln felt sharply the scarcity of money on the undeveloped frontier. Lincoln did not want Americans of the future to duplicate his frontier experience. He wanted them to have the benefit of opportunities and institutions which he had not, and among them were banks.

As an Illinois Whig legislator in 1835, Lincoln supported the establishment of the State Bank of Illinois. In the legislature, on January 11, 1837, he made his first widely reprinted speech, a defense of the Illinois Bank. He praised its ability to provide an elastic money supply, its usefulness in ending usury, and its safety as a depository for state funds. The Panic of 1837 forced the Bank to suspend specie payments—an action which made its charter liable to forfeiture. Lincoln supported successful moves to suspend that provision in 1837 and again in 1839. Since the legislature suspended the specie provision only until the next meeting of the legislature, determined Democrats in 1840 sought to adjourn the legislature on December 5 and reconvene on the 7th, which would force the Bank to resume specie payments and meet certain doom. Whigs tried to block the move by remaining away in numbers large enough to prevent the formation of a quorum. Lincoln was caught in the legislative hall by error and—in a celebrated case of political high jinks—departed by the window. The Whigs failed, but the Bank held on through 1841 with the help of another suspension. It failed finally in 1842.

As a dedicated Whig, Lincoln also did battle for the party's cherished principle of national banking. He heaped scorn on arguments that such a bank was unconstitutional, derided President Martin Van Buren's Subtreasury scheme as deflating the currency drastically by keeping the government's revenues locked up in "iron boxes," and championed the resurrection of a national bank. He campaigned strenuously for the Whig national ticket in 1840 on the banking issue, even though the party's standard-bearer, William Henry Harrison, dodged the issue: "I am not a Bank man." By the late 1840s, however, Lincoln recognized that politically the "question of a national bank is at rest" and was not likely to be revived. His personal views did not change.

As President, Lincoln had little time for domestic economic matters during the Civil War, but he did seize the opportunity to provide crucial support for Treasury Secretary Salmon P. Chase's plan to establish a national banking system. At first Lincoln rather cautiously justified the system as necessary for the war effort, but after its establishment he came to praise it as a permanent blessing which at last established a national currency and controlled the money supply.

SOURCES: G. S. Boritt's *Lincoln and the Economics of the American Dream* (Memphis: Memphis State University Press, 1978) is definitive on this and other economic questions.

See also CHASE, SALMON PORTLAND; ECONOMICS; FESSENDEN, WILLIAM PITT; McCULLOCH, HUGH.

Banks, Nathaniel Prentiss (1816–1894) Union general. Banks was born in Waltham, Massachusetts, where at an early age he worked in a cotton mill. The "Bobbin Boy of Massachusetts" became a Democratic politician, entering the United States House of Representatives, but soon was opposing the Kansas-Nebraska Bill. Shortly afterward he joined the Know-Nothing (American) party, and he became a Republican in 1856. He was elected Speaker of the House in that year and, in a brilliant political maneuver, became the presidential nominee of the North Americans (the Know-Nothing party having split into northern and southern factions). He quickly withdrew and threw his support to the Republican nominee, John C. Frémont, thus forging the Republican-nativist alliance which would sweep the Presidency four years later.

From 1858 to 1860 Banks was the Governor of Massachusetts. He was among those New England men "of Democratic antecedents" whom Lincoln suggested to Vice President–elect Hannibal Hamlin for the Cabinet, but Hamlin and Massachusetts antislavery radicals disliked Banks. Lincoln appointed him Major General of Volunteers after war broke out. Banks was a political general with almost no military experience.

The Bobbin Boy went first to Maryland, where he arrested various officials suspected of disloyalty, including nine members of the Maryland legislature. In 1862 he fought "Stonewall" Jackson's forces in Virginia, with the lack of success customarily experienced against that great adversary, and on December 17, 1862, he replaced Benjamin F. Butler in New Orleans as commander of the Department of the Gulf.

Thinking that "a clear majority of the people . . . opposed . . . the war" in the Confederacy, Banks assumed that it would be as easy to restore Louisiana to loyalty as it had been to keep Maryland in the Union. Remove the influence of a few rabid secessionists and otherwise pursue more moderate policies than his predecessor, and "you would have a population in all of these States . . . loyal and true to the Government." Banks quickly aligned himself with local moderate Unionists under the leadership of Michael Hahn. He was opposed by conservatives and a radical group sustained by the patronage of Salmon P. Chase's Treasury Department. The latter group particularly disliked Banks's Negro policies, initiated on January 30, 1863, which required blacks to work for pay on 1-year contracts with masters of their own choosing.

By spring President Lincoln was urging the raising of black troops, a task which Banks performed with alacrity. By summer Lincoln was happy to see steps taken toward reestablishing a loyal state government which would abolish slavery. But by November 5, 1863, the President was "bitterly" disappointed that more along these lines had not been done. Banks pleaded that he really did not control the situation or realize he was responsible for the political reorganization of the state. He shared power with the military governor to such a degree that Banks could not take responsibility for these political questions. He boasted that, were he given the power, the state could be reconstructed "with less public excitement than would attend the enactment of a 'dog law' in one of the Eastern States."

Banks did have military duties too. In the spring of 1863 they included helping Ulysses S. Grant open the Mississippi, which Banks's successful siege of Port Hudson (which fell on July 9, 1863) completed. Diplomacy rather than military considerations dictated his subsequent Texas campaign. "Recent events in Mexico," Lincoln explained on August 5, 1863, with French activities there in mind, ". . . render early action in Texas more important than ever." Banks wanted to move toward Mobile, but on Lincoln's orders he planted the flag in Texas.

On Christmas Eve 1863 the President told Banks "you are master of all" and ordered him to "give us a free-state re-organization of Louisiana, in the shortest possible time." Lincoln did not reject the slow efforts of the radical Free State Committee at work during Banks's absence in Texas, telling the general not to throw any of their useful work away, but he gave tremendous impetus to the moderate Banks-Hahn faction. Banks would not give the voters a chance to restore slavery. In December he said:

> Offer them a Government without slavery, and they will gladly accept it as a necessity resulting from the war. Other questions relating to the condition of the negro, may safely be deferred until this one is secured. If he gains freedom, education, the right to bear arms, the highest privileges accorded to any race and which none has yet proved itself worthy unless it be our own, his best friend may rest content for another year at least.

On January 11, 1864, Banks suspended the slavery provisions of the Louisiana constitution of 1853. Otherwise, under that constitution and the President's Proclamation of Amnesty and Reconstruction of December 8, 1863, he reorganized the government, calling for elections of state officers on February 22, 1864. Only white males qualified by the 1853 constitution who took the loyalty oath could vote. They would also elect delegates to a constitutional convention later in the spring. With about 20 percent of Louisiana's 1860 turnout, Hahn became governor. The voters and officeholders having taken an oath to support the government's antislavery measures, a free-state constitution was assured. The state "will confirm the absolute extinction of slavery," Banks told the President after the elections and, he added ambiguously, "provide for such extension of suffrage as will meet the demands of the age." He had thrown down the gauntlet to the Radicals and greatly widened the gap between the Unionist factions in the state. Lincoln backed Hahn with tremendous patronage powers.

In truth, Banks's conception of the government he had created is unclear. He seems to have seen it as providing "for the gradual restoration of power to the people" only, but "in such manner as to leave the control of affairs still in the hands of the commding General." "It is understood by the people," Banks insisted, "that Mr. Hahn represents a popular power entirely subordinate to the armed occupation of the state for the suppression of the rebellion and the full restoration of the authority of the government." He assured Lincoln that "The election perilled nothing—Had it resulted in the election of an opponent, he would be without power." Yet, after the ratification of the new constitution in September, Banks said: "History will record the fact that all the problems involved in restoration of States . . . have already been solved in Louisiana with a due regard to the elevation of the black and security of the white Race." He never said what would happen when the United States Army left and the Confederates returned. The opponents might well win. Would they be without power? Would the Negro's advance, left to the future, occur? Presumably, he retained his fundamental faith that most Southerners opposed the Confederate regime and merely needed a few new opinion leaders to guide them to free-state ideals. Optimism was his most salient trait.

In July 1864 Banks assured Lincoln that, though "At the beginning of the session negro suffrage was scarcely mentioned—To day it may be regarded as secure." The President urged Hahn privately to work for at least partial black suffrage, but Banks could persuade the constitutional convention only to empower the state legislature to authorize Negro suffrage. The constitution adopted on September 5, 1864, did abolish slavery. Lincoln had been "anxious that it . . . be ratified" and cracked the patronage whip ("let the civil officers in Louisiana, holding [office] under me, know that this, is my wish, and . . . let me know at once who of them openly declare for the constitution, and who of them, if any, decline to so declare").

In the spring of 1864, Banks had led an unsuccessful campaign on the Red River. He had still wanted to move toward Mobile, but General-in-Chief Henry W. Halleck wanted Shreveport. Critics who accused Banks of desiring the campaign to enrich himself on contraband cotton were off the mark, but the campaign was a disaster.

General E. R. S. Canby assumed most of Banks's military powers on May 19, 1864, and Banks left for Washington after the constitution passed in the fall to lobby for readmission of the state. He failed, blocked by Radical Republican opposition in Congress. After Lincoln's death, he maintained good enough relations with the Radicals to win election to the House in 1865, 1866, 1868, and 1870. He sharply opposed the conservative regime President Andrew Johnson supported in Louisiana. In 1872 Banks lost his bid for reelection when he switched to the Liberal Republican party. He continued to pursue an erratic political career by becoming a Democrat and again a Republican before his death.

SOURCES: Fred Harvey Harrington's *Fighting Politician: Major General N. P. Banks* (Philadelphia: University of Pennsylvania Press, 1948) is one of the better biographies of a collateral figure from Lincoln's period. *Abraham Lincoln and Reconstruction: The Louisiana Experiment* (Princeton, N.J.: Princeton University Press, 1948) by Peyton McCrary accuses Banks of deceiving Lincoln and executing a conservative coup in Louisiana. Though not always convincing, it does add essential information on the question. Banks's quotable letters to Lincoln about the "dog law" (December 6, 1863), offering only a government without slavery (December 30, 1863), suffrage fitting the demands of the age (February 25, 1864), gradual restoration of power (January 11, 1864), Hahn's power (March 6, 1864), history's verdict on Louisiana's reconstruction (September 6, 1864), and Negro suffrage (July 25, 1864) are in the Abraham Lincoln Papers, Library of Congress.

See also HAMLIN, HANNIBAL.

Barrett, Oliver Rogers (1873–1950) Greatest of the modern Lincoln collectors. Barrett was born in Jacksonville, Illinois, and raised in Pittsfield, Illinois. His father was a Methodist minister who had served with the Freedmen's Aid Society. In later life Oliver Barrett explained the origin of his interest in collecting Lincolniana as stemming from his being punished for misbehavior in grade school by being forced to sit next to the only Negro in the class. When he rushed home for sympathy, his mother talked to him about Lincoln and emancipation and promised to take him to Springfield. There the Lincoln home and tomb fired his imagination.

Barrett began collecting as a boy, sending a chain letter to eminent Americans asking for their autographs and requesting each to forward it to the next person on the list. His father had saved canceled stamps from the vast amount of Freedman's Aid Society mail he handled, and Barrett sold them and used the money to purchase autographs and letters.

In 1896 Barrett graduated from law school at the University of Michigan. He enlisted in the Fifth Illinois Volunteers for the Spanish-American War but saw no action. He practiced law on his return, and in 1905 he moved to Chicago to continue his practice. Collecting Lincolniana remained a passion. He wrote sparingly— an occasional book review and a denunciation of the Minor forgeries in 1928. He was a generous and helpful collector; he allowed Albert J. Beveridge and Carl Sandburg (among others) to use his collection for research.

And what a collection it was. When it was sold by Parke-Bernet Galleries in 1952, after Illinois citizens failed to raise $220,000 to purchase it for the Illinois State Historical Library, the collection contained one of the earliest examples of Lincoln's handwriting ("Abraham Lincoln his hand and pen he will be good but god

Oliver Rogers Barrett. (Courtesy of the Illinois State Historical Library)

knows When"), three of Mary Todd's earliest surviving letters, Lincoln's letters to Joshua Speed in the 1840s, books owned by Lincoln, Lincoln's letter to John D. Johnston about his father's last illness, Lincoln's scrapbook of the Lincoln-Douglas Debates (which sold to Alfred Whital Stern for $24,000), and numerous other famous manuscripts, relics, and books. The Parke-Bernet Galleries catalog for the sale is an important piece of Lincolniana in itself, and Barrett's collection is the only Lincoln collection on which an entire book has been written: Carl Sandburg's rambling and diffuse *Lincoln Collector: The Story of Oliver R. Barrett's Great Private Collection* (New York: Harcourt, Brace, 1949).

Barton, William Eleazer (1891-1930) Lincoln biographer. Barton was born in Sublette, Illinois, and graduated from Kentucky's Berea College (B.S., 1885; M.S., 1888). He became a Congregationalist minister, having graduated first in his class from Oberlin Theological Seminary in Ohio in 1890. He served as pastor in Robbins, Tennessee (1885–1887), Litchfield, Ohio (1887–1890), Wellington, Ohio (1890–1893), Boston (1893–1899), Oak Park, Illinois (1899–1924), and Nashville, where he lectured at Vanderbilt University and organized the Collegeside Congregational Church.

William Eleazer Barton

Barton's interest in Lincoln came late in life, after a long career as a writer and clergyman. Naturally, his first interest was Lincoln's religion, and his first book on Lincoln was *The Soul of Abraham Lincoln* (New York: George H. Doran, 1920). As a minister of a restrained religion, Barton was not surprised to find that Lincoln's religion existed outside any church. The denominations of Lincoln's frontier environment were given to the excesses of revivalism: "The preachers bellowed and spat and whined, and cultivated an artificial 'holy tone,' and denounced the Methodists and blasphemed the Presbyterians, and painted a hell whose horror even in the backwoods was an atrocity."

Soon Barton became interested in Lincoln's ancestry, and thereafter he devoted a large share of his attention to Lincoln's legitimacy (Barton said he was legitimate, without doubt) and to his mother's illegitimacy (Barton theorized that Nancy Hanks was the illegitimate daughter of Lucy Hanks). *The Paternity of Lincoln* (New York: George H. Doran, 1920), based on genealogical research in musty courthouse records, helped resurrect the reputation of Thomas Lincoln.

Barton was not at all pious or genteel as a biographer, and much of his work on Lincoln has the flavor of debunking about it. *The New York Times Book Review* noted that "He admires Lincoln, but there is no hero worship in his pages and rarely any enthusiasm in bestowing praise." His two-volume *Life of Abraham Lincoln* (Indianapolis, Ind.: Bobbs-Merrill, 1925), dedicated to Calvin Coolidge, was not the definitive work he hoped it would be. Paul M. Angle pointed out that there were 70 pages on ancestry and only 10 on Lincoln's relations with Congress. Barton discovered that Lincoln owned a German-language political newspaper in 1859–1860, and he never shrank from pointing out Lincoln's political machinations. He took the somewhat cynical view that Lincoln's famed attribute of clemency was on the whole unfortunate: "In the long run it had been better for the discipline of the army if he had kept his hands off except in cases where the mitigating circumstances were more pronounced than was usually the case." Professional historians, like Nathaniel W. Stephenson, found Barton's interests "antiquarian" and noted that, in dealing with matters after 1860, he was "out of his proper field."

A Beautiful Blunder (Indianapolis, Ind.: Bobbs-Merrill, 1926) pointed out the mistaken circumstances of Lincoln's famous Bixby letter. *The Women Lincoln Loved* (Indianapolis, Ind.: Bobbs-Merrill, 1927) questioned the "mushy lies" about Lincoln's involvement with Ann Rutledge and began a resurrection of Mary Todd Lincoln's reputation. Barton returned to more familiar territory in *The Lineage of Lincoln* (Indianapolis, Ind.: Bobbs-Merrill, 1929). *Lincoln at Gettysburg* (Indianapolis, Ind.: Bobbs-Merrill, 1930) examined in detail the circumstances of the Gettysburg Address. In truth, Barton was one of the last of the great amateur historians, uncertain of the context of Lincoln's political life and his Presidency. His works are little read today by Lincoln scholars. Benjamin P. Thomas has said aptly, "If he fell short of being a great historian, he was a great historical detective." Barton was most at home with the detailed analysis of some brief episode encrusted with myth over the years.

Barton also collected Lincolniana. At first he sought only a working library, but the collection grew to 4000 volumes, including a substantial part of John E. Burton's collection. Housed in his lifetime in the "Wigwam," a rustic study at his summer home in Foxboro, Massachusetts, the collection was placed by his heirs at the University of Chicago.

SOURCES: There is a fine appraisal of Barton and his work in Benjamin P. Thomas's *Portrait for Posterity: Lincoln and His Biographers* (New Brunswick, N.J.: Rutgers University Press, 1947). Paul M. Angle's review of *The Life of Abraham Lincoln* was in the *Bulletin* of the Lincoln Centennial Association for January 1926; Nathaniel Stephenson reviewed the same book in the New York *Sun* for April 11, 1925; and William MacDonald reviewed Barton's *President Lincoln* in the *New York Times Book Review* for February 12, 1933.

Bates, Edward (1793-1869) Attorney General in the Lincoln administration. Edward Bates was born in Virginia and moved to St. Louis in 1814, where he became a lawyer and politician. In 1847 his service as president of the Chicago River and Harbor Convention, which Lincoln attended, gave him national prominence.

A staunch Whig, Bates was slow to enter the Republican party. Between 1854 and 1856, he was a Know-Nothing. Even as the election of 1860 approached, Bates was hoping to unite nationalists of various party backgrounds by avoiding (and denouncing) agitation of the slavery issue in the hope that the Republicans would have to accept him as a candidate of strength. His presidential hopes were forwarded by the powerful Francis P. Blair family. By March 1860 the Bates-Blair group in Missouri took the name "Republican," and the Missouri state convention nominated Bates for the Presidency.

Bates's Republican credentials were questionable. Not until 1860 did he announce flatly, "I am opposed to the extension of slavery." Nevertheless, at the national Republican convention in Chicago he had the support of some prominent Republicans: Horace Greeley, who sought an alternative to his rival, William H. Seward; the Blairs; and Schuyler Colfax of Indiana, another former Know-Nothing. Their specific strategy was to make Bates the runner-up to Seward on the first ballot. Thereafter, Bates was to garner the former Seward delegates as they drifted away. Bates's mistake was to assume that only he and Seward were viable candidates; meanwhile, Lincoln's managers were gathering second-ballot votes. "We let Greeley run his Bates's machine but got most of them for a second choice," said Lincoln manager Leonard Swett. Lincoln's supporters stressed Bates's unpopularity with German voters because of his Know-Nothing background. And they stressed the weakness of his antislavery record; Bates insisted that only the extension of slavery, not its morality, was an issue (though he personally thought slavery a moral evil). On the first ballot, Bates got only 48 votes, and his total fell to 35 on the second (233 votes were necessary for nomination).

After Lincoln's nomination, Orville Hickman Browning, Lincoln's friend and a one-time Bates supporter, convinced Bates to support the party's nominee. On June 11, 1860, Bates endorsed Lincoln as "a sound, safe, national man" who "could not be sectional if he tried," but he did not campaign actively.

In a meeting in Springfield on December 15, 1860, Lincoln offered Bates an unspecified Cabinet post. When the administration took the reins of government, Bates became the Attorney General. He took a stern view of secession as itself a virtual firing of the first shot. In a March 15 Cabinet meeting, however, he cautioned against reprovisioning Fort Sumter. It was "not a question of lawful right nor physical power," both of which he thought adequate to hold the fort, "but of prudence & patriotism only." He feared that civil war "would soon become . . . social war, & . . . servile war, the horrors of which need not be dwelt upon." Besides, "in several of the misguided states . . . , a large proportion of the people are really lovers of the Union, & anxious to be safely back"; indeed, a "reaction has already begun." Yet two weeks later he was willing to support the President's decision to supply Sumter.

When war came, Bates advocated closing the Southern ports, protecting Washington and St. Louis, and controlling the Mississippi River. He wished "so to conduct the war, as to give the least occasion for social and servile war, . . . and to disturb as little as possible the accustomed occupations of the people." Southerners were "high spirited, and ready enough to fight, but impatient of control" and therefore susceptible to a rather passive Northern strategy of economic strangulation.

In constitutional matters Bates was conservative. Forced to defend Lincoln's suspension of the privilege of the writ of habeas corpus in the face of Roger B. Taney's hostile Merryman decision, Bates argued that the Constitution established three independently sovereign coordinate branches of government and the judiciary could not impede the executive's means of suppressing insurrections. Yet he remained somewhat in awe of Chief Justice Taney's reputation throughout his tenure in office and was the only member of the Cabinet to attend Taney's burial in 1864.

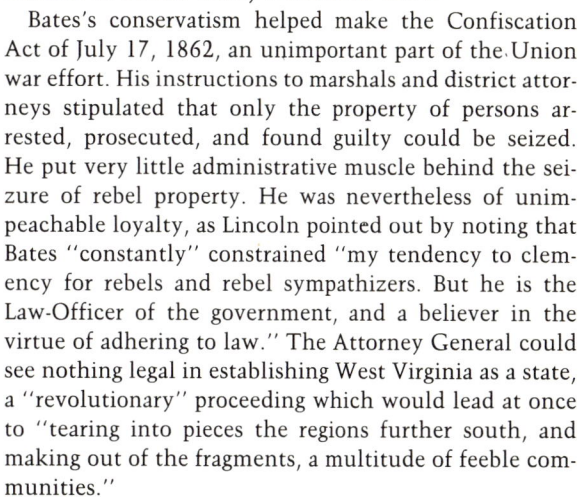

Bates's conservatism helped make the Confiscation Act of July 17, 1862, an unimportant part of the Union war effort. His instructions to marshals and district attorneys stipulated that only the property of persons arrested, prosecuted, and found guilty could be seized. He put very little administrative muscle behind the seizure of rebel property. He was nevertheless of unimpeachable loyalty, as Lincoln pointed out by noting that Bates "constantly" constrained "my tendency to clemency for rebels and rebel sympathizers. But he is the Law-Officer of the government, and a believer in the virtue of adhering to law." The Attorney General could see nothing legal in establishing West Virginia as a state, a "revolutionary" proceeding which would lead at once to "tearing into pieces the regions further south, and making out of the fragments, a multitude of feeble communities."

Bates gave unreserved support to Lincoln's Emancipation Proclamation when the President proposed the Proclamation on July 22, 1862. In part, his support was a function of his hope that Lincoln was more likely than Congress to provide for colonization of freed Negroes. Bates always opposed policies which might lead to Negro equality with whites in America and particularly disliked the employment of Negroes as soldiers, a policy which he thought tantamount to recognizing Negro equality. Despite that dislike, the Attorney General delivered an opinion to the President which suggested that Negro soldiers merited equal pay with whites. Lincoln ignored the opinion. In May 1864, when the administration learned of the Fort Pillow massacre, he reminded the President of his early warnings of "the great probability of such horrid results." Nevertheless, Bates saw no choice but to execute anyone involved in the massacre unless the Confederate government disavowed the act and surrendered the commanding officers.

Bates came to believe that Lincoln, though an admirable and conservative man, was too prone to compromise with the Radical Republicans. By 1863 he felt that the President was considering the "civil and political equality" of Negroes, aspects of citizenship which Bates, in an opinion written on November 29, 1862, did not deem essential trappings of citizenship for even a free-born Negro. Because of his close ties to Missouri, where Republicans had the bitterest intraparty struggles in the Union, Bates was especially hostile to Radicals and hopeful that Lincoln would side with the Missouri conservative Republicans. Lincoln was so disgusted with Missouri's factional disputes that he thought he had no friends in the state, as he told Bates in October 1863.

Bates repeatedly denounced "that class of politicians who are not ashamed to call themselves *Radicals*, and who . . . openly and contemptuously violate the constitution of their country." At times, he seemed to see Radical Republicans as an almost alien force, an emanation from radical Germans, who in 1863, seemed to be forming a "cabal" in order "to control, if possible, the Government of the Country, *as foreigners*." He always saw the Radicals as insincere politicians exploiting the Negro issue for party gain and essentially uninterested in the Negro's welfare. In Bates's mind, there was no such thing as Reconstruction, and his program for peace included simply universal amnesty, restoration of property rights, and the immediate resumption by rebel states of equal constitutional status in the Union.

In 1864 Bates supported Lincoln as "immeasurably preferable to his opponents—Our only chance of a return to law and order—our only means to keep down the reckless revolutionary spirit of the Radicals." He thought that the Baltimore convention which renominated Lincoln contained "some true, honest men" but "also a large amount of falsehood and treachery." It was "one of the few" conventions he ever knew "which did all that in it lay, to defeat its own nomination." Bates had suffered a stroke in May which affected his speech, and he was feeling "old, and . . . very old fashioned." "I belong to no party," he wrote on July 25, 1864. "When the Whig party committed suicide, in 1856, . . . I died with it."

Bates resigned from the Cabinet in November 1864. He hoped Lincoln would make him Chief Justice of the Supreme Court—he sought only "a brief term of service in that eminent position," mostly for the honor of it—but was disappointed. After Lincoln's assassination, he criticized the decision to try the alleged assassins by a military commission. Having returned to Missouri, he railed against martial law and Radical Reconstruction.

SOURCES: One of the less influential members of Lincoln's Cabinet, Bates has had great influence on historical writing on the period through his famous diary: Howard K. Beale, ed., *The Diary of Edward Bates, 1859–1866* (Washington: United States Government Printing Office, 1933). The only biography is Marvin R. Cain's *Lincoln's Attorney General: Edward Bates of Missouri* (Columbia: University of Missouri Press, 1965). Bates's letter to Lincoln on Fort Sumter (March 15, 1861), memorandum on strategy (April 15, 1861), opinion on West Virginia (December 27, 1862), opinion on Fort Pillow (May 4, 1864), denunciation of Radicals and the Baltimore convention (extracts from a letter to Titian J. Coffey, June 25, 1864), and request to be apppointed Chief Justice (October 13, 1864) are in the Abraham Lincoln Papers, Library of Congress.

See also HABEAS CORPUS.

Beard   See BEDELL, GRACE.

Grace Bedell as she looked about 10 years after writing her famous letter to Lincoln.

Bedell, Grace (1848–1936)   The impulsive 11-year-old girl who wrote a letter to Republican presidential nominee Abraham Lincoln suggesting that he grow a beard. Grace's father, Norman Bedell, a Republican stove and carriage maker in Albion and Westfield, New York, had carried home a campaign broadside which printed the Republican platform and the portraits of Lincoln and Hannibal Hamlin. Grace, two of whose older brothers were Democrats who teased her about her ardent Republicanism, was disappointed to find her hero's "face . . . so thin." On October 15, 1860, she wrote "Hon A B Lincoln" her famous letter recommending whiskers.

It cannot be said precisely that Grace's letter prompted Lincoln to grow his beard. His reply, written on October 19, far from saying that he would grow a beard, suggested that he doubted the wisdom of such action. "As to the whiskers," he wrote, "having never worn any, do you not think people would call it a piece of silly affect-[at]ion if I were to begin it now?" There were, however, many complaints about the portraits used in Lincoln's campaign, and some politicians even had the temerity to tell the candidate that he should grow whiskers and wear standing collars. By mid-November, Lincoln was letting his beard grow.

A fully bearded President-elect left Springfield for Washington on February 11, 1861. Five days later, the train stopped in Westfield, New York. Lincoln had spoken about the girl to George W. Patterson, a prominent Westfield Republican who boarded the train in northern Pennsylvania. When Lincoln appeared on the train platform, he dodged making a political address to the crowd of New Yorkers and called for his little correspondent from Westfield. When Grace appeared, he kissed her and said that he had taken her advice. Newspapers and humorists spread the story far and wide, but it was a temporary flutter, and the story was largely forgotten. Grace married George Billings after the Civil War, and in 1870 they moved to Kansas. There Billings farmed and became a banker in Delphos. The family's descendants are still bankers in Delphos.

John C. Power, the custodian of the Lincoln tomb, and William H. Herndon, Lincoln's law partner and biographer, resurrected the story in the 1870s and 1880s. In the 1930s George A. Dondero, a Michigan Congressman and Lincoln collector, gained possession of Grace's letter and willed it to the Burton Historical Collection of the Detroit Public Library, where it still rests. Lincoln's letter to Grace is currently in private hands; it sold for $20,000 in the 1960s, and it was offered for sale at $65,000 in 1976.

SOURCES: See Frederick L. Trump, *Lincoln's Little Girl* (Salina, Kansas: Heritage Books, [1977]).

Bennett, James Gordon (1795–1872)   Editor of the New York *Herald* during Lincoln's administration. One of the most powerful editors in the country, James Gordon Bennett was erratic in political preference, though he consistently opposed the antislavery movement. In 1856 the usually Democratic *Herald* supported Republican John C. Frémont, but in 1860 it supported Stephen A. Douglas. After Lincoln's nomination, Joseph M. Medill of the Chicago *Tribune* went to New York to persuade Bennett not to make mischief for the Republicans. He reported "his 'Satanic Majesty'" to be "too rich" and powerful to be influenced by promises of office, but he thought him susceptible to promises of "Social position"—invitations to "dinner or tea at the White house."

Bennett wrote to Lincoln occasionally during the war—significantly, almost always *in answer* to Lincoln's letters. Apologizing on September 28, 1861, for the denial of a pass to a *Herald* reporter, Lincoln promised Bennett "that the administration will not discriminate against the Herald, especially while it sustains us so generously, and the cause of the country so ably as it has been doing." In 1862 Bennett pledged his support for recruiting, for enlarging the army, and for operations in the field, but he was ominously silent about other administration policies. The *Herald* repeatedly attacked Lincoln's "nigger worshipping policy." Bennett got along rather well with Mrs. Lincoln, but his correspondence with the President was stiff and formal.

It is a myth that Lincoln "bought" the support of the *Herald* in 1864 by offering Bennett the Paris mission. The offer was made through intermediaries, and Bennett turned it down on March 6, 1865, because he was too old and felt that he could best improve America's relations with France through his newspaper. However, the *Herald* did not support Lincoln for the Presidency in 1864. It characterized Lincoln and his opponent George B. McClellan as "Two men of mediocre talent" and hoped almost to election day that the electoral college would choose Ulysses S. Grant for president.

SOURCES: Medill's letter to Lincoln about Bennett (June 19, 1860) is in the Abraham Lincoln Papers, Library of Congress. Bennett's course in 1864 is the subject of John J. Turner, Jr., and Michael D'Innocenzo's "The President and the Press: Lincoln, James Gordon Bennett and the Election of 1864," *Lincoln Herald*, LXXVI (Summer 1974), 63–69. They are doubtless correct that Lincoln never gained the *Herald*'s support, but they ignore the value of the *Herald*'s neutrality in the election. The best survey of Bennett's relationship with the administration is David Quentin Voigt's "'Too Pitchy to Touch'—President Lincoln and Editor Bennett," *The Abraham Lincoln Quarterly*, VI (September 1950), 139–161.

Berry, William Franklin (1811–1835) Lincoln's business partner in New Salem. William F. Berry was the son of a minister. He had attended Illinois College in Jacksonville and was a corporal in Captain Lincoln's company in the Black Hawk War. When they returned from the campaign, Berry bought James Herndon's share of a store he owned with his brother J. Rowan Herndon. Lincoln soon purchased the brother's share, and Berry and Lincoln were partners.

Berry was as poor as Lincoln, and both bought the "old stock of goods, upon credit." The store was not a "grocery" (where liquor was sold by the drink), but it doubtless handled liquor in larger quantities as most such stores did. On March 6, 1833, Berry and Lincoln were issued a tavern license, but Berry alone signed the bond for the license. Early in 1833, with their pay from service in the Black Hawk War, the partners went deeper

In a cartoon which comes close to foreshadowing the symbol of the Republicans, the elephant, cartoonist Frank Bellew lampooned James Gordon Bennett, easily recognized by his crossed eyes, for his vacillating course in 1864. After dumping Lincoln and Ulysses S. Grant, Bennett helps George B. McClellan mount the Herald elephant. This rare cartoon appeared in the New York humor magazine Phun.

into debt to buy the stock of Reuben Radford's store, recently vandalized by the Clary's Grove boys, from William G. ("Slicky Bill") Greene (who turned a quick profit in his sale to Lincoln and Berry).

Lincoln summarized the partners' experience succinctly: "they did nothing but get deeper and deeper in debt." Berry was reputedly a heavy drinker, and the partnership had disastrous consequences. In April 1833 Lincoln sold his share to Berry. The store, as Lincoln put it later in life, "winked out." Suits against the partners for failure to pay their debts resulted in judgments against Lincoln's personal property which took his horse and surveying instruments—returned to him by Greene and James Short after a sheriff's sale. Berry died in 1835, and the accumulated indebtedness of the partners, now entirely Lincoln's problem, amounted to a staggering $1100. Lincoln called it the "national debt" and was repaying those debts well into the 1840s.

SOURCES: See Benjamin P. Thomas, *Lincoln's New Salem* (Springfield, Ill.: Abraham Lincoln Association, 1934), and Harry E. Pratt, *The Personal Finances of Abraham Lincoln* (Springfield, Ill.: Abraham Lincoln Association, 1943). Zarel C. Spears and Robert S. Barton's *Berry and Lincoln, Frontier Merchants: The Store that "Winked Out"* (New York: Stratford House, 1947) is a labored but interesting defense of Berry, which belittles the "national debt" as a myth.

Beveridge, Albert Jeremiah (1862–1927) Politician and Lincoln biographer. The son of a Union soldier, Albert J. Beveridge was born in Ohio, grew up in Illinois, and graduated from Asbury College (now DePauw) in Indiana. He became a lawyer in Indianapolis and in 1899 was elected to the Senate. He was a Republican noted for his advocacy of imperialism and reform, and by 1912

Albert Jeremiah Beveridge

he was a Progressive. In 1916 he rejoined the Republicans. In 1919 he completed a widely acclaimed biography of John Marshall.

When he lost a race for the Senate in 1922, Beveridge turned to writing a biography of Lincoln, whom he saw as the natural heir of Marshall's nationalism. He immersed himself in original sources. In exchange for recommending the publication of Jesse W. Weik's *The Real Lincoln*, fellow-Republican Weik gave him access to the William H. Herndon collection of letters and reminiscences about Lincoln's early years. Collector Oliver R. Barrett allowed him to use his collection of Lincoln materials, and Beveridge used newspapers and published legislative journals as no Lincoln scholar had before. Robert Todd Lincoln, a conservative Republican, refused him access to his collection of his father's papers.

Beveridge was surprised to find how much "slush and rot" and "rubbish" had been written about Lincoln. He became convinced of the "truthfulness and trustworthiness" of Herndon, a faith which led him to be too harsh in judging Thomas Lincoln, to put too much credence in the Ann Rutledge romance, and to treat Mary Todd Lincoln unfairly even to the point of repeating the story that Lincoln left her at the altar on their wedding day. More important, Beveridge fell for Herndon's inflation of his own importance in Lincoln's life. Beveridge's dismay at Lincoln's "pettifogging" opposition to the Mexican War led him to endorse Herndon's complaints about Lincoln's opposition to the war. Herndon was pictured as the "carburetor in the great man's career," steering him more directly onto the antislavery path in the 1850s.

Beveridge was convinced that "the Lincoln of Illinois could not, by any possibility, have been the Lincoln of the Second Inaugural or the Gettysburg speech." When he explored Lincoln's career in the Illinois House of Representatives, Beveridge was surprised not only at the historians' neglect of the official sources for the period but also at Lincoln's narrow party regularity and political craftiness. Beveridge called the attempt to move the state capital to Springfield by promising support for a grandiose Internal Improvements Bill "a debauch of log-rolling." Lincoln was no leader; he "accurately registered . . . dominant popular thought and feeling."

Shocked by Lincoln's lack of nationalism in his term in the United States House of Representatives, Beveridge found that Lincoln still was not the heir of Marshall in the 1850s. The real nationalist appeared to be Stephen A. Douglas. Beveridge believed that Douglas had been "written down in order to write Lincoln up," and many readers agreed that Douglas was more the hero of Beveridge's biography than Lincoln. In part, Beveridge's fondness for Douglas was a function of his rather pro-Southern interpretation of the politics of the 1850s. Beveridge blamed the Civil War on abolitionist agitation, unnecessary in light of slavery's probable natural demise from economic inutility.

The work of an avowed imperialist, and one intensely committed to Anglo-Saxon supremacy, Beveridge's biography was deeply rooted in the racial verities of his day. He simply could not see heroism in Lincoln's antebellum career, for "the whole wretched mess would have been straightened out without the white race killing itself off, if the abolitionists had let matters alone." The nation, he thought, should not have been liable to sacrifice for the Negro.

Despite his reservations about it, Beveridge was the first to give Lincoln's early political career careful consideration. He had a passion for facts (as well as an amateur's faith that their accumulation would lead to truth without interpretive bias) which led to a notably rich account. His thoroughness led Beveridge to study Lincoln's times almost as carefully as the man himself, and the result was to bring the Lincoln theme squarely into the mainstream of American history as it was then being interpreted by professional scholars. His is still the best single account of Lincoln's life before the Presidency.

Tragically, Beveridge died before he could finish his biography. *Abraham Lincoln, 1809–1858* (Boston: Houghton Mifflin) appeared in two volumes posthumously in 1928.

SOURCES: Two excellent appraisals of Beveridge's work are in Benjamin P. Thomas, *Portrait for Posterity: Lincoln and His Biographers* (New Brunswick, N.J.: Rutgers University Press, 1947) and John Braeman, *Albert J. Beveridge: American Nationalist* (Chicago: University of Chicago Press, 1971).

Bible   *See* RELIGION.

Bibliography   Like Lincoln collectors, Lincoln bibliographers appeared almost immediately after the President's death. Indeed, they were often one and the same, and bibliographers most often saw their task as service to collectors. Less than six months after Lincoln's assassination, William V. Spencer published the first Lincoln bibliography as an appendix to his *Lincolniana* (Boston: privately printed, 1865).

Charles Henry Hart was an 18-year-old law student at the University of Pennsylvania when Lincoln was shot, and he began very soon to collect Lincolniana. By March 1866 Hart was suggesting to William H. Herndon that he add a bibliography of Lincolniana to his proposed biography of his famous law partner. Herndon liked the idea, but he moved much too slowly for young Mr. Hart, who entered a partnership with boastful collector Andrew H. Boyd to produce the *Memorial Lincoln Bibliography* (Albany: Andrew Boyd, 1870). It listed several hundred printed books and pamphlets as well as prints, medals, broadsides, and other ephemera. Hart had written many of the authors and publishers to find the number of copies printed.

Collectors, especially the so-called "Big Five" Lincoln collectors (Daniel Fish, William H. Lambert, Charles W. McLellan, Joseph B. Oakleaf, and Judd Stewart) continued to dominate bibliography. At the turn of the century Fish sought to systematize the collecting. Ruling out everything but books and pamphlets, he listed about 800 items in his *Lincoln Literature* (Minneapolis: Public Library Board, 1900). Aided by George Thomas Ritchie's *List of Lincolniana in the Library of Congress* (Washington, D.C.: Government Printing Office, 1903), he expanded his list to 1080 items in 1906 for a new edition of John G. Nicolay and John Hay's *Abraham Lincoln: Complete Works*, issued by the Francis D. Tandy Company.

Coping with the spate of publications prompted by the centennial of Lincoln's birth in 1909 led Oakleaf to compile a *Lincoln Bibliography* (Cedar Rapids: Torch Press, 1925) with 1576 titles not listed by Fish 19 years before. Only a year later, John W. Starr, Jr.'s *Bibliography of Lincolniana* (privately printed) noted another 380 titles.

All these early efforts paled by comparison with Jay Monaghan's massive *Lincoln Bibliography, 1839–1939*, 2 vols. (Springfield: Illinois State Historical Library, 1943–1945) with its 3958 titles found by research in numerous public and private collections. It remains the standard Lincoln bibliography for libraries, collectors, and bookdealers. For titles published since that time the collector must use the bibliographies published each year in *Lincoln Lore*, the monthly bulletin of the Louis A. Warren Lincoln Library and Museum.

Lincoln bibliographies are notorious for their inclusiveness, and their compilers generally admitted readily that the bulk of the items listed contained spurious, occasionally even worthless, information. Critical bibliographies are not plentiful. Except for Paul M. Angle's *Shelf of Lincoln Books* (New Brunswick, N.J.: Rutgers University Press, 1946), one is forced to consult the bibliographies in biographies of Lincoln. Among the best are those in Benjamin P. Thomas, *Abraham Lincoln: A Biography* (New York: Alfred A. Knopf, 1952), Richard N. Current, *The Lincoln Nobody Knows* (New York: McGraw-Hill, 1958), James G. Randall and Richard N. Current, *Lincoln the President*, 4 vols. (New York: Dodd, Mead, 1945–1955), Reinhard H. Luthin, *The Real Abraham Lincoln* (Englewood Cliffs, N.J.: Prentice-Hall, 1960), and G. S. Boritt, *Lincoln and the Economics of the American Dream* (Memphis: Memphis State University Press, 1978).

Biographers "Biographies as generally written are not only misleading, but false," Lincoln told his partner William H. Herndon, when he suggested that he read a biography of Edmund Burke.

> The author of this life . . . makes a wonderful hero out of his subject. He magnifies his perfections—if he had any—and suppresses his imperfections. . . . I've wondered why book-publishers and merchants don't have blank biographies on their shelves, always ready for an emergency; so that, if a man happens to die, his heirs or his friends, if they wish to perpetuate his memory, can purchase one already written, but with blanks. These blanks they can at their pleasure fill up with rosy sentences full of high-sounding praise. In most instances they commemorate a lie, and cheat prosperity out of the truth. History is not history unless it is the truth.

Lincoln's cynical assessment of biographers certainly applies to his earliest biographers, who wrote for campaign purposes in 1860. None of these has stood the test of time, and they are read today, if at all, only for insight on Republican campaign strategy and for the origins of Lincoln myths. In the latter respect one biography written in Lincoln's lifetime was important and paved the way for a nearly endless succession of popular writers. William Makepeace Thayer's *The Pioneer Boy, and How He Became President* (Boston: Walker, Wise, 1863) was a boy's life of Lincoln written "to show that 'the boy is father of the man,' showing the young that pluck and not luck makes the man, when it is accompanied with patience, perseverence, application sobriety, honesty, &c." Thayer was one of the more prolific producers of rags-to-riches success literature, and inspirational biographies of Lincoln, like Dale Carnegie's *Lincoln the Unknown* (New York: Century, 1932), continued to appear well into the twentieth century. Inspiration through the life of historical figures is no longer a staple in this age of the "antihero," but one can still get brief glimpses of the phenomenon in the regular appearance of two essentially spurious pieces of popular Lincolniana, the "You cannot" axioms and the "failure quiz." The former, originally written by a capitalist apologist, the Reverend William J. H. Boetcker, attach Lincoln's name to catchphrases he never spoke ("You cannot help the poor by destroying the rich"). The latter portray Lincoln as a failure who overcame the odds to reach success in 1860 (in fact, his early career was reasonably successful, and he lost only one election in his life by popular vote).

Serious biography began with Josiah G. Holland's hastily written *Life of Abraham Lincoln* (Springfield, Mass.: Gurdon Bill, 1866). In its uncritical acceptance of Republicanism and its antislavery zeal, it set the political tone of most Lincoln biographies until the twentieth century. Holland, however, had not known Lincoln in life, and since Lincoln was not a diarist and since many of his personal papers were still in the family's possession, the first era of Lincoln biography was dominated by men who had known him personally. Isaac N. Arnold utilized his political familiarity with Lincoln's life in his *History of Abraham Lincoln and the Overthrow of Slavery* (Chicago: Clarke & Co., 1866) and his later *Life of Abraham Lincoln* (Chicago: Jensen, McClurg, 1885), and Arnold's ardent antislavery convictions led him more and more to see Lincoln's life as a pilgrimage toward the Emancipation Proclamation. So uncomplicated was his picture of Lincoln's antislavery views that, as David M. Potter has said, the reader "would scarcely recognize that Lincoln was not an abolitionist himself."

Throughout the nineteenth century no biographer much complicated the simple political picture Arnold and Holland established. Complexities were seen only in the works of those Lincoln associates who chose to stress their knowledge of his personal life. Ward Hill Lamon helped discredit the facts that few wanted to believe in his somewhat unflattering *Life of Abraham Lincoln* (Boston: James R. Osgood, 1872) by choosing a Democrat as a ghostwriter, Chauncey F. Black. William H. Herndon and Jesse W. Weik's *Herndon's Lincoln: The True Story of a Great Life* (Chicago: Belford, Clark, 1889) reached only a limited audience because of the ineptitude of its publisher. And Henry Clay Whitney's

Life on the Circuit with Lincoln (Boston: Estes and Lauriat, 1892) failed to reach many readers because of its author's undisciplined intellect. Nevertheless, these three works were destined to exercise considerable influence on Lincoln's biography because of the richness and intimacy of their personal details. In this regard, Herndon's is still an absolutely indispensable work; knowledge of Lincoln's view of biography, to cite a pertinent example, comes only from that source. These men were Westerners, and their work gained in influence also because the earthy anecdotes they provided, in sharp contrast to the mid-Victorian pieties of Holland and his ilk, came to be useful to historians newly impressed around the turn of the century with the importance of the frontier in America's past. In sum, they helped shift the focus from Lincoln as a moral reformer to Lincoln as a robust specimen of the democratic west. They breathed life back into a figure in danger of becoming a statue, but they left biographers with a problem which went unresolved for many years. Herndon and Whitney knew Lincoln well only before he left Illinois, and their Western anecdotalism made him appear so folksy, if not crude, that his presidential greatness seemed unaccountable.

John G. Nicolay and John Hay, Lincoln's private secretaries in the Civil War years, provided the greatest analysis of Lincoln's Presidency in their huge *Abraham Lincoln: A History* (New York: Century, 1890). The only work based on Lincoln's private papers until after 1947 (when they were opened to the general public), Nicolay and Hay's history had the blessing of Lincoln's son Robert and was most decidedly "official." Even so, David M. Potter has noted that "the fullness and the candor of the record is astonishing." They rarely distorted the record or suppressed unpleasantnesses in the administration, but, as Potter notes, "they always defended that position whatever it might be." They also published the first extensive edition of Lincoln's works. Like *Herndon's Lincoln*, theirs is still a useful book, for their firsthand knowledge of the Lincoln administration was unsurpassed by any writer.

Herndon died in 1891, Lamon in 1893, Nicolay in 1901, and Whitney and Hay in 1905, and Lincoln biography thereafter lay in the hands of a new, post-Civil War generation. Uncritical acceptance of reminiscences, Herndon's great fault, became the target of numerous capable writers like Ida M. Tarbell. An enthusiastic journalist, she uncovered many new Lincoln sources, used them to great effect, and reached a large popular audience, in part through her writing ability and in part because she never seemed, as Herndon had, to belittle the sixteenth President. Her *Early Life of Abraham Lincoln* (New York: S. S. McClure, 1896) and her *Life of Abraham Lincoln* (New York: Doubleday & McClure, 1900) gave broad exposure to her view that the frontier environment of Lincoln's youth made him quintessentially American and therefore capable of leading a democratic nation through its worst test. "The horse, the dog, the ox, the chin fly, the plow, the hog," she wrote, "these companions of his youth became interpreters of his meaning, solvers of his problems in his great necessity, of making men understand and follow him." Hers was the most important influence on Illinois poet and journalist Carl Sandburg, whose *Abraham Lincoln: The Prairie Years* (New York: Harcourt, Brace, 1926), fully in the Tarbell tradition, was the beginning of the longest biography ever written of any American.

So explosive were the political issues of the Civil War that an Englishman, Godfrey Benson, Lord Charnwood, was the first to write a balanced book, asking what might be called the "hard" questions about Lincoln's statesmanship. Potter describes them this way:

> Did Lincoln temporize too much on slavery? Was there a quality of "cheap opportunism" in his political record? Did his policy at Fort Sumter differ from Buchanan's enough to justify the customary practice of gibbeting the silly old man while leaving Lincoln free from criticism? Was he, in the last analysis, responsible for precipitating the Civil War?

Charnwood concluded, more often than not, in Lincoln's favor, and in doing so he added a new dimension to Lincoln biography: he noted his universal significance, not as an American hero or the patron of a race in bondage, but as a symbol of democratic government everywhere. Charnwood's was to remain the best one-volume life of Lincoln for three and a half decades.

The future, however, did not lie with the Tarbells, Sandburgs, and British Lords—at least not entirely. They had the larger reading audiences perhaps, but they lost out in prestige to a new development in American biographical writing, the professional historian. Nathaniel W. Stephenson was a harbinger of this trend, but James G. Randall provided its first landmark book, *Constitutional Problems Under Lincoln* (New York: D. Appleton, 1926), and was for almost thirty years thereafter its chief spokesman and practitioner. His book was characteristic of the movement. Not a full biography at all, it was highly analytical and focused on a specialized problem somewhat removed from the layman's grasp.

Albert J. Beveridge was a crucial transitional figure. Not an academic professional, this former Republican Senator prided himself, and justifiably so, on his immersion in manuscript and newspaper sources and on his own thorough understanding of politics. His methods, in other words, were as professional as any academic's in his day, and he had professionals read his work in draft. The result, the posthumous *Abraham Lincoln, 1809–1858* (Boston: Houghton Mifflin, 1928), set a new standard for thoroughness in Lincoln biography. Even academic readers boggled at the "rivulet of text" in "a meadow of footnotes." Thematically, Beveridge and Stephenson offered a Lincoln for the Progressive Era, the heyday of American nationalism. Stephenson had a marked distaste for any opposition to Lincoln's Union-saving and Beveridge, an imperialist in his political career, detested any political move not calculated to strengthen American power. Since the Senator did not live to write on the Civil War period, this had the ironic effect of causing him to belittle Lincoln. Beveridge could not stomach Lincoln's opposition to the Mexican War or his apparent willingness to risk national unity to liberate the black race. Therefore, the real hero of his biography was Stephen A. Douglas, and Lincoln appeared as a somewhat narrowly partisan figure. The critical note was substantially new in treatments of Lincoln's Republican political milieu, especially by a Republican, and it was a harbinger of things to come in what Don E. Fehrenbacher calls the "golden age" of Lincoln scholarship.

That age was initiated symbolically in 1929 by the fiasco surrounding the *Atlantic Monthly*'s publication of Wilma Frances Minor's forgeries concerning the Lincoln-Ann Rutledge romance. The amateurs, Tarbell and Sandburg, fell for them, and the professionals, most importantly Paul M. Angle, the Executive Secretary of the Lincoln Centennial Association, denounced them roundly. The professionals won, Angle's organization became the Abraham Lincoln Association and the principal sponsor of scholarly editing and writing on Lincoln for about thirty years, and the romance of personal life took a back seat to monographs on Lincoln *and* some political or social subject or other.

Randall soon became a spokesman for the only school of interpretation of Lincoln and the Civil War to have a widely recognized name, Revisionism. Though Lincoln fared well at the hands of the Revisionists, the Republican party did not, and it was an interpretation fraught with possibilities for sharp criticism. Born of the American post-World War disgust for warfare and of the intense antiradicalism of its anti-Bolshevist conclusion, Revisionism pictured the Civil War as an unnecessary conflict brought on by bungling politicians and shrill radicals who exaggerated sectional problems for political gain. Compromise, Douglas, George B. McClellan, and the Northern Democratic party were its principal beneficiaries—none of them readily identifiable with Lincoln's affections—but Lincoln was saved from a general debunking by his unvindictive character. This made him the perfect foil of the Radical Republicans and their Reconstruction plans and saved him any substantial drop in esteem. Indeed, Edgar Lee Master's vitriolic *Lincoln the Man* (New York: Dodd, Mead, 1931) remains the only full-length biography of Lincoln thoroughly debunking in spirit. Occasionally Revisionism bordered on a sharply critical view of Lincoln, as when T. Harry William's *Lincoln and the Radicals* (Madison: University of Wisconsin Press, 1941) depicted him as the hapless victim of the Radicals, but most authors retained their admiration for him by seeing his assassination as severing him from the results of Republican policy after 1865. The greatest fruit of Revisionism and of the era of professionalism in Lincoln biography was Randall's four-volume biography, *Lincoln the President* (New York: Dodd, Mead, 1945–1955), completed after his death by Richard N. Current, and easily the finest biography of Lincoln ever written.

Early Revisionism was antipolitical. Beveridge, usually called the first Revisionist though he never heard the term so used, and Randall were both embarrassed by Lincoln's career in the Whig party. Williams faulted Lincoln for failing to master his party, but Reinhard H. Luthin, the last of the great Revisionists, was also the first to realize that Lincoln was a master politician and patronage wielder and to celebrate this trait. Benjamin P. Thomas's *Abraham Lincoln: A Biography* (New York: Alfred A. Knopf, 1952) replaced Charnwood's biography as the best single-volume life by embracing the important insights of Revisionism, the legitimacy of Democratic party opposition, for example, but avoiding any of its more tendentious assertions. Luthin also published a fine one-volume biography, *The Real Abraham Lincoln* (Englewood Cliffs, N.J.: Prentice-Hall, 1960), but it failed to receive its just acclaim because his writing style was unequal to Thomas's and because Revisionism was on the wane.

David Donald, the first Lincoln scholar to criticize Revisionism sharply, did so in part by asserting that Lincoln pragmatically mastered the inflexible Radicals. He went on to dismiss the Radical bogey as well, in *Lincoln Reconsidered: Essays on the Civil War Era* (New York: Alfred A. Knopf, 1956). The real death blow to Revisionism came from areas outside Lincoln scholarship. A new appreciation for the efforts of Northern reformers in Reconstruction, a new feeling after World War II that wars for oppressed races were worth fighting, and the civil rights movement of the 1950s changed perspectives. Revisionism retained some grip only by virtue of the antiradicalism of the Cold War, but things changed rapidly in the 1960s when, for the first time in three decades, substantial numbers of American reformers and social critics once again called themselves "radicals."

Harry V. Jaffa's *Crisis of the House Divided: An Interpretation of the Issues in the Lincoln-Douglas Debates* (Garden City: Doubleday, 1959) redrew the line of principle separating Douglas and Lincoln which Beveridge had obscured over thirty years before. Don E. Fehrenbacher's *Prelude to Greatness: Lincoln in the 1850's* (Stanford: Stanford University Press, 1962) gave renewed emphasis to Lincoln's antislavery convictions. Without quite duplicating the uncritical abolitionism of Isaac N. Arnold, scholarship began to draw Lincoln closer to the Radicals and principled antislavery men in his party, a movement which culminated in Stephen B. Oates's biography, *With Malice Toward None: The Life of Abraham Lincoln* (New York: Harper & Row, 1977).

Oates's enthusiasm and Fehrenbacher's sturdy, if judicious, admiration for Lincoln, however, were exceptions to the tone of academic scholarship on Lincoln in the 1960s and 1970s. Though no full-fledged biography embodied this view, the enthusiasms and disappointments of the 1960s led to the period of Lincoln's lowest esteem in a hundred years of historical writing. Lincoln's era was one of universal racism, and the sixteenth President was a man of his era. Civil rights activists found Lincoln's speeches unquotable for the cause of racial equality—to their surprise—and in shock liberal historians quickly demoted him to the malign mainstream of American history. Leon F. Litwack's *North of Slavery* (Chicago: University of Chicago Press, 1961) revealed the astonishing pervasiveness of racism in the North up to the Civil

War and claimed that Lincoln "accurately and consistently reflected the thoughts and prejudices of most Americans." *Ebony* editor Lerone F. Bennett answered the question "Was Abe Lincoln a White Supremacist?" in the affirmative in the February 1968 issue of his popular magazine for blacks. The modern civil rights era became a brief but dark Age of Animus against Lincoln.

The Watergate political crisis quickly revived the reputation of those Presidents once considered great, and "Honest Abe" became an important standard of rectitude for an era in which political virtue seemed to be declining. Careful research showed that Lincoln's antislavery views were genuinely liberal in their context of pervasive racism. Oates's biography, which was soon compared with Thomas's and Luthin's as among the best one-volume biographies, was an answer to the view of Lincoln taken in the Age of Animus.

No complete biography has appeared since, but G. S. Boritt's *Lincoln and the Economics of the American Dream* (Memphis: Memphis State University Press, 1978) returned to the part of Lincoln's life which Lamon, Herndon, and Beveridge had left in such an unappealing state, irreconcilable with any view of Lincoln's presidential greatness. By stressing the sophistication and consistency of Lincoln's devotion to the Whig vision of economic growth with its increased opportunities for the common man, Boritt depicted a newly unified portrait of Lincoln. Leaving behind the discomfort which liberal historians of the New Deal era had felt with Lincoln's devotion to the party of banks and tariffs, he showed that Lincoln was steadily devoted to principle throughout his political career. There was no gap between the frontier politician and the statesman of White House days.

SOURCES: See Benjamin P. Thomas, *Portrait for Posterity: Lincoln and His Biographers* (New Brunswick, N.J.: Rutgers University Press, 1947); David M. Potter, *The Lincoln Theme and American National Historiography* (Oxford: Clarendon Press, 1948); Don E. Fehrenbacher, *The Changing Image of Lincoln in American Historiography* (Oxford: Clarendon Press, 1968); and Mark E. Neely, Jr., "The Lincoln Theme Since Randall's Call: The Promises and Perils of Professionalism," *Papers of the Abraham Lincoln Association*, I (1979), pp. 10–70. Thayer's letter to Orville Hickman Browning, June 18, 1862, is in the Abraham Lincoln Papers, Library of Congress.

See also ANGLE, PAUL MCCLELLAND; ARNOLD, ISAAC NEWTON; AUTOBIOGRAPHY; BARTON, WILLIAM ELEAZER; BEVERIDGE, ALBERT JEREMIAH; CHARNWOOD, GODFREY RATHBONE BENSON, LORD; CODDING, ICHABOD; EISENSCHIML, OTTO; HAY, JOHN MILTON; HERNDON, WILLIAM HENRY; HESSELTINE, WILLIAM BEST; HOLLAND, JOSIAH GILBERT; HOWELLS, WILLIAM DEAN; LAMON, WARD HILL; LUTHIN, REINHARD HENRY; MASTERS, EDGAR LEE; NICOLAY, JOHN GEORGE; RANDALL, JAMES GARFIELD; RAYMOND, HENRY JARVIS; SANDBURG, CARL; SCRIPPS, JOHN LOCKE; STEPHENSON, NATHANIEL WRIGHT; STODDARD, WILLIAM OSBORN; TARBELL, IDA MINERVA; THOMAS, BENJAMIN PLATT; TYLER, LYON GARDINER; WEIK, JESSE WILLIAM; WILLIAMS, THOMAS HARRY.

Bixby Letter Letter of condolence written by President Lincoln on November 21, 1864, widely regarded as one of Lincoln's finest letters.

Massachusetts Governor John A. Andrew wrote the War Department on September 24, 1864, suggesting that the President write Mrs. Lydia Bixby, a Boston widow who, according to Massachusetts Adjutant-General William Schouler, had lost five sons in the war. On November 25 Schouler gave the widow Lincoln's letter. The Boston *Evening Transcript* printed it in the afternoon "second edition." Numerous other newspapers reprinted it after that date. The text of the letter is known only by the newspaper accounts; the original handwritten copy has never been found.

Confusion and mystery surround the letter. Schouler's information proved later to be incorrect. Of the five Bixby boys, only two died in combat. One was honorably discharged, one deserted, and one either deserted or died a prisoner of war. Even though no one knows what the original letter looked like, thousands of facsimiles in what appears to be Lincoln's handwriting exist. A New York City print dealer named Michael F. Tobin copyrighted a facsimile in 1891 and sold copies for $2. The proprietor of Huber's Museum, also in New York City, sold similar facsimiles for $1. Thereafter, numerous facsimiles were based on them.

Some people, most notably Nicholas Murray Butler in *Across the Busy Years*, have argued that John Hay, one of Lincoln's private secretaries, actually wrote the letter. There is not a scrap of reliable evidence to prove

The Huber's Museum "facsimile" of Lincoln's famous Bixby letter.

it. Butler was an unreliable witness on other Lincoln stories (see LINCOLN PAPERS), and John Hay himself in 1904 said in a letter to New Hampshire politician William E. Chandler that the "letter of Mr. Lincoln to Mrs. Bixby is genuine."

The greatest student of the letter's history, Boston journalist F. Lauriston Bullard, concluded not only that Lincoln wrote it but also that the "beauty of the letter is not destroyed by the fact that its premises were wrong." A reading of one of the facsimiles certainly proves the wisdom of Bullard's statement.

SOURCES: F. Lauriston Bullard's *Abraham Lincoln & the Widow Bixby* (New Brunswick, N.J.: Rutgers University Press, 1946) is definitive and makes fascinating reading in the bargain.

Black Hawk War A conflict with Sac and Fox Indians led by Chief Black Hawk in 1832. The war provided Abraham Lincoln with his only military experience before becoming commander in chief in the bloodiest war in American history.

When news reached New Salem that the Illinois governor had called for troops to fight the Indians, Lincoln was a clerk in a failing store and an announced candidate for the state legislature. He quickly enrolled in a militia company (on April 21, 1832) and was "to his own surprize," as he recalled later, "elected captain of it." The election gave him "much satisfaction." In fact, he said in 1859 that it was "a success which gave me more pleasure than any I have had since." It also gave him his first experience as a leader of men—over 60 of them. The election proved to be a better index of his popularity than of his military ability. One soldier recalled that Captain Lincoln was twice arrested, once for disobeying an order not to discharge a firearm near the camp and again for being unable to get his men, drunk on liquor stolen from the officers' quarters, to march. After his 30 days' enlistment expired, Lincoln reenlisted three times for a total of 51 days. He later recalled that he "went the campaign, served near three months, met the ordinary hardships of such an expedition, but was in no battle." Mustered out at Black River, Wisconsin Territory, a day after someone stole his horse, Lincoln walked most of the way to Peoria, paddled a canoe to Havana, and walked from there to New Salem. He received $125 and a land grant in Iowa Territory for his service.

In a speech in the United States House of Representatives on July 27, 1848, Lincoln belittled the extravagant claims made for the military heroism of Democratic presidential candidate Lewis Cass by recalling facetiously: "By the way, . . . did you know I am a military hero?" Lincoln made "charges upon the wild onions," had "a good many bloody struggles with the musquetoes," but he never "saw any live, fighting indians."

In an autobiographical statement in 1860, Lincoln recalled that having returned from the military campaign, he ran for the legislature, "encouraged by his great popularity among his immediate neighbors." The statement is misleading, for Lincoln had announced his candidacy long before the call for troops and the encouraging election as captain. In fact, his return from the campaign in July, near the August election day, prevented him from campaigning widely in the district and may have caused his defeat in the election.

SOURCES: See Benjamin P. Thomas, *Lincoln's New Salem* (Springfield, Ill.: Abraham Lincoln Association, 1934), and the interesting but less detailed account in Albert Beveridge, *Abraham Lincoln, 1809–1858*, 2 vols. (Boston: Houghton, Mifflin, 1928).

Blair, Francis Preston (1791-1876) Elder statesman and self-appointed adviser to the Lincoln administration. Blair was born in Virginia but spent most of his early career in journalism and politics in Kentucky. In 1830 President Andrew Jackson brought him to Washington

The Kaiser was "gratified"

A letter from the Kaiser

"His Majesty the Kaiser hears that you have sacrificed nine sons in defense of the Fatherland in the present war. His Majesty is immensely gratified at the fact, and in recognition is pleased to send you his photograph, with frame and autograph signature."

Frau Meter, who received the letter, has now joined the street beggars in Delmenhorst-Oldenburg, to get a living.

A letter from Lincoln

DEAR MADAM—I have been shown in the files of the War Department a statement of the Adjutant General of Massachusetts that you are the mother of five sons who have died gloriously on the field of battle. I feel how weak and fruitless must be any words of mine which should attempt to beguile you from the grief of a loss so overwhelming. But I cannot refrain from tendering to you the consolation that may be found in the thanks of the Republic they have died to save. I pray that our Heavenly Father may assuage the anguish of your bereavement and leave you only the cherished memory of the loved and lost, and the solemn pride that must be yours to have laid so costly a sacrifice upon the altar of freedom.

Buy Liberty Bonds to your UTMOST

LIBERTY LOAN COMMITTEE
Second Federal Reserve District

Paper is scarce. Don't destroy this hand-bill. Pass it on and help win the war.

American propaganda in World War I exploited the power of Lincoln's written words by contrasting the humane sentiments of the Bixby letter with a letter of condolence by Kaiser Wilhelm.

Blair, Francis Preston

to edit the *Globe*. President James K. Polk later forced him from the *Globe*, thereby alienating him from the Southern wing of the Democratic party. He became a Free-Soiler in 1848. From his country estate in Silver Spring, Maryland, Blair observed and occasionally manipulated national politics for the rest of his long life.

Blair became a Republican and was a delegate to the Chicago convention which nominated Lincoln for President. He supported Border State candidate Edward Bates for the nomination but, soon after Lincoln's nomination, was pressing advice on the candidate. He suggested that Lincoln's reply to the letter offering him the nomination should mention colonization in the American tropics as a way of avoiding the "irrepressible conflict." This would remove the cause of conflict (slavery) and keep Europe from turning our left wing by getting a foothold in Mexico. Mention of colonization might also "ward off the attacks, made upon us about negro equality." Lincoln, as he would on many other occasions, ignored the advice, but the same concatenation of ideas repeatedly appeared in Blair's correspondence with him. Blair also strongly opposed the inclusion of William H. Seward and Simon Cameron in the Cabinet, arguing that their inveterate taste for intrigue would sully Lincoln's reputation for honesty. His own son, Montgomery, became Postmaster General.

In the Sumter crisis Blair urged a policy of Jacksonian firmness; he equated surrender of the fort with surrender of the Union. Perhaps at Lincoln's instigation, Blair unofficially offered Robert E. Lee command of the Union army, the first of several behind-the-scenes missions he performed once the war began. He was a warm supporter of General George B. McClellan; he advocated the general's reinstatement as commander of the Army of the Potomac as late as the summer of 1864. At that time, without the President's knowledge, Blair apparently tried unsuccessfully to get McClellan to agree to spurn the Democratic presidential nomination in exchange for a renewed military commission from Lincoln. By 1864, however, the "Blair influence" on the Lincoln administration was well on the wane, and the old man failed to persuade the President later in the year to appoint Montgomery to the Supreme Court.

Blair retained his special interest in plans to colonize freed Negroes in Central America. He always held Thomas Jefferson's view that the white and black races could not prosper in the same society, and he continued to hope that a Central American colony would help the United States play a role in this hemisphere analogous to England's in India. He vigorously promoted Ambrose Thompson's Chiriqui Improvement Company colonization scheme. He thought the war surely doomed slavery to extinction, and in 1862 Lincoln asked Montgomery Blair to get his father to persuade Senator John J. Crittenden of Kentucky to support the President's plan for gradual emancipation with compensation in the Border States. Crittenden refused. In 1864 Blair supported an antislavery clause for the new Maryland constitution, but at the same time he was suggesting a Negro colony on the Rio Grande in Texas.

Blair's last great wartime mission involved slavery and Latin America, as usual. Prompted by Horace Greeley's interest in peace initiatives as well as by his own Southern background, the venerable Blair concocted a scheme to bring peace and reunion. Now that slavery was doomed, he thought, foreign war could reunite the country. He wanted to persuade Jefferson Davis to observe a truce and then launch a joint campaign (led, perhaps, by Blair's son, Francis Preston, Jr.) in which Union and Confederate troops would drive the French puppet Maximilian from the Mexican throne. Lincoln repeatedly put the old man off but finally gave him a pass to Richmond in December 1864. Blair met with Davis in private there on January 12, conferred again with Lincoln on the 18th, and returned to Richmond on the 20th. Blair's great fear was that the war was no longer a war "for slavery but monarchy" and that the Confederacy might league itself with France to gain its independence and bring monarchy to America. The war with France, which Blair thought inevitable, was not merely to drive European influence out of Mexico but also to extend the American "domain to the Isthmus." Davis thought reconciliation of North and South was impossible because of vindictive feelings born of Union invasion of the South, but he coyly showed some interest in the old man's scheme. Blair's negotiations led eventually to the futile Hampton Roads Peace Conference of February 3, 1865. Lincoln never showed any interest in the Mexican scheme and probably regarded the idea the way Blair feared he might—as "the dreams of an old man."

After the war Blair opposed Reconstruction and re-

Frank Leslie's Illustrated Newspaper of January 21, 1865, depicted Francis P. Blair as a granny.

A SELF-APPOINTED ENVOY.

turned to the Democratic party. He died at Silver Spring on October 18, 1876, a few months after he had professed a conversion experience.

SOURCES: See William Ernest Smith, *The Francis Preston Blair Family in Politics*, 2 vols. (New York: Macmillan, 1933). Blair's letter to Lincoln about the "irrepressible conflict" (May 26, 1860) and his bizarre memoranda of his negotiations with Jefferson Davis (January 12, 1865?) are in the Abraham Lincoln Papers, Library of Congress.

Blair, Montgomery (1813–1883) Postmaster General in President Lincoln's Cabinet. Montgomery Blair came from a distinguished Kentucky Democratic family. He graduated from West Point in 1835 and studied law at Transylvania University. In 1837 he moved to St. Louis, Missouri, and in 1853 to Maryland. Active in Democratic politics in Missouri, he joined the Know-Nothing (American) party in Maryland but left it in 1857 because of its silence on the slavery issue. In the same year he became counsel for Dred Scott. Three years later he helped John Brown secure defense counsel.

In 1860 Blair was a delegate to the Republican National Convention which nominated Lincoln for President, though he supported conservative Edward Bates for the nomination. Blair's importance as a former Democrat in the new party and his family's prominence in the Border States of Kentucky, Maryland, and Missouri led to his appointment to Lincoln's Cabinet, though many Republicans of Whig background preferred Maryland's Henry Winter Davis for the post.

Blair's father, Francis Preston Blair, had been a close ally of Andrew Jackson, and the family viewed secession as another Nullification crisis the solution to which should be stern and uncompromising threat of military force. Blair always thought that sucession was a minority movement in the South which held the essentially loyal masses in check by a "Military Government." Only the weak measures of the Buchanan administration allowed it to grow "to its present formidable proportions," he told the President on March 15, 1861, and all that was needed was to show that "Northern men" were not "deficient in the courage necessary to maintain the Government." That would shock the South back into the Union. Blair was the only Cabinet member who consistently urged reinforcing Fort Sumter. He had no confidence in General-in-Chief Winfield Scott. Blair reported that Lincoln thought Scott's course "shows that whilst no one will question his patriotism, the results are the same as if he was in fact treacherous." In later years, Blair blamed the war on those who delayed reinforcing Fort Sumter.

The "war does not seem greatly to add to the difficulties of the Post Office Department," Lincoln said accurately. Blair ran this easiest of departments well. He reduced the deficits, established military post offices, appointed stamp agents for the armies, helped develop indelible ink for canceling stamps, secured passage of a bill abolishing postmasters' franking privileges (though he defended Congress's privilege), worked to improve international mail, and urged the government to purchase the country's telegraph system.

At one time an ally of John C. Frémont, Blair soon judged Frémont incompetent and broke with him in 1861. Throughout the remainder of the war he was identified with the conservative wing of the Republican party. In the *Trent* crisis, he opposed from the start the arrest of the Confederate commissioners. He thought the admission of West Virginia as a state in 1863 was unconstitutional and unfair to the loyal people in the eastern part of the state. He opposed the banishment of Clement L. Vallandigham. In 1864 he advised the President not to execute Confederate prisoners in retaliation for the Fort Pillow massacre.

Despite his conservatism, Blair thought emancipation in the Gulf states inevitable as early as November 1861, but he always insisted that emancipation be accompanied by a program to colonize freedmen in Latin America. When Lincoln announced his plan for the Emancipation Proclamation to the Cabinet in July 1862, Blair feared the Proclamation's effect on the autumn elections. He nevertheless became quickly reconciled to the emancipation policy, though, like his father, he never thought that America could become a biracial country.

On October 3, 1863, Blair delivered a speech at Rockville, Maryland, which accused "ultra-Abolitionists" of supporting the "amalgamation" of "the black element with the free white labor of our land." He attacked Charles Sumner's theory that the seceded states had "committed suicide" and persisted in his belief that there was a loyal majority in the South with which the United States should never be at war. Although the speech was strongly worded and brought Blair the undying hatred of the Radical Republicans, Sumner assured Blair that he never took "any personal exception to your speech." On January 22, 1864, Blair spoke at Annapolis, Maryland, on "The Cause of the Rebellion and in Support of the President's Plan of Pacification," a plea for Democratic support of the administration.

Blair never trusted William H. Seward and came to hate Salmon P. Chase and Edwin M. Stanton. When Blair's brother Francis attacked Chase in a speech in the House of Representatives in February of 1864 for his "profligate" management of the Treasury, relations between the Blairs and the Radicals became even more strained. Montgomery continued to support emancipation but insisted in a letter of June 21, 1864, to William Lloyd Garrison's *Liberator* that separation of the races must follow emancipation. The Union (Republican) platform of 1864 called for harmony in the Cabinet—a plank widely construed as a demand for Blair's removal. The day after Frémont withdrew his third-party candidacy against Lincoln and George B. McClellan, the President asked Blair to resign. Blair did so on September 23, 1864. Lincoln never explained the reason, though Blair (and many others) thought the President wished "to appease the Fremonters and Radicals." Lincoln did affirm that the dismissal stemmed from "no dissatisfac-

Montgomery Blair at the beginning of the Lincoln administration.

tion of mine with you personally or officially." Blair was pleased by Lincoln's choice of William Dennison to succeed him as Postmaster General. He hoped to be appointed to the Supreme Court but was disappointed when Lincoln picked Chase later that year.

After the war, Blair supported Andrew Johnson, opposed Reconstruction, and soon returned to the Democratic party. He remained a Democrat the rest of his life and died while writing a biography of Andrew Jackson.

SOURCES: See William Ernest Smith, *The Francis Preston Blair Family in Politics*, 2 vols. (New York: Macmillan, 1933). Blair's letter to Lincoln about secession (March 15, 1861) and his memorandum on General Scott (March [?], 1861) are in the Abraham Lincoln Papers, Library of Congress.

See also CHANDLER, ZACHARIAH; FRÉMONT, JOHN CHARLES.

Bledsoe, Albert Taylor (1809–1877) Lincoln critic. Bledsoe was born in Kentucky, graduated from West Point, and became an Episcopal minister in 1835. He resigned from the ministry in 1839 and lived for most of the time until 1848 in Springfield, Illinois. There he practiced law as a partner of Lincoln's friend Edward D. Baker and was active in Whig politics; naturally, he came into contact with local Whig lawyer, Abraham Lincoln. For much of Lincoln's one term in the United States Congress, Bledsoe was the chief editorial writer for the *Illinois State Journal*, Springfield's Whig organ.

Bledsoe left Springfield for professorships of mathematics at the University of Mississippi (1848–1854) and the University of Virginia (1854–1861). While living in Springfield in 1848, he had voted against the Negro exclusion clause in the new state constitution, but he became a proslavery enthusiast and argued that the Bible sanctioned slavery. During the Civil War he served as the Confederacy's Assistant Secretary of War and did research in England which led to the publication in 1866 of *Is Davis a Traitor? or Was Secession a Constitutional Right Previous to the War of 1861?*, a classic defense of the Lost Cause.

In 1867 he founded the *Southern Review* in Baltimore and in it continued his Confederate apologetics. In April 1873 he published a long review of Ward Hill Lamon's *Life of Abraham Lincoln*. There he recalled, from his association with the man, that Lincoln was intelligent and honest in personal dealings, but he argued that Lincoln had a "thirst for distinction" which explained his duplicitous career as a politician whose "idol" was popularity. From Lamon he learned, he said, that Lincoln was a bastard and an infidel. Bledsoe claimed to have known Lincoln from the time when, as a Congressman unpopular for opposing the Mexican War, he "could not have been elected a constable or a justice of the peace." Yet Bledsoe had written editorials for the *Journal* which defended even Senator Thomas Corwin's more strident opposition to that war. He edited the *Southern Review* until his death.

SOURCES: See Harry E. Pratt, "Albert Taylor Bledsoe: Critic of Lincoln," in the *Illinois State Historical Society Transactions for the Year 1934* ([Springfield]: Illinois State Historical Library, n.d.). Bledsoe's vote on the constitution, March 6, 1848, is recorded in the Sangamon County Poll Books, Springfield Poll, Sangamon State University Archives, Springfield, Illinois.

Blind Memorandum A memorandum of August 23, 1864, in which Lincoln stated his fear that he might not win reelection. The President asked his Cabinet members to sign the back of a piece of paper without revealing the contents, which were:

> This morning, as for some days past, it seems exceedingly probable that this Administration will not be re-elected. Then it will be my duty to so co-operate with the President elect, as to save the Union between the election and the inauguration; as he will have secured his election on such ground that he can not possibly save it afterwards.

Written on the eve of the Democratic nominating convention, the memorandum was prompted by warnings from Thurlow Weed and Henry J. Raymond that the country was wild for peace and dismayed that Lincoln would seek peace only on terms of reunion *and* the death of slavery. The day after he wrote the memorandum he drafted a letter for Raymond to use in efforts to seek peace on terms of reunion alone. He never sent the letter.

The blind memorandum, along with the unsent letter written just after it, is a rare piece of evidence that Lincoln might have accepted peace without the abolition of slavery. In other words, it is a key document for those who see his overruling passion as the desire to save the Union. Yet it is clearly proof not of Lincoln's own desires, but of his depressed reading of public opinion in the hopeless summer of '64. If Union were all he could get, why certainly he would at least get that.

Repeatedly cited as proof of the likelihood of his defeat had military victories not intervened to save the administration before November, the memorandum is equally revealing of a point too often missed. Lincoln, like most Republican leaders, equated Democratic electoral victory with loss of the Union. That was a sincere fear which reached all the way to the Executive Mansion. It was not a cheap campaign tactic used to smear the loyal Democratic opposition and to avoid discussion of the subject that divided Republicans: what to do about the Negro in reconstructing the South after the war.

Blockade On April 19, 1861, President Lincoln issued a proclamation "to set on foot a blockade of the ports" from South Carolina to Texas. He added Virginia and North Carolina 8 days later. Realizing the importance of the economic base of modern warfare, Lincoln thus moved quickly to interdict foreign trade on over 3500 miles of Confederate coastline. Secretary of the Navy Gideon Welles, to whom the duty of enforcement fell, opposed the blockade in principle as improper in international law; he thought a nation could only close the ports of insurrectionary areas. A legal blockade, he and many others contended, was an aspect of war with a foreign nation and not of a domestic insurrection. In addition, only effective blockades were legal in international law; the United States itself had always opposed England's "paper blockades." With few more than 50 ships available for blockade duty at the beginning of the war, this was at first a serious problem. Nevertheless, Lincoln had the support of Secretary of State William H. Seward and Attorney General Edward Bates in establishing the blockade, which grew steadily in effectiveness as the North took advantage of its superior shipbuilding ability.

The dates of the blockade proclamations were to become the legal dates for the inception of the Civil War. Beginning in February 1863 the United States Supreme Court heard en bloc the *Prize Cases*, four cases involving ships seized as prizes early in the war under the President's proclamations (the *Amy Warwick*, the *Crenshaw*, the *Hiawatha*, and the *Brilliante*). Originally to be heard as early as March 18, 1862, the proceedings were delayed until Lincoln's three new appointees to the Court could participate in the deliberation. Arguing that the prizes were captured illegally because the President could not impose a blockade unless war had been declared, the ships' lawyers seemed to threaten the whole legality of the war. In a 5 to 4 decision, the Supreme Court upheld the prizes and the President's proclamations. Justice Robert C. Grier's majority opinion stated that the Court refused "to affect a technical ignorance of a war which all the world acknowledges to be the greatest civil war known in all the history of the human race" simply because Congress had not been in session to declare war in April 1861. The dissenters, including Chief Justice Roger B. Taney, argued that war existed only after July 13, 1861, when an act of Congress recognized a state of war. Significantly, no Justice argued that the war was illegal.

Declaring a blockade was one of several strong measures Lincoln took immediately after the fall of Fort Sumter before Congress was in session and for which he later asked congressional approval. The blockade was always one of the anomalous legal aspects of the Civil War. Lincoln's government never took the official view that the Confederacy was a legal belligerent in a war, yet a blockade was in international law strictly a measure of war. Most historians agree that the Union blockade was one of the most important factors determining the outcome of the war.

SOURCES: See J. G. Randall, *Constitutional Problems Under Lincoln*, rev. ed. (Urbana: University of Illinois Press, 1951).

Books The frontier society in which Lincoln grew up was not bookish. Books were scarce, and they never played a major role in his life. William H. Herndon noted that the mature Lincoln "never seemed to care to own or collect books."

It is not known when or how Lincoln learned to read, but he recalled in 1861 that in "the earliest days of my being able to read, I got hold of a small book . . . 'Weem's [sic] Life of Washington.'" He used the few textbooks, anthologies, and primers he could borrow from his neighbors.

Despite a culturally impoverished background, Lincoln had a reputation in New Salem, Illinois, as a reader. By his own recollection, "he studied English grammar" there, probably from Samuel Kirkham's *English Grammar*. When storekeeping failed and a postmaster's job proved not very remunerative, Lincoln learned surveying by studying "a little" Abel Flint's *System of Geometry and Trigonometry with a Treatise on Surveying* and Robert Gibson's *Theory and Practice of Surveying*. The first lawbook he read may have been *The Revised Laws of Indiana, Adopted . . . by the General Assembly . . . At Their Eighth Session*. But his real legal education came from William Blackstone's *Commentaries* (perhaps a copy bought at a sheriff's sale) and from books he borrowed from John Todd Stuart between 1834 and 1836: Joseph Chitty's *Precedents in Pleading*, Simon Greenleaf's *Treatise on the Law of Evidence*, and Joseph Story's *Commentaries on Equity*. Once he became a practitioner, however, he ceased to study law. Herndon, his partner, claimed that he "never knew him to read through a law book of any kind."

While practicing law on the Eighth Judicial Circuit, Stuart recalled, Lincoln "read hard books." After he served in Congress in 1849, Lincoln "studied and nearly mastered the Six-books of Euclid." Such reading was done "to supply the want" of education in his youth.

Most of the rest of Lincoln's reading was to a purpose, recalled Joseph Gillespie:

> Study with Mr. Lincoln was a business not a pleasure. He was extremely diligent when he had anything to do in preparing himself but when the task was done he betook himself to recreation. The information he gathered was in reference to special questions and not with a view of laying in a general store of knowledge expecting that he would have occasion to use it and yet his natural tastes and aptitudes led him to explore most of those departments of study which bore mainly on the practical affairs of life.

Lincoln knew little about history except the era of the American Revolution and the founding of the republic. When, at the Hampton Roads Peace Conference, R. M. T. Hunter told Lincoln that Charles I had entered into agreements with rebels, Lincoln is reported to have said, "I do not profess to be posted in history. . . . All I distinctly recollect about the case of Charles I, is, that he lost his head in the end." He did read lives of the Revolutionary heroes, George Washington and Patrick Henry. Apparently, he thought those very special events called forth something special in the men, for otherwise he found biography (as Herndon tells us) "as generally written . . . not only misleading, but false. The author . . . makes a wonderful hero out of his subject. He magnifies his perfections . . . and suppresses his imperfections. . . . In most instances they commemorate a lie, and cheat posterity out of the truth." Lincoln knew the Bible, of course, and read some eighteenth-century skeptics like Constantine Volney and Thomas Paine as well, but he did not read philosophy or theology after his thirties. Herndon noted that "if you wished to be cut off at the knee, just go at Lincoln with abstractions, glittering generalities, indefiniteness, mistiness of idea or expression." Witnesses disagree, but there is no direct evidence that he read novels, save perhaps *Don Quixote*. Of the classics, the great staple of the intellectual diet of Victorian gentlemen, Lincoln was largely ignorant, attaching little practical importance to knowing "the exact shade of Julius Caesar's hair."

Poetry was another matter. Lincoln was an ardent fan of Robert Burns and William Shakespeare and had an acquaintance with the work of several other poets. His sense of humor dictated a love of popular humorous writers.

Lincoln rarely devoured polemical or political literature in doses larger than the size of newspaper articles, but some of his reading after he was elected President was important. He used *The Life and Speeches of Henry Clay* (Philadelphia: J. L. Gihon, 1853) in the political campaigns of the 1850s and read Clay's speech on the Compromise of 1850 to prepare his First Inaugural Address. He also used Daniel Webster's reply to Hayne and Andrew Jackson's Nullification proclamation for the same speech (according to Herndon). He probably read Hinton R. Helper's *Impending Crisis*; he underlined the words, "Direct Government—over all of the people, by all the people, for all the people," in Theodore Parker's sermon, *The Effect of Slavery on the American People*; he complimented Charles Janeway Stillé for *How a Free People Conduct a Long War* (1862); and he thanked Charles P. Kirkland for his *Letter to . . . Benjamin R. Curtis . . . on the "Emancipation Proclamation"* (1862). George Livermore's *Historical Research: Opinions of the Founders of the Republic on Negroes as Slaves, as Citizens, and as Soldiers* (1862) helped persuade President Lincoln to accept blacks in the Union army.

Lincoln was a man of little formal education and a man of action with little time for reading. Herndon, who had one of the largest libraries in Illinois, thought his partner read little. Yet Robert T. Lincoln recalled of his father that he could "not remember ever seeing him without a book in his hand." From his earliest recollection, Robert remembered his father as "devoted to Shakespeare and Milton" and as reading Bunyan also. "In the later years of his life, he always had a Bible and a set of Shakespeare very near him, and went to them for relief at all times."

SOURCES: The great student of Lincoln's reading was David Mearns, whose article on Lincoln in Mearns, Arthur E. Bestor, and Jonathan Daniels, *Three Presidents and Their Books* (Urbana: University of Illinois Press, 1963), is without equal. Copies of books which Lincoln owned or used are rare and are scattered in many different collections. The Library of Congress owns Kirkham's *English Grammar*; the Louis A. Warren Lincoln Library and Museum owns *The Life and Speeches of Henry Clay*; and the Folger Shakespeare Library owns Lincoln's copy of Shakespeare's plays. A list of the books the Lincolns checked out of the Library of Congress was published in *Lincoln Lore*, Number 129, September 28, 1931. See also Mark E. Neely, Jr., "The President and the Historian: Lincoln and George Livermore," *Lincoln Lore*, Number 1621 (March 1973) pp. 1–4; "How a Free People Conduct a Long War," *Lincoln Lore*, Number 1634 (April 1974), pp. 1–4; and "Some Sober Second Thoughts about the New Constitutional History," *Lincoln Lore*, Number 1676 (October 1977) pp. 1–4. Robert Todd Lincoln's letter about his father's reading (to John F. Dillon, January 5, 1905 [copy]) is in the Robert Todd Lincoln Papers, Illinois State Historical Library.

See also CARROLL, ANNA ELLA; EDUCATION; GRAHAM, WILLIAM MENTOR; HUMOR; LIBRARY OF CONRESS; POETRY; SHAKESPEARE.

The famous actor John Wilkes Booth was much photographed. This portrait of him was taken by Charles D. Fredricks in New York City, perhaps in 1862.

Booth, John Wilkes (1838–1865) Actor who assassinated Abraham Lincoln. Booth was born 3 miles east of Belair, Maryland. He was the son of Junius Brutus Booth, an English tragedian who, having moved to America, owned a farm in Maryland which was worked with slaves. John attended school in Baltimore and later St. Timothy's Hall, an Episcopal military academy, in Catonsville, Maryland. At St. Timothy's he became an Episcopalian and a good shot; he learned to ride a horse on his father's farm.

In the 1850s Booth apparently became a Know-Nothing in politics. Late in the decade, he began a career upon the stage; he was especially popular in Richmond, Virginia. As a temporary member of a military unit called the Richmond Grays, he witnessed John Brown's hanging.

Booth opened in *Richard III* in New York on March 17, 1862. As an actor he was almost as successful as his brother Edwin and more so than his brother Junius Brutus, Jr. At 25 he had a large repertoire, including nine Shakespearean leading roles. He was no barroom loafer.

The handsome Booth was popular with the ladies and with his fellow actors generally. He was athletic and was noted for his boisterous stage sword fights and for his leaps and bounds. Appearances in Union-occupied New Orleans in the spring of 1864 were marred by throat problems, but reviews of later performances did not mention that apparently temporary affliction. His theatrical career was going well. He used some of his better than $20,000 a year income to speculate in Pennsylvania oil lands.

Politics began to interest Booth more than acting. The longest known Booth letter, given to his sister, Asia Booth Clarke in November 1864, reflected the prevailing rhetoric of the opposition to the Lincoln administration: "People of the North, to hate tyranny, to love liberty and justice, to strike at wrong and oppression, was the teaching of our fathers. The study of our early history will not let me forget it, and may it never." It also indulged in the aggressively racist proslavery argument typically forged in a slave state like Maryland: "This country was formed for the *white*, not for the black man. And, looking upon *African slavery* from the stand point held by the noble framers of our Constitution, I, for one, have ever considered it one of the greatest blessings (both for themselves and us) that God ever bestowed upon a favored nation. Witness heretofore our wealth and power; witness their elevation and enlightenment above their race elsewhere." John told his brother Edwin, who voted for Lincoln's reelection, that Lincoln would be made king of America.

In August or September 1864 Booth first spoke of a plan to kidnap the President. He hoped to carry out the plan while Lincoln rode to the Soldier's Home outside Washington. Then Booth would carry him to Richmond to exchange for Confederate prisoners of war. (General Ulysses S. Grant had ceased exchanging prisoners.) Just after the presidential election in 1864, Booth took up residence in the National Hotel in Washington. Outside Washington, in lower Maryland, Booth began to inquire about farm properties, but he was probably checking escape routes from Washington and seeking recruits to help kidnap the President. He first enlisted his old school chums Samuel B. Arnold and Michael O'Laughlin in the plot. He left for Montreal, where he sent his expensive theatrical wardrobe south on a blockade runner—proof that he expected to resume his acting career in Richmond after the crime. He may also have tried to contact Confederate agents in Canada.

Back in Washington, Booth enlisted other idlers and Southern sympathizers in his scheme, men who were not in any way his social equals: Lewis Thornton Powell, John H. Surratt, David E. Herold, and George A. Atzerodt. For some time early in 1865, Booth probably supported the lot of them in Washington, as they waited to kidnap the President. He maintained horses in Washington stables at the disposal of his friends. On March 17, 1865, they rode out to intercept the President's carriage on its way to a theatrical performance, but Lincoln was not in the carriage. Arnold and O'Laughlin abandoned the scheme at this time; Arnold had told Booth about a week before that his new idea of capturing the President at Ford's Theatre was impractical. Atzerodt and Powell continued to live off Booth's charity in Washington.

It was still too early in the warm season for the "tyrant" to be riding regularly to the Soldiers' Home to sleep at night, and Booth's little band was getting smaller—too small to bring off a kidnap plot. Richmond was seized, and only more desperate measures could now help the South. Booth considered the cause "almost lost," but only almost. By eliminating the most important members of the Washington government perhaps he could set in motion a revolution in the North that would allow the South to revive.

On the morning of April 14 Booth decided not to kidnap but to murder the President at a performance of *Our American Cousin* at Ford's Theatre. In the afternoon Booth apparently went to the theater, drilled a peephole through the door to the President's box, and prepared a brace to block the door against entry from the hall once he was inside. In a meeting at the Herndon House, where Powell had a room, at 8:00 p.m., Booth assigned roles to Powell, Atzerodt, and Herold. His accomplices were to murder the Vice President and also Secretary of State William H. Seward, long considered to be the strong man in the Lincoln administration.

Booth asked Edman Spangler, a scene-shifter at Ford's Theatre, to hold his horse behind the theater that night. Booth, who had been drinking heavily of late, took a drink before entering the theater. Armed with a single-shot Deringer pistol and a dagger, he approached the President's box from behind, closed and braced the door, shot Lincoln in the back of the head, and stabbed Major Henry R. Rathbone, the Lincolns' companion, in the arm. He leapt some 12 feet to the stage, snagging a spur in a Treasury Department flag which draped the President's box, and broke his left leg when he hit the stage. Most accounts agree that Booth shouted *"Sic semper tyrannis."* That would certainly be in keeping with the political preoccupations which drove Booth to his crime; for accusations of Republican tyranny had been the stock-in-trade of the Democratic party throughout the war. The theater was, to be sure, a self-dramatizing site for the actor's crime, and his leap from the box was in character with his athletic acting. Though idiosyncratic, there was no madness in choosing the theater for the assassination. It was a place he knew well, where he could perhaps expect help, and where Lincoln would not likely be guarded by his Union Light Cavalry escort (as he was on most carriage rides at that point in his administration).

Booth apparently rode over the Navy Yard Bridge out of Washington shortly after the murder, giving his real name to the sentry who stopped him temporarily. Herold followed shortly thereafter and overtook Booth somewhere outside Washington. They stopped in Surrattsville for whiskey and a carbine left at John M. Lloyd's tavern. Then they turned away from the Potomac toward the house of Dr. Samuel A. Mudd, for Booth's leg was causing him intense pain. They arrived about 4:00 a.m., April 15; Dr. Mudd fixed a splint for the "straight fracture of the tibia about two inches above the ankle. . . . not . . . a peculiarly painful or dangerous wound; there was nothing resembling a compound fracture." Booth and Herold gave false names at the doctor's house, according to Mudd.

About 12 hours later, Booth and Herold departed. They arrived at Samuel Cox's house in about 12 hours (on the 16th), having been lost in a swamp and led out by a black man named Oswald Swan. Cox was a wealthy Confederate sympathizer; he asked his devoted foster brother, Thomas A. Jones, to hide the two men and help them cross the river to Virginia.

Cox hid Booth and Herold for six days and five nights in a pine grove. Jones gave them food and newspapers; years later he recalled that Booth was anxious to read what was said about his deeds. On Friday, April 21, Jones felt this would be the night to cross. The Federal cavalry was supposed to be away on a wild-goose chase. Jones guided them to a boat, but they did not reach Virginia until the next night because a flood tide carried them 12 miles upstream from their destination, the house of Jones's friend Mrs. Quesenberry. Eventually Booth and Herold reached the farm of Richard H. Garrett. While they were sleeping in a tobacco barn early in the morning of April 26, they were surrounded by Union cavalry. Herold surrendered, but Booth refused to be taken alive. The soldiers set fire to the barn to smoke him out, but a shot, fired by Sergeant Boston Corbett, mortally wounded him. "Tell mother—

tell mother I die for my country," Booth gasped. About dawn, he died. There was no doubt about identity. One officer had a photograph of the famous actor, and articles belonging to Booth were taken from his clothes.

Booth's body was sewn in a blanket and carried to the *John S. Ide,* a steamer which transported it to Washington. There it was placed on the monitor *Montauk.* On April 27 an autopsy was performed. The body was identified by a panel of Booth's associates, including Dr. John F. May, who had removed a tumor from Booth's neck and recognized the scar. On the 27th the body was buried at the Washington Arsenal.

Booth kept a memorandum book during the period of the assassination and flight which was recovered at his death. It was not used as evidence at the trial of his accomplices but came to light in 1867, as the House Committee on the Judiciary gathered evidence for the impeachment trial of Andrew Johnson. The diary is self-dramatizing. Booth says he "rode sixty miles that night, with the bone of my leg tearing the flesh at every jump"; actually, Booth rode thirty miles, and Dr. Mudd said "there was nothing resembling a compound fracture." It also would have exonerated those who participated only in the kidnap plot from murder charges; for it states clearly that "until to day [Friday] nothing was ever *thought* of" killing the President. In trying the other conspirators, the government made no distinction between the kidnap and assassination plots, and therefore the prosecution had no desire to produce the diary as evidence. The defense, which could have learned of the book's existence from the newspapers, was remiss in not demanding to see the diary.

In February 1869 lame-duck President Andrew Johnson ordered Booth's remains delivered to Christ Church, Baltimore. On February 16 and 17 numerous persons, including a dentist, identified the decaying body, and on the 18th it was put in a vault in Green Mount Cemetery in Baltimore. On June 26, 1869, the Booth family had John's body interred with an Episcopal service performed by the Reverend Fleming James. James was forced to leave his post as assistant minister at St. Luke's Hospital, New York City, for performing the service.

SOURCES: Francis Wilson's *John Wilkes Booth: Fact and Fiction of Lincoln's Assassination* (Boston: Houghton Mifflin, 1929), though somewhat dated, is an intelligent biography full of quotations of the most important documents concerning Booth. Stanley Kimmel's *The Mad Booths of Maryland* (Indianapolis: Bobbs-Merrill, 1940) misses the mark in its emphasis on madness but contains a great deal of information unknown to Wilson. George S. Bryan's *The Great American Myth* (New York: Carrick & Evans, 1940) is at times a bit hard to follow, but it is still the best overall account of Booth's conspiracy. William Hanchett's "Booth's Diary," *Journal of the Illinois State Historical Society,* LXXII (February 1979), 39–56, is a definitive and clever history of Booth's famous and controversial memorandum book.

See also ASSASSINATION; ARNOLD, SAMUEL BLAND; ATZERODT, GEORGE A.; CORBETT, THOMAS P. ("BOSTON"); HEROLD, DAVID EDGAR; MUDD, SAMUEL ALEXANDER; O'LAUGHLIN, MICHAEL; *Our American Cousin*; POWELL, LEWIS THORTON; SPANGLER, EDMAN; SURRATT, JOHN HARRISON, JR.; SURATT, MARY EUGENIA (JENKINS); TRIAL OF THE ASSASSINS.

Borglum, John Gutzon de la Mothe (1867–1941)

Sculptor of the Mount Rushmore memorial. Borglum, who was born in Idaho, learned sculpting in Paris, where he was influenced by Rodin. One of his early patrons was Jessie Benton Frémont, the wife of Lincoln's old political rival, John C. Frémont. In 1907 Borglum began work on a beardless Lincoln head in marble strictly for his own satisfaction. He studied the life mask by Leonard W. Volk and produced a colossal head admired by Robert Todd Lincoln and Theodore Roosevelt. Eugene Meyer purchased it for $8000 and gave it to the United States Congress. It was placed in the Capitol rotunda in 1908. Years later a copy was placed at the entrance to Lincoln's tomb in Springfield. In 1910 Borglum received a commission to execute a heroic bronze statue of Lincoln for Newark, New Jersey. He hit upon the idea of portraying Lincoln seated on a park bench in the White House garden waiting for news from the front. Unveiled before the Newark courthouse in 1911, the statue gained immediate popularity in part because one could sit at the opposite end of the same bench with Lincoln.

Borglum was critical of plans for the Lincoln Memorial in Washington, D.C.; he argued that the rugged Westerner Lincoln was out of place in a Greek temple. When, in 1912, his second wife presented him with his first son, Borglum named him James Lincoln. He would be called "Lincoln." Borglum began to conceive grandiose designs in 1916. Asked to execute a face of Robert E. Lee on the side of Stone Mountain in Georgia, he decided to tell the story of the Confederacy by chiseling Lee, Jefferson Davis, "Stonewall" Jackson, and a host of other figures. World War I halted the project, and Borglum, who had been an ardent Progressive supporter of Theodore Roosevelt in 1912 and who was an aviation enthusiast, engaged in a dispute with President Woodrow Wilson over deficiencies in American production of airplanes.

In 1919 Borglum executed a bronze head of Lincoln for Samuel P. Colt, chairman of the board of the United States Rubber Company. The sculpture is now in the Detroit Institute of Arts. The Stone Mountain project came to a spectacular conclusion in 1925, when Borglum was, for all intents and purposes, fired from the task. He destroyed his models so that no other sculptor could finish the work. In spite of the bad publicity from the affair, South Dakotans engaged Borglum to do a colossal carving in the Black Hills. Borglum began work on models in 1925, when the United States Congress passed a bill to allow carving in the Harney National Forest. Funds were hard to come by, but President Calvin Coolidge's visits to the Black Hills in 1927 gave the first spur to fund raising. In 1929 Congress appropriated the first federal funds for the Mount Rushmore National Memorial Commission.

Borglum began work October 1, 1927. The project was not completed until shortly after his death in 1941, but he executed many other statues in that period, cold winters frequently halted work, and difficulties in raising money caused more delays than the weather. Borglum decided to sculpt four heads, Washington, Jefferson, Lincoln, and Theodore Roosevelt, in a Progressive Westerner's view of American history. It was a celebration of national unity and expansion, with Washington as the creator of the Union, Jefferson as the man who injected democracy and expanded the continent dramatically with the Louisiana Purchase, Lincoln as the preserver of the Union, and Roosevelt as the champion of the American West and the builder of the Panama Canal.

Not a single workman died in the construction process, and the work was completed for just under $1 million. President Franklin Delano Roosevelt placed the Memorial under the jurisdiction of the National Park Service. About 2 million people a year visit the memorial, which is located near Rapid City, South Dakota. The heads of the Presidents, visible from 60 miles away, are proportionate to men 500 feet tall.

SOURCES: See Willadene Price, *Gutzon Borglum: Artist and Patriot* (Chicago: Rand McNally, 1961).

Brady, Mathew B. *See* PHOTOGRAPHS.

Brenner, Victor David *See* LINCOLN PENNY.

Bright, John (1811–1889) Liberal Member of the British Parliament, industrialist, and Quaker; an ardent friend of the Lincoln administration during the Civil War. Bright corresponded regularly with Charles Sumner, Chairman of the Senate Committee on Foreign Relations, by which means Lincoln was apparently well acquainted with his views. As the owner of a textile mill in Lancashire, Bright represented an industry that was depressed by the Northern blockade which prevented Confederate cotton from reaching England. His support for the Union cause, in defiance of his economic self-interest and of his earlier pacifism during the Crimean War, was notable.

On April 15, 1863, Lincoln wrote for Bright sentiments condemning diplomatic recognition of any nation constructed "upon the basis of, and with the primary, and fundamental object to maintain, enlarge, and perpetuate human slavery." Sumner told Bright that Lincoln hoped to see such sentiments adopted in resolutions by public meetings in England. On June 30, 1863, John Arthur Roebuck introduced in Parliament a motion for Anglo-French recognition of the Confederacy. Bright attacked the motion in a thundering speech.

In December 1863 Lincoln was able to return the favor. He pardoned Alfred Rubery, the son of one of Bright's Birmingham constituents, who had been sentenced to 10 years in prison and a $10,000 fine for violation of the Confiscation Act of July 17, 1862. Rubery had been in league with a group of adventurers to sail the schooner *J. M. Chapman* from San Francisco as a Confederate privateer. Lincoln's pardon was meant "especially as a public mark of the esteem held by the United States of America for the high character and steady friendship of . . . John Bright."

The anteroom to Lincoln's White House office was decorated with a large photograph of Bright sent to Lincoln by an admirer of both men. When Lincoln was shot at Ford's Theatre in 1865, his wallet contained a newspaper clipping of John Bright's public letter endorsing Lincoln's reelection in 1864.

SOURCES: See J. G. Randall's "Lincoln and John Bright" in Randall, *Lincoln the Liberal Statesman* (New York: Dodd, Mead, 1947) and Mark E. Neely, Jr., "The Contents of Lincoln's Pockets at Ford's Theatre," *Lincoln Lore*, Number 1669 (March 1977), pp. 1–4.

See also CHAPMAN PIRATES.

Brooks, Noah (1830–1903) Journalist who was a friendly reporter of Lincoln's administration. Brooks was born in Castine, Maine, moved to Dixon, Illinois, in 1854, and met Lincoln in the Frémont campaign of 1856. After a brief stay in Kansas in 1857 as a "Free State" settler, he returned to Illinois and then moved to California in 1859. In 1862, after the death of his wife, he came to Washington to report on Lincoln's Presidency as a correspondent for the Sacramento *Daily Union*. He found the President's appearance already altered by the strain of responsibility: "His hair is grizzled, his gait more stooping, his countenance sallow, and there is a sunken, deathly look about the large, cavernous eyes."

Like Lincoln, a Whig turned Republican, Brooks was a friendly reporter of the Republican administration, and

John Bright was a peace-loving Quaker who led British opposition to the Crimean War. In 1864 a British cartoonist showed the irony in Bright's offering Lincoln the hand of friendship while the American President stands holding a dripping sword and treading on the Constitution. The dove of peace has become a buzzard.

Noah Brooks. (Courtesy of the Illinois State Historical Library)

Orville Hickman Browning

he enjoyed considerable intimacy with the President and Mrs. Lincoln. His 258 dispatches for the *Daily Union*, signed "Castine," are important sources for the day-to-day events of Lincoln's White House. Late in 1863 he gained appointment as a clerk in the House of Representatives. When he went to Chicago in 1864 to cover the Democratic nominating convention, Lincoln asked him to report to him by letter about the events there. Brooks reported a disturbing amount of enthusiasm for peace among the crowds that gathered to see the train carrying delegates to the convention; many were "blindly and ignorantly bawling for 'Peace.'" The crowd at the convention likewise applauded "peace men and measures and sentiments . . . to the echo, while patriotic utterances, what few there were, received no response from the crowd, though that is more noticeable among the outsiders than the members of the Convention." They vigorously applauded "'Dixie,' whenever it is played." These were not hopeful signs, but Brooks counted on the unifying effect on Republicans of at last having a specific Democratic opponent and platform on which to concentrate.

In 1865 Mrs. Lincoln and Dr. Anson G. Henry, an old Illinois associate of Lincoln's, worked to get Presidential secretary John G. Nicolay replaced by Brooks. Lincoln did announce a foreign appointment for Nicolay, but he never voiced his preference for a replacement.

Shortly after Lincoln's death, President Andrew Johnson appointed Brooks Naval Officer of the port of San Francisco, perhaps honoring a Lincoln pledge. In 1866, however, he removed Brooks in a purge of Radical Republican officeholders. Brooks admitted being a "'radical,' . . . if by that term is meant an adherence to the right, determination that equal and exact justice shall be done to all races, and denial to the rebels and rebellious States all political rights, forfeited by rebellion, until they have complied with conditions precedent."

Brooks sided with those who, after Lincoln's death, claimed that he was in all essential things a Christian. He stated that the President had told him that he prayed daily in the White House. "I have been driven many times upon my knees by the overwhelming conviction that I had nowhere else to go," Lincoln reputedly told Brooks. The California reporter surmised from such conversations that the President was seriously considering formal membership in a church.

In 1895 Brooks published *Washington in Lincoln's Time*, based on his Castine letters, a now standard source for information about the Lincoln White House.

SOURCES: Wayne C. Temple and Justin G. Turner's thorough biography of Brooks appeared serially in *Lincoln Herald* from volume LXXII (Fall 1970) through volume LXXIV (Winter 1972). *Mr. Lincoln's Washington: Selections from the Writings of Noah Brooks, Civil War Correspondent*, edited by P. J. Staudenraus (New York: Thomas Yoseloff, 1967), reprints some of the famous dispatches. See also William J. Wolf, *Lincoln's Religion* (Philadelphia: Pilgrim Press, 1970; originally published in 1959).

Brown University Lincoln Collection See MCLELLAN, CHARLES WOODBERRY.

Browning, Orville Hickman (1806–1881) Political associate and friend of Lincoln's. Browning, a Kentuckian by birth, attended Augusta College and was admitted to the bar in 1831, when he moved to Quincy, Illinois. Elected to the Illinois Senate in 1836, he served one term; he was conspicuous as a Whig who opposed the internal improvements system championed in the lower house by Abraham Lincoln, among others. Browning's district was located on the Mississippi River and therefore did not crave transportation improvements as desperately as Lincoln's central Illinois district. Like other Whigs, Browning supported the Illinois State Bank and favored the idea of a national bank. He advocated protective tariffs. In 1842 he was elected to a term in the Illinois House of Representatives, but he failed in a reelection race against Stephen A. Douglas. He ran again and lost in 1850 and in 1852.

Browning opposed the Kansas-Nebraska Act of 1854 and moved into Illinois's Republican party 2 years later. In 1856 he drafted the rather conservative state Republican platform and urged the nomination of conservative John McLean for President. Four years later he hoped for the nomination of Missouri's Edward Bates, the most conservative of the Republican hopefuls. He was a delegate to the national nominating convention in Chicago. Illinois's delegates were pledged to Lincoln, and Browning worked for Lincoln's nomination by stressing the candidate's opposition to nativism and his old Whig ties. Even after Lincoln's nomination, however, Browning thought that "we have made a mistake in the selection of candidates." The Quincy Republican was the natural choice to solicit Bates's support for the Republican ticket, and he procured from the conservative Missourian a public letter of endorsement. After Lincoln's election Browning unsuccessfully urged Bates's appointment as Secretary of State and Kentuckian Joseph Holt's selection as Secretary of War to conciliate the Border States. He also sought to keep ex-Democrat Norman B. Judd out of the Cabinet.

Lincoln gave Browning a draft of his First Inaugural Address, and the old Whig was in part responsible for what John G. Nicolay and John Hay called "the most vital change in the document." At his and William H. Seward's suggestion, Lincoln removed a provocative threat to "reclaim the public property and places which have fallen" in the seceded states. Browning advised the substitution of "hold, occupy and possess" for "reclaim."

It is ironic that Browning should be famous for that moderation of Lincoln's views in the Sumter crisis, for the threat of war on the whole brought out a radical streak in Browning. Even as he advised the President-elect not to threaten to "reclaim" Union forts, he admitted Lincoln's draft was right "On principle . . . as it now stands" and explained his reasoning for the change:

> In any conflict which may ensue between the government and the seceding States, it is very important that the traitors shall be the aggressors, and that they are kept constantly and palpably in the wrong.

The first attempt that is made to furnish supplies or reinforcements to Sumter will induce aggression by South Carolina, and then the government will stand justified, before the entire country, in repelling that aggression, and retaking the forts.

Browning's strategy for dealing with the Sumter crisis has often been taken as Lincoln's, and certainly Browning himself saw it that way. "Upon looking into the laws," he told the President 6 days after Sumter fell, "which clothe you with power to act in this emergency, I am not sure that you expected, or desired any other result." He was quite "sure the fall of Sumter has been of great advantage to us."

Months before Sumter fell, Browning had been so keen on "the duty of the government to protect its property" that he thought Lincoln might treat the seceding states "as territories" and organize new governments "accordingly." Actual warfare now brought a thunderous response. If Baltimore stood in the way of sending troops to Washington, he told Lincoln, it could be "laid in ruin." Before April was over he thought it likely that slaves would flock to the Union armies and inevitably "rise in rebellion." "The time is not yet," he added, "but it will come when it will be necessary for you to march an army into the South, and proclaim freedom to the slaves." Kentucky's "neutrality" was impossible, and Browning celebrated General John C. Frémont's emancipation proclamation for Missouri in the late summer of 1861. He thought Lincoln wrong to revoke it and to remove Frémont from command. Frémont's proclamation "does not deal with citizens at all," Browning remonstrated, "but with public enemies." International law had settled the question years ago. Grotius was wrong and Burlamaqui right: a state of war abolishes society and "gives . . . liberty to use violence *in infinitum.*" "All their property," Browning said, "is subject, to be . . . confiscated, and disposed of absolutely and forever by the belligerent power, without any reference whatever to the laws of society." Later, though, he acquiesced in Frémont's removal.

Browning sought appointment to the United States Supreme Court. In a somewhat embarrassed letter in April 1861 he told Lincoln that it was "an office peculiarly adapted to my tastes." Two months later Mrs. Browning informed the President of her husband's debilitating hernia and his modest economic circumstances. They owned "property enough to make us independent but that will be valuable only when we are under the sod." Browning was a prominent contender for the Court as late as the spring of 1862, but Lincoln never gave him the appointment.

After the death of Senator Stephen A. Douglas in June 1861, Governor Richard Yates appointed Browning to finish his term. In the Senate Browning defended the government's arbitrary arrests (against fellow Illinois Senator Lyman Trumbull's resolution demanding an explanation of them) and voted for the First Confiscation Act. But after April 1862 (when he voted to emancipate slaves in the District of Columbia) he grew suddenly and inexplicably conservative. He opposed the Second Confiscation Act and urged Lincoln to veto it, as it was a test "whether he was to control the abolitionists and Radicals or whether they were to control him." He admired Lincoln's letter answering Horace Greeley's "Prayer of Twenty Millions," and he opposed the Emancipation Proclamation, slowing down his campaigning for off-year congressional candidates when he learned of its issuance. He twice tried to get Lincoln to alter it.

There is no explaining the suddenness of his change, but it was a reversion to an accustomed conservatism rooted, in part, in old-fashioned racial views. In 1845 Browning became vice president of Illinois's Colonization Society, and he was still a colonizationist in the 1860s. He claimed always to have had "no doubt of the abstract injustice of human slavery," but in 1854 he still thought that "whilst the negroes remain in the country, the good of whites & blacks is alike consulted by preserving the present relations between them." Even in his brief period of radicalism, he thought emancipation of the slaves could be handled by giving "up the cotton states to them. Let them have the soil on which they were born—the climate which is congenial, the agriculture to which they are adapted." They could form "a Republic under the protectorate of this Government."

Browning grew increasingly disaffected with the administration politically. Many doubted whether he would support Lincoln's reelection. In September 1864 he told a correspondent that he had "never . . . been able to persuade myself that he [Lincoln] was big enough for his position." He respected presidential candidate George B. McClellan "personally," but he despised his platform, "which, in my opinion, looks only to separation and recognition of the Confederate Government." No one knows how he voted.

Browning and his wife remained personally friendly with the Lincolns. Browning was a frequent White House visitor in 1861 and 1862, and he and his wife stayed at the White House during Willie Lincoln's terminal illness. He was a pallbearer at the White House funeral services for the assassinated President.

In 1866 President Andrew Johnson appointed Browning Secretary of the Interior, and he remained in office to the end of Johnson's term. He fit in well with this anti-Reconstruction administration and became a Democrat in 1869. In the same year he was made a special attorney for the Chicago, Burlington, and Quincy Railroad, whose interests he served until his death in 1881 Gustave Koerner, a fellow Illinois Republican, remembered Browning's "conspicuous . . . ruffled shirt and large cuffs." Their relations had been pleasant enough, but Koerner would "have liked him better if he had been a little less conscious of his own superiority."

SOURCES: Maurice Baxter's *Orville Hickman Browning: Lincoln's Friend and Critic* (Bloomington: Indiana University Press, 1957) is a competent biography. *The Diary of Orville Hickman Browning*, edited in two volumes by Theodore Calvin Pease and James G. Randall (Springfield: Illinois State Historical Library, 1925) is an essential source for the politics of Lincoln's day. Browning's letters to Lincoln about revising the inaugural address (February 17, 1861), the benefits of Sumter's fall (April

18 and April 22, 1861), treating the seceded states as territories (January 15, 1861), and Frémont's proclamation (September 30, 1861) are in the Abraham Lincoln Papers, Library of Congress.

See also OWENS, MARY S.

Buchanan, James (1791–1868) Lincoln's immediate predecessor as President. Lincoln first met Buchanan in 1848, when he sought passports for constituents from Buchanan, who was then President James K. Polk's Secretary of State.

In the 1850s Lincoln was sharply opposed to Buchanan, whose platform, Lincoln argued, had a "tendency" to spread slavery's domain. In 1858 Lincoln charged that Buchanan conspired with Stephen A. Douglas, Franklin Pierce, and Roger B. Taney to nationalize slavery. Buchanan's role had been to "prepare the public mind" in his inaugural address in 1857 to accept a forthcoming Supreme Court decision (the Dred Scott decision) which would settle the question of slavery in the territories. Lincoln implied that President Buchanan already knew that the decision would favor slavery's extension. In truth, Buchanan and Douglas, far from being fellow conspirators, were bitter enemies, and in 1858 Douglas repeatedly charged that Lincoln's party conspired with the Buchanan wing of the Democratic party to unseat him from the United States Senate. Lincoln glossed over the differences between Douglas and Buchanan. He said the two men disagreed only in regard to the question of *fact* whether the Lecompton constitution for Kansas had been formed by the people; there was no difference in *principle* between them on the question of slavery's expansion.

Buchanan sought late in his administration to avoid confrontation with the South, at least until March 4, 1861, when Lincoln would assume office. The President's annual message to Congress of December 3, 1860, blamed the sectional crisis on antislavery agitation, but Buchanan warned the South that Lincoln's election the previous November was no provocation for secession. Even if Lincoln contemplated aggression on the South, and Buchanan did not think he did, Democrats in Congress and the Supreme Court would prevent it. "Let us wait for the overt act," he said. Buchanan believed that secession was not a legal right, but the Constitution granted the federal government no power to "coerce a State into submission." He recommended a convention to amend the Constitution to guarantee slavery where it already existed and to guarantee the rights of slave property in the territories until statehood; the people of a territory could decide at that point whether to retain slavery or not. He also recommended an amendment guaranteeing the enforcement of fugitive slave laws. Lincoln did not respond to the message publicly, but privately he affirmed his opposition to any concession on the territorial question.

After December 10 Buchanan refused to reinforce the federal forts in South Carolina, but he also refused to surrender Fort Sumter when South Carolina seceded on the 20th. On Christmas Day he halted the shipment of cannons from Pittsburgh to forts in Texas which were suspiciously unprepared to put them in place. Buchanan sent newspaper editor Duff Green to Springfield to persuade Lincoln to support calling a constitutional convention to resolve the crisis. Green met with Lincoln on the 28th, but the President-elect showed no interest in a convention.

As Southerners departed from Buchanan's Cabinet, men of sterner pro-Union sympathies replaced them. Buchanan's policies changed. After January 1, 1861, Buchanan decided to reinforce Fort Sumter, in Charleston harbor, with provisions and men. The steamer *Star of the West* attempted to do so but was repelled by shore batteries. Thereafter, the President's policy was to collect customs revenues from a vessel in the harbor (South Carolina had seized the federal customs house), defend public property if attacked, and avoid anything else that might cause war. Congress instituted an investigation of charges that former Secretary of War John Floyd had conspired to send large quantities of arms to Southern arsenals. In the end, Congress found that the South had received only its share or less of federal arms, but the investigation fed rumors that Buchanan's administration abetted secession.

On March 4, the day of the inauguration of the new President, Buchanan picked Lincoln up in his carriage. Accompanied by Senators Edward D. Baker and James A. Pearce, they chatted politely on the way to the Capitol and entered the Senate Chamber arm-in-arm. Two days later, Buchanan left Washington for his home, Wheatland, in Lancaster, Pennsylvania.

Buchanan carefully studied Lincoln's inaugural address and found in it the very policies he had been pursuing before leaving office: the Union was perpetual and

James Buchanan slumbers and John Floyd loots the treasury while Jefferson Davis and Alexander H. Stephens preach treason and the country splits. Lincoln calls men to serve sturdy Winfield Scott in this allegorical print published by Kimmel & Forster in 1865. Note the capitalists generously answering the call by emptying bags of money at Lincoln's feet.

secession illegal; the executive would defend public property but not attack the South; and the Constitution might be amended to guarantee slavery in the states. The partisan press did not recognize the similarities.

The morning he heard of the attack on Fort Sumter Buchanan wrote: "The Confederate States have deliberately commenced the civil war, & God knows where it may end." He never wavered in blaming the South for starting the war, and none of the five living ex-Presidents during the Civil War gave the administration firmer support. Most Republicans, however, blamed the war on the inaction, if not the deliberate conspiring, of the Buchanan administration. Wheatland had to be guarded by volunteers from the Masonic lodge in Lancaster. Even President Lincoln's first message to Congress charged that upon his arrival in Washington "a disproportionate share, of the Federal muskets and rifles" were in the South; that the Southern mints had a great deal of money; that the "Navy was scattered in distant seas"; and that Fort Pickens in Florida failed to be reinforced because of "some *quasi* armistice of the late administration." A Senate resolution of December 15, 1862, censured Buchanan for failing "to take necessary and proper measures to prevent" rebellion out of "sympathy with the conspirators and their treasonable project." The resolution did not pass, but Buchanan became obsessed with justifying his course in the secession crisis and eventually produced *Mr. Buchanan's Administration on the Eve of the Rebellion.* He finished the book in 1862 but delayed publication until 1866 "to avoid the possible imputation . . . that any portion of it was intended to embarrass Mr. Lincoln's administration."

Despite his feeling of persecution, Buchanan warned Democrats not to dally with nagging demands for peace initiatives, and he disagreed even with close friends in the party who thought the war was unconstitutional or that Lincoln had provoked it. "Mr. Lincoln had no alternative," Buchanan said, "but to defend the country against dismemberment. I certainly should have done the same thing had they begun the war in my time." He defended the draft when Pennsylvania's Democratic gubernatorial candidate, George Woodward, opposed it in 1863. Buchanan thought Lincoln's administration was guilty of "many clear violations of the Constitution," but he did not agree with Democratic opposition to administration war aims in 1864. After Lincoln won reelection, however, Buchanan did believe that the President should offer the enemy a "return to the Union just as they were before."

Buchanan never spoke ill of Lincoln. He thought him "an honest and patriotic man" and "a man of a kindly and benevolent heart and of plain, sincere and frank manners." After Lincoln's assassination Buchanan said that he had "felt for him much personal regard."

SOURCES: Philip Shriver Klein's *President James Buchanan: A Biography* (University Park: Pennsylvania State University Press, 1962) is definitive.

Burton, John Edgar (1847–1930) Millionaire Lincoln collector. John E. Burton was the son of a cobbler from New Hartford, New York. As a boy, Burton saw Lincoln when his train stopped in Utica on the way to his inauguration, and he always remembered the incident as sparking his interest in Lincoln.

Burton became a schoolteacher and then school principal in Richmond and Lake Geneva, Illinois. In 1872 he established the Geneva *Herald*. He became an agent for Equitable Life Insurance and later the general manager of the company's operations in Wisconsin, Minnesota, and northern Michigan. He invested in real estate, industry, and financial institutions. By investing in iron and copper mining in northern Wisconsin and Michigan in 1885, he made a fortune in 3 years. From his Milwaukee office, he branched out into California gold mines, Colorado and Mexican silver mines, tin mines in Alaska, and mahogany forests in Honduras. He was interested in coins and amassed a collection of 5000, some of them great rarities.

Burton claimed to have collected Lincolniana for 50 years, which would mean that he started in the 1860s. He acquired books, manuscripts, artifacts, relics, and pictures. In the heyday of Lincoln collecting, the "Big Five" collectors, who dominated the field, regarded his competition with curiosity and some jealousy. J. B. Oakleaf visited him in 1911 and reported to Daniel Fish that Burton lived "in a three story house, and the house is filled from top to bottom with books and curios of different things and every room is filled, with the exception of the sitting-room, the dining-room and the kitchen." Oakleaf thought him undiscriminating in classifying items as Lincolniana and reported "he doesn't know that exclusive Lincoln catalogues were Lincolniana. He did not consider Jap books Lincolniana." He noted as well that "He pays enormous prices for things and . . . seems to be quite a reader, so he knows about what is in them, but he has so many things that he calls Lincolniana that there would [be] no limit to a Lincoln collection if you should take such as he calls Lincolniana."

Burton amassed a library of 14,000 volumes, 2460 of which were devoted to Lincoln. He had begun to lose his economic empire in 1898, and was so hard-pressed financially by 1915 that he had to sell his collection at auction. The Anderson Galleries of New York handled the sale, which realized $11,126.35 for 2170 lots. He owned some great items: for example, two pages from Lincoln's Sum Book (among the earliest examples of Lincoln's writing), a presentation copy of the published version of the Lincoln-Douglas Debates (given by Lincoln to John H. Littlefield), and a rare pamphlet, *Reasons against the Re-Nomination of Abraham Lincoln* (1864).

Burton was enthusiastic and somewhat uncritical. Lincoln was frequently associated with local counsel in cases on the Eighth Judicial Circuit. In a letter attempting to sell some legal documents which were written and signed by Lincoln and by the associate lawyer in the case as well, Burton challenged "history, biography and bibliography to produce this simple fact hitherto unknown" that Lincoln "belonged to *six* law firms." He was a Republican in politics, a bimetallist in monetary

Butler, Benjamin Franklin

These two cartoons illustrate the opposing views of General Butler. The first, which appeared in Harper's Weekly on January 17, 1863, after Butler's removal from command in New Orleans, depicts the Massachusetts general as an efficient janitor. Indeed, Butler saw himself this way. Appalled at the stench of hot and humid New Orleans and fearing that Southerners counted on yellow fever to defeat the occupying Union army, Butler studied a history of the yellow fever epidemic of 1853, plotted the areas of the city where the outbreak was worst, put the unemployed poor of New Orleans to work cleaning up these areas, and in general attempted to "New Englandize" this old Southern port. He launched a similar program in occupied Norfolk. In the second cartoon Copperhead cartoonist Adalbert Johann Volck saw Butler, the enterprising political general, as "Spoons" Butler, the corrupt Yankee who stole the silverware from the homes of the Southern aristocracy. Volck brilliantly conceived of Lincoln as the impossible idealist Don Quixote (complete with a John Brown pike instead of a lance) accompanied by the sordid realist Benjamin F. Butler as Sancho Panza. Note the table knife in Butler's belt.

policy, and (late in life) an agnostic. Items from the Burton collection are now in many different collections.

SOURCES: See letters from Burton to T. B. Smalley, October 23, 1908, and J. B. Oakleaf to Daniel Fish, November 17, 1911, in the Louis A. Warren Lincoln Library and Museum, Fort Wayne, Indiana; *John E. Burton* (n.p., n.d.) a pamphlet at the Louis A. Warren Lincoln Library and Museum; and R. Gerald McMurtry, "John E. Burton: Lincoln Collector," *Lincoln Lore*, Number 1605 (November 1971), pp. 1–3.

Butler, Benjamin Franklin (1818–1893) Civil War general. Born in New Hampshire, Butler lived most of his life in Lowell, Massachusetts. He was a successful criminal lawyer, businessman, and Democratic politician. Though it would haunt him ever after, his decision to support Jefferson Davis for the presidential nomination in 1860 was not a profound index of his political ideas. Where Democrats were a hopeless minority, as in Massachusetts, the only hope for patronage from the national administration was if the Democrats won the Presidency, and that could happen, Butler thought, only if the nominee were acceptable to the South. Eventually, he supported John C. Breckinridge in the election of 1860.

A general of the Massachusetts militia, the impetuous Butler rushed his unit to Washington immediately after Fort Sumter fell. On May 13, 1861, largely on his own initiative, he seized Baltimore. Lincoln thereafter promoted him but allowed General Winfield Scott to relieve him of command there and send him to Fortress Monroe, Virginia. Almost immediately, Butler coined a term to refer to slaves used for insurrectionary purposes who subsequently escaped into Union lines: "contraband of war." Northern commanders could seize contraband, of course, but technically they had to return fugitive slaves. Thereafter, fugitive slaves in Union lines were popularly known as contrabands.

Authorized by Lincoln in the fall of 1861 to organize six New England regiments, Butler entered the first of countless controversies that would swirl about him and cause the President numerous headaches. He quarreled with Massachusetts Governor John A. Andrew over the right to appoint officers in the Massachusetts units he raised. In truth, Andrew misunderstood the purpose of raising the regiments, which at least in part was to get Democrats into the army and out of politics. Andrew's objections to appointing Democratic officers missed the mark, but the Governor did have the law on his side. Lincoln sent Butler to the Mississippi coast, where in May 1862 his troops occupied New Orleans. His occupation of the city was controversial in the extreme and earned him the nickname in the South of "the Beast." After the fall elections in 1862, the President removed Butler from the Department of the Gulf without explanation, though surely the general's confiscation of the property of foreign consuls in New Orleans, his reputation for corruption, and his inability to bring any military results further up the river influenced the Commander in Chief. Lincoln had word even from one of Butler's loyal associates, John W. Shaffer, that "Genl Butler is not much of a soldier."

Butler was a politician of considerable skill and importance, however, especially as a symbol of Democratic willingness to fight a Republican administration's war. Lincoln always treated him with respect. Butler also symbolized advanced policies toward the Negro, because he had begun to recruit them for military service while in New Orleans. In truth, Butler acted only when the administration, through Secretary of the Treasury Salmon P. Chase, appeared to encourage the move, but he acted in such a way as to gain the credit for himself. He was also a symbol of an uncompromisingly tough attitude toward disloyalty.

Lincoln more than once wavered in deciding what to do with Butler, buffeted probably by conflicting respect for the general's political following and his popularity with congressional Radicals on the Joint Committee on the Conduct of the War, on the one hand, and fears of his military incompetence, on the other. The President wrote but never issued an order to return him to his New Orleans command. Eventually Lincoln reassigned him to Fortress Monroe and command of the Department of Virginia and North Carolina in November 1863.

Butler claimed in later years that Lincoln invited him to be his running mate early in 1864, and he declined the offer. There is no firm documentation. Whatever the case, Butler's appraisal of Lincoln's abilities was not high. Though publicly he congratulated Lincoln on his renomination in 1864, privately he wrote his wife: "This country has more vitality than any other on earth if it can stand this sort of administration for another four years."

Military success again eluded Butler in Virginia, but controversy was his steady companion. When Mrs. J. Todd White passed through his lines to the Confederacy with a pass from Lincoln, a furor arose over the contents of her trunks. Mrs. White was a relative of Mrs. Lincoln, and newspapers in New York charged that she carried contraband goods in her baggage, which was protected from the customary inspection by Lincoln's pass. With his usual sharpness, Butler noted that the newspaper articles carried their own refutation: how could it be known that there was contraband in the baggage if, on the President's orders, there had been no inspection of it? Butler fully exonerated the President and told him to dismiss the incident from his thoughts. Surely, the controversial general said, the little episode could not trouble Lincoln much. Anyone as steeped in controversy as Butler was knew that this was a trifle.

Secretary of War Edwin M. Stanton sent Butler to New York City with 5000 troops to keep that Democratic stronghold, the site of enormous draft riots in the summer of 1863, calm at election time in November. Butler had become embroiled in a quarrel with Francis H. Pierpont, Governor of the Restored Government of Virginia, over their conflicting jurisdictions in general and over Butler's holding an election in Norfolk in particular. Lincoln let the election occur, though he doubted its propriety; but when Butler seemed ready to hold similar elections on Virginia's Eastern Shore at the end of the year, Lincoln sided with Pierpont. Butler, Lincoln said, could do whatever he saw was a military necessity under martial law, but he did not need the authority of an election to do it, and this was clearly an encroachment on civil powers. When General Ulysses S. Grant became exasperated over Butler's failure to capture Wilmington, North Carolina, in December, the political general's days were numbered. On January 7, 1865, he was relieved of command.

An important reminiscence in the *Autobiography and Personal Reminiscences of Major-General Benj. F. Butler: Butler's Book* (Boston: A. M. Thayer, 1892) claims that Lincoln discussed his desire to "get rid of the negroes," especially those "whom we have armed and disciplined," with Butler in 1865. Lincoln, Butler recalled, feared "a race war" and not "trouble with our white troops" after they were disbanded; for "all the intelligent men among them were good citizens or they would not have been good soldiers." He wanted Butler's advice concerning use of the navy, to be idled at war's end, for "sending all the blacks away." He needed Butler's "experience in moving bodies of men by water,—your movement up the James was a magnificent one," the President is alleged to have said. The anecdote is completely spurious. Butler was not in Washington at the time he claimed the interview occurred. Lincoln thought Negro soldiers especially deserving of privilege, not exportation. According to Gideon Welles's diary, Lincoln feared that "the disbanded armies would turn into robber bands and guerillas" in Virginia. And, whereas Butler had moved his troops up the James River successfully in May 1864, the campaign that followed was an unmitigated disaster which saw an inferior Confederate force bottle up and humiliate Butler's army. To have mentioned the campaign would have been to insult the general!

After the war Butler was for a time a leader of the Radical Republicans and the movement to impeach President Andrew Johnson. Thereafter he followed an erratic political course as, in succession, a Greenback, Democratic, and Anti-Monopoly party candidate.

SOURCES: A competent, readable, and perhaps overly sympathetic biography is Hans Louis Trefousse's *Ben Butler: The South Called Him BEAST!* (New York: Twayne, 1957). On Butler's recruitment of Negro soldiers in Louisiana see Peyton McCrary, *Abraham Lincoln and Reconstruction: The Louisiana Experiment* (Princeton, N.J.: Princeton University Press, 1978). See also Mark E. Neely, Jr., "Abraham Lincoln and Black Colonization: Benjamin Butler's Spurious Testimony," *Civil War History*, XXV (March 1979), 76–83.

See also ANDREW, JOHN ALBION; CAMERON, SIMON.

Butterfield, Justin *See* TAYLOR, ZACHARY.

C

Cabinet *See* BATES, EDWARD [Attorney General]; BLAIR, MONTGOMERY [Postmaster General]; CAMERON, SIMON [Secretary of War]; CHASE, SALMON PORTLAND [Secretary of the Treasury]; DENNISON, WILLIAM [Postmaster General]; FESSENDEN, WILLIAM PITT [Secretary of the Treasury]; McCULLOCH, HUGH [Secretary of the Treasury]; SEWARD, WILLIAM HENRY [Secretary of State]; SMITH, CALEB BLOOD [Secretary of the Interior]; SPEED, JAMES [Attorney General]; STANTON, EDWIN McMASTERS [Secretary of War]; USHER, JOHN PALMER [Secretary of the Interior]; and WELLES, GIDEON [Secretary of the Navy].

See also PRESIDENCY, POWERS OF.

Cabinet Crisis of December 1862 *See* CHASE, SALMON PORTLAND; RADICAL REPUBLICANS; SEWARD, WILLIAM HENRY.

Calhoun, John (1808–1859) Surveyor who employed young Abraham Lincoln as a deputy in Sangamon County. Calhoun was born in Boston and moved to New Salem in 1830. He served in the Black Hawk War and was appointed county surveyor. In 1833 he hired Lincoln as deputy surveyor, assigning him the northern part of the county (now Menard and southern Mason Counties). Lincoln knew nothing of surveying but "accepted, procured a compass and chain, studied Flint, and Gibson a little, and went at it." Calhoun chose to run for the state senate in 1835 rather than seek the surveyor's post (made elective that year). Lincoln stayed on in the job under Calhoun's successor, Thomas M. Neale. He surveyed several towns (New Boston, Bath, Albany, and Huron), numerous roads, and farm boundaries. All he said of the experience, however, was that it "procured bread, and kept soul and body together."

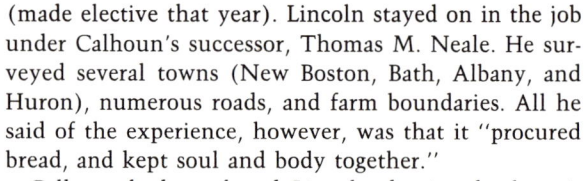

Calhoun had employed Lincoln despite the latter's politics; for Lincoln was already "an avowed Clay man" and Calhoun was a staunch Jacksonian Democrat. Their paths crossed again—as political rivals—when they spoke on opposite sides at a political rally on July 11, 1836. When Lincoln and Calhoun served in the state legislature at the same time (1839–1841), their views frequently clashed. Lincoln voted to table Calhoun's resolutions denying that Congress could abolish slavery in the District of Columbia, stating no objection to the annexation of Texas or the addition of slave states to the Union, and condemning the repeal of laws "which graduate the right of the citizens by the color of the skin." They took opposite sides on the tariff issue in debates in 1844.

Calhoun was Springfield's mayor from 1849 to 1851. In 1852 he lost a race for Congress against Richard Yates. In 1854 Lincoln and Calhoun clashed over the Kansas-Nebraska Act. In the same year, thanks to Stephen A. Douglas's influence, Calhoun became Surveyor General of Kansas and Nebraska Territory. In 1857 he was president of the constitutional convention which produced the divisive Lecompton constitution for Kansas. Calhoun favored submitting the whole constitution to the vote

John Calhoun. (Courtesy of the Illinois State Historical Library)

of the people, but he acquiesced in the final plan to submit to a vote only the question of legalizing slavery. When the legislature launched an investigation of the vote on the constitution, Calhoun left for Missouri and his clerk said that he had taken the returns with him. Later the returns were found buried in a candle-box, and even Lincoln referred to his old friend as "Candle-box" Calhoun. He was cordially despised by antislavery advocates in the North and died in Missouri in the shadow of this opprobrium. Yet he had opposed the extreme proslavery forces in Kansas and acquiesced only reluctantly in the compromise of partial submission of the constitution.

SOURCES: See J. G. Randall's biographical sketch in the *Dictionary of American Biography* (New York: Charles Scribner's Sons, 1958), II, 410–411. Calhoun's conservative resolutions on slavery appear in the *Journal of the House of Representatives of the Eleventh General Assembly of the State of Illinois* (Vandalia: William Walters, 1838), pp. 322–323.

Cameron, Simon (1799–1889) President Lincoln's first Secretary of War. Cameron was born in Pennsylvania, where he became first a newspaper editor and then a successful entrepreneur. His considerable wealth derived from construction contracts for canals and railroads which burgeoned in the era of internal improvements, from banking, from the iron industry, and from insurance. Though he always advocated tariffs for protection-mad Pennsylvania, his political career found him associated first with the Democratic party, then with Whigs, Native Americans, and protariff Democrats (who elected him to the United States Senate in 1845); with the Know-Nothing party in 1855; and finally with the Republicans, who kept his allegiance until his death. His wealth, his frequent changes of party, and the profits his bank gained from a settlement he negotiated as a state commissioner for Winnebago Indian claims in 1838 gave Cameron a reputation for dishonesty, political wire-pulling, and rapacious profiteering. Nevertheless, he influenced Pennsylvania politics as much as any single man from 1845 to 1889.

Cameron, who had been elected to the Senate again in 1857, was a contender for the Republican presidential nomination in 1860, but he did not have a firm hold even on the Pennsylvania delegation. On the first ballot at the nominating convention he was in third place behind William H. Seward and Lincoln. Many Pennsylvania delegates gave him initial backing only to ensure his support for the state gubernatorial ticket, which was headed by his factional enemy, Andrew G. Curtin. Curtin's henchman Alexander K. McClure later took credit for Pennsylvania's crucial second-ballot switch from Cameron to Lincoln, but some of Cameron's managers also pushed for the change. Cameron's men later claimed that Lincoln's managers, David Davis and Leonard Swett, had promised Cameron a Cabinet post in exchange. At most they may have promised Pennsylvania a place in the Cabinet. Cameron campaigned vigorously for Lincoln.

Cameron was so important in Pennsylvania that it would have been exceedingly difficult to give the state any office without giving it to him. He came to Springfield on December 30, 1860, and saw Lincoln. The President-elect was inundated with letters endorsing or opposing Cameron's appointment. In a long memorandum, Lincoln balanced charges of Cameron's corruption against letters of recommendation for him. The pros outweighed the cons, and on December 31 Lincoln told Cameron he would nominate him for the War Department or the Treasury. On January 2 Cameron's enemy McClure called on Lincoln, and the next day Lincoln withdrew his offer, partly because of his "interview with McClure," Lincoln explained, though the "more potent matter is wholly outside of Pennsylvania." Lincoln was "not at liberty to specify" the latter objection, and no one is sure what it was.

Cameron was crushed, but only temporarily. Though he was "galled by disappointment," as Francis P. Blair told Lincoln, when he heard of Maryland conspiracies

Simon Cameron, his reputation for corruption suggested by his appearance as a Winnebago chief, startles President-elect Lincoln, brilliantly depicted as a Puritan because of his reputation for honesty and moral rectitude. Henry Louis Stephens thus lampooned Cameron's visit to Springfield in the February 2, 1861, issue of Vanity Fair, *an American humor magazine modeled after London's* Punch.

ALARMING APPEARANCE OF THE WINNEBAGO CHIEF
CAMERON AT SPRINGFIELD.

CAMERON.—"YOU'VE SENT FOR ME, AND I'VE COME. IF YOU DON'T WANT ME, I'LL GO BACK TO MY WIGWAM."

to prevent Lincoln's inauguration, he went to Blair and told him "that if . . . there was danger to the Capitol he would go home & bring ten thousand men to see you inaugurated." In February opposition to Cameron within Pennsylvania collapsed out of fear that the state could put no one in the Cabinet but Cameron. Lincoln could find no firm evidence of corruption beyond what was in public print, and at the end of the month he saw Cameron in Washington. He needed an important former Democrat in the Cabinet, and after his inauguration the President nominated Cameron for Secretary of War.

With only about 90 employees, an army of less than 17,000 men, and not even an Assistant Secretary of War until August, Secretary Cameron faced an enormous task and, moreover, faced it bereft of any military knowledge to speak of. Greatly "influenced by the opinions of the Army officers," he thought at first that Fort Sumter had to be abandoned. More prescient was his advice that Lincoln call up more than the initial 75,000 men he asked for after the fall of Sumter.

Cameron's policies were less questionable than his administrative procedures, some of which were highly irregular. Because of his reputation for corruption, War Department contracts drew a firestorm of denunciation. When Cameron's annual report included a recommendation for freeing and arming slaves as soldiers, his days were numbered—particularly since the Secretary highhandedly sent copies of his report to key post offices for simultaneous distribution with Lincoln's annual report. When the government printer informed Lincoln of the contents of Cameron's report, Lincoln ordered the report's distribution halted and its contents altered, but the original report made its way into the newspapers anyway.

Cassius M. Clay's desire to resign from the Russian mission gave Lincoln the opportunity to get rid of Cameron by sending him to Moscow. The letter of dismissal (January 11, 1862) surprised and hurt Cameron because it was curt and failed to commend his previous service. Later, Lincoln antedated a letter accepting Cameron's resignation and praising his services as Secretary. The letter may have been written with some reluctance, but Lincoln faithfully defended Cameron from charges of corruption leveled by Congress in May. On May 26 Lincoln responded to a censure of Cameron by the House of Representatives, saying that the blame could not "rest exclusively or chiefly upon Mr. Cameron." Lincoln admitted that he and the other department heads "were at least equally responsible . . . for whatever error, wrong, or fault was committed." The President excused the War Department's careless practices as functions of the dire emergency.

Cameron left for Russia in May and was already back on furlough in November. He never returned to his foreign post, which he resigned the next February. His correspondence with Lincoln continued. Threatened with a civil suit brought by Baltimore citizens arrested by Federal authorities while he was Secretary of War, Cameron in the fall of 1863 pressured Lincoln to order treason trials for the Marylanders so that they would drop their suit. Pennsylvania politics were troubling him too. Though he had hoped for another nominee, he reluctantly supported Curtin's bid for reelection in 1863—but only because Curtin happened to be "the representative of the Loyalty of this state." Otherwise, many "good republicans and pious Christians . . . would see him in H__l first," Cameron said.

As early as June 1863 he was looking to Lincoln's reelection the next year, and he warned the President in September that Curtin wanted the nomination and would appeal for "contracts and jobs" in the meantime to aid his purpose by building a patronage machine. Like Lincoln, Cameron feared General George G. Meade would let Lee escape after Gettysburg, and wrote Lincoln a letter expressing "hope in God you will put forth your authority & order" reinforcements to Meade to press the offensive. The letter arrived at the White House only after Lee had escaped.

Though clearly getting back in the administration's good graces, Cameron's own political comeback was still in the future. In January 1863 he lost a bid for the Senate. He blamed his defeat on David Wilmot's treachery. Wilmot, Cameron told the President, had had his ally in the legislature vote for William D. Kelley; the result, the election of Democrat Charles Buckalew, was to send to Congress "an enemy of your Admin[istration]." He warned Lincoln repeatedly against similar treachery aimed at preventing the President's reelection. Cameron was "surprised to see what great exertions are being made *from Washington* and by men *in your apparent confidence* to create a reaction in our Legislature," which had endorsed Lincoln's renomination in January. But he assured Lincoln that "the D__l and all his imps cannot take Pennsylvania from you." All the officeholders in Philadelphia but the Collector of the Port, the Navy Officer, and the Navy Agent were against Lincoln, he warned.

Ever the careful politician, Cameron suggested to the President that the "German element of the republican party" felt "overlooked" for the Irish. They had some "cause of complaint," he chided, and deserved better—especially "when I remember at the beginning of the war how grandly they came to our rescue, and how glad all of us, at Washington were to receive them." He warned, too, against movements to postpone the Republican convention, saying it was "well known that Mr. Seward has never ceased to think he will succeed you, and that his faithful manager [Thurlow Weed] hopes to carry him into the Presidency next March, aided perhaps by the millions made in N. York [on] army & navy contracts." John A. Dix was another threat.

Lincoln trusted Cameron enough by 1864 that Cameron may have become the President's unofficial liaison to contact possible vice-presidential running mates. Such may have been the purpose of Cameron's visit to Benjamin F. Butler in March, though Butler extended the invitation and Cameron later asked to come to Washington to tell Lincoln what he had heard after "much pleasant conversation." Cameron claimed Lincoln urged him privately to support Andrew Johnson for Vice President. After the death of the first Vice President, Hannibal Hamlin, a controversy raged over his removal from the Lincoln ticket. Some discredit Cameron's statement about Lincoln's wishes as an attempt to put all responsibility on Lincoln for the selection of the ultimately extremely unpopular Johnson.

Cameron was named an honorary citizen pallbearer for Lincoln's funeral in Washington. Lincoln's widow regarded him as a special friend. She enlisted his willing aid in raising money to buy her a house in Chicago in 1866. Cameron failed to raise the substantial sum he hoped to, and after early 1867 Mrs. Lincoln ceased writing him. In 1870 he made an eloquent appeal in the Senate for a bill which gave Mrs. Lincoln a $3000 pension.

What Cameron thought of Lincoln is not precisely known. He seems to have enjoyed Lincoln's sense of humor and occasionally flavored his own letters to the President with wit. In 1864, for example, he sent Lincoln an article on how many Presidents had been reelected and added that his German neighbor had said of the list, that "all of them, who were good for anything were twice put in the place." On the other hand, when Ulysses S. Grant died in 1885, Cameron noted his "simple honesty—not cunning like . . . Lincoln."

SOURCES: Erwin Stanley Bradley's *Simon Cameron, Lincoln's Secretary of War: A Political Biography* (Philadelphia: University of Pennsylvania Press, 1966) provides adequate treatment of this difficult figure. Cameron's relationship with Mrs. Lincoln can be traced in Justin G. and Linda Levitt Turner, *Mary Todd Lincoln: Her Life and Letters* (New York: Alfred A. Knopf, 1972). Blair's letter to Lincoln about Cameron's reaction to threats on the Capital (January 14, 1861) and Cameron's letters to Lincoln about Sumter (March 16, 1861), Curtin's reelection (September 18, 1863), Meade (July 14, 1863), Pennsylvania's 1863 Senate race (January 13, 1863), "exertions . . . from Washington" (February 13, 1864), the "German element" (March 9, 1864), and Seward and Butler (March 29, 1864) are in the Abraham Lincoln Papers, Library of Congress.

See also CURTIN, ANDREW GREGG; DAVIS, DAVID; FELL, JESSE WILSON; MCCLURE, ALEXANDER KELLY; SWETT, LEONARD.

Carpenter, Francis Bicknell (1830–1900) Artist who painted the "First Reading of the Emancipation Proclamation of President Lincoln." Born on a farm near Homer, New York, Carpenter in 1844 served a 6-month apprenticeship with artist Sanford Thayer in Syracuse before commencing his career as a portrait painter. He was almost immediately successful, moved to New York City in 1851, and the next year was commissioned to paint a full-length portrait of Millard Fillmore. He painted President Franklin Pierce's portrait and in 1855 went temporarily to Washington to paint several famous political figures, including Horace Greeley and Lewis Cass.

Supported by patron Frederick A. Lane and given access to Lincoln through Representative Schuyler Colfax and Samuel Sinclair of the New York *Tribune,* Carpenter went to Washington February 4, 1864, to paint his famous picture. Representative Owen Lovejoy endorsed his purpose, and Lincoln allowed Carpenter to work in the White House. The artist set his large canvas up in the state dining room and frequently studied and sketched the President in his office while Lincoln conducted official business. Carpenter stayed in the White House until near the end of July 1864.

The result of this remarkable residence was not only a famous painting but also an important book, *Six Months at the White House with Abraham Lincoln.* Carpenter admitted that his book was "rambling and fragmentary." It was colored by a generally moralistic and antislavery point of view as well. But it is a valuable source for Lincoln's activities in the decisive year of his reelection, and it contains numerous anecdotes which are widely quoted by biographers and are available in no other source. Carpenter's book is the source of the story that Lincoln termed Lovejoy "the best friend I had in Congress," that he once wished that every Wall Street speculator in gold "had his *devilish* head shot off," and that, in reply to a clergyman who said that he hoped the Lord was on our side, Lincoln said, "it is my constant anxiety and prayer that *I* and *this nation* should be on the LORD'S *side."* Carpenter also included numerous Lincoln stories that he had heard from others, particularly about Lincoln's religious views, which seem more questionable than the stories Carpenter reported as an eyewitness. Numerous stories of Lincoln's knowledge of poetry and Shakespeare, of his reading habits (he never read a novel through in his life), and of his decision to emancipate the slaves are important sources for any Lincoln biographer.

Carpenter's painting, based on sittings and on photographs taken for him by cameramen from Mathew Brady's studios, was ready for viewing in the White House by July 22, 1864. Thereafter, it was exhibited in several cities in the United States and was copied in 1865–1866 by engraver Alexander Hay Ritchie for a popular $5 print distributed by printers Derby & Miller of New York City. Lincoln himself was the first subscriber to the engraving. Carpenter made numerous changes in the painting before Elizabeth Thompson of New York City purchased it for $25,000. In 1878 she presented it to the United States government. It hangs in the U.S. Capitol today.

Carpenter told Owen Lovejoy that "Most historical pictures (so called) are merely the fancy pieces of their authors." Inspired by John Ruskin to think that the "*portrait* is the only *true* historical picture," Carpenter nevertheless admitted his painting was a "mingling of fact and allegory." Apparently "the 'realistic' school of art, when applied to the illustration of historic events" allowed the painter to place "prominently in the foreground in attitudes which indicated their support of the measure" those who had long striven for the Proclamation. Likewise, he placed the "radical" group on the viewer's left and the more conservative on the right, with Lincoln "at the head of the official table, . . . nearest . . . the radical, but the uniting point of both." The details of the room were scrupulously copied, as the

Francis Bicknell Carpenter

Carroll, Anna Ella

KEY TO THE PICTURE

THE MEN
1. President Lincoln.
2. William H. Seward, Secretary of State.
3. Salmon P. Chase, Secretary of Treasury.
4. Edwin M. Stanton, Secretary of War.
5. Gideon Welles, Secretary of Navy.
6. Edward Bates, Attorney-General.
7. Montgomery Blair, Postmaster-General.
8. Caleb B. Smith, Secretary of Interior.

ACCESSORIES
9. Photograph of Simon Cameron, Ex-Sec. War.
10. Portrait of Andrew Jackson.
11. Parchment Copy of the Constitution.
12. Map of Seat of War in Virginia.
13. Map showing Slave Population in gradulight and shade.
14. War Department Portfolio.
15. Story's "Commentaries on the Constitution."
16. Whiting's "War Powers of the President."
17. New York *Tribune*.
18. Two volumes *Congressional Globe*.

The room is the Official Chamber of the White House, in which all Cabinet meetings are held, and in which the President receives calls upon official business.

Francis Bicknell Carpenter's famous painting, the basis of this popular print, was an ideological picture, showing the liberal members of the Cabinet on the viewer's left, and the more conservative on the right. Lincoln is in the center, but tending slightly to the liberal side. Simon Cameron's portrait on the wall at the far left appears on the liberal side because he was the first in the Cabinet to propose the use of Negroes as soldiers in the Union army.

key to the painting shows. The popular painting and engraving, therefore, were political works of art conveying a message of Lincoln's antislavery convictions. Mrs. Lincoln thought the Emancipation painting "very perfect" and Ritchie's engraving "quite equal to it."

Carpenter's book (after 1868 called *The Inner Life of Abraham Lincoln*) went through some 16 editions. Mrs. Lincoln became exasperated at Carpenter's claims to intimate knowledge of her husband and in 1867 said that he "never had a dozen interviews" with the President, that Lincoln complained "that C. presumed upon the privilege he had given C.," and that Carpenter "intruded frequently into Mr L's office, when time was too precious to be idled."

SOURCES: Francis B. Carpenter's *Six Months at the White House with Abraham Lincoln: The Story of a Picture* (New York: Hurd and Houghton, 1866) contains valuable and entertaining material. George Harvey Genzmer's biographical sketch of Carpenter in the *Dictionary of American Biography* (New York: Charles Scribner's Sons, 1958), II, 510, and F. B. Perkins's *The Picture and the Men* (New York: A. J. Johnson, 1867) are useful. A typed copy of Carpenter's letter to Lovejoy (January 5, 1864) is in the Louis A. Warren Lincoln Library and Museum. Mrs. Lincoln's letters to Derby & Miller about the engraving (June 3 [1866]) and to the H. C. Deming about Carpenter (December 16, [1867]) are in Justin G. and Linda Levitt Turner's *Mary Todd Lincoln: Her Life and Letters* (New York: Alfred A. Knopf, 1972).

Carroll, Anna Ella (1815–1893) Maryland-born Union propagandist and military writer. Anna E. Carroll claimed credit for influencing Lincoln's military strategy in the Civil War. Daughter of a prominent slaveholding family, she began her career as a publicist for the Know-Nothing (American) party in Maryland by writing two anti-Catholic books in 1856–1857. Principally through Edward Bates, a former Know-Nothing in Lincoln's Cabinet, she was brought to President Lincoln's attention.

When war broke out, Anna freed her family's slaves and began pamphleteering for the Union cause: *Reply to the Speech of the Honorable J. C. Breckinridge* (1861), a defense of Lincoln's war policies; *The War Powers of the General Government* (1861), another defense of Lincoln's policies as being entirely constitutional; *The Relations of the General Government to the Revolted Citizens. No Power in Congress to Emancipate Slaves or Confiscate Property* (1862), a reply to Senator Charles Sumner's speech for the Second Confiscation Act; and two letters to the New York *Times* (March 6 and 23, 1862) on colonization of Negroes and retention of states' rights. Thomas A. Scott, Assistant Secretary of War from August 3, 1861, to June 1, 1862, admitted encouraging their publication "under no special authority" but his own, and admitted giving her the impression that she would be compensated for the work. Attorney General Bates told Miss Carroll that the President was grateful for her reply to Breckinridge. She subsequently made known to Lincoln a plan costing $50,000 to write in Europe and circulate her work in Europe, which he rejected out of hand. Shortly after the rejection, on August 19, 1862, Lincoln wrote her:

"Like every thing else that comes from you I have read the address to Maryland with a great deal of pleasure and interest."

Anna Ella Carroll's most famous claim was to have inspired the western campaign of 1862 down the Tennessee and Cumberland Rivers rather than the Mississippi. There is much controversy about this point, but it is clear that the possibility of such a strategic move was widely recognized by various military authorities besides Miss Carroll.

After the war, Carroll pressed her claim for $5000 for publishing her pamphlets (she had received $1250, perhaps from Scott himself, for the reply to Breckinridge). She made numerous unsuccessful claims for money and recognition until her death, often with the support of Benjamin F. Wade, who backed her claims to have originated the idea for the Tennessee River campaign.

Miss Carroll's cause was taken up by feminist Sarah Ellen Blackwell, who published *A Military Genius: Life of Anna Ella Carroll of Maryland* in 1891. Miss Carroll's claims were clearly extravagant, but there is no doubting that her contribution has been slighted. Jay Monaghan's two-volume *Lincoln Bibliography, 1839–1939* fails to list any of her pamphlets as Lincolniana, though other defenses of presidential policies are so classified.

SOURCES: A defender of Miss Carroll is Marjorie Barstow Greenbie, *My Dear Lady: The Story of Anna Ella Carroll, the "Great Unrecognized Member of Lincoln's Cabinet"* (New York: Whittlesey House, 1940). Attackers are F. Lauriston Bullard, "Anna Ella Carroll and Her 'Modest' Claim," *Lincoln Herald*, L (October 1948), 2–10; Kenneth P. Williams's review of the Greenbie book in *Lincoln Herald*, LIV (Summer 1952), 54–56; and E. B. Long, "Anna Ella Carroll: Exaggerated Heroine?" *Civil War Times Illustrated*, XIV (July 1975), 28–35. No work seems definitive, and all the writers slight her political and social thought, which Lincoln seems to have appreciated.

When the popular women's magazine Godey's depicted Anna Ella Carroll near the end of the nineteenth century, she had become a feminist symbol. The woman in this poster, with the severely pulled-back hair and the masculine uniform, is not recognizable as the Anna Ella Carroll depicted in the J. C. Buttre engraving, based on a photograph by Mathew B. Brady.

Cartwright, Peter (1785–1872) Lincoln's opponent in the 1846 congressional election. Born in Virginia, Cartwright was taken to Kentucky at an early age, and there he underwent a conversion experience at the great western revival of 1801. He quickly became a circuit-riding preacher and delivered stunning performances in Kentucky, Tennessee, Indiana, Ohio, and Illinois. He stressed conviction and loathed theological education, but he did not condone the more extreme aspects of revivalism such as the barks, jerks, and trances.

In 1824 Cartwright moved to Sangamon County, Illinois, in order to "get clear of the evil of slavery" (he remembered in his 1857 *Autobiography*). He was elected to the lower house of the Illinois legislature in 1828, having entered politics, he claimed later, in order to oppose the forces in Illinois that wished to instate slavery in the state. When Cartwright won reelection in 1832, Abraham Lincoln was one of nine men who lost in the race for four seats in the same district. Cartwright was a Democrat, and, though he disliked slavery, he thought it best for the country "not to meddle politically with slavery" where it existed already.

In May 1846 the Seventh Congressional District Democrats chose Cartwright to run against Whig candidate Lincoln for the United States House of Representatives. Very little survives to suggest the nature of the campaign; the only report of a speech by Lincoln in the contest says that the candidate dealt principally with the tariff and closed with general remarks about Texas, Oregon, and the Mexican War. Shortly before election day Cartwright apparently spread the charge that his opponent was an infidel. Lincoln resented this "whispering" campaign against him and printed a broadside to answer the charge on July 31, 1846. In it he admitted that he was "not a member of any Christian Church" and that "in early life" he "was inclined to believe in what I understand is called the 'Doctrine of Necessity' " (fatalism). But he denied ever speaking "with intentional disrespect of religion," claimed to have given up arguing for fatalism "more than five years ago," and said that he "never denied the truth of the Scriptures." He affirmed that he would not himself "support a man for office, whom I knew to be an open enemy of . . . religion." The statement was published in newspapers only after the election was over.

Election day (August 3, 1846) saw Lincoln victorious; he got 6340 votes to Cartwright's 4829 votes (a Liberty Party candidate got 249). Lincoln carried Morgan, Scott, Cass, Mason, Menard, Tazewell, Logan, Putnam, and Sangamon Counties; Cartwright carried only the traditional Democratic strongholds of Marshall and Woodford Counties. Cartwright ran more poorly than previous Democratic candidates in this Whig district, even

Peter Cartwright. (Courtesy of the Lloyd Ostendorf Collection)

Catholicism

though Lincoln thought the religious question hurt him in some areas where he was not well known.

Fourteen years later, Lincoln could still recall that his majority was 1511 and that it was about double the customary Whig majority. Cartwright, by contrast, failed even to mention the election in his autobiography.

SOURCES: The only study of the election is Donald W. Riddle's *Lincoln Runs for Congress* (New Brunswick, N.J.: Rutgers University Press, 1948). See also Charles L. Wallis, ed., *Autobiography of Peter Cartwright* (New York: Abingdon Press, 1956).

Catholicism See KNOW-NOTHING PARTY; RELIGION.

Chandler, Zachariah (1813–1879) Republican Senator and Radical critic of Lincoln. Born in New Hampshire, Chandler in 1833 moved to Detroit, where he became a wealthy businessman. Originally a Whig, he was an early convert to the Republican cause. In 1857 he was elected to the United States Senate.

Chandler was Chairman of the Committee on Commerce while Lincoln was President. He grudgingly supported the first issuance of greenbacks and enthusiastically supported Treasury Secretary Chase's national banking plan. He was ready to go to war with England over the *Trent* crisis and envisioned the conquest of Canada as a result. He loathed the influence of Secretary of State William H. Seward over the President and supported the unsuccessful attempt to force Seward's removal from the Cabinet in December 1862.

A man of zealous patriotism, Chandler made speeches that dripped with careless denunciations of treason. In 1863 he said characteristically: "If I was President I would put Gov [Horatio] Seymour of New York in Fort Lafayette *at once* & hang a few Northern Traitors." As a member of the Joint Committee on the Conduct of the War, he denounced George B. McClellan bitterly and believed in Joseph Hooker's abilities. He wanted General George G. Meade removed after the Battle of Gettysburg for failure to follow up his victory. By 1865 he wanted to treat Confederate prisoners as Union prisoners were allegedly treated in the South, even "to the point of starvation."

Chandler thought Lincoln "as stubborn as a mule when he gets his back up"—a trait that worked to Radical advantage, he thought, when Lincoln got his back up on the Emancipation Proclamation. He always urged the removal of conservative Cabinet members and told the President in November 1863 that "we can carry every southern state as fast as occupied upon the platform of wages for labour & *poor mens rights*." Lincoln handled Chandler with gingerly respect, replying that he hoped "to 'stand firm' enough to not go backward, and yet not go forward fast enough to wreck the country's cause." Nevertheless, Chandler, who as early as 1861 had advocated a law forever forbidding high-ranking Confederates from holding federal office, came to disagree sharply with Lincoln over Reconstruction.

The differences were not sharp enough to drive Chandler into open opposition to Lincoln's reelection in 1864.

Zachariah Chandler

The Michigan Senator worked in August and September to remove Montgomery Blair from the Cabinet in order to mollify Radicals, like Benjamin F. Wade, who otherwise might not support the President in the election. Lincoln apparently demanded John C. Frémont's withdrawal from the presidential race in exchange. Chandler sought Wade's help in the bargain, but Wade stood clear. Chandler visited Frémont, but it is unclear whether the general's subsequent withdrawal from the campaign came as a result of Chandler's persuasion. The day after Frémont withdrew, Lincoln asked for Blair's resignation, and that request was more likely a result of Chandler's work.

Chandler canvassed for Lincoln's reelection—but strictly to prevent McClellan's election on a peace platform for the sake of the country and not for Lincoln's sake. He thought the Hampton Roads Peace Conference early in 1865 was "abominable . . . foolish, unauthorized, *unholy.*" He wasted few words in lamenting Lincoln's assassination. The "Almighty continued Mr. Lincoln in office as long as he was usefull," Chandler said, and he declined his appointment as one of the honor guard to accompany Lincoln's body to Springfield. On April 23, 1865, he said: "Had Mr. Lincoln's policy been carried out we should have had Jeff Davis[,] Toombs &c back in the Senate at the next session of Congress but *now* their chances to hang are better than for the Senate."

SOURCES: Sister Mary Karl George's *Zachariah Chandler: A Political Biography* (East Lansing: Michigan State University Press, 1969) is the standard modern biography, but it is marred by a distaste for its subject. On Chandler's role in the Frémont-Blair bargain see J. G. Randall and Richard N. Current, *Lincoln the President: Last Full Measure* (New York: Dodd, Mead, 1955).

Chapman Pirates Would-be Confederate privateers who were pardoned by President Lincoln. Kentucky-born Ashbury Harpending obtained a letter of marque from the Confederate government to outfit a vessel to capture a mail ship carrying one of the regular shipments of California gold to the East and convert it into a commerce raider. Enraged by the Emancipation Proclamation, he conspired with Kentucky-born Ridgely Greathouse and Englishman Alfred Rubery to sail the *J. M. Chapman* from San Francisco in the spring of 1863. On March 15, 1863, customs officers arrested Harpending, Rubery, and 18 others aboard the *Chapman*. The three leaders were indicted by a federal grand jury on August 11, 1863, for violating the Confiscation Act of July 17, 1862, by giving "aid and comfort" to the rebellion.

With Supreme Court Justice Stephen J. Field (as a circuit judge) and United States District Court Judge Ogden Hoffman presiding, a jury found Greathouse, Harpending, and Rubery guilty, and on October 16, 1863, Field sentenced each to 10 years in prison and a $10,000 fine.

On Senator Charles Sumner's advice, Lincoln pardoned Rubery on December 17, 1863, as a favor for British Liberal John Bright, who represented the district where the Englishman's mother lived. Harpending and Greathouse sought pardon under Lincoln's Proclamation of Amnesty and Reconstruction of December 8, 1863, aimed at Southerners and not at Northerners or those already convicted of crimes. Lincoln thought the amnesty oath should be taken voluntarily as a proof of loyalty and not as a means to escape a sentence already pronounced by a court. On February 15, 1864, however, Judge Hoffman pardoned Greathouse under the provisions of Lincoln's amnesty proclamation. Lincoln did nothing to alter the import of Hoffman's ruling, and on March 7, 1864, Harpending took the loyalty oath and was released. On March 26, 1864, Lincoln, perhaps under pressure from Radical Republicans, amended his proclamation to exclude persons "in military, naval or civil confinement or custody."

SOURCES: See Robert J. Chandler's excellent "The Release of the *Chapman* Pirates: A California Sidelight on Lincoln's Amnesty Policy," *Civil War History*, XXIII (June 1977), 129–143, and F. Lauriston Bullard's "Lincoln Pardons Conspirator on Plea of an English Statesman" in the *American Bar Association Journal*, March 1939.

Charleston, Illinois Site of the fourth Lincoln-Douglas Debate, September 18, 1858. Charleston was the county seat of Coles County, in eastern Illinois. A train carried 11 cars of people from Indiana for the event, and long processions brought the candidates to town. The Lincoln procession contained a float with 32 young women representing the states of the Union and the motto:

> Westward thy star of Empire takes its way,
> Thy Girls *Link-on* to Lincoln,—
> Their Mothers were for Clay.

Banners were plentiful; they included one showing Lincoln driving a team of oxen into Coles County when he entered Illinois almost 30 years before and another which stated: "This government was made for white men—Douglas for life." A crowd of perhaps 12,000, enormous for the times, thronged the county fairgrounds for the debate. The candidates were dusty from riding in the processions.

Douglas's assertions, made at Jonesboro 3 days before, that Lincoln stood for racial equality evidently bothered Lincoln. He did not respond at Jonesboro, but in Charleston he began with what has since become a much-quoted statement:

> I will say then that I am not, nor ever have been in favor of bringing about in any way the social and political equality of the white and black races,—that I am not nor ever have been in favor of making voters or jurors of negroes, nor of qualifying them to hold office, nor to intermarry with white people; and I will say in addition to this that there is a physical difference between the white and black races which I believe will for ever forbid the two races living together on terms of social and political equality. And inasmuch as they cannot so live, while they do remain together there must be the position of superior and inferior, and I as much as any other man am in favor of having the superior position assigned to the white race.

However, to assign "the superior position . . . to the white race" was not to say "the negro should be denied everything." Lincoln thought it "quite possible for us to get along without making either slaves or wives of negroes." Lincoln knew his audience well; 94.9 percent of Coles County's voters had voted to exclude Negroes from the state in 1848, and only 28.4 percent voted Republican in 1856.

Lincoln treated his racial views as a sort of aside and rushed on to the heart of his case: that Douglas, according to Lyman Trumbull, had plotted in 1856 to make a constitution for Kansas which would not be voted upon by the people. Lincoln's allegation hinged on a detailed history of a bill that to modern readers may seem tedious, but the newspaper account is punctuated with indications of audience applause.

Douglas hoped it would appear tedious, for his response began: "Let me ask you what questions of public policy relating to the welfare of this State or the Union has Mr. Lincoln discussed before you?" Douglas said that Trumbull's charge was a red herring brought up so "that I would be compelled to occupy my entire time in defending myself, so that I would not be able to show up the enormity of the principles of the Abolitionists." He would not "allow them to waste much of my time with these personal matters," he said, but he went on to deny the charge at great length, saying "it was taken for granted that the constitution would be submitted to the people whether the law compelled it or not." Douglas repeated his customary line: he did not conspire with Roger B. Taney, Franklin Pierce, and James Buchanan to nationalize slavery; Lincoln did conspire with Trumbull to abolitionize the Whig and Democratic parties; Lincoln was proabolition in the north, moderate in the middle, and conservative in the south of the state; and Douglas stood for white supremacy. He made special efforts to link his name with Whigs Daniel Webster and Henry Clay in trying to save the Union with the Compromise of 1850. Coles County had almost as many voters (28.4 percent) for the Whig-American ticket in 1856 as Republicans, and proving friendship for old Whigs was important.

In his rebuttal Lincoln denied that he wished to make citizens of Negroes, denied that there was *"any difference between my printed speeches north and south,"* explained the meaning of his "House Divided" speech, and focused considerable attention on a charge inserted briefly by Douglas that Lincoln unpatriotically opposed the Mexican War. Lincoln dismissed this "old charge" as a "lie." He led local politician Orlando B. Ficklin forward from his seat on the platform and insisted that he was present in Congress in 1848 and knew Lincoln always voted supplies for the soldiers even though he always voted against any resolution which "would indorse the origin and justice of the war." The embarrassed Ficklin, a friend of Lincoln's but a Democrat, said only that Lincoln had voted for the Ashmun amendment declaring the war "unnecessarily and unconstitutionally commenced by the President." Lincoln ended by reiterating Trumbull's charge that Douglas had supported the bill to impose a constitution on Kansas without a vote of the people.

That evening Richard J. Oglesby addressed Republicans for two more hours, while Democratic orators spoke to their supporters.

SOURCES: See Edwin Erle Sparks, ed., *The Lincoln-Douglas Debates of 1858* (Springfield: Illinois State Historical Library, 1908) and John M. Rozett, "Racism and Republican Emergence in Illinois, 1848–1860: A Re-Evaluation of Republican Negrophobia," *Civil War History*, XXII (June 1976), 101–115.

See also COLES COUNTY, ILLINOIS; FICKLIN, ORLANDO BELL; LINDER, USHER FERGUSON.

Charnwood, Godfrey Rathbone Benson, Lord (1864–1945)

Lincoln biographer. Lord Charnwood was born at Alresford, Hampshire, England. Oxford-educated, he was a lawyer, a member of the House of Commons (1892–1895), and, after 1911, a member of the House of Lords. What exactly impelled this English nobleman to write a biography of an American born in a log cabin is not clear, but some circumstances help explain his writing *Abraham Lincoln*, first published in England in 1916 and in America in 1917. In politics, Lord Charnwood was a Liberal. As a boy he read a biography of Lincoln by C. G. Leland which was memorable enough to him to be mentioned in the brief "Bibliographical Note" at the end of Charnwood's book. Perhaps most important was World War I, which brought a new enthusiasm for democratic government and a spirit of amicable kinship between Englishmen and Americans.

Charnwood's *Lincoln* lacked any basis in original research and relied on a relatively small number of standard works. It was not anecdotal, and it was less a fully rounded biography than a treatment of Lincoln as a public man. It was well written in a somewhat leisurely fashion but with an air of deep consideration. Lord Charnwood did not "shrink . . . from the display of a partisanship"—he frankly called the South's cause wrong—but he adhered to the view that the "true obligation of impartiality is that he [the author] should conceal no fact which, in his own mind, tells against his views." He accurately saw that Lincoln was "void of romantic fondness for vanished joys of youth." Somewhat less accurately, he pictured Lincoln's father as "a migrant" and noted that "unseemliness in talk of rough, rustic boys flavoured the great President's conversation through life." He called Lincoln's imposition of martial law on the North a usurpation of power.

Still, Charnwood pictured Lincoln as a great statesman and appreciated his common origins. In an ironic twist, he criticized an American critic of democracy, Henry Adams, by saying, "It is a contemptible trait in books like that able novel 'Democracy,' that they treat the sentiment which attached to the 'Rail-splitter' as anything but honourable." He stated simply that secession was a broadly popular movement for the sake of slavery, not a narrow conspiracy against the "real South" nor a movement for some other unspoken end. Lincoln's attempts to counter it, therefore, were noble, progressive, and somehow Christian. He praised Lincoln's abilities as a commander in chief, following a current of British military opinion at the time, and he did not belittle the Emancipation Proclamation. The Proclamation could be interpreted as a military measure only in law, he suggested. Though he repeated some spurious anecdotes and quotations, he often handled them well. Of the story of Lincoln's clemency for the sleeping sentinel William Scott, Charnwood concluded: "If the story is not true—and there is no reason whatever to doubt it—still it is a remarkable man of whom people spin yarns of that kind." A man of intense religious feeling and interests, Charnwood noted Lincoln's growth in that realm to the "language of intense religious feeling" in his Second Inaugural Address.

Charnwood kept in focus the meaning of Lincoln's efforts to save the Union. These were attempts to save democratic government for the whole world. He rightly stressed Lincoln's praise of Henry Clay, a patriot who "loved his country, partly because it was his own country, and mostly because it was a free country."

Abraham Lincoln was also colored by Charnwood's reading of James Bryce's *American Commonwealth*. From that critique of American politics came Lord Charnwood's hostility toward political parties and the spoils system. He saw party politics as avoiding serious issues and largely incapable of producing real leaders. Of Lincoln's election in 1860, he said that "the fit man was

Lord Charnwood addressing an audience in Springfield, Illinois, in October 1918. (Courtesy of the Illinois State Historical Library)

chosen on the very ground of his supposed unfitness."

New research and changing attitudes (Charnwood referred at one point to the "experience as to the relations between superior and inferior races, which is now at the command of every intelligent Englishman") have conspired to make Charnwood's book obsolete. But for several decades it was a great success. George Bernard Shaw told Lincoln collector Judd Stewart that there was "a cult of Lincoln in England, received of late from Lord Charnwood's very penetrating biography." Though obviously written for British readers, it was welcomed in America. And as late as 1947 Benjamin P. Thomas, an excellent judge of such matters, termed it "the best one-volume life of Lincoln ever written."

SOURCES: See Benjamin P. Thomas, *Portrait for Posterity: Lincoln and His Biographers* (New Brunswick, N.J.: Rutgers University Press, 1947). Shaw's letter is quoted in Frederick Hill Meserve's "My Experience in Collecting Historical Photographs and How That Life-time Adventure Led to Great Friendships," *Lincoln Herald*, LVI (Spring-Summer 1954), 19.

Chase, Salmon Portland (1808–1873) Secretary of the Treasury in the Lincoln administration. Salmon P. Chase was born in Cornish, New Hampshire. After his father died in 1817, he lived with his uncle, Episcopal Bishop Philander Chase, in Worthington Ohio. He became a devout Episcopalian who repeated psalms while bathing and dressing. He graduated from Dartmouth College in 1826. After teaching school briefly, he was admitted to the bar and moved to Cincinnati to practice law in 1830.

Chase became active in the antislavery movement in the 1830s, and by the end of the decade he had developed an influential argument that the United States Constitution was an antislavery document. He amassed the antislavery statements of the founding fathers, contending that the founders' intention had been to abolish slavery in the near future. They saw to it, he argued, that the Constitution never mentioned the word "slavery," and they meant the federal government to have nothing to do with maintaining the institution. For Chase, then, American history appeared to be a decline from the principles established by the founders. The decline began as early as 1793, when Congress passed a fugitive slave act that was, in Chase's view, unconstitutional because it involved the federal government in the capture of runaway slaves. He became known as the "attorney general for runaway negroes" because he took a number of famous cases in behalf of fugitive slaves. Abraham Lincoln developed a similar view of American history in the 1850s, but he was less pessimistic than Chase. Lincoln dated the decline only from the 1850s, and he was not inclined to see slavery in the District of Columbia or fugitive slave laws as unconstitutional. Chase also became alarmed much earlier than Lincoln at the aggressions of the "Slave Power." Chase heeded the warnings in a speech by Ohio Democratic Senator Thomas Morris in 1839 that a conspiracy by 1 percent of the nation's population—the "Slave Power"—was bent on undermining American liberties everywhere. Lincoln's fear of a conspiracy to nationalize slavery arose only in the 1850s. Both Chase and Lincoln differed from abolitionists, like William Lloyd Garrison, who held that the Constitution was a proslavery document.

Chase entered politics as a Whig but became a member of the Liberty party in 1841. His role in that radical party was essentially conservative: he strove to broaden the party's appeal by dropping its advocacy of clearly unconstitutional programs like the federal abolition of slavery in the states. He sought only "the absolute and unconditional divorce of the Government from slavery." Later he coined the even more influential slogan, "Freedom is national; slavery only is local and sectional."

In 1848 Chase became a leader in the Free Soil party and was elected the next year to the United States Senate by a coalition of Free Soilers and Democrats. He was a vociferous antislavery leader in the Senate and opposed the Compromise of 1850 and the Kansas-Nebraska Act of 1854. His attack on the latter, the "Appeal of the Independent Democrats," which he wrote with Joshua Giddings, he considered "the *most valuable*" of his works. It popularized the theory that the Kansas-Nebraska Act was part of a conspiracy to spread slavery over all the unsettled West. In 1855 and 1857 Chase was elected Governor of Ohio, the second time as a Republican. In 1856 he was an avowed candidate for the Republican presidential nomination. As would happen several times, his inability to control the Ohio party for his cause doomed him to failure.

Chase's role in the Republican party was the opposite of his role in the Liberty party. Now he was a radical among moderates. When Lincoln informed Chase in 1859 that the Ohio party's plank urging repeal of the Fugitive Slave Law was "damaging" the Republicans in Illinois and would "explode" the national party if even *"introduced"* as a subject for discussion in 1860, Chase replied that "a declaration in favor of the repeal of the Fugitive Slave Act of 1850 was indispensable." Despite this difference, Lincoln was grateful for Chase's "being one of the very few distinguished men, whose sympathy we in Illinois did receive [in 1858] . . . , of all those whose sympathy we thought we had reason to expect."

In 1860 Chase was one of Lincoln's rivals for the Republican presidential nomination. Again he failed to unite the Ohio delegation behind him, and his first-ballot showing was dismal (45 of 465 votes). The eventual switch of those votes to Lincoln's column helped Chase become Lincoln's Secretary of the Treasury in 1861. To assume the post, he resigned the Senate seat to which he had been reelected in 1860.

Chase's course in the secession crisis was a vacillating one. In January 1861 he warned Lincoln that the greatest danger was "the disruption of the Republican Party through Congressional attempts at Compromises." In the showdown over Fort Sumter, however, Chase at first told the President, on March 19, that if the attempt to reinforce the fort "will so inflame civil war as to involve an immediate necessity for the enlistment of armies and the expenditure of millions I cannot advise it." Ten days later he was "in favor of maintaining Fort

Salmon Portland Chase

Pickens and just as clearly in favor of provisioning Fort Sumter" even at the risk of war. For a time he had toyed with the idea that, if secession were limited to seven states, the seceding states could go in peace; for they would soon be back, chastened, and the cause of liberty be all the stronger for it.

Though in the early months of the administration Chase was an influential Cabinet member, his relationship with the President was never close and harmonious. As early as March 21, 1861, he complained to Lincoln that "Ohio has very little considering her population & Republican vote and character in comparison with New York or Pennsylvania." Chase never got along with New Yorker William H. Seward, and they squabbled over patronage appointments from March 1861 to the end of Chase's tenure as Secretary. By December 1862 those differences provoked a crisis in Lincoln's Cabinet. A congressional Republican delegation that thought Seward a drag on the administration sought a reconstruction of the Cabinet; the delegation's members had apparently been fed anti-Seward information by Chase. Lincoln arranged a meeting on December 19 with the delegation in the presence of all the Cabinet members except Seward. Chase was thus forced to commend Cabinet harmony in the face of men to whom he had probably complained of Cabinet disharmony. On the 20th the embarrassed Secretary of the Treasury tendered his resignation. Seward had already offered his. The President refused both requests and maintained the careful factional balance in the party by keeping both men.

Chase was the most radical member of Lincoln's official family. In April 1861 he urged the President to take strong military steps to prevent the Maryland legislature from passing a secession ordinance. He urged the disastrous appointment of Irvin McDowell as commander of the Army of the Potomac and, after McDowell's defeat at Bull Run, welcomed the advent of General George B. McClellan. He became critical of McClellan only after the general seemed too slow to attack the enemy in 1862. On the whole, he disliked the "Regular Army Officers" who reduced "the contest with the Rebels to a regular system and take out of it the largest part of its moral element by repressing all Anti-Slavery sentiment." "Proslavery sentiment," Chase said, "inspires rebellion; let antislavery sentiment inspire suppression."

In later years Chase recalled:

> Until long after Sumter I clung to my old ideas of non-interference with slavery within the state limits. That the United States Government under the war powers might destroy slavery I never doubted. I only doubted the expediency of the exercise.

His doubts soon faded, however, and in May 1862 he differed with Lincoln's intention to revoke General David Hunter's emancipation order in Hunter's Southern military department. He never thought that Lincoln's Emancipation Proclamation went far enough, and he repeatedly suggested that the exemptions of conquered areas of Virginia and Louisiana be removed. Chase's advice caused Lincoln to alter a passage in the preliminary Emancipation Proclamation which sounded like an invitation to servile insurrection, and Lincoln incorporated a closing suggested by Chase which invoked the "favor of Almighty God."

Chase had immense responsibilities at the Treasury. He oversaw the financing of an enormous war, at first principally by means of loans to the government. By late 1862 New York financier Jay Cooke marketed the loans. As sources dried up and the price of gold (which rises with lack of faith in the government) rose higher and higher, he resorted to printing money. He endorsed making "greenbacks" legal tender only reluctantly. (In 1870 he would deliver the Supreme Court decision declaring the Legal Tender Act of 1862 unconstitutional.) He devised the national banking system of February 25, 1863, in order to increase the sale of government bonds to banks and to ensure a national currency rather than the fluctuating variety of notes issued by state banks. He retained the belief that a "return to specie payments, . . . at the earliest period compatible with due regard to all interests concerned should ever be kept in view." He knew, and repeatedly told Lincoln, that "above all we need victories to inspire confidence." He loathed gold speculators. Gold was "unaccountably high" early in 1863, and in the spring of 1864 it continued to advance. Chase now desired taxation equal to one-half of the amount of current expenditures and revision of the national banking system so that it taxed state bank notes out of existence. Congress was unwilling to raise taxes in an election year, but it did revise the banking system. Military victories eventually salvaged government finances, but not until Chase left the government.

In addition to financial sophistication, Chase's job required great organizational ability and hard work. Clerks in the department increased from 383 to over 2000 in number, which forced Chase to allow women to be clerks. Hundreds of appointive offices were at his command in the many customs houses, treasury offices, and internal revenue offices throughout the country. Before war's end the New York Customs House alone employed more than 1000 persons. Chase insisted on controlling the appointments himself and was rarely overruled by the President. He told Lincoln frankly in the spring of 1863 that he sought "fit men for responsible places, without admitting the right of Senators or Representatives to control appointments for which the President & the Secretary . . . must be responsible" and that otherwise he felt he could not "be useful to you or the country in my present position." On May 11, 1863, Chase offered to resign because Lincoln appointed a new collector at Puget Sound before the Secretary was able to examine protests against the old collector from Lincoln's old friend Anson G. Henry. The difference was patched up, but difficulties over the New York Customs House grew from late winter to early summer of 1864. Finally, Lincoln stated in June that, because of complaints from his supporters in New York, he could not sustain Chase's most recent nominee for a post there, Maunsell B. Field as assistant treasurer. On June 29 Chase resigned, and this time Lincoln accepted his resignation.

Lincoln noted in his letter accepting Chase's resignation that their relations had "reached a point of mutual embarrassment" that could not be "overcome." There were greater differences between them than one New York appointment. Chase's opinion in 1862 that West Virginia statehood was both constitutional and expedient agreed with Lincoln's decision not to veto the statehood bill, but thereafter they seldom agreed. In a public "Letter . . . to the Loyal National League" of New York on April 9, 1863, Chase said of slavery, "What matter how it dies?—whether as a consequence or object of the war, what matter? Is this a time to split hairs of logic?" The President was never willing to state that emancipation was an *object* of the war. In the fall, the open hostility of Montgomery Blair toward Chase erupted into a serious issue when Blair's brother Francis sharply criticized Chase in a speech in the House of Representatives. Though Chase told the President that the draft Proclamation of Amnesty and Reconstruction gave him "very great satisfaction," he offered some criticism. He suggested that the exceptions for Louisiana and Virginia in the Emancipation Proclamation be revoked, that "no suggestion be made of any apprenticeship of the freedmen or other special legislation for them," and that nothing be said of admitting Senators and Representatives before "the reconstruction of the States." In the Cabinet discussion Chase alone suggested that the provision for reconstructing the states by loyal white voters only be changed to allow loyal black voters. Chase was suspicious of General Ulysses S. Grant and wished that General William T. Sherman commanded his army. Even Chase's daughter Kate was a bone of contention. Mrs. Lincoln was jealous of the wide swath she cut in Washington society.

Chase's radicalism grew into ambition to succeed Lincoln as the Republican presidential nominee in 1864. On February 20 of that year, in the midst of the difficulties over the New York Customs House, a movement to substitute Chase for Lincoln surfaced prematurely with the newspaper publication of the Pomeroy Circular. Chase claimed no prior knowledge of the circular, but public reaction to his seeming disloyalty to the President deflated the Chase boom. On February 25 a Republican caucus of the Ohio general assembly endorsed Lincoln's renomination. Lincoln rejected Chase's offer to resign from the Cabinet. On March 5 Chase withdrew his name from consideration for the Presidency in a public letter. He was in the Cabinet long enough to recommend retaliation for the Fort Pillow massacre in May by executing an equivalent number of Confederate officers (not enlisted men, "for the slaveholding class, which furnishes such officers, holds very cheap the lives of the nonslaveholding classes which furnish the privates"). In June he resigned for good.

Chase campaigned for Lincoln later in the year, and Lincoln appointed him Chief Justice of the United States Supreme Court to succeed Roger B. Taney, who died on October 12, 1864. Chase's appointment, though likely from the start, came only on December 6, 1864, apparently after Lincoln received assurances that Chase would not use the Court as a route to the Presidency. Chase thus achieved a final victory over Montgomery Blair, who also desired the appointment.

Chase had at one time been satisfied with suffrage for the "more intelligent" freedmen and Negro veterans, but by April 1865 he was "convinced that universal suffrage is demanded by sound policy & . . . justice alike." He differed sharply with Lincoln's Reconstruction policies in Louisiana, believing General Nathaniel P. Banks, Lincoln's commander there, should have worked through the liberal Free State Committee. On the 11th and 12th he told Lincoln to urge Louisiana's legislature to grant black suffrage and advocated its use in all reconstructions to follow.

Despite his early radicalism on Reconstruction and his willingness to retaliate for Southern "enormities," Chase dragged his feet in holding the federal circuit court trial of Jefferson Davis in Richmond until President Andrew Johnson pardoned all participants in the rebellion on Christmas Day, 1868. As presiding officer at Johnson's impeachment trial, Chase likewise surprised many by insisting on strict courtroom procedure. When Republicans showed little interest in him as a presidential candidate in 1868, Chase flirted with a Democratic nomination, but again Ohio sealed his doom by going for Horatio Seymour. In 1872 he was available as a Liberal Republican nominee, but the party showed little interest.

SOURCES: The best treatment of Chase's prewar antislavery career is Eric Foner's *Free Soil, Free Labor, Free Men: The Ideology of the Republican Party before the Civil War* (New York: Oxford University Press, 1970). David Donald appraises his role in Lincoln's Cabinet with balance and distinction in the "Introduction" to *Inside Lincoln's Cabinet: The Civil War Diaries of Salmon P. Chase* (New York: Longmans, Green, 1954). James G. Randall's biographical sketch of Chase in the *Dictionary of American Biography* (New York: Charles Scribner's Sons, 1958), II, 27–34, is above average in quality. Chase's letters to Lincoln about the Fugitive Slave Act (June 13, 1859), opposing compromises with secession (January 28, 1861), Fort Sumter (March 24, 1861), Ohio appointments (March 21, 1861), "Regular Army Officers" (November 9, 1861), gold and the need for victories (February 23, 1863), "fit men for responsible places" (March 2, 1863), Lincoln's Amnesty Proclamation (November 25, 1863), Fort Pillow (May 6, 1864), and Reconstruction (April 11 and April 12, 1865) are in the Abraham Lincoln Papers, Library of Congress. That collection also contains his memorandum on Finances ("return to specie payments," December 1862 [?]) and his "Letter . . . to the Loyal National League" (April 9, 1863).

See also HENRY, ANSON G.; POMEROY CIRCULAR.

Chicago Convention, 1860 *See* ELECTION OF 1860; DAVIS, DAVID; WIGWAM.

Chicago Historical Society Repository of probably the largest permanent Lincoln exhibit in the country. The Society elected Abraham Lincoln an honorary member in 1861, 5 years after its founding. Its first great Lincoln holding was the original draft of the Emancipation Proclamation. The document was deposited there by Thomas Bryan, president of the Chicago Soldier's

Home, who had purchased it for $3000 at the Northwestern Sanitary Fair of 1863. The Proclamation and the rest of the Society's collection burned in the Chicago Fire of 1871.

In 1882 the Society attempted to acquire one of the greatest Lincoln collections by asking Robert Todd Lincoln to deposit his father's papers there. Robert showed interest but consulted John G. Nicolay, who was then using the papers to write a biography of Abraham Lincoln. Nicolay apparently advised Robert against the move. When the Society put together a temporary exhibit of Lincoln prints in 1909, so many schoolchildren visited that Librarian Caroline McIlvane argued it as proof of the need for an Abraham Lincoln room.

Such a room became a real possibility only in 1920, when the Society entered into a complex contract to purchase the collection of Charles F. Gunther (1837–1920), a German immigrant who, after service as a civilian purchasing steward for the Confederate government, became a wealthy candy manufacturer. Gunther's remarkably eclectic collection contained, in addition to such curiosities as the alleged skin of the serpent which tempted Eve, a substantial number of choice Lincoln items: the bed on which Lincoln died, the Lincolns' piano, furniture from the Lincolns' Springfield home, the President's letter of April 7, 1865, to General Grant about pressing for General Lee's surrender (Let the *thing* be pressed"), and Lincoln's carriage.

A wonderful addition to the Society's collection was a series of dioramas constructed by 50 skilled craftsmen working from 1939 to 1941. The dioramas were a project of the Museum Extension Program of the Works Progress Administration. They depict scenes of Lincoln's life from his birthplace cabin to Ford's Theatre, embodying about 6000 figures ranging in height from ½ inch to 19 inches. In 1950 the Society brought together for a temporary exhibit all five of the known copies of the Gettysburg Address in Lincoln's hand—the only time that has ever been done.

Under director Clement Silvestro the Society began building a Lincoln gallery to bring the famous Lincoln artifacts together in a chronologically arranged display. The gallery was opened in 1973. The exhibit, in its 4000 square feet, includes the dioramas, materials from the Gunther collection, portraits of Lincoln by Thomas Hicks and George P. A. Healy, Lincoln's letter to Stephen A. Douglas making arrangements for their debates, a reconstruction of the Lincoln birthplace cabin, and many other campaign items, pictures, and personal family relics. The Society's library contains important research materials; they include the papers of John J. Hardin, the best source of information on Illinois Whig politics in the 1840s.

The Chicago Historical Society's collecting policy now focuses more exclusively on materials relating to the history of Chicago. It allows for an upgrading of existing exhibits in other areas, but its emphasis on Lincolniana is clearly reduced.

SOURCES: See Clement M. Silvestro, "The Candy Man's Mixed Bag," *Chicago History*, II (Fall 1972), 86–99, and Paul M. Angle, *The Chicago Historical Society, 1856–1956: An Unconventional Chronicle* (New York: Rand McNally, 1956).

Chicago *Press and Tribune* See MEDILL, JOSEPH MEHARRY.

Chicago River and Harbor Convention The Convention, which was held July 5 to 7, 1847, provided the occasion for Lincoln's first visit to Chicago. The Congressman-elect attended the convention to help protest President James K. Polk's veto of a bill to improve rivers and harbors. The subject of internal improvements was a dear one to the man who would be Illinois's only Whig member of the Thirteenth Congress, and on July 6 he addressed the convention—the first time he had ever addressed an audience of politicians of national prominence. Although his speech was not recorded, Horace Greeley noted in the New York *Tribune* for July 17, 1847, that Lincoln, "a tall specimen of an Illinoian, . . . spoke briefly and happily in reply to" David Dudley Field of New York. Field had argued for a limitation of river and harbor improvements to those which were national in scope. He denied the right of the federal government to improve navigation on the Illinois River (which runs through one state only) or the Hudson River above a port of entry.

Though not recorded, the nature of Lincoln's reply is not hard to imagine. Less than a year later he would tell Congress that, though there was "some degree of truth" in this argument, "No commercial object of government patronage can be so exclusively *general*, as to not be of some peculiar *local* advantage; but, on the other hand, nothing is so *local*, as to not be of some general advantage." Even the Navy, obviously instituted for general protection of American commerce, was "of some peculiar advantage to Charleston, Baltimore, Philadelphia, New-York and Boston, beyond what it is to the interior towns of Illinois." Conversely, the Illinois and Michigan Canal, entirely within Illinois, was of such general advantage that "sugar had been carried from New-Orleans through this canal to Buffalo in New-York." Lincoln believed "that if both the nation and the states would, in good faith, in their respective spheres, do what they could in the way of improvements, what of inequality might be produced in one place, might be compensated in another, and that the sum of the whole might not be very unequal."

SOURCES: See Robert Fergus's compilation of documents about the convention in Fergus's Historical Series, No. 18, *Chicago River-and-Harbor Convention, An Account of Its Origin and Proceedings* (Chicago: Fergus Printing Company, 1882) and G. S. Boritt, *Lincoln and the Economics of the American Dream* (Memphis: Memphis State University Press, 1978).

Chicago *Times*, Suppression of the On June 1, 1863, General Ambrose E. Burnside issued General Order No. 84 for the Department of Ohio, which included Chicago. The third article of that order "suppressed" the Chicago *Times* for "the repeated expression of disloyal and incendiary sentiments." Editor William Fiske Storey's *Times* had opposed emancipation as "a criminal wrong" and criticized the arrest of Democrat Clement L. Vallandigham. The Chicago Board of Trade and Y.M.C.A. had been boycotting the paper, and the Chicago and Galena Railroad had forbidden its sale on their trains. Illinois Governor Richard Yates had urged its suppression about a year before. Soldiers seized the *Times* office on June 3.

Lincoln advised revoking the order before he knew of the seizure, but overruling Burnside's action, once the action had been taken, was a difficult matter. Gideon Welles noted that the "President—and I think every member of the Cabinet—regrets what has been done, but as to the measures which should now be taken there are probably differences." Welles did not think that the administration could well disavow the acts and call Burnside to account. Lincoln confessed to being "embarrassed with the question between what was due to the Military service on the one hand, and the Liberty of the Press on the other." However, a telegram from Senator Lyman Trumbull and Congressman Isaac N. Arnold, forwarding an account of a protest meeting, "turned the scale." On June 4 Lincoln revoked Burnside's order.

Lincoln said about a year later that he was "far from certain . . . that the revocation was not right," but his order was far from popular. Congressman Arnold intimated that he was the focus of much criticism for his role in the revocation, and the charge that he caused the revocation (which he denied) was used against him when he sought renomination in 1864. The Chicago *Tribune*, a Republican organ, called the revocation "a triumph of treason." Most historians since Lincoln's day, however, have cited the revocation of Burnside's order as important evidence of Lincoln's deep respect for civil liberties even in the midst of unprecedented crisis.

SOURCES: See Robert S. Harper, *Lincoln and the Press* (New York: McGraw-Hill, 1951).

See also ARNOLD, ISAAC NEWTON; NEWSPAPERS.

Chicago *Tribune* *See* MEDILL, JOSEPH MEHARRY.

"Chicken Bone" Case When a chimney collapsed on Samuel G. Fleming and broke both of Fleming's legs, in Bloomington, Illinois, in October 1855, Drs. Thomas P. Rogers, Jacob R. Freese, and Eli K. Crothers set the legs. Later they found that the right leg was crooked and would thereafter be shorter than the left. When Fleming was advised to have the leg rebroken and reset, he thought the operation would be too painful, and he refused it. However, on March 28, 1856, he sued Drs. Rogers and Crothers for $10,000 damages.

Lincoln was among the six attorneys retained for the defense. After delaying the trial a year, he argued that the middle-aged Fleming was lucky to walk, the bones of older people being brittle and less capable of mending. He demonstrated his point by using chicken bones, those of young chickens being rather elastic but those of older ones brittle. The case resulted in a hung jury, postponement of retrial, and eventually the dismissal of the case on March 15, 1858, when the parties to the suit reached agreement out of court. The defendants paid the fees.

SOURCES: See Harry E. Pratt, "The Famous 'Chicken Bone' Case," *Journal of the Illinois State Historical Society*, XLV (Summer 1952), 164–167.

Chiniquy, Charles Paschal Telesphore (1809–1889) The principal source of allegations that Abraham Lincoln's assassination was a Jesuit plot. Chiniquy did know Lincoln, having engaged him as an attorney in Urbana, Illinois, in 1856 in a slander suit, but he was not an intimate, and Lincoln did not reveal his religious ideas even to his closest friends. Chiniquy was a Catholic priest when he met Lincoln, but he left the church in 1860 and later became a Presbyterian and an anti-Catholic publicist and lecturer. His autobiography *Fifty Years in the Church of Rome*, published in 1885, alleged that he saw President Lincoln on three occasions, and that on two of these Lincoln stated that Jesuits had tried to kill him in Baltimore and were still trying to do so, that there was a Roman conspiracy against the United States, and that the Pope and Jesuits had been behind French intrigue in Mexico and the draft riots in New York. But Chiniquy's letters to Lincoln preserved in the Library of Congress have a stiff and formal tone and never mention any meetings between the two men except the one in 1856.

SOURCES: Joseph George, Jr.'s. "The Lincoln Writings of Charles P. T. Chiniquy," *Journal of the Illinois State Historical Society*, LXIX (February 1976), 17–25, is a definitive and interesting refutation of Chiniquy's claims. It traces the history of the use of the story in anti-Catholic literature as well.

Charles Paschal Telesphore Chiniquy. (Courtesy of the Illinois State Historical Library)

"Chronicles of Reuben" *See* GRIGSBY, AARON.

Civil Liberties *See* CHICAGO *Times*; HABEAS CORPUS; NEGROES; NEW YORK *World*; NEWSPAPERS; VALLANDIGHAM, CLEMENT LAIRD.

Clary's Grove Boys A group of rowdy settlers from about three miles west of New Salem who were friends of Lincoln as a young man. In 1819 John Clary had settled in the grove that would bear his name, the first settler in the part of Sangamon County which would later form Menard County. The Clary's Grove boys represented a rougher frontier, the so-called second frontier of mobile homesteaders, who preceded the third (or post-) frontier of towns and cities represented by Lincoln and the rest of New Salem's residents. They seemed happy-go-lucky and boisterous to New Salem residents. By the time Lincoln moved to New Salem, they were led by John ("Jack") Armstrong. Soon after his arrival Lincoln wrestled Armstrong to a draw, which seems to have brought him the undying friendship of the Clary's Grove frontiersmen. Lincoln associated as easily with these men as with New Salem's staider merchants and doctors.

At the outbreak of the Black Hawk War in 1832, many of the Clary's Grove boys joined a local militia unit and were instrumental in electing Lincoln captain (Armstrong became sergeant of the company). Thus the Clary's Grove boys had a hand in, as Lincoln put it many years later, "a success which gave me more pleasure than any I have had since."

In later years the boys spurned Lincoln for the Democratic party. The six Clarys who showed up at the polls when Lincoln ran for Congress in their district in 1846 voted for his opponent, Peter Cartwright.

SOURCES: See Benjamin P. Thomas, *Lincoln's New Salem* (Springfield, Ill.: Abraham Lincoln Association, 1934) and Geoffrey C. Ward, *Lincoln and the Right to Rise* (Springfield, Ill.: Sangamon State University, 1979). A Petersburg poll book for August 3, 1846 (in the Louis A. Warren Lincoln Library and Museum, Fort Wayne, Indiana) proves the Clarys were Democrats.

See also ARMSTRONG, JOHN ("JACK"); NEW SALEM.

Clay, Cassius Marcellus (1810–1903) Minister to Russia for most of the Civil War. Clay was born at his father's estate, White Hall, in Madison County, Kentucky. He graduated from Yale College in 1832 and returned to Kentucky, where he studied law briefly and then entered politics as a Whig. He developed a characteristically Whig passion for internal improvements and industrial development of the South and a hatred of slavery well out of character for the son of a large slaveholder. His stormy career included numerous duels and bowie knife brawls and a military record in the Mexican War distinguished for bravery.

Once he had seen the industrial prosperity of Connecticut, Clay blamed slavery for keeping the South economically inferior to the North. Slavery "degrades the mechanic, ruins the manufacturer, lays waste and depopulates the country" he said in an 1840 campaign speech. He insisted that, though emancipation was just, he supported it most of all because it would dignify and liberate free white labor. Abolitionists were "incendiaries," and Negroes lacked "self reliance—we can make nothing out of them. God has made them for the sun and the banana!" As proslavery opinion hardened in the South in the 1840s, even that moderate message was deemed incendiary. Clay's peculiar status as an antislavery Southerner, his considerable abilities as a polemical speaker and writer, and the suppression of his newspaper, *The True American,* by a Lexington mob in 1845 made him nationally famous.

Clay hoped for the Republican vice-presidential nomination in 1860, but Lincoln's nomination doomed him. He ran a poor second to Hannibal Hamlin. "It became a necessity to chose a vice P. from the North East, and of democratic antecedents," he admitted to Lincoln on May 21, adding his jovial congratulations: "Nature does not aggregate her gifts: and as some of us are better looking men than yourself; we must cheerfully award you the post of honor!" He campaigned in Indiana, assuring voters that Republicans were opposed to abolitionism and Negro equality. He lowered his sights to a Cabinet appointment; but his reputation as an extremist made him of no use as a sop to Southerners, and the Republican party in Kentucky was too feeble otherwise to demand recognition in the President's official family. He tried to convince Lincoln that the party promised him the War Department back in 1856 and petulantly described himself as *"ignored . . . censured* and *deserted."*

Clay admitted that he would settle for a foreign mission—but only England or France. Hoping to soften his radical image, in January he showed an interest in Charles Francis Adams's plan for compromise with the South, the only one which would allow "Southern union men to come to the support of the administration without incurring sectional persecution." He visited Washington only to find "all here fixed against any movement towards concession" except for "a few of Mr. Seward's friends" and a handful of other politicians. "The truth is," he told Lincoln on February 6, 1861, ". . . the more we concede the more will be demanded."

Clay was full of ideas and advice. In February he thought a wise policy would be to "let disunion fever run its course," get Maryland "by purchase or conquest," gain Canada by negotiation with England, admit Canada as two states, form a treaty with England "against the Despotisms," form a protectorate over or gain a treaty with Mexico, and receive any of the seceding states which will come back as free states. We "will be *stronger* than *now!*" he exclaimed to the beleaguered President. In March he suggested a referendum "for or against the union" in the Southern states, the United States to grant independence if the states chose it by popular vote.

Lincoln ignored Clay's advice, but Secretary of State William H. Seward gave Clay the mission to Spain. The impoverished Clay accepted only on the promise of an increased salary and quickly gave it up when circumstances forced Seward to send Carl Schurz to Spain. Clay got Russia instead. Before he left, he organized a battalion to guard the Capitol and swaggered about Washington, as John Hay remembered, like something off the cover of a cheap romance.

On his way to Russia in May, the mercurial reformer changed his mind and asked for a major general's commission in the regular army, arguing that "Volunteers *must* have confidence in their leaders." Lincoln and Seward ignored the request, and Clay proceeded on his roundabout route to Russia via London and Paris. He was shocked to find that England "hoped for our ruin," and he wrote an irresponsible article for the London *Times* in which he claimed the war was an antislavery war and warned England to side with her natural ally or beware the consequences.

Russia was friendly to the United States (because she, too, hated and feared Great Britain), and Clay was well received there. Rather abruptly, early in 1862, Lincoln made Clay a major general of volunteers to make room in Russia for his departing Secretary of War, Simon Cameron. Cameron told Clay he would stay only long enough to save face, and the Kentuckian gladly withdrew with the administration's promise that he could return to Russia when Cameron vacated the post. Clay returned to the United States in the summer of 1862 and quickly began criticizing Lincoln for moving too slowly against slavery. The President acknowledged the criticism by sending Clay to sound out opinion in the Kentucky legislature on a possible emancipation proclamation for the seceded states. Clay told Lincoln that "you may not always represent my special views," but he promised and continued to give support. Never too keen on a military command (the good ones seemed already taken and the war might be over too soon to make his fame on the field, Clay reasoned), the Kentucky agitator offered to resign his commission on September 29, 1862, to take effect when Cameron resigned the Russian mission. He returned to St. Petersburg in 1863 and remained in that office for 6 years.

Events quickly passed Clay by. As early as September 6, 1863, he told his friend Salmon P. Chase, "If 'Uncle Abe' desires it, I rather think he deserves another term"—probably not what the ambitious Secretary of the Treasury wanted to hear. Once emancipation was effected, Clay himself had no platform but reunion. In 1863 he criticized Charles Sumner's "state suicide" theory by saying, "After the rebels are disarmed, the states and their rights *revive,* except so far as individuals may be affected by legal procedure." Such was the essence of his beliefs from then on. He was a critic of Reconstruction and moved first into the Liberal Republican party and next into the Democratic.

In 1862 Lincoln told Orville Hickman Browning that Clay had a "great deal of conceit and very little sense." The President's opinion never changed. Clay, shortly before his death in 1903, was judged a lunatic by a Kentucky court.

SOURCES: See David L. Smiley, *Lion of White Hall: The Life of Cassius M. Clay* (Madison: University of Wisconsin Press, 1962). Clay's letters to Lincoln congratulating him for his nomination (May 21, 1860), about his claims on the post of Secretary of War (January 10, 1861), on compromise and the future of the Union (February 6, 1861), urging a referendum on Union (March 23, 1861), about English opinion (July 25, 1861), and noting differences in his views and Lincoln's (August 13, 1863) are in the Abraham Lincoln Papers, Library of Congress.

Clay, Henry (1777–1852) Abraham Lincoln's "beau ideal of a statesman." William H. Herndon, Lincoln's law partner, could recall only two historical figures he had ever heard Lincoln praise: Thomas Jefferson and Henry Clay.

The precise origins of Lincoln's admiration for Clay are unknown; but when Lincoln entered politics at the age of 23, he was already "an avowed Clay man." A Kentuckian by birth, he had a natural tie with Kentucky's famous Senator and presidential contender. More important, Clay's ambitious platform for government-fostered economic development, which he called "The American System," seemed to the youthful Illinois politician the perfect solution to the problems of the underdeveloped West. Clay, despite his Southern origins, his personal status as a slaveowner, and his dislike of abolitionists, was an advocate of gradual emancipation of America's slaves and of colonization of the freedmen—both positions which Lincoln would adopt, the former very early in his career. Clay was also a nationalist and a lover of the Union, as Lincoln proved to be as well. Clay, as Lincoln understood him, never allowed his love of the Union to outweigh his love of freedom. His "ruling passion," Lincoln said in his eulogy of Clay in 1852, was "a love of liberty and right, unselfishly, and for their own sakes." That passion always qualified Clay's nationalism, Lincoln insisted: Clay "loved his country partly because it was his own country, but mostly because it was a free country."

Lincoln's identification with Clay was no simple matter of political gain. As early as 1832 Jacksonians outnumbered Clay men in Illinois, and Lincoln's support of the Kentuckian for the Presidency in 1832 and 1844 was in vain. Clay's principles attracted the youthful Illinois politician, but Lincoln did not borrow them altogether uncritically. Clay's economic ideas were appealing to him, but Lincoln was very slow to adopt Clay's view that "circumscribing the executive power" was the "most important" Whig tenet. In fact, Lincoln first mentioned the executive veto in 1844 and adopted the Whig theory of the Presidency only in 1848. Ironically, he adopted it as a defense of Zachary Taylor, who had defeated Clay for the Whig presidential nomination that year.

Even Clay's economic ideas were too Eastern-oriented for a prairie politician, and Lincoln generally argued for easier terms for purchasing Western lands than Clay did. Internal improvements, a national bank, and tariffs, on the other hand, were staples of Clay's and Lincoln's platforms alike. Lincoln had, if anything, more affection for the tariff because it was essential to fund internal improvements if high prices for government-owned Western lands did not. As a member of the younger generation of Whigs, Lincoln also put more emphasis on the sheer economic benefits to the working man of the Whig platform. Clay, the old "War Hawk" of 1812, tended to emphasize the platform's importance for national strength and independence.

In 1848 Clay was again hopeful for the Whig presidential nomination, but Lincoln became one of the earliest and most active supporters of Zachary Taylor's nomination. Lincoln claimed that he did so "not because I think he would make a better president than Clay, but because I think he would make a better one than Polk, or Cass, or Buchanan, or any such [Democratic] creatures, one of whom is sure to be elected, if he is not."

Lincoln's eulogy on Clay in 1852 stressed Clay's devotion to the cause of liberty and carried a stern warning, in Clay's words, to proslavery advocates. Throughout the rest of that decade, and especially in the famous debates of 1858, Lincoln and Stephen A. Douglas engaged in an elaborate contest to prove themselves and their parties the true disciples of Clay. With the votes of old Whigs in central Illinois crucial to success as parties reformed in the mid-1850s, Douglas claimed Clay's mantle as the Great Compromiser. In fact, even though

Douglas knew very well that the Democrats "gave twice as many votes [as the Whigs] in both Houses of Congress" for the measures comprising the Compromise of 1850—and that he had himself played the key role in delivering them—he nevertheless gave Clay more credit for the compromise than he deserved in an effort to show his devotion to the Kentuckian's principles. He also accused Lincoln of "cutting Clay's throat" in 1848; having "fought long enough for principle," Lincoln then urged Whigs to "fight for success" by going for Taylor. Lincoln cast suspicion on Douglas, Clay's "life-long enemy," who now sought political "profit" by appearing to defend Clay against Lincoln, his "life-long friend." Lincoln did not respond to the charges about 1848, but he could truthfully say, "I can express all my views on the slavery question by quotations from Henry Clay." And he did so repeatedly, carrying a book of Clay's speeches with him and quoting passages which showed that Clay thought slavery "a universally acknowledged curse" which ought ultimately to disappear from America, that Clay criticized the justification for enslaving Negroes on "their alleged intellectual inferiority to the white races," and that Clay believed the institution ought never to be introduced into new societies. In truth, Lincoln exaggerated Clay's antislavery sentiments, which the Great Compromiser muffled from the 1830s to 1849, the period in which he was a serious presidential contender.

As late as the presidential campaign of 1860, Clay's legacy was still a matter of serious concern to Lincoln. When John Hill circulated a pamphlet entitled *Opposing Principles of Henry Clay, and Abraham Lincoln,* Lincoln began in September to compose a long answer to it, which he inexplicably abandoned.

In 1864 Secretary of the Navy Gideon Welles was present to hear Lincoln recall that, when he prepared his eulogy on Clay in 1852, he could find no model for such an address in Clay's own works. Secretary of State William H. Seward, also a former Whig, explained that "Clay's self-esteem was so great, that he could tolerate no commendation of others." Welles added that both Lincoln and Seward considered Clay and Daniel Webster "hard and selfish leaders, whose private personal ambition had contributed to the ruin of their party." It must be remembered, however, that Welles was a former Democrat with little liking for the great Whig leaders who had once inspired Lincoln and Seward.

SOURCES: The only book on the subject is Edgar DeWitt Jones's *The Influence of Henry Clay upon Abraham Lincoln* (Lexington, Ky.: The Henry Clay Memorial Foundation, 1952), a rather slight work. It must be supplemented by the keen insights on aspects of the relationship by G. S. Boritt in *Lincoln and the Economics of the American Dream* (Memphis: Memphis State University Press, 1978) and George M. Fredrickson in "A Man but Not a Brother: Abraham Lincoln and Racial Equality," *Journal of Southern History,* XLI (February 1975), 39–58. Lincoln's copy of Clay's speeches is in the Louis A. Warren Lincoln Library and Museum, Fort Wayne, Indiana.

See also NEGROES.

Clemency During his Presidency, Abraham Lincoln pardoned 375 offenders convicted by civil courts and refused pardons in another 81 cases. The bulk of the crimes for which civil offenders were forgiven were treason, counterfeiting, stealing from the mails (180), murder and manslaughter (28), larceny (25), assault and battery (19), violations of revenue laws (15), mutiny (12), theft (12), engaging in the slave trade (4), opposing enlistments (4), and embezzlement (4). Refusals of pardon included cases of counterfeiting (20), larceny (16), manslaughter (7), arson (7), serving on a slave ship (3), perjury (3), and treason (1). Excluding 75 war-related pardons, Lincoln's 300 pardons for nonmilitary offenses exceed President James Buchanan's 141 and President Franklin Pierce's 175.

Records for clemency in military cases are not as complete. For the period from March 1863 to April 1865, there are at least 225 surviving Lincoln letters and telegrams which were sent to military commanders to suspend sentences or request information about persons sentenced. Pardons were not usually issued wholesale, but in August 1862, on the recommendation of Secretary of War Edwin M. Stanton, Lincoln pardoned 96 soldiers in the District of Columbia penitentiary who were serving what Congress considered long sentences for trivial crimes. One soldier, for example, was serving a year's sentence for stealing a shirt and a pair of drawers.

Lincoln considered most cases individually. Youth was always an extenuating factor. "I am unwilling for any boy under eighteen to be shot," Lincoln wrote General George G. Meade on October 8, 1863. Lincoln also considered economic distress as a mitigating factor: "I do not like the punishment of withholding pay—it falls so very very hard upon poor families." The government's interest as well as abstract justice was served by some of Lincoln's rules. Lincoln noted that "when neither incompetency, nor intentional wrong, nor real injury to the service is imputed—In such cases it is both cruel and impolitic, to crush the man and make him and his friends permanent enemies to the administration, if not to the government itself." He recognized the injustice of inconsistency, too, and, for example, established a rule which would "allow all females, with ungrown children of either sex, to go South, if they desire, upon absolute prohibition of returning during the war; and all to come North upon the same condition of not returning during the war, and the additional condition of taking the oath [of allegiance]."

The most memorable instances of clemency involved stays of executions of soldiers. Lincoln became so famous for such clemency even in his own time that in 1863 Francis De Haes Janvier published a poem, "The Sleeping Sentinel," which celebrated the President's alleged last-minute carriage ride, pardon in hand, to stay the execution of Vermont soldier William Scott, who was sentenced to die for sleeping while on guard duty. The fabled event probably never occurred; no written evidence of Lincoln's pardon of Scott has been found.

Nevertheless, Lincoln was famous among hard-bitten generals and sentimental common people alike for pardoning convicted soldiers. General William T. Sherman wrote in 1864 that "we all know that it is very hard for the President to hang spies, even after conviction, when a troop of friends follow the sentences with earnest . . . appeals." Secretary of the Navy Gideon Welles considered it "Sometimes . . . a weakness" that Lincoln was "always disposed to mitigate punishment, and to grant favors." Yet even Lincoln did not grant them all. He allowed slave-trader Nathaniel Gordon to hang on February 21, 1862, despite the earnest appeals of "a large number of respectable citizens." He ignored the appeals of 6 Senators and 91 Congressmen and let the young son of a wealthy and socially prominent Virginia family, John Y. Beall, hang for sabotage on February 25, 1865. And he was notably tougher on officers than on enlisted men: of 59 convictions involving officers in the last half of 1863, 14 were given more severe punishments by the President than by their courts-martial. Only a select few cases reached his eyes through pardon clerk Edmund Stedman, who recalled,

> My chief, Attorney [General Edward] Bates, soon discovered that my most important duty was to keep all but the most deserving cases from coming before the kind Mr. Lincoln at all; since there was nothing harder for him to do than to put aside a prisoner's application and he could not resist it when it was urged by a pleading wife and a weeping child.

Some cynics hold with reporter Donn Piatt that

> There was far more policy in this course than kind feeling. . . . He knew that he was dependent upon volunteers for soldiers, and to force upon such men as those the stern discipline of the Regular Army was to render the service unpopular. And it pleased him to be the source of mercy, as well as the fountain of honor, in this direction.

Yet Lincoln is too often on record as opposing revenge in all matters to be judged as merely politic in his mercy. He wanted "no motive of revenge, no purpose to punish merely for punishment's sake," he told Stanton, and when the subject of Confederate war crimes came up in a Cabinet meeting at the end of the war, Lincoln is reported by Gideon Welles to have said, characteristically, that he "was particularly desirous to avoid the shedding of blood, or any vindictiveness of punishment. He gave plain notice that morning that he would have none of it. No one need expect that he would take any part in hanging or killing these men, even the worst of them. 'Frighten them out of the country, open the gates, let down the bars, scare them off,' he said, throwing up his hands as if scaring sheep." Schuyler Colfax's recollection of Lincoln's remarks about clemency are widely quoted: "Some of my generals complain that I impair discipline by my frequent pardons and reprieves; but it rests me after a hard day's work that I can find some excuse for saving some poor fellow's life, and I shall go to bed happy tonight as I think how joyous the signing of this name will make himself, his family and friends."

SOURCES: The great student of Lincoln's clemency was Jonathan T. Dorris; see his "President Lincoln's Clemency," *Lincoln Herald*, LV (Spring 1953), 2–12, and *Pardon and Amnesty under Lincoln and Johnson: The Restoration of the Confederates to Their Rights and Privileges, 1861–1898* (Chapel Hill: University of North Carolina Press, 1953). The hard-boiled view is taken by William E. Barton in his chapter on "Justice and Mercy" in the second volume of *The Life of Abraham Lincoln* (Indianapolis: Bobbs-Merrill, 1925). Richard N. Current's *The Lincoln Nobody Knows* (New York: McGraw-Hill, 1958) gives a balanced general appraisal of the subject in the chapter entitled "The Tenderhearted."

See also INDIANS; HOLT, JOSEPH; PROCLAMATION OF AMNESTY AND RECONSTRUCTION; RECONSTRUCTION.

Codding, Ichabod (1811–1866) Antislavery lecturer and Congregationalist minister. Codding was born in Bristol, New York, attended Middlebury College in Vermont, and held successive pastorates in several Illinois towns in the 1840s and 1850s. He was typical of the earliest converts to the Republican party: a warmly antislavery man, an evangelical Protestant, and an offshoot of New England culture. He lectured widely in opposition to the Kansas-Nebraska Act and helped form the early Republican party in Illinois. At a convention in Springfield on October 4 and 5, 1854, Codding and his cohorts nominated Lincoln for the Republican State Central Committee. Lincoln was not present at the convention, and when asked to attend a committee meeting in November, he wrote Codding, saying that he was "perplexed some to understand why my name was placed on that committee." Lincoln supposed his "opposition to the principle of slavery . . . as strong as that of any member of the Republican party," but he thought that the party found "the *extent* to which I feel authorized to carry that opposition, practically; . . . not at all satisfactory." Almost two years passed before Lincoln called himself a Republican. In the celebrated debates of 1858, Stephen A. Douglas tried to associate Lincoln's name with Codding's.

Despite their obvious ideological differences, Codding wrote a campaign biography of Lincoln in 1860, *A Republican Manual for the Campaign* (Princeton, Ill.: "Republican" Book and Job Printing Office). In it, Codding tried to attract antislavery radicals to Lincoln's camp and apologized for the candidate's views on racial equality, the Fugitive Slave Law, and the possibility of admitting a new slave state into the Union. These were necessary compromises in "acting with masses of men, as we must in this country, if we act at all, politically." Codding also placed great stress on Lincoln's belief in "the irrepressible conflict" between free and slave societies.

The pamphlet is one of the great rarities in Lincolniana (only seven copies were known in 1962), and Ernest Wessen, the premier student of Lincoln campaign biographies, asserted that Republicans must have suppressed the biography because of its radicalism.

SOURCES: See Ernest Wessen, "Campaign Lives of Abraham Lincoln, 1860," in *Papers in Illinois History and Transactions for the Year 1937* (Springfield: Illinois State Historical Society, 1938), pp. 188–220, and R. Gerald McMurtry, "Codding's 'Republican Manual for the Campaign—1860,'" *Lincoln Lore*, Number 1490 (April 1962), pp. 1–3.

Coles County, Illinois The home of Lincoln's parents after his departure to find a career. Located in east-central Illinois, Coles County became the home of Thomas and Sarah Bush Lincoln in 1831. Discouraged by the hard winter of 1830–1831, they were on their way back to

Indiana when they stopped in Coles County and decided to stay. After living in the Buck Grove and Muddy Point neighborhoods within the county, Thomas settled at Goosenest Prairie in 1837 on 40 acres of land owned by his stepson John D. Johnston. In 1840 Thomas exchanged land for 80 acres next to Johnston's farm; and at the end of the year he purchased Johnston's land, giving him 120 acres of land in Coles County of which he was full owner. Apparently, he owned the 80-acre tract until his death, but in 1841 he sold the 40-acre tract to his son for $200. Since Abraham allowed Thomas and Sarah control of the property after the sale, the $200 was in fact a gift of the money to his parents, who had fallen into financial difficulty. In truth, Thomas had numerous difficulties in Coles County; he was defendant in five lawsuits, four of which he lost.

Although Coles County was not a part of the Eighth Judicial Circuit, it was not far away and, between 1841 and 1848, when Shelby County was part of the circuit, adjoined it. During that period especially, Lincoln took a good bit of legal work in Charleston, the county seat of Coles, and thus visited the county frequently. The famous Matson slave case was tried in Coles County in 1847. In 1858 one of the debates between Lincoln and Stephen A. Douglas was held in Charleston.

Thomas Lincoln died at his Goosenest Prairie home in 1851. Sarah continued to live in Coles until her death in 1869. Lincoln's last visit to the county was from January 30 to February 1, 1861, when he came to bid his stepmother good-bye before going to Washington to assume the office of the President of the United States.

On March 28, 1864, six soldiers and three civilians were killed in Charleston in a riot which occurred on court day when the local Democratic Congressman was to give a speech. It was the largest battle fought between soldiers and civilians in the North over an issue other than the draft. Fifteen of the "Copperhead" rioters were imprisoned in Fort Delaware, Delaware. Influenced in part by advice from local friends and relatives, Lincoln ordered the 15 returned to Coles; 13 were released, and 2 stood trial in Illinois, only to be acquitted. The release came on November 4, 1864, or 4 days before the presidential election, a timing that suggests that political considerations worked on Lincoln as much as the advice from Coles County which had been pouring in on him all summer.

Lincoln inherited the 80-acre plot when his father died and promptly sold it for $1 to John D. Johnston, his stepbrother. Lincoln owned the 40-acre farm all his life.

The cabin in which Thomas lived was eventually sold for $10,000 to the Abraham Lincoln Log Cabin Association in 1902. The group of Chicago promoters displayed the cabin near the Columbian Exposition in Chicago in 1893, and it disappeared thereafter. The State of Illinois acquired the 80-acre farm and 6 of Abraham Lincoln's 40 acres in 1929 and 1930. The Civilian Conservation Corps made the land into a park that was dedicated in 1936 as the Lincoln Log Cabin State Park. The remaining 34 acres of Lincoln's land were acquired by the Abraham Lincoln Land & Cattle Company, which sold deeds to one square inch of Lincoln's "Forgotten Farm" for $5 each. In its 1977 Christmas catalog the Neiman-Marcus department store in Dallas, Texas, advertised marble deeds to one square inch for $100 and copper deeds for $300.

SOURCES: Charles H. Coleman's *Abraham Lincoln and Coles County, Illinois* (New Brunswick, N.J.: Scarecrow Press, 1955), though dull reading, is carefully researched and provides detailed information on Lincoln's connections with this Illinois county.

See also CHARLESTON, ILLINOIS; FICKLIN, ORLANDO BELL.

Collections, Institutional *See* BARTON, WILLIAM ELEAZAR [UNIVERSITY OF CHICAGO]; CHICAGO HISTORICAL SOCIETY; FORD'S THEATRE; HENRY E. HUNTINGTON LIBRARY; ILLINOIS STATE HISTORICAL LIBRARY; LIBRARY OF CONGRESS; LINCOLN MEMORIAL SHRINE; LINCOLN MEMORIAL UNIVERSITY; LOUIS A. WARREN LINCOLN LIBRARY AND MUSEUM; MCLELLAN, CHARLES WOODBERRY [BROWN UNIVERSITY]; OAKLEAF, JOSEPH BENJAMIN [INDIANA UNIVERSITY].

Collections, Personal *See* BARRETT, OLIVER ROGERS; BARTON, WILLIAM ELEAZAR; BURTON, JOHN EDGAR; CHICAGO HISTORICAL SOCIETY [Charles F. Gunther]; FISH, DANIEL; ILLINOIS STATE HISTORICAL LIBRARY [Henry Horner]; LAMBERT, WILLIAM HARRISON; LIBRARY OF CONGRESS [Alfred Whital Stern]; MCLELLAN, CHARLES WOODBERRY; MESERVE, FREDERICK HILL; OAKLEAF, JOSEPH BENJAMIN; OLDROYD, OSBORN HAMILTON INGHAM.

Colonization Abraham Lincoln's proposed solution to America's race problem from the 1850s until 1863 or 1864. Lincoln's plan was to have the government subsidize the "voluntary emigration" of free blacks from the United States to "their long lost fatherland" or to some other place "situated within the tropics." Henry Clay, from whom Lincoln derived many of his political ideas, had been an ardent proponent of colonization. Lincoln read Clay's famous address on the subject delivered before the American Colonization Society in 1827. His eulogy on Clay in 1852 particularly praised Clay's efforts for colonization.

By the 1850s attempts to resettle free Negroes in Liberia had shown that African colonization was impractical because it was too expensive and because the Negroes were reluctant to go. Lincoln was aware of the difficulties. In 1854 he said that he had "high hope . . . in the long run," but "sudden execution" of the scheme was impossible because there was "not surplus shipping and surplus money enough." In 1862 he told a delegation of black leaders that he realized that "unwillingness" to emigrate stemmed from a desire to "remain within reach of the country of your nativity."

Despite the acknowledged impracticality, Lincoln as President breathed life back into the waning colonization movement. His first annual message to Congress included a recommendation that free blacks and those to be freed by the recent Confiscation Act should be colonized "in a climate congenial to them." By that time Lincoln was convinced that Central America or the West Indies offered suitable opportunities. Prompted by the President, Congress in 1862 passed a bill for emancipation in the District of Columbia which included $100,000 for voluntary colonization of the freedmen to Haiti or Liberia. On July 17, 1862, another congressional act provided $500,000 for colonization of freedmen liberated by the Second Confiscation Act.

The President spent only $38,000 of the $600,000 available to him for colonization. He attempted first to colonize Negroes in Chiriqui, Colombia (on the Isthmus of Panama), lured by promises of the Chiriqui Improvement Company's chief promoter, Ambrose Thompson, that rich coal deposits would make the colony work. Members of the Cabinet except for the Secretary of the Interior regarded Thompson as a sleazy operator; the Smithsonian Institution judged the coal deposits to be overrated; and Secretary of State William H. Seward noted the protest of neighboring Latin American governments and convinced Lincoln to cancel the project. Lincoln's second attempt involved Bernard Kock's promotional scheme for Cow Island, off Haiti. Lincoln signed a contract to colonize Negroes there the day before he issued the Emancipation Proclamation, and, in April 1863, 453 Negroes sailed for the island. Disease and poor preparations made the expedition a disaster, and in February 1864 Lincoln ordered a transport to bring 368 disgusted colonists back. On July 1, 1864, Lincoln's private secretary John Hay noted "that the President has sloughed off the idea of colonization."

Interpretations of the significance of Lincoln's interest in colonization differ. Of course, colonization was a profoundly racist movement which, whatever the degree of humanitarianism or paternalism motivating its adherents, could not envision America as anything but an all-white country in the future. Some argue that the small expenditure of available funds and the general feebleness of the effort indicate that Lincoln used colonization politically to soothe white fears of the possible influx of Negroes into the North after emancipation; yet he said nothing about it publicly after the issuance of the Emancipation Proclamation on January 1, 1863. Others argue that his willingness to be involved with slippery operators like Thompson and Kock betrays a deep pessimism and profound personal fear about the ability of America to become a biracial society. In short, the moves seem to be desperate, yet Lincoln certainly did not spend with desperation. Only one thing is certain: when Lincoln accepted freedmen as soldiers on January 1, 1863, he guaranteed a biracial future for the country because no President could ask a man to fight for his country and then tell him it was no longer his country. By the end of his administration Lincoln definitely had "sloughed off" the idea.

SOURCES: See Benjamin Quarles, *Lincoln and the Negro* (New York: Oxford University Press, 1962), a balanced account, and the more speculative article by G. S. Boritt, "A Voyage to the Colony of Lincolnia," *The Historian*, XXXVII (August 1975), 619–632.

See also BUTLER, BENJAMIN FRANKLIN; NEGROES.

Commander in Chief Abraham Lincoln's preparation to direct the bloodiest war in American history was almost nil and fell far short of the military experience of his adversary in the contest, Jefferson Davis. The Confederate President was a West Point graduate, a Mexican War hero, and a recent Secretary of War. Lincoln's limited experience, almost 30 years before the war, as a volunteer in the Black Hawk War was so farcical that Lincoln himself had made fun of it in a speech in Congress. Nevertheless, President Lincoln, "in terms of time, and probably in terms of mental intensity," as G. S. Boritt puts it, concentrated his attention more on the Union war effort than on any other aspect of policy.

Lincoln's first strategic ideas, as reported by his secretary John Hay, were, "always leaving an opportunity for change of mind, to fill Fortress Monroe with men and stores, blockade the ports effectually, provide for the entire safety of the Capital, keep them quietly employed in this way, and then go down to Charleston and pay her the little debt we are owing her" [for the capture of Fort Sumter]. Lincoln had imposed a blockade of Southern ports on April 19 without the advice of any military authorities. All commentators give him high marks for realizing the importance of utilizing Northern naval superiority in that way. Concern for the security of the Capital would be a continuing theme in Lincoln's strategic thinking; on that he gets lower marks. The rest of the plan was notably deficient in that it proposed action in only one theater.

When Winfield Scott, the general-in-chief, suggested a plan to seize the Mississippi River, blockade Southern ports, and wait for the slowly strangling Confederacy to sue for peace. Lincoln rejected it but learned from it the strategic importance of the Mississippi Valley. Thereafter, his plans generally contained moves for both the eastern and western theaters. Lincoln tried to gain a picture of the whole war effort as early as June 22, 1861, when he requested reports of the number of men enlisted in Federal and state forces, their location, their state of readiness, their arms and ammunition, and the number, description, and position of all war vessels and transports. Calculations of numerical superiority would shape much of the President's strategic thinking.

Lincoln was particularly quick to grasp the numerical imperative of having Democrats as well as Republicans support and participate actively in the war effort. He awarded civil offices almost exclusively to Republicans, but military appointments went to Republicans and Democrats alike. He paid attention, too, to ethnic groups, being careful to appoint Irish-American and German-American generals. Yet Lincoln was much less sensitive than the last wartime commander in chief, James K. Polk, to the political threat posed by a successful general in high command. Though General George B. McClellan more than once pressed his conservative polit-

Commander in Chief

ical ideas on the President, Lincoln ignored them and retained him in command until he proved incapable of pressing a decisive offensive campaign. Having heard rumors that General Joseph Hooker thought "that both the Army and the Government needed a Dictator," President Lincoln appointed Hooker to command and merely wrote a fatherly letter, saying: "What I now ask of you is military success, and I will risk the dictatorship." Lincoln never believed in the Radical Republican view of generalship which saw a man's ability to fight as a function of his political enthusiasm for the administration cause. He never linked McClellan's failure as a commander, for example, to his Democratic affiliation.

Unfortunately, Lincoln had to serve for all too much of the war as both commander in chief and chief of staff. When the war began, no one in the country had commanded more than a 14,000-man army (Ulysses S. Grant would hold sway over more than half a million by war's end), and there was no organization of high command suited to the vast size of Civil War armies and the vast scale of operations. Winfield Scott was too old and infirm to command, and Lincoln's attempts to find another general-in-chief came to nothing until 1864.

Lincoln's first choice was George B. McClellan, who replaced Scott on November 1, 1861. When McClellan commenced a long-awaited campaign in Virginia in the spring of 1862, Lincoln realized that the general could not exercise direct field command of a campaign and keep the West in view as well. Therefore, on March 11 he removed him from supreme command, leaving him in command of the Army of the Potomac. Lincoln replaced McClellan with General Henry W. Halleck, a scholarly soldier and the dean of American military theoreticians at the time. Halleck exercised the powers of general-in-chief only until the end of August 1862, when the Union defeat at the Second Battle of Manassas (or Bull Run) unnerved him and, as Lincoln told his secretary John Hay, "he broke down—nerve and pluck all gone—and has ever since evaded all possible responsibility—little more since that than a first-rate clerk." After that, and before Ulysses S. Grant's emergence as general-in-chief early in 1864, Halleck served as a conduit for communication between the President and his generals, but there was no general-in-chief. Lincoln himself supplied what little coordination there was among the various theaters of military operations.

Thus Lincoln, like James Madison and James K. Polk before him, supplied a good deal of the strategic thinking for the nation's armies. That was no easy task for a man who readily admitted his lack of technical military knowledge, and the President made his fair share of mistakes. Still, he learned fast. He possessed the stern will necessary in a commander in chief. So great was Lincoln's reputation for granting clemency in the cases of individual soldiers convicted of one military transgression or another that some were fooled then (and still are now) into thinking him too tender-hearted to wage successful war. Feebleness in confronting a national enemy and mercy for individual weakness are two different things, and Lincoln could be tough. Secretary W. O. Stoddard's reminiscences of the mood of the White House after the defeat of General Ambrose Burnside at Fredericksburg in 1862 reveal this side of Lincoln's character:

> We lost fifty per cent. more men than did the enemy, and yet there is sense in the awful arithmetic propounded by Mr. Lincoln. He says that if the same battle were to be fought over again, every day, through a week of days, with the same relative results, the army under Lee would be wiped out to its last man, the Army of the Potomac would still be a mighty host, the war would be over, the Confederacy gone, and peace would be won at a smaller cost of life than it will be if the week of lost battles must be dragged out through yet another year of camps and marches, and of deaths in hospitals rather than upon the field. No general yet found can face the arithmetic, but the end of the war will be at hand when he shall be discovered.

On July 23, 1861, Lincoln wrote some "Memoranda of Military Policy Suggested by the Bull Run Defeat." His strategic ideas now included not only controlling Manassas in Virginia and keeping the line open from there to Washington but also moving on Memphis and East Tennessee in the West. He had a special fondness for plans to free Unionist East Tennessee. On occasion that politically dictated objective overshadowed important military considerations, but its inclusion in the memoranda was a sign of the President's growing awareness of the necessity for overall strategic thinking for all theaters.

As early as January 13, 1862, Lincoln had arrived at a broad strategic plan for the Union war effort. As he wrote to General Don Carlos Buell, with a copy directed to General Halleck,

> [his] general idea of this war [was] that we have the *greater* numbers, and the enemy has the *greater* facility of concentrating forces upon points of collision; that we must fail, unless we can find some way of making *our* advantage an over-match for *his*; and that this can only be done by menacing him with superior forces at *different* points, at the *same* time; so that we can safely attack, one, or both, if he makes no change; and if he *weakens* one to *strengthen* the other, forbear to attack the strengthened one, but seize, and hold the weakened one, gaining so much.

This deceptively simple strategic understanding defied the military wisdom of the day as derived from the great interpreter of Napoleon's military genius, the Baron Jomini, who stressed concentration of forces for the offensive.

McClellan had followed Jomini's dictate in his earliest recommendation for a huge army of 273,000 men to invade Virginia from the sea, take Richmond, and seize other major cities in succession. Such a force was so far beyond the government's organizational ability early in 1861 that it never received serious consideration. Lincoln only reluctantly agreed to McClellan's next plan, to attack Richmond from the east with the much smaller Army of the Potomac landed from the sea. Lincoln preferred attacking the Confederate army at Manassas, which was an early sign of his predisposition toward seeking the enemy's army rather than its capital. Despite agreeing to McClellan's plan, Lincoln's concern for the

Commander in Chief

Copperhead cartoonist Adalbert Johann Volck depicted Lincoln as a comedian. The ridiculous puppets are Secretary of War Simon Cameron (hanging on the wall), Secretary of the Navy Gideon Welles (rowing a boat), General Benjamin F. Butler (leaning against the wall), and (left to right in front) Generals John C. Frémont, Winfield Scott, and George B. McClellan. Radical Republican and Secretary of the Treasury Salmon P. Chase is the sinister puppeteer in the rear.

Northern capital poisoned his relations with McClellan.

The President felt the political pressure for military action so keenly that he issued an impractical general order on January 31, 1862, for a general movement of all forces against the enemy to begin on Washington's birthday. When McClellan finally did move, Lincoln insisted that an adequate force be left behind to protect Washington. Severe disagreement ensued over the numbers left to protect the Capital. The dispute hinged on how near Washington a force had to be to count as protection. Lincoln did not recognize the value of a force far away in the Shenandoah Valley, the route to attack Washington that Jubal A. Early would use in 1864. McClellan, on the other hand, did little to educate his commander in chief in regard to the ability of far-flung forces to guard the attack routes. In the end, Lincoln withheld a 30,000-man corps from McClellan's drive up the Peninsula on Richmond.

McClellan's slow movements exasperated the President, who told the general on April 9, 1862, "it is indispensable to *you* that you strike a blow." When Lincoln added, "*I* am powerless to help this," he revealed a sense of frustration that occasionally led him to consider taking the field himself. Indeed, in May during a visit to the front, the President actually helped plan an attack on Norfolk.

Before the Peninsular campaign Lincoln detached General Blinker's 10,000 men to help General John C. Frémont in western Virginia take East Tennessee. The number was too small to give Frémont the prize but large enough to have been a help to McClellan. The political bait of loyalist Tennessee, though, Lincoln found hard to resist. Lincoln finally relieved McClellan of command for good in the fall of 1862 (just after the off-year election day) because he was too slow in pursuing the Confederate army he had stopped at the Battle of Antietam.

Lincoln decided to accept Negro soldiers in the Union army on January 1, 1863. This move altered the arithmetic of war more heavily in the North's favor but led some commentators to fear the war would become a barbarously desperate contest. It was probably Lincoln's boldest move as commander in chief (leaving aside the Emancipation Proclamation itself, which Lincoln issued under the war powers of the President).

By June 10, 1863, Lincoln had arrived at another important strategic assumption: "I think *Lee's* Army, and not *Richmond*, is your true objective point," he told General Joseph Hooker. "Fight him when opportunity offers," Lincoln said pointedly, and he said much the same thing to other commanders to the end of the war. This imperative made the President discontented even with so great a success as the Battle of Gettysburg. About a week after that battle the President wrote a letter to the victorious General George G. Meade which, though he never sent it, betrayed his aggressive nature. Lincoln was "oppressed" by evidence that Meade was "not seeking a collision with the enemy." The "golden opportunity" to end the war was "gone," and Lincoln was "distressed immeasureably because of it."

Partisans of the view that Lincoln was a military genius fault him for assenting, early on, to plans (like McClellan's) which he did not really like. Yet they compliment his willingness to allow General Grant to pursue an unorthodox strategy in the Vicksburg campaign, which Lincoln "feared . . . was a mistake." "I was wrong," he admitted generously to Grant in a letter of July 13, 1863.

Grant's ascendance led to the creation of the most successful command structure devised during the Civil War. Early in 1864 Grant became general-in-chief. He made strategic plans for all theaters of the war, although his headquarters were with the Army of the Potomac in Virginia. By retaining General Meade as commander of the Army of the Potomac, however, Grant was free enough really to be a general-in-chief. General Halleck remained in Washington as an efficient and lucid liaison between the Commander in Chief and Grant on the one hand, and Grant and his seventeen departmental commanders on the other.

Grant's *Memoirs*, published in 1886, gave the impression that Lincoln remained a hopeless and even willing *naif* in military affairs who happily turned all military decisions over to the general he could trust to fight—Grant. In truth, the congruence of Grant's strategic thinking with Lincoln's led the President to interfere little with Grant's plans, but he did occasionally disagree with Grant and suggest military actions. Proof of their like-mindeness lies in an entry in John Hay's diary for April 30, 1864:

> The President has been powerfully reminded, by General Grant's present movements and plans, of his (President's) old suggestion so constantly made and as constantly neglected, to Buell & Halleck, et al., to move at once upon the enemy's whole line so as to bring into action to our advantage our great superiority in numbers. Otherwise by interior lines & control of the interior railroad system the enemy can shift their men rapidly from one point to another as they may be required. In this concerted movement, however, great superiority of numbers must tell: as the enemy, however successful where he concentrates, must necessarily weaken other portions of his line and lose important positions. This idea of his own, the Pres^t recognized with especial pleasure when Grant said it was his intention to make all the line useful—those not fighting could help the fighting. "Those not skinning can hold a leg," added his distinguished interlocutor.

This cannot be reconciled with Grant's claim that when Lincoln "had . . . become acquainted with the fact that a general movement had been ordered all along the line, . . . [he] seemed to think it a new feature in war." Grant's memory was faulty and self-serving here.

Courage is a necessity in any commander, and some faulted Lincoln for lacking it. McClellan and many commentators since have felt the President was "scared" by Confederate threats on Washington. Yet his orders to troops delegated to protect Washington were rarely defensive in tone. He detached troops to the Washington area to *destroy* the enemy that threatened it. At Fort Stevens in the summer of 1864 Lincoln exposed himself to the fire of Early's troops unnecessarily but courageously. With becoming modesty, Lincoln himself once noted that his courage seemed to measure up to that of the battlefield commanders. "I who am not a specially brave man," he told Hay, "have had to sustain the sinking courage of these professional fighters in critical times."

SOURCES: T. Harry Williams's *Lincoln and His Generals* (New York: Alfred A. Knopf, 1952) argues the most vigorous case for Lincoln's military genius. A briefer summary of the arguments pro and con, and a balanced appraisal of their merit, is in Chapter VI of Richard N. Current's *The Lincoln Nobody Knows* (New York: McGraw-Hill, 1958). Some useful and original insights on the foundations of Lincoln's strategic thinking lie in Chapter XVIII of G. S. Boritt's *Lincoln and the Economics of the American Dream* (Memphis: Memphis State University Press, 1978).

See also BLACK HAWK WAR; CARROLL, ANNA ELLA; CLEMENCY; EMANCIPATION PROCLAMATION; GRANT, ULYSSES SIMPSON; HOOKER LETTER; MCCLELLAN, GEORGE BRINTON; PRESIDENCY, POWERS OF; SCHURZ, CARL.

Committee on the Conduct of the War, Joint

A congressional committee established on December 10, 1861, in the wake of a Union defeat at Ball's Bluff, "to inquire into the conduct of the present war." The chairman was Senator Benjamin F. Wade of Ohio, and it is generally agreed that the Committee's investigations and reports reflected the views of his Radical wing of the Republican party. The other two original Senate members were Andrew Johnson of Tennessee and Zachariah Chandler of Michigan. House members were George Washington Julian (Indiana), John Covode (Pennsylvania), Daniel Gooch (Massachusetts), and Moses Odell (New York). Though Wade was always chairman, the membership changed a bit over the years, and Senators Joseph A. Wright (Indiana), Benjamin F. Harding (Oregon), and Charles R. Buckalew (Pennsylvania) served on the Committee as did Representative Benjamin F. Loan (Missouri). The Committee's sessions were secret.

The Committee always urged a more vigorous prosecution of the war, favored politically Radical generals, and attempted to discredit conservative generals. It was able at times to influence President Lincoln. After Committee members called on the President on December 31, 1861, to complain of General George B. McClellan's inactivity, Lincoln wrote the general a letter the very next day saying the Committee were "in a perfectly good mood" and "rapidly coming to think of the whole case as all sensible men would." When Lincoln ordered the creation of four corps in McClellan's Army of the Potomac on March 8, 1862, he was instrumenting a favorite scheme of the Committee. The Committee shared the President's anxiety about defense of the Capital and recommended the retention of forces from the Army of the Potomac to protect Washington during McClellan's Peninsular campaign of 1862, an action of Lincoln's which outraged McClellan.

The Committee had no executive powers whatever, and its influence on the President was greatest when Lincoln shared their views anyway (as in his rising distrust of McClellan's abilities). Lincoln finally dismissed McClellan after the Battle of Antietam while the Committee was not in session; he arrived at that decision alone. Likewise, the Committee was unable to influence the President to restore one of its favorites, General Benjamin F. Butler, to command over occupied New Orleans. Lincoln remained firm in his dismissals of Generals John C. Frémont, Ambrose E. Burnside, and Joseph Hooker from high commands, though the Committee gathered favorable testimony in their behalfs.

The Committee doubtless troubled the President at times but never as much as historians of the 1940s and 1950s claimed. The story that Lincoln had to appear personally before the Committee to defend his wife from malicious allegations of disloyalty to the Union gained wide acceptance in those years, but it is completely without foundation.

The Committee was reconstituted by the Thirty-eighth Congress in 1863 and was active throughout the war as an investigative and propaganda-producing agency, but its influence was limited, especially after General Ulysses S. Grant assumed overall command of Union armies. From time to time, it broke its rule of

Confiscation Act of July 17, 1862

This rare, overly complicated, and somewhat confused cartoon, published by E. H. T. Nichols in Massachusetts in 1863, suggests that the Committee on the Conduct of the War did a hatchet job on McClellan in its reports. (Library of Congress)

THE FOUR YEARS CONTRACT AND ITS PROGRESS.

secrecy and published reports. Eventually, eight volumes of testimony from its hearings and other reports were published by the Government Printing Office (1863–1866); they are a valuable resource for military historians.

SOURCES: T. Harry Williams depicted Lincoln as the victim of a wildly irresponsible Committee on the Conduct of the War in *Lincoln and the Radicals* (Madison: University of Wisconsin Press, 1941). A valuable corrective is Hans L. Trefousse's "The Joint Committee on the Conduct of the War: A Reassessment," *Civil War History*, X (March 1964), 5–19. See also Mark E. Neely, Jr., "Abraham Lincoln Did NOT Defend His Wife Before the Committee on the Conduct of the War," *Lincoln Lore*, Number 1643 (January 1975), pp. 1–4.

Confiscation Act of July 17, 1862 Commonly called the "Second Confiscation Act." The Act was aimed at both mitigating the punishment for treason and punishing adherents of the rebellion by confiscating their property. Since many Congressmen felt that thousands of Southerners were guilty of treason and since the only punishment for treason was death, the act allowed traitors to be punished by fine and imprisonment and, more important, distinguished between treason and engaging in insurrection. The last-named crime was made punishable by up to 10 years' imprisonment, $10,000 fine, and, at the discretion of the court, liberation of the rebel's slaves, if any. In effect, this act treated the Confederates as both traitors and legal belligerents and refused, as the Lincoln administration generally did, to adhere to any rigid constitutional philosophy of the Civil War.

The confiscatory aspects were considered far more important, and much of the argument over the bill concerned whether the threat of property loss would bring rebels back to loyalty or tend to keep them in rebellion longer. The property of officers of the Confederate government, civil or military, was made immediately liable to seizure. The much larger class of supporters of the rebellion had to be warned by proclamation and given 60 days to return to loyalty before courts could confiscate their property. Confiscation proceedings could be in rem proceedings, court actions without the personal appearance of the accused.

President Lincoln objected to proceedings in rem, and he hoped that reasonable time would be given for the accused to appear in court. He thought that the bill's provision for forfeiture of property *forever* was unconstitutional; he saw it as being in effect an attainder or corruption of blood whose punishment reached beyond the life of the guilty party. Bills of attainder were explicitly forbidden by the Constitution. Lincoln's threat to veto the bill led Congress to pass an explanatory joint resolution forbidding any forfeiture beyond the life of the accused. Lincoln signed the bill but took the peculiar course of sending his prepared veto message to Congress to become a part of the record.

In fact, very little property was confiscated as a result of the act. Attorney General Edward Bates tended to the view that the law should affect only persons arrested, prosecuted, and convicted of crimes listed in the act. He put very little effort into enforcement.

The act was widely regarded as an antislavery measure because of its provision for freeing the slaves of those "engaged in rebellion." And it has often been argued since that Congress had already done as much or more to free slaves as Lincoln did months later with his more famous Emancipation Proclamation. However, such is clearly not the case. The courts were the enforcement arm of the Confiscation Act through actions brought by the Attorney General and his marshals and district attorneys, which were lacking in the war-torn South.

Though the emancipation clause was separate from the confiscation and treason clauses, the act prescribed absolutely no means of enforcement. It declared "forever free" slaves taking refuge in the lines of the army from "persons . . . in rebellion," but there was no way to determine who the owners were and what their loyalties were. It was a dead letter from the start, and Lincoln claimed that no slave was ever freed by the Second Confiscation Act. The Emancipation Proclamation involved no cumbersome and impractical judicial proceedings. The army became the means of enforcement; where it succeeded in vanquishing Confederates, slaves were freed.

SOURCES: See J. G. Randall, *Constitutional Problems Under Lincoln*, rev. ed. (Urbana: University of Illinois Press, 1951).

Congressman Lincoln *See* CARTWRIGHT, PETER; MEXICAN WAR.

Conkling, James Cook (1816–1899) Lincoln's friend and neighbor. James C. Conkling was born in New York City, graduated from Princeton in 1835, and moved to Springfield in 1838, where he practiced law. Like Lincoln, Conkling was a Whig. In 1841 he married Mercy Ann Levering. Mercy was a close friend of Mary Todd's, who called her "Dearest Merce" in her early letters. According to Mary, Mercy sought "good morals & Religion" in a mate. She apparently found them in Conkling.

Conkling was elected mayor of Springfield in 1844 and to the Illinois House of Representatives in 1851. He became a Republican and campaigned for Lincoln in Pennsylvania in 1860, where he was allied with supporters of Simon Cameron's bid for a place in Lincoln's Cabinet. During the war he served as agent for the state of Illinois in handling accounts with the national government and visited Washington occasionally. In 1862 he urged Lincoln to select Mackinaw City as a site for fortification on the Great Lakes, in part because he had invested $18,000 in the city in the preceding 5 years.

James Cook Conkling. (Courtesy of the Lloyd Ostendorf Collection)

In August 1863 Conkling invited Lincoln to speak at a massive Union rally in Illinois. Lincoln could not attend but sent a famous letter, written on August 26 and read by Conkling at the rally on September 3. The forceful letter addressed the President's critics: "to be plain, you are dissatisfied with me about the negro." The Emancipation Proclamation was fully constitutional within the commander in chief's powers in time of war, Lincoln insisted. More than a year and a half of war without it had failed to suppress the rebellion, and Lincoln knew "that some of the commanders of our armies in the field who has given us our most important successes, believe the emancipation policy, and the use of colored troops, constitute the heaviest blow yet dealt to the rebellion; and that, at least one of those important successes, could not have been achieved when it was, but for the aid of black soldiers." To those "who will not fight to free negroes" Lincoln said: "Whenever you shall have conquered all resistance to the Union, if I shall urge you to continue fighting, it will be an apt time, then, for you to declare you will not fight to free negroes." Whatever Negro soldiers did left "just so much less for white soldiers to do, in saving the Union."

> But negroes, like other people, act upon motives. Why should they do any thing for us, if we will do nothing for them? If they stake their lives for us, they must be prompted by the strongest motive—even the promise of freedom. And the promise being made, must be kept.

Things were looking better. "The Father of Waters again goes unvexed to the sea," Lincoln said, thanking the Union soldiers and not forgetting "Uncle Sam's Webfeet." When victory came,

> then, there will be some black men who can remember that, with silent tongue, and clenched teeth, and steady eye, and well-poised bayonet, they have helped mankind on to this great consummation; while, I fear, there will be some white ones, unable to forget that, with malignant heart, and deceitful speech, they have strove to hinder it.

Lincoln thought Conkling "one of the best public readers" he knew, but he still advised him to "Read it very slowly."

In 1848 Conkling had been one of the few in Springfield to vote against a clause in the proposed state constitution to exclude Negroes from Illinois. His ardent antislavery convictions led him to praise Lincoln's letter and to hope that Union military success would leave "no question as to the condition and rights of 'American citizens of African descent.'"

In the summer of 1864, Conkling sought appointment to office in Europe, and Lincoln gave him an introduction to the Secretary of State on July 29. Conkling worked for Lincoln's reelection and warned the President against third-party movements of "faint hearted, weakkneed politicians who are afraid of the popularity of McClellan." He pressed Lincoln again for a European appointment after the election, but none came.

After the war, Conkling served another term in the Illinois House, continued his successful law practice and business interests, and was a member of the National

Lincoln Monument Association. He served as a pallbearer at the funeral of Mary Todd Lincoln in 1882.

SOURCES: Conkling's letters to Lincoln about the Illinois rally (September 4, 1863) and third-party movements (September 6, 1864) are in the Abraham Lincoln Papers, Library of Congress. Mary Todd Lincoln's letters to Mercy are in Justin and Linda Levitt Turner's *Mary Todd Lincoln: Her Life and Letters* (New York: Alfred A. Knopf, 1972). Conkling's vote against Negro exclusion is recorded in the Sangamon County Poll Books, Springfield Poll, March 6, 1848, Sangamon State University Archives, Springfield, Illinois.

Conscription President Lincoln was the first American President to resort to a national draft to raise soldiers for war (though President Jefferson Davis requested and obtained a draft for the Confederacy earlier, in the spring of 1862). It replaced a volunteer system only when volunteering failed to bring the numbers of men necessary. To be drafted, therefore, carried something of a stigma, for it implied that one was not patriotic enough to volunteer.

When Lincoln's call for 300,000 volunteers on July 1, 1862, met with disappointing response, the President, prompted by Secretary of War Edwin M. Stanton, chose to interpret his powers under the Militia Act of July 17, 1862, broadly. That act allowed him to issue rules to cover defects in state laws for raising soldiers. He interpreted those powers to include the ability to draft soldiers from states unable to raise their quota of volunteers. On August 4 Stanton ordered a draft of as many as 300,000 men to meet deficiencies in quotas under the July 1 call for volunteers.

On March 3, 1863, Congress provided a Conscription Act to replace the rather casually instituted draft of 1862. The law made all able-bodied male citizens and aliens who had declared intentions to be citizens, between the ages of 20 and 45, liable to be drafted for up to 3 years' military service. The country was divided into districts, and federal officials in each district administered the enrollment and draft. Draft quotas were apportioned by population of the states, and volunteers were credited to each state's quota. A draftee might escape service by providing a willing substitute or by paying a $300 commutation fee. The exemptions were accepted practices in the militia system which preceded the draft. The President always allowed a considerable period of time between the call for troops and the actual day of the draft. On that day a blindfolded federal official chose names from a wheel placed in a public place in each district where the quota was not filled. The real purpose of the draft was to spur volunteering *to avoid the draft* in the time between the call for troops and the actual spinning of the wheel in any location.

Lincoln was beseiged with requests to delay or suspend the draft in one state or another throughout the war. A typical response was the one he gave New Jersey's Governor Joel Parker on July 20, 1863: "It is a very delicate matter to postpone the draft in one State, because of the argument it furnishes others to have postponements also. If we could have a *reason* in, one case, which would be good if presented, in all cases, we could act upon it." There was considerable negotiation and adjustment of state quotas during Lincoln's Presidency.

When the provost marshal began choosing names for the draft in New York City in the hot July of 1863, simmering resentment burst into the flames of riot. From July 13 to 15 working-class mobs made up largely of young Irish-American men terrorized New York City, killing, looting, and burning. Negroes and Horace Greeley were the special objects of their hatred; they burned a Negro orphan asylum and stoned the offices of the New York *Tribune*. Federal troops, militia, police, naval personnel, and a company from West Point quelled the disturbances. About 117 people were killed.

On August 3, 1863, New York's Democratic Governor Horatio Seymour, who thought conscription unconstitutional, asked that the draft be suspended in his state. He complained of partisanship in assigning quotas and suggested that conscription should await a Supreme Court test of its constitutionality. Lincoln refused to suspend the draft. He did "not object to abide a decision of the United States Supreme Court" on the constitutionality of the draft, but he could not afford "to lose the *time* while it is being obtained." The President protested that the enemy "drives every able bodied man . . . into his ranks, very much as a butcher drives bullocks into a slaughter-pen." Lincoln reduced some quotas, agreed to have a commission investigate inequities in New York's quotas, and sent General John A. Dix, a New York Democrat, to command Union troops in the state. But the draft resumed—without incident—on August 19.

In September Lincoln was much vexed by judges whose writs of habeas corpus discharged draftees, and he prepared an opinion on conscription which was not published in his lifetime. He called complaints of the draft's unconstitutionality "false arguments with which to excuse ourselves for opposing such disagreeable things." In fact, this was "the first instance . . . in which the power of congress to do a thing has ever been questioned, in a case when the power is given by the constitution in express terms." Congress had simply exercised its powers "to raise and support armies." Lincoln did "not say that all who would avoid serving in the war, are unpatriotic; but I do think every patriot should willingly take his chance under a law made with great care in order to secure entire fairness." As to complaints that the commutation fee favored "the rich against the poor," the President claimed that the $300 fee was in fact a ceiling price which protected the ability of the man of moderate means to purchase a substitute. Without it, the rich would soon bid up the price of substitutes out of range for many. None, he noted, objected to the provision for substitutes, as it was "in accordance with an old and well known practice, in the raising of armies." "Are we degenerate?" Lincoln asked. "Has the manhood of our race run out?"

Lincoln never issued the opinion and instead suspended the writ of habeas corpus on September 15 for, among others, draftees or draft resisters. On June 8,

Constitution of the United States

1864, Lincoln recommended that Congress end the $300 commutation provision; Congress did so on July 4, 1864. Substitution remained legal, however, and President Lincoln paid for a "substitute" or "representative recruit" for himself, John Summerfield Staples of Stroudsburg, Pennsylvania.

Altogether, 46,347 draftees and 117,986 substitutes were inducted; they represented 6 percent of the total Union forces in the war. The principal effect of conscription was to encourage volunteering.

SOURCES: The chapter on "Lincoln and Seymour" in J. G. Randall's *Lincoln the President: Midstream* (New York: Dodd, Mead, 1953) gives a fine glimpse at the difficulties in New York from Lincoln's perspective. It used to be thought that many more than 117 died in the New York City draft riots; for revision to the lower figure and other important revisions see Adrian Cook, *The Armies of the Streets: The New York City Draft Riots of 1863* ([Lexington]: University Press of Kentucky, 1974). For legal problems see J. G. Randall, *Constitutional Problems Under Lincoln*, rev. ed. (Urbana: University of Illinois Press, 1951). See also John M. Taylor, "Representative Recruit for Abraham Lincoln," *Civil War Times Illustrated*, XVII (June 1978), 34, 35.

See also STANTON, EDWIN MCMASTERS.

Constitution of The United States Abraham Lincoln's Whig and antislavery political heritage shaped his attitude toward the Constitution more than his profession as a lawyer. The Whig party generally took a broad view of what the Constitution allowed the federal government to do. If this was Whiggery, Lincoln was thoroughly Whiggish. For example, he thought a national bank constitutional because it was a "necessary and proper" instrument for Congress to safeguard and disburse the funds it collected under its explicit powers to "lay and collect taxes." Like most Whigs he interpreted the "general welfare" clause liberally. Therefore, Lincoln argued that no man "clear on the . . . expediency" of internal improvements "needs feel his conscience much pricked upon" the question of constitutionality. Lincoln seemed largely indifferent to, if not impatient with, constitutional arguments on the great economic questions of his Whig years; indeed, James K. Polk's indulgence in such "abstractions" clearly disgusted him.

Lincoln was, however, even as a Whig, a stickler on one constitutional point. Opposition to the Mexican War was an article of Whig faith generally, and Lincoln quite agreed that the war was "unconstitutional and unnecessary." In a quarrel over this with his law partner, William H. Herndon, Lincoln argued that a President could not order the invasion of another country because he deemed it necessary to repel an invasion by that country. The President could not be the *"sole"* judge of the "necessity" of this:

> The provision of the Constitution giving the war-making power to Congress, was dictated . . . by the following reasons. Kings had always been involving and impoverishing their people in wars, pretending generally . . . that the good of the people was their object. This, our Convention understood to be the most oppressive of all Kingly oppressions; and they resolved to so frame the Constitution that *no one man* should hold the power of bringing this oppression upon us. But your view destroys the whole matter, and places our President where kings have always stood.

Lincoln did not take the Constitution lightly; he merely interpreted it liberally. And he seems to have been led by Polk's transgressions to his strongest affirmation that the Constitution was not to be trifled with. On June 20, 1848, he stated his conservative view of amendments to the document:

> As a general rule, I think, we would [do] much better [to] let it alone. No slight occasion should tempt us to touch it. Better not take the first step, which may lead to a habit of altering it. Better, rather, habituate ourselves to think of it, as unalterable. It can scarcely be made better than it is.

In the 1850s Lincoln interpreted the Constitution as most antislavery moderates did. Unlike abolitionists who saw the document as a covenant with death because it protected the institution of slavery in the Southern states, Lincoln saw it as a reluctant guarantor of the slave interest which existed at the government's formation. The document betrayed the antislavery sentiments of its authors by hiding slavery "away, . . . just as an afflicted man hides away a wen or a cancer, which he dares not cut out at once, lest he bleed to death; with the promise, nevertheless, that the cutting may begin at the end of a given time." Like most Republicans, he attributed great importance to the absence of any explicit mention of slavery or the Negro race in the document. He argued that it was a sign that the Constitution's authors looked forward to the day when, with slavery eradicated by time, there would be "nothing in the constitution to remind them of it."

The Dred Scott decision of 1857 forced Lincoln to argue that a single Supreme Court decision did not necessarily decide a question of constitutionality for all departments of the government. Other factors determined the decisiveness of a Supreme Court's will, and Lincoln said simply that the Constitution would have to be "better construed than . . . in that decision." He did insist, to the discomfiture of his rival Stephen A. Douglas, who defended the decision, that the Court's view that the Constitution positively affirmed the right of property in slaves would as easily eradicate antislavery measures enacted by state legislatures as by territorial ones or by Congress, because the Constitution was the supreme law of the land.

Lincoln's Cooper Institute speech (February 27, 1860), his principal introduction to Eastern voters and an important document in his subsequent presidential campaign, was a carefully researched proof that the framers of the Constitution were antislavery men. Far from affirming that Congress had no power to prevent the spread of slavery to new territories, the framers in fact were overwhelmingly on record in support of that power.

As an antislavery man, Lincoln had a natural affinity not for the Constitution (with its compromising protections of the slave interest) but for the Declaration of Independence. There is no evidence that Lincoln ever read the *Federalist* papers, the classic commentary on the Constitution; he said repeatedly that the Declaration of Independence was the source of his political ideas. In the secession crisis of 1860–1861, Lincoln seems clearly to have stressed the importance of the Declaration rather than the Constitution. He attributed "our great prosperity" to "the *Constitution* and the *Union*," but "even these," he wrote, "are not the primary cause." He pointed to "something back of these, entwining itself more closely about the human heart. . . . the principle of 'Liberty to all.'" He thought the "*expression* of that principle, in our Declaration of Independence, was most happy, and fortunate." The Union and the Constitution were the adornments and preservers of that principle; but they were made for it, and not vice versa.

Lincoln's First Inaugural Address was a conservative document which retained his "philosophical" distinction between Union, Constitution, and Declaration of Independence as a chronological distinction. "The Union is much older than the Constitution," he said, tracing its origins to 1774. It was "matured and continued by the Declaration of Independence in 1776" and finally made "more perfect" by the Constitution of 1787. Later, he would return (most significantly, at Gettysburg) to dating the country's birth from 1776, and he *never* gave primacy to the Constitution as America's fundamental document. The Inaugural Address showed other earmarks of Lincoln's old constitutional ideas. The first draft stated that he was "not much impressed with the belief that the present Constitution can be improved." Though he thought it best not to amend the document, he was willing to allow the passage of an amendment guaranteeing slavery where it already existed in the Southern states. He continued to believe that the sectional crisis was, like the Bank war of his Whig days, not really a constitutional crisis. He denied "that any right, plainly written in the Constitution, has been denied" to the seceding states; in fact, he could not think of "a single instance in which a plainly written provision of the Constitution has ever been denied." The conflict was over the right or wrong of slavery. He did argue that the Constitution made "the Union of these States . . . perpetual" because "Perpetuity is implied, if not expressed, in the fundamental law of all national governments." Therefore, "in view of the Constitution . . . , the Union is unbroken," he insisted, and secession was plainly illegal. Despite his clear constitutional duty to enforce the laws, he would not "force obnoxious strangers" on the South as officeholders or otherwise force the issue.

After war broke out, Lincoln delivered a less conciliatory rebuttal to secessionist constitutional ideas in his July 4, 1861, message to Congress. He noted that the secessionists described their movement as secession rather than rebellion for good reason: "they knew they could never raise their treason to any respectable magnitude, by any name which implies *violation* of law." Thus "they commenced by an insidious debauching of the public mind" to argue that secession was constitutional because the states made the Union in the first place. Lincoln held that no state had ever "been a State *out* of the Union" and that the "original ones passed into the Union even *before* they cast off their British colonial dependence." Texas, the only state ever to be an independent republic, renounced its independence upon entering the Union by acknowledging the supremacy of the United States Constitution. Talk of state "sovereignty" disgusted him. A "sovereignty," Lincoln said, was "A political community, without a political superior." Only Texas was *ever* such a sovereign community. The Union gave the others "their independence, and their liberty." He resolved "This relative matter of National power, and State rights, as a principle" into "the principle of *generality*, and *locality*." States were merely local governments. "This," he said with finality, "is all there is of original principle about it." The South had "sugar-coated" rebellion.

It became almost immediately clear that the Constitution was of less importance to Lincoln than the Union. As early as May 4, 1861, the President enlarged the army by calling for volunteers without any congressional authorization. On July 4 Lincoln asserted that his actions, "whether strictly legal or not," were matters of "public necessity" which Congress "would readily ratify." They were not "beyond the constitutional competency of Congress." Lincoln never believed that his suspension of the privilege of the writ of habeas corpus violated any law; the Constitution was "silent as to . . . who, is to exercise the power" of suspension. On the average, any group of 2000 Americans in 1865 contained at least one person who had been arrested arbitrarily during the Civil War and held for some time by military authorities with no charges being pressed. This was the issue which, more than any other, gave the Democrats their charge that Lincoln was a tyrant. He never granted

Pittsburgh painter David G. Blythe showed President Lincoln hobbled in trying to crush the dragon of rebellion by the overscrupulous constitutionalism of the Democratic party in this 1862 work. (Courtesy of the Museum of Fine Arts, Boston)

Cooper Institute Speech

that he did anything unconstitutional in this area, and, though he was not one to take liberty lightly, he could never

> appreciate the danger . . . that the American people will, by means of military arrests during the rebellion, lose the right of public discussion, the liberty of speech and the press, the law of evidence, trial by jury, and Habeas corpus, throughout the indefinite peaceful future . . . , any more than I am able to believe that a man could contract so strong an appetite for emetics during temporary illness, as to persist in feeding upon them through the remainder of his healthful life.

Military conscription and the Emancipation Proclamation, two other measures that Democrats regularly denounced as unconstitutional, Lincoln also thought clearly constitutional. Other actions, "some of which," the President candidly admitted to Congress in May of 1862, "were without any authority of law," caused less excitement and less organized opposition.

When Lincoln stretched the constitutional powers of the President, he did so, not for his own aggrandizement, but to save the Union. Proof of this lies in the administration's willingness to hold the election of 1864. There was never any serious consideration of postponing that divisive political contest because of the existence of war. Contemporary Democratic charges that Lincoln was a tyrant (as well as the worries of historians living in the 1920s and 1930s that Lincoln provided a model for dictators) were misplaced. No dictator worthy of the name would have missed the opportunity the war afforded to perpetuate his power by "postponing" the election until the crisis was over. Lincoln had no taste for wandering in "the boundless field of absolutism."

Nor are those arguments persuasive which find Lincoln more a nationalist than a humanitarian because he was more willing to stretch the Constitution in order to save the Union than to stretch it to free the slaves. He feared that the Supreme Court might rule the Emancipation Proclamation inoperative after the war was over, and that impelled him to support something he had never had much taste for, an amendment to the Constitution. The proposed Thirteenth Amendment abolishing slavery was a part of Lincoln's 1864 political platform.

Historians agree, by and large, that Lincoln personally moderated the excesses his broad construction of the Constitution allowed. He restrained zealous commanders from abusive arrests. Though he signed the order suppressing the New York *World*, the suppression of the Chicago *Times* was an act of a military commander which Lincoln revoked, though somewhat hesitantly. More importantly, he allowed newspapers equally outspoken against the administration and the war to continue publication. Given the enormity of the crisis he faced, historians agree that civil liberties fared better under Lincoln than under twentieth-century presidents facing less drastic wars. His wartime Presidency treated the Constitution much as Lincoln had always treated it: as a document which left great powers for practical ends and as a means to embody the promise of liberty in the Declaration of Independence in a strong and unified nation.

SOURCES: For Lincoln's early views see G. S. Boritt, *Lincoln and the Economics of the American Dream* (Memphis: Memphis State University Press, 1978). On the Presidency see J. G. Randall, *Constitutional Problems Under Lincoln*, rev. ed. (Urbana: University of Illinois Press, 1951), and Randall's "The Rule of Law under Lincoln," in *Lincoln the Liberal Statesman* (New York: Dodd, Mead, 1947).

See also BATES, EDWARD; CHICAGO *TIMES*, SUPPRESSION OF THE; CONSCRIPTION; COOPER INSTITUTE SPEECH; DRED SCOTT DECISION; EMANCIPATION PROCLAMATION; FUGITIVE SLAVE LAW; HABEAS CORPUS; NEW YORK *WORLD*; NEWSPAPERS; PRESIDENCY, POWERS OF; REPUBLICAN PARTY; SLAVERY; SUPREME COURT; TANEY, ROGER BROOKE; THIRTEENTH AMENDMENT.

Cooper Institute Speech The address that introduced Abraham Lincoln to Eastern Republicans, February 27, 1860. In October 1859 Lincoln was invited to speak for a $200 fee at Henry Ward Beecher's famous Plymouth Church in Brooklyn. He agreed to speak in February "provided they would take a political speech, if I could find time to get up no other." As he was "not a professional lecturer" and thought his only lecture "rather a poor one," he soon decided to make it a political speech.

Lincoln's partner William H. Herndon had advised Lincoln to go, thinking "it was a move against [William H.] Seward," the front-runner for the Republican presidential nomination. Herndon was probably right. James S. Briggs, who wrote the initial telegram inviting Lincoln to speak, was the Eastern manager of Salmon P. Chase's attempt to gain that same nomination. The Young Men's Republican Union, which eventually sponsored Lincoln's speech, had on its board of advisers Horace Greeley, William Cullen Bryant, and other New York Republicans who opposed Seward's nomination.

Lincoln did considerable research for the speech in his own copy of Jonathan Elliott's six-volume *Debates . . . on the Federal Constitution* and in other sources at the state library. He left Springfield on February 23. The speech was scheduled for the 27th.

When he arrived in New York City, Lincoln learned that the site would be the Cooper Institute rather than Plymouth Church. Escorted to the platform in the evening by David Dudley Field, another anti-Seward Republican, Lincoln rose in a wrinkled and ill-fitting new suit to speak to an audience of some 1500 who had each paid 25 cents admission.

The speech was primarily an attack on the views of Stephen A. Douglas and Roger B. Taney that the founding fathers had not launched this country in an antislavery direction. Lincoln examined the public careers of the 39 men who signed the Constitution of the United States and discovered that 21, a clear majority, at some time or another voted to let Congress regulate slavery in the territories. Likewise, the same Congress which voted to forbid slavery from the Northwest Territory also formulated the first ten amendments to the Constitution, and the Fifth Amendment could hardly have been meant by them—as Taney said it was in the Dred Scott decision—as a prohibition of Congress's ability to regulate slavery in the territories. Lincoln concluded: *"As those fathers marked it [slavery], so let it be again marked, as an evil not to be extended, but to be tolerated and protected only because of and so far as its actual presence among us makes that . . . a necessity."* Thus Lincoln could say "to the Southern people" that the Republican party was not "revolutionary, destructive, or something of the sort" but adhered "to the old and tried" policy of the fathers toward slavery.

Lincoln denied any connection between Republicans or Republican policies and John Brown's raid on Harper's Ferry, and he belittled the raid itself as "so absurd that the slaves, with all their ignorance, saw plainly enough it could not succeed." He described Southern threats to secede if a Republican were elected President as a "rule or ruin" philosophy.

Lincoln concluded with a "few words to Republicans." Though these words began with a plea to *"do nothing through passion and ill temper,"* Lincoln's conclusion was actually a plea to hold firm to Republican principles and not a plea for conservatism. And Lincoln asserted that principles indeed were at stake. "Their thinking it [slavery] right, and our thinking it wrong, is the precise fact upon which depends the whole controversy." His final words were an admonition against "groping for some middle ground between the right and the wrong": "LET US HAVE FAITH THAT RIGHT MAKES MIGHT, AND IN THAT FAITH, LET US, TO THE END, DARE TO DO OUR DUTY AS WE UNDERSTAND IT."

The audience applauded and cheered. Greeley's New York *Tribune* stated that "No man ever before made such an impression on his first appeal to a New York audience." The *Tribune* published the address in full, made the text available to other papers, and published a pamphlet version. When Lincoln returned home on March 14 after a speaking tour of New England, he had the speech printed as a pamphlet by the *Illinois State Journal*. Cephas Brainerd and Charles C. Nott of the Young Men's Republican Union of New York published a pamphlet version in which they carefully annotated Lincoln's historical assertions and which Lincoln supervised.

Lincoln told his wife that the speech "went off passably well and gave me no trouble whatever." It was widely circulated as campaign literature.

SOURCES: The fullest treatment is in Benjamin Barondess, *Three Lincoln Masterpieces: Cooper Institute Speech, Gettysburg Address, Second Inaugural* (Charleston: Education Foundation of West Virginia, 1954). The copy editor of the New York *Tribune* apparently threw the original manuscript of the speech away.

Copperheads *See* HABEAS CORPUS; VALLANDIGHAM, CLEMENT LAIRD; WOOD, FERNANDO.

Corbett, Thomas P. ("Boston") (1832–?) The slayer of Lincoln's assassin. Corbett was born in England but "reborn" as a converted evangelical Christian in Boston, from which he took his new name. He came to New York with his parents in 1839 and became a hatter in Troy. He moved to New York City and married, but his wife died in childbirth. In 1857 he was working as a hatter in Boston. He was an eccentric man, wearing his hair very long because, one acquaintance said, Christ was always pictured with long hair. In 1858 he castrated himself to avoid sinful temptation by women.

Corbett rushed to the colors as soon as the war began, enlisting in the 12th New York Militia on April 19, 1861. He reenlisted three times, eventually becoming Sergeant in Company L, 16th New York Cavalry. He showed great courage in battle but was captured on June 24, 1864, and sent to the notorious Andersonville prison.

Corbett was one of 26 cavalrymen from the 16th New York selected by Lieutenant Edward P. Doherty on April 24, 1865, to pursue John Wilkes Booth. In the early morning of April 26, they arrived at the Virginia farm of Richard Garrett, where the assassin and David E. Herold were hiding. When Booth refused to surrender, the tobacco barn where he hid was fired. Before he was driven out by the smoke and flames, a shot rang out, and Booth fell, mortally wounded. Corbett admitted to his officers that he had killed Booth, because "Providence directed me." He was arrested but spared court-martial by Secretary of War Edwin M. Stanton on the grounds that the "rebel" was dead and the "patriot" lived. Corbett shared the reward for Herold and Booth's capture with the rest of the men in the unit, a share of $1653.85. On August 17, 1865, he was mustered out of service with the rest of the 16th New York Cavalry.

Boston Corbett

Corbett returned to his trade in Boston and then in Danbury, Connecticut. After residence in Camden, New Jersey, he moved to Concordia, Kansas, in 1878, where he had a homestead and continued lay-preaching as a revivalist. He was appointed assistant doorkeeper of the Kansas House of Representatives in Topeka in 1887. When he broke up a meeting in the legislative hall with a revolver, he was arrested, adjudged insane, and committed to the Topeka Asylum for the Insane. In 1888 he escaped to Neodesha, Kansas, where he told an old war buddy that he was going to Mexico. He was never heard from thereafter.

Those fond of finding bizarre associations with the Lincoln assassination mention Corbett's insanity often. However, he was a hatter for most of his life, and insanity was an occupational hazard because of the use of mercury in that trade.

SOURCES: On Corbett, as on all others associated with the assassination, see George S. Bryan, *The Great American Myth* (New York: Carrick & Evans, 1940). See also Byron Berkeley Johnson, *Abraham Lincoln and Boston Corbett* (Waltham, Massachusetts: privately printed, 1914).

Corning, Erastus, Letter to *See* HABEAS CORPUS.

Crittenden, John Jordan (1787-1863) Kentucky Senator. Widely regarded as the heir to Henry Clay's principles, Crittenden likewise fell heir to some of Abraham Lincoln's admiration for Clay. By 1847, when Lincoln and Crittenden were serving in the Thirtieth Congress, both men favored Zachary Taylor's nomination for President on the Whig ticket—"although he [Crittenden] does not expressly say so," as Lincoln noted. Clay's decision to seek the same nomination caused a rift with Crittenden and, some historians say, Lincoln concluded from it that Clay was willing to sacrifice his party for personal ambition.

The first bill voting supplies for the soldiers in Mexico in 1846 began with a preamble blaming Mexico for the war with the United States. Crittenden voted "aye, except for the preamble." He continued to vote supplies but was otherwise a critic of the war, which he said "should not be waged for the acquisition of territory." He was willing to accept a territorial accession, "of more limited extent" than that which President James K. Polk sought, in settlement of American claims against Mexico. Lincoln too opposed the war, and when Usher F. Linder objected that he should act more like Crittenden, Lincoln replied somewhat testily:

> Please wherein is my position different from his? Has *he* ever approved the President's conduct in the beginning of the war, or his mode or objects in prossecuting it? Never. He condemms both. True, he votes supplies, and so do I. What, then, is the difference, except that he is a great man and I am a small one?

After the Taylor campaign, sectional issues drove Lincoln and Crittenden further and further apart. In 1858 Lincoln heard that the Kentuckian was supporting Stephen A. Douglas against Lincoln for the Senate. "I do not believe the story," Lincoln told Crittenden. "It is not in character with you as I have always estimated you," but, though confirming the story "would pain me much," Lincoln said, "I should still continue your friend and admirer." Crittenden thought Douglas's opposition to the Lecompton constitution for Kansas "was full of sacrafice, & full of hazard, yet he took it, and he defended it, *like a Man.*" Crittenden "could not but wish for his success." He endorsed Douglas. In the ensuing debates with his archrival, Lincoln noted sarcastically that "Judge Douglas is very fond of complimenting Mr. Crittenden in these days." Crittenden's endorsement of Douglas spoiled Lincoln's chances to claim that he occupied good old Whig ground in opposing Douglas's Kansas-Nebraska Act. When, near election day, the Saint Louis *Missouri Republican* alluded to Lincoln's earlier correspondence about Crittenden's views, Crittenden wrote Lincoln to disclaim any role in giving the story to the press. "It never occurred to me to cast any blame upon you," Lincoln replied, though he admitted that "the use of your name contributed largely" to Douglas's victory. T. Lyle Dickey, a disgruntled old Whig who supported Douglas, had secured Crittenden's letter endorsing Douglas in August. He withheld it from publication until a week before the election, when it would damage Lincoln's cause the most. Speaking in Cincinnati the next year, Lincoln referred to the support of Douglas in the previous campaign by "a Senator from Kentucky, whom I have always loved with an affection as tender and endearing as I have ever loved any man."

In 1860 Crittenden supported the Constitutional Union ticket and, after Lincoln's election provoked the secession crisis, strove mightily to assume Clay's mantle as the great compromiser of sectional difficulties. Crittenden proposed a compromise based on extending the Missouri Compromise line to the Pacific and amending the Constitution to guarantee slavery in the states where it already existed. Lincoln opposed the proposed compromise because the first proposition allowed slavery to expand anew. Even so, Lincoln considered naming Crittenden to fill the seat of Supreme Court Justice John A. Campbell, who was to resign to return to Alabama. Salmon P. Chase opposed this attempt to placate the South; Campbell decided not to resign; and, once there was a vacancy, the war was on and Lincoln felt no need to appease the South.

Crittenden served in the House of Representatives while Lincoln was President, but it was his efforts in 1861 to keep Kentucky in the Union which most pleased Lincoln. A defender of Kentucky's position as a "neutral," Crittenden was also among the men who formed a Union Defense Committee to supply arms smuggled by the Lincoln administration to Unionist groups in Kentucky. By late summer Lincoln no longer agreed to follow Crittenden's advice not to establish recruiting in Kentucky. In November the Kentucky Congressman still had enough influence to procure the release of Kentucky Governor Beriah Magoffin's brother from Fort Lafayette. (The brother eventually fled to the Confederacy.) An omen of what would prove an inseparable gulf between Crittenden and the President lay in the former's letter to Lincoln of November 26, 1861, suggesting that Lincoln "say nothing on the subject of slavery or slaves" in his annual message to Congress.

Against Crittenden's advice, Lincoln in the next spring offered compensation to any state freeing its slaves. Crittenden thought Kentucky had done enough to prove her loyalty, and he opposed the Emancipation Proclamation, the formation of West Virginia, the confiscation acts, and the use of Negro soldiers to defend the "liberties of the white man."

In his last speech, delivered in May 1863 as he ran for Congress, Crittenden called Lincoln a "most well-meaning and excellent man." He died before election day.

SOURCES: See Albert D. Kirwan's solid *John J. Crittenden: The Struggle for the Union* ([Lexington]: University of Kentucky Press, 1962). Crittenden's letters to Lincoln about Douglas (July 29, 1858) and about his annual message (November 26, 1861) are in the Abraham Lincoln Papers, Library of Congress.

Crook, William Henry (1839-1915) Washington, D.C. policeman. For the last few months of Lincoln's life William H. Crook was a guard at the White House. In November 1864 four policemen were detailed by the

Washington chief of police to guard the President around the clock. One of these original guards, Thomas Pendel, became a doorkeeper at the White House, and on January 4, 1865, Crook replaced him as guard. Armed with revolvers, the guards worked in shifts, two from 8 a.m. to 4 p.m., one from 4 p.m. to 12 p.m., and one from 12 p.m. to 8 a.m. The guards dressed in plain clothes and accompanied the President whenever he left the White House, walking beside him like "any other . . . casual friend, office-seeker, petitioner, adviser." The existence of the guards was little known in Lincoln's day because the President, said Crook, "did not want it blazoned over the country that it had been found necessary to guard the life of the President of the United States from assassination." From January 9 until February 1 Crook was on duty from 4 p.m. to 12 p.m. and accompanied the President each night on his customary trip to the War Department to get the latest news by telegraph from the front. From February 1 until February 15, Crook took the 12 p.m. to 8 a.m. shift, and from February 15 on, he had day duty. Crook's reminiscences, *Through Five Administrations*, contained a few interesting glimpses of White House life and a startling charge: that guard John F. Parker was derelict in his duty the night of Lincoln's assassination. It was Crook's view that if Parker had been at his post, Booth could not have killed Lincoln.

SOURCES: Compiled and edited by Margarita Spalding Gerry, *Through Five Administrations* (New York: Harper and Brothers, 1910) makes interesting reading.

Curtin, Andrew Gregg (1815?–1894) Governor of Pennsylvania during the Civil War. Curtin, who was born in Bellefonte, Pennsylvania, became a lawyer in 1839. He was a Whig and adhered to that party through 1856, being a latecomer to Republican ranks. After he lost a bid for the United States Senate in 1855, he and the Know-Nothing candidate for that seat, Simon Cameron, developed a mutual hatred that would mar Republican politics in Pennsylvania throughout the Civil War.

Lincoln was introduced to the Cameron-Curtin feud before he met Curtin. Curtin ran for governor on the People's party ticket in 1860 (Pennsylvania was too conservative for the party to embrace the "Republican" name), but the party sent delegates to the Republican nominating convention in Chicago. The delegates were pledged to support Cameron for President on the first ballot. At the convention Curtin helped Lincoln indirectly by impressing on the delegates his own inability to carry the state if William H. Seward were the presidential candidate. The New Yorker was sound on the tariff, the overriding passion of Pennsylvania politics, but he was an anathema to former Know-Nothings; and it was clear that Pennsylvania's Republicans had to have the Know-Nothings' votes. On the second ballot Pennsylvania went for Lincoln, but the reward of a Cabinet post would go to Cameron rather than to Curtin's faction.

Curtin defeated Democrat Henry D. Foster in the important October gubernatorial race, which was taken as a bellwether of the presidential election to come. Curtin stressed the tariff (though Foster did not oppose it) and largely ignored the slavery issue. His henchman, Alexander K. McClure, captured the state organization from the Cameron forces by a maneuver which brought complaints even to nominee Lincoln. "I am slow to listen to criminations among friends," Lincoln said, "and never expouse their quarrels on either side. My sincere wish is that both sides will allow by-gones to be by-gones, and look to the present & future only."

Curtin supported William L. Dayton and later Thaddeus Stevens for Lincoln's Cabinet. In truth he sought anyone who could frustrate Cameron's chances of representing Pennsylvania and New Jersey in Lincoln's official family. He urged Edward Bates for Secretary of State, because William H. Seward and his manager Thurlow Weed were Curtin's enemies as well. In December he told the President-elect that he wanted to make his inaugural address conform to Lincoln's views. On December 21 Lincoln told him "to express, without passion, threat, or appearance of boasting, but nevertheless, with firmness, the purpose of yourself, and your state to maintain the Union at all hazzards." Curtin's address on January 15 stated it as "the first duty of the national authorities to stay the progress of anarchy and enforce the laws."

By February Curtin was convinced that Cameron had given Lincoln a bad impression of him, but Lincoln assured him it was not so. They met on Washington's birthday in Harrisburg, where both delivered speeches. Lincoln was en route to Washington for his inauguration.

Four days before Fort Sumter fell, Lincoln impressed on the Governor "the necessity of being *ready.*" When war broke out, Curtin urged its vigorous prosecution and began strenuous efforts—which would continue for 4 years—to rally Pennsylvania's manpower to the cause. Like governors of other Northern states which bordered slave states, he sought an aggressive policy toward the Border States and abetted the formation of West Virginia. His recommendation of George B. McClellan, along with that of Ohio Governor William Dennison, brought important Republican backing for McClellan's elevation to command of the Union armies. When McClellan proved slow to attack, Curtin remained faithful; he assured the President on March 3, 1862, that "Whatever may be the sentiment at Washington the Army and the masses of the people have entire confidence in the fidelity and ability of General MLelland."

Though he always pressed a vigorous war policy and at times offered Lincoln more men than he could take, Curtin was otherwise a rather conservative Republican. His rousing patriotic harangues almost never mentioned slavery. He informed Lincoln that taxation for the war effort was "a delicate question in Pennsylvania." The draft, too, was "very odious in the State," and Curtin engaged in bitter disputes with Secretary of War Edwin M. Stanton over Pennsylvania's quotas. He did not actually protest either policy, but he did disavow any connection with the government's arbitrary arrests and told his legislature that only Congress could suspend the privilege of the writ of habeas corpus.

Andrew Gregg Curtin. (Courtesy of The Historical Society of Pennsylvania)

Curtin, Andrew Gregg

After Lincoln promised him a "first class" mission abroad in the event of his retirement from office, Curtin announced in April 1863 that his health was too poor to allow him to run for reelection. Cameron would have liked nothing better than to have Curtin out of the country and planned to help nominate another, but, when the Democrats nominated the able conservative George W. Woodward, most Pennsylvania party leaders saw Curtin as the only possible candidate around whom they could rally to win the governorship. In August he accepted renomination. He told Lincoln that in "the cities and towns the changes are all in our favor, but in the country, remote from the centres of intelligence, the Democratic leaders have succeeded in exciting prejudice and passion, . . . and the changes are against us." Curtin did everything he could to obtain furloughs for his supporters in the army and waged a strong campaign. Cameron backed him reluctantly for the Union's sake; and despite McClellan's endorsement of Woodward, Curtin won.

Curtin's second term was marked by wrangles with the War Department over quotas and pay for Pennsylvania soldiers and recruiting, but he always protested their equity, not the overall burden. In fact, in 1864 Lincoln turned down an offer of more men from Curtin because, as the Governor put it, Lincoln "did not desire, without actual necessity, to further exhaust her [Pennsylvania's] laboring population, on which . . . the Government depended so largely for coal, iron, and other material aid."

Cameron and Curtin joined forces to gain an endorsement of Lincoln's reelection by the Pennsylvania legislature in January 1864. Later, however, Curtin joined those who wished to postpone the Republican convention, which was sure to nominate Lincoln unless delayed. Cameron whispered that Curtin wanted Lincoln's job, and Thurlow Weed told Seward in September that Curtin was only "luke-warm" for the cause.

Curtin supported ratification of the Thirteenth Amendment and, after Lincoln's death, supported the Fourteenth Amendment. He advocated Reconstruction as a legitimate exercise of Congress's constitutional ability to guarantee a republican government for the states. He turned down the offer of a foreign mission from Andrew Johnson because of disagreements with Johnson's conservative Reconstruction policies. In 1872 he became a Liberal Republican and eventually moved into the Democratic party.

SOURCES: There is no biography of Curtin, and one must use William B. Hesseltine's *Lincoln and the War Governors* (New York: Alfred A. Knopf, 1948), which takes a low view of Curtin's abilities, and the blatantly hagiographic William H. Egle, ed., *Andrew Gregg Curtin: His Life and Services* (Philadelphia: Avil Printing, 1895). Curtin's letters to Lincoln praising McClellan (March 3, 1862), on taxation (June 28, 1862), about the draft and changes in the country and cities (September 4, 1863), about his rejected offer of more men (June 6, 1864), as well as Weed's letter to Seward about Curtin's lukewarm attitude (September 18, 1864), are in the Abraham Lincoln Papers, Library of Congress.

See also CAMERON, SIMON; MCCLURE, ALEXANDER KELLY.

D

Davis, David (1815–1886) Lincoln's legal associate, friend, and campaign manager in 1860. Davis was born in Maryland, the posthumous child of Ann Mercer and David Davis. His mother lived on her father's plantation, which employed more than a dozen slaves. After she married Franklin Betts, Davis went to live in Annapolis with his uncle, the Reverend Henry Lyon Davis, the father of Henry Winter Davis. From the minister, David absorbed a dislike of Jacksonian democracy, admiration for Henry Clay, and moderate views on slavery. Reverend Davis taught his slaves to read, emancipated them when they reached the age of 25, and colonized them in Liberia.

After a sordid court dispute with the Reverend Davis over David's inheritance, Betts sent the boy to New Ark Academy (1826–1828) and to Kenyon College in Gambier, Ohio (1828–1832). Davis graduated from college and studied law with Henry W. Bishop, in Lenox, Massachusetts. He studied law less than a year at New Haven Law School in Connecticut and moved to Illinois. In 1836 he settled in Bloomington, where he took over the law practice of Jesse W. Fell. By 1838 his prospects had improved enough that Judge William Perrin Walker of Massachusetts allowed Davis to marry his daughter Sarah.

Davis's attraction to the Whig party was inherited from his uncle, but the party's ambitious platform of economic development meshed perfectly with the young lawyer's view of the West. "I am satisfied," he wrote in 1840, "that no professional man ought ever to locate himself in a country purely agricultural. It is only where manufacturing or commercial business is done, that a lawyer can expect always to have plenty to do." Like many Whigs, Davis blamed Democratic control of Illinois politics on corruption and the Irish vote. "If the *Irish* did not vote more than *3 times*," he complained, "we could easily carry the State." In 1844 he won election to the state legislature, but he despaired over the results in the national election, blaming James K. Polk's victory on the defection of abolitionists from the Whigs. "The abolitionists," he swore, "are hereafter and forevermore shut out of the pale of my sympathy."

Politics and the law brought Davis into contact with Lincoln as early as 1835. He soon recognized Lincoln's considerable abilities, writing in 1844 that "Lincoln is the best Stump Speaker in the State—worked on a farm at 8 dollars a month until he was 22. He shows the want of early education but he has great powers as a speaker." Davis shared Lincoln's dislike of the Mexican War and refused an invitation to speak at an enlistment rally in Bloomington. He hoped that the war would "open the eyes of the American People to the iniquities of Loco Focoism," and he despaired at "the sacrifice of human life—mourning families and all the evils and miseries attendant on war."

Early in 1848 he visited Lincoln in Washington, perhaps to solicit the Congressman's support for his nomination as candidate for judge of Illinois's Eighth Judicial Circuit. Lincoln remained neutral in the contest because Davis's rival was Benjamin S. Edwards, Mrs. Lincoln's

David Davis. (Courtesy of the Lloyd Ostendorf Collection)

brother-in-law's brother. That did nothing to diminish Davis's dislike of Mary Lincoln. "I don't fancy his wife and the family of Todds," Davis had said in 1847. He thought Lincoln, however, "a very pure and upright man."

Davis won election as circuit judge in 1848. He had occasionally appeared in court with and against Lincoln in the past, but beginning in 1849, Lincoln frequently appeared before him as judge. Davis decided cases for and against his old friend's clients. Together, the two men and other lawyers made the 3-month ride around the circuit each spring and fall. Davis recalled that "Lincoln was happy, as happy as *he* could be, when on this circuit—and happy no other place." After 1853 railroads lessened the time Davis and Lincoln spent on the circuit.

Lincoln and Davis were closely allied in politics by this time. Davis opposed the Kansas-Nebraska Act of 1854 and worked for Lincoln's election as an anti-Nebraska Senator in 1855. When Lincoln threw his support to Lyman Trumbull to avert a Democratic victory, Davis was bitter toward the Anti-Nebraska Democrats and began a long feud with Trumbull and his manager Norman B. Judd, both former Democrats. Because of their mutual dislike of Judd and Trumbull, Davis became a political ally of Chicago's John Wentworth.

Despite his distrust of Irishmen, Davis was never tempted to join the Know-Nothing party, which he thought had a "mean, narrow and selfish" platform. He became a Republican with the greater part of Illinois's Whigs in 1856, primarily because of the "outrages in Kansas & the general conduct of the administration, with the attack on Mr. Sumner." "Bleeding Kansas" and the caning of Senator Charles Sumner "made abolitionists of those, who never dreamed they were drifting into it."

Davis clung to his judgeship and therefore could not campaign actively for Lincoln in his friend's 1858 bid for the Senate, but he wrote letters and consulted regularly with Illinois Republicans in an effort to get Lincoln elected. He warned the candidate in August that "Among all the Kentuckians it is industriously circulated that, *you favor negro* equality." Republicans "should distinctly & emphatically disavow *negro suffrage*, Negro holding office, serving on juries & the like." After Lincoln was defeated, Davis assured him, "You have made a noble canvass . . . which, if unavailing in this State . . . has earned you a national reputation." He blamed the loss on the "Pharisaical old Whigs in the central counties," on T. Lyle Dickey's letter from John J. Crittenden endorsing Douglas, and on Horace Greeley and William H. Seward for encouraging Republicans not to oppose Douglas.

Davis and Lincoln continued a close political association; and when Lincoln gained the presidential nomination in 1860, Davis became, for all intents and purposes, his manager. At the Republican convention in Chicago, Davis rented two rooms at the Tremont House and gathered Lincoln's friends to work on the delegates. He tried mainly to gather pledges of support for Lincoln as the second choice of most delegations. He concentrated efforts on the Pennsylvania and Indiana delegates, as those two states were essential for Republican success in the election in the fall. He repeatedly told Lincoln not to come to Chicago, and he worked until he was "nearly dead with fatigue." Though Davis's efforts were masterful, there is no evidence to confirm Mrs. Walter Q. Gresham's claim, made years later, that Davis obtained Indiana's support by promising Caleb Blood Smith a Cabinet post. Davis's assurances of support for a Cabinet post for Pennsylvania's Simon Cameron appear to have been stronger, though they fell short of pledging Lincoln to it.

After Lincoln's nomination, Davis and Leonard Swett contacted Thurlow Weed, William H. Seward's manager, to invite him to meet with Lincoln in Springfield. Once Seward's men were assured that they would not be proscribed for opposing Lincoln at the convention, the major problem Davis faced was attracting the former Know-Nothing voters to the Republican cause. This he did by sending Orville Hickman Browning to get Edward Bates's endorsement of Lincoln and by contacting his cousin Henry Winter Davis and other former Know-Nothing leaders. Davis thought the Republican National Committee should concentrate on Pennsylvania and Indiana, both of which held state elections a month before the presidential election. In the summer Davis went to Indiana, Pennsylvania, and New York to confer with Republican leaders. In Pennsylvania he assured Simon Cameron of Lincoln's soundness on the tariff and gave him notes of early Lincoln speeches to prove it. By August, Davis was certain of victory: he thought all the East was safe (except perhaps Rhode Island), Pennsylvania was safe, and only Indiana seemed doubtful.

After Lincoln's election, Davis had considerable influence on Cabinet selections and other appointments. He thought Lincoln must include three Cabinet members from slave states. He recommended Nathaniel P. Banks as New England's representative in the Cabinet, and, of course, he urged Lincoln to appoint Caleb Smith and Cameron. His influence was not great enough, however, to gain his cousin's appointment as Postmaster General. Lincoln wanted Davis himself to become Commissary General, but General Winfield Scott persuaded him that the job should go to a military man.

Throughout Lincoln's term in office, Davis opposed the influence of his old enemy, Trumbull, and a new one, Salmon P. Chase. That made him an ally of Thurlow Weed, likewise a staunch opponent of Chase and the Radical wing of the Republican party. Davis's influence on the administration declined after 1861; in part that was because Davis wished Lincoln to move more forcefully against Chase's faction, something the President would not do. On the great political issue of the Civil War, emancipation, Davis was too closely aligned with conservatives in the Republican party to have much influence on Lincoln. Though he had always hated "the wild and disorganizing schemes of the political abolitionists," Davis nevertheless had a respectable antislavery record. As early as 1844, he had voted in the Illinois legislature to hear a petition to repeal all Illinois laws making distinctions between white and black people. He voted against a bill to imprison Negroes in the state who could not produce proof they were freemen. He led the movement to use the capitol for the organizational meeting of the local colonization society, of which he became a member. As a member of the convention which drafted the 1848 Illinois constitution, he fought the article which excluded free Negroes from Illinois.

When Lincoln announced the preliminary Emancipation Proclamation, Davis was involved in Leonard Swett's campaign for Congress in Lincoln's old district. The "Proclamation seems to take well," Davis observed at first, but Swett, who supported the Proclamation, lost. Davis grew fearful. When the Illinois legislature appeared ready to pass a resolution saying the Proclamation must be rescinded or the war stopped, Davis urged Lincoln to modify the Proclamation. The President refused.

Davis aspired to become a federal judge in Chicago and was somewhat surprised when Lincoln decided to appoint him to the Supreme Court. He was appointed on October 19, 1862. In his years on the court (1862–1877) he gained a reputation as a civil libertarian, primarily from the majority decision he wrote in *Ex parte Milligan* (1866). The case stemmed from the arrest of Indiana Democratic politician Lamdin P. Milligan for conspiring to seize United States arsenals, free Confederate prisoners, and join the Old Northwest to the Confederacy. A military commission sentenced him to death. Sitting on the United States Circuit Court in Indianapolis in 1865, Davis referred Milligan's appeal for a writ of habeas corpus to the Supreme Court. On December 17, 1866, Davis's opinion declared that "Martial rule can never exist where the [civil] courts are open," even in wartime.

After Lincoln's assassination, his widow and his son Robert asked Davis to become executor of the estate. Though Davis managed the estate well, this was an unfortunate episode for him. He had never liked Mrs. Lincoln, and she quickly grew to dislike him for stating frankly the size of the estate and thus diminishing her chances to receive charity. She tried to keep her sizable debts secret from the Judge. Davis did attempt for Mrs. Lincoln's sake to discourage William H. Herndon from spreading the story that Lincoln's only true love had been Ann Rutledge. For a time Davis held the Lincoln papers in Bloomington until Robert decided to allow John G. Nicolay and John Hay to use them for a biography of Lincoln. Davis increased the estate from about $85,000 to $110,000 before distributing it in thirds to Mary, Robert, and "Tad." He refused any compensation for his work. In 1875 he concurred in Robert's anguished decision to have his mother committed for insanity. Robert came to regard him "as a second father."

Davis followed an erratic political course after the Civil War. He blamed President Andrew Johnson's "obstinacy & combativeness" for the failure of the Southern states to ratify the Fourteenth Amendment, but he could not stomach black suffrage ("degraded ignorance" at the polls, he called it). Radical Republican attacks on the Supreme Court in Reconstruction drove him politically rightward. He opposed Johnson's impeachment in 1868 and by 1872 was a candidate for the Liberal Republican presidential nomination. In 1877 he was elected to the Senate and refused to enter either party's caucus there. He voted for the Democratic party in 1880 and for the Republican party in 1884.

Davis's wife died in 1879, and four years later he married Adeline Burr, 25 years younger than he. He retired from the Senate the same year, returned to Bloomington, and died there in 1886.

SOURCES: Willard L. King's *Lincoln's Manager: David Davis* (Cambridge: Harvard University Press, 1960) is a solid biography which quotes heavily from Davis's papers. Davis's letters to Lincoln about Kentuckians in 1858 (August 3, 1858) and about Lincoln's "noble canvass" and the "Pharasaical old Whigs" (November 7, 1858) are in the Abraham Lincoln Papers, Library of Congress.

Debates, Lincoln-Douglas A series of formal political debates between Abraham Lincoln and Stephen A. Douglas in a campaign for the United States Senate in 1858. The debates launched Lincoln to national fame. Many presidential campaigns in American history are less well known than the 1858 campaign for Senator from Illinois.

As an acknowledged leader of the Illinois Republicans with Whig antecedents, Lincoln was the natural candidate for the Senate. Illinois already had a Republican Senator, Lyman Trumbull, of Democratic antecedents. Besides, Lincoln was known to be a great campaigner. It would take hard campaigning to beat Douglas, who was already a two-term Senator and an important national figure in the Democratic party.

A peculiar circumstance shaped the nature of the contest. In the congressional session of 1857–1858, Douglas had opposed President James Buchanan, a fellow Democrat, for refusing to require the submission of the proslavery Lecompton constitution to the vote of the people of Kansas. In fighting the Lecompton constitution, Douglas had joined forces with Republicans in Congress. Douglas's value as a thorn in the side of proslavery Democrats led some Republicans to urge that his reelection be unchallenged. Illinois Republicans in general, and Lincoln in particular, took a dim view of surrendering party leadership to a man with whom they had battled all of their political lives. Illinois Republicans defiantly closed ranks behind Lincoln, scorned the advice of Eastern Republicans like Horace Greeley, who had come to admire Douglas, and on June 16, 1858, endorsed Lincoln for Senator. That was only the second time in American history a senatorial candidate had been so "nominated." Senators were chosen by the state legislature; Lincoln's name appeared on no ballot; and there was nothing binding in the "nomination." The real electoral contest was for 87 seats in the Illinois legislature.

Lincoln knew he must show that a gulf of principle separated his Republicanism from Douglas and the Democracy. Douglas's "popular sovereignty" gave Western territories the choice of allowing or forbidding slavery, but many Douglas supporters thought it would as surely

Debates, Lincoln-Douglas

This is the only surviving broadside related to the Lincoln-Douglas campaign of 1858. (Courtesy of the Illinois State Historical Library)

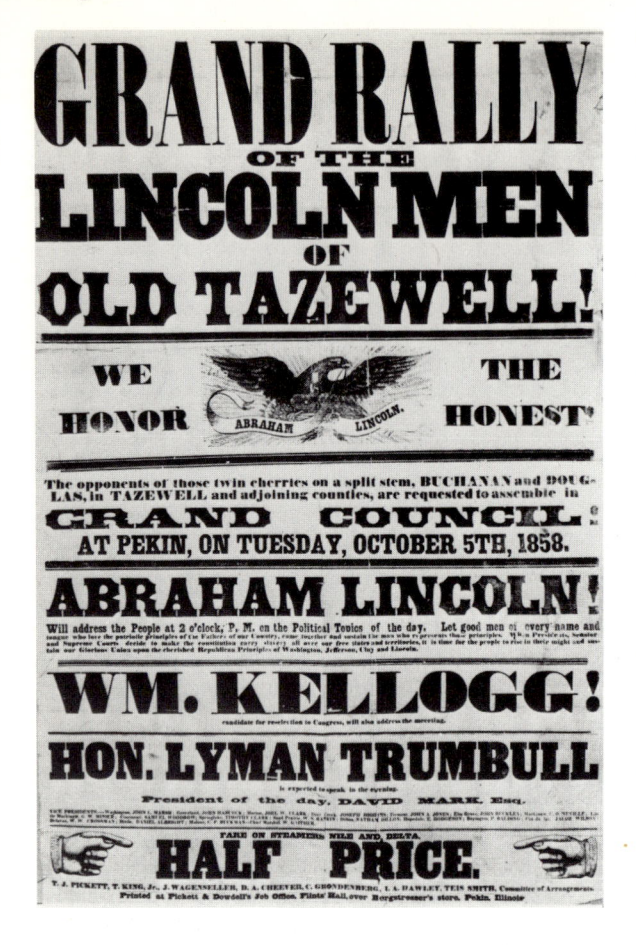

work to make the territories free as the congressional prohibition of slavery in the territories which Lincoln championed. Geography and climate, they thought, dictated that slavery would never take profitable root in the arid West; the people there would never vote to embrace a useless institution. Some Lincoln scholars, most notably Albert J. Beveridge, came to see Douglas as a greater, more practical man than Lincoln in these debates, for popular sovereignty would result in free territories and, as Douglas claimed, keep the nation from splitting in two in rancorous arguments over slavery in Congress. Such interpretations ignore the moral issues Lincoln stressed and focus only on policy differences.

Douglas attracted attention wherever he went. Like all underdog candidates, Lincoln wished to share Douglas's audiences. He appeared in Chicago and Springfield to make speeches at the same time Douglas did. Finally, Lincoln challenged Douglas to debate on the same platform. On July 24 he wrote Douglas, asking him to agree "to divide time, and address the same audiences during the present canvass." Douglas was not about to surrender all the advantage of his fame, but he feared Republicans would call a complete rejection cowardice. He promptly agreed to meet for one debate in each of the nine congressional districts except the two where they had already met (Chicago and Springfield). On July 30 Douglas set the times and places: Ottawa, August 21; Freeport, August 27; Jonesboro, September 15; Charleston, September 18; Galesburg, October 7; Quincy, October 13; and Alton, October 15. They would alternate opening and closing the debates; each time, there would be a 1-hour opening speech, a 1½-hour answer, and a ½-hour rebuttal by the first speaker.

Detailed descriptions of the individual debates will be found herein under the town's names. An overview suggests two general points. First, Douglas did not succeed in his main strategy of making Lincoln appear to be too radical on the slavery question. However, he did force Lincoln to enunciate precisely how far he would go to help the Negro. Douglas's charge that Lincoln catered his remarks on slavery to suit the latitude of the area of the state in which he spoke was not entirely true. Lincoln proved willing enough to express his opposition to racial equality in the northern (Republican) part of Illinois. On the other hand, he did tend to muffle his insistence on the natural rights (short of civil and political rights) guaranteed to all men in the Declaration of Independence in areas of heavy Southern origin and orientation (Charleston and Jonesboro). His statements on race became a bit more conservative as the debates progressed. By focusing at Jonesboro on inconsistencies in past Democratic platforms and at Charleston on the detailed legislative history of a bill to settle the Kansas controversy, Lincoln managed not to mention the Declaration of Independence at all.

Second, simply by not being completely vanquished (in the eyes of public opinion), Lincoln, in a sense, won the debates. He succeeded in another sense as well. His first speech revealed that it was his plan to show that Douglas's popular sovereignty, by being based on professed indifference to whether slavery was "voted up or voted down," had a tendency "to the *perpetuity and nationalization of slavery.*" The latter point he could never prove, but Douglas did say in the next-to-the-last debate (Quincy): "If we will stand by that principle [of letting each State decide], then Mr. Lincoln will find that this republic can exist *forever* [emphasis added] divided into free and slave States, as our fathers made it and the people of each State have decided." This may have been a slip of the tongue brought about by a too-neat reversal of the language of Lincoln's "House Divided" speech, but it serves to point up the real moral distinction Lincoln was able to make between Douglas and the Republicans. Douglas did not treat slavery as though it were wrong, and he refused ever to say whether he thought it was wrong or not.

Of course, the modern tendency to see this moral distinction must not lead one to exaggerate the high-mindedness of the debates. The debaters often dwelled on narrow questions, shirked answers, claimed relationships with heroes like Henry Clay and the founding fathers, accused each other of entering conspiracies, and in general sought political advantage where they could find it. In fact, some scholars argue that Lincoln's decision to take the offensive at Freeport by accusing Douglas of conspiring with Roger B. Taney, James Buchanan, and Franklin Pierce to nationalize slavery was the most important move he made. In a state in which 70 percent of the voters had voted to exclude Negroes from the state in the constitution of 1848, appeals for sympathy for the Negro's humanity were likely to fall on deaf ears. But fears of Southern arrogance, power, and aggressiveness were another matter altogether, and Republicans had great success in appealing to fears that the "Slave Power" would destroy white rights as well as black.

The debates drew enormous crowds—for example, over 10,000 in Ottawa, a town of only some 6000 population. The general attentiveness of the audiences for 3 hours of political debate speaks well for the political interest and sophistication of the nineteenth-century American electorate, but it should not be exaggerated. Lincoln commented after the first debate that there "was a vast concourse of people—more than could [get] near enough to hear." Some came for pageantry more than politics, and indeed the atmosphere of politics in Lincoln's day was much like that of a football game today. Banners painted with slogans and caricatures decorated the buildings, and long parades brought the speakers to town. Lincoln's escort to Charleston, for example, included the Bowling Green Band from Terre Haute, Indiana, and a large float containing 32 young ladies in white dresses, each carrying the flag of a different state. The procession was almost a mile long.

In one sense, Lincoln certainly lost the debates, for the election did not send enough Republicans to the legislature to elect him Senator. Though the Republicans outpolled Douglas's forces by a slight margin (about 125,000 to 121,000 for Douglas and 5000 for the Buchanan Democrats), legislative apportionment gave the Democrats 46 legislators and the Republicans only 41. There were 13 holdover Senators, however, and even a proportion of Republicans exactly corresponding to the vote would not have made Lincoln Senator. He was temporarily crushed: "I now sink out of view, and shall be forgotten."

Yet Lincoln did well enough that Illinois Republicans began to tout him for the Presidency in 1860. He himself knew he had performed well, for in the same gloomy letter quoted above he added: "I believe I have made some marks which will tell for the cause of civil liberty long after I am gone." Just 18 days after the election, he began gathering newspaper clippings of the speeches in order "to preserve a set of the last debates." He put together a scrapbook of his own speeches as they appeared in the Republican Chicago paper and Douglas's as they appeared in the Democratic Chicago paper. Certainly no one preserves proof of his own defeat for publication! Lincoln turned down one initiative to publish in 1858, but Oran Follett of Sandusky, a founder of the Republican party in Ohio, secured the scrapbook for Follett, Foster and Company. Lincoln instructed that the speeches be printed "without any comment whatever." *The Political Debates Between Hon. Abraham Lincoln and Hon. Stephen A. Douglas* appeared in 1860 and quickly became a best seller (over 30,000 copies in a matter of months).

Lincoln was given 100 copies for distribution to friends, and presentation copies of the book are much-sought-after rarities. To date, 19 have been found, all but one of them inscribed in pencil. The ink is badly smeared on the one copy signed with a pen, and it is assumed that the porous paper of the book forced Lincoln to sign them in pencil after one try with ink. Presentation copies sell for over $2000. Lincoln's scrapbook was owned by Oliver R. Barrett and was sold in 1952 for $26,400 to Alfred Whital Stern, whose collection is now in the Library of Congress.

SOURCES: Much of the best literature on the debates is recent. Harry V. Jaffa's *Crisis of the House Divided: An Interpretation of the Issues of the Lincoln-Douglas Debates* (New York: Doubleday, 1959) turned interpretation of the event around and stressed the differences of principle between the two men; it is essential, but difficult, reading. Much crisper, but also scholarly and much more astute about Illinois politics, is Don E. Fehrenbacher's *Prelude to Greatness: Lincoln in the 1850's* (Stanford: Stanford University Press, 1962). A useful narrative of the campaign is Richard Allen Heckman's *Lincoln vs. Douglas: The Great Debates Campaign* (Washington, D.C.: Public Affairs Press, 1967); though lucid, this account lacks drama and analytical complexity. Collectors and bibliophiles will want to read Jay Monaghan's "'The Lincoln-Douglas Debates,'" *Lincoln Herald*, XLV (June 1943), 2–11, and Harry E. Pratt, "Lincoln Autographed Debates," *Manuscripts*, VI (Summer 1954), 194–201. A good edition of the speeches themselves is Paul M. Angle, ed., *Created Equal? The Complete Lincoln-Douglas Debates of 1858* (Chicago: University of Chicago Press, 1958). An excellent brief treatment which stresses the importance of the conspiracy charge is Chapter XIII of David M. Potter's *The Impending Crisis, 1848–1861* (New York: Harper & Row, 1976). For local arrangements and press opinion, see Edwin Erle Sparks, ed., *The Lincoln-Douglas Debates of 1858* (Springfield: Illinois State Historical Library, 1908).

See also ALTON, ILLINOIS; CHARLESTON, ILLINOIS; CRITTENDEN, JOHN JORDAN; DOUGLAS, STEPHEN ARNOLD; FREEPORT, ILLINOIS; FREEPORT QUESTION; FUGITIVE SLAVE LAW; GALESBURG, ILLINOIS; GREELEY, HORACE; "HOUSE DIVIDED" SPEECH; JONESBORO, ILLINOIS; MEDILL, JOSEPH MEHARRY; OTTAWA, ILLINOIS; QUINCY, ILLINOIS; RAY, CHARLES HENRY; TRUMBULL, LYMAN; WHITE, HORACE.

Declaration of Independence *See* CONSTITUTION OF THE UNITED STATES; JEFFERSON, THOMAS; NATIONALISM.

Democracy *See* REPRESENTATIVE GOVERNMENT.

Dennison, William (1815–1882) Montgomery Blair's successor as Postmaster General in Lincoln's Cabinet. Dennison, who was born in Cincinnati, graduated from Ohio's Miami University in 1835. He became a lawyer, railroad promoter, bank president, and, generally, a successful businessman. In politics he was a Whig with a strong antislavery bent. He was an early convert to the Republican party.

In 1859 Dennison defeated Democrat Rufus P. Ranney in the gubernatorial election. Ohio's Republican party was one of the more radical ones in the Old Northwest, and Dennison followed the party line as a candidate by expressing sympathy for Ohioans recently convicted of aiding the escape of a fugitive slave. Dennison's first

William Dennison

personal contact with Lincoln resulted from his invitation to the President-elect to stop in Columbus en route to his inauguration. Even before that meeting he had urged Montgomery Blair's appointment as Secretary of War.

Though willing to adopt a "conciliatory tone" in his annual message to the legislature in January 1861, Dennison generally opposed compromise in the secession crisis and reported to Lincoln that even Democrats in Ohio favored reinforcing Forts Sumter and Pickens. "If blood must flow," he told the President two days before Confederates fired on Fort Sumter, "better for it to flow at Charleston than at Washington."

The Governor responded with alacrity to Lincoln's call for troops, but, like other governors, Dennison had his administrative troubles with mobilization. He was the first prominent Republican to call George B. McClellan to Lincoln's attention and was instrumental in gaining his appointment as a major general. He resisted overtures to cooperate with Kentucky to negotiate a reconciliation of the states and urged instead a military occupation of the key cities in Kentucky. Lincoln ignored the advice and followed a policy of allowing Kentucky to be "neutral." Dennison also abetted the formation of West Virginia. As his term neared its close, on the strength of rumors that other Northern governors had similar offers from the President, he requested a major general's commission. Lincoln did not grant it. Seeking a loyal Democrat and wary of criticism of Dennison's early attempts at mobilizing the state, Ohio Republicans nominated David Tod for governor in 1861. Despite those rebuffs Dennison remained thoroughly loyal to the Ohio party and to President Lincoln.

In 1863 Dennison instructed Lincoln to "regard the [gubernatorial] nomination of [John] Brough by the State Convention . . . as an earnest approval of the most vigorous policy for prosecuting the War & not as a disapproval of the policy of General Burnside," who had recently ordered the arrest of Ohio Democrat Clement L. Vallandigham. Governor Tod had been criticized for encouraging arbitrary arrests. Dennison was somewhat provincial in his zeal for the national cause, telling Lincoln that "we can raise troops much more rapidly in the West to defend the West." He admired the President's Proclamation of Amnesty and Reconstruction and the new high command system of March 1864.

At the same time Dennison was already certain of Lincoln's renomination. He never flirted with the Chase boom and was surprised at how soon Chase left the race for the nomination. He urged the President to announce publicly his "approval of the bill or resolution . . . for amending the Constitution for general emancipation." Dennison was presiding officer at the Baltimore convention which renominated Lincoln. He kept the President informed of developments in Ohio, assuring him that McClellan's nomination met with little enthusiasm from Ohio's peace-oriented Democrats and keeping him abreast of rumors about a Republican movement to replace Lincoln with Benjamin F. Butler. On September 24 Dennison got his reward: appointment as Postmaster General.

In Washington Dennison was regarded, more or less, as Ohio's representative in the Cabinet. Through him passed the many recommendations from Ohio for Noah Swayne and Salmon P. Chase as successor on the Supreme Court to Chief Justice Roger B. Taney. After Lincoln's assassination Dennison soon became an enemy of Andrew Johnson's Reconstruction policies and resigned in disgust in 1866. He returned to Ohio, his business interests, and state Republican politics.

SOURCES: See Eugene H. Roseboom, *The Civil War Era: 1850–1873; A History of the State of Ohio, Volume IV* (Columbus: Ohio State Archaeological and Historical Society, 1944) and Homer Carey Hockett's sketch in the *Dictionary of American Biography* (New York: Charles Scribner's Sons, 1958), III, 241–242. Dennison's letters to Lincoln about his "conciliatory tone" (January 7, 1861), Fort Sumter (April 10, 1861), Brough (June 18, 1863), Western troops (July 30, 1862), and the Thirteenth Amendment (March 12, 1864) are in the Abraham Lincoln Papers, Library of Congress.

Depression *See* PSYCHOLOGY.

Descendants Of Abraham and Mary Lincoln's four sons, only one lived to maturity. Robert Todd Lincoln (1843–1926) married Mary Harlan (1847–1937) in 1868. They had three children, Jessie, Abraham, and Mary. Abraham ("Jack") Lincoln died in 1890 at age 17. Mary (1869–1938) became the wife of Charles Bradley Isham in 1891. Their son, Lincoln Isham, born in 1892, died in Dorset, Vermont, in 1971. His marriage to Leahalma Correa was childless. Jessie (1875–1948) eloped with a college football player and sportsman from Mount Pleasant, Iowa, Warren Wallace Beckwith, in 1897. They had two children, Mary Lincoln Beckwith and Robert Lincoln Beckwith, before their divorce in 1907. Jessie lived with her parents until she remarried in 1915; her second husband was an explorer and geographer named Frank Edward Johnson. The marriage was childless and ended in divorce in 1925. The next year she married Robert J. Randolph, by whom she had no children.

Mary Lincoln Beckwith (1898–1975), Abraham Lincoln's great-granddaughter, never married. Her brother, Robert Lincoln Beckwith (b. 1904), twice married (to Mrs. Hazel Holland Wilson and to Annemarie Hoffman), had no children either and is the last direct descendant of Abraham Lincoln. Like most of the other Lincoln descendants before him, he is wealthy, leads a quiet life, and avoids the public gaze.

Diary of a Public Man Published in the *North American Review* in 1879; purported to be a firsthand account of the "intimate history" of events in New York and Washington between December 28, 1860, and March 15, 1861. The "diary" included accounts of three interviews with Abraham Lincoln and is the locus for several famous anecdotes about Lincoln: that he called Senator

Charles Sumner of Massachusetts "my idea of a bishop," that he wore black gloves in atrocious bad taste at an opera performance in New York City, and that archrival Stephen A. Douglas held Lincoln's hat while the President delivered his First Inaugural Address. After some thirty years of work, Frank Maloy Anderson wrote *The Mystery of "A Public Man": A Historical Detective Story* (Minneapolis: University of Minnesota Press, 1948) and proved that the account of one Lincoln interview was certainly fictitious (since it placed on the scene men who were probably elsewhere at the time) and that the other two were doubtful. Anderson destroyed the "diary" as a source of information on Lincoln, though many historians had used it for almost 70 years. He cast doubt on much of the rest of the "diary" and suggested a plausible author, one Samuel Ward, a Washington lobbyist and gadfly.

SOURCES: Roy N. Lokken's "Has the Mystery of 'A Public Man' Been Solved?" *Mississippi Valley Historical Review*, XL (December 1953), 419–440, gives "no" for an answer and casts some doubt on Anderson's book but not enough to revive using the "diary" as a source.

Diller, Isaac Roland (?–1891) Brother of Lincoln's Springfield druggist Roland Weaver Diller. Diller was born in Pennsylvania, fought in the Mexican War, and moved to Springfield, where he became a successful real estate agent. A prominent Democrat, he served as Springfield's postmaster. Partly as a reward for loyalty and partly to squelch a feud between Diller and Charles H. Lanphier, editor of the Democratic *Illinois State Register*, Diller gained appointment in 1857 as United States consul to Bremen on the recommendation of Stephen A. Douglas.

Lincoln's election meant Diller's removal from Germany, but by August 1862, the enterprising Diller was proposing to the President a scheme to develop a new gunpowder. Through connections in Germany, Diller had a one-third interest in a gunpowder invented by a German chemist. It relied on chlorates, which were plentifully available in the United States, rather than saltpeter, which was acquired principally from India through Great Britain. Lincoln showed keen interest but drove a hard bargain in December 1862: the government would pay the expenses, up to $5000, of developing 1000 pounds for testing. If tests proved the merit of the powder, Diller would then get $150,000. Results of tests in June of 1863 were marvellous, but the powder was dust only and had to be granulated for safe storage and movement. Experiments with 40 pounds of grains in October 1863 were not successful, and Diller returned to Springfield and the real estate business before the war's end.

SOURCES: Robert V. Bruce's *Lincoln and the Tools of War* (Indianapolis: Bobbs-Merrill, 1956) is excellent on the Diller episode as on all others having to do with inventions under the Lincoln administration. Diller's politics are mentioned in David E. Meerse, "Origins of the Buchanan-Douglas Feud Reconsidered," *Journal of the Illinois State Historical Society*, LXVII (April 1974), 163–164, 170–171.

Diplomacy *See* SEWARD, WILLIAM HENRY.

Dole, William Palmer (1811–1889) Commissioner of Indian Affairs in the Lincoln administration. William P. Dole was born in Danville, Vermont, but moved West at an early age. Eventually he settled in southern Indiana, where he became a successful merchant and politician. He moved to Paris, Illinois, in 1854. He became a Republican and was a delegate to the Republican convention which nominated Lincoln for President. He worked with David Davis to gain Indiana's and Pennsylvania's delegates for Lincoln. His reward was appointment as Commissioner of Indian Affairs in the Department of the Interior.

Although Dole had no special experience in Indian relations, President Lincoln left Indian matters in his hands. There was nothing original about Dole's policies, but both principle and practical politics led him generally to follow the more humane strands of policies established by his predecessors. In the spring of 1861 he urged a military campaign to protect the loyal Indians in Indian Territory, fearing that, left to the influence of Confederates, many of the Indians would side with the enemy. That provided the first of his many differences with the War Department, which refused to commit soldiers to the expedition. Though reluctant at first, by late in the year Dole was willing to employ Indians as soldiers. Many Westerners opposed the policy and so did the War Department, which did not allow it. Confederate influence grew strong, and loyalist Indians were driven out of the Territory into Kansas. For many, that meant being driven into starvation or freezing to death. Dole eventually gained approval of expeditions to return the loyal Indians to the Territory and to arm some of them. Most, however, did not return until 1864, and too late in the year to plant crops.

The most serious problem Dole faced was in Minnesota, where difficulties with the Sioux erupted into warfare late in the summer of 1862. The rebellion was quelled in the fall; but when a military commission sentenced 307 Sioux warriors to hang for their "murders" and "outrages" (a Victorian code word for "rapes"),

Isaac Roland Diller. (Courtesy of the Illinois State Historical Library)

William Palmer seated in front of a tent in Minnesota in 1862. Presidential secretary John G. Nicolay stands at Dole's left.

Dole's conscience was troubled. "I cannot reconcile it to my sense of duty to remain silent," he told Interior Secretary Caleb Blood Smith, who forwarded Dole's letter to the President. In it Dole characterized "an indiscriminate punishment of men who have laid down their arms and surrendered themselves as prisoners" as "revenge" rather than "deserved punishment." True, these people were "a wild, barbarous, and benighted race," but this helped suggest the appropriate punishment. Since Indians followed their leaders "almost superstitiously," it would be enough to hang the leaders; all the braves would feel it deeply. In the end President Lincoln followed an even more humane policy, leaving only 38 to hang, all of them guilty of rapes or massacres of innocent whites.

Despite his conventionally low opinion of Indian civilization, Dole's views were far removed from the widely held idea that the only good Indian was a dead one. His principal interest was in "concentration": gathering the tribes on a few reservations far removed from white civilization, which seemed always to corrupt them with liquor and to exploit them for their land. Left to themselves, they could "gradually become accustomed to a settled mode of life while learning the arts and advantages of civilization." "Severalty," a policy of dividing the reservations into parcels of land for individual ownership, and the encouragement of agriculture and animal husbandry would accelerate the process of growth in self-reliance and industrious habits. So would an improvement in schools for the Indians on the reservations.

Dole's ideas were thoroughly civil in nature, and the Commissioner was repeatedly at loggerheads with the Army; he disliked military solutions to Indian problems. Both the Army and white Westerners frequently viewed the Lincoln administration as "soft" on Indians. Often, however, Dole had to leave Indian relations to military or local authorities, and one result was the bloody massacre of Arapahoes and Cheyennes at Sand Creek in Colorado Territory on November 29, 1864.

Dole had other than Indian matters to preoccupy him; in 1864 he was deeply involved in political affairs. He attempted to patch up a factional feud in the Republican party in Kansas. After investigating the New York political scene in 1864, Dole told Interior Secretary John P. Usher that he found "considerable opposition to Mr. Lincoln" in the offices of *The Independent*, an antislavery newspaper. Only Henry Ward Beecher of those "folks" was for Lincoln, though Theodore Tilton was "not *against*" Lincoln. Even those who supported the President wanted the Cabinet reorganized. Dole worked to get the powerful New York Customs House behind Lincoln's drive for reelection. "Mr Lincoln," he warned, "must let these *Treasury people* know that *he* and not Mr Chase appointed them." He recommended dismissing Hiram Barney, the collector of the port. When Simeon Draper became collector of the port and promised in September to get the New York appointees behind Lincoln, Dole told the President that he had known things would work out in this important bastion of party jobs. Early in 1864 he had warned Lincoln about the movement to nominate Salmon P. Chase and later apprised him of rumors of a movement to make Benjamin F. Butler the nominee.

Dole was obviously a capable politician, and part of his success was attributable to his flexibility. He thought some Indian tribes more ready for severalty than others, and he recognized that different policies on slavery were fit for different states. The West, and Kansas in particular, feared slavery in Missouri as a threat to its own freedom. In 1862 Dole advised Lincoln to follow an antislavery policy in Kansas which would, he knew, be inappropriate in Maryland or Kentucky. Dole said "god speed" to antislavery moves in Missouri but did "not feel so about Kentucky, and not much so about Maryland & Virginia." He had "no disposition at all to interfere with it in any other slave state except it gets in our way."

Dole remained in office under Andrew Johnson only a brief time. Replaced in the summer of 1865, he chose to remain in Washington, D.C., where he died 24 years later.

SOURCES: See Donovan L. Hofsommer, "William Palmer Dole, Commissioner of Indian Affairs, 1861–1865," *Lincoln Herald*, LXXV (Fall 1973), 97–114, and the more hostile David A. Nichols, *Lincoln and the Indians: Civil War Policy and Politics* (Columbia: University of Missouri Press, 1978). Dole's letters to Smith about the Sioux prisoners (November 10, 1862), to Lincoln about antislavery sentiment in Kansas (February 3, 1862), and to John P. Usher about New York's Customs House (February 20, 1864) are in the Abraham Lincoln Papers, Library of Congress.

See also INDIANS.

Douglas, Stephen Arnold (1813–1861) Lincoln's archrival in Illinois politics. Stephen A. Douglas was born in Vermont. His father died while he was an infant, but he received a better formal education than Lincoln, including a smattering of classical learning. After living in Canandaigua, New York, from 1830 to 1833, Douglas left for the West and eventually settled in Jacksonville, Illinois. He was admitted to the bar in 1834.

Douglass (he spelled his name with two *s*'s in his early years) became a Jacksonian Democrat at a young age and helped organize the local Democratic party on the issue of a national bank in 1834. He drafted the law which made the office of Illinois state attorney elective and was subsequently elected to that office in 1835. He recognized the need for a state bank (despite his antibanking sentiments) and did not exude any Jacksonian animosity toward speculation. He noted that the "most money is made here by speculating in Lands" and encouraged a correspondent: "With the capital you can bring with you, you will be able to make a fortune in Lands without laboring any yourself." He had none of the nostalgia for a simpler noncommercial republic which marked the thought of some older Jacksonians. An ardent organizer, he helped introduce the convention system for party nominations in Morgan County in 1835. Only 5 feet 4 inches tall, Douglas was already so important in politics that he was called the "Little Giant."

Stephen Arnold Douglas

Douglas gained election to the Illinois House of Representatives in 1836, and he introduced an internal improvements bill that was not considered ambitious enough by more development-minded legislators. He voted for the more ambitious plan in 1837, as did Lincoln, but Douglas claimed later, when the internal improvements system collapsed, that he did so only because his constituents instructed him to vote for it. He opposed linking the Illinois State Bank to the improvements system.

In March 1837 Douglas resigned from the House to accept President Martin Van Buren's offer to become Register of the Springfield Land Office. In 1838 he ran for Congress against Lincoln's law partner, John Todd Stuart. Lincoln noted it only by saying, "We have adopted it as part of our policy here, to never speak of Douglass at all. Is'nt that the best mode of treating so small a matter?" Stuart won by 36 of 36,495 votes. Two years later Lincoln and Douglas met several times in debates in the presidential campaign of 1840.

Late in 1840 Douglas lobbied for a bill to increase the size of the Illinois Supreme Court from four to nine members. Since the new members would be elected by the Democratic legislature, the Democrats would gain a two-to-one majority on the Court, which had been dominated by Whigs before the legislation. When the bill passed in 1841, Douglas was named to the court. Lincoln denounced the reorganization "as a party measure for party purposes" which crushed "the independence of the Judiciary." Douglas moved to Quincy because he was assigned to the Fifth Judicial Circuit.

In 1842 Douglas tried for the United States Senate but lost to Sidney Breese in a close vote in the legislature. In 1843 he ran for Congress against Orville Hickman Browning. In the campaign he affirmed his belief in hard money, his opposition to a national bank, his support of a tariff for revenue only, and his opposition to the distribution of the federal surplus to the states. Douglas won, resigned his Supreme Court seat, and began his national political career.

In the House of Representatives Douglas supported bills to provide river and harbor improvements for the West; he distinguished between improving natural waterways and constructing "artificial works." He became a rabid expansionist and opposed Martin Van Buren's nomination in 1844 when Van Buren proved cool toward Texas annexation. Texas and Oregon (with its boundary to the northernmost 54°40' line) were, Douglas claimed, like husband and wife, not to be separated as objects of United States policies. He wanted to "make the area of liberty as broad as the continent itself." When President James K. Polk vetoed a Western river and harbors bill and settled for the 49° Oregon boundary, Douglas was as far from the Democratic administration as he would ever get, but in the end Polk came to trust him as one of his more devoted supporters—largely because Douglas was a staunch defender of the administration's policies in the Mexican War. Douglas went a good deal farther than Polk. He wished to acquire more territory than that ceded in the Treaty of Guadalupe Hidalgo (against which he voted), but he did not go as far as Illinois's fervently "all Mexico" Democrats. He was already hoping to purchase Cuba from Spain. He advocated a Pacific railroad and the granting of lands west of the Missouri River to actual settlers.

In 1847 he married Martha Martin, daughter of a North Carolina planter. They moved from Quincy to Chicago. His father-in-law's will left a plantation with more than 100 slaves to Martha, and Douglas gained 20 percent of the property's income as its administrator.

Twice reelected to the House, in 1847 Douglas won election to the Senate and became Chairman of the Committee on Territories. In organizing the new lands in the West, Douglas for a time urged extending the Missouri Compromise line to the Pacific, but less on principle than as the speediest practical way to get on with settling the territories. "All I ask is action," he said characteristically, "and I will cheerfully vote for any bill approved by a majority of the Senate." He loathed extremists, Northern and Southern alike, whose agitation of the slavery question slowed the business of expanding the area of freedom from sea to sea and beyond.

In 1850 Douglas arrived at the idea of "popular sovereignty" as the solution to the problem of slavery in organizing new territories. He saw it as a practical and democratic solution and predicted that the climate of the plains would dictate the formation of free states there. The area of freedom would continue to expand and might even lead the Upper South to emancipation. It was up to the inhabitants of the territories themselves to decide what their domestic institutions should be. The principle was embodied in the bills organizing the New Mexico and Utah Territories, part of the great Compromise of 1850. In the Senate Douglas played the key role in getting the compromise package through. Henry Clay's omnibus compromise bill, which brought together all the controverted sectional issues of the moment in one package, failed because it also brought together the enemies of each part of the compromise. Douglas, by breaking the bill into parts and submitting them separately, broke up the opposition. He was modest about his achievement; and because his Senate campaign against Lincoln in 1858 depended on getting the support of old Whigs in Illinois, he tended to exaggerate Henry Clay's role in the compromise and picture himself as a follower of the great Whig reconciler. As a result, Douglas's crucial role in the compromise was obscured for over 100 years.

Only 37 years old in 1850, Douglas had rapidly assumed public prominence. He was widely considered the embodiment of "Young America," a nebulous movement in the Democratic party against old fogies in politics and for nationalism and expansion. "He was with the Young America movement more than he was of it," says Douglas's able biographer Robert W. Johannsen. A sign of the vast ideological gulf that separated Lincoln and Douglas was Lincoln's view of Young America, which he lampooned in 1859:

He owns a large part of the world, by right of possessing it; and all the rest by right of *wanting* it, and *intending* to

Douglas, Stephen Arnold

have it. As Plato had for the immortality of the soul, so Young America has "a pleasing hope—a fond desire—a longing after" teritory. He has a great passion—a perfect rage—for the "*new*"; particularly new men for office, and the new earth mentioned in the revelations, in which, being no more sea, there must be about three times as much land as in the present. He is a great friend of humanity; and his desire for land is not selfish, but merely an impulse to extend the area of freedom. He is very anxious to fight for the liberation of enslaved nations and colonies, provided, always, they *have* land, and have *not* any liking for his interference. As to those who have no land, and would be glad of help from any quarter, he considers *they* can afford to wait a few hundred years longer. In knowledge he is particularly rich. He knows all that can possibly be known; inclines to believe in spiritual rappings, and is the unquestioned inventor of "*Manifest Destiny.*" His horror is for all that is old, particularly "Old Fogy"; and if there be any thing old which he can endure, it is only old whiskey and old tobacco.

His broad popularity led Douglas to dream of a presidential nomination in 1852, but he made the mistake of letting his intentions be known too soon, and his rivals quickly united opposition to him. In 1853 his wife died.

Zeal for a railroad route to the Pacific and pleas from settlers made the organization of Nebraska Territory, something in which Douglas had been interested since 1844, an increasingly pressing matter. Early efforts showed that most resistance to organizing bills came from Southerners—for an obvious reason. The Missouri Compromise had closed the area, which lay entirely above the 36°30' line, to slavery. Douglas decided that the principle used in the Compromise of 1850 must be applied to Nebraska. As Chairman of the Senate Committee on Territories, he wrote the first draft of a Nebraska bill by himself and, as he boasted, "passed" the eventual Kansas-Nebraska Act largely by himself. In the original bill, however, he neither affirmed nor repealed "the 8th section of the Missouri act," which forbade slavery above the 36°30' line in the Louisiana Purchase (except for Missouri). Both supporters and opponents saw to it that the Kansas-Nebraska Act more explicitly made that section "inoperative and Void" (though the act steered clear of the explicit word "repeal"). There was nothing in this that did violence to Douglas's original intentions. He meant from the start for the new territory to be organized on the new principles of the Compromise of 1850, and he was simply unrealistic in thinking that he could skirt the Missouri Compromise—replace it but not talk about it. Although the Kansas-Nebraska Act, signed into law May 30, 1854, had to satisfy Southern opponents of the territory's organization, Douglas resented charges that it was a Southern measure or that the South dictated its provisions. He thought of it entirely as a Western measure.

Out west in Illinois, Abraham Lincoln was "thunderstruck" by the act. He had been losing interest in politics before the bill's passage, but now he was more interested than ever. He attacked Douglas in speech after speech for turning his back on the Missouri Compromise restriction, which Douglas had once called "a sacred thing, which no ruthless hand would ever be reckless enough to disturb." Lincoln argued that the Compromise of 1850 had nothing more to do with the Nebraska Territory than it had with the territories of the moon and saw a covert desire to spread slavery to fresh territory in the removal of the Missouri Compromise restriction. And Lincoln's was not the only violent reaction to Douglas's Kansas-Nebraska Act. "I could travel from Boston to Chicago by the light of my own effigy," Douglas commented.

Immediately, Douglas moved from the very embodiment of the new to the opponent of all new enthusiasms in politics. He hated the allied army of "isms" of the age, Know-Nothingism, abolitionism, Anti-Nebraskaism, and, especially, Republicanism. In reaction, he became less flexible. Popular sovereignty, conceived as a practical solution to impractical sectional demands that blocked American expansion, itself became a more rigid demand. In 1856 Douglas began to say that the Constitution demanded popular sovereignty as a principle of territorial organization. He now argued that Congress's right to govern the territories was derived from the power to admit new states. Territories were incipient states and were therefore fully equal. The organic act for a territory could not impair that equality by keeping the territory from forming and regulating its own domestic institutions. Congress "must leave the people entirely free to" do so. The language of the Kansas-Nebraska Act now added a "must." Popular sovereignty was no longer a good solution; it was the only legal one.

Douglas was again a contender for the Democratic presidential nomination in 1856. Having learned his lesson in 1852, he now held back coyly from an overt quest for the office. James Buchanan, absent in England as minister to the Court of St. James, was untouched by the troubles in Kansas after the Kansas-Nebraska Act caused warring groups of proslavery and antislavery men to rush to the territory. Democrats united on him because he lacked a controversial record. Douglas failed to get vital support from the states of the Old Northwest because of opposition from Indiana's Jesse Bright, Douglas's rival in the Senate for leadership of the region. Most of his support came from the South. The Democratic platform did endorse the principles of the Kansas-Nebraska Act, but with a continuing ambiguity about *when* popular sovereignty could be exercised, in the territorial stage or when the territory applied for statehood.

In 1856 Douglas married Adele Cutts, a Catholic grandniece of Dolley Madison. Douglas himself was not a particularly religious man. His biographer says "he leaned toward the Baptists." Widowerhood had exaggerated Douglas's slovenly Western habits: tobacco, whiskey, and careless dress. Those habits and Douglas's social graces in general improved quickly after the marriage.

Douglas endorsed the Dred Scott decision, which ruled congressional interference with slavery in the territories unconstitutional. Chief Justice Roger B. Taney also stated in an *obiter dictum* that the territorial legislature could not exclude slavery either, a notion which Douglas swept aside as early as 1857 by saying that odious laws could never be enforced among a hostile populace. By refusing to pass the "appropriate police regulations" to maintain slavery, they could as effectively exclude slavery as if the legislature forbade it altogether. He was particularly pleased by the decision's denunciation of Negro citizenship in the United States. Negroes were an inferior race, he believed, and incapable of self-government. They were not for that reason doomed to slavery everywhere, but they should be allowed only those rights consistent with the welfare of the community in which they resided. He accused opponents of the Dred Scott decision of desiring Negro equality. When Lincoln answered Douglas's arguments later, he said Douglas used "counterfeit logic" in arguing that "because I do not want a black woman for a *slave* I must necessarily want her for a wife."

Douglas's relationship with the Buchanan administration was shaky from the start, and Kansas affairs made it downright hostile. In 1857 the proslavery party in Kansas formed a state constitution, the Lecompton constitution, which was so proslavery that it had no prayer of passage if submitted to the people. Therefore, the convention provided for no submission to popular vote. Douglas's ally in Kansas, John Calhoun, salvaged a compromise whereby Kansas voters could vote for the constitution with slavery or the constitution without slavery. Douglas did not approve of the idea; it was not popular sovereignty, which, he insisted, required voting on the whole constitution. The administration supported it. Don E. Fehrenbacher has described the anomaly of Douglas's behavior:

> The Little Giant had long since come to be regarded as one of the managers of American politics—pragmatic and flexible, an architect of compromise and always a loyal party man. Now, suddenly, he appeared as a party insurgent and a doctrinaire, taking an inflexible stand on principle and in the end rejecting a compromise that satisfied even many of his fellow insurgents.

The South was shocked; many Southerners felt they had lost their last friend in the North.

The resulting dispute with the administration and with Southern leaders made Douglas something of a hero among many of his old Republican enemies. That development worried Lincoln. He wanted Douglas's Senate seat in 1858, and the idea of Republican defections to Douglas by reason of Douglas's anti-Southern stand was frightening. Horace Greeley praised Douglas effusively and urged Republicans in Illinois not to oppose him. Lincoln was worried enough to send William H. Herndon to talk to Douglas and Greeley. Herndon concluded that Illinois was to be "*huckstered* off" by the national leaders. Lincoln took a more moderate and modest view. Greeley's support of Douglas stemmed from a belief that the Senator's "superior position, reputation, experience, and *ability*, if you please, would more than compensate for his lack of a pure republican position" and do "more good, than . . . the election of any one of our better undistinguished pure republicans."

This ticklish situation dictated part of Lincoln's strategy in the Senate campaign and the famous Lincoln-Douglas Debates of 1858. Lincoln stressed the gap in moral principles that separated Douglas from Republicans. In his effort at polarization he was largely successful. Douglas, following a tendency that began at least in 1856 when he insisted on the constitutional imperative of popular sovereignty, gave his territorial solution an increasing rigidity. He insisted in the next-to-the-last debate (at Quincy) that popular sovereignty meant that "this republic can exist forever divided into free and slave States, as our fathers made it." He had come a long way from his 1850 vision of a free West leading at least the upper South to emancipation. When Lincoln asked at Freeport whether the Dred Scott decision did not obliterate popular sovereignty, Douglas replied with what became widely known as the "Freeport Doctrine." Yet it was merely the position he had taken as early as a year before: local police regulations could keep slavery out anyway.

The Freeport question was more significant as part of Lincoln's strategy to take the offensive against Douglas, and the most important part of that offensive was the charge that Douglas had conspired with Pierce, Buchanan, and Taney to nationalize slavery. For his part, Douglas charged that the Republicans favored racial equality, and he repeatedly stressed his soundness on the racial question: "This government was established on the white basis. It was made by white men, for the benefit of white men and their posterity forever and never should be administered by any except white men." Democrats won enough seats in the legislature that, with the holdovers in the Illinois Senate, they easily elected Douglas to his third term in the United States Senate.

The Lecompton struggle alienated Southerners from Douglas's cause, from the Democratic party, and from the Union. As the Illinois Senator began to think of the 1860 presidential nomination, he could find plenty of delegate strength in the North, but the South was now cold to him. The Democratic convention at Charleston, South Carolina, in April adopted a platform reaffirming the 1856 platform. Douglas approved it. Delegations from eight slave states promptly walked out. Douglas could not muster votes equal to two-thirds of the original convention number, and the convention was adjourned to Baltimore in June.

Meanwhile, Douglas's friends hoped the Republicans would nominate William H. Seward and drive conservative and moderate Republicans into the Little Giant's camp. Douglas knew that Lincoln's nomination would mean a tough campaign against the ablest debater he had ever faced; he thought no stronger nomination could have been made. Southern delegates bolted the Baltimore convention in June, and Douglas was unanimously nominated by the remaining delegates. The Democratic party had split. The seceding delegates nominated John C. Breckinridge for President and Joseph Lane for Vice President. Douglas's running mate was Herschel V. Johnson of Georgia. Breaking with tradition, Douglas chose to campaign actively.

By midsummer Douglas may well have suspected that Lincoln was sure to win. When, late in August, the Little Giant turned south to campaign, his speeches changed in tone; they were more pleas for the Union than for his own election. "There is no evil . . . for which disunion is a legitimate remedy," he argued. Secession, if attempted, should be treated as Andrew Jackson treated Nullification in 1832. When results of state elections in Pennsylvania and Indiana in October guaranteed Lincoln's success, Douglas told his secretary, "Mr. Lincoln is the next President. We must try to save the Union. I will go South." There he pleaded once again for Union. He received 1,365,976 votes, about 29 percent of the total. Over 87 percent of his votes came from free states, and most of his Southern votes came from Border States. He got only Missouri's electoral votes and part of New Jersey's.

After secession, Douglas supported the Crittenden compromise, which was based on the idea of extending the Missouri Compromise line to the Pacific. He himself still preferred popular sovereignty, though now he suggested its exercise only after a territory reached a population of 50,000. Before that, slavery would be admitted; afterward, the territory would be admitted as a state automatically when it had population enough to merit a Representative in Congress. His position on the Negro hardened. He recommended an amendment to the Constitution limiting the ability of states and territories to legislate in regard to the Negro. They should never vote or hold office. Free Negroes would be colonized at the discretion of the states and by federal money. On January 3, 1861, he gave a speech strongly in favor of coercing the seceded states. "Coercion is the vital principle upon which all Government rests," he said. But he pleaded also for compromise by reviving the Missouri Compromise line. "You have sung paens enough in its praise," he chided the Republicans, "and uttered imprecations and curses enough on my head for its repeal, . . . to justify you now in claiming a triumph by its reestablishment." Elihu Washburne told Lincoln the speech "was utterly infamous and damnable, the crowning atrocity of his life."

There was no coldness in Douglas's reception of Lincoln in Washington. Some reporters were surprised at his seeming closeness to the administration, at least socially. In the Senate he defended Lincoln's First Inaugural Address as a peace-minded document. He assumed that Fort Sumter would not be reinforced or supplied. He began to toy with the idea of a brief peaceable separation followed by reconstruction as preferable to war. He hoped for more from William H. Seward than from Salmon P. Chase and Montgomery Blair.

Two days after Sumter fell, George Ashmun pleaded with Douglas to call on Lincoln and pledge his support. Douglas did so. Later, he headed west to bring a message of solidarity against the traitors. In Springfield, on April 25, he urged his countrymen to put aside partisan differences and unite to save the government and the Union. In Chicago, on May 1, he insisted: "Every man must be for the United States or against it. There can be no neutrals in this war, *only patriots—or traitors.*" It was one of his rare quotable statements. An excellent speaker and debater, Douglas usually shaped his rhetoric somewhat narrowly to the purpose at hand. The outbreak of war proved to be Douglas's most memorable moment. He died on the morning of June 3, leaving as his last words of advice to his sons: "Tell them to obey the laws and support the Constitution of the United States." He had never been baptized by the rites of any church.

Douglas has always suffered by association with Lincoln's fame. It is hard to remember that, when Lincoln debated Douglas in 1858, he was essentially attempting to share the limelight that Douglas, the most famous politician in America at the time, naturally attracted. Lincoln's later fame eclipsed Douglas's, and it was not until the twentieth century that the Little Giant received the attention from historians that was his due. In the 1920s, Lincoln biographer Albert J. Beveridge was the first to see that Douglas had been "written down in order to write Lincoln up." Douglas's prestige soared until well after World War II. The modern civil rights era, however, has made his white supremacist stand appear most unattractive, and his reputation has fallen from its heights of the 1920s and 1930s.

SOURCES: Robert W. Johannsen's *Stephen A. Douglas* (New York: Oxford University Press, 1973) is massive and definitive. Some interesting insights are in Don E. Fehrenbacher's *The Dred Scott Case: Its Significance in American Law and Politics* (New York: Oxford University Press, 1978).

See also ALTON, ILLINOIS; BEVERIDGE, ALBERT JEREMIAH; CHARLESTON, ILLINOIS; DEBATES, LINCOLN-DOUGLAS; *DRED SCOTT* V. *SANDFORD;* EDUCATION; ELECTION OF 1860; FREEPORT, ILLINOIS; FREEPORT QUESTION; FUGITIVE SLAVE LAW; GALESBURG, ILLINOIS; JONESBORO, ILLINOIS; KANSAS-NEBRASKA ACT; MISSOURI COMPROMISE; OTTAWA, ILLINOIS; "POPULAR SOVEREIGNTY"; QUINCY, ILLINOIS; SLAVE TRADE.

Douglass, Frederick (1817–1895) Former slave who became an abolitionist editor and speaker. On three occasions Douglass was a visitor in Lincoln's White House. He was not an ardent Republican. Though he at first applauded Lincoln's presidential nomination as that of a "radical republican . . . fully committed to the doctrine of the irrepressible conflict," emphasis on Lincoln's conservatism in the campaign afterwards gave him pause. Douglass voted for a radical abolitionist candidate as a gesture, hoping that Lincoln would be the winner among the candidates who had a real chance. Lincoln's conciliatory First Inaugural Address disgusted him.

With the outbreak of war, Douglass declared, "The slaveholders themselves have saved our cause from ruin!" Immediately, he began to urge the use of Negroes as soldiers and to stress that slaves were the "stomach of this rebellion." Lincoln summoned the first Negro delegation ever to have a formal meeting with an American President in August 1862. He stated that "the war could not have had an existence" without slavery and the black race, and he asked the delegates to lead blacks in support of his colonization efforts. Douglass despaired. Lincoln was telling "the poor negro that 'he was the cause of the war.'"

Frederick Douglass

The preliminary Emancipation Proclamation fired Douglass's zeal for the conflict, his "interest in the success of the North" before that being "largely due" to the belief that somehow the war would mean the end of slavery. Even so, the meeting at Tremont Temple in Boston on January 1, 1863, to receive word that the Proclamation was officially in effect was a tense one, Douglass remembered; blacks were "by no means certain" that Lincoln would go through with it. Douglass celebrated "the extinction of Slavery, even from a military necessity." Despite its limitations, the Proclamation made the war in the eyes of the world "no longer a mere strife for territory and dominion, but a contest of civilization against barbarism."

Douglass leapt to the fray; he energetically recruited black soldiers in the summer and spring of 1863. In August, however, his enthusiasm vanished with Lincoln's failure to promise retaliation in the face of Confederate threats to enslave captured Negro soldiers. On August 10, 1863, Senator Samuel Pomeroy took Douglass to see Lincoln at the White House. There Douglass was received "precisely as one gentleman would be received by another. He [Lincoln] extended to me a cordial hand, not too warm or too cold." Douglass complained that black soldiers received less pay than white, that the government offered them no protection from enslavement in the event of capture, and that Negro soldiers deserved promotions for service just as white soldiers did. Lincoln responded candidly that "they had larger motives for being soldiers than white men; that they ought to be willing to enter the service upon any conditions." He suggested, however, that the pay differential was a temporary concession to prejudice. He showed no taste for retaliation, a "terrible remedy," and said that he had evidence that Negro prisoners were being treated as prisoners of war. And he expressed a willingness to sign any officer's commission for a Negro soldier recommended by the Secretary of War.

Douglass went almost immediately to see Secretary of War Edwin M. Stanton. He asked for a commission as assistant adjutant general to recruit black soldiers in the South. Stanton apparently promised the commission. Later, Douglass was offered $100 a month plus expenses for the work, but he never received a military commission. He refused to go south, but he continued his public support of black recruiting.

In the bleak August of 1864, when Lincoln's hopes for the Union cause were at low ebb, the President summoned Douglass to the White House. In a meeting on August 19, while the Governor of Connecticut waited his turn outside Lincoln's office, the President expressed fears that he would be unable to continue an antislavery war and asked Douglass's opinion of a remarkable plan to spread word of the Emancipation Proclamation to slaves in the South. In Douglass's words, Lincoln wanted to "warn them as to what will be their probable condition should peace be concluded while they remain within the Rebel lines, and more especially to urge upon them the necessity of making their escape." Douglass suggested the outlines for implementing such a scheme in a letter to Lincoln on August 29, but its implementation proved unnecessary when Lincoln's political prospects improved in the fall. Douglass shrewdly remarked in later years that the plan was "evidence conclusive on Mr. Lincoln's part that the proclamation, so far at least as he was concerned, was not effected merely as a 'necessity.'"

Douglass supported Lincoln's reelection in 1864, though he did not campaign actively because Republicans "did not wish to expose themselves to the charge of being the 'N—r' party." He heard Lincoln's Second Inaugural Address, which he admired a great deal, and he daringly decided to make an unprecedented appearance at the postinauguration reception in the White House. Two policemen tried to bar his entry on the grounds that no blacks were allowed, but word from Lincoln gave entry to "my friend Douglass," as the Negro abolitionist said Lincoln referred to him. He proceeded through the receiving line without incident.

At inaugural ceremonies, on April 14, 1876, for a Lincoln statue in Washington paid for by contributions from freedmen, Douglass delivered a stunning oration. "Abraham Lincoln was not, in the fullest sense of the word, either our man or our model," he said. "He was preeminently the white man's President." He was "willing . . . to . . . postpone, and sacrifice the rights of humanity in the colored people to promote the welfare of the white people of this country." He was "an American of the Americans." White people "are the children of Abraham Lincoln. We are at best only his step-children." The "Union was more to him than our freedom or our future." He ended the oration, however, with praise of Lincoln's actions amidst great prejudices and difficulties.

Douglass remembered that in Lincoln's "company I was never in any way reminded of my humble origin, or of my unpopular color." In 1867 he offered to lecture in Mrs. Lincoln's behalf. She eventually refused the offer but let it be known that she would be pleased to have him visit her in Chicago. And though his 1876 oration left it to *white* people "to sound his praises, to preserve and perpetuate his memory, to multiply his statues, to hang his pictures on your walls," Douglass had the famous portrait engraving of Lincoln by William Marshall on his own study wall.

SOURCES: A solid survey of Douglass's relationship with Lincoln is Christopher N. Breiseth's "Lincoln and Frederick Douglass: Another Debate," *Journal of the Illinois State Historical Society*, LXVIII (February 1975), 9–26, but there is no substitute for Douglass's own eloquence in *The Life and Times of Frederick Douglass, . . . Written by Himself* (London: Christian Age, 1882) and in his unforgettable *Oration . . . Delivered on the Occasion of the Unveiling of the Freedmen's Monument in Memory of Abraham Lincoln* (Washington, D.C.: Gibson Brothers, 1876).

Draft   *See* CONSCRIPTION.

Draft Riots   *See* CONSCRIPTION.

Drama See *Abe Lincoln in Illinois*; DRINKWATER, JOHN.

Dreams See PSYCHOLOGY.

Dred Scott* v. *Sandford The 1857 Supreme Court decision in the celebrated Dred Scott case provided the primary focus of the Lincoln-Douglas Debates in 1858. Chief Justice Roger B. Taney wrote the majority opinion, which ruled that Negroes could not be United States citizens (and therefore capable of suing in a federal court). He also ruled that Congress could not, as it had attempted to do in establishing the Missouri Compromise line, exclude slavery from the territories. Dred Scott, therefore, was a slave despite his temporary residence on free soil in the Louisiana Territory.

Lincoln's first response to the decision came in a speech in Springfield on June 26, 1857, where he sided with the dissenting opinions of Justices John McLean and Benjamin R. Curtis. Lincoln had "respect for the judicial department of government" to the degree that "its decisions on Constitutional questions, when fully settled, should control, not only the particular cases decided, but the general policy of the country, subject to be disturbed only by amendments of the Constitution." But he quibbled over what constituted full settlement of a question. It was not, he said, merely the majority opinion of the Court. It depended on "circumstances": degree of unanimity among the judges, lack of "partisan bias," "accordance with legal public expectation, and with the steady practice of the departments throughout our history," and lack of error in citing "historical facts." Even if "wanting in some of these," the decision would be decisive if "it had been before the court more than once, and had there been affirmed and re-affirmed through a course of years." By these criteria the Dred Scott decision conspicuously failed to be decisive, and Lincoln simply said it was not "a settled doctrine for the country."

Lincoln particularly quarreled with Taney's insistence "at great length that negroes were no part of the people who made, or for whom was made the Declaration of Independence, or the Constitution of the United States." Curtis pointed to five states where Negroes were voters in 1787, and Lincoln eloquently attacked Taney's assumption, "as a fact, that the public estimate of the black man is more favorable *now* than it was in the days of the Revolution":

This assumption is a mistake. In some trifling particulars, the condition of that race has been ameliorated; but, as a whole, in this country, the change between then and now is decidedly the other way; and their ultimate destiny has never appeared so hopeless as in the last three or four years. In two of the five States—New Jersey and North Carolina—that then gave the free negro the right of voting, the right has since been taken away; and in a third—New York—it has been greatly abridged; while it has not been extended, so far as I know, to a single additional State, though the number of the States has more than doubled. In those days, as I understand, masters could, at their own pleasure, emancipate their slaves; but since then, such legal restraints have been made upon emancipation, as to amount almost to prohibition. In those days, Legislatures held the unquestioned power to abolish slavery in their respective States; but now it is becoming quite fashionable for State Constitutions to withhold that power from the Legislatures. In those days, by common consent, the spread of the black man's bondage to new countries was prohibited; but now, Congress decides that it *will* not continue the prohibition, and the Supreme Court decides that it *could* not if it would. In those days, our Declaration of Independence was held sacred by all, and thought to include all; but now, to aid in making the bondage of the negro universal and eternal, it is assailed, and sneered at, and construed, and hawked at, and torn, till, if its framers could rise from their graves, they could not at all recognize it. All the powers of earth seem rapidly combining against him. Mammon is after him; ambition follows, and philosophy follows, and the Theology of the day is fast joining the cry. They have him in his prison house; they have searched his person, and left no prying instrument with him. One after another they have closed the heavy iron doors upon him, and now they have him, as it were, bolted in with a lock of a hundred keys, which can never be unlocked without the concurrence of every key; the keys in the hands of a hundred different men, and they scattered to a hundred different and distant places; and they stand musing as to what invention, in all the dominions of mind and matter, can be produced to make the impossibility of his escape more complete than it is.

It is grossly incorrect to say or assume, that the public estimate of the negro is more favorable now than it was at the origin of the government.

Lincoln's next public pronouncement on the case, in his famous "House Divided" speech of June 16, 1858,

In this inspired cartoon published in 1860, Dred Scott plays the tune to which the four presidential candidates dance with their telltale partners. At the upper left, John C. Breckinridge dances with "Old Buck" (President James Buchanan). Stephen A. Douglas dances with a squatter sovereign at lower left, and John Bell, whose Constitutional Union party included the remnants of the Know-Nothing party, takes a turn with a true native American. Lincoln's partner is a Negro. In the highly partisan atmosphere of nineteenth-century America, it was rare to find a cartoon as evenly balanced as this one. (Library of Congress)

was different in emphasis. Now locked in a duel with Stephen A. Douglas for a United States Senate seat, Lincoln began to avoid discussion of Negro citizenship (a sensitive issue in negrophobic Illinois). He argued that there appeared to be a conspiracy to nationalize and perpetuate slavery. It began with Douglas's Kansas-Nebraska Bill, and Presidents Franklin Pierce and James Buchanan furthered it by urging deference to the upcoming decision. The Dred Scott decision itself fulfilled half the goal of nationalizing slavery and prepared the country for "another Supreme Court decision, declaring that the Constitution of the United States does not permit a *state* to exclude slavery from its limits." In the campaign that followed, which included the famed Lincoln-Douglas Debates, Lincoln continued to emphasize the idea of a conspiracy to nationalize slavery. For years historians overlooked the conspiracy charge and overemphasized Lincoln's Freeport question of August 27, 1858, which demanded that Douglas explain how popular sovereignty in the territories was congruent with Taney's decision. If Congress could not prohibit slavery in the territories, presumably territorial legislatures, which derived their powers from Congress, could not either. Douglas answered then, as he had before, that local police regulations were essential to slavery and that the territorial government could fail to enact them and, in effect, exclude slavery.

The decision was clearly a shock to Lincoln, and he saw in it an important landmark in America's decline from the political principles of the founding fathers. Though claiming at times that he first heard the idea that "the Declaration of Independence has no application to the negro" from "the lips of Judge Douglas," by 1860 Lincoln admitted that "Judge Taney might have first broached the doctrine" and "Douglas possibly got it from him." In his First Inaugural Address, with Taney at his side and memories of the Dred Scott decision in mind, Lincoln warned that

> if the policy of the government, upon vital questions, affecting the whole people, is to be irrevocably fixed by decisions of the Supreme Court, the instant they are made, in ordinary litigation between parties, in personal actions, the people will have ceased, to be their own rulers, having, to that extent, practically resigned their government, into the hands of that eminent tribunal.

Too democratic to believe in judicial sovereignty, Lincoln was nonetheless too conservative and legalistic to attack judicial supremacy, and he expressed no desire to make "any assault upon the court, or the judges." His view was not that there was some superior political tribunal but that, over time and with the government in different hands, the Court might well reverse itself, as it had in the past on other questions.

SOURCES: Don E. Fehrenbacher's *The Dred Scott Case: Its Significance in American Law and Politics* (New York: Oxford University Press, 1978) is definitive and brilliant.

See also DEBATES, LINCOLN-DOUGLAS; FREEPORT QUESTION; "POPULAR SOVEREIGNTY"; SUPREME COURT OF THE UNITED STATES; TANEY, ROGER BROOKE.

Drinkwater, John (1882–1937) British poet and playwright. Drinkwater wrote *Abraham Lincoln* (1918), a play about Lincoln's presidential years. He knew of Lincoln from his college days, but he was doubtless influenced to write the play by the success of fellow countryman Lord Charnwood's biography of Lincoln, which was published in 1916. The play opened at the Birmingham Repertory Theatre and moved to Hammersmith, a London suburb, where it was very successful. In 1919 it opened in America with Frank McGlynn in the title role.

The play first shows Lincoln in Springfield humbly accepting his presidential nomination. In Washington he exerts his leadership by handling Southern envoys who have come to talk to Secretary of State William H. Seward under the mistaken impression that he is the real power behind the throne. Lincoln convinces a grateful black man (who speaks a strange pidgin English) that revenge on his masters is not right. He announces his Emancipation Proclamation to a bickering Cabinet. He advises General Ulysses S. Grant to make his terms of surrender generous. The play concludes at Ford's Theatre. Through it all, Lincoln's magnanimous but forceful character is the central focus.

Drinkwater made no attempt at "local color." Nevertheless, his play was successful in America too, in part because of the new atmosphere of cooperation between England and America which resulted from World War I. William E. Barton criticized the play for depicting Lincoln as "a cock-sure Abolitionist, who foresees the Civil War as the inevitable result of his Abolitionism, and who deliberately forces it for the sake of the freedom of the slave." Southerners likewise were critical of *Abraham Lincoln* and were not mollified by its celebration of Lincoln's policy of mercy and lack of vindictiveness toward the Confederacy.

SOURCES: Barton's review, "The Errors of Mr. Drinkwater," appeared in the Boston *Evening Transcript*, January 24, 1920.

Dry Tortugas *See* FORT JEFFERSON.

Dubois, Jesse Kilgore (1811–1876) Close political associate of Lincoln's. Jesse K. Dubois was born in Lawrence County, Illinois, and in 1834 he became the only member of the state legislature younger than fellow Whig Representative Abraham Lincoln. He was reelected in 1836, 1838, and 1842. In 1841 he was a Harrison appointee in the land office in Palestine, Illinois, but he resigned after Harrison's death in protest against John Tyler's policies.

Lincoln met Dubois at the legislature and always remembered that he had "the elegant manners of a Frenchman, from which nation he had his descent." Both were devoted Whigs, and Dubois was again in public life when the next Whig President, Zachary Taylor, appointed him Receiver of Public Moneys at Palestine. A zealous partisan, Dubois was removed when Democratic President Franklin Pierce assumed office in 1853.

"*I am for you against the world,*" Dubois told Lincoln

Jesse Kilgore Dubois. (Courtesy of the Lloyd Ostendorf Collection)

late in 1854, when the latter aspired to the United States Senate. After the failure of Lincoln's bid in 1855, Dubois was still closely associated with Lincoln in the Republican party, being the nominee for state auditor in the 1856 election.

Dubois won and, as state auditor, maintained considerable important contact with Lincoln, both politically and in official business. As a counsel for the Illinois Central Railroad in 1857, for example, Lincoln asked Dubois "as a friend" to accept a $90,000 cash payment to the state in lieu of the larger tax assessment the state auditor thought due. Cash was scarce in this depression year, and Dubois evidently took the money and promised not to sue the railroad for the larger sum until 1859. Also in 1857 Dubois followed Lincoln's advice to allow banks to circulate notes given them by the auditor even though the value of the bonds they deposited with the auditor in exchange for the notes had declined well below the reserve level the legislature wished banks to maintain. In Lincoln's opinion the law applied only to banks asking for new notes for circulation.

In 1860 Dubois was an ardent supporter of Lincoln's drive for the Presidency. With David Davis he was one of the most active managers of Lincoln's interests at the Republican nominating convention in Chicago. Dubois won reelection when Lincoln won the Presidency.

An old friend and an active political henchman, Dubois expected to have some considerable influence with the Lincoln administration. But he was a man of narrow horizons who had hardly been out of his native state since his birth. He made impossible demands. He was furious when Lincoln refused to appoint his son-in-law, James S. Luse, to the Northern Superintendancy of Indian Affairs in Minnesota. Such a move, Lincoln explained, would be "unprecedented" in the face of objections from every Republican member of the Minnesota delegation to Washington. "I am sorely disappointed in all my expectations from Washington," Dubois told Lincoln. Dubois's *"heart was set"* on this request because he wished to see his daughter, who he said was dying, move to "the healthy climate of Minnesota" and perhaps prolong her life. The best Lincoln could do was to appoint Luse postmaster in Lafayette, Indiana, where he edited a newspaper. "I placed . . . too high an estimate on my *relations* with you, and Did not *know* my *position*," Dubois snorted. Lincoln had not, the auditor complained, "appointed a single man from Illinois that was originally your friend." For a considerable time to come, Dubois's recommendations came to Lincoln with pettish asides ("not that I expect any attention will be paid to what I may say because emanating from me," for example).

Still, Dubois's recommendations kept coming to the President. They tended to be provincial and narrowly partisan. Illinois mobilized as rapidly as any state, Dubois protested, yet got no help from the President's paymasters and mustering officers. When Illinois Governor Richard Yates joined with Dubois and others of Lincoln's local Republican friends to demand that John Pope be promoted from captain of volunteers to a general in the regular army, Lincoln declared that he had never done such a thing and could not in this case either. Dubois thought that the "Proslavery sentiments of our leading Generals" kept the army from fighting with true heart. He loathed West Point graduates and felt that too many Democrats were at the heads of armies.

One of Dubois's protests, though more painful to Lincoln perhaps than any other, got results. With other Republicans, he complained that Lincoln's brother-in-law, Ninian W. Edwards, appointed commissary in Springfield, was surrounded by associates guilty of "stupendous and unprecedented frauds" and gave contracts for supplying the army to friends of Joel A. Matteson, a Democrat with a reputation for corruption. By June 1863 Lincoln complained that his old Springfield friends were "harrassing" him, and eventually he replaced Edwards. When Dubois and Illinois Secretary of State Ozias M. Hatch made a recommendation for Quartermaster General, thinking erroneously that the office was vacant, Lincoln replied: "What nation do you desire Gen. Allen to be made Quarter-Master-General of? This nation already has a Quarter-Master-General." The Illinoisans complained that the letter "read harshly," and Lincoln explained that its tone had been "jocular."

There was no doubting Hatch's loyalty or ardor for the cause. In the spring of 1863 he joined other Illinois Republicans in requesting that four regiments be raised in Illinois to enforce martial law should the Democratic legislature severely impede the war effort. Lincoln approved the plan but rescinded his order when tensions in the state eased. Despite his differences with Lincoln, Dubois was an early advocate of Lincoln's reelection. He warned Lincoln of Salmon P. Chase's designs on the presidential nomination by sending him a copy of the Pomeroy Circular in February of 1864.

Dubois had ambitions of his own for 1864. He wanted the Republican gubernatorial nomination, but so did Richard J. Oglesby. Dubois told Lincoln in April, "I am now fighting the heaviest battle I have ever fought" and declared that he was "the only candidate for Governor in the State that has taken open ground for you in Public, and I find myself opposed by the whole military and official Patronage of the General Government." Hatch also begged Lincoln to intervene to avoid an ugly feud, but Lincoln refused. Dubois lost the nomination to Oglesby. He was nevertheless loyally working for Lincoln later in the year and was trying to get Illinois soldiers furloughed to vote in the November election.

Dubois was a member of the National Lincoln Monument Association. He accumulated considerable property and died at his home near Springfield in 1876.

SOURCES: Dubois's letters to Lincoln offering support in 1854 (November 21, 1854), about his disappointment over Luse (March 27, 1861), about his low position with Lincoln (April 6, 1861), making a recommendation to which Lincoln would surely pay no attention (June 8, 1861), about proslavery generals (October 6, 1862), and begging support in the gubernatorial contest (April 15, 1864) are in the Abraham Lincoln Papers, Library of Congress. See also the sources for HATCH, OZIAS MATHER.

Duel   *See* SHIELDS, JAMES.

E

Eckert, Thomas Thompson (1825–1910) Chief of the War Department telegraph staff for most of the Civil War. Eckert, who was born in Ohio, worked with telegraph companies before the war; though when the war broke out, he was managing a gold mine in North Carolina. He moved back to Ohio and entered the military telegraph service. Shortly after Edwin M. Stanton became Secretary of War, Eckert became chief of the War Department telegraph office, located by the spring of 1862 in the old library room adjoining the Secretary's office. The location of the office was symbolic of the close control Stanton exercised over the telegraph and of the importance and responsibility of Eckert's position.

Lincoln went to the telegraph room regularly to read the telegrams from the front, because there was no telegraph service at the Executive Mansion. The telegraph room was a welcome haven from the crush of office seekers and callers at the White House, and in that room Lincoln wrote the first draft of the Emancipation Proclamation on foolscap half sheets provided by Eckert in June 1862. The President came to know Eckert well and to trust him; he sent Eckert to meet the Confederate peace commissioners before the Hampton Roads Peace Conference in February 1865. Lincoln invited him to attend the performance of *Our American Cousin* on April 14, 1865. Eckert declined because Stanton, who probably wished to discourage the President's appearance at the crowded theater, said that he could not spare Eckert from work that night.

Eckert served briefly as Assistant Secretary of War and resigned in 1867 to join the Western Union Telegraph Company. He served with other telegraph companies, but eventually he became president of Western Union in 1893 and chairman of the board in 1900.

SOURCES: David Homer Bates's *Lincoln in the Telegraph Office* (New York: Century, 1907) gives important anecdotes of this part of Lincoln's Presidency.

Economics Lincoln's economic ideas looked forward to America's commercial future and never harked back to his log cabin origins. In fact, they were aimed at remedying the faults of the hardscrabble frontier environment of his youth. He was attracted to the Whig party in his early twenties by the ambitious Whig program for economic development of the West. His early political career in the Whig party identified him with the Second Bank of the United States, internal improvements, the tariff, and the Illinois State Bank. Taken as a whole, that vision of government-fostered banks, canals, turnpikes, railroads, and increased manufacturing amounted to a developer's dream. Consistent with that forward-looking economic platform, Lincoln showed a persistent interest in technological innovation. He even patented an invention of his own in 1849.

Lincoln's promotion of economic development was rooted in a capitalistic vision of America as a land of nearly limitless economic opportunity. In the 1850s, when he saw slavery as challenging the North's economic system, Lincoln's speeches were studded with defenses of the free-labor capitalistic assumptions behind the North's economic institutions. Arguing in 1856 that

Thomas Thompson Eckert

the North offered more to the working man because it did not have a permanent class of laborers, Lincoln said: "The man who labored for another last year, this year labors for himself, and next year will hire another to labor for him." He believed that success in such a system was strictly a function of individual effort and virtue. "If any continue through life in the condition of the hired laborer," he said, "it is not the fault of the system, but because of either a dependent nature which prefers it, or improvidence, folly, or singular misfortune." He defended capital flatly in 1859:

> That men who are industrious, and sober, and honest in the pursuit of their own interests should after a while accumulate capital, and after that should be allowed to enjoy it in peace, and also if they should choose, when they have accumulated it, to use it to save themselves from actual labor and hire other people to labor for them is right.

About such a system, he concluded, "I make no complaint."

Lincoln never forgot that "at an early age I was myself a hired laborer, at $12 a month." He sympathized with labor and disliked the "exclusive silk-stocking whiggery . . . of the nice exclusive sort." He recognized the primacy of labor in his first annual message as President in 1861: "Labor is prior to, and independent of, capital. Capital is only the fruit of labor, and could never have existed if labor had not first existed. Labor is the superior of capital, and deserves much the higher consideration." He told an audience of striking workers in New Haven, Connecticut, in 1860 that he was *glad to see that a system of labor prevails in New England under which laborers CAN strike* when they want to." Like his celebrations of opportunity in the capitalistic system, these defenses of labor were elicited by the challenge of slave labor. Though frequently cited by conservative or radical groups as Lincoln's philosophy of capital-labor relationships, neither class of statements can be understood properly without keeping in mind their context: Lincoln's war, not on labor or capital, but on slavery.

Lincoln never expressed any nostalgia for a pastoral America; on the contrary, he complained that agriculture was the sector of the economy which had profited least from labor-saving technological innovations. In an age when farmers constituted the bulk of the electorate, Lincoln was no agrarian. Addressing the Wisconsin Agricultural Society in 1859, he said, "I presume I am not expected to employ the time assigned me, in the mere flattery of the farmers, as a class. My opinion of them is that, in proportion to numbers, they are neither better nor worse than any other people."

SOURCES: See G. S. Boritt's *Lincoln and the Economics of the American Dream* (Memphis: Memphis State University Press, 1978).

See also BANKING; FINANCES, PERSONAL; INVENTION; RAILROADS; REPUBLICAN PARTY; TARIFF; WHIG PARTY.

Education Abraham Lincoln was among the American Presidents with the least formal education. After attending "A.B.C. schools" for "short periods" in Kentucky, Lincoln "went to A.B.C. schools by littles" in Indiana—altogether, his schooling "did not amount to one year." "There was absolutely nothing to excite ambition for education" on the frontier of Lincoln's youth. He "picked up" more "from time to time under the pressure of necessity," but he regarded his education as "defective." He called himself "uneducated," and he was so regarded by most educated people of his day. The true sign of education then was classical learning, but in rustic Indiana, "If a straggler supposed to understand latin, happened to sojourn in the neighborhood, he was looked upon as a wizzard." Lack of education, however, did not make Lincoln anti-intellectual. He always expressed regret at his want of education.

Lincoln was largely self-educated, and much of his learning came relatively late in life. He learned grammar only after he was 23 and had left the home of his illiterate parents. He was almost 40 when he "studied and nearly mastered the Six-books of Euclid." He carefully pointed out that he "did not read [law] with any one." To get the books and read them was "the main thing."

Proof of his regret at his lack of education lies in Lincoln's first political platform (1832):

> Upon the subject of education, not presuming to dictate any plan or system respecting it, I can only say that I view it as the most important subject which we as a people can be engaged in. That every man may receive at least, a moderate education, and thereby be enabled to read the histories of his own and other countries, by which he may duly appreciate the value of our free institutions, appears to be an object of vital importance, even on this account alone, to say nothing of the advantages and satisfaction to be derived from all being able to read the scriptures and other works, both of a religious and moral nature, for themselves. For my part, I desire to see the time when education, and by its means, morality, sobriety, enterprise and industry, shall become much more general than at present, and should be gratified to have it in my power to contribute something to the advancement of any measure which might have a tendency to accelerate the happy period.

Lincoln never delivered on that platform. His record on education in the Illinois House from 1834 through 1841 was lackluster. In 1840 he introduced a resolution to require examination of Illinois teachers whose schools received public funds. Otherwise, he was never in the forefront of pressing for improvement in Illinois's educational system, and his record was poorer than that of Stephen A. Douglas, a former schoolteacher. Lincoln supported spending only the interest earned from lands set aside for public schools; Douglas urged using the entire school fund immediately. Two factors restricted Lincoln's generosity toward Illinois's schools. Particularly after 1837, Lincoln felt confined by Illinois's disastrous finances brought on by the collapse of the internal improvements system he had worked for. And wealthy Sangamon County did not need the funds other parts of Illinois needed; it had many schools.

As President, Lincoln had little to do with educational policy, which was largely locally controlled. He did urge General Nathaniel P. Banks to include education for young blacks in his plans to reconstruct Louisiana. And

*Far Left:
Lincoln's fabled self-education so engaged the imagination of genre painter Eastman Johnson that in 1868 he painted the Boyhood of Lincoln, perhaps the most famous and appealing rendering of this familiar aspect of the Lincoln myth.*

his Proclamation of Amnesty and Reconstruction of December 8, 1863, stipulated that returning disloyal states had to make some provision for the education of freedmen.

SOURCES: In *Lincoln's Preparation for Greatness: The Illinois Legislative Years* (Norman: University of Oklahoma Press, 1965), Paul Simon made the startling discovery that Lincoln was never a leader in promoting education.

See also BOOKS; GRAHAM, WILLIAM MENTOR; INDIANA; KENTUCKY.

Edwards, Ninian Wirt (1809–1889) Son of Illinois Territorial Governor Ninian Edwards. Ninian W. Edwards was born in Kentucky and graduated from Transylvania University. While a junior at the university, in 1832, he married Elizabeth P. Todd. Elizabeth, then 16 years old, was an older sister of the girl who would marry Abraham Lincoln.

The Edwardses moved to Springfield, Illinois, in 1835, and in 1836 Ninian served with Lincoln in the Illinois legislature as a fellow Whig. Both were reelected in 1838, but in 1840 the Sangamon County Whig convention, dominated by rural delegates, ignored Edwards. According to Lincoln, Edwards was "verry much hurt." Lincoln reported him "a little mortified" at being left out again in 1842, but he went "for the ticket without complaint."

In 1839 Mary Todd came to live with her sister and brother-in-law in Springfield. The Edwardses were socially prominent, and life in the home was gay. Lincoln courted Mary there, but the Edwardses apparently opposed their marriage. Mrs. Edwards recalled years later that Lincoln was fascinated with Mary's conversational ability but was himself "not sufficiently educated & intelligent in the female line" to "hold a lengthy conversation with a lady." Mrs. Edwards saw "no congeniality—no feelings, &c. alike" between them. Since Edwards was Mary's guardian, his objections may have been decisive in causing Mary and Lincoln to break off their engagement in 1841. He later recalled Lincoln as a "mighty rough" and "not a warm hearted man." Also, social distinctions were important for Edwards, whom Usher F. Linder described as hating "democracy . . . as the devil is said to hate holy water." After Lincoln and Mary were reconciled, however, their wedding took place in the Edwards home, on November 4, 1842.

After election to the Illinois Senate in 1844 and to the Illinois House in 1848 and again in 1850, Edwards became a Democrat, a move which "deeply mortified" Lincoln (according to David Davis). As a result, Edwards was "a Douglas man" in the period when Lincoln rose to national prominence as an antislavery man. In 1855 Edwards supported Joel Matteson for the United States Senate over Lyman Trumbull and Lincoln, though he later claimed that Lincoln would have been his first choice if Lincoln had had a chance to win. Edwards borrowed $1500 from Lincoln in 1860, but he still supported Stephen A. Douglas for President.

Once Lincoln was elected President, Edwards belittled their political differences. He disagreed only "in relation to the *propriety* of Congressional interference in the Territories." He deemed the constitutional right to interfere settled by long practice, but he thought it better to "leave the question to the people immediately interested." He also told Lincoln repeatedly that he had stated publicly "that if there was a man living without a fault I believed you were that man."

Edwards's loan from Lincoln was a symptom of a severe "pecuniary embarrassment" which caused Edwards to seek an office from his brother-in-law. Lincoln said that he would not deprive Edwards "of a chance to make something, if it can be done without injustice," and on August 8, 1861, he made him a captain and commissary of subsistence. Lincoln also asked him to report on the propriety of the government's entering into a contract with the Chiriqui Improvement Company for Latin American coal and a possible colonization site for free Negroes. Edwards endorsed the project.

Lincoln knew that his brother-in-law kept his "official record dryly correct" as commissary of subsistence, letting his contracts to the lowest bidder, but Springfield's Republicans howled with indignation when Democrat Joel Matteson benefited from a contract. They charged Edwards with making $15,000 from his office. Edwards explained to the President that he had been able to retire $13,000 of his indebtedness, but he did it by spending $600 instead of $3000 or $4000 to live each year and by means of the rise in rents on his property. Lincoln did "not suppose Mr. Edwards has, at this time of his life, given up his old habits, and turned dishonest," but he did feel that Edwards did not care whether he provoked Lincoln's old friends and harassed the President with squabbling. On June 22, 1863, under pressure from

Ninian Wirt Edwards. (Courtesy of the Lloyd Ostendorf Collection)

other old Springfield friends, Lincoln replaced Edwards at Springfield with George R. Weber. By that time, his brother-in-law explained, he could "do without" the office, though he had "needed it very much" when he asked for it in 1861.

Mrs. Edwards had come to Washington to stay with Mrs. Lincoln after the death of Willie Lincoln in 1862. Their friendship continued despite the early strains over Mary's choice of husband and Lincoln's later troubles with Ninian over subsistence contracts. When Mrs. Lincoln was adjudged insane in 1875, she lived from the autumn of that year until June of the next at the Edwards home. When the verdict was reversed in June, she remained at the Edwards home only until fall, when she went to Europe. Upon returning in 1880, she again took up residence with the Edwardses. Their grandson, Edward Lewis Baker, Jr., became a great favorite of the eccentric widow. She died in their home in 1882.

SOURCES: Ruth Painter Randall's *Mary Lincoln: Biography of a Marriage* (Boston: Little, Brown, 1953) carefully describes the pre- and postwar Lincoln-Edwards relationship. Edwards's letters to Lincoln about their political differences (December 26, 1860), about thinking Lincoln "without a fault" and needing an office (June 18, 1863), and about his personal finances (July 27, 1863) are in the Abraham Lincoln Papers, Library of Congress. Lincoln's reaction to Edwards's becoming a Democrat is in Willard H. King, *Lincoln's Manager: David Davis* (Cambridge: Harvard University Press, 1960).

Effie Afton Case Officially called *Hurd* v. *Rock Island Bridge Company*, the *Effie Afton* case of 1857 was one of Lincoln's most celebrated legal efforts. On May 6, 1856, the river steamship *Effie Afton* ran into the piers of the railroad bridge over the Mississippi River between Rock Island, Illinois, and Davenport, Iowa. The ship caught fire and was a total loss. Her owner and captain, John S. Hurd, sued the Rock Island Bridge Company for $50,000 damages, claiming the bridge was a hazard to navigation. The Chicago, Rock Island, and Pacific Railroad Company retained Lincoln, Norman B. Judd, and Joseph Knox of Rock Island as defense attorneys.

The lengthy trial commenced in Chicago on September 8, 1857. Lincoln had examined the accident site, and he relied on his knowledge of river travel in developing the argument. His summation stressed the narrow ground that the burden of proof was on the plaintiffs to show that the boat had been managed with reasonable skill and care. He noted that a good pilot would have studied the currents around the bridge the day before, while the *Effie Afton* was docked. He took broader ground as well. He argued the importance of rail transportation to the continued growth of the West. Already rail traffic was greater than river traffic, and the bridge, therefore, should be an acceptable part of the landscape. The trial ended in a hung jury and dismissal by the judge. Lincoln's case was notable for its careful technical preparation and for the way in which his vision of Western development informed his innovative argument for the importance of rail transportation.

Lincoln's fee in the case is unknown.

Otto Eisenschiml. (Courtesy of Mr. and Mrs. Benjamin J. Gingiss)

SOURCES: John J. Duff's *A. Lincoln: Prairie Lawyer* (New York: Rinehart, 1960) has an excellent chapter on this famous case.

Eighth Judicial Circuit Because of small population, most Illinois counties could not sustain a full-time judge, and the state supreme court justices twice a year made a circuit of local county seats to try cases. From 1839 through 1857, Sangamon County was a part of the Eighth Judicial Circuit. Its boundaries changed from time to time, but from 1843 to 1853 the circuit comprised 14 counties which the judge (and the lawyers from Springfield) visited in this order: Sangamon, Tazewell, Woodford, McLean, Logan, DeWitt, Piatt, Champaign, Vermilion, Edgar, Shelby, Moultrie, Macon, and Christian. The area (about the size of Maryland) included more than 10,000 square miles, over a fifth of the area of the whole state. The lawyers were on the road almost 3 months, traveling by horse or buggy and stopping at the county seats for court terms of 2 days to 1 week. Lincoln traveled the 400-mile circuit twice a year, beginning customarily in March and September; he could return to Springfield for weekends when the county seat was nearby. From 1841 to 1848, Lincoln practiced mostly before Supreme Court Justice Samuel H. Treat. Illinois added elected circuit judges in its new constitution; after that, Lincoln practiced mostly before Judge David Davis.

Isaac N. Arnold called Lincoln "the strongest jury lawyer in the state." Lincoln was an excellent circuit lawyer. He worked in association with local lawyers on particular cases. Though Lincoln signed the pleadings in such cases "Lincoln and _____," the local lawyers were not his partners in the sense William H. Herndon was. But they were his friends, companions, and, often, political allies. The lawyers who traveled the circuit enjoyed a convivial camaraderie of storytelling and conversations in the nights spent in crude country taverns far away from the comforts of home.

Improvements in transportation (Lincoln could reach every circuit town by train in 1857) and a decrease in the size of the circuit made the duty less onerous in the 1850s. Lincoln always traveled the circuit himself and left areas not on the circuit and the office work to his partner. From 1853 to 1857 the circuit comprised only Sangamon, Champaign, Vermilion, DeWitt, McLean, Tazewell, and Logan counties, and it shrank more after that.

SOURCES: The lore of the circuit is vast. See Henry C. Whitney, *Life on the Circuit with Lincoln* (Boston: Estes and Lauriat, 1892) and Trevor N. Hill, *Lincoln the Lawyer* (New York: Century, 1906).

See also LAW PRACTICE.

Eisenschiml, Otto (1880–1963) The most controversial—and one of the most influential—of the students of the Lincoln assassination. Eisenschiml was born an American citizen in Austria. After earning a degree in chemical engineering at the Polytechnic School of Vienna in 1901, he emigrated to America and became a successful chemical consultant for businesses and later the president of the Scientific Oil Compounding Company.

Wealth gave Eisenschiml freedom to dabble in history, which he thought unduly unscientific as usually written but which offered him the fame that chemical engineers could never gain for their discoveries. Puzzled by General Ulysses S. Grant's refusal to attend the theater on the night of Lincoln's assassination, Eisenschiml decided that the general's excuse was flimsy and that he must have been ordered secretly not to go by the only man besides Lincoln from whom he took orders: Secretary of War Edwin M. Stanton. For years he labored to prove that Stanton, hoping to establish the policies of the Radical Republicans, engineered the plot to assassinate President Lincoln.

Eisenschiml first argued his thesis in *Why Was Lincoln Murdered?* (New York: Little, Brown, 1937). He pointed to the poor police record of Lincoln's guard John F. Parker, who was never punished for his negligence at Ford's Theatre; to Stanton's closing all the roads out of Washington save the one by which John Wilkes Booth escaped; to the failure of the telegraph that night; to the shooting of Booth without orders; to hooding the other captured conspirators so they could not talk; to the imprisonment of the conspirators who were not hanged away from public contact on Dry Tortugas; and other details to prove that Stanton might have been covering up a crime he himself instigated.

The Eisenschiml conspiracy theory gained wide exposure. The book in which it was expounded was a Book-of-the-Month Club selection, and other books, television dramas, and a motion picture *(The Lincoln Conspiracy)* perpetuated the idea into the 1970s. Its popularity, however, was a function of the gap between professional history and the popular mind. J. G. DeRoulhac Hamilton sneered at the book of the "Viennese Chemist" as "four hundred and thirty-eight dreary pages of rambling and disconnected implication and innuendo." Advances in the study of Reconstruction and the Radical Republicans closed the gap between Lincoln and his liberal critics— thought to be an inseparable gulf in Eisenschiml's day— and left Stanton motiveless. Even the facts of the thesis began to disappear: only the commercial, and not the military, telegraph had failed, for example, and some of the conspirators (John H. Surratt and Samuel Bland Arnold) lived as free men into the twentieth century and were anything but silenced.

SOURCES: William Hanchett's "The Eisenschiml Thesis," *Civil War History*, XXV (September 1979), pp. 197–217, is a definitive and amusing refutation of the thesis.

Election of 1860 The election of 1860, which made Lincoln President, was a momentous one for the nation's history, but it was not an especially suspenseful contest. In fact, when the Democratic party split into Southern and Northern factions in June, each with its own presidential candidate (John C. Breckinridge and Stephen A. Douglas, respectively), many assumed it to be a foregone conclusion that the Republicans would win.

The first candidate nominated, John Bell, led the Constitutional Union party, the remnants of the old Whig and Know-Nothing (American) party organizations; his only platform was the Constitution. The Republican convention met in Chicago on May 16 to choose a candidate who could hold the 11 states John C. Frémont had carried as the first Republican presidential nominee in 1856 and add one of the following combinations: Pennsylvania with Illinois, Indiana, or New Jersey, or all three of those states without Pennsylvania. All the critical states bordered on slave states, and that factor dictated the choice of a moderate Republican who was sound on slavery without being shrill. He must also be acceptable to the many Know-Nothings who had become Republicans since 1856. William H. Seward was widely regarded as the most likely nominee, though Salmon P. Chase, Edward Bates, and Simon Cameron had substantial support. Lincoln was not even mentioned as a likely candidate among eight Republicans in D. W. Bartlett's *Presidential Candidates: Containing Sketches . . . of Prominent Candidates for the Presidency in 1860* (New York: A. B. Burdick: 1859), but his able managers (David Davis, Leonard Swett, Norman B. Judd, Stephen T. Logan, Jesse W. Fell, and Ward Hill Lamon) pursued a strategy of making him everybody's second choice. His relative obscurity gave him few enemies at the convention.

The Republican gubernatorial candidates in Indiana and Pennsylvania were adamant that Seward could not carry their crucial states, the outcome in which was particularly important because their state elections took place in October, a month before the presidential election. Seward had a reputation for radicalism on the slavery question and, as a long-time champion of Catholic rights in New York, was an anathema to former Know-Nothings. Chase was likewise too radical on the slavery question; Cameron had a reputation for corruption; and Bates was far too lukewarm an antislavery man, having declared for Republican principles only shortly before the convention. Seward led on the first and second ballots, but Lincoln quickly became the second choice of many and won on the third ballot. Hannibal Hamlin, an Easterner and a former Democrat, balanced the ticket as his running mate. The party's platform was more moderate than in 1856 and reached out for voters on issues other than slavery, with planks for a protective tariff, a homestead act, and a transcontinental railroad. It reaffirmed the rights of immigrants. The Republican party was no longer a stridently one-issue party.

By "the lessons of the past, and the united voice of all discreet friends, I am neither [to] write or speak a word for the public," Lincoln wrote a political associate, and he held to that custom. Lincoln's name did not even appear on the ballot in states south of Virginia and Kentucky, and the Republican campaign—waged by speakers, newspapers, and massive rallies and parades by Wide-Awakes—was aimed principally against Douglas in the Northern states, a factor which served to keep Southern voters in ignorance of the Republican candidate and to allow the propagation of the idea that Lincoln

Election of 1860

Political parades were especially elaborate in the giant metropolis of New York, where these floats, mostly anti-Republican in content, were parts of a great "Union" torchlight procession late in October. The illustrations appeared in Frank Leslie's Illustrated Newspaper on November 3, 1860.

was an abolitionist threat to Southern institutions. Likewise, Northerners learned little of the serious gulf that separated them from Southerners, who were preoccupied in their region with a campaign mainly between Bell and Breckinridge. Douglas waged the first campaign of national speaking by an American presidential candidate, heroically carrying even into the South his message that Lincoln's election would not justify secession.

With knowledge of the momentous consequences of the election, it is hard to recover any sense that the election did not necessarily focus attention on those issues. Yet it was a campaign like any other and stressed parades by marching groups and popular symbols like "Honest Abe" and the "Rail Splitter." As heirs of the Whigs, the Republicans stressed the enthusiastic mass campaign techniques popularized by the Whigs in 1840.

Lincoln had won the nomination, in part because of his appeal in the doubtful states. His lifelong devotion to tariffs, along with the Republican platform's declaration for the tariff, was decisive in Pennsylvania. Also, his image of moderation on the slavery question was significant in Indiana, where politician Richard W. Thompson, nominally a Constitutional Unionist, apparently helped Constitutional Unionists to go into the Republican camp.

After the voting on November 6, Lincoln won with

39 percent of the popular vote (or 1,866,452 to 1,376,957 for Douglas, 849,781 for Breckinridge, and 588,879 for Bell). As James G. Randall has pointed out, Lincoln won less because his opponents were divided than because his voters were concentrated in populous states with large electoral votes. The electoral vote was 180 for Lincoln, 72 for Breckinridge, 39 for Bell, and 12 for Douglas. In the popular vote the ratio of Lincoln's vote to Douglas's was about 180 to 130, but in the electoral vote, 180 to 12. Had all the popular votes against Lincoln been united on a single candidate, Lincoln would still have won in the electoral college, 169 to 134, losing only California, Oregon, and the rest of New Jersey's votes in this scheme. Thus the attempts at forming "fusion" tickets against Lincoln in New York, New Jersey, Rhode Island, and Pennsylvania, though greatly feared by the Republicans, could not alter the final result. Nevertheless, the Democratic party was still strong, getting 47.6 percent of the national vote and 44.7 percent of the vote in the states that would not secede (down only slightly from an average of 48.7 percent and 45.7 percent, respectively, in contests from 1840 through 1856).

The most ominous feature was the sectional nature of Lincoln's vote. Of the states that would constitute the Confederacy only Virginia gave the Republican candidate any votes, and those mostly from the part that would in turn break off to become West Virginia. By contrast, Breckinridge, the most Southern candidate, received 278,000 votes in the free states.

Lincoln was not especially popular in cities. He lost seven of the eleven Northern cities of 50,000 or greater population, a sign of his lack of appeal to Catholic immigrants and mercantile communities tied to the South by trade. Modern scholars find considerable diversity in the voting behavior of the large German-American community, but most agree that Protestant Germans were more susceptible to Republican appeals than Catholic Germans.

The election of 1860, despite (as Don E. Fehrenbacher puts it) the pall of inevitability which hung over it, was a critical one, not only because civil war followed it but also because it signaled the emergence of an era of Republican dominance in national politics. The realignment of voters begun in 1856 was complete. There

THE 1860 ELECTION RETURNS

	Popular vote				Electoral vote			
States	Abraham Lincoln, Republican	Stephen A. Douglas, Democrat	John C. Breckinridge, Democrat	John Bell, Constitutional Union	Lincoln and Hamlin	Douglas and Johnson	Breckinridge and Lane	Bell and Everett
Alabama	—	13,651	48,831	27,875	—	—	9	—
Arkansas	—	5,227	28,732	20,094	—	—	4	—
California	39,173	38,516	34,334	6,817	4	—	—	—
Connecticut	43,792	15,522	14,641	3,291	6	—	—	—
Delaware	3,815	1,023	7,337	3,864	—	—	3	—
Florida	—	367	8,543	5,437	—	—	3	—
Georgia	—	11,590	51,889	42,886	—	—	10	—
Illinois	172,161	160,215	2,404	4,913	11	—	—	—
Indiana	139,033	115,509	12,295	5,306	13	—	—	—
Iowa	70,409	55,111	1,048	1,763	4	—	—	—
Kentucky	1,364	25,651	53,143	66,058	—	—	—	12
Louisiana	—	7,625	22,861	20,204	—	—	6	—
Maine	62,811	26,693	6,368	2,046	8	—	—	—
Maryland	2,294	5,966	42,482	41,760	—	—	8	—
Massachusetts	106,533	34,372	5,939	22,331	13	—	—	—
Michigan	88,480	65,057	805	405	6	—	—	—
Minnesota	22,069	11,920	748	62	4	—	—	—
Mississippi	—	3,283	40,797	25,040	—	—	7	—
Missouri	17,028	58,801	31,317	58,372	—	9	—	—
New Hampshire	37,519	25,881	2,112	441	5	—	—	—
New Jersey	58,324	62,801	—	—	4	3	—	—
New York	362,646	312,510	—	—	35	—	—	—
North Carolina	—	2,701	48,539	44,990	—	—	10	—
Ohio	231,610	187,232	11,405	12,194	23	—	—	—
Oregon	5,270	3,951	5,006	183	3	—	—	—
Pennsylvania	268,030	16,765	178,871	12,776	27	—	—	—
Rhode Island	12,244	7,707	—	—	4	—	—	—
South Carolina*	—	—	—	—	—	—	8	—
Tennessee	—	11,350	64,709	69,274	—	—	—	12
Texas	—	—	47,548	15,438	—	—	4	—
Vermont	33,808	8,649	1,866	217	5	—	—	—
Virginia	1,929	16,290	74,323	74,681	—	—	—	15
Wisconsin	86,110	65,021	888	161	5	—	—	—
	1,866,452	1,376,957	849,781	588,879	180	12	72	39

* Electors were appointed by the legislature.

Election of 1864

would not be another major shift in the ways social classes and ethnic groups voted until the 1890s. And the two parties which emerged successfully from the 1850s, the Democratic and the Republican, became fixed and dominant features on the American political landscape.

SOURCES: For a succinct and thoughtful treatment see the chapter on the election in David M. Potter's *The Impending Crisis, 1848–1861* (New York: Harper & Row, 1976). Reinhard H. Luthin's *The First Lincoln Campaign* (Cambridge: Harvard University Press, 1944) provides a more detailed study of the election state by state. See James G. Randall's chapter on the election in the first volume of *Lincoln the President: Springfield to Gettysburg* (New York: Dodd, Mead, 1945) and Joel H. Silbey, *A Respectable Minority: The Democratic Party in the Civil War Era, 1860–1868* (New York: W. W. Norton, 1977). Also useful are Don E. Fehrenbacher, "The Election of 1860," in *Crucial American Elections* (Philadelphia: American Philosophical Society, 1973) and Frederick C. Luebke, ed., *Ethnic Voters and the Election of Lincoln* (Lincoln: University of Nebraska Press, 1971).

See also DAVIS, DAVID; "RAIL SPLITTER"; "WIDE-AWAKES"; WIGWAM.

Election of 1864 "The most remarkable fact about the 1864 election," says historian Harold M. Hyman, "is that it occurred." Deciding matters of state by ballot was rare enough; deciding them by ballot in wartime was practically unheard of.

Abraham Lincoln may have thought that the most remarkable fact about the election was that he won it. He certainly did not think he would win in the summer before. On August 23, 6 days before the Democrats met in Chicago to nominate George B. McClellan, Lincoln wrote: "This morning, as for some days past, it seems exceedingly probable that this Administration will not be re-elected. Then it will be my duty to so co-operate with the President elect, as to save the Union between the election and the inauguration; as he will have secured his election on such ground that he can not possibly save it afterwards." Lincoln folded the memorandum and had his Cabinet sign it without seeing the contents. With the Union's peril in mind and with hopes of attracting more voters, Republicans ran as the Union party in 1864.

No President since Andrew Jackson had won reelection, and there were some feeble attempts to replace Lincoln as Republican nominee in 1864. When the Union party met in Baltimore in June, however, Lincoln had the nomination sewn up on the first ballot. The convention nominated Andrew Johnson, the war Governor of Tennessee, to replace Vice President Hannibal Hamlin as Lincoln's running mate. The move made the party genuinely "Union," at least at the top, for it united Democrat Johnson and Republican Lincoln. The platform urged war until the South surrendered, a constitu-

THE 1864 ELECTION RETURNS

States	Popular Vote — Abraham Lincoln, Republican (UNION)	Popular Vote — George B. McClellan Democrat	Soldiers' Vote — Abraham Lincoln	Soldiers' Vote — George McClellan	Electoral Vote — Lincoln and Johnson	Electoral Vote — McClellan and Pendleton
California	62,134	43,841	2,600	237	5	—
Connecticut	44,693	42,288	—	—	6	—
Delaware	8,155	8,767	—	—	—	3
Illinois	189,487	158,349	—	—	16	—
Indiana	150,422	130,233	—	—	13	—
Iowa	87,331	49,260	15,178	1,364	8	—
Kansas†	14,228	3,871	—	—	3	—
Kentucky	27,786	64,301	1,194	2,823	—	11
Maine	72,278	47,736	4,174	741	7	—
Maryland	40,153	32,739	2,800	321	7	—
Massachusetts	126,742	48,745	—	—	12	—
Michigan	85,352	67,370	9,402	2,959	8	—
Minnesota†	25,060	17,375	—	—	4	—
Missouri	72,991	31,026	—	—	11	—
Nevada	9,826	6,594	—	—	2*	—
New Hampshire	36,595	33,034	2,066	690	5	—
New Jersey	60,723	68,014	—	—	—	7
New York	368,726	361,986	—	—	33	—
Ohio	265,154	205,568	41,146	9,757	21	—
Oregon	9,888	8,457	—	—	3	—
Pennsylvania	296,389	276,308	26,712	12,349	26	—
Rhode Island	14,343	8,718	—	—	4	—
Vermont	42,422	13,325	243	49	5	—
West Virginia	23,223	10,457	—	—	5	—
Wisconsin	79,564	63,875	11,372	2,458	8	—
	2,213,665	1,802,237	116,887	33,748	212	21

* A Nevada elector (1 of 3) died before the election.
† The army vote from Minnesota and Kansas was too late to be counted.

tional amendment to end slavery, redress for any violation of the laws of war perpetrated upon black soldiers, more foreign immigration, a transcontinental railroad, and economy in government. One plank condemned attempts by European powers to establish monarchical governments in the Western hemisphere, a reference to French intervention in Mexico. Still another called for "harmony . . . in the National Councils," a plank widely interpreted as a call for the resignation of the conservative Postmaster General Montgomery Blair.

About a week before the Republican convention, the "Radical Democrats," led by Missouri German-Americans, met in Cleveland and nominated John C. Frémont for President. Some Democrats and Radical Republicans were present, but there were few Republicans of any prominence there.

Despite the tenor of his secret memorandum, Lincoln was not pitted against a Democratic opponent who would, if elected, give up the Union. George B. McClellan was a nationalist, and Lincoln probably knew it. Indeed, his memorandum said only that the candidate would have gained the nomination in such a way that he could not save the Union. On this point, Lincoln was very near the mark. After McClellan gave a speech at West Point in June which was a strong endorsement of the war, Ohio Democrat S. S. Cox warned him that it "will give you the election, but it does not help to the nomination."

The Democrats chose a war candidate and a peace platform. Yet even the peace plank, after declaring the war a failure, insisted only that "efforts be made for a cessation of hostilities, with a view of an ultimate convention of the States, or other peaceable means, to the end that, at the earliest practicable moment, peace may be restored on the basis of the Federal Union of the States." In other words, reunion was the goal of peace men too. And General McClellan in his statement accepting the nomination a week later, chose simply to ignore the platform and argue for a vigorous prosecution of the war as the best way to save the Union. The Democratic nominee, and especially the platform, reunited and invigorated the Republicans, who had degenerated into factional squabbling largely because they had no opponent to focus on. Frémont withdrew from the race on September 22, and Lincoln asked for Blair's resignation the next day. Republican unity was complete.

Most historians agree that the election was decided by two factors: (1) military victories, especially General William T. Sherman's capture of Atlanta on September 2, and (2) Republican campaign strategy, which played down the race issue and Reconstruction and claimed that Democrats were disloyal and treasonous "Copperheads." Historians have interpreted the Republican campaign strategy cynically as an attempt to smear the Democrats—an admittedly loyal opposition—with the disloyalty issue merely because they were critical of some acts of the administration. Likewise, historians have seen the Democrats as sincerely conservative doubters of the constitutional looseness of President Lin-

Although Americans voted with paper ballots in the 1860s, there really was no secret ballot. Harper's Weekly revealingly showed that the ballot receptacles were identified by party. Harper's also revealed its pro-Republican sentiments in this and other supposedly reportorial illustrations. Solid bourgeois citizens vote the Republican ticket, but a simian Irishman, goaded by a fat party boss, votes the Democratic ticket.

coln. A further tendency is to exempt Lincoln himself from the bad implications of both charges. On the one hand, he is pictured as triumphing personally by his popularity with the common man, though his own party had little enthusiasm for him. Thus he is rarely tarred with the charge of running a smear campaign himself. On the other hand, most constitutional historians agree that Lincoln stretched the Constitution as much as any President but that he did it not for personal gain, but rather for the sake of saving the Union.

The cynical interpretations of the election are clearly wrong. In the first place, Lincoln himself sincerely believed, at least in August, that the future of the Union itself was at stake. This is the often ignored import of the famous blind memorandum, which is usually cited only to show that Lincoln was in real danger of losing and knew it. But it also shows that he thought the Democratic platform would be so constituted that the candidate "can not possibly save it [the Union] afterwards." In the second place, the libertarian issues the Democrats stressed (well buttressed by appeals to race prejudice) were the only issues left to them by 1864. Loyal as they were, the Democrats could criticize only the alleged inefficiency of the Republican administration's handling of the war. The party's old Jacksonian appeals to economic discontent were useless in the face of high employment in the tight wartime economy. So the Democrats complained bitterly of Lincoln's suspension of the privilege of the writ of habeas corpus, arbitrary arrests, and press censorship. The Democrats in the North were probably no more sincere, and no less, than the many former Whigs in the Confederacy, led by Alexander H. Stephens, who bitterly criticized their President, Jefferson Davis, a former Democrat, for being a tyrant and military usurper. They were probably no more sincere, and no less, than the Republicans who feared that Democrats endangered the Union by opposing the administration. Among those Republicans was certainly the incumbent President, who had said in 1863: "The man who stands by and says nothing, when the peril of his government is discussed, can not be misunderstood. If not hindered, he is sure to help the enemy. Much more, if he talks ambiguously—talks for his country with 'buts' and 'ifs' and 'ands.'"

McClellan won only three states—Delaware, New Jersey, and Kentucky—but he gained 45 percent of the popular vote. After the election Lincoln showed a shrewd understanding of its meaning:

> We can not have free government without elections; and if the rebellion could force us to forego, or postpone a national election, it might fairly claim to have already conquered and ruined us. . . . It has demonstrated that a people's government can sustain a national election, in the midst of a great civil war.

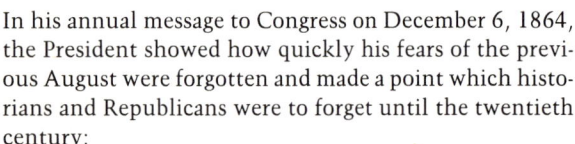

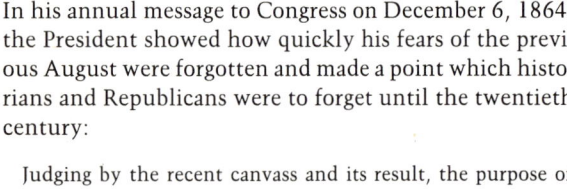

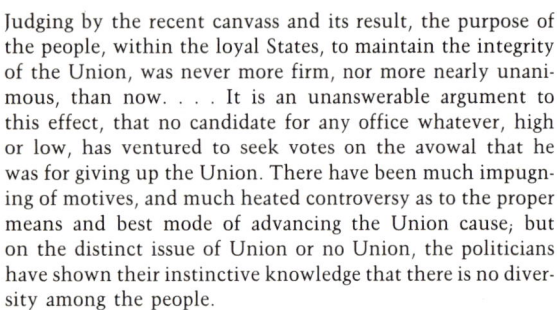

In his annual message to Congress on December 6, 1864, the President showed how quickly his fears of the previous August were forgotten and made a point which historians and Republicans were to forget until the twentieth century:

> Judging by the recent canvass and its result, the purpose of the people, within the loyal States, to maintain the integrity of the Union, was never more firm, nor more nearly unanimous, than now. . . . It is an unanswerable argument to this effect, that no candidate for any office whatever, high or low, has ventured to seek votes on the avowal that he was for giving up the Union. There have been much impugning of motives, and much heated controversy as to the proper means and best mode of advancing the Union cause; but on the distinct issue of Union or no Union, the politicians have shown their instinctive knowledge that there is no diversity among the people.

The election was not without great significance, even though the Union itself was never at issue. The Democratic platform pledged the party "to preserve . . . the rights of the States unimpaired" and did not mention slavery. McClellan showed no inclination to ignore this plank. Had he won, slavery would doubtless have survived the war, and the history of American racial relations might be a good deal more like South Africa's than was in fact the result.

In terms of electoral behavior the election was much less significant. Most historians agree that the principal party realignment occurred in the 1850s, and Democrats and Republicans by and large retained their traditional classes of voters thereafter. The turnout was larger than in 1860, and Lincoln got a greater percentage of the popular vote. He did rather better in the cities than he had in 1860, but he still did not do well. Catholic immigrants and urban working classes still tended to vote Democratic. Eleven states allowed voting in the field, and Lincoln saw to it that some soldiers returned home briefly to vote in those states that had no such provisions. Republicans captured the soldier vote by an overwhelming margin. Above all else the Republican party established its staying power, and though the Democrats were clearly a minority to be respected at the polls, Republican dominance of future national elections would last almost until World War I.

SOURCES: William Frank Zornow's *Lincoln and the Party Divided* (Norman: University of Oklahoma Press, 1954) is so marred by its hostility to Radical Republicans that it makes the contest within the Republican party seem more important than the one between the Republicans and the Democrats. Harold M. Hyman's "Election of 1864" in the second volume of Arthur M. Schlesinger, Jr., et al., eds., *History of American Presidential Elections, 1789–1968* (New York: Chelsea House, 1971) and the treatment in Peter J. Parish's *The American Civil War* (New York: Holmes & Meier, 1975) are balanced, succinct accounts.

See also BLIND MEMORANDUM; FRÉMONT, JOHN CHARLES; McCLELLAN, GEORGE BRINTON.

Ellsworth, Elmer Ephraim (1837–1861)

Young favorite of Lincoln's and the first commissioned officer to die in the Civil War. Ellsworth was born in Saratoga County, New York. Of humble origins, he restlessly sought advancement in life. In his search he moved to New York City, Chicago, and, eventually, Springfield, Illinois, where in 1860 he read law in Lincoln's office. He had been a patent solicitor and was noted as a skilled Zouave drill instructor. In the summer of 1860, he toured 20 cities with the U.S. Zouave Cadets of Chicago, having written a *Manual of Arms for Light Infantry* published in the same year. His crack troop made him something of a sensation, and he later made political speeches for Lincoln's presidential campaign.

The Lincolns developed a great fondness for Ellsworth, and the President-elect asked the young man to accompany him on his inaugural trip to Washington. Ellsworth did so and sought appointment as a clerk in the War Department in Washington. Lincoln made such a recommendation on March 5, 1861, but on March 18 made Ellsworth Adjutant and Inspector General of Militia. Ellsworth wished to establish a Bureau of Militia in the War Department.

When war broke out, Ellsworth abandoned bureaucracy for war and rushed to New York City, where, armed with a letter of recommendation from the President, he quickly organized the 1100-man Fire Zouaves, a volunteer unit recruited from New York's firemen. The 11th New York Volunteer Infantry (usually called the Fire Zouaves) departed New York for Washington on April 29, were sworn in in an elaborate ceremony observed by the President on May 5, and helped put out a fire on May 7.

When Virginia seceded on May 23, Ellsworth readied his men to take Alexandria, which was just across the Potomac from Washington (a rebel flag was visible from the White House). On entering Alexandria the next day, Ellsworth removed the flag from the Marshall House hotel. The hotel's proprietor, James W. Jackson, shot him and was shot in turn by Corporal Francis E. Brownell of Ellsworth's unit. Jackson was celebrated in the South as the first martyr for Southern independence.

The young officer's body lay in state in the East Room of the White House the next day, when Lincoln wrote the first of the famous letters of condolence he would write in the tragic years to come. He told Ellsworth's parents that "our affliction here, is scarcely less than your own" and referred to Ellsworth as "my young friend, and your brave and early fallen child." Ellsworth's body lay in state in New York City Hall and in the Capitol at Albany before burial in Mechanicville, New York. Lincoln appointed his father captain in the Ordnance Department to alleviate the family's financial stress.

Ellsworth and his avenger Brownell were early sensations in the war. No fewer than 52 different print portraits of Ellsworth were issued, along with at least 6 different prints of the death scene. 12 existing Ellsworth photographs were reproduced many times.

SOURCES: Ruth Painter Randall's *Colonel Elmer Ellsworth: A Biography of Lincoln's Friend and First Hero of the Civil War* (Boston: Little, Brown, 1960) is solid but ignores the symbolic uses of Ellsworth's image after his death. See also "Ellsworth was 'Golden Boy'; Death Made Him a Martyr of the North," *New York State and the Civil War*, II (June 1962), pp. 1–17, and Winfred Porter Truesdell, *Catalog Raisonne of the Portraits of Col. Elmer E. Ellsworth* (Champlain, N.Y.: The Print Connoisseur, 1927).

Emancipation Proclamation The Presidential proclamation that, on January 1, 1863, freed the slaves in the unconquered Confederacy. The Proclamation was the most important and most controversial executive document of Abraham Lincoln's Presidency.

Such a document was undreamed of by Lincoln when the Civil War began. Republicans had always held that the Constitution protected slavery in the states, and only a few, like Senator Charles Sumner, thought immediately after the fall of Fort Sumter that the war powers of the President made such a move possible. The President himself clearly thought it unconstitutional throughout 1861. When he revoked an emancipation proclamation for Missouri issued in August by General John C. Frémont, he did so in part because he feared its effect on the slaveholding Border States still loyal to the union, especially Kentucky. But he also did so because he thought "the liberation of slaves, is . . . not within the range of *military* law, or government necessity." "Can it be pretended that it is any longer the government of the U.S.—any government of Constitution and laws,—wherein a General, or a President, may make permanent rules of property by proclamation?" Lincoln exclaimed. He would "not say Congress might not with propriety pass a law, on the point," but he ruled it out of the realm of possibility for himself. In sum, Lincoln thought it both unconstitutional and inexpedient.

Ironically, by failing in his Peninsular campaign in Virginia in the late spring of 1862, General George B. McClellan, who opposed emancipation, caused Lincoln to change his mind about the expediency of emancipation. And expediency was without doubt the most important factor, as Lincoln explained to a Kentuckian 2 years later: "When, in March, and May, and July 1862 I made earnest, and successive appeals to the border states to favor compensated emancipation, I believed the indispensable necessity for military emancipation . . . would come, unless averted by that measure." Lincoln claimed "not to have controlled events" but confessed "plainly that events have controlled me." He said repeatedly that the results of the war were "fundamental and astounding" and "not what either party, or any man devised, or expected" at its beginning. Wars make many actions expedient which are unthinkable in peacetime.

The War Powers of the President, by William Whiting, a War Department solicitor, probably changed Lincoln's mind in regard to the constitutional question. Whiting argued in the first edition of his work, in 1862, that Lincoln's powers were as sweeping as those of any ruler whose country had been invaded by a foreign power and included the right, as commander in chief, to emancipate the enemy's slaves. Whiting relied on arguments ex-President John Quincy Adams had developed over 20 years before.

Lincoln wrote a draft of a proclamation in June. He apparently read it first to Vice President Hannibal Hamlin on June 18, 1862. He told Secretary of State William H. Seward and Secretary of the Navy Gideon Welles about it on July 13, as the three rode in a carriage to the funeral of Secretary of War Edwin M. Stanton's son. He read the document to the assembled Cabinet on July 22. The members were stunned. Even Secretary of the Treasury Salmon P. Chase, the most radical member of the Cabinet, said that the document went beyond anything he had comtemplated. Seward said that the Proclamation would be inexpedient at the time because it would appear as a "last measure of an exhausted govern-

British cartoonist John Tenniel presented what was probably the dominant view of the Emancipation Proclamation in England: it was Lincoln's last desperate trump card and was fraught with explosive potential for both sides in the war. The cartoon appeared in Punch *on October 18, 1862. Tenniel's hostility to the Lincoln administration, evident in the contrasting characterizations of the rather elegant Southerner and the awkward Northern President, mellowed in time, and he drew one of the most famous funerary cartoon tributes to Lincoln after his assassination.*

Emancipation Proclamation

ment, a cry for help, the government stretching forth its hands to the Ethiopia, instead of Ethiopia stretching forth her hands to the government." Postmaster General Montgomery Blair, who arrived late, thought it would cause the Republicans to lose the fall elections and might drive the Border States into the Confederacy. Lincoln took Seward's advice and decided to wait for a Northern victory.

Victory did not come for 2 months, and in the meantime Lincoln made several public statements which seemed to indicate that he had little or no intention of freeing the slaves. The most famous of these, a public letter in answer to Horace Greeley's editorial "Prayer of Twenty Millions," stated flatly that the President's policy on slavery was entirely a function of what he thought necessary to save the Union. He would free some, all, or none of the slaves if he thought any of those moves would save the Union. He would act differently only when he thought current policies a failure. Most antislavery men were disappointed, but a few shrewd ones noted that, since not freeing the slaves had not brought victory, Lincoln might try freeing them. Few noted the important point that the letter expressed no doubts on the constitutionality of such an act—proof that Lincoln had changed his mind since the time of Frémont's proclamation (those constitutional doubts had been expressed only in a private letter). On September 13, he told a delegation of Chicago Christians that he did "not want to issue a document that the whole world will see must necessarily be inoperative, like the Pope's bull against the comet." But when General McClellan checked the Confederate invasion of Maryland at Antietam on September 17, 1862, Lincoln decided the time had come. Five days later he issued what is called the preliminary Emancipation Proclamation. The slaves in any state not back in the Union by January 1 would be forever free.

Though Lincoln received "commendation in newspapers and by distinguished individuals . . ., the stocks . . . declined," and troops came "forward more slowly than ever." The Republican party did poorly in the off-year elections in October and November. After Christmas, Lincoln asked for suggestions from the Cabinet and wrote a draft of the final Proclamation which he finished on the morning of January 1. After the customary New Year's reception, the President signed the Proclamation. His hand was aching from the 3 hours of handshaking, and he took special pains to write a steady signature so that no one would think him shaky in his resolve to issue the document. He had added a closing (suggested by Chase) which invoked the "gracious favor of almighty God." He omitted a section regarded as an invitation to slave rebellion which had promised that the government would "do no act or acts to repress such persons . . . in any efforts they may make for their actual freedom" (again on Chase's recommendation as well as Seward's, Welles's, and Edward Bates's). He also added a clause accepting former slaves in the armed services, in part because he had read, on Christmas Day, George Livermore's book on the use of black soldiers in the American Revolution. (Sumner had seen to it that Lincoln saw the book.)

In recent years the Emancipation Proclamation has been criticized as a reluctantly issued document without humanitarian motivation, a document written "with all the moral grandeur of a bill of lading." Indeed, it is not one of Lincoln's more readable pieces, and Karl Marx was correct in reflecting on the Proclamation this way: "All Lincoln's Acts appear like the mean pettifogging conditions which one lawyer puts to his opposing lawyer. But this does not alter their historic content." Yet it surely was not politically motivated; in fact, it was issued in defiance of political advice which proved to be accurate. The argument that a really decisive battle unlike the one at Antietam might have caused Lincoln never to issue the Proclamation is so conjectural as to be almost unanswerable, but it certainly can be said that Lincoln was not personally reluctant to issue the document. He had been ready in July, and he had always insisted that the impediments were constitutional and political; his personal wish, as he told Greeley on August 22, 1862, was "that all men every where could be free." Some have seen the document as a diplomatic weapon. If it was, it misfired. William Gladstone, British Chancellor of the Exchequer and a Liberal leader, made a speech just two weeks after the announcement of the preliminary Emancipation Proclamation in which he said: "We may anticipate with certainty the success of the Southern States sofar as regards their separation from the

Lucius Stebbins copyrighted this print, entitled "Reading the Emancipation Proclamation," in 1864. Published in Hartford, Connecticut, the print reflected the favorable interpretation of the document as a humanitarian act. A handsome blue-and-gold-covered pamphlet advertised the print, saying: "The internal view of the Cabin is true to nature. The stone chimney, garret, ladder, side of bacon, rough cradle, piece of sugar cane and cotton balls, &c., all combine to give a correct idea of the slaves' home."

North." Prime Minister Lord Palmerston called the Proclamation "trash," proof that the United States government was "utterly powerless and contemptible." And Foreign Secretary John Russell saw it as an invitation "to acts of plunder, of incendiarism, and of revenge."

It is widely argued that the Proclamation was ineffectual, that it actually freed not a single slave, nor did anything more than Congress had already done. In fact, Lincoln and Seward thought it had freed at least 200,000 slaves by February 1865. They were freed, of course, by the advent of Union armies in parts of Southern territory. That might have led to their freedom under the Confiscation Act of 1862 anyway, but Lincoln said that not a single slave had been freed by that act. The real enforcement of the Confiscation Act depended on court proceedings to prove the disloyalty of the slaves' masters, and courts were very scarce on battlefields. To be sure, the Proclamation exempted the areas of the Confederacy already controlled by Union military forces at the time of its issuance, but Lincoln insisted: "The original proclamation has no constitutional or legal justification, except as a military measure. The exemptions were made because the military necessity did not apply to the exempted localities." To abandon that footing would put the President "in the boundless field of absolutism."

Lincoln reluctantly donated the historic draft of the final Proclamation to the Northwestern Sanitary Fair in Chicago in 1863. Thomas B. Bryan bought it for $3000 and in turn donated it to the Soldiers' Home in Chicago. Later it was deposited in the Chicago Historical Society, and it burned in the Chicago Fire of 1871. The first draft of the preliminary Proclamation was given to the Albany Army Relief Bazaar in 1865. Abolitionist Gerrit Smith purchased it for $1000 and gave it to the United States Sanitary Commission. The New York Legislature bought it, and it is now in the New York State Library.

SOURCES: Astonishingly, there is only one modern study, *The Emancipation Proclamation* (Garden City, N.Y.: Doubleday, 1963), a small book by John Hope Franklin written without using the Abraham Lincoln Papers in the Library of Congress. It gives a succinct survey of the genesis, content, and immediate reception of the historic document. Charles Eberstadt's *Lincoln's Emancipation Proclamation* (New York: privately printed, 1950) traces the history of the various drafts and lists the printed facsimiles of the document issued in Lincoln's lifetime. Richard Hofstadter denounced the document for lacking "moral grandeur" in *The American Political Tradition and the Men Who Made It* (New York: Alfred A. Knopf, 1948).

See also CONFISCATION ACT; CONSTITUTION OF THE UNITED STATES; DOUGLASS, FREDERICK; FRÉMONT, JOHN CHARLES; GREELEY, HORACE; NEGROES; PROCLAMATION OF AMNESTY AND RECONSTRUCTION; SLAVERY; THIRTEENTH AMENDMENT.

Everett, Edward *See* GETTYSBURG ADDRESS.

Executive Mansion The Lincolns' home from March 1861 until the President's assassination. The White House was both office and residence during the most important period of Abraham Lincoln's life. It was rather dilapidated when the Lincolns moved in, and Mary had little trouble spending a special congressional appropriation to fix the place up. Shopping sprees to the Northeast in May and in August quickly exhausted the $20,000 budget on carpets, furniture, drapes, and an $1100 "solferino and gold" set of presidential china, 666 pieces from Limoges, France. She raced to complete the redecoration for the Washington social season, which began in December with a dress reception (called a "levee") in the White House. Her extravagance exceeded the appropriation by $6700. Lincoln exploded. As Commissioner of Public Buildings Benjamin Brown French related the story, the President exclaimed that "it would stink in the nostrils of the American people to have it said that the President of the United States had approved a bill overrunning an appropriation of $20,000 for *flub dubs*, for this damned old house, when the soldiers cannot have blankets." Congress quietly appropriated the extra money the next year.

For the most part, life in the White House was hard. Lincoln usually rose at 7 a.m. and worked a couple of hours before breakfast with his family in the private rooms on the second floor of the west wing. The east wing held Lincoln's office, which was also the Cabinet room. There, the President worked at a table. The pigeonholes in a large desk were stuffed with letters and documents. Though three secretaries were on the staff for most of the war, the administration keep no systematic letter books. The room was lighted by ceiling gas jets and warmed by the fire from a marble-manteled fireplace. About the only decoration was an oil portrait of Andrew Jackson. Maps often lay on the long Cabinet table or were pinned to the walls.

The White House was jammed much of the time with visitors, many of whom were seeking offices, favors, or pardons from the President. There were so many visitors, in fact, that Lincoln quickly altered his policy of unlimited visiting hours; he opened his doors to visitors at 10 a.m. and closed them at 1 p.m. on Mondays, Wednesdays, and Thursdays and at 12 noon on Tuesdays and Fridays (at which time the Cabinet met). Cabinet members, Senators, and Representatives (in that order) had priority, but throngs of ordinary citizens tried to see

The Executive Mansion as it looked while Lincoln was President. A statue of Thomas Jefferson stands in front.

the President—and succeeded if they could wait long enough in the crowded corridor outside the office. Only military officers were forbidden entry; they had to have written permission from the Secretary of War even to come to Washington. A guard in the corridor, Louis Bargdorf, took visitors' cards, and private secretary John G. Nicolay, with an office adjoining the President's, screened the visitors. There was a doorman, Edward Moran, on the first floor, but the public rooms were open at all times. The hordes of visitors were the most prominent phenomenon of Lincoln's White House; he considered his contacts "public opinion baths."

The public almost crowded private life out. When the President went to lunch, he made his way through the usually jammed public corridor to the private rooms in the west wing. In 1864 new doors and partitions allowed him to get from his office to the private rooms without going through the public corridor. In the winter, public receptions were held Tuesday evenings and Saturday afternoons. Souvenir hunters often took pieces of the carpet and draperies as mementoes of their visit, which kept the appearance of the Executive Mansion rather shabby. The Lincoln children had numerous pets, including goats, in the White House, which must not have enhanced the mansion's appearance either.

The White House had no telegraph service, so Lincoln usually went to the War Department late each night to read the telegrams from the front. After November 1864, one of four Washington policemen in plain clothes but armed with a revolver accompanied him on these walks. Those trips and a daily carriage ride with his wife at 4 p.m. were Lincoln's only regular departures from the Executive Mansion.

The Lincolns dined at 6 p.m. unless there was a state dinner, which began at 7:30 p.m. Wine was served at the latter occasions; accounts vary in regard to whether Lincoln ever drank any himself. Except for such occasions and for the reception night, Lincoln usually returned to his office to work until about 11 p.m. Some evenings he spent in his office in enjoyable conversation with old Illinois friends like Ward Hill Lamon, Orville Hickman Browning, and Elihu Washburne. Secretary of State William H. Seward and a handful of Senators and Congressmen were regular visitors as well—including Harvard-educated Charles Sumner. Secretaries John Nicolay and John Hay lived in the White House but dined in hotels. Their assistant, William O. Stoddard, lived in town.

Social life at the White House fell to a minimum after Willie Lincoln died in February 1862. Mrs. Lincoln discontinued the band concerts, but the President reinstated them on Lafayette Square across from the White House. Mrs. Lincoln did not put her mourning away until 1865. By then, everyone seemed tired. Nicolay and Hay, who did not get along well with Mrs. Lincoln, were seeking foreign appointments. Stoddard fell ill, was replaced by Edward Duffield Neill, and then left to become a federal marshall in Arkansas.

After Lincoln's assassination, his body lay in state in the East Room of the White House on April 19, when a funeral service was read.

SOURCES: "Profile of a President," Chapter XIX in Benjamin P. Thomas's *Abraham Lincoln: A Biography* (New York: Alfred A. Knopf, 1952), is a lively treatment of the Lincoln's White House unequaled in the vast Lincoln literature. Harry E. Pratt and Ernest E. East's "Mrs. Lincoln Refurbishes the White House," *Lincoln Herald*, XLVII (February 1945), 13–22, contains interesting details.

See also HAY, JOHN MILTON; CROOK, WILLIAM HENRY; GRIMSLEY, MRS. HARRISON; KECKLEY, ELIZABETH; LINCOLN, MARY TODD; NICOLAY, JOHN GEORGE; SOLDIERS' HOME; STODDARD, WILLIAM OSBORN.

F

Family *See* DESCENDANTS; GENEALOGY; HANKS, DENNIS FRIEND [cousin]; HANKS, JOHN [cousin]; JOHNSTON, JOHN DAVIS [stepbrother]; LINCOLN, MARY TODD [wife]; LINCOLN, NANCY HANKS [mother]; LINCOLN, ROBERT TODD [son]; LINCOLN, SARAH BUSH JOHNSTON [stepmother]; LINCOLN, THOMAS [father]; LINCOLN, THOMAS ("TAD") [son]; LINCOLN, WILLIAM WALLACE ("WILLIE") [son].

Fatalism *See* PSYCHOLOGY.

Fell, Jesse Wilson (1808–1887) Illinois land speculator, lawyer, and politician. Jesse W. Fell was born in Chester County, Pennsylvania. Admitted to the bar in Ohio in 1832, he became the first lawyer in Bloomington, Illinois, in 1833. He met Abraham Lincoln, who was then serving his first term in the Illinois House of Representatives, in the winter of 1834–1835 while lobbying in Vandalia for local Bloomington interests.

Raised on a farm and always longing to go into the nursery business, Fell never cared much for indoor work. He abandoned law for real estate, selling his practice to David Davis in 1836. He was a successful land speculator but suffered heavily in the panic of 1837, declared bankruptcy in 1841, and started a new legal career after that date. In 1844 he began farming and returned to Bloomington in 1851, where he dabbled in journalism, resumed land speculation, and promoted railroad development. A man of great energy, he founded towns, charitable institutions, schools, and newspapers.

Fell was a Henry Clay Whig, which brought him, immediately upon entering Illinois, into contact with John Todd Stuart. Stuart introduced him to Lincoln, and the two Whigs had a long political association. Fell's views were close to Lincoln's on many points. In 1845 Fell recommended taxation to pay Illinois's debt and stave off repudiation in his *Copy of a Letter upon State Repudiation, Jesse W. Fell to the Senate and House of Illinois, 1845*; Lincoln had for some time advocated the unpopular solution of taxation for the same reason. Fell shared Lincoln's dislike of the Mexican War, a *bête noire* to Whigs everywhere, and in 1848 he sent Congressman Lincoln a petition for peace to be read in the United States House of Representatives. Fell's mother was a Hicksite Quaker, and he therefore shared Lincoln's dislike of the expansion of slavery.

Like Lincoln, Fell became a Republican. In 1856, though a supporter of Leonard Swett in the local race for the Republican nomination for Congress, Fell quickly endorsed the eventual nominee, radical Owen Lovejoy, and thereby gained his political friendship. Yet on the whole, Fell was identified with the fortunes of fellow Bloomington resident David Davis, who was more conservative than Lovejoy on the slavery question. His politic nature helped make Fell secretary of the party's state central committee in 1856 and 1860. In one respect, he was incapable of bridging gaps in the Republican party: he retained a fondness for men who had been

Jesse Wilson Fell. (Courtesy of the Illinois State Historical Library)

Fellowships, Lincoln

Whigs (like Davis and Lincoln) and a dislike of former Democrats. He became a factional enemy, therefore, of Norman B. Judd, and in 1861 he wrote a letter urging President-elect Lincoln not to take Judd into the Cabinet because he was disliked by the Whig element in the Republican party.

In addition to influencing Cabinet selections, Fell is famous for three things. First, in 1859 he requested an autobiography of Lincoln for use among Eastern voters, who knew little or nothing about Lincoln's life. The brief and modest autobiography Lincoln sent on December 20 was forwarded immediately to a Pennsylvania friend of Fell's and was widely reprinted in newspapers in that key state. It is one of the more important sources of information on Lincoln's family history and early life.

Second, Fell was among the group of Illinois men who worked hard in Chicago in 1860 to gain the Republican presidential nomination for Lincoln. In a letter about the convention written on January 2, 1861, Fell said that "no improper pledges, so far as I know or believe, were asked—as I am very sure they were not, and could not be, given." For his own efforts, Fell was rewarded by being appointed a paymaster in the Regular Army on June 30, 1862. Lincoln obviously felt strongly about the appointment, for he told the Secretary of War, "I wish nothing to interfere with this."

Third, Fell became embroiled in the controversy that raged over Lincoln's religious views after Lincoln's death. In a statement he made to William H. Herndon in 1870, later used by Ward Hill Lamon and by Herndon in their biographies of Lincoln, Fell said that Lincoln's Christianity could be "summed up . . . in these two propositions: the Fatherhood of God, and the brotherhood of man." Perhaps they could be, but it should be carefully noted that Fell inherited from his mother distinctly liberal religious leanings, became a founder of the Unitarian church in Bloomington, and, Herndon says, gave Lincoln a set of the works of Unitarian luminary William Ellery Channing. The simple creed Fell described was certainly that of a Unitarian; whether it was Lincoln's also is a matter of considerable doubt and controversy.

Fell had little contact with Lincoln during the Civil War, though in 1863 he advised that Kentucky was so opposed to emancipation that to raise 20,000 more soldiers from that state would be to raise 20,000 soldiers for the Confederacy, for they would surely desert to the other side. After the war he continued his promotional activities and his work in behalf of the Republican party. He became a Liberal Republican in 1872 and championed David Davis for the party's presidential nomination (against Norman Judd's favorite, Lyman Trumbull). Both Davis and Trumbull failed, and Fell supported Horace Greeley in the election. In 1877 he aided Davis's election to the United States Senate. He died in 1887.

SOURCES: *The Life of Jesse W. Fell* by Frances Milton I. Morehouse (Urbana: University of Illinois, 1916) is a slender biography, particularly weak on politics. Fell's role in the controversy over Lincoln's religion is discussed in William J. Wolf's *The Almost Chosen People: A Study of the Religion of Abraham Lincoln* (Garden City, N.Y.: Doubleday, 1959).

See also AUTOBIOGRAPHY.

Fellowships, Lincoln Private societies formed to celebrate and learn about Lincoln's life. The fellowships have evolved in various ways. The first was the Lincoln Association of Jersey City, New Jersey, which has held a Lincoln banquet every year since 1865. The Abraham Lincoln Association, founded in Springfield, Illinois, in 1908, was by far the most important group (see entry herein). The Old Salem-Lincoln League (1917) of Petersburg, Illinois, spearheaded the restoration of Lincoln's New Salem. Many groups followed, but none evolved, as the Abraham Lincoln Association did, into a research and publishing organization. The others met from one to twelve times yearly to hear Lincoln students, authorities, collectors, and buffs speak.

The Lincoln Fellowship of Wisconsin, founded in 1940, still meets yearly and publishes its annual address. The Lincoln Group of Boston (1938) still meets four times a year. Other fellowships founded were the Lincoln Club of Los Angeles (1921), the Lincoln Group of Delaware (1929), the Lincoln Group of Chicago (1931), the Lincoln Association of Ohio (1935), the Lincoln Group of Southern California (1935), the Lincoln Group of the District of Columbia (1935), the Lincoln Club of Long Beach (California, 1937), the Detroit Lincoln Group (1939), the Cincinnati Lincoln Fellowship (1941), the Lincoln Memorial Association of Redlands (California, 1941), and the Lincoln Group of New York (1978). The Fellowships have declined in number in recent years, and some mentioned above are no longer active.

SOURCES: For information on active groups write the Louis A. Warren Lincoln Library and Museum, 1300 S. Clinton Street, Fort Wayne, IN 46801.

See also ABRAHAM LINCOLN ASSOCIATION.

Fessenden, William Pitt (1806–1869) Lincoln's Secretary of the Treasury for eight months. Fessenden was an illegitimate child born in New Hampshire but raised in Maine. He graduated from Bowdoin College and became a lawyer (1827). He lived most of his mature life in Portland, where he became an active Whig politician.

Fessenden was elected to the United States Senate in 1854 and very quickly voiced sharp opposition to the Kansas-Nebraska Bill. He became a Republican, was reelected Senator in 1859, and was pleased when his rival for Republican leadership in Maine, Hannibal Hamlin, became a vice-presidential candidate in 1860, for it removed Hamlin from state politics. He opposed compromise in the secession crisis and urged Lincoln not to take Simon Cameron into his Cabinet.

Fessenden became Chairman of the Senate Finance Committee. His views were characterized by general support for Treasury Secretary Salmon P. Chase's policies, though he voted reluctantly for the bill which allowed issuing legal-tender notes and tended to advocate stiffer taxation in its stead. Likewise, he reluctantly supported the National Currency Act of 1863, which established a national banking system, under pressure from Lincoln and Chase. Missouri Senator John B. Henderson noted that the "able" Fessenden went "as far in extreme notions looking to the protection of the Treasury as any gentleman in Congress."

Fessenden thought little of Lincoln's abilities at first and felt the President was the mere tool of William H. Seward. Early in 1862 he quipped that "If the President had his wife's *will* and would use it rightly, our affairs would look much better." On December 18 and 19, 1862, he participated in the movement of Republican Senators to force Seward's removal. When the movement failed, he blamed "the weak squeamishness of our friend Chase. . . . He will never be forgiven . . . for deliberately sacrificing his friends to the fear of offending his and their enemies." He disliked the suppression of civil liberties in the North, but in public he always defended the President on this score. He thought Lincoln "McClellan-mad" as well and wished that general removed long before he was.

Lincoln apparently regarded Fessenden as something of a Radical, though most historians since have deemed him a moderate Republican. The son of an abolitionist, Fessenden did not follow in his father's footsteps. He did criticize Lincoln's revocation of John C. Frémont's emancipation order in 1861 as "a weak and unjustifiable concession to the Union men of the border States." He voted for the second Confiscation Act only reluctantly and worked with other members of Congress to meet President Lincoln's objections to the bill. He realized that Lincoln was sure to win the Republican nomination for 1864 and stayed clear of the Chase movement. He thought the President's Proclamation of Amnesty and Reconstruction of December 8, 1863, too weak, but he thought the Wade-Davis Bill too radical and was not present for the roll-call vote on it. Gradually, he had become more reconciled to Lincoln's leadership, recognizing that "the people have a strong faith in his honesty of purpose."

When Chase left the Cabinet at the end of June 1864, Fessenden reluctantly succeeded him as Secretary of the Treasury. Fessenden did not seek to issue more legal-tender notes and instead initiated more large government loans. He tried to market them through the national bank system and at first spurned the services of financial wizard Jay Cooke, a Philadelphia financier who had been broker for previous government bond-selling drives. On January 28, 1865, Fessenden reinstated Cooke as general agent for selling government loans, in part because of Lincoln's advice. Such advice came rarely. Fessenden characterized the President late in the summer of 1864 as

> too busy looking after the elections to think of anything else. I am glad it is so, for the less he interferes in other matters the better for all concerned. Yet he is a man of decided intellect and a good fellow, able to do well any one thing if he was able or content to confine his attention to that thing until it was done. In attempting to do too many things he botches them all.

On March 3, 1865, Fessenden, who had been reelected to the Senate in January, resigned his Cabinet post to reclaim his seat in Congress. He maintained a moderate course during Reconstruction, and he worked to compromise differences between President Andrew Johnson and Congress until Johnson's vetoes of the Freedmen's Bureau and Civil Rights Bills. Thereafter, he broke with the President but voted "not guilty" at Johnson's impeachment trial in 1868.

SOURCES: Charles A. Jellison's *Fessenden of Maine: Civil War Senator* (Syracuse, N.Y.: Syracuse University Press, 1962) is bland but competent. Frances Fessenden's *Life and Public Services of William Pitt Fessenden* (Boston: Houghton, Mifflin, 1907) reprints some interesting letters. Senator Henderson's characterization of Fessenden is in his letter to Edward Bates (July 18, 1862), Abraham Lincoln Papers, Library of Congress.

Ficklin, Orlando Bell (1808–1886)

An Illinois legal associate of Lincoln's. Ficklin, a Kentuckian by birth, in 1830 graduated from Transylvania Law School and moved to Illinois. He settled in Charleston (in Coles County) in 1837. He was elected to the Illinois House of Representatives in 1834, 1838, and 1842 and served as a United States Congressman from 1843 to 1849 and from 1851 to 1853.

RUNNING THE "MACHINE".

This Currier & Ives cartoon of the 1864 presidential campaign featured Secretary of the Treasury William Pitt Fessenden, who continued to grind out paper money from [Salmon P.] "Chase's Patent Greenback Mill." Lincoln appears as a shallow jokester oblivious to the chaos of incompetences. Stanton boasts of minuscule victories, and Secretary of the Navy Gideon Welles seems simple-minded. Secretary of State William H. Seward demands the arrest of someone who "has called me 'A Humbug,'" a reference to Seward's alleged boast of being able to have anyone thrown into federal prison merely by ringing a little bell.

Fillmore, Millard

Orlando Bell Ficklin. (Courtesy of the Illinois State Historical Library)

Ficklin met Lincoln in Vandalia in 1835, when both men were serving as freshmen Whig legislators. He became a Democrat in 1842, but legal work brought the two men together occasionally even when politics tended to separate them.

During Lincoln's Charleston debate with Stephen A. Douglas on September 18, 1858, Ficklin sat on the platform with the speakers. When Lincoln answered Douglas's charge that he had opposed his country's cause in the Mexican War, he pushed Ficklin forward and insisted that the Charleston resident knew he had voted for supplies for the soldiers even while he attacked the war as unconstitutional and unnecessary. Ficklin, who had served in Congress with Lincoln during the war, replied: "Mr. Lincoln and myself are just as good personal friends as Judge Douglas and myself." He recalled only that Lincoln had voted for George Ashmun's amendment calling the war unconstitutional and unnecessary. In the debate in Alton on October 15, Douglas noted the inconclusiveness of Ficklin's remarks.

In July 1864 Ficklin visited Washington to plead with President Lincoln for the release of Charleston citizens involved in a bloody riot with drunken Union veterans on March 28. Lincoln had almost been ready to turn the two indicted men over to the authorities and send the rest home when he received a thick military report which cast doubt on the innocence of all 15 men then imprisoned in Fort Delaware. Ficklin replied that the evidence in the report was "not only wholly ex parte but was taken when the town was a military Camp & the whole community was excited beyond description." Ficklin denounced "all resistance to or violation of law as much as any one can," but he was sure trials or taking new evidence would establish "the innocence of those not indicted." When that brought no response, Ficklin on September 10 sent Lincoln a letter from Thomas A. Marshall, "than whom no more ultra Republican lives in this latitude," which stressed "the insignificance & want of influence & of consequence of the . . . Coles Co prisoners." "Is the government afraid of a trial in open day?" he chided. Lincoln did not act until November 4, and then he followed his original inclination: he turned the two men indicted over to local authorities and released the rest.

After Lincoln's death Ficklin recalled his former associate as "a case lawyer" unsurpassed when he thought he was in the right and as a "statesman . . . deeply imbued with the principles of Henry Clay, but . . . conscientiously opposed to slavery all his life." Lincoln's true views supported "compensated emancipation," for Lincoln "did not wish to see rich men made poor by having their negroes freed without compensation."

SOURCES: There is a good sketch of Ficklin in Charles H. Coleman, *Abraham Lincoln and Coles County, Illinois* (New Brunswick, N.J.: Scarecrow Press, 1955). Usher F. Linder assessed Ficklin's personality in his *Reminiscences of the Early Bench and Bar of Illinois* (Chicago: Chicago Legal News Company, 1879). Ficklin's letters to Lincoln about the evidence in the Charleston riot case (July 22, 1864) and about Thomas A. Marshall's views (September 10, 1864) are in the Abraham Lincoln Papers, Library of Congress.

Fillmore, Millard (1800–1874) Whig President (1850–1853). Millard Fillmore received Lincoln's support as Zachary Taylor's vice-presidential running mate in 1848. By 1856, however, Lincoln opposed Fillmore, now the Know-Nothing (American) party's nominee for President, and supported John C. Frémont, the first Republican presidential candidate. Lincoln accused Fillmore of straddling the vital issue of the day, slavery in the territories. He ridiculed Fillmore's willingness on the one hand to condemn the Democrats for allowing slavery into the territories with the Kansas-Nebraska Act and on the other to vow not to interfere with slavery in the territories thus opened. "Fillmore," Lincoln quipped, ". . . will go out of this contest the most national man we have. He has no prospect of having a single vote on either side of Mason and Dixon's line, to trouble his poor soul about." He equated a vote for Fillmore with a vote for James Buchanan, the Democratic candidate, because Fillmore had no chance to carry Illinois and Buchanan could win by splitting the opposition. Mrs. Lincoln, on the other hand, found her "weak woman's heart . . . too Southern in feeling, to sympathise with any but Fillmore, I have always been a great admirer of his, he made so good a President & and is so just a man & feels the *necessity* of keeping foreigners, within bounds."

"I see by the papers this morning, that Mr. Fillmore

Henry Louis Stephens, hearing of Franklin Pierce's proposal that the five living ex-Presidents convene to suggest a compromise solution for the war, depicted Lincoln's living predecessors in office as haggling spinsters actually responsible for the war. Millard Fillmore himself is indecisive. The cartoon appeared in Vanity Fair on May 11, 1861.

refuses to go with us," Lincoln noted on June 5, 1860. Lincoln was by that time the Republican presidential nominee. Fillmore had no use for the Republicans, who refused to compromise with the South and refused as yet to guarantee the execution of the fugitive slave laws. He also found fault with the Democrats, particularly with President Buchanan's refusal to "coerce a state" when South Carolina seceded. The secession convention, the ex-President thought, should have been treated as an "unlawful assembly" of men "conspiring to commit treason." On February 17, 1861, the Fillmores, who lived in Buffalo, New York, took Lincoln, on his inaugural journey, to Buffalo's First Unitarian Church. In the evening the two men went to a public meeting in behalf of Indians.

When war broke out, Fillmore rushed to the colors. On April 16, 1861, he led a pro-Union demonstration in Buffalo and pledged $500 to support the families of volunteers. He quickly organized the Union Continentals, a group of old but distinguished Buffalo citizens, who performed ceremonial functions, gave to charity for volunteers, and generally increased war spirit. He also badgered Washington officials for guns and men to defend Buffalo and the Erie Canal from possible British invasion from Canada, which he feared was invited by the weakened condition of the United States.

In 1863 Fillmore wrote the President to ask for a court of inquiry in the case of his nephew, First Lieutenant George M. Fillmore, who was dismissed from the army for intemperance. Lincoln asked the Judge Advocate General to investigate, but no action was taken. Whether or not this sharpened Fillmore's initial distrust of the Republicans for causing what the ex-President regarded as an unnecessary war and heightened his war-weariness, in February 1864 he made a sudden about-face. At the Great Central Fair of the Ladies Christian Commission, he declared the war a failure. Peace would require that "much must be forgiven, if not forgotten." When the North conquered the Confederate armies, it should restore the South "to all their rights under the Constitution." This was an election year, and Fillmore, fearing "military despotism," decided that there must be a change in administration. He privately supported George B. McClellan before the Democratic convention nominated the general for President and openly endorsed him afterward. Republican indignation against Fillmore ran high.

When Lincoln was assassinated, Fillmore was out of town and unable to drape his doorway in mourning. An irate townsman smeared the doorway with ink. When Fillmore returned, he showed the proper mourning symbols and headed the committee which met the Lincoln funeral train and escorted it to Buffalo.

SOURCES: Robert G. Rayback's *Millard Fillmore: Biography of a President* (Buffalo, N.Y.: Henry Stewart, 1959) devotes a chapter to Fillmore's life during the sectional crisis and the Civil War.

Finances, Personal Although the poverty of Lincoln's youth has been somewhat exaggerated—in an 1814 tax book his father stood fifteenth in taxable wealth among 98 persons listed—his father was not able to give him any advantages in the race of life. Until he was 21, the wages Lincoln earned as a farmhand and flatboatman were legally his father's. In 1831 he earned the first money of his own by working for $12 a month to build a flatboat to take produce to New Orleans for frontier merchant Denton Offutt. He earned $10 a month when he guided the boat to New Orleans. Offutt then made Lincoln a clerk in a general store in New Salem, but the store failed in 1832. Joining to fight in the Black Hawk War that year was an economic necessity for the jobless Lincoln. When he returned, Lincoln became a partner in a general store with William F. Berry. They went in debt to purchase the stock and went deeper and more hopelessly in debt while Berry drank himself to death and neglected the business. By 1835 Lincoln's indebtedness and the debt of his partner (which Lincoln assumed when Berry died) was probably about $1100, a sum so large that Lincoln referred to it humorously as the "National Debt." Fees he earned as New Salem's postmaster and as deputy surveyor for the county merely "kept soul and body together."

Politics helped get Lincoln out of debt. Elected to the first of four consecutive terms in the state legislature in 1834, Lincoln benefited from the $3 per day salary and $3 per 20 miles travel allowance to and from Vandalia (each raised to $4 in his second term).

Even more important was the practice of law which Lincoln commenced in 1837. Lincoln had three partnerships in succession, but in all of them the business was built on the same principle: small fees of $10 or $20 and a large number of cases. In one day his firm might well have 10 or more cases called in court. With his first partner, John Todd Stuart (1837–1841), and his third, William H. Herndon (1844–1861), he split fees evenly; he may have got only a third of the fee in cases with his second partner, Stephen Trigg Logan (1841–1844). As early as the 1840s Lincoln's income from the law was probably a respectable $1500 to $2000 a year. "The matter of fees is important," Lincoln chided would-be lawyers; and though his own fees were not high, he was zealous in collecting them and at times resorted to suits to claim his fees.

By the mid-1840s Lincoln had probably paid off his debt. After he returned from Congress in 1849, he began to lend money at 10 percent interest. He speculated a bit in property, mostly town lots. After the failure of the State Bank of Illinois in 1842, Lincoln used the Springfield Marine and Fire Insurance Company as the next best thing to a bank, and Robert Irwin, the company's cashier, was Lincoln's financial agent until Lincoln's death.

When Lincoln paid attention to his practice, his income was substantial. Though fees continued to be typically under $100 in the 1850s, his work for the Illinois Central Railroad was lucrative, and in 1857 he asked, and received after a suit, an enormous $5000 fee in a tax case for the railroad against McLean County. But he often neglected his practice for politics, which, since he held no office in the 1850s, was nothing but a drain on his finances. He served as a presidential elector in 1840, 1844, 1852, and 1856. The duty required extensive traveling and speaking, as did his own political efforts. For the most part, he financed his campaigns out of his own pocket. The 1858 campaign for the Senate against Stephen A. Douglas left Lincoln "absolutely without money . . . for even household expenses." He talked often in his life of having to return diligently to legal work to replenish his resources after periods of political activity. His presidential campaign was another matter. In it, a group of 10 Illinois Republicans subscribed about $12,500 at various times to pay for campaign expenses, though Lincoln did not travel himself or do any public speaking.

When Lincoln left for Washington, his estate was about $15,000; when he died a little over 4 years later, it amounted to over $85,000. The difference was for the most part the money he saved from his $25,000 annual salary as President. He did most of his banking at Riggs & Co., and he was sufficiently indifferent to money that he left four of his salary warrants uncashed in his desk and no will at his death. He had, Herndon said years later, "no avarice of the *get* but he had the avarice of the *keep.*" And his reputation for honesty in money matters was well earned. The forerunner of the credit-rating firm of Dun & Bradstreet called Lincoln "Trustw[orth]y," "a G[oo]d man & to be relied on."

At Lincoln's death, his widow and his son Robert made David Davis administrator of the estate. Davis increased the estate to over $110,000 before relinquishing his duties in 1867, when the estate was divided equally among Mrs. Lincoln and sons Thomas and Robert.

SOURCES: Harry E. Pratt's *The Personal Finances of Abraham Lincoln* (Springfield, Ill.: Abraham Lincoln Association, 1943) is definitive. See also Ann M. Scanlon, "Dun & Bradstreet's Credit Rating of Abraham Lincoln," *Lincoln Herald*, LXXVII (Summer 1975), 124.

First Inaugural Address Lincoln's First Inaugural Address, delivered on March 4, 1861, was written in Springfield in January. By way of preparation, according to William H. Herndon, Lincoln used "Henry Clay's great speech delivered in 1850; Andrew Jackson's proclamation against Nullification; . . . a copy of the Constitution . . . and Webster's reply to Hayne."

Lincoln had the first draft set in type by the *Illinois State Journal* and circulated copies to David Davis, Orville H. Browning, Francis P. Blair, and William H. Seward. Browning and Seward offered important suggestions for revision. Lincoln accepted some of them and made revisions of his own before he delivered the address. The revisions made it a more conciliatory document, and J. G. Randall said truly "that Lincoln in Washington was more moderate than Lincoln in Springfield." The change was probably largely a result of Seward's influence; Seward suggested many little changes "in their general effect tending to soothe the public mind."

The address began by trying to calm Southern fears of aggressive Republican intentions. Lincoln omitted an original assertion of intent to abide by the Republican platform (at Seward's suggestion) and began by repeating his assurance that he had "no purpose, directly or indirectly, to interfere with the institution of slavery in the States where it exists." Near the end of the speech he expressed his lack of objection to a constitutional amendment guaranteeing that the federal government would never so interfere, and he mentioned favorably the possibility of a convention to amend the Constitution (another Seward idea). He also affirmed the constitutional necessity to enforce the return of fugitive slaves.

Lincoln asserted "that in contemplation of universal law, and of the Constitution, the Union of these States is perpetual" and that therefore he considered "the Union . . . unbroken." He argued that the Union was "much older than the Constitution," having been formed not in 1787 but in 1774 by "the Articles of Association." This is the only document in which Lincoln so dated the origin of the United States. Customarily, he dated its birth in 1776, and even here he noted that it "was matured and continued by the Declaration of Independence of 1776." Secession was "lawfully" impossible, and he had, by oath, to "take care, . . . that the laws of the Union be faithfully executed in all the States."

Having said that, Lincoln, as David M. Potter put it, quickly explained "that he would temporarily suspend the operation of the authority which he had so firmly asserted." He declared his intention only "to hold, occupy, and possess the property, and places belonging to the government" and eliminated (at Browning's suggestion) his statement that he would "reclaim" federal property. "Where hostility to the United States, in any interior locality" prevented local residents from holding federal offices, Lincoln would not "force obnoxious strangers among the people for that object." He would send the mails, "unless repelled."

Lincoln denied that "any right, plainly written in the Constitution," had been violated. Surely, there was no cause for secession, "the central idea" of which, anyway, was "the essence of anarchy" and would lead only to more and more secessions and fragmentation. He rejected the notion of allowing the Supreme Court to decide the important constitutional questions at issue as a surrender by the people of their right "to be their own rulers" and a practical resignation of "their government, into the hands of that eminent tribunal."

Lincoln's famous closing, suggested by Seward and improved stylistically by Lincoln, underlined the overall point of the speech, its appeal to the idea of Union:

> I am loth to close. We are not enemies, but friends. We must not be enemies. Though passion may have strained, it must not break our bonds of affection. The mystic chords of memory, stre[t]ching from every battle-field, and patriot grave, to every living heart and hearthstone, all over this broad land, will yet swell the chorus of the Union, when again touched, as surely they will be, by the better angels of our nature.

Newspaper reaction to the speech was predictably partisan, and Lincoln's address did little to calm the secessionist forces in the South.

SOURCES: John G. Nicolay and John Hay's third volume of *Abraham Lincoln: A History* (New York: Century, 1890) treats the genesis of the speech thoroughly. David M. Potter's analysis in *Lincoln and His Party in the Secession Crisis* (New Haven: Yale University Press, 1942) emphasizes the conciliatory nature of the speech. J. G. Randall's treatment in volume one of *Lincoln the President: Springfield to Gettysburg* (New York: Dodd, Mead, 1945) is succinct and offers a compact survey of reactions to the address.

Fish, Daniel (1848–1924) One of the "Big Five" who dominated Lincoln collecting at the turn of the century. Daniel Fish was born on a farm in Cherry Valley, Illinois, and educated in the public schools in Winnebago County. On January 4, 1864, he enlisted in the 45th Illinois Infantry. Mustered out on July 12, 1865, he moved to Iowa, where he became a lawyer. He moved to Minnesota in 1872, briefly edited the Delano *Eagle*, and became probate judge in Wright County (1876–1879). In 1880 he moved to Minneapolis, where he served as counsel for several important corporations. In 1901 he served as chairman of a commission to revise and codify the laws of Minnesota. From 1914 to 1921 he was a district judge.

Fish was 44 years old when an invitation to give a speech on Lincoln to the men's club of the Park Avenue Congregational Church first prompted him to seek materials on the sixteenth President. From that time on he was "bitten by the bug of Lincoln bibliomania." By 1909 he had amassed a collection of well over 1000 books and pamphlets as well as a modest collection of manuscripts and memorabilia. His greatest contribution was his compilation of the *Lincoln Bibliography: A List of Books and Pamphlets Relating to Abraham Lincoln* (New York: Francis D. Tandy, 1906). This was "the first comprehensive bibliography of Lincolniana," in Lincoln bibliographer Jay Monaghan's words, and it established the definitions and standards for classifying Lincolniana. It became the guidebook for many collectors. A realist, Fish admitted that he "could pick out fewer than a hundred titles containing everything of substance in the whole 1400," but he got "lots of fun out of the effort to gather up the whole outfit." He could casually refer to his collection as his "Lincoln rubbish," but he could also say: "As a son of Illinois and a boy soldier of the Union," he "rejoiced to contribute in this humble way to the continued fame of his great compatriot and commander, whose matchless qualities of heart and brain are celebrated in a special literature, more copious and more brilliant than the life of any other American has evoked."

Fish died on February 9, 1924, and was buried on Lincoln's birthday. In 1930 the Lincoln National Life Insurance Company acquired his collection, which is now the basis of the Louis A. Warren Lincoln Library and Museum in Fort Wayne, Indiana.

SOURCES: See Jay Monaghan, *Lincoln Bibliography, 1809–1939*, 2 vols. (Springfield: Illinois State Historical Library, 1943–1945). All the Fish quotations but the last are from his letter to I. N. Phillips, April 22, 1909, in the Louis A. Warren Lincoln Library and Museum. The last is from Fish's *Lincoln Literature* (Minneapolis: Public Library Board, 1900).

Daniel Fish in his office.

Florville, William See NEGROES.

Ford, Thomas (1800–1850) Governor of Illinois and early historian of the state's politics in the era of Lincoln's legislative career. Thomas Ford was born in Fayette County, Pennsylvania, but moved to Illinois in 1804. He was the half brother of prominent Illinois Democrat George Forquer and became Forquer's law partner in Edwardsville (1825–1829). Afterward he was state's attorney in Galena and Quincy (1829–1835), circuit judge (1835–1837), judge of the Chicago municipal court (1837–1839), circuit judge again (1839–1841), and state supreme court judge (1841–1842). When Democratic gubernatorial candidate Adam W. Snyder died in 1842, Ford was quickly chosen to replace him and won election. As governor, he dealt sternly with financial depression and the effects of the failure of the internal improvements system of which Lincoln had been a principal supporter. Before his death from tuberculosis, Ford completed his *History of Illinois from Its Commencement as a State in 1818 to 1847*.

Thomas Ford. (Courtesy of the Illinois State Historical Library)

Although he scarcely mentioned Lincoln (and then misspelled his name as "Abram"), the picture of Illinois politics in Ford's *History of Illinois* (1854) has been adopted by many Lincoln biographers and historians—to the detriment of Lincoln's reputation. Ford held "that a public man will scarcely ever be forgiven for being right when the people are wrong." Illinois's politicians courted popularity at the expense of the public good. "Surly and stubborn wisdom stood no chance for office"; the people preferred "men who were loved for their gaiety, cheerfulness, apparent goodness of heart, and agreeable manners." The "race of politicians" was "more numerous and more popular . . . than the race of statesmen." Newspapers exploited political excitement, for editors knew "that their most profitable harvest is during an excited contest."

The advent of national parties meant that local officials were chosen by their reputations on national issues, and the people rarely "elected members of the legislature with reference to any well-defined notions of State policy." The disastrous internal improvements scheme was not so much the people's folly as the result of "logrolling" in the state legislature. Ford singled out Sangamon County's "Long Nine" for bargaining to vote for internal improvements for any area whose representatives would in turn support the removal of the state capital from Vandalia to Springfield.

In truth, the Long Nine voted together on only 5 of 25 roll calls in which logrolling was possible. Ford had a peculiarly jaundiced view of party politics. He had spent most of his career as a judge, well removed from the customary means of legislative management. He became governor not by working his way up through the political system, but almost by accident and at the very last minute. He was shocked by the unfamiliar workings of the political system in the legislature. That shock and his terminal illness made his history a sour affair indeed.

SOURCES: Ford's cynical book was published after his death (Chicago: S. C. Griggs, 1854). Lincoln apparently read the book, because he referred to it in the Lincoln-Douglas Debates. Paul Simon's *Lincoln's Preparation for Greatness: The Illinois Legislative Years* (Norman: University of Oklahoma Press, 1965) refuted the logrolling charge. "The Illinois Bookshelf," *Journal of the Illinois State Historical Society*, XXXVIII (March 1945), 99–104, carefully explains the reasons for Ford's jaundiced view of party politics. See also Mark E. Neely, Jr., "A 'Great Fraud'? Politics in Thomas Ford's *History of Illinois*," *Lincoln Lore*, Number 1687 (September 1978), pp. 1–4.

Ford's Theatre The theater on 10th Street, between E and F Streets, in Washington, D.C., that was the site of Lincoln's assassination. Theatrical manager John T. Ford built the theater in 1863 on the ashes of another theater of his, a converted Baptist church which burned down. The theater could pack in as many as 1700 Washington theatergoers a night. After John Wilkes Booth shot President Lincoln at Ford's Theatre on April 14, 1865, Secretary of War Edwin M. Stanton had guards placed at the theater. Desiring no symbolic or commercial exploitation of the assassination site, Stanton worked to prevent the theater from opening again. When owner Ford announced his intention to reopen the theater in June 1865, public outrage led the government to rent the building from Ford at $1500 a month. Soon the government purchased the building for $100,000 and converted it into a three-floor office building. It held the Record and Pension Bureau of the War Department. All three floors collapsed in 1893, killing 22 people.

In 1932 Congress appropriated money to convert Ford's Theatre, used only for storage after its transfer from the War Department in 1928, into a museum to house Osborn H. Oldroyd's outstanding Lincoln collection. It remained a museum until 1964, when it was closed to be restored by the National Park Service to look as it did when Booth shot Lincoln. The Ford's Theatre Society raised enough money to make the theater a place for performances once again, and it reopened in 1968. The museum was placed in the basement, and it is now one of the most popular Lincoln sites in the country.

SOURCES: The National Park Service provides an informative pamphlet on *Ford's Theatre and the House Where Lincoln Died* by Stanley W. McClure; the price is available from the Superintendent of Documents, Washington, DC 20402.

See also OLDROYD, OSBORN HAMILTON INGHAM.

The exterior of Ford's Theatre as it looked at the time of Lincoln's assassination.

Forney, John Wien or Wein (1817–1881) Philadelphia journalist and editor of the nearest thing to an administration organ during the Civil War. John W. Forney was, for much of his early career, a Democrat identified with the ambitions of James Buchanan. When Buchanan became President, Forney failed to receive the reward he thought his due, and, when Stephen A. Douglas broke with Buchanan over Kansas policy in 1857, Forney became a Douglas supporter. In 1860 Forney's Philadelphia *Press* supported Douglas for President. The editor later told Lincoln that he thought he "could better promote" Lincoln's election "by standing up for Douglas" and splitting the Democrats than by running "forward into a direct support" of Lincoln. Whatever the case, by December 1860, he was definitely a Republican, and early the next year he defended Lincoln from the charge that the President-elect entered Washington for his inauguration disguised in a Scotch cap and cape.

Forney claimed in later years that Lincoln reached out to him for support by writing him a letter commending his opposition to Buchanan and that he replied by recommending Horace Greeley for the Cabinet. In truth, Forney's letter about Greeley, dated November 12, 1860, does not appear to be an answer to a letter from Lincoln. Ten days later he urged Pennsylvania's Simon Cameron for the Cabinet (though Cameron had defeated Forney in a race for the Senate in 1857) and reminded Lincoln of the satisfaction the appointment would give "to those large interests that look to the Tariff as their whole political creed." In 1861 Forney failed to be elected Clerk of the House of Representatives, but in the summer Lincoln "took the trouble to call upon Senators, and to insist" that Forney be elected Secretary of the Senate, a post he held until 1868.

Soon Forney was working closely with the administration; he wrote an article based upon Lincoln's "suggestions" as early as August 1861. Forney brought into line not only his Philadelphia paper but also his Washington paper, the *Sunday Morning Chronicle*, which on November 3, 1862, became the *Daily Morning Chronicle*. Each day, 10,000 copies of the *Chronicle* went to the Army of the Potomac. Forney was constantly urging more recognition of Democrats who supported the war effort, but publicly he hewed faithfully to the administration's policies with never a critical editorial. Two of his sons received military commissions, but the editor described his Washington newspaper to Lincoln as "a loyal paper, honestly conducted, and steadily devoted to you and your policy, without being concerned in a single 'job' (except Job Printing)."

Forney seems to have relished his role as a wielder of influence with the administration. He wrote numerous letters of introduction to the President, sent frequent recommendations for office, and asked many favors for friends. He did not always get his way. He "begged" Lincoln to appoint a Democrat to replace Philadelphia's deceased Federal District Attorney, but Lincoln did not. Gradually, Forney complained in 1864, "the old Whig party, and the old Bell & Everett party consumed all the offices" in Philadelphia. Still, Forney had influence as great as that of any editor. He persuaded Lincoln to keep the Philadelphia postmaster from using his patronage against the reelection of Congressman William D. Kelley in 1864, and he had Lincoln ask the Treasury Secretary to allow a Philadelphia merchant to receive a shipment of cotton from one of his Arkansas debtors in the same year. He had frequent interviews with the President and was careful to write nothing of which the administration would disapprove. When he prepared an article in 1864 proving that Republican control of the House of Representatives would mean that George B. McClellan could not be elected President even if he could throw the election into the House, Forney thought it a "snorter" but promised Lincoln: "I will not print till I see and read it *to you*."

In 1864 Forney went to great lengths for Lincoln's reelection. He campaigned in Pennsylvania and joined with a partner to buy a formerly Democratic newspaper in Reading, a move which made the partners responsible for a debt of $8000. He was especially delighted to see that "the *rich* men: men who have never before taken any part except to vote, and many . . . old Democrats" were the "most active" for Lincoln's reelection. Despite his role as champion of loyal Democrats, Forney's opinions on slavery seem to have tended in a radical direction. He admired Edwin M. Stanton but was detested by Montgomery Blair. When Blair left the Cabinet in 1864, Forney hoped for "an *ultra radical*" replacement. However, he had had no trouble defending Lincoln's policies before the Emancipation Proclamation.

Forney became a critic of President Andrew Johnson. In 1870 he returned to Philadelphia from Washington. By 1880 he had also returned to the Democratic party.

SOURCES: Forney's letters to Lincoln about Douglas, his election as Senate Secretary, and Philadelphia patronage (October 24, 1864), about Greeley (November 22, 1860), about the suggested article (August 16, 1861), and about the "*rich* men" and the "snorter" (September 24, 1864) are in the Abraham Lincoln Papers, Library of Congress. He wrote *Anecdotes of Public Men* (New York: Harper & Brothers, 1873). Though weak on the Civil War years, Roy F. Nichols's sketch of Forney in the *Dictionary of American Biography* (New York: Charles Scribner's Sons, 1958), III, 526–527, is an otherwise able treatment of a man curiously neglected by biographers.

Fort Jefferson Place of imprisonment for Dr. Samuel A. Mudd, Samuel Arnold, Michael O'Laughlin, and Ed-

John W. Forney. (Courtesy of The Historical Society of Pennsylvania)

Fort Jefferson National Monument. (Courtesy of the National Park Service)

man Spangler, who were convicted of conspiring with John Wilkes Booth, Lincoln's assassin. Built in 1846 to protect the Gulf of Mexico, Fort Jefferson is a giant six-sided polygon enclosing most of a 16-acre island called Garden Key, which is one of seven coral islets called the Dry Tortugas. Garden Key lies almost 70 miles west of Key West, Florida.

The fort was never finished but was garrisoned during the Civil War. After the war, it served as a prison for political prisoners. The Lincoln conspirators were sentenced first to the Albany penitentiary, but Secretary of War Edwin M. Stanton persuaded President Andrew Johnson to send them to Fort Jefferson, beyond the jurisdiction of any civil courts, out of fear that the civil courts might review the legality of the military trial of Booth's associates. They remained there from July 1865 until February 1869, when President Johnson pardoned the survivors.

The advent of rifled artillery had made Fort Jefferson useless militarily, and hurricane damage and a yellow fever epidemic led to its abandonment in 1874. It was declared a national monument in 1935. Accessible only by plane or boat, it is one of the most unusual sites maintained by the National Park Service. Information about it is available from the Superintendent, Everglades National Park, Box 279, Homestead, FL 33030.

Fort Pillow Massacre The killing on April 12, 1864, of a substantial part of a Federal garrison in Tennessee by soldiers under Confederate General Nathan Bedford Forrest. The "massacre" became a sensation because many of the Union soldiers were black. Six days later President Lincoln acknowledged that the "painful rumor" of the slaughter of unarmed men trying to surrender was "true I fear." It naturally led to "some anxiety in the public mind whether the government is doing its duty to the colored soldier." Lincoln admitted his responsibility for the use of Negro soldiers "to the American people, to the christian world, to history, and on my final account to God." But retaliation against Confederate prisoners would be "too cruel a mistake" if the rumor proved false. He would await the results of a thorough investigation, but if the massacre were proved to have happened, "the retribution shall . . . surely come."

By May 3 Lincoln was "quite certain" that a massacre occurred. While waiting for a final report, he asked for written opinions from the Cabinet. Four (William H. Seward, Salmon P. Chase, Edwin M. Stanton, and Gideon Welles) were for selecting hostages; three (John P. Usher, Edward Bates, and Montgomery Blair) recommended revenge only on the actual perpetrators of the massacre. The recommendations ranged in tone from the antislavery rage of Chase (who recommended retaliation against Confederate officers only, because they held the lives of privates supplied by the nonslaveholding classes cheap) to Bates's revulsion at entering a "compact . . . for mutual slaughter" or a "cartel of blood and murder." The Cabinet were genuinely perplexed and apparently decided to make the officers who commanded the massacres outlaws to be tried for murder if captured.

Despite his early promise of retribution, Lincoln was less excited than his Cabinet. On May 17 he drafted a letter instructing the Secretary of War to set aside a number of captured Confederate officers equal to those murdered (adopting Chase's view of the responsibility of the slaveholding class). As "blood can not restore blood, and government should not act for revenge," Lincoln sought Confederate assurance that no similar action would occur before returning those officers to their status as prisoners of war. Confederate prisoners equal in number to captured Negro soldiers would be set aside for exchange. If there were no response, he would assume the Negroes were murdered or returned to slavery and take appropriate action.

Nothing came of his letter. Indeed, there is no evidence Lincoln finished it or that Stanton received it. As John G. Nicolay and John Hay put it, Grant's "Wilderness Campaign . . . crowded out of view and consideration a topic so difficult and so hazardous as wholesale retaliation." There "could be little doubt toward which [view] the kind heart of the President would incline."

SOURCES: John G. Nicolay and John Hay in *Abraham Lincoln: A History*, 10 vols. (New York: Century, 1890), VI, 477–484, give unsurpassed treatment of the event. Albert Castel's "The Fort Pillow Massacre: A Fresh Examination of the Evidence," *Civil War History*, IV (March 1958), 37–50, weighs the question of the existence and extent of the massacre.

See also BATES, EDWARD; BLAIR, MONTGOMERY; CHASE, SALMON PORTLAND; SEWARD, WILLIAM HENRY; STANTON, EDWIN MCMASTERS; USHER, JOHN PALMER; WELLES, GIDEON.

Fort Stevens *See* WASHINGTON, D.C.

Fort Sumter *See* SUMTER CRISIS.

Francis, Simeon (1796–1872) Editor of the Whig newspaper in Springfield, Illinois. Simeon Francis, who was born in Connecticut, published the Buffalo, New York, *Emporium* until 1828. When the anti-Masonic movement swept the area, Francis, a Mason, had to cease publication. In 1831 he settled in Springfield, where he published the *Sangamo Journal* (later the *Illinois State Journal*). The newspaper often opened its pages to Lincoln and vehemently supported the Whig cause. So vehement was it, in fact, that in 1840 Stephen A. Douglas attempted to cane Francis on the street—an occupational hazard of the highly partisan journalism of Lincoln's day. After Lincoln's engagement to Mary Todd fell through, Francis and his wife played a key role in getting them back together in 1842. In 1849 Lincoln worked to gain Francis's appointment as Secretary of Oregon Territory from the Zachary Taylor administration, noting that the editor had "for a long time desired to go to Oregon" and that his "good business habits are proved by the facts, that the paper has existed

Simeon Francis. (Courtesy of the Illinois State Historical Library)

eighteen years, all the time weekly, and part of it, triweekly, and daily, and has not failed to issue regularly in a single instance." Lincoln noted also that Francis had "advanced to the meridian of life without ever before asking for an office."

Francis did not receive the appointment and remained editor of the *Journal*. As the Whig party collapsed, he resisted "from policy and principle" giving the paper's support to the Know-Nothing (American) party, which was rapidly gathering support among old Whigs. In 1856 the Know-Nothings were cheered to hear that two young men planned to establish a new paper in Springfield. Francis feared that he could not sustain the paper in the face of the competition and sold out in June. He was angered that Lincoln, Stephen T. Logan, and other old Whig friends did not come around to promise to stand by him in a struggle with the proposed new paper.

Francis entered business but was badly hurt in the aftermath of the 1857 depression, and in 1859 he left for Oregon. Lincoln thought selling the paper and moving were both mistakes, and told Francis so. Nevertheless, before he left, Francis wrote an article for the *Journal*'s new editors promoting Lincoln for President in 1860. Francis became editor of the *Oregon Farmer*. In 1861 Lincoln appointed him an Army paymaster at Fort Vancouver, Washington Territory. He served until 1870, retired on half-pay, and died in Portland.

SOURCES: See the brief biographical sketch in Newton Bateman and Paul Selby, eds., *Historical Encyclopedia of Illinois* (Chicago: Munsell Publishing, 1900) and Francis's letter to Lincoln (December 26, 1859) about the Know-Nothings in the Abraham Lincoln Papers, Library of Congress.

Freedom of Speech   *See* HABEAS CORPUS; VALLANDIGHAM, CLEMENT LAIRD.

Freedom of the Press   *See* NEWSPAPERS.

Freeport, Illinois   Site of the second and most famous of the Lincoln-Douglas Debates, August 27, 1858. Freeport, in Stephenson County, was about 100 miles west of Chicago. The area was Republican in sentiment; it was represented in Congress by Elihu B. Washburne. Trains offering special excursion fares brought thousands to Freeport from Galena, Rockford, Chicago, and other northern Illinois towns. Crowd estimates ran as high as 15,000, about double the normal population of the town. Douglas arrived the night before and was greeted by a large torchlit procession. Lincoln arrived the next morning. The weather was cloudy, cool, and damp.

Some of Lincoln's political friends had thought their candidate was too defensive in the first debate (in Ottawa), and in this one he came out swinging. He answered the seven questions Douglas had asked at the end of the Ottawa debate: (1) The South was entitled by the Constitution to a fugitive slave law, and Lincoln was not about "to introduce it as a new subject of agitation." (2) Lincoln would dislike "to be put in a position of having to," but he would vote to admit a new slave state if the people there chose slavery after a territorial stage without slavery. (3) Therefore, he would vote to admit any new state with any constitution its people really wanted. (4) Though he would "be exceedingly glad to see slavery abolished in the District of Columbia," Lincoln would not urge the abolishment without allowing a vote on it by the people of the District. He would favor gradual emancipation with compensation to the masters. (5) Lincoln had never thought of abolishing the domestic slave trade. If, after study, he decided that abolition was constitutional, he would urge it only "upon some conservative principle," as he had urged abolition in the District of Columbia. (6) Lincoln affirmed that it was the *"right* and *duty* of Congress to prohibit slavery in all the United States Territories." (7) He would not oppose the "honest acquisition of" new territory, but an important consideration in any such possible acquisition would be the potential for aggravating the slavery controversy. Lincoln noted proudly that he was willing to give these answers "to a vast audience . . . strongly tending to Abolitionism."

Lincoln then asked his own questions: (1) Would Douglas vote to admit Kansas as a state before she had the population required for other territories to request statehood in the past? (2) Could the people of a territory really keep slavery out if, as Douglas had repeatedly affirmed, the Dred Scott decision were valid? (3) Would Douglas support a Supreme Court decision "that States can not exclude slavery from their limits"? (4) Did Douglas favor "acquiring additional territory, in disregard of how such acquisition may affect the nation on the slavery question"? Lincoln reiterated his charge that Douglas had falsely connected him with radical Republican resolutions drawn up in Illinois in 1854.

Douglas answered the questions. (1) If Kansas "has population enough to constitute a slave State, she has people enough for a free State." (2) Local police regulations could keep slavery out of a territory no matter what the Dred Scott decision said about Congress's inability to do so. (3) A Supreme Court decision forbidding states to exclude slavery was "not possible" and "would be an act of moral treason that no man on the bench could ever descend to." (4) To "increase, and multiply, and expand, is the law of this nation's existence," Douglas thundered. Adopting the doctrine of popular sovereignty would keep the slavery question from being a consideration in acquiring any new territory.

On his last visit to Freeport, Douglas charged, he had seen black abolitionist Frederick Douglass riding in a carriage with the wife and daughter of the white owner of the carriage, who was driving. That, he suggested, typified Republican radical policies. Douglas explained that he had erred about the 1854 Republican resolutions only in regard to the "spot" where they were drawn up, using a word which called to mind Lincoln's "Spot Resolutions," in opposition to the Mexican War. Besides, Republicans pledged to similar principles in other localities had voted for Lincoln for Senator in 1855. He renewed his charge that Lincoln and Lyman Trumbull had conspired to abolitionize the Whig and Democratic parties, respectively, in order to become Illinois's Senators.

Lincoln replied that his principles were well known. There were "minor differences," Lincoln admitted, between Republicans in the northern and southern parts of the state, but the two groups were united in the important resolve to oppose "a design to nationalize and perpetuate slavery." Lincoln used half his rebuttal time to argue that Douglas had accused others of conspiring to overthrow the right to exclude slavery from the territories when he was hoping to gain Republican support. Now, Lincoln said, "he is crawling back into his old camp, and you will find him eventually installed in full fellowship among those whom he was then battling, and with whom he now pretends to be at such fearful variance."

SOURCES: See Edwin Erle Sparks, ed., *The Lincoln-Douglas Debates of 1858* (Springfield: Illinois State Historical Library, 1908).

See also DEBATES, LINCOLN-DOUGLAS; FREEPORT QUESTION.

Freeport Question Asked of Stephen A. Douglas by Abraham Lincoln at Freeport, Illinois, on August 27, 1858, during the second Lincoln-Douglas Debate. It was the second in a series of four "interrogatories" and read thus: "Can the people of a United States Territory, in any lawful way, against the wish of any citizen of the United States, exclude slavery from its limits prior to the formation of a State Constitution?" The Dred Scott decision, which Douglas endorsed, had stated that Congress could not forbid slave property from entering the territories. Lincoln's question was meant to embarrass Douglas by showing that popular sovereignty in the territorial stage, before statehood, was impossible. Douglas's answer was that slavery was always sustained by local police regulations or slave codes, and that the territorial legislature could exercise local control and effectively exclude slavery by refusing to enact such regulations.

After the campaign a story emerged that Lincoln's advisers had thought their candidate should not ask the question for fear an affirmative answer would make Douglas look more like a free-soiler and thus all the more popular with Illinois's antislavery voters. Lincoln is reputed to have said, "I am after bigger game. The battle of 1860 is worth a hundred of this." In other words, he was sacrificing his chances for the Senate in 1858 and looking ahead to the presidential election in 1860. He would ruin Douglas with the Southern wing of the Democratic party, whose support was necessary for Douglas to win the Presidency in 1860. Lincoln could then win the larger prize in 1860.

There is not a shred of reliable evidence for the story, and it is utterly implausible in view of Lincoln's historical circumstances. Joseph M. Medill, editor of the Chicago *Press and Tribune*, claimed in 1895 to have advised Lincoln not to ask the question. But the Abraham Lincoln Papers at the Library of Congress, opened in 1947, contain a letter from Medill to Lincoln urging him to ask Douglas, "What becomes of your vaunted popular sovereignty in [the] Territories since the Dred Scott decision?" Horace White, who covered the debates for the Chicago *Press and Tribune*, also endorsed the "bigger game" story, claiming that Charles H. Ray, a *Press and Tribune* editor, described the conference to him. Ray, however, was on a business trip to the East at the time of the conference. The whole story is implausible because in 1858 Lincoln was hardly a presidential hopeful; it was his showing *in* the debates that made him one. Moreover, as Don E. Fehrenbacher says, "if Lincoln did propose to knock Douglas out of the presidential race, there was scarcely a better way of doing it than by ousting him from the Senate; for such a defeat on his home grounds would have been a staggering blow to the Little Giant's prestige."

To a substantial degree, Douglas had already burned his bridges to Southern support for the Presidency by opposing the Lecompton constitution for Kansas. Lincoln realized that as early as July; for he wrote to Henry Asbury, "He cares nothing for the South—he knows he is already dead there."

Lincoln asked the questions for the same reason he asked other questions of Douglas: He thought the answer would embarrass Douglas, and Lincoln's advisers felt their candidate needed a more aggressive image. Lincoln argued repeatedly in later debates that there was surely something unconstitutional about arguing for local legislation that prevented the exercise of a constitutional right—in this case, the right to carry slave property to the territories. He also argued that Douglas was saying that a territorial legislature, which derived its powers from Congress, could do what Congress itself could not do. The importance of the Freeport Question has been greatly exaggerated; it was only one question among several in the Lincoln-Douglas Debates.

SOURCES: There is a lucid and brilliant summary of the issues involved in and the literature on the Freeport Question in Don E. Fehrenbacher, *Prelude to Greatness: Lincoln in the 1850's* (Stanford: Stanford University Press, 1962).

Frémont, John Charles (1813–1890) General and Republican political rival of Abraham Lincoln. Frémont parlayed his fame as a Western explorer into the Republican nomination for the Presidency in 1856. Lincoln made some 50 speeches for Frémont in the campaign.

When Lincoln formed his administration four years later, it was clear that Frémont merited an office. Secretary of State William H. Seward suggested him for the Cabinet; Lincoln had thought of him for such an office but "not very definitely." Lincoln proposed him as minister to France, but Seward opposed the appointment; he feared Frémont would be involved in personal financial dealings in Paris, and he also discounted Frémont's loyalty for reason of the man's birth and education in South Carolina. On July 3, 1861, Lincoln appointed Frémont commander of the Department of the West, with headquarters at St. Louis. In a very brief period, General Frémont lost all of his standing with the Lincoln administration. The press unfairly blamed him for military defeats in Missouri. Many found him to be inaccessible, surrounded as he was by a comic-opera staff of foreign officers of improbable rank and title, and to be haphazard if not corrupt as an administrator.

President Lincoln became alarmed at Frémont's conduct when the general issued an order on August 30, 1861, which declared martial law in Missouri, threatened to court-martial and shoot citizens found with arms in their hands, and ordered the confiscation of the property and the freeing of slaves of active enemies of the Union. On September 2 Lincoln, fearing Frémont's proclamation might "ruin our rather fair prospect for Kentucky," ordered the general not to shoot anyone without his permission and requested that he alter his emancipation proclamation to conform with law "as of your own motion." Frémont told the President that he had "felt the position bad and saw danger." On the night of the 29th he had decided "upon the proclamation & the form of it." He had written it the next morning and had it printed the same day, acting "without consultation or advice with any one."

Frémont argued that the proclamation "was as much a movement in the war as a battle is" and said the President must "openly direct" him "to make the correction." Were he to "retreat" of his own accord, Frémont explained, "it would imply that I myself thought it wrong and that I had acted without reflection which the gravity of the point demanded." Lincoln quickly accepted the challenge and insisted that he change the order. Mrs. Frémont had hastened to Washington to remonstrate with Lincoln and bring her husband's message of refusal. The meeting was not a pleasant one, and Lincoln protested against "being understood as acting in any hostility toward" her husband.

If he had not been before, the proclamation made Lincoln receptive to Frémont's critics, the most virulent of whom was Francis P. Blair, Jr. Blair was Frémont's rival for control of Union sentiment in Missouri and the brother of Lincoln's Postmaster General Montgomery Blair. Earlier, relations between the Blairs and Frémont had been cordial. Francis P. Blair, Frank's father, had requested that Mrs. Frémont, the daughter of Missouri politician Thomas Hart Benton and a power to reckon with in the state, use her influence to make his son a major general of volunteers. By September Frémont had arrested Francis Blair, Jr., and threatened him with court martial. Blair, writing directly to his brother, the Postmaster General, rather than to his military superiors or the Secretary of War, had accused Frémont of military incompetence and financial corruption. He charged that Frémont had established "about his Head Quarters in the City of St. Louis, a barricade, whereby information absolutely indispensible to the public service was repelled and shut out from his mind." Montgomery Blair was closer to the President than Frémont was, and on the same day that Lincoln forced Frémont to change his proclamation the President also sent the Postmaster General and Montgomery Meigs to investigate the commander of the Department of the West. Lincoln's justifications for the informal investigation echoed General Blair's complaints. Lincoln felt Frémont needed "assis-

As early as October 26, 1861, Frank Leslie's Illustrated Newspaper *saw in Frémont's proclamation an attempt to reach for the 1864 Republican presidential nomination. President Lincoln's elbow rests firmly on the Constitution—unlike, the cartoon implies, Frémont's daring proclamation.*

LINCOLN—" Well, Master Fremont, that's rather a long reach, ain't it? You might fetch it with your sword, perhaps, in the proper time, but it isn't ripe yet."

tance" because he was "losing the confidence of men near him, whose support any man in his position must have to be successful." "His cardinal mistake," Lincoln added, "is that he isolates himself, & allows nobody to see him."

After further investigation by Secretary of War Simon Cameron, Congressman Elihu B. Washburne, and General Lorenzo Thomas, Lincoln relieved Frémont of command on October 24, 1861. That and the revocation of Frémont's proclamation were the most sensational political acts of the first year of the Lincoln administration. Many antislavery advocates, Westerners, and German-Americans saw Frémont as a martyr. Montgomery Blair worked feverishly and furtively to undo Frémont's reputation by proving that the general benefited directly from the corruption in letting military contracts under his command. In December he tried to procure testimony that Frémont had been involved in fraud before the war. "I do not want my name . . . brought out in the matter," Blair added. After Frank Blair attacked Frémont's Missouri campaign in a vicious speech in Congress on March 7, 1862, Lincoln felt it necessary to restore Frémont to command—this time, to the Mountain Department of Virginia. There Frémont unsuccessfully faced "Stonewall" Jackson in the Shenandoah Valley in May and June. When John Pope, a personal enemy, became commander of a consolidated Army of Virginia that included Frémont's forces as a corps, Frémont resigned.

The millionaire Frémont resumed business pursuits. He was especially interested in the movement to build a railway to the Pacific. In a public letter of April 24,

French, Daniel Chester

1863, he stated that it would be a good idea "to occupy immediately upon the work of the road, large bodies of the men who are freed by the President's Proclamation [of Emancipation]." Many of the freedmen would "soon require some provision to be made for them," and this would get them to the underpopulated West, which he thought well adapted to cultivating cotton, raising stock, and mining precious minerals. That summer, Frémont suggested that all the black soldiers should be concentrated in the West for a military campaign on the Mississippi Valley.

When the boom to make Salmon P. Chase Republican nominee failed in March 1864, Republican opponents of Lincoln began to focus their attention on Frémont. On May 31 a convention representing discontented Radical Republicans, German-Americans, and some War Democrats nominated Frémont for President. Frémont charged: "Today we have in this country the abuses of a military dictation without its unity of action and vigor of execution." His platform was radical, but he repudiated a plank calling for confiscation of rebel property and its distribution to Union soldiers and sailors. Lincoln evidently had little fear of this third-party threat, having told John Hay 9 days before the nomination that Frémont was "like Jim Jett's brother. Jim used to say that his brother was the damndest scoundrel that ever lived, but in the infinite mercy of Providence he was also the damndest fool."

Lincoln heeded Radical Republican opinion, however, and obtained Montgomery Blair's resignation from the Cabinet on September 23, 1864. The President may have extracted a promise of Frémont's withdrawal from the campaign as the price for removing Blair. The day before Blair's resignation Frémont had withdrawn from the presidential race with a grudging statement that Republicans must unite to defeat Democratic nominee George B. McClellan, who would restore slavery if he won the election; nevertheless, Frémont added, he considered the administration "politically, militarily, and financially a failure, and . . . its necessary continuance . . . a cause of regret for the country."

Frémont returned to railroad promotion, and in a disastrous series of ventures lost most of his enormous fortune by 1873. Tainted somewhat with financial corruption, the general lived out his life in relative poverty.

SOURCES: Allan Nevins's *Fremont: The West's Greatest Adventurer*, 2 vols. (New York: Harper & Brothers, 1928) is a readable and balanced biography. Lincoln's remark about Jim Jett's brother is in Tyler Dennett, ed., *Lincoln and the Civil War in the Diaries and Letters of John Hay* (New York: Dodd, Mead, 1939), p. 183. Frémont's letter to Lincoln about the proclamation (September 8, 1861), Frank Blair's charges (October 2, 1861), and Frémont's letter about the Pacific railroad (April 24, 1863) are in the Abraham Lincoln Papers, Library of Congress. Montgomery Blair's letter about Frémont's corruption (to H. L. Dawes, December 22, 1861) is in the Louis A. Warren Lincoln Library and Museum, Fort Wayne, Indiana.

See also BROWNING, ORVILLE HICKMAN; CHANDLER, ZACHARIAH; ELECTION OF 1864; SLAVERY.

French, Daniel Chester   *See* LINCOLN MEMORIAL.

Fugitive Slave Law   Lincoln's view of the Fugitive Slave Act of 1793 was simple, relatively consistent, and a hallmark of his Republicanism. He regarded the law as something which "springs of necessity from the fact that the institution [of slavery] is amongst us," and, therefore, as something about which, he told William H. Seward in 1861, "I care but little." He was much more interested in what would eventually remove slavery itself from the United States. Moreover, the Constitution required that "the fugitive slave *'shall be delivered up,'* " and Lincoln granted Congress the necessity of passing a law to effect the obligation. He carefully noted, however, that the word "slave" was not used in the clause in the Constitution—a sign to him that the founders were embarrassed even to mention the institution. Lincoln's own resolution to abolish slavery in the District of Columbia, submitted to Congress on January 10, 1849, included a provision for means to "deliver up to their owners, all fugitive slaves escaping into said District." As a lawyer, he took either side in cases involving fugitive slaves, despite his antislavery convictions.

The new, sterner Fugitive Slave Act that was a result of the Compromise of 1850 was never a favorite with him, but Lincoln wasted little time railing against it. In 1854 he said that, if "called upon by a Marshal, to assist in catching a fugitive slave, I should suggest to him that others could run a great deal faster than I could." He never believed private persons should be required to assist in executing the law. But he insisted that he would grant the South "any legislation for the reclaiming of their fugitives, which should not, in its stringency, be more likely to carry a free man into slav-

Lincoln's willingness to accept his constitutional duty to enforce the Fugitive Slave Law was the butt of this cartoon by Henry Louis Stephens in Vanity Fair, *September 15, 1860. Lincoln promises William L. Yancey, a leader of Southern secession, that he will take care of his fugitive slave "nag" if Yancey will let him have the United States "stables" in peace.*

ery, than our ordinary criminal laws are to hang an innocent one."

In the 1858 campaign against Stephen A. Douglas for the Senate, Lincoln repeatedly stated that he was not for unconditional repeal of the Fugitive Slave Act and not interested in injecting the law as a fresh topic of controversy in the slavery crisis. Though "distasteful" to him, he would in Congress vote for a fugitive slave law as a constitutional duty. He willingly admitted that unfriendly legislation by a state could not override the fugitive slave clause of the Constitution. He linked the admission to pointing out that unfriendly legislation could not, as Douglas claimed, keep slavery out of the territories if the Dred Scott decision were correct.

In 1859 Lincoln stressed Republican adherence to his view of the Fugitive Slave Act as essential to keeping the party together for its highest duty of putting slavery itself on the road to ultimate extinction. When the Ohio Republican party declared for repeal of the law, Lincoln wrote Salmon P. Chase that the Ohio platform would "explode" the national party and make the cause "hopeless" in Illinois. There such a platform would be regarded as opposed to and disregarding "the constitution itself." Chase did not agree.

Lincoln's First Inaugural Address reaffirmed his willingness to enforce the Fugitive Slave Act. Once the war began, Lincoln was less willing to enforce the law. He "was puzzled, for a time, as to denying the legal *rights* of those citizens who remained individually innocent of treason and rebellion" and who demanded return of their fugitive slaves. But he soon came to the view (expressed in a letter of November 20, 1862) that "I may as well surrender this contest, directly, as to make any order, the obvious purposes of which would be to return fugitive slaves.

See also MATSON SLAVE CASE; STANTON, EDWIN MCMASTERS.

Funeral On the day Lincoln died, Surgeon General Joseph K. Barnes supervised an autopsy. The bullet was removed; it was flattened and chipped by its passage through Lincoln's skull. Harry P. Cattell of Brown & Alexander, undertakers, embalmed the body in the President's Room of the west wing of the White House. The embalmer drained the blood, removed body parts that might decay easily, and used a chemical which more or less petrified the corpse.

Washington officials wanted Lincoln buried in the Capitol, but a Springfield delegation persuaded Mrs. Lincoln to choose their Illinois home (for a time, she considered Chicago). The National Lincoln Monument Association purchased a lot on the site of the present Illinois Capitol.

Secretary of War Edwin M. Stanton arranged the itinerary of the funeral train which would carry Lincoln's body back to Springfield. He by and large duplicated the route of the 1861 inaugural train but left Pittsburgh and Cincinnati off and added Chicago.

On Tuesday, April 18, 1865 Lincoln's body, clad in his Second Inauguration suit, was laid in a $1500 open casket in a catafalque in the East Room of the White House. At noon on Wednesday, April 19, the first of many funeral services for Lincoln occurred. The Reverend Phineas D. Gurley preached the funeral sermon. Robert Todd Lincoln was present, but Mrs. Lincoln and Tad stayed away. At 2 p.m. a hearse carried the body in a long procession to the Capitol, where the open coffin was on view the rest of that day and all the day following.

Early on the morning of Friday, April 21, the body was placed on a train along with Willie's coffin, which had been disinterred, at Mrs. Lincoln's request, to be buried with his father's coffin in Springfield.

Listed below are the times of arrival and departure for major stops, the locations where the remains were on view, and the orator, if any:

April 21.	8:00 a.m.	Leave Washington
	10:00 a.m.	Arrive Baltimore, Maryland Merchants' Exchange rotunda
	3:00 p.m.	Leave Baltimore
	8:20 p.m.	Arrive Harrisburg, Pennsylvania Hall of the House of Representatives
April 22.	11:00 a.m.	Leave Harrisburg
	4:30 p.m.	Arrive Philadelphia, Pennsylvania Independence Hall
April 24.	4:00 a.m.	Leave Philadelphia
	10:00 a.m.	Arrive New York City City Hall rotunda George Bancroft
April 25.	4:15 p.m.	Leave New York City
	6:20 p.m.	Arrive Garrison's Landing (opposite West Point)
	10:55 p.m.	Arrive Albany, New York Assembly Chamber of the Capitol
April 26.	4:00 p.m.	Leave Albany
April 27.	7:00 a.m.	Arrive Buffalo, New York St. James Hall
	10:00 p.m.	Leave Buffalo
April 28.	7:00 a.m.	Arrive Cleveland, Ohio Public Park
	Midnight	Leave Cleveland
April 29.	7:30 a.m.	Arrive Columbus, Ohio State Capitol rotunda Job E. Stevenson
	8:00 p.m.	Leave Columbus
April 30.	7:00 a.m.	Arrive Indianapolis, Indiana State House
	Midnight	Leave Indianapolis
May 1.	11:00 a.m.	Arrive Chicago Court House rotunda
May 2.	9:30 p.m.	Leave Chicago
May 3.	9:00 a.m.	Arrive Springfield, Illinois Representatives' Hall of the State House
May 4.		Matthew Simpson

Practically every town on the route prepared a funeral arch, tolled bells, fired salutes, and turned out large delegations of mourners to watch the train pass (at less than 5 miles per hour). Richmond, Indiana, for example, estimated its mourners at a number greater than the town's population of 12,000—at 3:15 a.m.! Ex-Presidents James Buchanan and Millard Fillmore saw the train. Although the body lay in state in Buffalo, there was no formal procession there, since that city had already had its ceremonies on April 19. In Indianapolis Governor Oliver P. Morton failed to give his oration because of heavy rains. In New York City the local government's attempt to prevent black delegations from participating in the procession was thwarted only by special order of Secretary of War Stanton. Altogether the train traveled 1662 miles and arrived only 1 hour late in Springfield.

Around noon on Thursday, May 4, the coffin was sealed. Lincoln's body was carried in a long procession to Oak Ridge Cemetery, where it was placed in a temporary vault. Methodist Bishop Matthew Simpson delivered the funeral oration. The dramatic 16-day-long funeral launched the Lincoln legend.

SOURCES: John C. Power's *Abraham Lincoln: His Great Funeral Cortege, from Washington City to Springfield, Illinois, with a History and Description of the National Lincoln Monument* (Springfield, Ill.: privately printed, 1872) is a wonderfully detailed and loving account of Lincoln's amazing funeral. One of the finest picture books on Lincoln is *Twenty Days* by Dorothy Meserve Kunhardt and Philip B. Kunhardt, Jr. (New York: Harper & Row, 1965), which chronicles the assassination of Lincoln and the 20 days that followed it.

See also TOMB.

G

Galesburg, Illinois Site of the fifth Lincoln-Douglas Debate, October 7, 1858; situated in the west-central part of the state. The crowd of 15,000 or more that jammed the campus of Knox College to see the debate, despite heavy rains the day before and a raw wind on the day of the debate, was probably the largest for any of the debates. Galesburg was more Republican in sentiment than Charleston or Jonesboro, the two sites immediately preceding it in the series. Republican banners, one of which read: "Small-fisted Farmers, Mud Sills of Society, Greasy Mechanics, for A. Lincoln," dominated the setting.

Perhaps because the local postmaster had been a victim of the patronage feud between President James Buchanan and Stephen A. Douglas over the Lecompton constitution for Kansas, Douglas spent over a third of his time explaining his stand on that issue, his opposition to the English Bill (a compromise solution to the Lecompton controversy), and his feeling of persecution aroused by the cooperation of disgruntled Buchanan Democrats with Lincoln's campaign for the Senate. He concluded with his customary emphasis: the Republicans and Lincoln stood for abolitionism in the northern part of the state and white supremacy in the southern part; Douglas stood for white supremacy and local control of the Negro population by whatever means a state thought best.

As he had not done in Jonesboro or Charleston, Lincoln answered Douglas's assertion that the Declaration of Independence did not apply to Negroes by saying that to deny its application was to muzzle the cannon of liberty that thunders every July 4th. He denied that the Compromise of 1850 set a pattern for the future in its principle of popular sovereignty. It was, rather, a part of a specific compromise balanced against other concessions.

Lincoln dwelled on Douglas's assertion in a previous speech that he "don't care whether Slavery is voted up or down." This was logical, only "if you do not admit that Slavery is wrong." Lincoln thought it impossible "to institute any equality between right and wrong." He denounced as a fraud and forgery certain antislavery resolutions reputed by Douglas to have been Republican resolutions passed at a meeting at which Lincoln was in attendance. Douglas had admitted his error, but Lincoln strongly hinted that Douglas had perpetrated the fraud. Lincoln attacked Douglas's acceptance of the Dred Scott decision despite his party's willingness in the days of Andrew Jackson to ignore the Supreme Court. By not criticizing it, Douglas would surely lead the country, though he might not mean to, to a decision that would nationalize slavery and allow it to go not only into the territories but everywhere. He also attacked Douglas's stand for the acquisition of new territory. Lincoln was "not generally opposed to the acquisition of additional territory" *as long as* it did not "aggravate this slavery question amongst us."

Genealogy

Douglas replied to a now-rowdy audience that Lincoln's inclusion of the Negro in the Declaration of Independence was his Chicago platform; in Charleston he had not dared say the same thing. The mistaken resolutions were a matter of honest error, and Lincoln was stooping to a personal quarrel in accusing him of forgery. And he described Lincoln's criticism of the Dred Scott decision as an invitation to mob rule.

Lincoln was not as defensive about Republican views on the Negro as he had been at Charleston. Before this more friendly audience, and on the campus of antislavery-oriented Knox College, Lincoln stressed instead Douglas's inability to distinguish morally between slavery and freedom.

SOURCES: For local color see Edwin Erle Sparks, ed., *The Lincoln-Douglas Debates of 1858* (Springfield: Illinois State Historical Library, 1908).

See also DEBATES, LINCOLN-DOUGLAS.

Genealogy "My grandfather went from Rockingham county in Virginia, to Kentucky, about the year 1782; and, two years afterwards, was killed by the indians. We have a vague tradition, that my great-grand father went from Pennsylvania to Virginia; and that he was a quaker. Further back than this, I have never heard any thing." Written in March 6, 1848, to Solomon Lincoln of Hingham, Massachusetts, Lincoln's statement of his ancestry was never much improved upon in his own lifetime. In 1859 Lincoln said with more certainty that his ancestors were Quakers, but he also reported that an "effort to identify them with the New-England family of the same name ended in nothing more definite, than a similarity of Christian names in both families, such as Enoch, Levi, Mordecai, Solomon, Abraham, and the like." About his mother's ancestry Lincoln never wrote at length; he knew only that she too was born in Virginia.

Lincoln was correct about his Pennsylvania Quaker ancestry, but his earlier ancestors were New England Puritans. His original American progenitor was Samuel Lincoln of Hingham, Massachusetts, who came to the new world before 1640 in the great Puritan migration of the 1630s. Of his mother's ancestry—the Hanks family—little more is known for certain than what Lincoln knew. He may have suspected that she was illegitimate, and modern genealogists disagree on this point. No documents have been uncovered to prove the point conclusively one way or another.

Lincoln seems to have had a normal curiosity about his ancestry and helped people who wrote to him for information on the subject. Yet his interest never equaled that of the numerous students of his genealogy who, especially from 1900 to 1940, scoured courthouses and engaged in bitter disputes over his ancestry. Louis A. Warren spent most of his career in the Lincoln field on the subject, and William E. Barton published a substantial volume and numerous articles on it as well—as did many other writers and researchers of less ability than they had. Lincoln's interest did not stem from the same assumptions that impelled the genealogists. The great unwritten assumption of most genealogical research was that acquired characteristics could be inherited. Although it is now biologically discredited, the idea nevertheless motivated students who thought that study of Lincoln's ancestry would somehow prove something essential about the man himself. Lincoln, however, was a firm believer in the ability of the individual to make of himself what he would by his own enterprise and was quite content to admit even in materials to be used for campaign biographies that his parents came "of undistinguished families—second families, perhaps I should say."

SOURCES: Waldo Lincoln's *History of the Lincoln Family: An Account of the Descendants of Samuel Lincoln of Hingham, Massachusetts, 1637–1920* (Worcester, Mass.: Commonwealth Press, 1923) is exhaustive and contains a detailed index of names, but it is a rare book. On the controversies over Lincoln's ancestry see Benjamin P. Thomas, *Portrait for Posterity: Lincoln and His Biographers* (New Brunswick, N.J.: Rutgers University Press, 1947).

Generals   See COMMANDER IN CHIEF.

Gentry, Matthew   See INDIANA.

Gentryville   See INDIANA.

German-Americans   See IMMIGRANTS.

Gettysburg Address   Lincoln's most famous speech. The speech, on November 19, 1863, had its origins in a sanitary problem on the Gettysburg battlefield. The shallow graves were in danger of being uncovered by autumn rains, and several states thought their fallen heroes deserved a more suitable burial. At the instigation of Gettysburg citizen David Wills, the Commonwealth of Pennsylvania bought seventeen acres of the battlefield and had a cemetery designed. Wills planned a ceremony for November to dedicate the grounds.

Edward Everett, the former president of Harvard and a famed orator, was to be the featured speaker. Wills invited President Lincoln as an afterthought on November 2, well over a month after he had invited Everett. Lincoln accepted with probably less than 2 weeks left in which to compose his address.

The President took a train to Gettysburg the night before the ceremony. It is almost certain that he did not write the speech on the back of an envelope on the train ride. The first page of the earliest existing draft is written neatly in ink on ruled White House stationery. The address appears on no envelope or scrap of paper, and a 1 hour 10 minute jolting railroad trip provided no opportunity for the neat hand or the careful elo-

Edward Everett, the other orator at Gettysburg.

Lincoln rode in this parade down Baltimore Street in Gettysburg to the cemetery where he gave his famous address. (U.S. Signal Corps Photo No. 111-B-357 [Brady Collection] in the National Archives)

quence. Lincoln did apparently finish writing the address at Wills's house.

After a long procession on Thursday morning, the 19th, Lincoln waited for Everett, who was ½ hour late, and then sat through the old orator's courtly 2-hour-long speech. Lincoln's own address lasted about 2 minutes and was over before many of the 15,000 people present realized that he had begun to speak. Nevertheless, it was recognized immediately by men of letters as a masterpiece. Everett himself wrote Lincoln the next day: "I should be glad, if I could flatter myself that I came as near the central idea of the occasion, in two hours, as you did in two minutes." Henry Wadsworth Longfellow told the editor of *Harper's Weekly* on the same day that he found the address "admirable." *Harper's* called the address as "simple and felicitous and earnest a word as was ever spoken," and in sharp contrast to Everett's "smooth and cold" speech. Josiah Gilbert Holland of the Springfield, Massachusetts, *Republican* called the speech "a perfect gem" and said that "the rhetorical honors of the occasion were won by President Lincoln." In less than 2 years Ralph Waldo Emerson would say that Lincoln's "brief speech at Gettysburg will not easily be surpassed by words on any recorded occasion." Lincoln himself seems to have thought his Second Inaugural Address his best speech, and indeed the popular fame of the Gettysburg Address came after his death. Some 35 lithographed and engraved copies of the Emancipation Proclamation were printed before 1866, but one searches in vain for any similar decorative editions of the Gettysburg Address published in Lincoln's lifetime.

The address has been variously interpreted, but its meaning seems clear enough within the context of Lincoln's political thought. Lincoln dated the founding of the country "Four score and seven years" before 1863—that is, in 1776. He always thought the Declaration of Independence of 1776 the fundamental document of the nation's history and saw all American history as an attempt to live up to the promise embodied in its statement that all men are created equal. The Gettysburg Address stated simply that the reason for the deaths on the battlefield was the preservation of the nation dedicated to that proposition. The ceremonies, Lincoln said, could add no luster to that sacrifice but should lead Americans to dedicate themselves to finishing the work those heroes began.

Though there are controversies over the circumstances of the composition of the address, over the speed with which its worth was recognized, and over the exact meaning of the address, there is no controversy over its standing as one of the grandest examples of American letters. The existing handwritten copies of the address are regarded as national treasures. Two copies are in the Library of Congress; one is in the Lincoln Room of the White House; one is in the Cornell University Library; and one is in the Illinois State Historical Library.

SOURCES: A lucid treatment based on the most reliable sources is David C. Mearns and Lloyd A. Dunlap, *Long Remembered: Facsimiles of the Five Versions of the Gettysburg Address in the Handwriting of Abraham Lincoln* (Washington, D.C.: Library of Congress, 1963). The only book-length treatment is Louis A. Warren's *Lincoln's Gettysburg Declaration: "A New Birth of Freedom"* (Fort Wayne, Ind.: Lincoln National Life Foundation, 1964). Other sources are Benjamin Barondess, *Three Lincoln Masterpieces: Cooper Institute Speech, Gettysburg Address, Second Inaugural* (Charleston: Education Foun-

Globe Tavern

The first draft of the Gettysburg Address was begun in ink on ruled Executive Mansion stationery and finished in pencil, beginning at the end of the first page. The second page was probably written at David Wills's house in Gettysburg. The neat writing and the straight lines are proof that Lincoln did not compose the speech on the train ride. (Library of Congress)

dation of West Virginia, Inc., 1954) and Allan Nevins, ed., *Lincoln and the Gettysburg Address: Commemorative Papers* (Urbana: University of Illinois Press, 1954).

Globe Tavern   See SPRINGFIELD, ILLINOIS.

Goose Nest Prairie   See COLES COUNTY, ILLINOIS.

Graham, William Mentor (1800–1886)   Graham was aptly named for the role he claimed as Abraham Lincoln's teacher while he resided in New Salem. He was born in Kentucky but moved to Illinois in 1826, where he lived about a mile west of New Salem and was the local schoolteacher. In a letter to William H. Herndon on May 29, 1865, Graham said that Lincoln lived with him for about 6 months in 1833 and that he "commenced the study of English grammar with me." Graham also claimed to have "taught him the rules of surveying." There was not a single grammar book in New Salem, but Graham directed Lincoln to a copy of Samuel Kirkham's *English Grammar in Familiar Lectures* owned by a man 6 miles away. "I think I may say," Graham recalled, "that he was my scholar and I was his teacher." Although Graham's statements, made over 30 years after the events, are riddled with errors, Lincoln did study grammar and surveying about the time Graham mentioned, and he may well have sought and obtained the local schoolteacher's help.

Graham was a Democrat who voted for James K. Polk in 1844. In 1846, when Lincoln ran for Congress against Peter Cartwright, he voted for Cartwright. During the Civil War, however, he was a sturdy supporter of the Union cause. His cousin, Mary Owens Vineyard (whom Lincoln had once courted), threatened "never" to "call me cousin again" if Graham voted for Lincoln in 1864, but he did vote for his old pupil.

Graham taught in various rural Illinois schools until his seventy-ninth year. He died in South Dakota.

SOURCES: Kunigunde Duncan and D. F. Nickol's *Mentor Graham: The Man Who Taught Lincoln* (Chicago: University of Chicago Press, 1944) is thoroughly unreliable, but it is the only biography of Graham. The book pictures Graham as a Whig and political friend of Lincoln's, but a Petersburg poll book for August 3, 1846 (and another for November 4, 1844),

William Mentor Graham. (Courtesy of the Illinois State Historical Library)

in the Louis A. Warren Lincoln Library and Museum, Fort Wayne, Indiana, proves him a Democrat. Graham letters are very rare, but an interesting one about the election of 1864 (quoted above) was excerpted in pages 6 and 7 of the *Americana Mail Auction* catalog for April 20, 1975.

Grant, Ulysses Simpson (1822–1885) General-in-chief of the Union armies at the end of the Civil War. Grant was born in Ohio and named Hiram Ulysses. He graduated in the lower half of his West Point class in 1843 (where his name was changed, partly by clerical error) and served with distinguished gallantry in the Mexican War. He gave up his commission in 1854, having recently received a warning from his commanding officer about his excessive drinking.

When war broke out in 1861, Grant, who had pursued several not very successful civilian careers, was a clerk in a leather goods store in Galena, Illinois. He was anxious to join the army and was finally commissioned colonel of the 21st Illinois Volunteers by Governor Richard Yates. By August he was a brigadier general. By capturing Fort Henry and Fort Donelson and more than 12,000 men in Tennessee in February 1862, Grant gave the North its first smashing victory and for the first time came to Lincoln's attention. The President recommended his appointment as major general of volunteers.

By March, Grant was in trouble. Never much of a letter writer, he seemed to be failing to inform his commanding officer of his movements. In truth, a disloyal telegraph operator was at the root of the problem. In April he fought the Battle of Shiloh, the first battle of the war to produce great casualties. Rumors that Grant's misconduct was the reason for the high casualty rate reached the President. General Henry W. Halleck, Grant's commanding officer, defended his subordinate, though he had his private doubts about Grant's abilities anywhere but on the field of battle.

As Lincoln began to plan the campaign to capture the Mississippi River line, he overlooked Grant for two political generals: Nathaniel P. Banks and John A. McClernand. By early 1863, however, Halleck convinced Lincoln that Grant should direct the Vicksburg campaign. Grant's first attempt failed, as did several others in the winter and spring which involved cutting canals. In March Secretary of War Edwin M. Stanton sent newspaperman Charles A. Dana (ostensibly as a commissioner to the army) to make regular reports on Grant to him and Lincoln. Dana's reports assuaged any fears Stanton and Lincoln may have had that Grant had lapsed into his old drinking habits. Lincoln, however, did grow impatient with the campaign, and he wanted Grant to move his army south of Vicksburg to join with Banks's forces. Grant ran a fleet down the river past the Confederate forts, marched his army south on the opposite bank, and transported his troops across the river in the boats. However, he did not march south to join Banks but instead turned north to lay siege to Vicksburg. By May 26 Lincoln saw that the campaign was "one of the most brilliant in the world." Vicksburg fell on July 4, 1863, and 9 days later Lincoln wrote Grant a frank letter of thanks. Noting that he could not recall "that you and I ever met personally," Lincoln praised the general's "almost inestimable service." Lincoln added that he had agreed that Grant should move south of Vicksburg, but he had little faith that the expedition thereafter would succeed and had thought Grant should join Banks downriver. "I now wish," Lincoln concluded, "to make the personal acknowledgment that you were right, and I was wrong." Grant became a major general in the regular army.

Grant had shown Lincoln many qualities that the President admired in a commander. In answering a complaint about the failure of the transfer of some troops from Grant to Ambrose E. Burnside on July 27, Lincoln explained with pointed language: "Gen. Grant is a copious worker, and fighter, but a very meagre writer, or telegrapher." Although he had great confidence in Grant, he did not fail to overrule the general on occasion. When Grant suggested a campaign to capture Mobile, the President vetoed it; he said that men the general wanted for the campaign must be sent to Texas, which appeared to be threatened by the presence of French forces in Mexico. Lincoln's confidence was unshaken, and in October he put Grant over all the departments and armies from the Alleghenies to the Mississippi (except Banks's command in the Southwest).

Grant began to think in grand strategic terms. In the winter of 1863–1864, after a victorious campaign for Chattanooga, he was still keen on an overland campaign to capture Mobile and from there invade Alabama and Georgia. Lincoln, Stanton, and Halleck feared laying Tennessee open to invasion by focusing attention so far south and agreed only if Grant arranged to push the remaining Confederate forces out of Tennessee and north Georgia. Grant revised the plan to include moves from Chattanooga on north Georgia and from New Orleans on Mobile, but there were not in Lincoln's opinion enough troops in the West to accomplish two major objectives at once. For the East, Grant recommended a seaborne invasion of North Carolina to threaten Richmond's communications. Halleck suggested that Lincoln would not like it. Lincoln wanted Robert E. Lee's army destroyed; he was not interested in maneuvers to gain Richmond.

These discussions of strategy by mail were preliminaries to Grant's appointment as general-in-chief of all Union armies. Before the appointment Grant apparently made it clear that he had no aspirations for the Presidency in 1864. In February Congress revived the rank of lieutenant general, last held by Winfield Scott and before that only by George Washington. Grant received his commission at Washington on March 9, 1864. At a reception at the White House the night before, he met his commander in chief for the first time. Grant had not been a "Lincoln man" before the war. Originally sympathetic with the Whig party, Grant had been a Know-Nothing for one week. He had read the Lincoln-Douglas Debates and supported Stephen A. Douglas for President in 1860.

In his *Memoirs*, published in 1886, Grant exaggerated

Ulysses Simpson Grant

his own independence and Lincoln's lack of military knowledge. He gave the impression that Lincoln professed complete ignorance of military affairs, suggested a bad strategic plan which Grant charitably ignored, and expressed a desire not even to know what Grant's plans were. In a letter to Grant written on April 30, 1864, Lincoln said, "The *particulars* [emphasis added] of your plans I neither know, or seek to know." He wished "not to obtrude any constraints or restraints upon" Grant, but he followed events closely and, when necessary, intervened in military planning. The principal reason that Lincoln interfered very little with Grant was that, after the feelers about his strategic ideas of the previous winter, the two thought similarly about strategy. Grant's plan to send Benjamin F. Butler toward Richmond from the James River, to instruct General George G. Meade to follow Lee wherever he went, and to send William T. Sherman to attack Atlanta was congruent with Lincoln's idea that there should be a general move to attack the enemy's armies on all fronts. On the same day he wrote his letter to Grant, Lincoln told private secretary John Hay that he recognized his own plans in Grant's: "Those not skinning can hold a leg."

Grant rarely wrote directly to Lincoln. Instead, he communicated with General Halleck, now a sort of liaison between the government and Grant and between Grant and his 17 department commanders—who were controlling over half a million soldiers. But Lincoln read the orders and commented on them when occasion warranted it. Grant failed to bring Lee to a decisive battle in the Wilderness campaign in the spring, and he decided to move south of the James River and seize Petersburg, the key to rail communications with Richmond. When he made his move south of the James, Lincoln telegraphed: "I begin to see it; you will succeed."

In July, Lee sent General Jubal A. Early up the Shenandoah Valley to threaten Washington in hopes Grant would shift attention away from Petersburg. Grant showed little interest, but Lincoln urged him to come himself to Washington to destroy Early's army, though he did not order him to do so. Grant decided later to coordinate Washington-area armies under General Philip Sheridan in order to destroy Early's army rather than merely fend it off. Lincoln suggested that "it will neither be done nor attempted unless you watch it every day, and hour, and force it." Grant took the hint and came to Washington to coordinate planning for the campaign. Previously, in July, Lincoln had read Grant's dispatch to General Sherman suggesting a "desparate effort" to seize a good position at Petersburg. Lincoln cautioned him against making an effort "desparate in the sense of great loss of life." This was the summer before a presidential election, and Lincoln could ill afford any staggering casualties. Nevertheless, neither man was panicked by rumors that a new draft call for soldiers would be heavily resisted in the war-weary North. Grant refused to send troops to meet the threat of draft resistance. Lincoln agreed with the policy: "Hold on with a bulldog gripe, and chew & choke, as much as possible."

Lincoln admired Grant's dogged persistence, and Grant smoothed relations further by his willingness to stand clear of political problems. When Grant began to get peace feelers, Lincoln told Stanton to order him not to discuss "any political questions," only the "capitulation of General Lee's army." By and large, Grant complied. Of course, Lincoln and Grant had their differences, particularly over the removals of political generals like Banks and Butler and over the abilities of General George H. Thomas. Lincoln was reluctant to remove any of the three and forced Grant to have good military reasons for doing so or to take responsibility for the removals by himself. In Thomas's case, Grant was on the brink of removing the general when Thomas scored a resounding victory at Nashville.

Grant attended Lincoln's last Cabinet meeting, on April 14, 1865. After it, he explained that he and Mrs. Grant could not accept Lincoln's invitation to go to Ford's Theatre that night because they wanted to leave as quickly as possible to see their sons in New Jersey.

SOURCES: T. Harry Williams's *Lincoln and His Generals* (New York: Alfred A. Knopf, 1952) argues a case for the great military abilities of both Lincoln and Grant with clarity. Grant's *Personal Memoirs*, 2 vols. (New York: Charles L. Webster, 1886) are themselves models of clear writing.

Greeley, Horace (1811–1872) Editor of the New York *Tribune* during the Lincoln administration. Greeley first saw Abraham Lincoln at the Chicago River and Harbor Convention of 1847, where both protested President James K. Polk's opposition to internal improvements. Greeley noted in the *Tribune* that Lincoln spoke "briefly and happily" in answer to David Dudley Field—one of the earliest mentions of Lincoln in a national newspaper. The *Tribune* was read by Whigs in many states. Lincoln had confidence enough in his opinion on the Mexican War to write "Friend Greeley" on June 27, 1848, and point out that the *Tribune* attributed to Whigs a position which most Whigs did not hold. The Nueces River was not the boundary of the Texas republic; rather, "the boundary of Texas extended just so far as American settlements taking part in her revolution extended" and thus included "one or two points, beyond the Nueces." Lincoln also sent the editor a copy of his speech in Congress on the Mexican War.

Ten years later Greeley and Lincoln were at odds on another matter. The New York editor so admired Stephen A. Douglas's opposition to the Buchanan administration that he wished Illinois's Republicans would not oppose his bid for reelection to the United States Senate. Most Illinois Republicans, and especially Lincoln (who was running against Douglas), were of another mind. Lincoln, however, refused to believe stories that Greeley had made a deal with Douglas. He believed that Greeley was "incapable of corruption, or falsehood"; Greeley doubtless thought Douglas's abilities compensated for his "lack of a pure republican position." Greeley admitted having met with Douglas but denied making a deal. His support of the Republican cause in Illinois was lackluster at best, however, and Lincoln feared the influence of the *Tribune's* lukewarm articles, which he knew to be "extensively read in Illinois." Greeley felt that Illinois had "spurned and insulted" Republicans from other states and "thrown a load upon us that may . . . break us down." Illinois "might get through," he told Joseph M. Medill, if "Lincoln would fight up to the work," but "if he apologizes, and retreats, and defines, he is lost." Greeley would "keep neutral."

On February 27, 1860, Greeley was on the platform with Lincoln at the Cooper Institute, and the *Tribune* said of Lincoln's address on that occasion that "No man ever before made such an impression on his first appeal to a New York audience." The *Tribune* also printed the speech in pamphlet form, but Greeley did not support Lincoln for the presidential nomination. He supported Edward Bates, in part because of that candidate's credentials as a conservative nationalist and in part because he harbored a grudge against the front-running Republican hopeful, William H. Seward. In 1854 Seward's manager, Thurlow Weed, had ignored Greeley's desire to run for lieutenant governor and helped his rival at the New York *Times*, Henry Jarvis Raymond, gain the office. While attending the Chicago nominating convention as an Oregon delegate, Greeley worked hard to thwart Seward's hopes and thus, indirectly, helped Lincoln gain the nomination.

Greeley regarded Lincoln as a mediocrity but campaigned loyally for the Republican ticket. After Lincoln's election, the New York editor went to Springfield on a lecture tour, and there on February 5, 1861, he saw Lincoln. Greeley urged no compromise with the South on slavery extension, opposed Simon Cameron's appointment to the Cabinet, and advocated the appointments of Salmon P. Chase and Schuyler Colfax to the Cabinet. Greeley would consistently oppose the influence of Seward and Weed on patronage in New York, and he suggested to the President in 1861 that a representative of each faction take turns choosing appointees for a list of jobs remaining after Lincoln made his personal choices. When Lincoln sneaked into Washington for his inauguration, Greeley commented, "Lincoln is true and right, but not a Jackson or Clay, as his dodge through Maryland lamentably shows."

Greeley's attitude toward secession was strange and vacillating. He thought that the cotton states should be allowed to "go in peace," but only because his confidence in the underlying national loyalty of the Southern masses made him believe that they would soon rejoin the Union. Not advocating coercion, he nevertheless opposed any compromise on political principles with the South. Once war broke out, Greeley sought its vigorous prosecution and was critical of Lincoln's policy of conciliation toward the Border States. But he was given to periods of bitter defeatism, the first of which led him to write the President on July 29, 1861, to inform him, "You are not considered a great man." Greeley felt that "peace with the Rebels at once and on their terms" might be necessary.

Lincoln supplied the *Tribune* with inside information on the administration through Robert J. Walker, and Greeley staunchly supported the administration in re-

In 1860 Currier & Ives cartoonist Louis Maurer made Horace Greeley an essential part of his anti-Lincoln cartoons. Easily identified by his white duster with its pockets crammed with newspapers or pamphlets, Greeley symbolized the "lunatic fringe" of the Republican reform impulse. Linked with the ominous figure of a Negro, he suggested the threat that the Republican party would bring black equality. The third essential element, a rail, suggested the meaningless stress on Lincoln's humble origins.

turn until 1862, when he became a shrill advocate of emancipation. On August 20, 1862, his *Tribune* editorial, "Prayer of Twenty Millions," made a demand for emancipation which the President could not ignore. Lincoln's August 22 letter in response, which declared that the administration's policy was to save the Union by freeing all the slaves, some of them, or none, is considered to be Lincoln's classic statement of his constitutional duty:

I have just read yours of the 19th. addressed to myself through the New-York Tribune. If there be in it any statements, or assumptions of fact, which I may know to be erroneous, I do not, now and here, controvert them. If there be in it any inferences which I may believe to be falsely drawn, I do not now and here, argue against them. If there be perceptable in it an impatient and dictatorial tone, I waive it in deference to an old friend, whose heart I have always supposed to be right.

As to the policy I "seem to be pursuing" as you say, I have not meant to leave any one in doubt.

I would save the Union. I would save it the shortest way under the Constitution. The sooner the national authority can be restored; the nearer the Union will be "the Union as it was." If there be those who would not save the Union, unless they could at the same time *save* slavery, I do not agree with them. If there be those who would not save the Union unless they could at the same time *destroy* slavery, I do not agree with them. My paramount object in this struggle *is* to save the Union, and is *not* either to save or to destroy slavery. If I could save the Union without freeing *any* slave I would do it, and if I could save it by freeing *all* the slaves I would do it; and if I could save it by freeing some and leaving others alone I would also do that. What I do about slavery, and the colored race, I do because I believe it helps to save the Union; and what I forbear, I forbear because I do *not* believe it would help to save the Union. I shall do *less* whenever I shall believe what I am doing hurts the cause, and I shall do *more* whenever I shall believe doing more will help the cause. I shall try to correct errors when shown to be errors; and I shall adopt new views so fast as they shall appear to be true views.

I have here stated my purpose according to my view of *official* duty; and I intend no modification of my oft-expressed *personal* wish that all men every where could be free.

The Battle of Gettysburg snapped Greeley out of another spell of defeatism and brought rapprochement with the administration until early 1864. Greeley began opposing Lincoln's renomination in February of that year. The editor's predilection for peace proposals increased in the summer, in part as a way to prove that the South wanted war no matter what, in part because of his defeatism, and in part because of his loathing of war. When the *Tribune*'s editor showed an interest in negotiation with Confederate agents in Canada across from Niagara Falls, Lincoln on July 9, much to Greeley's surprise and dismay, authorized Greeley to deal with them himself if they had official credentials and if they would agree to "the restoration of the Union and abandonment of slavery."

Greeley disingenuously failed to explain to the Confederates that emancipation was a sine qua non; and when they asked for safe conduct passes to Richmond to get authorization, Lincoln responded with another famous letter "To Whom it may concern" (on July 18) guaranteeing safe conduct for anyone willing to treat for peace on the basis of reunion and emancipation. Greeley and Lincoln's secretary John Hay met with the agents on the 20th, and the Confederates claimed that Lincoln had betrayed them by demanding emancipation. Greeley's rival Raymond then called for publication of the correspondence about the abortive Niagara Falls conference. On August 5, Greeley agreed. Lincoln agreed, too, as long as defeatist passages in Greeley's letters about "our bleeding, bankrupt, almost dying country" be censored. Lincoln also wanted to delete passages "which present the carrying of elections as a motive of action." Greeley had suggested that Confederate refusal to accept a peace offer might throw North Carolina elections to the powerful Unionist party there. Greeley did not agree to the censorship.

Greeley participated in the late summer movement led by Henry Winter Davis to call a new convention and nominate a new candidate, but when it failed, he fought loyally and fiercely for Lincoln's election. Though he had at first spoken carelessly of hanging traitors, Greeley became an advocate of forgiveness toward the South; his old faith in the loyalty of the Southern masses reasserted itself. As early as December 1862 he urged peace terms of general amnesty for Confederates coupled with general emancipation and the assumption of $400 million of the Confederate debt, terms he advocated consistently through the war. He applauded Lincoln's Proclamation of Amnesty and Reconstruction of December 8, 1863, steered clear of the Wade-Davis manifesto (even though it came at a time when he was thoroughly at odds with Lincoln), and criticized Lincoln's mild Second Inaugural Address for being too warlike. He came to recognize the forgiving nature of Lincoln's attitude toward the South and saw Lincoln's death as a blow to the South itself. He also came at last to appreciate the martyred President's greatness.

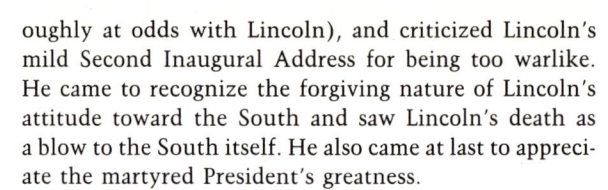

SOURCES: Glyndon G. Van Deusen's *Horace Greeley: Nineteenth Century Crusader* (New York: Hill and Wang, 1964; originally published in 1953) is a masterful, breezily written, but somewhat hostile biography. Lincoln's copy of Greeley's letter to Joseph M. Medill about the 1858 election (July 24, 1858) and Greeley's defeatist letter of July 29, 1861, are in the Abraham Lincoln Papers, Library of Congress.

See also RAYMOND, HENRY JARVIS.

Grigsby, Aaron (1801–1831) Abraham Lincoln's brother-in-law. Aaron Grigsby moved with his parents from Kentucky to Indiana in 1815. The Lincolns settled within 3 miles of the Grigsby home. Aaron married Lincoln's sister Sarah on August 2, 1826, and the couple lived on a farm near the Lincolns. On January 28, 1828, Sarah died in childbirth.

Several old settlers from southern Indiana, questioned after Lincoln's death, recalled that Lincoln apparently blamed Sarah's death on Grigsby's neglect and that his relations with the Grigsbys were thereafter rather cool. When two Grigsby boys got married and had a reception the same night, pranksters, perhaps instigated by Lincoln, played a joke which assigned the bridegrooms to the wrong rooms and wives. Lincoln is said to have written a satire on the affair, called "The Chronicles of Reuben," in mock-Biblical style.

On September 11, 1830, Aaron Grigsby married Margaret Miller. He died the next year, leaving an estate valued at nearly $300 and including a horse, cows, sheep, geese, hogs, and chickens.

SOURCES: See Louis A. Warren, *Lincoln's Youth: Indiana Years, Seven to Twenty-one, 1816–1830* (New York: Appleton, Century, Crofts, 1959).

Grimsley, Elizabeth Todd (1825–1895) Mrs. Grimsley, *nee* Elizabeth J. Todd, was Mary Todd Lincoln's cousin. Born in Edwardsville, Illinois, "Cousin Lizzie" was a favorite friend in Mary Todd's girlhood and was bridesmaid at her wedding in 1842. Elizabeth married Harrison Grimsley, a Whig merchant, in Springfield in 1846. When the Lincolns went to Washington in 1861, Mrs. Grimsley and others of Mary's Illinois relatives joined them. Mrs. Grimsley remained for 6 months to help Mary adjust to life in the White House and then returned to Illinois. Her reminiscence of that stay, "Six Months in the White House," first published in the *Journal of the Illinois State Historical Society*, XIX (October 1926–January 1927), 43–73, gives some vivid glimpses of the private and social side of White House life before the death of Willie Lincoln afflicted the family. The reminiscence does not mention that Mrs. Grimsley sought the job as postmistress in Springfield, an appointment Lincoln feared to make because he had al-

Elizabeth Todd Grimsley

ready given so many jobs to his wife's relatives and those of Illinois Republican Senator Lyman Trumbull. She did not get the job and asked again in vain in 1864. She sought her son John's appointment to the Naval Academy from Lincoln in 1863.

Elizabeth and Mary apparently corresponded often, but only one of Mrs. Lincoln's letters to this "noble, good woman" survives. Its gossipy content suggests that they were intimate friends. After Willie Lincoln died early in 1862, Mrs. Lincoln did not write her cousin until the fall of 1864—a sign of her severe affliction.

In 1865 Harrison Grimsley died and 2 years later Elizabeth married Springfield Presbyterian minister John H. Brown. In 1871, when Tad Lincoln died, Mrs. Brown cared for Mrs. Lincoln in Chicago, when her husband then had a church. He died in 1872, and she died 23 years later in Duluth, Minnesota.

Elizabeth owned the famous "carpetbag letters," a batch of Lincoln manuscripts which Lincoln left with her when he went to Washington. She gave five of them to friends, but a maid mistakenly burned the rest as trash.

SOURCES: See Roy P. Basler, *President Lincoln Helps His Old Friends* (Springfield, Ill.: Abraham Lincoln Association, 1977) and Justin G. and Linda Levitt Turner, *Mary Todd Lincoln: Her Life and Letters* (New York: Alfred A. Knopf, 1972).

H

Habeas Corpus President Abraham Lincoln first suspended the privilege of the writ of habeas corpus on April 27, 1861, "at any point on or in the vicinity of the military line . . . between the City of Philadelphia and the City of Washington." He allowed commanding General Winfield Scott to make arrests without specific charges in that area in order to prevent secession-minded Marylanders from interfering with the Capital's communication with the North. The tense situation in Maryland just after the fall of Fort Sumter led to several sensational arrests by military authorities: the Baltimore marshal of police George P. Kane, Baltimore Mayor William Brown, and, on September 17, nine members of the Maryland legislature and the chief clerk of the Maryland Senate (the last-named group from fear that, if allowed to attend the legislative session, they might well vote to take the state out of the Union). But the most important arrest proved to be that of an obscure Southern sympathizer named John Merryman on May 25. Sitting as a federal circuit court judge, Chief Justice Roger B. Taney of the United States Supreme Court issued a writ of habeas corpus demanding that the military authorities "have . . . the body of" Merryman in court to "make known the day and cause of the capture and detention." The military authorities refused. In *Ex parte Merryman* Taney argued that only Congress could suspend the privilege of the writ and that the President, though sworn to "take care that the laws be faithfully executed," had broken the laws himself. Individual freedom from arbitrary arrest became the most important constitutional issue in the early part of the Civil War; the larger majority of the loyal North, both Democrats and Republicans, acknowledged that secession was not a constitutional right.

Taney suspected that Lincoln might arrest him, but, by and large, the President ignored him and his decision, averting what could have become a debilitating constitutional crisis. In a message to Congress on July 4, 1861, President Lincoln answered Taney (without mentioning his name) by asking whether "all the laws, *but one*, [were] to go unexecuted, and the government itself to go to pieces, lest that one be violated?"

Doubt about the constitutionality of the suspension stemmed from the ambiguous language of the Constitution, which states only that "The Privilege of the Writ of Habeas Corpus shall not be suspended, unless when, in Cases of Rebellion or Invasion the public Safety may require it." The document does not say *who* may suspend the privilege, Congress or the President, but most of the American legal authorities who had thought about it before the war believed with Joseph Story that only Congress had the power. Lincoln answered Taney in his July 4 message before he received the written opinion of his Attorney General Edward Bates. That opinion, dated July 5, argued that the government's three branches were "co-ördinate and coequal, that is, neither being Sovereign, each is independent in its sphere." Thus, "the judgment of one of them is not binding upon the other two" in interpretations of the Constitution.

Far more influential was an able defense of the Presi-

"THE LITTLE BELL," 1861-65.

"MY LORD, I can touch a bell on my right hand, and order the arrest of a citizen of Ohio; I can touch a bell again, and order the imprisonment of a citizen of New York; and no power on earth, except that of the President, can release them. Can the Queen of England do so much?"

Secretary Seward to Lord Lyons, see page 13.

William H. Seward's alleged boast of his power to make arbitrary arrests provided ammunition for critics of the Republicans during the war and for years to come. "The Little Bell" was the frontispiece of John A. Marshall's American Bastile, first published in 1869 in Philadelphia. This history of sensational arbitrary arrests of many apparently innocent Democratic politicians and partisans was in its eighth edition by 1871.

133

Habeas Corpus

dent by a Philadelphia octogenarian lawyer named Horace Binney in a widely circulated pamphlet, *The Privilege of the Writ of Habeas Corpus under the Constitution* (Philadelphia: C. Sherman and Son, 1862). Whereas Taney had stressed British example in Parliament's exclusive ability to suspend the writ, Binney stressed the irrelevance of England's example. England had no written constitution, and Parliament's control stemmed from fears of the monarch. America, with an elected president, had no such problem. The controversy excited lawyers and politicians; more than 40 separately published answers to Binney's pamphlet appeared.

The issue was important not for abstract constitutional reasons alone, but because of the continuing effect of arbitrary arrests on the lives of American citizens. On September 24, 1862, and again on September 15, 1863, Lincoln suspended the privilege of the writ "throughout the United States." Some of the citizens arrested were spies and saboteurs, but others landed in federal prisons for "political" crimes—opposing the war effort of the Lincoln administration in words rather than deeds. There is no exact record of the total number arrested during the Civil War, but the commissary general of prisoners listed 13,535 citizens arrested from February 1862 to April 1865. Many were arrested before those dates, and there are no records for those arrested by naval authorities or for those in state prisons. Easily one American in every 1500 was arrested during the war. The State Department controlled arrests until February 14, 1862 (probably because Lincoln did not trust Secretary of War Simon Cameron to handle internal security); after that, the President shifted authority to the War Department. Persons arrested were usually held for a period of weeks and released without a trial, but they languished in prison long enough to cause Democrats to refer to Fort Lafayette, Fort McHenry, Fort Warren, and the Old Capitol Prison as "American bastilles."

The arbitrary arrests gave rise to the charge that President Lincoln was a "tyrant," yet he was often in the position of restraining the power of the military in arresting suspects. For example, he discouraged General Scott from ordering the arrest of members of the Maryland legislature in a letter of April 25, 1861. In a memorandum written in May, he said, "Unless the *necessity*

President Lincoln presides over the burial of the Constitution in this cartoon from the 1864 presidential campaign. The cartoon suggests the centrality of civil libertarianism to the Democratic party in that year and singles out the War Democrats, led by hearse-driver Edwin M. Stanton, for special blame in subverting traditional American liberties. The baby under Henry Ward Beecher's arm is a reminder of the other issue that always lurked in Democratic charges against the Lincoln administration—race.

for these arbitrary arrests is *manifest,* and *urgent,* I prefer they should cease." The arrests of the Maryland legislators in September, like many other arrests, were more acquiesced in than instigated by the President.

Lincoln's warnings against abuses of the power and his reluctance to use it for personal aggrandizement should not blind one to the fact that Lincoln used the power willingly and forthrightly defended its use. His letter of June 12, 1863, to Erastus Corning and others was a bold defense of the suspension of the privilege in the face of sharp Democratic criticism. Lincoln claimed to be "thoroughly imbued with a reverence for the guaranteed rights of individuals." He was "slow to adopt the strong measures, which by degrees I have been forced to regard as being within the exceptions of the constitution, and as indispensable to the public Safety." But he characterized Northern libertarian dissent as something on which the Confederacy depended when the states seceded:

> Under cover of "Liberty of Speech" "Liberty of the Press" and *"Habeas corpus"* they hoped to keep on foot amongst us a most efficient corps of spies, informers, suppliers, and aiders and abettors of their cause in a thousand ways. They knew they had friends who would make a question as to *who* was to suspend it; meanwhile their spies and others might remain at large to help on their cause. Or if, as has happened, the executive should suspend the writ, without ruinous waste of time, instances of arresting innocent persons might occur, as are always likely to occur in such cases; and then a clamor could be raised in regard to this, which might be, at least, of some service to the insurgent cause.

Arbitrary arrests were a tough and deliberate war policy of the Lincoln administration, and Democratic criticism was not pursuing a will-o'-the-wisp. The tendency of Democrats to interpret the President's motive as tyrannical was surely off the mark, however. And the fact of the matter is that wartime economic prosperity and Lincoln's skillful handling of the explosive race question robbed the Democrats of their stock arguments against Republicans. Civil libertarian dissent was the only effective weapon left in their political arsenal.

On March 3, 1863, Congress passed a Habeas Corpus Indemnity Act which stated that "during the present rebellion, the President . . . is authorized to suspend the privilege of the writ of *habeas corpus* in any case throughout the United States or any part thereof." Interpreted by some as a reaffirmation of Congress's right in the matter and by others as acquiescence in what the President had already done, the act did attempt to regularize and control arbitrary arrests by requiring the Secretaries of State and War to furnish lists of prisoners to federal judges within 20 days of the arrests.

SOURCES: See J. G. Randall, *Constitutional Problems Under Lincoln*, rev. ed. (Urbana: University of Illinois Press, 1951), and Harold M. Hyman, *A More Perfect Union: The Impact of the Civil War and Reconstruction on the Constitution* (New York: Alfred A. Knopf, 1973). Bates's opinion of July 5, 1861, is in the Abraham Lincoln Papers, Library of Congress.

See also CONSTITUTION OF THE UNITED STATES; PRESIDENCY, POWERS OF THE; VALLANDIGHAM, CLEMENT LAIRD.

Halstead, Murat (1829–1908) Cincinnati *Commercial* reporter. Halstead covered all four of the national nominating conventions in 1860, and he published his reports as a book. He was cynical about politics, terming nominating conventions mere caucuses of "rottenness and corruption." He described Lincoln's nomination as "the triumph of availability over pre-eminence in intellect and unrivalled fame." Halstead attributed Lincoln's victory to the gubernatorial candidates who feared defeat in their states if William H. Seward were the Republican nominee and to the pro-Lincoln galleries in Chicago. But he was unaware of the work of Lincoln's managers—David Davis, Leonard Swett, and others.

A loyal Republican, Halstead was much too independent and acerbic to enter political life, and in a letter shown to Lincoln by Henry Villard he stated flatly: "Mr. Lincoln has no office within his gift for which I am competent that I would accept. . . . I never expect a particle of the patronage." He did occasionally try to press advice on the President (through Salmon P. Chase or John G. Nicolay). In the spring of 1863 he excitedly told Chase that General U. S. Grant was "a jackass in the original package," sure to be defeated. He strongly urged that Grant's and Ambrose E. Burnside's armies be united under General William Rosecrans to attack the Confederate center in the West up the Tennessee River.

Halstead remained active in journalism through the turn of the century. Driven into the Liberal Republican movement in 1872 by his continuing revulsion at Grant, then President, he returned to the Republican fold and wrote compaign biographies of William McKinley and Theodore Roosevelt.

SOURCES: William B. Hesseltine reprinted Halstead's widely quoted coverage of the 1860 conventions in *Three Against Lincoln: Murat Halstead Reports the Caucuses of 1860* (Baton Rouge: Louisiana State University Press, 1960). Halstead's letter to Chase (April 1, 1863) is in the Abraham Lincoln Papers, Library of Congress.

Murat Halstead. (Courtesy of the Cincinnati Historical Society)

Hamlin, Hannibal (1809–1891) Lincoln's first Vice President. Hamlin was the son of a prominent Maine physician and Federalist. His brother was a Whig, but Hannibal became a Jacksonian Democrat. Educated briefly at Hebron Academy, Hamlin taught school and published a Democratic newspaper before studying law with Samuel C. Fessenden, a renowned abolitionist in Portland, Maine. He was admitted to the bar in 1833 and practiced law in Hampden, Maine. In 1835 he was elected to the Maine House of Representatives. He was generally hostile to paper money issued by banks; he disliked slavery ("a curse, a moral wrong") and abolitionism alike. He hoped to "confine it [slavery] within as narrow a compass as possible to prevent it from spreading." He led a movement to abolish capital punishment in Maine in 1837.

Hamlin first won election to Congress in 1843, and in 1844 he joined the fight against the Gag Rule, which prevented debate on antislavery petitions. He also op-

Hannibal Hamlin

posed a national bank and tariffs (except on Maine products like cordwood and potatoes). Reelected in 1844, he opposed dueling and Texas annexation (unless part of the slave territory was reserved for free territory), but he urged immediate "reoccupation" of the Oregon Territory. He supported the building of a transcontinental railroad, though he otherwise opposed internal improvements at federal expense. In 1846 and 1847 he supported the Wilmot Proviso.

In 1847 Hamlin resumed his place in the Maine House of Representatives; in the next year he was elected to the United States Senate. He opposed the Compromise of 1850 on President Zachary Taylor's grounds and advised the Whig President on Maine patronage. With Free-Soil party support, he was reelected to the Senate in 1851, but in the next year he stumped Maine for Democratic presidential candidate Franklin Pierce. Though he opposed the Kansas-Nebraska Act of 1854, he remained a Democrat until June 1856, when he turned Republican. He was elected Governor in that year and Senator again in 1857.

In May 1860 he became Lincoln's running mate. His candidacy balanced the former Whig Westerner with a former Democrat from the East, and was acceptable to Lincoln's rival Seward. He first corresponded with Lincoln in June. Lincoln and Hamlin met in Chicago from November 22 to 24, 1860, to discuss Cabinet selections. Lincoln allowed Hamlin to choose the New England representative for the Cabinet from a list of four: Charles Francis Adams, Nathaniel P. Banks, Amos Tuck, and Gideon Welles. In December Hamlin conferred with New England politicians about the selection. At first he leaned toward Adams: he was able, had a prestigious name, and had "a fortune of one or two Millions of dollars, which would give great confidence to the commercial and financial public—Those are timid elements in our community, and it does seem to me that it will be wise indeed to have Some man of fortune in your cabinet for the purpose of giving confidence in the quarter indicated." Adams, however, was much too close to Seward to serve in the same Cabinet. Hamlin did not care for Banks, "a man of decided ability, but . . . *wonderfully* cold and selfish." Once Adams was ruled out, Welles was Hamlin's preference. Hamlin thought the Secretary of War should be a Southerner and supported Welles's suggestion of Montgomery Blair for that post. He thought Simon Cameron would be a "ruinous" appointment.

Hamlin feared that the Buchanan administration connived at acts of "treason," and he supported an unyielding stand in the Sumter crisis that followed in the spring. His important role was over, and he quickly became a typically powerless Vice President, complaining to Jessie Benton Frémont in 1862 that he disapproved of the "slow and unsatisfactory movements of the Government" but was "not consulted at all." He was often absent from his job as President of the Senate and spent considerable time in Maine. For 2 months in 1864 he even served a tour of garrison duty with the Maine Coast Guards. Hamlin thought the President too slow to move against slavery and claimed, in later years, that he had been the first to be shown Lincoln's Emancipation Proclamation (as early as June 18, 1862). When the Proclamation was issued, he complimented the President for "the great act of the age."

Hamlin controlled little patronage and had a serious falling out with Welles over the Secretary's refusal to establish a prize court in Portland, Maine. At the Republican convention in Baltimore, in 1864, Hamlin lost the vice-presidential nomination to Andrew Johnson on the first ballot. There is no direct evidence of Lincoln's role in this change, but many would agree with Ward Hill Lamon's recollection that Lincoln wanted War Democrat Johnson but worked for his nomination only secretly in order not to give offense to New England. Hamlin showed no outward and immediate signs of disgruntlement and campaigned in the fall for the Lincoln-Johnson ticket.

In August 1865 President Johnson appointed Hamlin collector of the Port of Boston. Believing that "treason is a crime to be punished, and that is the only *security* for the future," Hamlin was soon horrified by Johnson's Reconstruction policy. He kept his job only a year. He supported the Fourteenth Amendment, though he would have preferred a clause guaranteeing the vote to veterans of any color, and he hoped for Johnson's impeachment. In 1869 he returned to the Senate and became a loyal supporter of President Ulysses S. Grant. Reelected in 1875, he served out his term and was appointed minister to Spain by Secretary of State (and Maine political ally) James G. Blaine.

Despite political differences, Hamlin admired Lincoln and called him, in 1881, "one of the most distinguished [men] of all times and all nations." He thought him "systematic and industrious" in discharging public duties, humorous, and unassuming. He ranked the Emancipation Proclamation, of course, as the most important act of Lincoln's life. Of Mrs. Lincoln, however, he was none too fond; he complained in 1865 that she was a "mere snob."

SOURCES: See Charles Eugene Hamlin, *The Life and Times of Hannibal Hamlin* (Cambridge: Riverside Press, 1899) and H. Draper Hunt, *Hannibal Hamlin of Maine: Lincoln's First Vice-President* (Syracuse, N.Y.: Syracuse University Press, 1969), a competent biography. Hamlin's letters to Lincoln about Adams (December 10, 1860), Banks (December 14, 1860), Cameron and Blair (December 27, 1860), and the Emancipation Proclamation (September 25, 1862) are in the Abraham Lincoln Papers, Library of Congress.

See also CAMERON, SIMON; MCCLURE, ALEXANDER KELLY.

Hampton Roads Peace Conference A secret meeting on February 3, 1865, of Abraham Lincoln and William H. Seward with three Confederate peace commissioners, Vice President Alexander H. Stephens, R. M. T. Hunter, and John A. Campbell. The conference grew out of a scheme initiated by Francis Preston Blair, an old-time Democratic politician friendly with the Lincoln administration. Blair had known Jefferson Davis before the war, and on January 12, 1865, he used a pass secured from Lincoln to visit the Confederate President in Richmond. He proposed that Davis give up slavery and Southern independence to send an army to drive the French out of Mexico and assume a temporary dictatorship over the unstable republic. That, Blair thought, would end the American Civil War by uniting North and South against French imperialism. It would also add new territory to the South which would serve to balance the superiority of the North. Davis was noncommittal. He did not trust Seward, and he did not know Lincoln.

President Lincoln sent Blair back to Richmond on January 20 with his reply: "I have constantly been, am now, and shall continue ready to receive any agent whom he [Davis], or any other influential person now resisting the national authority, may informally send to me, with the view of securing peace to the people of our one common country." Davis selected critics of his administration, among whom none had been more vociferous than his own Vice President, to meet Lincoln and Seward. His letter of appointment, however, instructed the commissioners to discuss "securing peace to the two countries" (the United States and the Confederacy). In truth, Davis and Lincoln were no closer to agreement than they had been in 1861, and the conference was doomed to failure before it began. The commissioners were really seeking an armistice, not a peace based on reunion.

The meeting took place at Hampton Roads, Virginia, aboard the steamship *River Queen*. Seward stipulated that no notes be taken. Common political heritage helped break the ice: Hunter, Stephens, Seward, and Lincoln had at one time been members of the Whig party. After reminiscing about old Whig days, the conference began in earnest. Lincoln showed no interest in the Mexican scheme, and he repeatedly asserted that no agreements on any such project could be reached without first obtaining from the South an unconditional pledge of loyalty to the Union.

Inevitably, the subject of emancipation arose. Lincoln and Seward agreed that the courts would ultimately decide the fate of the slaves not actually freed by the Union armies (all but 200,000, they estimated). As the Emancipation Proclamation was a war measure, it was likely to have no effect in peacetime. Seward mentioned the Thirteenth Amendment, which would abolish slavery, and inferred that it too was a war measure which could be blocked if the Southern states hurried back into the Union and refused to ratify it. Stephens later claimed that Lincoln then urged him to go home to Georgia and gain the ratification of the amendment *prospectively*, to take effect 5 years later. Lincoln promised to compensate slaveholders $400 million for their loss.

On this last point Stephens's memory was certainly in error. As soon as Lincoln returned to Washington he did indeed draft a plan to distribute $400 million in 6 percent bonds to the 15 slave states in proportion to their slave population. Half would be paid on April 1, 1865, if the South rejoined the Union, and half on July 1, 1865, provided the Thirteenth Amendment was ratified by that date. Thus Lincoln's plan called for ratification in 5 *months*, not 5 years. Stephens, however, wrote his account of the conference, the only lengthy one in existence, in 1870, 5 years after the event. It was easy for this Georgia proslavery thinker, after 5 years of Reconstruction conflicts over civil and voting rights for Negroes, to write, nostalgically, as though Lincoln would never have condoned the events of the preceding 5 years of Southern history, indeed, would just be getting around to freeing the slaves. This clearly erroneous reminiscence serves to cast doubt on any part of Stephens's account of the conference which might be susceptible to pro-Confederate bias.

The conference ended after 4 hours of discussion. President Davis felt that Lincoln had offered only unconditional surrender, and he used the results of the conference to show that the South must continue to fight; Lincoln would offer it no real peace terms. When Congress requested a report on the conference from Lincoln, the President responded with the formal correspondence leading up to it and little more than the bare statement: "The conference ended without result."

SOURCES: Edward Chase Kirkland's *The Peacemakers of 1864* (New York: Macmillan, 1927) is a solid, if somewhat dated, study of the conference and other peace initiatives in the Civil War. Like all accounts, it relies too uncritically on Alexander H. Stephens's recollection of the conference in *A Constitutional View of the Late War Between the States*, II (Philadelphia: National Publishing Company, 1870), 589–625.

See also BLAIR, FRANCIS PRESTON; STEPHENS, ALEXANDER HAMILTON.

Hanks, Dennis Friend (1799–1892) Lincoln's mother's cousin. Hanks was born in Hardin County, Kentucky, the illegitimate son of Nancy Hanks, an aunt of the Nancy Hanks who was Lincoln's mother. In 1817 he came to southern Indiana with the Sparrow family, who also were relatives of Nancy Hanks Lincoln. Despite their difference in age, the loneliness of the wilderness made young Abraham and Dennis close companions. When Lincoln's mother and the Sparrows died of "milk sickness" in 1818, Dennis moved in with the Lincolns and slept in the loft of the cabin with Abraham. In 1821 he married Sarah Elizabeth Johnston, daughter of Thomas Lincoln's second wife, Sarah Bush Johnston. Hanks moved with the Lincoln party to Illinois in 1830, but thereafter he parted ways from Abraham.

Hanks settled in Charleston, Coles County. In 1836 he was a codefendant with Thomas Lincoln in a suit brought against him, Thomas Lincoln, and others for failure to pay debts incurred in the lease of a saw and grist mill. From 1844 to 1846 his daughter Harriet apparently boarded with Abraham and Mary Lincoln in Springfield to better her education. In 1851 Lincoln represented Hanks in a suit against William B. White.

While Lincoln was President, Hanks and John J. Hall, the son of Lincoln's stepsister Matilda Johnston Hall, argued over the responsibility for caring for Lincoln's aged and ill stepmother. Lincoln sent Hanks $50 for her use. In acknowledging the money Hanks said that

Dennis Friend Hanks

Sarah was a "mity childish heep of truble to us." In May he visited Lincoln in Washington, in part to discuss the President's stepmother and in part to plead for the release of men arrested for rioting against Union soldiers in Charleston on March 28. Lincoln released the prisoners much later during the summer, and Hanks's pleas were probably not decisive. Since his wife was dying, Hanks tried to get Hall, then living on land Lincoln had purchased for his stepmother's use, to care for Sarah. Hall claimed that he had cared for her all along and that Dennis pocketed the money Lincoln sent for her use. After Lincoln's death, Hanks joined others in purchasing and displaying publicly a cabin near Decatur in which Lincoln had lived briefly.

Hanks was a cobbler. Tradition has it that all the Hankses were democrats, but in 1843 Dennis voted for Whig Justin Harlan over Democrat Orlando B. Ficklin for Congress. Hanks himself ran for Recorder in the same contest and was probably a Whig like Thomas Lincoln, who voted for him. He may have turned Republican later. His wife sought an appointment for him as postmaster from President Lincoln, and this sort of request was rarely made by members of the opposite party. He died in 1892, run down by a carriage while he returned from a celebration of the anniversary of the passage of the Thirteenth Amendment.

SOURCES: William H. Herndon, Lincoln's law partner and early biographer, thought Hanks an outrageous liar. And Hanks's testimony, in the Herndon-Weik Collection, Library of Congress, is indeed riddled with inaccuracies. For information on Hanks see Charles H. Coleman's, *Abraham Lincoln and Coles County, Illinois* (New Brunswick, N.J.: Scarecrow Press, 1955). Hanks's vote for Harlan is recorded in a Charleston Poll Book, August 7, 1843, in the Louis A. Warren Lincoln Library and Museum, Fort Wayne, Indiana.

Hanks, John (1802–1889) Lincoln's mother's cousin. Abraham Lincoln met John Hanks in 1822 when Hanks moved from Kentucky, where he had been born, to southern Indiana. He lived off and on in the Lincoln household there. In 1826 Hanks returned to Kentucky and in 1828 moved to Illinois, settling in Macon County near Decatur. Though illiterate, he apparently lured the Lincolns west by getting word to them of Illinois's fertile soil and absence of "milk sickness" (which had killed Nancy Hanks Lincoln). The Lincolns moved to Macon County in 1830, and Abraham and John briefly hired out to split fence rails. Denton Offutt, a pioneer-merchant, hired them a year later to take a flatboat of produce to New Orleans. Hanks later claimed that the sight of the horrors of slavery in New Orleans forged Lincoln's antislavery convictions, but Lincoln stated in an 1860 autobiography written for John Locke Scripps that Hanks turned back at St. Louis and did not make the trip to New Orleans.

Hanks joined the gold rush to California in 1850 and returned to Illinois in better financial condition in 1853. As Lincoln's political career began to prosper shortly thereafter, Hanks was merely an observer; he was a Democrat. However, before the Republican State Convention met in Decatur in May of 1860, a Republican lawyer from Decatur, Richard J. Oglesby, contacted Hanks and took him (at the party's expense) to get some of the black walnut and honey locust rails Hanks had split with Lincoln 30 years before. On May 8 Oglesby announced to the convention that an "old Democrat" would make a contribution to the convention, and Hanks came down the aisle with Isaac Jennings, carrying two rails and a banner which said: "ABRAHAM LINCOLN The Rail Candidate For President in 1860 Two rails from a lot of 3,000 made in 1830 by John Hanks and Abe Lincoln, whose father was the first pioneer in Macon County." Hanks became so famous for his role in creating the "Rail Splitter" candidate that he sold rails from the old farm all over the country at a dollar per rail. That year, Hanks voted Republican.

When Lincoln visited Coles County to bid his stepmother farewell before leaving for Washington, Hanks accompanied him from Decatur. In September 1861 he sought a government appointment from President Lincoln through Oglesby, but his illiteracy disqualified him. It was no barrier to military service, however, and the 59-year-old Hanks had become a wagoner in the Twenty-first Illinois Volunteer Infantry that summer. He was discharged in 1864.

Hanks attended Lincoln's funeral in Springfield and has the dubious distinction of being among the earliest to capitalize on his association with the martyred President by displaying relics associated with Lincoln. With Dennis Hanks and James Shoaff he purchased the Lincoln cabin in Macon County, had it disassembled, and displayed it at a Sanitary Fair in Chicago in June. They displayed the cabin on the Boston Common later in the summer. Sales of souvenir canes made from Lincoln rails were brisk. After display in Barnum's Museum in New York City, the cabin disappeared from history.

When interviewed about Lincoln by William H. Herndon in 1865, Hanks, then 63 years old, recalled Lincoln as a hard-working youth who read books at every opportunity. He remembered young Abraham's pulling fodder for a neighbor from whom he had borrowed a life of Washington which got wet on a bookshelf close to the cabin window. Lincoln was "always a Whig; so was his father before him." Hanks's oft-quoted but dubious remembrance of the encounter with slavery in New Orleans stated: "Lincoln saw it, his heart bled, said nothing much, was silent from feeling, was sad, looked bad, felt bad, was thoughtful and abstracted. I can say knowingly that it was on this trip that he formed his opinions of slavery; it ran its iron in him then and there—May 1831." At the end of the interview Herndon wrote in his notes: "I can say that this testimony can be implicitly relied on. Mr. Lincoln loved this man, thought him beautiful, honest, and noble. Lincoln has stated this to me over and over again."

Hanks returned to Decatur in 1865 and lived in retirement there until his death in 1889.

SOURCES: See Marilyn Gahm Ames, "John Hanks, Lincoln's Rail Splitter Cousin," unpublished master's thesis, Illinois State University, 1974, and R. Gerald McMurtry, "The Lincoln Cabin on Boston Common," *Lincoln Lore*, Number 1449 (November

John Hanks

1958), pp. 1–3. John Hanks's famous recollections of Lincoln are printed in Emanuel Hertz's *The Hidden Lincoln: From the Letters and Papers of William H. Herndon* (New York: Viking, 1938).

See also RAIL SPLITTER.

Hardin, John J. **(1810–1847)** Mary Todd Lincoln's cousin and Abraham Lincoln's Whig rival in the Seventh Congressional District of Illinois. John J. Hardin was born in Frankfort, Kentucky, the son of a United States Senator. He graduated from Transylvania University, was admitted to the Kentucky bar in 1831, and established a law practice in the same year in Jacksonville, Illinois, the seat of Morgan County. He was a major general in the Illinois militia and mustered in Abraham Lincoln's company in the Black Hawk War in 1832. In 1836 Morgan County sent Hardin to the lower house of the Illinois legislature, where, unlike Lincoln, he opposed the internal improvements bill and voted consistently to move the state capital from Vandalia to Jacksonville. In 1838 and in 1840 he was reelected to the Illinois House. Both men left the state legislature at the same time. In September 1842 Hardin intervened to avert a threatened duel between his friend Lincoln and Democrat James Shields over the satirical "Rebecca letters."

Lincoln, Hardin, and Edward D. Baker were the acknowledged leaders of the Illinois Whig party, the strength of which was concentrated by 1843 in one congressional district, the Seventh, in which all lived. Both Lincoln and Hardin regarded Baker as the man to beat for the 1843 Whig nomination for Congress. Lincoln lost Sangamon County's support to Baker, and Baker, in turn, lost the nomination to Hardin. Hardin was younger than Lincoln and had served one term less in the state legislature, but he had opposed the failed internal improvements system. He was a critic of tighter party organization and especially of the convention system for nominations, of which Lincoln was an outspoken supporter. Hardin worried that Sangamon's Whigs might not support him warmly in the election, but Lincoln assured him that he could "dismiss all fears on that subject." However, Lincoln himself voted only for minor offices and did not vote for Hardin.

In Congress Hardin voted against the Gag Rule, which prevented debate on antislavery petitions, and gave his maiden speech, studded with impressive statistics, in favor of river and harbor improvements for the West. The latter was proof that Hardin was a good, development-minded Whig despite his opposition to the Illinois internal improvements system. "A few years ago," he told a correspondent in 1844, "the [Illinois] Legislature was Internal Improvement mad—Now it is *Retrenchment mad*." Hardin was for claiming a more northerly boundary for Oregon than England seemed willing to grant, but the young Congressman cast a skeptical eye on the "great effort amongst the locos [Democrats] to make capital out of the Texas question." "From the first," he told a friend, "I have been openly against it [the annexation of Texas], but in common with the Northern Whigs we have been quiet in order to enable the southern Whigs to act in a body with us." As the only Whig Congressman from Illinois, Hardin worked indefatigably to frank and distribute documents and speeches all over the state for the 1844 presidential election.

Meanwhile, Seventh District Whigs chose Baker as Hardin's successor in keeping with a resolution put forward at the Pekin convention of 1843, which had nominated Hardin. The resolution pointed to Baker as a worthy candidate for Congress in 1844 and thus cleared the way for a succession without divisive squabbling among the party leaders. At that time Lincoln had apparently suggested to Baker and Hardin that the three should agree to one term in order to prevent dividing the Whigs.

By the time Lincoln's turn came around in 1846, the incumbent Baker was "certainly off the track" (Lincoln had it in writing), but, he added, "I fear Hardin intends to be on it." As he angled for delegates' votes for the 1846 district convention, Lincoln insisted that "nothing be said against Hardin . . . nothing deserves to be said against him. Let the pith of the whole argument be 'Turn about is fair play.' " Nevertheless, Hardin still sought the nomination, and Lincoln would not yield. To do so when neither or both had been to Congress was one thing, but to "yield to Hardin under present circumstances, seems to me as nothing else than yielding to one who would gladly sacrifice me altogether."

Lincoln's suspicions were confirmed when Hardin proposed a new system for nominating candidates, a sort of preferential primary in which Whigs would determine their counties' choices on one day of voting. Lincoln sniffed in it a system less catered to making nominations more democratic than to increasing Hardin's chances of gaining the nomination. In a long letter to Hardin written on January 19, 1846, he noted that Hardin's proposal that candidates be pledged not to electioneer outside their home counties gave a decided advantage to Hardin, who had already been to Congress and was, therefore, well known all over the district. If more democracy were really Hardin's desire in reforming the convention system, Lincoln pointed out, a crucial need was to reapportion the weight given each county in the final decision. This Hardin had not proposed, and in all cases but one, the undervalued counties were the ones where Hardin had the least strength. Without acrimony or personal criticism, Lincoln rejected the proposal. "Turnabout" proved a persuasive argument with Whig leaders in the district, and Hardin withdrew his candidacy on February 16. Before that, however, Hardin had inspired an article in the *Morgan Journal* which, with "utter injustice," Lincoln thought, suggested that Lincoln had gone after the nomination by means of "management," "maneuvering," and "combination."

Lincoln won election in 1846, but Hardin was already pursuing another path to prominence. Even as the Texas question seemed to threaten war with Mexico, Hardin had said, "Though not agreeing with the administration on all points of domestic policy, yet in our foreign rela-

John J. Hardin. (Courtesy of the Illinois State Historical Library)

tions I acknowledge no fealty to any party but our country." Soon after war broke out, he was elected colonel (June 30, 1846) of the First Illinois Regiment of Volunteers. He was killed in combat at the Battle of Buena Vista on February 23, 1847.

SOURCES: See Donald W. Riddle, *Lincoln Runs for Congress* (New Brunswick, N.J.: Rutgers University Press, 1948). Hardin's letters to S. T. Matthews about internal improvements and retrenchment mania (January 3, 1844), to C. D. Drake about Democrats' capitalizing on the Texas question (April 9, 1844), and to D. A. Smith about his opposition to Texas annexation (April 26, 1844) are in the Hardin Papers, Chicago Historical Society.

Hardin County *See* KENTUCKY.

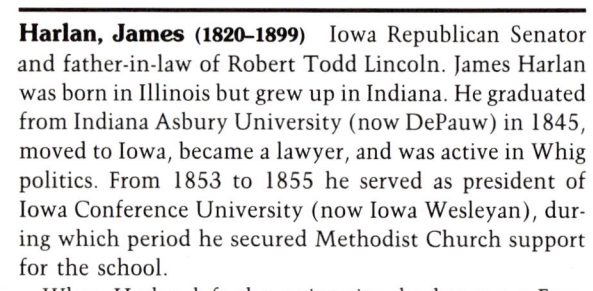

Harlan, James (1820–1899) Iowa Republican Senator and father-in-law of Robert Todd Lincoln. James Harlan was born in Illinois but grew up in Indiana. He graduated from Indiana Asbury University (now DePauw) in 1845, moved to Iowa, became a lawyer, and was active in Whig politics. From 1853 to 1855 he served as president of Iowa Conference University (now Iowa Wesleyan), during which period he secured Methodist Church support for the school.

When Harlan left the university, he became a Free-Soil Senator and later a Republican, winning reelection in 1860. Though he wrote Lincoln to advise on Cabinet selections and oppose the choice of Simon Cameron, he did not meet the President-elect until March 2, 1861, when Lincoln consulted him about the Cabinet in person.

As a Senator, Harlan advocated typically Republican measures: homestead legislation, land grants for agricultural colleges, and a Pacific railroad. He took special interest in the last-named and was influential in gaining legislation for the road which benefited Iowa. During the Civil War, he advocated confiscation legislation and was an early champion of arming the slaves of both loyal and disloyal masters. In a meeting with Lincoln to urge the use of black soldiers in June 1862, he was told that such a policy would endanger the loyalty of the all-important Border States. He afterward gave a speech on the question meant more for the President's ears than the Senate's. His arguments for the policy were hardly idealistic: "Why may not their bodies be made food for powder and lead as well as those of your sons and brothers?" In speaking in behalf of a constitutional amendment to abolish slavery, however, Harlan argued that Negroes could take care of themselves and had in Liberia demonstrated a capacity for self-government.

Harlan headed the Republican Congressional Committee for the campaign of 1864. His speech, *The Constitution Upheld and Maintained*, widely circulated as a campaign pamphlet, defended emancipation, arbitrary arrests, and suppression of newspapers as legitimate constitutional measures. Lincoln rewarded his diligent work on March 9, 1865, with an appointment as Secretary of the Interior. Washington observers had expected the appointment when they saw Robert Todd Lincoln escort Mary Harlan, the Senator's daughter, to the inaugural ball. Only insiders knew that his appointment was a sop to the Methodists, long disappointed at their treatment by the Lincoln administration. Harlan did not actually assume the duties of office until after Lincoln's death.

Harlan was a member of the congressional committee which escorted Lincoln's remains to Springfield, and he served as president of the short-lived Lincoln Monument Association, organized to establish a Lincoln monument in Washington. He broke with Andrew Johnson over Reconstruction and resigned his Cabinet post in July 1866. He returned to the Senate for one term and then to his old post at Iowa Wesleyan College.

In 1868 Robert Lincoln married Mary Harlan in the Harlan home in Washington. Later, the Lincolns frequently spent their summers in the Harlan home in Mount Pleasant, Iowa. One-third of the sizable estate of Lincoln's last direct descendant, Robert Lincoln Beckwith, will go to Iowa Wesleyan.

SOURCES: There is no adequate biography, but there is some useful information in Johnson Brigham's *James Harlan* (Iowa City: State Historical Society of Iowa, 1913). See also R. Gerald McMurtry, "The Harlan-Lincoln Tradition at Iowa Wesleyan College," *Lincoln Herald*, XLVIII (October 1946), 11–21.

See also SIMPSON, MATTHEW.

Harris, Clara *See* RATHBONE, HENRY RIGGS

Hatch, Ozias Mather (1814–1893) A political associate of Lincoln's. Hatch was born in New Hampshire but moved in 1836 to Griggsville, Illinois, where he entered the general merchandising business. From 1841 to 1848 he was clerk of the circuit court of Pike County; afterward he and his brother Reuben ran a general store in Meredosia, Illinois. In 1850 he was elected to the Illinois House of Representatives as a Whig. He thereafter was prominent in Illinois's Know-Nothing (American) party. He would retain his nativist prejudices; in 1861 he complained that it was "lamentable . . . that there are very few fighting Union men in Mo. that are not Germans." Like Lincoln, Hatch was never a member of a church.

Lincoln's association with Hatch began in 1856. Both men were Republicans by then, and Hatch was the candidate for Illinois Secretary of State. The Republican state ticket was successful in 1856 and again in 1860, when Hatch was reelected to the same office.

Lincoln appointed Reuben Hatch as Assistant Quartermaster of Volunteers, and Ozias Hatch's letters to Lincoln generally concerned appointments to office. In July 1861 Hatch joined other Republicans in protesting the possible appointment of Lincoln's brother-in-law Ninian W. Edwards as commissary in Springfield. Hatch and the State Auditor, Jesse K. Dubois, thought Edwards was surrounded by associates guilty of "stupendous and unprecedented frauds." Edwards did nothing in office to change their minds. For almost 2 years, Hatch complained of Edwards's corruption. "Fortunes" were being made improperly in letting contracts for the troops' sub-

James Harlan

Ozias Mather Hatch. (Lloyd Ostendorf Collection)

sistence. Though Hatch admitted that he could not prove fraud and avoided saying that Lincoln's relative was himself dishonest, he knew for "certain," he said, that contracts went "to men, that denounce your administration, and sympathize with rebels." He thought Edwards a tool of Democrat Joel A. Matteson. Lincoln removed Edwards from the Springfield office and made another appointment.

By June 15, 1863, Lincoln was complaining that his old Springfield friends were "harrassing" him because of Edwards, and the tone of his correspondence with Hatch became strained. When Hatch and Dubois, thinking erroneously that Quartermaster General Montgomery Meigs had resigned, recommended Robert Allen for that office, Lincoln replied tartly (September 15, 1863): "What nation do you desire Gen. Allen to be made Quarter-Master-General of? This nation already has a Quarter-Master-General." Hatch and Dubois protested that the letter "read harshly," and Lincoln explained (September 22, 1863) that his letter had been "jocular."

As the Illinois Secretary of State, Hatch played a major role in mobilizing the state for war; he refused to keep the fees which accrued to his office for commissions for Illinois soldiers. He was a staunch Unionist of antislavery convictions. In March 1863 he joined Dubois, William Butler, and Governor Richard Yates in requesting that four regiments be raised in Illinois to enforce martial law in the state if the legislature abolished the governor's control of the militia, resisted the draft, and refused to return deserters to the army. Lincoln approved the plan, and Secretary of War Edwin M. Stanton ordered the raising of four regiments. Stanton rescinded the order at the end of March, when political tensions in Illinois eased. In 1864 Hatch asked Lincoln to intervene in Dubois's favor to avoid an "ugly contest" within the party for the gubernatorial nomination between "Uncle Jesse" and Richard J. Oglesby. Lincoln refused to intervene. Hatch worked for Lincoln's renomination and reelection.

When his term expired, Hatch retired from public life and engaged in banking, farming, and railroad interests. He had been a member of the committee on arrangements for Lincoln's funeral in Springfield and was an active member of the National Lincoln Monument Association. He died a prosperous man in Springfield.

SOURCES: There is a biographical sketch of Hatch in the *Biographical Dictionary . . . of the Representative Men of the United States: Illinois Volume*, ed. by John Moses (Chicago: Lewis Publishing Co., 1896). Hatch's letters to Lincoln mentioning Germans (August 17, 1861); about Ninian W. Edwards (July 1, 1861 ["stupendous . . . frauds"], October 21, 1861 [about Matteson], May 25, 1863 ["Fortunes . . . to men, that . . . sympathize with rebels"]); and about the legislature's probable disloyal acts (March 1, 1863) are in the Abraham Lincoln Papers, Library of Congress. John P. Senning's "The Know-Nothing Movement in Illinois," *Journal of the Illinois State Historical Society*, VII (April 1914), 9–33, notes Hatch's Know-Nothing affiliation. See also Roy P. Basler, *President Lincoln Helps His Old Friends* (Springfield, Ill.: Abraham Lincoln Association, 1977).

Hay, John Milton (1838–1905) President Lincoln's secretary and later his biographer. John Hay was born in Salem, Indiana, and grew up in Warsaw, Illinois. He attended a private academy in Pittsfield, Illinois, in 1851 and there met John G. Nicolay, a local newspaperman; theirs would be a lifelong friendship. Hay attended a "college" in Springfield, and in 1855 entered Brown University as a sophomore. He did well academically and was class poet.

Hay returned to Illinois in 1858 and the next year entered the law office of his uncle Milton Hay. He met Lincoln, and he renewed his friendship with Nicolay, now a clerk in the office of the Illinois Secretary of State. After Nicolay became Lincoln's secretary and the volume of mail increased after Lincoln's election, he chose Hay to help, and Hay retained the job until Lincoln's death.

The work was taxing. With Nicolay, Hay screened visitors, read mail, prepared a daily news summary, and acted as messenger. He went through it all with the ironic humor of youth; he referred to the President as the "Tycoon" or the "Ancient." When time permitted, he kept a diary. Those sporadic notes and his letters of the time are important sources for the inner history of the Lincoln administration. An early doubter of General George B. McClellan's abilities, Hay traced that general's downfall in interesting detail; the diary is a key source for Lincoln's attitude toward McClellan. Other vignettes of White House life are unforgettable: Benjamin F. Butler denouncing Jews (King John "fried them in swine's fat"); Lincoln describing John C. Frémont as a dangerous man but for his lack of ability ("like Jim Jett's brother . . . the damndest scoundrel that ever lived, but in the infinite mercy of Providence . . . also the damndest fool"); and Hay himself telling Nicolay he would rather "make the tour of a smallpox hospital" than take a letter asking a military favor to Secretary of War Edwin M. Stanton. His hostility to Radical Republicans, whom he called "Jacobins," still influences the literature on Lincoln.

Like Nicolay, Hay was occasionally entrusted with errands above the clerical level. In the spring of 1863 he went to South Carolina. Early in 1864 he went to Florida to try to enlist enough repentant Confederates to take Lincoln's loyalty oath and elect Hay to the House of Representatives. Hay could not enroll enough voters. He visited St. Louis to investigate General William S. Rosecrans's allegations that the disloyal Order of American Knights posed a serious threat; Hay and Lincoln concluded that the threat was not serious. Hay also accompanied Horace Greeley at his meeting with the Confederate peace commissioners in Canada on July 20, 1864.

The work grew more tedious, and Hay bridled at living in the same house with Mrs. Lincoln; "the Hell-Cat," he called her. By March 1865 Hay had obtained an appointment as Secretary of Legation in Paris. He remained to get the new office staff in working order and was, therefore, still in Washington when Lincoln was shot. He was at the bedside when the President died.

Hay served in several foreign posts until 1870. He took a job with the New York *Tribune* and left it in

John Milton Hay

1875, about a year after his marriage to Clara Stone, the daughter of a wealthy Cleveland family.

In the early 1870s he began to work with Nicolay on an authorized biography of Abraham Lincoln based on private papers lent Nicolay by Lincoln's son Robert. Hay was a proven writer with several published works to his credit, but Nicolay had been a journalist; the two shared the writing responsibilities so equally that it is impossible to tell who wrote which section. They exchanged and criticized each others' drafts, checked sources, and carefully proofread their manuscript. The work was laborious, especially since Hay, in the 15-year period of work on the 10-volume history, moved to Washington from Cleveland, had a famous house built there, served (after November 1878) as Assistant Secretary of State, and wrote an anonymous novel, *The Bread-Winners* (1884).

In 1885 *The Century Magazine* gave Nicolay and Hay $50,000 to serialize the work. About half of the work had appeared in serial form by 1890, when *Abraham Lincoln: A History* was published as a book. Hay warned Nicolay that the "war has gone by," and he attempted to tone down some of the more critical characterizations of Lincoln's enemies. The writers made changes demanded by Robert Lincoln, but, on the whole, their view of his father was so favorable that Robert seems to have asked for little in that vein. Hay characterized their approach to General McClellan by saying that they should "*seem* fair to him, while we are destroying him." He found "enough in Chase's letters abusing Lincoln behind his back for a quiet scorcher." With Stephen A. Douglas, they were gentler; they forgave Douglas much for his support of the Union in the secession crisis.

By the end Hay was sick of the project. Still, the coauthors managed to produce a two-volume set of Lincoln's works, which printed many previously unknown manuscripts, in 1894. With that, Hay was through with writing history and went on to make it himself as Ambassador to the Court of St. James and Secretary of State under Presidents William McKinley and Theodore Roosevelt.

About a decade before he began work as Lincoln's "official" biographer, Hay assessed Lincoln's character for a more iconoclastic biographer, William H. Herndon. From a clerk's point of view, Lincoln was "extremely unmethodical" and broke "through every regulation as fast as it was made." He found Lincoln "very abstemious, ate less than anyone I know," and he never drank alcoholic beverages, "not from principle, but because he did not like wine or spirits." An aspiring author himself, Hay noticed that the President "read very little" and frequently scoffed that he knew more than many authors did about their subjects. "It is absurd to call him a modest man," Hay said. "No great man was ever modest." And Lincoln's unconscious arrogance in intellectual matters was what men like Salmon P. Chase and Charles Sumner could never forgive. At the end of this gloves-off sketch of his former boss, Hay characterized Lincoln as "Republicanism incarnate." "As . . . Republicanism is the sole hope of a sick world," he added, "so Lincoln, with all his foibles, is the greatest character since Christ."

SOURCES: Tyler Dennett's edition of *Lincoln and the Civil War in the Diaries and Letters of John Hay* (New York: Dodd, Mead, 1939) is a crucial source for the history of the Lincoln administration. On the writing of the monumental history of the Lincoln administration, still an important source for the period, see Benjamin P. Thomas, *Portrait for Posterity: Lincoln and His Biographers* (New Brunswick, N.J.: Rutgers University Press, 1947). Hay's letter to Herndon (September 5, 1866) appears in Emanuel Hertz, *The Hidden Lincoln: From the Letters and Papers of William H. Herndon* (New York: Viking, 1938), pp. 307–308.

See also BIOGRAPHERS; EXECUTIVE MANSION; NICOLAY, JOHN GEORGE.

Health *See* PHYSICAL CHARACTERISTICS.

Helm, Emilie Todd (1836–1930) Mary Todd Lincoln's half sister. Emilie Todd was born in Lexington, Kentucky; she was the daughter of Robert Smith Todd and Elizabeth Humphreys Todd and the fifteenth of Robert Smith Todd's 16 children. Since Mary left home when Emilie was only 3 years old, the younger sister did not know her well. Mary's rare visits to Lexington and Emilie's 6-month stay in Springfield in the winter of 1854–1855 provided their only acquaintance before the Civil War.

In 1856 Emilie married Benjamin Hardin Helm (1831–1863), a West Point graduate from a distinguished Kentucky family. The Civil War added deep political differences to the physical gap that separated the half sisters. Although President Lincoln had Helm appointed an Army paymaster after the fall of Fort Sumter, Helm declined the commission on April 27 and joined the Confederate Army; he became a brigadier general in 1862. Emilie lived with relatives in Selma, Alabama, while her husband was away. General Helm was killed at the battle of Chickamauga in September 1863. On September 24 Lincoln wrote Mary, who was visiting New York City, a letter describing the battle and mentioned incidentally that her brother-in-law had been killed in it.

Lincoln answered earnest appeals from the South to allow Emilie, who had attended her husband's funeral in Atlanta, to pass through Union lines in order to return, with her children, to her mother in Lexington. Lincoln's pass, dated October 15, allowed Mrs. Robert S. Todd "to go south and bring her daughter, Mrs Genl B. Hardin Helm, with her children, North to Kentucky." Mrs. Helm came through the lines but was stopped at Fortress Monroe, apparently because she refused to take a loyalty oath. The President had her sent to Washington.

Mrs. Helm, with her daughter Katherine, stayed in the Executive Mansion for some time. Lincoln, according to Orville Hickman Browning, was not anxious to have it known that a Confederate general's widow resided in the President's house. The same embarrassing circumstance made it perilous for Lincoln to help Mrs. Helm gain protection of stores of cotton in which she had an economic stake. Nevertheless, on December 14, Lincoln drew up an amnesty declaration for her, premised on her taking a loyalty oath, and added to it a P.S.: "Mrs. Helm claims to own some cotten at Jackson, Mississippi, and also some in Georgia; and I shall be glad, upon either place being brought within our lines, for her to be afforded the proper facilities to show her ownership, and take her property."

There is no evidence Mrs. Helm ever took the oath, but she had arrived in Lexington by December 20. Immediately, she wrote the President, "again throwing myself upon your kindness," and asked to be allowed to give clothes to Confederate prisoners at Camp Douglas. She promised to "try not to *overstep* the limits" she "should keep," but apparently she did so. On August 8, 1864, Lincoln instructed General Stephen G. Burbridge, Union commander in Kentucky, that he did "not intend to protect her against the consequences of disloyal words or acts, spoken or done by her since her return to Kentucky." Lincoln's pass applied to the trips only, though Mrs. Helm had apparently used it to prevent her arrest. She said in later years that the existence of this letter surprised her, as she never had any trouble with the Union authorities.

Emilie returned to Washington in the fall of 1864. After this second visit, "long tedious unproductive and sorrowful," she wrote a vengeful letter to the President. Her mother was ill, in shock from the death of Mrs. Helm's brother Levi Todd, who died "from utter want and destitution"; he was "another sad victim to the powers of more favored relations." With this "dreadful lesson" in mind, she added, Lincoln should give "consideration to my petition to be permitted to ship my cotton & be allowed a pass to go South to attend to it." She reminded him "that your *minnie bullets* have made us what we are" and gave her "that additional claim" on him. She apologized only for being "a woman almost crazed with misfortune." That entreaty failed also, and in January she asked Montgomery Blair's influence in recovering the cotton.

Mrs. Helm did not recover her cotton—though, according to Browning, Lincoln charged two agents dealing in Southern cotton to make some arrangement with her. The cotton burned accidentally. Mrs. Helm bought a home in Madison, Indiana, and earned her livelihood as a musician. She returned eventually to Louisville and then moved to Elizabethtown, Kentucky, where she was appointed postmistress by means of Robert Todd Lincoln's influence—despite her "undoubted anti-republican affinities (to put it no stronger)." Finally, she resided near Lexington and died there in 1930.

Before Mrs. Helm's death, her daughter Katherine published *The True Story of Mary, Wife of Lincoln* (New York: Harper & Brothers, 1928), based on family recollections, Mrs. Helm's diary, and articles Mrs. Helm had written on her relationship with the Lincolns. This somewhat saccharine defense of Mary Lincoln is not altogether reliable, but it provides important intimate glimpses of the domestic life of the Lincolns. From her visit to Springfield in 1854–1855, Mrs. Helm recalled a generally warm family life and some of Mrs. Lincoln's sparkling wit. Mrs. Helm's record of her visit to Washington in 1863 gave a more chilling picture of Mrs. Lincoln after the death of her son Willie. Emilie and Mary were drawn together by their mutual bereavements and largely maintained silence over political differences. One night, Mrs. Helm said, Mary Lincoln came to her to tell her that Willie lived and comforted her; he came to the foot of her bed every night, sometimes with his brother Eddie.

Emilie Todd and Ben Hardin Helm. (Courtesy of the Lloyd Ostendorf Collection)

SOURCES: See R. Gerald McMurtry, *Ben Hardin Helm: "Rebel" Brother-in-Law of Abraham Lincoln—with a Biographical Sketch of His Wife and an Account of the Todd Family of Kentucky* (Chicago: Civil War Round Table, 1943) and Ruth Painter Randall, *Mary Lincoln: Biography of a Marriage* (Boston: Little Brown, 1953). Mrs. Helm's letters to Lincoln of December 20, 1863, and October 30, 1864, are in the Abraham Lincoln Papers, Library of Congress. A copy of Robert's letter about her post office appointment (to J. Proctor Knott, May 7, 1881) is in the Robert Todd Lincoln Papers, Illinois State Historical Library, Springfield, Illinois.

Henry, Anson G. (1804–1865) Lincoln's doctor and close Whig political associate. Anson G. Henry was born in Richfield, New York, where he received a common-school education and studied medicine with a doctor. After he completed his medical study in Cincinnati in 1827, he restlessly moved from place to place and job to job and finally settled in Springfield, Illinois, in 1833.

Henry was an extremely active Whig, an ardent promoter of internal improvements, and (in 1837) one of three commissioners to oversee building the new state capitol. Like Lincoln, with whom he became well ac-

Anson G. Henry. (Courtesy of the Lloyd Ostendorf Collection)

Henry, Anson G.

quainted, he was an advocate of temperance and of strong party organization, something which other Whigs were slow to realize was crucial to winning elections. As late as 1844 he complained that "Our system of organization is progressing, but more slowly than I could wish. . . . Our party can beat the world in the way of bragging & talking, but when it comes to the more important & substantial part of business they are most sadly remiss." He worked strenuously for the election of William Henry Harrison in 1840, and Lincoln felt that his work merited the reward of a post office appointment. Lincoln urged the appointment on Congressman John Todd Stuart, mentioning also that it would keep the doctor in Springfield and his medical advice was "necessary to my existence" (Lincoln was in a period of depression brought on by the breaking of his engagement to Mary Todd). Henry failed to get the office, but he remained in Springfield and continued to labor for the Whig cause.

In 1842 Dr. Henry was one of the organizers of the Springfield Henry Clay Club. When he sent a list of Whig voters to Congressman John J. Hardin on November 11, 1843, he wrote:

> You need not expect Stuart, [Edward D.] Baker or Lincoln to do this kind of work for the party. I am the only working man of *this sort* in Springfield. I have all my life beat the bush for others to catch the bird, and as I am a Whig from principle, I shall continue . . . to labour faithfully for the triumph of those principles, without hope of fee or reward.

In 1844 he was president of Sangamon County's Whig convention and chairman of the State Central Committee. He labored tirelessly; he pressed merchants to sell Whig Almanacs ("A Locofoco [Democrat] will read an almanac when they would not read any thing else"); and he sought enough subscribers to warrant establishing a German-language party newspaper. Thinking (and hoping) that Martin Van Buren would be the Democratic presidential nominee in 1844, Dr. Henry felt the Whigs could win on the tariff issue. "Lincoln," he reported, "has proved conclusively that the English are now flooding this country with tracts & money to break down the present Whig tariff. *We all believe it.*"

Henry pushed Lincoln's nomination for Congress in the *Tazewell Whig* in 1845. (He had moved to Pekin, perhaps because of an oversupply of physicians in Springfield.) Lincoln won the seat the next year; and before he could take his seat in December 1847, the Mexican War posed special difficulties for Western Whigs. Dr. Henry helped raise a military company in the Pekin area. Like most Whigs he did not like the war, but he thought Henry Clay went too far toward proposing a Whig stand against taking any Mexican territory as indemnity for the war. The "no territory" doctrine, he warned Congressman Lincoln, would "beat us as a party for years to come." Henry could not "honestly go with" the party on that question; he apparently resigned as editor of the *Tazewell Whig* on account of it; and he had "great anxiety" to know Lincoln's stand on the war. If Lincoln adopted Clay's position, Henry warned, "It would be painful in the extreme to part company with you after having fought with you side by side so long. But . . . I shall at the polls . . . sustain Mr. Polk." Even before he received Henry's letter, Lincoln had demonstrated their like-mindedness by voting against a "no territory" resolution. Henry wanted free territory to offset Texas and said he would not vote a dollar to carry on the war without the Wilmot Proviso.

In 1848 Henry moved back to Springfield. He and Lincoln were ardent supporters of Zachary Taylor and stumped the northern counties of the district in the fall for "Old Rough and Ready." Lincoln worked for a year to get Henry a job from the Taylor administration; he expressed his "peculiar anxiety" for the doctor, who had "done more disinterested labor in the Whig cause, than any other one, two, or three men in the state." Of "all those whom I have desired should receive appointments from this Administration," he said, "Dr. Henry . . . is No. One with me." On June 24, 1850, Henry was appointed Indian agent for the Oregon Territory.

Henry did not go to Oregon until 1852, and then he went as leader of a party of emigrants from Springfield. For 9 years thereafter, he farmed, practiced medicine, and dabbled in Western politics. He opposed the Kansas-Nebraska Bill and, rather late, became a Republican. He helped Edward D. Baker, also transplanted from Illinois to Oregon, become Senator in 1860. The year before, Henry had reassured Lincoln, upon reading the debates with Stephen A. Douglas, that he had not "sunk out of sight" after losing to Douglas. Henry thought, however, that Douglas "yields *in reality*, all you contend for," and Henry toyed with the idea of becoming a Democrat because of the peculiarities of Oregon politics. He opposed adopting Know-Nothing principles in the Republican party. With Lincoln as President and Baker as Senator, Henry expected at last to get his reward for years of political labor. He was "doing little or nothing," he told Lincoln in June 1861; his "services" were available "at a moment's notice." He was appointed Surveyor General of Washington Territory, but Baker and Henry were disappointed. The President, "although my very good friend and yours still," Baker wrote, had "not done what you or I would have expected." Even so, Henry's job in Olympia paid $3000 a year.

Holding office was to bring Dr. Henry still more vexations and disappointments. He expected great reforms in Indian affairs under the new President, but Lincoln's superintendent in Henry's area insulted the Methodist Church, was under indictment for fornication and adultery, and undid "the little good that had been done by our Democratic predecessors." Henry traveled to Washington to see the President in February 1863; by then he was embroiled in a feud with Victor Smith, the customs collector for Puget Sound. Smith had been editor of the Cincinnati *Commercial* and was an old friend of Treasury Secretary Salmon P. Chase, who refused to remove him. When Lincoln finally removed him in Chase's absence, Chase submitted his resignation in protest. Henry continued to complain vehemently of Smith's influence and the Chase appointees in the Territory generally. He became a bitter foe of those who sought to replace Lincoln with Chase in 1864. A good friend of Mrs. Lincoln's, Henry surmised that "scandalous reports" about her that she thought were circulated by Seward in 1863 were actually circulated by the Treasury Department's minions. When Lincoln won reelection in 1864, Henry's appetite for office had grown. He set out for Washington again in December, this time encouraged by Mrs. Lincoln and therefore certain that he could get the mission to Honolulu and perhaps even a Cabinet post. He arrived in February and by April 1865 he focused his hopes on the office of Commissioner of Indian Affairs, but Lincoln would not remove the politically astute William P. Dole.

Before Henry returned to Washington and his surveyor's job, the President was shot. Henry consoled Mrs. Lincoln and remained in Washington 6 weeks to help her over the worst. He also tried his chances for the Indian Affairs job with the new President. Failing also with Andrew Johnson, he set out for the West Coast and drowned when the ship on which he sailed sank off northern California. Mary Todd Lincoln wrote Eliza Henry, the doctor's wife: "We have both been called upon to resign, to our Heavenly Father, two of the best men & the most devoted husbands, that two unhappy women, ever possessed. . . . We consider that we have lost our best & dearest friend."

SOURCES: Harry E. Pratt wrote an excellent biographical sketch of Dr. Henry in an article in two parts: "Dr. Anson G. Henry: Lincoln's Physician and Friend," *Lincoln Herald*, XLV (October 1943), 3–17; (December 1943), 31–40. Henry's complaints about Whig organization (letter to John J. Hardin, February 13, 1844), endorsement of Whig almanacs (letter to John J. Hardin, January 6, 1844), and his report of Lincoln's stand on the tariff in 1844 (letter to Hardin, March 25, 1844) are in the John J. Hardin Papers, Chicago Historical Society. His letters to Lincoln on the Mexican War (December 29, 1847) and on the debates with Douglas (February 15, 1859), his letter to Dole about hopes for Indian reform (October 28, 1861), and his letter to Isaac Newton Arnold on "scandalous reports" about Mrs. Lincoln (April 21, 1864) are in the Abraham Lincoln Papers, Library of Congress.

Henry E. Huntington Library and Art Gallery

Repository of the best Lincoln collection west of the Mississippi River. Huntington (1850–1927), a railroad magnate, began collecting seriously after he retired from business in 1910. Rare books, particularly early English ones, were his specialty, but he began purchasing Lincolniana at the sale of William H. Lambert's collection in 1914. (Among other things, he bought Lincoln's hilarious letter to Mrs. O. H. Browning about Mary Owens, 22 letters from Lincoln to Lyman Trumbull, and a scrapbook of newspaper clippings of Lincoln's speeches of the 1854 to 1858 period that Lincoln compiled and later gave to J. N. Brown.) In the same year he bought the private papers of Ward Hill Lamon from dealer George D. Smith. He purchased 66 Mary Todd Lincoln letters and 52 letters by John Hay about the monumental Hay-Nicolay biography of Lincoln. His major book purchase was the collection of Judd Stewart, one of the "Big Five" Lincoln collectors, which Huntington bought from Stewart's heirs in 1922. Until his death in 1927, Huntington added Lincolniana to the collection, but the library in San Marino, California, has added only modestly to the Lincoln holdings since Huntington established it in 1919.

SOURCES: See Lyle H. Wright, "Famous Lincoln Collections: The Huntington Library," *Abraham Lincoln Quarterly*, I (June 1941), 323–330. For information write the Huntington Library, Art Gallery, Botanical Gardens, San Marino, CA 91108.

Herndon, William Henry (1818–1891)

Lincoln's law partner and biographer. Herndon was born in Kentucky but went to Illinois with his family in 1820; he settled in Springfield in 1823. His father, a successful merchant, sent him to Illinois College in Jacksonville. The year Herndon spent there (1836–1837), though in the preparatory rather than the collegiate department, gave him a taste for books and learning, apparently made him a Whig in politics (unlike his father, who was an active Democratic politician), and exposed him to strong antislavery opinions.

Herndon became a clerk in Joshua Speed's store in Springfield in 1837 and there gained close acquaintance with Lincoln. Both slept above Speed's store. Herndon began to study law in 1841 and became Lincoln's partner the year Herndon was admitted to the bar (1844). Why Lincoln chose him is a mystery to this day; Herndon himself, when asked for Lincoln's reasons, said, "I don't know and no one else does." Herndon managed the office and did much of the research work of looking up precedents. He did not travel the Eighth Judicial Circuit, though he came to handle most of the work in Menard County. It was a true partnership, however, for both men argued cases in court, and they split their fees equally.

Herndon thought of himself as a Southerner, but he "always turned *New-Englandwards*" for his ideas. He accumulated one of the largest private libraries in Springfield, and he cultivated epistolary friendships with Eastern intellectuals, especially Theodore Parker, to whom he wrote numerous letters. His political ideas developed a New England flavor. He became a shrill advocate of temperance, was president of the Springfield Temple of Honor (a prohibition group) in 1855, and as mayor of Springfield in the same year was noted primarily for establishing prohibition in the town. He did not run for reelection.

Though Herndon claimed to have been an abolitionist from an early age, there is no contemporary evidence to support the claim. He did not goad Lincoln into his famous antislavery career in the mid-1850s. His claim to have forged Lincoln's name without his knowledge to the call for a Republican Convention in May 1856 (the beginning of Illinois's Republican party) is doubtful. Lincoln had been the only participant who was not a newspaper editor at the convention the preceding February which established a committee to call the May

William Henry Herndon. (Courtesy of the Lloyd Ostendorf Collection)

convention. The call for that convention was surely no surprise. In 1856 Herndon was a Republican presidential elector and gave numerous speeches for the Frémont ticket. In 1857 Illinois's first Republican Governor, William H. Bissell, rewarded Herndon for his efforts by appointing him a state bank commissioner, a lucrative ($1000 per year) post he held through 1865.

Herndon's Republicanism was of a violently denunciatory and radical stripe. He told Parker in 1857 that "the Northern institutions and the Southern are founded on ideas exactly opposite and antagonistic, and . . . the logic thereof impels the people in opposite directions." That necessitated one of three things: "(1) The South may conquer the North; (2) The North may conquer the South; (3) The two may separate without a fight." In 1858 he thought that "the only way to right ourselves is through bloody Revolution." Those ideas were far different from his partner's and would grow more so; it is little wonder that he admired the "House Divided" speech, the most radical speech of Lincoln's pre-Presidential career. Despite his Republican radicalism and his interest in fugitive slave cases in Springfield in this period, Herndon's views rarely showed humanitarian sympathy for the black man (whom he almost invariably called "the nigger"). In 1848 he had voted for the article in the Illinois constitution which excluded free blacks from settling in the state. Herndon's real fear was that toleration of Negro slavery could soon lead to white slavery, as he told Parker early in 1858:

> Let me ask you a terrible question: "Is not Wendell Phillips's idea about niggers and the Union the only way to cut the knot? Will not this people be compelled to *cut through the Constitution* to reach the nigger, and break his chains so as to keep the white man free?"

Herndon grew fearful in 1858 that Eastern Republicans would sell Illinois out and support Stephen A. Douglas for the Senate because, even though he was a Democrat, Douglas was locked in a bitter brawl with President James Buchanan and the Southern wing of the party over the Lecompton constitution in Kansas. He was amazed when Senator Douglas began to send him documents. Herndon worked hard for and closely with Lincoln in the famous 1858 campaign against Douglas.

After Lincoln lost, Herndon's importance as a political ally began to wane. As the Republican party grew more conservative to attract votes in the 1860 presidential campaign, Herndon became irrelevant—even embarrassing. He disliked former Democrat Norman B. Judd for refusing to support Lincoln for Senator back in 1855, and 5 years later he leveled accusations against Judd for using party funds for personal business. Judd was an important Republican organizer and a contender for the gubernatorial nomination. He protested to Lincoln, and Lincoln got Herndon's "solemn pledge to say nothing of the sort in the future." No Herndon letter which advocates Lincoln's nomination for President in 1860 exists, and, though Herndon may have been present at the convention that nominated Lincoln, he played no important role there.

His contacts with Lincoln diminished further. The candidate moved into an office in the State House after his nomination. Herndon no longer saw him daily in the law office. In fact, as Henry Clay Whitney said, after 1860 Lincoln "took no advice, and sought no counsel from . . . Herndon." Lincoln did bid his partner an affectionate farewell when he left Springfield, lectured him on his occasional drunkenness, and stated a preference for maintaining the law partnership.

In the secession crisis Herndon sought no compromise with the South. When war came, he was the staunchest of patriots and quickly came to see the salvation of the Union as inextricably linked to the destruction of slavery. He came to that conclusion far sooner than his partner did, and Herndon was privately critical of Lincoln's revocation of General John C. Frémont's emancipation proclamation for Missouri. He thought Lincoln moved too slowly against slavery and handled the South altogether too tenderly: "Does he suppose he can crush—squelch out this huge rebellion by pop guns filled with rose water [?]"

Herndon did not apparently seek an appointment from Lincoln with any ardor. In January 1862 he did go to Washington to seek a job, but not for himself. Herndon's wife had died in 1861; and in seeking the hand of Anna Miles, Herndon agreed with Anna's brother-in-law to ask for an office for him in exchange for his influencing Anna toward the marriage. The President was amused and found a job in an Indian agency; Herndon married Anna in 1862. In 1863 he rejected a temporary job on a commission to St. Louis. He hinted indirectly at desiring an office in 1864; but Lincoln did nothing, and his partner never complained. In truth, Herndon was not exactly Lincoln's partner by that time; as early as 1862 he had entered an informal arrangement with a new partner, Charles S. Zane.

"Lincoln's death was the most important event in Herndon's life," says Herndon's biographer David Donald. Immediately, Herndon became a sought-after interviewee. Quickly he realized that he could use the knowledge of Lincoln which others sought from him (and which he almost always shared generously, even effusively) to write his own book on Lincoln. To that end he began doing research in 1865, particularly on the years of Lincoln's life about which he knew little (before 1837 and after 1860). He sent queries by mail and had local Republican lawyers interview people who remembered Lincoln in southern Indiana. He began to hear tales of the low morality of the Hanks family, especially from Kentuckian John B. Helm.

Dennis Friend Hanks proved to be a loquacious witness. Conflicting statements puzzled Herndon, however, and he resolved the problems as a lawyer rather than a historian might—by seeking to interview the witnesses in person and judge them by looking them in the eye. In the fall of 1865 he traveled to southern Indiana and eastern Illinois. In Petersburg, near the site of New Salem, he heard of Ann Rutledge for the first time. He uncovered Lincoln's courtship of Mary Owens and located and interviewed Mary by mail. He interviewed

Lincoln's stepmother and even his wife, though she never liked Herndon, never had had him to the house for dinner, and had snubbed him on his one trip to Washington. He finished his research by the end of 1866. Though reminiscences, often of events long-distant in time, these interviews are the most important source for Lincoln's early life to this day.

Herndon delivered a series of lectures on Lincoln in Springfield, the first being held on December 12, 1865, and the second on December 26. They were candid but vague. Lincoln "read *less* and thought *more* than any man in America," the bookish Herndon reported. He was not "warm, & all heart"; reason dominated him. He was ambitious. He even had "greed for office." He was not "a technical Christian." Herndon gave his third lecture on January 23, 1866. It continued a principal theme, that Lincoln was not a man of heart. Otherwise, Herndon thought, the casualties of the war for the *"one idea and one purpose"* which seized Lincoln *"as it were insanely, . . . namely the Union and its preservation"*— would have unstrung him.

When J. G. Holland's biography of Lincoln appeared in 1866, its emphasis on Lincoln's being a Christian statesman shocked Herndon and so angered him that he quarreled the rest of his life with the pious writers who stressed Lincoln's religious nature. On November 16, 1866, he delivered his most famous and contentious lecture "Abraham Lincoln. Miss Ann Rutledge. New Salem. Pioneering, and THE Poem." There he first articulated his theory of Lincoln's life: disappointment at the death of the sweetheart of his youth, Ann Rutledge, made Lincoln a melancholy man who led a tragic life guided by the morbid sentiments of his favorite poem, "Oh, why should the spirit of mortal be proud." Robert Todd Lincoln, who had found nothing objectionable in the earlier lectures, despite their definite tendency away from hero worship, now thought that "Mr. Wm. H. Herndon is making an ass of himself." Mrs. Lincoln was mortified at the lecture's implication about the unhappiness of her marriage. By March 4, 1867, she articulated privately the essence of the case argued by most of those who disliked Herndon then and have ever since: "This is the return for all my husband's kindness to this miserable man!" she exclaimed to David Davis. "Out of pity he took him into his office, when he was almost a hopeless inebriate and . . . he was only a drudge, in the place." She thought him "a dirty dog," as did many other Lincoln associates, admirers, and Republicans. The religious were angered even more. The Reverend James Smith, once the Lincolns' minister in Springfield, shuddered at Herndon's making Lincoln's children the "sons of a man who never loved their mother."

Herndon's reputation as a Lincoln authority fell, as did his fortunes generally. He had hated the law for over a decade, and his practice deteriorated steadily— especially after he inherited a farm 6 miles north of Springfield in 1867. A great lover of nature (unlike his former law partner), he began to neglect his practice for farming. An agricultural depression impoverished him. He sold copies of what he called his Lincoln Records, the research notes for his book, to Ward Hill Lamon in 1869 for $2000 in cash and a $2000 note. The book was further away than ever. In 1865 he had told Lincoln he was "a sober man, and will keep so the balance of my days." That resolve faltered, and he took to drinking heavily.

Poverty changed Herndon's political outlook. In 1870 he announced that Lincoln had misled him into believing in protective tariffs; now he was for free trade. In 1866 he had supported Reconstruction and denounced Andrew Johnson's claim to be following Lincoln's policies as a "wilful and premedi[t]ated lie." He had supported Grant for President in 1868, but by 1872 he was a Liberal Republican. He denounced monopolies repeatedly, but his anti-inflationism kept him away from many Western radical groups. He became a Democrat in 1874. In about a year he would abandon his hard-money ideas for greenbacks and inflation. He retained his detestation of orthodox religion and mustered one more Lincoln lecture in 1873, on Lincoln's religion. It was an attack on James Reed's pious defense of Lincoln's Christianity in an article in *Scribner's Monthly* that year. Herndon wrote regularly to religious free thinkers, though he was never an athiest or even an agnostic himself.

In 1881 Herndon quit drinking and tried to pull himself together. He looked over his dormant correspondence and responded to a letter written by Jesse W. Weik. That chance occurrence put him in touch with a young man capable of writing the nearly forgotten Lincoln biography. Their collaboration produced *Herndon's Lincoln: The True Story of a Great Life*, which appeared in 1889. The book disappointed Herndon's financial hopes for it (he repeatedly told Weik that he was in it for "the dimes"), but it immortalized him as a Lincoln biographer.

Herndon's Lincoln is still an important source for Lincoln's life, but it must be used cautiously. Herndon knew very little about Lincoln's Kentucky years, and what the book says on that part of Lincoln's life is nearly worthless. The book stresses Lincoln's "Western-ness" and especially his rise from an early "putrid" environment to greatness. It thus considerably underestimates Thomas Lincoln's character and station in life and overestimates the importance of Lincoln's frontier heritage. Written while Herndon was a Democrat, the book undervalues Lincoln's Republican (and Whig) economic ideas, though Weik was a staunch Republican. The emphasis on Ann Rutledge is out of all proportion to the documentary evidence for the romance and is generally agreed to be Herndon's way of explaining Lincoln's marriage to a woman Herndon could not stomach. Finally, it exaggerates Herndon's importance as an influence in Lincoln's political life. On the other hand, the book tells much about Lincoln's personal habits and tastes during the period from 1837 to 1860 that is unobtainable from any other source.

SOURCES: David Donald's superb biography *Lincoln's Herndon* (New York: Alfred A. Knopf, 1948) can be supplemented by reading many of Herndon's eccentric and unforgettable letters

David Edgar Herold

William Best Hesseltine. (Courtesy of the University of Wisconsin—Madison Archives)

in Joseph Fort Newton's *Lincoln and Herndon* (Cedar Rapids, Iowa: The Torch Press, 1910). Herndon's vote on the Illinois constitution in 1848 is recorded in the Springfield Poll, Sangamon County Poll Books, Sangamon State University Archives, Springfield, Illinois. For the process of writing *Herndon's Lincoln* see WEIK, JESSE WILLIAM.

See also BEVERIDGE, ALBERT JEREMIAH; BIOGRAPHERS; HOLLAND, JOSIAH GILBERT.

Herold, David Edgar (1846–1865) Coconspirator with John Wilkes Booth, the assassin of Abraham Lincoln. Herold was the son of a government naval stores clerk. He lived with his widowed mother and several sisters in Washington and worked briefly as a pharmacist's clerk. Booth met him in 1863 while purchasing drugs to treat a growth on his neck.

Herold was fond of sport, gunning, and dogs, and Booth recruited him for his plot to kidnap President Lincoln because of his knowledge of lower Maryland gained on hunting trips. When the plot turned to assassination, Booth probably assigned Herold the job of guiding Lewis Thornton Powell out of Washington. He was seen only once on the night of the assassination, as he fled Washington by the same Navy Yard bridge over which Booth had escaped somewhat earlier. Stopped by a guard, Herold gave his name as "Smith," said that he had been in bad company, and reported that he was going home to White Plains, Maryland. Somewhere along the 13-mile route to Surrattsville, he overtook Booth. At the Surratt tavern they picked up a carbine and whiskey from the drunken proprietor. Then they rode to Dr. Samuel A. Mudd's home near Bryantown. Herold gave his name as "Huston" and Booth's as "Tyson" or "Tyser" and asked the doctor to set Booth's broken leg. The two men fled from Mudd's house the next afternoon. For 6 days, Thomas A. Jones, a Confederate mail runner in Maryland, took care of the fugitives.

On April 21 Jones procured a skiff for use by the two men in crossing the Potomac to Virginia. They could not cross until the 22d. Eventually, Booth and Herold stopped at the farm of Richard H. Garrett, 3 miles from Port Royal. On April 26, Federal soldiers under Lieutenant Edward P. Doherty of the 16th New York Cavalry and Lieutenant Colonel Everton J. Conger and Lieutenant Luther Baker formerly of the 1st District of Columbia Cavalry surrounded the tobacco barn where Herold and Booth slept. Summoned to surrender, Herold did so while Booth called to the soldiers that his companion had had nothing to do with the crime.

Herold's case was hopeless, and his lawyer, Frederick Stone, could only call witnesses to attest to his being so triflingly boyish in character that he had no political opinions. The witnesses said that he was easily led; one guessed him to have the mentality of an 11-year-old. Reporter Ben: Perley Poore described him as "a doltish, insignificant-looking young man . . . with a slender frame and irresolute, cowardly appearance." On June 30 a military court sentenced him to death. He was hanged on July 7.

In 1869 Herold's body was removed from the Washington Arsenal warehouse and reinterred in Washington in an Episcopal service.

SOURCES: See George S. Bryan, *The Great American Myth* (New York: Carrick & Evans, 1940); Benn Pitman, ed., *The Assassination of President Lincoln and the Trial of the Conspirators* (Cincinnati, Ohio: Moore, Wilstach & Baldwin, 1865); and Ben: Perley Poore, *The Conspiracy Trial for the Murder of the President*, 3 vols. (Boston: J. E. Tilton, 1865).

See also ASSASSINATION; BOOTH, JOHN WILKES; TRIAL OF THE ASSASSINS.

Hesseltine, William Best (1902–1963) Historian. William B. Hesseltine was born in Virginia, received his undergraduate education at Washington and Lee University, earned a master's degree at the University of Virginia, and was granted a doctorate by Ohio State University. He was, with Lincoln biographer J. G. Randall, a leader of the school of historical thought called Revisionism. His first Lincoln book was *Lincoln and the War Governors*, published by Alfred A. Knopf in 1948. It pictured Lincoln as the political master of the difficult wartime governors and as "the architect of a new nation" which conquered states' rights in both the South and the North. Juggling the many Northern governors with skill, Hesseltine's book is still the best treatment of Lincoln's relations with the Northern states, but it greatly exaggerates the decline of the power of states *vis-à-vis* the federal government.

The theme of nationalism grew steadily in Hesseltine's thought. He repeatedly stressed that Lincoln never mentioned the word "nation" in his First Inaugural Address, though he referred 20 times to "Union." With the Gettysburg Address's affirmation that the United States was a "new nation," the word "nation" began to replace "Union" in Lincoln's thinking, Hesseltine argued. When he wrote *Lincoln's Plan of Reconstruction* (Tuscaloosa, Ala.: Confederate Publishing Company) in 1960, Hesseltine still stressed the theme of Lincoln's "war against the states." He also shared the general Revisionist view that Lincoln's Reconstruction plans were "pragmatic and realistic" unlike those of the Radical Republicans, who succumbed to "the epidemic of hate-psychosis that paralyzed the[ir] reasoning powers." The book noted that Lincoln had several different plans; and by treating them as responses to the changing situation during the Civil War, Hesseltine provided what is still the best overview of Lincoln's Reconstruction policies.

Hesseltine wrote many other historical works, but he is best known for his influence on young scholars. In his seminar at the University of Wisconsin, where he taught from 1932 until his death, he trained many of the great modern Civil War and Reconstruction historians. Among them were T. Harry Williams (author of *Lincoln and the Radicals* and *Lincoln and His Generals*), Richard N. Current (author of *The Lincoln Nobody Knows* and *Lincoln and the First Shot*), Kenneth Stampp (author of *The Era of Reconstruction*), and Frank Klement (the leading student of Northern "Copperheads").

SOURCES: Current wrote an obituary, "William Best Hesseltine, 1902–1963," for *Lincoln Herald*, LXVI (Spring 1964), 14.

Hildene See LINCOLN, ROBERT TODD.

Holland, Josiah Gilbert (1819–1881) Coeditor of the Springfield, Massachusetts, *Republican* and early Lincoln biographer. Josiah G. Holland came from pious New England stock. An ardent Republican, he was chosen to deliver the eulogy for the observance of Lincoln's funeral in Springfield, Massachusetts. His eulogy showed an Easterner's view of Lincoln. He called Lincoln "nature's nobleman, with nature's manners, springing directly from a kind and gentle heart." He confessed that "it took us all a long time to learn to love" Lincoln, "Unattractive in person, awkward in deportment, unrestrained in conversation, a story-lover and a story-teller." But Lincoln's great achievements, the "destruction of the rebellion and the destruction of slavery," were the work of "a simple, honest, Christian heart."

A shrewd publisher commissioned Holland, a facile writer, to write a biography of Lincoln. He completed it in a few months by consulting campaign biographies, studying published sources, and making a lightening research trip to the West. He spent two days in Springfield, where William H. Herndon talked to him and introduced him to some of Lincoln's associates. The resulting book, *The Life of Abraham Lincoln* (Springfield, Mass.: Gurdon Bill, 1866), was an extension of the themes Holland developed in his eulogy. Holland admitted his "personal partiality for Mr. Lincoln" and his "thorough sympathy with the political principles" of the Republican party. He knew that his book would only "satisfy an immediate want" and become at most a tributary "to that better and completer biography" which a later generation would produce.

The Life of Abraham Lincoln retained the hostility to the frontier seen in Holland's eulogy and described a good deal of "the pioneer spirit" as "simply a spirit of shiftless discontent." Holland attributed Lincoln's shortcomings to his early frontier environment, made young Abraham very precocious, and exaggerated the amount of his reading. Above all, he stressed the theme that Lincoln was "developed by the providence of God." "Mr. Lincoln," he wrote, "will always be remembered as eminently a Christian President." The religious sentimentality of the book exasperated William H. Herndon and made him want to strike back at the pious myth makers. Years later, Herndon told Isaac N. Arnold that Holland had asked him, "What about Mr. Lincoln's religion." Herndon had answered, *"The less said the better."* And Holland, Herndon recalled, had replied " 'O never mind,' . . . with a wink. 'I'll fix that.' "

Holland became the editor of *Scribner's Monthly*, where he reviewed the next important book on Lincoln, Ward Hill Lamon's *Life of Abraham Lincoln* in August 1872. Holland attacked Lamon for making Lincoln a hypocrite by depicting him as privately skeptical but publicly orthodox in religion. Moreover, he thought that the story of Lincoln's domestic difficulties, even if true, was best left unwritten, at least until his widow and child were dead. In short, Lamon's book lacked what this proper New Englander valued highly: "delicacy" and "decency." Benjamin P. Thomas characterizes Holland's work as "presenting the Mid-Victorian conception of Lincoln as a model youth, who forged to the top through sheer merit and the force of high ideals." The book quickly sold over 100,000 copies.

SOURCES: See Benjamin P. Thomas, *Portrait for Posterity: Lincoln and His Biographers* (New Brunswick, N.J.: Rutgers University Press, 1947) for a rather unsympathetic treatment. More favorable is Paul M. Angle's *A Shelf of Lincoln Books* (New Brunswick, N.J.: Rutgers University Press, 1946). See also David Donald, *Lincoln's Herndon* (New York: Alfred A. Knopf, 1948) and J. G. Holland, *Eulogy on Abraham Lincoln, . . . Springfield, Mass., April 19, 1865* (Springfield, Mass.: L. J. Powers, 1865). Thomas calls the book "Mid-Victorian" in *Abraham Lincoln: A Biography* (New York: Alfred A. Knopf, 1952), p. 524.

Holt, Joseph (1807–1894) Judge Advocate General under President Lincoln. Joseph Holt, who was born in Kentucky, became a lawyer, newspaperman, and Democratic politician noted for his oratory. He practiced law in Kentucky and later in Mississippi with great success. After the death of his first wife, Holt married the daughter of Kentucky politician Charles A. Wickliffe; and in 1856 he worked diligently enough for the Democratic presidential campaign to be appointed commissioner of patents by President James Buchanan. In 1859 he became Postmaster General in the rather pro-Southern Cabinet and was himself an avowed opponent of "coercion" of seceding states.

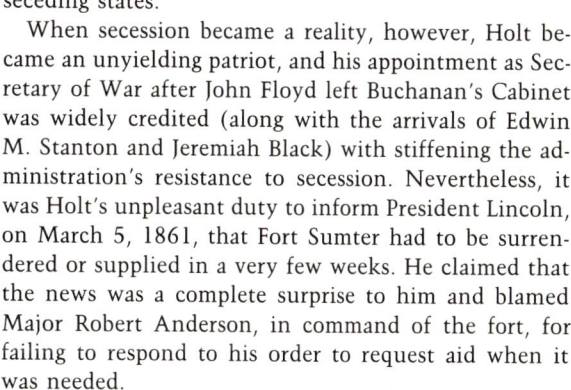

When secession became a reality, however, Holt became an unyielding patriot, and his appointment as Secretary of War after John Floyd left Buchanan's Cabinet was widely credited (along with the arrivals of Edwin M. Stanton and Jeremiah Black) with stiffening the administration's resistance to secession. Nevertheless, it was Holt's unpleasant duty to inform President Lincoln, on March 5, 1861, that Fort Sumter had to be surrendered or supplied in a very few weeks. He claimed that the news was a complete surprise to him and blamed Major Robert Anderson, in command of the fort, for failing to respond to his order to request aid when it was needed.

When civil war began, Holt's patriotism grew absolutely fervid. His *Letter . . . upon the Policy of the General Government . . . and the Duty of Kentucky in the Crisis*, written to James Speed on May 31, 1861, and *The Fallacy of Neutrality. An Address . . . at Louisville, July 13th, 1861* were perhaps the most broadly circulated Union propaganda of the early months of the war. With hot eloquence, Holt spelled out the practical meaning of Union for Kentucky and for the country as a whole. Disunion would mean national weakness, standing armies and incessant wars, expensive frontier fortifications, commerce ruined by loss of natural channels of trade, continuing dissolution after the example of secession, revolution, and eventual despotism, and "above all, humiliation . . . for having failed in their great mission to demonstrate before the world the capacity of our race for self-government."

There was nothing original in that—very little, in fact, that Lincoln had not said in his First Inaugural Address—

Josiah Gilbert Holland

but Holt stated it with such forceful and flag-waving clarity that it doubtless reached a broader audience. There was an element of cunning practicality, too, in his arguments for Kentucky's remaining in the Union. Now a secure interior state, she would become a frontier state, if she seceded, a highway for fugitive slaves to a North as foreign as Canada, a member of a hapless "self-disintegrating league," and a pauper forced to pay direct taxes to support a Confederacy opposed on principle to raising money by the tariff.

President Lincoln was impressed by Holt's role in arousing Northern patriotism. He found jobs for Holt investigating contracts. The accession of his former associate Stanton to the position of Secretary of War surely helped Holt as well, and on September 3, 1862, the President made him the first Judge Advocate General of the Army. His Democratic credentials were important, for he would be handling political prisoners arrested arbitrarily in the North.

Problems of disloyalty in the North led to his two most important wartime actions. Early in 1864 he successfully argued the Clement Vallandigham case before the United States Supreme Court, which adopted his view that it had no jurisdiction in appeals from decisions of military tribunals. In the autumn of that year, on orders from Stanton, he investigated Northern secret societies. The resulting *Report of the Judge Advocate General on "The Order of American Knights," Alias "The Sons of Liberty," a Western Conspiracy in Aid of the Southern Rebellion,* issued as a pamphlet on the eve of the presidential election, was a sensation. More than any other single document, the report created the myth of a vast organized disloyal opposition in the North. Glossing over the curious circumstance that the organization apparently had three different names (depending on the witness), Holt boldly charged that Vallandigham led the northern wing and General Sterling Price the southern wing of a 500,000-man, paramilitary organization dedicated to slavery, states' rights, and secession. Part of the report's success is attributable to its unflinching willingness to name names and point to specific actions. This organization, Holt charged, circulated such antiadministration pamphlets as *Abraham Africanus* and the *Lincoln Catechism.* It was behind the antimilitary riot in Charleston, Illinois, the previous March. Its membership was concentrated in Indiana (75,000–125,000), Illinois (100,000–140,000), Ohio (40,000–70,000), Missouri (20,000–40,000), and Kentucky (40,000–70,000). Democrats considered the report a partisan electioneering document, and historians since have agreed that the Order of American Knights had many fewer members than Holt alleged. Vallandigham said the charges against him were "absolute falsehoods and fabrications from beginning to end."

In his day-to-day reviews of courts martial, Holt was an uncompromising opponent of treason. "*Theoretically,*" he said in 1861, "we have been treating the rebels as traitors & criminals; it is quite time that we should treat them as such *practically.*" Denunciations of a convicted person as an "arch-fiend of treason" came easily to the Judge Advocate General; and when convinced of guilt, he was ferocious, as in the case of John Y. Beall. "Beall," Holt said, "fully deserves to die a felons death, and the summary enforcement of that penalty is a duty which Government owes to society." Yet, unless Lincoln's reputation for mercy is unmerited, Holt had a more reasonable side to his nature. Time after time the President, faced with a plea for a pardon, wrote: "Judge Advocate General please examine and report on this case." More often than not, Lincoln followed Holt's advice, and that advice often was to remit punishment. Thus the President worked closely with Holt and seems to have esteemed him highly—but not highly enough to make him his vice-presidential running mate. "Mr. Holt is a good man," Lincoln said when his name was mentioned for that position in 1864, "but I had not heard or thought of him for V. P." When Edward Bates resigned as Attorney General later that year, Lincoln offered Holt the post. Holt turned Lincoln down, apparently because he doubted his courtroom ability in arguing before the Supreme Court after so long an absence from practice. He praised fellow Kentucky Unionist James Speed as a candidate for the post.

Holt at first had little enthusiasm for emancipation. He denounced John C. Frémont's emancipation order for Missouri in 1861. Negroes were "a population unprepared for freedom & whose presence could not fail to prove a source of painful apprehension if not of terror to the homes & families of all." But he became reconciled to emancipation and by war's end celebrated it and urged, on the evening of Lincoln's assassination, "guarantees . . . against the re-establishment of slavery, through some cunningly devised system of tutelage." He also foresaw the necessity of vigorous Reconstruction measures: "If a loyal population cannot be found to put the machinery of State government into operation, then let us wait and see if the next will not be a wise and better generation. In the meanwhile, let these former States be subjected to military rule."

Joseph Holt (center) with Henry A. Bingham (left) and Henry L. Burnett, the prosecutors in the trial of Lincoln's assassins.

Lincoln's assassination brought out Holt's stern streak and his penchant for finding conspiracies as perhaps no event before had. He was the prime mover behind the idea of trying the alleged conspirators by military commission. He wanted to make the commission's sessions completely secret, and he believed deeply that the assassins were Jefferson Davis's minions. Stanton made him the government's chief prosecutor, though John A. Bingham did most of the arguing in the courtroom. Holt pursued the theory of a Confederate plot at the expense of a thorough investigation of the real conspirators, and eventually, at the expense of justice itself. Some who helped Booth escape were never prosecuted. Holt gathered the evidence to prove a Confederate conspiracy; in the end the "evidence" proved to be flimsy and circumstantial, when it was not downright perjury. His alleged failure to show President Andrew Johnson the commission's recommendation for commuting Mary Surratt's death sentence led to a bitter feud between him and Johnson and troubled Holt the rest of his life.

Holt remained Judge Advocate General until 1875.

SOURCES: Mary B. Allen's sketch of Holt in the *Dictionary of American Biography* (New York: Charles Scribner's Sons, 1958), V, 181–183, is important because Allen wrote a lengthy study of Holt's career, a doctoral dissertation. Frank L. Klement criticized Holt's *Report* on the Order of American Knights in *The Copperheads in the Middle West* (Chicago: University of Chicago Press, 1960). Holt's Reconstruction views appear in his *Remarks . . . at a Dinner in Charleston, South Carolina, on . . . 14th April, 1865* (Washington, D.C.: Gibson Brothers, 1865). His letters to Lincoln protesting Frémont's proclamation (September 12, 1861), mentioning an "arch-fiend of treason" (June 14, 1862), and urging Beall's execution (February 17, 1865) are in the Abraham Lincoln Papers, Library of Congress, as is his letter to Schuyler Colfax (December 2, 1861) about treating the rebels as traitors *"practically."* On the assassination trial see Harold M. Hyman and Benjamin P. Thomas, *Stanton: The Life and Times of Lincoln's Secretary of War* (New York: Alfred A. Knopf, 1962).

See also SURRATT, MARY EUGENIA; TRIAL OF THE ASSASSINS.

Homes   *See* EXECUTIVE MANSION; INDIANA; KENTUCKY; NEW SALEM, ILLINOIS; FINANCES, PERSONAL; SPRINGFIELD, ILLINOIS.

Honesty   *See* FINANCES, PERSONAL.

Hooker Letter   Abraham Lincoln's letter written, on January 26, 1863, to General Joseph Hooker on the occasion of Hooker's appointment to command the Army of the Potomac. Hooker had been an ambitious corps commander in the same army when it was commanded by Ambrose E. Burnside. He had clashed so frequently with his superior that Burnside sought to dismiss him on January 23 for criticizing his superior officers. President Lincoln refused to approve Burnside's order and instead replaced Burnside with General Hooker.

On January 26, 1863, Lincoln met with Hooker in Washington to iron out difficulties between the new commander of the Army of the Potomac and the general-in-chief, Henry W. Halleck. The two officers hated each other, and Hooker in effect reported directly to President Lincoln. In addition to his well-merited reputation for intriguing against his superior officers, Hooker, according to rumor, had expressed opinions in the wake of the disaster at the Battle of Fredricksburg in December indicating that he thought the country needed a dictator. Before he left for his army, Lincoln gave Hooker this now famous letter:

> I have placed you at the head of the Army of the Potomac. Of course I have done this upon what appear to me to be sufficient reasons. And yet I think it best for you to know that there are some things in regard to which, I am not quite satisfied with you. I believe you to be a brave and skilful soldier, which, of course, I like. I also believe you do not mix politics with your profession, in which you are right. You have confidence in yourself, which is a valuable, if not an indispensable quality. You are ambitious, which within reasonable bounds, does good rather than harm. But I think that during Gen. Burnside's command of the Army, you have taken counsel of your ambition, and thwarted him as much as you could, in which you did a great wrong to the country, and to a most meritorious and honorable brother officer. I have heard, in such way as to believe it, of your recently saying that both the Army and the Government needed a Dictator. Of course it was not *for* this, but in spite of it, that I have given you the command. Only those generals who gain successes, can set up dictators. What I now ask of you is military success, and I will risk the dictatorship. The government will support you to the utmost of it's ability, which is neither more nor less than it has done and will do for all commanders. I much fear that the spirit which you have aided to infuse into the Army, of criticising their Commander, and withholding confidence from him, will now turn upon you. I shall assist you as far as I can, to put it down. Neither you, nor Napoleon, if he were alive again, could get any good out of an army, while such a spirit prevails in it.
>
> And now, beware of rashness. Beware of rashness, but with energy, and sleepless vigilance, go forward, and give us victories.

In April the general showed the letter to newspaper correspondent Noah Brooks, describing it as "just such a letter as a father might write to his son." When Lincoln's old friend Anson G. Henry saw the letter that April, he was so moved that he told his wife that it "ought to be printed in letters of Gold—It will be read by our posterity with greater veneration for its author than has ever been shown for any thing written by Washington, or any other man. It breathes a spirit of Patriotic devotion to the country, and a spirit of frankness & candor worthy of Mr. Lincoln's character, and is peculiarly his own."

SOURCES: William E. Barton's *Abraham Lincoln and the Hooker Letter: An Address* (New York: Bowling Green Press, 1928) contains an excellent facsimile of the letter and an interesting discussion of its composition. See also Paul M. Angle's *Abraham Lincoln's Letter to Major General Joseph Hooker Dated January 26, 1863* (Chicago: Caxton Club, 1942). The original letter is now in the Library of Congress.

Horner, Henry   *See* ILLINOIS STATE HISTORICAL LIBRARY.

"House Divided" Speech Lincoln's concluding speech, on June 16, 1858, at the Illinois Republican State Convention. The convention had nominated Lincoln to run for the United States Senate against Stephen A. Douglas. Although the speech addressed questions raised by the Dred Scott decision of 1857, Lincoln had already attacked that decision in public about a year previously; and this time he aimed not at Chief Justice Taney, but at Senator Douglas. It was an answer in particular to Douglas's new-found appeal among antislavery men for his opposition to the Buchanan administration and the Lecompton constitution for Kansas. The seemingly radical doctrine of the speech that "A house divided against itself cannot stand" has often been compared to William H. Seward's "irrepressible conflict" doctrine and, indeed, disturbed Lincoln's Republican friends to whom he read the speech in private before its final delivery.

The speech was Lincoln's most radical pronouncement on the sectional question in the 1850s. Yet the real import of the doctrine and of the whole speech that flowed from it was aimed, not at the South, but at Douglas and at any Republicans tempted to support him: if the country could not "endure, permanently half *slave* and half *free*," then Douglas's mediatory policy of allowing the people in the territories themselves to choose slavery or freedom was dodging a crucial moral choice. Moreover, Lincoln pointed out, the policy of not caring "whether slavery be voted *down* or voted *up*" actually aided the cause of making the country all slave rather than all free.

That proposition was the heart of Lincoln's argument in the speech. Almost three-fourths of the speech was devoted to suggesting for the first time in Lincoln's speeches a conspiracy among Douglas, Franklin Pierce, James Buchanan, and Roger B. Taney to nationalize slavery. The progress of the conspiracy, as Lincoln saw it, had been simple. First, Douglas's Kansas-Nebraska Act opened territories previously closed to slavery to the possibility of its establishment. Then Presidents Pierce and Buchanan prepared the public mind to accept the pending decision in the Supreme Court on the status of slavery in the territories. Finally Chief Justice Taney's decision forbade the exclusion of slavery from the territories. An indifferent North following Douglas's " 'care not' policy" would "ere long, see . . . another Supreme Court decision, declaring that the Constitution of the United States does not permit a *state* to exclude slavery from its limits." "We shall *lie down* pleasantly dreaming that the people of *Missouri* are on the verge of making their State *free;* and we shall *awake* to the *reality*, instead, that the *Supreme* Court has made *Illinois* a *slave* State."

Republicans and Democrats, even those like Douglas opposed to the Southern wing of the Democratic party, did not agree on *principles*, Lincoln charged, and "Our cause, then, must be intrusted to, and conducted by its own undoubted friends . . . who *do care* for the result."

The "House Divided" speech embodied the two points Lincoln would stress in his campaign against Douglas: the gulf of moral principle that separated Republicanism from "popular sovereignty" and the charge that Douglas conspired to nationalize slavery. It was the keynote speech of the Lincoln-Douglas Debates.

SOURCES: The chapter on the speech in Don E. Fehrenbacher's *Prelude to Greatness: Lincoln in the 1850's* (Stanford: Stanford University Press, 1962) is definitive.

Howells, William Dean (1837–1920) Campaign biographer of Lincoln; later, a famed novelist and literary critic. *The Lives and Speeches of Abraham Lincoln and Hannibal Hamlin*, published for the 1860 presidential campaign, was Howells's first prose work. Based in part on research and interviews by a law student named James Quay Howard, whom Howells sent to Springfield, the book had a curious history. The publisher, Follett, Foster & Company, was so swamped with orders for its first Lincoln best seller, a book reproducing the text of the Lincoln-Douglas Debates, that it could not produce Howells's biography on schedule. Fearing competition, the publisher rushed a 25-cent paperback 170-page version of the 400-page book into production; it is a rarity much sought after by book collectors. The 400-page cloth version appeared by July and sold well.

Follett, Foster & Company advertised the volume as "Authorized by Mr. Lincoln," an announcement which "astounded" the candidate. Lincoln wrote an *"Especially Confidential"* letter to an Ohio Republican saying that he *"authorized nothing."* He had refused to look at the proof sheets in order "to maintain the position of truly saying I never saw . . . any part of their work, before it's publication." The book included a serious error, the statement that a Republican convention in Springfield in 1854 passed radically antislavery resolutions. In fact, Lincoln had repeatedly stressed in his debates with Douglas in 1858 that the resolutions were the product of a meeting in Kane County, Illinois, and expressed radical sentiments not present in appreciable force in the party's state convention 2 years later. Later editions corrected the error, and the edition containing an errata slip at page 74 is another book collector's rarity.

Quite by chance, Samuel C. Parks, an Illinois Republican associate of Lincoln's, asked the candidate to correct any errors in his copy of Howells's biography. Lincoln made over a dozen corrections, and the book, now owned by the Illinois State Historical Library, is the most important Lincoln campaign biography in existence. It is assumed that most of what Lincoln did not change is true.

Howells, a reporter and editorial writer for the Columbus *Ohio State Journal* at the time he wrote the biography, was soon rewarded for his efforts. After Lincoln's election, he went to Washington and impressed Lincoln's secretary John G. Nicolay with his claim for reward. He became consul at Venice, a post he held throughout the war. (Appointments to office were a customary form of government patronage of the arts in nineteenth-century America.)

Howells never met Lincoln, and he lived to regret

it. He recognized in Howard's notes "the charm of the material; the wild poetry of its reality." When Lincoln became a great man, Howells realized that he had "missed the greatest chance of my life in its kind."

SOURCES: Ernest James Wessen's "Campaign Lives of Abraham Lincoln, 1860" in *Papers in Illinois History* (Springfield: Illinois State Historical Society, 1938) contains a meticulous study of the Howells biography. A facsimile of the copy corrected for Parks was published by the Abraham Lincoln Association in 1938. It contains an introduction which carefully notes the few known errors in the book Lincoln failed to correct.

Humor "The continual interweaving of good fun in his writings and speeches shows that humor was no mere technique, but a habit of his mind," biographer James G. Randall accurately said of Lincoln. Even when using extreme caution in sifting the evidence of his humor, one cannot escape the conclusion that Lincoln was, especially for his era, a singularly humorous man.

Lincoln's father was reputedly a good storyteller, and there is evidence of Abraham Lincoln's humor from the earliest examples of his writing through the Civil War. Copybooks written when he was in his mid-teens contain humorous verses like this one:

Abraham Lincoln is my name[e]
And with my pen I wrote the same
I wrote in both hast and speed
and left it here for fools to read

He doubtless derived some of his humor from standard joke books like John Mottley's *Joe Miller's Jests* and James Quinn's *Quinn's Jests or the Facetious Man's Pocket Companion*. As a young legislator in Illinois, Lincoln often showed his ability to use humorous anecdotes to advantage. Replying to criticism for being willing to put Illinois further in debt to save its internal improvements system, Lincoln told the story of

an eccentric old bachelor who lived in the Hoosier State. Like the gentleman from Montgomery [Lincoln's opponent in the House debate], he was very famous for seeing *big bugaboos* in every thing. He lived with an older brother, and one day he went out hunting. His brother heard him firing back of the field, and went out to see what was the matter. He found him loading and firing as fast as possible in the top of a tree.

Not being able to discover any thing in the tree, he asked him what he was firing at. He replied a squirrel—and kept on firing. His brother believing there was some humbug about the matter, examined his person, and found on one of his eye lashes a *big louse* crawling about. It is so with the gentleman from Montgomery. He imagined he could see squirrels every day, when they were nothing but *lice*.

The clerk who recorded the debates noted that the "House was convulsed with laughter."

Lincoln's humor was flavored with the atmosphere of his frontier youth in Indiana. It also tended to be self-deprecating and thus fully in keeping with his reputation for humility. He made light of Democratic presidential candidate Lewis Cass's military reputation in 1848 by recalling his own military career

By the way, . . . did you know I am a military hero? Yes sir; in the days of the Black Hawk war I fought, bled, and came away. Speaking of Gen: Cass' career, reminds me of my own. I was not at Stillman's defeat, but I was about as near it, as Cass was to Hulls surrender; and, like him, I saw the place very soon afterwards. It is quite certain that I did not break my sword, for I had none to break; but I bent a musket pretty badly on one occasion. . . . If Gen: Cass went in advance of me in picking huckleberries, I guess I surpassed him in charges upon the wild onions. If he saw any live, fighting indians, it was more than I did; but I had a good many bloody struggles with the musquetoes.

Lincoln answered most requests for autobiographical information with equal humor and humility. He sent Charles Lanman a 49-word autobiography in response to Lanman's request for information for his *Dictionary of Congress* in 1858. It included this description of his schooling: "Education defective." When Jesse W. Fell asked for information on which to base a campaign biography late in 1859, Lincoln concluded the notes with this "personal description": "I am, in height, six feet, four inches, nearly; lean in flesh, weighing, on an average, one hundred and eighty pounds; dark complexion, with coarse black hair, and gray eyes—no other marks or brands recollected." He apologized for the brevity of the autobiography by saying, "There is not much of it, for the reason, I suppose, that there is not much of me."

Storytelling and good humor were essential to vanquish the boredom of riding the Eighth Judicial Circuit in Illinois. Lincoln's cronies on the circuit made his humor legendary. After Ward Hill Lamon tore the seat of his pants in front of a courthouse, the other lawyers circulated a petition for contributions to repair the trousers, but Lincoln protested, "I can contribute nothing to the end in view." Such humor made Lincoln a most welcome comrade as the lawyers whiled away the hours in lonely inns.

On rare occasions Lincoln's humor could verge on sharp ridicule. In the Lincoln-Douglas Debates of 1858, he at one point accused his rival's argument of being

Harper's Weekly, as early as March 2, 1861, depicted Lincoln as a jokester unaware of the serious plight of the Constitution and the Union (seen through the window passing in a hearse). Lincoln had a sense of humor, but, despite the wineglass in his hand in this cartoon, he did not drink.

OUR PRESIDENTIAL MERRYMAN.
"The Presidential party was engaged in a lively exchange of wit and humor. The President Elect was the merriest among the merry, kept those around him in a continual roar."—*Daily Paper*

"as thin as the homeopathic soup that was made by boiling the shadow of a pigeon that had starved to death." Matters of state occasionally took a "jocular" form: the President, on September 15, 1863, responded to a recommendation for office by two old Illinois friends, who erroneously believed the Quartermaster General had retired, by writing: "What nation do you desire Gen. [Robert] Allen to be made Quarter-Master-General of? This nation already has a Quarter-Master-General." The Illinoisans took offense, and Lincoln had to explain that he thought they "knew me well enough to understand" the humorous intent. When an office-seeker boasted that he was a direct descendant of John Randolph of Roanoake, Lincoln knew enough Washington scuttlebutt to recall that Randolph had been notoriously impotent. The President scrawled on the letter: "A direct descendant of one who never was a father." When Stephen A. Douglas's brother-in-law, an army officer, got into trouble for peering over a transom at a lady who was undressing, Lincoln suggested to John Hay that he "should be elevated to the peerage." After receiving a rambling legalistic opinion which ultimately recommended that the President take no action on a problem, Lincoln filed it away after writing these words on it: "Profoundly laid by."

Though the cover illustration showed Lincoln's splitting the Union with a joke, Lincolnana was not hostile to the President, and it was one of the earliest joke books to attempt to print stories Lincoln actually told. Most early joke books on Lincoln merely attached Lincoln's name to standard minstrel jokes.

In keeping with the times, much of Lincoln's humor involved ethnic groups of low status in American society, Irishmen and Negroes. In a speech on internal improvements in the House of Representatives on June 20, 1848, Lincoln argued that the government should finance them directly and not rely on "tonnage duties" collected on traffic after the improvements were built: "How could we make any entirely new improvement by means of tonnage duties? . . . The idea that we could, involves the same absurdity as the irish bull about the new boots. 'I shall never git em on' says Patrick 'till I wear em a day or two, and strech em a little.' " Secretary of the Navy Gideon Welles recalled Lincoln's statement about the Dominican problem of 1864, when Spain appeared to be trying to recover the republic and Negroes desired United States intervention to help the black republic. The administration needed the friendship of both Spain and black Americans, and Lincoln told the Cabinet the story of a black preacher who had warned his friend, "There are two roads for you, Joe. . . . One . . . leads straight to hell, de odder right to damnation." Joe replied: "I go troo de wood." Lincoln added: "I . . . shall neither go for Spain nor the Negro, but shall take to the woods."

Lincoln enjoyed the popular humorous writers of his day: Orpheus C. Kerr, the pseudonym (a pun on "office seeker") for Robert H. Newell; Petroleum V. Nasby, the pseudonym of David Ross Locke; and Artemus Ward, the pseudonym of Charles Farrar Browne. He began the Cabinet meeting at which he revealed the Emancipation Proclamation for the first time by reading Ward's "High Handed Outrage in Utica."

Considerable dispute rages over whether Lincoln told risqué jokes or smutty stories. There are persuasive witnesses for both sides but little direct evidence. He wrote one humorous piece which involved such spoonerisms as *"bass-ackwards,"* *"Jass-ack,"* *"tow-curd,"* and *hat* and *farty."* In 1860 Lincoln's friend, Ward Hill Lamon, "thinking that being a candidate for a little office like that which you are running for, has not at all blunted your appreciation for the *rediculous*," sent a poem about the Democratic nominations, which read in part:

And when they got to Charleston, they had to,
    as is wont
Look around to find a chairman, and so they took
    a Cu-
    -shing, who is known throughout the land
As most prodigious "pumpkins" when the niggers
    is on hand

Then, an ultra southern platform, they made and
    tried to pass
When up jumped all the Douglas men and quickly
    showed their as-
    -tonishment, at proceedings such as these,
For a platform made to suit the South, the
    North would never please

And they made another, that on it, all might sit
When the South got mad as fury and swore they'd
    on it sh-
    -ow that down among the chivalry in their peaceful
    sunny land

There was not a single Cotton State on its planks
would stand

When Douglas found his chances were scarcely
worth a shuck
He bade his Delegates, go home, to take a
little fu-
-rther time, in order as you see
To meet again in Baltimore on some one to agree

Lincoln lived in the Victorian Era, an age of religious earnestness, and a sense of humor in statesmen was rare. Lincoln's humor was legendary in his own time. Robert M. DeWitt's *Old Abe's Joker, or Wit at the White House*, a 10-cent paperback published in New York in 1863 and sold at railway stations, was the first book to capitalize on the fact that "Wit at the White House is in full blow." *Lincolnana; or the Humors of Uncle Abe* by "Andrew Adderup" was a similar celebration of the President's humor, as was *Old Abe's Jokes, Fresh from Abraham's Bosom, Containing All His Issues, Excepting the "Greenbacks," to Call in Some of Which This Work is Issued*. The latter, published in 1864, was practically a campaign biography, interspersing jokes with praise of the President quoted from the contemporary press.

Lincoln's humor was far from universally admired. Hugh McCulloch, later Lincoln's Secretary of the Treasury, was shocked on his first meeting of the President to find Lincoln telling jokes while the country fell apart. The political opposition repeatedly cited his relish for humor as proof that Lincoln was too small a man for the job, a mere frontier joker incapable of grasping or surmounting the grave national crisis. When word reached the press that Ward Hill Lamon sang "Picayune Butler," a nonsense song, while he and the President visited the Antietam battlefield in 1862, it became a national issue used against the President in editorials in 1864. Lincoln even drafted a long answer to the charge, though it was never released to the press.

In the twentieth century, Lincoln's humor became one of his most endearing qualities. Along with his democratic manners, it made Lincoln an approachable and lovable national saint. Even in his own time, the trait was exaggerated. White House secretary William O. Stoddard noted that the President had never even heard "a vast number of so-called jokes, attributed to him." This exaggeration has increased in modern times, and many of the widely circulated examples of Lincoln's humor are completely mythical.

SOURCES: See "The Gift of Laughter" in J. G. Randall's *Lincoln the President: Midstream* (New York: Dodd, Mead, 1952) and Mark E. Neely, Jr.'s "The Presidential Apotheosis" in *Every Four Years* (Washington, D.C.: Smithsonian Exposition Press, 1980).

See also MUSIC; OWENS, MARY S.

Huntington Library See HENRY E. HUNTINGTON LIBRARY AND ART GALLERY.

Hurd v. Rock Island Bridge Company See EFFIE AFTON CASE.

"Hypo," Hypochondria See PSYCHOLOGY.

I

Illinois *See* COLES COUNTY, ILLINOIS; NEW SALEM, ILLINOIS; SANGAMON COUNTY, ILLINOIS; SPRINGFIELD, ILLINOIS.

Illinois Central Railroad Case *See* MCLEAN COUNTY TAX CASE.

Illinois State Historical Library Repository of one of the most outstanding collections of Lincolniana in the world. From the time of its founding in 1889 the library actively sought Lincolniana, though by 1940 it owned only 200 Lincoln letters and documents. In the next 30 years, the number was increased by over 1000. The holdings include one of the five handwritten copies of the Gettysburg Address; it was purchased in 1944 for $60,000 raised by nickel donations from Illinois schoolchildren and a $10,000 contribution from Marshall Field III. The important document was acquired while Paul M. Angle was the library's head (1932–1945). Under the administration of Harry E. Pratt (1951–1956), an important group of Lincoln letters was purchased from the collection of Oliver R. Barrett for $76,076. It included Lincoln's letters to his intimate friend Joshua Fry Speed.

In 1940 the library acquired its principal holdings of printed Lincoln materials: the collection of Henry Horner. Born in Chicago in 1879, Horner became a lawyer in partnership with Frank A. Whitney, the son of Lincoln's friend Henry C. Whitney. That association bred Horner's interest in collecting Lincolniana, an interest that persisted through five consecutive terms as judge of the probate court of Cook County and two terms as Governor of Illinois, and that existed despite Horner's being a lifelong Democrat. Horner's collection contained more than 6000 items, including a copy of Joseph G. Baldwin's *Flush Times of Alabama and Mississippi*, a humorous book which Lincoln read; rare campaign biographies; and Isaac N. Arnold's annotated copy of his own *History of Abraham Lincoln, and the Overthrow of Slavery*. Horner gave his collection to the library while suffering from a terminal illness in 1940.

Numerous relics and artifacts—paintings from life by George H. Story and William Cogswell, the doorplate from Lincoln's home, and Lincoln's shaving mirror, for example—are also located in the great Springfield collection. The private papers of many of Lincoln's most important personal and political associates supplement the Lincoln collections, and the library continues to add important Lincoln-related items. In 1979 Robert Lincoln Beckwith gave the library the 46 letterbooks of Lincoln's son Robert.

The library is located in new quarters (dedicated in 1970) beneath the restored Old State Capitol in Springfield. Its staff edits the quarterly *Journal of the Illinois State Historical Society*. The present head, whose title is State Historian, is William K. Alderfer. James T. Hickey is curator of the Lincoln collection. The Illinois State Historical Society is a department of the library. For more information write the Illinois State Historical Library, Old State Capitol, Springfield, Illinois 62706.

Immigrants "In regard to the Germans and [other] foreigners, I esteem them no better than other people, nor any worse," said President-elect Abraham Lincoln in Cincinnati on February 13, 1861. His statement succinctly and candidly expressed his sentiments toward immigration. If anything, it underestimated the value that Lincoln placed on immigration to the United States, for he tended to look upon it favorably as a source of population growth and consequently of economic development and prosperity.

Such were not the sentiments of all Americans in Lincoln's day, and among his immediate political associates his views were notably liberal on the subject. The Whig party, of which Lincoln was a member "from its birth to its death," was tainted with nativist dislike of immigrants, especially Catholic ones. Lincoln's Whiggery was exceptional on that score. When news of serious anti-Catholic and antiforeigner riots in Philadelphia reached Springfield in 1844, Lincoln called a public meeting to condemn the mob and deny Whig responsibility. The meeting adopted Lincoln's resolutions, which declared "the guarantee of the rights of conscience, as found in our Constitution, . . . sacred and inviolable, . . . no less to the Catholic than to the Protestant." The immigrant should gain citizenship after "some reasonable test of his fidelity to our country and its institutions" and after dwelling "among us a reasonable time to become generally acquainted with the nature of those institutions."

Political animosity toward foreigners, especially Catholics, crested in the mid-1850s with the formation of the powerful Know-Nothing party, the fastest growing political party in the East by 1855 and a major contender with Lincoln's Republican party everywhere to become the principal opposition of the Democratic party. Lincoln detested the proscriptive principles of the Know-Nothings and said so repeatedly in private. His public denunciations were fewer and quieter because many of his personal and political friends in Springfield had joined the Know-Nothings and because the Republican party clearly needed their support to beat the Democrats. Lincoln never thought of American citizenship as an inherited status but rather as something easily obtained by embracing the principles of freedom which were the country's true foundation. Thus he told a polyglot audience in Chicago on July 10, 1858:

> We have besides . . . men . . . descended by blood from our ancestors . . . perhaps half our people who are not descendants at all of these men, . . . men who have come from Europe—German, Irish, French and Scandanavian—men that have come from Europe themselves, or whose ancestors have . . . and settled here, finding themselves our equals in all things. If they look back through this history to trace their connection with those days by blood, they find they have none . . . , but when they look through that old Declaration

The London Illustrated News, *in September 1864, depicted the recruiting of Irish and German immigrants for the Union army immediately upon their landing in New York. Note that bounties are advertised in both English and German.*

of Independence they find that those old men say that "We hold these truths to be self-evident, that all men are created equal," and then they feel that that moral sentiment . . . evidences their relation to those men, . . . and that they have a right to claim it as though they were blood of the blood, and flesh of the flesh of the men who wrote that Declaration . . . , and so they are.

Lincoln cultivated close political relationships with influential German-Americans. In May 1859 he purchased the *Illinois Staats Anzeiger*, a German-language newspaper in Springfield, from Theodore Canisius and gave Canisius control of it as long as he supported the Republican party. With other Republican strategists, he realized the value of sending popular German speakers like Carl Schurz to areas of heavy German population. Lincoln rewarded his German-American friends liberally; he gave the post of minister to Spain first to Carl Schurz and later to Gustave Koerner. He made Schurz a major general, and he carefully watched and aided the careers of important generals of German-American stock.

Lincoln also appointed Irish-American generals, but his political contacts with Irish politicians were and always had been minimal. The Irish were the steadiest of Democratic voters throughout Lincoln's era. Like most former Whig politicians, Lincoln occasionally blamed political failures on "colonizing" Irish voters. Shortly before election day in his 1858 contest for the Senate with Stephen A. Douglas, Lincoln had told Norman B. Judd of his "high degree of confidence that we shall succeed, if we are not over-run with fraudulent votes to a greater extent than usual." Lincoln had seen "Celtic gentlemen, with black carpet-sacks in their hands" in several tight districts. They were suspiciously hanging "about the doggeries." The candidate feared that they would lie about their residence and vote in the close districts. He was so alarmed that he suggested planting "a true man, of the *'detective'* class . . . among them in disguise, who could, at the nick of time, control their votes." The letter, often quoted to show Lincoln's willingness to play the most rough-and-tumble game of politics, also reveals the ease with which Whig-Republican politicians fell into stereotyping Irish-Americans as the pawns of Democratic bosses, as men so poor they could carry their belongings in carpetsacks, and as heavy drinkers.

Before the Civil War, Lincoln saw America as "comparatively a new country" in which immigrants should be welcome: "If they can better their condition by leaving their old homes, there is nothing in my heart to forbid them coming; and I bid them all God speed." The war discouraged immigration. Lincoln showed little sympathy for immigrants who claimed exemption from the draft as aliens but also voted as or declared intentions to become citizens. A proclamation of May 8, 1863, was aimed at limiting any such abuses, but 7 months later Lincoln accused some immigrants of evading military duty. At the same time he urged Congress to encourage immigration. An act of July 4, 1864, did so by allowing employers to bring foreign workers to America under contract and to deduct transportation costs from future wages. Lincoln later urged Congress to guard against frauds under that law and proclaimed immigrants "one of the principal replenishing streams . . . appointed by Providence to repair the ravages of internal war and its wastes of national strength and health." To do so the government must show that "it neither needs nor designs to impose involuntary military service upon those who come from other lands to cast their lot in our country." Thus the President was always willing to allow unnaturalized aliens to escape the dreaded draft.

SOURCES: For an able and original treatment of the subject see Richard N. Current, *Unity, Ethnicity, & Abraham Lincoln* (Fort Wayne, Ind.: Louis A. Warren Lincoln Library and Museum, 1978).

See also KNOW-NOTHING PARTY; KOERNER, GUSTAVE PHILIPP; RELIGION; SCHURZ, CARL.

Inaugural Addresses *See* FIRST INAUGURAL ADDRESS; SECOND INAUGURAL ADDRESS.

Inaugural Journey On the inaugural journey, February 11, 1861 to February 23, 1861, Lincoln broke the long official silence he had maintained during and after the presidential campaign. The itinerary for his trip to Washington for his inauguration was apparently arranged by William H. Seward with railroad official W. S. Wood. Announcements in the newspapers indicated that the trip would be nonpartisan in nature, demonstrations by Republican Wide-Awake groups would be "objectionable," and there would be no military escort on the train.

Lincoln departed from Springfield's Great Western depot on February 11. Of his immediate family only Robert boarded there. A number of army officers, Todd relatives, and aids and friends accompanied him. Among the last named were secretaries John G. Nicolay and John Hay, political associates Norman B. Judd and Ward Hill Lamon, and Elmer Ellsworth. The train made brief stops, and Lincoln appeared on the platform at Tolono and Danville, Illinois, at the Indiana state line, and at Lafayette, Thorntown, and Lebanon, Indiana, before reaching the first important stop at Indianapolis. From the balcony of the Bates House that night, Lincoln delivered a short prepared address which hinted that the country's "holding its own forts, or retaking those forts which belong to it" would not constitute "coercion or invasion of any State." He also attacked the idea of the "sacredness of a State"; a state was what the Constitution and the Union made it. Mrs. Lincoln with Willie and Tad joined the Presidential party at this stop.

Lincoln left Indianapolis on the 12th, appeared briefly at Lawrenceburg, Indiana, and arrived at Cincinnati the same day. There his remarks were somewhat more conciliatory, though he swore that he would not perform "treachery" to the Republican party and "shift the ground upon which" he had been elected. In a speech to German-Americans, Lincoln stressed "that the working men are the basis of all governments," that he was "for those means which will give the greatest good to the greatest number," and that it was not in his "heart to throw aught" in the way of foreigners "to prevent them from coming to the United States."

Lincoln left Cincinnati on the 13th and stopped briefly in London, Ohio, before addressing the state legislature in Columbus. In apparently extemporaneous remarks, Lincoln belittled the crisis by saying that "there is no more than anxiety, for there is nothing going wrong" and "there is nothing that really hurts anybody." Those remarks were widely quoted in the press to show that Lincoln was insensitive and unequipped to cope with the secession crisis.

Lincoln reached Pittsburgh on the 14th after brief stops in Newark, Cadiz Junction, Steubenville, and Wellsville, Ohio, and in Rochester, Pennsylvania. In a speech in Pittsburgh on the 15th, Lincoln described the nation's crisis as an "*artificial one . . . gotten up . . .* by designing politicians." And he spoke briefly on the tariff, a subject which always concerned Pennsylvanians. His remarks were vague and he claimed ignorance of details, but he reaffirmed Republican devotion to the protective principle.

From Pittsburgh the Presidential party traveled to Cleveland, having stopped briefly at Alliance, Ohio. In Cleveland on the 15th Lincoln complained of fatigue and reiterated his view that the crisis was artificial. He left the same day, traveling through Ravenna, Hudson, Painesville, Ashtabula, and Conneaut, Ohio; Erie, Pennsylvania; and Westfield and Dunkirk, New York. He made brief remarks at all those places and in Westfield kissed Grace Bedell, who had urged him to grow a beard. He stopped in Buffalo for the weekend and left on Monday, February 18, for Albany (with brief appearances in Batavia, Rochester, Clyde, Syracuse, Utica, Little Falls, Fonda, and Schenectady). His remarks were generally conciliatory and unspecific in regard to policy.

Citizens of Troy, Hudson, Poughkeepsie, Fishkill, and Peekskill saw the President-elect on the 19th, the day he arrived in New York City. His remarks began to take on a less compromising tone. Replying to New York Mayor Fernando Wood on the 20th, Lincoln spoke of the Union as the ship of state and liberty as its precious cargo, making it clear that "a ship" is "made for the carrying and preservation of the cargo."

After stopping briefly in Jersey City, Newark, and New Brunswick on the 21st, Lincoln reached Trenton the same day. In a speech to the New Jersey Senate, he recalled reading Mason Weems's *Life of Washington* as a boy and thinking that the country's fathers fought for "something . . . more than National Independence," for "something that held out a great promise to all the people of the world to all time to come." Lincoln struck a stern note when he told the General Assembly, "The man does not live who is more devoted to peace than I am. . . . But it may be necessary to put the foot down firmly." The remark brought prolonged cheering. He reached Philadelphia the same day, and on the next day (Washington's birthday) he spoke at Independence Hall. Again he stressed that what had kept the country "so long together" was more than national independence; it was the promise of liberty in the Declaration of Independence. Lincoln said that he would "rather be assassinated on this spot" than surrender the principle.

Assassination was on Lincoln's mind. The night before (the 21st), detective Allan Pinkerton, Norman Judd, and railroad executive S. M. Felton had urged Lincoln to sneak into Washington to avoid assassination in Baltimore. Lincoln insisted on completing his scheduled appearances in Philadelphia and Harrisburg on the 22d. The train stopped in Leaman Place and Lancaster on the way to Harrisburg. When Seward's son Frederick told him that General Winfield Scott's detectives had corroborated a Baltimore plot, Lincoln agreed to go to Washington, unannounced, by a night train. He arrived there at 6 a.m. on the 23d.

SOURCES: William E. Baringer gives the trip its fullest treatment in *A House Dividing: Lincoln as President Elect* (Springfield, Ill.: Abraham Lincoln Association, 1945).

See also BALTIMORE PLOT; BEDELL, GRACE; SPRINGFIELD, ILLINOIS.

Indiana Abraham Lincoln lived a quarter of his life in Indiana, having moved there with his parents, in the autumn of 1816, when he was 7 years old. Years later, Lincoln recalled that his father came to Indiana "chiefly on account of the difficulty in land titles in K[entuck]y" and "partly on account of slavery." The Land Ordinance of 1785 subdivided Indiana neatly into sections by government survey, and the Northwest Ordinance of 1787 outlawed slavery there. The Lincolns settled near Little Pigeon Creek in western Perry (now Spencer) County.

Abraham was a boy "raised to farm work," and, since he was "large for his age," he "had an axe put into his hands at once; and . . . he was almost constantly handling that most useful instrument—less, of course, in plowing and harvesting seasons." He remembered Indiana as "a wild region, with many bears and other wild animals still in the woods," and his life in the "unbroken wilderness" was a fight "with the trees and logs and grubs."

Lincoln lived to regret the lack of opportunity for education in the crude frontier state. "There was absolutely nothing to excite ambition for education," he remembered, and he belittled the "schools, so called," in which "no qualification was ever required of a teacher, beyond *readin'*, *writin'*, and *cipherin'*, to the Rule of Three." Lincoln attended *ABC* schools "by littles." His Hoosier schoolmasters were Andrew Crawford, James Swaney, and Azel W. Dorsey. Lincoln attended the *ABC* schools for less than a year altogether. He later expressed amazement that, when he left Indiana, "somehow, I could read, write, and cipher to the Rule of Three." But "that was all," and he admitted that "when I came of age I did not know much." In 1860 Lincoln felt that what he had "in the way of education" he had "picked up" since his Indiana years.

Lincoln found it difficult to wax nostalgic about his

hardscrabble years in Indiana. When he returned to the state in 1844 to campaign for Henry Clay, he visited his old home and over a year later wrote a poem which began this way:

> My childhood-home I see again,
>   And gladden with the view:
> And still as mem'ries crowd my brain,
>   There's sadness in it too.

The stanzas that followed referred "To woods, and fields, and scenes of play/ And school-mates loved so well," but dwelt mainly on the madness of Matthew Gentry, a "fortune-favored child," three years older than Abraham, who went berserk before Lincoln's eyes. Lincoln could not help but complain that death tore "more blest ones hence" but left poor Matthew "ling'ring here." He doubtless had in mind also the death of his mother from "milk sickness" in 1818 and the death of his sister in childbirth in 1828. He experienced his own brush with death at age 10, when a horse kicked him in the head and left him unconscious for a time. Still, he could recall the rough good times on the frontier and wrote at about the same time a humorous poem about a boisterous "Bear Hunt" that put the "woods . . . in a roar" with a "merry *corps*" of hunters; it made the usually quiet and solitary forest "alive with fun."

On March 1, 1830, the Lincolns left Indiana for Illinois; they were lured by word from John Hanks that the soil was good and there was no milk sickness. Two years after he left the state, Lincoln published his first political platform. It recommended "good roads" and "clearing of navigable streams" for "thinly populated countries" as well as better educational opportunities. In other words, his earliest political platform, indeed his subsequent devotion to the Whig party, with its ambitious programs for economic development of the West, was an attempt to remedy the faults of his Indiana experience: too much wilderness and too little education. Lincoln would return to Indiana only in 1844, 1859, and 1861. Significantly, when he spoke in Indianapolis in 1859, he remarked, as the newspaper reported, that the "scenes he passed through to-day are wonderfully different from the first scenes he witnessed in the State of Indiana."

Because of lack of documentation for these early years in Lincoln's life, it has always been easy to overlook the 14 years Lincoln spent in the Hoosier state. Indiana was herself slow to capitalize on the part she played in Lincoln's life. It was 1878 before P. E. Studebaker of South Bend had a marble slab placed on Nancy Hanks Lincoln's weed-covered grave. Around the turn of the century, interest in the site revived and some steps were taken to mark and preserve the site, but it was 1926 before the Indiana Lincoln Union was established to plan a suitable national memorial. By 1932 their work resulted in establishing Lincoln State Park and the Nancy Hanks Lincoln State Memorial, which were finally built and landscaped as Depression relief measures. The National Park Service showed interest in the site in the 1960s and now operates a "living historical farm" called the Lincoln Boyhood National Memorial. It is marked on maps as Lincoln City, 2 miles east of Gentryville and 4 miles south of Dale.

SOURCES: Louis A. Warren's *Lincoln's Youth, Indiana Years, Seven to Twenty-one, 1816–1830* (New York: Appleton, Century, Crofts, 1959), the only full-length book on the subject, paints too rosy a picture of the Indiana years. Lincoln's own recollections of these years suggest a different picture; see his autobiographies written for Jesse W. Fell, December 20, 1859, and for John Locke Scripps, ca. June 1860, in Lincoln's *Collected Works*. The second chapter of the first volume of Albert J. Beveridge's *Abraham Lincoln, 1809–1858* (Boston: Houghton, Mifflin, 1928) contains a sober view of the Indiana years.

See also BOOKS; GRIGSBY, AARON; LINCOLN, SARAH BUSH JOHNSTON; LINCOLN, THOMAS; MORTON, OLIVER PERRY; NEW ORLEANS, LOUISIANA; POETRY.

Indians In 1786 Abraham Lincoln's grandfather was killed by Indians "not in battle, but by stealth, when he was laboring to open a farm in the forest." As a result, Lincoln's father became "a wandering laboring boy, and grew up litterally without education." When, in 1832, Indian trouble struck Illinois, 23-year-old Abraham Lincoln joined a militia company to fight the Sac and Fox Indians under Chief Black Hawk, but he saw no "live, fighting Indians."

Despite the bitter experience with Indians he could recall from his personal family history and his otherwise typical frontier experiences, Abraham Lincoln never showed the frontiersman's customary hostility toward Indians. A campaign biography written in 1860 and carefully corrected by Lincoln is the source of a story that Lincoln protected the life of an old Indian who came into camp with a safe-conduct pass during the Black Hawk War.

As President, Lincoln left Indian affairs largely to his Indian commissioner, politician William P. Dole. Though treaties obliged the government to protect the Five Civilized Tribes in Indian Territory (Oklahoma),

Hanging Indians, not pardoning them, was matter for celebration in the nineteenth-century American West. The hanging of the 38 Sioux Indians in Mankato, Minnesota, inspired this later beer advertisement. The depiction of the hanging was based on a lithograph printed in 1863.

the Lincoln administration at first abandoned the reservations to the Confederacy. Many loyal Indians fled to Kansas. Later the administration sought to regain the Territory and authorized (January 2, 1862) the use of Indians as soldiers in the campaign. On September 12, 1862, Cherokee leader John Ross visited Lincoln to explain that his alliance with the Confederacy had been a function of Northern refusal to live up to its treaty obligations to protect the reservations. A congressional bill in 1864 required Lincoln to order the removal of the refugees from Kansas back to Indian Territory.

Indian policy was forced upon Lincoln's attention in August 1862, when a Sioux rebellion broke out in Minnesota. White soldiers crushed the rebellion, and General H. H. Sibley established a military commission which sentenced 303 Sioux warriors to death for "participation in . . . murders and outrages [rapes]." Lincoln discussed the events in Minnesota with his Cabinet (October 14, 1862) and directed Sibley to execute no one without his sanction. He demanded the records of the trials and instructed two War Department lawyers to go over them carefully to determine which Indians had participated in rapes and massacres as opposed to pitched battles with white soldiers. Popular opinion in Minnesota demanded the execution of all the Indians, and Governor Alexander Ramsey, military officers, and other state officials threatened that outraged public opinion would take revenge on all the Indians if the President did not permit their hanging.

Indian Commissioner Dole and Minnesota Episcopal Bishop Henry B. Whipple were among the very few who urged that most of the Indians should be treated as prisoners of war and not as murderers. Whipple had met with Lincoln in September to plead for reform of the Indian system; he saw corruption of the system as giving the Indians cause for wars such as the one in Minnesota. On December 11, 1862, Lincoln announced his decision to the Senate: "Anxious to not act with so much clemency as to encourage another outbreak on the one hand, nor with so much severity as to be real cruelty on the other," he would pardon all but 39, of whom 2 were guilty of rapes and 37 others of participation in "massacres" rather than "battles." At the last minute another was pardoned, and 38 Indians were hanged on December 26 at Mankato, Minnesota. Congress compensated Minnesotans for losses in the war; the pardoned men remained prisoners; the Sioux were removed from the state (along with the Winnebagoes, who had not participated in the uprising); and only the Chippewas, a tribe of special interest to Bishop Whipple, remained in Minnesota.

With Indian affairs forced to his attention, Lincoln came to endorse reform in his annual message to Congress of December 1, 1862. Secretary of the Interior Caleb B. Smith and Commissioner Dole added details to the sketchy plan; they endorsed the treatment of Indians as "wards" of the government rather than as members of independent nations, payments to Indians in goods rather than cash, and increased encouragement of agriculture. Lincoln reiterated his endorsement of reform in his annual message in 1863, but the pressures of war and reelection in 1864 diverted his attention from Indian affairs. The Department of Interior and the military followed a policy of "concentration"; the hope was to gather the tribes in New Mexico Territory and California on a small number of reservations. It was the Sand Creek massacre of Indians by white militia in Colorado Territory in November 1864 which moved Congress to debate reforms which would be instituted under President Ulysses S. Grant long after Lincoln's death.

Lincoln's view of Indians, though kindly and sympathetic for a son of the frontier, was conventional for his day. Meeting with a group of chiefs on March 27, 1863, Lincoln pointed to the contrast between the numerous and prosperous "pale-faced people" and the Indians. The reasons for the differences were simple, he thought; whites "cultivate the earth, produce bread, and depend upon the products of the earth rather than wild game for a subsistence." And, even with the Civil War raging, he was able to say, "we are not, as a race, so much disposed to fight and kill one another as our red brethren."

SOURCES: David A. Nichols, *Lincoln and the Indians: Civil War Policy and Politics* (Columbia: University of Missouri Press, 1978).

See also DOLE, WILLIAM PALMER.

Internal Improvements *See* CHICAGO RIVER AND HARBOR CONVENTION; ECONOMICS; INDIANA; LONG NINE; RAILROADS; WHIG PARTY.

Inventions Lincoln the "Rail Splitter" had no nostalgic fondness for the back-breaking methods of labor of his frontier past. His longing for technological innovation

Indian delegations were regular visitors to the White House. In 1862 Mathew Brady photographed Comanche chieftains in the White House conservatory with Mrs. Lincoln (right) and John G. Nicolay (center). (Courtesy of the Lloyd Ostendorf Collection)

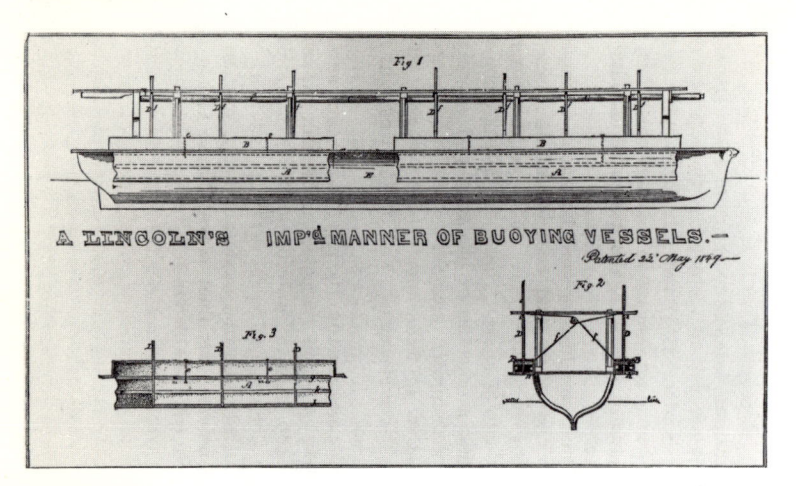

Facsimile of patent drawing of Lincoln's invention.

was as strong as his hope for economic development of the West.

Lincoln proved to be the only President ever to own a patent. Returning via the Great Lakes from a session of Congress, he had been impressed when empty barrels and boxes were used to float a vessel run aground in shallow water. The event sparked an interest which lingered from his youthful days when he had rescued a boat hung up on the fickle waters of the Sangamon River. Back home in Illinois, Lincoln got the assistance of a local mechanic and constructed a model of a boat equipped with "buoyant chambers" attached to "sliding spars." A system of pulleys would at once cause the chambers to fill with air and the spars to force them into the water to float the beleaguered vessel. Reversing the procedure would secure the chambers high on the hull and collapsed into a small space. Taking his model to Washington himself and employing patent attorney Z. C. Robbins, Lincoln applied for a patent on March 10, 1849. He received Patent No. 6469 but never realized anything from his device—probably because the weight of the apparatus could cause the problem he was trying to solve.

Inventions nevertheless continued to fire Lincoln's imagination, and political success did not crowd the subject out of his mind. Early in 1858 he delivered a lecture in Bloomington, Illinois, on "Discoveries and Inventions." He revised it and delivered it again in 1859. The lecture cited "the introduction of Patent-laws" along with the development of writing and printing and the discovery of America as three of the most important discoveries and inventions "in the world's history."

As President, Lincoln could indulge his fondness for new technology in ways that affected the lives—and deaths—of thousands of Americans. General James W. Ripley, the Army's Chief of Ordnance, took a dim view of inventions for new weapons. He felt that they merely added to the clutter which prevented standardization of weapons and ammunition and that even promising innovations could hardly be developed fast enough to affect the war's outcome. Lincoln took a far different view. The year 1861 was a sort of *annus mirabilis* in American weapons technology, and the President himself aided the testing and occasionally forced the Army to use such innovations as balloons for aerial reconnaissance, Christopher Spencer's breech-loading rifles, and a "coffee-mill" machine gun. He favored breech-loading rifled artillery and ironclad naval vessels as well.

In 1862 the President was more cautious about overriding the stodgy Ordnance officers, but his interest in innovative weaponry persisted until after the summer of 1863. He lost interest, partly because Ripley's retirement removed the major obstacle to Regular Army consideration of new weapons and partly because the war seemed more certain to come to an end before new weapons could help.

SOURCES: William H. Herndon's brief account of the origins of Lincoln's invention (in his *Life of Lincoln*, originally published in 1889, ed. by Paul M. Angle [Cleveland: World Publishing, 1965]) has not been much improved upon. Robert V. Bruce's *Lincoln and the Tools of War* (Indianapolis: Bobbs-Merrill, 1956) is a superb treatment of Lincoln's Presidential role in opening doors for inventors. The patent model for Lincoln's own invention is in the Smithsonian Institution, Washington, D.C.

Irish-Americans   See IMMIGRANTS.

J

Jefferson, Thomas In 1854 Lincoln said that Jefferson "was, is, and perhaps will continue to be the most distinguished politician of our history." He showed considerable familiarity with Jefferson's views and works. The best evidence is his reference in an 1858 speech to a Jefferson letter "to be found in the seventh volume of his correspondence, at page 177." His earliest invocation of the third President's name was in a Whig circular of 1843, in which Lincoln quoted Jefferson's letter to Benjamin Austin (January 9, 1816) in favor of domestic manufacturing. Five years later, Lincoln was willing to quote Jefferson's views on internal improvements to show that "on the question of *expediency*" he favored them, though Jefferson thought an amendment to the Constitution necessary to spend the national Treasury surplus in support of them. In the same year, Lincoln noted that, though Jefferson thought the bill establishing the first Bank of the United States unconstitutional, he recommended that President George Washington not veto it unless he was quite certain that it was flagrantly unconstitutional. Doubtful cases demanded restraint on the veto power out of respect for the coequal status of the legislative branch.

Jefferson's similar views on the power of the United States Supreme Court—that it was not the sole arbiter of constitutionality—drew Lincoln's praise in the late 1850s. The conflict over the Dred Scott decision of 1857 found Lincoln in the position of criticizing the Court's decision and, somewhat hesitantly, the Court itself. To make it the final arbiter in every case of questionable legislation without respect to the quality and nature of the Court's particular decision was to turn the country over to the "despotism of an oligarchy," Lincoln thought.

When Lincoln so used Jefferson's views, it was primarily to confute his Democratic opponents with the opposing opinions of the man *they* claimed to be their party's founder. Lincoln never precisely granted that claim. After he became a Republican, Lincoln said only "*If* [italics added] the two leading parties of this day are really identical with the two in the days of Jefferson and Adams, they have performed about the same feat as the two drunken men" who in a comical brawl had somehow exchanged overcoats by the end of the fight. Lincoln was confident that the Republican party was true to Jeffersonian principles.

But Jefferson meant more to Lincoln than an occasional source of doctrines to confuse the Democrats. As the author of the Declaration of Independence, he was the source of Lincoln's basic political ideas. In a letter to the organizers of a Jefferson birthday celebration in Boston in 1859, Lincoln noted Jefferson's importance this way:

> One would start with great confidence that he could convince any sane child that the simpler propositions of Euclid are true; but, nevertheless, he would fail, utterly, with one who should deny the definitions and axioms. The principles of Jefferson are the definitions and axioms of free society.

Questioning Jefferson's declaration that "all men are created equal" was to Lincoln a new, dangerous, and decadent development of the mid-1850s, and much of his argument with Stephen A. Douglas in that decade concerned the meaning of Jefferson's legacy to their age. Lincoln, of course, seized on those Jefferson texts which seem to point to a policy of restriction of slavery extension in order to lead to the ultimate extinction of the institution. To counter Douglas's indifference to whether a territory adopted slavery or not, Lincoln reminded Douglas that Jefferson "trembled for his country when he remembered that God was just." As the author of the Northwest Ordinance of 1787, Jefferson originated "the policy of prohibiting slavery in new territory." Lincoln esteemed Jefferson most for having "in the concrete pressure of a struggle for national independence by a single people, had the coolness, forecast, and capacity to introduce into a merely revolutionary document, an abstract truth, applicable to all men and all times," the doctrine of equality in the Declaration of Independence.

But the Jeffersonian legacy was more ambiguous than Lincoln realized. Jefferson's antislavery principles were most often uttered in private, and the author of the Northwest Ordinance was also the opponent of the Missouri Compromise because it restricted the spread of slavery. His image as Virginian and slaveholder loomed too large during the Civil War to allow his use as an effective symbol. As President, Lincoln rarely mentioned him, though he continued to revere the document Jefferson wrote, the Declaration of Independence.

Jews Lincoln's era was sufficiently prejudiced that even as tolerant a man as Lincoln could refer to Americans as "a Christian people" (in his "Order for Sabbath Observance" of November 15, 1862). The law concerning military chaplains required that they be "regular ordained ministers of some Christian denomination," a fact which led Secretary of War Simon Cameron to reject Arnold Fischel's application for appointment as chaplain of the Cameron Dragoons of New York. President Lincoln wrote Dr. Fischel on December 14, 1861, saying that he would "try to have [Congress provide] a new law broad enough to cover what is desired by you in behalf of the Israelites." Such a new law passed on March 12, 1862.

The most notorious example of anti-Semitism produced by the war was General Ulysses S. Grant's Order No. 11 of December 17, 1862, which expelled "The Jews, as a class," from the Department of the Tennessee for "violating every regulation of trade established by the Treasury Department." Jews were outraged by "this inhuman order," but a telegram to Lincoln brought no response. Attorney General Edward Bates, "feeling no particular interest in the subject," later passed a letter protesting the order on to the President. On January 3, 1863, Caesar J. Kaskel of Paducah, Kentucky, called on the President to protest the order, and the next day General-in-Chief Henry W. Halleck revoked Grant's order. He explained on January 21 that the President objected to proscribing "an entire religious class, some of whom are fighting in our ranks."

Andrew Johnson

Lincoln's tolerance extended to his personal relationships. Two of his Jewish friends were Abraham Jonas and Isachar Zacharie. Jonas was a political associate from Quincy, Illinois; the two had more than once worked closely together against the Democrats. Lincoln called him "one of my most valued friends" and presented him a copy of the published version of the speeches in the Lincoln-Douglas Debates. On the recommendation of their mutual political friend, Orville Hickman Browning, Lincoln appointed Jonas postmaster at Quincy in 1861, and in 1864 he allowed Jonas's son Charles, a Confederate soldier who was then a Union prisoner, to visit his dying father. Lincoln allowed the widowed Mrs. Jonas to complete her husband's term in the post office.

Isachar Zacharie, a chiropodist who operated on Lincoln's feet in 1862, gained the President's confidence enough to be sent twice to New Orleans, which had a large and influential Jewish community, on mysterious missions for the President. After the Battle of Gettysburg and the fall of Vicksburg, Lincoln sent Zacharie to Richmond, again on a mysterious mission, to consult with Confederate leaders, perhaps about a peace plan in which the North would assume the Confederate debt. In 1864 Zacharie worked zealously for Lincoln's reelection.

SOURCES: Bertram W. Korn's *American Jewry and the Civil War* (New York: Atheneum, 1970; originally published 1951) is definitive. Abraham Jonas's copy of the *Political Debates Between Hon. Abraham Lincoln and Hon. Stephen A. Douglas in . . . 1858* is in the Illinois State Historical Library, Springfield. Bates's nonchalant letter about Grant's order (to Lincoln, January 12, 1863) is in the Abraham Lincoln Papers, Library of Congress.

Johnson, Andrew (1808–1875) Lincoln's second Vice President. Johnson was born in Raleigh, North Carolina, but moved to Tennessee with his mother and stepfather in 1826. Eventually he settled in Greenville in his adopted home of East Tennessee. He entered politics and soon became a Jacksonian Democrat, served in the House of Representatives (1843–1853), was twice Governor of Tennessee (elected in 1853 and 1855), and was elected United States Senator in 1857. Poverty-stricken as a youth and residing in the part of Tennessee not wedded to plantation slavery, Johnson was widely regarded as the champion of the Southern small farmer and the rabid foe of the planter aristocracy, though he defended slavery and owned slaves himself.

Alone of the Senators from states that seceded, Johnson retained his seat and spoke forcefully for the Union. In December 1861 his loyalty was rewarded when he became a member of the Joint Committee on the Conduct of the War. Lincoln and Johnson had met when they were members of the same Thirtieth Congress (1847–1849), and in the Civil War they shared at least one passionate desire: to liberate East Tennessee, whose "loyal people . . . would rally" to the Union cause, Lincoln felt sure. In January 1862 Lincoln expressed "distress . . . that our friends in East Tennessee are being hanged and driven to despair, and . . . are thinking of taking rebel arms for the sake of personal protection." News that the Army could not well invade East Tennessee, Lincoln felt, would cause Johnson to "despair—possibly resign" to save his family "somehow, or die with them." After Ulysses S. Grant's victories at Forts Henry and Donelson in February and the flight of Confederate armies from western Tennessee, Lincoln appointed Johnson military governor of the state. Though Confederates still occupied East Tennessee, Lincoln was anxious to restore the state to the Union politically and on July 3 was already explaining to Johnson: "If we could, somehow, get a vote of the people of Tennessee and have it result properly it would be worth more to us than a battle gained. How long before we can get such a vote?"

Johnson was hopeful, but many a bitter struggle lay ahead, and he repeatedly nagged Lincoln (as on August 9, 1863), "Now is the time for an entrance into East Tennessee." He never thought General Don Carlos Buell, Union commander in Tennessee, "the man to redeem East Tennessee," and indeed Buell took little interest in a campaign in that part of the state. When, on September 11, 1863, it appeared to Lincoln that "All Tennessee is now clear of armed insurrectionists," the President hastened to remind Johnson "that it is the nick of time for re-inaugurating a loyal State government." He suggested that the "re-inauguation must not be such as to give control of the State, and it's representation in Congress, to the enemies of the Union," that Johnson should exclude from the process all but "such men only as can be trusted for the Union," and that he must "trust that your government, so organized, will be recognized here, as being the one of republican form."

Lincoln also reminded Johnson to "Get Emancipation into your new State government—Constitution." Indeed, having heard the previous March that Johnson had "at least *thought* of raising a negro military force," Lincoln had strenuously urged him to do so. Johnson was no friend of the Negro, but he hated slavery as the basis of the Southern aristocracy and told Lincoln on September 17, 1863, "I have taken decided ground for . . . immediate emancipation," having abandoned his previous support for "gradual emancipation" only. Johnson worked to raise black soldiers from Tennessee slaveholders (Tennessee was exempted from the Emancipation Proclamation of January 1, 1863). When a constitutional convention established through Johnson's work moved to abolish slavery in Tennessee in January 1865, Lincoln thanked Johnson and the convention.

Johnson thus pursued policies obnoxious to western Tennessee, and all along he assumed sweeping powers and used them sternly to restore the state. He justified his military government by pointing to the clause in the Constitution guaranteeing a republican form of government to the states; he found in that clause "all power necessary & proper to secure to the people of Tennessee a republican form of government." He hoped, however, that Lincoln would "not be committed [to] the proposition of states relapsing into Territories & sold as such," and he cheered Lincoln's veto message on the Wade-Davis Bill.

Apparently at Lincoln's instigation, Johnson became his running mate in 1864. Three days before the nomination Ward Hill Lamon told John Hay he thought "Lincoln rather prefers Johnson or some other War Democrat as calculated to give more strength to the ticket," but Lincoln was publicly noncommittal. When Johnson appeared in Washington in March 1865 for the inauguration, he was exhausted and ill, and a brandy taken to fortify him turned his swearing-in into a grotesque rambling which embarrassed or shocked everyone present. When Lincoln was shot, Johnson also was a target of the assassination, but George A. Atzerodt lost his courage and did not even attempt to kill the Vice President. Johnson assumed the Presidency and, early in May, issued a proclamation for the arrest of Jefferson Davis and other Confederate officials for conspiring to assassinate Lincoln and William H. Seward. He later claimed not to have seen a plea for clemency for Mrs. Surratt signed by five of the nine judges in the trial of the conspirators and allowed her to hang. Judge Advocate General Joseph Holt disputed the claim for years afterwards. Before leaving office, Johnson pardoned the conspirators who were still in prison.

Most politicians expected Johnson to be tougher on the South than Lincoln would have been. Claiming to be following Lincoln's plan of Reconstruction, Johnson was true to a notion he had as early as November 24, 1863, that slavery was destroyed and "there is no good reason . . . for destroying the states to bring about the destruction of slavery." He worked for immediate restoration of the seceded states to the Union. He sustained conservative Southern regimes with government patronage. As Peyton McCrary says of Johnson's policies in Louisiana, "When Andrew Johnson assumed the presidency in 1865 he pursued a reconstruction policy antithetical to that of his predecessor, if viewed in terms of its impact on the party system rather than in light of superficial constitutional similarities." Johnson's conflict with the Republican Congress over this question led to his impeachment in 1868. He returned to the Senate in 1875.

SOURCES: There is no adequate biography of Johnson, and most modern historians focus on Johnson's conduct of office after Lincoln's death. Clifton R. Hall's *Andrew Johnson, Military Governor of Tennessee* (Princeton, N.J.: Princeton University Press, 1916), though dated, is useful for the years before Lincoln's death. Johnson's letters about East Tennessee (to Lincoln, August 9, 1863), about Buell (to Lincoln, July 10, 1862), about emancipation and guaranteeing a republican form of government (to Lincoln, September 17, 1863), and about rebel states as territories and destroying the states (to Montgomery Blair, November 24, 1863) are in the Abraham Lincoln Papers, Library of Congress. Peyton McCrary's book is *Abraham Lincoln and Reconstruction: The Louisiana Experiment* (Princeton, N.J.: Princeton University Press, 1978).

Johnston, John Davis (1811–1854) Lincoln's improvident stepbrother. John D. Johnston was the youngest son of Sarah Bush Johnston, Abraham's stepmother. When Lincoln's father Thomas returned from Kentucky to Indiana with his new wife in 1819, John came with them. Two years younger than Abraham, John and he were doubtless childhood chums.

Johnston moved with the Lincolns to Illinois in 1830 and accompanied Abraham on a flatboat trip to New Orleans in 1831. When they returned, Lincoln settled in New Salem, but Johnston went to Coles County to live with Thomas Lincoln. There he married Mary Barker in 1834. From 1837 to 1840 Johnston and Thomas Lincoln lived in the same cabin on 40 acres of land which Johnston owned. In 1840 Johnston sold his land to Thomas but continued to live on the farm.

As he explained to his stepbrother in 1848, Johnston avoided paying his debts "by not having any property." He was constantly in financial distress, and his influence on Lincoln's father was not good; he involved Thomas Lincoln as a defendant in at least four lawsuits in Coles County which they lost. Johnston's attempts to get money from Abraham produced a correspondence which documents Johnston's improvident character and his stepbrother's sturdy dedication to the work ethic. Having asked Lincoln for $80 in 1848, Johnston received a rejection and a lecture on the virtues of work. "I doubt whether since I saw you," Lincoln answered, "you have done a good whole day's work, in any one day." Johnston's problem was not that he was *lazy*," Lincoln continued, but that he was an "idler"; that is, he did not "much dislike to work" but he never felt like working for the amount he could earn. In other words, he had a get-rich-quick desire that led to a habit of "uselessly wasting time." Lincoln cautioned him against schemes for wealth without work, going "off to . . . the lead mines [in Illinois], or the gold mines" in California. Lincoln offered to match any wages Johnston earned by steady labor over several months to pay his debts. Lincoln thought he needed the "habit" of diligent work for his own sake and for the sake of his children.

Lincoln's fears proved to be well-founded. Johnston had eight children, several of whom later ran afoul of the law. One was simply a thief. Nevertheless, Johnston refused to work even on Lincoln's generous terms. Lincoln was exasperated by his stepbrother but felt genuine affection for him—he called Johnston "brother" in his letters. When Thomas Lincoln died in 1851, Abraham sold 80 acres he inherited from his father to Johnston for $1. Within a year, despite Lincoln's sharp advice to the contrary, Johnston sold the land. Lincoln considered his stepbrother's desire to move west "utterly foolish." "If you intend to go to work," Lincoln chided, "there is no better place than right where you are; if you do not intend to go to work, you cannot get along any where." Johnston must "*face* the truth—which truth is, you are destitute because you have *idled* away all your time. . . . *Go to work* is the only cure for your case." Instead, in 1852 Johnston moved to Arkansas, only to return to Coles County within a year. He died in 1854. His personal property was worth $55.90.

SOURCES: There is a good portrait of Johnston in Charles H. Coleman's *Abraham Lincoln and Coles County, Illinois* (New Brunswick, N.J.: Scarecrow Press, 1955).

Thomas A. Jones

Joint Committee on the Conduct of the War
See COMMITTEE ON THE CONDUCT OF THE WAR, JOINT.

Jones, Thomas A. (?–1895) Aided John Wilkes Booth's escape after the assassination of President Lincoln. Jones was an agent for the Confederate "mail" between Baltimore and Richmond. His farm stood on a hill about 2½ miles from the Potomac on the Maryland side. He deposited dispatches and newspapers to be picked up by Confederate signal corpsmen, and he ferried passengers across the river.

Although he declared that he had no connection with Booth's plots, Jones claimed many years later that Confederate sympathizers in Charles County had heard by December 1864 that Lincoln would be kidnapped while riding without escort near the Navy Yard and that John Wilkes Booth was involved. No contemporary evidence supports Jones's claim.

Jones himself became involved only after Booth left Dr. Samuel A. Mudd's house for the house of Samuel Cox on April 16, two days after the assassination. Jones was Cox's foster brother; Cox asked him to care for Booth and accomplice David E. Herold until they could be ferried across the Potomac to Virginia. Jones explained his willingness to help this way: "Murderer though I knew him to be, his condition so enlisted my sympathy in his behalf that my horror of his deed was almost forgotten in my compassion for the man." For 6 days, Jones sheltered Booth and Herold and took food and newspapers (Booth "seemed very desirous to know what the world thought of his deed") to their hiding place. He did so either out of pity or out of loyalty to the Confederacy, for he was passing up a $100,000 reward for Booth's capture. If he was loyal to the Confederacy, he was loyal indeed. The Confederate States of America owed him $2,300 in wages, and the Confederate bonds in which he had invested $3000 were worthless. He was loyal also to Cox, "the best friend I ever had"; and since Cox had charged him with Booth's care, "nothing," Jones recalled, "would have tempted me to betray him."

On April 21 Jones took Booth and Herold to the river, gave them food, and put the two in a skiff he had procured. He showed them the way to Virginia and directed them to a woman who would take them in. Booth gave Jones $18 for the boat.

Though arrested, Jones was never tried or called as a witness at the trial of the assassins. He took a federal job in the Navy Yard in Washington. After he was dismissed from his job in 1889, he wrote a book, *J. Wilkes Booth. An Account of His Sojourn in Southern Maryland* (Chicago: Laird & Lee, 1893), which is among the most important accounts of Booth's escape. It has been reprinted, but the original edition is quite a rare book.

SOURCES: A sympathetic account of Jones's role is in George S. Bryan's *The Great American Myth* (New York: Carrick & Evans, 1940).

Jones, Thomas Dow (1808–1881) Sculptor. Thomas D. Jones was born on a farm in Oneida County, New York, moved to Ohio in 1837, and learned his trade by chiseling gravestones. He established a studio in Cincinnati in the early 1840s and gained a number of commissions for busts of prominent politicians, most of them Whigs. He executed busts of Salmon P. Chase (1858) and Thomas Ewing (1859). Armed with letters of introduction from Chase and Ewing and commissioned by Robert M. Moore and other Cincinnati Republicans, Jones arrived in Springfield on Christmas Day 1860 to sculpt a bust of Abraham Lincoln.

Lincoln granted Jones daily sittings of 1 hour at Jones's temporary studio in Springfield's St. Nicholas Hotel. Lincoln read his mail and composed speeches to be delivered on his journey to Washington for his inauguration. Jones tried to put Lincoln at ease by exchanging a few humorous anecdotes at the beginning of each session. Jones found Lincoln "a subject of great interest, but a very difficult study"; on first meeting he was reminded of "a rough block, of the old red primitive sand-stone." He saw "hard and rugged lines upon his face," but the anecdotes "much improved the plastic character of his features." Jones sought to avoid Lincoln's face in repose, "hard, liney, . . . care worn," and to capture it "illuminated with thoughts or emotions," when "it is everything one could desire." He thought the bust a great success, and Lincoln, when shown the preliminary results, said simply, "I think it looks very much like the critter." Jones remained in Springfield well past Lincoln's departure; he finished his work by August 24, 1861. Jones saw the "firmness of a Jackson" in Lincoln, and his bust is somewhat Jacksonian in flavor as well as neoclassical in form (though Lincoln is clothed in modern dress).

Jones fared poorly with his sculpture. He received only $20 from his patron, Moore. Although Moore raised further funds, he spent them on an unsuccessful trip to Washington to procure a political appointment. Jones tried to get an office too; he asked Salmon P. Chase, then Secretary of the Treasury, to inquire about an appointment as consul to Rome. When that failed, Jones inquired about a lesser consular post in Italy, still with no results. He made very few plaster copies of his bust, but one found its way to the Red Room of the White House, where it was on view while Lincoln was President. On March 6, 1865, Lincoln reminded Secretary of State William H. Seward to "watch for chances" to give Jones one "of those moderate sized consulates which facilitates artists a little [in] their profession," but the sculptor never became a consul.

After Lincoln's death, Jones failed to capitalize on the many demands for likenesses of Lincoln by casting his life-size bust. Instead, he was at work on a cabinet-size bronze bust of Lincoln, stamped "1864" and patented August 8, 1865. The Ohio Monumental Association chose Jones to execute a memorial to Lincoln and Ohio veterans. The Lincoln was a heroic-size marble version of Jones's original Lincoln bust from life, and the monument was dedicated in the rotunda of the state capitol on January 19, 1871.

SOURCES: The definitive work is Wayne C. Temple's *Abraham Lincoln and Others at the St. Nicholas* (Springfield, Ill.: St. Nicholas Corporation, 1968). His "Lincoln as seen by T. D. Jones," *Illinois Libraries*, LVIII (June 1976), 447–456, reprints three important Jones letters and Jones's "Recollections of Mr. Lincoln," originally published in the Cincinnati *Commercial*, October 18, 1871, p. 4.

Plaster copy of Thomas Dow Jones's neoclassical bust of Lincoln, sculpted from life.

Jonesboro, Illinois Site of the third and southernmost of the Lincoln-Douglas Debates. Sparsely populated Union County, in which Jonesboro is situated, could muster only about 1500 people to watch the debate on September 15, 1858.

The area was heavily Democratic in sentiment. Republicans had never gained more than 17.4 percent of the congressional district's vote, and John C. Frémont received only 3.8 percent of the vote there in 1856. Douglas performed well for his willing audience on the hot day. His opening remarks accused Lincoln and Lyman Trumbull of conspiring in 1854 to "abolitionize" the Whig and Democratic parties, respectively, in order to unite the North in one overwhelming party which would send both men to the United States Senate. Douglas also initiated a charge which would stick and would influence literature on the debates for years. He said that the Republican party was boldly abolitionist in northern Illinois, "bleached and . . . paler" in central

Illinois, where they were merely "anti-Nebraska men," and "in this neighborhood" content to talk "about the inexpediency of the repeal of the Missouri compromise" and to appeal to the *"free democracy."* Much of his own appeal in this speech was aggressively racist. Republicans "brought [Negro] Fred [erick] Douglass to Freeport . . . in a carriage driven by the white owner, the negro sitting inside with the white lady and her daughter." He accused Lincoln of denouncing the Dred Scott decision "mainly because it deprives the negro of the rights of citizenship." Douglas held "that this government was made . . . by white men, for the benefit of white men . . . , and should be administered by white men and none others." He denounced Lincoln's "House Divided" speech also.

Lincoln could not possibly gain enough votes for Republicans to carry the district, but he could be hurt by significantly altering the positions he took in areas of the state more friendly to him politically. He replied that, but for Douglas's Kansas-Nebraska Act, the American house would be nearer all free and not divided, as the founding fathers had intended. He denied the existence of a bargain with Trumbull. Relying on careful research, Lincoln answered the charge of trimming principles to regional prejudices by saying that Douglas quoted local Republican resolutions and acted as though Lincoln must be responsible for every word uttered by any Republican. To counter, Lincoln quoted numerous Democratic resolutions from Illinois which urged excluding slavery from the territories. He spent the rest of his time arguing that "popular sovereignty," Douglas's idea for settling the problem of the territories, would not work because the Supreme Court in the Dred Scott decision made it unlawful to exclude slave property from a territory. Finally, he asked Douglas a new question: would he vote for congressional legislation to protect slave property in a territory? Lincoln did not respond to Douglas's talk of white supremacy; he did not stress the doctrine of equality in the Declaration of Independence.

Some of the Democratic resolutions Lincoln quoted had been used against Douglas before, and the Little Giant could point out their nonrepresentative nature or his own denunciations of them when issued. He reiterated his charge that Lincoln could not stand by the antislavery principles of his party as enunciated by Republicans in northern Illinois. He answered Lincoln's new question by saying that the Democracy was pledged to noninterference by Congress in the territories. And Douglas added that, even if the Supreme Court guaranteed the ability to take slaves to a territory, only local police legislation could keep it there; thus, local control could drive it out.

Douglas was greeted by enormous cheers from the rather partisan crowd, and Lincoln appears to have been disturbed by the debate. The next day, he wrote a letter apologizing to a Republican associate for a slip of the tongue that might have been construed as an insult. And he wrote Elihu B. Washburne to ask whether Douglas was correct in saying that Washburne was "every where, pledging . . . unconditionally against the admission of any more Slave States."

The debate did little to alter the political complexion of the Jonesboro area. Republicans did not even run any candidates for the state legislature in Union County, and the statewide ticket garnered less than 15 percent of the vote in the district.

SOURCES: John Y. Simon's "Union County in 1858 and the Lincoln-Douglas Debate," *Journal of the Illinois State Historical Society*, LXII (Autumn, 1969), 267–292, is definitive.

Judd, Norman Buel (1815–1878) Lincoln's Republican political associate and minister to Prussia. Judd was born in Rome, New York, where he became a lawyer. In 1836 he moved to Chicago; there he continued to practice law and became a prominent Democrat. He was a member of the Illinois Senate from 1844 to 1860. An attorney for the railroads in private life, Judd was noted in Illinois public life for measures promoting railroad growth.

Judd became an Anti-Nebraska Democrat in 1854, and his refusal (and that of other Anti-Nebraska Democrats) to vote for Whig Abraham Lincoln for United States Senator in 1855 forced Lincoln to throw his support to Anti-Nebraska Democrat Lyman Trumbull. Many Illinois Whigs who later joined Judd in the Republican party never forgave him for his role in that contest, but Lincoln was willing to let bygones be bygones. Judd later explained to Lincoln, "I thought then that a position in which I could not be howled down as having joined the 'Whig party' was the best for the future." Judd became a prominent Republican; he served as chairman of the state central committee (1856–1861) and on the National Republican Committee (1856–1861).

In 1858 Judd presented the letter to Stephen A. Douglas which resulted in the Lincoln-Douglas Debates. Lincoln consulted him before the famous Freeport debate, and Judd urged Lincoln to make his opening "a Series of Charges against Douglass leaving all Statement of your own views for your reply." Lincoln's defeat left Judd "blue," and he complained of the party's unpaid bills. Lincoln "at least made a national reputation that cannot be taken away," he noted.

Judd hitched his political wagon to that reputation. In 1859 he became embroiled in a bitter political feud with Chicago Republican John Wentworth, who charged, among other things, that Judd had served Lincoln poorly in 1858 as well as 1855. Delicate negotiations and Judd's considerable pressure on him led Lincoln to provide a statement testifying to Judd's faithful service. The Wentworth-Judd feud was patched up enough to allow Wentworth's election as mayor in March 1860. As Lincoln had feared, his statement in Judd's behalf led in turn to hints of trouble within the Republican state convention at Decatur in 1860. Judd's enemies, now "pretty bitter towards" Lincoln, might seek to kill Lincoln's presidential nomination by supporting either William H. Seward or Edward Bates. Lincoln asked Judd on February 9, 1860, to "help me a

Norman Buel Judd from a photograph by John Corbutt, circa 1867–1868. (Courtesy of the Chicago Historical Society)

little in this matter, in your end of the vineyard." At the same convention Judd sought the Republican nomination for governor against Leonard Swett and Richard Yates but "was left standing out in the cold at Decatur." Lincoln had stood aloof from the contest. The Wentworth feud was not over; Judd asked Lincoln to "allow Cook Co. to deal with him" and to extend no "olive branch to him."

At the behest of his advisers, Lincoln reminded Judd of the importance of having the Republican national convention in Illinois, and Judd is credited with bringing it to Chicago by virtue of his position on the national committee. He nominated Lincoln at the convention, seated the delegations to Lincoln's advantage, and worked hard for the victory. Opposed by Leonard Swett and David Davis, however, he failed to gain a Cabinet post as a reward. Jesse W. Fell's letter of January 2, 1861, dashed his chances if he ever had any. Professing no personal animosity, Fell pointed out Judd's unacceptability to old Whig elements in the Illinois Republican party and argued that, with an Illinoisan at the helm, there was no need for a Cabinet representative from Illinois at all. Though not invited to join the Cabinet, Judd was asked to accompany Lincoln on his inaugural journey. He received two warnings from Allan Pinkerton of a plot to kill Lincoln in Baltimore and was privy to the plan which had Lincoln pass secretly through Baltimore to Washington in the night. On March 8, 1861, Lincoln appointed him minister to Berlin.

Judd's political views smacked of his Democratic antecedents. In June 1860 he had advised Lincoln to work for three policies: (1) the "seperation of the races" by a "peaceful exodus" of the "Servile race" (otherwise there would be "no permanent peace . . . or servile insurrection [would] blacken some of these States"), (2) the "peaceful acquisition of the unoccupied Mexican territory," and (3) the annexation of Canada. When war began, he urged "Aggression" as "the only policy now," and the logic of events led him to celebrate emancipation and the use of Negro troops. By 1863 he seems to have dropped his insistence on colonization of Negroes, and he foresaw the use of "colored soldiers" to "administer the south" in Reconstruction. In 1864 he told the President, "you belong in principle to the radicals although in execution your caution leads many people to call you conservative." He applauded Salmon P. Chase's exit from the Cabinet to the Supreme Court in 1864 as ridding Lincoln of factional trouble in his official family and at the same time strengthening the antislavery sentiment on the bench—"to save judicially, what you have decreed administratively."

Lincoln lent Judd money and tried to help him with his troublesome son Frank, who fell in with bad company in Europe in 1863 and was led to "dissipation more with women than wine." Judd wished Frank away from Europe and under salutary military discipline. Lincoln arranged Frank's appointment to West Point, but young Judd enlisted instead, served under aliases, and was twice spared from being shot for desertion by President Lincoln.

Andrew Johnson removed Judd from his Prussian post. After his return, Judd enjoyed a primary victory over his old rival Wentworth and was elected to Congress in 1866.

SOURCES: Judd's role in Illinois politics from 1854 to 1860 is best treated in Willard L. King's *Lincoln's Manager: David Davis* (Cambridge: Harvard University Press, 1960) and in Don E. Fehrenbacher's *Chicago Giant: A Biography of "Long John" Wentworth* (Madison, Wis.: The American History Research Center, 1957). Judd's letters to Lincoln about his vote for Trumbull in 1855 (December 11, 1859), about the Lincoln-Douglas Debates (September, 1858), about the debates' aftermath (November 18, 1858), about Decatur and Wentworth (May 28, 1860), about his political views (June 6, 1860), about aggression (April 21, 1861), about Negro soldiers and his son (August 27, 1863), about Lincoln's conservatism (January 4, 1864), and about Chase (December 28, 1864) are in the Abraham Lincoln Papers, Library of Congress.

See also FELL, JESSE WILSON; TRUMBULL, LYMAN.

K

Kansas-Nebraska Act The issue that renewed Abraham Lincoln's declining interest in politics. The Kansas-Nebraska Act was largely the work of Senator Stephen A. Douglas. It provided for the organization of the Nebraska Territory, which, in turn, was part of the original Louisiana Purchase. The bill passed on May 30, 1854.

From the start, Douglas intended to organize the territory according to the principles of the Compromise of 1850, which had left it up to the inhabitants of the New Mexico and Utah Territories to decide whether they would legalize slavery or not. Nevertheless, the first version of the bill reported from Douglas's Committee on Territories neither affirmed nor repealed the eighth section of the act enabling Missouri to enter the Union—the section which banned slavery above the 36° 30' line in the rest of the Louisiana Purchase. Still, the act clearly would supersede the restriction in the Missouri Compromise.

When some Senators insisted on an explicit repeal of the Missouri Compromise restriction, Douglas conferred with President Franklin Pierce and others and decided to state that the eighth section of the Missouri Act was "inoperative" ("repeal" was a blunt word they wished to avoid). Southern pressure shaped the eventual wording of the bill, and Southern resistance to earlier efforts to organize Nebraska Territory had prompted Douglas to seek some new approach to settling the slavery question there. But for the most part Douglas wrote and passed the bill by himself. He had intended the "popular sovereignty" doctrine in the Compromise of 1850 to be the solution to future sectional questions in the territories.

Lincoln was at once "astounded," "thunderstruck," "stunned;" he "reeled and fell in utter confusion" but "rose . . . fighting." The Kansas-Nebraska Act seemed to be something completely new, the abrogation of long-settled American principles. He was aroused "as he had never been before" by a political question and rushed back into politics.

Lincoln immediately interpreted the act as *intended* to spread slavery into Kansas. Why else tear down a "restrictive fence" Douglas "had solemnly pledged himself to sustain"? To believe otherwise simply because the act did "not require slaves to be sent there" was to be "a knave and a fool." It was an ignoble law, "descending from the high republican faith of our ancestors, to . . . declare by the highest act of our government that we have no longer a choice between freedom and slavery—that both are equal with us—that we yield our territories as readily to one as the other!" He dismissed the idea that climate would keep slavery out anyhow; several slave states extended above the 36° 30' line. To apply popular sovereignty to Nebraska was not the intention of those who voted for the Compromise of 1850: "Now I insist this provision was made for Utah and New Mexico, and for no other place whatever. It had no more direct reference to Nebraska than it had to the territories of the moon." He probed the ambiguity of the Kansas-Nebraska Act which allowed it to unite

Northern and Southern Democrats: precisely when would the people in the territory vote on slavery—when 10 people were there or 50,000? By 1855 he saw the act as "conceived in violence, passed in violence, . . . maintained in violence, and . . . executed in violence." It did not represent popular will. Even Democrats disliked it. Lincoln had heard that a caucus of Democrats in the Illinois legislature at the time the bill was being discussed in Congress found only 3 of about 70 in favor of the measure. And the masses "were even, nearer unanamous against it."

By 1858 Lincoln was arguing that the Kansas-Nebraska Act was "the beginning of a conspiracy" to make slavery "perpetual, national and universal." The "Nebraska doctrine" was meant "to *educate* and *mould* public opinion . . . to not *care* whether slavery is voted *down* or voted *up*," Lincoln argued in his "House Divided" speech. Afterward Presidents Pierce and James Buchanan prepared public opinion for Roger B. Taney's Dred Scott decision, declaring congressional interference with slavery in the territories unconstitutional. The next step would be a court decision forbidding the states from prohibiting slavery.

The conspiracy charge rested in part on a close knowledge of the history of the Kansas-Nebraska Bill. Lincoln claimed that Douglas left a "niche . . . to put that Dred Scott decision in" by saying in the act:

> It being the true intent and meaning of this act not to legislate slavery into any Territory or State, nor to exclude it therefrom; but to leave the people thereof perfectly free to form and regulate their domestic institutions in their own way, subject only to the Constitution of the United States.

Douglas certainly did not foresee the Dred Scott decision of 3 years later, but the clause referring to the Constitution was important. It was a veiled reference to the Supreme Court and was necessary to gain Southern support for the bill, for some Southerners believed that congressional interference with slavery in the territories was illegal and would be so declared by the Court. Moreover, the wording maintained the essential ambiguity of popular sovereignty: Northerners like Douglas thought territorial governments would keep slavery out, but Southerners thought popular sovereignty would not be exercised until the territory formed a constitution and applied for admission as a state, giving slavery a chance to gain a foothold. Lincoln also claimed that he had "always been puzzled to know what business the word 'State' had in that connection." The act concerned not states, but territories. Lincoln argued that Douglas thereby readied the country for the anticipated *"other half"* of the Dred Scott decision, a new decision preventing legislatures from prohibiting slavery in the states. The inclusion of the word "State" was apparently inadvertent, and certainly harmless and valid (it was not the act's intention to legislate slavery in any state); but after the Dred Scott decision and in the fevered anxiety over what appeared to be an aggressive "slave power," it looked ominous.

In 1858 Lincoln added a new argument against the act. Introduced, according to Douglas, to alleviate agitation over slavery, the Kansas-Nebraska Act, Lincoln insisted, in fact ended a period of quiet following the Compromise of 1850 and ushered in 4 years of turmoil.

Douglas did not introduce the Kansas-Nebraska Act as a Southern measure, and he always resented imputations that he had done so. It was to him a Western measure which was fair to the South so that Western expansion, the real business of America, could be got on with. Lincoln regarded it differently, but it would be dangerous to charge him with a steadily conscious distortion of Douglas's motives. There is no evidence that Lincoln did not sincerely believe even the specious charge of conspiracy with Pierce, Buchanan, and Taney to nationalize slavery. Lincoln never took the really low road of attack, which indulged in charging Douglas with trying to increase the value of his deceased wife's Mississippi plantation.

In recent years, too, emphasis on the importance of the Kansas-Nebraska Act in causing the formation of the Republican party has diminished. The coalition that would become that party was already forming on other issues in some areas slightly before 1854, and the number who became Republicans immediately after the passage of the act was very small. Indeed, Lincoln was not one of them. "Bleeding" Kansas and the caning of Charles Sumner probably made more Republican voters. But there is no diminishing the importance of the Kansas-Nebraska Act in Lincoln's life. Lincoln simply thought at first that he could resist it effectively as a Whig.

SOURCES: See Robert W. Johannsen, *Stephen A. Douglas* (New York: Oxford University Press, 1973).

See also DOUGLAS, STEPHEN ARNOLD; MISSOURI COMPROMISE; "POPULAR SOVEREIGNTY."

Keckley, Elizabeth (1818?–1907) Mrs. Lincoln's mulatto dressmaker and confidante. Elizabeth Keckley was born a slave in Dinwiddie Courthouse, Virginia; her master was a Burwell. Her parents were Agnes Hobbs and George Pleasant (or possibly her white master). Hobbs and Pleasant were forced to separate. Elizabeth says in her autobiography that she was first lashed at age 4. She had an illegitimate child by a white man named Alexander Kirkland. While still a slave, she became a seamstress in St. Louis. James Keckley, her husband for 8 years, was also a slave; he was so dissipated that she eventually deserted him.

In 1855 Mrs. Keckley bought her own and her child's freedom for $1200 supplied by grateful customers. She left St. Louis in 1860 and eventually established herself as a "modiste" in Washington, D.C., where Jefferson and Varina Davis were among her elite customers. Another customer introduced her to Mrs. Lincoln, who liked her work and liked her personally as well; she recognized Mrs. Keckley almost immediately as "a very remarkable woman." Mrs. Keckley made many of Mrs. Lincoln's clothes and was frequently at the Executive Mansion.

Mrs. Lincoln came to regard Mrs. Keckley as a confidante, and the seamstress had knowledge of Mrs. Lin-

Elizabeth Keckley

coln's foibles and of domestic life in the Lincoln White House unknown to almost anyone else. She knew Mrs. Lincoln's likes and dislikes. Mary was jealous of Lincoln's attentions, no matter how trifling, to any other woman. She thought Salmon P. Chase and William H. Seward were not to be trusted, regarded Andrew Johnson as a "demagogue," George B. McClellan as a "humbug," and Ulysses S. Grant as a "butcher." Mrs. Keckley is the source of two widely quoted stories about Lincoln. The one, an example of his humor, was his comment on Mrs. Lincoln's train: "Whew! our cat has a long tail to-night." The other, more chilling, concerned his fears for Mary's sanity after the death of Willie Lincoln: "Mother, do you see that large white building on the hill yonder [the lunatic asylum]? Try and control your grief, or it will drive you mad, and we may have to send you there."

Mrs. Keckley's own son was killed in battle, and she was sensitive to the plight of her race. She helped organize the Contraband Relief Organization to aid freedmen in the North, for she believed Northerners were cold, would blame Negroes for the war, and would regard them as "an idle, dependent race." She herself admitted that "dependence had become a part of their second nature."

Mrs. Lincoln became especially dependent on her talented seamstress from the time of the President's assassination until 1868. Mary had revealed to Mrs. Keckley in 1864 that she owed $27,000 in debts to cloth and clothing merchants—of which the President knew nothing. She was miserably anxious for his reelection; a loss would mean the end of the extension of credit and, consequently, Lincoln's knowledge of her deceit. When the President died, his widow, prostrated by grief, was saddled with the debts. Mrs. Keckley said they amounted to $70,000 by then, but Mrs. Lincoln later ridiculed that figure. Mrs. Keckley consoled Mrs. Lincoln in the White House, accompanied her on her return to Illinois, and remained with her in Chicago until her inability to pay forced Mrs. Keckley to go back to her business in Washington.

In 1867 Mrs. Lincoln found her economic circumstances so straitened that she decided to sell much of her wardrobe in New York. She wanted to do so in secret and relied on Mrs. Keckley to join her in New York City to help. Mrs. Keckley's reminiscences are the principal source of information on the ensuing "Old Clothes Scandal." The seamstress joined Mrs. Lincoln, who was registered as Mrs. Clarke in the shabby St. Denis Hotel. Eventually they contacted W. H. Brady and S. C. Keyes, who promised to raise $100,000 if Mrs. Lincoln gave up the idea of anonymity. She agreed and wrote letters for them to show Republican politicians who, Brady and Keyes assured them, would never let her suffer that way. They were wrong. Next, they got the bereaved widow to agree to publish letters in the New York *World* and display the clothes publicly for sale in New York. Mary left for Chicago after charging Lizzie, her "best living friend," with seeing to the details. People came and gawked, but they did not buy. With only vague promises of future reward, Mrs. Lincoln begged Mrs. Keckley to remain in New York to see to the sale. A scheme to send circular letters signed by prominent men failed, and eventually the seamstress agreed to Brady and Keyes's last plan, sending the clothes on tour. Mrs. Lincoln was horrified and, fortunately, authorities in Providence, Rhode Island, the first stop, refused to agree to the display. In the spring of 1868 the trunks of clothes, minus only a few garments sold, were returned to Mrs. Lincoln.

Mrs. Keckley worked at her miserable task faithfully and even proposed a scheme of her own to get Frederick Douglass and H. H. Garnet, Negro leaders, to lecture for Mrs. Lincoln. Douglass did not want the movement to be strictly a black one, and Mrs. Lincoln was reluctant as well. The scheme fell through. But Mrs. Keckley was not to be without some compensation. While she labored to sell the old clothes in New York, she also dictated her memoirs to a ghost writer, possibly James Redpath or Hamilton Busbey. In 1868 the New York firm of G. W. Carleton & Co. published *Behind the Scenes. Or, Thirty Years a Slave, and Four Years in the White House.* The revelations about the old clothes scandal and the publication of Mrs. Lincoln's letters to her seamstress without her permission brought even more humiliation to Mary and ended her friendship with the woman to whom Mary thereafter referred only as "the colored historian."

Mrs. Keckley claimed that the letters were published without her knowledge and that she planned to share her profits from the book with Mrs. Lincoln. Apparently there were no such profits; the book, after some sensationally denunciatory reviews, did not sell well. It may even have hurt her dressmaking business. Mrs. Keckley gave up sewing and became an instructor in domestic arts at Wilberforce University in Xenia, Ohio. Though she paid for her room and board, she died in the Home of Destitute Colored Women and Children in Washington and left that institution her small estate.

After her death, Mrs. Keckley came near to losing her historical identity altogether. An Associated Press story in 1935 claimed that there was no Elizabeth Keckley and that *Behind the Scenes* was actually the work of journalist Jane Swisshelm. John E. Washington, who later wrote a book about Negroes who knew Lincoln, corrected the error in an article in the Washington *Evening Star.*

SOURCES: See Justin G. and Linda Levitt Turner, *Mary Todd Lincoln: Her Life and Letters* (New York: Alfred A. Knopf, 1972) and John E. Washington, *They Knew Lincoln* (New York: E. P. Dutton, 1942).

Keene, Laura   See ASSASSINATION.

Kentucky   Abraham Lincoln's earliest recollection of his youth was of the Lincoln homestead on Knob Creek in Kentucky, but that farm was not his birthplace. Instead, Lincoln was born on February 12, 1809, in a log cabin 3 miles south of Hodgenville, Kentucky, on the south fork of Nolin Creek. That was in Hardin (now

Kentucky

Larue) County. In 1811 the Lincolns moved to the Knob Creek farm, a 230-acre spread which Abraham's father purchased. Abraham and his older sister Sarah "were sent for short periods, to A.B.C. schools, the first kept by Zachariah Riney, and the second by Caleb Hazel." Lincoln was only 7 years old when he and his family moved to Indiana "partly on account of slavery; but chiefly on account of the difficulty in land titles in K[entuck]y," as he recalled in 1860.

Difficulties with land titles were plentiful in Kentucky, and Thomas Lincoln had more than his fair share of them. Inaccurate private surveys and conflicting government land policies made Kentucky a crazy-quilt of overlapping claims. Thomas Lincoln owned three farms while he lived in Kentucky. The first proved to have fewer acres than he thought, and he sold it at a loss in 1814 after 11 years of ownership. The second (on which Abraham was born and which Thomas owned concurrently with the first from late 1808) became the object of litigation, and another claimant sued to dispossess him of the third one, on Knob Creek.

That was enough to drive anyone out of the state, and the recollection that slavery played a role in their removal to Indiana came only after Lincoln was active in the political antislavery cause. Nevertheless, slavery may well have genuinely troubled Thomas. In 1811 Hardin County had 1007 slaves and only 1627 white males over 16 years of age. The Lincolns attended the Little Mount (Baptist) Church, which had been founded in 1811 by former South Fork Church members who had left their church as a result of a controversy over slavery.

Since Lincoln left Kentucky when he was 7, one should not exaggerate the influence of his early environment. On the other hand, he married a Kentuckian, his three law partners were born in Kentucky, his best friend (Joshua Speed) was a Kentuckian, and his political hero (Henry Clay) was a Kentucky Senator. When he ran for Congress in 1846, over 80 percent of Springfield voters who came from Kentucky voted for him.

Sentimental regard for his native state probably did not dictate the importance Kentucky assumed in the early strategic and political thinking of the Lincoln administration. On June 4, 1860, after a suggestion that "a visit to the place of my nativity might be pleasant," Lincoln responded, "Indeed it would. But would it be safe? Would not the people lynch me?" By then he was the Republican nominee for President and none too popular in the Border State with the largest slave population. Kentucky had 225,483 slaves, more than three states which seceded. Lincoln judged Kentucky sentiment well. In November the state gave him only 1364 votes.

Once war broke out, a major policy of the Lincoln administration was to keep Kentucky's political hostility from driving the state into the Confederacy; the North could ill afford the loss of her nearly 1,150,000 population. Combined with the population of the other three Border States she might take with her (Maryland, Missouri, and Delaware), Kentucky's secession would swell the Confederacy's white population by almost half. Little wonder Lincoln told Orville Hickman Browning on September 22, 1861, that "to lose Kentucky is nearly the same as to lose the whole game."

Kentucky's Governor Beriah Magoffin was a Democrat of decidedly pro-Southern sentiments, but the legislature was not in session when, after the fall of Fort Sumter, President Lincoln announced measures to coerce the Confederate states. Magoffin swore that Kentucky would supply no soldiers "for the wicked purpose of subduing her sister states," and he called for the legislature to meet on May 6. When the legislature did meet, it followed policies suggested by John Jordan Crittenden, the heir of Henry Clay's mantle of compromise and Union-saving. It announced a policy of neutrality: Kentucky would help neither side but would stand ready as "mediator" for reunion. Lincoln had promised Kentucky Unionist Garrett Davis that he would send no troops through the state if Kentucky showed no signs of resisting Federal authority. Secretly, Lincoln supplied arms to pro-Union groups in Kentucky led by William Nelson, Crittenden, Davis, and Lincoln's old friends, Joshua and James Speed.

Constitutionally, neutrality violated Lincoln's oath to execute the laws of the Union, and in his first message to Congress (July 4, 1861), he said so: "It recognizes no fidelity to the Constitution, no obligation to maintain the Union; and while very many who have favored it are, doubtless, loyal citizens, it is, nevertheless, treason in effect." Constitutional scruple and victorious strategy were two different things, however, and throughout the summer Lincoln kept Federal troops out of the state. John C. Frémont nearly upset the policy by issuing his emancipation proclamation for Missouri on August 30, and Lincoln expressed as his principal motive in revoking it that the proclamation would lose Kentucky. The revocation allowed Lincoln to cling to his policy until Confederate forces occupied Columbus, Kentucky, early in September. Thus Union soldiers were not the first to "invade" Kentucky, and the legislature raised the United States flag over the capital on September 7.

Governments and lines on a map are not altogether indicative of loyalty, and Kentucky would furnish some 40,000 men to the Confederacy along with about

Lincoln's birthplace cabin, a humble building with a controversial history, as it looked about a century after Lincoln lived in it.

100,000 for the Union. Yet they are powerful factors, and Lincoln knew by December 3, 1861, that "Kentucky, . . . for some time in doubt, is now decidedly, and, I think, unchangeably, ranged on the side of the Union."

As soon as Lincoln became President, Dr. George Rodman recognized the historical value of the birthplace cabin and purchased the farm in March 1861. He moved the cabin to his own neighboring farm, and controversy still rages over its precise original location. In 1895 New Yorker A. W. Dennett purchased the cabin and returned it to the Lincoln farm. The cabin was dismantled several times for display at expositions throughout the country. It was subsequently stored on Long Island until the Lincoln Farm Association purchased it in 1906. The association, formed in 1904 by the editor and publisher of *Collier's Weekly*, raised money to purchase the birthplace for a national memorial. In 1911 the Lincoln Farm Association completed a granite and marble building, designed by John Russell Pope, to hold the cabin. Five years later the association donated the cabin and the land around it to the United States government. The National Park Service now administers the Abraham Lincoln Birthplace National Historic Site, located 3 miles south of Hodgenville, Kentucky.

SOURCES: Louis A. Warren's *Lincoln's Parentage and Childhood: A History of the Kentucky Lincolns Supported by Documentary Evidence* (New York: Century, 1926) is by far the most important book on the subject. Warren added a valuable supplement in *The Slavery Atmosphere of Lincoln's Youth* (Fort Wayne, Ind.: Lincolniana Publishers, 1933). James A. Rawley gives a capable summary of the Kentucky issue for the Lincoln administration in *Turning Points of the Civil War* (Lincoln: University of Nebraska Press, 1966).

See also SPEED, JAMES; SPEED, JOSHUA FRY.

Know-Nothing Party The Know-Nothing (American) party emerged in opposition to the Democratic party in about 1854 as thousands of Irish refugees from the potato famine and Germans escaping the political turmoil of the 1848 revolutions concluded their 5-year naturalization period and began to vote in American elections. The party, called the American party by its members but the Know-Nothing party by its opponents, opposed immigrant political power—especially if the immigrants were Catholics. It arose at the same time that the Republican (or Anti-Nebraska) party formed and became its major competitor for the votes of persons who were not Democrats.

Lincoln at first belittled the importance of the Know-Nothings while affirming rather quietly his opposition to any group which "had for its object interference with the rights of foreigners." He blamed false charges that Richard Yates was a Know-Nothing, and consequent fear among English-born Whigs in Morgan and Scott Counties, for defeating Yates's attempt to gain reelection to the House of Representatives in 1854. Lincoln took a keen interest in the election because Yates was an Anti-Nebraska man running in Lincoln's own congressional district. By the summer of 1855, Lincoln was no longer underestimating the power of Know-Nothingism, and he knew it would be essential to absorb the Know-Nothing votes in the Anti-Nebraska organization. He told Owen Lovejoy in August: "Until we can get the elements of this organization, there is not sufficient materials to successfully combat the Nebraska democracy with." Lincoln admitted that in his own area "they are mostly my old political and personal friends; and I have hoped their organization would die out without the painful necessity of my taking an open stand against them." Even Lincoln's wife supported Know-Nothing candidate Millard Fillmore for the Presidency in 1856 in part because she felt "the *necessity* of keeping foreigners, within bounds."

Lincoln loathed the party's principles. When his old friend Joshua Speed asked him whether he was a Know-Nothing, Lincoln replied:

I am not a Know-Nothing. That is certain. How could I be? How can any one who abhors the oppression of negroes, be in favor of degrading classes of white people? Our progress in degeneracy appears to me to be pretty rapid. As a nation, we began by declaring that *"all men are created equal."* We now practically read it "all men are created equal, *except negroes."* When the Know-Nothings get control, it will read "all men are created equal, except negroes, *and foreigners, and catholics."* When it comes to this I should prefer emigrating to some country where they make no pretence of loving liberty—to Russia, for instance, where despotism can be taken pure, and without the base alloy of hypocracy.

Nevertheless, because he knew that the Anti-Nebraska party had to absorb the Know-Nothings to beat the Democrats, Lincoln repeatedly expressed no objection to "stand with any body who stands right." He was willing to cooperate with Know-Nothings as "opponents of slavery extension." He always seemed to think such fusion simpler than it actually turned out to be.

In the presidential campaign of 1856 Lincoln characterized the Know-Nothings as "an ephemeral party" which "would soon pass away," but 2 years later he was still worrying about "some effort to make trouble out of 'Americanism.'" As a practical problem, it would not disappear. He spoke frankly to German-American Gustave P. Koerner of gaining German voters for the Republicans while "Others of us must find the way to save as many Americans as possible."

That would be the Republican strategy for 1860. Lincoln's own nomination was aided considerably by the unacceptability of William H. Seward, his chief competitor, to former Know-Nothings. Seward was a stanch opponent of the Know-Nothings who had worked with Catholic Archbishop John Hughes to give public money in New York to parochial schools. Lincoln, though privately opposed to Know-Nothingism, had made few public denunciations of the party, and former Know-Nothings found him much more acceptable. When Abraham Jonas told him of accusations—which were false—that Lincoln had been in a Know-Nothing lodge in Quincy, Illinois, Lincoln denied it flatly, but he admitted that probably better men than he had been in such lodges. And he warned against being forced "to openly deny this charge, by which some degree of offence would be given to the Americans." It "must not publicly appear that I am paying any attention to the charge." Most historians now agree that Lincoln's strategy was correct. The margin of difference between Republican loss in 1856 and Lincoln's victory in 1860 was supplied in large measure by accessions to the party from Know-Nothings.

Lincoln's own relationship to the party is clear. He despised Know-Nothing principles. He so despised them, in fact, that he consistently underestimated their staying power. He seemed always surprised that the movement had "not yet entirely tumbled to pieces." Yet he was practical enough to realize that the Republicans must absorb the Know-Nothings—without accepting their principles. He did little in public to offend Know-Nothings, and, characteristically, as President he duly rewarded William W. Dannenhower, "the only marked representative of the American organization in Ills. who co-operated with us in 1858 & 1860," with a government office.

SOURCES: Although it underestimated Lincoln's personal detestation of Know-Nothing principles, Charles Granville Hamilton's little-known *Lincoln and the Know Nothing Movement* (Washington, D.C.: Public Affairs Press, 1954) was among the first to stress the importance of former Know-Nothings to Lincoln's victory in 1860. Michael F. Holt's "The Politics of Impatience: The Origins of Know Nothingism," *Journal of American History*, LX (September 1973), 309–331, and his "The Antimasonic and Know Nothing Parties" in Arthur M. Schlesinger, Jr., ed., *History of U.S. Political Parties, 1789–1860*, 4 vols. (New York: Chelsea House and R. W. Bowker, 1973), I, 575–737, are definitive.

See also IMMIGRANTS.

Koerner, Gustave Philipp (1809–1896) Lincoln's second minister to Spain. Koerner was born in Frankfurt-am-Main, became a lawyer, and participated in a revolt in 1833. Wounded, he fled eventually to America, where he settled in Belleville, Illinois. He practiced law, became active in Democratic politics, and served on the Illinois Supreme Court (1845–1850) and as lieutenant governor (1852–1856).

Opposed to the Kansas-Nebraska Act, Koerner became an Anti-Nebraska Democrat and, by the summer of 1856, a Republican. After Stephen A. Douglas's break with the Buchanan administration, he wrote a widely circulated article which argued that Douglas sold out his political principles for Southern support for the Presidency in 1854 and then, facing reelection in Illinois in 1858, was mending his fences with local voters by opposing Buchanan and the Lecompton constitution. Koerner believed his article led to his selection as president of the Republican state convention of 1858, which nominated Lincoln for the United States Senate. He witnessed only the Alton debate between Douglas and Lincoln, but he followed the famous campaign closely. He noted that Douglas "frequently lost his temper, made unguarded statements of facts which he had to take back," and "roused the existing strong prejudices against the negro race to the highest pitch." He felt that Lincoln's Freeport question sealed Douglas's "doom for the Presidency forever," and he accused Douglas of "almost criminal efforts to reach the dazzling prize of the Presidency."

In 1860 Koerner found the "German element" especially enthusiastic for William H. Seward's nomination for President. Lincoln, who had known Koerner socially and professionally for years, named him a delegate-at-large to the national Republican nominating convention in Chicago. As a member of the platform committee, Koerner insisted on a repudiation of the amendment to the Massachusetts constitution excluding foreign-born citizens from voting or holding office until 2 years after naturalization. He also spoke to the Indiana delegates in support of Lincoln's candidacy, arguing that they should not support Edward Bates because his previous Know-Nothing affiliation would lose the critical German vote in the states of the Old Northwest. After Lincoln's nomination Koerner advised Mrs. Lincoln not to serve alcoholic beverages to the committee which came to Springfield to notify Lincoln officially.

Many assumed that Koerner would be sent as minister to Berlin, and when Lincoln instead sent Norman B. Judd, whom Koerner had supported for a Cabinet post, Koerner was embarrassed. He complained to the President that his health had been "shattered by the 3 terrible last campaigns" and that he was "being considered every where as neglected & orphaned by your administration." He served a "short and entirely unheroic" stint as aide-de-camp to General John C. Frémont, whom he thought Lincoln should not dismiss because his name had a magical appeal to Missouri's German-Americans. In Koerner's view Lincoln gave a disproportionate share of political rewards to German-Americans like Carl Schurz who had supported Seward rather than Lincoln at the Republican convention in 1860. Despite Koerner's disgruntlement, Lincoln still managed to use Koerner almost as an ambassador to America's population of German extraction. In January 1862 the President sent him to patch up a dispute between Generals Henry W. Halleck and Franz Sigel. When Schurz resigned as minister to Spain in order to take a military commission, Lincoln nominated Koerner for the post (June 16, 1862). Koerner accepted, but he would have preferred the mission to Berlin or Vienna.

Relations between the United States and Spain had been amicable, and Koerner was able to keep them that way despite his inability to speak Spanish (French sufficed as the language of diplomacy). Koerner returned from Spain in the summer of 1864; he brought his family back to stay because social life was too expensive in Madrid. He himself came back to attend to his financial affairs, which were in disarray because his agent to collect his debts in the United States had died. Democrats charged that Koerner abandoned official business in Spain because Lincoln ordered him home "to regulate the Dutch" for the fall presidential election. Koerner was so sensitive to the charge that he deliberately hung back from the political stump.

Nevertheless, Koerner kept in touch with German-American politics. He felt that the discontent with Lincoln among German-Americans did not run deep, that

Gustave Koerner

Radicals opposed to Lincoln had "no political sense, nor were they able to manage a campaign," and that, "although some . . . blamed him for being too conservative, they would support no one but him." Only in St. Louis were the leaders so discontented that they would vote Democratic.

Koerner resigned his foreign post on December 20, 1864, and he was in America when the President was shot. He felt that Lincoln's assassination somewhat blunted the "spirit of moderation and willingness to forgive shown to the conquered South by the loyal people of the North." "The rebels had lost their best friend, was the general expression," he said. Koerner was a pallbearer at Lincoln's funeral in Springfield.

After the war, Koerner recalled, Reconstruction might have been averted "if the South had behaved with the least discretion and prudence." However, black codes "which soon would have placed most of the free negroes under a sort of Mexican peonage" provoked Northern acts to protect the freedmen, and those acts were justified because "Practically the former rebel States formed at this time merely a territory." Discontent with the corruption of the Grant administration led Koerner to the Liberal Republicans by 1872 and to the Democrats by 1876. He had never shed his basic Democratic leanings; he called "the Republicans of Democratic antecedents . . . firmer and more energetic in facing the rebellion."

Koerner thought Lincoln "somewhat in advance of the masses" but aware that he must attain his goals "step by step." He admired Lincoln for his fairness and honesty; he thought, for example, that Lincoln could easily have charged the Illinois Central Railroad twice his $5000 fee for winning the McLean County tax case. Though on friendly terms with Lincoln, Koerner recognized that he was not "really capable of what might be called warm-hearted friendship."

SOURCES: *The Memoirs of Gustave Koerner, 1809–1896: Life-sketches Written at the Suggestion of His Children*, edited by Thomas J. McCormack, 2 vols. (Cedar Rapids, Iowa: Torch Press, 1909) is the most valuable source for Koerner's life. Koerner's letters to Lincoln about being orphaned by the administration (April 5, 1861) and about regulating the "Dutch" in 1864 (September 22, 1864) are in the Abraham Lincoln Papers, Library of Congress.

L

Labor *See* ECONOMICS.

Lambert, William Harrison (1842–1912) One of the "Big Five" Lincoln collectors. Lambert, who was born in Reading, Pennsylvania, interrupted his study of the law to become a soldier in the Civil War and was brevetted major in 1865 for "gallant and meritorious conduct during the war." He went by the title the rest of his life. Upon returning from the war, he felt it too late in life to enter law practice and instead became the manager of the New York Mutual Life Insurance Company's agency in Philadelphia. In 40 years of work he built up one of the largest agencies in the country.

When his father gave Lambert a copy of J. G. Holland's biography of Lincoln, he inspired a career of more than 40 years of collecting. Lambert did not pay fabulous prices, but he sought materials steadily and diligently. He owned several books from Lincoln's own library, the bookcase, table, and chair from Lincoln's law office, chairs from the White House library, numerous manuscripts (including 22 letters from Lincoln to Lyman Trumbull and Lincoln's letter to Orville Hickman Browning explaining his revocation of General John C. Frémont's emancipation proclamation in Missouri), over 300 funeral sermons, and an excellent collection of books and pamphlets. As even his fellow collectors (and competitors) admitted, he had the greatest Lincoln collection outside the Lincoln family itself. He was also a noted collector of Thackeray materials.

Despite his successful business career and his public service activities, Lambert was a knowledgeable collector who read books as well as collected them—as his various public addresses on Lincoln showed. He stuck close to the documentary record, and though his addresses were never tolerant of Lincoln's critics, they did not grasp at unlikely anecdotes to answer the criticisms. Even *The Faith of Abraham Lincoln: An Address before the Presbyterian Social Union of Philadelphia, February 22, 1909* relied substantially on Lincoln's own writings to prove—what devout Presbyterian Lambert wanted to—that Lincoln was a man of Christian faith. Lambert was also a generous collector; he exchanged materials with other collectors and allowed scholars to use his collection.

In 1906 a fire in Lambert's library in Germantown, Pennsylvania, destroyed most of the law office and White House furniture and many of the books from Lincoln's library. The fire occurred in the summer, luckily enough, a season when Lambert always placed most of his manuscripts in a safe in Philadelphia. After Lambert's death, the collection was sold at auction by the Anderson Galleries in New York City in 1914.

SOURCES: See *In Memoriam: William Harrison Lambert . . .* (New York: The Lincoln Fellowship [of New York], 1912).

William Harrison Lambert

Lamon, Ward Hill (1828–1893) Illinois lawyer whom President Lincoln described as "my particular friend." Ward Hill Lamon was born in Virginia, moved in 1837 to Danville, Illinois, where he became a lawyer, and

Lamon, Ward Hill

Lincoln called burly Ward Hill Lamon "Hill."

in the 1850s rode the Eighth Judicial Circuit with Lincoln and David Davis. From 1852 to 1857 he was Lincoln's associate in Vermilion County cases. Lamon worked for Lincoln's election to the United States Senate in the campaigns of 1854–1855 and 1858. He disliked more radically antislavery Republicans like Owen Lovejoy. He labored for Lincoln's presidential nomination and election in 1860 and accompanied the President-elect on his inaugural journey to Washington. Lamon was Lincoln's only companion on the secret midnight trip through tough, pro-Southern Baltimore. He acted as bodyguard, armed with a slungshot, two revolvers, a knife, and brass knuckles.

Lincoln appointed Lamon Marshal of the District of Columbia in April 1861. Lamon performed various ceremonial duties, kept the local prison, and served unofficially and occasionally as the President's bodyguard. He raised a brigade of loyal Virginians near his old home and commanded them in the field from June to December 1861. In 1863 he was marshal-in-chief of the procession at Gettysburg before Lincoln's famous address and introduced the President on the platform.

More than anyone else, Lamon fretted over the President's personal safety. As early as August 11, 1861, he feared "Eavesdroppers and traitors lurking about the White House" and told the President to allow no one upstairs where his office was located "except such as you permit after their sending up their cards." He recommended employing "a secret Detective" to ferret out disloyalty in the Executive Mansion. In 1864 he became so distressed over the bitterness of the opposition to Lincoln and over the President's carelessness about exposing himself to the public that he drafted a letter of resignation in protest. In April he offered to arrest a Maryland Congressman who, according to a newspaper report, gave a speech which *"acquiesced in the doctrine of Secession."* "I may not be mighty in Counsel," the fiery Lamon told the President, "but *might be useful in a fight."*

According to Leonard Swett, Lamon did not sleep at home in the politically agitated fall of 1864 but instead went to the White House around 10:00 p.m. to watch the house and grounds. According to White House secretary John Hay, Lamon slept outside Lincoln's door on election night, curled up on blankets on the floor and wearing a brace of pistols and knives. On December 10 he chided Lincoln for going "unattended to the Theatre—when I say you went unattended I mean that you went alone with Charles Sumner & a foreign Minister—neither of whom could defend themselves against an assault from any able-bodied woman in this City." Five days later he told John G. Nicolay to see that Lincoln "dont go out alone either in the day or night time." On April 11, 1865, the President sent Lamon to Richmond to investigate conditions for reconstruction of the state; therefore, he was out of town when Lincoln was murdered. He returned to be marshal of the civil part of the state funeral.

Though Lincoln doubtless had enjoyed the burly Virginian's company in Washington—his beautiful singing and his scatological sense of humor—"Hill" had been something of a political liability. Lamon was a Republican and enforced the Fugitive Slave Act with too much zeal to satisfy antislavery General James Wadsworth, who accused him of holding Negroes in the jail on suspicion of being fugitives. In 1862 the President had to work out a compromise with Lamon, the civil authorities, and Wadsworth, the military commander of the District. Congressmen also accused him of profiting illicitly from his marshalship and the operation of the District of Columbia jail.

In June 1865 Lamon resigned as Marshal of the District of Columbia. After unsuccessfully seeking to be appointed governor in the Idaho and Colorado Territories, he entered law practice in Washington with Charles E. Hovey and Jeremiah S. Black, a former member of James Buchanan's Cabinet. In 1869, with his partner's son Chauncey Black, he acquired transcripts of William H. Herndon's notes for a biography of Lincoln for $2000 in cash and a $2000 note. Black would write the book, relying on Lamon's memory, Herndon's notes, and Lamon's name as author—for Black was a Democrat whose name would have aroused immediate suspicion of the book's worth.

Lamon's *Life of Abraham Lincoln* appeared in 1872, the first debunking biography of the sixteenth President. It noted that Lincoln's mother carried her mother's maiden name and hinted that the record of the marriage of Thomas Lincoln and Nancy Hanks was suspiciously hard to locate. Lamon and Black questioned Lincoln's piety, said Lincoln liked dirty stories, and called his marriage an "affliction." The book received hostile reviews, angered many of Lincoln's friends, and sold only about 1900 copies. James Russell Lowell typified refined opinion when he said that the "author was a vulgar man and vulgarized a noble subject." Robert Todd Lincoln refused even to open the book's covers and avenged his father when, as Secretary of War in 1883, he blocked Lamon's appointment as postmaster in Denver.

SOURCES: The only extended biographical treatment of this obscure man of limited abilities is Lavern M. Hammond's "Lincoln's Particular Friend" in Donald F. Tingley, ed., *Essays in Illinois History in Honor of Glenn Huron Seymour* (Carbondale: Southern Illinois University Press, 1968). Benjamin P. Thomas's *Portrait for Posterity: Lincoln and His Biographers* (New Brunswick, N.J.: Rutgers University Press, 1947) chronicles the origins of and the conflicts surrounding Lamon's biography of Lincoln. See also Albert V. House, Jr., "The Trials of a Ghost-Writer of Lincoln Biography: Chauncey F. Black's Authorship of Lamon's Lincoln," *Journal of the Illinois State Historical Society*, XXXI (September 1938), 262–296. Lamon was by no means a man of letters. His *Life of Abraham Lincoln* (Boston: James R. Osgood, 1872) had to be ghost-written, and his *Recollections of Abraham Lincoln, 1847–1865* (Chicago: A. C. McClurg, 1895) was pieced together and heavily edited by his daughter Dorothy Lamon Teillard. The second edition (1911) contains a biographical memoir of Lamon. The Lamon papers are at the Henry E. Huntington Library, San Marino, California. Lamon's letters to Lincoln about White House eavesdroppers (August 11, 1861) and to Nicolay about Lincoln's safety (December 15, 1864) are in the Abraham Lincoln Papers,

Library of Congress. James Russell Lowell's letter about Lamon's book (to James A. Manson, May 11, 1881) is in the Louis A. Warren Lincoln Library and Museum, Fort Wayne, Indiana.

See also HUMOR; MUSIC.

Land Office *See* TAYLOR, ZACHARY.

Law Practice Penniless and unemployed in 1832, Abraham Lincoln "thought of trying to study law" but "rather thought he could not succeed at that without a better education." Two years later, in the midst of a campaign for the Illinois legislature, fellow Whig candidate John Todd Stuart encouraged Lincoln to undertake the study. Lincoln borrowed books from Stuart—probably those he recommended later to similar young students: "Blackstone's Commentaries, Chitty's Pleading's . . . Greenleaf's Evidence, Story's Equity, and Story's Equity Pleading's"—but "studied with nobody." Working alone in New Salem between legislative sessions, Lincoln learned enough, in an era in which there were no state bar exams and only one law school west of the Appalachians, to be licensed to practice on September 9, 1836, after Sangamon Circuit Court gave him a certificate of good character on March 24, 1836. It is doubtful that he underwent even the informal examination by practicing attorneys later required in Illinois. On March 1, 1837, the Supreme Court clerk entered his name on the roll of attorneys.

Lincoln entered practice with Stuart in Springfield in the spring of 1837. In 1841 he left Stuart to practice with Stephen Trigg Logan. In 1844 Lincoln began practicing with William Henry Herndon, his partner the rest of his life. Those offices did not employ secretaries or clerks, and only occasionally did young men temporarily studying law in the offices take any of the burden of book fetching and precedent searching.

For the most part Lincoln learned law by practicing it. Even his second partner claimed Lincoln knew very little law when he first joined the firm. Throughout his career Lincoln had a varied practice involving disputes over property and debts, murders, rapes, divorces, and slander. He was involved primarily in litigation and appellate work. He had little office practice (contracts, papers of incorporation, and arrangements for sale of land). Because of his limited legal training and generally nonbookish approach to law, Lincoln showed his greatest ability in persuading juries. Most of his courtroom eloquence, however, is lost to history because lower courts did not employ stenographers. He was not at all squeamish about criminal law, though it formed only a small part of his practice, and some of his more famous cases were murder cases. Nor did he have to be convinced of his client's innocence or the righteousness of his cause. Henry B. Truett, whom Lincoln defended on a murder charge, undoubtedly killed the victim and was a man of somewhat questionable reputation. And Lincoln took the master's side in the famous Matson fugitive slave case.

Lincoln was a successful lawyer with a large practice. The firm of Lincoln and Logan, for example, in one 11-day period in March 1844, took court action in an average of seven cases a day. In 1853 Lincoln and Herndon were involved in 34 percent of the cases before the Sangamon County Circuit Court in Springfield. Lincoln was not a "corporation lawyer" in any modern sense of the term, though he performed work for large corporations and collected his largest fee, slightly over $5000 (split two ways as always), from the Illinois Central Railroad. By the middle of the 1850s Lincoln was certainly one of the greatest lawyers in Illinois, but his reputation did not reach much beyond the state; the *McCormick* v. *Manny & Company* case was his only famous out-of-state case. Much of his practice was in the small-town county courthouses of the Eighth Judicial Circuit surrounding Springfield. He was involved in well over 200 Illinois Supreme Court cases.

The only contemporary picture of the interior of the Lincoln-Herndon law office, drawn for Frank Leslie's Illustrated Newspaper, December 22, 1860.

Lincoln freely admitted that he was "not an accomplished lawyer." He generally took more interest in politics than law, except perhaps between 1849 and 1854, when he "went to the practice of the law with greater earnestness than ever before." In that brief period "his profession . . . almost superseded the thought of politics in his mind."

Long experience in the law bred in Lincoln strong opinions about the proper conduct of lawyers. He well knew that there was "a vague popular belief that lawyers are necessarily dishonest," and Lincoln advised any "young man choosing the law for a calling" to "resolve to be honest . . . ; and if . . . you cannot be an honest lawyer, resolve to be honest without being a lawyer." He urged lawyers never to "stir up litigation"; he knew there would "still be business enough." He admitted that the "matter of fees is important," but he rarely, if ever, claimed an "exorbitant fee" and built his own practice on modest fees charged to an abundance of clients. Though not at all orderly himself, he knew that the "leading rule for the lawyer, as for the man of every other calling, is diligence." Speaking "should be practised and cultivated," but "speech-making" could not be relied on as a substitute for "the drudgery of the law." In sum, he thought, a "moral tone ought to be infused into the profession" to drive any litigious "knave" out of it.

SOURCES: The best study of Lincoln's legal mind and practice is John P. Frank's *Lincoln as a Lawyer* (Urbana: University of Illinois Press, 1961). John J. Duff's *A. Lincoln: Prairie Lawyer* (New York: Rinehart, 1960) takes a chronological case-by-case approach and is a model of clarity. A useful and lively brief treatment is *Lincoln and the Law: Lincoln's Law Office* (Springfield, Ill.: Sangamon State University, 1978), a pamphlet available from the Illinois State Museum Society, Spring and Edwards Streets, Springfield, IL 62706. The Lincoln-Herndon office from the period 1844–1847 is located at Sixth and Adams Streets in Springfield and has been restored for public visits.

See also ARMSTRONG, WILLIAM "DUFF"; "CHICKEN BONE" CASE; CONSTITUTION OF THE UNITED STATES; *DRED SCOTT* V. *SANDFORD*; *EFFIE AFTON* CASE; EIGHTH JUDICIAL CIRCUIT; FINANCES, PERSONAL; HERNDON, WILLIAM HENRY; LOGAN, STEPHEN TRIGG; *MCCORMICK* V. *MANNY & COMPANY*; MCLEAN COUNTY TAX CASE; MATSON SLAVE CASE; RAILROADS; STUART, JOHN TODD; SUPREME COURT OF THE UNITED STATES; TANEY, ROGER BROOKE; TRAILOR MURDER CASE; TRUETT MURDER CASE; WHITNEY, HENRY CLAY.

Libraries   *See* COLLECTIONS, INSTITUTIONAL.

Library of Congress
The world's largest library. The Library contains one of the largest collections of Lincolniana in the world. That seems especially appropriate, since President Lincoln himself used the Library of Congress; more than 125 books were charged out to him during his administration. Unfortunately, it is quite impossible to tell which works were for his own use and which for the use of his family and secretaries. Most of them probably were not for Lincoln himself (only Mrs. Lincoln, for example, could have read the works in French, and Lincoln had little time to read the likes of Victor Hugo's works).

For the President, the Library was not only a handy collection of books but also a patronage plum. At the urging of Indiana Republicans Caleb Blood Smith, William P. Dole, and Senator Henry S. Lane, Lincoln appointed as Librarian Dr. John G. Stephenson, a physician from Terre Haute. Stephenson was no librarian and appointed Ainsworth Rand Spofford as his assistant to run the institution. Stephenson resigned in 1864, and Lincoln made Spofford his successor. The Library then had about 70,000 books, a number that it now acquires every 10 days.

The Library grew rapidly after the Civil War, and the richness and depth of its collections have always had the power to astonish. Lincoln collectors and bibliographers took note in 1903, when George T. Ritchie published *A List of Lincolniana in the Library of Congress*. It contained many entries unknown to Lincoln bibliographer Daniel Fish. The Library's future as a key repository of Lincoln materials was assured in 1919, when Robert Todd Lincoln deposited his father's papers there, by far the largest collection of letters to Lincoln anywhere. In 1953 Alfred Whital Stern donated his large Lincoln collection (some 7000 pieces) and an endowment for "perpetual enlargement." Those two major accessions, and other acquisitions over the years, make the collection astoundingly rich in Lincolniana. Two of the five handwritten copies of the Gettysburg Address typify the quality of the collection, and the quantity of prints, cartoons, photographs, broadsides, and collateral collections makes it essential to almost any serious study of Lincoln. For years the presence of outstanding Lincoln authorities like David C. Mearns and Roy P. Basler on the Library's staff guaranteed the professional care and increase of its Lincoln holdings.

SOURCES: See *A Catalog of the Alfred Whital Stern Collection of Lincolniana in the Library of Congress* (Washington, D.C.: Library of Congress, 1960); Constance Carter, "John Gould Stephenson: Largely Known and Much Liked," *Quarterly Journal of the Library of Congress*, XXIII (April 1976), 77–92; and John Y. Cole, "Ainsworth Rand Spofford: The Valiant and Persistent Librarian of Congress," ibid., 93–116. Louis A. Warren's "Borrowed Books in the White House," *Lincoln Lore*, Number 129 (September 28 1931) is useful.

See also LINCOLN PAPERS.

Lincoln, Edward Baker   *See* DESCENDANTS.

Lincoln, Mary Todd (1818–1882)
Abraham Lincoln's wife. Mary Ann Todd was a Kentuckian. She was the daughter of Eliza Parker and Robert Smith Todd, who had six children survive infancy (Elizabeth, Frances, Levi O., Mary, Ann, and George R. C. Todd). Robert Smith Todd's second marriage to Elizabeth Humphreys produced Mary's eight half brothers and half sisters (Margaret, Samuel B., David H., Martha, Emilie, Alexander H., Elodie, and Katherine Todd)—some of whom Mary "never knew since they were infants, and scarcely then."

Mary's parents were scions of important families in Kentucky and were socially prominent. Mr. Todd was a well-to-do banker, merchant, and lawyer in Lexington. He was also a Whig politician, a stanch supporter of Henry Clay and of Kentucky's 1833 law forbidding the importation of slaves into the state for sale.

Mary remembered her childhood as "desolate." Her mother died when she was 6, and she never got along well with her stepmother. Her "early home," she said, "was truly at a *boarding* school." She attended Dr. John Ward's academy and the select finishing school of Madame Victorie Mentelle. After 4 years at Madame Mentelle's she visited Springfield, Illinois, in 1837 and returned to Lexington for two further years of study at Dr. Ward's academy.

In 1839 she went again to Springfield. There she lived with her older sister Elizabeth, who was now married to Ninian Wirt Edwards, son of Illinois's Territorial Governor. They too were prominent in society, and Mary moved immediately in the highest social circles. She met rising politician Abraham Lincoln, and they were soon engaged to marry. But on what Lincoln called the "fatal first of Jany. '41," the engagement was broken. The reasons for the break are unknown, though it is likely that Edwards, Mary's guardian, opposed the marriage because of Lincoln's inferior social position. In later years, Edwards remembered Lincoln as a "rough" man at that time.

Whatever the reason for the broken engagement, no contemporary evidence supports the story that Lincoln never showed up at the altar on the wedding day. And much evidence points to the devastating effect of the break on both Mary and Abraham. On January 23 Lincoln described himself to his law partner as

> the most miserable man living. If what I feel were equally distributed to the whole human family, there would not be one cheerful face on the earth. Whether I shall ever be better I can not tell; I awfully forebode I shall not. To remain as I am is impossible; I must die or be better, it appears to me.

Mary was depressed well into the summer. The couple achieved a reconciliation in 1842. Apparently they courted at the house of Simeon Francis, editor of Springfield's Whig newspaper, another sign that the Edwardses were a problem for them. By late summer, Lincoln and Mary were engaged in some high jinks, the satirical "Rebecca letters," which practically forced Lincoln into a duel with James Shields. Lincoln wrote one of the letters, which made fun of Shields and Democratic doctrine; Mary and her friend Julia Jayne wrote another. It must be said that Lincoln's "Rebecca" letter was abusive enough to provoke Shields's challenge. The one written by Mary and Julia Jayne and a satirical poem which appeared at the same time, probably also by the women, merely complicated the patching up of the quarrel. Lincoln took full blame for the letters and, in a rare show of chivalry, did not reveal the female coauthors. On November 4, 1842, the Episcopal Reverend Charles Dresser married Mary and Abraham in the Edwards home.

The Lincolns boarded in the Globe Tavern for $4 a week, quite a decline in status for Mary. There their first child, named Robert Todd for her father, was born on August 1, 1843, 3 days less than 9 months after their marriage. Thereafter, Lincoln usually called her "Mother." She called him "Mr. Lincoln" or "Father." These were years of hard work for Mary, Lincoln being absent on the legal circuit for about 6 months out of the year. His diligence considerably improved their finances, however, and in 1844 Lincoln purchased for $1200 and the transfer of a city lot, their first and only house. On March 10, 1846, Edward Baker Lincoln, named for Lincoln's Whig political crony Edward D. Baker, was born.

When Lincoln went to Washington to assume a seat in the House of Representatives in 1847, Mary and the children went along. After a time, they left the Congressman alone in Washington, in part because Lincoln thought Mary "hindered me some in attending to business." Once she was gone, in the spring of 1848, Lincoln found that "having nothing but business—no variety" made life "exceedingly tasteless." By June, Mary wished to return with the boys. Lincoln agreed—if she would "be a *good girl* in all things"—and expressed his desire to see her and the "dear—*dear* boys very much."

The tone of their correspondence shows that Lincoln and Mary had their fair share of disagreements, but probably no more than are incidental to any long marriage. There is no reliable evidence that their marriage was especially stormy. Mary frequently suffered from headaches, and her husband was not only absent a great deal of the time but also probably somewhat deficient in the social graces to which she was accustomed. His illiterate and semiliterate relatives and Mary were simply in-

Mary Todd Lincoln's earliest portrait, a daguerreotype taken by N. H. Shepherd in Springfield in 1846. A companion picture of her husband, also his first photograph, was taken at the same time. The two portraits hung in the Lincolns' home in Springfield.

Lincoln, Mary Todd

compatible, and she had very little contact with them. Thomas and Sarah Lincoln, for example, were not present at the wedding and never saw the grandchildren.

On February 1, 1850, the first of many severe tragedies struck the Lincoln household: Eddie died. That Mrs. Lincoln was profoundly affected is obvious from changes in her religious life soon thereafter. Consoled by the Reverend James Smith of Springfield's First Presbyterian Church, she ceased to attend Episcopal services (a practice she had adopted while living with the Edwardses) and in 1852 became a member of the Presbyterian Church. Within three months of Eddie's death, the Lincolns conceived another child, William Wallace Lincoln, born December 21, 1850. This son was named after Mrs. Lincoln's brother-in-law, Dr. Wallace, who had married her sister Frances and also lived in Springfield. The Lincolns' last child, Thomas, named for Lincoln's father, who had died 2 years previously, was born on April 3, 1853. The Lincolns called him "Tad" because his father compared his large head and small body as a baby to the proportions of a tadpole. Both Mary and Abraham proved to be extremely indulgent parents.

Mrs. Lincoln followed her father's Whig political preferences (another solid bond, like their common Kentucky backgrounds, between Abraham and Mary). She was not as fast as Lincoln, however, to adopt Republican principles. She had to explain to her Kentucky relatives in 1856 that Lincoln, though "a *Fremont* man" was not like "so many of those, who belong to *that party*, an *Abolitionist.*" All he wanted was to prevent slavery's extension and "let it remain, where it is." Even this was too much for Mrs. Lincoln's "weak woman's heart," which was "too Southern in feeling, to sympathize with any but Fillmore," the Whig and Know-Nothing candidate. She agreed with him in "the *necessity* of keeping foreigners, within bounds." Mary's Know-Nothing proclivities differed sharply from her husband's views; Lincoln flatly despised Know-Nothing principles. Her views seem to have stemmed from nothing deeper than a housekeeper's difficulties in dealing with Irish servant-girls.

Though Mrs. Lincoln may have hindered Abraham's work at times, she never interfered with his political ambitions. It was with high hopes, then, that she went to Washington in 1861. (She joined Lincoln's inaugural train in Indianapolis and parted his company in Pennsylvania when he was smuggled into Washington to avoid assassination.) The move had its anxieties, too. Though Mary was well educated and aristocratic within her limited Western surroundings, she was provincial, had traveled little (though she loved to travel), and feared to disappoint the East. As she told her Washington seamstress, Elizabeth Keckley, she felt that the eyes of the nation would be upon her, and "The very fact of having grown up in the West, subjects me to more searching observation." This anxiety exaggerated an unfortunate strain in her character which made it difficult for her to think and act rationally about money. She was alternately miserly and extravagant, and Washington life became for her a gigantic, and often socially and politically embarrassing, spending spree. She insisted on finery in dress far exceeding anything she had exhibited in Springfield, and in the first year of the administration she exceeded by $6700 a $20,000 appropriation to redecorate the shoddy Executive Mansion. President Lincoln was mortified, though Congress quietly made up the difference with two deficiency appropriations. Instead of causing her to contract expenditures, the incident seems to have led her to the disastrous practice of keeping her enormous debts secret from the President.

Despite her own anxieties, the considerable hostility of the rather pro-Southern Washington socialites to the first Republican administration, and the doubts of the East in general, Mary Lincoln performed her social functions adequately. At the weekly Friday levees, she stood to the right and somewhat behind Lincoln, nodding to most guests to avoid the paralyzing ordeal of hundreds of grasping hands, but special guests were brought to her for closer personal introductions. In managing the Executive Mansion she had her friends and her detractors. Even her defenders, like William O. Stoddard and Commissioner of Public Buildings Benjamin Brown French, admitted that she was hard to deal with at times. John G. Nicolay and John Hay, the President's secretaries, disliked her intensely; Hay always referred to her as "the Hell-cat."

Mrs. Lincoln's relatives were a severe trial for the President, though he treated them well in the distribution of patronage. Ninian W. Edwards as commissary of subsistence aroused the ire of many of Lincoln's close political friends in Springfield. Lincoln gave offices to Dr. Wallace's brother as well as to cousin Lockwood Todd and Charles S. Todd, a distant relative of Mary's. Cousin Elizabeth Todd Grimsley sought an office in vain. Lincoln offered Ben Hardin Helm, Emilie Todd's husband, a commission which Helm rejected to join the Confeder-

Mary Todd Lincoln, taken by Mathew Brady in Washington, probably in 1861. This is the only photograph of Mary showing her profile.

ate Army. The Confederacy enjoyed the military services of Helm, N. H. R. Dawson (who married Elodie Todd), Alexander Todd, Sam Todd, George Todd, and David Todd. That factor made Mrs. Lincoln the unfortunate focus of rumors of lack of loyalty. After Helm's death in battle, Lincoln aided his widow with passes through the lines. He also granted passes (but not an interview) to Martha Todd White, Mary's half sister, and newspapers reported that she used them to smuggle medicines to the Confederacy.

Mary had her own influence on the President, of course. When a schoolmaster from Kentucky wrote her to request a pass for a mother in Georgia to go through the lines to pick up her young child, she gave the letter to the President, who wrote on it: "The writer of this, an old man, was a Sunday School-teacher of Mrs. L. and she would be glad for him to be obliged—I know no other reason." The pass was granted. In more important matters her opinion had no weight. She distrusted William H. Seward and Salmon P. Chase and thought little of General Ulysses S. Grant's talents. Indeed, her judgment of men was not the best. She was susceptible to flatterers and courtiers, like Henry Wikoff and the scheming White House gardener John Watt. They were close to her, but the President banished the one and fired the other early in 1862 for leaking administration secrets to a newspaper. On the other hand, she formed a warm friendship with the distinguished Charles Sumner, which may have helped Lincoln's relations with that touchy intellect (and would benefit Mrs. Lincoln later in life).

After Willie died in the White House on February 20, 1862, Mrs. Lincoln was never quite the same again. She never again went into the rooms where he died and was embalmed. Mrs. Edwards came east for a time to console her, but she was almost inconsolable. She fell prey for a time to a new group of bad influences, spiritualist mediums, who promised to put her in touch with her lost children. Correspondent Noah Brooks exposed a medium named Colchester as a fraud in the summer of 1862 and threw him out of the Executive Mansion, but Mrs. Nettie Colburn Maynard retained some influence for a time. Mary apparently told Emilie Todd Helm late in 1862 that Willie's spirit came to the foot of her bed at night, but in 1869 Mary emphatically denied that she was a spiritualist. She did not resume social activities until 1863.

Mrs. Lincoln's loyalty was beyond question. The enemy were "rebels" and "traitors," and by all reports Mary Lincoln became an ardent abolitionist, more zealously antislavery than her husband. The influence of Sumner and that of her mulatto seamstress, Elizabeth Keckley, who became a confidante of hers, doubtless sped the change. She retained her Southern prejudices to some degree, however; when she recommended Mrs. Keckley for a job, she described her as "very industrious," "although colored."

The other significant change, aside from her increasing irrationality in money matters, was a growing distance from her husband and an increasingly unhappy outlook on life. The President worked long hours, and Mrs. Lincoln traveled a good deal in the Northeast to escape the sorrows, heat, and allegedly unhealthy climate of Washington. She feared that if Lincoln lost the 1864 election, he would discover her debts. Even Mary recalled that in their last carriage ride together, on the afternoon of the day Lincoln was assassinated, he insisted that they "must *both*, be more cheerful in the future— between the war & the loss of our darling Willie—we have both, been very miserable."

The assassination plummeted Mary into a grief so deep that she could take no part in any of the funeral ceremonies. Indeed, she did not leave the Executive Mansion for Chicago until May 22, more than a month after the assassination. Her bereavement and anxieties over her debts made her wretched and dominated the subject matter of her letters until her death.

Mary's trials continued. In 1866 William H. Herndon aired his theory that Ann Rutledge was the great love of Lincoln's life. In 1867, when her problems in money matters were fast growing into an obsession, Mary tried to sell her old clothes in New York, a humiliating spectacle which exasperated Robert Lincoln. In 1868 Elizabeth Keckley published a memoir which focused on the "Old Clothes scandal" and forever lost her Mrs. Lincoln's friendship. Indeed, Mrs. Lincoln shunned old friends and the public gaze in general and often traveled incognito and used false names. In 1868 she escaped to Germany with Tad. She returned in 1871; and Tad died on July 15, soon after their return.

Mary Todd Lincoln's last photograph, taken perhaps 10 years before her death, allegedly by a spiritualist photographer who added a ghostly image of her husband to the print. The hand of Lincoln, however, is smaller than Mary's.

Mrs. Lincoln had no real financial problems by this time. Her share of Lincoln's sizable estate, a $3000-a-year pension granted by Congress at Charles Sumner's insistance in 1870, and her half of Tad's share of the estate made her a wealthy woman. But she did not realize it. Her alternating extravagance and niggardliness continued. Other signs of instability developed. After she expressed fears that Robert, a robustly healthy and successful lawyer, was in danger of dying, he began to fear her sanity impaired. In 1875, after consulting with David Davis and John Todd Stuart, he caused his mother to stand trial for insanity. The court judged her insane and committed her to a private sanitarium called Belleview in Batavia, Illinois. The night after the trial she tried to commit suicide. Robert gained control of her finances; he returned useless and gaudy jewelry (incompatible with the mourning apparel she always wore), some of which she had taken on approval and refused to return or pay for. Her fear of fire had caused him to worry that she might leap from a building, and when she packed for Batavia, Robert discovered her baggage consisted of numerous carpet sacks, each with a footstool in it.

After less than 4 months in Belleview, Mrs. Lincoln was released to the custody of the Edwardses. On June 15, 1876, a second trial judged her sane. She fled in the fall to France, leaving her financial affairs to be handled by Springfield banker Jacob Bunn. Her health declined seriously, and she returned to the Edwards home in 1880. In 1881 she patched up some of her differences with Robert. In January 1882 Congress raised her pension to $5000 and donated $15,000 to her.

Mary did not get to enjoy the money. She stayed alone in a room in the Edwards house. With the shades pulled at all times, it was only dimly lit by candles. On July 16, 1882, she at last realized her often expressed wish to join her beloved husband and children in death.

SOURCES: An overly defensive but solidly researched biography is Ruth Painter Randall's *Mary Lincoln: Biography of a Marriage* (Boston: Little, Brown, 1953). Justin G. and Linda Levitt Turner's *Mary Todd Lincoln: Her Life and Letters* (New York: Alfred A. Knopf, 1972) is the essential source for her letters and contains thoughtful and well-written sections linking the letters together. W. A. Evans's *Mrs. Abraham Lincoln: A Study of Her Personality and Her Influence on Lincoln* (New York: Alfred A. Knopf, 1932) and William H. Townsend's *Lincoln and the Bluegrass: Slavery and Civil War in Kentucky* ([Lexington]: University of Kentucky Press, 1955) are useful for understanding the Todd family, but there is no thorough and reliable work on the subject. Roy P. Basler's *President Lincoln Helps His Old Friends* (Springfield, Ill.: Abraham Lincoln Association, 1977) shows Lincoln's indulgence of his Todd relatives. All of these works were written before the acquisition of the Robert Todd Lincoln Papers by the Illinois State Historical Library. The papers contain some interesting information on Mrs. Lincoln's later life, some of which was used here. President Lincoln's endorsement for Mrs. Lincoln's Sunday school teacher, December 10, 1863, belongs to the Louis A. Warren Lincoln Library and Museum, Fort Wayne, Indiana, and was previously unpublished.

See also EDWARDS, NINIAN WIRT; EXECUTIVE MANSION; GRIMSLEY, ELIZABETH TODD; HELM, EMILIE TODD; KECKLEY, ELIZABETH; LINCOLN, ROBERT TODD; WIKOFF, HENRY.

Lincoln, Nancy Hanks (1784–1818) Abraham Lincoln's mother. Nancy Hanks Lincoln was born in Virginia. Lincoln said that both his parents came "of undistinguished families—second families, perhaps I should say," but precisely which undistinguished family his mother came from is shrouded in mystery. When and how she came to Kentucky are unknown. On June 10, 1806, Thomas Lincoln obtained a marriage bond to wed Nancy Hanks. Richard Berry, her guardian, was the bondsman. Two days later they were married. She died in Indiana on October 5, 1818, of "milk sickness," a disease contracted by drinking the milk of cows which had grazed on poisonous white snakeroot.

Lincoln wrote almost nothing about his mother. She died when he was 9 years old, and he probably knew very little about her background, especially since his father quickly remarried. Descriptions of her from reminiscences vary widely. She was illiterate and signed legal documents with a mark.

An enormous controversy raged for more than 50 years after publication in the 1870s and 1880s of William Henry Herndon's assertion that Nancy was illegitimate. Herndon rested his claim on an alleged conversation with Lincoln early in the 1850s in which Lincoln said that his mother was illegitimate. No documents have been discovered which give conclusive proof one way or another.

SOURCES: Among modern scholars only Louis A. Warren argues her legitimacy (in *The Lincoln Kinsman*, Number 33 [March 1941]). See also William E. Barton, *The Lineage of Lincoln* (Indianapolis: Bobbs-Merrill, 1929).

Lincoln, Robert Todd (1843–1926) The first child of Abraham and Mary Todd Lincoln and the only one to live to maturity. Robert Todd Lincoln was born in the Globe Tavern in Springfield, Illinois. His parents, as Abraham Lincoln himself admitted, "never controlled him much." He studied in the college preparatory department of Illinois State University at Springfield but in 1859 he failed the entrance examination for Harvard University. To make up his deficiencies, he enrolled in Phillips Exeter Academy in Exeter, New Hampshire, in September 1859, and the improved preparation enabled him to enter Harvard in the fall of 1860. He accompanied his father on part of the inaugural trip to Washington, was present at the inauguration, and visited the Executive Mansion on vacations.

Robert graduated from Harvard in 1864; he ranked thirty-second in a class of ninety-nine. After a brief stint at Harvard Law School, he was appointed captain and assistant adjutant general of volunteers on General U. S. Grant's staff (February 11, 1865), in accordance with an arrangement made by his father. Lincoln, in part because of Mary's fears, did not "wish to put him in the ranks" and offered to pay Robert's wages himself. Robert was present at Robert E. Lee's surrender to Grant and breakfasted with his father the day Lincoln was assassinated. In the end, he knew very little of his father's

Presidency because he "was very little in Washington while he was there."

With the help of David Davis, Robert assumed considerable responsibility for the family and for his father's estate. All in all, he inherited $138,901.54, including a third of Lincoln's original estate, half of his brother's estate at his death in 1871, and his mother's estate after her death in 1882.

Robert lived with his mother in Chicago until the spring of 1867, when he began making his own way in the world. He was admitted to the Illinois Bar on February 25, 1867, and became a successful lawyer. In 1872 he established a partnership with Edward Swift Isham; the firm became Isham, Lincoln, and Beale in 1887. He married Mary Eunice Harlan, the daughter of Iowa Republican politician James Harlan, in 1868. The union bore three children: Mary (born October 15, 1869), Abraham ("Jack") (born August 14, 1873), and Jessie Harlan (born November 6, 1875). His wife was sickly and, even more so than he, shunned publicity and photographers.

Robert's mother proved to be a severe burden. Embarrassed by her many letters begging money from President Lincoln's political friends and mortified by her attempt to sell her old clothes in 1867, Robert found it "very hard to deal with one who is sane on all subjects but one," money. By 1875 he feared "probable tragedy" in his mother's bizarre behavior and instigated an insanity hearing, at which he gave emotional testimony leading to her brief commitment to a private institution for the insane. His mother bought gaudy jewelry which she would never wear because she dressed always in black mourning, took expensive jewelry on approval and neither paid for it nor returned it, carried large amounts of securities on her person, and had a fear of fire that might have caused her to leap from a building. When she packed to go to the asylum, she filled numerous carpet sacks with footstools. She hated Robert for his part in the insanity trial and thought he was trying to get her money.

Robert followed his father's political preference and was, throughout his life, a rock-ribbed and regular Republican. He supported Reconstruction; as late as 1874 he expressed disgust at the prospect of being taxed to compensate slaveowners for the loss of their slave property. When he campaigned for the Republicans in 1884, he was still waving the "bloody shirt," stressing murders and intimidations of Republican voters and politicians in the South (which he compared to the Massacre of St. Bartholomew), the prospect of paying pensions to Confederate veterans, and the vanity of having spilled "so much precious blood" for this result. He also stressed the virtues of protectionism, especially for the "working classes—farmers and mechanics," whose wages were protected by tariffs from competition with cheap foreign labor. The campaigns of the 1890s showed him a believer in "sound money" (the gold standard for currency).

As early as 1877 Robert turned down President Rutherford B. Hayes's offer to appoint him Assistant Secretary of State; he felt that he must continue to build up his law practice. In 1880 he supported Grant's drive for an unprecedented third term, and a year later President James A. Garfield made him Secretary of War (partly to appease the disappointed Grant faction in the party). Robert was in the train station when Garfield was shot, and he kept in close touch with the White House during the President's long and agonizing slide to death through the late summer of 1881. Robert suspected that a lawyer he had known in Chicago who was also assassin Charles Guiteau's brother-in-law might have been aware of Guiteau's intentions before the crime occurred, but discreet inquiries to inspectors in the Chicago post office proved the suspicion groundless. He thought, quite correctly, that no attention should be paid to Guiteau's claims to have been a "Stalwart," that is, an opponent of Republicans who advocated civil service reform. Guiteau was a madman, not a disappointed office seeker. When inquiries were made about a heavy military guard for Garfield's successor, President Chester A. Arthur, Robert replied:

In my father's time, . . . the situation was very different, and it was at one time supposed that an attempt would be made to abduct him and hold him as a hostage. It was for this reason that he was guarded.

I have no doubt that President Arthur will take care of himself; but he is undoubtedly liable to be killed by some crazy person or by a fanatic who would be willing to do

Robert Todd Lincoln as a student at Harvard. Lloyd Ostendorf discovered this previously unpublished photograph. (Courtesy of the Lloyd Ostendorf Collection)

the deed for the notoriety which might be gained thereby.
As things go in this life, it is impossible to thoroughly guard against these classes of people.

Lincoln remained as Secretary of War until the end of Arthur's administration, the only such holdover from Garfield's Cabinet.

In 1884 there was a presidential boom for him, but Lincoln never became a major contender—in part because of his own reluctance to seek the office he called "a gilded prison." However, he never categorically ruled out the possibility of accepting the Presidency—it was "a duty . . . imposed upon a man which he could not honorably avoid"—and his name was mentioned again in 1888 as a possible candidate. In 1889 President Benjamin Harrison appointed him minister to England, a post he held until 1893.

When he received an honorary degree from Harvard in 1893, Robert spoke at the annual dinner of Harvard alumni and denounced Illinois Governor John P. Altgeld's pardon of the Haymarket Riot anarchists. He did not share his father's sympathy for labor, and he admired his friend John Hay's antilabor novel *The Bread-Winners*. He came to dislike Theodore Roosevelt intensely, supported William Howard Taft in 1912, and denounced Roosevelt's attempt to link his "New Nationalism" with the ideals of Abraham Lincoln. "The Government under which my father lived," Robert wrote angrily in a rare public letter, "was . . . a republic, or representative democracy, checked by the Constitution which can be changed by the people, but only when acting by methods which compel deliberation and exclude so far as possible the effect of passionate and short-sighted impulse." A government "in which the people act in a mass directly on all questions and not through their chosen representatives—is an unchecked democracy, a form of Government so full of danger, as shown by history, that it has ceased to exist except in communities small and concentrated as to space." Roosevelt's ideas constituted "a revolution" and could "lead to attempted dictatorships." The Gettysburg Address was not a call for unchecked democracy, Robert believed, and Abraham Lincoln's criticism of the Dred Scott decision sought only a reversal by a future Supreme Court, not a popular recall of the decision or the judges who made it. Robert was a harsh critic of Woodrow Wilson and supported Warren G. Harding for President in 1920.

After his return from England in 1893, Lincoln was increasingly absorbed in business affairs. In 1897, after the death of his friend George Pullman, he became temporary president of the Pullman Palace Car Company. From 1901 to 1911 he was president of that company. In testimony before the Federal Commission on Industrial Relations in 1915, Lincoln admitted that Pullman car porters had a job that was a "blind alley" paid primarily by tips rather than wages, an "arrangement . . . not nice . . . at all."

Robert's outburst against Roosevelt's use of Lincoln's image was unusual, but he always scrupulously, if quietly, protected his father's reputation. As early as 1866 he felt that William H. Herndon was "making an ass of himself" in his attempt to produce an "honest" biography of Abraham Lincoln. Herndon thought "Bob" hated him "religiously . . . for telling the naked truths about his noble father." Robert controlled his father's Presidential papers and allowed only John Hay and John G. Nicolay to use them. The collaborators began work late in 1872 or early in 1873 to produce *Abraham Lincoln: A History* (1890), a biography written, as Hay said, "in a spirit of reverence and regard," dedicated to and approved by Robert before publication. Robert later willed his papers to the Library of Congress with the stipulation that they not be opened until 21 years after his death.

Robert took a keen private interest in what was said and written about his father—and even in how his father was represented in art. He was a sharp-tongued critic of Lincoln sculpture and repeatedly told those who asked him, that his favorite portrait of Abraham Lincoln was G. P. A. Healy's, which he himself owned. He told a military historian in 1881 that he had "pretty strong feelings" on the subject of George B. McClellan's removal from command. The historian thought the only justification for President Lincoln's interference with McClellan lay in "the existence of precedents during the war of 1812 or the war with Mexico." Robert was interested in such precedents only "if a precedent for General McClellan as a Commander-in-Chief could be found, —certainly not otherwise."

Despite his care for his father's good name, Robert never trafficked in his fame. In addition to having a "repugnance to what is called 'public life' that is almost morbid," he never desired "a nomination which I could not honestly feel was gained by my own merit." Many think him more his mother's son, and he has come to be called "Robert Todd Lincoln" although he always went by "Robert T." or "R.T." He was also his father's son, especially in the genial sense of humor he displayed to those who knew him intimately.

Robert suffered severe disappointments in his own family. His wife was neurasthenic and reclusive, and his only son, "Jack," died young (on March 5, 1890) of blood poisoning from an infected carbuncle. His daughter Jessie eloped in 1897 with an Iowa Wesleyan football player named Warren Beckwith (of whom Robert disapproved). He rallied from those trials—as well as the earlier deaths of all his brothers, his father's assassination, and his mother's insanity—and lived a comfortable and determinedly "normal" life. He enjoyed golf and amateur astronomy and loved his gracious summer home, "Hildene," in Manchester, Vermont. He lived to attend the dedication of the Lincoln Memorial in Washington, D.C., in 1922. Four years later he died quietly in his sleep at Hildene. He is buried in Arlington National Cemetery.

SOURCES: John S. Goff's biography, *Robert Todd Lincoln: A Man in His Own Right* (Norman: University of Oklahoma Press, 1969), was written before the Illinois State Historical Library in Springfield obtained Robert's letter books. From those letter books and the clippings in that collection come Robert's version of his mother's insanity (letter to Leonard Swett, May 25, 1884), 1884 campaign views (clipping), suspicions about

Lincoln, Sarah Bush Johnston (1788–1869)

Abraham Lincoln's stepmother. Sarah Bush was born in what is now Elizabethtown, Kentucky. Her father, Christopher Bush, seems to have prospered in Kentucky, but her first husband, Daniel Johnston, whom she married in 1806, was a ne'er-do-well. He appeared on the delinquent tax list for Hardin County in 1806, and the county court noted that he was "Without funds" when a creditor pressed suit to collect a debt in 1810. In 1814 he was appointed Hardin County jailer. He died in 1816, leaving Sarah, in the words of local historian Samuel Haycraft, "an honest poor widow."

Widower Thomas Lincoln set out for Elizabethtown in 1819, married Sarah on December 2, and returned to Indiana with her. It must have been a shock for the bride. In 1865 Sarah recalled the country as "wild, and desolate." The children who awaited her, "Abe" (as she called him) and his sister Sarah, had to be "dressed . . . up" to look "more human," but the log cabin was "good . . . , tolerably comfortable." The family was large; it included Thomas and Sarah, Abraham, Dennis Hanks, Sarah Lincoln, Elizabeth Johnston, John D. Johnston, and Matilda Johnston, the last three being Sarah Bush's children by her previous marriage. Illiterate herself, she seems to have marveled at and respected Abraham's studious habits. She defended her husband from charges made later that he discouraged Abraham's education. She gave other indications of loyalty to Thomas; in 1865 she told an interviewer that she wished she had died when her husband did, 14 years earlier.

Sarah repeatedly asserted that "Abe was a good boy," and she grew to love him more than her own son, John. After Abraham left home on his own, Mrs. Lincoln "saw him every year or two" in Coles County, Illinois, where she lived from 1831 until her death. Lincoln attended to her welfare as best he could from a distance. After Thomas died in 1851, Lincoln retained a 40-acre plot of land in his own name "for Mother while she lives," and he discouraged John D. Johnston from selling the other 80 acres of the Lincoln homestead in Coles "on *Mother's* account." Abraham saw his stepmother last on January 31 and February 1, 1861, when he came to bid her farewell before going to Washington for his inauguration. When she recalled the visit for an interviewer after her stepson's death in 1865, she wept. Sarah died in 1869.

Lincoln said of his stepmother that "she proved a good and kind mother" to him, and he referred to her as "Mother" in his letters. Their relationship was excellent, by all reports, and Mrs. Lincoln considered her stepson a model child who was always honest, witty, and "diligent for knowledge"; he never needed "a cross word." She recalled that her mind ("what little I had") and his "seemed to run together," and that disingenuous tone was typical of her character. In all the vast literature of controversy over Lincoln's early years, there is hardly an unkind word about Sarah Bush Johnston Lincoln.

SOURCES: Louis A. Warren's *Lincoln's Youth, Indiana Years, Seven to Twenty-one, 1816–1830* (New York: Appleton, Century, Crofts, 1959) contains much information on Sarah's early years. Her late years are best followed in Charles H. Coleman's *Abraham Lincoln and Coles County, Illinois* (New Brunswick, N.J.: Scarecrow Press, 1955). Sarah's own touching and revealing statement about her son is reproduced in Emanuel Hertz, *The Hidden Lincoln: From the Letters and Papers of William H. Herndon* (New York: Viking Press, 1938).

Sarah Bush Johnston Lincoln

Lincoln, Thomas (1776 or 1778–1851),

Abraham Lincoln's father. Thomas Lincoln moved from Rockingham County, Virginia, to Kentucky in the 1780s. His father, Abraham Lincoln, "was killed by Indians, . . . when he was laboring to open a farm in the forest." As a result, Thomas was "even in childhood . . . a wandering laboring boy, and grew up litterally without education." In 1802 he moved to Hardin County, Kentucky, where, one year later, he purchased a 238-acre farm for £118. Four years later he married Nancy Hanks. Their first child, a daughter named Sarah, was born a year later. In 1808 Thomas bought a 300-acre farm on Nolin Creek. There, on February 12, 1809, Abraham Lincoln was born. A third child, named Thomas, died in infancy.

Numerous documents from Kentucky courthouses prove that Thomas Lincoln was a responsible middling citizen on a rough and poor frontier. He appears too often in those documents as a wage earner, a jury member, a petitioner for a road, or a guard for county prisoners to have been what many later writers claimed he was: a shiftless ne'er-do-well of no ambition who discouraged his promising son from reading. To be sure, Thomas "never did more in the way of writing than to bunglingly sign his own name," as his son recalled years later, but he could read a little, was a skilled carpenter, and was a property owner. He purchased still another farm in Kentucky in 1815—for cash. That was the Knob Creek farm to which the Lincolns moved as renters in 1811 and which was the first home a mature Abraham Lincoln could remember. Thomas was a member of the Little Mount Separate Baptist Church.

Thomas fell victim to Kentucky's chaotic land laws. The title to each of the three farms he purchased there proved defective. He lost land or money in each case and in disgust moved to Indiana in 1816 because there the land was surveyed by the federal government under the Land Ordinance of 1785 for the Northwest Territory. Abraham claimed many years later that his father moved from Kentucky "partly on account of slavery," which was outlawed in Indiana. It is possible. Hardin County had 1007 slaves and only 1627 white males over 16 in 1811. The Little Mount Separate Baptists had broken with the regular church over slavery. And Thomas was a common laborer forced to compete for wages against wageless workers.

In Indiana the Lincolns settled by the Little Pigeon Creek near Gentryville, and Thomas resumed farming. He soon put his unusually tall 8-year-old son to work, planting, harvesting, and wielding an axe. Nancy Lincoln died in 1818, and the resourceful Thomas remarried within a year; he chose a widow from Elizabethtown, Kentucky, Sarah Bush Johnston. In 1823 he became a member of the Little Pigeon Baptist Church "by letter" (of reference from his Kentucky church). By 1827 he owned 100 acres of land outright, and 2 years later he began building a new and better cabin. News from John Hanks that Illinois had fertile soil and was free of the disease that had killed the first Mrs. Lincoln lured Thomas west before he finished the cabin.

Thomas sold his land and moved first to Macon County (1830) and eventually to Coles County, Illinois (1831). His son left home to make his way in the world, but Thomas lived in Coles County the rest of his life. His record as a citizen in Illinois seems less commendable than that in Kentucky and Indiana. He was a defendant in five lawsuits, four of which he lost. In all the suits but one, John D. Johnston, his stepson and a notorious idler, was a codefendant. Johnston was obviously a bad influence. By 1841 Thomas owned 120 acres in Illinois, but within a year he had to sell a third of his land to his son to get out of financial difficulty. In 1848 he had to procure $20 from Abraham to save the rest of his land from forced sale. He died in 1851.

Although Thomas's status as a respectable citizen while he raised Abraham is now secure from his detractors, there is considerable controversy over the relationship between father and son. There is almost no direct evidence of a strong bond of affection between the two. Abraham never wrote anything complimentary about his father. The unflattering allusions to Thomas's lack of education and bungling signature, for example, were written by Abraham. The son, too, noted that he learned grammar only "After he . . . had separated from his father." Warned that his father was dying in 1851, Abraham explained to Johnston that Mary Todd Lincoln's illness would prevent his coming to see his father. "Say to him," Lincoln instructed Johnston, who wrote and read letters for the illiterate Thomas, "that if we could meet now, it is doubtful whether it would not be more painful than pleasant."

Despite the substantial evidence of a falling out between Thomas and Abraham, the father did leave a mark on his famous son. Thomas was by all accounts well liked by his neighbors, and he was a good storyteller; so was his son. Thomas's evident dislike of slavery created an atmosphere in Lincoln's youth that would allow Abraham to say many years later that he could not remember a time when he was not antislavery in sentiment. Moreover, Thomas was a Whig in politics. When he had Johnston write Abraham for $20 in 1848, Thomas told him: "I am glad that I have lived to see anuther Whig Presedent alected & hope live to see monarcha or Locofoco principals crmble to dust be of good cheer four you ar on a good caus and I think old Zak will make all things right."

SOURCES: Louis A. Warren resurrected Thomas Lincoln's reputation in *Lincoln's Parentage and Childhood: A History of the Kentucky Lincolns Supported by Documentary Evidence* (New York: Century, 1926). He continued his theme, less successfully, in *Lincoln's Youth, Indiana Years, Seven to Twenty-one, 1816–1830* (New York: Appleton, Century, Crofts, 1959). Charles Coleman's *Abraham Lincoln and Coles County, Illinois* (New Brunswick, N.J.: Scarecrow Press, 1955) covers Thomas's years of decline thoroughly.

See also COLES COUNTY, ILLINOIS; INDIANA; KENTUCKY; PSYCHOLOGY.

Lincoln, Thomas ("Tad") (1853–1871) The Lincolns' youngest son. Thomas was named after Abraham Lincoln's father but nicknamed "Tad" because as a baby he looked like a tadpole, with a head too large for his body. He enjoyed the privilege of being the son of a "most indulgent parent," according to William H. Herndon, and was noted for his mischievous nature. White House secretary John Hay recalled that Tad "had a very bad opinion of books, and no opinion of discipline." Even his mother thought of him as "a *marked character.*" He had crooked teeth, a serious speech impediment, and a lisp.

The Lincoln childrens' play took its flavor from contemporary events and most frequently involved war. The boys viewed the war from their father's vantage point,

Far Left: The boys took the themes of their play from their father's grim work. Here is Tad Lincoln in a Union officer's uniform.

shortly after the death of "Eddie" Lincoln. He was named for his Uncle William Wallace, who married Mary Todd Lincoln's sister Frances. William H. Herndon recalled that Lincoln "was the most indulgent parent I have ever known," and that his boys "were absolutely unrestrained in their amusement." "Willie," as the Lincolns called him, seems to have had a happy youth. Mrs. Lincoln noted, too, that he was "a most peculiarly religious child." He was more studious than his brother Tad and wrote several letters which have survived. In 1862 he fell ill with a "bilious fever," as doctors described it, and died in the White House on February 20. His death greatly affected Mrs. Lincoln, who interpreted it as God's punishment for her being "so wrapped up in the world, so devoted to our own political advancement." She occasionally visited spiritualists who claimed to bring her messages from her dead son. Mrs. Lincoln recalled that her husband took more interest in religion after Willie's death.

Willie was buried in Oak Hill Cemetery in Georgetown after services conducted by the Reverend Phineas D. Gurley. After Lincoln's assassination, Willie's casket was exhumed, his remains were carried on the Lincoln funeral train, and they were buried in his father's tomb in Springfield.

SOURCE: See Ruth Painter Randall, *Lincoln's Sons* (Boston: Little, Brown, 1955).

and their play included grim parallels with the President's role in enforcing or remitting military discipline. A soldier doll named Jack was regularly "executed" for desertion or sleeping on guard duty and was once pardoned in a note by the President. Tad also shared his father's love of the theater.

What little tendency the Lincolns had toward disciplining Tad vanished at the death of his brother Willie in 1862. Tad was the only boy left at home, and he was smothered with affection. He was not forced to study, and he had numerous pets, including a pony and two goats. As late as 1866 he still could not write—despite being tutored in Washington.

After Lincoln's assassination, Tad's life took a turn for the worse. The boy was the constant companion of his mother, now a sad and unstable woman who said in 1867, "Only my darling Taddie prevents my taking my life." Tad testified at the trial of John H. Surratt in 1867. He finally attended school in Chicago (1866–1868) and learned his letters. Boarding school at Dr. Hohagen's Institute in Frankfurt, Germany (1868–1870), apparently cured him of his speech impediment. Thereafter, he had a tutor in England. He returned to America with his mother in May 1871 and died later that year, of, from all appearances, tuberculosis.

SOURCES: See Ruth Painter Randall's somewhat saccharine *Lincoln's Sons* (Boston: Little, Brown, 1955).

Lincoln, William Wallace ("Willie") (1850–1862)
Lincoln's third son. William Wallace was conceived very

Willie Lincoln in Springfield in 1860.

Lincoln Herald See LINCOLN MEMORIAL UNIVERSITY.

Lincoln Heritage Trail Established in 1963 to promote tourism in Kentucky, Indiana, and Illinois. The trail marked highways in three states on or near sites visited by or routes traveled by Abraham Lincoln. The Lincoln Heritage Trail Foundation, supported by money from the three states' departments of tourism, some individual contributors, and—until recently—the American Petroleum Institute, distributed brochures featuring historical and tourist attractions on the routes and courted newspaper travel writers to promote the trail. Charles Warnick, who was director of the Kentucky Department of Public Information's Tourist and Travel Division in 1963, admitted that the Trail "will not attempt to follow exactly in the footsteps of the Lincoln family's migrations," and several communities felt unjustly slighted by the routes designated. Information on the Trail is available from the Lincoln Heritage Trail Foundation, 702 Bloomington Road, Champaign, IL 61820.

Lincoln Highway America's first coast-to-coast paved road. The Lincoln Highway was the brainchild of the original promoter of Miami Beach, Carl Graham Fisher. That Indiana native—the builder of the Indianapolis Speedway—first revealed his plan in 1912. With no federal highway funds and little state money devoted to highways, he proposed formation of the Lincoln Highway Association to raise $10 million from the automobile industry and other private sources. Fisher kept pictures of Lincoln and Napoleon on his bedroom walls and wanted to name the road after Lincoln. The Lincoln Highway Association was formed in 1913. Since Fisher did not seek federal money, he ignored a suggestion to call the road the Thomas Jefferson Highway in order to get Southern support in Congress. Fisher's plan was to supply materials with the $10 million and let states and counties anxious to have the road go through their area meet the construction costs. The route, from New York to San Francisco, was chosen for directness and had no association with Lincoln's homes or travels. The road was completed in 1923 by the federal government, and it thereby lost its identity as a memorial to Abraham Lincoln. On modern maps it follows for the most part U.S. Route 30 through the Middle West and Interstate 80 in the West.

SOURCES: See Joe McCarthy, "The Lincoln Highway," *American Heritage*, XXV (June 1974), 32–37, 89.

Lincoln Lore See LOUIS A. WARREN LINCOLN LIBRARY AND MUSEUM.

Lincoln Memorial In 1901 Congress created a commission to recommend plans for revitalizing Washington, D.C. Architects Daniel H. Burnham and Charles F. McKim, immortalized by their work for the Columbian Exposition in Chicago in 1892–1893, landscape architect Frederick Law Olmsted, Jr., and sculptor Augustus St. Gaudens recommended extending the Mall from the Washington Monument to the Potomac River and erecting a Lincoln memorial at the end opposite the Washington Monument. Congress debated and delayed, and the plan was complicated by an alternative proposal to memorialize Lincoln by building a national highway from Washington to Gettysburg.

Two Illinois members of Congress, Joseph G. Cannon and Shelby M. Cullom (who had known Lincoln), guided through the legislation which created the bipartisan Lincoln Memorial Commission, headed by President William Howard Taft. After consulting the Fine Arts Commission, they selected architect Henry Bacon (1866–1924), a disciple of McKim's, and Bacon's friend Daniel Chester French (1850–1931) to produce a suitable sculpture of Lincoln. Bacon's architectural design, after many changes from his original conception, was well under way when French received his commission and began work on a statue in 1914. Ground had been broken for the memorial on Lincoln's birthday that same year.

Modeled on a Greek temple, the Memorial had 36 Doric columns outside to symbolize the states of the Union at Lincoln's death. It was made of white Colorado Yule marble. The base was 204 feet long and 134 feet wide; the columns were 44 feet high.

In that enormous structure, French was to place a bronze statue about 12 feet high. He was well qualified for the task, being generally considered America's greatest sculptor at the time. He had already executed a bronze Lincoln for the grounds of the Nebraska state capitol in Lincoln (unveiled in 1912). When French and Bacon placed a 10-foot plaster model in the Memorial, however, they saw immediately that it was far too small and that bronze would not do. French could work in marble, but cost was a problem—the 28 blocks of Georgia marble and carving by the famed Piccirilli brothers alone would equal his $45,000 fee. In 1917 the Commission granted French a $43,400 supplement.

French made a seated Lincoln 19 feet high and resting on an 11-feet-high base. It was meant to show the strength and confidence of the war President. French had studied Lincoln photographs for his earlier Lincoln work, and he used the Leonard Volk mask for Lincoln's face. He found the Volk hands unsatisfactory, however, and modeled Lincoln's hands on casts of his own.

The statue was completed and the Memorial dedicated on May 30, 1922, but French was not happy. The glare from the marble floor and the reflecting pool outside lighted Lincoln's face directly from the front and gave the face a ghostly and startled appearance. French needed lighting from above. After several experiments, the General Electric Company devised a satisfactory system of artificial lighting for which Congress appropriated the money in 1926. Altogether the Memorial cost about $3 million.

A New York art critic named Royal Cortissoz, who occasionally wrote inscriptions for public monuments, devised the eloquent inscription in the Memorial: "IN

THIS TEMPLE AS IN THE HEARTS OF THE PEOPLE FOR WHOM HE SAVED THE UNION THE MEMORY OF ABRAHAM LINCOLN IS ENSHRINED FOREVER."

SOURCE: See Michael Richman, "The Long Labor of Making Nation's Favorite Statue," *Smithsonian*, VII (February 1977), 54–61.

Lincoln Memorial Shrine The shrine, which is located in Redlands, California, about 70 miles east of Los Angeles, was the gift of Mr. and Mrs. Robert Watchorn to the city of Redlands. Mr. Watchorn was born in England in 1858. A coal miner from the age of 11, he moved to America in 1880. He became an American citizen, secretary of the United Mine Workers, Chief Factory Inspector of Pennsylvania (1891–1895), Commissioner of Immigration on the Canadian border (1898–1905), United States Commissioner of Immigration (1905–1909), and treasurer of the Union Oil Company (1909–1915). From 1916 to 1944 he was president of the Watchorn Oil and Gas Company and amassed a considerable fortune. Redlands was his winter home.

Watchorn collected Lincolniana; his prize possession was George Grey Barnard's marble bust of Lincoln, which he purchased for $10,000 in 1920. The shrine, dedicated in 1932, is a memorial to Emory Ewart Watchorn, the Watchorns' son, who was killed in World War I. It houses the Barnard bust and a substantial collection of books, pamphlets, pictures, and manuscripts on Lincoln and the Civil War.

For information on the Redlands shrine, contact the Archivist and Head of Special Collections, A. K. Smiley Public Library, 125 West Vine Street, P.O. Box 751, Redlands, CA 92373. The shrine is maintained by income from Watchorn's endowment, by the A. K. Smiley Public Library, and by public donations.

Lincoln Memorial University The university, in Harrogate, Tennessee, near the Cumberland Gap, is unique: a college in the South, not primarily for black students, named for a hero of the Union. The explanation lies in the political geography of the Confederacy, the mountain areas of which were often bastions of Unionist sentiment in opposition to the lowland slave areas. Mountainous East Tennessee was just such a bastion.

In 1890 the Reverend Arthur A. Myers, a Congregationalist minister sent to Kentucky by the American Missionary Association, established a school, later named Harrow Academy, for the poor children of the economically depressed region. In 1895 General O. O. Howard, a Civil War general who had led Union forces in East Tennessee in 1863, addressed Harrow's graduating class. He decided to help the institution become a college to be named after Abraham Lincoln, thus fulfilling the wish Howard said he had heard Lincoln express to help the loyal mountain people in Tennessee. On February 12, 1897, Lincoln Memorial University was chartered "to make education possible to the children of the humble, common people of America, among whom Abraham Lincoln was born, and whom he said God must love because he made so many of them." The university was a monument also to sectional reconciliation. A former Confederate colonel served as vice president of the charter committee, and the charter described the school as "an expression of renewed good will and fraternal feelings between the people of sections of this country once opposed to each other in civil war." The first building of the college's campus was called "Grant-Lee Hall."

In 1928 the university established a Lincoln Room in which to display documents, artifacts, and memorabilia of President Lincoln. Some items had already been collected by John Wesley Hill, a Methodist minister and influential board member and fund raiser for the university. J. B. Oakleaf, a famous Lincoln collector, headed a committee to solicit donations for the collection, often duplicates from the large private collections. In 1937 R. Gerald McMurtry joined the history department at the school and became the driving force behind cataloging, displaying, and systematically building the Lincoln and Civil War collection. He remained until 1956. In 1977 the Abraham Lincoln Library and Museum, a separate building for the collection made possible by a gift from fried chicken magnate Harlan D. Sanders, was dedicated. The institution publishes the only quarterly journal devoted to Lincoln studies, *Lincoln Herald*.

Far Left: Daniel Chester French's statue in the Lincoln Memorial.

SOURCES: Joseph E. Suppiger's *Phoenix of the Mountains: The Story of Lincoln Memorial University* (Harrogate, Tenn.: Lincoln Memorial University Press, 1977) describes the school's founding and history. Weldon E. Petz's *In the Presence of Abraham Lincoln* (Harrogate, Tenn.: Lincoln Memorial University, 1973) highlights the rarities in the Lincolniana collection, several in four-color illustration. For a subscription to *Lincoln Herald* write Lincoln Memorial University Press, Abraham Lincoln Library and Museum, Harrogate, TN 37752.

Lincoln Papers A large collection of letters, most of them written to Abraham Lincoln when he was President, now housed at the Library of Congress. After the President's assassination, David Davis, administrator of the estate, selected Lincoln's private secretaries, John G. Nicolay and John Hay, to get his papers in order for shipment to Springfield, Illinois. Since the administration of Washington, a President's papers had been considered his private property. Robert Todd Lincoln took charge of his father's papers and refused from the start to allow biographers to use the papers because "many documents . . . would be damaging to men now living." Boxed and sealed, the Lincoln papers rested in a vault in a bank in Bloomington, Illinois, Davis's hometown.

In 1874 Nicolay and Hay began work in earnest on their long-contemplated history of the Lincoln administration, and Robert consented to let them use the papers. That year the papers arrived in Washington, where Nicolay, in the spare time left over from his government job, began getting them in order. They formed the basis of Nicolay and Hay's monumental *Abraham Lincoln: A History* (1890). In 1894 the collaborators published most of the Lincoln letters from the collection in *Abraham Lincoln: Complete Works*. The papers remained in Nicolay's home in Washington, D.C.

After Nicolay died in 1901, the papers, separated into Lincoln manuscripts and letters to Lincoln, were stored, respectively, in a vault of the National Capital Bank and the vaults of the State Department, of which John Hay was now the head. The Librarian of Congress asked Robert to deposit the papers there. Robert replied that he would have left them to his son, but, since his son was dead, he would "select some depository for them, just what it will be I am not yet prepared to say." When Hay died in 1905, Robert took the papers to his office in Chicago. When he retired from the presidency of the Pullman Company in 1911, he moved to Washington. There he kept the papers, taking them with him in eight trunks on his frequent trips to "Hildene," his summer home in Manchester, Vermont. In those years, he went through his father's papers. In 1919 he deposited the papers, sealed, at the Library of Congress; there was no public announcement. In a will written later that year, he bequeathed them to the United States. In 1923 he imposed a restriction that the papers could not be opened to the public until 21 years after his death. His reasoning had not changed: he did so "because said papers contain many references of a private nature to the immediate ancestors of persons now living, which, in my judgment, should not be made public." Robert died in 1926; the papers would be opened in 1947.

Robert's secretiveness about the papers bred fevered suspicions about their contents. The suspicions erupted into wild allegations in 1937, when Frederick Coykendall, a collector, alleged in *The Collector, A Magazine for Autograph and Historical Collectors* that Horace Gedney Young, a golf partner of Robert Lincoln, had discovered Robert in the act of destroying papers which "contained the documentary evidence of the treason of a member of Lincoln's cabinet." Soon, Nicholas Murray Butler, president of Columbia University, confirmed the story. Young, Butler said, had informed him, and he rushed to save the trunk of papers from the fire for the Library of Congress. Emanuel Hertz published Butler's story in *The Hidden Lincoln: From the Letters and Papers of William Herndon* (1938). Butler repeated the story, with embellishments and details, in *The Saturday Evening Post* of February 11, 1939, though he denied therein that the reason was that the papers "contain evidence of the charge which has since been made, that Secretary Stanton conspired to wreck Lincoln's policies and to bring about his murder." The story, despite the distinguished status of its perpetrators, is purest bunk. Butler dated the event at 1923, 4 years after Robert had deposited the papers in the Library of Congress, and he mentioned only one trunk, failing to account for the other seven trunks of papers. However, Robert apparently did sift the collection and may have destroyed some personal family letters.

On July 26, 1947, the papers were opened before a group of distinguished Lincoln scholars. Press coverage was extensive. By and large, the event was anticlimactic. It was a scholar's collection; there was no scent of treason or bastardy in the papers. Scholars have since put the papers to good use, but the collection is far from exhausted.

The Lincoln Papers contain mostly letters to Lincoln. Lincoln's own letters and speeches are available in Roy P. Basler's definitive *Collected Works of Abraham Lincoln*, 9 vols. (New Brunswick, N.J.: Rutgers University Press, 1953–1955). The *Supplement, 1832–1865*, ed. by Roy P. Basler (Westport, Conn.: Greenwood Press) appeared in 1974.

SOURCES: David C. Mearns's *The Lincoln Papers*, 2 vols. (New York: Doubleday, 1948) is definitive. The papers themselves are readily available for use at the Library of Congress or on microfilm (97 reels) at many scholarly libraries in the country.

Lincoln Penny Issued on August 2, 1909; the first American coin to bear the likeness of a President on its face. President Theodore Roosevelt, who admired Lincoln and wished to improve the artistic merit of the country's coins, asked Victor David Brenner, a Jewish immigrant from Russia, to execute the work in honor of the centennial of Lincoln's birth. Brenner had worked on a Panama Canal Medal with Roosevelt's likeness on it in 1908, and when he showed the President his Lincoln bas-relief modeled from a photograph borrowed from Harvard professor Charles Eliot Norton, Roosevelt knew he had his man. Brenner suggested its appropriateness for the penny rather than a coin of larger denomination, because the penny was the coin of Lincoln's "plain people."

The Lincoln penny created quite a sensation in 1909. Some saw in it a tendency toward the monarchical practice of putting the features of a head of state on coins. Many Southerners resented the choice of Lincoln. But the biggest controversy resulted from the placement of

Brenner's initials, V. D. B., on the reverse of the coin. Although not the first coin signed by an artist, it was the first widely circulated coin so struck, and many protested the self-advertisement. So great was the protest, in fact, that President William Howard Taft's Secretary of the Treasury, Wayne McVeagh, ordered removal of all but the "B" from the coin within a week of issue. Only 22,350,000 "V. D. B." pennies were struck.

Brenner's original design of the reverse with "two heads of wheat to show that in America there is plenty" was changed in 1959 in honor of the sesquicentennial of Lincoln's birth. It now shows an image of the Lincoln Memorial.

SOURCES: Willard B. Gatewood wrote a substantial and amusing article on this seemingly rather slight subject, "The Lincoln Penny: 'Mid-Summer Madness' of 1909," *Lincoln Herald*, LXVII (Fall 1965), 119–123. For a checklist of other Lincoln medals see Robert P. King, *Lincoln in Numismatics* (Reprinted by the Token and Medal Society, 1966).

Linder, Usher Ferguson (1809–1876) Early political and legal associate of Lincoln's. Linder, who was born in Elizabethtown, Kentucky, moved to Illinois and eventually settled in Charleston in Coles County in 1838. He spent a brief but fateful period in Alton in 1837. There he became a leader of the citizens opposed to the establishment of a newspaper by abolitionist Elijah Lovejoy. Linder was serving as Illinois attorney general at the time, but he played a role out of keeping for the state's chief law enforcement officer. He engineered the takeover of antislavery meetings by skillful use of parliamentary methods. He urged and gained passage of a formal resolution by a public meeting which stated that Lovejoy should under no circumstances be allowed to establish a newspaper. In his *Reminiscences*, written almost 40 years later, Linder was careful to point out that he was out of town when a mob killed Lovejoy.

A Democrat until 1838, Linder became a Whig in that year, only to go back to the Democracy in the 1850s. He was elected to the Illinois legislature in 1836, 1846, and 1850. From 1838 to 1860 he practiced law "on the Wabash circuit." He became acquainted with Lincoln when both men served in the state legislature. They clashed bitterly over the issue of the Illinois State Bank. When Linder moved to Coles County, Lincoln was on occasion associated with him in legal cases tried in the county seat.

Even when they became party allies, Lincoln and Linder had their political differences. A residue of Linder's original Democratic leanings showed in his uneasiness with the Whig party's opposition to the Mexican War. On February 20, 1848, Lincoln had to tell Linder not to say that President James K. Polk was not to be condemned for the way he prosecuted the Mexican War. "By justifying Mr. Polk's mode of prossecuting the war," Lincoln wrote, "you put yourself in opposition to Genl. Taylor [the Whig presidential hopeful] himself, for we all know he has declared for, and, in fact originated, the defensive line policy." Besides, to defend Polk would gain some Democrats but lose many Whigs; going for Zachary Taylor whole hog would keep all the Whigs and gain a few Democrats too. Linder was hardly satisfied, and Lincoln had to write again to tell him it was impossible to elect Taylor without opposing the war. Whigs "are compelled to *speak*," Lincoln said on March 22, "and their only option is whether they will . . . tell the *truth*, or tell a foul, villainous, and bloody falsehood." Nor should he be squeamish about siding with abolitionists who supported Taylor, Lincoln added; they had supported William Henry Harrison in 1840, the only year the Whigs had won the Presidency.

Linder's hatred of abolitionism led him back to the Democracy and thus to the support of Stephen A. Douglas against Lincoln in their famous 1858 race for the United States Senate. He opposed Lincoln in 1860 as well. He was bitterly opposed to emancipation but considered secession as treason and was a War Democrat. His son Daniel was a Confederate soldier. In 1863 Daniel was captured and imprisoned in Maryland. In answer to Usher's plea, President Lincoln had him released and sent home to his parents.

In 1860 Linder moved to Chicago, but he did not fare well there. In the spring of 1864 he wrote Lincoln to ask for an office. The tone of the letter suggests the bond of good humor which joined the two men despite their political differences:

> In the revolutions of the wheel of fortune I have often been at the top—and as often at the bottom—In other words I have been, now, four years at this place, and notwithstanding I have exerted a dilligence and prudence hardly common to me, no prosperous wind has yet filled my sail—but the whole bag full have steadily set against me.

Lincoln did not offer Linder a job. On April 17, 1865, Linder addressed a special meeting of the Chicago Bar Association in memory of Abraham Lincoln.

Linder's lot did not much improve. In 1874 he began writing his *Reminiscences*. He died 2 years later, and the book was published posthumously in 1879.

SOURCES: The best secondary source is Charles H. Coleman, *Abraham Lincoln and Coles County, Illinois* (New Brunswick, N.J.: Scarecrow Press, 1955), but he ignores the Lovejoy incident. For that, see Leonard L. Richards, *"Gentlemen of Property and Standing": Anti-Abolition Mobs in Jacksonian America* (New York: Oxford University Press, 1970). Linder's own disjointed *Reminiscences of the Early Bench and Bar of Illinois* (Chicago: Chicago Legal News Company, 1879) contains some wonderful anecdotes about Lincoln's associates. See George K. Holbert, "Lincoln and Linder in Kentucky," *Lincoln Herald*, XLIV (June 1942), 2–3, 10–12, and "Lincoln and Linder in Illinois," *Lincoln Herald*, XLIV (October–December 1942), 2–5. Linder's letter requesting a job from the President (March 26, 1864) is in the Abraham Lincoln Papers, Library of Congress.

See also MATSON SLAVE CASE.

Literature *See* BOOKS; EDUCATION; POETRY; SHAKESPEARE.

Lloyd, John Minchin (?–1892) Principal government witness against Mary Surratt at the trial of Lincoln's alleged assassins. Lloyd rented Mrs. Surratt's tavern in Surrattsville and her farm late in 1864. About

Logan, Stephen Trigg

Stephen Trigg Logan. (Courtesy of the Illinois State Historical Library)

5 or 6 weeks before the assassination, John H. Surratt, Mary's son, accompanied by David E. Herold and George A. Atzerodt, left two Spencer carbines, a box of ammunition, a long rope, and a monkey wrench with Lloyd, who, with Surratt, hid them in the tavern building. On the night of April 14, 1865, at about midnight, Herold and John Wilkes Booth stopped at the inn. Herold asked the sleepy and confused proprietor for the things hidden in the tavern. Lloyd gave Herold a carbine and a package given him by Mrs. Surratt earlier that day.

On May 13 at the trial of the alleged conspirators Lloyd testified that Mrs. Surratt had told him on the Tuesday before the assassination that the "shooting-irons" would be wanted soon. On Friday, the day of the assassination, he added, she had given him a package containing a field glass and told him the "shooting-irons" would be called for that night. Another key government witness, Louis J. Weichmann, who disliked being blamed for Mrs. Surratt's hanging, claimed in later years that Lloyd's testimony hanged her. He pictured Lloyd as a responsible witness, "a very plain and unpretentious individual, but abundantly able to run the farm and sell whiskey to his neighbors." The defense showed, however, that Lloyd was anything but a solid citizen. Attorney Frederick Stone got Lloyd to admit on the stand that he "was right smart in liquer that afternoon, and after night got more so." Defense counsel also showed that Lloyd at first denied to detectives that two men had stopped at his tavern on the night of the assassination. He admitted on the stand that Booth, whom Lloyd did not recognize, had told him on the very night that "we have assassinated the President and Secretary Seward." Yet he had not gone to the authorities.

In 1867 Lloyd reluctantly testified again at the trial of John H. Surratt. Defense counsel, arguing that Lloyd's testimony was born of fear of what the government might do to him, elicited from Lloyd an admission that an interrogating officer before the first trial had told him he was guilty of a capital offense. Lloyd admitted to being a very heavy drinker and to being so drunk on April 14 that he felt sick when he lay down. Drink, he also admitted, "makes me forget a great many things." He had also been drinking when he met Mrs. Surratt on the Tuesday before the assassination. In addition to being a drunkard, the witness was also a brawler. On April 14 Lloyd returned to Surrattsville from testifying in the trial of a man who had tried to stab him. After the trial, he drank and played cards and nearly "got into a fuss" with his card-playing companion. Lloyd's unimpressive character is the principal reliance of all those who argue that Mrs. Surratt was innocent.

Lloyd died in Washington, D.C.

SOURCES: Benn Pitman, *The Assassination of President Lincoln and the Trial of the Conspirators* (Cincinnati, Ohio: Moore, Wilstach & Baldwin, 1865) and the *Trial of John H. Surratt* 2 vols. (Washington, D.C.: Government Printing Office, 1867) contain Lloyd's testimony. Weichmann's assessment is in *A True History of the Assassination of Abraham Lincoln and of the Conspiracy of 1865*, ed. by Floyd E. Risvold (New York: Alfred A. Knopf, 1975).

See also SURRATT, MARY EUGENIA; TRIAL OF THE ASSASSINS; WEICHMANN, LOUIS J.

Logan, Stephen Trigg (1800–1880) Abraham Lincoln's second law partner. Stephen T. Logan was born in Kentucky and first practiced law there. Impoverished by lending money to friends who failed in business, he left Kentucky in 1832 to recoup his fortunes in Springfield, Illinois. He resumed practice the next year and was elected by the Illinois legislature as judge of the First Judicial Circuit in 1835. He resigned in 1837 because the salary was too low.

Logan met Lincoln in 1832, when Lincoln was running for the legislature. Over 40 years later he recalled that Lincoln "was a very tall and gawky and rough looking fellow then—his pantaloons didn't meet his shoes by six inches," but he "made a very sensible speech." Both men were Whigs. Lincoln "was as stiff as a man could be in his Whig doctrines," Logan remembered.

Lincoln became Logan's partner in 1841, in part because Logan's previous partner, Edward D. Baker, was reckless in money matters. According to Logan, Lincoln's "knowledge of law was very small" at the time. Lincoln's previous partner, John Todd Stuart, did not study the law much, and Lincoln, Logan claimed, only began to study law and develop "considerable ambition in the law" under his tutelage. Like Baker, Lincoln was important "in getting the good will of juries." He was never "much of a reader." The partnership was successful but was amicably dissolved in 1844, when Logan wished to bring his son David into the firm.

Lincoln and Logan were close political associates in the 1840s. Logan was elected to the Illinois legislature in 1842, 1844, and 1846. In 1847 he was a member of the state constitutional convention. A year later he lost to Thomas L. Harris in a race for Lincoln's seat in Congress—a loss that is often incorrectly blamed on the alleged unpopularity of Lincoln's opposition to the Mexican War, a record Logan had to defend. Logan's opportunity to run for the seat stemmed from Lincoln's decision not to run for reelection in order "to keep peace among our friends" and share the opportunities for office in the only Whig district in the state. Lincoln's decision had nothing to do with his record on the war. Logan was, as Thomas Drummond recalled, "by nature and temperament unfitted to become a successful politician." His voice was high-pitched and unsuitable for stump speaking. Lincoln refused to speculate at length on the cause of Logan's defeat and said simply that "a good many Whigs, without good cause, . . . were unwilling to go for Logan." Besides, Harris was a war hero, and many Whig voters had served with him in Mexico. Lincoln unsuccessfully urged Logan's appointment as a federal judge after Zachary Taylor's election.

Logan ran successfully for the state legislature again in 1854; but when he lost an election for judge on the state supreme court a year later, Lincoln commented that he was "worse beaten than any other man ever was since elections were invented." Logan served as a delegate to the Republican national nominating convention in 1860. He was a delegate to the Washington Peace Conference in February 1861, and President Lincoln appointed him to a commission to investigate claims against the government in Cairo, Illinois, in 1862.

By the time of the Civil War, Logan had amassed wealth enough to retire from politics and from active legal practice. The precise nature of his political opinions late in his life is unknown, but some considered him anything but an ardent supporter of the war effort. William H. Herndon thought that, like other "monied men," he was "old & timid—disturbed and terrified." Logan wrote President Lincoln only a few formal lines to recommend judges' appointments during the war. He had been one of the few citizens of Springfield to vote against the article in the state constitution of 1848 which excluded Negroes from Illinois, but the *Illinois State Journal* noted that in late life, "Like many others, he was puzzled by the question of Reconstruction, . . . and for a time was claimed to be in harmony with the Democratic party, but of late years has been pronounced and unswerving in his Republicanism."

Herndon pictured Logan as a "cold, avaricious, . . . mean" man, and even friends admitted that he "was not a man who 'wore his heart upon his sleeve.'" Like Lincoln, he was not a member of a church, though many described him as a good Christian.

SOURCES: The only biographical material of note is in *Memorials of the Life and Character of Stephen T. Logan* (Springfield, Ill.: H. W. Rokker, 1882). Logan's reminiscences of Lincoln, which may well exaggerate his own role in making a good lawyer of Lincoln, were recorded by Herndon in 1875 and are available in the *Lincoln Centennial Association Bulletin*, Number 12 (Sept. 1, 1928), pp. 1–3, 5. Herndon's letter to John G. Nicolay mentioning Logan's confused political opinions during the Civil War (August 1, 1861) is in the Abraham Lincoln Papers, Library of Congress.

Long Nine A group of legislators elected to represent Sangamon County in the Illinois legislature in 1836. All nine—Abraham Lincoln, Ninian W. Edwards, Andrew McCormick, Daniel Stone, Robert L. Wilson, Job Fletcher, Archer G. Herndon, John Dawson, and William F. Elkin—were around 6 feet tall and inclined toward Whig principles in politics. The "long nine" was a nickname for a naval gun in Lincoln's era. Herndon and Fletcher were senators; the rest, representatives. Lincoln was the youngest of the group. The Long Nine were together only until the special legislative session of July 10, 1837, in which Stone, who had resigned to become a judge, was replaced by Edward D. Baker, only 5 feet 8 inches tall.

In the 1836–1837 legislative session the Long Nine supported important legislation: the move of the state capital from Vandalia to Springfield and the Internal Improvements Act. Illinois historian Thomas Ford charged the Long Nine with logrolling—that is, with trading their powerful bloc of votes for internal improvements benefiting localities whose representatives would support the move of the capital to Springfield in return. However, on eight roll calls on amendments extending internal improvements schemes, the seven house members of the Long Nine voted as a unit on only two. John J. Hardin, whose district benefited from one of the two amendments supported by the Sangamon County seven, voted against Springfield on all four ballots on moving the capital. The Long Nine did not trade internal improvements benefits for capital relocation.

SOURCES: Paul Simon disproved the logrolling charge in *Lincoln's Preparation for Greatness: The Illinois Legislative Years* (Norman: University of Oklahoma Press, 1965).

"Lost Speech," Lincoln's Speech that Lincoln delivered on May 29, 1856, at the conclusion of the Illinois Republican state convention in Bloomington. The speech was so captivating, apparently, that no one even took full notes on it. William H. Herndon "attempted for about fifteen minutes," he recalled, "as was usual with me then to take notes, but at the end of that time I threw pen and paper away and lived only in the inspiration of the hour."

Henry Clay Whitney later claimed to have made notes on the occasion, and in 1896 he sold *McClure's Magazine* the text of the speech, which the magazine published in its September issue. Joseph M. Medill, who had heard the speech, endorsed it as a "close reproduction," but John G. Nicolay, who also had heard it, thought it spurious. Nicolay was vindicated in 1930 when a brief account of the speech was found in the Alton *Courier* of June 5, 1856. The description differed so markedly from Whitney's version that no one now accepts Whitney's account.

The contemporary newspaper account said that Lincoln stressed that the *"Union must be preserved in the purity of its principles as well as in the integrity of its territorial parts."* And Lincoln apparently noted an ominous increase in the "sentiment in favor of white slavery" in the slave states and implied that it was growing in the national Democratic party.

SOURCES: See Benjamin P. Thomas, *Portrait for Posterity: Lincoln and His Biographers* (New Brunswick, N.J.: Rutgers University Press, 1947) and [Paul M. Angle], "Lincoln's 'Lost Speech,'" *Bulletin of the Abraham Lincoln Association*, Number 21 (December 1930), pp. 3–5.

Louis A. Warren Lincoln Library and Museum A memorial formed in 1928 by the Lincoln National Life Insurance Company in Fort Wayne, Indiana. When the company was founded in 1905, Secretary Arthur F. Hall wrote Robert Todd Lincoln a letter describing the company and requesting a photograph of his father to appear on the company's letterhead. Lincoln replied on August 3, 1905, that he found "no objection whatever to the use of a portrait of my father upon the letterhead of such a life insurance company named after him as you describe." Once the fledgling company became successful, Hall, now president, brought Louis A. Warren to Fort Wayne to establish some sort of memorial to Lincoln. Warren, a Christian minister in Zionsville, Indiana, and author of *Lincoln's Parentage and Childhood: A History of the Kentucky Lincolns Supported by Documentary Evidence* (New York: Century, 1926), decided to establish a library; it was called the Lincoln Historical Research Foundation. Warren purchased the library of one of the "Big Five" Lincoln collectors, Judge Daniel Fish. He began publishing *Lincoln Lore*, a weekly "clip sheet" intended to supply "fillers" for newspapers, in 1929. Warren was surprised when people began saving the fillers rather than throwing them away. He made speaking tours of the country in and around February. In 1932 the Company renamed the institution The Lincoln National Life Foundation.

R. Gerald McMurtry, once an employee of the Foundation and later the builder of the Lincoln collection at Lincoln Memorial University, became the Director of the Lincoln National Life Foundation in 1956 and held the position until his retirement in 1972. McMurtry stressed museum items more than his predecessor had, and he changed *Lincoln Lore* into a four-page monthly bulletin. In 1977 the foundation was named after its first director.

The Louis A. Warren Lincoln Library and Museum, still located in the home office of its patron, the Lincoln National Life Insurance Company, now offers a museum with 60 Lincoln exhibits arranged in chronological order to tell the full history of Lincoln's life. The museum displays Lincoln's copies of Mason Locke Weems's *Life of Benjamin Franklin* and of the *Life and Speeches of Henry Clay*, Lincoln manuscripts, a Lincoln shawl in superb condition, a patent model of the Manny reaper, and a flag that draped the President's box at Ford's Theatre. The library contains 10,000 books and pamphlets on Lincoln, 6000 portraits (including Lincoln's last portrait painted from life, by Matthew Wilson for Gideon Welles), numerous original photographs, manuscripts written by Lincoln and his close contemporaries, broadsides, and numerous statues and statuettes (including rare pieces by Vinnie Ream, Thomas D. Jones, and Leonard W. Volk). *Lincoln Lore*, the oldest continuously published periodical devoted to Lincoln studies, is still available from the institution. In 1978 the museum instituted an annual Lincoln lecture, called the R. Gerald McMurtry Lecture, which brings an outstanding authority to deliver an original paper on Lincoln each May. The lecture is published in pamphlet form. Like most other materials from the institution, it is distributed free of charge. The address of the museum and library is 1300 South Clinton Street, Fort Wayne, IN 46801.

Louisiana See BANKS, NATHANIEL PRENTISS; NEW ORLEANS, LOUISIANA.

Lovejoy, Owen (1811-1864) Illinois abolitionist and early Republican. Owen Lovejoy was born in Maine but moved to Alton, Illinois, in 1836 to prepare for the ministry with his brother Elijah. When Elijah was killed by an antiabolition mob the next year, Owen vowed by Elijah's body never to forsake the cause sprinkled with his brother's blood. He became a minister in the Congregational church in Princeton, Illinois. He and Ichabod Codding led Illinois's small abolitionist movement. He was a typical member of the Liberty party: a Protestant minister with abolitionist convictions.

The Kansas-Nebraska Act moved many Illinois citizens nearer Lovejoy's extreme dislike of the "Slave Power," if not nearer his abolitionist convictions, and in 1854 Lovejoy was elected to the Illinois House of Representatives. He tried to form a third party called "Republican" that year which would include Abraham Lincoln, but Lincoln spurned the movement. Lovejoy voted for Lincoln for Senator on the first three of ten ballots in the Illinois legislature in 1855. In 1856, when the Republican organization in Illinois was successfully forged, Lovejoy was conspicuously absent from membership on the state central committee—a sign that this Republican party would be dominated by moderates.

Lincoln disliked Lovejoy's abolitionist views and said "it turned me blind" after hearing that the Princeton minister had won the nomination for the Third Congressional District over Lincoln's friend Leonard Swett. Many of Lincoln's close political associates, especially David Davis, detested Lovejoy, but Lincoln was quick to realize Lovejoy's appeal in the Third District and the value to the party of his supporters' enthusiasm. He advised Davis that it was "best to let the matter stand," but T. Lyle Dickey, another old Whig, maintained an independent candidacy in the district until almost the middle of September. Davis told Dickey that "Bleeding Kansas" and the caning of Charles Sumner had "made abolitionists of those, who never dreamed they were drifting into it." Lovejoy won by more than 6000 votes.

When Lovejoy ran for reelection in 1858, Lincoln secretly warned him of possible factional trouble in his district. Davis, Swett, and Ward Hill Lamon hoped in vain for another nominee. Lovejoy sent a copy of his acceptance speech to Lincoln. It was a clear declaration of Republican orthodoxy: "I am content to fight slavery in modes pointed out in the Constitution, and in those modes only." When charged " 'why, you have changed, you are not as radical and rabid as you used to be,' my uniform reply has been," Lovejoy said, "it is no matter who has changed, so that we are all right and all together *now*." The speech was also a wholehearted endorsement of Lincoln for the Senate "because he is a true hearted man, and . . . , come what will, unterrified by power, unseduced by ambition, he will remain true to the great principles upon which the Republican party is organized." Lovejoy concluded by saying that "whoever is in Abraham's bosom cannot, I think, be far from the Senate." He won reelection. He epitomized the issue between Lincoln and Stephen A. Douglas by complimenting Lincoln for showing "that the mistake of Judge D. was that he made slavery a *little* thing when it was a great thing." By 1860 his district was so secure that he stumped the whole state for the Republican ticket and won reelection by a large margin as well.

In Congress Lovejoy was an uncompromising foe of secession and an early advocate of emancipation and the use of Negro soldiers. In 1861 he abstained from voting on the Crittenden resolution, which declared that the war's purpose was not to overthrow slavery. He introduced the bill—in 1862—which finally redeemed the Republican pledge to exclude slavery from the territories. He opposed the return of fugitive slaves by the Union armies, supported homestead legislation, but was

Owen Lovejoy. (Courtesy of the Lloyd Ostendorf Collection)

a bitter opponent of the Pacific railroad bill. Fellow Congressmen regarded him as a radical or fanatic, but he was occasionally capable of compromise. He voted for a resolution of March 6, 1862, suggested by Lincoln, to compensate slaveholders in states which voluntarily abolished slavery. He answered Northern fears of an influx of free Negroes by vowing to "let them stay where they are and work under the stimulus of cash instead of . . . the lash." Running in a newly redrawn district in 1862, Lovejoy rarely mentioned emancipation and stressed his support of a vigorous prosecution of the war.

Lovejoy's relations with President Lincoln seem rarely to have been strained. A speech to the Emancipation League in New York City on June 12, 1862, typified his careful policy of cooperation with the President: "If he does not drive as fast as I would, he is on the right road, and it is only a question of time." That fall he asked John W. Forney to seek a letter from Lincoln endorsing Lovejoy's reelection. Forney admitted to the President that Lovejoy was "a little too extreme in some of his opinions," but asked Lincoln for a letter for Lovejoy to exhibit "to a few of your friends." Lovejoy often defended Lincoln's moral sincerity; he told William Lloyd Garrison in 1864 that the Emancipation Proclamation was "not extorted . . . by . . . outward pressure." He introduced painter Francis B. Carpenter to Lincoln to facilitate Carpenter's commemorating in oils the first reading of the Emancipation Proclamation to the Cabinet. When Lovejoy died in 1864, Lincoln described his acquaintance with the abolitionist as "quite intimate" and marked by "increasing respect and esteem, ending, with his life, in no less than affection on my part." He was, Lincoln said, "my most generous friend."

SOURCES: The only biography is Edward Magdol's *Owen Lovejoy: Abolitionist in Congress* (New Brunswick, N.J.: Rutgers University Press, 1967). David Davis's letter to Dickey is quoted in Williard L. King, *Lincoln's Manager: David Davis* (Cambridge: Harvard University Press, 1960), p. 114. Lovejoy's nomination acceptance speech (June 30, 1858) and his letter about Lincoln and Douglas (August 4, 1858) are in the Abraham Lincoln Papers, Library of Congress, as is Forney's letter asking Lincoln to endorse Lovejoy (October 21, 1862).

Luthin, Reinhard Henry (1905–1962) One of the most underrated Lincoln biographers. Reinhard H. Luthin was born in New York City; his ancestors were Union veterans from Missouri. He received a doctor's degree from Columbia University, where he was a student of Allan Nevins. He taught at Columbia and later at Duke University, Barnard College, Trinity College, and the University of Pittsburgh. He wrote his first Lincoln article in 1941 and with Harry J. Carman published *Lincoln and the Patronage* (New York: Columbia University Press) in 1943. That remarkable book paved the way for a new appreciation of Lincoln as a statesman because and not in spite of his skill and diligence as a party politician. While James G. Randall was attempting to prove that President Lincoln was great because "he was less of an intense party man than he had been in earlier days," Luthin and Carman were compiling an encyclopedic account of political appointments from the diplomatic corps to local postmasters and federal marshals. The book foreshadowed the Lincoln books of the late 1940s and 1950s which celebrated political realism; Luthin and Carman, in fact, characterized Lincoln as "a practical man, reared in the realism of the frontier."

Luthin shared the Revisionist slant of his generation in disliking the Radical Republicans. *Lincoln and the Patronage* argued that Lincoln used the patronage against the Radicals late in his administration, and Luthin's next book, *The First Lincoln Campaign* (Cambridge: Harvard University Press, 1944) downplayed the importance of antislavery sentiment in the early Republican party. It was a more conventionally Revisionist work; it stressed the importance of local economic issues, like the tariff in Pennsylvania, to the party's success, and it saw slavery as a plaything for emotional exploitation by politicians. It also shared the predilection of Luthin's first book for focusing on party and factional deals; Luthin described Lincoln's nomination as the triumph of availability. Prodigiously documented, like all of Luthin's work, it is still the best book on Lincoln's nomination and election, and in its state-by-state approach it prefigured the political analysis of historians of the 1970s.

In 1960 Luthin published *The Real Abraham Lincoln* (Englewood Cliffs, N.J.: Prentice-Hall). This large one-volume biography continued Professor Luthin's attempt, begun in *Lincoln and the Patronage,* to "shed light on the real Lincoln." Like other books written in the 1950s, it stressed Lincoln's conservatism. Unlike many works on Lincoln by academic historians, it focused considerable attention (about 10 percent of the book) on the assassination. Wisely ignoring the innuendos of Otto Eisenschiml, this section is still the best brief account of the assassination. And *The Real Abraham Lincoln*, though not as well written as Benjamin P. Thomas's *Abraham Lincoln: A Biography* (New York: Alfred A. Knopf, 1952) or Stephen B. Oates's *With Malice Toward None: The Life of Abraham Lincoln* (New York: Harper & Row, 1977), is regarded among experts as one of the best modern one-volume biographies of Lincoln. It never reached the broad audience Thomas's work did, however.

When he died, Professor Luthin was at work on a book which would have continued his lifelong interest: "A Century of Lincoln: Fact, Fiction and Folklore."

SOURCES: Arnold Gates, who knew Luthin personally, wrote a brief biographical sketch, "Dr. Reinhard Henry Luthin, 1905–1962," in *Lincoln Herald,* LXV (Spring 1963), 20–21.

See also BIOGRAPHERS.

Lyceum Address Lincoln's second published speech of substantial length. The speech was given at Springfield's early cultural institution, the Young Men's Lyceum, on January 27, 1838. The subject of Lincoln's address, "The Perpetuation of Our Political Institutions," was suggested by recent lynchings in Vicksburg and St. Louis (and perhaps by the murder of abolitionist

Reinhard Henry Luthin. (Courtesy of the Columbiana Collection, Columbia University)

Elijah Lovejoy in Alton, Illinois, on November 7, 1837). The speech was very much in the law-and-order vein. It denounced the "mobocratic spirit" apparent in these crimes as evidence of a "growing disposition to substitute the wild and furious passions, in lieu of the sober judgment of Courts." Without lamenting the particular victims of the crimes, Lincoln perceived an internal threat to the republic in the spirit which was far more dangerous than the external threat of "some transatlantic military giant" like Napoleon. The young lawyer's prescribed remedy has been much quoted: "Let reverence for the laws, be breathed by every American mother, to the lisping babe, that prattles on her lap—let it be taught in schools, in seminaries, and in colleges;—let it be written in Primmers, spelling books, and in Almanacs;—let it be preached from the pulpit, proclaimed in legislative halls, and enforced in courts of justice. And, in short, let it become the *political religion* of the nation; and let the old and the young, the rich and the poor, the grave and the gay, of all sexes and tongues, and colors and conditions, sacrifice unceasingly upon its altars."

In 1962 Edmund Wilson's *Patriotic Gore: Studies in the Literature of the American Civil War* (New York: Oxford University Press, 1962) noted Lincoln's curious concern in the speech that "men of ambition and talents" might not find satisfaction for their "ruling passion" in "supporting and maintaining an edifice that has been erected by others" in the heroic times of the American Revolution. "Towering genius," Lincoln said, "disdains a beaten path," and it would not be "unreasonable . . . to expect, that some man possessed of the loftiest genius, coupled with ambition sufficient to push it to its utmost stretch" might so crave distinction as to "have it, whether at the expense of emancipating slaves, or enslaving freedmen." Wilson suggested that "Lincoln . . . projected himself into the role against which he is warning them." But these words take on extraordinary importance only from the perspective of knowledge of Lincoln's later career. The only solid evidence of the 29-year-old Lincoln's ambition in the speech is its uncharacteristic lack of homespun language. Its somewhat inflated style is not equal to Lincoln's later speeches.

The Lyceum Address is better understood as a young lawyer's call for orderly procedures in an unruly republic and as the classic document of Lincoln's early intellectual style, before he became an impassioned political foe of slavery. "Passion has helped us," Lincoln concluded, "but can do so no more. It will in future be our enemy. Reason, cold, calculating, unimpassioned reason, must furnish all the materials for our future support and defence."

SOURCES: See George M. Fredrickson, "The Search for Order and Community," in Cullom Davis et al., eds., *The Public and the Private Lincoln* (Carbondale: Southern Illinois University Press, 1979), pp. 86–98.

Mc

McClellan, George Brinton (1826–1885) Union general and Lincoln's Democratic rival for the Presidency in 1864. McClellan was the son of a successful Philadelphia doctor. After graduating from West Point in 1846, he served on Winfield Scott's staff in the Mexican War. In 1855 he traveled to Europe to study the armies of the Continent. He became chief engineer on the Illinois Central Railroad in 1857 and met Lincoln in 1858, but he supported Stephen A. Douglas in the famous contest for the Senate that year. He became president of the eastern division of the Ohio and Mississippi Railroad.

When war broke out, McClellan was living in Cincinnati, Ohio. He gained a major general's commission and the only military victories of 1861 in a small campaign in western Virginia. On July 22 Lincoln, seeking a general to reorganize Union forces in the Department of the Potomac after their defeat at Bull Run and possibly to become Winfield Scott's successor as general-in-chief, summoned McClellan to Washington. The young general's Democratic loyalties did not bother Lincoln, who knew he must have Democrats in the armies in order to win the war. Besides, Republican Governors William Dennison and Andrew G. Curtin recommended McClellan strongly.

"By some strange operation of magic," McClellan told his wife, "I seem to have become the power of the land." Such rapid success was heady. "The people call on me to save the country," he wrote. "I must save it, and cannot respect anything that is in the way." His plans were grandiose. An army of 273,000 men (the largest army commanded by any living American general had been General Scott's 14,000 in the Mexican War) should invade Virginia from the sea, take Richmond, and move on to seize other major cities. He did not shy away from

A two-faced McClellan stands on a rickety Democratic platform supported by the devil, Jefferson Davis, Clement Vallandigham, and Fernando Wood in this Currier & Ives cartoon issued for the campaign of 1864. The ape-like figure at right was a standard Republican depiction of an Irish workingman and, because of the Irish Catholics' overwhelming preference for the Democratic party, a standard depiction as well of a Democratic voter.

THE CHICAGO PLATFORM AND CANDIDATE.

political questions; he recommended an alliance with Mexico in order to ensure the success of an attack launched from Kansas and Nebraska on Texas. Even before Lincoln called him to Washington, McClellan had issued proclamations in western Virginia promising that his army would not interfere with slavery and would put down any slave insurrections. Confident that he voiced the Commander in Chief's views, he sent copies to Lincoln. He went over Scott's head and communicated directly with the President.

McClellan worked hard, organized well, and grew in popularity among his troops. A 70,000-man army was ready in the fall, but McClellan waited. In October Lincoln informed him of political pressures to advance. McClellan felt hampered by Scott's authority. On November 1 Lincoln made McClellan general-in-chief. The general's relations with the President were awkward at best. McClellan regarded Lincoln with condescension as a "rare bird." When the President, Secretary of State William H. Seward, and Presidential secretary John Hay called on McClellan on November 13, the general was not at home. They waited. He returned and went to bed without seeing them. McClellan resented Lincoln's suggestions about strategy. The "rare bird" soon became "the original Gorilla."

What kept McClellan from action were reports, from detective Allan Pinkerton, which exaggerated the size of the enemy's army. When the general fell ill with typhoid fever in December, Lincoln began to fear the army would never move. McClellan got out of bed in mid-January, and on the 31st Lincoln issued General War Order Number One for a general movement of army and naval forces against the enemy to begin on or before February 22.

McClellan had a plan, which he was slow to reveal to Lincoln, that called for moving his troops to Urbana and working along the lower Chesapeake line to attack Richmond from the east. Lincoln wanted him to attack the Confederate army at Manassas, but he yielded to McClellan's judgment. Relations between the two men improved, but Lincoln expressed his doubts about McClellan's plan again in March. McClellan then submitted his plan to his division commanders. Lincoln abided by an 8 to 4 decision in favor of the scheme, but he ordered a reorganization of the army from 12 divisions into 4 corps without consulting the general. Lincoln also stipulated that if McClellan changed his base of operations, he must leave behind a large enough force to protect Washington.

On March 11, 1862, when McClellan had finally taken to the field, Lincoln removed him from supreme command; he thought the general could not run a campaign and control strategic movements in the rest of the country simultaneously. Confederate movements made McClellan's Urbana plan impossible, but he clung to the idea of attacking Richmond from the east and decided to move up the Peninsula, between the York and James rivers.

Misunderstandings about the size of force necessary to defend Washington poisoned relations between Lincoln and McClellan and, according to some, undermined the Peninsula campaign. McClellan's generals had agreed that 40,000 to 50,000 men were necessary to protect Washington. By his own calculations, McClellan left many more than that but only 29,000 in the immediate Washington defenses. The general knew that soldiers at other points far away—in the Shenandoah Valley, for example—effectively defended Washington. The President did not understand that idea, and McClellan, who wrote much but divulged little of his plans, did nothing to alleviate Lincoln's anxieties. The President withheld a corps of 30,000 men from the campaign. McClellan was furious. Men or no, Lincoln said, "you must act." A few days later, assured Washington was secure, Lincoln compromised and released 11,000 of the 30,000 men. McClellan wanted still more. Lincoln began to worry about "indefinite procrastination," and his tone became testy. "Is anything to be done?" he asked. McClellan began to feel that the "hounds" in Washington opposed his success.

As a battlefield commander, McClellan showed a tendency to write nervous and rambling reports on the eve of battle. He told the President and Secretary of War that defeat would be *their* fault and victory *his* achievement. He also disliked casualties. After the Battle of Fair Oaks (Seven Pines) he told his wife: "Victory has no charms for me when purchased at such cost." "Every poor fellow that is killed or wounded," he said, "almost haunts me!" While he fought the Seven Days' battles of late June, McClellan became so distraught at the "many dead and wounded comrades" that he wrote the Secretary of War: "You have done your best to sacrifice this army." The telegraph office deleted the sentence from McClellan's telegram, and Lincoln and Stanton did not see it for months. McClellan fought defensively with a somewhat defeatist attitude born of paranoia about lack of support from Washington and exaggerated claims that Confederate forces were twice as numerous as his own. (In truth, McClellan's army numbered about 115,000; the Confederate army numbered about 88,000.)

The Seven Days ended indecisively on July 1. Within the week the President visited McClellan at Harrison's Landing. The general handed Lincoln a letter recommending that the war be waged against the Confederate armies only, not against the Southern people and not against slavery.

In August McClellan withdrew the Army of the Potomac from the Peninsula under orders from General Henry W. Halleck, now general-in-chief. McClellan disliked the idea, because his army was only 25 miles from Richmond, as close as it would get to the Confederate capital until 1864. Ordered to cooperate with General John Pope's Army of Virginia near Manassas, McClellan dragged his feet and demanded assurances that he would be in command if he operated with Pope. He suggested that he could concentrate his forces to help Pope or "leave Pope to get out of his scrape" and use the Army of the Potomac to secure Washington. Lincoln was shocked by McClellan's statement about Pope. On August 30–31, 1862, Pope suffered defeat at the Second Battle of Bull Run; he was relieved and sent west. Lincoln in part blamed McClellan for Pope's failure but relied on him to make the army ready for others to lead it to victory. McClellan assumed command of all forces in the Washington area.

The Confederate invasion of Maryland in September made McClellan a field commander again. When a Union soldier found a carelessly dropped set of Robert E. Lee's orders, McClellan was in possession of vital knowledge about the unconcentrated state of Lee's forces. At Antietam (Sharpsburg) on September 17, he stopped the Confederate invasion. Lincoln was anxious for a quick follow-up which would destroy Lee's army, but McClellan did not move. The President visited him on the battlefield the first week of October to urge movement. McClellan still did not move. When he complained of needing fresh horses, the President was exasperated: "Will you pardon me for asking what the horses of your army have done since the battle of Antietam that fatigue anything?" On November 7, after the off-year elections, Lincoln replaced McClellan with Ambrose E. Burnside. The President told Francis P. Blair that General McClellan simply had the "slows."

Ironically, McClellan's overzealous report that his victory at Antietam was "complete" prompted Lincoln to issue the preliminary Emancipation Proclamation. Three days afterward, McClellan wrote his wife that he could not "make up my mind to fight for such a cursed doctrine as that of a servile insurrection." He considered the Proclamation "infamous in the extreme," but he was silent in public.

Though several Democratic groups extended invitations to him, McClellan avoided public political statements until the fall of 1863. Then he wrote to Charles J. Biddle endorsing Judge George W. Woodward for Governor of Pennsylvania. Woodward, an opponent of conscription, was widely regarded as a representative of the "peace" wing of the Democratic party. McClellan made a rare public appearance on June 15, 1864, when he delivered a dedicatory oration for a monument site at West Point. In it he stated his stanchly Unionist views. The only alternative to "suppression" of the rebellion was "destruction of our nationality." Ohio Democratic politician S. S. Cox noted that the speech "will give you the election but it does not help to the nomination." Cox had told John Hay previously that the letter endorsing Woodward was essential for the nomination, though McClellan "lost some prestige" by it. Like Cox, many Democratic leaders had assumed since late 1863 that their party would nominate McClellan for President in 1864. In July 1864 Francis P. Blair met with McClellan in New York to persuade the general to withdraw his name from consideration for the nomination in exchange for a new command in Virginia. McClellan refused. Blair's son Montgomery was Lincoln's Postmaster General, but the elder Blair denied that the President had anything to do with his mission.

McClellan felt that the original object of the war, the preservation of the Union, had been lost sight of in favor of "other issues . . . which either should be entirely secondary, or are wrong or impossible of attainment." He thought, as he said in a private letter, that Democrats who urged an armistice were "fools" who would "ruin the country." After the speech at West Point, the more radical peace wing of the party looked to another nominee, possibly Governor Horatio Seymour of New York. McClellan had too much strength, however, and he received the nomination on the first ballot on August 31, 1864.

Lincoln, who suspected that McClellan would be the nominee, had written a blind memorandum on the 23d stating his belief that, if he lost his bid for reelection (which seemed "exceedingly probable"),

> Then it will be my duty to so cooperate with the President elect, as to save the Union between the election and the inauguration; as he will have secured his election on such ground that he can not possibly save it afterwards.

Indeed, the Democratic platform, dictated by the wing of the party opposed to McClellan, declared the war a "failure" and urged "immediate efforts . . . for a cessation of hostilities, with a view to an ultimate convention of the states, or other peaceable means, to the end that . . . peace may be restored on the basis of the federal Union of the States."

Lincoln judged the platform correctly but misjudged McClellan. The general wavered only briefly in his Union sentiments. He prepared four drafts of his letter accepting the nomination, and the first discussed a suspension of hostilities for "negotiation and mutual explanations." The second draft contained similar statements, but Democratic fund-raiser August Belmont insisted that there could be no cessation of hostilities without a preceding guarantee from the South of reunion. McClellan's third draft mentioned cessation only "as soon as it is clear, or even probable, that our . . . adversaries are willing to negotiate upon the basis" of reunion. The fourth and final draft was even tougher; it was a clear and ringing defense of the idea that a vigorous prosecution of the war was the only route to reunion.

McClellan apparently thought slavery a national evil which weakened the country, but he opposed "forcible abolition" as an "object of the war or a necessary condition of peace and reunion." His first draft stated "frankly to the Southern people" that he would not "wage war for the abolition of slavery." The final letter of September 8 did not mention slavery at all.

In accordance with the custom of the day, McClellan did no campaigning, and his defeat in November was hardly attributable to any failings of his own. The principal factor was Northern battlefield successes in the South; these saved the administration from the wrath of a war-weary North. McClellan carried only Delaware, Kentucky, and New Jersey. He resigned his commission on election day.

McClellan liked President Andrew Johnson's policies much better than Lincoln's, and he even complimented Johnson in a letter in 1866. From 1878 to 1881 McClellan was Democratic Governor of New Jersey.

SOURCES: For McClellan's relationship with the Lincoln administration, see T. Harry Williams, *Lincoln and His Generals* (New York: Alfred A. Knopf, 1952). For a defense of McClellan and the best treatment of his political life see William Starr Myers, *A Study in Personality: General George Brinton McClellan* (New York: D. Appleton-Century, 1934). Charles R. Wilson's "McClellan's Changing Views on the Peace Plank of 1864," *American Historical Review*, XXXVIII (April 1933), 498–505, gives the best account of McClellan's political opinions at the time of the 1864 election. The general's memoirs, entitled *McClellan's Own Story* (New York: Charles L. Webster, 1887), contain many revealing letters.

See also COMMANDER IN CHIEF; ELECTION OF 1864; PINKERTON, ALLAN.

McClure, Alexander Kelly (1828–1909) Journalist and Pennsylvania Republican politician and organizer. McClure wrote his first letter to Lincoln on June 16, 1860, and he met Lincoln face to face only in January of the next year. However, as a delegate to the Republican National Convention of 1860, he had helped switch Pennsylvania delegates from support of Simon Cameron to Lincoln instead of William H. Seward. McClure's close ally and Pennsylvania's Republican nominee for governor, Andrew G. Curtin, thought he would surely lose the state if Seward were the nominee. McClure's first letter to Lincoln reminded the candidate of the importance of the tariff issue in the Keystone State. During the ensuing campaign, as chairman of the People's State Central Committee, McClure regularly informed Lincoln of the progress of Pennsylvania's organization for the election. McClure succeeded in establishing an organization in each of the state's 2000 electoral districts.

McClure's first visit with Lincoln, on January 2, 1861, had as its object keeping his rival Cameron out of the Cabinet. The day after the meeting Lincoln told Cameron he was withdrawing his offer of a Cabinet position, "partly" because of his interview with McClure. McClure was so opposed to Cameron that he was willing to see Pennsylvania ignored in the Cabinet selections rather than have Cameron be the choice. In the end Lincoln did appoint Cameron Secretary of War, in part because McClure had to admit that he and his political allies could not "make or sustain specific charges [of corruption against Cameron] beyond public records."

McClure was a state senator and owner of the *Franklin Repository*, the influential Republican newspaper in his hometown, Chambersburg. Philadelphia editor John W. Forney warned Lincoln that "McClure is a man of power, talent, wealth, and sagacity, and should be always so regarded." McClure was an active ally of Governor Curtin in organizing the state for war, and he felt the terrors of war keenly because Chambersburg was more than once invaded by Confederates and was burned in 1864. Alarmed at Robert E. Lee's invasion of Pennsylvania in 1863, McClure urged Lincoln to restore General George B. McClellan to command. Pennsylvanians were "paralyzed for want of confidence & leadership," McClure complained. He feared that General George G. Meade would be defeated and "revolution threatening us with anarchy" would follow. Lincoln replied simply: "Do we gain anything by opening one leak to stop another?" In August 1864 McClure begged Lincoln to exempt Franklin County from its proportion (800) of his call for troops because the local economy was terribly shaken by the ravages of war.

McClure was a delegate to the Baltimore convention which renominated Lincoln in 1864. Almost 30 years later he engaged in a bitter controversy with John G. Nicolay over Lincoln's role in replacing Hannibal Hamlin with Andrew Johnson as his running mate. McClure claimed that Lincoln personally expressed to him his wish to do so. Nicolay claimed that Lincoln was officially neutral and personally inclined toward Hamlin's retention.

The letters which McClure and Nicolay exchanged were published as an appendix to McClure's book, *Abraham Lincoln and Men of War-Times* (Philadelphia: Times Publishing, 1892). The book is an important source for the political aspects of the Lincoln administration and is especially valuable for its estimate of Lincoln's relations with Pennsylvanians like Curtin, Cameron, and Thaddeus Stevens.

SOURCES: McClure's letters to Lincoln about the tariff (June 19, 1860), about charges against Cameron (January 9, 1861), about reinstating McClellan (June 30, 1863), and about the threat of revolution without McClellan (July 1, 1863) are in the Abraham Lincoln Papers, Library of Congress, as is Forney's letter (September 24, 1864) about McClure.

McCormick v. Manny & Company In 1854 Cyrus H. McCormick sued J. H. Manny & Co., for violating a patent on his famous reaper; the trial lasted from September 20 to October 2, 1855. The Manny interests retained Lincoln, probably because they wanted "local" counsel for a case they thought would be tried in Chicago. However, the case was moved to Cincinnati, and Lincoln was not found to be useful by Manny's distinguished battery of Eastern lawyers: George Harding, Peter H. Watson, and Edwin M. Stanton. He wrote a brief which was never used, attended court, and received a fee, but he played no role in the courtroom. The court found no patent infringement.

It is without doubt true that Manny's attorneys snubbed the unknown and unneeded Lincoln, but the story that Stanton threatened to abandon the case if that Illinois "giraffe appeared in the case" rests on flimsy evidence.

SOURCES: See Benjamin P. Thomas and Harold M. Hyman, *Stanton: The Life and Times of Lincoln's Secretary of War* (New York: Alfred A. Knopf, 1962) and R. Gerald McMurtry "The Manny Reaper: Some Background Information on the Case of McCormick v Manny, 1855," *Lincoln Lore*, Number 1516 (June 1964), pp. 1–4. A manufacturer's model of the Manny reaper is on display in the Louis A. Warren Lincoln Library and Museum, Fort Wayne, Indiana.

McCulloch, Hugh (1808–1895) Comptroller of the Currency and Secretary of the Treasury in the Lincoln administration. Hugh McCulloch was born in Kennebunk, Maine, attended Bowdoin College, studied law in Boston,

Alexander Kelly McClure. (Courtesy of the Historical Society of Pennsylvania)

and moved in 1833 to Fort Wayne, Indiana. There he became the manager of the Fort Wayne branch of the Bank of the State of Indiana, a position he held from 1835 until 1856, when he became president of the parent bank in Indianapolis.

McCulloch was active in the Whig party, but he was tolerant of party opposition and his memoirs are marked by a lack of partisan fervor. Though a conservative man, he became a Republican and opposed slavery. In later years he recalled that, at the time of emancipation, "the prevailing opinion of Northern men was, that the colored people would rapidly decline in numbers, and pass away, as has been the case with the Indians; or be scattered over the country where laborers were scarce." He always thought whites were "the superior race in intelligence and energy" and inevitably "the dominant race."

McCulloch became a member of Lincoln's administration because of his financial expertise. As president of a large and sound state bank, McCulloch opposed the introduction of the national banking system in 1863, but Secretary of the Treasury Salmon P. Chase nevertheless persuaded him to become Comptroller of the Currency and oversee the establishment of the new banking system.

The circumstances of McCulloch's appointment as Secretary of the Treasury in March 1865 were complicated, but his financial expertise seems once again to have been the dominant factor. President Lincoln first offered the post to Edwin D. Morgan of New York, who refused. Lincoln next chose McCulloch. New York's Thurlow Weed claimed that he had a brief Sunday morning visit with McCulloch and pronounced him acceptable before Lincoln sent McCulloch's name to the Senate for confirmation. McCulloch had been warmly recommended by the two preceding Treasury Secretaries, Chase and William Pitt Fessenden.

McCulloch was a conservative in economic matters, but he was flexible enough to resist the truly bearish forces on Wall Street. During the war, at least, he steered a middle course. "I had before me yesterday," McCulloch wrote on March 28, 1865, "two gentlemen of distinguished reputation, as writers upon Finance:—Mr. Carey, of Philadelphia, and Mr. Hazard, of Rhode Island. The former is of the opinion that the country can only be saved from utter ruin by an increase of Paper Money; the latter argues, that unless the currency be rapidly curtailed, we shall have, in a short period, a financial collapse. My own opinion is, that both are equally in error." He apparently had free rein: "Financial matters had not been discussed at the Cabinet meetings before I became Secretary, and they were not as long as I continued in office." He could be daring; for example, he chose to buy United States bonds with Treasury money at the time of Lincoln's assassination to avert panic on Wall Street. A day after the assassination McCulloch saw the smooth transition of power to a new President as proof of "the permanence of our institutions, . . . an event that would have shaken any other country to the centre does not even stagger for a moment a Government like ours."

McCulloch played his most important role in American history as Andrew Johnson's Secretary of the Treasury. He battled Congress in an attempt to retire the greenbacks issued by the government during the Civil War. After he left the Cabinet, in March 1869, he became a partner in a London banking house with Jay Cooke, with whom he had worked closely during the Civil War. (Cooke acted as broker of government bonds, on the sale of which he took a personal commission.) McCulloch served briefly from 1884 to 1885 as President Chester A. Arthur's Treasury Secretary. He retired to "Holly Hill" in Prince George's County, Maryland, and died there in 1895.

McCulloch was not much impressed at his first meeting with Lincoln in 1861: "I was surprised that he should relate anecdotes when the Government . . . seemed to be in imminent peril." His opinion of Lincoln rose with increased contact but never quite as high as he made it appear in the memoirs he published late in life. In his private letters he was critical; he told his wife in 1864 that Lincoln was "not exactly my man for the Presidency a second time." After Lincoln was shot, McCulloch noted that his relations with President Johnson "are cordial and intimate, rather more so I think than they would have been with Mr. Lincoln."

SOURCES: McCulloch's memoirs are *Men and Measures of Half a Century* (New York: Charles Scribner's Sons, 1888). His papers are at the Lilly Library, Indiana University, Bloomington, Indiana. From that collection came these letters quoted above: ("writers upon Finance") Hugh McCulloch to D. W. Bloodgood, March 28, 1865, copy in Secretary of Treasury copybook, vol. A, page 12; ("permanence of our institutions") Hugh McCulloch to John A. Stewart, April 16, 1865, copy in Stewart and Van Dyck copybook, vol. I, pages 110–111; ("not exactly my man") Hugh McCulloch to Susan Mann McCulloch, September 25, 1864; and ("cordial and intimate") Hugh McCulloch to Susan Mann McCulloch, May 7, 1865.

Hugh McCulloch

McCullough Letter Written on December 23, 1862, to Fanny McCullough; acknowledged to be one of the greatest letters of condolence ever written. Fanny was the daughter of William McCullough, once the clerk of the McLean County Circuit Court in Bloomington, Illinois. Her father knew Abraham Lincoln and David Davis well. One of her sisters was married to William Orme, a partner of Lincoln's friend Leonard Swett and a close associate of Davis's.

William McCullough, despite poor vision and the loss of his right arm, enlisted and was elected Lieutenant Colonel of the Fourth Illinois Cavalry. On December 5, 1862, he was killed in battle in Mississippi, and rumor soon had it that grief was about to endanger his daughter's sanity. As early as December 14 Lincoln was urged, probably by Davis, to write Fanny. Davis reminded him again after the 21st that he had "promised the other day that he would." The letter Lincoln finally wrote was eloquent:

> It is with deep grief that I learn of the death of your kind and brave Father; and, especially, that it is affecting your young heart beyond what is common in such cases. In this sad world of ours, sorrow comes to all; and, to the young,

it comes with bitterest agony, because it takes them unawares. The older have learned to ever expect it. I am anxious to afford some alleviation of your present distress. Perfect relief is not possible, except with time. You can not now realize that you will ever feel better. Is not this so? And yet it is a mistake. You are sure to be happy again. To know this, which is certainly true, will make you some less miserable now. I have had experience enough to know what I say; and you need only to believe it, to feel better at once. The memory of your dear Father, instead of an agony, will yet be a sad sweet feeling in your heart, of a purer, and holier sort than you have known before.

Please present my kind regards to your afflicted mother.

Fanny recovered and later married Frank D. Orme. She died in 1920, apparently still in possession of the letter. Eventually, the letter was sold by Chicago dealer Ralph G. Newman to a private collector for $60,000, the highest price ever paid for a Lincoln letter.

SOURCES: See Carl Haverlin, *A. Lincoln's Letter to Fanny McCullough* ([Chicago]: Ralph Geoffrey Newman, Inc., 1968).

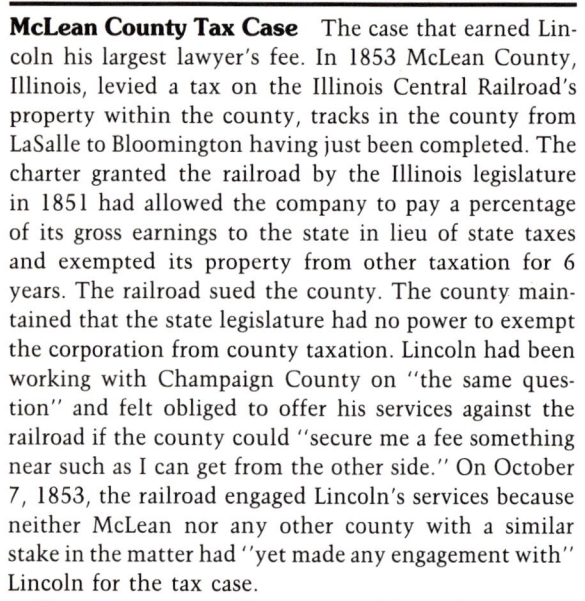

Charles Woodberry McLellan. (McLellan Lincoln Collection, The John Hay Library, Brown University)

McLean County Tax Case The case that earned Lincoln his largest lawyer's fee. In 1853 McLean County, Illinois, levied a tax on the Illinois Central Railroad's property within the county, tracks in the county from LaSalle to Bloomington having just been completed. The charter granted the railroad by the Illinois legislature in 1851 had allowed the company to pay a percentage of its gross earnings to the state in lieu of state taxes and exempted its property from other taxation for 6 years. The railroad sued the county. The county maintained that the state legislature had no power to exempt the corporation from county taxation. Lincoln had been working with Champaign County on "the same question" and felt obliged to offer his services against the railroad if the county could "secure me a fee something near such as I can get from the other side." On October 7, 1853, the railroad engaged Lincoln's services because neither McLean nor any other county with a similar stake in the matter had "yet made any engagement with" Lincoln for the tax case.

The case went quickly on appeal from the McLean County Circuit Court, where Lincoln lost, to the Illinois Supreme Court. Lincoln and James F. Joy argued that the real conflict lay between the county and the state, not the county and the railroad. They were opposed by Stephen T. Logan and John Todd Stuart, Lincoln's former law partners. The Supreme Court ruled, in the company's favor, that the state could exempt the corporation from uniform taxation and that the county therefore could not tax the railroad. The case, often called the "McLean County Tax Case," was officially described as *Illinois Central Railroad Company* v. *The County of McLean and George Parke, Sheriff and Collector.*

Lincoln asked a staggering fee of $5000 because he thought that the court's decision "was worth half a million dollars to" the railroad. Indeed, the decision may have kept the railroad from being ruined by taxation in its infancy, but the Illinois Central at first refused to pay Lincoln, for such a fee seemed unprecedentedly large for a Western lawyer. Lincoln sued the company for his fee and easily won a judgment in his favor in June 1857. The company had proved unwilling to contest the issue further in order not to have Lincoln in opposition to them as a politician or as a lawyer in future cases. Lincoln, as usual, gave half the fee to his partner, William H. Herndon, who had done research for the case. Because of confusion over the amount of Lincoln's original retainer, the company paid fees of $5050 altogether. Lincoln invested his share in land.

SOURCES: See John J. Duff, *A. Lincoln: Prairie Lawyer* (New York: Rinehart, 1960) for a brief treatment, but the best study is Robert M. Sutton, "Lincoln and the Railroads of Illinois," in O. Fritiof Ander, ed., *Lincoln Images: Augustana College Centennial Essays* (Rock Island, Ill.: Augustana College Library, 1960), pp. 41–60.

See also LAW PRACTICE; RAILROADS.

McLellan, Charles Woodberry (1836–1918) One of the "Big Five" who dominated Lincoln collecting around the turn of the century. Charles W. McLellan was the only great Confederate Lincoln collector. Born in Beverly, Massachusetts, he moved to Springfield, Illinois, in 1856; there he was a bank clerk until 1860. In later years he claimed to have been present when Lincoln received the telegram notifying him of his presidential nomination in 1860. McLellan, who was interested in the cotton brokerage business, moved South and served in the commissary department of the Confederate Army. After the war he moved to New York and entered the banking business.

In 1893 McLellan purchased a copy of William H. Herndon's biography of Lincoln. The book aroused his interest, and he began to collect Lincolniana. After his retirement in 1906, he concentrated on it heavily. His son, Hugh, aided him. He collected books, manuscripts, and prints, and he was especially noted for obtaining European works and periodical literature on Lincoln. (The latter was usually scorned by collectors in his day.) In some 20 years of collecting, McLellan amassed about 6000 items.

In 1923 John D. Rockefeller, Jr., a graduate of Brown University (1897) purchased the McLellan collection and donated it to his alma mater. The collection was housed in special rooms in the John Hay Library. Rockefeller also provided funds to add to the collection in future years. By 1948 the Brown University Lincoln collection had grown to include 22,000 items (9000 books, 3800 broadsides and leaflets, 3600 pictures and prints, and 1700 manuscripts).

The McLellan Lincoln Collection contains several famous Lincoln documents, including the so-called "Meditation upon the Divine Will," a fragment written in 1862. Brown also owns Lincoln's "To whom it may concern" letter, written for Horace Greeley's use in the summer of 1864, which stated conditions for peace as "the integrity of the whole Union, and the abandonment of slavery." Some of the earliest examples of Lincoln's handwriting, including the muster roll of "Abraham Lincoln, Capt.," in the Black Hawk War, are in the collection. Three portraits of Lincoln by artists who were his contemporaries, Elizabeth Croasdale, William Cogswell, and Peter Baumgras, as well as two large deathbed paintings by Alonzo Chappel and Alexander H. Ritchie, are the highlights of a substantial pictorial collection. The finest piece of sculpture is a Lincoln statuette by Truman H. Bartlett.

McLellan's periodical collection was sold separately to Albert H. Greenly of New York City. Greenly added to it and subsequently donated it to the William Clements Library at the University of Michigan.

SOURCES: See Edna M. Worthington, "Famous Lincoln Collections: Brown University," *Abraham Lincoln Quarterly*, I (December 1940), 210–215; Edith R. Blanchard, "The McLellan Lincoln Collection," *Books at Brown*, IV (January 1947), no pagination; and Marion E. Brown, "Abraham Lincoln, Capt.'" *Books at Brown*, XVI (1953/54), 1–7.

M

Manny Reaper Case See McCormick v. Manny & Company.

Marfan's Syndrome See Physical Characteristics.

Masters, Edgar Lee (1869–1950) Poet and Lincoln hater. Masters was born in Garrett, Kansas, but he grew up in Lincoln country: Petersburg and Lewistown, Illinois. He attended Knox College in Galesburg, Illinois, studied law in his father's office, and became an attorney in Chicago. He gave up the law for a literary career, his most famous work being the *Spoon River Anthology* (1914), which included this stirring epitaph for Ann Rutledge:

> Out of me unworthy and unknown
> The vibrations of deathless music;
> "With malice toward none, with charity for all."
> Out of me the forgiveness of millions toward millions,
> And the beneficent face of a nation
> Shining with justice and truth.
> I am Anne Rutledge who sleep beneath these weeds,
> Beloved in life of Abraham Lincoln,
> Wedded to him, not through union,
> But through separation.
> Bloom forever, O Republic,
> From the dust of my bosom!

By 1931, when he published *Lincoln: The Man* (New York: Dodd, Mead), Masters had changed his mind about Ann Rutledge and about Abraham Lincoln as well.

Edgar Lee Masters. (Courtesy of the Illinois State Historical Library)

He described Ann's importance and Lincoln's high reputation as largely mythical. Lincoln was "profoundly ashamed of the poverty of his youth" and therefore married for money and leagued himself politically with the privileged classes in the Whig party. Though "mannerless" and "unkempt," Lincoln was no hail-fellow-well-met democrat; he was "cold" and no one called him "Abe." There "was no time when he was not thinking of his career." His mind was "lazy," and he knew little of the history of his country and its institutions. He was a "slick" and "crafty" politician.

Masters relied on the recent Albert J. Beveridge biography of Lincoln and the older work by William H. Herndon for the facts to support his hostile portrait of Lincoln's personality. For his appraisal of Lincoln's Presidency, he relied on his own political prejudices. He was a Democrat and thought Thomas Jefferson was America's greatest statesman. He loathed the Republican party, war (which made "brutes of those who practice it"), and the Christian religion.

Lincoln could and should have avoided the Civil War, Masters argued, but instead invaded and conquered the South. He obliterated states' rights and with them the true Republic. Lincoln wedded religious cant to conservative politics ("Hebraic Puritanism") and ushered in the forces of industrial plutocracy, prohibition, and political corruption.

Masters's attack on Lincoln was a part of the antiwar mood of the post–World War I era and of his own assault on small-town (Spoon River) America. It was a function, too, of his nostalgic Jeffersonianism (though in this Masters was hardly consistent, living much of his life in Chicago and moving to New York City when his writing career became a success). Predictably, *Lincoln: The Man* received one of its few favorable reviews from the professional cynic H. L. Mencken (in the New York *Herald Tribune*, February 8, 1931). Lincoln "turned his back on the Jacksonian tradition and allowed himself to be carried out by the tide that was eventually to wash away the old Republic altogether and leave in its place a plutocratic oligarchy hard to distinguish from the Roman," Mencken said. Lincoln's "most memorable feat," Mencken added in praise of Masters's book, "was his appointment of the Lord God Jehova to the honorary chairmanship of the Republican National Committee." The Bill of Rights, Mencken added, "has never recovered" from Lincoln's repressive administration.

Schoolteachers, Boston booksellers, preachers, and Lincoln admirers denounced the book in dozens of articles, sermons, and letters to the editor. California Republican Congressman Joe Crail introduced a bill to ban the "obscene, lewd, lascivious, filthy, and indecent" book from the U.S. Mails. Many saw the book as another in a series of debunking biographies fashionable in the 1920s.

Lincoln: The Man was, in fact, the high tide of the debunking spirit in American biography between the World Wars. The popular Lincoln books and plays of the Depression era praised Lincoln, and predictions that this "Copperhead" biography would not damage his reputation proved true. Even Masters himself by 1944 could write an article on "Abe Lincoln's New Salem" which noted that "Lincoln's career is more magical, more dramatic, than Washington's or Jackson's." He wrote the article for, of all things, *The Rotarian* (LXXIV [February 1944], 32–33)!

Masters died penniless in a rest home outside New York City in 1950.

SOURCES: See Mark E. Neely, Jr., "Lincoln and the Hateful Poet," *Lincoln Lore*. Number 1696 (June 1979), pp. 1–4.

Matheny, James Harvey (1818–1890) Best man at Lincoln's wedding in 1842. James H. Matheny was a political associate of Lincoln's in the Whig party. He served in the convention that drafted the Illinois constitution of 1848 and voted against the clause which excluded Negroes from entering the state. Matheny did not become a Republican as early as Lincoln did, and he supported Whig presidential nominee Millard Fillmore in 1856. Lincoln apparently opposed Matheny's nomination for Congress by Anti-Nebraska forces in that year, but in 1858 he supported Matheny as a candidate likely to draw votes from both "Frémont and Fillmore men." Lincoln's "difficulty" with "Jim" in 1856 had been "on a point . . . since measurably superseded by the Dred Scott decision, and he is with us on that." In the Lincoln-Douglas Debates Douglas quoted Matheny, Lincoln's "especial confidential friend for the last twenty years," as alleging in an 1856 speech that Lincoln, Lyman Trumbull, and the "Abolitionists" conspired to send Trumbull to Congress, give the legislature to the abolitionists, and send Whig Lincoln to the Senate. Douglas cited Matheny's speech as evidence that Trumbull doublecrossed Lincoln and the Whigs and gained the Senate himself. Lincoln denied the charge.

Matheny served as an officer in the Civil War. He practiced law after the war; and in 1873 he was elected judge of Sangamon County, an office he held until his death in 1890.

SOURCES: Matheny's letter about Lincoln's wedding (to Jesse W. Weik, August 21, 1888) is in the Herndon-Weik Collection, Library of Congress. Matheny's vote on the constitution of 1848 is recorded in the Sangamon County Poll Books, Springfield Poll, March 6, 1848, Sangamon State University Archives, Springfield, Illinois.

Matson Slave Case A hearing, in 1847, for a writ of habeas corpus in behalf of Jane Bryant and her four children. Jane Bryant and her children were slaves of Robert Matson, a Kentucky planter who owned land in Coles County, Illinois. Matson brought slaves to farm the land each year but always returned after harvest; he thus avoided any claim that they were permanent residents on free soil and therefore free. Matson employed Jane's husband Anthony, a freed slave, as a permanent overseer on the Illinois farm, and when Anthony began to fear that Matson would sell Jane and his children to a plantation further south, he sought the help of local antislavery men, Hiram Rutherford and Gideon M. Ashmore, who harbored Bryant's family. Matson employed lawyer Usher F. Linder, who had the slaves confined to jail in Charleston, the Coles County seat. Ashmore and Rutherford obtained a writ of habeas corpus, and on October 16, 1847, a hearing was held before Judges Samuel H. Treat and William Wilson.

Lincoln came to Coles County and was also engaged on Matson's side. Opposing attorneys Orlando B. Ficklin and Charles H. Constable argued that the Northwest Ordinance of 1787 and the Illinois state constitution made the slaves free by virtue of their residence on free soil. Lincoln apparently argued that, following a long-accepted custom, Jane Bryant was a seasonal worker and was in no way a "resident" of the state. The judges ruled for the slaves and declared them free.

Though the anomaly of the involvement by the Great Emancipator on the side of a slaveholder has attracted wide attention over the years, the legalities involved have generally been ignored. The difference between a slave's "domicile" and "sojourn" in a free state was a commonplace distinction in American jurisprudence. Pennsylvania, for example, allowed a master a 6-month sojourn and New York a 9-month sojourn with his slaves without affecting the slaves' status. Lincoln and Linder had the law on their side but not the judges. Indeed, in 1843 the Illinois Supreme Court had affirmed a master's right of sojourn in the state with his slaves, saying that to deny it would "tend greatly to weaken, if not to destroy the common bond of union amongst us." In the 1840s, however, New York and Pennsylvania re-

James Harvey Matheny by Springfield photographer C. S. German.

Medill, Joseph Meharry

voked their sojourning laws, and other courts in other Northern states began to rule that slaves became free merely by touching free soil. Treat and Wilson were following a new trend in Northern jurisprudence—a trend which outraged the South.

SOURCES: See John J. Duff, *A. Lincoln: Prairie Lawyer* (New York: Rinehart, 1960), but the crucial distinction between "sojourn" and "domicile" is explained in Don E. Fehrenbacher's *The Dred Scott Case: Its Significance in American Law and Politics* (New York: Oxford University Press, 1978).

Medill, Joseph Meharry (1823-1899) Editor of the Chicago *Tribune*. Medill was born in Canada but moved to Ohio. After practicing law briefly, he became active in Whig journalism. He was one of the founders of Ohio's Republican party. In 1855, with Charles H. Ray, he bought a controlling interest in the Chicago *Tribune*.

Medill first heard Lincoln speak in Bloomington, Illinois, in 1856 and "took a liking" to him. He supported Lincoln for the Senate in 1858 and became alarmed at reports that some Eastern Republicans thought the Illinois party should not oppose Stephen A. Douglas's bid for reelection to the Senate. In July he forwarded to Lincoln a letter from Horace Greeley which complained of the Illinois Republicans' rejection of Douglas. Greeley's letter expressed fears that Lincoln, "if he apologises, and retreats, and defines, . . . is lost." Medill met with Norman B. Judd, Leonard Swett, and other Lincoln advisers before the Freeport debate with Douglas in August. Medill advised Lincoln to "Put a few ugly questions at Douglas," to ask him, "Do you care whether Slavery be voted up or down[?]" He urged him to ask whether, having acquiesced in the Dred Scott decision, Douglas "will . . . acquiesce in the other half of that decision when it comes to be applied to the States, by the Same court?" In other words, said Medill, "give him h–l." Medill was nothing if not bold, and he told Lincoln, who was campaigning for Republicans in Ohio in 1859, to "talk out as boldly as you please."

In 1860 Medill supported Lincoln for the presidential nomination, though he had been receptive sometime before to the movement to nominate Salmon P. Chase. He worked to turn the Ohio delegation to Lincoln's column at the Republican nominating convention. Afterward he went to New York to persuade maverick Democrat James Gordon Bennett of the New York *Herald* not to make mischief for the Republican cause.

After Lincoln's election Medill urged "a *Jackson* policy toward the Disunionists." He supported Chase for Secretary of State, and he thought there should be some Southern men in the Cabinet. He also aided Norman Judd's bid for a Cabinet post. He strongly opposed Simon Cameron's appointment. Medill became increasingly exasperated at Lincoln's Cabinet selections, at the slow pace of the war once it began, and especially at Lincoln's slowness to move against slavery. His letters became shrill: "for God's sake and your country's sake rise to the realization of our awful National peril," he told Lincoln early in 1862; Lincoln should not shape policies merely to "placate a few hundred Kentucky slave-masters."

After the Emancipation Proclamation, Medill was less critical, but he had lost most of whatever influence he ever had with Lincoln. When he traveled to Washington in May 1863 to protest the provision for the $300 commutation fee in the draft law, he tried to call on Lincoln four times but was not received. Still, he showered Lincoln with advice, urging more rapid recruitment of Negro soldiers and the identification of the administration with the Radical faction in Missouri. He strongly endorsed Lincoln's 1863 Proclamation of Amnesty and Reconstruction. He realized as early as December of that year that Lincoln could not be beaten for the Republican presidential nomination in 1864; therefore, he turned a deaf ear to the Chase boom. He still hoped that Lincoln would purge his Cabinet of its conservatives—Montgomery Blair, John P. Usher, Edward Bates, and Gideon Welles. After Lincoln's reelection, Medill commended the choice of Chase for the Supreme Court but urged the appointment of Benjamin F. Butler as Secretary of War. He supported the Thirteenth Amendment and championed higher taxation rather than more expansion of the currency to finance the war. Medill told Lincoln characteristically on January 15, 1865: "Don't be in too much hurry for Peace. Don't *coax* the rebel chiefs, but pound them a little more."

After the war Medill wrote the minority-representation clause in the Illinois constitution of 1870, urged civil service reform, and served as mayor of Chicago after the great fire of 1871. He acquired a controlling share of the stock of his beloved *Tribune* in 1874 and set the newspaper's tone of nationalism and militant expan-

Joseph Meharry Medill, circa 1891-1892. (Courtesy of the Chicago Historical Society)

Polycarp Von Schneidau photographed Lincoln with a copy of the Chicago Press and Tribune in Chicago on July 11, 1858.

sionism. He lived long enough to give hearty support to the Spanish-American War.

SOURCES: Medill's views are readily ascertainable in letters to Lincoln in the Abraham Lincoln Papers in the Library of Congress. See especially those of August 1858 ("ugly questions"), September 10, 1859 ("talk out . . . boldly"), December 18, 1860 ("a *Jackson* policy"), February 9, 1862 ("for God's sake"), May 15, 1863 (conscription), and January 15, 1865 ("Don't *coax* the rebels"). Lincoln's copy of the Greeley letter is dated July 24, 1858. The Chicago *Tribune* published *Joseph Medill: A Brief Biography and an Appreciation* in 1947.

"Meditation on the Divine Will" See PSYCHOLOGY.

Melancholia See PSYCHOLOGY.

Mentelle, Madame Victorie See LINCOLN, MARY TODD.

Merryman Decision See HABEAS CORPUS.

Meserve, Frederick Hill (1865–1962) America's first great photograph collector. Meserve was born in Boston, the son of a Civil War Union officer. After the war he lived in several states where his father served as a Congregationalist minister. He attended Colorado College and the Massachusetts Institute of Technology, and he was an executive in the textile firm of Deering, Milliken & Co. in New York City.

Meserve first became interested in old photographs in 1897, when he sought illustrations for a book about his father's Civil War experiences. He began to purchase and study photographs. In 1902 he bought the negatives which Mathew Brady, the great Civil War photographer, had been forced to give E. & H. T. Anthony and Company in settlement of his debts. Meserve purchased the negatives from Anthony Scoville and Company, the successors to the Anthony brothers. He acquired about 10,000 negatives of portraits from Lincoln's era. Seven were negatives of photographs of Lincoln himself. Meserve worked night after night to identify the portraits. Over the years he added thousands of photographs to the collection—75,000 theatrical photographs in 1918 alone.

Meserve is best known for his work with Lincoln photographs. In the course of collecting and trading he became acquainted with the "Big Five" Lincoln collectors and corresponded with Robert Todd Lincoln and Ida M. Tarbell. In 1911 he published a book of 100 Lincoln photographs, which he believed to be all the known poses. Each picture in the book was a photograph pasted to the page; 100 copies of the book sold quickly at $35 a copy.

The great reception of his privately printed work led Meserve to prepare a 28-volume set of historical photographs. He eventually included about 8000 photographs of some 6000 subjects, mostly contemporary with Lincoln. The sets, which cost about $5000 when they were new, are extremely rare. He published four supplements to the 1911 *Photographs of Abraham Lincoln* (1917, 1928, 1952, and 1955) and added what he thought were 30 new Lincoln portraits. Meserve's photographs were consulted by many famous Lincoln sculptors, including Daniel Chester French, Victor David Brenner, and Gutzon Borglum. His collection is still in private hands; it is the property of Philip B. Kunhardt, Jr., Meserve's grandson.

Like all pioneers, Meserve made errors (in identifying distinct poses and dates of sittings) which have been corrected by later students. The most notable of the students are Stefan Lorant, author of *Lincoln: A Picture Story of His Life,* revised ed. (New York: W. W. Norton, 1969) and Lloyd Ostendorf, author (with Charles Hamilton) of *Lincoln in Photographs: An Album of Every Known Pose* (Norman: University of Oklahoma Press, 1963). Nevertheless, Meserve made photographs and the art of identifying them an integral part of the world of Lincolniana.

SOURCES: See Lloyd Ostendorf, "Frederick Hill Meserve," *Lincoln Herald,* LXIV (Fall 1962), 140–146.

See also PHOTOGRAPHS.

Mexican War (1846–1848) Like most other members of the Whig party, Abraham Lincoln opposed the Mexican War. He chose the war as the subject on which he hoped "to distinguish" himself in the House of Representatives. Lincoln arrived in Washington for his first term in national office in December 1847, and on the 22d he introduced a series of resolutions that are now called "the Spot Resolutions." The resolutions asked President James K. Polk to designate the precise spot where American blood had been shed on American soil and had thereby provoked the war with Mexico. On January 3, 1848, Lincoln joined a House majority in voting to amend a resolution of thanks to General Zachary Taylor to say that his victories came "in a war unnecessarily and unconstitutionally begun by the President of the United States." Then on January 12 (the printed versions of the speech were misdated the 14th) Lincoln delivered a long speech on the Mexican War.

A peace treaty was almost at hand, but Lincoln's speech dwelled on the origins of the war. Lincoln argued that the boundary of Texas was neither the Rio Grande (where the war began) nor the Nueces, but a line between the two rivers extending just so far as Texan control extended when Texas succeeded in her revolution against Mexico in 1836. Thus the war did not begin on American soil. It was, rather, a war of conquest to gain territory. Lincoln suspected that President Polk felt that "the blood of this war, like the blood of Abel, is crying to Heaven against him."

Though he thought the war unconstitutional and unnecessary, Lincoln gave "some votes . . . of doubtful propriety" for supplies for the soldiers in the field. He thus followed the course taken by most Whigs, who criticized the war as unjust but who did not go so far as to refuse money for military appropriations. As a Westerner from a rabidly expansionist state, Lincoln did

Frederick Hill Meserve

not go as far as many Eastern Whigs in opposing territorial expansion. He wanted no territory that extended "so far South, as to enlarge and agrivate the distracting question of slavery," but he felt that some accessions of Mexican land were "a sort of necessity." He voted against a Whig no-territory resolution as early as January 3, 1848. (He was with an overwhelming 137 to 41 majority.) And he championed Zachary Taylor's "defensive line strategy," which called for United States forces to hold territory gained thus far but to cease hostilities unless further attacked by Mexican forces.

Illinois Democrats attacked Lincoln's antiwar stand vigorously, but there was no significant Whig opposition to his stand—except from Lincoln's law partner William H. Herndon, who in later years spread the myth that he warned Lincoln against committing "political suicide" by opposing a war that his patriotic Illinois constituents supported. Lincoln would have encountered significant Whig opposition at home had he gone for the no-territory scheme, as his close political ally Anson G. Henry had warned him on December 29, 1847: "If this no Territory doctrine is to be made the test of Whiggery I shall retire from all participation in the coming canvass with the firm conviction that Locofocoism [the Democratic party] will continue triumphant." Lincoln, however, steered clear of this dangerous ground, and Herndon's doubts about Lincoln's stand were not representative of Illinois Whigs in general.

Nor did Lincoln ever argue, as many antislavery Whigs did, that the war was a conspiracy to gain territory for slavery. Although he voted repeatedly for the principle of the Wilmot Proviso, which would have barred slavery from any territory acquired as a result of the Mexican War, Congressman Lincoln did "not believe with many . . . fellow citizens that this war was originated for the purpose of extending slave territory." He thought it "a war of conquest brought into existence to catch votes." He felt that President Polk started the war to distract attention from his unpopular settlement of the Oregon boundary far south of the 54°40′ line Western expansionists desired. Nor was Lincoln's opposition to the war notably internationalist in flavor. His Whig friend David Davis heard veterans report that Mexico was "not worth fighting about . . . the people never can be amalgamated with us," and Lincoln himself in later years noted that enterprising "yankees, almost instantly, discover[ed] gold in California, which had been trodden upon, and over-looked by Indians and Mexican greasers, for centuries."

Lincoln did not run for reelection to the House. In 1858 Stephen A. Douglas claimed that Lincoln's Mexican War stand made him so unpopular that he dared not run, but Lincoln explained the real reason succinctly in his 1860 autobiography written for John Locke Scripps: "This was determined upon, and declared before he went to Washington, in accordance with an understanding among whig friends, by which Col. [John J.] Hardin, and Col. [Edward D.] Baker had each previously served a single term in the same District." Whigs rotated the candidacy for the Representative from this lone Whig district in Illinois. After his single term, Lincoln retired in order to keep peace among his friends. Until recently, most historians have repeated Douglas's charge.

SOURCES: See G. S. Boritt, "A Question of Political Suicide: Lincoln's Opposition to the Mexican War," *Journal of the Illinois State Historical Society*, LXVII (February 1974), 79–100, and two articles by Mark E. Neely, Jr., "Lincoln and the Mexican War: An Argument by Analogy," *Civil War History*, XXIV (March 1978), 5–24, and "James K. Polk," in G. S. Boritt, ed., *Painful Story: Lincoln, Tennessee, and the Civil War* (Memphis, Tenn.: Memphis State University Press, 1981). Anson G. Henry's letter to Lincoln is in the Abraham Lincoln Papers, Library of Congress.

See also LINDER, USHER FERGUSON; LOGAN, STEPHEN TRIGG; TEXAS ANNEXATION.

Military Thought   See COMMANDER IN CHIEF.

Milligan Case   See HABEAS CORPUS.

Mills, Clark (1810–1883) Sculptor. Clark Mills was born in Onondaga County, New York; but he worked first in sculpture in South Carolina, where he found his first patron. Commissioned to execute an equestrian statue of Andrew Jackson in 1848, Mills pioneered in bronze casting in the United States. His Jackson (1853) was successful enough to lead to requests for copies for New Orleans (1856) and Nashville (1880). President Lincoln could see the original across the street from the Executive Mansion every day. Congress commissioned Mills to cast a statue for the Capitol dome and to execute an equestrian Washington for the Capitol. He established a studio outside Washington.

On February 11, 1865, Mills made the second and last life mask of Lincoln; he utilized an innovative method which required only a half hour from the subject and was much less painful than the process Lincoln had suffered through for sculptor Leonard W. Volk. Mills never used the mask for a sculpture, though he was planning a huge Lincoln monument when he died. After his death his son Theodore gave plaster impressions of the mask to John Hay and the Smithsonian Institution. The original cast of the mask was recently discovered and is now in the collection of Lloyd Ostendorf of Dayton, Ohio.

SOURCES: See Harold Holzer and Lloyd Ostendorf, "Sculptures of Abraham Lincoln from Life," *Antiques*, CXIII (February 1978), 382–394.

Minor Forgeries   See RUTLEDGE, ANN.

Missouri Compromise A congressional compromise that was worked out from 1819 to 1821. By it, Missouri was allowed to enter the Union as a slave state and slavery was banned in the rest of the Louisiana Purchase above the 36°30′ line. Territories south of the line were free to have slavery. Repeal of the compromise by Stephen A. Douglas's Kansas-Nebraska Act in 1854 revived

A plaster copy of Mills's life mask of Lincoln.

Abraham Lincoln's "interest in politics." The Kansas-Nebraska Act allowed the residents of those territories, which lay above the Missouri Compromise line, to choose whether to have slavery or not by "popular sovereignty." This was only the last of many attempts by Douglas to solve the problem of slavery in the territories.

For a time Douglas had advocated extending the Missouri Compromise line to the Pacific. A bill he proposed to organize Oregon Territory in 1848 "hereby revived, and declared to be in full force and binding, for the future organization of the Territories of the United States" the antislavery provision of the Missouri Compromise. When he opposed the Wilmot Proviso in 1849, Douglas praised the Missouri Compromise as a measure that had "harmonised and tranquilised the whole country" and that "had become canonised in the hearts of the American people, as a sacred thing, which no ruthless hand would ever be reckless enough to disturb." Lincoln, of course, reproached Douglas for his inconsistency, but the Little Giant had always been less interested in the principle than in the practical result of finding a speedy solution to the slavery question, which otherwise paralyzed territorial organization.

Lincoln opposed repeal of the Missouri Compromise restriction because it allowed slavery to spread to areas where it had previously been banned and thereby reversed the progress of American history toward the ideal of equality in the Declaration of Independence. He called the Missouri Compromise "a real Compromise between two parties—the north and south—in which each had yielded something it had contended for, and obtained something it desired." The North, having yielded its part already, felt betrayed now that the South was to be exempted from yielding its part. Restoring the line, Lincoln said, would "thereby reinstate the spirit of concession and compromise—that spirit which has never failed us in past perils, and which may be safely trusted for all the future."

In truth, the Missouri Compromise was always a means of "*Slavery prohibition*" during Lincoln's active political career. It was this more than its nature as a compromise that appealed to him. Lincoln had never supported *extending* the line to the Pacific to settle the problem of slavery in other territories. To oppose its extension was, of course, not to oppose its operation in the Nebraska Territory, as Lincoln frequently pointed out. But he was always more interested in its practical operation as an antislavery measure in Kansas than in its spirit of compromise. He ended his campaign against Douglas for the Senate in 1858 by saying he would settle for a restoration of the compromise line *and* of the national faith that slavery was to be tolerated where it already existed but never spread.

In the secession crisis of 1860–1861 Lincoln opposed the resurrection of the Missouri Compromise line and its extension to the Pacific. In that crisis it would have been a genuine compromise measure, for it would have caused the North to concede territory it thought forever free from the intrusion of slavery. Lincoln's devotion to the Missouri Compromise in the mid-1850s was more a sign of his antislavery convictions than of his love of Union-saving compromises.

SOURCES: See Robert W. Johannsen, *Stephen A. Douglas* (New York: Oxford University Press, 1973).

Morton, Oliver Hazard Perry Throck (1823–1877)

War Governor of Indiana. Oliver P. Morton was born in Salisbury, Wayne County, Indiana. He attended Miami University in Ohio and returned to his home state, where he became a successful lawyer. He entered politics as a Democrat but in 1854 opposed the Kansas-Nebraska Act and joined the People's party, the forerunner of the Republican party in Indiana. In 1856 he was the unsuccessful candidate for governor on the Republican ticket. Four years later Henry S. Lane displaced Morton as the Republican candidate for governor, probably because the party needed a former Whig at the head of the ticket to attract the votes of old Whigs who had moved into the Know-Nothing (American) party. Morton ran for lieutenant governor. He and Lane agreed that if the Republicans carried the legislature, Lane would go to the United States Senate and Morton would succeed him as governor. Despite his later reputation for radicalism, Morton toyed with the idea of having the party abandon the issue of slavery to advocate expansion into Mexico. Both he and Lane agreed that the nomination of William H. Seward for President, with his reputation for antislavery zeal and his record of opposition to Know-Nothing principles, would ruin the state ticket in Indiana. When Republicans carried the state, Morton became governor as planned.

Morton viewed the Old Northwest as potentially the biggest loser by secession, which he feared would isolate the interior states from coastal trade. He therefore opposed any concessions to the South. He only reluctantly sent delegates to the Washington Peace Conference early in 1861. He feared that Pennsylvania's Republicans would lead a movement to grant concessions to the South. He told Lincoln that the Pennsylvania party differed from Western Republicans because it was "largely made up of commercial and protective tariff" men who were indifferent to the party's other principles. Morton himself appointed a delegation pledged not to compromise.

Morton first met Lincoln when the President-elect stopped in Indianapolis on February 11, 1861, on his way to Washington for his inauguration. Thereafter he corresponded frequently with Lincoln. Governor Morton became, after the firing on Fort Sumter, one of the most energetic and efficient leaders of mobilization. He constantly urged on Lincoln a more vigorous prosecution of the war. Feeling that Indiana bordered the dangerously disloyal part of Kentucky (whereas lucky Ohio bordered the more loyal eastern part), Morton had no use for Lincoln's toleration of Kentucky's neutrality in the early months of the war. He badgered the administration to rush troops and arms to stave off the threat from Kentucky, but Lincoln coolly informed him that he could see no threat greater than the one before Washington.

Oliver Perry Morton

Morton, Oliver Hazard Perry Throck

Morton complained that his dispatches were "not highly honored." "If I have done anything the Government dont like charge it to me & dont let the state suffer," he pleaded, but Lincoln's policy did not change.

Morton was so energetic in supplying troops that Lincoln on November 10, 1861, expressed "some alarm lest we get more men than we can arm, provide & pay." Morton's energy often bordered on the frantic. As early as June 1862 he warned Lincoln and Secretary of War Edwin M. Stanton that secret organizations with as many as 10,000 members threatened to thwart the war effort in Indiana, and he urged "immediate, vigorous and effective steps . . . to break up these unlawful and dangerous combinations." In particular, he wanted 10,000 weapons sent to Indiana to arm a home guard militia.

On October 7, 1862, Morton told Lincoln that the war must be won within 60 days or the North would face financial collapse (as people rebelled against the flood of paper money) and foreign powers would recognize the Confederacy. He loathed "cold, professional" generals and urged Lincoln to place at the head of the armies men whose hearts were in the cause, whatever their military expertise.

When Democrats recovered control of the Indiana legislature in the 1862 elections, Morton became increasingly fearful. As the legislature met early in 1863, he told Lincoln tales of conspiracies to form a Northwest Confederacy which would offer the South peace and reunion by leaving New England out of the reconstructed United States. Democratic leaders from Pennsylvania and New York, including Governor Horatio Seymour, were in on the plot, he said. Morton urged a campaign to gain control of the Mississippi River and thereby retain the fragile loyalty of the West. Doubting the loyalty of the opposition, Morton was in no mood to cooperate with the stiffly partisan Democratic legislature. When the legislature threatened to pass a bill which would take the governor's military powers away and place them in a four-man committee, Republicans walked out, a quorum could not be formed, and the legislature adjourned. It would not meet again until 1865, when the Republicans regained a majority.

The legislature adjourned without passing necessary revenue measures, and Morton daringly proceeded to finance the state's war effort by borrowing from bankers, loyal county governments, and the War Department. He kept the funds in a safe in his office and disbursed them without going through the Democratic state treasurer and auditor. Morton was virtually the state's dictator.

Governor Morton's concern about disloyalty in his state increased. The commander of the District of Indiana, Henry Carrington, kept a close watch on the activities of allegedly disloyal groups, especially the Sons of Liberty. In August 1864 Morton apparently decided to make some arrests. When Carrington balked, he was replaced by Alvin P. Hovey, who had Harrison Dodd arrested and tried by military commission for conspiring to release prisoners of war at Camp Morton. In September others were arrested, including Lambdin P. Milligan, for treasonous activities. The trials took place in October in the midst of the heated 1864 political campaigns, about which Morton—and President Lincoln—were very worried.

Morton worked to delay the unpopular draft in his state and to get Indiana soldiers furloughed from General William T. Sherman's army to vote in the state elections in October. Sherman was not very helpful and stated flatly that any delay in the draft would cause soldiers to vote against the administration. On September 19 Lincoln wrote Sherman a letter which perfectly reflected Morton's view of the disloyalty of the opposition in Indiana:

> The State election of Indiana occurs on the 11th. of October, and the loss of it to the friends of the Government would go far towards losing the whole Union cause. The bad effect upon the November election, and especially the giving the State Government to those who will oppose the war in every possible way, are too much to risk, if it can possibly be avoided. The draft proceeds, notwithstanding its strong tendency to lose us the State. Indiana is the only important State, voting in October, whose soldiers cannot vote in the field. Any thing you can safely do to let her soldiers, or any part of them, go home and vote at the State election, will be greatly in point. They need not remain for the Presidential election, but may return to you at once. This is, in no sense, an order, but is merely intended to impress you with the importance, to the army itself, of your doing all you safely can, yourself being the judge of what you can safely do.

Sherman needed the soldiers, but Morton did obtain furloughs for sick and wounded soldiers to come home to vote.

The timing of the Sons of Liberty arrests and Morton's obvious anxiety about the election have led to charges that the Indiana treason trials were orchestrated largely for political effect. Whatever the case, Morton did stress the loyalty issue in his campaign for reelection and won in November. The treason trials resulted in death sentences for three men including Milligan, whose appeal to the Supreme Court resulted in a postwar decision that was a landmark for American civil liberties (*Ex parte Milligan*). Morton at first urged the executions be carried out, but by May 1865, after a conversation with Supreme Court Justice David Davis, he asked for commutation of the death sentences. He did not want Indiana to be the first state to have military executions of its civilians.

After Lincoln's assassination, Morton soon became critical of Andrew Johnson, and as a Senator from 1867 to his death he worked for stern Reconstruction measures. Severe paralysis and his early death ended his hopes for the Presidency.

SOURCES: There is no modern biography of Morton, but valuable information on the man is available in Kenneth M. Stampp, *Indiana Politics During the Civil War* (Indianapolis: Indiana Historical Bureau, 1949), William B. Hesseltine, *Lincoln and the War Governors* (New York: Alfred A. Knopf, 1948), and Gilbert R. Tredway, *Democratic Opposition to the Lincoln Administration in Indiana* ([Indianapolis]: Indiana Historical Bureau, 1973). Morton's letters to Lincoln about Pennsylvania's willingness to compromise (January 29, 1861), to Thomas A.

Scott urging him not to let the state suffer (September 25, 1861), to Lincoln about his "not highly honored" dispatches (September 26, 1861), to Stanton about "unlawful and dangerous combinations" (June 25, 1862), and to Lincoln about "cold, professional" generals (October 7, 1862) are in the Abraham Lincoln Papers, Library of Congress.

Mount Rushmore See BORGLUM, JOHN GUTZON DE LA MOTHE.

Mudd, Samuel Alexander (1833–1883) Maryland physician and farmer who treated John Wilkes Booth for a broken leg on the night of Lincoln's assassination. Mudd was the son of Henry Lowe Mudd, a wealthy Maryland planter and slave owner. He attended St. John's College in Frederick, Maryland, graduated from Georgetown College in the District of Columbia, and also graduated from the Baltimore Medical College (now the University of Maryland in Baltimore) in 1856. Upon his graduation his father gave him a 218-acre farm which Mudd operated with 11 slaves. He once wounded one of his disobedient slaves with a shotgun blast. In 1857 he married Sarah Frances Dyer. The Mudds were Catholics. Dr. Mudd thought secession a legal right, and he was pro-Southern during the Civil War.

John Wilkes Booth, claiming he was in the neighborhood to buy a horse, spent the night at the Mudds' house 30 miles south of Washington in November 1864. Dr. Mudd met Booth again in Washington on December 23, 1864, apparently by accident. They had a brief meeting in a hotel room with John H. Surratt. Otherwise, the Mudds claimed—and there was no conclusive proof to the contrary—that Dr. Mudd did not see Booth again until about 4 a.m., April 15, 1865, when the assassin, perhaps in false whiskers, appeared with a broken leg at the doctor's door. Mudd set Booth's leg and prepared a splint. Before Booth and his companion David E. Herold left in the afternoon, Mudd made crutches for Booth.

Detectives arrived to question Mudd on the 18th, Mudd having told his second cousin Dr. George Mudd on the 16th to contact the authorities about the two mysterious strangers. On April 24 Mudd was arrested. He was tried as a conspirator in the assassination of Abraham Lincoln. Louis J. Weichmann, a principal government witness, claimed that Mudd had conferred with Booth and John Surratt in Washington sometime in mid-January 1865. He was mistaken about the date, but the meeting did occur, and Mudd had not admitted it when interrogated before the trial. *Two* previous meetings with Booth made Mudd's claim not to have recognized Booth on April 15 unbelievable to the military commission which tried the conspirators.

At best, Mudd was an uncooperative witness. At worst, given the evidence available today, the historian might call him an accessory after the crime. Mudd did not report the Saturday (April 15) appearance of Booth and Herold at his home until Sunday. Mudd claimed that he grew suspicious only after the strangers had gone. He may have failed to report his suspicions, as his wife claimed, because he did not want to leave her alone at home with dangerous felons in the neighborhood. He lied about his second meeting with Booth, however, and that may have been for the reason that his claim not to have recognized him on April 15 would otherwise have been unbelievable. Mudd's defense attorney, General Thomas Ewing, Jr., admitted of the doctor: "His family being slaveholders, he did not like the anti-slavery measures of the Government," and the doctor had been evasive when questioned by Federal authorities. General Ewing sought to prove that Booth had not spent the night at the Mudd home in 1864.

Sentenced on June 30, 1865, to life at hard labor, Dr. Mudd was imprisoned at Fort Jefferson. The Secretary of War allowed him to communicate by mail with his wife. He did not in fact work at hard labor but served instead as nurse and steward in the prison hospital. On September 25, 1865, he attempted to escape on the United States Transport *Thomas A. Scott*. He failed and thereafter suffered more severe treatment—leg chains, confinement, and hard outdoor labor. The escape attempt coincided roughly with the arrival of black soldiers to guard Fort Jefferson's prisoners. Mudd bewailed the "degraded condition" of prisoners guarded by a "set of ignorant, prejudiced and irresponsible beings of the unbleached humanity." When President Andrew Johnson received Mrs. Mudd's letter of December 22, 1865, describing her husband's treatment, he ordered better treatment for Mudd and other conspirators at Fort Jefferson.

In 1866 Mudd hoped for release because of the Supreme Court's decision in *Ex parte Milligan*, which declared illegal the trials of civilians by military courts when civil courts were open. Mudd and his partisans judged that the President's continuing inaction was a function of his fear of reprisal from party and public opinion; they thought him personally convinced that Mudd had been unjustly convicted. An attempt to have Mudd released on a writ of habeas corpus after the Milligan decision failed. In 1867 Mudd began to work in the carpenter's shop and occupied his "time principally in making little boxes, ornamenting them with different colors and varieties of wood."

Mudd hoped that he would be called to be tried with John H. Surratt in 1867, but he was not. When the existence and contents of Booth's diary were revealed in May 1867, Mudd felt that the diary would have exonerated him at the trial.

Late in the summer of 1867 yellow fever broke out in the prison. Mudd hoped that it would mean the prisoners' removal to a different location. He took over the fort hospital in September after the post doctor died of the disease. Eventually, Mudd himself was stricken but recovered. A petition to the government, citing Dr. Mudd's services, was signed by every noncommissioned officer and soldier in the garrison.

In February 1869 Mudd was pardoned by President Andrew Johnson. He returned to Maryland to farm and practice medicine, but he did not entirely regain his old practice. He was elected to the Maryland legislature

Samuel Alexander Mudd

as a Republican in 1876. On January 10, 1883, he died of pneumonia.

Dr. Richard D. Mudd of Saginaw, Michigan, has worked for many years to clear his grandfather's name of any complicity in Booth's assassination plot. He has gained resolutions from six state legislatures declaring Mudd's innocence. In 1975 the State of Maryland, which passed one of the resolutions in 1973, purchased the Mudd home in Bryantown to be maintained as a museum.

SOURCES: There is a collection of Mudd's letters from prison in Nettie Mudd's *The Life of Dr. Samuel A. Mudd* (New York: Neale Publishing, 1906). Hal Higdon's *The Union vs. Dr. Mudd* (Chicago: Follett Publishing, 1964) is a well-written and balanced account. Higdon concludes that Mudd probably recognized Booth when he set his leg, then delayed reporting the event and lied to escape implication in the assassination plot.

Museums *See* COLLECTIONS, INSTITUTIONAL.

Music Unlike the theater, music did not figure especially prominently in Abraham Lincoln's life. Lincoln could not read music, play an instrument, or sing. Nevertheless, he still enjoyed music when performed, and he heard a great deal of it in Washington once he became President.

The most important musical incident in Lincoln's life occurred near the Antietam battlefield on October 3, 1862. As he rode in an ambulance to reach troops he was to review, Lincoln asked Ward Hill Lamon to sing one of his sad little songs. Lamon sang one of the President's melancholy favorites about the passing of time, "Twenty Years Ago," and then sang a couple of nonsense tunes to cheer him up. One of them was a tune in Negro dialect called "Picayune Butler."

This 1864 political cartoon published in New York linked the Antietam battlefield incident to the all-important soldier vote. Lincoln clutches a scotch-plaid cap—a reminder of the story that he sneaked into Washington in disguise for his inauguration in 1861.

In December a New York newspaper printed a story that Lincoln inappropriately called for a "jolly" song while on the "sanguinary" field of Antietam. Another version appeared in the London (England) *Standard* soon thereafter. By 1864 the opposition press widely circulated the story that Lincoln had called for a vulgar Negro tune while in the midst of the dead bodies that littered the Antietam battlefield. The story stood unchallenged until Francis B. Carpenter attacked it in 1867, after the fifth anniversary of the battle revived the story. It was not refuted until the publication in 1895 of Ward Hill Lamon's *Recollections of Abraham Lincoln, 1847–1865*. That book reprinted in facsimile a refutation of the story written by Lincoln for Lamon in September 1864 to give to the press; Lincoln decided ultimately not to release it for publication.

While he was President, the musical group Lincoln heard most often was the Marine Band (directed by Francis Scala), which played every Saturday afternoon in the summer on the lawn of the Executive Mansion (except in 1862 after Willie Lincoln's death and in 1863, when it played at Lafayette square opposite the White House). The piece of music he heard most often, as was the case with most Presidents, was "Hail to the Chief." Patriotic tunes and popular excerpts from operas were other Marine Band staples. Lincoln saw his first full opera, *Un Ballo in Maschera*, in New York City on February 20, 1861, on his way to his inauguration. He saw several other operas in Washington, especially after 1862, when operatic activity increased in the Capital.

As was true of his taste in poetry, Lincoln liked melancholy songs about the passage of time. After he heard singing chaplain Charles C. McCabe sing "The Battle Hymn of the Republic" at the second anniversary meeting of the United States Christian Commission on February 2, 1864, Lincoln shouted "Sing it again!" He was apparently moved to tears by it. At the third anniversary meeting on January 29, 1865, Lincoln heard Philip Phillips sing "Your Mission," was deeply moved, and requested that it be sung again. The "Marseillaise" and the "Soldiers' Chorus" from Faust were other favorites. The last music Lincoln heard was "Hail to the Chief," played when he entered Ford's Theatre on the fateful night of April 14, 1865.

Asked about Lincoln's favorite song in later years, Robert Todd Lincoln said that he did "not know that my father had any special predilection for any particular hymn, song or music. Although many years have elapsed, I think I should remember such a thing if it had been at all pronounced, but I do not."

SOURCES: Kenneth A. Bernard's *Lincoln and the Music of the Civil War* (Caldwell, Idaho: Caxton Printers, 1966) is definitive and gives many interesting glimpses of the social side of White House life. A copy of Robert Todd Lincoln's letter to Isaac L. Rose about Lincoln's taste in music (February 13, 1902) is in the Robert Todd Lincoln Papers, Illinois State Historical Library, Springfield.

N

National Lincoln Monument Association See TOMB, THE LINCOLN.

Nationalism As the savior of the Union during the Civil War, Abraham Lincoln has been considered by many to be the supreme nationalist in American history. Confederate Vice President Alexander H. Stephens said of Lincoln in 1870 that the "Union with him in sentiment rose to the sublimity of a religious mysticism." Yet there was little that was mystical about Lincoln's nationalism.

In his youth Lincoln learned affection for America's historical heroes by reading books like Mason Locke Weems's *Life of Washington*. The disappointments of his early years on the hardscrabble frontier of Indiana quickly drove him to find political solutions to the deprivations of the wilderness, and Lincoln was identified almost from the start of his public career with ambitious programs calling for national support of economic development. His early political hero was Henry Clay, whose American System embodied a nationalistic vision of a United States welded together and made strong by complementary regional economic specialization: tariff-nurtured factories in the East linked by improved transportation to Western foodstuffs and, to some degree, to Southern crops. Lincoln saw no imperative for territorial expansion in his nationalism and joined most Whigs in denouncing the Mexican War.

The political issues of the mid-1850s and 1860s provoked Lincoln's most important statements about the American nation. Like most moderate antislavery men, Lincoln saw no conflict between antislavery convictions and love of the Union. His nationalism was old-fashioned and generally identified the American nation with the principles expressed in Thomas Jefferson's Declaration of Independence. He said repeatedly that American history began with that Declaration, it was not a product of slow growth since 1607, nor did it begin with the Constitution of 1787. Lincoln told Joshua Speed in 1855 that "As a nation, we began by declaring that *'all men are created equal.'*" Though as a lawyer he knew better, as a politician his enthusiasm for the Declaration of Independence led him to speak of it as though it were a fundamental legal document like the Constitution. In denouncing the Dred Scott decision in 1858, he suggested that "If that declaration [of Independence] is not the truth, let us get the Statute book, in which we find it and tear it out!" In the calm of private reflection Lincoln knew that the principle of the Declaration "has not been made one of legal obligation" but was actually an ideal to which the nation was to aspire steadily through its history.

Some Americans thought of the nation as a Protestant country, and that idea reached a potent culmination in the mid-1850s in the growth of the nationalistic anti-Catholic and anti-immigrant Know-Nothing (American) party. Lincoln despised the party's principles (though he cooperated with its members to form an antislavery coalition which could beat the Democrats in 1860). He

215

never saw anything religiously exclusive about America. In fact, he argued in 1858 that immigrants who could point to no connection by "blood" with the men of the Revolution could gain "relation to those men" by embracing the ideal of the equality of all men expressed in the Declaration of Independence—"they have a right to claim it as though they were blood of the blood, and flesh of the flesh of the men who wrote that Declaration." Such was not the case with black men. Like Henry Clay, Lincoln was an advocate of colonization, the voluntary removal of black people from America. Colonization was rooted in the idea that America must be an all-white country.

In his Peoria speech of 1854 Lincoln had described his policy of preventing the extension of slave territory as the way to save the Union so "as to make, and to keep it, forever worthy of the saving." The Civil War severely tested the firmness of his conception of the American nation. For the most part he remained remarkably true to his early view. In the secession crisis Lincoln's speeches and writings consistently maintained his view that the essence of the American nation was the promise of equality in the Declaration of Independence and that without that promise America was not America at all. Or to put it in the political parlance of 1861, without it, the Union was not worth saving.

At Independence Hall in Philadelphia, on February 22, 1861, Lincoln asked "what great principle or idea . . . kept this Confederacy so long together. It was not the mere matter of the separation of the colonies from the mother land; but something in that Declaration giving liberty, not alone to the people of this country, but hope to the world for all future time." He seemed to value liberty more than mere national sovereignty:

> I understand a ship to be made for the carrying and preservation of the cargo, and so long as the ship can be saved, with the cargo, it should never be abandoned. This Union should likewise never be abandoned unless it fails and the probability of its preservation shall cease to exist without throwing the passengers and cargo overboard. So long, then, as it is possible that the prosperity and the liberties of the people can be preserved in the Union, it shall be my purpose at all times to preserve it.

Lincoln's First Inaugural Address was one of his longest speeches on American nationhood. Facing a serious Southern independence movement which took the Union lightly, he avoided dwelling on the origins of the Union in an earlier independence movement. As a concession to the immediate crisis, he said that the "Union is much older than the Constitution." He argued that the Union was formed in 1774 "by the Articles of Association," "matured and continued by the Declaration of Independence in 1776," and further matured by the Articles of Confederation and the Constitution. This was one of the rare occasions when Lincoln thought of some date other than 1776 as the foundation of the American nation. The address also stressed the necessity and practical advantages of Union. Unlike a married couple who could be divorced, "Physically speaking, we cannot separate," Lincoln told the Southerners. Intercourse between North and South would continue. "Can aliens make treaties easier than friends can make laws?" Lincoln asked. The "central idea of secession, is the essence of anarchy," he added, and Southern separation could lead only to further separations and chaos.

After the Emancipation Proclamation Lincoln reverted to dating American nationhood from 1776. Thus the first words of the Gettysburg Address are of crucial importance—the fathers founded the country "Four score and seven years ago"—that is, 87 years before 1863, or 1776. Despite his warnings against anarchy, Lincoln seldom interpreted the war as a simple defense of government authority. The "gigantic Rebellion" was "an effort to overthrow the principle that all men were created equal."

The Constitution never figured in Lincoln's thought as *the* fundamental American document. The Declaration of Independence held that place in his thought. Therefore, he did not hesitate to violate the Constitution, especially for the sake of saving the precious principles of the Declaration of Independence and the Union which embodied those principles. He did not do so lightly—hence his insistence on issuing the Emancipation Proclamation as a military act of the commander in chief. But faced with rebellion, he took some actions, "otherwise unconstitutional," which were necessary to save the Union. Nor was this a mere propping up of authority; the Union, for Lincoln, was the embodied experiment of republican principles. The war was "essentially a People's contest." Maintaining the Union was

> maintaining in the world, that form, and substance of government, whose leading object is, to elevate the condition of men—to lift artificial weights from all shoulders—to clear the paths of laudable pursuit for all—to afford all, an unfettered start, and a fair chance, in the race of life. Yielding to partial, and temporary departures, from necessity, this is the leading object of the government for whose existence we contend.

Lincoln's nationalism was distinctly old-fashioned; its greatest statement, the Gettysburg Address, called simply for a "new birth of freedom," that is, a rededication to the principles of the country's founders. His political thought never departed from the old Lockean universe of natural rights. In 1858 Lincoln described the territories as places where "a state of nature *does* exist." In laying the foundations of society there, he insisted "that the declaration of the equality of all men shall be kept in view, as a great fundamental principle."

SOURCES: See Mark E. Neely, Jr., "Abraham Lincoln's Nationalism Reconsidered," *Lincoln Herald*, LXXVI (Spring 1974), 12–28.

Negroes Abraham Lincoln rarely mentioned race in his correspondence and speeches until the 1850s. He made it clear that he was morally opposed to slavery as early as 1837, and his legal work brought him into contact with free Negroes seeking to escape reenslavement in the 1840s. Those contacts did not lead Lincoln to deep ruminations on race any more than his other legal work led him to study and reflect on criminology or the nature of private property.

Doubtless Henry Clay was an important early influence on Lincoln's views, but Clay's legacy was ambiguous. Clay urged gradual emancipation coupled with colonization to Africa. He refused to discuss Negro "inferiority" in categorical terms (thereby avoiding a word that Lincoln would likewise avoid, "inherent") and referred to blacks' "alleged intellectual inferiority." Clay admitted their humanity as "rational beings, like ourselves, capable of feeling, of reflection, and of judging of what naturally belongs to them as a portion of the human race." He attributed the necessity of colonization not to the depraved nature of the black man but to the universal "prejudice" of the white man—"and what man, claiming to be a statesman, will overlook or disregard the deep-seated and unconquerable prejudices of the people?" That factor, if nothing else, "would forever prevent the two races from living together in a state of cordial union."

Whatever the extent of Lincoln's knowledge of Clay's works (augmented by preparation for delivering a eulogy of Clay in 1852), his racial views in the 1850s bore a striking similarity to Clay's. His Clay eulogy is the first indication that he supported colonization, though he may well have approved of the idea for some time before. The passage of the Kansas-Nebraska Act early in 1854 caused Lincoln to reflect deeply on slavery, and that in turn caused him to do some thinking about race:

> If A. can prove, however conclusively, that he may, of right, enslave B.—why may not B. snatch the same argument, and prove equally, that he may enslave A?—
> You say A. is white, and B. is black. It is *color*, then; the lighter, having the right to enslave the darker? Take care. By this rule you are to be slave to the first man you meet, with a fairer skin than your own.
> You do not mean *color* exactly?—You mean the whites are *intellectually* the superiors of the blacks, and, therefore have the right to enslave them? Take care again. By this rule, you are to be slave to the first man you meet, with an intellect superior to your own.

Like Clay, Lincoln was never willing to grant that the Negro was "not a man"; even Southerners "felt satisfied that the creatures had mind, feeling, souls, family affections, hopes, joys, sorrows—something that made them more than *hogs* or *horses*." Yet he shrank from recommending freeing the slaves and making "them politically and socially, our equals." In his Peoria speech on October 16, 1854, he said:

> My own feelings will not admit of this; and if mine would, we well know that those of the great mass of white people will not. Whether this feeling accords with justice and sound judgment, is not the sole question, if indeed, it is any part of it. A universal feeling, whether well or ill-founded, cannot be safely disregarded. We can not, then make them equals.

Lincoln continued to dwell on the Negro's humanity as the reason the Negro could not be treated as ordinary property like hogs or horses in America's territories, but he came no closer in the 1850s to deciding the proper station of the Negro after emancipation.

After his earliest denunciations of the Kansas-Nebraska Act, Lincoln's statements on race were most often answers to race-baiting by his Democratic opponents, especially Stephen A. Douglas, who exploited those feelings "of the great mass of white people" of which Lincoln was keenly aware. Lincoln believed that thousands turned away from the Republican party in the 1856 election because of this low "demagougeism": "We were constantly charged with seeking an amalgamation of the white and black races ["amalgamation" was the pre-Civil War word for "miscegenation"]; and thousands turned from us, not believing the charge (no one believed it) but *fearing* to face it themselves." Lincoln answered this charge with the common Republican argument that there could be no amalgamation in the territories if there were no slavery there, for only slavery brought Negroes in substantial enough numbers to intermarry with whites and "amount to much in the way of mixing blood." For once, though, Lincoln agreed with Douglas—"a thousand times agreed"—that amalgamation should be prevented.

Beyond numerous expressions of the view that his humanity did not require that the Negro be allowed to intermarry with whites, the clearest statement of Lincoln's racial views came in Charleston, Illinois, on September 18, 1858, in the fourth Lincoln-Douglas Debate:

> I will say then that I am not, nor ever have been in favor of bringing about in any way the social and political equality of the white and black races,—that I am not nor ever have been in favor of making voters or jurors of negroes, nor of qualifying them to hold office, nor to intermarry with white people; and I will say in addition to this that there is a physical difference between the white and black races which I believe will forever forbid the two races living together on terms of social and political equality. And inasmuch as they cannot so live, while they do remain together there must be the position of superior and inferior, and I as much as any other man am in favor of having the superior position assigned to the white race.

This statement, by and large, endorsed the legal and constitutional racial discrimination of Illinois in the 1850s, but not entirely. Negroes, for example, could not serve as witnesses in Illinois courts; Lincoln mentioned only juror status. Negroes, in fact, could not even enter the state; in 1857, Lincoln discussed the future of Kansas Territory and admitted that a "few free colored persons may get into the free States." Of course, he was not drafting a code, and such omissions may mean little. In 1859 he criticized Israel Washburn for objecting "to the Oregon constitution because it excludes free negroes." Still, this was the maximum he would grant the opposition, and it was a far cry from the Democratic policy he characterized as an effort to "crush all sympathy" for the Negro "and cultivate and excite hatred and disgust against him." He was concerned mainly that the Negro have the right to the bread he earned by the sweat of his brow.

Lincoln was well aware that the history of the black race in the United States had not shown progress. Denouncing the Dred Scott decision in a Springfield speech

Negroes

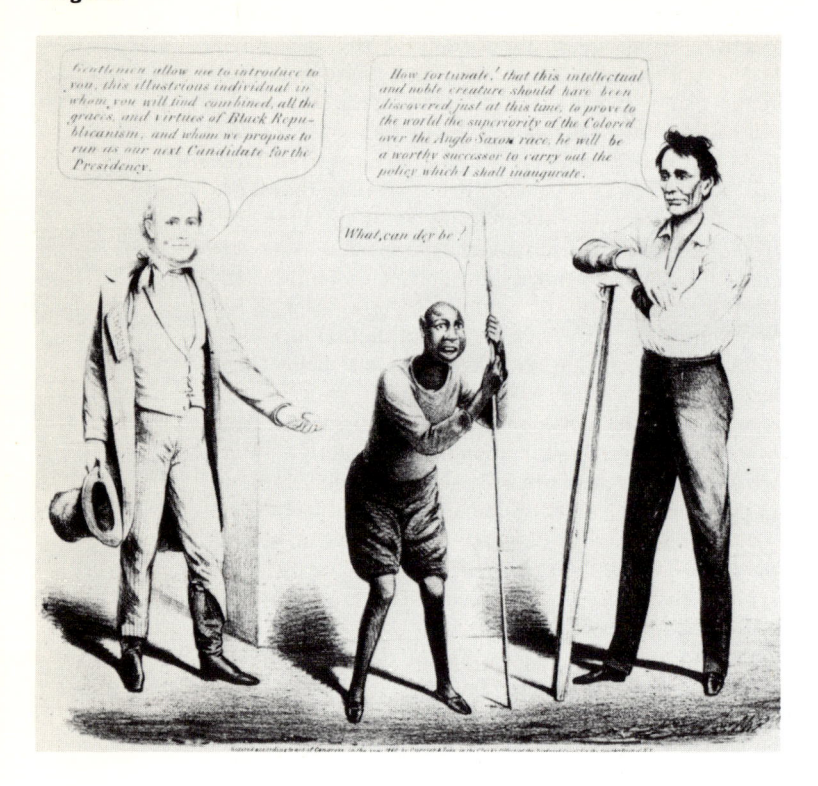

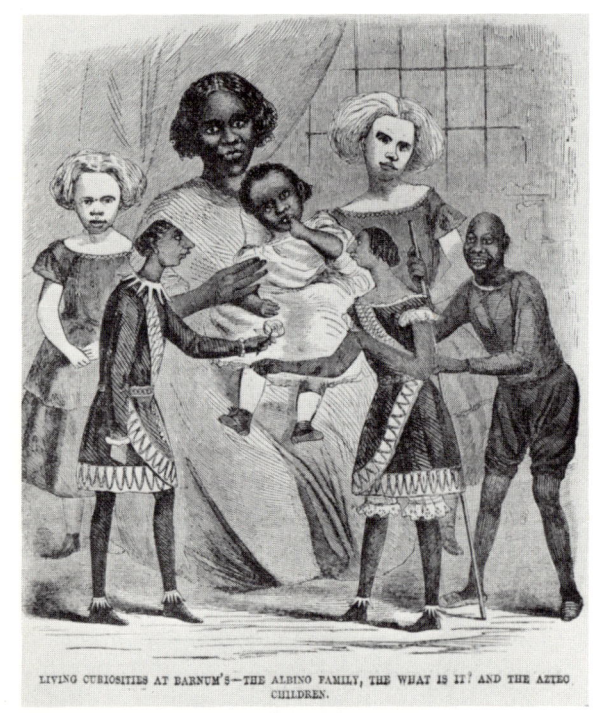

This cruel cartoon by Currier & Ives's Louis Maurer capitalized on the latest sensation at Phineas T. Barnum's museum of curiosities in New York City to add special power to what had become the standard elements in Maurer's anti-Lincoln cartoons. Horace Greeley as a lunatic reformer, Lincoln in a workingman's blouse, carrying a rail, and a black man were the staples of these cartoons, but here Maurer brilliantly makes the black man Barnum's "What Is It?"—a misshapen African pygmy from Barnum's freak show. The message was the same as in most anti-Republican cartoons and literature of the 1860 election: the Republicans really care about nothing but the Negro.

Frank Leslie's Illustrated Newspaper advertised the freaks in P. T. Barnum's Museum in December 1860. The "What Is It" was obviously copied from this picture for the cartoon entitled "An Heir to the Throne."

on June 26, 1857, he dwelled especially on the erroneous assumption in Chief Justice Roger B. Taney's opinion "that the public estimate of the black man is more favorable *now* than it was in the days of the Revolution."

> In some trifling particulars, the condition of that race has been ameliorated; but, as a whole, in this country, the change between then and now is decidedly the other way; and their ultimate destiny has never appeared so hopeless as in the last three or four years. In two of the five States—New Jersey and North Carolina—that then gave the free negro the right of voting, the right has since been taken away; and in a third—New York—it has been greatly abridged; while it has not been extended, so far as I know, to a single additional State, though the number of the States has more than doubled. . . . All the powers of earth seem rapidly combining against him. Mammon is after him; ambition follows, and philosophy follows, and the Theology of the day is fast joining the cry.

The Civil War profoundly altered what Lincoln was "in favor of bringing about" for the Negro. He instrumented immediate emancipation without compensation in the Emancipation Proclamation. According to private secretary John Hay, he had "sloughed off that idea of colonization" by July 1, 1864. Accepting Negroes as soldiers in the Union army (after January 1, 1863) guaranteed America's biracial future. One could not ask a man to fight for his country and then tell him it was not his country. The President twice recommended making voters of Negroes in Louisiana—that is, of the "very intelligent" Negroes and "those who have fought gallantly in our ranks." There can be no doubting this change, but considerable controversy rages over whether Lincoln's sincere personal views of the race changed along with the alteration in what he thought politically viable or necessary.

Lincoln's work for colonization, for example, continued through the time of the issuance of the Emancipation Proclamation, though after 1862 he never again said anything about colonization publicly. In his annual message of December 1, 1862, he repeated his assurance that he "strongly" favored colonization, but he added a careful rebuttal to one "objection urged against free colored persons remaining in the country":

> If there ever could be a proper time for mere catch arguments, that time surely is not now. In times like the present, men should utter nothing for which they would not willingly be responsible through time and in eternity. Is it true, then, that colored people can displace any more white labor, by being free, than by remaining slaves? If they stay in their old places, they jostle no white laborers; if they leave their old places, they leave them open to white laborers.

Lincoln added this argument as well:

> But it is dreaded that the freed people will swarm forth, and cover the whole land? Are they not already in the land? Will liberation make them any more numerous? Equally distributed among the whites of the whole country, and there would be but one colored to seven whites. Could the one, in any way, greatly disturb the seven? There are many communities now, having more than one free colored person, to seven whites; and this, without any apparent consciousness of evil from it.

On the other hand, less than 4 months previously, Lincoln had told a Negro delegation at the White House:

> You and we are different races. We have between us a broader difference than exists between almost any other two races. Whether it is right or wrong I need not discuss, but this physical difference is a great disadvantage to us both, as I think your race suffer very greatly, many of them by living among us, while ours suffer from your presence. In a word we suffer on each side. If this is admitted, it affords a reason at least why we should be separated.

And separation to Lincoln still meant voluntary black removal from the country.

As President, Lincoln's personal acquaintance with members of the black race increased. In Illinois, he had known William de Fleurville (or William Florville, as he called himself when Lincoln knew him), a black Haitian barber who met Lincoln in New Salem. Florville was Lincoln's barber in Springfield, and he apparently engaged Lincoln's services as attorney to help him manage his tax payments on lots he owned in Bloomington. In Washington, the White House servants were Negroes—William Slade, manager of the staff, valet, and messenger for Lincoln; Cornelia Mitchell, the cook; Peter Brown, butler and waiter; and others. For the first time in his life, however, Lincoln encountered Negroes who were not servants or menials. Abolitionist Frederick Douglass visited the White House and recalled years later that in all his interviews with Mr. Lincoln, he "was impressed with his entire freedom from popular prejudice against the colored race." And Lincoln's signing a bill to establish diplomatic ties with Haiti and Liberia brought black diplomats to Washington for the first time.

All that may have had some effect. Lincoln noticed that the "District of Columbia, and the States of Maryland and Delaware" had more Negroes than he had seen back in Illinois. "The District," he went on, "has more than one free colored to six whites; and yet, in its frequent petitions to Congress, I believe it has never presented the presence of free colored persons as one of its grievances." Despite the changes in racial policy forced by the Civil War and his increased familiarity with Negro problems, Lincoln may never have made up his mind in regard to the race—at least, not in a way for which he would "willingly be responsible

The word "miscegenation" was coined during the Civil War by Democrats critical of Republican policy on race. This 1864 cartoon, published in New York by Bromley & Co., envisioned a millennium of race-mixing if President Lincoln were reelected. Charles Sumner introduces Lincoln to a black woman, and Horace Greeley dines with another. (Library of Congress)

through time and in eternity." However, he does seem to have decided that there would long be a black presence in America. When he recommended Negro suffrage to Louisiana Governor Michael Hahn on March 13, 1864, he especially commended the case of the Negro soldiers, because they "would probably help, in some trying time to come, to keep the jewel of liberty within the family of freedom."

Because Lincoln shared many of the common racial assumptions of his era, his words proved inadequate to the modern civil rights era of the 1960s. Disappointed liberals soon began picturing him as a racist, even a "Honkie." Such terminology is anachronistic, however, and it is only fair to judge Lincoln by the standards of his own day. By those standards, he was clearly not a radical on the race question, and just as clearly a liberal.

SOURCES: Benjamin Quarles's *Lincoln and the Negro* (New York: Oxford University Press, 1962) is a balanced survey of the subject. Don E. Fehrenbacher's article, "Only His Stepchildren: Lincoln and the Negro," *Civil War History*, XX (December 1974), 293–310, embodies fresh insights, as does George M. Fredrickson's "A Man but Not a Brother: Abraham Lincoln and Racial Equality," *Journal of Southern History*, XLV (February 1975), 39–58. *They Knew Lincoln* by John E. Washington (New York: E. P. Dutton, 1942) describes Lincoln's personal contacts with Negro servants and citizens.

See also ANDREW, JOHN ALBION; BIOGRAPHERS; BROWNING, ORVILLE HICKMAN; COLONIZATION; CONSTITUTION OF THE UNITED STATES; DOUGLASS, FREDERICK; *DRED SCOTT* v. *SANDFORD*; EMANCIPATION PROCLAMATION; FRÉMONT, JOHN CHARLES; RECONSTRUCTION; SLAVERY.

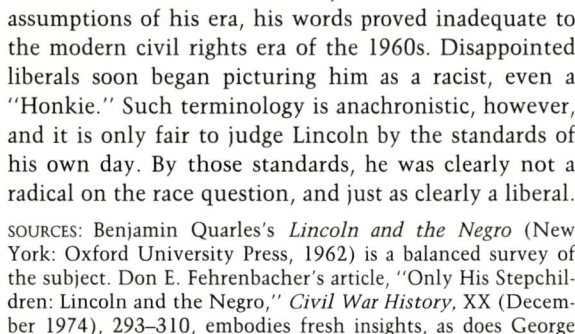

Edward Duffield Neill. (Courtesy of the Minnesota Historical Society)

Neill, Edward Duffield (1823–1893) For about a year, a secretary in Lincoln's White House. Born in Philadelphia, Neill graduated from Amherst College, attended Andover Theological Seminary, and entered the Presbyterian ministry. He moved eventually to St. Paul, Minnesota, where he was an active pastor, educator, and historian.

During the Civil War, Neill served as chaplain of the First Minnesota Volunteer Infantry and as chaplain of the United States Military Hospital in Philadelphia, established and headed by his brother John. When White House secretary William O. Stoddard suffered a prolonged illness, John G. Nicolay, who knew of Neill from having used Neill's *History of Minnesota* (1858) to prepare for negotiating an Indian treaty in that state in 1862, obtained Neill's appointment as a clerk in the Interior Department. Neill took over Stoddard's job of signing land patents for the President and also assumed Stoddard's other clerical and messenger duties in the Executive Mansion. He remained as a secretary under President Andrew Johnson. Unlike many Lincoln administration holdovers, Neill stayed on to the end of Johnson's term, in part because he believed that Johnson's conciliatory Reconstruction policy followed Lincoln's plans. He opposed Negro suffrage and the imprisonment of Jefferson Davis. Residence in the Washington area also allowed him to pursue his interest in American colonial history. He published four books before leaving in 1869 to become consul in Dublin. In 1871 he returned to Minnesota, where he founded Macalester College.

Neill greatly admired Lincoln. Though somewhat pompous himself, he appreciated Lincoln's refusal to use "great, swelling words." He never heard Lincoln speak of himself as the President. Good humor pervaded the Lincoln administration. When, after the Hampton Roads Peace Conference, Secretary of State William H. Seward sent a black servant with a gift of champagne to the Confederate commissioners aboard a steamboat, the Secretary shouted to the commissioners: "Keep the champagne, but return the negro."

Neill marveled at Lincoln's capacity for work amidst distractions and in the sultry Washington summers. The President conferred with Cabinet members even while his barber gave him a shave in his office. Neill commented on Lincoln's accessibility, as did most White House insiders. "No one," the secretary said, "was too poor to be received." Lincoln once called his office hours, Neill added, "the Beggars' Opera."

SOURCES: See Theodore C. Blegen, ed., *Abraham Lincoln's Mailbag: Two Documents by Edward D. Neill, One of Lincoln's Secretaries* (St. Paul: Minnesota Historical Society, 1964).

Nevada The focus of considerable attention in 1864, the presidential election year in which it entered the Union as a state. One way to add electoral votes to Lincoln's column was to add states to the Union which were sure to go Republican. Nevada was such a state, and Territorial Governor James W. Nye worked with Secretary of State William H. Seward to get Nevada into the Union in time to add its three electoral votes to Lincoln's total. When Lincoln estimated the election results on October 13, 1864, he figured his margin at but three electoral votes, and Nevada's additional three would surely have been a nice cushion for so close an election.

Congress moved the date of Nevada's constitutional referendum from October 11, 1864, to September 7, when the constitution was indeed ratified. But the President, despite Seward's urging, was slow to proclaim Nevada's statehood. He insisted on seeing a copy of the constitution as ratified, though he had seen a draft before the ratification. Nye sent him a copy by telegraph (it cost the government a whopping $4303.27). Lincoln still did not proclaim Nevada a state until October 31, just 8 days before the election. He received Nevada's electoral votes, but nothing in his actions indicated special anxiety that the state be admitted before election day.

In 1898 journalist Charles A. Dana, an Assistant Secretary of War in the Lincoln administration, argued that Nevada statehood was a pet project of the President's, instigated in order to gain votes for the passage of the Thirteenth Amendment in the House of Representatives. Dana, however, confused events of January 1865, when the Amendment passed the House, with the period almost a year earlier when Nevada's enabling act passed Congress.

SOURCES: See J. G. Randall and Richard N. Current, *Lincoln the President: Last Full Measure* (New York: Dodd, Mead, 1955) and Earl S. Pomeroy, "Lincoln, the Thirteenth Amend-

New Almaden Mine A giant quicksilver mine in California that became the focus of an alleged scandal in the Lincoln administration and almost caused the Republicans to lose California. The mine was the object of long-protracted legal disputes between the New Almaden Company, which operated the mine, and the Quicksilver Mining Company, an Eastern company which claimed ownership. By an 1863 Supreme Court decision, the mine appeared to be rightfully the property of the Quicksilver interests. Informed, apparently by Interior Secretary John P. Usher and Attorney General Edward Bates, that the New Almaden Company held the mine in defiance of law, Lincoln signed a writ on May 8, 1863, ordering the surrender of the mine to the United States through Lincoln's agent, his old Illinois friend Leonard Swett. In truth, still another dispute concerning title to the land on which the mine was located was pending before the Court, and the New Almaden Company had through it yet another chance to lay claim to the mine.

Swett arrived in California in July with the Quicksilver president, but the superintendent of the mine refused to surrender the property. Protests against the action poured into Washington; they warned Lincoln that miners throughout California feared that the writ betokened a government plan to take over California mines located on lands in the public domain. Those fears were hurting the Republican cause in the California gubernatorial campaign being waged at the same time. A public letter from Lincoln to Republican gubernatorial candidate Frederick Low reassured Californians that the writ had "no reference to any other mines or miners." Lincoln had suspended the writ on July 15 anyway, "simply to keep the peace." The letter calmed California opinion and probably helped make Low the governor.

The administration came under considerable suspicion of shady financial involvement in the dispute. Secretary of War Edwin M. Stanton, for example, had long been involved in the New Almaden legal dispute, and Leonard Swett seems almost certainly to have gone to California not only as the government's agent but also on retainer from the Quicksilver Mining Company. He was, as his friend David Davis said, "crazy to make money." The New Almaden interests charged that he was speculating in Quicksilver stock with his insider's information. A compromise settlement allowed the Quicksilver Company to purchase the mine from the New Almaden Company in 1863.

In March 1864, Attorney General Bates argued the government's case in a further dispute of the Quicksilver claim. He argued that the mine should revert to public ownership, but the Supreme Court ruled in favor of the Quicksilver claim.

SOURCES: The most careful work is Leonard Ascher's "Lincoln's Administration and the New Almaden Scandal," *Pacific Historical Review*, V (March 1936), 38–51, but there is essential information in Milton H. Shutes's *Lincoln and California* ([Stanford]: Stanford University Press, [1943]).

New Orleans, Louisiana Abraham Lincoln made two trips to New Orleans early in his life. In 1828 James Gentry, who owned a store near the Lincolns' farm in southern Indiana, hired Abraham, then 19 years old, to accompany his son Allen Gentry on a flatboat carrying produce to New Orleans. He guaranteed return passage on a steamboat and paid Lincoln $8 a month. Lincoln remembered one event from the trip vividly all his life. Trading "along the Sugar coast" on the Mississippi River near New Orleans, "they were attacked by seven negroes with intent to kill and rob them. They were hurt some in the melee, but succeeded in driving the negroes from the boat, and then 'cut cable' 'weighed anchor' and left." The trip was otherwise uneventful, apparently. Lincoln and Gentry sold the produce and the boat and returned to Indiana. The whole trip probably took about 2 months.

In the spring of 1831 merchant Denton Offutt hired Lincoln (recently moved to Illinois), John Hanks, and John D. Johnston as his crew to take a flatboat of produce to New Orleans from Springfield. Offutt had trouble procuring a boat and eventually hired the three to build one at Sangamo Town, near Springfield. When they had difficulty in bringing some rather wild hogs on board, Offutt hit on the idea of sewing their eyes shut. Lincoln helped him, but in their "blind condition" the hogs "could not be driven out of the . . . field they were in." The men then tied the hogs and hauled them aboard in carts. Lincoln remembered the episode as "ludicrous," but it embarrassed his son Robert, who had it suppressed from the edition of Lincoln's works edited by John G. Nicolay and John Hay.

John Hanks later made this second trip to New Orleans famous by claiming that the crew saw a mulatto girl sold at auction in New Orleans. Lincoln, Hanks recalled, was so outraged that he swore he would hit slavery and "hit it hard" if he ever got the chance. However, Lincoln noted in an 1860 autobiography that Hanks did not make the journey to New Orleans, "but having a family, and being likely to be detained from home longer than at first expected, had turned back from St. Louis." He could not possibly have witnessed the incident, and there is no reliable evidence that it occurred.

Lincoln returned by steamboat to St. Louis and from there on foot to New Salem, Illinois, where he settled. Offutt had been so impressed with the abilities of his lanky crewman that he asked Lincoln to work as a clerk for him in New Salem.

New Salem, Illinois Lincoln's home from July 1831 to April 15, 1837. James Rutledge and John M. Camron founded the town in 1829, damming the Sangamon River to provide power for a lumber and grist mill. The mill was a success, and soon Camron and Rutledge had lots surveyed and sold. Local settlers dreamed of making the Sangamon navigable by steamboats, the key to the future commercial success of the town. In the spring of 1832, the *Talisman*, a river steamer from Cincinnati, made the trip to New Salem and fueled enthusiasm for the town's future; a consequent influx of settlers took the town's population to perhaps 25 families at its peak early in 1833. There was a blacksmith, a hatter, a tanner, a wheelwright, a cooper, a tavern, stores, and doctors but no church, though religious services were conducted in private homes. Homes were log houses rather than cabins.

Denton Offutt, a frontier merchant, brought Lincoln to New Salem to act as clerk in a store he established in September 1831 and to manage the mill, which Offutt rented. The store failed in less than a year, leaving the rootless Lincoln little choice but to join the militia to fight in the Black Hawk War in April 1832. When he returned in the summer, he was "without means and out of business," as Lincoln recalled in later years. He "studied what he should do—thought of learning the black-smith trade—thought of trying to study law— rather thought he could not succeed at that without a better education." But he shared the optimism of New Salem's "boom" atmosphere and entered a partnership in a store on credit with William F. Berry. Lincoln spent his Black Hawk War pay (and went deeper into debt) in January 1833 to buy still more stock for the store. The Lincoln and Berry store, however, soon "winked out."

Lincoln had already entered the political life of the frontier town; he announced his candidacy for a seat in the state legislature on March 9, 1832, about 7 months after his arrival as a stranger in the town. Already "an avowed Clay man," Lincoln issued a platform which declared as his principal object "the improvement of Sangamo river" and eschewed the tempting project of a railroad because of the "heart appalling shock accompanying the account of its cost." Fully half of his platform announcement dealt with improving the river for navigation, which Lincoln, like most of New Salem's hopeful citizens, thought "completely practicable."

Lincoln's platform also denounced "the practice of loaning money at exorbitant rates of interest," and indebtedness would soon become a serious problem for him. By 1834 he was being sued for failure to pay his debts. Though the store had failed, he had other means of making a living. On May 7, 1833, he was appointed New Salem's postmaster even while Andrew Jackson was President, "the office being too insignificant, to make his politics an objection." The income was insignificant, too, though the job allowed him to send and receive letters free and to receive a daily newspaper free. It was illegal to send letters for others free, but Lincoln did that too. He remained in the job until the post office was removed to Petersburg on May 30, 1836. In 1833 John Calhoun appointed Lincoln deputy surveyor of Sangamon County, again despite his politics (Calhoun was an ardent Jacksonian). The job merely "procured bread, and kept soul and body together."

Politics and law would be Lincoln's avenue of success and his way of leaving New Salem. He returned too late from the war in 1832 to campaign thoroughly. But he had "rapidly made acquaintances and friends" in the town and carried his local precinct 277 to 7, though he lost the election. He ran again in 1834, with the support of both pro- and anti-Jackson men, and won. During the campaign, Springfield's John Todd Stuart, a fellow Whig candidate, encouraged Lincoln to study law. He borrowed books from Stuart's office and read them, alone, in New Salem. In 1836 he ran for the legislature and won again, this time polling the highest number of votes of all the Sangamon County candidates. Politics and exposure to greater men in the capitol at Vandalia doubtless inspired Lincoln to study for a legal career (he was officially enrolled as an attorney on March 1, 1837) and to leave New Salem (on April 15, 1837) for Springfield.

Lincoln's move was part of a general exodus from New Salem. The river was not navigable; the last attempt to get steamboat access failed in 1836. A fresh promotion of Petersburg, just 2 miles away, succeeded, and New Salem lost its post office to that town. In 1839 Petersburg became the county seat of the new Menard County, which was carved out of Sangamon County and included, of course, New Salem. The few remaining residents moved to Petersburg.

In 1906 William Randolph Hearst addressed the Old Salem Chautauqua, founded in 1897. Inspired by his visit to the site of New Salem, he bought the site for $11,000 and gave it in trust to the old settlers' organization. In 1917 Petersburg citizens founded the Old Salem Lincoln League, which began to collect information on and promote restoration of the town. A year later the Illinois legislature voted to take over the site, make it a state park, and restore the buildings. Restoration began in 1932 with modern methods of research, and the result was New Salem State Park, a popular historic site, about 20 miles northwest of Springfield.

The importance of the park as a tourist attraction may have served to inflate the importance of New Salem in treatments of Lincoln's life, at the expense especially of Vandalia. Nevertheless, the spirit of the frontier town was important, for the town's citizens never judged Lincoln a failure despite his frequent changes of occupation. Even when the sheriff seized his horse and surveying instruments for nonpayment of debts in 1834, a neighbor, James Short, bought Lincoln's personal property for $81.00 at the sheriff's sale and generously returned it to him. Though he came to the village without status or kinship ties, Lincoln quickly built a successful political career on the friendship of local residents. He had genuine affection for the town; in 1860 he recalled that 28 years earlier he had stayed in New Salem, though unemployed and penniless, because he "was anxious to remain with his friends who had treated him with so much generosity."

SOURCES: An excellent pamphlet, Geoffrey C. Ward's *Lincoln and the Right to Rise* (Springfield, Ill.: Sangamon State University, 1978), is available from the Illinois State Museum Society, Spring and Edwards Streets, Springfield, IL 62706. The fullest treatment remains Benjamin P. Thomas's lively and scholarly

Lincoln's New Salem (Springfield, Ill.: Abraham Lincoln Association, 1934).

See also ARMSTRONG, JOHN ("JACK"); BERRY, WILLIAM FRANKLIN; CLARY'S GROVE BOYS; EDUCATION; GRAHAM, WILLIAM MENTOR; OFFUTT, DENTON; RUTLEDGE, ANN.

New York *World*, Suppression of the (May 18, 1864) The only instance in which President Lincoln himself signed an order for the suppression of a newspaper.

On May 18 the New York *World* and the New York *Journal of Commerce*, both Democratic newspapers, published what purported to be a presidential proclamation calling for a day of fasting and prayer and for a draft of 400,000 men. The proclamation was an ingenious forgery written by newspapermen Joseph Howard and Francis A. Mallison. Howard imitated Lincoln's style, and the two distributed the bogus proclamation on Associated Press paper at 4 a.m., when the sharper editors were not at work. Even so, only the two papers fell for the ruse; the others in the city found fault with the handwriting. When news of the proclamation reached Washington, Secretary of State William H. Seward immediately sent out an explanation. Apparently at Seward's urging, Lincoln signed an order for the military arrest of the editors, proprietors, and publishers of the two papers on the 18th. Secretary of the Navy Gideon Welles immediately assumed that the bogus proclamation was a plot of rebels and gold speculators (the price of gold quickly rose 10 percent). Several arrests were made, but Manton Marble, editor of the *World*, could not be located. The offices of the papers were closed and occupied by soldiers.

General John A. Dix, commanding the Department of the East, conducted a speedy and thorough investigation which quickly proved that the two unfortunate Democratic newspapers were dupes of a scheme got up by Howard and Mallison to raise the price of gold. The perpetrators bought gold on Tuesday and planned to sell on Wednesday the 18th when the bogus proclamation caused the price to rise. With arrests made and confessions procured by the 21st, the War Department allowed the newspapers to resume publication.

Howard, ironically, was apparently a Republican. He remained under military arrest at Fort Lafayette until his minister, Henry Ward Beecher, asked the President to intervene. On August 23, 1864, Lincoln ordered Howard to be released.

SOURCES: Robert S. Harper gives the incident full treatment in *Lincoln and the Press* (New York: McGraw-Hill, 1951).

Newspapers "I think newspapers were had in Indiana as early as 1824 and up to 1830 when we moved to Illinois. Abe was a constant reader of them," said Lincoln's stepmother in 1865. Lincoln continued to read newspapers avidly until the Presidency so absorbed his time that he had to rely on news summaries provided by his secretaries and clippings sent to him by politicians.

The press was essentially a political institution in Lincoln's day. Almost every newspaper received direct subsidy from a political party or survived financially because a party encouraged its supporters to be subscribers. Naturally, politicians subscribed to and read newspapers regularly. One of the principal benefits of Lincoln's appointment as New Salem's postmaster in 1833 was the perquisite of receiving a newspaper free of charge. Besides, he could read the other newspapers that arrived in the mail office before the recipients picked them up. As Lincoln grew more prosperous and more deeply involved in politics, he subscribed to many newspapers. "Now are you going to take another worthless little paper?" his wife exclaimed in 1857, when Lincoln subscribed to still another short-lived frontier sheet. Like many Whigs all over the country, he read Horace Greeley's New York *Tribune*. As a Republican, he became a steady reader of the Chicago *Press and Tribune* (later, the Chicago *Tribune*).

Lincoln subsidized the party press and at one time even owned a newspaper. In 1857 he subscribed $500 to help circulate the St. Louis *Missouri Democrat* in central and southern Illinois. Two years later he purchased the presses and type to establish a German-language Republican newspaper in Illinois to be edited by Theodore Canisius. He occasionally contributed articles to the friendly *Sangamo Journal* (later, *Illinois State Journal*) in Springfield.

As President, Lincoln utilized the customary methods of controlling the press. Always an advocate of giving government advertising to politically friendly newspapers, he exercised that power as Chief Executive. However, he did allow government advertising to go to Republican newspapers which supported other potential Republican nominees in 1864. He humored the independent newspapers (like the New York *Herald*) that might say something in his behalf, but he knew that much of the partisan press was committed to the other party and "persistently garbled, and misrepresented what I have said."

President Lincoln also tolerated control of the press by extraordinary means. Military news from Washington was censored. After February 1862, the War Department rigidly regulated the Washington telegraph. Military news (and secrets) appeared in papers nevertheless, but reporters had to send such stories by mail or via the telegraph wires of New York or some city other than the capital.

The President himself had no active role in censorship, but the suspension of the privilege of the writ of habeas corpus permitted arrests of editors (like other citizens) without the preferring of charges. Lincoln himself rarely took a direct hand in muzzling the press. He revoked the military suppression of the Chicago *Times* in 1863, a little reluctantly. With less reluctance, he ordered the New York *World* suppressed in 1864 for publishing a bogus presidential proclamation. For the most part, however, the President tolerated any political abuse of the administration in the press. Samuel Medary's Columbus, Ohio, newspaper, *The Crisis*, called Lincoln a "half-witted usurper," and such views were commonly expressed in other Democratic newspapers. Lincoln expressed his view succinctly to General John M. Schofield on October 1, 1863:

> You will only arrest individuals, and suppress assemblies, or newspapers, when they may be working *palpable* injury to the Military in your charge; and, in no other case will you interfere with the expression of opinion in any form, or allow it to be interfered with violently by others. In this, you have a discretion to exercise with great caution, calmness, and forbearance.

Lincoln died in 1865 with nine old newspaper clippings in his brown leather wallet.

SOURCES: See Robert S. Harper, *Lincoln and the Press* (New York: McGraw-Hill, 1951) and Mark E. Neely, Jr., "The Contents of Lincoln's Pockets at Ford's Theatre," *Lincoln Lore*, Number 1669 (March 1977), pp. 1–4.

See also BENNETT, JAMES GORDON; BROOKS, NOAH; CHICAGO *TIMES*, SUPPRESSION OF THE; FORNEY, JOHN W.; FRANCIS, SIMEON; GREELEY, HORACE; MEDILL, JOSEPH MEHARRY; NEW YORK *WORLD*, SUPPRESSION OF THE; RAY, CHARLES HENRY; RAYMOND, HENRY JARVIS; SCRIPPS, JOHN LOCKE; WHITE, HORACE.

Nicolay, John George (1832–1901) President Lincoln's private secretary and biographer. John G. Nicolay was born in Essingen, Bavaria, but came to America with his family in 1838. In 1848 he went to work as a printer's devil for the Pittsfield (Illinois) *Free Press*, a Whig newspaper; eventually he became the paper's owner. He sold the paper in 1856, and in 1857 he became a clerk in the office of his friend Ozias M. Hatch, the Illinois Secretary of State. Both men were then firm Republicans. As Lincoln was an "assiduous student of election tables," which were kept by the Secretary of State, Nicolay met Lincoln in the secretary's office.

In 1858 Nicolay compiled a campaign pamphlet, *The Political Record of Stephen A. Douglas*. He attended the Chicago convention which nominated Lincoln for the Presidency as a correspondent for the *Missouri Democrat* and hoped afterward to write a campaign biography of Lincoln. The job fell to others, but shortly after the nomination Lincoln made him his secretary, a post he would hold until Lincoln's assassination.

Nicolay was the perfect secretary—loyal, quiet, a listener rather than a talker, a man who never said anything that was quotable (except in the private letters he wrote to his fiancee, Therena Bates). While living in Pittsfield, he had met and formed a friendship with John Hay, who was attending a private academy there. After Lincoln's election, when the mail increased greatly over the preelection rate of 50 letters per day, he asked Hay to help. Both men accompanied Lincoln on his inaugural journey, and both served as his secretaries in Washington.

Nicolay took occasional notes on conversations with the President, and Hay kept a diary; it is likely that they planned to write a book on Lincoln from the start. Nicolay (Lincoln called him that) and Hay screened most of Lincoln's many White House visitors, sorted much of his mail, prepared a daily news summary, and occasionally wrote letters for Lincoln. They lived in the White House but took their meals in town. The life was grueling and lonely, and Nicolay's spirits rose and fell with the fortunes of the administration. Nicolay agreed with Lincoln in 1861 that General John C. Frémont should be dismissed, he thought England's attitude toward America contemptible, and he thought Simon Cameron incompetent for his duties as Secretary of War.

In the summer of 1862 the President sent Nicolay to Minnesota to help Indian Commissioner William P. Dole settle a treaty with Chief Hole-in-the-Day. That was the first of several duties Nicolay performed which went well outside the secretarial realm. The next summer he went to Colorado Territory to negotiate with the Utes.

In his public demeanor Nicolay was reserved and, when necessary, a little forbidding. Privately, his letters sparkled with wit and irony. He and Hay referred to Lincoln as "the Tycoon," and Nicolay expressed his dismay with General George B. McClellan's performance by saying it was "rather a good thing to be a major general—one can take things so leisurely."

Nicolay warned Lincoln of the Pomeroy Circular and referred to Salmon P. Chase's appointees as the "Treasury rats." He admired the President's "magnanimity" in forgiving Chase's ambition to displace Lincoln in the White House and appointing Chase to the Supreme Court in 1864. In fact, he greatly admired Lincoln in almost all respects and carefully protected the President's reputation. He fretted when a ghost-written manuscript might be auctioned as a genuine Lincoln document at the Sanitary Fair in New York in 1864, and he personally scotched the rumor that Mrs. Lincoln's sister, Mrs. J. Todd White, carried contraband quinine to the Confederacy with a pass signed by Lincoln. Lincoln sent Nicolay to the Baltimore convention in 1864 to watch over his renomination; later, the President trusted his secretary to go to New York City to deal with the controversial appointments in the Custom House and with the testy Thurlow Weed.

Mrs. Lincoln did not like Nicolay, and the strain of the job as well as the prospect of Union victory led him to seek a foreign appointment. He had been studying French while in the White House. On March 11, 1865, he was appointed consul resident in Paris. He remained in Washington to finish some work. He was on a cruise when Lincoln was assassinated and returned to get the martyred President's papers in order.

Nicolay remained in Paris until President Ulysses S. Grant removed him in 1869. He did some free-lance writing, tried newspaper work again, and applied for the consulship in Bogotá in 1872. (He argued that Grant needed to please Lincoln's old friends with that appointment, for central Illinois was fast turning Liberal Republican in sentiment.) He did not get the Bogotá post, but he was appointed Marshal of the United States Supreme Court.

The job was perfect. It brought him to Washington, where the sources for a book on the Lincoln administration were available, and it was sinecure enough to give

John George Nicolay

him plenty of time for research. Soon he was badgering Robert Todd Lincoln to entrust his father's papers to him so that he and Hay could write a proper biography. By 1874 Robert had done so, and within a year Nicolay and Hay were at work on the monumental history which would preoccupy them for the next decade and a half.

Nicolay's infant son died in 1877. His wife died in 1885. Through it all Nicolay labored, with failing eyesight and poor health, on the gigantic manuscript. He and Hay came to distrust interviews and sought documents for everything. Nicolay jealously guarded their territory and more than once discouraged Robert from releasing any of the Presidential papers for publication by others. In 1885 *The Century Magazine* offered the coauthors $50,000 to serialize their work, as well as royalties when the work was published in book form. They accepted, and from October 1886 to January 1890, about half the book appeared in serial form. *Abraham Lincoln: A History* was published in 1890 in 10 substantial volumes. For so large a work it was quite a success; it sold 5000 copies in a short time.

Nicolay and Hay carefully wrote, rewrote, and checked sources. No one knows which man wrote which part. Of course, it was "court history" in a sense. Robert T. Lincoln approved the drafts of the manuscript, and the authors made what changes he demanded (especially by way of making Lincoln's parents and frontier youth appear more respectable). They vilified Lincoln's opponents, from Jefferson Davis to McClellan and Chase. Nicolay was particularly zealous in his detestation of the Confederates. He thought Robert E. Lee should have been shot. Hay thought so too but realized that "The war has gone by" and that the authors must muffle some of their denunciations of Lincoln's enemies. The *Century* editor, Richard Watson Gilder, also tried to cool their partisanship and begged for more details of Lincoln's personality and everyday life. On the whole, however, the authors ignored his advice and stuck to the high road of political and administrative history. For all its bias, the book was one of the greatest historical products of its era and is still a necessary source for Lincoln biographers.

In 1894 Nicolay and Hay produced a two-volume set of Lincoln's works which included many previously unpublished manuscripts. After that, Hay was through with history, but Nicolay was at work on a one-volume condensation of the *History* when he died.

SOURCES: Helen Nicolay, John's daughter, wrote a useful biography, *Lincoln's Secretary: A Biography of John G. Nicolay* (New York: Longmans, Green, 1949). On the writing of the monumental *Abraham Lincoln: A History* see Benjamin P. Thomas, *Portrait for Posterity: Lincoln and His Biographers* (New Brunswick, N.J.: Rutgers University Press, 1947).

See also BIOGRAPHERS; EXECUTIVE MANSION; HAY, JOHN MILTON.

O

Joseph Benjamin Oakleaf

Oakleaf, Joseph Benjamin (1858–1930) One of the "Big Five," who dominated the field of Lincoln collecting at the turn of the century. He became interested in collecting Lincolniana when he read the serialized version of John G. Nicolay and John Hay's *Abraham Lincoln: A History* in *Century Magazine.*

Born in Moline, Illinois, Oakleaf was the son of Swedish immigrants. He became a lawyer in 1886. As city attorney in the 1890s, he established a good reputation when he forced railroads to bring their crossings down to grade level in the town. He was a Lutheran in religion and a Republican in politics.

Oakleaf delivered a number of addresses on Lincoln, generally celebratory in nature and shallow in content. His greatest contribution was his *Lincoln Bibliography* (Cedar Rapids, Iowa: Torch Press, 1925), which listed some 1576 titles not in Daniel Fish's 1906 bibliography.

As a collector, Oakleaf began by attempting to obtain the books referred to in Nicolay and Hay's footnotes. He collected mostly printed materials and refused to pay high prices for rare items; he learned quickly that with patience he could often get an item later for little or nothing.

In 1942 Indiana University purchased the Oakleaf collection. It is now the basis of the Lincoln collection at the Lilly Library, the rare book and manuscript library at the University. Remarkably, it has never been fully catalogued.

SOURCES: See J. L. McCorison, Jr., "The Great Lincoln Collections and What Became of Them," *Lincoln Herald*, L–LI (December 1948–February 1949), 2–16, 36.

Offutt, Denton (ca. 1803/1807–ca. 1860) The man who brought Abraham Lincoln to New Salem. In 1831 Offutt, "an entire stranger," hired Lincoln, John D. Johnston, and John Hanks to help navigate a flatboat loaded with produce from Beardstown, Illinois, to New Orleans. Offutt had trouble procuring a boat and in March hired the three for $12 a month each to build a boat at Sangamo Town. They started the voyage, but the boat hung up on a mill dam near New Salem. Lincoln freed the boat in an ingenious manner, and Offutt "conceived a liking" for him. Offutt also conceived a liking for New Salem. He thought that the new town would be accessible by steamboat up the Sangamon River, if improved, and it therefore appeared likely to have commercial possibilities.

Offutt "contracted with" Lincoln "to act as clerk . . . on his return from New-Orleans, in charge of a store and Mill at New-Salem." Lincoln returned to the town in July 1831; Offutt came later with supplies procured in St. Louis; and the store opened in September. Offutt boasted so of Lincoln's cleverness and strength that the local wrestling champion, "Jack" Armstrong, challenged Lincoln to a match. Offutt wagered with Armstrong's partisan William Clary on the outcome. The match was a draw, but it gave the Clary's Grove boys, rough frontiersmen who lived near New Salem, respect for this new man in town.

By the spring of 1832, Offutt's store was failing, and Lincoln decided to join the militia for the Black Hawk War. Offutt closed the store, gave up the mill, moved from New Salem, and vanished from Lincoln's life to reappear briefly in 1861, his "property . . . lost," seeking an office in Louisiana from President-elect Lincoln. There is no evidence of his appointment.

New Salem schoolteacher William Mentor Graham remembered Offutt as "an unsteady, noisy, fussy and rather brutal man, wild and unprovidential." But he was, in the words of Benjamin P. Thomas, "the discoverer of Lincoln."

SOURCES: See Benjamin P. Thomas, *Lincoln's New Salem* (Springfield, Ill.: Abraham Lincoln Association, 1934). The letter asking for an office is printed in Roy P. Basler, *President Lincoln Helps His Old Friends* (Springfield, Ill.: Abraham Lincoln Association, 1977). Graham's letter is reproduced in Kunigunde Duncan and D. F. Nickols, *Mentor Graham: The Man Who Taught Lincoln* (Chicago: University of Chicago Press, 1944).

See also CLARY'S GROVE BOYS; NEW SALEM, ILLINOIS; NEW ORLEANS, LOUISIANA.

Oglesby, Richard James (1824–1899) Personal friend and political associate of Lincoln. Oglesby was born in Kentucky and settled eventually in Decatur, Illinois, where he practiced law. He was first a Whig and then a Republican in politics. In 1858 he ran for Congress and lost, but he ran well in a customarily Democratic district. In 1860 he devised the idea to make Lincoln the "Rail Splitter" candidate for the Presidency. He was elected to the state senate the same year but resigned when war broke out to serve as colonel of the 8th Illinois Volunteers. After fighting at Fort Donelson, he was promoted to brigadier general by Lincoln. On October 3, 1862, he was wounded at the Battle of Corinth, and President Lincoln solicitously asked General Ulysses S. Grant about the extent of the wounds to his "intimate personal friend." Oglesby returned to the army and became a major general, only to resign in May 1864 to run for Governor of Illinois.

In the preceding February, Ozias M. Hatch had asked Lincoln to intervene to prevent an ugly contest between Oglesby and Jesse K. Dubois for the Republican gubernatorial nomination. Both men were friends of Lincoln's, and the President apparently refused to intervene. Oglesby gained the nomination and won the election. After his victory he told Lincoln that the people of Illinois broadly endorsed the President but thought that "your only fault seems to have been a somewhat too much indulging in clemency to traitors and their confederates under your power." Oglesby explained that "there is manifestly a verry general disposition amongst the people to compel the rebels to submit humbly to the Laws without a single indulgence."

Oglesby became an ardent supporter of Reconstruction; he believed that the only cure for the nation's ills lay in "the ascendancy and the control" of the South by "Southern loyal and Union men." He was elected Governor two more times and served one term as Senator from Illinois. He was president of the National Lincoln Monument Association and gave the dedicatory address at the unveiling in Springfield on October 15, 1874.

SOURCES: There is no biography of Oglesby. The letter advising Lincoln against too much clemency (November 20, 1864) is in the Abraham Lincoln Papers, Library of Congress. The letter about Reconstruction (to H. B. Moore, March 4, 1867) is in the Louis A. Warren Lincoln Library and Museum, Fort Wayne, Indiana. There is a substantial collection of Oglesby's papers at the Illinois State Historical Library, Springfield.

See also "RAIL SPLITTER."

O'Laughlin (or O'Laughlen), Michael (?–1867) A coconspirator with John Wilkes Booth in the plot to kidnap President Lincoln. In his youth O'Laughlin was a Baltimore neighbor and schoolmate of Booth's. He served in the Confederate army until about the time of the Battle of Antietam, when he returned home, probably because of poor health. He entered the produce and feed business with his brother, and on June 16, 1863, he took the oath of allegiance. His brother sold the business in the fall of 1863, but Michael remained in Washington to receive orders supplied by his brother in Baltimore until March 1865. He then returned to Baltimore and boarded with his brother-in-law, P. H. Maulsby.

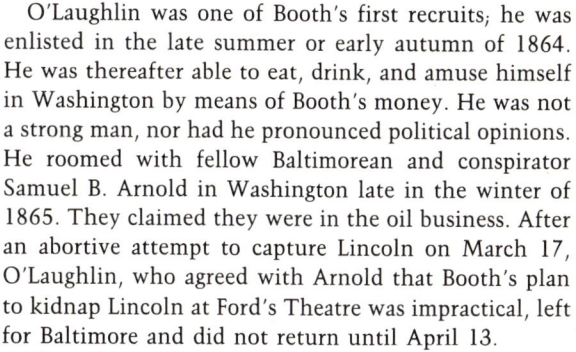

O'Laughlin was one of Booth's first recruits; he was enlisted in the late summer or early autumn of 1864. He was thereafter able to eat, drink, and amuse himself in Washington by means of Booth's money. He was not a strong man, nor had he pronounced political opinions. He roomed with fellow Baltimorean and conspirator Samuel B. Arnold in Washington late in the winter of 1865. They claimed they were in the oil business. After an abortive attempt to capture Lincoln on March 17, O'Laughlin, who agreed with Arnold that Booth's plan to kidnap Lincoln at Ford's Theatre was impractical, left for Baltimore and did not return until April 13.

That O'Laughlin returned at that ominous time was completely fortuitous. He went to Washington with three companions to view the illumination celebrating Union victory. He attempted to see Booth, but apparently only to collect money he had lent the actor; Booth had by then spent most of his savings on the plot. O'Laughlin and his companions were to return to Baltimore on the 14th, but one of the group persuaded the others to stay over so he could visit a woman. On the night of the assassination, O'Laughlin, dressed in a purple and green plaid suit, drank 10 ales with his friends and was very merry. He returned to Baltimore the next day, fled his residence out of consideration for his mother, and on Monday surrendered voluntarily to the authorities.

Ben: Perley Poore described O'Laughlin as "a rather small, delicate-looking man, with rather pleasing features, uneasy black eyes, bushy black hair, a heavy black mustache and imperial, and a most anxious expression of countenance, shaded by a sad, remorseful look." His capable lawyer, Walter S. Cox, proved that he had an ironclad alibi for the evening of the assassination and that he was not, as charged, lying in wait to murder General Ulysses S. Grant. However, the prosecution refused to believe that a plot to kidnap rather than murder the President ever existed. The principal evidence against him, Samuel Arnold's oral confession, gave him connection enough with the conspirators for the military

Michael O'Laughlin

Richard J. Oglesby. (Courtesy of the Lloyd Ostendorf Collection)

commission to sentence him to life imprisonment at hard labor.

With Arnold, Edman Spangler, and Samuel A. Mudd, O'Laughlin was sent to Fort Jefferson. There he died on September 23, 1867, the victim of a yellow fever epidemic that swept the prison.

SOURCES: See Benn Pitman, *The Assassination of President Lincoln and the Trial of the Conspirators* (Cincinnati, Ohio: Moore, Wilstach & Baldwin, 1865), and Ben: Perley Poore, *The Conspiracy Trial for the Murder of The President*, 3 vols. (Boston: J. E. Tilton, 1865).

See also ASSASSINATION; TRIAL OF THE ASSASSINS.

Old Clothes Scandal *See* KECKLEY, ELIZABETH.

Old State Capitol *See* SPRINGFIELD.

Oldroyd, Osborn Hamilton Ingham (1842–1930) Lincoln collector. Osborn H. I. Oldroyd was born in Ohio (his initials spell the state's name). While running a newstand in Mount Vernon, Ohio, in 1860, he read a campaign biography of Lincoln which sparked his interest. He enlisted in the Twentieth Ohio Infantry in 1861, saw considerable action, was wounded, and was honorably discharged in 1865. After the war he served as assistant steward of the National Soldiers Home in Dayton and for 8 years as steward at the Dayton insane asylum. He was already collecting items having to do with Abraham Lincoln. He married a woman from Springfield, Illinois, and in 1883 rented Lincoln's home, where he lived for 10 years. Robert Todd Lincoln gave the home to the state of Illinois in 1887, but Oldroyd remained as custodian.

In 1893 he moved with his now large Lincoln collection to Washington, where he lived in the Petersen house, where Lincoln died. He displayed his collection there. Automobile magnate Henry Ford attempted to buy Oldroyd's collection for $50,000, a move which prompted Republican Representative Henry R. Rathbone, son of Lincoln's guest in the box at Ford's Theatre on the night of the assassination, to sponsor a bill in the United States Congress to match Ford's offer. The United States government purchased the collection for $50,000 in 1926. Oldroyd became curator emeritus of the collection.

In 1932 money was appropriated to convert Ford's Theatre into a museum to hold Oldroyd's collection, which contained Lincoln letters, furniture from the Lincoln home and from his law office, cartoons, books which Lincoln owned as well as books about Lincoln, a woolen shawl which belonged to Lincoln, and a spur said to have been worn by John Wilkes Booth on the night of the assassination. It is still the basis of the collection in the Ford's Theatre Museum maintained by the National Park Service.

SOURCES: See William Burton Benham, *Life of Osborn H. Oldroyd: Founder and Collector of Lincoln Mementos* (Washington, D.C.: privately printed, 1927).

See also FORD'S THEATRE; PETERSEN HOUSE.

Osborn Hamilton Ingham Oldroyd

Oregon Territory *See* MEXICAN WAR; TAYLOR, ZACHARY.

Ottawa, Illinois The site of the first Lincoln-Douglas Debate, August 21, 1858. The town, which lies 80 miles southwest of Chicago, was a Republican stronghold represented in Congress by Illinois's most radical Republican officeholder, Owen Lovejoy. Trains carried people to Ottawa at special half-rate excursion fares from Chicago, Rock Island, Joliet, and other towns. Reporters, unable to get hotel rooms, slept on couches the night before. A crowd of 10,000 or 12,000 people thronged the public square of this town of at most 6000 residents. The weather had been dry, and the crowd stirred great clouds of dust as the speakers mounted the platform at 2:00 p.m. in a bright sun. There were no seats or bleachers for the audience.

Douglas opened the debate with charges that would form much of the material of the six debates to follow. He claimed that Lincoln and Lyman Trumbull had conspired to abolitionize the Whig and Democratic parties, respectively, in order to become Illinois's Senators. He accused Lincoln of supporting the most radical formulation of Republican policies in Illinois. As basis for the claim he cited a set of resolutions drawn up in 1854 in opposition to the Fugitive Slave Act, the admission of any new slave state to the Union, slavery in the District of Columbia, and the acquisition of any new territory unless slavery were excluded therefrom. He threatened to cite the same resolutions in "Egypt," the far-southern part of Illinois, to see how Lincoln would respond away from his radical friends in the northern part of the state. Douglas also accused Lincoln of "taking the side of the common enemy against his own country" in the Mexican War. He described Lincoln's "House Divided" speech, which opened the campaign, as "revolutionary and destructive of the existence of this Government." And he carefully reminded his antislavery audience that "Slavery is not the only question which comes up in this controversy. There is a far more important one to you, and that is, what shall be done with the free negro?" Lincoln, Douglas charged, opposed the Dred Scott decision because "it deprives the negro of the rights and privileges of citizenship," and Republican success would allow "the free negroes to flow in, and cover your prairies with black settlements." Do you, Douglas asked, "desire to turn this beautiful State into a free negro colony"? Douglas affirmed his belief that "this government was made on the white basis. . . . by white men, for the benefit of white men and their posterity for ever."

After denying any connection with the radical resolutions Douglas had quoted and denying any conspiracy with Trumbull to abolitionize the old party system, Lincoln dwelt at length on "that general abolition tilt" Douglas seemed to find in his views. "I am no longer a young man," said Lincoln, as he put on spectacles to read at length from his Peoria Speech of 1854. Then he had said that if "all earthly power were given me,

I should not know what to do, as to the existing institution" of slavery. His "own feelings" would not allow him to free the slaves and make them, "politically and socially, our equals." Lincoln added to those familiar remarks this rejection of racial equalitarianism:

> There is a physical difference between the two [races], which in my judgment will probably forever forbid their living together upon the footing of perfect equality, and inasmuch as it becomes a necessity that there must be a difference, I, as well as Judge Douglas, am in favor of the race to which I belong having the superior position.

Owen Lovejoy sat on the platform, but there are no descriptions of his expression during those remarks. Lincoln even stated that Lovejoy had had a hand in the radical resolutions Douglas had quoted; and by denying any connection with them himself, Lincoln put some distance between his own views and Lovejoy's. Lincoln used the term "nigger" twice in the speech, something he did very rarely.

Not all of Lincoln's speech was defensive. He charged that Douglas's policies, intentionally or unintentionally, would lead "to the *perpetuity and nationalization of slavery."* He strongly hinted that Douglas had conspired to do that. After all, the Kansas-Nebraska Act had a sort of "niche" in it for the Dred Scott decision, which came 3 years later. Lincoln cast suspicion on Douglas's respect for the finality of the Dred Scott decision by pointing to the fact that "his great prototype, Gen. Jackson, did not believe in the binding force of decisions" of the Supreme Court. Lincoln concluded by appealing to the memory of "Henry Clay, my beau ideal of a statesman." When Douglas "says that the negro has nothing in the Declaration of Independence," Lincoln chided, he contradicted Clay, who "plainly understood the contrary."

In his rebuttal Douglas dwelt on the 1854 resolutions; he pointed out that Lincoln dodged saying whether he believed in them or not. He claimed that Lincoln did not answer the questions he asked and promised to ask them again in Freeport, the site of the next debate. Douglas concluded by denying that he had conspired with anyone to nationalize slavery.

Douglas had made an error which would dog his steps for the rest of the campaign. The radical resolutions had been drawn up at a meeting at which Lincoln was not present, and Lincoln was never pledged to support them. Capitalizing on fears of black equality, however, was something Douglas would do throughout the campaign.

Lincoln had had a sense of great anticipation before the debate. A somewhat deferential tone runs through his speech that was not present later. "I know the Judge is a great man, while I am only a small man," Lincoln said on the platform, "but *I feel that I have got him."* Republicans in the crowd seemed to agree, and when the debate ended, Lincoln was carried away on the shoulders of part of the throng that surrounded him. He showed obvious relief afterward; a day later he told the editor of the Urbana *Union,* "Douglas and I, for the first time this canvass, crossed swords here yesterday; the fire flew some, and I am glad to know I am yet alive." Richard Yates told Lincoln, "We were *well satisfied* with you at Ottawa, Dug evidently felt bad."

Some Republican leaders were less impressed with Lincoln's performance. Abolitionist Theodore Parker thought "Douglas had the best of it." He put the hard questions about slavery to Lincoln, and Lincoln "made a technical evasion" by saying the resolutions were not his. Next time, Lincoln would answer Douglas's questions; but after consultation with other Republican leaders, he would also put questions to Douglas at Freeport which would alter the somewhat defensive tone of his performance.

SOURCES: See Edwin Erle Sparks, ed., *The Lincoln-Douglas Debates of 1858* (Springfield: Illinois State Historical Library, 1908). Parker's letter to Herndon is quoted in Joseph Fort Newton, *Lincoln and Herndon* (Cedar Rapids, Iowa: Torch Press, 1910). Yates's letter (August 26, 1858) is in the Abraham Lincoln Papers, Library of Congress.

Our American Cousin

The play Lincoln attended the night of his assassination. Tom Taylor, a British playwright, wrote the comedy, but actress Laura Keene first produced it, in New York City, in 1858. By 1865 it had played in Washington several times. Walt Whitman characterized the play as a "piece . . . in which, among other characters, so call'd, a Yankee, certainly such a one as was never seen, . . . in North America, is introduced in England, with a varied fol-de-rol of talk, plot, scenery, and such phantasmagoria as goes to make up

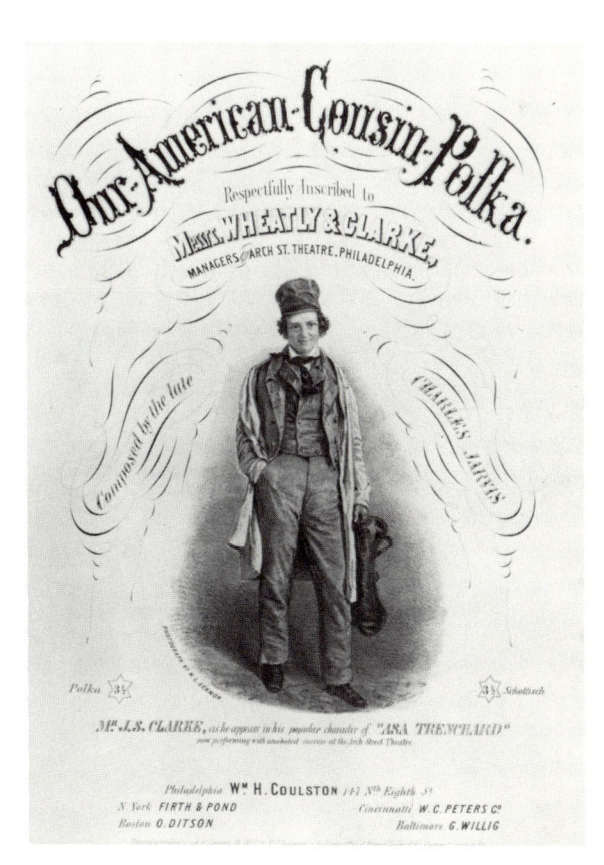

Our American Cousin was already an extremely popular play in America long before President Lincoln decided to go to see it on April 14, 1865. This piece of sheet music published in Philadelphia in 1858 capitalized on its popularity.

a modern popular drama." In truth, the American character, Asa Trenchard, did not make the play popular. Americans liked the English character, a "silly ass" named Lord Dundreary. Mrs. Mountchessington, a gold-digging Englishwoman, wishes to marry her daughter to Trenchard, who is thought to be wealthy but has, in fact, given up his fortune.

Accounts disagree in regard to the visibility of Lincoln's face to the audience during the play, but those witnesses who claimed to have seen the President during the performance agree that he laughed as though he enjoyed it.

SOURCES: See George S. Bryan, *The Great American Myth* (New York: Carrick & Evans, 1940).

Owens, Mary S. (1808–1877) The only well-documented romantic interest in Abraham Lincoln's life before Mary Todd. Mary S. Owens was born in Green County, Kentucky. She later described her father as "a gentleman of considerable means." She was, her son recalled, "polished in her manners, pleasing in her address," and she "had received a good education." In 1833 she visited her sister, Mrs. Bennett Abell, in New Salem, Illinois, and met Lincoln. Three years later, Mrs. Abell returned the visit and lightheartedly told Lincoln she would bring Mary back if he would marry her. Lincoln agreed, probably lightheartedly as well. Mary's return visit lasted from November 1836 to the spring of 1838, but Lincoln left to attend the legislature in December 1836 and moved to Springfield on April 15, 1837, and they were seldom together.

The ensuing correspondence between Mary and Lincoln revealed a troubled relationship. On December 13, 1836, Lincoln wrote Mary that he had "not [been] pleased since I left you," but on May 7, 1837, he warned her that if she "cast her lot" with him, she "would have to be poor without the means of hiding your poverty." On August 16, 1837, he wrote, just after parting from her again, that she could dismiss him from her thoughts "forever," if she wished. "If it suits you best to not answer this—farewell—a long life and a merry one attend you." Finally, in the fall of 1837, he made a formal proposal of marriage; to his surprise, she turned him down.

Lincoln may never have known why Mary rejected him, and later generations certainly would not have known either had not William H. Herndon, gathering materials for a biography of Lincoln in 1866, sought Mary Owens out. Somewhat reluctantly, she corresponded with Herndon and explained simply that "Lincoln was deficient in those little links which make up the chain of woman's happiness." His "training had been different from" hers; "hence there was not that congeniality which would otherwise have existed." She recalled that he had failed to help her cross a "bad branch" when riding with friends. The "other gentlemen were very officious in seeing that their partners got over safely," but Lincoln rode ahead, "never looking back to see how I got along." They did see "eye to eye" in politics, "though since then we differed as widely as the South is from the North."

After leaving New Salem, Mary married Jesse Vineyard (1841) and had five children. She was widowed in 1862 and lived in Weston, Missouri, when Herndon wrote her.

Lincoln had recalled the ill-starred match in a letter written to Mrs. Orville Hickman Browning, appropriately enough, on April Fools' Day in 1838. He claimed to have been shocked when Mary (whose name is not mentioned in the letter) returned in 1836; suddenly her proportions seemed Falstaffian and her appearance "weather-beaten . . . in general." Nothing, he thought, "could have commenced at the size of infancy, and reached her present bulk in less than thirty-five or forty years," though she was only twenty-eight. He determined to live up to his bargain anyway and was astonished when she "actually rejected me with all my fancied greatness." Only then, Lincoln said, "for the first time," did he begin "to suspect that I was really a little in love with her."

Though Herndon did not grasp it, his documenting the Lincoln-Owens courtship, which began only a year after Ann Rutledge's death, was an important step in deflating the Ann Rutledge myth. Mary Owens told Herndon that she could "not recollect of ever hearing him [Lincoln] mention her [Ann Rutledge's] name."

SOURCES: There is no better account than that of the man who pieced the story together; see Paul M. Angle, ed., *Herndon's Life of Lincoln* (Cleveland, Ohio: World Publishing, 1949). The last word on the romance is R. Gerald McMurtry's careful appendix to Olive Carruthers's novel, *Lincoln's Other Mary* (Chicago: Ziff-Davis Publishing, 1946).

P

Paine, Lewis Thornton *See* POWELL, LEWIS THORNTON.

Palmer, John McAuley (1817–1900) Illinois Republican associate of Lincoln's. Palmer was born in Kentucky but moved to Illinois with his father in 1831; he settled in Carlinville in 1839 and became a lawyer. Though a Democrat, he opposed Stephen A. Douglas's Kansas-Nebraska Bill in 1854. Lincoln urged him to oppose the local Democratic candidate for Congress, pointing out that Palmer's opposition to the bill had surely robbed him of the nomination and election to Congress, but he failed to draw Palmer into the Anti-Nebraska coalition. As a state senator in 1855, Palmer played a major role in electing Lyman Trumbull to the United States Senate; he and four other Anti-Nebraska Democrats spoiled Lincoln's bid for that seat by refusing to vote for any Whig. In 1856 he became a Republican.

At the Republican National Convention in Philadelphia in 1856, Palmer urged Lincoln's nomination for Vice President. Recognizing the debt he owed Lincoln for causing him to lose the race for the Senate in 1855, Palmer vigorously supported Lincoln's campaign against Douglas for the Senate in 1858. He attributed Lincoln's defeat to being "betrayed by the eastern Republicans" who did not wish to oppose Douglas, now temporarily cooperating with Republicans against the Buchanan administration. Lincoln expressed confidence that Palmer and other ex-Democrats had worked as hard as ex-Whigs to put him in the Senate. When Palmer ran unsuccessfully for the House in 1859, Lincoln urged his election as a "good and true" Republican. Palmer was a moderate Republican in the 1850s; he attempted to make the new party stand "for free homes for free white people." In 1860 Palmer introduced the resolution at the Illinois state Republican convention endorsing Lincoln for the Presidency, and, as a delegate to the national convention in Chicago, he worked for Lincoln's nomination.

When war broke out, Palmer joined the army. He asked for and eventually received from Lincoln an appointment as brigadier general. He served in Missouri, at Stone River, and at Chickamauga, becoming a major general. He loathed the aristocratic airs and tendencies to Caesarism among his fellow generals, especially West Pointers, and resigned in 1864 after a dispute over rank with General William T. Sherman.

Palmer seems never to have wavered in his support of Lincoln, though he became increasingly Radical in political opinion. At times he feared that "the restoration of the Union as it was," a Union with "its foundations in consent," was impossible and that a military aristocracy and proscription of civil liberties might "convert this constitutional republic into despotism." Palmer saw the South as needing a fundamental reorganization of society. There was a "natural antagonism" of the "poorer classes" to the "rich" in the South, but the poor there lacked leadership. In Tennessee, he saw a quarter of the people impoverished utterly by the war and allowed by their leaders to "wander homeless" when there were "farms enough in middle Tennessee, deserted by their rebel owners, to give temporary homes to thousands." Appointed by Lincoln as military commander in the Department of Kentucky in February 1865, Palmer replaced the Radical General S. G. Burbridge, who had enrolled Negroes for the army and quarreled bitterly with conservative Governor T. E. Bramlette. "A native of Kentucky with all the contempt of my race against Negroes," Palmer had told Lyman Trumbull as early as December 28, 1861, he was nevertheless ready to "raise and command a Brigade of them" if foreign intervention threatened to give victory to the Confederacy. Palmer soon became identified with Radical policies to free Kentucky's slaves as well. He admitted that his policies were "high-handed" and "unsupported by any considerable portion of the people." By 1866 he could see "no remedy for the evils which exist here [in the South] other than the complete enfranchisement of the negroes."

In 1868 Palmer was elected Governor of Illinois. He abandoned his Reconstruction Radicalism and the Republican party, became a Liberal Republican in 1872, and eventually returned to the Democratic party. He served as a Democrat in the United States Senate after 1891. In 1896 he ran for President as a Gold Democrat.

SOURCES: George Thomas Palmer, *A Conscientious Turncoat: The Story of John M. Palmer, 1817–1900* (New Haven, Conn.: Yale University Press, 1941) quotes some useful letters at length, but there is no satisfactory biography. Palmer's revealing letter to Trumbull (December 28, 1861) about his racial views is in the Abraham Lincoln Papers, Library of Congress.

Pardons *See* CLEMENCY.

Parker, John Frederick A Washington, D.C., policeman who was President Lincoln's bodyguard the night Lincoln was assassinated. In trouble with the force repeatedly, Parker, on August 3, 1863, was reported absent 41 of 82 days and was charged with inefficiency. He got off with a warning. On April 2, 1864, he was charged with insubordination, using disrespectful language, and neglect of duty. Four days later the Police Board recommended his dismissal, but he was reinstated on December 1, 1864. Parker was one of four plainclothesmen assigned to guard the White House, fears for the President's safety having been aroused by the excited presidential campaign that autumn.

On the night of the assassination Parker watched the President's party from the coach to the theater door and took a seat outside the box in the vestibule for a time. History knew nothing of Parker until 1910, when White House guard William H. Crook revealed that Parker had abandoned his seat so he could see the play, thereby allowing John Wilkes Booth to go unchallenged into the President's box. On May 1, 1865, Parker was charged with neglect of duty. Records of the Police Board trial have not survived, but on June 2, 1865, the charge was dismissed. Mary Lincoln's confidante, Elizabeth Keckley, claimed later that Mrs. Lincoln blamed Parker for complicity in the crime. Finally, in 1868, he was dismissed from the force for sleeping on duty.

Though much has been made of Parker's dereliction of duty, in truth he may have stopped Booth, who showed his card to someone before going up to the box. Lincoln's well-known fondness for actors was likely to have caused any guard to let Booth in to see the President anyway.

SOURCES: A balanced appraisal is George S. Bryan's *The Great American Myth* (New York: Carrick & Evans, 1940). See also William Hanchett, "The Eisenschiml Thesis," *Civil War History*, XXV (September 1979), 197–217.

Patronage Although Lincoln had no executive experience before becoming President, he had long realized the importance of organization to political success. And he knew that the reward of appointive office held political organizations together.

The Whig party in part grew from criticism of the organizational methods of the Democratic party, and Whigs therefore tended to be reluctant to adopt those methods. Among Illinois Whigs, Lincoln and his close political allies like Anson G. Henry were leaders in urging better organization, which Lincoln knew was the party's only hope of success in his overwhelmingly Democratic state.

In 1840 Lincoln wrote a confidential circular for the Whig state committee suggesting that the way to "overthrow the *trained bands* that are opposed to us, whose salaried officers are ever on the watch, and whose misguided followers are ever ready to obey their smallest commands" was "to organize the whole State." The letter recommended the establishment of committees in every county to canvass voters to determine their preferences. When Democrats seized on the circular as a campaign issue, Lincoln responded: "*They* set us the example of organization; and we, in self defense, are driven into it. . . . Let them *disband* their double-drilled-army of 'forty thousand office holders.'" Lincoln continued to "justify . . . urge. . . . organization on the score of necessity." Still, he was Whig enough to tell John Todd Stuart, while advising him on local appointments after William Henry Harrison's election as President, "I am, as you know, opposed to removals to make places for our friends." He insisted on having some reason beyond mere partisan identification for removing officeholders.

Lincoln's Whig campaign address in 1843 continued to stress the necessity of organization. He favored the convention system for nominations, and he urged Whigs to run candidates for Congress in every district in the state, "regardless of the chances of success." He was still ahead of average Whig sentiment on those questions and "got thunder" as his "reward" for writing the address. When he served in the House of Representatives (1847–1849), Lincoln did what he could to gain offices and appointments for Whig allies, but there was little he could do. President James K. Polk was a Democrat and "could hardly be expected to give them to whigs, at the solicitation of a whig Member of Congress." Things changed with the election of Whig Zachary Taylor. Lincoln promised offices, for example to Walter Davis: "When I last saw you I said, that if the distribution of the offices should fall into my hands, you should have *something*." In the end he shared a good deal of the power of distribution with incoming Whig Congressman Edward D. Baker of Galena. When he recommended a Whig appointee as Springfield's postmaster, Lincoln admitted that the only objection to the Democratic incumbent was that he was "an active partizan in opposition to us." Lincoln would "give no opinion . . . as to whether he should or should not be removed." He did not say, as he had said to Stuart almost a decade before, that such men should not be removed.

Since he did not run for reelection, Lincoln himself began to think of receiving a patronage appointment. But, he said frankly, "there is nothing about me which would authorize me to think of a first class office; and a second class one would not compensate me for being snarled at by others who want it for themselves." Eventually, Lincoln did become an aspirant for appointment to the lucrative General Land Office. He admitted that his major competitor, Justin Butterfield of Chicago, was "qualified to do the duties of the office," as were "quite one hundred Illinoisans." Lincoln argued that the office "should be so given as to gratify our friends, and to stimulate them to future exertions." Butterfield "fought for Mr. Clay against Gen Taylor to the bitter end," and it would "now mortify me deeply," Lincoln said, "if Gen. Taylors administration shall trample all my wishes in the dust."

Taylor's weak partisanship gave Lincoln a new appreciation of the importance of the patronage. Taylor, Lincoln realized, "will not go the doctrine of removals very strongly." Leaving many Democratic incumbents in office, Lincoln insisted, gave "the greater reason, when an office or job is not already in democratic hands, that it should be given to a Whig." If *less* than this is done for our friends, I think they will have just cause to complain." The appointment of Butterfield doubtless accelerated Lincoln's appreciation for distributing the

This woodcut from Frank Leslie's Illustrated Newspaper, November 24, 1860, *comes as near to showing Lincoln distributing patronage as any contemporary illustration. Between his election and inauguration, Lincoln occupied an office in the Illinois State Capitol, where he greeted the many visitors who trekked to Springfield to recommend appointments to office.*

HON. ABRAHAM LINCOLN, THE PRESIDENT ELECT, RECEIVING HIS VISITORS IN THE GOVERNOR'S ROOM IN THE STATE HOUSE, SPRINGFIELD, ILL.—From a Sketch by our Special Artist, Mr. Henri Lovie.

patronage to friends as the ultimate bond of party loyalty.

Lincoln was out of office and largely uninvolved in patronage matters for more than a decade before becoming President in 1861. He brought with him to the office the traditional habits of a good party man who had been toughened by the unhappy experience of the Taylor administration. That experience was reinforced by the organizational needs of a new party, the Republican, now enjoying its first taste of national office. Lincoln was widely criticized for spending too much time on petty patronage matters while the nation fell apart into civil war. However, the Republican party was only 6 years old and was as yet a loose coalition of former Whigs, former Democrats, and former Know-Nothings. Lincoln had to exercise great care in distributing the patronage to keep the new coalition together. For that task Lincoln was peculiarly well equipped; for although no one appreciated loyalty more than he, Lincoln was also free of any vindictive spirit. When Republicans who had supported other candidates than Lincoln at the nominating convention in 1860 worriedly wrote him, Lincoln responded that such things were "not even remembered by me for any practical purpose." He would not go "back of the convention, to make distinctions among its' members."

Personal loyalty was one thing, but party loyalty was quite another. Lincoln initiated the most sweeping removal of federal officeholders in the country's history up to that time. Of 1520 presidential officeholders, 1195 were removed; and since most Southern offices were left unfilled, that was almost a complete overturn. He appointed Republicans to almost all of the jobs. Lincoln's administration, the President explained frankly in 1862, "distributed to its' party friends as nearly all the civil patronage as any administration ever did."

Lincoln observed "Senatorial courtesy"; that is, he consulted Republican members of the upper house about major appointments for their states. For minor offices he generally chose appointees suggested by Republican members of the lower house. Governors and influential party bosses like Thurlow Weed in New York also had their say in the distribution of offices. The President made little effort to evaluate the candidates suggested by others. Thus he wrote the Secretary of the Treasury on July 18, 1862: "Mr. Senator Doolittle informs me that the Wisconsin delegation have unanimously recommended persons for assessors and collectors throughout their State, and that the paper showing this is filed with you. If so, I am in favor of adopting their 'slate' at once, and so disposing of one State."

Lincoln used similar channels of "courtesy" in distributing military commissions, but in that realm the appointments went to men of both parties. Lincoln knew that Democratic support was essential to win the war, and he never believed the argument, a favorite of Radical Republicans, that generals fought better when their hearts were in the contest and they ardently endorsed the administration's antislavery measures.

Nepotism was a common practice throughout the administration. Many of Mrs. Lincoln's relatives held political appointments. The Lincolns' own son Robert gained a military commission. The President knew that too much of the practice could hurt him. John Todd Stuart, for example, pressed the appointment of one of Lincoln's cousins to the Springfield post office. The President had already rewarded Illinois Senator Lyman Trumbull's relatives, and Lincoln wroteStuart on March 30, 1861: "Will it do for me to go on and justify the declaration that Trumbull and I have divided out all the offices among our relatives?" The practice was traditional and common. Every member of Lincoln's Cabinet had family members on the federal payroll or had relatives who received military commissions. Secretary of State William H. Seward's case was typical: his three sons were Assistant Secretary of State, Army paymaster, and brigadier general of volunteers. His nephew was consul general in Shanghai.

Though Lincoln maintained his thoroughly partisan record in appointments throughout the war, he also maintained his record of lack of vindictiveness. He never used the patronage to punish Radical Republicans or to build a machine committed to him personally and to his reelection in 1864. He tended to accept the recommendations of the majority faction of the party in each state, whether that faction was committed to him or not, or to give appointments to all factions in a state ("justice to all").

Abraham Lincoln led a new party in the heyday of party politics before civil service reform was a reality or even an issue. He brought to this traditional partisan atmosphere a record of party loyalty and a strong belief in party organization. Keeping the Republican party together in the midst of the worst political crisis in American history was perhaps the major political achievement of his administration.

SOURCES: Harry J. Carman and Reinhard H. Luthin's *Lincoln and the Patronage* (New York: Columbia University Press, 1943) is a superb study of presidential patronage; it is marred only by its hostility to the Radical Republicans. Prodigiously researched, it is an encyclopedic reference for the relationship to Lincoln of the many obscure names that appear in the Presidential correspondence.

See also COMMANDER IN CHIEF; RADICAL REPUBLICANS; SCHURZ, CARL; TAYLOR, ZACHARY.

Payne, Lewis Thornton   *See* POWELL, LEWIS THORNTON.

Peoria Speech   Lincoln's "first great speech," according to biographer Albert J. Beveridge. The 3-hour address, delivered on October 16, 1854, was apparently the same speech Lincoln had given 12 days earlier in Springfield, but it takes its name from Lincoln's later delivery in Peoria because a complete text appeared in the Springfield newspaper only after the Peoria speech. Accounts of the Springfield reading are sketchy.

Lincoln was running for a seat in the Illinois House

of Representatives. Senator Stephen A. Douglas's Kansas-Nebraska Act was the big issue in the campaign, and, though Douglas was not Lincoln's opponent, all Anti-Nebraska men were in some sense running against Douglas. Lincoln and Douglas agreed on a debate format beforehand, and the Peoria speech was an evening answer to Douglas's speech delivered in the afternoon.

Lincoln's speech protested the repeal of the Missouri Compromise by the Kansas-Nebraska Act. He considered the Missouri Compromise line, which separated territory that was free from that in which slavery might be permitted in the balance of the Louisiana Purchase, sacred. Lincoln ridiculed Douglas's excuses for repeal. The device of "popular sovereignty" in the Compromise of 1850, for example, in no way supplanted the Missouri Compromise line; the two compromises dealt with entirely different territories.

Lincoln focused his attack on the principle behind the repeal and stressed the moral questions involved in the expansion of slavery. The principle behind the act, Lincoln argued, was completely new and utterly repugnant. He rejected as a *"lullaby"* the argument that slavery could never exist in Nebraska Territory even if the law allowed it. Neither latitude nor climate nor the institutions of states geographically near the Territory clearly guaranteed that slavery could not survive there. Conversely, the record of statutory prohibition of slavery from territories was perfect: it had never failed to keep a territory from legalizing slavery when it became a state. In the last analysis, Lincoln contended, all of his differences with Douglas were rooted in a fundamental disagreement about the Negro. It was true, he admitted, that it was just for the Southerner to be allowed to take his slave to Nebraska if the Northerner could take his hog there—"if there is no difference between hogs and negroes." Lincoln refused to deny the humanity of the Negro and insisted that even Southerners did not. In their contempt for slave dealers, in their willingness to ban the slave trade as piracy, and even in their allowing free Negroes to exist ("We do not see free horses or free cattle running at large"), they too recognized "that the poor negro has some natural right to himself," that he was in fact human. And "If the negro is a *man*, why then my ancient faith teaches me that 'all men are created equal;' and that there can be no moral right in connection with one man's making a slave of another."

For all of its principled ardor against the Kansas-Nebraska Act, the speech showed Lincoln's customary moderation toward the South and his ambiguity in regard to race. Southerners were "just what we would be in their situation." Lincoln admitted that "they are no more responsible for the origin of slavery, than we."

> I surely will not blame them for not doing what I should not know how to do myself. If all earthly power were given me, I should not know what to do, as to the existing institution. My first impulse would be to free all the slaves, and send them to Liberia,—to their own native land. But a moment's reflection would convince me, that . . . this . . . is impossible. . . . What then? Free them all, and keep them among us as underlings? Is it quite certain that this betters their condition? . . . Free them, and make them politically and socially, our equals? My own feelings will not admit of this; and if mine would, we well know that those of the great mass of white people will not.

At this early date in his antislavery career, Lincoln clearly valued national unity more highly than the freedom of the Negro race. "Much as I hate slavery," he said, I would consent to the extension of it rather than see the Union dissolved, just as I would consent to any GREAT evil, to avoid a GREATER one." His opposition to slavery's expansion even retained some racist appeal; he wanted to see the territories become "the happy home of teeming millions of free, white, prosperous people, and no slave amongst them."

The speech was notable for joining moral indignation over the expansion of slavery with patriotic appeals to the founders of the Republic. The result was to legitimize the antislavery movement as conservative and thoroughly American. Lincoln clearly conveyed the impression that popular sovereignty was "NEW." It departed from the wishes of the country's founders. "I love the sentiments of those old-time men," Lincoln said, and by pointing to Thomas Jefferson's Northwest Ordinance, and especially to the Declaration of Independence, he suggested that Douglas had departed from "our ancient faith." The "policy of prohibiting slavery in new territory originated," Lincoln said, "with the author of the declaration of Independence." A famous passage near the end of the speech combined these elements powerfully:

> Our republican robe is soiled, and trailed in the dust. Let us repurify it. Let us turn and wash it white, in the spirit, if not the blood, of the Revolution. Let us turn slavery from its claims of "moral right," back upon its existing legal rights, and its arguments of "necessity." Let us return it to the position our fathers gave it; and there let it rest in peace. Let us re-adopt the Declaration of Independence, and with it, the practices, and policy, which harmonize with it. Let north and south—let all Americans—let all lovers of liberty everywhere—join in the great and good work. If we do this, we shall not only have saved the Union; but we shall have so saved it, as to make, and to keep it, forever worthy of the saving. We shall have so saved it, that the succeeding millions of free happy people, the world over, shall rise up, and call us blessed, to the latest generations.

Lincoln won election to the Illinois House, but he quickly resigned his seat. A member of the Illinois House was ineligible for the United States Senate, and his campaigning against Douglas had convinced him that he might well aim higher, at a seat in the Senate.

See also MISSOURI COMPROMISE; "POPULAR SOVEREIGNTY."

Petersen House The house where Abraham Lincoln died. The Petersen house was located across the street from Ford's Theatre. After John Wilkes Booth shot Lincoln in the theater on April 14, 1865, the unconscious

Philately

Far Right: The first photograph of Lincoln, and the only original daguerreotype, was taken when he was 37 years old. The Library of Congress owns the original.

President was taken to it, and there he died the next morning at 7:22.

William Petersen, a Swedish tailor, had built the house on 10th Street, N.W., in 1849. Both Petersen's shop and the family's living quarters were located in the house, and the extra rooms were rented to boarders. At the time of Lincoln's assassination, William T. Clark, once a soldier in the Thirteenth Massachusetts Infantry and now a clerk at the Quartermaster General's Office, was renting the room to which Lincoln was taken.

In 1878 the house was sold to Mr. and Mrs. Louis Schade. The Schades rented the building to the Memorial Association of the District of Columbia in 1893 to house Osborn H. Oldroyd's outstanding Lincoln collection. In 1896 the government purchased the house for $30,000. Oldroyd's museum remained in the Petersen house until 1932, when it was moved to Ford's Theatre. Five women's patriotic organizations then refurnished the house to look as it did the night Lincoln died. It is now administered by the National Park Service and is a popular Lincoln site.

SOURCES: The National Park Service provides an informative pamphlet on *Ford's Theatre and the House Where Lincoln Died* by Stanley W. McClure; the price is available from the Superintendent of Documents, Washington, D.C. 20402.

See also OLDROYD, OSBORN HAMILTON INGHAM.

Philately *See* POSTAGE STAMPS.

Photographs Although Abraham Lincoln was a modest man and anything but vain about his appearance, he nevertheless sat for photographers on more than 60 occasions. Well over 100 different photographs resulted from Lincoln's sittings. Logically, most of these date from the last 7 years of his life, that is, from 1858 through 1865. Before Lincoln's famed debates with Stephen A. Douglas in 1858, few people wanted his likeness. Afterward, and especially after Lincoln became President, the demand was practically insatiable.

Far Right: The second photograph of Lincoln, taken by Alexander Hesler in Chicago 11 years after the first, was one of the very few poses available when Lincoln ran for the Presidency in 1860 and was widely copied in campaign items.

A photograph then was not the easy proposition it is today. Cameras required long exposures and still subjects. Photographers typically supported their standing subjects with a hidden metal brace, the base of which is often visible at the subject's feet. The first photograph of Lincoln, a daguerreotype, was made around the time of Lincoln's election to Congress in 1846 by N. H. Shepherd of Springfield. At that early stage in photography, a sitting was a rare occurrence for anyone and was typically linked to a special event in the subject's life. Since photography had been introduced in western America only in 1840, Lincoln's daguerreotype is practically as early in his life as possible. (A companion portrait of his wife, by far the handsomest of her ever made, was taken at the same time.) The next surviving photograph of Lincoln was taken 11 years later, and there is no evidence that any others were taken in the intervening period—further proof that fame came late for Lincoln. The rather dishevelled 1857 likeness, by Alexander Hesler of Chicago, Lincoln thought "a very true one; though

Physical Characteristics

Far Left: Robert Todd Lincoln told collector Frederick Hill Meserve that this photograph was "the most satisfactory likeness" of his father.

my wife, and many others, do not." Lincoln's "impression" was "that their objection arises from the disordered condition of the hair." As always in dealing with portraits of himself, Lincoln stated, "My judgment is worth nothing in these matters."

Lincoln posed for a few more photographs, usually at the request of some particular person, before 1860, when the purpose of his sittings changed dramatically: he now needed campaign photographs. The tousled-hair picture would never do for a presidential candidate. While in New York to deliver his Cooper Institute Address in February 1860, Lincoln visited Mathew Brady's studio, where the great photographer produced what became the most popular campaign photograph by far: a portrait of Lincoln as a statesman and gentleman. Like many Lincoln photographs of the presidential period, prints of it were carefully touched up or dressed up with phony backgrounds. Other photographs were commissioned to provide models for campaign medals or for lithographs and engravings to be bound in campaign biographies or copied for campaign distribution. Portrait painters in oils worked from photographs then, as they do now when painting portraits of famous but busy men. Even portraits of Lincoln painted from life were often based on brief sittings with the President and much longer study of photographs.

In Washington there was greater opportunity for sittings than in Illinois, and Lincoln sat numerous times for photographs—so often, in fact, that it is hard to determine the purpose of many of the poses save to serve as portraits for the photographers to sell. Most who purchased the photographers' wares bought *carte-de-visites*, paper prints mounted on stiff card, about 2¼ by 4 inches. They were most often placed in parlor albums. Lincoln occasionally signed such pictures (and on rare occasions, larger ones) to give to friends or political supporters.

Robert Todd Lincoln preferred the photograph of his father taken by Anthony Berger at the Brady gallery in Washington on February 9, 1864—the famous pose which later became the model for the engraving on the $5 bill. Yet the portrait is very unusual in one respect: Lincoln's hair is parted on the right rather than the left.

Lincoln was never photographed with his wife, probably because of the great difference in their height. Mrs. Lincoln was more rarely photographed than her husband. The demand for her likeness was not nearly as great, and she seems to have thought photographs made her hands look large.

Lincoln never grinned in his photographs. Victorian gentlemen were supposed to be earnest, not frivolous. But there is a hint of a smile in the photograph of Lincoln taken by Alexander Gardner in February 1865. One photograph of the assassinated President lying in state has survived.

To mention the subject of Lincoln photographs is to call to mind the name of Mathew Brady, but that genius of early photography in America also had a genius for self-promotion. Alexander Gardner took almost three times as many pictures of Lincoln as Brady took, and Anthony Berger also took more than Brady.

SOURCES: The best book on the subject is Charles Hamilton and Lloyd Ostendorf's *Lincoln in Photographs: An Album of Every Known Pose* (Norman: University of Oklahoma Press, 1963), but Stefan Lorant also did important work with Lincoln photographs. See his *Lincoln: A Picture Story of His Life*, rev. ed. (New York: W. W. Norton, 1969). The finest reproductions available in published form appear in James Mellon's *The Face of Lincoln* (New York: Viking, 1980).

See also MESERVE, FREDERICK HILL; PHYSICAL CHARACTERISTICS.

Physical Characteristics "I am, in height, six feet, four inches, nearly; lean in flesh, weighing, on an average, one hundred and eighty pounds; dark complexion, with coarse black hair, and grey eyes—no other marks or brands recollected." Thus Lincoln described himself, with characteristic humor, on December 20, 1859, on the brink of his career in the national limelight. As a youth he was large for his age, and the frontier labors of wielding an axe and farming gave him remarkable physical strength all his life. His health appears to have been excellent. Only occasional letters refer to periods of illness—the customary colds and flu, doubtless. He was very ill in the White House shortly after the trip to deliver the Gettysburg Address (November 19, 1863), he suffered from varioloid, a mild form of smallpox. A note declaring his inability to attend a Cabinet meeting over a week later is written in an uncharacteristically shaky hand. He did not smoke, drink, or chew tobacco and was temperate in all things, including eating; he seems to have been a light eater who was largely indifferent about food.

After Lincoln's reelection, Harper's Weekly used his fabled height to celebrate the country's having Lincoln longer as President. American cartoonists did not utilize caricature a great deal until after the Civil War. Most cartoons depended on likenesses slavishly copied from photographs and depended on improbable situations and lengthy balloons of language for their humor.

UNCLE ABE– "*Sambo, you are not handsome, any more than myself, but as to sending you back to your old master, I'm not the man to do it—and what's more, I won't.*"—(*Vide President's Message.*)

Lincoln's fabled ugliness provided ammunition for cartoonists throughout the war. On December 24, 1864, Frank Leslie's Illustrated Newspaper joined Lincoln and the Negro in the brotherhood of ugliness and commended one of Lincoln's repeated assurances, that he would not renege on the promise of freedom made in the Emancipation Proclamation.

Lincoln's contemporaries deemed him an ugly man. Usher F. Linder, for example, recalled the fabled homeliness of Illinois lawyer Archibald Williams by saying that he surpassed even Lincoln in that regard. Lincoln was himself anything but vain about his personal appearance. Early in 1860 he did not have a single photograph at his disposal to send political admirers.

The lack of photographs, a severe liability by the 1860s when campaigns demanded images of the candidates for lithographs, engravings, medals, and political literature of all kinds, was quickly remedied; and, from the more than 100 different photographs, Americans now have an accurate idea of Lincoln's appearance. Moreover, sculptors Leonard W. Volk and Clark Mills made life masks which supplied posterity with the exact dimensions and features of Lincoln's head. Even his foot size is known from a diagram that Lincoln traced for a shoemaker. Only his teeth and smile are a mystery. Victorian gentlemen never appeared in portraits with a grin; the long exposures necessary for photographs in Lincoln's day made holding a smile difficult.

In recent years some doctors have argued that Lincoln suffered from Marfan's syndrome, a congenital disease with symptoms that include "tallness, loose jointedness, a dolichocephalic skull, a high arched palate, arachnodactyly, pigeon breast or pectus excavatum, kyphosis,

Franklin Pierce

poor muscle tone, scant subcutaneous fat, pes planus, and large deformed ears." Victims rarely reach old age and are susceptible to heart disease. Analysis of Lincoln must be confined to examination of photographs of him fully clothed, of physical descriptions by his associates, and by genealogical evidence. Yet almost nothing is known about Lincoln's mother, not even the rudiments of her physical appearance; his physical vigor was diminished by the strain of the Presidency only to a normal degree; and his powerful hands were anything but spidery (a symptom which gives the disease its name, arachnodactyly). Fortunately, Volk made casts of Lincoln's hands as well as his face, and the evidence for Lincoln's suffering from the disease is at best inconclusive.

SOURCES: See Charles Hamilton and Lloyd Ostendorf, *Lincoln in Photographs: An Album of Every Known Pose* (Norman: University of Oklahoma Press, 1963); A. B. Loveman et al., "Marfan's Syndrome: Some Cutaneous Aspects," *Archives of Dermatology*, LXXXVII (April 1963), 64–71; and "A Famous Case of Marfan's Syndrome," *Pfizer Spectrum*, XI (November–December, 1963), 94–96.

See also BEDELL, GRACE; PHOTOGRAPHS; PORTRAITS; PSYCHOLOGY; TEMPERANCE.

Pierce, Franklin (1804–1869) President of the United States from 1853 to 1857 and sharp critic of the Lincoln administration. Pierce was one of five surviving ex-Presidents during the Civil War.

A Democrat, Pierce had been the object of Lincoln's partisan denunciation many times. When Pierce ran for the Presidency in 1852, Lincoln ridiculed "the attempt to set him up as a great general" as "simply ludicrous and laughable" in light of the fact that his Whig opponent was General Winfield Scott, the greatest American general of the pre–Civil War era. Lincoln likewise accused Pierce of being "the steady, consistent enemy of western improvements" at government expense. In 1856 Lincoln said Pierce was in "the cat's paw," probably a reference to his being the tool of proslavery interests, and "a shelled pea's Pod," discarded by his party in 1856 for the unpopularity he gained by defending the party's pro-Southern policies. Two years later Lincoln, in his "House Divided" speech, accused Pierce of conspiring with Stephen A. Douglas, James Buchanan, and Roger B. Taney to nationalize slavery.

On January 6, 1860, Pierce wrote Jefferson Davis a letter describing him as the best Democratic candidate for President that year. As events turned out, Pierce favored John C. Breckinridge's nomination but quickly endorsed Stephen A. Douglas when the Democratic convention in Pierce's home state, New Hampshire, nominated Douglas for President. Pierce regarded Lincoln's subsequent election as a "distinct and unequivocal denial of the coequal rights" of the states. He urged the North to repeal its personal liberty laws (which frustrated enforcement of the Fugitive Slave Act) and begged the seceded states to give the North 6 months to right its wrongs against the South. If there were no results, then the South could depart in peace. The Northern states were "the first wrong doers." After Fort Sumter fell and Pierce heard rumors of a proposed Confederate attack on Washington, he declared that the flag must be upheld if the South attacked.

Within a few months Pierce became a bitter opponent of the war. On a trip to Michigan and Kentucky, he glorified the Union and the Constitution but ignored the war. He was overheard saying that arbitrary arrests, like that of his friend James G. Berret, might lead to civil war in the North. A New Hampshire newspaper editor urged Lincoln to watch Pierce's movements in Kentucky, but the President replied: "I think it is well that P. is away from the N.H. people. He will do less harm anywhere else; and, by *when* he has gone, his neighbors will understand him better." Secretary of State William H. Seward, then in charge of military arrests of persons suspected of disloyalty, was less restrained. Warned by an anonymous letter that "President P—— . . . has drawn many . . . men" into a "secret league, the object of which [is] to overthrow the Government," Seward demanded an explanation from Pierce. The ex-President received Seward's letter on Christmas Eve. He replied indignantly, and Seward quickly apologized. After much controversy in the press and in Congress, the letter accusing Pierce of treason was shown to be a hoax. Dr. Guy S. Hopkins of North Branch, Michigan, had written the letter to prove how ludicrously willing the "treason-shrieking" Republicans were to exploit such insubstantial accusations.

In a remarkable act of compassion, Pierce, who had witnessed the horrible death of his own 11-year-old son in a railroad accident in 1853, wrote President Lincoln a letter of condolence on March 4, 1862, for the loss of his 11-year-old son Willie.

Despite that touching act of personal kindness, Pierce's opposition to the war grew apace. He saw Lincoln as a tyrannical usurper who crushed civil liberties. He loathed the Emancipation Proclamation as the triumph of Charles Sumner and the abolitionists; Lincoln, "to the extent of his limited ability and narrow intelligence [was] their willing instrument" in thus inviting "servile insurrection." To his wife, Pierce vowed never to "justify, sustain, or in any way or to any extent uphold this cruel, heartless, aimless unnecessary war. Madness and imbecility are in the ascendant." On July 4, 1863, he delivered a speech in Concord, New Hampshire, declaring the attempt to maintain the Union by war "futile." Only "peaceful agencies" would work.

Northern resentment at Pierce's views ran high. In 1863 Union soldiers found his 1860 letter to Jefferson Davis. A lithographed copy of it circulated widely. A pamphlet likened him to Benedict Arnold. Veterans so resented his antiwar stand that New Hampshire gave Pierce's political career no recognition in a plaque or monument until 50 years after the Civil War.

SOURCES: Roy F. Nichols's excellent biography, *Franklin Pierce: Young Hickory of the Granite Hills*, 2d ed., revised (Philadelphia: University of Pennsylvania Press, 1958) should be supplemented by two references to Pierce in J. G. Randall's *Lincoln the President: Midstream* (New York: Dodd, Mead, 1952), pp. 35–36, 195–197.

Pigeon Creek See INDIANA.

Pinkerton, Allan (1819–1884) Detective and Union spy. Pinkerton was born in Glasgow, Scotland, and he moved to America in 1842. After experience in law enforcement in Illinois, he founded a detective agency in Chicago. Successful work for the Adams Express and various railroads gave him a national reputation.

The Philadelphia, Wilmington & Baltimore railroad employed Pinkerton early in 1861 to ferret out plots by Maryland secessionists to sabotage the railroad's property. In the course of the investigation, Pinkerton agent Timothy Webster accidentally discovered evidence of a plot to assassinate President-elect Lincoln as he passed through Baltimore to Washington for his inauguration. Pinkerton informed his employer, S. M. Felton, the railroad's president, who agreed that the information should reach the Presidential party.

On February 21, 1861, Pinkerton gave the information to Norman B. Judd, a Chicago politician traveling with Lincoln's party, and Judd, Pinkerton, and Felton warned Lincoln to go immediately to Washington. With speeches to make in Philadelphia and Harrisburg the next day, Lincoln refused. The plot was confirmed by detectives working for Winfield Scott, however, and the next day Lincoln agreed to Pinkerton's plan to travel secretly through Baltimore that night and arrive early in Washington. A female Pinkerton agent arranged for a sleeping car for her "invalid brother," and only burly Ward Hill Lamon accompanied the President-elect. In

President Lincoln posed with Allan Pinkerton, then the chief of Secret Service for the Army of the Potomac, on his visit to General McClellan's headquarters at Antietam on October 3, 1862.

later years, Lamon, insulted by reading that Pinkerton thought him "a brainless egotistical fool," claimed that there was no assassination plot. Yet evidence of one had been strong enough to alarm detectives working independently of Pinkerton's agents.

When war began, Pinkerton attempted to capitalize on his acquaintance with the President by offering himself and 16 to 18 agents for secret service work. Lincoln apparently rejected the offer, and Pinkerton subsequently went to work for General George B. McClellan, at first in the Department of the Ohio and then in Washington after McClellan was appointed to command the Army of the Potomac. Pinkerton was a detective, not an intelligence man, and his gross overestimates of the size of Confederate forces are widely credited with discouraging McClellan's aggressiveness (though McClellan did not blame Pinkerton, or even mention him, in his memoirs).

Pinkerton also supplied McClellan with reports on the movements and moods of Lincoln and his Cabinet. The detective was more adept at flattery than spying, and he consistently reported McClellan's good standing with the President right up to the time of his dismissal in the autumn of 1862. In later years Pinkerton claimed to be an old friend of Lincoln's, but in fact he had told McClellan he was "prejudiced" against Lincoln.

Pinkerton gleaned some of his information from Presidential secretaries John G. Nicolay and John Hay, but in his interviews with Lincoln, the President seems to have handled the detective well. Lincoln appears always to have exemplified an attitude of trust in McClellan all the while trying to ascertain from Pinkerton the condition of the general's army and his willingness to advance.

SOURCES: James D. Horan and Howard Swiggett's *The Pinkerton Story* (New York: G. P. Putnam's Sons, 1951) though poorly written, was apparently based on documents from the Pinkerton company's files not available elsewhere. The definitive edition of documents on the Baltimore plot is Norma B. Cuthbert's *Lincoln and the Baltimore Plot, 1861* (San Marino, Calif.: Henry E. Huntington Library, 1949).

See also BALTIMORE PLOT.

Poetry The oldest existing examples of Abraham Lincoln's handwriting—from copybooks written when he was 15 to 17 years old—contain, in addition to arithmetic exercises, some pieces of childish doggerel:

> Abraham Lincoln
> his hand and pen
> he will be good but
> god knows When

and

> Abraham Lincoln is my nam[e]
> And with my pen I wrote the same
> I wrote in both hast and speed
> and left it here for fools to read

Another piece of verse from the same source, less often quoted, reveals something of what was to be a lifelong taste in poetry for Lincoln:

> . . . Time What an emty vaper
> tis and days how swift are swift as an indian arr[ow]
> fly on like a shooting star the presant moment Just
>   [is here]
> then slides away in h[as]te that we [can] never
>   say they['re ours] but [only say] th[ey]'re past

He liked humor, as the first two verses show, but he had an especial liking—almost a passion—for poems on melancholy themes.

Lincoln's favorite poet was Shakespeare, but next to the Bard he like Robert Burns best. Numerous associates testify to that. It is probable that he read Burns even as a youth in Indiana and memorized poems that he could quote the rest of his life. Even at 51, he marveled at an acquaintance who had "seen and known a sister of Robert Burns" and insisted that he "must tell me something about her when we meet again." Asked to attend the annual meeting of Washington's Burns Club in 1865, Lincoln responded with a hastily written sentiment:

> I can not frame a toast to Burns. I can say nothing worthy of his generous heart and transcending genius. Thinking of what he has said, I can not say anything which seems worth saying[.]

Lincoln's favorite poem was William Knox's *Mortality, or Oh, Why Should the Spirit of Mortal Be Proud?*, which he first encountered at about the time of his move to Illinois and embraced fondly in 1845, when he saw it again "in a straggling form in a newspaper." "I would give all I am worth, and go in debt," Lincoln said, "to be able to write so fine a piece as I think that is." Modern critics do not share Lincoln's view, and without doubt the poem appealed to him especially because of its melancholy sentiments. The poem closes with these lines, which are similar in sentiment to those Lincoln copied as a child:

> 'Tis the twink of an eye, 'tis the draught of a
>   breath,
> From the blossom of health to the paleness of death,
> From the gilded salon to the bier and the shroud—
> Oh, why should the spirit of mortal be proud!

Lincoln did not learn who the author was until he was President.

Lincoln tried his own hand at the art. "Feeling a little poetic" one evening in 1846, he wrote "My childhood-home I see again." He had campaigned in Indiana 2 years before, and that visit recalled fond memories of "woods, and fields, and scenes of play." Yet much of the poem dwelt on the madness of young Matthew Gentry, the son of a prominent local merchant near Lincoln's home in Indiana, who went mad:

> Poor Matthew! Once of genius bright,—
>   A fortune-favored child—
> Now locked for aye, in mental night,
>   A haggard mad-man wild.

That same poetic year Lincoln also wrote "The Bear Hunt," a rollicking poem about a lively chase through the Indiana woods. Once the bear is killed, a dog grows brave, and

> He growls, and seizes on dead bear,
>   And shakes for life and death.
>
> And swells as if his skin would tear,
>   And growls and shakes again;
> And swears, as plain as dog can swear,
>   That he has won the skin.
>
> Concieited whelp! we laugh at thee—
>   Nor mind, that not a few
> Of pompous, two-legged dogs there be,
>   Conceited quite as you.

By many reports President Lincoln was fond of Thomas Hood's *The Haunted House* and of another melancholy poem, Oliver Wendell Holmes's *The Last Leaf*. In later years Holmes proudly recalled Massachusetts Governor John A. Andrew's report that Lincoln recited *The Last Leaf* to Andrew from memory.

The Battle of Gettysburg inspired Lincoln's last poetry. On July 19, 1863, he wrote a few lines of doggerel revealing the high glee which the Northern victory aroused in the President:

> In eighteen sixty three, with pomp, and mighty swell,
> Me and Jeff's Confederacy, went forth to sack Phil-del,
> The Yankees they got arter us, and giv us particular hell,
> And we skedaddled back again, and didn't sack Phil-del.

SOURCES: For the most part Lincoln's taste in poetry is a matter of reports from friends and associates like John Hay, John G. Nicolay, Noah Brooks, and William Henry Herndon. See *Lincoln's Favorite Poets* by David J. Harkness and R. Gerald McMurtry (Knoxville: University of Tennessee Press, 1959).

See also SHAKESPEARE.

Political Parties *See* KNOW-NOTHING PARTY; PATRONAGE; REPUBLICAN PARTY; WHIG PARTY.

Political Philosophy *See* CONSTITUTION OF THE UNITED STATES; JEFFERSON, THOMAS; NATIONALISM; REPRESENTATIVE GOVERNMENT; REPUBLICAN PARTY; WHIG PARTY.

Polk, James Knox *See* MEXICAN WAR.

Pomeroy Circular A printed letter circulated in February 1864 to perhaps 100 Republican politicians. The circular urged the nomination of Salmon P. Chase for President rather than the renomination of President Lincoln. Kansas Senator S. C. Pomeroy signed the letter, which was marked "Private" and was mailed from Washington, D.C. While extolling Chase's presidential qualifications, the letter stated that Lincoln's reelection was "practically impossible" and that, if Lincoln were to win, the war might "continue to languish during the whole administration." Government patronage, it charged, was so inflated by war that only the one-term principle for Presidents could insure the country against executive despotism. The letter was provoked, it said, by "movements recently made throughout the country, to secure the renomination of President Lincoln"; organization was necessary before it was "too late."

The Pomeroy circular is famous because it had an effect precisely opposite from the one intended; it killed Chase's chances for the nomination in 1864. Many people thought it unseemly for a Cabinet member to appear to be conspiring against the man who had given him his job. Chase claimed no knowledge of the circular until he saw it printed in a Washington newspaper on February 20, but he nevertheless offered his resignation. Lincoln responded to Chase's offer by saying that he had heard of the circular but had not read it; friends, he said, "bring the documents to me, but I do not read them; they tell me what they think fit to tell me, but I do not inquire for more." Chase remained in the Cabinet, and the correspondence between Lincoln and Chase was published in the Washington *Chronicle* on March 8.

Many newspapers printed the contents of the circular by February 22, and shortly thereafter resolutions in support of the President's renomination abounded. A telling blow to Chase's fortunes came on February 25, when a Republican caucus in the general assembly in Ohio, Chase's home state, was in favor of renomination of the President. On March 5 Chase wrote a letter to James C. Hall of Toledo asking that "no further consideration be given to my name."

In the New York *Times* of September 15, 1874, J. M. Winchell of Hyde Park, New York, took issue with the story of the circular as told in J. W. Schuckers's *Life and Public Services of Salmon Portland Chase*. Winchell claimed that he had been secretary of the national committee formed to promote Chase's candidacy, that he wrote the circular to force Chase to cease vacillating and capitalize on his popularity to seize the nomination, and that *"Mr. Chase was informed of this proposed action and approved it fully."*

SOURCES: J. G. Randall and Richard N. Current give the Pomeroy circular careful treatment in *Lincoln the President: Last Full Measure* (New York: Dodd, Mead, 1955), pp. 98–108.

"Popular Sovereignty" Stephen A. Douglas's solution to the problem of slavery in the territories. The expression "popular sovereignty" was first made famous by Lewis Cass. In his campaign for the Democratic presidential nomination in 1848, Cass announced his views on slavery's expansion in a public letter written to A. O. P. Nicholson in December 1847. Since slavery did not exist in the Mexican cession and the Constitution could not establish it there, it was best to

> Leave to the people, who will be affected by this question, to adjust it upon their own responsibility, and in their own manner, and we shall render another tribute to the original principles of our government, and furnish another guaranty for its permanence and prosperity.

Douglas at the time generally championed an extension to the Pacific of the Missouri Compromise line, which would ban slavery above 36°30′ latitude. He clearly recognized the right of Congress to settle the question of slavery in the territories, though by 1849 he thought as a matter of policy the effort should not be made by the North.

"Popular Sovereignty"

Douglas announced his version of the doctrine of popular sovereignty in an 1850 speech. The North had a right to regulate slavery in the territories through Congress, but it should not do so because it embittered the South and threatened disunion. The South wrongly insisted on a right to dictate policies in the territories, in which it had as much at stake as the North. The only people with a genuine right to dictate policy in the territories were the people who lived there. The "great and fundamental principle of free government" was that "each community shall settle this and all other questions affecting their domestic institutions by themselves, and in their own way."

When Douglas applied his new principle to Nebraska Territory in the Kansas-Nebraska Act, negating the Missouri Compromise line, Abraham Lincoln reacted strongly. His interest in politics, which had been dwindling, was renewed. His mind boggled at the notion that the principle of prohibition of slavery in the Northwest Ordinance of 1787 and in the Missouri Compromise ban above 36°30′ in the Louisiana Territory was "*now* called an infraction of the sacred right of self-government." To apply the idea that settlers could determine their own domestic policies in territories "bought and paid for" by Congress was absurd. Popular sovereignty was a "new-fangled" doctrine "invented in these degenerate latter days to cloak the spread of slavery." No territory with 50,000 inhabitants would legalize slavery unless it were already there, and it could not be there if Congress's prohibition of it in the Missouri Compromise were not repealed. Thomas Jefferson never thought he was violating the sacred principle of self-government when he banned slavery in the Northwest Territory, and Jefferson's ideas were the very axioms of self-government.

The sacred right of self-government ended where another man's rights were involved, and the right to slavery in the territories was such a right only if the Negro was not a man but a mere piece of property. This "application of the right of self-government" enabled "the first FEW, to deprive the succeeding MANY, of a free exercise of the right of self-government." Besides, slavery was not a local institution. Everyone in the North had a stake in keeping the territories free for homes of free white men in the future. Everyone in the North had a stake in preventing the creation of new slave states which got greater proportional representation in Congress (by counting three-fifths of their slaves in apportionment) and thus diminished the right to self-government of every man in a free state. Lincoln most frequently denied with bitter irony that the right to make a slave of another man was a "sacred right of self-government."

After 1857 Lincoln often called popular sovereignty "squatter sovereignty"; he equated it with the notion that people who "squatted" on Western lands (but had no legal right of ownership by purchase) had the right of possession. When the Dred Scott decision the same year affirmed the rights of Southerners to take their slaves to the territories, Lincoln argued that it eradicated popular sovereignty because local will could not keep slavery out. Douglas argued (as early as 1857 but most spectacularly in the Freeport debate with Lincoln on August 27, 1858) that, whatever the Supreme Court said about "the abstract question whether slavery may or may not go into a territory," the people there had "the lawful means to introduce it or exclude it as they please, for the reason that slavery cannot exist a day or an hour anywhere, unless it is supported by local police regulations." Unfriendly legislation would as effectively keep slavery out as a direct exclusion. Lincoln noted that thereafter Douglas said that "the Constitution does not carry Slavery into the Territories of the United States beyond the power of the people legally to control it, as other property." Controlling, Lincoln said, was not excluding, and Douglas used the word because he, like "all lawyers," knew that a legislature cannot do indirectly what it cannot do directly. The "Dred Scott court" would never uphold such exclusion.

"Popular Sovereignty" was widely lampooned as "squatter sovereignty"—hence this cartoon of Stephen A. Douglas as a ragged and surly frontier ruffian ready to defend his "right" by force. The cartoon appeared in Vanity Fair, February 4, 1860.

THE ORIGINAL SQUATTER SOVEREIGN.

Douglas certainly never meant popular sovereignty as a cloak for slavery. That was most evident when he introduced the principle in 1850. Then he had told Southern Senators that "the cause of freedom has steadily and firmly advanced, while slavery has receded in the same ratio," so that equality between the sections was no longer possible. Popular sovereignty, too, would result in the expansion of the area of freedom. The area between the Mississippi River and the Pacific Ocean would hold 17 new free states; nature herself would keep slavery out of those arid regions. Before long, he hoped, Delaware, Maryland, Virginia, Kentucky, Missouri, North Carolina, and Tennessee would adopt gradual emancipation and become free states as well. Yet this was by far the most pro-Northern interpretation Douglas made for the doctrine, and by 1858 he advertised popular sovereignty as a doctrine of sectional balance which would preserve the spirit of compromise in the Constitution and allow the country to go on forever, part slave and part free. Thus Lincoln attacked popular sovereignty not in 1850 but in 1854 and after, when it had become increasingly favorable toward the interests of the South. After 1854 the South appeared to be reneging on its part of the compromise precisely when its provisions began to hurt the South's interests for the first time.

SOURCES: See Robert W. Johannsen's *Stephen A. Douglas* (New York: Oxford University Press, 1973).

Portraits Lincoln sat for numerous paintings from life, the first 10 almost immediately after his nomination for the Presidency in 1860. Typically, the artists had commissions from Republican patrons to make likenesses suitable as models for mass-produced lithographs and engravings to be circulated in the campaign. Although campaign pictures, banners, broadsides, and medals had been widely used in American politics since the Harrison "log cabin" campaign of 1840, their use was not second nature to many politicians even 20 years later. Illinois organizer Norman B. Judd, for example, told Lincoln in 1860: "I am coming to believe, that likenesses spread broad cast, are excellent means of electioneering." Yet when asked for a photograph, Lincoln, even though he was an experienced politician and a contender for the Republican presidential nomination, found himself without "a single one now at my control."

Lincoln as nominee posed special problems for distributors of campaign pictures: his nomination was a great surprise to everyone; he had not held national office for over a decade; he had never held any office higher than Representative, and he held that for only one term. Furthermore, he was widely reputed to be ugly.

Alban Jasper Conant, commissioned by St. Louis railroad executive William M. McPherson, sought to capture Lincoln's smile in a painting. That would correct what Conant regarded as unskillful in the work of the photographers: harsh lighting and inflexible poses served to accentuate "the deep, repellent lines in his face, giving it an expression easily mistaken for coarseness that well accorded with the prevalent disparagement of his character." Conant's portrait is now owned by the Philipse Manor Hall in Yonkers, New York.

Charles Alfred Barry was commissioned by Boston printmaker John H. Bufford, who wanted a likeness on which to base a campaign lithograph. The recently rediscovered crayon original, together with Joseph E. Baker's lithographic adaptation, shows a romantic portrait of a rugged Westerner that was suggestive to the Boston *Transcript* of Andrew Jackson's "firmness." Republican Judge John M. Read of Philadelphia paid miniaturist John Henry Brown to execute a miniature as the basis for another campaign print. Read admonished Brown to make Lincoln "good looking whether the original would justify it or not"; Lincoln thought the resulting likeness "an excellent one." The National Portrait Gallery in Washington owns the miniature; Samuel Sartain made the mezzotint engraving based on it.

Other early portraits were by George Peter Alexander Healy (original in the Corcoran Gallery of Art, Washington, D.C.), George Frederick Wright (University of Chicago), Thomas Hicks (Chicago Historical Society), and Jesse Atwood (Lilly Library, Indiana University, Bloomington). For many of these portraits, Lincoln sat while reading his mail in an improvised office in the Illinois State Capitol in Springfield.

When Lincoln grew his beard, he made all those efforts obsolete. This and the accomplishments of the administration, especially the issuance of the Emancipation Proclamation, led to the production of more portraits. Though a busy President, Lincoln was the subject of paintings in Washington by Healy again (location unknown), George Henry Story (Illinois State Historical

Charles Alfred Barry saw Jacksonian firmness in the Republican nominee from Illinois.

Postage Stamps

G. P. A. Healy's seated Lincoln was Robert Todd Lincoln's favorite portrait of his father. Lincoln heirs eventually deeded the portrait to the White House. (The White House)

Lewis Thornton Powell

Library, Springfield), Edward Dalton Marchant (Union League Club of Philadelphia), James Read Lambdin (present whereabouts unknown), William F. Cogswell (White House Historical Association), Pierre Morand (sketches in the Missouri Historical Society and elsewhere), Samuel B. Waugh (Pennsylvania Academy of Fine Arts, Philadelphia), and Matthew Wilson, who painted the last Lincoln portrait from life, dated April 1865 (Louis A. Warren Lincoln Library and Museum). Francis Bicknell Carpenter immortalized his Lincoln portrait (which hangs in the Capitol) with a book about Lincoln's sittings for it called *Six Months in the White House.*

Lincoln associates then and critics now generally agree that none of the likenesses is distinguished. Presidential secretary John G. Nicolay noted that "Lincoln's features were the despair of every artist who undertook his portrait." Walt Whitman, who saw Lincoln several times, termed all the "current portraits . . . failures." White House secretary John Hay said simply: "There are many pictures of Lincoln; there is no portrait of him."

SOURCES: Harold Holzer's "Out from the Wilderness—Contemporary Portraits of Abraham Lincoln," *The Connoisseur,* CXCIX (October 1978), 124–131, and "How the Printmakers Saw Lincoln: Not-So-Honest Portraits of 'Honest Abe,'" *Winterthur Portfolio,* XIV (Summer 1979), 143–170, are vital and lively sources for this subject. See Rufus Rockwell Wilson, *Lincoln in Portraiture* (New York: Press of the Pioneers, 1935).

See also CARPENTER, FRANCIS BICKNELL; PHOTOGRAPHS.

Postage Stamps Abraham Lincoln served as postmaster of New Salem, Illinois, from May 7, 1833, to May 30, 1836, and, though his term predated the use of postage stamps on letters, it seems especially appropriate that his likeness should appear on many different United States postage stamps (and on those of many foreign countries as well). The United States Post Office Department issued the first Lincoln stamp late in 1865, a 25-cent red stamp for mailing newspapers and periodicals where payment could not be collected at the destination. About a year after Lincoln's death, the Post Office Department issued a black 15-cent postage stamp, the first of many Lincoln stamps for regular mail. If it was commemorative of his death, the Department made no effort to announce it. A 90-cent carmine-and-black stamp issued in 1869 is among the rarest of Lincoln stamps; only 47,460 of the expensive stamps were issued.

Thereafter so many stamps bore Lincoln's likeness that in 1962 a group formed the Lincoln Society of Philately for stamp collectors especially interested in Lincoln stamps. The society's bulletin, the bimonthly *Lincoln Log,* ceased publication in 1977.

SOURCES: See Randle Bond Truett, *Lincoln in Philately* (Washington, D.C.: privately printed, 1959).

Powell, Lewis Thornton (1845–1865) A coconspirator with John Wilkes Booth, the assassin of President Lincoln. Lewis Powell was also known by aliases, Lewis Paine (or Payne) or Wood. He was the son of a Baptist clergyman from Florida. Born in Alabama, he was superintending his father's plantation when the Civil War began. He enlisted in the Second Florida Infantry. At the Battle of Murfreesboro in 1863, one of his brothers was killed and another was maimed for life. Powell was wounded, taken prisoner at Gettysburg, and made a nurse in a Gettysburg hospital. After being moved to another hospital in Baltimore, he escaped and joined a Confederate cavalry unit under John Singleton Mosby. Despairing of the Confederate cause, he took the oath of allegiance (using the name "Paine") in January 1865. He went to Baltimore to board with the family of Margaret Branson, a nurse he had worked with in Pennsylvania.

Ben: Perley Poore described Powell as "very tall, with an athletic, gladiatorial frame." He displayed a "massive robustness of animal manhood in its most stalwart type." He had "unflinching dark gray eyes, low forehead, massive jaws, compressed full lips, small nose with large nostrils, and stolid, remorseless expression." His hands were soft, not those of a laborer, and one side of his head appeared a good deal larger than the other. While at the Branson boarding house, this large and violent man was reported to military authorities for beating a Negro maid. (He "threw her on the ground and stamped on her body, struck her on the forehead, and said he would kill her," said a witness at his trial.)

Powell probably met Booth while he was serving with Mosby, and Booth probably recognized him later in Baltimore. Whatever the mechanism of acquaintance, Booth's money was a welcome sight to the unemployed Powell, who was recruited for the abduction plot in

March. Powell's powerful frame was obviously useful, especially when Booth contemplated kidnapping Lincoln in Ford's Theatre by lowering him over the side of the box seat some 13 feet above the stage. Powell participated in the abortive attempt of March 17 to kidnap Lincoln as the President rode in a carriage to the outskirts of Washington. Thereafter, he spent about a week in Baltimore and returned to live at Booth's expense in the Herndon House in Washington.

At an 8 p.m. meeting in the Herndon House on April 14, Booth assigned Powell the task of assassinating Secretary of State William H. Seward. While Booth shot Lincoln, Powell appeared at Seward's house masquerading as a messenger with medicine from Seward's doctor (a stratagem devised by David E. Herold to capitalize on Powell's experience as a nurse). Seward was convalescing from a carriage accident, but his son Frederick refused entry to Powell, who insisted he had medicine for the Secretary. Powell then pistol-whipped Frederick Seward to unconsciousness and stabbed the Secretary of State several times with a Bowie knife. Seriously injured, Seward was saved from death by a heavy neck brace he wore as a result of his accident, by rolling off the bed onto the floor, and by the efforts of his nurse, George T. Robinson, who suffered several knife wounds also. Powell knocked Seward's son Augustus down and wounded a State Department messenger on his way out. He escaped on a horse he had waiting outside the residence. Two hours later he abandoned the horse.

On the night of April 17, officers arrested the occupants of Mary Surratt's boarding house. While they were at the house, Powell appeared at the door with a pickax on his shoulder and a cap made out of his drawers or the sleeve of his shirt. He asked whether he was to start digging a gutter the next day. Mrs. Surratt denied knowing him or sending for him, and he was arrested on the spot as a suspicious character. Only later did authorities realize he was Powell. Ten men split a $5000 reward for his capture.

Powell proved to be a remarkably stoic prisoner. He did not have a bowel movement from April 29 until June 2. Defense attorney W. E. Doster attempted an insanity defense for Powell which failed. In his final argument before the military commission that tried the conspirators, Doster argued that the simple Confederate soldier had been brutalized by proslavery propaganda and an inherently violent social system, by warfare, and by economic hardship. On June 30, however, Powell was sentenced to hang. He died on the gallows on July 7. His body was buried in the old penitentiary yard of the Washington Arsenal and moved to "Warehouse 1" on the arsenal grounds in 1867.

SOURCES: See Benn Pittman, ed., *The Assassination of President Lincoln and the Trial of the Conspirators* (Cincinnati, Ohio: Moore, Wilstach & Baldwin, 1865); Ben: Perley Poore, *The Conspiracy Trial for the Murder of the President,* 3 vols. (Boston: J. E. Tilton, 1865), and Leon O. Prior, "Lewis Payne, Pawn of John Wilkes Booth," *Florida Historical Quarterly,* XLIII (July 1964), 1–20.

See also ASSASSINATION; TRIAL OF THE ASSASSINS.

Presidency, Powers of the "The Presidency," Abraham Lincoln said in 1850, "is no bed of roses. . . . No human being can fill that station and escape censure." Lincoln, in his long political apprenticeship in the Whig party had lost any grand illusions he may have had about the highest office in the land. The Whig party, born of opposition to a strong President (Andrew Jackson) and nearly always opposed to the administration in power, was little prone to exaggerate the majesty of the office. Whigs tended to think of the President as a glorified clerk who should follow the will of Congress, administer the laws, and not interfere with the legislative power.

Lincoln himself came rather late to the Whig conception of the office. Only in 1848, when he campaigned for Zachary Taylor, who had no platform and very weak partisan identification, did he extol the virtues of the Whig theory. A President who doubts the constitutionality of a bill but is not sure of it, Lincoln argued, should not "veto it, . . . but is to defer to congress, and approve it." Though in "a certain sense, and to a certain extent, he is the representative of the people," the President cannot "know the wants of the people, as well as three hundred other men, coming from all the various localities of the nation." The Whig party "maintained for years that neither the influence, the duress, or the prohibition of the Executive should control the legitmately expressed will of the people."

Taylor's election, however, came at a time when Lincoln was most sensitive to executive usurpations of power. Lincoln thought that President James K. Polk's ability to maneuver Congress into a declaration of war against Mexico placed "our President where kings have always stood." Lincoln was led to the most extreme statement of the Whig view he ever made by his sharp distaste for the Mexican War. Once in office, President Taylor seemed to Lincoln to be carrying the Whig idea too far. Lincoln warned Secretary of State John M. Clayton that the President must not appear "a mere man of straw." Lincoln understood the popular power of Jackson's conception of the office. Taylor, Lincoln said, "must occasionally say. . . , 'by the eternal,' 'I take the responsibility.' Those phrases were the 'Samson's locks' of Gen. Jackson, and we dare not disregard the lessons of experience." Lincoln's failure to receive an appointment to the General Land Office from Taylor, who may have favored Lincoln for the post but deferred to Cabinet advice to appoint someone else, doubtless intensified his conviction that a President should exercise his will.

As President, Lincoln proved Whiggishly reluctant to use, or even threaten to use, the veto power. He directly vetoed only two minor pieces of legislation and used the pocket veto only twice also. "My political education," Lincoln told a Pittsburgh audience on February 15, 1861, "strongly inclines me against a very free use of any of these means [recommending legislation, the veto, or indirect influences], by the Executive, to control the legislation of the country." He rarely drafted or recommended legislation and as rarely utilized his powers

Presidency, Powers of the

The title page of this anti-Lincoln satirical piece, issued for the campaign of 1864, showed Lincoln with a crown—a reference to his enlargement of the powers of the Presidency.

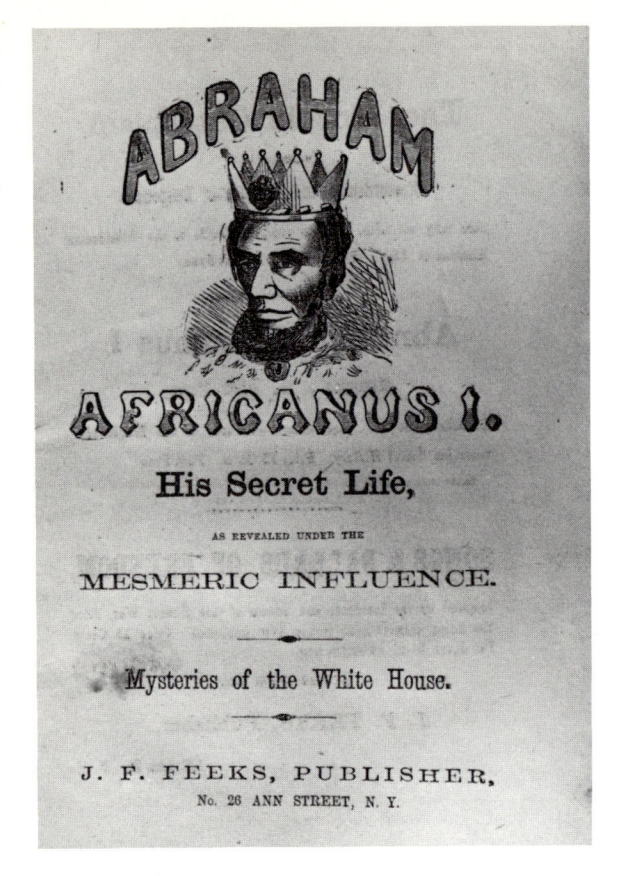

to help or hinder legislation through Congress. The Republican complexion of Congress during his administration generally made it easy for him passively to sign whatever bills Congress put on his desk.

Disunion, however, brought out the Jackson in him. Indeed, Lincoln thought immediately of that great opponent of Nullification as he prepared to assume office; he used Jackson's speech on Nullification to prepare his First Inaugural Address. And he referred to his stern predecessor when he replied to a group of conservative Baltimore citizens alarmed at the passage of Federal troops through their state to protect Washington:

> The rebels attack Fort Sumter, and your citizens attack troops sent to the defense of the Government, and the lives and property in Washington, and yet you would have me break my oath and surrender the Government without a blow. There is no Washington in that—no Jackson in that—no manhood nor honor in that. . . . Our men are not moles, and can't dig under the earth; they are not birds, and can't fly through the air. There is no way but to march across, and that they must do. . . . Go home and tell your people that if they will not attack us, we will not attack them; but if they do attack us, we will return it, and that severely.

Lincoln could risk putting his major rivals for the Republican presidential nomination—William H. Seward, Edward Bates, Salmon P. Chase, and Simon Cameron—in his Cabinet in part because he planned to make the important decisions himself. He had recognized the importance of executive will more than 10 years earlier:

> It is said Gen. Taylor and his officers held a council of war, at Palo Alto . . . ; and that he then fought the battle against

unanimous opinion of those officers. This fact (no matter whether rightfully or wrongfully) gives him more popularity than ten thousand submissions, however really wise and magnanimous those submissions may be.

President Lincoln did not shrink from exerting his will. Within days of the firing on Fort Sumter he enlarged the army without congressional authorization, spent money for purposes other than those designated by Congress, and suspended the privilege of the writ of habeas corpus. He awaited congressional approval after the fact, noting "that nothing has been done beyond the constitutional competency of Congress"—a remarkable equation of executive and legislative powers. He admitted that some of his actions were "without authority of law." As he explained in 1863, he was "thoroughly imbued with a reverence for the guarranteed rights of individuals" and "was slow to adopt the strong measures, which by degrees I have been forced to regard as being within the exceptions of the constitution, and as indispensable to the public safety." On the habeas corpus privilege, he was anything but slow. Conscription, the Emancipation Proclamation, and novel Reconstruction measures followed by degrees—too slowly to suit the Radical Republicans but much too fast for the Democratic opposition. The President's war powers seemed to him greater than Congress's; the Emancipation Proclamation was in effect when he stated his view that Congress could not abolish slavery.

Though they disagree on the constitutionality of the measures, all modern students agree with Lincoln's assessment that his administration used "strong measures." His strong successors in the Presidency have shared the view, generally in an effort to hide their own vigorous measures behind Lincoln's venerable mantle. Theodore Roosevelt chided President Woodrow Wilson by saying that Washington and Lincoln "did not 'keep us out of war.'" Roosevelt identified strongly with what he called "the Lincoln-Jackson" school of the Presidency. Harry Truman claimed that Lincoln "exercised the powers of the President to meet the emergencies with which he was faced"—largely without limit. "He had the guts to go ahead and do what he thought was the right thing at a time when he had a great big opposition," Truman added.

American historians have generally agreed with the Presidential assessments. In a 1969 poll of 571 historians, Lincoln ranked first in "general prestige" (a position he held in more informal surveys by Arthur M. Schlesinger in 1948 and 1962). In "strength of action" he ranked second only to Franklin Delano Roosevelt, and in "presidential activeness" he stood eighth (behind Franklin Roosevelt, Theodore Roosevelt, Jackson, Lyndon Johnson, Truman, John F. Kennedy, and Woodrow Wilson). He ranked first in administration "accomplishments."

In very recent times, some historians have been careful to note that Lincoln's strong measures, instituted without congressional advice or approval, were not precedents for similar actions by modern Presidents in wars against foreign nations. The Civil War was not a foreign war, and the justification of Lincoln's measures was his constitutional oath to "take care that the Laws be faithfully executed." Lincoln on occasion boldly took the position that to save the whole of the Constitution, he had temporarily to violate part of it.

SOURCES: See especially J. G. Randall's "The Rule of Law Under Lincoln" in his *Lincoln the Liberal Statesman* (New York: Dodd, Mead, 1947), pp. 118–134; David Donald's "Abraham Lincoln: Whig in the White House" in his *Lincoln Reconsidered: Essays on the Civil War Era* (New York: Vintage Books, 1961), pp. 187–208; Curtis P. Nettels's letter to the editor, *Presidential Studies Quarterly*, IX (Winter 1979); Richard N. Current's "The Lincoln Presidents," ibid., 25–35; and Gary M. Maranell's "The Evaluation of Presidents: An Extension of the Schlesinger Polls," *Journal of American History*, LVII (June 1970), 104–113.

See also COMMANDER IN CHIEF; CONSCRIPTION; CONSTITUTION OF THE UNITED STATES; HABEAS CORPUS; NEWSPAPERS; SLAVERY.

Proclamation of Amnesty and Reconstruction

December 8, 1863. President Lincoln's plan for reconstructing the Union by "ten percent" governments was announced in his annual message to Congress. Lincoln offered amnesty and the restoration of property rights to participants in the rebellion who would take an oath to support the Constitution thereafter and obey all acts of Congress and proclamations of the President affecting slavery. Lincoln affirmed that "while I remain in my present position I shall not attempt to retract or modify the emancipation proclamation; nor shall I return to slavery any person who is free by the terms of that proclamation, or by the acts of Congress." Certain groups were excepted from the amnesty: Confederate civil and diplomatic officers, Confederate military officers above colonel or naval officers above lieutenant, those who had left the United States judiciary or Congress to aid the rebellion, commissioned officers who had left the United States Army or Navy to aid the rebellion, and those who treated Negro or white prisoners "otherwise than lawfully as prisoners of war."

To restore a seceded state to the Union, Lincoln declared, no fewer than 10 percent of the people who voted in 1860 must take the oath. When they organized a government republican in form, it would be recognized and its representatives readmitted to Congress. The state had to recognize the freedom of and provide for the education of the slaves, but Lincoln would allow any other policies "consistent, as a temporary arrangement, with their present condition as a laboring, landless, and homeless class." Lincoln admitted that his was not the only plan possible and that Congress had the ultimate constitutional power to admit Representatives.

Lincoln's secretaries recalled that the "reception of the message was extremely pleasing to the President. A solution of the most important problem of the time, which conservatives like [James] Dixon and Reverdy Johnson thoroughly approved, and to which Mr. [Charles] Sumner made no objection, was of course a source of profound gratification." Antislavery men were particularly pleased by its assertion of the irrevocability of the Emancipation Proclamation (though Lincoln admitted the Supreme Court might alter it).

There was at this point no major gap between Radical Republicans in Congress and the President on the issue of Reconstruction, and it is an error to exaggerate the conservatism of Lincoln's 10 percent plan. It showed that the war had changed his view of the underlying loyalty of the Southern masses. In his first message to Congress in 1861, Lincoln had expressed his doubt "whether . . . a majority of the legally qualified voters of any State, except perhaps South Carolina, . . . favor . . . disunion." By the end of 1863 he knew that it would be difficult to find even 10 percent of the Southern voters still loyal to the Union. This was a wartime plan meant to lure the small minority of wavering Confederates to the Union side. What it most clearly revealed of Lincoln's vision of the future was that the postwar reunited country should be slaveless.

SOURCES: There is a superb analysis of the proclamation in Herman Belz, *Reconstructing the Union: Theory and Policy During the Civil War* (Ithaca: Cornell University Press, 1969).

See also BANKS, NATHANIEL PRENTISS; RADICAL REPUBLICANS; RECONSTRUCTION; WADE DAVIS BILL.

Prohibition *See* TEMPERANCE.

Psychology

Since Lincoln's parents were illiterate and left no rich record of his youth and since Abraham was himself a notoriously shut-mouthed man, it has always proved extremely difficult to plumb Lincoln's psychology. As many of his associates agreed, Lincoln revealed his inner thoughts to no one. Most of his surviving correspondence is political in nature and contains only a handful of letters to or from his wife. Any conclusions about aspects of Lincoln's psychology, then, are tentative at best.

Certainly the best documented and most widely famed attribute was a streak of melancholy in his nature. Lincoln commented on periods of melancholy himself on several occasions and referred to it as the "hypo" (for "hypochondria"). "That gives me the hypo whenever I think of it," he told Mary S. Owens on May 7, 1837, in reference to the possibility of her moving away from Illinois with her sister. Difficulties in courtship brought on the most severe attacks of melancholy. When, on January 1, 1841, he and Mary Todd broke off their engagement, Lincoln was plummeted into despair. He felt that his doctor was at that time "necessary to my existence." He had too little "composure" even to write a long letter to his law partner. He interrupted his labors in the state legislature, and he described himself as

> the most miserable man living. If what I feel were equally distributed to the whole human family, there would not be one cheerful face on the earth. Whether I shall ever be better I can not tell; I awfully forbode I shall not. To remain as I am is impossible; I must die or be better, it appears to me.

He recovered to marry Miss Todd on November 4, 1842, but he experienced periods of melancholy, though none as deep as this one, the rest of his life.

In part Lincoln coped with his tendency to depression in the manner suggested by the above letter, with ironic humor. His difficult youth on the frontier gave him an essentially tragic outlook on life. "How true it is," he said late in September 1841, while "the 'Blues'" were still very much on his mind, "that 'God tempers the wind to the shorn lamb,' or in other words, that He renders the worst of human conditions tolerable, while He permits the best, to be nothing better than tolerable." Death was an ever-present frontier companion. When he was 9 years old, his mother died in an epidemic that took others close to the family. His older sister died while he was a teenager, and Lincoln himself had a brush with death, in 1819, when a horse kicked him in the head and rendered him unconscious and, to all appearances momentarily, dead. When he thought of his childhood in Indiana, the mature Lincoln thought of death, as in this poetry he wrote in 1846:

> The friends I left that parting day,
> How changed, as time has sped!
> Young childhood grown, strong manhood gray,
> And half of all are dead.
>
> I hear the loved survivors tell
> How nought from death could save,
> Till every sound appears a knell,
> And every spot a grave.
>
> I range the fields with pensive tread,
> And pace the hollow rooms,
> And feel (companion of the dead)
> I'm living in the tombs.

Such experiences taught him, however, that "in the dep[t]h and even the agony of despondency, . . . verry shortly you are to feel well again." In addition to the value of humor, Lincoln learned the therapeutic value of work. He advised his friend Joshua Speed, in an agony of doubt over marriage, to "avoid being *idle*." In "case my mind were not exactly right," Lincoln said, "I would immediately engage in some business."

The philosophical expression of Lincoln's tendencies toward depression and of his occasional preoccupation with death was fatalism, a doctrine to which Lincoln was attracted off and on throughout his life. Explaining his religious views in 1846, he admitted "that in early life I was inclined to believe in what I understand is called the 'Doctrine of Necessity'—that is, that the human mind is impelled to action, or held in rest by some power, over which the mind itself has no control." He said that he had "entirely left off" the "habit of arguing thus" for "more than five years." He did not say, however, that he no longer believed it. As President, Lincoln resumed thinking along similar lines. "I claim not to have controlled events, but confess plainly that events have controlled me," he said on April 4, 1864. He had made a similar statement privately perhaps 2 years before, in what is called his "Meditation on the Divine Will," a title his biographers gave the undated fragment:

> The will of God prevails. In great contests each party claims to act in accordance with the will of God. Both *may* be, and one *must* be wrong. God can not be *for*, and *against* the same thing at the same time. In the present civil war it is quite possible that God's purpose is something different from the purpose of either party—and yet the human instrumentalities, working just as they do, are of the best adaptation to effect His purpose. I am almost ready to say this is probably true—that God wills this contest, and wills that it shall not end yet. By his mere quiet power, on the minds of the now contestants, He could have either *saved* or *destroyed* the Union without a human contest. Yet the contest began. And having begun He could give the final victory to either side any day. Yet the contest proceeds.

And the same view provided the central message of Lincoln's Second Inaugural Address:

> Each [side] looked for an easier triumph, and a result less fundamental and astounding. Both read the same Bible, and pray to the same God; and each invokes His aid against the other. . . . The prayers of both could not be answered; that of neither has been answered fully. The almighty has His own purposes.

Frontier primitivism gave Lincoln a slightly superstitious nature. "I always was superstitious," Lincoln admitted to Speed, and this trait revealed itself particularly in his belief in dreams. "Think you better put 'Tad's' pistol away," Lincoln wrote Mary on June 9, 1863. "I had an ugly dream about him." A dream of sailing on a ship near mysterious shores often preceded good news from the front, Lincoln reported. Ward Hill Lamon claimed that, shortly before his assassination, Lincoln described a dream in which he visited the corpse of the President laid out in the White House.

Lincoln was reluctant to speak of his parents. He wrote almost nothing about his mother, and, if William H. Herndon can be believed, the reticence stemmed from his fear that she was illegitimate. His stepmother proved to be "good" and "kind" to him, but his relations with his father were not the best. His few written statements about his father were uncharitable to say the least (his father could do no "more in the way of writing," Lincoln said on one occasion, "than to bunglingly sign his own name"). Warned that the old man was dying in 1851, Lincoln did not free himself to visit him, feeling "that if we could meet now, it is doubtful whether it would not be more painful than pleasant." Thomas Lincoln had never met Mary, visited Springfield, or seen his grandchildren.

Lincoln's ability to cope with whatever melancholy afflicted him late in life was great. Through humor, fatalistic resignation, and, perhaps, some religious feeling, he became his wife's principal prop in the losses of their children Eddie and Willie. Likewise, no melancholy ever interfered with his ability to work in the White House (as it had briefly in the Illinois legislature 20 years before). John Hay, the only person close to Lincoln in the Presidential years who kept a diary, consistently reported the President in good spirits and in complete control of events. As for his superstition, it was not a controlling force by then either. No careful lawyer who dreams of his own death fails, as Lincoln failed, to write a will.

SOURCES: To date, psychobiographies of Lincoln have been unmitigated disasters. There are hopeful signs, however, in Charles B. Strozier's "The Search for Identity and Love in Young Lincoln," in Cullom Davis et al., eds., *The Public and the Private Lincoln* (Carbondale: Southern Illinois University Press, 1979), pp. 3–19.

See also HUMOR; RELIGION; SPEED, JOSHUA FRY.

Q

Quincy, Illinois Site of the sixth Lincoln-Douglas Debate, October 13, 1858. Quincy is in Adams County, in west-central Illinois. The county was Democratic, though not overwhelmingly so, and it had for a time been Stephen A. Douglas's home district. When the Little Giant arrived on the night of the 12th, a torchlit procession perhaps a half-mile long accompanied him to his quarters at the Quincy House. A long procession guided Lincoln to the home of Orville Hickman Browning the next day. The parade included a "model ship on wheels drawn by four horses and labeled 'CONSTITUTION.'" A live raccoon (the symbol of the old Whig party) was at the helm—a sign that the two candidates would be vying for the support of conservative former Whigs in the area. A crowd of about 12,000 thronged the public square for the debate at 2:30 that afternoon.

Lincoln in the opening speech denied that he uttered different principles for different latitudes in the state. He quoted his statement in opposition to civil rights for Negroes made in the Charleston debate and noted its close similarity to what he had said in the first debate in Ottawa, where the leader of Illinois's radical antislavery men, Owen Lovejoy, sat on the very platform with him. He repeated his charge that abolitionist resolutions Douglas had previously imputed to the Republicans were a "forgery."

Lincoln continued to stress the idea that slavery was a moral wrong to be dealt with by halting its growth but not without "due respect to the actual presence of it amongst us and the difficulties of getting rid of it in any satisfactory way." Republicans, Lincoln assured the audience, would attack slavery only where the Constitution allowed, in the territories. So restrained were the Republicans, he added, that they did not attack slavery in one place where the Constitution clearly permitted such an attack, the District of Columbia. He refuted Douglas's charge in the preceding debate that Republican criticism of the Dred Scott decision constituted a threat of mob law, but his language was carefully convoluted: "We propose so resisting it as to have it reversed if we can, and a new judicial rule established upon this subject." Republicans, Lincoln concluded, dealt with slavery as a wrong; Douglas "has the high distinction, so far as I know, of never having said slavery is either right or wrong."

Douglas took pains to prove that his use of the erroneous Republican resolutions was an honest error and pointed to Lincoln's earlier attempt to prove a conspiracy among Douglas, Franklin Pierce, James Buchanan, and Roger B. Taney to reopen the territories to slavery as a similarly false charge of conspiracy. He chided that Lincoln would not say whether he would vote to admit as a state a territory which chose a slave constitution. He continued to argue that Lincoln ignored the words he had uttered at Chicago urging the people to "discard all this quibbling about this man and the other man—this race and that race and the other race being inferior, and therefore they must be placed in an inferior position." No matter what Lincoln said at Ottawa, the Chicago speech contradicted his statement in Charleston "in favor of the superior position being assigned to the white man." He repeated, as he did in every debate in the series, the charge that Lincoln's "House Divided" speech was "making a war upon slavery." How else could he put it "in a course of ultimate extinction"? Douglas now added a new and ingenious argument:

> He first tells you that he would prohibit slavery everywhere in the territories. . . . When he thus gets it confined, . . . the natural laws of increase will go on until the negroes will be so plenty that they cannot live on the soil. He will hem them in until starvation seizes them, and by starving them to death, he will put slavery in the course of ultimate extinction . . . he can extinguish it only by extinguishing the negro race. . . . This is the humane and Christian remedy that he proposes for the great crime of slavery.

Douglas refused to "argue the question whether slavery is right or wrong" because he would be "discussing a question that we have no right to act upon." He pressed Lincoln for more clarity in regard to how he would reverse the Dred Scott decision. Constitutionally, Douglas knew, "From that decision there is no appeal this side of Heaven." Douglas reaffirmed his "Freeport Doctrine" that slavery could be excluded from a territory despite the Dred Scott decision simply by the territory's refusing to pass local police laws to protect the property. He continued to link his name with that of Whig hero Henry Clay by saying "that I sustained Clay's compromise measures on the ground that they established the principle of self-government in the territories." He spent over 20 percent of his time on an essentially intraparty Democratic feud with James Buchanan over popular sovereignty. He concluded with a warning against discussing "the morals of the people" of the slave states, for which "they are accountable to God and their posterity and not to us." Thereby Americans would preserve peace and "this republic can exist forever divided into free and slave States, as our fathers made it."

Lincoln's rebuttal seized immediately on Douglas's announcement "here to-day, to be put on record, that his system of policy in regard to the institution of slavery *contemplates that it shall last forever."* Lincoln invoked Jacksonian doctrine that "each man was bound to support the Constitution 'as he understood it' " to suggest how he would change the Dred Scott decision—the same way the Democrats reversed "the decision of that same Court in favor of the constitutionality of the National Bank." Lincoln explained that his inclusion of Negroes in the Declaration of Independence was holding the same "sentiments that Henry Clay used to hold" that the principle that *"men are created equal"* should be kept in view "in the *original construction* of society." Precisely this was this case "where the soil is clean and clear," as in the territories. And this did not mean "that I want a negro wife." Lincoln ended with his charges of forgery and conspiracy to nationalize slavery. That evening Republican speaker Carl Schurz addressed Quincy's German-Americans in German to end a long day of high political excitement.

The Quincy debate was important in two respects, both largely marginal to the bulk of the arguing. Douglas's charge that Republican plans to confine slavery would lead to the extinction of the Negro race was an argument he failed to develop later. It might have embarrassed Republicans, who always left to the imagination the exact way their platform would end slavery. And Douglas's careless statement that the Republic could remain forever half free and half slave clearly delighted Lincoln. On the whole, the Quincy debate was not distinguished for its high-minded exploration of important issues. A correspondent for the *Missouri Democrat*, for example, complained: "It is certainly to be regretted that the canvass in Illinois has turned so much on personal issues."

SOURCES: See Edwin Erle Sparks, ed., *The Lincoln-Douglas Debates of 1858* (Springfield: Illinois State Historical Library, 1908).

R

Radical Republicans Radicalism in mid-nineteenth century American politics was a function of one's stance on the slavery question; the more zealously antislavery a person was, the more radical he was. Before the Civil War, the more nearly one approached abolitionism, the more radical one was. Abolitionists were so radical that many did not vote for either the Democratic or Republican parties, since both parties were pledged not to interfere with slavery in the states, where the Constitution protected it. Despite Democratic accusations that the Republican party, the more liberal of the two on the slavery question, was an abolition party, neither abolitionists nor Republicans so regarded it. That party never pledged to do more than halt the expansion of slavery to new areas.

Still, there were Republicans who maintained good relations with the abolitionists despite their differences over the constitutional accessibility of slavery to congressional interference. When the Civil War broke out, the more zealously antislavery Republicans, who wanted the administration to move more quickly and decisively to abolish slavery, came quickly to be regarded by their enemies, and in many cases to regard themselves, as radicals. The hostile New York *Herald* may have coined the term which was often used to describe them when it blamed those politicians who screamed "On to Richmond" for the defeat at Bull Run. The *Herald* denounced a "Jacobin club" for that overzealousness, and Lincoln's secretary (and, later, biographer) John Hay referred to the Radicals as Jacobins ever after. Historians most often call them the Radical Republicans, a phrase which gained wide usage during Reconstruction, after Lincoln's death. Lincoln himself rarely used either term in his speeches or letters. In 1864, in fact, he told campaign biographer Henry J. Raymond that the attribution of the phrase *"the Jacobinism of Congress"* to Lincoln in a conversation was erroneous: "I do not remember using [it] literally or in substance, and . . . I wish [it] not to be published in any event."

Historians from the 1920s through the 1950s—most notably the greatest Lincoln biographer, James G. Randall—pointed to the President's differences from the Radical Republicans as the most serious problem of his administration. David Donald, himself a student of Randall's but the first historian to attack his view, described the older view this way in 1956:

> . . . Abraham Lincoln was an astute, farseeing statesman who would have won the war with expedition and ended it without bitterness. For the North he proposed malice toward none and charity for all; for the Negro, freedom, a gradual emancipation, possibly continuing till 1900; for the Southern whites, compensation for their slaves and amnesty for their rebellion in return for future loyalty. . . .
>
> But these plans were frustrated, not so much by the Southerners, not even by the Democrats, but by a small yet articulate and potent group within the President's own party. These were the antislavery extremists, the "Jacobins," the Radicals. . . .
>
> The abolitionist principles that these Radicals so piously announced were only a front for their real purposes. "Their main characteristics," according to J. G. Randall, "were anti-

Radical Republicans

slavery zeal as a political instrument, moralizing unction, rebel-baiting intolerance and hunger for power." . . . these unsavory Radicals were the advance agents of industrialism, which was about to take over the government of the United States and pervert it for selfish ends. . . . the Radicals intended to enact a high protective tariff that mothered monopoly, to pass a homestead law that invited speculators to loot the public domain, and to subsidize a transcontinental railroad that afforded infinite opportunities for jobbery.

Secession and the withdrawal of Southern Congressmen from Washington gave the Radicals a chance to enact their program, but an early end of the fighting might imperil their schemes. . . .

At every turn, then, these Radicals harassed the President. They meddled with military affairs and prolonged the war. They interfered with civilian administration and tried to wreck the Cabinet. They forced through brutal measures of confiscation which retarded the progress of pacification. They stressed the abolition issue at the cost of dividing Northern sentiment and prolonging Southern resistance. They opposed Lincoln's renomination in 1864, and even after he was officially selected by the Republican party as its standard-bearer, they attempted to force his withdrawal and to run another, more Radical candidate in his stead. In 1865 they were ready to frustrate Lincoln's plans for speedy, peaceful reconstruction, just as they did, in fact, override those of his successor.

Historians now disagree on the degree of cohesiveness and unity among the Radicals, and they have always disagreed on the membership of the group. However, practically all include Senators Charles Sumner, Benjamin F. Wade, Zachariah Chandler, and Henry Wilson, Representatives George W. Julian, William D. Kelley, Thaddeus Stevens, Owen Lovejoy, and Henry Winter Davis, Generals Benjamin F. Butler, John C. Frémont, and David Hunter, and agitator Wendell Phillips. Within the administration itself, only Salmon P. Chase was consistently Radical, though Secretary of War Edwin M. Stanton frequently cooperated with Radicals in Congress.

Few of the accusations against the Radicals will stand close scrutiny. Some of the charges are inconsistent. John Codman Ropes, later a military historian of the Civil War, noted as early as January 1, 1863, that "The cry of the so-called radical party has always been to push forward, do something—yet the uniform charge against them has been that they wish to prolong the war till Slavery be overthrown." Likewise their vaunted power seems inconsistent with their small numbers and allegedly unrepresentative opinions. Though some point to the Joint Committee on the Conduct of the War as the locus of their power, that congressional body, though radical enough in opinion, was merely investigatory and advisory in nature, had no enforcement powers, and in fact achieved its ends—removing General George B. McClellan, for example—only when they coincided with the President's wishes. It was frustrated when they did not; no matter what it did, for example, it could never get General Butler reinstated to command in Louisiana after his removal in 1862.

Lincoln felt Radical pressure. As he told Border State Congressmen, reluctant to institute the President's compensated emancipation plan, on July 12, 1862: "The pressure, in this direction [emancipation], is still upon me, and is increasing." Repudiating the emancipation schemes of generals like David Hunter "gave disatisfaction, if not offence, to many whose support the country can not afford to lose." Pressure was one thing, but control was another. John Hay told fellow secretary John G. Nicolay on September 11, 1863: "You may talk as you please of the Abolition Cabal directing affairs from Washington. . . . The old man sits here and wields like a backwoods Jupiter the bolts of war and the machinery of government with a hand equally steady & equally firm."

It is best not to confuse peripheral Civil War issues with the essence of Radicalism in that period: zeal to eliminate slavery. The Radicals had no peculiar views on military efficiency except to think that generals who had their hearts in the effort—in their view, that is, antislavery Republicans—would fight best. A generally critical attitude toward the administration's war effort was widely held by Republicans and especially Democrats of all hues of opinion in periods of few Union victories. Likewise, beyond the generally capitalistic economic views common to most Republicans, and Democrats for that matter, Radicals agreed on no coherent economic program. Butler, Stevens, and Wade were inflationists; other Radicals like Lovejoy and Sumner feared inflation. They did not agree on tariff policy or banking. Stevens, like most Pennsylvania Republicans, was a high-tariff man and disliked Chase's national bank policies. Chase, Julian, and Lovejoy were low-tariff men. Sumner devised the first bill for federal regulation of the railroads; other Radicals helped vote it down.

Vindictiveness and brutality were matters of individual temperament. In general, the Republican party was at least as anti-Southern as it was antislavery, and some

Charles Sumner was the symbolic head of the Radical wing of the Republican party, and before the Civil War he appeared in political cartoons only as a reminder of the dangerously radical nature of Republican policies on race. The war enhanced the Radicals' reputation, and this cartoon for the campaign of 1864 proudly depicted Sumner as one of the patriots upholding the Republican platform. (Library of Congress)

Radicals, like some conservatives and moderates, were more vindictive than others. Lincoln was notable for his lack of personal condemnation of Southern slaveholders and for his lack of feelings of vindictiveness toward Confederates. Some Radicals were like him in that. Sumner opposed retaliation against Confederate prisoners of war and introduced resolutions to forbid the display in the Capitol of battle paintings showing some Americans victorious over other Americans. Chase made it difficult to bring Jefferson Davis to trial after the war; Wilson aided Davis and former Confederate Vice President Alexander H. Stephens while they were imprisoned; Stanton ordered Davis's manacles removed; and Wade opposed hanging Mary Surratt.

On the all-important issue of slavery itself, the Radicals did differ from Lincoln and always felt that they were in advance of him on the question. Most Radicals were disgusted by Lincoln's revocation of Frémont's emancipation proclamation for Missouri in September 1861. Wade thought it "could only come of one, born of 'poor white trash' and educated in a slave State." Yet the matter of difference was never as great as the differences between almost any Republican and almost any Democrat. Senator Sumner said twice that the distance between him and the President was not great. *"The Presdt. tells me,"* he said in December 1861, "that the question between him & me is one of 4 weeks or at most 6 weeks, when we shall all be together." And he told Massachusetts Governor John Andrew, "He tells me that I am ahead of him only a month or six weeks." As disgusted as Wade had been with the Frémont imbroglio, he recovered when Lincoln announced the preliminary Emancipation Proclamation: "Hurrah for Old Abe and the *proclamation.*" Radicals found little fault with that move and many other moves that Lincoln made; they would simply have made them sooner.

Radical differences from Lincoln on Reconstruction, too, have been exaggerated. Lincoln's Proclamation of Amnesty and Reconstruction of December 8, 1863, pleased most of the party, Radicals included. His policies in occupied Louisiana *dis*pleased most of the party, moderates included. The Wade-Davis Bill, which Lincoln gave a pocket veto, passed with the votes of all Republican Senators and with all Representatives but six—five of whom were from the slave-holding Border States. Even after that disagreement, Lincoln in December 1864 agreed to a compromise in which he would approve a revised Wade-Davis Bill if Congress would recognize his reconstructed governments in Louisiana and Arkansas. Much of the Reconstruction disagreement focused on the relative power of Congress or the Executive to instrument plans. The disagreement persisted, but on other questions the Radicals would not be a unit until Andrew Johnson's obstinacy and Southern reluctance to make concessions forced them together—after Lincoln's death. The fact of the matter was that Republicans agreed substantially on slavery and disagreed on the Negro. Radical opinion varied from the equalitarianism of Stevens, who insisted on being buried in a Negro cemetery, to the insolent racism of Wade, who complained about Washington food, "cooked by Niggers until I can smell and taste the Nigger . . . all over."

The differences between Lincoln and the Radicals have been most overdrawn in the realm of politics. Radical assaults on Lincoln's Cabinet were no different from conservative assaults; they more often had to do with place, person, and power than issues. The famed so-called Radical assault of December 1862, fed by Chase and aimed at the moderate William H. Seward, was not strictly a Radical attempt. All but two members of the Republican caucus endorsed it, and conservative Jacob Collamer led the delegation which asked Lincoln to reshape his Cabinet in the crisis. The longer Montgomery Blair remained in Lincoln's Cabinet, the more his bitter factional rival for leadership of the Maryland Republican party, Henry Winter Davis, associated with Radicals and adopted their ideas. Discontent with the idea of renominating Lincoln for 1864 was not confined to Radicals. Many Republicans, including Lincoln himself, feared he could not win reelection, and that fear always spurs shopping around for available alternatives. In the end Radicals voted for Lincoln. They felt more at home with any Republican than with the Democratic nominee, McClellan.

Conversely, Lincoln saw his role as party leader as one of unifying the young party for the crisis which would test its ability to govern. Doctrinal purity—except in opposition to slavery's expansion—was never his purpose. As he told Henry Winter Davis on March 18, 1863, "the supporters of the war should send no man to congress who will not go into caucus with the unconditional supporters of the war, and abide the action of such caucus. . . . Let the friends of the government first save the government, and then administer it to their own liking." Lincoln's patronage policies never consistently favored either Radicals or conservatives; they favored unity and, where the party was badly split, the apparent majority. Lincoln, in his own words, was "for the regular nominee in all cases." If Radicals were regular nominees, as were Julian and Kelley in 1864, he rebuked factional rivals who might use the powers of their appointive offices against them. In states where the more conservative Republicans dominated and thereby received administration support, Lincoln tried to be fair. In Maryland he got Blair and Davis to agree on a compromise slate of potential officeholders for Baltimore. Even in states where he favored conservatives in the face of bitter Radical denunciation, as in Missouri, which sent the only anti-Lincoln delegation to the 1864 Republican nominating convention, Lincoln said of the malcontents that they were "utterly lawless—the unhandiest devils in the world to deal with—but after all their faces are set Zionwards."

SOURCES: David Donald's important essay, "The Radicals and Lincoln," is in his *Lincoln Reconsidered* (New York: Alfred A. Knopf, 1956). Donald advanced his argument in sophistication with "Devils Facing Zionwards," in Grady McWhiney, ed., *Grant, Lee, Lincoln and the Radicals: Essays on Civil War Leadership* ([Evanston, Ill.]: Northwestern University Press, 1964), where he was answered by the most eloquent spokesman of the old school, T. Harry Williams, in an essay called "Lincoln and the Radicals: An Essay in Civil War History and Historiography." A useful survey is Hans L. Trefousse, *The Radical Republicans: Lincoln's Vanguard for Racial Justice* (New York: Alfred A. Knopf, 1969). See also Herman Belz, *Reconstructing the Union: Theory and Policy during the Civil War* (Ithaca, N.Y.: Cornell University Press, 1969).

See also ABOLITIONISM; CHANDLER, ZACHARIAH; CHASE, SALMON PORTLAND; COMMITTEE ON THE CONDUCT OF THE WAR, JOINT; RECONSTRUCTION; REPUBLICAN PARTY; SUMNER, CHARLES; WADE, BENJAMIN FRANKLIN.

"Rail Splitter" Lincoln's nickname as a presidential candidate in 1860. The nickname was the brainchild of Richard J. Oglesby. At the Republican State Convention in Decatur, Illinois, on May 9, 1860, Oglesby announced that an old Illinois Democrat wished to come forward with a contribution. Oglesby had spoken to John Hanks before the convention met, and he and Hanks went together to Macon County. There, Hanks recalled, he and Lincoln had split 3000 rails for a fence just after the Lincolns moved to Illinois in 1830. Hanks, the "old Democrat," identified two rails, and he and Oglesby carried the rails secretly to Decatur. At the appointed moment, Hanks and another man carried the rails into the convention with a banner stretched between them which read: ABRAHAM LINCOLN/The Rail Candidate/FOR PRESIDENT IN 1860/Two rails from a lot of 3,000/ made in 1830 by Hanks and Abe Lincoln/—whose father was the first pioneer/ of Macon County." Lincoln was present and responded that, though these might not be the identical rails, he had indeed split rails there.

The effect was electric. The idea quickly caught on as a symbol of Lincoln's candidacy, a symbol reminiscent of the log cabin used to great effect in William Henry Harrison's presidential campaign in 1840. A campaign newspaper published in Chicago from June 23 to October 27, 1860, was named *The Rail Splitter*, as was a Cincinnati newspaper published from August 1 to October 27. Political cartoonists and makers of campaign trinkets capitalized on the rail as a quickly recognizable symbol of this Western candidate whose origins were genuinely humble.

SOURCES: See Wayne C. Temple, *Lincoln the Railsplitter* (La Crosse, Wis.: The Willow Press, 1961).

See also HANKS, JOHN.

This newspaper broadside urged Republicans to subscribe to a campaign paper named for the best-known aspect of Lincoln's personal history in 1860.

Railroads Abraham Lincoln's first political platform, announced in the *Sangamo Journal* in March 1832, noted that "No other improvement that reason will justify us in hoping for, can equal in utility the rail road." Yet, though "our imaginations may be heated at thoughts of it," Lincoln argued that the cost of a railroad from the Illinois River to Springfield was too great, and "the improvement of Sangamo river is an object much better suited to our infant resources."

At the time, the United States had little more than 20 miles of track, and Lincoln would look forward as an Illinois legislator—perhaps too hopefully—to the time when his state would have much more (as indeed Illinois did in 1860, with some 3000 miles of railroads). The Internal Improvements Act, forged in the legislature in the winter of 1836–1837 with Lincoln's help, envisioned 1300 miles of railroad built at public expense. The plan proved too ambitious; only 24 miles had been built by 1840, when financial difficulties halted the improvements. With other Illinois members of Congress, both Whig and Democratic, Lincoln supported legislation as a member of the House of Representatives in 1848 which would grant public lands to the state to fund railroad construction, though nothing was achieved during his term.

Back in Illinois in the 1850s Lincoln became increasingly involved as a lawyer in cases which stemmed from the burgeoning rail traffic in the state. He accepted cases for and against the railroads, but some of his greatest successes came as a lawyer for the Illinois Central Railroad and other rail companies in the state. Indeed, for much of the time from 1853 to 1860 he was on retainer for the Illinois Central, tried numerous cases for it, and turned down considerable "business against the road" from which he "could have realized several hundred dollars." His work as attorney for the railroad in the McLean County Tax Case (1854–1856) saved the railroad, Lincoln thought, "half a million dollars" and gained him the largest fee he ever earned, slightly over

$5000. He had been willing to work for the other side, but county authorities moved too slowly to retain him.

Lincoln had to sue to get his large fee, but the railroad proved willing enough to pay in the end, in part because it did not wish to see Lincoln's talents used against it in further litigation. The Illinois Central acted wisely. Lincoln was soon instrumental in preventing the State of Illinois from taxing the road for an amount greater than the maximum of 7 percent of gross earnings specified in the railroad's 1851 charter, now expired. The road agreed to pay a substantial part of the 7 percent in cash, a scarce commodity after the Panic of 1857, in exchange for a postponement of legal action by the state until 1859. Lincoln's friendship with State Auditor Jesse K. Dubois surely helped. In the meantime new legislation took the decision on the valuation of the railroad's property for tax purposes from Dubois to the Illinois Supreme Court, where Lincoln in 1860 won a decision which allowed the railroad to pay taxes on a value of $5 million rather than the $20 million assessment of 1857. The report of the case was not published until 1863, when Lincoln was far away in the White House. Although it never became a major issue in the 1858 Senate campaign, Stephen A. Douglas's hints that Lincoln was too cozy with the railroads led Lincoln to defend his work for them in a speech in Carthage on October 22.

Lincoln's work in the *Effie Afton* Case for the Chicago, Rock Island, and Pacific Railroad in 1857 resulted in a dismissal of a $50,000 damage suit against the road brought by the master of a ship, the *Effie Afton*, which was lost as a result of a collision with the piers of the railroad's bridge across the Mississippi. Lincoln's argument included a stress on the greater importance of railroads than river transportation to the future growth and prosperity of the West.

Lincoln was comfortable with the plank of the Republican platform of 1860 which stressed the importance of building a railroad to the Pacific. He signed legislation in 1862 which chartered the Union Pacific Railroad Company to build a railroad and telegraph line to the Pacific. Grenville Dodge, an engineer and railroad promoter, recalled Lincoln's belief in the road "not only as a military necessity, but as a means of holding the Pacific Coast to the Union." Lincoln's platform in 1864 again endorsed the project, but, long before the road was completed, the assassinated President's body journeyed by train to final rest in Springfield.

SOURCES: See John W. Starr, Jr., *Lincoln and the Railroads* (New York: Dodd, Mead, 1927), Norman Graebner, "The Apostle of Progress," in Cullom Davis et al., eds., *The Public and the Private Lincoln: Contemporary Perspectives* (Carbondale: Southern Illinois University Press, 1979), pp. 71–85, and, especially, Robert M. Sutton, "Lincoln and the Railroads of Illinois," in O. Fritiof Ander, ed., *Lincoln Images: Augustana College Centennial Essays* (Rock Island, Ill.: Augustana College Library, 1960), pp. 41–60. Charles Leroy Brown's "Abraham Lincoln and the Illinois Central Railroad, 1857–1860," *Journal of the Illinois State Historical Society*, XXXVI (June 1943), 121–163, should be supplemented with G. S. Boritt's "Honest Abe Lincoln? The Lawyer-Politician on the Eve of His Election to the Presidency," a paper read at the meeting of the American Historical Association in 1978, and his *Lincoln and the Economics of the American Dream* (Memphis: Memphis State University Press, 1978).

See also ECONOMICS; *EFFIE AFTON* CASE; MCLEAN COUNTY TAX CASE; WHITNEY, HENRY CLAY.

Randall, James Garfield (1881–1953) The greatest Lincoln scholar of all time. Randall was born in Indianapolis, received his undergraduate training at Indiana University, and earned his doctorate in history at the University of Chicago, where he studied with William E. Dodd. Randall taught in Virginia for 8 years, lectured briefly for the Committee on Public Information, and worked for the Shipping Board during and immediately after World War I. In 1920 he accepted an assistant professorship at the University of Illinois for a salary of $2500. He published his first book, *Constitutional Problems Under Lincoln* (New York: D. Appleton) in 1926. Writing in what he called "this year of dictatorships," Randall argued that Lincoln "was driven by circumstances to the use of more arbitrary power than perhaps any other President has seized." Lincoln's government was conspicuous for its "irregular and extralegal characteristics," and "the 'rule of law' largely broke down." But Lincoln's "humane sympathy, . . . [and] dislike of arbitrary rule" saved America from dictatorship.

Though interested in Lincoln from boyhood, Randall considered himself a constitutional historian and did not decide to do biographical work on Lincoln until 1927–1928. He felt in 1929 that "historians have not yet rescued his personality from the myth & fiction with which it is encrusted." He delivered a now famous paper at the annual meeting of the American Historical Association in 1934 entitled "Has the Lincoln Theme Been Exhausted?" Published in the *American Historical Review* in 1936, the article suggested that the "hand of the amateur has rested heavily upon Lincoln studies."

From 1930 to 1936 Randall wrote a textbook, *The Civil War and Reconstruction*, but he began work on what he called "a very solid book on Lincoln" immediately after publication of the text in 1937. *Lincoln the President: Springfield to Gettysburg* (New York: Dodd, Mead) appeared in two volumes in 1945. Based on careful research, the work interpreted Lincoln from the standpoint of "Revisionism," which viewed the Civil War as a needless war brought on by a "blundering generation" of politicians who exaggerated minor sectional differences. The problem of slavery in the territories, he held, was a pseudoproblem inflated by bombastic rhetoric. Reasonable men, Randall explained, should have seen that slavery could never exist in the arid plains of the unorganized territories. *Lincoln the President* was remarkable, too, for its defense of George B. McClellan as a capable general, the savior of the Union at Antietam, a man who differed little from Lincoln's moderate views on sectional questions and love of the Union, and a victim of the political wrath of the Radical Republicans. Throughout the work, the real villains were these Radi-

James Garfield Randall. (Courtesy of the Illinois State Historical Library)

cals: "the conservative Lincoln, President of the dis-United States, found among his own Republicans almost a greater vexation than among those of the opposite party, or even among enemies in arms." Randall had an undisguised hostility to the Republican party after Lincoln and thought that the

> true party alignment, if there had to be parties, would have been moderate liberals on one side (nonvindictive Republicans together with the main body of the Democrats), and on the other side Republican Jacobins [Radicals] mustering under such a leader as [Thaddeus] Stevens or [Benjamin] Wade. . . . The Northeast would thus have had less directing influence, big business would have had smaller opportunity in the exploitive sense, and the party associated with Lincoln would have had larger influence in his own section, the Middle West.

In his next book, *Lincoln and the South* (Baton Rouge: Louisiana State University Press, 1946) Randall carried the same themes to an extreme. Randall argued that Lincoln would not have reconstructed the South, as the Radical Republicans did after the war. He pointed especially to the fact that many of Lincoln's friends and political associates later rebelled against the Republican party and became Liberal Republicans in 1872 or even Democrats. "If one looks for the complete opposite of Lincoln's policy and programs," Randall wrote, "he finds it not among the Democrats, but among the Jacobins." "One does not need to belabor the point," he added, "that the postwar Republican party was no longer a Lincoln party."

Although Randall saw Lincoln as "conservative" vis-à-vis the Radicals, he pictured Lincoln as a political liberal. *Lincoln the Liberal Statesman* (New York: Dodd, Mead, 1947) was a collection of Randall's essays gathered to prove that Lincoln was "a tough-minded liberal realist" who "reacted with a kind of Jeffersonian liberalism to problems and conditions in American society." Randall was embarrassed by Lincoln's "favoring of the . . . 'Bank of the United States'" and defending protective tariffs with "meaningless verbalisms" in his early political career. These faults he attributed "largely to his attachment to the Whig party." In later life, Lincoln rose above party and became a statesman. "Human rights meant more to him than profits," Randall argued, and his "philosophy of man and the state did not begin and end with *laissez faire*." He was friendly toward labor, "Racial bigotry did not control Lincoln's mind," and he was an internationalist, showing "a vigorous sympathy for democracy in other lands."

Lincoln the President: Midstream (New York: Dodd, Mead, 1952) benefited from research in the Abraham Lincoln Papers at the Library of Congress, opened in 1947. This volume was heavily biographical, with chapters on Lincoln's White House routine, domestic life, gift of laughter, and personal appearance to Washington visitors and correspondents. *Lincoln the President: Last Full Measure* (New York: Dodd, Mead, 1955) was completed by Richard N. Current after Randall's death. Southern historian Avery O. Craven noted that Randall and Current were "unashamed admirers of the President," but he admitted that *Lincoln the President* was "one of the truly great biographical undertakings of our time." In a 1952 poll of 103 American historians asked to rate 69 biographies of American figures written between 1920 and 1950, *Lincoln the President* ranked behind only Douglas S. Freeman's *R. E. Lee* and Samuel Eliot Morison's *Admiral of the Ocean Sea*. Like those works, Randall's biography is a masterpiece.

SOURCES: Much biographical information on Randall is available in Ruth Painter Randall's autobiography, *I Ruth, Autobiography of a Marriage* (Boston: Little, Brown, 1968). Avery Craven's review is in the *Mississippi Valley Historical Review*, XLIII (June 1956), 128–129, and the poll is in John Walton Caughey's "Historian's Choice: Results of a Poll on Recently Published American History and Biography," ibid., XXXIX (September 1952), 289–302. See also Mark E. Neely, Jr., "The Lincoln Theme Since Randall's Call: The Promises and Perils of Professionalism," *Papers of the Abraham Lincoln Association*, I (1979), 10–70.

Rathbone, Henry Riggs (1837–1911) Lincoln's guest at Ford's Theatre on the night of his assassination. Rathbone was born in Albany, New York. After his father's death, his mother married Ira Harris, who replaced William H. Seward in the United States Senate when Seward entered Lincoln's Cabinet. Mrs. Lincoln remembered Harris as "an intimate friend, of my beloved husband, in Washington . . . *always* a welcome guest at the Executive Mansion." Mrs. Lincoln also regarded Senator Harris's daughter, Clara, as "a dear friend." Rathbone joined the volunteer infantry in 1861 and rose to the rank of major (brevet) by 1865.

After others rejected the Lincolns' invitation, Major Rathbone and his stepsister, Clara, agreed to attend the performance of *Our American Cousin* at Ford's Theatre on April 14, 1865. Both were in the President's box when Booth shot Lincoln. Rathbone, who was seated about 8 feet from Lincoln, rose to stop the assassin, who stabbed him in the upper left arm with a dagger. Booth escaped over the box railing despite Rathbone's continued attempts to grasp him, but Rathbone's efforts may have spoiled the athletic actor's leap (which resulted in Booth's breaking his leg). The major later assisted the distraught Mary Todd Lincoln across the street to the Petersen house, where her unconscious husband had been carried. Rathbone then fainted from loss of blood.

In 1867 Rathbone married his stepsister. Twenty years later President Grover Cleveland appointed him consul to Hanover, Germany. There Rathbone, Clara, and their three children lived until 1894, when Rathbone, who had become mentally ill, apparently grew jealous of his wife's attentions to the children and murdered her. German authorities convicted him of murder and committed him to an asylum for the criminally insane, where he died in 1911.

Rathbone's son, Henry, became a Democratic Congressman from Illinois and took an active interest in Lincoln memorials; he introduced, in 1926, the bill to purchase the Oldroyd Lincoln collection that is the basis of the museum at Ford's Theatre.

Henry R. Rathbone

Mrs. Henry R. Rathbone

SOURCES: See R. Gerald McMurtry, "Major Rathbone and Miss Harris: Guests of the Lincolns in the Ford's Theatre Box," *Lincoln Lore*, Number 1602 (August 1971) pp. 1–3.

Ray, Charles Henry (1821–1870) Journalist. Charles H. Ray was born in Norwich, New York, but moved west in 1843. He met Abraham Lincoln in 1845 in Springfield, where he briefly edited a temperance newspaper. In 1847 he moved to Galena; until 1854 he edited the Galena *Jeffersonian*, a Democratic newspaper. He strongly opposed the Kansas-Nebraska Act, and in 1855, with Joseph M. Medill, he bought a controlling interest in the Chicago *Tribune*. Ray was no admirer of Irish Catholics or Germans, and the *Tribune* was already a Know-Nothing paper, but he soon saw that the Anti-Nebraska coalition would need to attract Protestant German voters. He was a founder of the Republican party in Illinois. In 1858 the *Tribune* merged with the *Daily Democratic Press* to become the Chicago *Press and Tribune*. (The name was changed to Chicago *Tribune* in the fall of 1860.)

As early as 1858, Ray was pressing Lincoln for notes for a short biography. Lincoln refused, and the editor judged Lincoln's reluctance due to reticence about his humble origins. The *Press and Tribune* covered the Lincoln-Douglas Debates carefully; it sent a shorthand expert, Robert R. Hitt, to record the speeches accurately. Ray told Congressman Elihu B. Washburne, "When you see Abe at Freeport, for God's sake tell him to 'Charge Chester! Charge!' Do not let him keep on the defensive." After Lincoln's defeat Ray felt "like h-ll," but Lincoln was hopeful that "we shall have fun again. Douglas managed to be supported both as the best instrument to *put down* and to *uphold* the slave power; but no ingenuity can long keep these antagonisms in harmony."

Ray was active in promoting Lincoln's presidential nomination in 1860. In the subsequent campaign the *Tribune* followed an anti-Catholic but pro-German line. Ray had little influence on Lincoln after the election; he found the President to be "most uncommunicative." He opposed Simon Cameron's appointment to the Cabinet, sought rewards for German-Americans who supported the Republican ticket, and urged the appointment of *Tribune* editor John Locke Scripps as Chicago postmaster, an appointment which Lincoln made and which, doubtless, aided the *Tribune* financially. Ray, in general, supported the President but thought he moved much too slowly toward emancipation.

With emancipation achieved, Ray felt less committed to journalism. In the summer of 1863, his wife died. In the fall he sold his interest in the *Tribune*. Early in 1865 he sought permission to trade with the Confederate states in noncontraband goods. Lincoln gave him the permit, in part because Illinois Governor Richard J. Oglesby preferred to see Ray out of the state rather than reestablished in journalism in Chicago and provoking schisms in the party.

SOURCES: Ray was not *The Man Who Elected Lincoln*, but Jay Monaghan's biography of Ray, so entitled, is a useful survey of the journalist's career (Indianapolis: Bobbs-Merrill, 1956).

Raymond, Henry Jarvis (1820–1869) Editor of the New York *Times* during Lincoln's Presidency. Henry J. Raymond was a politician (Whig turned Republican) as well as a journalist. Long an ally of William H. Seward, he was a rival of fellow editor Horace Greeley of the New York *Tribune*. At the Republican nominating convention in Chicago in 1860, he worked hard for Seward's nomination; Greeley did all he could to prevent it. After Seward's defeat, Raymond, with Seward's knowledge, blamed the defeat on Greeley's personal hatred for Seward. He claimed that the *Tribune* editor perfidiously posed as Seward's friend while he told the delegates that Seward was unelectable. The charge greatly widened the factional split in New York's Republican party.

Raymond was slower than Seward to endorse Lincoln. A moderate Republican who insisted that the sectional crisis was a struggle for power with a Southern minority that had too long dominated American politics, he thought emphatically that the moral issue of slavery was subordinate to the practical question of power. He convinced himself that Lincoln was "eminently conservative" and campaigned vigorously for him. Raymond himself won election to the New York Senate, where he served as speaker.

After the election Raymond pressed Lincoln to make a public statement indicating that the South misunderstood the Republican party's intentions. Lincoln refused in a strongly worded letter that argued that "Party malice" was too pronounced to make of his remarks anything but capital for "political fiends." When Raymond sent him a letter from a Mississippi friend who thought Lincoln threatened the South's institutions, Lincoln dismissed the Southerner as "a very mad-man." The editor urged opening the doors to "the Union men of the

Charles Henry Ray. (Courtesy of the Chicago Historical Society)

Louis Maurer depicted Raymond as a somewhat insignificant follower of James Watson Webb of the New York Courier and Enquirer in this Currier & Ives poster cartoon published around September 1860. "The Great Exhibition of 1860" attributed Lincoln's studied silence in the presidential campaign to orders issued from the real power in the Republican party, William H. Seward of New York. Lincoln, characteristically in shirtsleeves and astride a rail, danced to the tune of the New York newspapers. The organ grinder is Horace Greeley of the Tribune.

South," Seward's principal strategy for dealing with the secession crisis.

The *Times* proved to be the administration's steadiest supporter in New York City. It condoned the suspension of the privilege of the writ of habeas corpus, arbitrary arrests, and the revocation of General John C. Frémont's emancipation proclamation for Missouri. When one of the paper's editorials criticized Lincoln's proposal for compensated emancipation for the Border States as doomed to failure because it was too expensive, Lincoln told Raymond in a letter of March 9, 1862, that the cost of one-half day of the war would pay for all of Delaware's slaves at $400 a head. The editor responded on March 15, saying that he had been out of town but the minute he saw the editorial he ordered the paper to sustain Lincoln's plan *"without qualification or cavil."* He deemed the plan "a master-piece of practical wisdom and sound policy."

Raymond was much less enthusiastic about the Emancipation Proclamation. After the President announced the preliminary Proclamation, on September 22, 1862, and Republicans lost the fall elections in New York, Raymond suggested that the final form of the proclamation should be a military order to generals to free the slaves of rebels. It should not be the more sweeping proclamation Lincoln had promised. The practical effect would be the same, for slaves could be freed only where Union armies held sway, and Raymond felt that "any attempt to make this war *subservient* to the sweeping abolition of slavery" would "destroy the Union." Lincoln politely acknowledged the advice, but he did not alter the form of the Proclamation.

In 1864 Raymond wrote a campaign biography of Lincoln, the *History of the Administration of President Lincoln* (New York: Derby & Miller, 1864). Even though he felt that Secretary of War Edwin M. Stanton helped other papers' reporters while his had trouble getting permission to go into the field, Raymond remained steadily in Lincoln's column. He became an important agent for Lincoln's renomination at the Baltimore convention and served as chairman of the party's national committee. He raised money vigorously. By August 22 he feared that the Republicans would surely lose unless Lincoln made a bold move to prove it untrue "that we are not to have peace *in any event* under this administration until Slavery is abandoned." He suggested proposing peace to Jefferson Davis on the basis of Union only. Lincoln drafted a proposal but in a meeting with Raymond on August 25 convinced him that it would be an error. Raymond's pessimism had led Lincoln to draft his famous blind memorandum of August 23, saying that his reelection was unlikely and that he would work with the victor to save the Union before leaving office. When Lincoln won reelection, Raymond was elected to the House of Representatives.

After Lincoln's death Raymond expanded his campaign biography into *The Life and Public Services of Abraham Lincoln* (New York: Derby & Miller, 1865), an undistinguished biography which mostly stitched together Lincoln's state papers. In Congress Raymond followed an erratic but largely conservative course on Reconstruction.

SOURCES: Francis Brown's *Raymond of the Times* (New York: W. W. Norton, 1951) attributes too much political independence to Raymond but is a readable biography.

Reading   See BOOKS.

"Reaper Case"   See MCCORMICK V. MANNY & COMPANY.

"Rebecca Letters"   See LINCOLN, MARY TODD; SHIELDS, JAMES.

Reconstruction   The term usually applied to the period in American history immediately after Lincoln's assassination and extending to 1877. Although Lincoln died before he could deal with the problem of reconstructing Southern loyalty to the Union *in peace*, he repeatedly faced the problem of undermining Southern loyalty to the Confederacy *in war*, a problem definitely akin to Reconstruction as it is commonly understood. Moreover, considerable Confederate territory fell into Union hands before he died, and Lincoln played a large and direct role in reconstructing loyalty to the Union in those areas.

Like many other Republicans, Lincoln underestimated the depth and extent of secessionist feeling in the South. Even after war broke out in 1861, he had little comprehension of the size of the problem he faced. His April 15 call for volunteers stipulated but 3 months' service. Secretary of State William H. Seward thought, even after the Battle of Bull Run in June, that Unionists in the South might rise in revolt against secession. In his first message to Congress, on July 4, 1861, Lincoln stated that "it may well be questioned whether there is, to-day, a majority of the legally qualified voters of any State, except perhaps South Carolina, in favor of disunion. There is much reason to believe that the Union men are in the majority in many, if not in every other one, of the so-called seceded States." In December the President still worried about using "radical and extreme measures, which may reach the loyal as well as the disloyal" in the Confederate States.

By 1862 some areas of Confederate territory were in Union hands. Lincoln at first thought loyalty in those areas might be reconstructed simply by appointing military governors to rally local Unionist sentiment; in the spring and summer of 1862, he appointed Andrew Johnson in Tennessee, General George F. Shepley in Louisiana, Edward Stanly in North Carolina, and General John S. Phelps in Arkansas. He considered Reconstruction as a political form of making war. On July 3, 1862, he told Johnson, "If we could, somehow, get a vote of the people of Tennessee and have it result properly it would be worth more to us than a battle gained." In early September 1863, when Tennessee was temporarily clear of Confederate forces, Lincoln urged Johnson to reinaugurate "a loyal State government," being careful to include in the process "such men only as can be trusted for the Union." In Louisiana, Lincoln cautioned against a mere "movement of our military and quasi-military authorities there"; he insisted on reliance on loyal *local* inhabitants as well. An election in two districts in Louisiana in 1862 sent Benjamin Flanders and Michael Hahn to the House of Representatives. Military reverses and political resistance in Tennessee halted Johnson's work, but in Louisiana George F. Shepley and Nathaniel P. Banks, the area's military commander, worked to organize elections in the fall of 1863. Lincoln expressed bitter disappointment in November that so little progress had been made, and in the end the Congressmen elected in Louisiana in 1863 were denied seats in the House. Reconstruction was even more difficult now since Lincoln wanted the states to adopt constitutions abolishing slavery. (Tennessee and occupied Louisiana had been excluded from the Emancipation Proclamation.)

Disappointment and a realization that Unionist sentiment was scarcer than he imagined led Lincoln officially to assume control of Reconstruction himself by means of the Proclamation of Amnesty and Reconstruction of December 8, 1863. In it he recognized that amnesty must be offered to some who would swear an oath of future loyalty. Past disloyalty must be ignored in order to find a nucleus of voters in any state equal in number to even 10 percent of the voting populace in 1860. Before such a group could begin to restore a state, it must swear to obey all future Presidential proclamations and acts of Congress affecting slavery. The new state constitution must also outlaw slavery. This was still a wartime plan. Any government resting on so few must of necessity really be sustained by the occupying army, and an oath guaranteeing future loyalty was a meaningful act only while the Confederacy still threatened to reoccupy the area. Lincoln believed genuinely in the meaningfulness of repentence, however, and the plan was hardly punitive; only certain high-ranking Confederate officials were exempted from the possibility of amnesty. Lincoln received "not a single objection" to the plan "from any professed emancipationist."

On Christmas Eve Lincoln assured Banks, "you are master of all" and demanded "a free-state re-organization of Louisiana, in the shortest possible time." In elections held on Washington's Birthday in 1864, under Lincoln's amnesty plan, about 20 percent of Louisiana's 1860 voting totals were reached. The realism of Lincoln's plan was vindicated, especially since the total fell in later elections. Louisiana became the prime focus of Lincoln's Reconstruction policy. Quietly he urged local authorities to work to admit very intelligent Negroes and Negro veterans to the suffrage in the new constitution, but the constitution adopted on September 5, 1864, merely abolished slavery and *allowed* the legislature to permit Negro suffrage. Meanwhile, some Congressmen had become critical of the conservative government elected in Louisiana and put forward a different plan of Reconstruction embodied in the Wade-Davis Bill of July 2, 1864.

Lincoln refused to sign the bill, in part because the bill effectively repudiated the existing loyal governments of Louisiana and Arkansas and in part because he did not think Congress could mandate the abolition of slavery. The bill would have done more than assert Congress's role in the Reconstruction process; it would also have essentially postponed any Reconstruction until the war was over (to be precise, until 50 percent of a state's population took the loyalty oath).

At the Hampton Roads Peace Conference on February 3, 1865, President Lincoln revealed his magnanimity by suggesting that Southerners might earn compensation for their loss of slave property by quickly ceasing hostilities, reentering the Union, and ratifying the Thirteenth Amendment abolishing slavery. In any case, he demanded unconditional loyalty to the Union as the precondition of peace for the rebel states. The conference was fruitless.

Lincoln's last speech (April 11, 1865) dealt with Reconstruction and the criticism leveled at the way his plan had worked in Louisiana. Lincoln admitted that it "would be more satisfactory" if the new government rested on more than "only about twelve thousand" people (more than double the 10 percent required). He also admitted, for the first time publicly, a personal preference that the franchise be "conferred on the very intelligent [Negroes], and on those who serve our cause as soldiers." Yet he argued that Louisiana could be sooner brought "into proper practical relation with the Union . . . by *sustaining*" rather than by "*discarding* her new

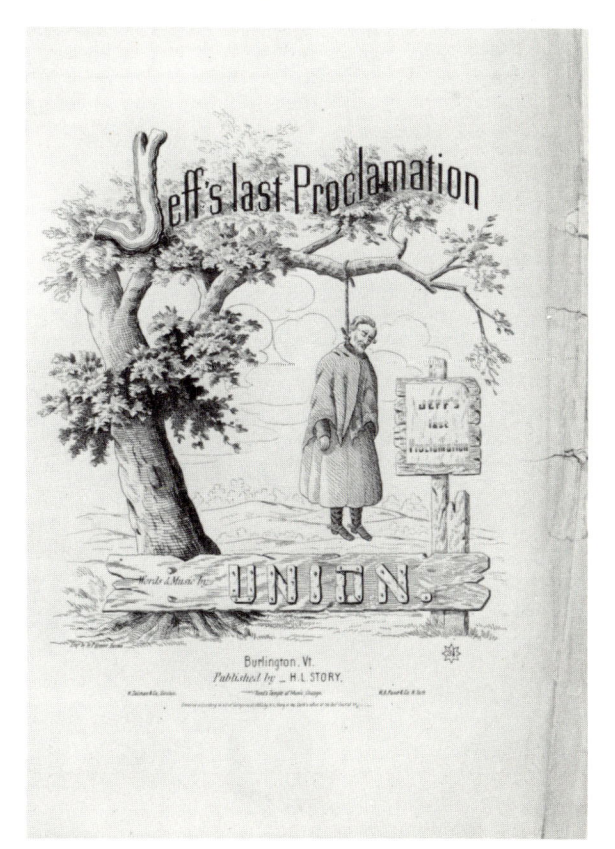

The lithographed cover of this piece of sheet music published in 1865 shows the strong popular sentiment for revenge on the leadership of the Confederacy. The motif of Jefferson Davis's hanging appeared also in numerous patriotic envelopes sold by Northern stationers during the Civil War.

Redlands Shrine

State Government." To spurn the 12,000 who had agreed to end slavery in Louisiana and resume loyalty to the Union would be "to disorganize and disperse them" rather than to "encourage the hearts." The "colored man" would sooner attain the franchise "by saving the already advanced steps toward it, than by running backward over them." The new government might only be "as the egg is to the fowl," but "we shall sooner have the fowl by hatching the egg than by smashing it."

Lincoln was never inflexibly pledged to any plan, his own included, and he had admitted that the Wade-Davis Bill embodied "one very proper plan." On the day of his assassination, he agreed to a plan submitted by Secretary of War Edwin M. Stanton for military occupation of Virginia and North Carolina, though he stipulated that the plan could not ignore existing state boundaries in establishing military districts.

No myth has a stronger hold on the popular mind than the assertion that John Wilkes Booth's bullet killed the best friend the South ever had. Yet the mildness of Lincoln's plans for Reconstruction may well have been a lure to get a warring people back. What he would have done in peacetime remains unknown.

SOURCES: A difficult and somewhat speculative subject, Lincoln and Reconstruction is treated in William B. Hesseltine's *Lincoln's Plan of Reconstruction* (Tuscaloosa, Ala.: Confederate Publishing Company, 1960) and Peyton McCrary's *Abraham Lincoln and Reconstruction: The Louisiana Experiment* (Princeton, N.J.: Princeton University Press, 1978). J. G. Randall's argument in *Lincoln and the South* (Baton Rouge: Louisiana State University Press, 1946) that Lincoln's friends who survived him left the Republican party over Reconstruction is answered by Mark E. Neely, Jr.'s "The Lincoln Theme since Randall's Call: The Promises and Perils of Professionalism," *Papers of the Abraham Lincoln Association*, I (1979), 10–70.

See also BANKS, NATHANIEL PRENTISS; GREELEY, HORACE; HAMPTON ROADS PEACE CONFERENCE; JOHNSON, ANDREW; PROCLAMATION OF AMNESTY AND RECONSTRUCTION; RADICAL REPUBLICANS; RANDALL, JAMES GARFIELD; STEPHENS, ALEXANDER HAMILTON; WADE-DAVIS BILL.

Redlands Shrine *See* LINCOLN MEMORIAL SHRINE.

Religion Though many denominations have claimed him since his death, Abraham Lincoln was not a member of any church during his lifetime. His parents, Thomas and Nancy Lincoln, were members of the Little Mount Baptist Church in Kentucky. After the family's move to Indiana, Thomas was active in founding the Pigeon Creek Baptist Church. Abraham's older sister, Sarah, became a member in 1826.

On his own in New Salem, Illinois, Lincoln probably read Thomas Paine's *Age of Reason* and Constantine de Volney's *Ruins*, rationalistic books of the Enlightenment, and took positions in local philosophical debates which led the pious to call him an "infidel." When the impoverished young lawyer and state legislator moved to Springfield in 1837, he at first did not attend any of the town's five churches "because," he told Mary Owens, "I am conscious I should not know how to behave myself." In a speech before the Young Men's Lyceum of Springfield in 1838, he still praised "Reason, cold, calculating, unimpassioned reason." In 1841, while recovering from a spell of deep depression caused by the breakup of his engagement to Mary Todd, Lincoln thanked a friend for the gift of a Bible, saying, "I intend to read it regularly." "I doubt not," he added, "that it is really . . . the best cure for the 'Blues' could one but take it according to the truth." Episcopal clergyman Charles Dresser married Mary and Abraham in 1842.

Lincoln's unorthodox religious views hurt his political career. In 1843 he complained that in a recent contest political enemies "every where contended that no ch[r]istian ought to go for me, because I belonged to no church, was suspected of being a deist, and had talked about fighting a duel." Running for Congress against Methodist circuit rider Peter Cartwright in 1846, Lincoln faced a "whispering" campaign accusing him of infidelism. After the election, newspapers published a handbill which is one of the most important documents for Lincoln's religious views:

> A charge having got into circulation in some of the neighborhoods of this District, in substance that I am an open scoffer at Christianity, I have by the advice of some friends concluded to notice the subject in this form. That I am not a member of any Christian Church, is true; but I have never denied the truth of the Scriptures; and I have never spoken with intentional disrespect of religion in general, or of any denomination of Christians in particular. It is true that in early life I was inclined to believe in what I understand is called the "Doctrine of Necessity"—that is, that the human mind is impelled to action, or held in rest by some power, over which the mind itself has no control; and I have sometimes (with one, two or three, but never publicly) tried to

This rare cartoon suggested that Lincoln's conditions for Reconstruction as written in his famous "To whom it may concern" letter would backfire. The dog at lower right is Edwin M. Stanton. (Library of Congress)

The SPORTSMAN upset by the RECOIL of his own GUN. (Jo. Miller)

maintain this opinion in argument. The habit of arguing thus however, I have, entirely left off for more than five years. And I add here, I have always understood this same opinion to be held by several of the Christian denominations. The foregoing, is the whole truth, briefly stated, in relation to myself, upon this subject.

I do not think I could myself, be brought to support a man for office, whom I knew to be an open enemy of, and scoffer at, religion. Leaving the higher matter of eternal consequences, between him and his Maker, I still do not think any man has the right thus to insult the feelings, and injure the morals, of the community in which he may live. If, then, I was guilty of such conduct, I should blame no man who should condemn me for it; but I do blame those, whoever they may be, who falsely put such a charge in circulation against me.

When the Lincolns' young son Edward died in 1850, the Reverend James Smith of Springfield's First Presbyterian Church consoled Mrs. Lincoln. She joined the church; her husband rented a pew and attended more regularly.

In Washington, the Lincoln family attended the Reverend Phineas D. Gurley's New York Avenue Presbyterian Church. The death of 11-year-old son William in 1862 heightened the Lincolns' religious interests. Mrs. Lincoln even attended seances and dabbled in spiritualism; her husband occasionally attended also—but mostly to protect her. Mary said that her husband was "never a technical Christian," but that he "first seemed to think about the subject when our boy Willie died, and then more than ever about the time he went to Gettysburg." Biblical and religious references in his state papers, thanksgiving proclamations, and speeches of the Civil War period are numerous, and they are distinguished by their humility. Lincoln was careful never to say with smug assurance that God was on the North's side; rather, he entertained the notion that "it is quite possible that God's purpose is something different from the purpose of either party."

Lincoln's religious views were related most closely to his private life; the milestones of his spiritual career were the depression over his broken engagement, the death of Eddie, and the death of Willie. He did not mix religion and statesmanship and therefore proved to be remarkably tolerant. Even when many of his political associates became members of the anti-Catholic Know-Nothing party in the mid 1850s, Lincoln spurned their course as violating the spirit of the Declaration of Independence. Likewise, when he learned that General Ulysses S. Grant had expelled Jewish traders from his army in Tennessee in 1862, President Lincoln had the order revoked.

No one can be certain what Lincoln's religious views were, because Lincoln did not talk openly about such things even with his intimate friends. David Davis, his campaign manager and long-time friend, admitted, "I don't know anything about Lincoln's religion, nor do I think anybody else knows anything about it." Mary Todd Lincoln described Lincoln's religion best by saying that her husband was truly religious but that his religion was "a kind of poetry in his nature."

SOURCES: William J. Wolf's *Lincoln's Religion*, orig. pub. 1959 as *The Almost Chosen People: A Study of the Religion of Abraham Lincoln* (Philadelphia: Pilgrim Press, 1970) is a balanced appraisal of the subject based on reliable sources. A popular account, based on a less critical use of the sources, is Elton Trueblood's *Abraham Lincoln: Theologian of American Anguish* (New York: Harper and Row, 1973). A classic on the early years is Louis A. Warren's *The Slavery Atmosphere of Lincoln's Youth* (Fort Wayne, Ind.: Lincolniana Publishers, 1933). See also Edgar DeWitt Jones, *Lincoln and the Preachers* (New York: Harper and Brothers, 1948); William E. Barton, *The Soul of Abraham Lincoln* (New York: George H. Doran, 1920); and Chapter III in Richard N. Current, *The Lincoln Nobody Knows* (New York: McGraw-Hill, 1958).

See also BROOKS, NOAH; CARTWRIGHT, PETER; CHINIQUY, CHARLES PASCHAL TELESPHORE; FELL, JESSE WILSON; HERNDON, WILLIAM HENRY; JEWS; KNOW-NOTHING PARTY; PSYCHOLOGY; SIMPSON, MATTHEW; THANKSGIVING PROCLAMATION.

Representative Government Abraham Lincoln believed in democratic government. "I go for all sharing the privileges of the government," he announced in his 1836 platform, "who assist in bearing its burthens. Consequently I go for admitting all whites to the right of suffrage, who pay taxes or bear arms, (by no means excluding females.)." He saw representatives in legislatures as mere stand-ins for their constituents, instruments for finding the people's will when it was impractical to assemble the people themselves. In 1836 he told voters:

If elected, I shall consider the whole people of Sangamon my constituents, as well those that oppose, as those that support me. While acting as their representative, I shall be governed by their will, on all subjects upon which I have the means of knowing what their will is; and upon all others, I shall do what my own judgment teaches me will best advance their interests.

In his early political career, a test of the principle of representative government came in the conflict between Whigs and Democrats over the "doctrine of instructions," that is, the notion that a Representative was obliged to vote in Congress the way his constituents instructed him. In 1848 Lincoln told the United States House of Representatives that instruction was "the primary, the cardinal, the one great living principle of all Democratic representative government—the principle, that the representative is bound to carry out the known will of his constituents." Lincoln was a good Whig and was fully aware that instruction was part of the Democratic party's creed. In 1854 he argued that "If this State should instruct [Democrat Stephen A.] Douglas to vote for the repeal of the Nebraska Bill, he must do it, for 'the doctrine of instructions' was a part of his political creed." Nevertheless, he did not share with some Whigs an elitist dislike of instruction and a preference for relying on the uninstructed conscience of the legislator.

Lincoln believed strictly in the principle of equal numerical apportionment of representation. In 1841 he told the Illinois General Assembly that representation must be apportioned at the ratio of 1:12,000 for this reason:

If we . . . give each county a representative, we must begin with the county which has 750 inhabitants; and as the republican principle of representation according to numbers, will not be denied as proper for the basis of our action, we must then give a representative . . . for every 750 in the state. This by calculating, would be found to give a house of representatives of almost 650 members. Such a proportion . . . would not be tolerated by the house.

In 1850 Lincoln noted that even on questions as important as slavery, the Wilmot Proviso, and the Compromise of 1850, if "the wish of my district . . . shall be known to me, that wish shall govern me." Lincoln could "exercise my own judgment" only if "that wish shall not be known to me."

Ultimately, Lincoln's faith in representative government was rooted in his democratic faith that the common man did not need elites to govern him. There were plenty of capable representatives available. In 1861 he said confidently:

> there are many single Regiments whose members, one and another, possess full practical knowledge of all the arts, sciences, professions, and whatever else, whether useful or elegant, is known in the world; and there is scarcely one, from which there could not be selected, a President, a Cabinet, a Congress, and perhaps a Court, abundantly competent to administer the government itself.

SOURCES: See Mark E. Neely, Jr., "Lincoln's Theory of Representation: A Significant New Lincoln Document," *Lincoln Lore*, Number 1683 (May 1978), pp. 1–3.

See also LINCOLN, ROBERT TODD.

Republican Party Abraham Lincoln spent less than one-third of his political life in the Republican party. But he won the Presidency as a Republican, and it is as a Republican that he has been most remembered and written about. Even though he was a Whig for more than twice the time he was a Republican, it is wrong to think of Lincoln as a reluctant Republican. Some politicians took the Republican label as early as 1854; Lincoln adopted it only in 1856, but he was not dragging his feet. The party formed with greater rapidity in some states than in others, Lincoln was committed to the Republican organization as soon as it became a statewide force in Illinois, and in fact he was one of the party's principal organizers in that state.

The Whig cause was so hopeless in Illinois by 1852 that Lincoln, though a presidential elector for Winfield Scott that year, by his own admission "did less than in previous presidential canvasses." The passage of the Kansas-Nebraska Act early in 1854 sparked a renewed interest in politics for Lincoln. Opposition to that measure caused some radical antislavery men in Illinois to try to form a new political organization under the Republican label in that year, but Lincoln saw nothing inconsistent with Whiggery in opposing the Kansas-Nebraska Act. He ran for the state legislature as an Anti-Nebraska Whig. When a group of radicals heard his October 4 speech in Springfield against the Kansas-Nebraska Act, they placed his name on the list of names of the Republican state central committee without his knowledge. Lincoln did not attend the meeting of this abortive group in Chicago, and he recognized a considerable difference in attitude between his own and the group's goals. As he told one of the Republican organizers, Ichabod Codding, in November, "I suppose my opposition to the principle of slavery is as strong as that of any member of the Republican party; but I had also supposed that the *extent* to which I feel authorized to carry that opposition, practically, was not at all satisfactory to that party." As he told his old friend Joshua Speed almost a year later, he did "no more than oppose the *extension* of slavery."

Lincoln was an active candidate for the United States Senate. Voting took place in the state legislature in February 1855, and Lincoln failed to be elected by the Anti-Nebraska majority because five Anti-Nebraska Democrats refused to vote for a Whig. He threw his support to Anti-Nebraska Democrat Lyman Trumbull (who won) and learned for the first time that the Whig party would probably be unable to absorb the Anti-Nebraska sentiment. Through most of 1855 he still considered himself a Whig, but he was not forced so to label himself very often because it was an off year in Illinois politics. Lincoln knew also that victory for Illinois's Anti-Nebraska forces would require the absorption of those politicians and voters who had joined the Know-Nothing party. "Know-nothingism," Lincoln told Republican Owen Lovejoy on August 11, 1855, had "not yet entirely tumbled to pieces," and he knew the Anti-Nebraska forces could "not get them so long as they cling to a hope of success under their own organization." He feared that "an open push . . . now, may offend them" and "prevent our ever getting them." Lincoln was ready to "'fuse' with any body . . . on ground which . . . is right," and he thought "the opponents of slavery extension" could fuse effectively "if it were not for this K.N.ism."

Early in 1856 there was still no statewide Republican organization in Illinois. But this was a presidential election year, and the pressure of that impending event, along with the steady erosion of Know-Nothing strength, precipitated the fusion for which Lincoln himself had been ready in 1855. A group of antislavery newspaper editors called a meeting in Decatur for Washington's Birthday. Their purpose was to arrange for a state convention, and Lincoln was the only prominent politician present. The editors and Lincoln called for a state convention to meet in Bloomington on May 29. That convention selected candidates, drafted a platform, and heard a Lincoln speech allegedly so stirring that reporters were too entranced to take notes (it is called, therefore, his "Lost Speech"). This organization contained all the essential elements of Illinois's Republican party, and Lincoln played a key role in putting them together. He went on that year to give more than 50 speeches for Republican presidential nominee John C. Frémont, but he still avoided the Republican name; instead he identified with the "Fremont men" or the "anti-Nebraska men." In Illinois the name itself still smacked of the radicalism of abolitionists like Ichabod Codding.

Lincoln's opinions were representative of the Republican party's in general. That party, a loose amalgam of anti-Democratic voters, contained a spectrum of opinion, of course, but the whole spectrum was quite different from Democratic opinion. It was to the left of Democratic opinion on the slavery question, and Lincoln's views approximated its middle.

All that united the leaders of the Republican party was opposition to expansion of slavery. Radical Republicans believed in the complete denationalization of slavery, that is, in attacking slavery wherever the Constitution allowed Congress to do so—in the territories, in the District of Columbia, in the Fugitive Slave Act, even in the interstate slave trade. They tended to think of the slavery issue as the only one of importance. Conservatives in the party thought slave expansion an important enough issue, but primarily because, if allowed, it promised to increase the "Slave Power's" sway in the national government. That power had too long blocked the economic policies of homestead legislation, protective tariffs, and improvements, like the Pacific railroad, which required the support of the national government. The conservatives desired to halt the Slave Power now in order to get on with the important economic legislation that American economic development and national power required.

Moderates shared with conservatives a belief that issues other than slavery were important, but they shared with radicals in the party a belief that the slavery question must be met head on immediately and that, after meeting the problem, the country would be on its way eventually to a slaveless future. Moderates like Lincoln, therefore, argued that slavery was a moral evil, not just an economic one, and that the institution must be put on the road to "ultimate extinction" by cutting off its access to fresh territories, which were necessary to the continued existence of an inefficient labor system which mined the soil.

To be sure, a majority of Republicans shared an economic vision not unlike Lincoln's, because a majority had, like Lincoln, been Whigs before becoming Republicans. Abolitionists dwelled on the sin of slavery and radical Republicans on the blighting effects of slavery on black souls. Lincoln always stressed the moral idea too, but he joined more moderate and conservative Republicans in seeing slavery as the underpinning of a society completely inconsistent with the American dream of individual economic mobility. Thus slavery was a violation not only of the abstract principle of equality in the Declaration of Independence but also of the way that principle operated to improve each American's life and with that the whole of American society. The "principle of 'Liberty to all,'" Lincoln wrote early in 1861, was "the principle that clears the *path* for all—gives *hope* to all—and, by consequence, *enterprize*, and *industry* to all." Soon after the passage of the Kansas-Nebraska Act, he noted the superiority of government based on the "equal rights of men." The "fruit is before us," he said. "Look at it, in it's aggregate grandeur, of extent of country, and numbers of population—of ship, and steamboat, and rail[road]."

Louis Maurer, the star cartoonist for the Currier & Ives firm, captured the popular view of the Republican party as a party of radical reform on the lunatic fringe of American politics in this 1860 cartoon. A Mormon, an advocate of women's rights, a champion of free love, a Negro, and a communist follow Lincoln, held aloft by Horace Greeley on a symbolic rail. A similar cartoon had been issued in 1856 with Republican presidential nominee John C. Frémont as the leader of the motley crew of crank reformers. (Library of Congress)

Lincoln and other Republicans were genuinely surprised and alarmed by new developments in the politics of slavery, the Kansas-Nebraska Act, the violent struggle for control of Kansas, and the Dred Scott decision. For the first time Lincoln felt that the assumptions which had underlaid his Whig economic views were genuinely challenged by new theories that free labor was not necessarily the best system. Therefore, it was as a Republican that he most often articulated those philosophical assumptions. In Milwaukee in 1859, for example, he attacked the "mud-sill" theory that a substratum of labor underlies all successful societies, that laborers are fixed in that condition for life, and that the condition of slaves and hired laborers is equally bad. Lincoln argued that "labor is prior to, and independent of, capital" and "the superior . . . of capital." A "large majority" of laborers were neither owned nor hired by capital, and, where the free labor system prevailed,

> The prudent, penniless beginner in the world, labors for wages awhile, saves a surplus with which to buy tools or land, for himself; then labors on his own account another while, and at length hires another new beginner to help him. This . . . is *free* labor—the just and generous, and prosperous system, which opens the way for all—gives hope to all, and energy, and progress, and improvement of condition to all. If any continue through life in the condition of the hired laborer, it is not the fault of the system, but because of either a dependent nature which pefers it, or improvidence, folly, or singular misfortune.

Though Lincoln himself tended not to denounce Southern society as much as other Republicans denounced it, the corollary of such views was that the South was a retrograde society, little improved over what nature gave her, with an indolent labor force, uneducated, and without hope for the future. Lincoln himself noted that "now, especially in these free States, nearly all are educated."

Republicans differed over how best to organize their own superior society, and though many shared Lincoln's old Whig views of economic development, those views had to be kept in the background in order to hold the new alliance of former Whigs and former Democrats together. If ever the party appeared to be merely an attempt to revive Whiggery under another name, it would lose its essential minority of former Democrats.

The Republicans lost the presidential race with Frémont in 1856 and won it with Lincoln in 1860. The difference lay in broadening their base of appeal in those years without at the same time losing the attributes which distinguished them from the Democratic party. Lincoln aimed at widening the gulf of principle separating Republicans and Democrats in his famed campaign for the Senate against Stephen A. Douglas in 1858. He stressed Douglas's Democratic indifference to the morality of the slavery question by saying that the doctrine of popular sovereignty embodied a "don't care" attitude toward whether slavery was made legal in a territory or not. And he stressed the importance of the Republican party's principled opposition as insurance that the Republicans alone could be relied upon to resist the increasing aggressions of the Slave Power. In fact, he said, popular sovereignty was a way to soften up the North and make it indifferent and unvigilant, so that the Slave Power could use its tool, the Democratic party, to spread slavery not only to the territories but also to the Northern states where slavery was illegal. The aggressiveness of slavery showed a conspiratorial pattern that Lincoln claimed was a clear indication that the next step would be another Supreme Court decision, similar to the Dred Scott decision, which would declare it impossible to outlaw slavery even in the *states*. In all this, however, he never went beyond the main Republican principle—opposition to the *extension* of slavery only. Also, he never so stated the question of the morality of slavery as to put the focus solely on the plight of the black man himself. In his last debate with Douglas, at Alton, Lincoln said:

> Now irrespective of the moral aspect of this question as to whether there is a right or wrong in enslaving a negro, I am still in favor of our new Territories being in such a condition that white men may find a home—may find some spot where they can better their condition—where they can settle upon new soil and better their condition in life.

The genius of Republican doctrine was that it appealed both to those who hated slavery for the black man's sake and to those who hated it because it *brought* black men to the territories. Most Republicans, Lincoln included, did little or nothing to dispel that ambiguity.

Other Republicans sought to maintain the party's distinctiveness and to broaden its appeal in ways of which Lincoln disapproved. He warned Salmon P. Chase in 1858 that the Ohio party's addition of a plank to repeal the Fugitive Slave Act would "explode the [next Republican National] convention and the party." He opposed the Massachusetts law, passed by Republicans with Know-Nothing roots, which excluded naturalized citizens from the franchise for 2 years.

Lincoln's nomination in 1860 was the victory of a Republican moderate. His stress on the moral nature of the slave question appealed to the radicals. His refusal to broaden the attack to include things like the Fugitive Slave Act appealed to conservatives and moderates, as did his long and consistent record as a Whig on economic questions. William H. Seward's principal drawbacks as a potential nominee for the party were his steady record of opposition to nativism and his reputation for radicalism on the slavery question. Lincoln opposed nativism too—enough so that he worked well with Republicans of German descent like Carl Schurz and Gustave Koerner—but his sharpest denunciations were in private letters. His public record was sketchy enough that former Know-Nothings—especially the large body in all-important Pennsylvania—had no objection to him. He certainly had no problem with the 1860 platform's call for a Pacific railroad, homestead legislation, and a tariff, but he let his Whig background stand as mute testimony. Lincoln himself said nothing to give former Democrats the impression that the party would revive Whiggery.

As President of the United States Lincoln was also the symbolic head of the Republican party, and he obeyed an unwritten sense of duty that dictated an obligation to help party unity and strength. He proudly proclaimed that his administration "distributed to it's party friends as nearly all the civil patronage as any administration ever did," and he tried "to deal fairly with all men and all shades of opinion among our friends." Military appointments were another matter, and Lincoln recognized the necessity of making Democratic appointments to ensure Democratic support for the war.

As President, Lincoln was also able to continue his prewar policy of silence on economic questions. He was preoccupied with the war. Besides, with the Southerners withdrawn from Congress, he had, as G. S. Boritt says, "the pleasure of signing into law much of the [economic] program he had worked for through the better part of his political life."

In 1864 Lincoln was the candidate of the "Union" rather than the Republican party. This was a policy much like the one he followed in military appointments, an attempt to attract War Democrats to his column. Ideologically and structurally, it apparently had little impact on the Republican party. It did, however, point the way toward Lincoln's future image as a national hero. By the middle of the twentieth century, Lincoln became as much the hero of Democrats as Republicans, and his image has lost most of its partisan cast.

SOURCES: Don E. Fehrenbacher clearly and brilliantly details Lincoln's entrance into the Republican party in *Prelude to Greatness: Lincoln in the 1850s* (Stanford: Stanford University Press, 1962). The spectrum of opinion in the antebellum party, and Lincon's place on that spectrum, is astutely delineated in Eric Foner's wonderful book *Free Soil, Free Labor, Free Men: The Ideology of the Republican Party before the Civil War* (New York: Oxford University Press, 1970). Michael F. Holt's insights on the structure of that party are not to be ignored and are most easily accessible in *The Political Crisis of the 1850s* (New York: John Wiley & Sons, 1978). And G. S. Boritt's *Lincoln and the Economics of the American Dream* (Memphis: Memphis State University Press, 1978) expands and elaborates Foner's views, extends them brilliantly into the Civil War era, and explains precisely the relationship between Lincoln's Whiggery and his Republicanism.

See also CHASE, SALMON PORTLAND; ELECTION OF 1860; ELECTION OF 1864; PATRONAGE; RADICAL REPUBLICANS.

Reputation *See* BIOGRAPHERS; MASTERS, EDGAR LEE; PRESIDENCY, POWERS OF THE; TYLER, LYON GARDNER.

Revisionism *See* BIOGRAPHERS; RADICAL REPUBLICANS; RANDALL, JAMES GARFIELD.

Rock Island Bridge *See* EFFIE AFTON CASE.

Rutledge, Ann (1813–1835) Reputedly the object of Lincoln's earliest romantic interest. Ann Rutledge was born in Kentucky but moved to Illinois, where her father, James Rutledge, was one of the founders of New Salem. When Abraham Lincoln came to the village in 1832, he boarded for a time at Rutledge's tavern and met Ann. She was engaged to John McNamar, who had assumed the name McNeil when he came west to seek his fortune. The Rutledges moved to a farm 7 miles north of New Salem at Sand Ridge, but Lincoln could visit them there when he was traveling the county as a surveyor. McNamar left for the East and remained a suspiciously long time. In the summer of 1835 Ann contracted a "fever" and died. Lincoln was, by many later reports, grief stricken.

From this meager factual record has been woven one of the most fantastic romantic tales in all of American folklore. For the most part the elaboration of the romance was the work of William H. Herndon as he interviewed old Illinois settlers in 1865–1866 for a biography of his long-time law partner, Abraham Lincoln. There was one earlier mention of a Lincoln-Rutledge romance in the February 15, 1862, issue of the *Menard Axis*, the newspaper in Petersburg, Illinois, a town near the site of New Salem (by then, long since abandoned). The editor, John Hill, was the son of Sam Hill, who had lived in New Salem. He was a Democrat and used the story of Lincoln as a lovesick swain to belittle the Republican President. He had heard the story from his father.

Herndon heard the story from former residents of New Salem and was intrigued by it because it seemed to explain what had always been mysteries to him: Why was Lincoln given to spells of melancholy and why did he marry Mary Todd, a woman whom Herndon loathed? On November 16, 1866, Herndon announced his theory in a lecture in Springfield: The tragic death of Lincoln's only true love had blighted his life, had made him fatalistic, had led him to marry someone he did not love, but had also driven him to great heights in politics.

Mary Todd Lincoln was horrified and insulted by the tale, which she considered a complete fabrication, but numerous Lincoln biographers believed it and repeated it well into the twentieth century. A great turning point came in 1928 when Wilma Francis Minor published "Lincoln the Lover" in the December issue of the highly respected *Atlantic Monthly*. She claimed to have papers handed down in her family that were love letters from Lincoln to Ann and other letters that mentioned the romance. The letters were clumsy forgeries, and they were denounced as such by numerous scholars and collectors including Paul M. Angle, Worthington C. Ford, Louis A. Warren, and Oliver R. Barrett. The *Atlantic* continued to publish the series of articles, but the April 1929 issue included a rebuttal by Angle called "The Minor Collection: A Criticism." Thereafter, the importance of the alleged romance diminished in Lincoln scholarship, and the romance is now regarded as unproved and its profound effect on Lincoln's later life as completely disproved.

SOURCES: J. G. Randall's "Sifting the Ann Rutledge Evidence," in *Lincoln the President: Springfield to Gettysburg* (New York: Dodd, Mead, 1945) II, 321–342, capably weighs the controversy. Don E. Fehrenbacher's *The Minor Affair: An Adventure in Forgery and Detection* (Fort Wayne, Ind.: Louis A. Warren Lincoln Library and Museum, 1979) carefully narrates the bizarre case of forgery which consigned the Ann Rutledge story to oblivion among Lincoln scholars.

See also HERNDON, WILLIAM HENRY; OWENS, MARY S.

S

Sandburg, Carl (1878–1967) Poet and immensely popular Lincoln biographer. Carl Sandburg was born and raised in Galesburg, Illinois, where Civil War veterans, old friends of Lincoln, and memorials to the Lincoln-Douglas Debate at Galesburg piqued his interest in the sixteenth President. He graduated from Lombard College in Galesburg in 1902 and wrote his first essay on Lincoln, "The Average Man," in 1906–1907. Sandburg's interests turned to politics. He became a member of the Social Democratic party and began to write numerous pieces for socialist causes in Milwaukee. He moved to Chicago and in 1914 published his first poetry.

Throughout the period of his greatest poetic productivity (1914–1923), Sandburg collected information on Lincoln. After beginning work on what he first conceived as a boys' book on Lincoln, by 1923 Sandburg was writing in earnest what he quickly realized would be more than a juvenile book. He first delivered the manuscript to his publisher, Harcourt, Brace, in 1924, but revisions delayed the publication of his two-volume *Abraham Lincoln: The Prairie Years* until 1926. The books covered Lincoln's life up to 1861. Sandburg's portrait of a folksy Lincoln was widely praised for rendering the "real" Lincoln, not a cold statue or a model for Sunday School class. Sandburg wrote poetically and relied upon the accumulation of a mass of details of frontier life and anecdotes about Lincoln.

In 1928 Sandburg began work on *Abraham Lincoln: The War Years*, a four-volume work published 11 years later. The huge opus, containing more words than Lincoln's collected works or Shakespeare's, again relied on a massive accumulation of details and myriads of quotations from contemporaries. It had no single theme, was less lyrical than *The Prairie Years*, and seemed to readers

Carl Sandburg in front of Gutzon Borglum's bust of Lincoln.

266

to give almost a journalistic chronicle of the developing Lincoln administration. Historian Charles A. Beard, who liked the books, said they were "more like a diary or saga" than systematic history. Sandburg presented Lincoln again as a man, a beleaguered human being facing a crisis of immense proportions. He stressed the President's vilification in the contemporary press and especially by the Radicals of his own party. The books pictured Lincoln as both a stern war leader and a personally forgiving man.

Sandburg's *Abraham Lincoln* was widely hailed as a literary masterpiece, though critic Edmund Wilson dismissed *The Prairie Years* as "corn" and was tempted "to feel that the cruellest thing that has happened to Lincoln since he was shot by Booth has been to fall into the hands of Carl Sandburg." Even professional historians, slow to praise the work of amateurs, commended the books, despite their many errors both of fact and interpretation. Paul M. Angle, with whom Sandburg wrote a book on Mrs. Lincoln in 1932, and Milo M. Quaife did admit that the books were much too loose to be considered biography. The reason for the literary praise was Sandburg's skill as a writer; Lincoln biographer J. G. Randall said in 1942 that Sandburg's made all other Lincoln books "dull or stupid by comparison." The reason for the historical praise was Sandburg's long period of work on the biography during which he accumulated a great mass of details in notes in cigar boxes. Finally, Sandburg's interpretation fit the political and social spirit of the 1920s and 1930s.

Sandburg's Lincoln was Middlewestern and liberal. In 1941 Sandburg, who had long since abandoned socialism for the New Deal, said that he studied Lincoln "in the hope of getting a better understanding of this man who the Republican party and the G. A. R. and the preachers magnified until he was too big to see." He found Lincoln's picture on the walls of politicians and big businessmen who "do not understand him and probably would not approve of him if they did." Lincoln's long allegiance to the Whig party, the party of banks and industrial development, received only passing mention, and Sandburg stressed Lincoln as an embodiment of democracy. Relying heavily on Walt Whitman's contemporary interpretations, Sandburg said that "For Whitman, Lincoln was a great voice and a sublime doer in the field of democracy. He regarded both Lincoln and himself as foretellers of a New Time for the common man and woman."

Informed by Ida M. Tarbell's favorable view of the frontier's influence of Lincoln, Sandburg made Lincoln a homespun and rumpled son of the prairie. "Like him," Sandburg said, "I am a son of the prairie, a poor boy who wandered over the land to find himself and his mission in life." Critics who thought Sandburg captured the real Lincoln mistook Western earthiness for realism. Edmund Wilson thus shrewdly objected that Lincoln's writings "do not give the impression of a folksy and jocular countryman swapping yarns at the village store or making his way to the White House by uncertain and awkward steps or presiding like a father, with a tear in his eye, over the tragedy of the Civil War." Sandburg frequently compared Franklin D. Roosevelt to Lincoln. Writing to the President in 1935, Sandburg said, "you are the best light of democracy that has occupied the White House since Lincoln." In an essay on Lincoln in *There Were Giants in the Land* (New York: Farrar & Rinehart, 1942), he drew a close parallel between the two beleaguered wartime presidents, Lincoln and Roosevelt.

Sandburg repeated as fact numerous folk tales about the young Lincoln. The great symbol of his gullibility on this score was his emphasis on the romance of Lincoln and Ann Rutledge, something Sandburg regretted after Paul M. Angle proved that the romance was undocumented. Sandburg soft-pedaled Lincoln's racial views and exaggerated his differences with the Radical Republicans. He also exaggerated Lincoln's popularity with the people, despite all the quotations from hostile partisans, and failed to come to grips with the importance of political parties and religion in Lincoln's America. After all, Sandburg "wanted to take Lincoln away from the religious bigots and the professional politicians and restore him to the common people."

Nevertheless, Sandburg did immerse himself in the published sources, and he used the great private collection of Oliver R. Barrett to advantage. Above all, his Lincoln fit the spirit of the troubled and depression-ridden 1930s by affirming that democracy could survive periods of crisis and produce leaders equal to the demands of even the most trying times. Around Lincoln, Sandburg wrote in *The War Years*, "gathered some of the hope that a democracy can choose a man, set him up high with power and honor, and the very act does something to the man himself, raises up new gifts, modulations, controls, outlooks, wisdoms, inside the man, so that he is something else again than he was before they sifted him out and anointed him to take an oath and solemnly sign himself for the hard and terrible, eye-filling and center-staged, role of Head of the Nation." Stephen Vincent Benét, writing in the *Atlantic Monthly*, called *The War Years* a "good purge for our own troubled time and for its more wild-eyed fears." Sandburg's *Abraham Lincoln* was not analytical, had no scholarly apparatus, and used only a poet's criteria for evidence, but, as Henry Steele Commager stated in the Winter 1940 issue of *The Yale Review*, Sandburg's secret was that he "realized that Lincoln belongs to the people, not to the historians."

SOURCES: See Benjamin P. Thomas, *Portrait for Posterity: Lincoln and His Biographers* (New Brunswick, N.J.: Rutgers University Press, 1947) and Alfred Haworth Jones, *Roosevelt's Image Brokers: Poets, Playwrights, and the Use of the Lincoln Symbol* (Port Washington, N.Y.: Kennikat Press, 1974). Edmund Wilson's criticism appears in his *Patriotic Gore: Studies in the Literature of the American Civil War* (New York: Oxford University Press, 1962).

Sangamon County, Illinois Lincoln's home from 1831 until 1861. At its formation in 1821, Sangamon County was twice the size of Rhode Island—a vast but sparsely settled empire in central Illinois. Lincoln first entered the county in 1831 via the Sangamon River, as most of the earlier settlers had. He was in a canoe en route to Springfield to procure produce to take to New Orleans for pioneer merchant Denton Offutt. After his return from the South in July, Lincoln settled in New Salem, which was northwest of Springfield. By that time Sangamon County was the most populous county and the premier agricultural region of Illinois. The county's residents were among the wealthier in a poor state. Early settlers had been primarily Kentuckians, Tennesseans, and Virginians or their descendants; Northerners filtered in later.

As soon as political parties formed in Illinois in the mid-1830s, Sangamon showed anti-Democratic leanings; 62 percent of the voters in 1836 were anti–Van Buren men, and almost 55 percent voted for Whig John Todd Stuart for Congress 2 years later. Lincoln began his legislative career in 1834 as a representative of Sangamon County in the Illinois House of Representatives. In four successive terms he served the county's interests well, particularly by obtaining in 1837—with eight other tall Sangamon legislators nicknamed "The Long Nine"—a law to move the state capital from Vandalia to Springfield. Soon afterward, Lincoln made Springfield his home; it became the capital 2 years later (July 4, 1839). The county remained 60 percent Whig throughout the 1840s. (Lincoln got over 64 percent of the county's vote when he ran for Congress in 1846.)

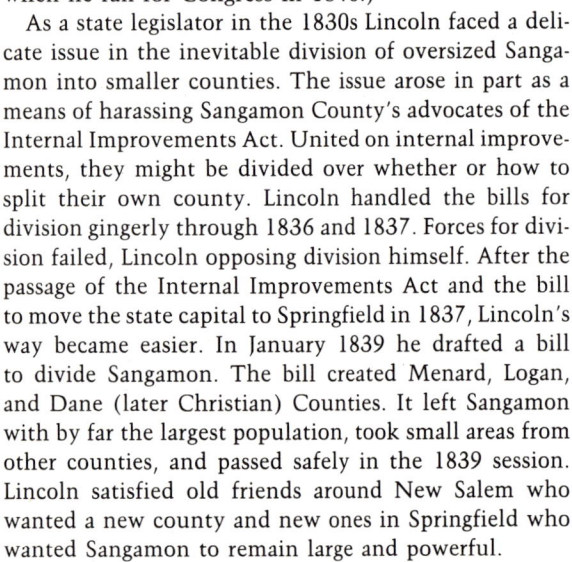

As a state legislator in the 1830s Lincoln faced a delicate issue in the inevitable division of oversized Sangamon into smaller counties. The issue arose in part as a means of harassing Sangamon County's advocates of the Internal Improvements Act. United on internal improvements, they might be divided over whether or how to split their own county. Lincoln handled the bills for division gingerly through 1836 and 1837. Forces for division failed, Lincoln opposing division himself. After the passage of the Internal Improvements Act and the bill to move the state capital to Springfield in 1837, Lincoln's way became easier. In January 1839 he drafted a bill to divide Sangamon. The bill created Menard, Logan, and Dane (later Christian) Counties. It left Sangamon with by far the largest population, took small areas from other counties, and passed safely in the 1839 session. Lincoln satisfied old friends around New Salem who wanted a new county and new ones in Springfield who wanted Sangamon to remain large and powerful.

Sangamon County remained stanchly Whig until 1854. By then, however, new issues and alignments changed its politics sharply. The influence of Southern origins in the population was visible in the county's vote on the constitutional provision to exclude Negroes from settlement in Illinois in 1848. Over 78 percent of Sangamon's voters supported exclusion (above the 70 percent average for Illinois as a whole). After the party realignments of the mid-1850s Sangamon voted Democratic, generally by less than 55 percent. In the 1856 presidential election, Republican John C. Frémont ran third (1174) to Democrat James Buchanan (2475) and Whig-American Millard Fillmore (1612). Lincoln failed to carry his own county in the presidential elections of 1860 and 1864. By the time Lincoln left for Washington, Sangamon County was, politically, no longer Lincoln country.

SOURCES: The best treatments of Sangamon's division are in William E. Baringer's *Lincoln's Vandalia: A Pioneer Portrait* (New Brunswick, N.J.: Rutgers University Press, 1949) and Harry E. Pratt's "Lincoln and the Division of Sangamon County," *Journal of the Illinois State Historical Society*, XLVII (Winter 1954), 398–409. The best discussion of the region's political geography is in Donald W. Riddle's *Lincoln Runs for Congress* (New Brunswick, N.J.: Rutgers University Press, 1948). Other useful sources are Theodore Calvin Pease, *Illinois Election Returns, 1818–1848* (Springfield: Illinois State Historical Library, 1923) and Arthur Charles Cole, *The Era of the Civil War* [*The Centennial History of Illinois, Volume Three*] (Springfield: Illinois Centennial Commission, 1919).

Schurz, Carl (1829–1906) Important Republican leader of the German-Americans during the Civil War. Carl Schurz was born near Cologne, Germany. He became a revolutionary in 1849 and fled, eventually, to America after the revolution failed. He lived in Philadelphia from 1852 to 1855 and then moved to Watertown, Wisconsin. His antislavery convictions led him into the Republican party, which used him especially for speaking to German-American voters. Lincoln complimented Schurz for his speech of January 4, 1860, at Springfield, Massachusetts; it was an attack on Stephen A. Douglas's doctrine of popular sovereignty. At the Republican convention that year, Schurz supported William H. Seward for President; but immediately after Lincoln's nomination, he promised to "do the work of a hundred men for Abr. Lincolns election." Lincoln replied that Schurz's support of Seward was "not even remembered by me for any practical purpose"; he would not go "back of the convention, to make distinctions among its' members."

Schurz headed "the foreign department" of the Republican Central Committee. He organized German, Norwegian, and Dutch speakers, dispatched them to appropriate districts, and did a great deal of speaking himself, especially in the critical states of Indiana and Pennsylvania. When Lincoln won election, Schurz wrote: "Yours, dear Sir, is the greatest mission that ever fell to the lot of mortal man: the restoration of original principles in the model Republic of the world." In the secession crisis he urged no surrender of Republican principles; he suggested that Lincoln "overawe the border-states" by having the Republican governors organize their state militias on the Ohio and Susquehanna Rivers. He advocated reinforcement of Fort Sumter in April and told Lincoln "to make short work of the secession movement and then to make front against the world abroad."

Despite his being 20 years Lincoln's junior and his never having held elective office, Schurz was full of advice for the President throughout the war years. After the military defeats of the summer of 1861, he explained a proper military policy. His ideas were not the sort that endear an officer to his men. He would not let soldiers lie down on their faces during an artillery barrage: "there never was a battle won by troops crawling upon their bellies. Soldiers go into battle not only for the purpose of shooting but also of being shot at." True, "we may . . . lose now and then a few more men, but we shall gain immensely as far as the morale of our forces is concerned." Having fought in a revolutionary army himself, Schurz always put great emphasis on the ardor and political purity of officers. After Republican defeats in the 1862 elections, Schurz bluntly told the President that the "defeat of the Administration is the Administration's own fault." It "admitted its professed opponents to its counsels" and "placed the Army . . . into the hands of its enemy's." "Let us be commanded by generals whose heart is in the war," Schurz said, and if "West-Point cannot do the business, let West-Point go down. Who cares?"

Lincoln was less a partisan than Schurz, and the latter's postelection letter prompted a sharp response from the President. The Republicans were a minority party and could not win the war without the help of Democrats. Schurz had not protested military appointments for Democrats when they were made, the President continued, and neither had most Republicans. Even General George B. McClellan "was first brought forward by the Republican Governor of Ohio, & claimed, and contended for at the same time by the Republican Governor of Pennsylvania."

Lincoln had other problems with the peppery and outspoken German-American. Though Schurz seemed interested in military command, Lincoln rewarded his campaign efforts in 1861 by making him minister to Spain—a choice dictated by Schurz's political importance at home and not by his appropriateness as a minister to that conservative, counterrevolutionary monarchy. By January 1862 Schurz had returned to the United States. He resigned the Spanish post in April and became a brigadier general in John C. Frémont's army in the summer. He defended Frémont's actions in the valley campaign against "Stonewall" Jackson (Frémont was a great favorite with the German-American community), distinguished himself at Second Bull Run, and became a major general on March 14, 1863. Lincoln's request for this promotion—coupled with recommendations for other German leaders, Franz Sigel and Julius Stahel—"may seem rather large," Lincoln explained to his Secretary of War, but "any thing less is too small." Thereafter Lincoln had trouble finding a command commensurate with Schurz's rank. General Schurz quarreled with his superiors, especially O. O. Howard, Joseph Hooker, and Henry W. Halleck. (Schurz thought Halleck was prejudiced against Germans.) He fought at Chancellorsville and at Gettysburg, but by early 1864 his difficulties with Hooker led him to seek a role in the canvass for Lincoln's reelection rather than on the battlefield.

Schurz's importance always stemmed from his role as a leader of German-Americans. When he sought promotion to major general in 1863, he reminded Lincoln of his "influence with a large class of citizens, which would undoubtedly be impaired by a letting down and might otherwise become useful to the public interest at a critical moment." When his promotion seemed stymied by being tied to similar promotions for other less competent German officers, however, Schurz complained that he had "become something of an American and not altogether dependent upon the endorsement of any class of foreign born people." When Hooker reorganized his army in 1863 and Schurz lost command of the XI Corps, two-thirds German, he told Lincoln that the soldiers "as well as the German population in this country" expected "the only compact representation of the 90 or 100,000 Germans who have entered the Army, would remain in the hands of one of their own." And he complained, "We have always been outsiders in this Army, we never belonged to the family, and I have no doubt this Army will see us leave without regret, provided our place be filled by an equal number of American troops."

When Schurz proposed campaigning for Lincoln in 1864, the President was willing to accept his help but, for undisclosed reasons, would not allow him to come to Washington to confer with him during the summer. Schurz felt banished from the Capital, but he campaigned vigorously; he denounced peace men in a speech at Philadelphia on September 16, 1864. After the election, Schurz wrote Lincoln a letter which foreshadowed one of the great interests of his subsequent long political career, civil service reform. He denounced "the system called rotation in office" as one that "has done more than anything else to demoralize the body politic." And he urged Lincoln not to turn men out of office in the traditional postelection way.

SOURCES: There is no modern biography of Schurz. The Schurz letters to Lincoln pledging support after the convention (May 22, 1860), describing Lincoln's "mission" (November 7, 1860), advising Lincoln to "make short work of secession" (April 5, 1861), describing a soldier's role in battle (August 13, 1861), about the 1862 elections (November 8, 1862), reminding Lincoln of his influence with Germans (February 14, 1863), saying he was "something of an American" (March 11, 1863), about the unfortunate XI Corps (April 6, 1863), and about rotation in office (December 1, 1864) are in the Abraham Lincoln Papers, Library of Congress.

Scott, Winfield (1786–1866) General-in-chief of the United States Army when Lincoln assumed the Presidency. Scott had been a hero of the Mexican War and an active Whig politician. In 1852, when he was the Whig presidential nominee, Lincoln was an elector on the Scott ticket, "and did something in the way of canvassing, but owing to the hopelessness of the cause in Illinois, . . . did less than in previous presidential canvasses."

Lieutenant General Scott was a focus of much attention in the secession crisis of 1860–1861. While James Buchanan was still President, Scott generally advocated a vigorous policy of reinforcing federal forts so that they could not be taken "by surprise or *coup de main.*" That view and others he committed to paper on October 24, 1860, and sent to Lincoln after the November election. There was much in them to arouse concern about the old general. Scott thought that "the right of secession

Winfield Scott

may be conceded" but "instantly balanced" by the government's right to use force to keep its territory should an interior state secede and isolate a coastal state. Moreover, he said, reuniting our territory would cause such a terrible war that perhaps a dissolution into four sectional confederacies would be a "smaller evil." He described at some length the curious composition of one of the possible confederacies which would contain seven slave states as well as free states of the Old Northwest—a sign that he was viewing his confederacies as an alternative for serious contemplation. Scott added that he never voted but that his sympathies were "with the Bell and Everett ticket." Lincoln acknowledged the views politely, but he must have been somewhat shaken by their erratic content. He more than once informed the general that he would have to retake any forts surrendered before the President-elect assumed office. In late January Lincoln sent a representative to test Scott's loyalty. The general was, after all, a Virginian—and a Virginian who had contemplated what the country would be like after a successful secession. Lincoln was apparently satisfied by what he learned.

Indeed, Scott's performance until the President arrived was more than satisfactorily loyal. Though he "eschew[ed] the idea of invading a seceded State," he repeatedly advised Buchanan to reinforce the forts and reminded him just before South Carolina's secession that President Andrew Jackson had sent troops to Charleston harbor even before the announcement of Nullification. Scott's efforts to gain permission to send reinforcements to Fort Sumter came to nothing.

By the time Lincoln was heading for Washington, the situation had changed radically. Scott worked hard to make the Capital secure for the new President's inauguration, and was among those who advised Lincoln to enter Washington surreptitiously to avoid assassination. By that time, however, Scott was in close contact with Senator William H. Seward, who was soon to become Secretary of State. Seward had been so influential over Scott in the past that in 1852 Lincoln had had to defend Scott from charges of being "wholly under the control of Seward of New York."

On March 3 Scott outlined four possible plans for the President; significantly, he submitted them through Seward. Three were so obviously undesirable that he was in fact recommending only the first: to form a "Union party," endorse the Crittenden compromise, and pursue a generally conciliatory course toward the South. The other three were to let the South depart in peace, to conquer her by "invading armies" (a feat which would require 2 or 3 years and "a Wolfe, a Desaix, or a Hoche, with 300,000 disciplined men" and would leave 15 "devastated *provinces*" to be "held, for generations, by heavy garrisons"), or to collect tariff duties outside Southern ports (or close or blockade them). Scott was fiercely loyal; he reportedly told one questioner that anyone interfering with the electoral count "should be lashed to the muzzle of a twelve-pounder gun and fired out of a window of the Capitol" to "manure the hills of Arlington with fragments of his body." But he had bad news for President Lincoln: the garrison at Fort Sumter would be out of key provisions in as few as 26 days. It could not be saved without 25,000 men with 6 or 8 months training and special legislation from Congress, which was not in session. He told President Lincoln this bad news a week after the President, in his First Inaugural Address, had promised to hold federal property in the seceded states. Scott even drafted an order for Sumter's evacuation. He repeatedly recommended withdrawal thereafter but was gathering scattered troops to protect the Capital.

Scott was too old, fat, dizzy, and gouty to mount a horse, and his days as general-in-chief were numbered; but his long military experience was important in the early days of the war. His so-called "Anaconda plan" recommended an enveloping of the enemy by a blockade of Southern coasts, a vigorous move down the Mississippi River from Cairo to New Orleans, and a passive strangulation thereafter. The plan was too passive to suit Lincoln, but from it the President did begin to learn the strategic importance of the Mississippi for cutting the Confederacy in two.

Scott did not get along well with General George B. McClellan, on whose plans he commented unfavorably as early as May 2, 1861. McClellan had proposed to capture Richmond by marching over the mountains from the west with 80,000 men. Scott saw little to recommend in these *"break-down* marches," in ignoring the use of waterways to envelop the enemy, and in so riling western Virginia politically that a sure Unionist bastion would join the rebellion. Serious disagreements with McClellan began in August, when Scott submitted his resignation because the young general sent letters over his head to Cabinet members and to the President, letters in which he sought to "decide all the greater war questions" without the general-in-chief. Lincoln managed to keep Scott on until October 31, when Scott resigned and was replaced, the next day, by McClellan. Lincoln consulted Scott at West Point the next summer, having himself come to disagree with McClellan over the placement and number of forces necessary to protect Washington while the Army of the Potomac campaigned in Virginia.

Scott showed considerable flexibility and moderation in retirement. He wished the administration well. In March 1862 he commended the President's plan for compensated emancipation in the loyal slave states and reminded him, through Seward, that New York Senator Rufus King had in 1825 devised a plan "pledging the public domain, after the discharge of the national debt, to such states as might adopt a system of slave emancipation." Contrary to his early doomsday talk of needing 2 or 3 years and a general as great as Wolfe to defeat the South, he actually thought the war constantly on the brink of being won. On April 28, 1862, he sent Seward a plan for Reconstruction ("early" suppression of the rebellion then being "inevitable") which would offer general amnesty with about 150 to 250 persons excepted, of whom the President should execute no more than a tenth.

Scott retired to write his memoirs. He lived to view Lincoln's remains in New York City after the President's assassination.

SOURCES: Scott's letters to Lincoln giving his "Views" (October 29, 1860), endorsing a "Union party" (March 3, 1861), about McClellan's plans (May 2, 1861), and protesting McClellan's going over his head (August 12, 1861) are in the Abraham Lincoln Papers, Library of Congress. So are the two letters to Seward (March 8, 1862 and April 28, 1862). See Charles Winslow Elliot's substantial biography, *Winfield Scott: The Soldier and the Man* (New York: Macmillan, 1937).

See also BALTIMORE PLOT; COMMANDER IN CHIEF; SUMTER CRISIS.

Scripps, John Locke (1818–1866) Journalist and early campaign biographer of Lincoln. Scripps was born in Missouri but moved to Illinois. He settled in Chicago in 1847. There he worked for the Chicago *Tribune* and in 1852, with William Bross, established the *Daily Democratic Press*. He became a Republican, but he was a moderate and warned Lincoln on June 22, 1858, that his "House Divided" speech aroused objections from Kentucky friends "who want to be Republicans, but who are *afraid* we are not sufficiently conservative." Those friends thought the speech threatened "to make war upon the institution [slavery] in the States where it now exists." Lincoln replied in a letter not for publication that he never intended any such threat.

On July 1, 1858, the *Press* united with the *Tribune* to form the Chicago *Press and Tribune*. Scripps remained as an editorial writer, and the paper was closely allied to Lincoln's political fortunes. On July 3, 1858, Scripps apologized for having already divulged Lincoln's upcoming "charge of conspiracy against [Stephen A.] Douglas when you next meet him on the stump." He pleaded for more guidance in the future in regard to Lincoln's plans.

In June 1860 Scripps elicited from Lincoln a long autobiographical statement to serve as the basis for a campaign biography. Scripps planned a 96-page work, but the newspaper's editor, Joseph M. Medill, wanted the pamphlet published in New York by Horace Greeley's *Tribune*. That paper insisted on a 32-page work. Poor planning also forced Scripps to cut four of the last eight pages, which, he admitted, caused him to botch his treatment of the Lincoln-Douglas Debates and the conclusion. Time did not permit him to submit the manuscript for Lincoln's approval before publication in July.

In 1861 Lincoln appointed Scripps postmaster of Chicago, a job which kept him from editorial work. Disagreements thereafter occasionally arose. For example, Scripps objected to Lincoln's revocation of John C. Frémont's emancipation proclamation for Missouri in 1861 as "a backward step"; he felt that the war would inevitably see either slavery or the national government destroyed.

Scripps wanted to run for Congress in 1864, and he entered into a bitter feud with Chicago's incumbent Republican Congressman Isaac N. Arnold. In July Arnold complained to Lincoln that Scripps used the post office's more than 100 appointees against him. Lincoln admonished Scripps in a letter delivered by Arnold, and Scripps wrote a stinging reply to Lincoln. Lincoln answered that it had been his general policy to ask postmasters not to use their offices against incumbent Republicans. The Scripps-Arnold feud threatened Republican control of the district, and in the end the convention compromised on John Wentworth as its nominee.

SOURCES: Scripps's letters about the "House Divided" speech (to Lincoln, June 22, 1858), about the conspiracy charge against Douglas (to Lincoln, July 3, 1858), and about Frémont (to Lincoln, September 23, 1861) are in the Abraham Lincoln Papers, Library of Congress. The famous campaign biography is reprinted with a careful introduction explaining its genesis in John Locke Scripps, *Life of Abraham Lincoln*, edited by Roy P. Basler and Lloyd Dunlap (Bloomington: Indiana University Press, 1961).

See also ARNOLD, ISAAC NEWTON; AUTOBIOGRAPHY.

Sculptors *See* BORGLUM, JOHN GUTZON DE LA MOTHE; LINCOLN MEMORIAL; MILLS, CLARK; TOMB, THE LINCOLN; VOLK, LEONARD WELLS.

Secession *See* NATIONALISM; SUMTER CRISIS.

Second Inaugural Address Lincoln's address on March 4, 1865, was the shortest inaugural address yet delivered by an American President. Almost nothing is known of the manner or time in which Lincoln composed the speech.

The address had the character, not of a forecast of administration policies, but of a philosophical rumination on the meaning of the Civil War. Friend and foe alike commented on its religious—even "theological"—nature. Many newspapers remarked that it was in a style "Lincolnian" and unique, and it seems best to quote the inimitable address rather than to paraphrase it:

> At this second appearing to take the oath of the presidential office, there is less occasion for an extended address than there was at the first. Then a statement, somewhat in detail, of a course to be pursued, seemed fitting and proper. Now, at the expiration of four years, during which public declarations have been constantly called forth on every point and phase of the great contest which still absorbs the attention, and engrosses the enerergies [sic] of the nation, little that is new could be presented. The progress of our arms, upon which all else chiefly depends, is as well known to the public as to myself; and it is, I trust, reasonably satisfactory and encouraging to all. With high hope for the future, no prediction in regard to it is ventured.
>
> On the occasion corresponding to this four years ago, all thoughts were anxiously directed to an impending civil-war. All dreaded it—all sought to avert it. While the inaugeral address was being delivered from this place, devoted altogether to *saving* the Union without war, insurgent agents were in the city seeking to *destroy* it without war—seeking to dissol[v]e the Union, and divide effects, by negotiation. Both parties deprecated war; but one of them would *make* war rather than let the nation survive; and the other would *accept* war rather than let it perish. And the war came.
>
> One eighth of the whole population were colored slaves, not distributed generally over the Union, but localized in the Southern part of it. These slaves constituted a peculiar and powerful interest. All knew that this interest was, some-

how, the cause of the war. To strengthen, perpetuate, and extend this interest was the object for which the insurgents would rend the Union, even by war; while the government claimed no right to do more than to restrict the territorial enlargement of it. Neither party expected for the war, the magnitude, or the duration, which it has already attained. Neither anticipated that the *cause* of the conflict might cease with, or even before, the conflict itself should cease. Each looked for an easier triumph, and a result less fundamental and astounding. Both read the same Bible, and pray to the same God; and each invokes His aid against the other. It may seem strange that any men should dare to ask a just God's assistance in wringing their bread from the sweat of other men's faces; but let us judge not that we be not judged. The prayers of both could not be answered; that of neither has been answered fully. The Almighty has His own purposes. "Woe unto the world because of offences! for it must needs be that offences come; but woe to that man by whom the offence cometh!" If we shall suppose that American Slavery is one of those offences which, in the providence of God, must needs come, but which, having continued through His appointed time, He now wills to remove, and that He gives to both North and South, this terrible war, as the woe due to those by whom the offence came, shall we discern therein any departure from those divine attributes which the believers in a Living God always ascribe to Him? Fondly do we hope—fervently do we pray—that this mighty scourge of war may speedily pass away. Yet, if God wills that it continue, until all the wealth piled by the bond-man's two hundred and fifty years of unrequited toil shall be sunk, and until every drop of blood drawn with the lash, shall be paid by another drawn with the sword, as was said three thousand years ago, so still it must be said "the judgments of the Lord, are true and righteous altogether."

With malice toward none; with charity for all; with firmness in the right, as God gives us to see the right, let us strive on to finish the work we are in; to bind up the nation's wounds; to care for him who shall have borne the battle, and for his widow, and his orphan—to do all which may achieve and cherish a just, and a lasting peace, among ourselves, and with all nations.

Luckily, Lincoln misread a letter from Thurlow Weed, commending another recent public statement by Lincoln, as a compliment on his inaugural address and wrote him explaining his own feelings about it. Lincoln expected it "to wear as well as—perhaps better than—any thing I have produced; but I believe it is not immediately popular." The reason was simple: "Men are not flattered by being shown that there has been a difference between the Almighty and them." But to "deny it," Lincoln stated, "is to deny that there is a God governing the world."

Lincoln somewhat underestimated the immediate reception of his speech. Democrats disliked it, but most Republican newspapers praised it. Charles Francis Adams, Jr., told his father, the minister to Great Britain, that the "rail-splitting lawyer" proved himself "one of the wonders of the day." "Once at Gettysburg and now again on a greater occasion he has shown a capacity for rising to the demands of the hour which we should not expect from orators or men of the schools," Adams continued. "This inaugural strikes me in its grand simplicity and directness as being for all time the historical keynote of the war."

On April 10, 1865, Lincoln gave the original handwritten manuscript to John Hay. Hay's heirs later gave it to the Library of Congress.

SOURCES: Benjamin Barondess surveys the reaction of the contemporary press to the Second Inaugural Address in *Three Lincoln Masterpieces: Cooper Institute Speech, Gettysburg Address, Second Inaugural* (Charleston: Education Foundation of West Virginia, 1954).

Secretaries, Private *See* HAY, JOHN MILTON; NEILL, EDWARD DUFFIELD; NICOLAY, JOHN GEORGE; STODDARD, WILLIAM OSBORN.

Seward, William Henry (1801–1872) Lincoln's Secretary of State. Seward was born in Orange County, New York, and was educated at Union College. He established a law practice in Auburn, New York, in 1822, and Auburn was thereafter his home. He moved from the National Republican to the Antimasonic to the Whig party, serving as state senator (1830–1834) and governor (1838–1842). He championed government-financed internal improvements, prison reform, and improved education as well as schools for immigrants taught in their own language by teachers of their own religious faith. He considered his views too advanced for great popularity in the Whig party. From 1830 on, he was closely associated with Thurlow Weed, who was known as "The Dictator" in New York politics.

Seward had no sympathy for those who hated "men for the marks which God set upon them to commend them to our pity and our care." No radical equalitarian, he nevertheless had a paternalistic attitude toward Negroes which made him an early antislavery advocate and a defender of free Negroes and fugitive slaves in court cases. Elected to the United States Senate in 1849, Seward opposed the Compromise of 1850, saying that a "higher law than the Constitution" demanded the exclusion of slavery from territories as yet untainted by it. That memorable phrase, and another in 1858 describing the sectional controversy as an "irrepressible conflict" gave him a reputation for antislavery radicalism.

Seward became a Republican in 1855, but Weed, thinking the party's defeat inevitable, held him back from serious contention for the Republican presidential nomination the next year. In 1860 Seward was the front-runner for the nomination, but he lost to Lincoln because of his reputation for radicalism in the West and because of his reputation for sympathy toward Catholics in the East. The Republicans focused their strategy on winning four states they had lost in 1856: Indiana, Illinois, Pennsylvania, and New Jersey. The New Yorker's dalliance with Stephen A. Douglas in 1858 earned Illinois's resentment, and Indiana's Republicans thought the state could not be carried with so radical an Easterner as the standard-bearer. Pennsylvania Republicans, for whom the votes of former Know-Nothings were crucial, found Seward unacceptable. Horace Greeley, once his political ally, opposed him at the Chicago convention too. An irreparable rift between Greeley and Seward did not, however, appear until after the convention, when

Seward blamed Greeley's opposition on resentment at having received no offices from Seward and Weed in the past. Seward supported Lincoln and made a speaking tour of the West in the autumn.

On December 8, 1860, Lincoln asked Seward to become Secretary of State. After thinking the offer over for more than two weeks and sending Weed to Springfield to discuss Seward's "unsettled views" on the offer, the New Yorker finally accepted. He urged John C. Frémont's appointment as Secretary of War (though he would later oppose Lincoln's suggestion of making him minister to France because Frémont had private business to attend to in Paris and, as a South Carolinian by birth and education, might not be loyal enough). But primarily Seward sought a Whiggish Cabinet and a Cabinet which symbolized Republican conciliatoriness toward the South. For the latter policy he and Weed urged the appointment of two non-Republican Southerners to the Cabinet, but Lincoln made an offer to only one, John A. Gilmer of North Carolina, who eventually rejected the offer. For the former policy Seward, without actually urging Simon Cameron's appointment, suggested that he would "dread exceedingly" to have any of Cameron's friends hostile to the administration. Cameron's political antecedents were mixed but were not as clearly Democratic as Salmon P. Chase's, and Seward and Weed sought to keep Chase and ex-Democrat Montgomery Blair out of the administration.

Weed was nakedly opposed to giving former Democrats a large share of the spoils, but Seward more suavely cloaked his policy as one which sought a "strong" Cabinet for a national crisis rather than one which balanced all the "little factions" in order to strengthen the Republican party. Back in 1850 the New York Senator had thought the Union so strong that there was no need to compromise on slavery. Unlike Lincoln, he tended to believe that dry weather and poor soil would keep slavery out of the unsettled West. Since 1858 he had blamed the northern Democratic party more than the South for the controversy over slavery. By the secession crisis of 1860–1861, however, Seward was one of the few Republicans who took threats of disunion seriously as something more than bluster, bluff, and blackmail.

By March 2, Seward's plans had so far failed that he tried to back out of his acceptance of a Cabinet post. He had not changed Lincoln's "compound Cabinet," but he did considerably soften the tone of the President's inaugural address: he persuaded Lincoln to drop a reaffirmation of the Republican platform for an assurance that he had no designs on slavery in the states and to mention favorably a national constitutional convention to solve sectional problems. After a long conversation with the President following the inaugural ceremonies, Seward reconsidered and on March 5 agreed to be Secretary of

Louis Maurer's cartoon, published by Currier & Ives in 1860, shows Seward's being thrown overboard from the Republican ship of state by Horace Greeley, Edward Bates, and Francis Preston Blair. Lincoln, who refers to his experience as a flatboatman, takes over the tiller, and James Watson Webb, editor of the New York Courier and Enquirer, warns of dangers ahead. Only the Negro has a life preserver as the ship of state sinks, and the nineteenth-century cartoon equivalent of Uncle Sam, at right, warns that the ship will sink unless the Negro is thrown overboard.

Seward, William Henry

State after all. Seward's role up to this point is bafflingly enigmatic and baldly duplicitous. He established surreptitious contact with Edwin M. Stanton, who kept him apprised of the secrets of President James Buchanan's Cabinet and, knowing that Lincoln recognized his handwriting, "for prudence" refused to sign the letters in which he told Lincoln what he learned thereby.

Seward remained in Lincoln's Cabinet in part because he felt that his departure would otherwise "leave the country to chance." Thus his passion for conciliating the South was now highlighted by his feeling that he was the only member of the administration who *could* do so. When Lincoln sought the Cabinet's opinion on reinforcing Fort Sumter, the Secretary of State on March 15 declared his opposition to any move that might provoke war. The fort was a useless symbol of federal "authority and sovereignty" which would fall to Southern assault as soon as word leaked out, as it surely would, that a relief expedition was on its way. He admitted that conciliation "tends to demoralize the Republican party," but the Union was "inestimable and even indispensable to the welfare and happiness of the whole country, and to the best interests of mankind." Time would see the "blind unreasoning popular excitement" for disunion subside, but military coercion would drive the Border States into the arms of the secessionists and civil war would make "reunion . . . hopeless, at least under this administration, or in any other way than by a popular disavowal, both of the war and of the administration which commenced it." War would arouse an opposition party that would offer peace and would profit politically by reunion. Unlike Montgomery Blair, who saw secession as a minority coup, Seward saw it as a "popular" sway of unreason. He was somewhat self-contradictory in putting faith in Southern devotion to Union "even in South Carolina" on the one hand, and fearing disunion because of the fragility of that sentiment in the Border States on the other. He did not put as much stress as Blair did on the element of political "terror" which "suppressed and silenced" that sentiment "for a time."

Committed to conciliation and feeling that he would be the power behind the throne, Seward made a careless promise to three Confederate commissioners that Fort Sumter would be evacuated. But by March 29, when Lincoln polled the Cabinet again, the Secretary of State was the only one who opposed resupplying the garrison. Seward became increasingly desperate, and on April 1 he wrote a memorandum which accused Lincoln of being "without a policy either domestic or foreign," suggested demands for explanations from Spain and France, and urged convening Congress to declare war against Spain and France if their explanations were not "satisfactory." Threat of foreign war would reunite the sections and change *"the question before the Public from one upon Slavery, or not Slavery* for a question upon *Union or Disunion."* The President might "devolve . . . on some member of the Cabinet" the execution of the policy. Lincoln replied that there *was* a policy, and, if a new one were to be executed, "I must do it." Only Seward's secrecy and aggressiveness suggest the sinister interpretation that he tried to sabotage the Sumter relief expedition by signing his own rather than the President's name to the order detaching the warship *Powhatan* for the task. The order countermanded a previous order of the President's, and the ship's commander did not think an order from the Secretary of State should countermand one from the President.

Two weeks after Sumter fell, Seward still thought the crisis might "blow over." He was wrong, but his optimism proved a tonic throughout the war. He never suffered Lincoln's occasional melancholy over the hopes of the Union cause. And Seward proved to be a stern and uncompromising foe once war began in earnest. As head (until February 1862) of the government's program to arrest disloyal persons in the North, the Secretary of State—perhaps because of his fear that an antiwar party would rise in the North—was zealous. His actions gave rise to a story that Seward boasted that "he could ring a little bell and cause the arrest of a citizen" anywhere in the country. The opposition used the story, but there is no proof of its accuracy. Seward's letter to ex-President Franklin Pierce in December 1861, in which he demanded an explanation of allegedly disloyal activities, was prompted by an anonymous letter written as a hoax. Seward apologized quickly, but his reputation for dictatorial methods increased.

President Lincoln interfered little in foreign policy. He did soften Seward's toughly worded instructions of May 21, 1861, to Charles Francis Adams, minister to England, and he saw to it that the English foreign minister did not see them. Otherwise, Seward's bluster of the period from April to June 1861 convinced England that recognition of the Confederacy would mean war. Later, the Secretary of State proved more willing to compromise, and in the *Trent* crisis of November and December 1861 he acceded to British demands despite American public opinion. He convinced France, too, that recognition meant war, but he later spoke more truculently in public about French intervention in Mexico than he did in private conversations with French authorities. By 1864 he was sufficiently weaned from his idea that foreign war would unite the country not even to entertain seriously any threat to France's Mexican policy.

Seward was the most important member of Lincoln's Cabinet; he gave advice on many matters even as he conducted the bulk of foreign policy. Lincoln heeded Seward's advice to delay the Emancipation Proclamation until after a Union victory. Seward saw no merit for foreign policy in the proposed proclamation, which he thought might bring European intervention out of fear that servile insurrections in the Confederacy would bring anarchy and an end to cotton supplies for 60 years. Lincoln valued Seward enough by December 1862 to protect him from an attempt by disgruntled Republican Senators to oust him from the Cabinet. (Although Democrats saw Seward as the manipulative evil genius behind all the too-vigorous policies of the Lincoln administration, many Republicans saw him as the evil genius who palsied the administration's will to fight.) Later that month Seward was one of three Cabinet members who urged recognition of West Virginia as a state. Throughout the war the President and the Secretary of State worked well together and got along amiably in private moments (despite Seward's and Mrs. Lincoln's mutual dislike).

Although late in the war Montgomery Blair became the favorite target of Radical Republican critics of the administration, Seward continued to pursue his moderate course. In May 1864 he advised Lincoln to "give the insurgents an opportunity to deny the charge" that they sanctioned the Fort Pillow massacre, but he did say that Confederate prisoners equal in number and rank to the Union soldiers killed should be "set apart and held in rigorous confinement" pending the explanation. The Secretary of State was a conduit for various peace and Reconstruction proposals that came to the administration as Confederate military fortunes declined. In April he told a Southerner that no armistice was possible and that "a fundamental principle in negotiating" reunion must be "that Slavery . . . be abolished and all slaves must be made unconditionally free, although it is not intended to say that laws might not be proposed by the States, not inconsistent with the freedom of the slaves, with a view to alleviate the inconveniences of a sudden and universal emancipation." At the Hampton Roads Peace Conference of February 3, 1865, Seward is said to have described not only the Emancipation Proclamation but also the Thirteenth Amendment as war measures, and practically invited the South to kill the latter by a speedy return to the Union. The account, however, comes from an unreliable Confederate source.

John Wilkes Booth included Seward as a target of his assassination plot. On the night of April 14, 1865, Lewis Thornton Powell seriously injured Seward, who was in bed recovering from a carriage accident. The Secretary eventually recovered, and he finished his term under President Andrew Johnson. He was conspicuously conservative in Reconstruction, being fundamentally willing to sacrifice protection of the freedmen for the sake of national unity.

In April 1873 Charles Francis Adams delivered a eulogy which pictured Seward as the self-sacrificing mastermind of the Lincoln administration. Gideon Welles, who had had nothing but distrust of his fellow Cabinet member, rushed to Lincoln's defense with *Lincoln and Seward*, a book which showed Lincoln's hand even in Seward's realm of foreign policy and asserted Lincoln's mastery and Seward's secondary role. Of the secondary roles, however, Seward's was by far the largest.

SOURCES: Glyndon G. Van Deusen's *William Henry Seward* (New York: Oxford University Press, 1967) is a biography of quality. On Seward's enigmatic role while Lincoln was President-elect see Daniel W. Croft's lucid article, "A Reluctant Unionist: John A. Gilmer and Lincoln's Cabinet," *Civil War History*, XXIV (September 1978), 225–249. Seward's letters to Lincoln on his "unsettled views" (December 16, 1860) and on his dread of alienating Cameron's friends (January 15, 1860), Leonard Swett's letter to Lincoln about Seward's preference for a strong Cabinet (December 31, 1860), and Seward's unsigned letter to Lincoln about Buchanan (December 29, 1860), his opinion on Fort Sumter (March 15, 1861), his notorious memorandum of April 1 (April 1, 1861), his opinion on the Fort Pillow massacre (May 4, 1864), and his memorandum on Cornelius Wendell and Southern peace initiatives (April 19, 1864) are in the Abraham Lincoln Papers, Library of Congress.

See also ADAMS, CHARLES FRANCIS; PIERCE, FRANKLIN; POWELL, LEWIS THORNTON; *TRENT* AFFAIR.

Shakespeare Despite his "defective" education, Abraham Lincoln's acquaintance with the plays of Shakespeare apparently stemmed from early age. William Scott's *Lessons in Elocution*, which Lincoln probably used as a schoolboy in Indiana, reprinted several soliloquies from Shakespeare, including one of Lincoln's favorites, "O, my offence is rank," from *Hamlet.*

Lincoln's first opportunity to see Shakespearean plays came only when he was President. He attended the theater on several occasions, and his taste for Shakespeare became something of a national news item in 1863 after the President saw James H. Hackett as Falstaff in *King Henry IV*. Hackett then sent the President a copy of his book *Notes and Comments on Certain Plays and Actors of Shakespeare* on March 20. Lincoln replied on August 17, telling the actor that "For one of my age, I have seen very little of the drama." He admitted that he had never read some of Shakespeare's plays, "while others I have gone over perhaps as frequently as any unprofessional reader." He liked plays with political themes, mentioning "Lear, Richard Third, Henry Eighth, Hamlet, and especially Macbeth. I think nothing equals Macbeth." He added that "Unlike you gentlemen of the profession, I think the soliloquy in Hamlet commencing 'O, my offence is rank' surpasses that commencing 'To be, or not to be.'"

Hackett wasted little time in using Lincoln's letter in a self-promoting broadside. The press seized on the affair and ridiculed the audacity of the backwoods President's expressing his critical opinions on Shakespeare. Hackett wrote to apologize, and Lincoln responded in a letter marked "Private": "Those comments constitute a fair specimen of what has occurred to me through life. I have endured a great deal of ridicule without much malice; and have received a great deal of kindness, not quite free from ridicule. I am used to it."

Lincoln's secretary, John Hay, recalled that the President "read Shakespeare more than all other writers together." The President had a habit of cornering a secretary and reading passages of Shakespeare aloud to him. He was critical. He preferred the histories and tragedies to the comedies and thought the comedies had to be seen in performance to be appreciated. He thought Hackett misread a line in a performance as Falstaff and thought actors generally misinterpreted Richard III's first speech, missing the "repressed hate and jealousy" in it, as he told White House portraitist Francis B. Carpenter. Lincoln also told Carpenter, "It matters not to

Shakespeare

One of several political cartoons to capitalize on public knowledge of Lincoln's fondness for the theater and Shakespeare, this rare undated lithograph made the move from depicting Lincoln with black men to depicting him as a black man himself. Benjamin F. Butler appears as Falstaff, in the background, and Charles Sumner stands behind a wastebasket full of discarded texts from America's past. Secretary of War Stanton converses with Secretary of State Seward, who cannot get the "little bell" he uses to have citizens arbitrarily arrested to ring. Secretary of the Navy Welles, almost always depicted as incompetent, dozes in the corner. The references to Andrew Johnson and the Monroe Doctrine probably indicate that the cartoon was issued for the campaign of 1864.

This fine cartoon seized on Lincoln's reputation for joke-telling as well as for liking Shakespeare to suggest that Democratic nominee George B. McClellan would beat Lincoln in the election of 1864.

me whether Shakespeare be well or ill acted; with him the thought suffices."

SOURCES: A pioneering work is R. Gerald McMurtry's "Lincoln Knew Shakespeare," *Indiana Magazine of History* XXXI (December 1935), 266–277. Roy P. Basler has a chapter on the subject in *A Touchstone for Greatness: Essays, Addresses, and Occasional Pieces about Abraham Lincoln* (Westport, Conn.: Greenwood Press, 1973). See also Don E. Fehrenbacher, "Lincoln and the Weight of Responsibility," *Journal of the Illinois State Historical Society*, LXVIII (February 1975) 45–56.

Sherwood, Robert See ABE LINCOLN IN ILLINOIS.

Shields, James (1806–1879) Illinois Democratic rival of Lincoln's. Shields was born in Ireland. He settled eventually in Kaskaskia, Illinois, and by 1836 he was a Democratic member of the legislature. As state auditor in 1842, he ordered that depreciated Illinois State Bank notes be accepted by the state's revenue collectors only at actual value. Whigs protested, and a satirical letter of August 27, 1842, written by a widow named "Rebecca" in the *Sangamo Journal*, alluded to the order and described Shields as "a conceity dunce." Shields sought "Rebecca's" identity from editor Simeon Francis and learned it was Abraham Lincoln.

Before Shields could challenge Lincoln, another insulting "Rebecca" letter, this one written by Mary Todd and Julia Jayne, claimed that Rebecca could fight with Shields on an equal footing if he donned petticoats or she, britches. Shields's seconds eventually challenged Lincoln to a duel. Lincoln offered to admit authorship and to explain that the letter was written "wholly for political effect." If Shields were unsatisfied by this offer, Lincoln said, he would accept the challenge. The fight would be with "Cavalry broad swords of the largest size." A plank, 10 feet long, "firmly fixed on edge, on the ground," would be "the line between us which neither is to pass his foot over upon forfeit of his life."

Shields was much shorter than Lincoln, but the absurdity of the conditions failed to dissuade the fiery Irishman. The two men met across the Mississippi River from Alton because dueling was illegal in Illinois. Seconds and John J. Hardin and Dr. R. W. English, mutual friends of the would-be combatants, patched up the feud before the duel began. Lincoln was considerably embarrassed for the rest of his life that he had agreed to fight a duel. When Lincoln and Mary were married, they agreed never to mention it again.

Governor Thomas Ford appointed Shields to the Illinois Supreme Court in 1843 and later entrusted him with the manuscript of his *History of Illinois*, an important source for Illinois political history during Lincoln's early career. Shields devotedly saw it through to publication in 1854. Shields was wounded in the Mexican War and returned to Illinois to be elected United States Senator in 1849, a phenomenon Lincoln cynically described as "a fruit of the glorious Mexican war." In 1855 Lincoln aspired to Shields's seat, but both men were defeated, Lyman Trumbull being chosen by the legislature in a complicated and bitter election. Shields was later elected Senator from Minnesota and subsequently moved to California, "sick and tired of public life."

Shields was depressed by "the struggles of parties in this country almost as shamefully selfish as the wretched struggles of degenerated factions in Mexico." In 1860 he vowed never to *"help . . . impose a Northern man on the South as President."* The South, he felt, was "acting in self-defense." He personally preferred Stephen A. Douglas for President, but since Douglas was unacceptable to the South, he reluctantly supported John C. Breckinridge. When war broke out, he was managing a mine in Mexico, but he quickly offered his services to the United States government. Republicans accused him of disloyalty for his pro-Southern statements in 1860, but Lincoln appointed him brigadier general of volunteers on August 19, 1861, partly to satisfy Irish-Americans. Shields resigned his commission in 1863. He later served as a United States Senator from Missouri (1879).

SOURCES: On the Lincoln-Shields duel, see Paul M. Angle, *"Here I Have Lived": A History of Lincoln's Springfield* (New Brunswick, N.J.: Rutgers University Press, 1935), and James E. Myers, *The Astonishing Saber Duel of Abraham Lincoln* (Springfield, Ill.: Lincoln-Herndon Building Publishers, 1968). A newspaper clipping entitled "Out of His Own Mouth" in the Abraham Lincoln Papers, Library of Congress, reveals Shields's political views in 1860.

Simpson, Matthew (1811–1884) Methodist bishop who conducted the services at Lincoln's funeral in Springfield. Simpson was an ironic choice for the funeral role: he had spent much of the war criticizing Lincoln's indifference toward Methodists in distributing the patronage. The administration made no appointment on a par with the Buchanan administration's sending Indiana Methodist Joseph A. Wright as minister to Berlin. In July 1861 Henry C. Whitney overheard the President's recommendation of one man for office: "the fact that he was urged by the Methodists should be in his favor, as they were 'complaining some of us.'" In the autumn, Simpson gained an audience with the President through Simon Cameron to complain of the relative paucity of appointments from his church in light of the church's numerical superiority in the American population at large.

Simpson did exert some influence in appointments through Senator James Harlan, Secretary of War Edwin M. Stanton, and Secretary of the Treasury Salmon P. Chase. His attempt to see a list of Post Office Department appointees designated by religion provoked a nasty confrontation with Montgomery Blair, who refused flatly and ever after carried the church's enmity. Simpson's son gained a commission from Stanton, and Lincoln appointed John Evans, a Methodist friend of Simpson's, Governor of Colorado Territory.

Methodists still felt they lacked a first-class appointment from the Lincoln administration, and so large a group could hardly be ignored in an election year. In June 1864 Lincoln asked Bishop Simpson to stand in for him at the opening of the Philadelphia Sanitary Fair. Simpson and other Methodist bishops were not ap-

Matthew Simpson

peased, but they adopted a strategy of concentrating their strength on gaining a Cabinet appointment for Harlan, a graduate of Indiana Asbury University (now DePauw) while Simpson was president of the university. By December, prospects looked good for Harlan's appointment.

The Methodist bishops were also interested in regaining control of the property of the Methodist Episcopal Church, South, in occupied areas. Stanton abetted but Lincoln apparently took a dim view of their efforts. In 1865 the President upheld an order by Governor Andrew Johnson which would restore the McKendree Methodist Church of Nashville to the Southern Methodist bishop, minister, and trustees of the church.

Simpson's differences with Lincoln were matters of power and prestige and not of ideology and purpose. The bishop's speeches and sermons were stridently patriotic and endorsed the important policies of the administration, especially emancipation. Speaking in New York City just five days before the election of 1864, Simpson painted a hopeful picture of the condition of the Union and praised emancipation and the work of Negro soldiers, who, he thought, deserved a state of their own in the Southwest after the war. Simpson was invited to preach in the Capitol on the Sunday after Lincoln's inauguration.

After Lincoln's assassination, members of the Cabinet chose Simpson to take charge of the funeral services. He delivered a prayer at the Washington services and a famous eulogy at Lincoln's burial in Springfield on May 4. Simpson called Lincoln "no ordinary man" and felt that he "was especially singled out to guide our government in these troublesome times." He admitted that he could not "speak definitely" about Lincoln's "religious experience," because "acquaintance with him did not give me the opportunity to hear him speak on those topics." He suggested that "Traitors will probably suffer by the change of rulers, for one of sterner mould, and who himself has deeply suffered from the rebellion, now wields the sword of justice." Simpson himself urged that former members of Congress who became Confederates be tried and punished and that "every officer educated at the public expense" who did the same "be doomed to a traitor's death." Simpson closed with a famous passage:

> Chieftain, farewell! The nation mourns thee. Mothers shall teach thy name to their lisping children. The youth of our land shall emulate thy virtues. Statesmen shall study thy record and learn lessons of wisdom. Mute though thy lips be, yet they still speak. Hushed is thy voice, but its echoes of liberty are ringing through the world, and the sons of bondage listen with joy. Prisoned thou art in death, and yet thou art marching abroad, and chains and manacles are bursting at thy touch. Thou didst fall not for thyself. The assassin had no hate for thee. Our hearts were aimed at, our national life was sought. We crown thee as our martyr, and humanity enthrones thee as her triumphant son. Hero, Martyr, Friend, FAREWELL!

The eulogy was an indication of Simpson's future course as a supporter of Reconstruction and a critic of Andrew Johnson, when the new President proved not to be "of sterner mould."

SOURCES: Robert D. Clark's *Life of Matthew Simpson* (New York: Macmillan, 1956) has an eye-opening appraisal of Lincoln's relations with the Methodists.

Sioux Uprising   *See* INDIANS.

Slave Trade   The slave trade, both African and domestic, and the men who participated in it were objects of moral loathing for Abraham Lincoln. Slaveholders, Lincoln thought, were not morally different from Northerners—circumstances made them what they were. Slavetraders were another matter. Domestic slave-dealers brought out in Lincoln a rare vituperative denunciation in his 1854 Peoria speech. They were "sneaking" individuals, "native tyrants"; they crawled up to their customers who shunned the "snaky contact" of shaking hands with these dishonest men. Lincoln had decades of national feeling against the African slave trade on his side; Congress itself in 1820 had classed the trade "with piracy and murder" as a "capital" crime.

The increasing extremism of the politics of sectionalism in the 1850s led to some talk among Southerners of reopening the African slave trade (forbidden by Congress in 1808), but Lincoln did not see the movement as a serious new threat to American freedom. He felt that any chance of reopening the African slave trade was, at worst, well in the future. He did not attack the domestic slave trade at all. They were important in his political thought in the 1850s mainly as moral examples for arguments on other questions.

The African slave trade first became a frequent subject of Lincoln's political discourse in 1854, when he attacked the Kansas-Nebraska Act. In answer to the argument "that the slaveholder has the same right to take his negroes to Kansas that a freeman has to take his hogs and horses," Lincoln pointed to the Southern slaveholders' own refusal "to associate with" domestic slave-dealers "or let their families associate with his family." That was surely proof that treating "droves of negroes . . . precisely like droves of horses" was morally repugnant even to slaveholders. Lincoln's political enemy was not the South but Stephen A. Douglas of Illinois, and the African slave trade figured as an important debating point with Douglas. Douglas opposed the revival of the African slave trade, but Lincoln asked repeatedly from 1854 on, "how can he resist it? . . . he has labored to prove it a *sacred right* of white men to take negro slaves into the new territories. Can he possibly show that it is *less* a sacred right to *buy* them where they can be bought cheapest?" There was, as Lincoln had said at Peoria in 1854, no way to distinguish between the two "on any moral principle."

Lincoln used the argument repeatedly in 1858 to show the importance of treating the question of the expansion of slavery as a moral one. Douglas's response was to argue that the prohibition of the African slave trade had been a compromise of the Constitution to keep the Union together. He argued that he maintained the spirit of compromise in his view that the people of the territories could decide whether to exclude or allow slavery in their new polities. Lincoln responded with an argument he used repeatedly in 1859 and 1860. The Constitution merely stated that the slave trade could not be halted before 1808. It extracted no promise in exchange for tolerating it to that point; it did not require its abolition even in 1808. True, the fathers of the Republic gave proof of their moral hatred of slavery and their expectation that it should eventually become extinct in America by showing that the people even without constitutional prohibition would abolish the trade as soon as they could; they merely felt that the large commercial interests involved needed and deserved 20 years to adjust to sure doom. The country's fathers thus expected the slave trade to die and allowed Congress to prevent it after 1808, just as they expected slavery to shrink, not expand, and allowed Congress to prevent it in the territories.

As an existing fact of illegal commerce rather than a moral example for argument, the African slave trade to Lincoln was an object of occasional consideration. In 1854 he thought that the trade "is not yet effectually suppressed" and pointed to the exceptional increase of black population as proof. As President he showed his detestation of the African slave trade by refusing to commute to life imprisonment the death sentence of Nathaniel Gordon, who was convicted of participating in the African slave trade on November 30, 1861. Despite numerous appeals, Lincoln allowed him to hang on February 21, 1862 (he did grant him a brief stay of execution on February 4 so that he could prepare for his fate). A new treaty with Great Britain to halt the trade gained Lincoln's hearty support in 1862.

The legal domestic slave trade, so long tolerated by the American government, met less stern treatment. Lincoln pardoned William Yocum, "unquestionably guilty" of returning a slave in United States military service to his master, in March 1864, because what Yocum had done "was perfectly lawful, only a short while before" and was "the single instance" of the crime Lincoln knew of. Secretary of War Edwin M. Stanton was outraged. To give "a colored man under his [Yocum's] command into the hands of a slave dealer to be sold" was a crime "greater than that of the African Slave trader."

SOURCES: Ronald N. Satz's "The African Slave Trade and Lincoln's Campaign of 1858," *Journal of the Illinois State Historical Society*, LXV (Autumn 1972), 269–279, ignores Lincoln's earlier focus on the issue in 1854.

Slavery Abraham Lincoln was a native of a slave state. Hardin County, Kentucky, where he was born in 1809, contained 1007 slaves and 1627 white males above the age of 16 in 1811. His father's brother Mordecai owned a slave. His father's uncle Isaac may have owned over 40 slaves. The Richard Berry family, with whom Lincoln's mother Nancy Hanks lived before her marriage to Thomas Lincoln, owned slaves. Thomas and Nancy Lincoln, however, were members of a Baptist congregation which had withdrawn from another church because of opposition to slavery. That helps explain why Lincoln could say, in 1864, that he was "naturally anti-slavery" and could "not remember when I did not so think, and feel." In 1860 he claimed that his father left Kentucky for Indiana's free soil "partly on account of slavery."

Nothing in Lincoln's political career is inconsistent with his claim to have been "naturally anti-slavery." In 1836 resolutions condemning abolitionism, declaring that the Constitution sanctified the right of property in slaves, and denying the right of Congress to abolish slavery in the District of Columbia came before the Illinois House. Lincoln was one of six to vote against them (77 voted in favor). Near the end of the term, March 3, 1837, Lincoln and fellow Whig Dan Stone wrote a protest against the resolutions which stated that "the institution of slavery is founded on both injustice and bad policy." Lincoln and Stone agreed that abolitionism was more likely to exacerbate than abate the evils, and they asserted the right of Congress to abolish slavery in the District of Columbia (though the right should not be exercised without the consent of the District's citizens). Congress, of course, had no right to interfere with slavery in the states. In 1860 Lincoln could honestly point to the consistency of his antislavery convictions over the last 23 years. That early protest "briefly defined his position on the slavery question; and so far as it goes, it was then the same as it is now."

In his early political career in the 1830s and 1840s, Lincoln had faith in the benign operation of American political institutions. Though "opposed to slavery" throughout the period, he "rested in the hope and belief that it was in course of ultimate extinction." For that reason, it was only "a minor question" to him. For the sake of keeping the nation together, Lincoln thought it "a paramount duty" to leave slavery in the states alone. He never spelled out the basis of his faith entirely, but he had confidence that the country was ever seeking to approximate the ideals of the Declaration of Independence. All men would be free when slavery, restricted to the areas where it already existed, exhausted the soil, became unprofitable, and was abolished by the slaveholding states themselves or perhaps by numerous individual emancipations. Reaching that goal, perhaps by the end of the century, required of dutiful politicians only "that we should never knowingly lend ourselves directly or indirectly, to prevent . . . slavery from dying a natural death—to find new places for it to live in, when it can no longer exist in the old." Slavery already existed in Texas, and Lincoln was indifferent to the issue of Texas annexation. But as a Congressman during the Mexican War, Lincoln supported the Wilmot Proviso because it would prevent the growth of slavery in parts of the Mexican cession where the institution did not already exist. He still considered slavery a "distracting" question, one that might destroy America's experiment in popular government if politicians were to "enlarge and agrivate" it either by seeking to expand slavery or to attack it in the states.

Lincoln became increasingly worried in about 1850 when he read John C. Calhoun's denunciations of the Declaration of Independence. Similar denunciations by a Virginia clergyman upset him more. Such things undermined his confidence because they showed that some Americans did not wish to approach the ideals of the Declaration of Independence; for some, those ideals were no longer ideals at all. But these were the statements of a society directly interested in the preservation of the institution, and Lincoln did not become enough alarmed to agitate the slave question. He began even to lose interest in politics.

The passage of Stephen A. Douglas's Kansas-Nebraska Act in 1854 changed all that. Lincoln was startled when territory previously closed to slavery was opened to the possibility of slavery's introduction by local vote. He was especially alarmed at the fact that the change was promoted by a Northerner with no direct interest in slavery to protect.

In 1841 Lincoln had seen a group of slaves on a steamboat being sold south from Kentucky to a harsher (so he assumed) slavery. Immediately after the trip he noted the irony of their seeming contentment with their lot. They had appeared to be the happiest people on board. After the Kansas-Nebraska Act, he wrote about the same episode, still vivid to him, as "a continual torment to me." Slavery, he said, "has, and continually exercises, the power of making me miserable."

Lincoln repeatedly stated that slaveholders were no worse than Northerners would be in the same situation. Having inherited an undesirable but socially explosive political institution, Southerners made the best of a bad situation. Like all Americans before the Revolution, they had denounced Great Britain's forcing slavery on the colonies with the slave trade, and even in the 1850s they admitted the humanity of the Negro by despising the Southerners who dealt with the Negro as property, pure and simple: slave-traders. But he feared that the ability of Northerners to see that slavery was morally wrong was in decline. That, almost as surely as disunion, could mean the end of the American experiment in freedom, for any argument for slavery which ignored the moral wrong of the institution could be used to enslave any man, white or black. If lighter men were to enslave darker men, then "you are to be slave to the first man you meet, with a fairer skin than your own." If superior intellect determined masters, then you were to be slave "to the first man you meet, with an intellect superior to your own." Once the moral distinction between slavery and freedom were forgotten, nothing could stop slavery's spread. It was "founded in the selfishness of man's nature," and that selfishness could overcome any barriers of climate or geography. By 1856 Lincoln was convinced that the "sentiment in favor of white slavery . . . prevailed in all the slave state papers, except those of Kentucky, Tennessee and Missouri and Maryland."

The people of the South had "an immediate palpable and immensely great pecuniary interest" in the question; "while, with the people of the North, it is merely an abstract question of moral right." Unfortunately, the latter formed a looser bond than economic self-interest in $2 billion worth of slaves. And the Northern ability to resist was steadily undermined by the moral indifference to slavery epitomized by Douglas's willingness to see slavery voted up or down in the territories. The Dred Scott decision in 1857 convinced Lincoln that the Kansas-Nebraska Act had been the beginning of a conspiracy to make slavery perpetual, national, and universal. His "House Divided" speech of 1858 and his famous debates with Douglas stressed the specter of conspiracy.

Lincoln's claims in behalf of the slaves were modest and did not make much of the Negro's abilities outside slavery. The Negro "is not my equal . . . in color, perhaps not in moral or intellectual endowment," Lincoln said, but "in the right to put into his mouth the bread that his own hands have earned, he is the equal of every other man, white or black." Lincoln objected to slavery primarily because the institution violated the doctrine of the equality of all men announced in the Declaration of Independence. "As I would not be a *slave*, so I would not be a *master*," Lincoln said. "This expresses my idea of democracy. Whatever differs from this, to the extent of the difference, is no democracy."

Lincoln had always worked on the assumption that the Union was more important than abolishing slavery. As long as the country was approaching the ideal of freedom for all men, even if it took 100 years, it made no sense to destroy the freest country in the world. Lincoln's growing perception that the country might not be approaching that ideal somewhat confused his thinking. In 1854 he admitted that as "Much as I hate slavery, I would consent to the extension of it rather than see the Union dissolved, just as I would consent to any GREAT evil, to avoid a GREATER one." As his fears of a conspiracy to nationalize slavery increased, he ceased to make such statements. In the secession crisis he edged closer toward making liberty more important than the Union. In New York City on February 20, 1861, President-elect Lincoln said:

> There is nothing that can ever bring me willingly to consent to the destruction of this Union, under which . . . the whole country has acquired its greatness, unless it were to be that thing for which the Union itself was made. I understand a ship to be made for the carrying and preservation of the cargo, and so long as the ship can be saved, with the cargo, it should never be abandoned. This Union should likewise never be abandoned unless it fails and the probability of its preservation shall cease to exist without throwing the passengers and cargo overboard. So long, then, as it is possible that the prosperity and the liberties of the people can be preserved in the Union, it shall be my purpose at all times to preserve it.

The Civil War saw Lincoln move quickly to save the Union by stretching and, occasionally, violating the Constitution. Since he had always said that constitutional scruple kept him from bothering slavery in the states, it is clear that early in the war he was willing to go much further to save the Union than he was willing to go to abolish slavery. Yet he interpreted it as his constitutional duty to save the Union, even if to do so he had to violate some small part of that very Constitution. There certainly was no constitutional duty to do anything about slavery. For over a year, he did nothing.

On August 22, 1862, Lincoln responded to criticism from Horace Greeley by stating his slavery policy:

> If there be those who would not save the Union, unless they could at the same time *save* slavery, I do not agree with them. If there be those who would not save the Union unless they could at the same time *destroy* slavery, I do not agree with them. My paramount object in this struggle *is* to save the Union, and is *not* either to save or to destroy slavery. If I could save the Union without freeing *any* slave I would do it, and if I could save it by freeing *all* the slaves I would do it; and if I could save it by freeing some and leaving others alone I would also do that. What I do about slavery, and the colored race, I do because I believe it helps to save the Union; and what I forbear, I forbear because I do *not* believe it would help to save the Union. I shall do *less* whenever I shall believe what I am doing hurts the cause, and I shall do *more* whenever I shall believe doing more will help the cause. I shall try to correct errors when shown to be errors; and I shall adopt new views so fast as they shall appear to be true views.
>
> I have here stated my purpose according to my view of *official* duty; and I intend no modification of my oft-expressed *personal* wish that all men every where could be free.

The preliminary Emancipation Proclamation, announced just one month later, was avowedly a military and not a humanitarian act, and Lincoln boasted of his consistency 2 years later by saying, "I have done no official act in mere deference to my abstract judgment and feeling on slavery."

Nevertheless, he had changed his mind in some regards. Precisely 1 year before he issued the preliminary Emancipation Proclamation, Lincoln had criticized General John C. Frémont's emancipation proclamation for Missouri by saying that "the liberation of slaves" was a question "*purely political*, and not within the range of *military* law, or necessity."

> If a commanding General finds a necessity to seize the farm of a private owner, for a pasture, an encampment, or a fortification, he has the right to do so, and to so hold it, as long as the necessity lasts; and this is within military law, because within military necessity. But to say the farm shall no longer belong to the owner, or his heirs forever; and this as well when the farm is not needed for military purposes as when it is, is purely political, without the savor of military law about it. And the same is true of slaves. If the General needs them, he can seize them, and use them; but when the need is past, it is not for him to fix their permanent future condition. That must be settled according to laws made by lawmakers, and not by military proclamations. The proclamation in the point in question, is simply "dictatorship." It assumes that the general may do *anything* he pleases—confiscate the lands and free the slaves of *loyal* people, as well as of disloyal ones. And going the whole figure I have no doubt would be more popular with some thoughtless people, than that which has been done! But I cannot assume this reckless position; nor allow others to assume it on my responsibility. You speak of it as being the only means of *saving* the government. On the contrary it is itself the surrender of the government. Can it be pretended that it is any longer the government of the U.S.—any government of Constitution and laws,—wherein a General, or a President, may make permanent rules of property by proclamation?
>
> I do not say Congress might not with propriety pass a law, on the point, just such as General Fremont proclaimed. I do not say I might not, as a member of Congress, vote for it. What I object to, is, that I as President, shall expressly or impliedly seize and exercise the permanent legislative functions of the government.

Critics could call this inconsistent with his own later Proclamation; Lincoln's admirers have called it "growth." Whatever the case, just as Lincoln's love of Union caused him to handle the Constitution somewhat roughly, so his hatred of slavery led him, more slowly, to treat the Constitution in a manner inconceivable to him in 1861. Emancipation, if somewhat more slowly, was allowed about the same degree of constitutional latitude the Union earned in Lincoln's policies.

The destruction of slavery never became the avowed object of the war, but by insisting on its importance, militarily, to saving the Union, Lincoln made it constitutionally beyond criticism and, in all that really mattered, an aim of the war. In all practical applications, it was a condition of peace—and it was so announced in the Proclamation of Amnesty and Reconstruction of December 8, 1863, and repeatedly defended in administration statements thereafter. He reinforced this fusion of aims by insisting that the Confederacy was an attempt to establish "a new Nation . . . with the primary, and fundamental object to maintain, enlarge, and perpetuate human slavery," thus making the enemy and slavery one.

Only once did Lincoln apparently change his mind. In the desperately gloomy August of 1864, when defeat for the administration seemed certain, Lincoln bowed to pressure from Henry J. Raymond long enough to draft a letter empowering Raymond to propose peace with Jefferson Davis on the condition of reunion alone, all other questions (including slavery, of course) to be settled by a convention afterward. Lincoln never finished the letter, and the offer was never made. Moreover, as things looked in August, Lincoln was surrendering only what he could not keep anyway. He was so convinced that the Democratic platform would mean the loss of the Union, that he vowed in secret to work to save the Union before the next President came into office in March. In that he could hope for some cooperation from Democrats, for they professed to be as much in favor of Union as the Republicans. Without the Union, slavery could not be abolished anyhow, and the Democrats were committed to restoring slavery.

Lincoln had made abolition a party goal in 1864 by making support for the Thirteenth Amendment a part of the Republican platform. The work he performed for the amendment after his election proved that his antislavery views had not abated. Near the end of his life, he repeated in a public speech one of his favorite arguments against slavery: "Whenever [I] hear any one, arguing for slavery I feel a strong impulse to see it tried on him personally."

Smith, Caleb Blood

SOURCES: Lincoln's collected works are essential for his own views, and Louis A. Warren's *The Slavery Atmosphere of Lincoln's Youth* (Fort Wayne, Ind.: Lincolniana Publishers, 1933) explains the origins of those views as well as any existing work.

See also ABOLITION; CONSTITUTION OF THE UNITED STATES; DOUGLASS, FREDERICK; EMANCIPATION PROCLAMATION; LINCOLN-DOUGLAS DEBATES: NATIONALISM; NEGROES; THIRTEENTH AMENDMENT.

Caleb Blood Smith

Smith, Caleb Blood (1808–1864) Lincoln's first Secretary of the Interior. Caleb B. Smith was born in Boston, Massachusetts, but moved at an early age to Cincinnati. He was admitted to the bar in Connersville, Indiana, where he began to practice law in 1828. He was active and successful as a Whig politician (especially because of his abilities as an orator), and he was typically internal-improvements-minded.

Smith was entering his fourth term in the House of Representatives when Lincoln came to Washington for his only term in that body. Smith represented a safe Whig district which contained a substantial number of Quakers, and he was the most consistent and vociferous opponent of the Mexican War from a state west of Ohio. Although he was more opposed to territorial expansion than Lincoln was, he came around to Lincoln's view that some territorial acquisition as a result of the war would be necessary. Both men worked for Zachary Taylor's election in 1848. When Lincoln sought the appointment as Commissioner of the General Land Office from the Taylor administration, Smith at first aided Lincoln's successful opponent Justin Butterfield and later wrote a not very helpful—or honest—letter supporting Lincoln's candidacy for the office.

Smith and Lincoln left the House for good in 1849. Smith, who was active in railroad management and legal work, moved eventually to Indianapolis to practice law. He became a leading Indiana Republican and a delegate to the Chicago convention that nominated Lincoln for President in 1860. Smith seconded Lincoln's nomination; and the Indiana delegation, which went to the convention uncommitted to any candidate, proved to be as solidly for Lincoln as the Illinois delegation—because, some said, David Davis promised Smith a Cabinet post. Lincoln did make Smith the Secretary of the Interior on Davis's recommendation, but he had considered South Bend's Schuyler Colfax for the position as well. In the end he told Colfax he chose Smith because Colfax was young and had a very promising career before him, and "With Smith, it is now or never."

Smith's conservatism showed itself soon in the Sumter crisis. Although most of the Cabinet were influenced by the military opinions against relieving the fort, Smith believed those few who thought relief possible—and advised against moving to help the garrison in Fort Sumter anyway. Fort Sumter was unessential to enforcing the laws; the expedition would be bloody in result at best; and South Carolina should be forced to be the aggressor by resisting some essential law enforcement if civil war were to start. Smith changed his mind before a relief expedition was sent.

The Secretary of the Interior ran a department in which the work was not greatly augmented by the war. Even so, Smith apparently disliked the job, and declining health led him to consider resigning early in 1862. But he wanted to move to a federal judgeship, and one did not become available in Indiana until the end of that year.

Smith grew to be very critical of General George B. McClellan's "imbecility," and he disliked Secretary of State William H. Seward. His only important influence on administration policy stemmed from his zeal for colonization. He was the prime supporter of the Chiriqui Improvement Company's scheme to mine coal for the Navy with colonized Negroes, and he repeatedly pressed the scheme despite stubborn opposition from Navy Secretary Gideon Welles. Also, he was adamantly opposed to using Negroes as soldiers in the Union army.

Smith became increasingly disaffected and felt that Cabinet meetings were useless because the President made all the important decisions for himself. "Smith has no faith & no hope," David Davis commented. Lincoln appointed him Judge of the Indiana District in December and on the 31st he resigned his Cabinet post. Davis thought Smith lacked "heart" and "sincerity." His Assistant Secretary, John P. Usher, was his successor.

SOURCES: There is no biography of Smith, but Louis J. Bailey's "Caleb Blood Smith," *Indiana Magazine of History*, XXIX (September 1933), 213–239, is a character sketch adequate for this colorless and not well-liked man. See also Willard L. King, *Lincoln's Manager: David Davis* (Cambridge: Harvard University Press, 1960); Mark E. Neely, Jr., "Lincoln and the Mexican War: An Argument by Analogy," *Civil War History*, XXIV (March 1978), 5–24; and Donald W. Riddle, *Congressman Abraham Lincoln* (Urbana: University of Illinois Press, 1957).

Soldiers' Home President Lincoln's "summer White House." Established in 1851 for invalid and disabled soldiers, the United States Soldiers' Home was located on a tree-shaded hill 3 miles beyond the city boundary of Washington. Its location made it considerably cooler in the summer than the steamy Capital, and President James Buchanan was the first President to sleep at the home in that miserable season. The Lincolns spent their first Washington summer in the White House, but in 1862, 1863, and 1864 they moved to the Soldiers' Home in mid-June or early July and remained apparently until November. There were four buildings on the grounds, and the Lincolns occupied the same stone cottage Buchanan had. Lincoln rode the 4 miles from the White House to the Home each summer evening, occasionally alone on horseback but usually in a carriage with a small cavalry escort. The daily trip was a security problem. A would-be assassin shot a hole through Lincoln's hat on one of his trips to the Home, apparently, and John Wilkes Booth's plot to kidnap the President hinged on his ability to capture Lincoln on one of the President's trips to or from the Home.

SOURCES: See R. Gerald McMurtry, "The Soldiers' Home: The Lincolns' Summer Retreat," *Lincoln Lore*, Number 1589 (July 1970), pp. 1–3.

This print shows the Soldiers' Home as it looked in 1863. The "President's Villa," the Anderson Cottage, is the second building from the left.

Spangler, Edman ("Edward") (?–1871) Sceneshifter at night and assistant carpenter in the day at Ford's Theatre. Spangler came originally from York, Pennsylvania, but he lived most of his life in Baltimore. He worked off and on for 4 years for the Fords during the Civil War. When the theater closed for the summer, he vacationed in Baltimore, crab fishing. In 1864 he buried his wife in Baltimore. John T. Ford characterized Spangler as a "very good-natured, kind, willing man" and "a very good, efficient drudge," though he occasionally drank too much. Something of a loner, he slept at the theater. In Baltimore he had been a member of the Know-Nothing (American) party, but he was not notable for strong political sentiments while he lived in Washington.

John Wilkes Booth, Ford testified, "was a peculiarly fascinating man who controlled the lower class of people, such as Spangler belonged to, more . . . than ordinary men would." Like most of the theater's employees, Spangler was well acquainted with Booth. He had worked for Booth's father and had known John as a boy. He frequently took care of Booth's horse.

On the night of Lincoln's assassination, Spangler was on duty as one of the scene-shifters on the side of the stage where the President's box was located. Booth sent word he wanted Spangler to hold his horse. Spangler went to the rear door and took the reins. But he could not stay, and he asked "Peanut John" Burroughs, stage doorkeeper and handbill distributor for the theater, to hold the horse. Spangler returned to his station and was there when the shot rang out. Booth escaped across the stage, ran out the back door, and knocked Burroughs down when he seized his horse.

Spangler was arrested and tried as a conspirator in the assassination. The government's principal witness against him was Jacob Ritterspaugh. He testified that Spangler hit him on the mouth and said, "Don't say which way he went," after Ritterspaugh had chased Booth. Thomas Ewing, Jr., Spangler's lawyer, found witnesses who said that Ritterspaugh had changed his story after a month of imprisonment and intimidation by detectives. Immediately after the event, he had said only that Spangler hit him and said, after Ritterspaugh had insisted the escaping man was Booth, to shut up because he did not know for certain who the man was. From his position to the side of the stage Spangler himself could not have seen Booth. The military commission that tried the alleged assassins found Spangler guilty of aiding Booth's escape and sentenced him to 6 years at hard labor.

Spangler was imprisoned at Fort Jefferson with Dr. Samuel A. Mudd, Michael O'Laughlin, and Samuel B. Arnold. In 1869 President Andrew Johnson pardoned him, and he returned to Maryland to live with Dr. Mudd, to whom he had become attached during their imprisonment. Spangler performed carpentry chores, and Mudd gave him 5 acres of land to farm. About 18 months after his return, however, Spangler died.

SOURCES: Spangler's story is told in a brief manuscript found by Dr. Mudd in Spangler's trunk and printed by Nettie Mudd

Edman Spangler

James Speed

Speed, James (1812–1887) Lincoln's second Attorney General. James Speed was born and lived most of his life in Kentucky, near Louisville. A college graduate who had studied law at Transylvania University, he was a Whig in politics but with decidedly antislavery leanings—which doomed him in Kentucky to but one term in the state legislature before the Civil War. His brother Joshua was Lincoln's best friend in his early life, and James probably met Lincoln when the Illinois lawyer visited Joshua in Kentucky in 1841. James Speed was a Democrat by the late 1850s, but he told Lincoln in 1859, "I would not have sorrowed at your election to the U.S. Senate—I feel that our rights and institutions would not have been in jeopardy in your hands."

Elected to the Kentucky Senate in 1861, Speed became a leader of pro-Union activities in Kentucky. While the state maintained a precarious "neutrality" in the early weeks of the war, Speed was among those working directly with President Lincoln to smuggle arms into the state for pro-Union groups. Though his protest was less vigorous than Joshua's, he did tell Lincoln that General John C. Frémont's proclamation freeing rebel slaves in Missouri "will be condemned by a large majority of [the] Legislature & people of Kentucky." Yet within 4 months he himself had introduced in the Kentucky legislature "a bill to confiscate the estates of rebels." In a letter to Lincoln describing the bill, he warned "how sensitive our people are" upon the subject of slavery but prophesied that a "growing hatred of the southern traitors in Kentucky . . . must soon embrace the institutions" of the South. In July 1862 Lincoln apparently showed Speed a draft of his proposed Emancipation Proclamation, known at that time only to the Cabinet. Speed's somewhat confused response was that the "negro can not be emancipated by proclamation," that Kentucky's loyal men would nevertheless "not be moved by any thing that may be done with the negro," and that "If the negro is to be free he must strike for it himself."

Far Right: Joshua and Fanny Speed

Speed's legislative term ended in 1863, but in November of the next year Lincoln selected Speed to replace Edward Bates as Attorney General (after Joseph Holt refused the job). Though some have seen little more in the appointment than cronyism, Joshua Speed was probably more accurate when he said that his brother was "appointed . . . as a representative man of the party for freedom in the slave States." In March, shortly before Lincoln died, Speed noted that "great suffering is still in store" for the South unless the people "frankly and fully acknowledge the freedom of the black man and give to him the chance for improvement and elevation." After Lincoln's murder, Speed quickly became a Radical Republican, advocated Negro suffrage, and broke with the conservative Andrew Johnson administration. He resigned in protest in July 1866 and went to Louisville, where he established a successful law practice. His attempt to win election to the United States Senate in 1867 failed.

In later years Speed was sensitive to criticism of his argument for trying the "fiends" who killed Lincoln by military commission and was involved in an unfortunate dispute with Joseph Holt over the allegation that President Andrew Johnson saw a recommendation for mercy for Mary Surratt and ignored it.

Speed called Lincoln "the best and greatest man I ever knew."

SOURCES: See James Speed, *James Speed: A Personality* (Louisville, Ky.: Press of John P. Morton, 1913) and the *Address of Hon. James Speed Before the Society of the Loyal Legion, at Cincinnati, May 4, 1887 . . . [on] Abraham Lincoln* (Louisville, Ky.: John P. Morton, 1888). Both are disappointing in content. They are supplemented here by Speed's letters to Lincoln in the Abraham Lincoln Collection, Library of Congress: on Lincoln as Senator (November 15, 1859), on Frémont (September 2, 1861), on confiscation and slavery in Kentucky (December 22, 1861), and on the Emancipation Proclamation (July 28, 1862).

Speed, Joshua Fry (1814–1882) Lincoln's only intimate friend. Speed, like Lincoln, was a Kentuckian (born and raised near Louisville) who moved to Springfield, Illinois (in 1835). There he became a partner in a general store and met Lincoln on April 15, 1837, when the young lawyer arrived in Springfield from New Salem and was seeking lodging. Speed offered Lincoln his room above the store, and for four important years, the young men slept in the same bed. Both were Whigs in politics; both were not conventionally religious; and both were seeking—rather uncertainly—marriage. They became fast friends.

Speed moved back to Kentucky in 1841, the year in which Lincoln's engagement to Mary Todd was broken, and Lincoln's letters to his friend at that critical juncture provide probably the most intimate glimpses into Lincoln's personality in all of Lincoln's vast, but largely political and businesslike correspondence. Lincoln was severely depressed by the unfortunate turn in his personal affairs, and, for relief, he visited "Farmington," the Speed home near Louisville, in August and September. Upon his return, he expressed appreciation for the gift of a Bible from Speed's mother Lucy ("I doubt not that it is really, as she says, the best cure for the 'Blues' could one but take it according to the truth"). Thereafter, the correspondence focused on Speed's courtship of Fanny Henning. Lincoln's letters discuss "forebodings . . . peculiar" to the two men about marriage. Speed and Fanny were married on February 15, 1842, and on October 5, 1842, Lincoln pressed Speed for an answer to the question whether he was "glad" to be "married as you are." On November 2, Lincoln married Mary Todd. Seven of the letters to Speed bear the signature "Lincoln" rather than the customary "A. Lincoln"—another sign of the intimacy of the friendship.

Time and distance took their toll, however, and by 1846 Lincoln noted "the suspension of our correspondence" and warned against "allowing a friendship, such as ours, to die by degrees." Speed was a farmer—an occupation of little interest to Lincoln—until 1851, when he entered the real estate business in Louisville with his brother-in-law James Wittenning. He was successful and grew wealthy. He served one term in the Kentucky legislature at the same time Lincoln was in the United States House of Representatives, but the two men grew apart politically as slavery became an increasingly important issue in American politics. In a long (and now famous) letter written on August 24, 1855, Lincoln responded to Speed's suggestion that "in political action now, you and I would differ." Lincoln argued that Southerners little appreciated "how much the great body of the Northern people do crucify their feelings" to maintain a union with slaveholders, that there would be no fair decision on slavery in Kansas, that the Kansas-Nebraska Act was "conceived in violence, passed in violence, is maintained in violence, and is being executed in violence," and that he was "not a Know-Nothing." By 1860 Speed could congratulate Lincoln on his nomination for the Presidency only as a "warm personal friend," for he was an avowed "political opponent."

When sectional controversy erupted into war, Speed remained loyal to the Union and was instrumental in smuggling arms supplied by President Lincoln to Unionists in Kentucky while the state maintained a policy of "neutrality." On questions involving slavery Speed remained conservative. He vigorously protested John C. Frémont's emancipation order in Missouri as a policy that "will hurt us in K[entuck]y" because "All of us who live in Slave states whether Union or loyal have great fear of insurrection." He was "so much distressed" by the Proclamation that he was "unable to eat or sleep." Nevertheless, he told Lincoln that, though most would balk at freeing slaves, he would remain loyal. And he did so remain even after the Emancipation Proclamation was issued. He acted as an unofficial coordinator of Union activities in Kentucky and as a liason with the Lincoln administration.

After the war, Speed wrote nine letters about Lincoln to William H. Herndon, and late in life he delivered an address containing his "Reminiscences of Abraham Lincoln" (published in Louisville by John P. Morton in 1884 as *Reminiscences of Abraham Lincoln and Notes of a Visit to California: Two Lectures*). The reminiscences are notable for an anecdote about Lincoln's religion. Finding Lincoln reading the Bible in the summer of 1864, Speed stated that he had not "recovered" from his youthful "skepticism." The President responded: "You are wrong Speed, take all of this book upon reason that you can, and the balance on faith, and you will live and die a happier and better man."

SOURCES: There is no satisfactory biography, but the *Filson Club History Quarterly*, XVII (April 1943) devoted an entire issue to Robert L. Kincaid's sketch of "Joshua Fry Speed—1814–1882: Abraham Lincoln's Most Intimate Friend" and conveniently reprinted the famous Lincoln letters to Speed. (The letters were given by Speed to Herndon, acquired years later by collector Oliver R. Barrett, and sold at the famous Barrett sale to the Illinois State Historical Library for $35,000.) The letters to Lincoln congratulating Lincoln on his nomination (May 19,1860), protesting Frémont's proclamation (September 1, 1861), and complaining of being "unable to eat or sleep" (September 3, 1861) are in the Abraham Lincoln Papers, Library of Congress.

Spencer County See INDIANA.

Spiritualism See RELIGION.

"Spot Resolutions" See MEXICAN WAR.

Springfield, Illinois Lincoln's hometown from 1837 to 1861. Springfield was founded in 1821, but it was little more than a village of about 600 inhabitants when Lincoln moved to Illinois in 1830. Like the rest of central Illinois, however, it grew rapidly thereafter, and its population reached 2579 in 1840. The state legislature's decision in 1837 to move the state capital there from Vandalia by July 4, 1839—a measure of which Lincoln was an important supporter—assured Springfield's future.

That Lincoln moved to Springfield on April 15, 1837, was a matter of economic necessity. He had to move somewhere. New Salem had always been too small to support a lawyer, and the town was failing anyway. He had an offer to enter a law partnership with John Todd Stuart, a fellow Whig legislator who lived in Springfield, and he took it. He roomed with Joshua Speed above Speed's store. Lincoln was awed at first by Springfield's grandeur as compared with New Salem. He immediately noticed "a great deal of flourishing about in carriages here" and was keenly aware of his own poverty by contrast. After 3 weeks in town he felt "quite as lonesome here as . . . anywhere in my life" and noted, "I have been spoken to by but one woman since I've been here, and should not have been by her, if she could have avoided it." He was staying away from church "because I am conscious I should not know how to behave myself."

Springfield, Illinois

Lincoln was poor and lonely, but his isolation was mainly a function of his newness in town. He entered Springfield with important status relatively assured. He was a prominent man's law partner, and he was already a two-term member of the state legislature. After the initial adjustment to new surroundings, he entered a rather select social circle led by Ninian Wirt Edwards, the son of Illinois's Territorial Governor, and his wife Elizabeth Todd Edwards, a cousin of Lincoln's law partner John Todd Stuart. Lincoln met Mary Todd while she was living with the Edwardses, her sister and brother-in-law, in 1839 or 1840. Even without wealth Lincoln's social connections were good enough to win Mary Todd's hand in marriage, though the Edwardses at first apparently opposed the match. The Lincolns, after their marriage on November 4, 1842, boarded at the Globe Tavern, a two-story wooden inn, for $4 a week.

Law and politics brought Lincoln substantial income and greater status. Springfield was a haven for lawyers because Illinois's highest court was located there, but Lincoln still had to seek business outside the capital by riding the Eighth Judicial Circuit for court days at surrounding counties. The town was politically congenial for him. Strongly Whiggish and heavily populated with former Kentuckians like Lincoln, Springfield's voters went for Henry Clay over James K. Polk 1031 to 758 (a negligible 15 voted for the Liberty party) in 1844. When Lincoln ran for Congress 2 years later, Springfield gave him 919 votes, more than double the 450 they gave his Democratic opponent Peter Cartwright. In 1848 the city went for Zachary Taylor, 1100 votes to Lewis Cass's 699 (and a minuscule 39 for Free-Soiler Martin Van Buren).

In 1844 Lincoln purchased the only home he ever owned—a house on the corner of Eighth and Jackson Streets—for $1200 and a piece of property worth $300. His income from the law allowed him to live comfortably, if not extravagantly, thereafter. In 1856 the Lincolns added a second story for $1300. There was a great deal of building in Springfield at the time, for the town was growing rapidly. The population grew almost as much between 1848 and 1850 as it had between 1840 and 1848; in 1850 it was 4533. The fifties were even better, and Springfield's population reached 9320 by the end of the decade. A key to the growth was the completion before 1850 of the Sangamon and Morgan Railroad west through Jacksonville to Naples and the Illinois River, a fast link to the Mississippi River and St. Louis. By 1855 railroads linked Springfield to Alton to the south, Chicago to the north, Urbana to the east, and Quincy to the west.

Population growth and the change in political issues in the 1850s altered Springfield's politics. No longer was it so near Lincoln's own politics. In 1848 the town had voted 772 to 148 for the article in the state's new constitution which excluded Negroes from settlement in Illinois. Among the handful of opponents of the measure were many of Lincoln's close political friends like Stephen T. Logan, Anson G. Henry, Edwards, and Simeon Francis. In the presidential election of 1856 Springfield cast 912 votes for Democrat James Buchanan, 549 for Republican John C. Frémont, and 403 for Whig-American Millard Fillmore. The close margin over Buchanan arrived at by adding the Fillmore and Frémont votes together typified the elections to come. In 1860 Lincoln carried his hometown with 1395 votes to Stephen A. Douglas's 1326, John C. Breckinridge's 31, and John Bell's 16. Four years later he beat McClellan by only 10 votes, 1324 to 1314.

As President, Lincoln did not forget his Springfield friends; he appointed many of them to offices, but there was no satisfying them. He was a national figure now, and he had important offices to fill and a whole country to satisfy. Some friends, like Anson G. Henry, thought the offices they received were less than they deserved. "Springfield is my home," the President said in 1863, "and there, more than elsewhere, are my life-long friends." But "for now nearly two years," they "have been harrassing me," he said, about his appointment of Ninian Wirt Edwards as a commissary of subsistence. Lincoln felt that he had "borne a fair share" of the burden of bickering among his old associates.

The real affection Lincoln felt for Springfield was beautifully expressed on February 11, 1861, his last day in his hometown, as he departed by train for Washington:

> My friends—No one, not in my situation, can appreciate my feeling of sadness at this parting. To this place, and the kindness of these people, I owe every thing. Here I have lived a quarter of a century, and have passed from a young to an old man. Here my children have been born, and one is buried. I now leave, not knowing when, or whether ever, I may return, with a task before me greater than that which rested upon Washington. Without the assistance of that Divine Being, who ever attended him, I cannot succeed. With that assistance I cannot fail. Trusting in Him, who can go with me, and remain with you and be every where for good, let us confidently hope that all will yet be well. To His care commending you, as I hope in your prayers you will commend me, I bid you an affectionate farewell.

Boston photographer John Adams Whipple photographed the Lincoln home in Springfield in the summer of 1860. Lincoln and his sons Tad and Willie are at the corner of the fence.

SOURCES: The only history of Lincoln's Springfield is Paul M. Angle's *"Here I Have Lived": A History of Lincoln's Springfield, 1821–1865* (New Brunswick, N.J.: Rutgers University Press, 1935), now out of date and undistinguished by modern standards for community studies. The election statistics for the 1840s are from the manuscript election returns for Sangamon County in the Archives of Sangamon State University, Springfield.

Stanton, Edwin McMasters (1814–1869)

Lincoln's second Secretary of War. Stanton was born in Steubenville, Ohio. He attended Kenyon College and became a lawyer in 1836. He gained success at the law rapidly; he moved to Pittsburgh for a larger practice in 1847 and to Washington, D.C., in 1856 for an extensive practice before the United States Supreme Court. Stanton first met Lincoln as an associate counsel in the case of *McCormick* v. *Manny* in 1855. Stanton, one of the most eminent lawyers in America, clearly snubbed the unproven Illinois lawyer, but the evidence that he called Lincoln a "giraffe" is not convincing.

Stanton was a Democrat but was not particularly active in politics. Nevertheless, when President James Buchanan reorganized his Cabinet on December 20, 1860, he made Stanton Attorney General. Stanton helped stiffen the President's resistance to pleas to surrender Fort Sumter to South Carolina and surreptitiously leaked information about Cabinet meetings to Republicans through an intermediary of William H. Seward's.

When Buchanan left office, Stanton remained in Washington. His opinion of Lincoln, now President, was unchanged. Finding "no token of any intelligent understanding by Lincoln, or the crew that govern him," Stanton was so fearful that Washington would be taken by the Confederates that he sold his government bonds. After George B. McClellan became commander of the Army of the Potomac, he and Stanton became friends. They saw eye to eye on Lincoln's "painful imbecility."

Stanton served as legal adviser to Secretary of War Simon Cameron; and when Lincoln removed Cameron from office on January 13, 1862, Stanton was appointed in his place. The appointment resulted in part from a rare instance of agreement between Seward and Salmon P. Chase, both of whom urged Stanton's name on the President. Stanton proved to be the right man for the job. He was all business, and he worked quickly to turn the somewhat muddled bureaucracy in the War Department into an efficient organization. Stanton doubled the size of the War Department building and quickly received authorization to appoint 2 more Assistant Secretaries of War, 49 clerks, 4 messengers, and 2 laborers. He regularized the procedure for letting contracts and greatly dispelled the atmosphere of "shoddy" and corruption which had surrounded the department under Cameron's management. Stanton controlled the Washington telegraph and used the railroads effectively, but he was otherwise unreceptive to technological innovations in weaponry. He worked long hours, and his ordinarily "bearish manner" grew worse under the strain.

Stanton was no optimist, but many of his errors as Secretary of War (for example, shutting down government recruiting offices in the spring of 1862) stemmed from his belief that the war would not be long in duration. The Secretary of War grew to dislike McClellan's inaction, and the President began to rise in Stanton's esteem when he discoverd that Lincoln too was disgusted with McClellan's slowness to attack.

Stanton was stern and pragmatic in all things having to do with achieving Union victory. When the President sought his opinion on the formation of West Virginia, Stanton wrote a very brief letter supporting statehood; he said flatly that it was both constitutional and expedient. He felt no necessity to answer the many doubts expressed about the move: "The present good is real and substantial, the future may safely be left in the care of those whose duty and interest may be involved in any possible future measures of legislation." He tended to oppose Lincoln's recommendations of clemency, saying to the President in a typical case involving a Missouri Confederate prisoner in 1863: "If such offenses are to be taken out of the general rule of captives of war what should not be? He stands good at least for the release of one Union soldier from bondage." Stanton repeatedly refused requests to alter state quotas or delay the dreaded military draft, and he advised Lincoln in a characteristic note late in the war that he should ignore Congressman William D. Kelley's request to delay the draft a week in Philadelphia "unless you are prepared to give it up altogether." Members of Congress who courted popularity with their constituents by thus standing "between their constituents and the execution of the law" disgusted the Secretary of War.

Stanton took over from Seward all the administration's internal security measures soon after assuming office and therefore gained the reputation of being a tyrant. His zeal to win the war occasionally verged on ruthlessness. When the Confederacy released especially sickly

Edwin McMasters Stanton, a portrait by Henry Ulke. (Courtesy of National Portrait Gallery, Smithsonian Institution, Washington, D.C.)

Stanton, Edwin McMasters

and emaciated Union prisoners in 1864, he saw in them evidence of a "deliberate system" of starvation and cut rations distributed to Confederate prisoners by 20 percent. In 1863 and 1864 he used the power of the War Department to help the Republican party by furloughing clerks and soldiers to vote, favoring the partisan press with departmental advertising, and allowing military intimidation at the polls in Border States. Like Lincoln, Stanton favored generals who fought and won victories. He early recognized and gave free rein to the talents of Ulysses S. Grant. When Philip Sheridan, on his and Grant's orders, scorched the Shenandoah Valley in 1864, Stanton refused any but emergency rations to keep the inhabitants from starvation. The loyal, he reasoned, could come North to work, and the disloyal could "feed upon the enemy." Like Grant and Lincoln, he understood the nature of total war.

Stanton came from Quaker stock, but he had always been able to trim his antislavery opinions, some of them gained by reading William Lloyd Garrison's newspaper *The Liberator* while he was a college student, to the needs of the Democratic party. He was one of the earliest advocates of the use of Negro troops in the Civil War, and he helped write Cameron's report recommending their use in 1861. As early as March 1862, he seems to have allowed General David Hunter to recruit black soldiers in South Carolina without Lincoln's knowledge. When Lincoln announced to his Cabinet, on July 22, 1862, his intention to issue a proclamation of emancipation, Stanton was the only Cabinet member to urge him to issue it at once. The Secretary's advocacy of black troops was always a matter of practicality. Early in 1864, when Kentucky Governor Thomas E. Bramlette protested the recruiting of black regiments in his state, Stanton argued that the policy was "not only wise and expedient, but *necessary*": "In securing the navigation of the Mississippi River, . . . a force exceeding a hundred thousand men may . . . be . . . employed at places subject to yellow fever and other pestilential diseases fatal to whites. The medical statistics during this war have shown that from such diseases persons of African descent are exempt in a remarkable degree." Besides, there was, "in the public mind, a great mistake as to the number that can be raised of such troops; for in the rebel States the chief part of the able-bodied men have been withdrawn to the interior of Georgia, Alabama, and Texas and are not accessible to us, and hence the greater necessity for recruiting in Missouri, Kentucky, Maryland, and wherever they can be found within loyal States."

Practicality, too, dictated Stanton's views of recruiting in general. Admitting that "much difference of opinion" existed in regard to the question, Stanton pointed out to Lincoln on January 4, 1864:

> First. — That, . . . a large portion of the people in every State prefer the method of contributing their proportion of the military force by bounty to volunteers rather than by draft.
> Second. — That veteran soldiers who have become inured to service, even when paid bounty, constitute a cheaper force than raw recruits or drafted men without bounty.

Therefore the Secretary opposed Congress's attempts to limit bounty payments.

Lincoln worked more closely with Stanton than with any other member of the Cabinet for the simple reason that he was more preoccupied with the war than any other administration problem. The two worked well together, and Stanton gradually lost his early animosity toward Lincoln. The letters they exchanged at the end of the administration reveal their close relationship. While Lincoln was at the front in Virginia in the spring of 1865, the Secretary of War kept him apprised of the news from Washington in letters sprinkled with touching and light-hearted personal references. He noted ironically that "now you are away everything is quiet and the tormentors [Congressmen] vanished." He hoped "the present fine weather will afford you relaxation exercise and improved health." He warned Lincoln not to expose himself to the enemy.

As the organizer of internal security, Stanton was especially solicitous of the safety of the President, whose cavalry escort he increased after rumors of a plot to kidnap or kill the President reached him in 1864. In fact, he was the only Cabinet member who took the threat to Lincoln's safety seriously. On July 9, 1864, for example, he told Lincoln: "A fact that has just been reported by the Watchman of the Department, viz that your carriage was followed by a horseman not one of your escort and dressed in uniform unlike that used by our troops induces me to advise that your guard be on the *alert* tonight."

When Lincoln was assassinated, Stanton was inexhaustible in his efforts to capture the killers. He came very early to the conclusion that the assassination was a Confederate plot, and the belief guided his investigation and his preparation for the trial of the conspirators. He wanted no exploitation of the assassination for commercial ends or to provide tokens or symbols for the lost cause. Therefore, he forbade photographs of the President lying in state, closed Ford's Theatre, and had John Wilkes Booth's body buried in secrecy.

In order to assure that the conspirators did not escape punishment, Stanton advocated a military trial; but he did not go as far as Joseph Holt, who recommended that the trial be secret. Both Stanton and Holt relied on extremely questionable witnesses in an attempt to link the conspirators to Confederate agents in Canada. Stanton also apparently gave star witness Louis J. Weichmann a very stiff questioning which may have bordered on intimidation, but Weichmann in later years had nothing but praise for Stanton. In part, no doubt, that was due to Stanton's (and Holt's) efforts to get Weichmann a patronage job in the Philadelphia customs house. By military law, the prosecution should have produced Booth's diary as evidence, for the diary showed that the kidnap and murder plots were two different things. However, the government wished to ignore that distinction in order to punish all the conspirators, and the defense never called for it. Thus Booth's diary was not suppressed in the sense that it was withheld from defense demands.

After the war, Stanton remained in Andrew Johnson's Cabinet while advocating Reconstruction and coming into conflict with the President. He resigned in 1868, exhausted by his years of public life. He had given up a $50,000-a-year income for the $8,000-a-year job as War Secretary, and he was in too poor health to regain his income at the law afterwards. President Ulysses S. Grant appointed him to the Supreme Court, but he died before he could take office.

Stanton's differences with Lincoln have been exaggerated. The two differed greatly in personality, Stanton being duplicitous and impolite and brusque, but great policy differences did not separate them. Even on Reconstruction, they agreed in principle at the last Cabinet meeting on military occupation of Virginia and North Carolina, though Lincoln wanted Stanton to revise his plan so that it did not ignore existing state boundaries. The famous sentence, "Now he belongs to the ages," which Stanton is said to have uttered at Lincoln's death, is not as well documented as the fame of the quotation might suggest. But Stanton's deep feelings for the President are well established. Robert Todd Lincoln recalled "that for more than ten days after my father's death in Washington, he called every morning on me in my room, and spent the first few minutes of his visits weeping without saying a word."

SOURCES: Benjamin P. Thomas and Harold M. Hyman's *Stanton: The Life and Times of Lincoln's Secretary of War* (New York: Alfred A. Knopf, 1962) is a superb biography, well written, deeply researched, and judicious. Stanton's letters to Lincoln about West Virginia (December 26, 1862), clemency for a Missouri Confederate (August 19, 1863), the draft in Philadelphia (February 22, 1865), black troops in Kentucky (February 8, 1864), bounties (January 4, 1864), Lincoln's "tormentors" (March 25, 1865), and the weather (March 29, 1865) are in the Abraham Lincoln Papers, Library of Congress. Robert Todd Lincoln described Stanton's emotional state after the assassination in a letter to David H. Bates, October 2, 1911, Robert Todd Lincoln Papers, Illinois State Historical Library, Springfield.

Stephens, Alexander Hamilton (1812–1883) Vice President of the Confederacy. Stephens and Lincoln met when both were Whig members of the Thirtieth Congress (1847–1849). Lincoln heard Stephens speak against the Mexican War on February 2, 1848 and immediately wrote William H. Herndon:

> I just take up my pen to say, that Mr. Stephens of Georgia, a little slim, pale-faced, consumptive man, with a voice like [Stephen T.] Logan's has just concluded the very best speech, of an hour's length, I ever heard.
> My old, withered, dry eyes, are full of tears yet.
> If he writes it out any thing like he delivered it, our people shall see a good many copies of it.

Stephens in his speech denounced the Mexican War as a "wanton outrage upon the Constitution" for which President James K. Polk bore "all" the responsibility. He carefully defined the Texas boundary as lying between the Nueces and the Rio Grande, "just so far as her revolution successfully extended." And he turned the criticism of Polk into a paean of praise for General Zachary Taylor by denouncing as persecution the attempt of Polk's apologists to blame Taylor for advising the troop movement that started the war. When Stephens compared Polk's guilt to Cain's, his language came near Lincoln's own in his speech denouncing the war 3 weeks earlier. On all these points Lincoln and Stephens were in agreement, as were they also on their hopes to nominate Taylor for the Presidency. Lincoln and Truman Smith of Connecticut were the only Northern members of a group called the "Young Indians," early committed to Taylor, and of which Stephens was a member.

Political differences soon separated Lincoln and Stephens in the 1850s. Stephens was ardently proslavery and a stanch supporter of the Kansas-Nebraska Act. Antislavery convictions and a steady denunciation of that act made Lincoln famous. By the late 1850s Lincoln thought Stephens typified those Southern politicians eager to "sound the bugle for the revival of the slave trade, for the second Dred Scott decision, for the flood of slavery to be poured over the free States."

Stephens was nevertheless an opponent of immediate secession after Lincoln's election in 1860, and the President-elect wrote him to ask for a revised copy of a pro-Union speech Stephens delivered to the secession-minded Georgia legislature. Stephens's reply urged Lincoln to say a word "to save our common country." Lincoln answered (*"For your own eye only"*) on December 22, saying that the Republicans would not *"directly, or indirectly"* interfere with slavery in the states, but adding: "You think slavery is *right* and ought to be extended; while we think it is *wrong* and ought to be restricted. That I suppose is the rub. It certainly is the only substantial difference between us." Stephens's inflated reputation for Unionism even led to rumors that Lincoln would offer him a Cabinet post, an idea Lincoln thought absurd.

As Vice President of the Confederate States of America, Stephens soon became a leader of the opposition to President Jefferson Davis—a fact he tried to cover up in his two-volume *Constitutional View of the Late War Between the States* (1868–1870) by saying that his differences with Davis stopped far short of a feud. In fact, however, Stephens denounced the President bitterly; he described him in a typical letter of 1864 as "a weak timid aspirant for Military Domination." Opposition made Stephens something of a defeatist and a perennial advocate of peace negotiations with the North. In June 1863 he gained Davis's permission to go to Washington ostensibly to discuss prisoner exchanges but actually to see whether peace negotiations might start. Lincoln flatly refused to allow him to come, not wanting to give "quasi acknowledgement of the independence of the Confederacy" by receiving officially this commissioner of the "Confederate States." After the war, Stephens claimed that he had hoped for little from Lincoln's administration but thought his mission would work "through them, when the correspondence should be published, upon the great mass of the people in the

Alexander Hamilton Stephens

Northern States, who were becoming so sensitively alive . . . to the great danger of their own liberties." In other words, he had not sought peace so much as victory, to be gained by playing on Northern war-weariness. Whether that was true or not, Stephens's attempt worked on Horace Greeley. The *Tribune* editor repeatedly flayed Lincoln for refusing to receive Stephens and make at least a gesture toward peace.

In 1865 Davis once again sent Stephens and two other politicians north, this time to discuss terms of peace with Lincoln and Secretary of State William H. Seward at Hampton Roads. No notes were allowed at the conference, and Stephens gave, in his *Constitutional View of the Late War Between the States* in 1870, the only lengthy account of what was said at the 4-hour discussion on board the *River Queen* on February 3, 1865. Stephens recalled that Lincoln and Seward were inflexibly opposed to an armistice or any terms other than reunion. But he claimed that Seward suggested that the Confederate states reenter the Union quickly and thereby block passage of the Thirteenth Amendment abolishing slavery. Likewise, he remembered Lincoln's saying that a $400 million indemnity for freed slaves was possible and that Georgia could reenter the Union quickly by ratifying the Thirteenth Amendment "*prospectively*, so as to take effect—say in five years." In this statement, Stephens indulged in wishful thinking. Immediately after the conference Lincoln did draft a bond issue to reimburse Southern slaveowners contingent on ratification of the amendment in 5 *months*. (He also saw to it that Stephens's nephew, a prisoner of war, was exchanged.) By 1870, when he wrote the account, Stephens had deluded himself into thinking that Lincoln would never have allowed Georgia to experience what she had in the preceeding 5 years of Reconstruction— why, he would not even have abolished slavery until 1870, Stephens imagined.

Although he was among the first to create a mythical Lincoln who would not have reconstructed the South, Stephens was anything but kind to Lincoln in his *Constitutional View*. He commented favorably on Lincoln's personal characteristics, but he pictured the President as a Caesar destroying the Republic. He compared him to Danton and Robespierre in combining personal likableness with political destructiveness. Stephens's explanation for the paradox was this:

> I do not think that he intended to overthrow the Institutions of the country. I do not think he understood them or the tendencies of his acts upon them. The Union with him in sentiment, rose to the sublimity of a religious mysticism; while his ideas of its structure and formation in logic, rested upon nothing but the subtleties of a sophism!

SOURCES: The best biography is the oldest, R. M. Johnston and W. H. Browne's *Life of Alexander H. Stephens* (Philadelphia: J. B. Lippincott, 1878). Stephens's speech on the Mexican War is in *Cong. Globe*, 30 Cong. 1 Sess., Appendix, pp. 159–164. His *Constitutional View of the Late War Between the States*, 2 vols. (Philadelphia: National Publishing Company, 1868–1870) earned Stephens some $35,000 in royalties. The letter about Davis (to R. M. Johnston, August 26, 1864) is in the Papers of Alexander H. Stephens, Library of Congress.

See also HAMPTON ROADS PEACE CONFERENCE.

Stephenson, Nathaniel Wright (1867–1935) One of the first academic historians to write a biography of Lincoln. Stephenson was born in Cincinnati, Ohio, attended Indiana University, and worked as a newspaper man. Later he taught briefly at Yale and Columbia, edited the *Chronicles of America* series, experimented with history on film, and ended his career at Scripps College in Claremont, California.

In the period from 1918 to 1922 Stephenson published a book on the Confederacy, two books on Lincoln, and a book on the Mexican War. His most important book was *Lincoln: An Account of His Personal Life, Especially of Its Springs of Action as Revealed and Deepened by the Ordeal of War* (Indianapolis, Ind.: Bobbs-Merrill, 1922). Roy P. Basler, assessing the state of Lincoln scholarship in 1935, claimed that "Sandburg combined with Stephenson may be recognized as the best version of the private Lincoln; Charnwood, perhaps, has the best of the public Lincoln." Basler appreciated Stephenson's ability to capture Lincoln's "poetic" nature and his assertion that Lincoln was a man of stern will and inflexible purpose, and no mere political opportunist. David M. Potter in *The Lincoln Theme and American National Historiography* (Oxford: Clarendon Press, 1948) noted that, at "a time when Freudian interpretations" were all the rage, Stephenson "garnished his *Lincoln* . . . with psychoanalytical speculation." Potter also saw Stephenson as "one of the first writers to attempt an appraisal of the meaning of Lincoln's preservation of the Union."

Stephenson's *Lincoln* was a product of the era in which it was written in other respects as well. His article "Lincoln and the Progress of Nationality in the North" (1919) was a perfect epitome of the mind of the Progressive Era. He loved to pit Lincoln against the war profiteers, and he cited Lincoln's letter to William Kellogg of June 29, 1863: "Few things are so troublesome to the government as the fierceness with which the profits of trading in cotten are sought." Stephenson hated the "dreaming pacifists," who opposed World War I, and saw their counterparts in the cowardly Copperheads, whom he saw as victims of disordered psychology. He admired Lincoln's sympathy for labor and pointed to his remark in 1861 that "Labor is the superior of capital, and deserves much the higher consideration." Yet Stephenson hated socialism as "the political science of fairyland," and he pointed out that Lincoln opposed aristocracy, not private property. In keeping with the era's elitist admiration of the expert, he claimed that "Lincoln was not a friend of the plebiscite or of the referendum." Stephenson admired Lincoln's use of the power of the Presidency for military arrests. By ignoring the clamor over them, Lincoln "refused to be the mere spokesman of the people," said Stephenson; "there does not exist, probably, as a summary of Lincoln's basal attitude toward his own electorate, a better statement of fundamental theory than that immortal letter to the electors of Bristol signed by Edmund Burke."

Above all those erring groups, above plebiscitarian democracy, above labor, above capital, and above pacifists stood the nation. Stephenson claimed that "Lincoln in his vision of nationality had outstripped his time." Preoccupied with Lincoln's nationalism, he ignored Lincoln's opposition to the Mexican War in 1848 and doubted his wisdom in failing to act more vigorously to expel the French from Mexico during the Civil War. Reviewers like Arthur C. Cole recognized that Lincoln became in Stephenson's books "less the 'great Emancipator' " and "more the 'great Conciliator.' " Certainly, Stephenson's is the most nationalistic Lincoln portrait ever drawn.

SOURCES: Basler's appraisal is in *The Lincoln Legend: A Study in Changing Conceptions* (Boston: Houghton, Mifflin, 1935). Stephenson's "Lincoln and the Progress of Nationality in the North," first published in the *Annual Report of the American Historical Association for 1919*, I, 351–363, was deemed important enough to be reprinted by the Government Printing Office in 1923. Arthur C. Cole's review appeared in the *American Historical Review*, XXVIII (April 1923), 596.

Stern, Alfred Whital   See LIBRARY OF CONGRESS.

Stewart, Judd (1867-1919)   One of the "Big Five" Lincoln collectors who dominated Lincoln collecting around the turn of the century. Judd Stewart lived in Plainfield, New Jersey. Among the "Big Five," who tended to focus on printed materials and manuscripts, he was perhaps the least discriminating collector; he gathered medals, newspaper clippings, curios, and memorabilia in addition to books and letters. Nor was he a particularly astute judge of manuscripts. His pamphlet, *Some Lincoln Correspondence with Southern Leaders Before the Outbreak of the Civil War* (New York: privately published, 1909), contained alleged Lincoln letters to John J. Crittenden and Alexander H. Stephens that were proved by Worthington C. Ford in 1928 to be forgeries.

Stewart was a conservative Republican. Like Lincoln's son Robert, he took great exception to Theodore Roosevelt's use of Lincoln's words to support the Progressive platform in 1912, especially the party's plank urging the recall of Supreme Court decisions and its generally favorable attitude toward labor. Stewart published a shrilly worded pamphlet, *Abraham Lincoln on Present-day Problems and Abraham Lincoln as Represented by Theodore Roosevelt* (n.p., n.d.), which contrasted the two men sharply.

After his death, Stewart's heirs sold his collection to Henry E. Huntington. It now resides in the Henry E. Huntington Library and Art Gallery in San Marino, California. By the time of the purchase, the collection contained 3000 books, pamphlets, and broadsides, the proof of Lincoln's First Inaugural Address given to Orville Hickman Browning for revision, Lincoln's letter of condolence to the parents of Elmer E. Ellsworth, and some 50 Robert Todd Lincoln letters.

See also HENRY E. HUNTINGTON LIBRARY AND ART GALLERY.

Stoddard, William Osborn (1835–1925)   One of Lincoln's White House secretaries. Stoddard was born in Homer, New York, graduated from the University of Rochester, and moved to Illinois in 1858. There he soon became an editor of West Urbana's *Central Illinois Gazette*. A Republican in politics, he was among the earliest (1859) to promote Lincoln's presidential candidacy in his newspaper.

After Lincoln's election, Stoddard thought his work merited the reward of appointment as Lincoln's private secretary. He told Lincoln's law partner that he was "willing to begin 'on trial,' as the Dutchman took his wife," but his request languished for two months. In 1861 Lincoln appointed him to a clerkship in the Interior Department, where he signed presidential land grants. During the war there were not many to sign, and Stoddard served eventually in a White House office as an assistant to Presidential secretaries John G. Nicolay and John Hay. He gave the initial screening to the incoming mail, some 200 to 300 letters a day, throwing away the great quantity that came from cranks and lunatics. There were so many assassination threats that soon the idea had "no more scare in it." He performed other clerical and messenger duties as well.

Unlike Nicolay and Hay, Stoddard got along well with Mrs. Lincoln. He sympathized with her as the victim of ridiculous rumors that she fed secret information to her Confederate relatives, and he noted that her frequent visits to hospitals for the wounded were unattended by public relations fanfare.

Stoddard seems to have been very much a clerk and therefore to have had little important contact with Lincoln. Nevertheless, his *Inside the White House in War Times* (New York: Charles L. Webster & Co., 1890) contains some memorable vignettes of the Lincoln White House and is particularly good at describing the atmosphere of the tense and hard-working wartime administration.

In 1864 Lincoln appointed Stoddard United States Marshal for the Eastern District of Arkansas. In his book he claimed that Lincoln told him to "do all you can . . . to get the ballot into the hands of the freedmen! We must make voters of them before we take away the troops." And Stoddard was certainly Radical in his views on Reconstruction; he advocated a vigorous use of the Confiscation Act to break up "the old rebel aristocracy" and to encourage immigration to Arkansas by giving Union veterans the right to preempt forfeited Southern estates. After the failure of the Red River campaign, Stoddard told Lincoln that Union forces in Arkansas were "disorganized, demoralized, and in good part depopulated," without the strength "to maintain a healthy state government."

Stoddard resigned his post as marshal in 1866 and later engaged in business and inventing. He wrote over a hundred books, many of them children's books and several of them on Lincoln.

SOURCES: Stoddard's letters to William H. Herndon ("willing to begin 'on trial,' " December 27, 1860) and to Lincoln ("rebel

William Osborn Stoddard. (Lloyd Ostendorf Collection)

Stuart, John Todd

aristocracy," December 13, 1864, and "disorganized, demoralized," January 16, 1865) are in the Abraham Lincoln Papers, Library of Congress.

Stuart, John Todd (1807–1885) Abraham Lincoln's first law partner and political mentor. Like Lincoln, John Todd Stuart was a Kentuckian. The son of a Presbyterian minister, he attended Centre College in Danville, Kentucky. He was admitted to the bar in 1827, and a year later he became the sixth lawyer in Springfield, Illinois, a county seat of about 300 residents.

John Todd Stuart

While serving as a major in the Black Hawk War in 1832, Stuart met Captain Abraham Lincoln. When he returned from the war, he campaigned successfully to be one of four Representatives from Sangamon County to the Illinois General Assembly. Lincoln also campaigned for one of the seats but lost. In 1834 both ran successfully. At the legislature in Vandalia, Lincoln was Stuart's protégé; he drafted legislation which Stuart introduced and frequently, but by no means always, voted on the same side. Stuart soon became a Whig leader in the state and was nicknamed "Jerry Sly" for his considerable abilities at legislative management and political intrigue.

While they ran for the legislature together in 1834, Stuart encouraged Lincoln, who had earlier thought his education too meager to consider it, to study law. Stuart lent Lincoln the necessary books. Three years later, his partner, Henry E. Dummer, left to establish his own practice in Beardstown, and Lincoln became Stuart's partner in Springfield. Their office was located on the second floor of Hoffman's Row, a new building which contained several rooms for stores and offices. Stuart's interests ran heavily to politics in those years, and Lincoln carried a substantial burden of the practice. Stuart had run unsuccessfully for the United States House of Representatives in 1836, and in 1838 he ran again in a bitter but successful campaign against Stephen A. Douglas. The district contained 34 counties and half the territory of Illinois; canvassing kept the senior partner away from the office much of the time. When Stuart went to Congress in 1839, Lincoln wrote on a fresh page in the firm's account book, "Commencement of Lincoln's administration." Lincoln not only maintained the practice but wrote his partner frequently to keep him abreast of political developments at home. When Stuart returned in 1841, Lincoln left the firm to become the partner of Stephen T. Logan.

Stuart retained his seat in Congress in the 1841 election. When he returned from Washington in 1843, he formed a partnership with Benjamin S. Edwards which would last until his death.

Stuart served one term as a state senator from 1848 to 1852; but soon thereafter his political fortunes changed, and he and Lincoln parted ways politically. Lincoln became a Republican in 1856, but Stuart's "slight pro-slavery proclivities," as Lincoln termed them, prevented his joining the Republicans. In 1860 Stuart did not support Lincoln for President and he himself ran for governor on the Constitutional Union ticket and lost.

In 1862 Stuart announced that he would run for Congress in Illinois's Eighth Congressional District, saying he had been a member of no party since the demise of the Whigs. The Democrats endorsed him, and he ran against another Lincoln associate, Leonard Swett. Stuart was careful in the campaign to state his "unbounding confidence" in Lincoln's "personal integrity" while urging Lincoln to use only "the ample powers conferred upon him by the constitution, and repulse any resort to revolutionary means" to save the Union. The statement certainly implied criticism of the recently announced preliminary Emancipation Proclamation, which Swett endorsed. Stuart, as David Davis noted, "tried to dodge, and did not come out either for or against the Proclamation." He "talks but little but will spend a great deal of money," Davis added. Stuart won, 12,808 to 11,443, in a victory characterized by the New York *Times* as a "vote of want of confidence" in the President.

Though Stuart was now a member of the opposition to the administration, he was Lincoln's old law partner and Mrs. Lincoln's cousin, and he therefore enjoyed good social relations with the White House. In 1863 the President helped a relative of Stuart's reclaim her plantation in Arkansas.

Stuart's political views belonged to a bygone era. In 1864 he urged Millard Fillmore, the old Whig President, to seek the Democratic nomination for the Presidency. Fillmore opposed Lincoln but admitted to Stuart that he was "no candidate for popular favor." Stuart ran for Congress again that year and lost to Shelby M. Cullom. He returned to Springfield, his law practice, and his considerable involvement in civic and economic enterprises. After Lincoln's death, he became a director of the National Lincoln Monument Association and oversaw the erection of the Lincoln tomb. He died suddenly in 1885.

SOURCES: There is no adequate biography of Stuart. Paul M. Angle's *One Hundred Years of Law: An Account of the Law Office which John T. Stuart Founded in Springfield, Illinois, a Century Ago* (Springfield, Ill.: Brown, Hay and Stephens, 1928) contains a laudatory sketch that is skimpy on Stuart's politics. Harry E. Pratt's article on "The Repudiation of Lincoln's War Policy—Stuart-Swett Congressional Campaign," *Journal of the Illinois State Historical Society*, XXIV (April 1931), 129–140, is a solid account of Stuart's most important campaign. The David Davis quotations are from letters to William M. Orme, October 15 and 20, 1862, copies of which are in the Chicago Historical Society. On Stuart's views in 1864 see Harry E. Pratt, "Lincolniana Notes," *Journal of the Illinois State Historical Society*, XLVI (Autumn 1953), 302.

Sumner, Charles (1811–1874) Massachusetts Republican Senator during the Civil War. Sumner introduced himself to Lincoln the day after the President-elect arrived in Washington in 1861. Lincoln was a "seemingly untutored child of nature" to the learned and formal Sumner. A stanch opponent of compromise with the South in the secession crisis, Sumner lamented Secretary of State William H. Seward's willingness to compromise and praised Lincoln's First Inaugural Address as "best described by Napoleon's simile of 'a hand of iron and a velvet glove.'" Soon after the firing on Fort Sumter, Senator Sumner told the President that "under the war power the right had come to him to emancipate the slaves."

As Chairman of the Senate Committee on Foreign Relations, Sumner worked closely with Lincoln on foreign policy; he urged that Seward's belligerent memo of May 21, 1861, be softened in language and be shown only to Charles Francis Adams, the American minister in England, and not to the British Foreign Office. He urged the appointment of literary figures to foreign posts and was a major source of information on British opinion through his private correspondence with Englishmen, especially the Liberals John Bright and Richard Cobden. During the *Trent* crisis late in 1861, Sumner steadily argued that the captured Confederate emissaries, James M. Mason and John Slidell, must be allowed to go to Europe. Though he professed to be "no idolator of the Union," Sumner showed his patriotism by complaining only at home of the government's slowness to abolish slavery; his letters to Englishmen always described the United States as a nation at war with slavery itself.

Sumner felt that Lincoln moved too slowly to aid the black man; on September 17, 1861, he complained that the President's revocation of General John C. Frémont's emancipation proclamation for Missouri showed "how vain [it was] to have the power of a god and not use it godlike." Only what Frémont had done could save the Union, he told Lincoln almost a year later. *"Recruits will not do it. A draft will not do it."* As early as October 1861, Sumner said in a speech that rebellion and slavery were so closely linked that emancipation was a matter of "self-defense" for the nation. He felt strongly that British popular opinion so opposed slavery that a Union policy of emancipation would guarantee British opposition to the Confederacy. Still, Sumner never broke with the administration over slavery, and Lincoln is said to have told Sumner that "the only difference between you and me on this subject is a difference of a month or six weeks in time." And Sumner was pleased by Lincoln's plan of March 6, 1862, to offer federal aid to any state initiating a program of gradual and compensated emancipation. Lincoln's preliminary Emancipation Proclamation of September 22, 1862, pleased Sumner too, but the Massachusetts Senator blamed Seward for delay in issuing it. He participated in the unsuccessful move to force Seward's resignation from the Cabinet in December, arguing that some of the Secretary of State's diplomatic documents were inadequate. Sumner's relations with Lincoln remained stable, however, and on Christmas Day 1862 Lincoln consulted him on the wording of the final Emancipation Proclamation to be issued in a week. Lincoln agreed with Sumner to include a clause accepting Negro troops in the Union army.

Alternating confidence that Christian civilization would never go backward after the Proclamation and nagging fears that somehow it just might do so characterized Sumner's thought thereafter. In the summer he found "every where consternation at the idea that the Proclamation can be forgotten or abandoned." By autumn he professed "no fear that there can be any arrest of the judgment which Providence has entered already against Slavery." Yet he begged the President to state in his annual message that the Confederacy "for the first time in human history" was a nation seeking "'recognition' in the Christian Family, whose only declared reason of separate existence is the support of Slavery." This, he thought, would guarantee European neutrality.

Sumner disagreed with Lincoln on Reconstruction, in part because of his anxiety to ensure that "If the proclamation does not destroy slavery," the people of the rebel states must do it "previous to assuming the control of the State Governments." As early as February 11, 1862, Senator Sumner argued that the seceded states had committed suicide and their land and population were under congressional jurisdiction. This "state-suicide" theory aroused so much opposition that Sumner soon ceased advocating it; Republicans, he said, should not get "lost in a discussion, only worthy of schoolmen, on the metaphysical entity of a State." He applauded Lincoln's Proclamation of Amnesty and Reconstruction of December 8, 1863, principally because of its pledge never to renege on emancipation. However, he opposed the actual workings of Lincoln's Reconstruction policy in Louisiana and was one of the sternest opponents of recognizing that state's restored government.

Sumner held himself aloof from the controversies over the Republican presidential nomination in 1864, though other Radical Republicans sought some means to replace Lincoln as the nominee. He campaigned for Lincoln in the fall but thought that "many . . . are anxious to have it, understood, that they vote *against* McClellan rather than *for* Lincoln." Sumner saw the hand of Providence in the death of Chief Justice Roger B. Taney of the United States Supreme Court, and he repeatedly pressed for the appointment of Salmon P. Chase to fill Taney's place. New York Republican Edwin D. Morgan apparently persuaded the President to delay naming a successor until after the election. Sumner thought the naming should have been done "on the evening of Taney's funeral," and as soon as the election was over he told the President there could now be no reason for further delay. Still haunted by fears for the completeness and permanence of emancipation, the Massachusetts Senator felt it essential that the future composition of the Court guarantee the interpretation of the Constitution in favor of freedom rather than slavery.

In the same post-election letter urging Chase's speedy appointment, Sumner argued that all the slaves in the South were already free de jure and counseled the President against Southern moves "to substitute *prospective* Emancipation for *immediate*" to gain them "an opportunity of making terms." Sumner argued that there was no one in the Confederacy whom Lincoln could deal

Charles Sumner

with: Jefferson Davis and the rest of the members of his government were traitors. All the North could do was to press for military victory so that "the Unionists of the South can then show themselves." Besides, Sumner said, peace terms and Reconstruction were matters that belonged to Congress rather than the executive branch. *"Next to the Rebellion itself I most dread a premature State Govt. in a rebel State,"* Sumner told Lincoln. In keeping with that sentiment, Sumner was a major force in helping to kill the recognition of Louisiana in February 1865. Even after that he was still on good enough terms with the President to be invited to accompany the Lincolns to the inaugural ball on March 6, 1865.

Lincoln and Sumner were not as far apart on Reconstruction as some thought. Sumner believed that "The only Unionists of the South are black," and Lincoln was more concerned with the white "loyal minority," which he seemed to think might constitute 10 percent of the population. Still, neither believed, as conservative Montgomery Blair believed, that the majority in the South was really loyal but was held in subjection by secessionists. Sumner by 1865 wished universal enfranchisement of blacks, and Lincoln was willing to recommend only partial enfranchisement. Both were more interested in results than constitutional theory, but they disagreed thoroughly over the proper agency of Reconstruction. Sumner advocated Congress and Lincoln the Executive.

The night Lincoln was assassinated, Sumner rushed to his bedside and remained there until Lincoln's death in the morning. Mrs. Lincoln had always admired the Massachusetts Senator, and he had frequently been her escort on social occasions. He remained her steadfast champion after the war; he worked unsuccessfully to get her a $5000 pension in 1869 and succeeded in 1870 in securing passage of a bill for a $3000 pension.

Sumner also admired Abraham Lincoln. His eulogy on Lincoln, delivered in Boston on June 1, 1865, was called *The Promises of the Declaration of Independence.* In preparing the address, Sumner studied Lincoln's writings and discovered the degree to which the President's political thought, like his own, derived from the Declaration.

SOURCES: David Donald's *Charles Sumner and the Coming of the Civil War* (New York: Alfred A. Knopf, 1965) and *Charles Sumner and the Rights of Man* (New York: Alfred A. Knopf, 1970) are, though somewhat hostile to their subject, definitive. Sumner's letters to Lincoln about Frémont (August 29, 1862), about abandoning the Proclamation (August 7, 1863), about British recognition (November 30, 1863), and about Taney and prospective emancipation (November 20, 1864) are in the Abraham Lincoln Papers, Library of Congress, as is a memorandum, not in Sumner's hand, explaining his views on Reconstruction in 1862.

Sumter Crisis The incident which started the Civil War. The crisis began when South Carolina seceded on December 20, 1860. Fort Sumter, in Charleston harbor, became an irritating symbol of "foreign" authority. Lame duck President James Buchanan believed both secession and "coercion" of states unconstitutional, and he wanted nothing so much as to finish his term in peace. He did nothing when South Carolina seized unoccupied Fort Moultrie, Castle Pinckney, the customs house, the post office, the treasury, and the arsenal. He did nothing when South Carolina batteries fired on the unarmed steamer, *Star of the West,* coming to the harbor with supplies and men for the fort. He agreed not to reinforce Fort Pickens, off Florida, in exchange for Southern pledges not to attack that fort. But he refused Southern demands to withdraw the garrison from Fort Sumter. He succeeded in leaving office with the country at peace. Lincoln would have to solve the Sumter crisis.

In his inaugural address of March 4, 1861, Lincoln declared that he would "hold, occupy, and possess" federal installations still under federal control in the South, but he made no threats to take action. The first draft had said he would "reclaim the public property and places," but Orville Hickman Browning suggested the more conciliatory final wording. The day after the speech, Lincoln was jolted by a letter from Major Robert Anderson, commander at Fort Sumter, saying he had only 40 days' supply of food. General Winfield Scott advised Lincoln that relief was impossible, and Secretary of State William H. Seward desired evacuation of Sumter as a way of stalling until Southern lovers of Union came to their senses and nullified secession. Seward told Confederate commissioners that Lincoln would abandon the fort. Lincoln polled the Cabinet on March 15, asking whether it would be wise to attempt to supply Sumter, and only two thought it would be, Montgomery Blair and Salmon P. Chase. On March 29 Lincoln announced

Harper's Weekly completely misinterpreted the direction of the incoming administration in this cartoon published two days before Lincoln's inauguration. Henry Ward Beecher, following William H. Seward's "Higher Law" doctrine, refuses communion to slaveholder and father of his country George Washington. Lincoln is less prominent in the congregation than Seward. In truth, Seward was pursuing compromise with the South, and Lincoln quickly dominated his Cabinet.

NO COMMUNION WITH SLAVEHOLDERS.
"Stand aside, you Old Sinner! WE are HOLIER than thou!"

to the Cabinet that he would send only supplies, not reinforcements, to the fort and would let South Carolina Governor Francis W. Pickens know they were coming. Only Seward still opposed the idea. Ignoring much advice, Lincoln had taken control and pursued an independent course.

On April 1 Seward's memorandum, "Some Thoughts for the President's Consideration" recommended evacuating Sumter and retaining Fort Pickens, but the die was cast. There ensued a muddled period of preparation in which Lincoln confused the names of the warships *Powhatan* and *Pocahontas*. Seward, instructed to countermand the President's order, signed his own name, and the naval commander ignored the order on the assumption that Seward's order could not supersede the President's. The relief expedition sailed without the *Powhatan*.

In 1937 Charles W. Ramsdell argued that Lincoln deliberately provoked the South into firing the first shot in order to get world opinion on the side of the North. Lincoln knew the Confederates would resist any relief expedition, Ramsdell argued, and he pointed to an entry in Browning's diary for July 3, 1861, reporting that Lincoln had said of Sumter, "The plan succeeded, They attacked Sumter—it fell, and thus, did more service than it otherwise could." This secondhand report is the only such evidence and may take Browning's reasoning as Lincoln's own. The intense focus on the meaning of Lincoln's actions long obscured evidence that Confederate President Jefferson Davis was ready to fire the first shot before hearing of the Sumter relief expedition. Lincoln's note to Governor Pickens about the relief expedition was written on April 6, but on April 3 Davis had written a letter to General Braxton Bragg at Pensacola telling him to take Fort Pickens if suitable preparations had been made. Bragg was unready, and war began only when guns fired on Fort Sumter on April 12, 1861.

Ironically, ex-President Buchanan, whom Republicans accused of conniving at treason with the South, always held that he would "have done the same thing" that Lincoln did. His friend and Attorney General Jeremiah Black, however, maintained that Buchanan could not defend Lincoln's policy and his own at the same time:

> It is vain to think that the two administrations can be made consistent. The fire upon the Star of the West was as bad as the fire on Fort Sumter; and the taking of Fort Moultrie & Pinckney was worse than either. If this war is right and politic and wise and constitutional, I cannot but think you ought to have made it.

SOURCES: The literature on the Sumter crisis is large and good. See Charles W. Ramsdell, "Lincoln and Fort Sumter," *Journal of Southern History*, III (August 1937), 159–188; David M. Potter, *Lincoln and His Party in the Secession Crisis* (New Haven, Conn.: Yale University Press, 1942); Richard N. Current, *Lincoln and the First Shot* (Philadelphia: J. B. Lippincott, 1963); and, for a brief summary, Albert Castel, "Fort Sumter—1861," *Civil War Times Illustrated*, XV (October 1976), special issue. The Davis letter about Fort Pickens is discussed in Grady McWhiney, "The Confederacy's First Shot," *Civil War History*, XIV (March 1968), 5–14. As historians have moved away from the Revisionist idea that the war was a needless one brought on by blundering politicians, interest in the Sumter crisis has lessened; the particular incident which triggered the conflict has seemed less important than the larger social and political incidents which brought North and South to an apparently hopeless impasse.

See also BROWNING, ORVILLE HICKMAN; BUCHANAN, JAMES; SCOTT, WINFIELD; SEWARD, WILLIAM HENRY.

Supreme Court of the United States

Abraham Lincoln argued cases before the Illinois Supreme Court, but he never argued before the United States Supreme Court. The Court was an institution he regarded from afar. Though some conservative Whigs came increasingly to think of the Court as a brake on democracy, as a young Whig Lincoln apparently never regarded the Court in that way. In his Lyceum speech of 1838, Lincoln did say, "Let reverence for the laws . . . become the *political religion* of the nation," and he later chided Democrats for claiming the Second Bank of the United States was unconstitutional after "the most enlightened judicial tribunal in the world," the United States Supreme Court, had declared a national bank constitutional.

Lincoln changed his stance toward the Court as a result of the Dred Scott decision of 1857, and he was forced for the first time to think seriously about judicial review. Now critical of the Court, Lincoln became the target of Stephen A. Douglas's accusation that he urged policies (congressional exclusion of slavery from the territories) declared unconstitutional by the Supreme Court. Lincoln retorted repeatedly that Douglas had in the past ignored the Court's blessing of the Bank of the United States, and noted that Douglas's political heroes Andrew Jackson and Thomas Jefferson "were both against him on the binding political authority of Supreme Court decisions." But, Lincoln sighed, "I might as well preach Christianity to a grizzly bear as to preach Jefferson and Jackson to" Douglas.

Many Republicans, opposed to the Dred Scott decision but not wishing to appear opposed to the law of the land, dismissed the unpleasant parts of the Dred Scott decision as *obiter dicta*, personal opinions of Chief Justice Taney irrelevant to the binding law of the case, but Lincoln probed deeper. He admitted the Court's authority in the disposition of Dred Scott, but certain conditions had to be met in order for the Supreme Court to "control, not only the particular cases decided, but the general policy of the country."

> If this important decision had been made by the unanimous concurrence of the judges, and without any apparent partisan bias, and in accordance with legal public expectation, and with the steady practice of the departments throughout our history, and had been in no part, based on assumed historical facts which are not really true; or, if wanting in some of these, it had been before the court more than once, and had there been affirmed and re-affirmed through a course of years, it then might be, perhaps would be, factious, nay, even revolutionary, to not acquiesce in it as a precedent.
>
> But when, as it is true we find it wanting in all these claims to the public confidence, it is not resistance, it is not factious, it is not even disrespectful, to treat it as not having yet quite established a settled doctrine for the country.

Lincoln's hostility toward the Court would continue.

Supreme Court of the United States

The Supreme Court in 1865: Davis, Swayne, Grier, Wayne, Chase, Nelson, Clifford, Miller, Field, and (below) Catron. (Library of Congress)

Lincoln's First Inaugural Address did "not forget the position assumed by some, that constitutional questions are to be decided by the Supreme Court," but he warned "that if the policy of the government . . . is to be irrevocably fixed by decisions of the Supreme Court . . . the people will have ceased, to be their own rulers." He made no "assault upon the court, or the judges," but the speech certainly set an ominous tone for the administration's relations to a Court still headed by the author of the Dred Scott decision. In addition to Chief Justice Roger B. Taney, who thought a peaceful separation of the states better than "union . . . under a military government & a reign of terror," there were five justices already on the bench. New York Democrat Samuel Nelson had also hoped for a peaceful separation. Maine Democrat Nathan Clifford would support the military effort but not other measures of a Republican administration. Pennsylvania Democrat Robert C. Grier was thoroughly prowar. Two Southerners on the Court were very pro-Union. Both John Catron of Tennessee and John M. Wayne of Georgia had property confiscated by the Confederacy but remained on the bench. Justice John A. Campbell of Alabama resigned to join the Confederacy, making three vacancies on the Court (John McLean of Ohio died shortly after Lincoln's inauguration, and President Buchanan had left one seat vacant).

In 1861, then, the Court stood balanced at 3–3 in terms of likelihood of supporting vigorous war measures, and Lincoln had begun his tenure with a veiled threat against that body. Though relations between the President and the Supreme Court were often strained, there was never the confrontation one might have expected from those origins—for three reasons. First, by filling vacancies, Lincoln altered the political and ideological composition of the Court in his favor. Second, the Court exercised restraint in dealing with war issues. Third, the Northern Democratic party was largely loyal, and even its opposition stopped short of disloyalty in most cases.

President Lincoln appointed five persons to the Supreme Court over the course of his administration. Despite the Court's divided and lukewarm makeup, Lincoln was in no haste to fill the Court vacancies. He nominated the first of the five, antislavery Republican Noah H. Swayne of Ohio, on January 21, 1862. He nominated Iowa Republican Samuel Freeman Miller in July 1862. Two of Lincoln's personal friends from Illinois, David Davis and Orville Hickman Browning, were contenders for the third appointment. Lincoln finally nominated Davis on October 17, 1862.

Each of the nine Supreme Court Justices in Lincoln's day was also responsible for a Federal Circuit Court, a job which required much time and travel. The Supreme Court met one term a year. The limited staff of the Court consisted of a reporter, a clerk, a marshal, and a crier. The size of the country was fast outstripping the ability of the circuit courts to cope with it, and Lincoln's message to Congress in December 1861 suggested that the system be changed in one of three ways: first, by adding circuit judges and relieving Supreme Court Justices of the burden of that duty; second, by simply adding enough circuit judges to take some burden from the Justices; or, third, by abolishing the circuit courts altogether. Lincoln rejected the idea of increasing the Supreme Court's size to accommodate circuits for all parts of the country and insisted that "the Supreme Court be of convenient number in every event."

Some Republicans in Congress were more critical of the Court than Lincoln. Despite an initial conflict with Taney over the suspension of the privilege of the writ of habeas corpus (*Ex parte Merryman*, May 1861), Lincoln never mounted an assault on the Court. Senator John P. Hale, on the other hand, led a move to abolish the Court and appoint a new one altogether. Some other critics took encouragement from Lincoln's statement in his annual message about maintaining a "convenient number" on the Court, hoping to add more justices to outweigh the conservative incumbents' votes.

The attempts to abolish the Court never gained great support, but early in 1863, as the Court heard arguments in the first important war-related cases to come before them (the Prize Cases), Congress moved to create a tenth circuit and add a tenth Justice to preside over it and join the Court. Lincoln and the Republicans have been charged with "packing" the Court in this move, but the evidence is largely circumstantial. Distant California and Oregon badly needed a circuit court system. California was producing a number of important cases involving land and mining which hinged on peculiar land laws which the Court barely comprehended. Lincoln signed the bill creating the new circuit on March 3, 1863, a week before the decision in the Prize Cases, and nominated California's Stephen J. Field for the seat. Field was a stanch Unionist and was familiar with California's complicated land laws.

The Prize Cases involved the legality of seizures of ships under Lincoln's blockade proclamation issued after the fall of Fort Sumter and before Congress had met. The Court upheld the legality of those war measures by a 5 to 4 vote. Field had not yet assumed his place on the Court.

The Court upheld the administration in other important cases as well. In December 1863 it eschewed commenting on the constitutionality of the Legal Tender Act, the basis of the administration's war finance. In February 1864 it refused to overturn Clement L. Vallandigham's sentence by a military court for disloyalty, claiming no ability to review the decision of a military commission. The potential for conflict and confrontation was always present, however. Chief Justice Taney died with two undelivered and unfriendly decisions among his papers: one would have declared the Legal Tender Act unconstitutional, and the other would have declared military conscription illegal. On January 31, 1863, Attorney General Edward Bates discouraged Secretary of War Edwin M. Stanton from bringing the habeas corpus question before the Supreme Court because he feared an adverse decision. After the war, the Court decided in *Ex parte Milligan* (1866) that military trials while civil courts were open were illegal, thereby altering its stand in the Vallandigham case of the war years. In his majority opinion, David Davis characterized the Court's studied avoidance of hot political issues in wartime:

> the temper of the times did not allow that calmness in deliberation and discussion so necessary to a correct conclusion of a purely judicial question. *Then*, considerations of safety were mingled with the exercise of power.... *Now* that the public safety is assured, this question ... can be discussed ... without passion.

Chief Justice Taney died in October 1864, and once again Lincoln took his time in filling the vacancy. There seems to have been little doubt that Salmon P. Chase would be his choice, partly because of Chase's eminent qualifications and partly because he seemed to promise reliability should important administration measures like the Emancipation Proclamation come before the Court after the war. Lincoln hesitated until well after the November presidential election, apparently because he wanted assurances that Chase would not see the Court as a stepping-stone to the Presidency. Finally, on December 6, 1864, Lincoln nominated Chase for Chief Justice.

SOURCES: David M. Silver's *Lincoln's Supreme Court* (Urbana: University of Illinois Press, 1956) is a competent but bland survey of the subject. Though short, Don E. Fehrenbacher's "Lincoln and Judicial Supremacy: A Note on the Galena Speech of July 23, 1856," *Civil War History*, XVI (September 1970), 197–204, is definitive and clear on Lincoln's view of judicial review.

See also BLOCKADE; CONSTITUTION OF THE UNITED STATES; *DRED SCOTT V. SANDFORD*; HABEAS CORPUS; TANEY, ROGER BROOKE.

Surratt, John Harrison, Jr. (1832–1916) Confederate spy and accomplice of John Wilkes Booth. John, Jr., was one of John H. and Mary Surratt's three children. A student at St. Charles College in Maryland when the war broke out, he left school in July 1861 to become a courier "carrying dispatches to Confederate boats on the Potomac" and sending information regarding the movements of the United States soldiers stationed in Washington and elsewhere. He carried messages "sometimes in the heel of my boots, sometimes between the planks of the buggy," and he found the Federal detectives "stupid." Surratt thought the life fascinating and felt he "could not do too much or run too great a risk."

In the autumn of 1864 Surratt met John Wilkes Booth, who wanted to know about the route from Washington to the Potomac. Soon Booth revealed his plan to kidnap President Lincoln and exchange him for Confederate prisoners. At the time Surratt was dazzled by "the unparalleled audacity of his scheme," though in later years he admitted it was "a foolhardy undertaking." He joined Booth and his fellow conspirators.

After an unsuccessful attempt to kidnap Lincoln on March 17, 1865, the group split up and, Surratt claimed, he never saw another member of the group again—except one whom he ran into by chance on the streets of Washington on April 3, 1865. Surratt had been to Richmond and was on his way to Montreal with Confederate dispatches. In Canada General Edwin G. Lee directed Surratt to Elmira, New York, to sketch the Federal prison there. According to four witnesses at his 1867 trial, Surratt was in Elmira when the President was shot.

After Lincoln's assassination Surratt fled to Canada, from there to England, and finally to the Papal States, where, under the name John Watson, he enlisted as a Pontifical Zouave. A French Canadian Zouave, named Henri Belmont de Ste. Marie, informed on Surratt, and, despite the fact that the United States had no extradition treaty with the Vatican, the fugitive was arrested. On November 8, 1866, he escaped, but he was recaptured in Alexandria, Egypt, on the 27th. He was brought back to the United States to stand trial, on June 10, 1867, for murder before Judge George P. Fisher of the Supreme Court of the District of Columbia. The trial lasted until August 11, 1867, when the judge discharged the hung jury (four for conviction, eight for acquittal).

A free man, Surratt delivered a lecture on the conspiracy in Rockville, Maryland, on December 6, 1870. He boasted of his part in the abduction plot but claimed: "Such a thing as the assassination of Mr. Lincoln I never heard spoken by any of the parties. Never!" Nevertheless, he did recall one quarrel among the group over Surratt's suggestion that they should give up the plan because of government security measures. Booth said, "Well, gentlemen, if the worst comes to the worst, I shall know what to do." Four arose in protest, one saying, "If I understand you to intimate anything more than the capture of Mr. Lincoln I for one will bid you goodbye." Booth apologized, saying he had drunk "too much champagne."

Surratt defended himself from charges that he had deserted his mother in her hour of need, claiming that friends had kept news of Mrs. Surratt's fate from him by censoring newspapers in order to protect him. He lashed out at Louis J. Weichmann, John's former friend and a boarder at Mrs. Surratt's house. He had been a key government witness at the trial. Surratt said that Weichmann showed him files from his government job, knew all about the abduction plot, and begged to be a participant. He called Weichmann "a base-born perjurer,

John Harrison Surratt, Jr.

Surratt, Mary Eugenia (or Elizabeth) (Jenkins)

a murderer of the meanest hue." Surratt also said that the Confederate government knew nothing of their scheme and that he had heard of other plots against Lincoln.

Surratt explained his motive simply: "Where is there a young man in the North with one spark of patriotism in his heart who would not have with enthusiastic ardor joined in any undertaking for the capture of Jefferson Davis and brought him to Washington? . . . so I was led on by a sincere desire to assist the South in gaining her independence."

Surratt moved to Baltimore and became an auditor for the Old Bay Line (Baltimore Steam Packet Company).

SOURCES: Surratt's famous lecture is accessible in the appendix to Louis J. Weichmann's *A True History of the Assassination of Abraham Lincoln and of the Conspiracy of 1865*, ed. by Floyd E. Risvold (New York: Alfred A. Knopf, 1975). Other biographical information is in George S. Bryan's *The Great American Myth* (New York: Carrick & Evans, 1940).

Surratt, Mary Eugenia (or Elizabeth) (Jenkins) (1820 or 1823–1865)

In the oft-quoted words of President Andrew Johnson, as recalled by Joseph Holt, Mary Surratt "kept the nest that hatched the egg" of the Lincoln assassination. Educated at a Catholic female seminary in Alexandria, Virginia, Mary Jenkins married John H. Surratt in about 1835. She bore three children: Isaac (who became a Confederate soldier), Anna (who lived with her mother), and John Harrison Surratt, Jr. (a Confederate spy and a conspirator with John Wilkes Booth to kidnap President Lincoln). Her husband, who was the postmaster at Surrattsville, Maryland, died in 1862. Two years later she rented her tavern and farm to John M. Lloyd for $500 a year and moved to Washington. There she ran an eight-room boarding house on H Street. She had frequent visitors from the country around Washington, among them, John Wilkes Booth. Lewis Thornton Powell and George A. Atzerodt, two of Booth's coconspirators, also visited the boarding house.

Ben: Perley Poore described her as having "rather pleasing features, with dark gray eyes and brown hair." One of her boarders, a government clerk named Louis J. Weichmann, went with her to mass regularly ("at least every two weeks"). He characterized her as "exemplary and lady-like in every particular; and her conduct, in a religious and moral sense, altogether exemplary." At one time the Surratts had owned slaves, and her husband had been a secessionist sympathizer. Detectives found *carte-de-visite* photographs of General P. G. T. Beauregard, Jefferson Davis, Alexander H. Stephens, and John Wilkes Booth as well as a card "with the arms of the State of Virginia and two Confederate flags emblazoned thereon, with the inscription 'Thus will it ever be with tyrants, Virginia the Mighty, *Sic Semper Tyrannis*' " in her house. But they also found photographs of Union generals, and Anna Surratt said that her father had given the Confederate photographs to her before his death.

Lloyd claimed that he met Mrs. Surratt on the road to Washington on April 11, 1865, and that she asked him about the "shooting-irons" which John Surratt, David E. Herold, and George A. Atzerodt had hidden in the Surrattsville tavern. She told him, he testified later, that they would be needed soon. The buggy she rented to make the trip was paid for by John Wilkes Booth. Three days later she hired a buggy to go to Surrattsville to collect a debt from John Nothey. She asked her boarder, Weichmann, to drive her. She had received a letter that day from George H. Calvert, Jr., to whom she owed money for land her husband had purchased and sold to Nothey. The somewhat impecunious widow needed the money from Nothey to pay Calvert. She had seen Nothey about the debt on the 11th, but now she had to press him for the money. She left for Surrattsville at about 2:30 p.m. Booth had called on her before she left and given her a package containing a field glass to take to Surrattsville. According to Lloyd, she left the package with him and once again told him to have the firearms ready. Mrs. Surratt returned to Washington. That night Booth shot Lincoln.

Shortly after the shooting, detectives searched the boarding house and left. On the night of April 17 officers arrested Mrs. Surratt and her whole household. While the officers were there, Lewis Thornton Powell appeared at the door dressed as a workman wearing a cloth cap and carrying a pickax. He claimed that he had come to ask when to start work digging a gutter for Mrs. Surratt. Because of the late hour, the detectives were suspicious and decided to take him with the rest of the prisoners. Two of the arresting officers testified later that Mrs. Surratt swore she did not know the man when she saw him in the hall of her home.

Mrs. Surratt was confined in the Old Capitol Prison (the male prisoners were confined aboard government monitors) and later in the Old Penitentiary. She suffered terribly. She was apparently going through menopause, and her "womb disease" made her cell scarcely habitable. She never had to wear the uncomfortable canvas hood the male prisoners were forced to wear to keep them from communicating with other prisoners, but it is unclear whether she was placed in irons. She was eventually given a more comfortable cell and better food than the other prisoners received.

Frederick Aiken and John W. Clampitt were Mrs. Surratt's young lawyers at the conspiracy trial. A United States Senator from Maryland, Reverdy Johnson, also appeared as her attorney. On the first day of the trial he argued that a military commission had no right to try the alleged assassins. General Thomas M. Harris, a member of the military commission, impugned Johnson's loyalty, however, and thereafter the Senator played only a small role at the trial. The principal witnesses against Mrs. Surratt were John M. Lloyd, Louis J. Weichmann, and the officers who arrested her on the 17th. The defense proved that Lloyd was drunk when he saw Mrs. Surratt on the 14th and that her eyesight was very poor (hence her inability, they claimed, to recognize Powell in the dim hallway). Booth had given Weichmann the money to rent the carriage on the 11th; Mrs. Surratt did not know anything about it. Weichmann, the defense argued, was so cozy with the conspirators that it was hard to believe he was not a part of the plot himself. Numerous witnesses, including Weichmann, testified to Mrs. Surratt's good moral character, and her Maryland relatives and neighbors testified that she had never shown any disloyalty to the Union. Nevertheless, the commission found her guilty and sentenced her to hang.

Lawyers learned of the sentence on July 6; Mrs. Surratt was to hang the next day. Feverish efforts to save her ensued. Five of the nine members of the military commission recommended clemency because of her age and sex. Anna Surratt tried to see President Johnson. Stephen A. Douglas's widow pleaded with the President to give the poor widow more time. And Lewis Powell stated that she knew nothing of the conspiracy. Johnson never saw the commission's recommendation for clemency—or claimed he did not. In later years a bitter dispute arose between Johnson and Judge Advocate General Joseph Holt, who swore he showed the recommendation to the President. Whatever the case, Mrs. Surratt was hanged on July 7.

In February 1869 Anna Surratt made a successful request for her mother's remains, and Mrs. Surratt is now buried in Mount Olivet Cemetery in Washington, D.C. The Surrattsville tavern became a private residence shortly after the war was over and remained such until 1965, when the Maryland National Capital Park and Planning Commission acquired it. Information on tours of the house, located south of Washington near Andrews Air Force Base, is available by writing the Surratt House, 9110 Brandywine Road, Clinton, MD 20735 (the name of Surrattsville was changed to Clinton shortly after Lincoln's assassination). The boarding house on H Street still stands.

SOURCES: Guy W. Moore's *The Case of Mrs. Surratt: Her Controversial Execution for Conspiracy in the Lincoln Assassination* (Norman: University of Oklahoma Press, 1954) is a well-written, well-documented, and lucid summary of Mrs. Surratt's case. David Miller DeWitt did the ground-breaking work on her case in *The Judicial Murder of Mary E. Surratt* (Baltimore: John Murphy & Co., 1895). See also Benn Pitman, ed., *The Assassination of President Lincoln and the Trial of the Conspirators*, (Cincinnati, Ohio: Moore, Wilstach & Baldwin, 1865) and Ben: Perley Poore, ed., *The Conspiracy Trial for the Murder of the President*, 3 vols. (Boston: J. E. Tilton, 1865–1866).

Surveying See CALHOUN, JOHN.

Swett, Leonard (1825–1889) Devoted Republican political lieutenant of Abraham Lincoln. Leonard Swett was born in Maine, served in an Indiana regiment in the Mexican War, and moved eventually to Bloomington, Illinois. There he practiced law and rode the Eighth Judicial Circuit with his Bloomington friend, Judge David Davis, who introduced him to Lincoln in 1849.

Swett joined the forces opposed to the Kansas-Nebraska Act in 1854 and worked unsuccessfully to gain Lincoln a seat in the United States Senate "by giving away all but senator" to other groups in the coalition. Setting the tone for his future devotion to Lincoln's political cause, Swett told him in December of 1854 to *"use me in any way you may think you can."* In 1856 Swett sought the Republican nomination for Congress from his district but lost it to Owen Lovejoy. The defeat, Lincoln said, "turned me blind." Realizing the extent of Lovejoy's support in the district, however, Lincoln discouraged disgruntled conservative Republicans from running an independent candidate against the hotly antislavery Lovejoy. In 1860 Swett contended with Norman B. Judd and Richard Yates for the Republican gubernatorial nomination in Illinois, but he lost again and eventually threw his support to the victorious Yates.

In 1860 Swett was, with his friend Davis, one of the leaders most active in gaining Lincoln's presidential nomination in Chicago. Swett promised supporters of William H. Seward and Simon Cameron that they would be treated fairly by Lincoln if they would work for him as their second choice. But he and Davis apparently did not, as some have alleged since, promise Cameron a place in the Cabinet without Lincoln's knowledge. Swett admitted that the Cameron forces had a "right" to apply for office for their leader through him and Davis, for they had been in close contact at the convention, but he told Lincoln that he was "annoyed" that "these applications of Cameron's friends are made so prominently through Judge Davis & myself." These were not the words, surely, of a man who had promised Cameron the job, though he mildly endorsed Cameron for the Cabinet.

After the election, Swett went to Washington, where in late December and January he kept Lincoln in touch with important developments at the Capital. Swett communicated with Seward, Thurlow Weed, and Cameron, reported on preparations for the inauguration, and warned repeatedly that secession was a serious problem which threatened to engulf Virginia and Maryland. In truth, he had become Seward's mouthpiece; he argued for a "strong" Cabinet for the crisis rather than a Cabinet which conciliated the various Republican factions. Translated into party realities, that meant a Cabinet of former Whigs whom Seward could dominate. His own views on the Cabinet were flexible, but he opposed any appointment for Norman Judd, his old rival in Illinois.

Apparently Swett sought only modest rewards for his own efforts, although he complained to Ward Hill Lamon in April that he was "quietly wearing out my old clothes" and trying "to pay the debts I have made this campaign." When his partner William Orme went to Washington to urge an office for Swett, Lincoln winced. Swett urged Davis's appointment to the Supreme Court so strongly that in August 1861 he suggested that Davis's appointment would satisfy those of his friends who thought he should get an appointment too. In November Lincoln gave Swett an army staff appointment that was later canceled.

In 1862 Swett ran for Congress against Lincoln's first law partner, John Todd Stuart. Stuart dodged the issue of the Emancipation Proclamation, but Swett, David Davis observed, "endorses it, and argues it, as right and

Leonard Swett. (Courtesy of the Lloyd Ostendorf Collection)

constitutional under the war power." Swett campaigned hard but found that when he visited homes "on the road the women want to know when the war is going to close." He protested the shipment of Southern Negroes to Illinois as tending "to degrade white labor," and pressure on the War Department ended the practice about 3 weeks before the election. Feeling that the war took Republican voters from the polls to the front, the Republicans lacked confidence; Davis thought Swett lacked organization and "plan of campaign." Swett lost, 11,443 to 12,808, and the New York *Times* termed it a "vote of want of confidence" in President Lincoln.

Davis urged Lincoln to give the next foreign appointment to the devoted Swett and was surprised and a little digusted when Swett gave up "his Peru Mission" in 1863 to go to California to dispossess the New Almaden Mine for the New York–based Quicksilver Mining Company. "He is crazy to make money," Davis said. Swett was guaranteed $10,000 and could earn more if he was successful. He also acted as Lincoln's agent to seize the mine for the United States, and he became, as Lincoln told him, "the single one" to urge dispossession by the United States. Clearly Swett's personal pecuniary interest in the mission clouded his judgment. Lincoln chose to rescind the earlier decision to dispossess the mine, and a compromise transferred the mine to the Quicksilver Mining Company. Swett speculated in mining stocks, basing his operations on insiders' information about the disposition of the mine, but lost heavily.

Swett was a delegate to the Baltimore convention which renominated Lincoln in 1864 and worked for Lincoln's reelection. In the summer he asked Lincoln for an appointment on the Pacific Rail Road Commission, if appropriate legislation passed Congress, and he sought permission for his partner Orme to deal in confiscated Southern cotton.

In 1865 Swett moved to Chicago and became a successful criminal lawyer. He moved with Davis into the Liberal Republican party in 1872 but returned to the Republican fold later.

Swett described his relationship to Lincoln in a long letter written to William H. Herndon in 1866. He pictured Lincoln as anything but "frank, guileless, and unsophisticated." Lincoln looked far into the future and calculated being right in the long run. The "House Divided" speech, for example, was wrong for the 1858 campaign for the Senate, but it looked great with the ultimate triumph of the antislavery movement. Lincoln conducted the war on "the theory that but one thing was necessary, and that was a united North." Therefore Lincoln "was a trimmer, and such a trimmer the world has never seen." He "would always give more to his enemies than he would to his friends." He was "certainly a very poor hater." He "always told enough only of his plans and purposes to induce the belief that he has had communicated all, yet he reserved enough to have communicated nothing." But he was a trimmer only in dealing with men; he "never trimmed his principles." Lincoln did not believe in "political combinations" and did nothing to "help himself" gain renomination in 1864, though he wanted the nomination badly, more so than in 1860.

SOURCES: Willard L. King's *Lincoln's Manager: David Davis* (Cambridge: Harvard University Press, 1960) contains a great deal of information on Swett and quotes frequently from Swett's letters. The New Almaden episode is well described in Milton H. Shutes, *Lincoln and California* ([Stanford] Stanford University Press, 1943). See Harry E. Pratt, "The Repudiation of Lincoln's War Policy—Stuart-Swett Congressional Campaign," *Journal of the Illinois State Historical Society*, XXIV (April 1931), 129–140. Swett's letters to Lincoln about the Senate in 1854 (December 22, 1854), Lincoln's using him (December 1854), and being annoyed by Cameron's men (November 30, 1860) are in the Abraham Lincoln Papers, Library of Congress. His letter to Herndon is reprinted in Paul M. Angle, ed., *Herndon's Life of Lincoln* (Cleveland, Ohio: World Publishing, 1965), pp. 425–433.

See also NEW ALMADEN MINE; SEWARD, WILLIAM HENRY; STUART, JOHN TODD; WASHBURNE, ELIHU BENJAMIN.

T

Taft, Horatio Nelson The father of the favorite playmates of Willie and Tad Lincoln in Washington. A Democrat from New York, Taft was appointed Chief Examiner in the Patent Office by President James Buchanan. Horatio N. Taft, Jr., known as "Bud," and Halsey Cook Taft, known as "Holly," were 12 and 8 years old, respectively, when the Civil War began. Willie Lincoln was 10 and Tad was 7. The four boys became inseparable playmates watched over on occasion by the Taft boys' older sister Julia, 16. After Willie Lincoln's death in 1862, Mrs. Lincoln did not invite the Taft boys to the White House, apparently out of a desire not to be reminded of her lost son.

Charles Sabin Taft, the Taft children's half brother, was a surgeon in Judiciary Square Hospital in Washington and, by chance, one of the first doctors to reach Lincoln's box after the President was shot at Ford's Theatre.

SOURCES: Julia Taft Bayne wrote a memoir, *Tad Lincoln's Father* (Boston: Little, Brown, 1931), which is a principal source for anecdotes about the Lincoln children in the White House.

Taney, Roger Brooke (1777–1864) Chief Justice of the United States Supreme Court while Lincoln was President. Taney is famed for his decision in *Dred Scott* v. *Sandford* (1857). Though he had freed his own slaves in 1818, this son of a Maryland planter felt that slavery was necessary as long as Negroes were in the United States. He identified provincially with the South; he even spurned Newport as a summer resort on the ground that the South's Old Point Comfort was just as good. By the 1850s he was acting the role of a desperate defender of the faith in the face of certain knowledge that the "Constitution will undoubtedly be trampled under foot, and the Union will be [one] of power & weakness, like the Union of England & Ireland, or Russia & Poland." He feared that the "South is doomed to sink to a state of inferiority, and the power of the North will be exercised to gratify their cupidity & their evil passions, without the slightest regard to the principles of the Constitution." He knew "that nothing but a firm united action, nearly unanimous in every state can check northern insult & northern aggression."

The Dred Scott decision, which declared Negroes incapable of United States citizenship and the Missouri Compromise line unconstitutional, outraged Republicans. Lincoln came to believe that Taney "might have first broached the doctrine" that "the Declaration of Independence has no application to the negro." Though none would have said it but a few years before, by 1860 "half the people of this nation . . . [were] taking man from his kind and placing him among the brutes." Lincoln immediately sided with the dissenting opinions of Benjamin R. Curtis and John McLean and accused Taney of "partisan bias" and of basing his decision on "assumed historical facts which are not really true." Within a year, he was accusing Taney of conspiring with Stephen A. Douglas, James Buchanan, and Franklin Pierce to nationalize slavery. In the Lincoln-Douglas Debates, he warned

Roger Brooke Taney. (Courtesy of National Portrait Gallery, Smithsonian Institution, Washington, D.C.)

that the next step would be a second Dred Scott decision declaring that the Constitution forbids the states from excluding slavery from their limits.

Taney swore Lincoln in as President on March 4, 1861, and within months, they came into inevitable conflict. The Chief Justice believed that "there is no rightful power to bring back by force the states into the Union." In May, as a circuit judge, Taney issued his *Ex parte Merryman* decision, which denied that the President could suspend the privilege of the writ of habeas corpus; only Congress could do that. Taney sent his opinion to the President but, as far as is known today, received no direct reply. An indirect one came in the President's message to Congress of July 4, 1861, in which Lincoln vowed not to let "the government itself go to pieces" for the sake of an overscrupulous interpretation of one law.

Since Taney thought forcing the states back into the Union unlawful, it followed naturally that he tended to interpret the war as military usurpation. Already by June 12, 1861, he could tell ex-President Franklin Pierce that "a peaceful separation, with free institutions in each section, is far better than the union of all the present states under a military government & a reign of terror— preceded too by a civil war with all its horrors, and which end as it may will prove ruinous to the victors as well as the vanquished." On January 1, 1862, he refused to make the customary call on the President at the opening of the Court's term. He prepared drafts of opinions (never delivered) which declared conscription and government notes used as legal tender unconstitutional. It was widely feared among Republicans that he was itching to declare the Emancipation Proclamation illegal. By the summer of 1863 he thought that the "supremacy of the military power over the civil seems to be established."

When Taney died on October 12, 1864, many Republicans expressed relief. Senator Henry Wilson said that Taney "never gave one cheering word nor performed one act to protect or save" the Union. George Templeton Strong said simply: "Better late than never." Lincoln attended brief services for Taney in Washington, but Attorney General Edward Bates was the only member of Lincoln's Cabinet to attend the funeral in Frederick, Maryland.

SOURCES: Carl Brent Swisher's *Roger B. Taney* (New York: Macmillan, 1935) is a sympathetic biography which should be balanced with Don E. Fehrenbacher's *The Dred Scott Case: Its Significance in American Law and Politics* (New York: Oxford University Press, 1978) and his "Roger B. Taney and the Sectional Crisis," *Journal of Southern History*, XLIII (November 1977), 555–566.

Tarbell, Ida Minerva (1857–1944) Popular Lincoln biographer. Ida M. Tarbell was born in rural Pennsylvania. She graduated from Allegheny College in 1880, one of only five women in that coeducational institution at that time. Hoping for a career in botany, she abandoned that hope first for teaching and then for journalism. She was the associate editor of *The Chautauquan* for 8 years and worked thereafter for *McClure's Magazine*. Samuel Sidney McClure got her interested in Lincoln and set her at work gathering Lincoln materials. She wrote hundreds of letters and combed the countryside while the magazine published appeals for Lincolniana. In 1895 and 1896 *McClure's* published a series of her articles on Lincoln's life to 1858. The articles doubled the magazine's circulation from 125,000 to 250,000 in a matter of months. Readers loved her new finds: photographs, Lincoln's first speech, letters on his early political and legal career, his first vote, and his surveys. In 1898 and 1899 she published a second series on his later career.

From the successful articles grew Miss Tarbell's *Early Life of Abraham Lincoln* (New York: S. S. McClure, 1896) and *The Life of Abraham Lincoln*, 2 vols. (New York: Doubleday & McClure, 1900), containing a nearly 200-page appendix of newly discovered documents. Later she wrote her more famous muckraking *History of the Standard Oil Company* (1904), but she never abandoned the Lincoln theme. She wrote children's books, including the popular *Boy Scouts' Life of Lincoln* (New York: Macmillan, 1921). In 1924 she added *In the Footsteps of the Lincolns* (New York: Harper and Brothers), a survey of the migrations of the Lincoln family from seventeenth-century Massachusetts to Illinois. A feminist, though an opponent of women's suffrage, she took special pains to improve the image of Nancy Hanks Lincoln by arguing that Nancy was legitimate and the descendant of a respectable old family.

Miss Tarbell wrote in the heyday of Frederick Jackson Turner's frontier thesis, which argued that the frontier

Far Right: Ida Minerva Tarbell with Louis A. Warren in 1932.

experience had made America a democratic nation. Although there is no evidence she read Turner's work, she was the first to stress the benefits Lincoln derived from his frontier heritage. New England writers like J. G. Holland had pictured Lincoln as triumphing over his primitive environment, and Westerners like Ward Hill Lamon and William H. Herndon had lived too near the frontier to romanticize it. Lamon thought of Lincoln as a "diamond glowing on the dunghill." By contrast Miss Tarbell celebrated the "delights and interests the country offers a child." "The horse, the dog, the ox, the chin fly, the plow, the hog," she wrote, "these companions of his youth became interpreters of his meaning, solvers of his problems in his great necessity, of making men understand and follow him." In this way she became Carl Sandburg's chief inspiration, for, as he said, Ida Tarbell made interesting what had seemed before "drab and miserable beyond the fact." She also revised the reputation of frontiersman Thomas Lincoln, Abraham's father, whom she described as a responsible middling citizen and property owner. Nathaniel W. Stephenson's review of *In the Footsteps of the Lincolns* in *The New Republic* of August 6, 1924, was entitled "A Bourgeois Lincoln," revealing the undercurrent of resistance to her views in the debunking 1920s. He also noted her increasing sentimentality, especially about Lincoln's religion.

Miss Tarbell was not altogether uncritical; she questioned the stories of Lincoln's vow against slavery in New Orleans, and his failing to show up for his wedding in 1841. She was willing to admit that the Lincoln-Berry store in New Salem sold liquor by the drink. However, she swallowed whole Henry Clay Whitney's spurious version of Lincoln's "Lost Speech," and she never completely rejected the Ann Rutledge romance.

A Democrat who worked for the election of Al Smith and Franklin D. Roosevelt, Miss Tarbell was among the first to begin the process of de-Republicanizing Lincoln. Republican orators exploited Lincoln's name she said, but in their true ideas "They have denied him at every point."

Ida Tarbell was essentially a popularizer. Still, she was responsible for numerous documentary discoveries. She pestered other Lincoln authors and Lincoln's living contemporaries for information, but she was generous and not at all contentious; she always encouraged the publication of opinions contrary to her own. She was the first of the modern biographers in at least one sense: she was not of the generation which knew Lincoln personally as Herndon, Lamon, John G. Nicolay, and John Hay had known him. And in her quest for documentary sources and in her willingness to foster debate, she may have pointed the way forward even more.

SOURCES: There is an excellent and sympathetic appraisal of Ida Tarbell's work on Lincoln in Benjamin P. Thomas's *Portrait for Posterity: Lincoln and His Biographers* (New Brunswick, N.J.: Rutgers University Press, 1947).

Tariff As a good Whig, Abraham Lincoln naturally took an interest in protective tariffs. His interest developed only after some experience in politics, however, and none of his earliest surviving political platforms and speeches mentions the issue. In 1842 he signed a petition to Congress that stated very well the position he would argue at length in the coming years:

> The undersigned citizens of Sangamon County of the State of Illinois, respectfully request Congress to establish by law a TARIFF of duties, so as to prevent excessive importations of goods, and excessive exportations of specie; to create a Home market for agricultural productions; a Home demand for the skill and industry of our people; to raise revenue enough to relieve the nation from debt and to support the government, and so to foster our manufactures as to make our nation PROSPEROUS in Peace and INDEPENDENT in War.

Congress repealed the compromise tariff of 1833 in that year, and Lincoln showed great concern. He stressed the tariff's importance as a source of government revenue (and indeed it was a key source), argued that the only alternative to it was unpopular taxation, and relegated the protective principle to a secondary position as a concession to political reality in agrarian Illinois. Lincoln noted that a tariff was easy and cheap to collect; he contrasted the few customs officers necessary with "assessors and collectors, going forth like swarms of Egyptian locusts, devouring every blade of grass and other green thing." He argued that the burden of tariff duties fell "almost entirely on the wealthy and luxurious few, while the substantial and laboring many who live at home, and upon home products, go entirely free." In this way, it was really only a tax on "foreign luxuries— fine cloths, fine silks, rich wines, golden chains, and diamond rings."

In the presidential campaign of 1844, which was waged in great part over the issue of expansion in Oregon and Texas, Lincoln stuck with the tariff issue. He apparently argued that, historically, real wages rose when tariffs were high. Two years later the Walker Tariff, passed during the Democratic Polk administration, drastically lowered tariff rates. His interest in the subject increased,

In Pennsylvania, as always, "protection to American industry" played a major role in Republican campaign items, like this fine print published in Philadelphia in 1860.

and he began to develop new arguments. In fragmentary notes written in this period he spurned economic theory (mostly free trade in Lincoln's day) for historical experience and in a sophisticated argument claimed that high tariffs lowered the cost of consumer goods by lowering the labor cost. Tariffs allowed the development of home industries and thus saved the "*useless* labor" of transporting products across the seas and gave the "*useful* labor" of production its full reward. Increased domestic manufacturing would increase the domestic market for farm products. Free trade would reduce the country to an impoverished economy, "cold and still as death." He began to stress the strictly economic benefits and left behind the nationalistic argument of older Whigs, like Henry Clay, who believed that tariffs were necessary for a strong, independent country.

Lincoln never really got to use those arguments. While he was Congressman (1847–1849), the subject was quiet. Lincoln thought that paying the national debt created by the Mexican War would make "a modification of the existing tariff indispensable," and, of course, he wanted to see the adjustment made "with a due reference to the protection of our home industry." But in the ensuing presidential campaign of 1848, Whigs studiously avoided economic issues, and Lincoln followed their lead this time.

As events turned out, the tariff issue was dead for a long time to come, and Lincoln became reluctant to revive it. The Republicans, in their party's infancy, could not afford to raise issues which reminded the former Democrats in the party of their differences from the former Whigs. In Connecticut on March 6, 1860, Lincoln said that the "old question of tariff," though important, "cannot even obtain a hearing"; for "whether we will or not, the question of Slavery is *the* question." Lincoln's views had "undergone no material change upon that subject," he told one correspondent, and his protariff record was important in tariff-mad Pennsylvania in the autumn election. But Lincoln did not speak out on the subject.

Nor did President Lincoln's annual messages mention the subject. The Republican-controlled Congress of the Civil War period, however, raised tariffs to unprecedented heights, and Lincoln could have his tariffs and keep his peace too.

SOURCES: On the subject of Lincoln and the tariff, G. S. Boritt is the outstanding authority. See his *Lincoln and the Economics of the American Dream* (Memphis: Memphis State University Press, 1978).

Taylor, Zachary (1784–1850) Twelfth President of the United States. Taylor was Lincoln's choice for the Presidency long before he was nominated in 1848. He had never participated in political life—indeed, like many professional military officers he had never voted—and movements to nominate him for the Presidency in 1846 "were generally put forth as being of a no-party character." Lincoln backed Taylor in 1847, well before Taylor finally wrote a letter in April 1848 saying that he was "a Whig but not an ultra Whig."

Lincoln candidly explained that he supported Taylor "not because I think he would make a better president than [Henry] Clay, but because I think he would make a better one than" any of the Democratic candidates, "one of whom is sure to be elected, if he is not." Lincoln's belief that the Mexican War was "unconstitutional and unnecessary" did not trouble him in supporting a candidate who was, "par excellence, the hero of the Mexican War." On the contrary, he thought it took the Democrats "on the blind side" and turned "the war thunder against them." "The war is now to them," he explained, "the gallows of Haman, which they built for us, and on which they are doomed to be hanged themselves." Lincoln claimed to derive his own view of the proper resolution of the war from Taylor's "defensive line policy": maintain a defensive line until Mexico sued for peace and take "some territory," but none "extending so far South, as to enlarge and agrivate the distracting question of slavery."

With little known of Taylor's principles except that the general was not an "ultra Whig," Lincoln even drafted notes for the principles on which Taylor should stand. Taylor should not revive the question of a national bank nor veto a bill to revive it in the unlikely event that Congress chose to do so. He should advocate adjusting the tariff to gain money to pay for the war debt, with an eye "to the protection of our home industry." And he should maintain the defensive line policy.

Lincoln took an extremely active role in the presidential campaign. He worked with a committee of members of Congress to frank thousands of speeches and documents, campaigned in Maryland and Delaware, made

Far Right: Justin Butterfield, portrait by Oskar Gross. (Courtesy of the Chicago Historical Society)

a speaking tour of Massachusetts, and returned to campaign in Illinois as well. A principal issue in the contest was Taylor's alleged lack of principles, and Lincoln's speech in the House of Representatives, July 27, 1848—known sometimes as the "military coattails" speech—addressed that issue with pungent humor. Answering Democratic charges that Whigs were trying to ride into office on the coattails of a military hero who stood for nothing, Lincoln noted the hypocrisy of such a charge from the party of Andrew Jackson. He belittled efforts to glorify the military career of Democratic nominee Lewis Cass in a famous passage which also belittled Lincoln's own limited military experience:

> By the way, Mr. Speaker, did you know I am a military hero? Yes sir; in the days of the Black Hawk war, I fought, bled, and came away. Speaking of Gen: Cass' career, reminds me of my own. I was not at Stillman's defeat, but I was about as near it, as Cass was to Hulls surrender; and, like him, I saw the place very soon afterwards. It is quite certain I did not break my sword, for I had none to break; but I bent a musket pretty badly on one occasion. If Cass broke his sword, the idea is, he broke it in de[s]peration; I bent the musket by accident. If Gen: Cass went in advance of me in picking huckleberries [whortleberries], I guess I surpassed him in charges upon the wild onions. If he saw any live, fighting indians, it was more than I did; but I had a good many bloody struggles with the musquetoes; and, although I never fainted from loss of blood, I can truly say I was often very hungry. Mr. Speaker, if I should ever conclude to doff whatever our democratic friends may suppose there is of black cockade federalism about me, and thereupon, they shall take me up as their candidate for the Presidency, I protest they shall not make fun of me, as they have of Gen: Cass, by attempting to write me into a military hero.

Lincoln also defended Taylor's seeming lack of principles—even though he had himself hoped the general would make a statement on the bank, the tariff, and the war—by saying that Taylor's principle was to be guided by the will of Congress. Taylor would not ram a platform down the people's throats or veto what the people wanted, as expressed by their elected representatives in Congress. Lincoln admitted that he did not know Taylor's stance on the Wilmot Proviso but said that he hoped and believed that Taylor would not veto it if it passed Congress. Uncertainty on this question with Taylor was better than the certainty of Cass's position: "new wars, new acquisitions of teritory and still further extensions of slavery." In his campaign speeches for Taylor, Lincoln stressed the futility of antislavery advocates' voting for a third party, a strategy which would be sure to elect Cass and thereby extend slave territory.

With Taylor's election, Lincoln had hopes of some influence in appointments to office. His hopes in regard to Illinois's greatest patronage plum, the commissionership of the General Land Office in Washington, a lucrative post with responsibilities and powers just below Cabinet level, were dashed. Though Taylor and his Home (Interior) Secretary Thomas Ewing were willing to offer him the office, Lincoln was already committed to support another Illinoisan, Cyrus Edwards. Lincoln would apply for the office himself only if it appeared that Illinois could get it in no other way. A rivalry between Edwards and another Illinois hopeful snarled the appointment, and on June 2, 1848, Lincoln became an active applicant when he heard that the choice now lay between him and Justin Butterfield of Chicago. The latter was Lincoln's "personal friend" but had gained an appointment from Whig President William Henry Harrison (even though other Illinoisans had campaigned harder for Harrison) and had "fought for Mr. Clay against Gen Taylor to the bitter end" while Lincoln was working hard for Taylor's nomination. Butterfield got the job, because he had the support of Ewing (Taylor left great powers of appointment to his Cabinet) and, ironically, Henry Clay, with whom the new administration needed good relations. As a consolation, Lincoln was offered the secretaryship and then the governorship of the Oregon Territory, both of which he turned down flatly. Lincoln told one correspondent that it would mortify him deeply to lose to Butterfield, but after it was all over, he said that he was "not greatly dissatisfied."

Lincoln was mildly critical of Taylor's conduct of office. He felt that he looked too weak in leaving appointments so completely to the Cabinet, and he complained that administration printing was allowed to go to the local Democratic paper. After Taylor died suddenly in 1850, Lincoln gave a eulogy in Chicago (July 25, 1850) which noted that Taylor learned that the "Presidency . . . is no bed of roses." Significantly, however, Lincoln expressed his fear that "the one *great* question of the day, is not now so likely to be partially acquiesced in by the different sections of the Union, as it would have been, could Gen. Taylor have been spared to us." Thus Lincoln apparently endorsed Taylor's intransigent opposition to what would become, after the President's death, the Compromise of 1850. Death had been much on Lincoln's mind at the time, for his son Edward had died less than 6 months before the eulogy. He concluded the speech by saying that the deaths of great men remind "us, that *we*, too, must die" and by quoting his favorite poem, "Oh, why should the spirit of mortal be proud?"

In the Alton debate with Stephen A. Douglas in 1858, Douglas accused Lincoln of cutting Henry Clay's throat in 1848 and abandoning Whig principles for the hope of electoral success with Taylor. But Whigs in as hopelessly Democratic states as Illinois saw how acutely the party needed to capture the Presidency for survival. Lincoln learned some lessons from Taylor's Presidency which he did not mention in his eulogy. The Whig theory of the Presidency as properly a weak office Lincoln embraced for the first time in defending Taylor. Though he never abandoned the idea altogether, Taylor's apparent weakness in the Land Office imbroglio did cool Lincoln's ardor for the idea a bit. And Taylor's weak partisanship strengthened Lincoln's realization that patronage must go to the party faithful to keep the party from falling apart.

SOURCES: See Holman Hamilton, *Zachary Taylor: Soldier in the White House* (Indianapolis: Bobbs-Merrill, 1951) and Donald W. Riddle, *Congressman Abraham Lincoln* (Urbana: University of Illinois Press, 1857).

See also CLAY, HENRY; PATRONAGE; PRESIDENCY, POWERS OF THE; WHIG PARTY.

Technology   *See* INVENTIONS.

Temperance   "He never drank whiskey or other strong drink—," recalled Abraham Lincoln's stepmother, "was temperate in all things, too much so, I thought sometimes." There is very little evidence to contradict that statement, and what there is indicates only that Lincoln tried alcoholic beverages in his youth and in the White House may have occasionally sipped wine at state dinners. Lincoln found it easy to be temperate because he simply had no taste for alcohol. William H. Herndon recalled Lincoln's saying, "I am entitled to little credit for not drinking because I hate the stuff. It is unpleasant and always leaves me flabby and undone."

Corroboration of Herndon's recollection can be found in Lincoln's address to the Washington Temperance Society of Springfield (February 22, 1842), in which he said: "In my judgement, such of us as have never fallen victims, have been spared more from the absence of appetite, than from any mental or moral superiority over those who have." This statement also gives evidence of an attitude which has generally endeared Lincoln to writers on the subject: his complete lack of self-righteousness. To be sure, he advocated temperance. He considered alcoholism a "bondage" to be "broken," a vile "slavery" to be "manumitted," and a "tyrant" to be "deposed." Its use brought "want," "disease," and "sorrow." He associated it, as eighteenth-century reformers had, with the triumph of "passions" over "Reason." Yet his reliance was always on "*persuasion*, kind, unassuming persuasion," rather than on denunciation of drunkards and dram-sellers or on prohibition by law. In the address before the Washington Temperance Society he took special pains to denounce the "old school" of temperance reform: "Too much denunciation against dram sellers and dram-drinkers was indulged in." He did not consistently vote for temperance measures as a member of the Illinois legislature, and he had no part in the prohibition agitation of the 1850s (called the "Maine Law" agitation in Lincoln's day because Maine passed the first law prohibiting the sale or consumption of alcoholic beverages in 1851). On January 24, 1853, Lincoln joined in requesting the publication of a discourse by the Reverend James Smith, which denounced the use of alcohol and recommended prohibition. But to advocate publishing the address was not necessarily to advocate prohibition, especially since Smith had become a close personal comforter of the Lincolns after the death of their son Edward.

In the Lincoln-Douglas Debate at Ottawa Douglas accused Lincoln of having been "a flourishing grocery keeper in the town of [New] Salem." A "grocery" sold liquor by the drink and required a tavern license; the Lincoln-Berry general store, like all such stores, sold liquor in larger quantities. A tavern license in the name of Lincoln and Berry was issued on March 6, 1833, but Lincoln may have quit the partnership before the store became a tavern. His name but not his signature appears on the license, and he denied the accusation in 1858. Lincoln's denial avoided self-righteousness ("I don't know as it would be a great sin") and indulged in humor ("It is true that Lincoln did work . . . in a small still house, up at the head of a hollow.").

In the White House, the Lincolns served wine at state dinners, but John G. Nicolay recalled that Lincoln "never drank" and that "the only qualification that could possibly be made on this last point is that he did sometimes at his own dinner-table, and especially at state dinners, sip a little wine; but even that in a merely perfunctory way, as complying with a social custom and not as doing it from any desire or initiative or habit of his own."

SOURCES: William H. Townsend's *Lincoln and Liquor* (New York: Press of the Pioneers, 1934) is definitive. See also Helen Nicolay, *Lincoln's Secretary: A Biography of John G. Nicolay* (New York: Longmans, Green and Co., 1949). The controversial tavern keeper's bond is in the Illinois State Historical Library, Springfield.

"Ten Percent" Plan   *See* PROCLAMATION OF AMNESTY AND RECONSTRUCTION.

Texas Annexation   "[I]ndividually, I never was much interested in the Texas question," Lincoln told Williamson Durley on October 3, 1845. Lincoln had made a speech on May 22, 1844, expressing "the opinion, that Annexation at this time upon the terms agreed upon by [President] John Tyler was altogether inexpedient." He scoffed that the Democrats spoke of "nothing but Texas" in the campaign of 1844; he avoided discussing the issue and much preferred discussing the tariff.

Inasmuch as slavery already existed in Texas, Lincoln could not see how "annexation would augment the evil of slavery. . . . slaves would be taken there in about equal numbers, with or without annexation." On the other hand, he "never could see much good to come of annexation; inasmuch, as they [Texas] were already a free republican people on our own model." Even if more slaves were taken to Texas as a result of annexation, "still there would be just so many the fewer left, where they were taken from."

When Congressman Lincoln arrived in Washington in December 1847 to assume his seat in the House of Representatives, the annexation of Texas was no longer an issue. But the war that resulted from the annexation was a highly partisan issue, and Lincoln quickly joined his fellow Whigs in denouncing it. His opposition to the Mexican War hinged on the question of the location of the boundary between Texas and Mexico. In his famed "spot resolutions" of December 22, 1847, he took issue with President James K. Polk's contention that Mexico started the war "by invading the teritory of the State of Texas, striking the first blow, and shedding the blood of our *citizens* on *our own soil*." On January 12, 1848, Lincoln delivered his maiden speech in the House. In it he admitted that the boundary between

Texas and Mexico was a matter of dispute; Texas claimed the Rio Grande River, and Mexico, the Nueces. Lincoln said that the actual boundary was not a matter of mere claims one way or another but of the "actual *exercise* of jurisdiction"—that was "the very class or quality of evidence we want." Texas did exercise jurisdiction *beyond* the Nueces but not *to* the Rio Grande. Since no treaty had fixed the boundary, Texas's right rested "on revolution." In Lincoln's view, "just so far as she carried her revolution, by obtaining the *actual*, willing or unwilling, submission of the people, *so far*, the country was hers, and no farther." Lincoln's earlier resolutions clearly implied that General Zachary Taylor had encamped in a Mexican settlement on the east bank of the Rio Grande which had never "submitted themselves to the government or laws of Texas, or of the United States, by *consent*, or by *compulsion*, either by accepting office, or voting at elections, or paying taxes, or serving on juries, or having process served upon them, or *in any other way*." In fact, the peaceful Mexican settlement fled before the American Army, "leaving unprotected their homes and their growing crops." Zachary Taylor's Fort Brown "was built by that army, within a Mexican cotten-field, on which . . . a young cotton crop was growing and which crop was wholly destroyed." When the Mexicans "captured Capt. Thornton and his command," the incident which started the war, it was "within another Mexican field" and not in Texas at all.

Lincoln was precise about the boundary question, and he even wrote Horace Greeley, editor of the New York *Tribune*, to correct Greeley's assertion that "All Whigs . . . contended it [the boundary] stopped at the Nueces." Lincoln repeated "that the boundary of Texas extended just so far as American settlements taking part in her revolution extended; and that as a matter of fact those settlements did extend, at one or two points, beyond the Nueces, but not anywhere near the Rio Grande at any point."

See also MEXICAN WAR; STEPHENS, ALEXANDER HAMILTON.

Thanksgiving Proclamation Abraham Lincoln is generally credited with beginning the regular national observance of Thanksgiving on the last Thursday in November (set by Congress as the fourth Thursday in November in 1941). Much of the credit, however, should go to Sarah Josepha Hale, editor of the popular women's magazine, *Godey's Lady's Book*. She had long desired an annual day of national thanksgiving, and letters from her prompted two of Lincoln's nine proclamations of fasting, prayer, or thanksgiving.

Lincoln first proclaimed a national "day of humiliation, prayer and fasting" for "the last Thursday in September" on August 12, 1861, in response to a request from "a joint Committee of both Houses of Congress." He ordered government departments closed for a local day of thanksgiving on November 28, 1861. On April 10, 1862, he asked Americans to give thanks for recent "signal victories" at their next weekly worship. In response to a request from the Senate, Lincoln, on March 30, 1863, proclaimed "a day of national humiliation, fasting and prayer" for Thursday, April 30, 1863. Less than 2 weeks after the Battle of Gettysburg, Lincoln proclaimed "a day for National Thanksgiving, Praise and Prayer" for Thursday, August 6, 1863.

On September 28, 1863, Mrs. Hale wrote the President, suggesting *"a National and fixed Union Festival."* On October 3 Lincoln issued a proclamation "to set apart . . . the last Thursday of November next, as a day of Thanksgiving and Praise." This, the most famous of the proclamations, was written not by Lincoln but by William H. Seward. Gideon Welles noted in his diary on October 3 that Seward "read me the draft of a proclamation for Thanksgiving. I complimented the paper as very well done, and him for his talent in the preparation of such papers, which pleased him." John G. Nicolay wrote John Hay on April 1, 1864, saying that "the Mss. of the President's Thanksgiving Proclamation, which was written by Seward and is in his handwriting" had been sent to New York to be sold at a Sanitary Fair. Since the sale, the original document has disappeared.

On May 9, 1864, Lincoln called for "common thanksgiving and prayer" for recent successful army operations. On July 7, 1864, he proclaimed, at the request of the Senate and House of Representatives, "a day of national humiliation and prayer" for the first Thursday in August. He issued his last thanksgiving proclamation on October 20, 1864, again setting aside the last Thursday in November. Mrs. Hale had sent Seward a reminder on October 9 that the President should issue such a proclamation.

Sarah Josepha Hale

British cartoonist Matt Morgan saw Lincoln's Proclamation of Thanksgiving in 1863 as hypocritical. John Bull chides Lincoln: "Don't you think you had better wash off your war-paint before going to church, friend?"

Thirteenth Amendment

These documents have assumed great importance as sources for Lincoln's religious ideas, but their significance is exaggerated. Over half were written in response to demands for such days by others. The most important was certainly written by Seward for Lincoln. Indeed, the importance of an *annual* Thanksgiving to Lincoln is uncertain, as he nowhere mentioned the subject and had to be reminded by Sarah Hale in 1864, even after designating the last Thursday in November the year before. None of his proclamations called explicitly for an annual day of thanksgiving. Only one of the proclamations in Lincoln's handwriting exists today; and given Seward's role in drafting formal state papers, the authorship of the others should at least be closely examined. Of course, Lincoln signed them all, and they cannot be dismissed as unrelated to him.

Whatever their origin and authorship, the proclamations are remarkable for their lack of self-righteousness, their ability to see the war as an affliction for *national* sins, and their admission of national faults even in the midst of a grave crisis calling for extreme patriotism.

SOURCES: See J. G. Randall's "Lincoln and Thanksgiving," *Lincoln Herald*, XLIX (October 1947), 10–13.

Thirteenth Amendment The constitutional amendment that abolished slavery in the United States did not pass in Lincoln's lifetime. Though the Constitution had not been amended since 1804, Republicans introduced a resolution late in 1863 to amend it to end "slavery . . . except as a punishment for crime . . . within the United States." Requiring a two-thirds vote, it passed the Senate, 38 to 6, on April 8, 1864, but failed in the House, 93 to 65, on June 15, 1864. Only four Democrats in the lower house voted for it.

Even before the failure of the resolution in the House, Lincoln told Edwin D. Morgan, chairman of the Republican National Committee, to be sure that the antislavery amendment was a part of the party's platform. Lincoln ran for the Presidency in 1864 on that plank. This distinguished the Republicans sharply from the Democrats, who said nothing about slavery. Lincoln insisted that the amendment would help end the war because the Confederacy would no longer be able to look to the slaveholding Border States as possible allies.

Lincoln carried enough Republicans with him in the election to assure passage of the amendment resolution by the Thirty-ninth Congress. However, the Thirty-eighth Congress, which had already rejected it, had yet another session after his election. Lincoln pursued the resolution's passage by that same body. His annual message of December 6, 1864, stressed that it was "only a question of *time*" when the amendment would pass. The "sooner the better," Lincoln urged. The "voice of the people now, for the first time" had been heard. The Congress owed "some deference . . . to the majority, simply because it is the will of the majority" in a time of crisis demanding "unanimity of action." The "common end" was "maintenance of the Union," and the majority had clearly indicated that the amendment was "among the means to secure that end."

Most scholars agree that the amount of effort Lincoln put behind the amendment is proof, if any be needed, of the sincerity of his antislavery convictions. Lincoln spoke personally to some wavering Democrats in January 1865 and probably traded patronage for changes of votes. New York Democrat Moses F. Odell, for example, changed his vote from no to yes and gained appointment as Navy Agent in New York City at the end of the session. Other Democrats, merely by bowing to the inevitable, had the chance to rid themselves of the incubus of appearing otherwise to support slavery. On January 31, 1865, thirteen Democrats changed their votes, and the resolution passed the House by more than a two-thirds majority (119–56).

Lincoln exuberantly signed the resolution on February 1—exuberantly and unnecessarily, for the Supreme Court had long ago ruled that such resolutions were binding without the President's signature. That night, Lincoln told serenaders that "this measure was a very fitting if not an indispensable adjunct to the winding up of the great difficulty." This would "remove all causes of disturbance in the future." Lincoln hoped that all "would bear him witness that he had never shrunk from doing all that he could to eradicate Slavery by issuing an emancipation proclamation." Yet the Proclamation fell "far short" of the amendment and might be questioned as to legality in peacetime. Whatever the Emancipation Proclamation's weakness, the amendment would be "a King's cure for all the evils."

Twenty states ratified before Lincoln's assassination, but ratification by three-fourths of the states was not achieved until December 18, 1865.

SOURCES: See J. G. Randall and Richard N. Current, *Lincoln the President: Last Full Measure* (New York: Dodd, Mead, 1955), pp. 298–321.

See also CONSTITUTION OF THE UNITED STATES; SLAVERY.

Thomas, Benjamin Platt (1902–1956) Lincoln biographer. Benjamin P. Thomas was born in Pemberton, New Jersey. He earned his bachelor's degree in 1924 from the Johns Hopkins University, where he majored in economics. After a brief and unhappy stint as a bond salesman, he returned to graduate school at Johns Hopkins and earned a doctorate in history in 1929. His dissertation subject was "Russo-American Relations, 1815–1867." He taught for 3 years at Birmingham-Southern College in Alabama. In 1932 Thomas became executive secretary of the Abraham Lincoln Association in Springfield, Illinois.

The principal duty of the Association's secretary was research and writing. Thomas published *Lincoln's New Salem* (Springfield, Ill.: Abraham Lincoln Association) in 1934. No study of that part of Lincoln's early life has superseded it. In 1936 the Association published his *Lincoln: 1847–1853*, part of a continuing project to describe Lincoln's whereabouts and actions on every day of his life. Searching for evidence of Lincoln's daily activities, Thomas discovered hundreds of Lincoln documents and references to Lincoln in grimy Illinois court

Benjamin Platt Thomas. (Courtesy of the Illinois State Historical Library)

houses long thought to have been exhausted as repositories of Lincolniana.

Thomas's wife, the former Salome Kreider of Springfield, whom he married in 1929, came from a family of substance. By 1936 Thomas had had his fill of detailed and thankless research, and he left the Association to manage property and sell insurance. He operated a large farm successfully. He eventually became president of the Springfield Chamber of Commerce.

In 1944 Thomas returned to history. Rutgers University Press published his *Portrait for Posterity: Lincoln and His Biographers* (1947), which carefully assessed the contributions of the major Lincoln biographers from J. G. Holland to J. G. Randall. Thomas's book is still the basic source on the subject. His treatment of many individual works—those of John G. Nicolay and John Hay, of William E. Barton, and of Ida M. Tarbell, for example—is the best in print. But his decision to divide the authors into "realists" and "romanticists" was unfortunate, and it underrated the importance of modern methods of historical research in distinguishing the contributions of various authors. William E. Barton, for example, was the "first of the modern, thoroughgoing realists" for Thomas, but today he appears much more to have been the last of the great amateurs of the gentleman-*literatus* type.

The year 1950 saw the appearance of Thomas's *Theodore Weld: Crusader for Freedom* (New Brunswick, N.J.: Rutgers University Press). Poor sales convinced him never to write on another obscure figure and led him back to the Lincoln theme. Thomas wrote *Abraham Lincoln: A Biography* (New York: Alfred A. Knopf, 1952) in about 2 years. It was a masterpiece and a nonfiction best seller; it was proclaimed by *Time* magazine as "the best one-volume life of Lincoln since Lord Charnwood's." Thomas used the recently opened Abraham Lincoln Papers at the Library of Congress and benefited from numerous monographs on special subjects written by the professional scholars of the twentieth century. His book showed none of the coolness toward Lincoln that some works by the Revisionist academic scholars of his generation had, but it retained the Revisionist hostility to the Radical Republicans. He gave the race question less attention than the scholars who came after him. The book was less notable for innovative interpretation than for elegant and balanced synthesis—digestion of the best research and rendering of it in fluid and readable style. It is still regarded, with Reinhard Luthin's *The Real Abraham Lincoln* and Stephen B. Oates's *With Malice Toward None: The Life of Abraham Lincoln*, as one of the three best one-volume biographies of Lincoln.

Thomas began work on a biography of Edwin M. Stanton, but he discovered in 1956 that he had cancer of the throat and committed suicide.

SOURCES: See Paul M. Angle's "To the Memory of Benjamin Platt Thomas: 1902–1956" in his book *On a Variety of Subjects* (Chicago: Chicago Historical Society and The Caxton Club, 1974). Harold M. Hyman completed Thomas's biography, *Stanton: The Life and Times of Lincoln's Secretary of War* (New York: Alfred A. Knopf, 1962). The Modern Library keeps Thomas's wonderful Lincoln biography in print in an inexpensive edition.

Tobacco See PHYSICAL CHARACTERISTICS.

Todd Family See LINCOLN, MARY TODD.

Tomb, The Lincoln Located in Oak Ridge Cemetery, Springfield, Illinois; one of the most frequently visited Lincoln sites. A group of Illinois citizens formed the National Lincoln Monument Association shortly after Lincoln's death in April 1865, to make arrangements for his burial. The directors of the Association included several of Lincoln's personal associates, among them Richard J. Oglesby (president), John Todd Stuart, Jesse K. Dubois (vice president), and James C. Conkling. They quickly arranged for the construction of a temporary vault in the center of Springfield to hold the President's remains after their arrival from Washington and before the monument was finished. Mrs. Lincoln objected to the location even as a temporary resting place and insisted that her husband's remains rest at suburban Oak Ridge Cemetery.

When Lincoln's body came to Springfield, it rested first in the public receiving vault of Oak Ridge Cemetery on ground since purchased for the Illinois State Capitol. The directors still hoped to build a monument on the site of the first temporary vault, but Mrs. Lincoln remained adamant; and on June 14 the board voted to build at Oak Ridge. Before the end of the year a temporary vault at Oak Ridge was completed (to make possible the removal from the receiving vault). When Lincoln's

The Lincoln Tomb

remains were transferred, six of his associates viewed the remains to verify the identity of the corpse. Edward Baker Lincoln's remains were exhumed and placed in the vault with his father's body and that of his brother William Wallace Lincoln, which had come from Washington on the long funeral journey.

In 1868 the Association offered $1000 for the best design for a tomb. Of the many designs submitted, including plans by Leonard W. Volk, Thomas D. Jones, and Vinnie Ream, who had previously sculpted Lincoln likenesses, the board chose the design of Larkin G. Mead, a sculptor from Brattleboro, Vermont. Work on the monument began in 1869. The partially completed tomb received Thomas "Tad" Lincoln's remains after his death in July of 1871. In September President Lincoln's remains were transferred, his wooden casket replaced with a metal one, and the corpse once again viewed and identified. The tomb was finished that year, but the bronze Lincoln statue was not added until 1874.

Before funds were raised to add the last of the four bronze military groups on the tomb, a bizarre plot to steal Lincoln's corpse was discovered. Thieves planned to exchange Lincoln's body for the release of counterfeiter Benjamin Boyd from Joliet prison. A detective named Lewis C. Smegles, who had infiltrated the group, revealed the plot to the authorities. After that sensational event in 1876, Springfield citizens formed the Lincoln Guard of Honor to protect the remains as well as to conduct exercises on memorial days.

Mrs. Lincoln's body came to the tomb in 1882. Lincoln's remains were identified again in 1887 and in 1901. In 1895 the National Lincoln Monument Association gave the tomb to the State of Illinois, which provided a custodian. It was in bad repair and suffering from the faults of a poor original foundation. The state rebuilt all of the tomb but the shaft in 1900–1901 and increased the height of the shaft from the original 98 to 135 feet. Around the time of the centennial of Lincoln's birth, attendance at the tomb increased dramatically. The original monument contained a museum of Lincoln relics and curios which the state removed in a 1931 remodeling which turned the museum area into a more dignified reception area.

SOURCES: A visit to the Lincoln tomb is an appropriate conclusion to a day of visiting the many Lincoln sites in Springfield. A detailed history of the tomb and the plot to steal Lincoln's body is in John C. Power's works: *Abraham Lincoln: His Great Funeral Cortege, . . . With a History . . . of the National Lincoln Monument* (Springfield, Ill.: privately printed, 1872); *Abraham Lincoln: His Life, Public Services, Death and Great Funeral Cortege with a History . . . of the National Lincoln Monument* (Chicago: H. W. Rokker, 1889); and *History of an Attempt to Steal the Body of Abraham Lincoln . . .* (Springfield, Ill.: H. W. Rokker, 1890). See also Louis A. Warren, "The Plot to Steal the Lincoln Corpse," *Lincoln Lore*, Number 792 (June 12, 1944) and R. Gerald McMurtry, "The Attempt to Steal Lincoln's Body," *Lincoln Lore*, Number 1609 (March 1972), pp. 1–2, and "Viewing Lincoln's Remains," *Lincoln Lore*, Number 1611 (May 1972), pp. 2–3.

Trailor Murder Case On June 2, 1841, Archibald Fisher disappeared, not long after being seen in Springfield in the company of the Trailor brothers, Archibald, Henry, and William. Springfield citizens searched the area for Fisher's body but could not find it. After questioning, Henry Trailor confessed that his brothers had killed Fisher and that he had helped them dispose of the body in a pond. William and Archibald Trailor were charged with murder, and they retained Abraham Lincoln, Edward D. Baker, and Stephen T. Logan as defense counsel.

The trial began on June 18, and the defense produced only one witness, Dr. Robert Gilmore, who testified that Fisher was alive and residing in Gilmore's home at that very moment! The doctor said that Fisher suffered from periodic blackouts and could give no account of his whereabouts at the time of his disappearance. The defendants were acquitted. When Fisher came to Springfield later, he could give no explanation of the events. Lincoln had to sue to obtain his fee of $100 from William Trailor. As Lincoln said in 1846, "Much of the matter remains in mystery to this day."

SOURCES: See John J. Duff, *A. Lincoln: Prairie Lawyer* (New York: Rinehart, 1960); Paul M. Angle, *"Here I Have Lived": A History of Lincoln's Springfield, 1821–1865* (New Brunswick, N.J.: Rutgers University Press, 1935); and Roger W. Barrett, *A Strange Affair* (n.p.: privately printed, 1933).

Trent Affair A diplomatic crisis which nearly brought England to war with America. The affair began on November 8, 1861, when Captain Charles D. Wilkes, commander of the U.S.S. *San Jacinto*, captured two Confederate envoys, James M. Mason and John Slidell, aboard the British mail-packet, the *Trent*. Wilkes acted entirely without orders in removing the two envoys and their secretaries bound for England and France and bringing them back as prisoners to the United States. The act outraged British public opinion and certainly violated international law as the British government interpreted it: Wilkes could interfere with neutral shipping on the ground that it contained contraband of war only if he brought the *Trent* into port to be judged in an admiralty court. The British government demanded that the envoys be surrendered, and it made preparations for war. France backed England's demands completely.

The American reaction at first was to lionize Wilkes and cheer his defiance of John Bull. The Lincoln administration, however, maintained a studied silence. Only Navy Secretary Gideon Welles commended Wilkes's action in a public letter. Privately, Attorney General Edward Bates expressed his opinion that it was legal according to British precedents. Lincoln did not mention the crisis in his annual message to Congress in December. On the 18th of that month, the British ultimatum arrived. A week later, the President and Cabinet met to consider their response.

Inexperienced in foreign affairs, wanting to avoid a disastrous war with England, but fearful of public wrath if the administration appeared to back down in the face of a British threat, Lincoln favored ultimate arbitration by a neutral foreign power or powers. Apparently influenced by a letter from liberal John Bright, practically the only prominent British apologist for the United States in the crisis, the President wished to be heard by the British government and to submit any remaining differences to binding arbitration. The United States was "willing to make reparation" for an act done by an officer "without orders from, or expectation of, the government." That solution lacked the crucial speediness necessary to answer the complaint fully: England demanded an answer by December 30.

Secretary of State William H. Seward, alone of the Cabinet members, had an answer ready. He was prepared "cheerfully" to give the prisoners up. Seizing on the legal arguments of the British, Seward was willing to say that Wilkes had inadvertently broken a law by taking the men without also seizing the ship as a prize. Still, as he had studied his answer, Seward had been dogged by the fear of acceding to a British demand in the face of American public opinion. Charles Francis Adams, however, had given him a welcome solution. The learned minister to the Court of Saint James, by pointing to American protests of British violations of neutrality at sea during the Madison administration, showed Seward that by siding with Britain in this affair he was actually defending traditional American doctrines of the freedom of the seas. Salmon P. Chase and Bates, originally unwilling to surrender the envoys, were alarmed by the unanimity of British opinion and by France's siding firmly with Britain. The Cabinet and President agreed to Seward's suggestion on December 26, though Lincoln and some officers showed considerable anxiety about the effect on American opinion. Seward informed the British minister the next day. The British government, although it disagreed with much of the legal reasoning of Seward's dispatch, found the answer acceptable.

SOURCES: Norman B. Ferris's *The Trent Affair: A Diplomatic Crisis* (Knoxville: University of Tennessee Press, 1977) gives a lucid narrative of the crisis and is definitive.

Trial of the Assassins On May 1, 1865, President Andrew Johnson ordered the formation of a nine-man military commission to try the conspirators to assassinate President Lincoln and other government officers. The actual events of the trial (May 10 to June 30, 1865) have always been somewhat obscured by this single fact: though the civil courts were open, the civilians who allegedly conspired to assassinate the President and others were tried in a military court—before Army officers rather than civil judges and without a jury. The Supreme Court decision in *Ex parte Milligan* the next year would make any such trial illegal, but in 1865 the atmosphere of war made the military commission seem proper to many. To be sure, it had its critics, even among Republicans and close associates of Lincoln. Edward Bates protested the decision vigorously, and Orville Hickman Browning thought it clearly illegal. Gideon Welles and Hugh McCulloch preferred a civil trial also. Montgomery Blair, however, accepted its legality.

Secretary of War Edwin M. Stanton, having won crucial approval from Attorney General James Speed, managed to push through the idea of a military trial. President Johnson was persuaded, too. They wanted speedy proceedings and no leniency toward the conspirators—in part from fear of Radical Republican wrath. The real driving force behind the idea was Judge Advocate General Joseph Holt, a fierce and talented Unionist from Kentucky. The argument was simple: the conspirators killed the Commander in Chief. Holt wanted the tribunal to be entirely secret as well, but a storm of newspaper protests caused Stanton to overrule Holt on that point and allow limited access, record keeping, and eventual publication of officially approved transcripts of the trial. Navy Secretary Welles thought that the elimination of secrecy removed the most objectionable aspect of the proceeding.

Next to the very existence of the military commission, the most objectionable feature of the trial was the indictment, the theory of the prosecution. On May 2 President Johnson issued a proclamation for the arrest of former Confederate agents in Canada, Jacob Thompson, Clement C. Clay, Beverly Tucker, George N. Sanders, and William C. Cleary, for conspiring with Jefferson Davis to assassinate Lincoln and other United States officials. The sincerity of the prosecution, led by Judge Advocate General Holt with John A. Bingham and H. L. Burnett, immediately appeared doubtful. Jefferson Davis was arrested on the day of the tribunal's first meeting, yet he was imprisoned in Fortress Monroe and not brought to Washington to stand trial with his alleged coconspirators. Stanton and the President thought the evidence pointed to a Confederate conspiracy, but Holt held the idea most deeply of all and was led to accept the testimony of a notorious liar, Sanford Conover, who

This rare cartoon, published on June 7, 1865, in Washington, associated the defendants (the alleged assassins) with Jefferson Davis, following the theory of the prosecution. (Library of Congress)

claimed to be able to link the Confederates to Booth's plot. Conover was later convicted of perjury, and a group of witnesses whom he had instructed confessed to lying for government money. A substantial number of prosecution witnesses testified about Confederate war crimes, but the starving Union prisoners of Andersonville had absolutely nothing to do with John Wilkes Booth. Conversely, while the prosecution pursued the will-o'-the-wisp of Jefferson Davis's instigation of the murder, it ignored obvious witnesses and criminals, including those who had helped Booth escape and hide in Virginia.

The questionable nature of the military court itself and the wrongheaded prosecution theory made the trial by far the poorest follow-up to a Presidential assassination in American history. The defendants—George A. Atzerodt, David E. Herold, Lewis Thornton Powell (called by an alias, "Payne," throughout the proceedings), Mary E. Surratt, Samuel B. Arnold, Michael O'Laughlin (or O'Laughlen), Edman Spangler, and Samuel A. Mudd—were allowed civilian counsel (W. E. Doster for Powell and Atzerodt; Frederick Stone for Herold and Mudd; Walter S. Cox for O'Laughlin; Thomas Ewing, Jr., for Arnold, Spangler, and Mudd; Frederick A. Aiken for Mrs. Surratt and Spangler). Maryland Senator Reverdy Johnson also appeared for Mrs. Surratt, but the commission challenged his loyalty, and he chose not to harm his client by appearing further. His argument against the commission's jurisdiction was later read by another lawyer. The lawyers faced the military commission composed of David Hunter, Lew Wallace, August V. Kautz, Alvin P. Howe, Robert S. Foster, James A. Ekin, T. M. Harris, C. H. Tompkins, and David R. Clendenin.

There was no good way to defend Herold, Atzerodt, and Powell, who were doomed from the start and very likely knew it. Arnold and O'Laughlin were surely in on the abduction plot but just as surely not in on the assassination. The only doubt concerning Spangler's innocence sprang from testimony indicating he cleared Booth's escape route from the theater and hid the assassin's identity. Doctor Mudd and Mrs. Surratt, about whose guilt or innocence controversy rages to this day (with the heavy preponderance of opinion in their favor), seemed questionable on only two points. Mudd may have recognized Booth when he set his leg and may have been slow to tell authorities that Herold and Booth had slept in his house. Mrs. Surratt, convicted on the testimony of Louis J. Weichmann and John M. Lloyd, carried a package (useful later for Booth's escape) to the Surrattsville tavern for Booth on the day of the assassination. Mudd and Surratt seemed to have some chance of being acquitted. However, Mrs. Surratt's cause was hurt by the failure of her son John, Booth's closest associate in the abduction conspiracy, to come out of hiding to save her; her fate was hostage to his surrender. And Mudd proved to be suspiciously uncooperative under interrogation.

The government's case rested on obscuring the fact that there were two plots: the first to kidnap and the second to assassinate. The prosecution, therefore, had no desire to produce Booth's memorandum book, which dated the assassination idea as of April 14. The defense was remiss in not demanding it, for newspapers in New York had noted its capture.

On June 30, 1865, the military commission found all guilty of conspiring with the Confederates enumerated in Johnson's proclamation to murder Lincoln, Johnson, Seward, and Grant. Powell, Atzerodt, Herold, and Mrs. Surratt were to hang; O'Laughlin, Arnold, and Mudd were sentenced to life imprisonment at hard labor; and Spangler was given 6 years at hard labor. Five members of the commission recommended that the President commute Mrs. Surratt's sentence to life imprisonment. Johnson thought her guilty and denied that sex was any bar to hanging, but he claimed that Holt never showed him the recommendation for clemency. The sentences were carried out, though Spangler, Arnold, and Mudd were pardoned by Johnson in 1869.

The trial gained more critics when, 2 years later, a civil trial of John H. Surratt resulted in a hung jury.

SOURCES: David Miller DeWitt denounced the trial with eloquent invective in *The Assassination of Abraham Lincoln and Its Expiation* (New York: Macmillan, 1909) and in other books—from which assault defenders of the trial have never fully recovered. Benjamin P. Thomas and Harold M. Hyman, in *Stanton: The Life and Times of Lincoln's Secretary of War* (New York: Alfred A. Knopf, 1962), lay the bulk of the blame for the excesses of the trial on Holt rather than Stanton. Benn Pitman, the official recorder, called his *Assassination of President Lincoln and the Trial of the Conspirators* (Cincinnati, Ohio: Moore, Wilstach & Baldwin, 1865) "a great heap of rubbish." Ben: Perley Poore's *The Conspiracy Trial for the Murder of the President,* 3 vols. (Boston, J. E. Tilton, 1865) is likewise edited defensively for the reputation of the prosecution. Nevertheless, they give the substance of the cases for both sides.

See also ARNOLD, SAMUEL BLAND; ATZERODT, GEORGE A.; FORT JEFFERSON; HEROLD, DAVID EDGAR; HOLT, JOSEPH; LLOYD, JOHN MINCHIN; MUDD, SAMUEL ALEXANDER; O'LAUGHLIN (OR O'LAUGHLEN) MICHAEL; POWELL, LEWIS THORNTON; SPANGLER, EDMAN ("EDWARD"); SURRATT, JOHN HARRISON, JR.; SURRATT, MARY E.; WEICHMANN, LOUIS J.

Truett Murder Case The Truett case provided Lincoln with his most famous courtroom confrontation with Stephen A. Douglas. The murder occurred in Spottswood's Hotel in Springfield on March 7, 1838. There Henry B. Truett, Register of the United States Land Office in Galena, accused Dr. Jacob M. Early of writing a set of resolutions adopted at a Democratic meeting in Peoria which condemned Truett's conduct of the office and called for his removal. Early refused to answer the charge; Truett threatened him with a pistol; the doctor picked up a chair to protect himself; and Truett shot and killed him. Truett was indicted for murder on March 14.

The murder capped a long political feud. Truett, the son-in-law of William L. May, had gained his office through May's influence. May, however, became disaffected from the Democratic party because of President Martin Van Buren's fiscal policies, and the party wreaked its vengeance on Truett. Early, a warm Democrat, had challenged Ninian W. Edwards to a duel in 1836 and had been having sharp disagreements with Simeon Francis, editor of Springfield's Whig newspaper.

Douglas assisted the prosecutor in the trial, and Truett engaged five Whig lawyers to defend him: Lincoln, Edward D. Baker, John Todd Stuart, Stephen Trigg Logan, and Cyrus Walker.

The trial began on October 8, 1838. Logan's defense of Truett stressed Early's greater size and the threat presented by his wielding a chair. Lincoln made the summation to the jury. Logan characterized it as "short but strong and sensible." The verdict was "not guilty."

Thomas Ford, the able contemporary historian of Illinois, noted that in this early period "in all cases of murder arising from heat of blood or in a fight, it was impossible to convict. The juries were willing enough to convict an assassin, or one who murdered by taking a dishonorable advantage, but otherwise if there was a conflict and nothing unfair in it."

SOURCES: See Harry E. Pratt, "Abraham Lincoln's First Murder Trial," *Journal of the Illinois State Historical Society*, XXXVII (September 1944), 242–249.

Trumbull, Lyman (1813–1896) A political associate of Lincoln's. The descendant of a distinguished Connecticut family, Lyman Trumbull moved from his birthplace, Colchester, Connecticut, to the South in 1833. Admitted to the bar in Georgia, he moved in 1837 to Belleville, Illinois, where he practiced law and became an active Democrat. In 1840 he ran successfully for the lower house of the Illinois General Assembly and a year later had charge of a bill increasing the size of the Illinois Supreme Court which Abraham Lincoln bitterly opposed. As a Democrat from the southern part of the state, Trumbull opposed building the Illinois and Michigan Canal and fought the Illinois State Bank, both of which were championed by Lincoln.

Though political opponents, both men moved in the same social circles in Springfield. When Trumbull married Julia Jayne in 1843, Mrs. Lincoln was a bride's attendant. In 1846 Lincoln defended Trumbull before the Illinois Supreme Court from a suit to recover $400 which Trumbull had withheld as his fee for work performed on a digest of state laws while he was the Illinois Secretary of State (1841–1843).

Trumbull was a stanch Democrat who was identified with free trade, hard money, and opposition to all banks. He supported the Mexican War with gusto. However, he disliked slavery and worked from the late 1830s on to end Illinois's system of Negro indenture, a form of voluntary servitude.

Twice elected to the Illinois Supreme Court, Judge Trumbull served for 5 years; he resigned his position in 1853 to resume private law practice. He reentered politics a year later because of opposition to Stephen A. Douglas's Kansas-Nebraska Act. "I am surprised at myself," he told his brother, "and but for the slavery question . . . I should not have taken any active part in recent elections." He was soon the most prominent Anti-Nebraska Democrat from southern Illinois. In 1854 Trumbull won election over a Douglas Democrat for a seat in the Illinois House and became associated with John M. Palmer, Norman B. Judd, and Burton C. Cook, other Anti-Nebraska Democrats.

In 1855 he resigned his seat to run for the Senate against incumbent Democrat James Shields and Whig Abraham Lincoln. When Joel Matteson gained strength as a Democratic candidate, Lincoln threw his support to Trumbull, who won on the tenth ballot in the Illinois General Assembly. Lincoln had no choice if the Anti-Nebraska forces were to win the seat, because five Anti-Nebraska Democrats, associates of Trumbull's, refused to vote for an Anti-Nebraska Whig. Mrs. Lincoln never forgave Mrs. Trumbull for her husband's refusal to support Lincoln in earlier balloting and developed a hatred for Trumbull's lieutenant, Norman Judd, as well. Lincoln's lieutenant, David Davis, likewise developed a hatred for Trumbull and Judd.

Lincoln himself cooperated with Trumbull thereafter to steer the Anti-Nebraska forces on a moderate course, and he avoided Owen Lovejoy's call to form a new party in Springfield in 1855. Trumbull knew that the border warfare in Kansas would draw moderates to a new coalition, and in May 1856 he supported the call for a convention in Bloomington to form the Republican party.

Trumbull shared with Lincoln not only a moderate Republicanism but also a strong opposition to Stephen A. Douglas. When Douglas became an opponent of the regular Democracy of President James Buchanan, Trumbull joined Lincoln in resisting Republican efforts to support Douglas's senatorial campaign of 1858. Both men thought Douglas was not genuinely antislavery, that his acceptance of the Dred Scott decision proved it, and that the Dred Scott decision could not rightfully "lay down political doctrines" for the nation. Though he always insisted on the importance of Republican principles, Trumbull was a politician and did not ask for trouble. In June 1858 he told Lincoln that the "platform is a good one, & perhaps covers enough." It would "not do, of course, to get mixed up with the free negro question, & . . . it will be best to say nothing about the admission or non-admission of any more slave states." Lincoln did not himself ask Trumbull to come to Illinois to help him in his campaign against Douglas in 1858, but Trumbull came at the request of others—apparently, whether from dislike of campaigning or lukewarmness for Lincoln, somewhat reluctantly.

Trumbull proved to be a valuable asset. He bothered Douglas particularly with a charge that the Little Giant had once deliberately struck a clause requiring the submission of a draft constitution for Kansas statehood to a vote of the people. Lincoln adopted that charge in his own famous debates with Douglas in the campaign. After Lincoln's loss, Trumbull assured him of the steadfastness of his support in the campaign. "I am so constituted as to be incapable of practicing disguise and deceit if I would," Trumbull said. Lincoln in turn affirmed his political alliance with Trumbull: "I do not for a

Lyman Trumbull

moment doubt that you, Judd, Cook, Palmer, and the republicans generally, coming from the old democratic ranks, were as sincerely anxious for my success in the late contest, as I myself.... I can not conceive it possible for me to be a rival of yours, or to take sides against you in favor of any rival."

Throughout 1859 Trumbull kept Lincoln abreast of developments in Washington and of Douglas's actions, reassuring Lincoln that Douglas was bound to remain a Democrat and was every day less intimate with Republicans in Congress. As an old Democrat, Trumbull could not entirely resist the allures of expansionism, and he told Lincoln he was "inclined not to place myself against the acquisition of Cuba under any and all circumstances." Lincoln replied that Cuba did not seem to be much of an issue in Illinois, and Trumbull could safely follow that course. By late 1859 Trumbull was convinced that the Republicans had "about all we ever will from the old Whig element in central Ill—We must hereafter rely upon obtaining accessions from the young men & from the Democracy."

Trumbull had antislavery views that were much like Lincoln's. He thought "negro slavery.... an evil" but "never contended for giving the negro equal privileges with the white man." Both men advocated colonization. Yet Trumbull was unenthusiastic about Lincoln's presidential prospects early in 1860. "When urging your claims," he told Lincoln on April 24, "I am almost always met with the remark, 'if you are going to nominate a man of that stamp why not take Seward?'... from the fact, I suppose, that you have both given expression to a similar sentiment in regard to the ultimate extinction of slavery." Trumbull thought Seward could not win the election, however, and he leaned toward aged John McLean. "I wish to be distinctly understood as first & foremost for you," Trumbull added. Lincoln confessed that the "taste *is* in my mouth a little." He thought McLean's age a serious if not debilitating factor, and he added

> A word now for your own special benefit. You better write no letters which can possibly be distorted into opposition, or quasi opposition to me. There are men on the constant watch for such things out of which to prejudice my peculiar friends against you. While I have no more suspicion of you than I have of my best friend living, I am kept in a constant struggle against suggestions of this sort. I have hesitated some to write this paragraph, lest you should suspect I do it for my own benefit, and not for yours; but on reflection I conclude you will not suspect me.

Trumbull ceased talking of other candidates than Lincoln.

Trumbull rejoiced at news of Lincoln's nomination ("Glory to God, the country is safe"), reported that Benjamin F. Wade considered the election "settled" with Lincoln's nomination, and noted that even Southern Senators like Judah Benjamin and Robert Toombs were impressed with Lincoln's conservatism, fairness, and candor. After Lincoln's election, Trumbull tried to discourage Seward's appointment to the Cabinet and was sharply opposed to Simon Cameron's appointment. He urged Salmon P. Chase for the Cabinet and thought Montgomery Blair "about the only Southern man of Democratic antecedents" acceptable as Secretary of War (and a Southerner in that post, he thought, would be politic). He also sought a Cabinet post for his old ally Norman Judd.

Trumbull opposed any compromise in the secession crisis; he was especially suspicious of the stamina of Republicans "from the commercial portions of the country." He feared that President Buchanan was "in complicity with the disunionists." Lincoln inserted some soothing words to the South in a speech Trumbull gave in Springfield on November 20, 1860. By December Trumbull was so worried that he thought Lincoln should perhaps make a public statement which Southern Unionists could use to blunt secessionist accusations, but he soon returned to the view that silence was the President-elect's best policy. After South Carolina seceded, Trumbull declared that the "question is no longer about African Slavery, but whether we have a government capable of maintaining itself." After war broke out, he sought its vigorous prosecution and soon urged a resolution in the Senate for an advance on Richmond.

Trumbull was an effective and powerful Senator, and as chairman of the Judiciary Committee he was involved in the vital issue of civil liberties throughout the war. He had deep reservations about the President's suspension of the privilege of the writ of habeas corpus and worked for legislation to control arbitrary arrests in the North. He wrote the amendment to the first Confiscation Act which freed slaves employed to help the enemy's war effort. In 1862 he sponsored the second Confiscation Act, which freed the slaves of rebels but provided no machinery of implementation. The administration did not enforce the antislavery provision vigorously.

Trumbull's bill affirming the suspension of the privilege of the writ of habeas corpus but regulating the arrests resulting from the suspension became law on March 3, 1863. Despite his care for civil liberties in the North, Senator Trumbull shared Republican fears of Democratic disloyalty. In September 1862 he had told Lincoln that the Democratic party "in Ill.... is under the control of leaders who sympathise with the South & if they get control of the State, Ill.... will be paralyzed, if her influence is not thrown positively against the government." After General Ambrose E. Burnside suppressed the Chicago *Times* on June 1, 1863, Trumbull, with Chicago Congressman Isaac N. Arnold, asked Lincoln to revoke the order. The President said later that their request "turned the scale in favor of revoking the order." In 1864 and 1865 Trumbull worked for the passage of the Thirteenth Amendment to the Constitution.

Trumbull thought Lincoln "a most excellent and honest man," but lacking in talent for action and business. Relations between the two Illinoisans were not intimate. In 1862 Trumbull participated in the attempt by Republican Senators to force Lincoln to change the composition of his Cabinet. In 1864 he noted "a distrust and fear that he [Lincoln] is too undecided and inefficient to put down the rebellion," but friends persuaded him to drop any opposition to Lincoln's renomination.

After the war, Trumbull was reelected to the Senate and became a major architect of early Reconstruction. He was astonished when President Andrew Johnson vetoed his Freedmen's Bureau Bill and Civil Rights Bill. Trumbull joined the opposition to the President. In 1868, however, he voted to acquit Johnson of impeachment charges. In 1872 he joined the Liberal Republican movement and was a contender for the presidential nomination of that party. When his third term in the Senate ended, he retired to practice law in Chicago. He returned to the Democratic party in 1876 and in 1894 became a Populist. He died of cancer of the prostate 2 years later.

SOURCES: Mark M. Krug's *Lyman Trumbull: Conservative Radical* (New York: A. S. Barnes, 1965) is a well-written and solid political biography. Trumbull's letters to Lincoln about the "free negro question" (June 12, 1858), deceit (January 29, 1859), the "old Whig element" (November 23, 1859), Lincoln and Seward (April 24, 1860), Lincoln's nomination (May 18, 1860), Southern Senators (May 22, 1860), Republican sentiment for compromise (December 14, 1860), Blair (December 18, 1860), the government's "maintaining itself" (December 24, 1860), and Democrats in Illinois (September 7, 1862) are in the Abraham Lincoln Papers, Library of Congress.

Tyler, Lyon Gardiner (1853–1935) Lincoln hater. Lyon Gardiner Tyler was the son of President John Tyler. A graduate of the University of Virginia, he became a lawyer and educator. He was the president of William and Mary College.

Tyler had fled Virginia with his mother during the Civil War, and their home was eventually occupied by Negro troops. His father had cast his fortunes with the Confederacy, and he died in 1862 just before assuming a seat in the Confederate Congress. Lyon spent the rest of his life defending the Lost Cause by attacking Lincoln.

Tyler portrayed the old South as a democratic society with the leisure to produce an exceptional class of political leaders who were not aristocrats in any class sense. The North was much more the exemplar of aristocracy. The "difference between the rich and the poor," he wrote in 1917, "was always great in the North, and this difference has continued to grow deeper and wider, till in this day a perfect chasm exists between the multimillionaire and the poor man of the slums." He thought that the "South will never acquire real prosperity till it gets rid of the negro, who is as disturbing a factor now as he ever was." His desire was not "to restore slavery, but to scatter the negroes throughout the Union so that their influence will not be felt particularly in any one section."

A Confederate Catechism, which Tyler wrote in 1929, summarized his case succinctly. Lincoln "determined to make war in order to fix the tariff for protection forever on the South." He fought the war by barbarous means; he invited slave insurrection with his Emancipation Proclamation, which was strictly a military and not a humanitarian measure. The South fought to repel invasion, not to save slavery, which "in a short time would have met a peaceful and natural death with the development of machinery consequent upon Cyrus H. McCormick's great invention of the reaper." Tyler noted carefully that the "North has become ashamed of the manner in which the South has been treated and it is now pretty unanimous in calling Reconstruction 'a dark blot upon the history of the country,' but it tries to win over the South to recognizing Lincoln as a national hero by claiming that Lincoln was a friend of the South and that if Lincoln had survived the war, the South would have had no trouble." But Lincoln by freeing the negro "was the true parent of reconstruction, legislative robbery, negro supremacy, cheating at the polls, rapes of white women, lynching, and the acts of the Ku Klux Klan." The black man, barely raised from being "a barbarian and cannibal," was not ready for freedom. "The fact is that the South's taking ignorant negroes and making them work was no more criminal violation of democracy or self-government than the government is guilty of to-day in keeping the Porto Ricans and Filipinos under political slavery." Lincoln was the true autocrat who "treated the Constitution *as a doormat and wiped his feet upon it.*" He was utterly unlike Woodrow Wilson, "who has scrupulously consulted Congress on every important question concerning the war with Germany."

Tyler died on Lincoln's birthday in 1935.

SOURCES: See Michael Davis, *The Image of Lincoln in the South* (Knoxville: University of Tennessee Press, 1971) and Tyler's *The South and Germany* (Richmond, Va.: Whittet & Shepperson, 1917) and *A Confederate Catechism: The War of 1861–1865*, 5th ed. (Holdcroft, Va.: privately published, 1930).

U, V

Union See CONSTITUTION OF THE UNITED STATES; NATIONALISM.

Usher, John Palmer (1816–1889) Lincoln's second Secretary of the Interior. John P. Usher was born in New York, became a lawyer there, and moved to Terre Haute, Indiana, in 1839. His legal practice prospered. Since he worked in western Indiana and Lincoln worked often in eastern Illinois, the two lawyers became acquainted in the 1850s.

A Whig in politics, Usher was slow to join the Republicans; he did not do so until after the election of 1856. As a Republican, he clung to conservative policies and candidates; he supported Edward Bates for the presidential nomination early in 1860 but switched to Lincoln in the spring. On March 22, 1862, he became Assistant Secretary of the Interior—with heavy duties because of the indifferent administration of the Secretary, Caleb Blood Smith. His inside view of government made him cynical. "The war will never end," he wrote in 1862, "as long as there is any thing to steal." In October and November of that year, Usher investigated the damage claims and capital sentences arising from the Minnesota Sioux Uprising, and he recommended clemency and moderation.

Usher's racial views and his friendship with Terre Haute's Richard W. Thompson led him into considerable involvement with colonization schemes. He urged President Lincoln to settle blacks on the Chiriqui coast in Central America, and he was pleased to see "that very many consequential *niggers* from the North are manifesting a desire to go." But that would take care of only the small Northern black population. He devised a plan in 1862 "by which we can separate the two *races*" by accommodating the rest of America's black population on land in Texas confiscated from the Confederacy. Usher was also a vigorous advocate of a transcontinental railroad, and he attempted to influence the selection of a route that would benefit certain of his friends who were railroad promoters.

On January 8, 1863, Usher succeeded the unhappy Smith as Secretary of the Interior, more because of Indiana's political importance than Lincoln's personal preference. By relying on Leonard Swett, a friend of both Lincoln and Usher, as the government's agent, the Secretary exacerbated a serious crisis over federal control of the New Almaden Mine in California. Perhaps because he was wedded to the plans of his friend Thompson and the Chiriqui Improvement Company, Usher played a less enthusiastic role in the disastrous Cow Island colonization scheme of early 1864, and he deftly covered up a potential scandal even as he extricated the unfortunate colonists from their miserable would-be colony off the coast of Haiti.

Under Usher, Indian policy was marked by a continuation of removals (from Kansas and Minnesota) and by facilitating claims for railroad rights-of-way through reservations. Usher himself championed gathering the tribes on reservations in the Southwest, which he obvi-

John Palmer Usher

ously saw as a vast repository for America's unwanted peoples. While overseeing the efforts to build the transcontinental railroad, Secretary Usher did what he could to aid the Kansas route in which his friends were interested. He was himself a stockholder in the Union Pacific Railway Company—Eastern Division. In July 1864 Congress granted a federal subsidy to the Eastern Division's Kansas route.

Usher admired Lincoln and thought there was "not on earth a more guileless man, and but few of more wisdom." He ardently opposed Radical Republican moves to displace Lincoln in 1864 and warned against Salmon P. Chase's ambitions repeatedly. He was widely regarded as a nonentity, too small a man for so important a post, though harmless enough in himself. When another Hoosier, Hugh McCulloch, entered Lincoln's Cabinet in March 1865, Usher's days were numbered, and he was asked to resign by May 15 in order that there not be two men from the same state in the Cabinet. Lincoln quickly chose Senator James Harlan of Iowa to succeed Usher. After Lincoln's death Usher opposed President Andrew Johnson, whom he thought to be "in sympathy with the Copperheads." He was not ready "to submit to the government of rebels." Already on the board of directors of the Eastern Division by April 1865, he moved after his resignation to Lawrence, Kansas, where he became chief counsel of the Union Pacific Railroad, a position he held the rest of his life.

SOURCES: There is a slender but competent biography, *John Palmer Usher: Lincoln's Secretary of the Interior* by Elmo R. Richardson and Alan W. Farley (Lawrence: University of Kansas Press, 1960). Usher's letters to Richard W. Thompson about stealing (December 20, 1862) and colonization (September 17, 1862), to Allen Hamilton on Lincoln's character (February 4, 1863), and to Thompson about Andrew Johnson (July 6, 1866) are in the Louis A. Warren Lincoln Library and Museum, Fort Wayne, Indiana.

Vallandigham, Clement Laird (1820–1871) Ohio Democratic politician and the most famous Northern opponent of the Lincoln administration's war. Vallandigham was born in New Lisbon, Ohio, the son of a Presbyterian minister. He became a lawyer and, in 1845, the youngest member of the Ohio legislature. Consistently pro-Southern in his political views, he reluctantly supported Stephen A. Douglas for President in 1860. On November 2, 1860, he gave a speech at the Cooper Institute in New York City in which he said that he would never as a Representative in the Congress of the United States *"vote one dollar of money whereby one drop of American blood should be shed in a civil war."* In the midst of the secession crisis, on February 2, 1861, Vallandigham, now a member of the House of Representatives, recommended three constitutional amendments based on the idea of John C. Calhoun's "concurrent majority." He proposed the division of the Union into four quadrants, North, South, West, and Pacific, a majority vote in each of which was necessary to elect a President. Controversial legislation in Congress would need the approval of the majority of the Senators from each section. Secession of a state would be possible if the rest of the states in the quadrant agreed.

From the moment war broke out, Vallandigham consistently urged compromise and a cessation of hostilities as the only route to peace. In a meeting of the Democratic congressional caucus in July, Vallandigham was the only congressman to oppose coercion of the South.

Defeated by Republican Robert C. Schenck in an attempt at reelection in 1862, Vallandigham worked for the Ohio Democratic gubernatorial nomination and a resurrection of his political fortunes by becoming a martyr to the measures imposed in the North to enforce loyalty. General Ambrose E. Burnside, commander of the Department of the Ohio, in his General Order No. 38 issued on April 19, 1863, declared that "the habit of declaring sympathy for the enemy" would no longer be tolerated and that offenders would be arrested and tried as spies or traitors or banished "into the lines of their friends." On May 1 Vallandigham delivered a speech against the war at a rally in Mount Vernon, Ohio. A military spy took notes on the speech, and Burnside had Vallandigham arrested on May 6. The following day a military commission in Cincinnati convicted him of expressing treasonable sympathy for the enemy and sentenced him to close confinement in a Federal prison for the war's duration. In the trial Vallandigham was allowed counsel, could cross-examine witnesses personally, and could subpoena witnesses.

President Lincoln learned about the arrest and trial from the newspapers. He and all his Cabinet regretted the arrest but, as he told Burnside, "being done, all were for seeing you through with it." On May 19 Lincoln, taking his cue from Burnside's order, decided with his Cabinet to banish Vallandigham to the Confederacy. Burnside was miffed at the change in sentence but saw to it that "Valiant Val," as his partisans called him, was sent through Confederate lines in Tennessee.

Indignation meetings were held by Democrats all over the North, and President Lincoln felt compelled to answer the charges against him. He chose to answer the protest of a Democratic meeting held in Albany, New York, on May 16. On June 12, 1863, Lincoln drafted his famous public letter to Erastus Corning and others. In it the President protested that he was himself "thoroughly imbued with a reverence for the guarranteed rights of individuals" and, therefore, had been "slow to adopt the strong measures, which by degrees I have been forced to regard as being within the exceptions of the constitution, and as indispensable to the public Safety." He recalled that a timely arrest of Robert E. Lee would certainly have altered the course of the war; one could not always await an overt act of disloyalty. In fact, he said, "the time [is] not unlikely to come when I shall be blamed for having made too few arrests rather than too many." The Confederates had hoped all along "under cover of 'Liberty of speech' 'Liberty of the press' and 'Habeas corpus' . . . to keep on foot amongst us a most efficient corps of spies, informers, suppliers, and aiders and abettors of their cause in a thousand ways. . . . Or if, as has happened, the execu-

Clement L. Vallandigham, in a sympathetic portrait engraved in 1863 expressly for The Old Guard, an extreme antiadministration monthly published in New York City.

tive should suspend the writ, without ruinous waste of time, instances of arresting innocent persons might occur, as are always likely to occur in such cases; and then a clamor could be raised in regard to this, which might be, at least, of some service to the insurgent cause." Defending the idea of constructive treason in now-classic language and capitalizing on his own reputation for clemency, the President said: "Must I shoot a simple-minded soldier boy who deserts, while I must not touch a hair of a wiley agitator who induces him to desert? . . . I think that in such a case, to silence the agitator, and save the boy, is not only constitutional, but, withal, a great mercy." He carefully pointed out as well that Burnside and the Ohio federal district judge who upheld the conviction were Democrats, and he cited as precedent within that party's hallowed memory Andrew Jackson's declaration of martial law in New Orleans in 1812. John G. Nicolay and John Hay in their biography of Lincoln noted that "few of the President's state papers . . . produced a stronger impression upon the public mind than this." Moreover, his changing the sentence to banishment kept Vallandigham from martyrdom in prison and, as Nicolay and Hay shrewdly observed, "affected the popular mind as an event rather ridiculous than serious."

Vallandigham visited Richmond, ran the blockade, and took up residence in Canada. In June, Ohio Democratic leaders lost control of the party, and a stampede to Valiant Val gave him the gubernatorial nomination. He conducted his campaign from Canada and lost to John Brough. In February 1864 the United States Supreme Court in *Ex parte Vallandigham* ruled that it could not "review . . . the proceedings of a military commission."

Vallandigham returned illegally to Ohio the next summer. Though Governor Brough wanted him arrested, General Samuel P. Heintzelman, now military commander of the Ohio department, was less impetuous than Burnside and did not want to act without higher authority. Lincoln decided, upon the advice of his Cabinet, to take no official notice of the return, though he instructed Brough and Heintzelman to watch Vallandigham "closely." In part, the President thought, as Nicolay and Hay put it, that "it could not but result in benefit to the Union cause to have so violent and indiscreet a man go to Chicago [for the Democratic nominating convention] as a firebrand to his own party." Indeed Vallandigham did help write the so-called "peace plank" in the 1864 Democratic platform. In June an embarrassed Illinois Democrat wrote John Hay, "How much did you fellows give [peace Democrat] Fernandy Wood for importing him?"

Vallandigham viewed Lincoln's assassination as "the worst public calamity which could have befallen the country." He had become something of an admirer of the President's "liberal and conciliatory" Reconstruction policies. An opponent of Reconstruction after Lincoln, Vallandigham did accept the Emancipation Proclamation as a fait accompli, and in 1871 he urged an acceptance of the results of the war and a realignment of parties around living issues. In the same year he killed himself accidentally while demonstrating to a friend how a victim was killed in a murder case in which he was counsel for the defendant.

SOURCES: Frank Klement's *The Limits of Dissent: Clement L. Vallandigham & the Civil War* ([Lexington]: University of Kentucky Press, 1970), although more sympathetic than most accounts, is a judicious and scholarly biography. The hostile Nicolay and Hay have a perceptive chapter on the Vallandigham episode in Volume XII of *Abraham Lincoln: A History* (New York: Century, 1890). James G. Randall's *Constitutional Problems Under Lincoln* (rev. ed.: Urbana: University of Illinois Press, 1951), is clear on the legal issues in the case.

Vandalia, Illinois The capital during Lincoln's early political career. Vandalia was founded in 1819 and incorporated in 1820, when it replaced Kaskaskia as the state capital. Law stipulated that it serve as the seat of government until at least 1840. Located on the route of the uncompleted National Road (now U.S. 40), it was founded in anticipation of the northerly movement of population increase in Illinois.

Lincoln arrived in Vandalia in November 1834 to assume his seat as a freshman member of the lower house of the Illinois General Assembly. He roomed in an inn with John Todd Stuart; few legislators brought their families to Vandalia. The town had no more than 900 inhabitants, and the capitol, across the street from the public square, though a two-story brick building but 10 years old, was a dilapidated structure. Lincoln remained until the end of the regular session in February 1835. He returned in December for a special session of the legislature which ended in January 1836.

Like Kaskaskia, Vandalia was fast becoming the victim of the steady northward move of Illinois's population center. In the summer of 1836, Vandalia citizens began building a new state house to blunt criticism of the capital's location. When the Tenth General Assembly convened in December, the building was sufficiently complete to allow the legislature to meet on the second floor, though the first-floor government offices were not ready and the plaster was still wet. Lincoln, reelected that year, sat in the House of Representatives' chamber at the west end of the building. An internal improvements convention met simultaneously and gave a sign of the most significant work of this historic assembly, which passed Illinois's ill-fated Internal Improvements Act. In January 1837 Lincoln made his first published speech in that chamber in opposition to Usher F. Linder's assault on Springfield's State Bank of Illinois.

In the same session Lincoln and eight other tall legislators from Sangamon County called the "Long Nine" also led the movement which would end Vandalia's reign as state capital. When the session ended on March 6, Lincoln headed home to New Salem for the last time. He had recently been enrolled as an Illinois attorney in Vandalia, and he remained in New Salem only a short while before moving to Springfield, where he became John Todd Stuart's law partner. He would return to Vandalia only twice more for legislative sessions, for on July 4, 1839, Springfield would become the new capital.

In July 1837 Lincoln unexpectedly returned to Vandalia for a brief special session to deal with the results of the Panic of 1837. It endangered the ambitious internal improvements scheme he had championed in the preceding session. While Springfield prepared to become the capital, Lincoln was reelected and would return to Vandalia for the Eleventh General Assembly, the last to meet in that city.

When the state offices moved to Springfield in 1839, Vandalia saw its population fall to 600. It practically became a ghost town until it was revived by the advent of the Illinois Central Railroad line in 1852. In 1857 the county remodeled the old shell of the state house into a handsome courthouse. In 1919 the State of Illinois purchased the building, and in 1939 it completed a restoration of it as an historic site.

The importance of Vandalia as a temporary residence for Abraham Lincoln, who was there for about 44 weeks altogether, has generally been underestimated. That is largely due to the restoration and subsequent promotion of New Salem as a tourist attraction. Although Lincoln lived much longer in New Salem and had his home there, crucial events in his development occurred during his temporary residences in Vandalia. There he first learned the arts of government, gave his first published speech, first gained enough confidence to study law, and was admitted to the bar.

SOURCES: See William E. Baringer's *Lincoln's Vandalia: A Pioneer Portrait* (New Brunswick, N.J.: Rutgers University Press, 1949).

Vice Presidents See HAMLIN, HANNIBAL; JOHNSON, ANDREW.

Villard, Henry (1835–1900) A German-born journalist who settled eventually in Belleville, Illinois. Villard covered four of the Lincoln-Douglas Debates for the New York *Staats-Zeitung*. Having thus gained personal acquaintance with Abraham Lincoln, in 1860 he reported for the hostile New York *Herald* on the President-elect's activities from November 16, 1860, to the arrival of his inaugural train in New York City. Though the newspaper was vaguely Democratic, it apparently published Villard's sometimes admiring accounts of the President-elect without censorship. Villard at first thought Lincoln a "man of good heart and good intention" but "not firm." "The times demand a Jackson," he said. By the first week of December, however, he reported "dormant qualities in 'Old Abe' which occasion will draw forth, develop and remind people to a certain degree of the characteristics of 'Old Hickory.' " Villard's reports were occasionally erroneous, but are widely regarded as the most accurate and perceptive for an important period of Lincoln's life. Lincoln had, in his own words, "only a slight acquaintance with Mr. Villard."

SOURCES: In 1941 Harold G. and Oswald Garrison Villard excerpted the dispatches mostly for the descriptions of Lincoln's personal habits and traits in *Lincoln on the Eve of '61: A Journalist's Story by Henry Villard* (New York: Alfred A. Knopf).

Bronze castings made by Jules Berchem from Volk's original plaster mask and hands (from the private collection of O. Gerald Trigg). (Photograph by Scott Simpson)

For Cabinet and policy formation, the dispatches are best read in full in the *Herald*. William E. Baringer relied on them heavily for *A House Dividing: Lincoln as President Elect* (Springfield, Ill.: Abraham Lincoln Association, 1945).

Volk, Leonard Wells (1818–1895) Sculptor. Volk was born in Wellstown, New York. He learned stonecutting in his father's shop and in other retail establishments. He moved for a time to Illinois in 1852, where he met his wife's cousin, Stephen A. Douglas. Under Douglas's patronage, he studied sculpture in Rome from 1855 to 1857. Thereafter, he opened a studio in Chicago.

Volk met Lincoln during the famous Senate campaign against Douglas in 1858, and early in the spring of 1860 he persuaded Lincoln to sit in his Chicago studio. First, on March 31 he made a plaster life mask of Lincoln and made measurements of Lincoln's torso to produce a "Hermes" bust ("head, shoulders, and breast cut off below the pectoral muscles and without drapery or covering of any kind"), which he completed in April and patented on June 12, 1860. On May 18, 1860, Volk was in Springfield and presented a cabinet-sized copy of the life-sized Hermes bust (now lost) to Mrs. Lincoln. That was also the day on which Lincoln received the presidential nomination. Probably 2 days later, on May 20, Volk made plaster copies of Lincoln's hands. The right one was conspicuously swollen "on account of excessive hand-shaking the evening before" with the committee notifying him of his nomination and with the large crowd that congratulated Lincoln.

Volk made several different versions of his bust, including one cut off at the neck and another, with neoclassical drape, manufactured by the Hennecke

Henry Villard. (Courtesy of the Illinois State Historical Library)

Volk, Leonard Wells

Company of Chicago in the 1880s. In addition, other manufacturers apparently pirated his work and sold unauthorized copies.

The mask and hands provided the models for many a Lincoln statue by other sculptors, as well as a life-size statue of Lincoln by Volk for the Illinois State Capitol in Springfield (1876), and a heroic bronze statue of Lincoln for Rochester's Soldiers and Sailors monument. The latter, dedicated in 1892, cost $26,000. Volk modeled two different Lincoln statuettes in the 1870s to celebrate the Emancipation Proclamation; one of them was based on a famous full-length photograph of Lincoln probably taken at the sculptor's request.

In 1886 Richard Watson Gilder of the *Century Magazine* obtained subscriptions from 33 people to purchase the originals of the mask and hands from Volk's son Douglas; each subscriber in turn received a copy of the mask and hands executed by Augustus St. Gaudens. The originals were presented to the United States government and now rest in the Smithsonian Institution.

Art historians have not rated Volk's work highly. Lorado Taft's *History of American Sculpture* (1903), for example, complimented him only for faithful portraiture. But that has been all that mattered for Lincoln students, for Volk's mask and the busts based on it present, as Lincoln said to Volk, "the animal himself."

SOURCES: Volk wrote an article on "The Lincoln Mask and How It Was Made" for the *Century Magazine* of December, 1881. See also Harold Holzer and Lloyd Ostendorf, "Sculptures of Abraham Lincoln from Life," *Antiques*, CXIII (February 1978), 382–393. Modern copies of his mask, bust, and hands are still available from the Mazzolini Artcraft Company, 1607 E. 41st Street, Cleveland, Ohio.

W

Wade, Benjamin Franklin (1800–1878) Civil War Senator from Ohio and Radical Republican critic of Lincoln. Wade was famed for his outspokenness, which earned him the nickname "Bluff Ben." Born in Massachusetts, he settled eventually in Jefferson, Ohio, in the Western Reserve area heavily populated by transplanted New Englanders. Wade first became an antislavery Whig and later a Republican. He served in the United States Senate from 1851 to 1869.

An uncompromising foe of slavery, secession, and the Confederate States of America, Wade was generally critical of Lincoln's policies. As early as November 14, 1860, he urged, through a letter to Lyman Trumbull, that Lincoln say nothing by way of appeasing Southern secession bluster. He thought President James Buchanan was "doubtless guilty of treason" in handling the Sumter crisis. He was a factional rival of Salmon P. Chase in the Ohio Republican party, had done nothing to help Chase's bid for the Presidency in 1860, and was critical of Chase's appointment to Lincoln's Cabinet. If Ohio got a place in the Cabinet, Wade had told Lincoln, he preferred R. C. Schenck of Dayton or D. E. Carter of Cleveland. He also distrusted Secretary of State William H. Seward, but he had supported conservative Montgomery Blair for Attorney General.

When war broke out, Wade tried to enlist to fight, but his proposed volunteer unit was not needed. When Baltimore citizens fought Massachusetts troops on their way to protect Washington, his typically intemperate reaction was to say that Baltimore should be destroyed. Through the Joint Committee on the Conduct of the War, of which he was Chairman from its inception through the end of the war, he hounded conservative generals, promoted the cause of Radical generals, and vented his prejudices against West Point. In general, his view was that "mercy to traitors is cruelty to loyal men," and he always thought the administration too lenient in dealing with the rebellion and its sympathizers, though Lincoln's leniency "sprung from the best of motives."

By December 18, 1862, enough Senators shared Wade's views of Lincoln's overcaution and his hostility to Seward to provoke a Cabinet crisis. Wade was present only at the first meeting with Lincoln, on December 18. He complained of leaving "the direction of our military affairs in the hands of bitter and malignant Democrats." Most of the Senators were seeking Seward's removal, however, and Wade was absent the next night when Lincoln confronted his critics with all the members of the Cabinet except Seward.

"I am a Radical and I glory in it," Wade said in 1863, and by June 1864 he was in a position to oppose Lincoln's Reconstruction policies in a provocative manner. As Chairman of the Committee on Territories, he reported the Wade-Davis Bill and guided it to passage in the upper house. He stressed its importance as the only practical emancipation measure before the Congress after the failure of the proposed Thirteenth Amendment in the House on June 15 and after Andrew Johnson became Lincoln's running mate. Johnson, the war Governor of

Benjamin Franklin Wade

Tennessee, was a living embodiment of the executive branch's Reconstruction policy. Wade, who had a Whiggish distaste for a strong executive branch, pushed for a Reconstruction plan dominated by Congress. He wanted it badly enough to sacrifice the bill's provision for Negro suffrage (which he had supported in committee even though he advocated colonization and had promised Northerners that Negroes would remain in the South) in order not to arouse enough opposition to kill the bill. Only one Republican member of Congress from a free state voted against the bill; Republicans in Congress were united, Radical and conservative alike. Lincoln nevertheless gave the bill a pocket veto on July 4. Wade joined Davis in publishing the Wade-Davis manifesto on August 5. Davis wrote the document, which denounced Lincoln's "dictatorial usurpation" and urged the people to "consider the remedy for these usurpations," words with explosive meaning in the midst of Lincoln's campaign for reelection.

Wade met such a storm of abuse for his manifesto as an arrogant document which aided Democrats in an election year that he soon muffled his efforts to replace Lincoln with a more suitable Radical candidate. Eventually, he campaigned for Lincoln in Ohio and Pennsylvania, but privately he was still saying, "I wish the d——l had Old Abe."

After Lincoln's assassination, Wade became a vociferous critic of President Johnson's Reconstruction policies. He stanchly advocated Johnson's impeachment. Ironically, however, the fact that, as president pro tempore of the Senate, Wade would become President upon Johnson's removal, acted for several Senators as a deterrent from convicting Johnson at his impeachment trial.

SOURCES: H. L. Trefousse's *Benjamin Franklin Wade: Radical Republican from Ohio* (New York: Twayne, 1963) is a solid and readable biography.

See also COMMITTEE ON THE CONDUCT OF THE WAR, JOINT; RADICAL REPUBLICANS; WADE-DAVIS BILL.

Wade-Davis Bill Legislation aimed at establishing a congressional plan of Reconstruction different from Lincoln's, particularly as Lincoln's plan had been carried out in Louisiana. Congressman Henry Winter Davis of Maryland first introduced the bill in February 1864. Davis disliked the conservative regime in Louisiana and was angry that the President did not help him in his struggle with Montgomery Blair for control of the Maryland Republican party. Ohio Senator Benjamin F. Wade guided the bill to passage in the upper house.

Variously amended in its long legislative history, the final bill provided for the appointment by the President of a civil officer to administer the state in accordance with existing state laws (except laws relating to slavery) until half the prewar voting population of the state took an oath to support the United States Constitution and laws and proclamations concerning slavery issued during the war. Then those who subscribed to an "iron-clad" oath guaranteeing that they had never supported the rebellion would elect a convention to write a new state constitution, which must abolish slavery and repudiate the Confederate debt. The bill excluded from amnesty all Confederate and Confederate-state civil officers above ministerial rank and military officers ranking colonel or above. It excluded forever from United States citizenship those who held such offices and commissions after the passage of the bill. The Senate Committee on Territories, chaired by Wade, amended the bill to include Negroes in the reconstruction process. On July 1 the amendment failed, 24 to 5. Wade himself voted to include only white voters (though he had supported the amendment in committee) because, he said, adoption of the amendment would, in his judgment, have sacrificed the bill. The bill passed the House, 73 to 59, on May 4. It passed the Senate, 18 to 14, on July 2.

President Lincoln refused to sign the bill on July 4, and since the congressional session was over, the bill died of his pocket veto. He then took the unusual step of issuing a proclamation, on July 8, saying that he refused to sign the bill because (1) he did not wish "to be inflexibly committed to any single plan of restoration," (2) he did not want to repudiate the "governments, already adopted and installed in Arkansas and Louisiana," and (3) he did not wish "to declare a constitutional competency in Congress to abolish slavery in States." He noted, however, that he was "fully satisfied with the system for restoration contained in the Bill, as one very proper plan for the loyal people of any State choosing to adopt it." In part, Lincoln was bidding for party unity for his reelection campaign.

Though often pointed to as a drastic piece of legislation betokening an irreparable split between President and Congress or between Lincoln and the Radical Republicans, the Wade-Davis Bill was neither drastic nor irreconcilably distant from Lincoln's policies. Both agreed to exclude Negroes from reconstructing states, and both agreed on emancipation as a condition of reentry to the Union. Neither saw the South as mere territory. Davis's bill rested constitutionally on Congress's duty to guarantee a republican form of government to the states. The Wade-Davis Bill did exclude more classes of people from participation in Reconstruction and went well beyond the President in excluding some from citizenship forever. More important was the difference in the minimum number of citizens to reconstruct a state government. The President required only 10 percent who would promise future loyalty; Congress demanded that 50 percent promise future loyalty and that none who had ever been disloyal participate in reconstructing the government. Congress, in other words, wished to reconstruct only when the war was over, for 50 percent of prewar voters was an impossibly high figure to demand. Lincoln's plan was, at least in part, a wartime policy meant to give a rallying point of a 10 percent remnant courageous enough to renounce the Confederacy while it was still fighting the Union.

On August 5, 1864, the New York *Tribune* published the Wade-Davis manifesto, which denounced the pocket veto and pictured the President as a military tyrant imposing minority governments on the states. Often seen only as a sign of a widening gulf between Lincoln and the Radicals in Lincoln's own party which threatened his chances for reelection, the manifesto's disastrous effect on Radicals is rarely noted. However, Davis failed to gain renomination for the House, Wade was denounced in his home district in resolutions passed by the Ashtabula County Republican Convention, and even the *Tribune*, which published the manifesto, avoided endorsing the contents forthrightly.

SOURCES: The only accurate and detailed treatment of the Wade-Davis Bill is in Herman Belz's *Reconstructing the Union: Theory and Policy during the Civil War* (Ithaca, N.Y.: Cornell University Press, 1969).

Washburne, Elihu Benjamin (1816–1887) Illinois political associate of Lincoln. Elihu B. Washburne was born in Maine, attended the Harvard Law School, became a member of the Massachusetts bar, and moved to the Illinois lead-mining boom town of Galena in 1840. There he established a successful law practice, speculated in Western lands, and soon became an active Henry Clay Whig. Like his brothers Israel and Cadwallader, he gained considerable political prominence, but unlike them he added an "e" to Washburn as a link to his British forbears. Washburne was a member of the House of Representatives from 1853 to 1869.

Washburne met Lincoln in the Whig "log cabin" campaign of 1840, but their closest association came at the time of the formation of the Republican party and after. Washburne was a much earlier convert to the new party than Lincoln. As early as November 1854, he told Lincoln that every representative and senator sent to the state legislature from his northern Illinois district was a Republican. The new party's formation was slower in central Illinois, and Lincoln remained a Whig until 1856. Nevertheless, Washburne supported Lincoln's attempt to win a seat in the United States Senate in 1855. Washburne or one of his friends saw every member of the state legislature from his district and urged Lincoln's election. But he warned the candidate: "We are pretty ultra on the slave question . . . , and you will have to take pretty high ground." He encouraged Lincoln to describe his views on slavery so that he could show them to Salmon P. Chase and get Chase to write Free-Soilers in Washburne's district in Lincoln's behalf. From his Washington vantage point he also saw Ohio's Joshua Giddings. He reported him as being "your strongest possible friend" and willing to "walk clear to Illinois to elect you." He got Giddings to write two letters to urge Illinois radical Owen Lovejoy to support Lincoln. Washburne even suggested that legislator Wait Talcott procure Lincoln's legal services in a lawsuit over an alleged patent infringement, hoping that "that will be a good pull on him" to vote for Lincoln for Senator.

In 1858 Washburne again supported Lincoln for the Senate, though some said that he had been telling his friends not to oppose incumbent Democrat Stephen A. Douglas in the hope that Douglas would join the Republicans. Lincoln was "satisfied you have done no wrong" even before Washburne explained that he would welcome Douglas "as a valuable and indomitable ally" but that he "had no idea of making him Senator." Washburne discounted the view of some of Lincoln's friends "that the republicans outside the State were wanting to sell us out in Illinois." By May 31 he was telling Lincoln that Douglas had "ceased associating with our folks" and "is understood to repudiate all sympathy with republicans and desires no support from them."

Washburne reported that Lincoln's presidential nomination in 1860 was "so unexpected we could hardly believe it." He added that Douglas thought the nomination "the strongest that could have been made." As a member of the Republican Executive Congressional Committee for the campaign and as "an old friend of twenty years," Washburne devoted his "whole soul and energies to the campaign." He advised the candidate to "keep very quiet and out of the way as much as possible," and he kept Lincoln abreast of political developments throughout the country. In May, for example, he urged Lincoln to consider saying "nothing about the platform" in his letter of acceptance of the nomination so that former Know-Nothings in Pennsylvania "can support you without committing themselves to those planks" in the platform which affirmed the rights of immigrants. Lincoln ignored his advice.

Washburne's committee franked an average of 40,000 printed speeches a day. The Congressman added his own contribution to that campaign literature with a speech in the House on May 29, 1860, *Abraham Lincoln, His Personal History and Public Record*. The Republican Congressional Committee published it and sold the pamphlet for 50 cents per hundred. Washburne told Lincoln that it "was hastily got up," but he "thought it necessary . . . that your record while in Congress should be brought out in answer to the misrepresentations already made." A full page of the eight-page pamphlet explained that Congressman Lincoln had voted supplies and land bounties for the soldiers even though he opposed the Mexican War.

After Lincoln's election Washburne kept the President-elect apprised of developments in Washington. Early in December he warned him that Westerners considerably underestimated "the imminent peril" of secession. He recommended firmness in the face of the threat and reported that sentiment as the consensus of Republicans in Congress. Lincoln told Washburne to prevent "any of our friends from . . . entertaining propositions for compromise of any sort, on *'slavery extention.'* . . . On that point hold firm, as with a chain of steel." Washburne had good relations with General Winfield Scott and informed Lincoln of the general-in-chief's views on the federal forts located in seceded states. In January Washburne opposed moves toward compromise with the South on the part of William H. Seward and Thurlow Weed, and he warned Lincoln that his friend Leonard Swett was "the agent to be employed to get you into" the compromise scheme. Indeed, Swett did write Lincoln to encourage compromise with the South. Washburne characterized Swett's attempt to appear in Washington as "grand advisor to the King" as provoking "extraordi-

Elihu Benjamin Washburne

nary disgust." He opposed Simon Cameron and supported Salmon P. Chase for Lincoln's Cabinet.

Washburne warned repeatedly that there was evidence of a conspiracy to take Washington or prevent Lincoln's inauguration. He and three other Republicans employed New York detectives to investigate the possibility. When Lincoln arrived secretly in Washington for his inauguration, Washburne was the only man on the platform to greet him.

During the war, Washburne loyally supported the administration. He is best known for promoting the career of fellow Galena townsman Ulysses S. Grant, and he eventually proposed the bill which resurrected the rank of lieutenant general for Grant. His loyalty to Grant extended to that general's infamous order banning "Jews, as a class" from trading with his army; Washburne told Lincoln that he thought it "the wisest order yet made by a military Command."

Washburne was among the earliest to seek Lincoln's intentions in regard to his desire to run for the Presidency again in 1864. In that contest, he was once again a member of the congressional Republican committee which distributed campaign materials. He even procured $250 each from William H. Seward, Gideon Welles, Edward Bates, and Montgomery Blair for the circulation of campaign documents. Never overconfident, Washburne always held the view that "there is no telling who will be governor till after the election." He worried about Illinois in 1864 and was convinced that the state would be lost to the Republicans unless Lincoln furloughed a substantial number of soldiers to go home to vote.

After Lincoln's assassination Washburne soon became a violent critic of his successor, Andrew Johnson, and a proponent of Radical Reconstruction measures. He was an early supporter of Grant for the Presidency in 1868. Grant in turn made him minister to France.

SOURCES: Washburne's letters to Lincoln about "ultra" views in northern Illinois (December 19, 1854), Giddings (December 26, 1854), Wait Talcott (January 17, 1855), Douglas (May 2 and May 31, 1858), Lincoln's nomination (May 19, 1860), his own speech on Lincoln (May 30, 1860), Swett (January 7 and 20, 1861), Grant's anti-Semitic order (January 6, 1863), and his election philosophy (September 5, 1860) are in the Abraham Lincoln Papers, Library of Congress. The only biography is Gaillard Hunt, *Israel, Elihu and Cadwallader Washburne: A Chapter in American Biography* (New York: Macmillan, 1925).

Far Right: Immediately after Lincoln's assassination printmakers began to associate him with George Washington.

Washington, George Abraham Lincoln was acquainted with the life of Washington from "the earliest days of . . . being able to read." He read Mason Locke Weems's *Life of Washington* as a boy; some 40 years later he still recalled "all the accounts there given of the battle fields and struggles for the liberties of the country." It impressed him "that there must have been something more than common that those men struggled for. . . . something even more than National Independence; . . . something that held out a great promise to all the people of the world to all time to come."

Although he rarely quoted Washington, Lincoln seemed to have confidence that he knew Washington's words. In the Galesburg debate with Stephen A. Douglas on October 7, 1858, Lincoln defied "Judge Douglas to show that . . . Washington ever said" that the Negro was excluded from the promise of equality in the Declaration of Independence. Democrats, Lincoln noted, "delight to flaunt in our faces the warning against sectional parties given by Washington in his Farewell Address," but they ignored the facts that Washington signed an act enforcing the antislavery clause in the Northwest Ordinance 8 years before, that he "wrote LaFayette that he considered that prohibition a wise measure," and that he expressed "in the same connection his hope that we should at some time have a confederacy of free States."

In an order of November 15, 1862, for Sabbath observance in the army, President Lincoln recalled that Washington's "first General Order" had urged *"every officer and man . . . to live and act as becomes a Christian soldier defending the dearest rights and liberties of his country."* On another occasion Lincoln cited Washington's childless condition while urging free Negroes to migrate to Africa. Their sacrifice in leaving America would be like Washington's in the Revolution; he was "engaged in benefiting his race—something for the children of his neighbors, having none of his own."

Before his election to the Presidency, Lincoln's references to Washington had been somewhat vague or rather mechanically to the point. In 1842 he recommended invoking Washington's name only in "solemn awe." He noted repeatedly in the political struggles of the 1830s and 1840s that Washington had had no constitutional objections to a national bank. In the 1850s he frequently grouped Washington with Thomas Jefferson and James Madison as embodiments of the early republican spirit of opposition to slavery.

In the midst of the secession crisis Lincoln felt as close to Washington as he ever did. Leaving Springfield for his inauguration in 1861, he said that the task before him was "greater than that which rested upon Washington." Two days later, in Columbus, Ohio, he repeated the idea. Lincoln's realization that he might have to save the Union that Washington had founded foreshadowed the frequent comparisons of the two men during his Presidency and especially after his death. Typical was Schuyler Colfax's estimation that Lincoln "has had no parallel since Washington." To the end of the century eulogists praised Lincoln as having no equal except Washington. Theodore Roosevelt, for example, thought "Washington was, not even excepting Lincoln, the very greatest man of modern times." In the twentieth century, however, Lincoln's fame has eclipsed Washington's. In polls taken in 1948, 1962, and 1968, to sample opinion among American historians on the quality of American Presidents, Lincoln rated first and Washington second.

SOURCES: There are handy references to Lincoln's quotations about Washington in Edmond S. Meany's not altogether reliable *Lincoln Esteemed Washington* (Seattle, Wash.: Frank McCaffrey, 1933) and in R. Gerald McMurtry's "Lincoln Revered Washington," *Lincoln Lore*, Number 1536 (February 1966), pp. 1–4. Results of polls on Presidents can be found in Gary M. Maranell, "The Evaluation of Presidents: An Extension of the Schlesinger Polls," *Journal of American History*, LVII (June 1970), 104–113.

Washington, D.C. Abraham Lincoln first came to the nation's Capital in 1847 to serve in the House of Representatives. He left nothing to indicate what he thought of the place, though it seems that he did not think it particularly special. Like most Congressmen, the Illinois freshman lived in a boarding house inhabited by other members of Congress belonging to the same political party. Lincoln's residence was the house run by Ann G. (Mrs. Benjamin) Sprigg; it was full of Whigs. Unlike most Congressmen, Lincoln brought his family with him, but the arrangement did not work out well—perhaps because he thought his wife Mary "hindered me some in attending to business." After she and his boys left, however, he found his work "tasteless." "I hate to stay in this old room by myself," he said.

Like other Congressmen of antislavery convictions, Lincoln was appalled by the large presence of slavery in the Capital. Over a fourth of Washington's 50,000 inhabitants in the 1840s were black, and probably 10,000 of those Negroes were slaves. The city was a flourishing center for the domestic slave trade. On January 10, 1849, Lincoln introduced an amendment to a resolution which called for the abolition of slavery in the District of Columbia. The proposal bore the customary marks of Lincoln's moderation in regard to the question. Southern officers of the government could bring their slaves to Washington while in the city on business. Slaves born after January 1, 1850, would be free, but they were to be supported and educated in youth by their present owners in exchange for apprentice service. Slaves now resident in Washington would remain such, but their owners could receive compensation from the government for emancipating them. Washington authorities would have to return fugitive slaves escaping into the District. The bill would go into effect only if a majority of the District's voters endorsed the project in a referendum. Lincoln's support for the measure apparently melted away, and Lincoln dropped the matter.

After he left the Thirtieth Congress, Lincoln did not return to Washington until 1861. Well before he arrived to deliver his inaugural address, he received numerous warnings that a Southern plot was afoot to seize the Capital before he could take the oath of office. Some Republican leaders were so distrustful of the outgoing Buchanan administration that they urged Lincoln to come to Washington early in order to counteract disloyal movements there. Once the electoral college votes were officially counted, those fears subsided, but General Winfield Scott took care to have riflemen on the rooftops and cavalry at the intersections on inauguration day.

Lincoln was too busy as a wartime President and too unpretentious as a man to participate greatly in Washington society. Except for a daily carriage ride and daily walks to the War Department telegraph office, he hardly ever left the Executive Mansion. The social tone of the city's elite was decidedly Southern and hostile to Republicans. Culturally, the city did give Lincoln opportunity to see more theater than he ever could in the past, and he even attended operas there. But for the most part, Washington was the place in which he worked—and which he guarded.

Washington's strategic importance loomed large in Lincoln's mind—too large, some critics say. Though the President would quickly come to the conclusion that the destruction of the Confederate army and not the capture of Richmond was the principal objective in the

Under construction during most of Lincoln's Presidency, the uncompleted dome of the Capitol has been a favorite visual symbol of the "unfinished" nature of the American Union in the 1860s.

eastern theater of war, he never took the corresponding view that Washington's safety was unessential to Union success and subordinate to the other strategic movements of the Army of the Potomac. Whatever its strategic validity, his opinion about the importance of Washington was widely held in the North. Western Republicans from Orville Hickman Browning of Illinois to Benjamin F. Wade of Ohio were willing to see Baltimore destroyed if necessary to keep communications open to Washington. And Cabinet members as Western-minded as Edward Bates of Missouri thought the seat of government should be protected "cost what it may." On April 22, 1861, Lincoln himself gave a firmly worded reply to a Baltimore committee concerned about the passage of Union soldiers through their riot-torn city:

> You express great horror of bloodshed, and yet would not lay a straw in the way of those who are organizing in Virginia and elsewhere to capture this city. The rebels attack Fort Sumter, and your citizens attack troops sent to the defense of the Government, and the lives and property in Washington, and yet you would have me break my oath and surrender the Government without a blow. There is no Washington in that—no Jackson in that—no manhood nor honor in that. I have no desire to invade the South; but I must have troops to defend this Capital. Geographically it lies surrounded by the soil of Maryland; and mathematically the necessity exists that they should come over her territory. Our men are not moles, and can't dig under the earth; they are not birds and can't fly through the air. There is no way but to march across, and that they must do. But in doing this there is no need of collision. Keep your rowdies in Baltimore, and there will be no bloodshed. Go home and tell your people that if they will not attack us, we will not attack them; but if they do attack us, we will return it, and that severely.

Washington was surrounded by enemy territory or territory of doubtful loyalty (Maryland) and was within easy striking distance of the Confederacy. "I am, if not in *range*, at least in *hearing* of cannon-shot," the President explained to Indiana's panicky Governor Oliver P. Morton, who was worried about his state's proximity to doubtful Kentucky. This nearness to Confederate territory was a factor in Union strategy, though authorities differ in regard to the importance of the factor. Next to General George B. McClellan's slowness to move his army, the issue which led most to his falling from Lincoln's grace was the issue of guarding Washington. The retirement of McClellan's superior, Winfield Scott, in November 1861 was in part a result of McClellan's accusation that Scott left Washington insecure from attack, but thereafter McClellan generally took the view that the Army of the Potomac, no matter where it was, was the true defender of Washington. A relatively small garrison was adequate for the city's security otherwise. Lincoln, on the other hand, ordered McClellan on March 8, 1862, to leave "in, and about Washington, such a force as, in the opinion of the General-in-chief, and the commanders of all the Army corps, shall leave said City entirely secure." Lincoln and McClellan never agreed how near those men had to be to Washington to constitute an adequate defense, and the disagreement made their increasingly bad relations much worse.

Enough people shared Lincoln's view of Washington's importance to allow spending $1.4 million on fortifying the city during the war. Those forts, Lincoln's increased confidence in his commander (U. S. Grant), and perhaps an increased realization that Union armies in Virginia protected the Capital as well as garrisons could, made Lincoln very calm when a small army under Jubal A. Early arrived on the outskirts of the Washington defenses early in July 1864. On July 12 a coolly courageous and confident Lincoln was under Confederate sharpshooter fire at Fort Stevens, due north of Washington, D.C.—the only time during the war the President was so exposed.

Washington's proximity to disloyal territory was an important factor in bringing Lincoln's administration to its bloody conclusion. The President's fears, and those of others around him, had always been fears *for* Washington, not *of* it. The city's large black population and the dependence of much of its work force on the government seems to have made for a rather loyal city despite proximity to Virginia. But Maryland was a slave state, and it contained a large population of Southern sympathizers from whom an assassin could readily recruit allies. Most of John Wilkes Booth's fellow conspirators were from Maryland; only one, David E. Herold, was from Washington.

SOURCES: Margaret Leech's *Reveille in Washington, 1860–1865* (New York: Harper & Brothers, 1941) is a lively and detailed narrative of events in Lincoln's Washington. Benjamin Franklin Cooling's *Symbol, Sword, and Shield* ([Hamden, Conn.]: Archon Books, 1975) treats Washington's role in strategic planning by the Lincoln administration. Bates's memorandum on strategy, recommending saving Washington at all costs (April 15, 1861), is in the Abraham Lincoln Papers, Library of Congress.

See also EXECUTIVE MANSION; FORD'S THEATRE; LINCOLN, MARY TODD; LINCOLN, THOMAS ("TAD"); LINCOLN, WILLIAM WALLACE; LINCOLN MEMORIAL; MUSIC.

Webster, Daniel (1782–1852) Webster influenced Lincoln primarily by means of his famous reply to Robert Y. Hayne, a speech which, according to William H. Herndon, Lincoln "read when he lived at New Salem, and which he always regarded as the grandest specimen of American oratory." Lincoln may have seen Webster when he spoke in Springfield in 1837, but for the most part this Whig giant was as much a symbol to Lincoln as a reality. In 1848 Lincoln cited as proof of Whig patriotism in a war of which the party disapproved, the fact that "Clay and Webster each gave a son, never to be returned" in the Mexican War. In 1849 Webster backed Lincoln's rival Justin Butterfield for the General Land Office. That may have cooled Lincoln's admiration for Webster somewhat. Gideon Welles got the impression that Lincoln shared William H. Seward's feeling that Clay and Webster were "hard and selfish leaders, whose private personal ambition had contributed to the ruin of their party."

In the political contests of the mid-1850s, Illinois Democrats and Republicans alike vied to align themselves with the reputations of Clay and Webster in order to attract the votes of old Whigs. Lincoln noted in his 1854 Peoria speech that Stephen A. Douglas "invokes against me, the memory of Clay and of Webster." Lincoln protested that he had been "their life-long friend." "The truth is that some support from whigs is now a necessity with the Judge [Douglas], and for thus it is, that the names of Clay and Webster are now invoked." The same was true in the Lincoln-Douglas Debates of 1858. Douglas, in appealing to old Whigs, invoked the memory of Webster's and Clay's devotion to the Compromise of 1850. Ironically, he tended to exaggerate their roles at the expense of his own vital floor leadership in getting the essential votes for the compromise.

When Lincoln prepared his First Inaugural Address, he used in addition to Webster's reply to Hayne only two other speeches and a copy of the Constitution. As President, Lincoln was faced with a recommendation from the Massachusetts Republican delegation to remove Webster's son Fletcher, a Democrat, from his post as Surveyor of the Port of Boston—"a thing I hate to do," Lincoln told Secretary of the Treasury Salmon P. Chase. Massachusetts Congressman George Ashmun's request that Webster be retained saved Webster's job. In June, again at Ashmun's request, Lincoln persuaded Secretary of War Cameron to accept Webster's Twelfth Massachusetts Regiment into the service.

SOURCES: Richard N. Current's "Lincoln and Daniel Webster," *Journal of the Illinois State Historical Society*, XLVIII (Autumn 1955), 307–321, is definitive.

Weed, Thurlow (1797–1882) New York journalist and political organizer. Weed was born in Greene County, New York. In 1830 he established the Albany *Evening Journal* as an Anti-Masonic newspaper but soon became a Whig allied with William H. Seward. Both men became Republicans, but Weed held Seward back from contention for the party's presidential nomination in 1856 because he saw little hope for victory that year.

To Weed's surprise, 1860 proved not to be Seward's year either. After the New Yorker lost the Republican nomination to Lincoln, Weed had a 5-hour meeting with the nominee and "found Mr. Lincoln sagacious and practical." He worked for his election and again visited Lincoln, now President-elect, in December to discuss Cabinet appointments. Seeing secession as "a long contemplated Free Trade, African Slavery movement," Weed was "anticipating troubles not generally apprehended by our Friends." He urged the appointment of two Cabinet members from slave states. Lincoln was reluctant but finally contacted John A. Gilmer of North Carolina, who eventually rejected the offer. Weed was suspicious of Republicans of Democratic antecedents. They were "exacting and exclusive," whereas former Whigs worked "to divide power and patronage equitably"; "*They* take what we concede, and work, systematically and secretly to obtain as much more as possible." He objected to the proposed Cabinet's including former Democrat Montgomery Blair and a preponderance of men of Democratic backgrounds. Lincoln made it clear that Blair's appointment was decided and pointed out that, since as President *he* would attend Cabinet meetings, the former Whigs would exactly equal the number of former Democrats, 4 to 4. An organizer who knew the importance of patronage, Weed worried that former Democrats controlled the Treasury and Post Office Departments, which dispensed the bulk of government jobs. He was noncommital about Simon Cameron, though in August he had told Lincoln that Cameron was "by far the strongest man and best worker" in Pennsylvania.

Weed worried especially about New York City's huge and lucrative Customs House. He apparently assumed that he would have more influence in appointments than he had, and Lincoln on February 4, 1861, admonished him not to think of himself as the dictator of New York's federal patronage. The President would observe a policy of "justice for all"—including, though Lincoln did not mention him by name, the friends of Weed's arch-rival Horace Greeley.

Weed, like Seward, took secession seriously. He overcame the partisanship which characterized his intraparty views; he wanted "to meet Disunion as Patriots rather than as partisans—as a People rather than as Republicans." He urged a conciliatory policy "to hold the Border States," especially in order to ensure a quorum in Congress when the electoral votes were counted. In February, alarmed at rumors of a seizure of Washington to establish

Thurlow Weed and William H. Seward beg Lincoln to trust them to compromise the difficulties with the South, as Horace Greeley tries to get in the room to remind Lincoln to remain firm on the Republican platform written in Chicago. The cartoon, by Henry Louis Stephens, appeared in Vanity Fair, *March 2, 1861.*

"a Despotism . . . over the whole Union, with Breckenridge Dictator, Davis, Secretary of War, &c.," Weed was ready to go to New York City where troops were "in readiness." Like Seward, however, he wanted a generally conciliatory policy toward the South; he feared that if others joined the Gulf States in secession, "the Government can not obtain money to war with the whole South. If all those states go out the Capitalists, Merchants, &c &c will say 'let them alone.'"

Once war broke out, Weed sought a vigorous policy, especially "a prompt and stringent Blockade." His services were available to the administration, and Lincoln and Secretary of State Seward used them often. Lincoln asked Weed to persuade James Gordon Bennett to cease his policy of opposition to the administration in the pages of the New York *Herald*. In November 1861 Weed went to England and France with Catholic Archbishop John Hughes and Episcopal Bishop Charles P. McIlvaine to counteract Confederate propaganda in Europe. Just before he left, Captain Charles Wilkes captured two Confederate emissaries from the British ship *Trent*. Weed admitted that his "first feeling, on hearing that Mason and Slidell were captured [from the *Trent*], was one of joy and thanksgiving," but his "next suggested a question of right, or policy." He urged "magnamimity" on Seward; he told Lincoln to "turn, if needs be, . . . the other cheek." Otherwise, war was clearly a settled policy in England. He advised capturing Southern ports to restore the flow of cotton to Europe. Weed later *claimed* that he performed other services: at Lincoln's request he told New York Democratic Governor Horatio Seymour in December 1862 that the President would make way for him as his successor if he would follow a Unionist policy; he told General George B. McClellan the same thing in 1863 with equal lack of success; and, again at Lincoln's request, he raised $15,000 from contributors for an unspecified purpose.

While in England, Weed discovered, as he told Seward on February 4, 1862, that the famous British abolitionists like Lord Shaftesbury were "now with the South!" He was always skeptical of the radical antislavery wing of the Republican party. He cheered Lincoln's answer to Greeley's "Prayer of Twenty Millions" in August 1862; for he feared that the "ultras" were "getting the Administration into [a] false position." He always believed that "Democrats will prefer Party to Country if Abolition is thrust forward as a reason for Prosecuting the War." When he resigned as editor of the Albany *Evening Journal* in January 1863, he announced that his differences with his party "about the best means of crushing the Rebellion" were "radical and irreconsilable." On January 29 Lincoln wrote him that the resignation letter gave him "a good deal of uneasiness." "What does it mean?" he asked. Weed lamented "the malign influence" of abolitionist "fanatics . . . with the President," and in the summer and autumn of 1863 he devised a plan embodying four points to end the war: (1) at the first military victory, Lincoln should issue a proclamation of amnesty and pardon; (2) he should then declare a 90-day armistice; (3) states returning to the Union in that period would resume their prewar status; and (4) property in states still in rebellion after the armistice would be partitioned among the soldiers that conquered them. His scheme was as radical in terms of property rights as any antislavery scheme, but it lacked any radical racial goals. The plan had no influence on Lincoln.

In the fall Weed heard that Lincoln regarded his continuing feud with Greeley as "a *personal* quarrel . . . in which both were damaging our cause." Weed was insulted and reminded the President: "If, a year or more since, when ultra Abolition was rampant, I had not throttled it, rescuing Republican organizations from its incendiary influences, the North would have been fatally divided, and your power . . . fatally paralyzed." He complained to David Davis in the spring of 1864 that his friends in New York were "out in the cold," while "Nearly all the Officeholders appointed through our enemies, are now Mr. Lincoln's Enemies." He warned Lincoln that the New York Customs House was giving "Aid and Comfort" to his enemies who sought to make Salmon P. Chase the Republican presidential nominee. He could not understand, he told Davis, "*why* the President prefers his Enemies over his Friends, in this State." As the struggle for control of the Customs House grew more heated, Weed became involved in a libel suit; and one Rufus Andrews accused him of having said in a New York hotel that Mrs. Lincoln had been banished from Washington for treason. Andrews had been ousted from the position as Surveyor of the Port of New York by Weed's influence, and this was doubtless merely a desperate charge by a disappointed office seeker.

Despite sharp ideological and factional differences with the administration, Weed was in harness in 1864 for Lincoln's reelection campaign. He was in high glee when the Radical "conspiracy against Mr. Lincoln collapsed" in September. It had been "equally formidable and vicious." Knowing that he was "not satisfied with the President," they had come to recruit him, but, as Weed told Seward, "my objection to Lincoln is that he has done too much for those who now seek to drive him out of the Field." Accurately, he predicted in October that things would go well in "the Counties, but the Cities will give an ugly Vote."

Lincoln consulted Weed again in 1865, when he reformed his Cabinet. Weed recommended Edwin D. Morgan to succeed William Pitt Fessenden in the Treasury post, but Morgan declined to serve. The President saw to it that Weed met, conversed with, and reported his confidence in Hugh McCulloch, the eventual appointee. Weed admired Lincoln's Second Inaugural Address and hoped that its spirit of charity would pervade the questions of Reconstruction after his death.

SOURCES: The two-volume *Life of Thurlow Weed* (Boston: Houghton Mifflin, 1883) contains Weed's *Autobiography*, edited by his daughter Harriet A. Weed, and *A Memoir* by his grandson Thurlow Weed Barnes. The modern biography by Glendon G. Van Deusen, *Thurlow Weed: Wizard of the Lobby* (Boston: Little, Brown, 1947) is somewhat thin on the Civil War years. See also Mark E. Neely, Jr., "Thurlow Weed, the New York Customs House, and Mrs. Lincoln's Treason," *Lincoln Lore*, Number 1679 (January 1978), pp. 1–4.

Weed's letters calling secession a "Free Trade, African Slavery movement" (to Leonard Swett, December 2, 1860), about "exacting and exclusive" former Democrats (to Swett, January 20, 1861), about Cameron (to Lincoln, August 13, 1860), about meeting secession as "Patriots" (to Lincoln, December 11, 1860), about the "Border States" (to Lincoln, January 10, 1861), about the difficulties of fighting "the whole South" (to Lincoln, February 10, 1861), about the blockade (to Lincoln, May 4, 1861), about Mason and Slidell (to Seward, November 28, 1861), about British abolitionists (to Seward, February 4, 1862), about Lincoln's answer to Greeley (to Seward, August 23, 1862), about his quarrel with Greeley (to Lincoln, October 18, 1863), saying his friends were "out in the cold" (to David Davis, March 30, 1864), about Lincoln's preference for enemies over friends (to Davis, April 11, 1864), on the collapse of the Radical "conspiracy" (to Seward, September 10, 1864), and on predicting the city vote (to Lincoln, October 23, 1864) are in the Abraham Lincoln Papers, Library of Congress.

Weichmann, Louis J. (1842–1902) A key government witness at the trial of Lincoln's assassins. Weichmann was born in Baltimore, the son of a German tailor. He moved to Philadelphia in 1853 and attended Philadelphia's Central High School. After graduation in 1859, he entered St. Charles College in Maryland to prepare for the Catholic priesthood. There he met John H. Surratt, a fellow student. Weichmann left the seminary in 1862 and moved to Washington, D.C. In Washington he taught school until 1864, when he became a clerk in the War Department.

Through John Surratt, Weichmann came to be a boarder at the boarding house kept by Surratt's mother, and he met everyone involved in John Wilkes Booth's plot to kidnap President Lincoln. Weichmann always claimed not to have been a coconspirator, but he admitted under oath that he had once asked a Captain Gleason, also a clerk in the War Department, whether Lincoln could be captured. Weichmann claimed that it was a question prompted only by idle curiosity.

Arrested with the other members of Mrs. Surratt's household on April 17, 1865, Weichmann quickly became a prosecution witness. Though he later claimed that the testimony of John M. Lloyd hanged Mrs. Surratt, Weichmann's testimony was a key part of the prosecution case against her. On the day of the assassination and on the Tuesday before, Weichmann had driven Mrs. Surratt in a hired buggy to the tavern in Surrattsville that she rented to Lloyd. On the first trip, he testified, she had a conversation with Lloyd in tones so hushed he could not hear them (Lloyd testified that she asked about the "shooting-irons" hidden in the tavern). Before the second trip, Weichmann testified, Booth called at the boarding house, had a private conversation with Mrs. Surratt, and left a package with her to take to the tavern. (Booth asked for the package when he arrived at the tavern after killing Lincoln.) The defense challenged the significance of Weichmann's testimony on the ground that Mrs. Surratt had a pressing financial reason to make both trips. Weichmann also testified that Booth had met with Dr. Samuel A. Mudd in Washington in January, a meeting Mudd had not admitted took place when he was interrogated. Weichmann was wrong about the date (actually December 23), but the meeting did take place.

Judge Advocate General Joseph Holt, the government prosecutor, and Secretary of War Edwin M. Stanton got Weichmann a patronage job in the Philadelphia Customs House after the trial. Weichmann's pleas to be readmitted to preparation for the priesthood fell on deaf ears; the Catholic hierarchy, he suspected, took a dim view of his testimony against Mrs. Surratt, who also was a Roman Catholic. In November 1866 he was removed from the customs house job as a result of President Andrew Johnson's estrangement from the Republican party. In 1867 he testified at the trial of John H. Surratt. When Ulysses S. Grant became President, Weichmann got his patronage job back, again with the help of Holt and Stanton. In October 1886 he was again removed, this time by a Democratic administration. He moved to Anderson, Indiana, where his brother was a Catholic priest. He lived with his sister and brother-in-law, Mr. and Mrs. Charles O'Crowley, and established the Anderson Business College. He died there in 1902, having signed a deathbed statement that he had told the truth at the trial.

Weichmann's role in the trial had been an obsession all his life. While in Anderson, he left the Catholic Church because, he alleged, Catholics persecuted him for his role in testifying against Mary Surratt. He wrote a long book, not published until 1975, defending his role. Weichmann needed defense, for he has rarely been regarded as a very sympathetic character. John Surratt called him a liar and a coward who had begged to be in on the plot but was rejected because he could not ride and shoot. Historians of the assassination often apply adjectives like "feline" to him. Nevertheless, his testimony was balanced; he testified to Mrs. Surratt's good moral character, for example. And no one has ever effectively impugned the truthfulness of what he said.

SOURCES: See Floyd E. Risvold, ed., *A True History of the Assassination of Abraham Lincoln and of the Conspiracy of 1865* (New York: Alfred A. Knopf, 1975), the long-lost book by Weichmann. Risvold, who discovered the manuscript and bought it, is very partial to Weichmann, as most authors are not. For balance, check George S. Bryan, *The Great American Myth* (New York: Carrick & Evans, 1940).

See also TRIAL OF THE ASSASSINS.

Weik, Jesse William (1857–1930) William H. Herndon's collaborator on his famous biography of Lincoln. Weik was born in Greencastle, Indiana, and he lived there most of his life. He graduated from Indiana Asbury University (now DePauw) in 1875 and later earned a master's degree there. He was a Republican in politics and an enthusiastic admirer, from his student days on, of Abraham Lincoln.

When he was only 18 years old, Weik wrote Herndon requesting a Lincoln autograph. Herndon failed to reply until 6 years later, when he answered with a long letter about his project to write a Lincoln biography and with a Lincoln manuscript of more than ordinary significance. It was one of the earliest examples of his writing:

Jesse William Weik

Abraham Lincoln
his hand and pen
he will be good but
god knows When

In the meantime Weik had gained appointment as a pension agent for the Department of Interior. His work took him to Springfield, where he met Herndon in 1882 and saw his papers relating to Lincoln.

In 1885 poor health forced Weik to quit his job, and he looked to writing as a career. He returned to Greencastle; he planned to write an article on Lincoln with Herndon's help. Herndon agreed and began to send long, garrulous letters full of reminiscences of his old law partner. As the letters stretched out, Herndon became convinced that he and Weik should write a book. Weik leapt at the opportunity. In a sense, Herndon's letters became the famous biography of Lincoln, but only after Weik had selected from them, organized the material, added to it, and substantially rewritten it. "You must write," Herndon told his young collaborator, "& Ill give the facts." Herndon continued to write to Weik until his death in 1891.

As the team began seeking a publisher in 1886, Herndon sent Weik his collection of notes on Lincoln. Weik discovered some gaps in Herndon's research and tried to fill them in, notably by visiting Kentucky for reminiscences Herndon never collected. He began to lend money to the impoverished Herndon. In the summer of 1887 Herndon joined Weik in Greencastle to write the book above the grocery store–bakery established by Weik's father, which the son now operated. Herndon wrote rough and rambling drafts of chapters on particular subjects; Weik turned them into readable literature. In fact, he wrote the lion's share of the book. Probably about 80 percent of the manuscript was substantially the younger partner's work and was only based on Herndon's letters and papers.

When the book was finished in 1888, it went begging for a publisher. Weik employed an agent, Mrs. Gertrude Garrison. Reputable houses in that genteel age wanted nothing that smacked of the gloves-off approach of Ward Hill Lamon's earlier book on Lincoln. Finally, Belford, Clarke & Company, a publisher of low repute, agreed to take the manuscript. Weik signed the contract. The two men quarreled over the relative weight to be given Weik's efforts on the title page and in the preface. In the end, both names appeared, Weik's smaller than Herndon's, and the title was *Herndon's Lincoln: The True Story of a Great Life.* It was published in three volumes in 1889.

Shortly thereafter, Belford, Clarke & Company went bankrupt. Reorganized as the Belford Clarke Company, it put out a second edition in 1890 under a new contract again arranged by Weik. With the help of journalist Horace White, Weik obtained the plates from the inept first publishers and sold the book to Charles Scribner's Sons. Weik pressed Herndon to delete a few offensive passages. Herndon agreed. He died, thinking Scribner's would publish the book. But the firm got wind of Robert Todd Lincoln's objections to the book and backed out.

Gideon Welles

White helped Weik get D. Appleton & Company to publish the third edition in 1892.

Herndon owed Weik $650 the year he died. He never sold or formally gave his partner the collection of papers, but Weik had them in his possession and kept them. He helped other Lincoln writers with them over the years, including Ida M. Tarbell. He wrote occasional articles on Lincoln for popular magazines, but he did not put the papers to serious use for many years. In 1910 he tried to sell the collection but could not find a buyer at his price. In 1922 he wrote *The Real Lincoln* (Boston: Houghton, Mifflin), based on the papers; reviewers agreed that at most it supplemented *Herndon's Lincoln.* Albert J. Beveridge helped get it published and reviewed it favorably. His kindnesses helped him gain access to the papers for his own Lincoln biography.

When Weik died, he still had the papers. His heirs sold them to a manuscript dealer, and the Library of Congress acquired them in 1941. They are now called the Herndon-Weik Collection, and they constitute the principal source of information on Lincoln's early life.

SOURCES: Nothing surpasses David Donald's *Lincoln's Herndon* (New York: Alfred A. Knopf, 1948) in its treatment of Weik's important and often underestimated role in producing *Herndon's Lincoln.* Some supplemental information on Weik is available in Benjamin P. Thomas's *Portrait for Posterity: Lincoln and His Biographers* (New Brunswick, N.J.: Rutgers University Press, 1947).

See also HERNDON, WILLIAM HENRY.

Welles, Gideon (1802–1878) Lincoln's Secretary of the Navy. Gideon Welles was born in Connecticut. He was editor of the Hartford *Times,* and he became an ardent Jacksonian Democrat. The Kansas-Nebraska Act caused him to drift away from the Democrats, but he had no use for the party's major competitors in Connecticut, the "miserable" Know-Nothing party. A "proscription of men on account of birth is as odious certainly as that of color," Welles argued. By February 1856 he was helping to organize the Republican party in Connecticut. The Hartford *Evening Press,* which Welles established, became a principal party organ. His bid for the governorship on the Republican ticket in 1856 failed.

In 1860 Welles was chairman of the Connecticut delegation to the Republican national convention. He detested William H. Seward as the quintessential Whig whose 1858 "irrepressible conflict" speech had smeared every Democrat from Jefferson to Van Buren as proslavery. Welles was one of the earliest and steadiest opponents of Seward's nomination, but he supported Salmon P. Chase, a former Democrat, rather than the eventual nominee, Lincoln, a former Whig.

Welles became Secretary of the Navy because Lincoln, who may have preferred Nathaniel P. Banks for the post, left the choice for the traditionally New England department to Hannibal Hamlin. To satisfy Lincoln's constitutional propriety, Welles had first to pledge that he would support enforcement of the Fugitive Slave Act.

Welles at first thought Fort Sumter would have to be evacuated, but he supported its attempted reinforcement later. Though enforcing the blockade would become one of his major duties, Welles never thought the blockade justified in international law; he believed that legally the government could close the ports of only the insurrectionary states. Nevertheless, within 6 months of the war's beginning he had built up a respectable fleet to guard the South's 3500 miles of coastline. An able administrator, Welles chose probably the best subordinates in any department in the persons of Assistant Secretary Gustavus Vasa Fox (Montgomery Blair's brother-in-law and a favorite of Lincoln's) and Chief Clerk William Faxon (formerly business manager of the *Evening Press*). He tried, for the most part successfully, to keep politics out of the navy yards.

Welles was competent, but he was not adventurous. He was slower than his Confederate counterpart, Stephen R. Mallory, to realize that ironclad vessels were valuable, but he recommended their use in time to halt the Confederate *Virginia* (or *Merrimack*). He was quick to see the merits of eccentric John Ericsson's floating battery which would become the *Monitor*. Likewise, he was quick to see the merit of Fox's idea to capture New Orleans by sea, an idea which pleased the surprised President as well.

Though conservative on constitutional issues involving states' rights (he opposed West Virginia statehood, for example), Welles ordered the Navy to shelter and employ fugitive slaves as early as 1861. Not one of the most influential Cabinet members, Welles was nevertheless, with Seward, among the first to learn of Lincoln's intention to issue the Emancipation Proclamation. He thought the proclamation "safely within the President's war powers."

Welles's relations with Secretary of War Edwin M. Stanton were stiff and formal, to say the least, but Welles came to agree with Stanton and the President that General George B. McClellan wished "to outgeneral the Rebels, but not to kill and destroy them." He had numerous conflicts with Seward over foreign policy because his extremely anti-British views clashed with Seward's frequent duty to mollify British opinion. He approved of Captain Charles Wilkes's seizure of Confederate emissaries in the *Trent* crisis publicly, and he was the only Cabinet member to do so.

Welles's wife, Mary, and Mary Todd Lincoln became friends, partly because they shared the common experience of losing a young son to disease in Washington. Welles supported Lincoln steadily and had strayed so far from his early support of Chase that he was never seriously tempted in 1864 to seek another Republican nominee besides Lincoln. He took very little active role in the election, however. When Lincoln was shot, Welles's first response was, "Damn the Rebels, this is their work."

A leader of New England's more radical Republicans in 1860, Welles became increasingly disturbed by infringements of civil liberties in the North during the war and especially by threats to the power of states. He deplored the arrest of Clement L. Vallandigham (with the rest of the Cabinet and the President), but he endorsed measures to prevent the abuse of the privilege of the writ of habeas corpus to frustrate the war effort. He feared centralization of power in Washington, but in the Jacksonian tradition he respected executive power as much as legislative power. After Lincoln's death, Welles opposed Reconstruction measures. He became a Democrat in 1868 and a Liberal Republican in 1872.

After Charles Francis Adams suggested that Seward was the genius behind the Lincoln administration in a eulogy of Seward in 1873, Welles argued in *Lincoln and Seward* (1874) that Lincoln played a large role even in Seward's realm of foreign policy and played the largest role in the administration by far. He himself has played a larger role in historical writing than more influential Cabinet members because of the acerbic, gossipy, well-written, and frequently acute diary he kept from 1862 through the end of his years of public service.

The diary is one of the most important sources for study of the Lincoln administration. Only Welles and Seward were in the Cabinet for the whole of the Lincoln administration. The diary is the source of knowledge of innumerable ideas and attitudes in the White House. For example, Welles believed that West Point had fostered defensive attitudes out of a belief that America was not an aggressive nation and would always be resisting the attacks of monarchical governments. Welles was privy to Seward's (and perhaps Lincoln's) private opinion that Henry Clay had sacrificed the Whig party to personal ambition. The diary contains unforgettable (and almost always acid) character portraits from the "scheming jobbers" working for the Chiriqui colonization project to Senator Charles Sumner—"He would not only free the slaves but elevate them above their former masters, yet with all his studied philanthropy and love for the negroes in the abstract, is unwilling to fellowship with them, though he thinks he is." For several of the most important acts or events in the administration the diary is the major source of information, including the genesis of the Emancipation Proclamation (along with the essential memoirs of Francis Bicknell Carpenter) and the Cabinet crisis of December 1862. Characteristically, Welles shows the President as decidedly the controlling force in those episodes as in most others.

SOURCES: John Niven's *Gideon Welles: Lincoln's Secretary of the Navy* (New York: Oxford University Press, 1973) is better on administration than politics, but it is a solid biography in general. See also Howard K. Beale, ed., *The Diary of Gideon Welles*, 3 vols. (New York: W. W. Norton, 1960).

West Virginia Became a state during and as a result of the Civil War. Before Virginia seceded, a convention (irregularly attended) of the state's northwestern counties met to call for another convention in June in the event that Virginia did secede. After Virginia's secession ordinance of May 23, 1861, delegates were chosen by various means for the second convention to meet at Wheeling on June 11. Only two-thirds of the counties which would later constitute the new state had any representation at the convention, which appointed a temporary government with Francis H. Pierpont as Governor of "Virginia." A "reorganized legislature" met in July and elected United States Senators.

An August convention resolved to form a new state called "Kanawha" and provided for elections in October to vote on the proposition of forming a new state and to send delegates to a constitutional convention. By February 1862, a constitution was written for a new state, now to be called "West Virginia," and 18,862 voters ratified it on April 3 (only 514 voted in opposition). On May 13, 1862, the reorganized legislature of Virginia consented to the formation of the new state. That complied technically with the Constitution's requirement that no new state could be formed from an old one without the consent of the old state, but, of course, much of the old state (represented by the seceded government in Richmond) in no way passed judgment on the enterprise.

As required by the Constitution, Congress passed a bill to admit West Virginia, and in December 1862 Lincoln faced the question whether to sign it. He was apparently distressed by the problem and requested written opinions from his Cabinet, something he rarely did. William H. Seward, Salmon P. Chase, and Edwin M. Stanton supported statehood; they held that the loyal element in an insurrectionary state constituted the state. Chase said the constitutionality of West Virginia statehood was not as "technical as some may think," and he called the Virginia legislature which ratified the move "the only Legislature of the State known to the Union." Gideon Welles, Montgomery Blair, and Edward Bates opposed statehood as unconstitutional. Bates argued that Congress admits but does not *make* states; he called the formation of West Virginia "nothing less than attempted *secession*." If successful, it would tear "into pieces the regions further south" and produce "a multitude of feeble communities." Though willing to recognize the usefulness of the loyal government of Virginia for some purposes, Blair saw in the recognition of statehood only a technical legality. He denounced it as unfair: it was "no fault of the loyal people of [eastern] Virginia" that they were held in subjection and were unable to express their will on the subject.

Lincoln reasoned that "Doubtless among these nonvoters [for West Virginia statehood in eastern Virginia] were some Union men whose voices were smothered by the more numerous secessionists; but we know too little of their number to assign them any appreciable value." Practically, he questioned, "Can this government stand, if it indulges constitutional constructions by which men in open rebellion against it are to be accounted, man for man, the equals of those who maintain their loyalty to it?" Moreover, it was "expedient," tending "the more strongly to the restoration of the national authority throughout the Union." He signed the act on December 31, 1862.

The act required West Virginia to ratify a proposed clause in the state constitution providing for gradual emancipation as a condition of statehood. That condition having been met, Lincoln on April 20, 1863, proclaimed that West Virginia would be a state on June 20, 1863.

The irregularity of the statehood process for West Virginia seemed glaring when the Thirty-eighth Congress denied representation to the reorganized government of Virginia under Pierpont, which had moved from Wheeling to Alexandria because of West Virginia statehood. The government's representatives had been admitted in the preceding Congress (1861–1863) when Virginia's consent to West Virginia statehood had been necessary to comply with the Constitution.

SOURCES: A clear but critical evaluation of West Virginia statehood appears in J. G. Randall, *Constitutional Problems Under Lincoln*, rev. ed. (Urbana: University of Illinois Press, 1951). Chase's opinion on West Virginia, in a letter to Lincoln of December 29, 1862; Bates's opinion, dated December 29, 1862; and Blair's in a letter to Lincoln of December 26, 1862, are in the Abraham Lincoln Papers, Library of Congress.

Whig Party For years historians have been mystified by Abraham Lincoln's long association with the Whig party. His log cabin origins and his identification with the cause of the common man seemed at odds with that party's reputation for being the party of the bankers, the urban commercial classes, and the rich and conservative in general. As a result, his Whig years have been ignored or misunderstood as a period in his life when Lincoln was narrowly partisan and had not yet grown to greatness. Such views are unfair both to the Whig party and to Lincoln. The Whig years merit much attention. After all, Lincoln was a Whig for almost the entire life of that party, was a Whig more than twice as long as he was a Republican, and remained confident longer than many politicians that the Whig party could meet the sectional issues of the 1850s.

The reasons for Lincoln's becoming a Whig are not in the least mystifying. Most important, the party which opposed the Democracy of Andrew Jackson offered the solution to the deficiencies of the young politician's hardscrabble frontier youth in Indiana. Lincoln's earliest surviving political statement (a communication to the voters of Sangamon County, March 9, 1832) stressed "the public utility of internal improvements" to "the poorest and most thinly populated countries." Government sponsorship of roads and the clearing of navigable streams would bring prosperity and end rural isolation. He complained, too, of usurious rates of interest. Although in this early statement he recommended a law regulating interest rates, the need would soon lead him to take an interest in another staple of Whig doctrine: banks to provide currency and credit for commercial transactions. Thus the Whig party's vision of the economic development of the West seemed the perfect solution to the deficiencies of a backwoods environment which had made Lincoln all "too familiar with disappointments."

Though the party's principles were its most obvious appeal to Lincoln, two other factors cannot be discounted. Kentucky politician Henry Clay, who was Lincoln's "beau ideal of a statesman," summarized Whig principles eloquently as the "American System." And Lincoln probably inherited his early political leanings from his father Thomas Lincoln. Although reminiscences about Thomas's early political views differ, it is certain that in later life the elder Lincoln was a Whig, and that was probably his affiliation earlier as well. Lincoln's career in the Illinois General Assembly (1834–1841) was closely identified with the State Bank of Illinois and the Internal Improvements Act of 1837. National politics drew his attention to the protective tariff, which he advocated strenuously in the period from 1842 to 1847.

A peculiarity of Lincoln's Whiggery was his absorption with the issues of economic development summed up in the American System at the expense of other issues in which many Whigs were interested. The party began as a loose coalition of groups opposed to Andrew Jackson, a vigorous President who used the veto power spectacularly and who belonged to a well-organized party called "the Democracy" in Lincoln's day (Lincoln often called them the "Loco-Focos" or "Locos," a Whig tactic to identify the party with a radical working-class wing of the party so nicknamed in New York). Whigs generally favored a weak executive and bridled at the trappings of tight party organization. Lincoln did not. In 1840 he drew up a plan of campaign "to organize the whole state" with county, precinct, and section captains in each county. He was a member of the Whig State Central Committee for that historic campaign for William Henry Harrison, and in 1841, still on the committee, he recommended a state convention to nominate a gubernatorial ticket. He strenuously urged a convention system for nominations in an "Address to the People of Illinois" on March 4, 1843. Lincoln refused to speculate whether "the system is right in itself"; he claimed merely that "while our opponents use it, it is madness in us not to defend ourselves with it." He dwelt little on circumscribing executive power until 1848. Then the Whig candidate Zachary Taylor, not identified with any of the traditional Whig issues, ran a campaign which justified his lack of a statement of principles by urging that a President simply execute the expressed will of Congress. Lincoln argued for Taylor's principle during that campaign, but afterward he warned that the President must not appear "a mere man of straw." "He must occasionally say. . . , 'by the Eternal,' 'I take the responsibility.' Those phrases were the 'Samson's locks' of Gen. Jackson, and we dare not disregard the lessons of experience."

Whigs, particularly in the East, had a reputation for being uneasy with popular democracy. The road to election did not lie in opposing suffrage for the common man, but some Whigs devised an elitist doctrine of representation. The theory posited the elected representative as a check on the will of his constituents—not as a stand-in for the people who elected him, but as a man sifted out by the electoral process to speak his superior conscience. Many Whigs loathed the idea of "instruction," the notion that a constituency could instruct its representative how to vote on a particular issue. Lincoln, by contrast, stated in 1848 that "the primary, the cardinal, the one great living principle of all Democratic representative government [was] . . . the principle, that the representative is bound to carry out the known will of his constituents."

The Whig party was also tainted with nativism: dislike of immigrants, especially Catholic immigrants. Again Lincoln defied the pattern. When news of violent anti-Catholic rioting in Philadelphia in 1844 reached Springfield, Lincoln drafted the resolutions adopted by a Whig meeting which protested "all attempts to either destroy the naturalization laws or to so alter them, as to render admission under them, less convenient, less cheap, or less expeditious than it now is." The "guarantee of the rights of conscience" belonged "no less to the Catholic, than to the Protestant."

The Whiggish penchant for moralistic political issues was something Lincoln shared with the party in general. He was a temperance advocate (but an opponent of prohibition) and, throughout his career, an antislavery man. He, like other Whigs, showed little interest in territorial expansion, and as a member of Congress in 1848 he opposed the Mexican War as an unconstitutional and unnecessary war of conquest. However, he was a Westerner, and that colored some of his Whig positions. He did not at first oppose all expansion as weakening the intensity with which the already existing country could be improved (as many Eastern Whigs did), and he voted against a resolution for a peace settlement that would gain no territory as a result of the war. His close Whig friend, Anson G. Henry, warned him that going "against all Territory" would keep them "the minority party for a long time to come."

Although some leaders deserted the Whig party as early as 1854, Lincoln did not join the competing Republican organization until 1856—to some degree a sign of his lasting affection for his old party and belief in its ability to meet any issue. Whiggish economic ideas dominated Lincoln's mind until his death, but he showed a remarkable ability as President not to indulge any favoritism for old Whigs in the Republican party. He recognized the essential contribution of former Democrats to party victory and, later, the contribution of Democrats themselves to military victory.

Lincoln's affiliation with the Whig party had a lasting effect on writing about his life: it gave a false air of obscurity and failure to his career before the 1850s. Illinois was an overwhelmingly Democratic state, and Lincoln failed to gain national prominence because his party was not prominent enough to launch anybody out of its ranks to the governor's mansion or the United States Senate. However, *within* that party he was very successful. He quickly rose to a position of leadership in minority ranks in the Illinois legislature. By the early 1840s, he and Edward D. Baker and John J. Hardin were the three shining stars on the state's Whig horizon. When Hardin died in the Mexican War, Lincoln was one of the two most prominent Whigs in the state. But the paucity of Whig districts forced any Whig to sacrifice ambition to unity—thus Lincoln could not run for reelection to Congress in 1848 because of a previous agreement to allow another Whig to run in the most Whiggish district in central Illinois.

SOURCES: See G. S. Boritt, *Lincoln and the Economics of the American Dream* (Memphis: Memphis State University Press, 1978).

See also BANKING; CLAY, HENRY; ECONOMICS; MEXICAN WAR; PATRONAGE; PRESIDENCY, POWERS OF THE; RAILROADS; TARIFF; TAYLOR, ZACHARY.

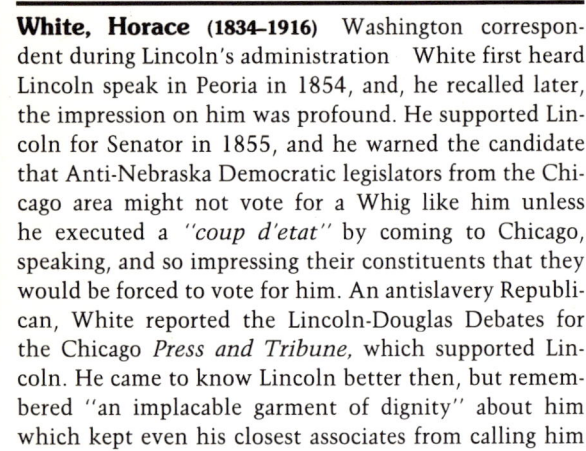

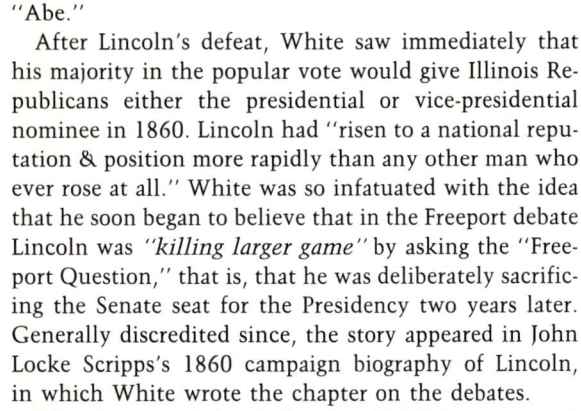

White, Horace (1834–1916) Washington correspondent during Lincoln's administration White first heard Lincoln speak in Peoria in 1854, and, he recalled later, the impression on him was profound. He supported Lincoln for Senator in 1855, and he warned the candidate that Anti-Nebraska Democratic legislators from the Chicago area might not vote for a Whig like him unless he executed a *"coup d'etat"* by coming to Chicago, speaking, and so impressing their constituents that they would be forced to vote for him. An antislavery Republican, White reported the Lincoln-Douglas Debates for the Chicago *Press and Tribune*, which supported Lincoln. He came to know Lincoln better then, but remembered "an implacable garment of dignity" about him which kept even his closest associates from calling him "Abe."

After Lincoln's defeat, White saw immediately that his majority in the popular vote would give Illinois Republicans either the presidential or vice-presidential nominee in 1860. Lincoln had "risen to a national reputation & position more rapidly than any other man who ever rose at all." White was so infatuated with the idea that he soon began to believe that in the Freeport debate Lincoln was *"killing larger game"* by asking the "Freeport Question," that is, that he was deliberately sacrificing the Senate seat for the Presidency two years later. Generally discredited since, the story appeared in John Locke Scripps's 1860 campaign biography of Lincoln, in which White wrote the chapter on the debates.

Like the rest of the *Tribune* staff, White supported Lincoln's presidential bid in 1860. He was a delegate to the Chicago convention that nominated Lincoln. White, with the rest of the paper's staff generally, strongly opposed Simon Cameron's appointment to Lincoln's Cabinet. The reporter told Lincoln in December that the story that $40,000 had been subscribed in a New Orleans hotel to reward the assassins of the Republican President- and Vice President-elect came from a reliable source. White himself already thought war "quite a probable event." He opposed any compromise with the South and told Lincoln that the mass of young men "will plunge into blood to the horses' bridles to defend your newly acquired prerogatives." After Fort Sumter fell, White told Presidential secretary John G. Nicolay: "He has kept his promise, and now we are keeping ours."

White was the *Tribune*'s Washington correspondent until 1863. He followed the paper's stoutly antislavery reporting slant, and he was even more critical in private of the President's slowness in moving toward emancipation than he was in public print. He quit the *Tribune* but remained in Washington. He turned a deaf ear to Radical Republican attempts to replace Lincoln as the party's nominee and supported Lincoln for the Presidency in 1864.

In 1890 White rewrote the chapter on the debates for the third edition of William H. Herndon and Jesse Weik's *Abraham Lincoln: The True Story of a Great Life* (New York: D. Appleton, 1892), and he helped get a publisher in the East for the floundering book.

SOURCES: In addition to being a solid biography of White, Joseph Logsdon's *Horace White, Nineteenth Century Liberal* (Westport, Conn.: Greenwood Publishing, 1971) does the best job of sorting out the complicated story of the Chicago *Tribune*'s relationship to Lincoln. White's letters to Lincoln about the "coup d'etat" (October 25, 1854), Lincoln's Presidential chances (November 5, 1858), probable war (December 11, 1860), compromise (December 22, 1860), and Lincoln's "promise" (April 19, 1861) are in the Abraham Lincoln Papers, Library of Congress.

White House *See* EXECUTIVE MANSION.

Whitman, Walt (1819–1892) The first great poet to write verse about Abraham Lincoln. Born on Long Island, Whitman lived in Brooklyn and various towns in New York, where he worked for several Democratic newspapers. He became a free-soil Democrat identified with New York's Barnburner faction after 1848. He had already published three editions of *Leaves of Grass* when he moved to Washington, D.C., in December 1862. Whitman was sympathetic to the Republicans by that time, but he denounced parties in general. He visited military hospitals regularly and was deeply moved by the sufferings of the common soldier. On January 24, 1865, he gained appointment as a clerk in the Indian office of the Department of Interior. He had prepared another book of poems by that year, *Walt Whitman's Drum Taps*, and he quickly added a *Sequel* in 1866 which contained four poems about the death of President Lincoln: "When Lilacs Last in the Dooryard Bloom'd," "O Captain! My Captain!" "This Dust Was Once the Man," and "Hushed be the Camps To-day."

Whitman never met Lincoln, though he saw him on numerous occasions in Washington and fancied Lincoln acknowledged him personally by nodding to him on the streets. He thought him "a curious looking man, very sad," but "a pretty big President." Between 1879 and 1890 he delivered a lecture on "The Death of Abraham Lincoln" to several audiences. He found Lincoln's Western nature appealing and celebrated his democratic leanings, the emancipation of the slaves, and his devotion to the Union. He accurately summarized the importance of Lincoln's death (and at the same time the role of his famous poems about Lincoln) when he said that the "final use of a heroic-eminent life—especially of a heroic-eminent death" was as "a cement to the whole people, subtler, more underlying than any thing in written Constitution, or courts or armies—namely, the cement of a death identified thoroughly with that people at its head, and for its sake. Strange (is it not?) that battles, martyrs, agonies, blood, even assassinations, should so condense—perhaps only really, lastingly condense—a nationality."

SOURCES: In a thorough but overly contentious book William E. Barton nearly exhausted the subject: *Abraham Lincoln and Walt Whitman* (Indianapolis: Bobbs-Merrill, 1928). George Frederickson's *The Inner Civil War: Northern Intellectuals and the Crisis of the Union* (New York: Harper & Row, 1965) gives a briefer and more sympathetic comparison of Whitman's political views with Lincoln's.

Whitney, Henry Clay (1831–1905) Lawyer and fellow traveler with Lincoln on the Eighth Judicial Circuit. Whitney was born in Detroit, Maine, but after several moves settled in Urbana, Illinois, in 1854. There he met Lincoln, and thereafter they were associated several times in legal cases at various county seats on the Eighth Judicial Circuit. Lincoln apparently thought well of the young lawyer's abilities, and he referred business to Whitney.

Both men were Whigs before they became Republicans. Whitney worked with Lincoln in politics soon after their meeting. He was especially active in the Senate campaign of 1858, which he regarded as essentially a popular contest between Lincoln and Stephen A. Douglas (though in fact it was numerous contests for seats in the Illinois legislature, which elected Senators). He warned Lincoln of a "dangerous" attack published in the Chicago *Times*, which claimed that as a Congressman in the 1840s Lincoln had voted against supplies for American soldiers fighting in Mexico. Whitney had heard the charge in a campaign 2 years previously, had spoken to Lincoln about it, and had subsequently denounced it as a lie. Yet, in 1858 he seemed unsure. Lincoln replied: "Give yourself no concern about my voting against the supplies, unless you ar[e] without faith that a lie can be successfully contradicted." Whitney himself helped contradict it by borrowing old copies of the *Congressional Globe* from the Chicago Historical Society and researching an answer for the (Republican) Chicago *Press and Tribune*.

Whitney watched Lincoln's interests closely. He was distrustful of former Democrats now working for Lincoln's election. He told Lincoln that Richard J. Oglesby "bears down on the Administration too much" (Douglas was opposed to the Buchanan administration, too) and urged Lincoln "to talk to him about it." He saw "danger" in Owen Lovejoy's strongly antislavery district. Following Lincoln's lead, Whitney accepted the invincibility of Congressman Lovejoy in the district, but he disliked the abolitionist candidates running for the state legislature in that district and feared that "the loss of two or three members of the Legislature through the greediness of those stinking abolitionists" might cost Lincoln's election to the Senate. At Whitney's urging, Lincoln wrote Lovejoy on the subject.

Whitney thought that the Illinois Central Railroad sought Douglas's election, and he hoped to "turn the hatred of the people to the I.C.R.Rd. against Douglas." Lincoln's own close ties with the Illinois Central were an obvious difficulty in this strategy, and later Whitney reported that the railroad president was coming to Chicago to promise the Chicago Republican leaders "that his Co. will not interfere with the Election." Whitney divined Douglas's strategy in the campaign: "to drive you from a *Conservative* position to one on the other extremes." Like other Republicans, Whitney told Lincoln "not to treat him tenderly." When the campaign was over, he sent Lincoln a set of the *Tribune*'s reports of his debates with Douglas. The clippings became part of the scrapbook which supplied the material for the published edition of the Lincoln-Douglas Debates.

Through their mutual friend David Davis, Whitney sought an office from Lincoln after he became President. Lincoln refused on several occasions, but eventually he made Whitney an Army paymaster, a position which Whitney held throughout the Civil War.

After the war Whitney moved to Kansas and then to Chicago, where, in a sensational divorce case in 1888, the wife of the man Whitney represented shot the lawyer in the courtroom. Badly wounded, Whitney sought a quieter life lecturing on Lincoln. His voice proved unequal to the task, and he decided to write a book. *Life on the Circuit with Lincoln*, published in 1892, relied on the biographies by Ward Hill Lamon and William H. Herndon, but for the years 1854 to 1861, when Whitney repeatedly saw Lincoln, his memory produced many rich and original anecdotes. Amidst the random, discursive, and often boring musings of Whitney's undisciplined mind (the book urged Robert T. Lincoln's election to the Presidency as a debt owed by America to his father), there were details which gave an authentic flavor of life on the Eighth Judicial Circuit and believable appraisals of Lincoln's lawyerly and personal manner available nowhere else. Whitney noted that his friends called him "Lincoln" (no one called him "Abe" to his face). He appraised Lincoln's legal career honestly and noted that the famed Springfield lawyer did not know things about case law which Whitney knew when first admitted to the bar. Moreover, "biographers, in a gush of enthusiasm," Whitney reported, "incline to inculcate the idea that Lincoln was wont to retire from every case in which he found himself to be wrong and to surrender up his fees"; this was "by no means the case." The book also contained a spurious text of a Lincoln speech at Urbana in 1854; Whitney simply copied Lincoln's Peoria speech and omitted parts of the introduction and conclusion. The book, watered down with rambling asides, sold poorly.

In 1896 Whitney sold *McClure's Magazine* the alleged text of Lincoln's "Lost Speech" at the Bloomington Republican convention of 1856. He claimed to have taken notes and reconstructed the speech from them. Most scholars now regard the result also as spurious, for it bears no resemblance to a brief newspaper account of the speech discovered in 1930.

Whitney published a book on *Marriage and Divorce*

(1894), lectured, moved to Salem, Massachusetts, and published occasional articles. In the end, he was sorry he "ever invested" in the Lincoln business.

SOURCES: Paul M. Angle carefully discusses the merits and failings of Whitney's *Life on the Circuit with Lincoln* in the 1940 edition published by the Caxton Printers, Caldwell, Idaho. Benjamin P. Thomas's *Portrait for Posterity: Lincoln and His Biographers* (New Brunswick, N.J.: Rutgers University Press, 1947) gives a similar assessment of Whitney's own work but adds an interesting discussion of Whitney's views on other Lincoln authors. Both books ignore Whitney's political opinions and his work for Lincoln reconstructed here from his letters to Lincoln about voting supplies for the Mexican War (June 23, 1858), Oglesby (July 24, 1858), Lovejoy's district (July 31, 1858), the Illinois Central (August 7, 1858 and September 23, 1858), and Douglas's strategy (August 7, 1858) in the Abraham Lincoln Papers, Library of Congress.

Wide-Awakes Groups of young Republicans formed into clubs for the election of 1860. The first group of Wide-Awakes was organized for the Connecticut gubernatorial campaign in Hartford in the spring, and it was quickly copied throughout the North in the summer. The clubs were semimilitary and marched with precision in torchlit campaign parades. Because their tin torches (which were suspended atop "rails" or poles) emitted sparks and splattered hot oil, the marchers wore distinctive uniforms of glazed caps and oilcloth capes to protect their clothing. The other parties quickly imitated the organizations. The Douglas Democratic clubs, for example, were known as "Little Giants."

The Wide-Awakes typified the ritualistic aspects of nineteenth-century American politics. In America, political pageantry more or less took the place that religious rituals occupied in the Catholic countries of Europe. Politics in the nineteenth century were also entertainment. The rallies, long speeches, and parades provided the excitement and color that modern sports events supply for many Americans.

Previously unpublished, this is the only known photograph of a Wide-Awake club in full marching regalia. Note the large Lincoln banner in the rear.

"SEE THEM ON THEIR WINDING WAY."
MOHAWK WIDE AWAKES AND BAND
Parade, In honor of the Republican Victories, November, 1860.

Photograph by Stanton.

Wigwam The temporary auditorium in which Abraham Lincoln was nominated for the Presidency in 1860. Republicans subscribed $5000 in April to put up a rough, two-story wooden structure, "The Great Wigwam," at Market and Lake Streets in Chicago for the national nominating convention. Reminiscent of the political symbolism of the great Whig "log cabin" campaign of 1840, the Wigwam measured 100 by 180 feet and held the 466 delegates, dozens of representatives of the press, over 1000 people seated in an upstairs gallery, and perhaps as many as 8000 spectators on a series of landings. The acoustics were good, and everyone could see the speaker's platform.

The Wigwam, like the "Wide-Awake" marching groups, quickly became a successful symbol of a boisterous Republicanism. The state nominating convention held at Decatur, Illinois, early in May had also met in a Wigwam; it was built of wood and canvas. There Lincoln had received his first presidential nomination.

The Chicago Wigwam was finished in the nick of time. Dedicated on May 12, it was ready for the convention which met 4 days later. Converted into stores for a time, the Wigwam was apparently torn down before the Chicago fire of 1871. Another building now stands at 333 West Lake Street where it once stood. A plaque placed on the building by the Chicago chapter of the Daughters of the American Revolution on February 12, 1909, notes the site's significance.

SOURCES: See William Eldon Baringer, "Campaign Technique in Illinois—1860," *Illinois State Historical Society Transactions for the Year 1932* ([Springfield]: Illinois State Historical Library, n.d.), pp. 203–281.

Wikoff, Henry (1813–1884) A regular visitor in Mrs. Lincoln's "salon" in the first year of the administration. Henry Wikoff was born in Philadelphia. His wealthy family sent him to Yale, from which he was expelled; he earned his degree from Union College. He traveled frequently to Europe and lived the life of a cosmopolitan courtier; among many others, he met Louis Napoleon and Lord Palmerston. He was a facile writer known especially for *My Courtship and its Consequences*, the story of his abduction of a wealthy sweetheart and his subsequent imprisonment in Italy.

"The Chevalier," as Wikoff was called, had, according to newspaperman John W. Forney, "seen more of the world than most men, . . . mingled with society of every shade and grade, . . . tasted of poverty and affluence, talks several languages fluently, is skilled in etiquette, art, and literature, and, without proclaimed convictions, is a shrewd politician, who understands the motives and opinions of others." A regular visitor at the White House while James Buchanan was President, Wikoff quickly became a favorite of Mrs. Lincoln's and a frequent visitor in the Republican White House too. A friend of James Gordon Bennett of the New York *Herald*, he had brought about a reconciliation between Buchanan and that testy editor in 1856, and his connection with the *Herald* continued, though secretly, while he frequented the Lincoln White House.

Late in 1861 Wikoff telegraphed the *Herald* part of Lincoln's annual message before it was presented to Congress, an offense serious enough to cause his subpoena before the House Judiciary Committee on February 10, 1862. His refusal to reveal his source led to his arrest for contempt of Congress. Confinement in Old Capitol Prison loosened his tongue, and he claimed he gained his information from White House gardener John Watt. Watt was fired that month, and Wikoff was banished from the White House social circle.

The irrepressible Wikoff continued his career of hanger-on in the highest social circles. He became an intimate of Louis Napoleon and, after Napoleon's fall from power, the intermediary between the ex-Emperor and any American who wished to see him.

SOURCES: See John W. Forney, *Anecdotes of Public Men* (New York: Harper & Brothers, 1873); Frank Maloy Anderson, *The Mystery of "A Public Man": A Historical Detective Story* (Minneapolis: University of Minnesota Press, 1948); and Ruth Painter Randall, *Mary Lincoln: Biography of a Marriage* (Boston: Little, Brown, 1953).

Williams, Thomas Harry (1909–1979) Historian. Williams was born in Vinegar Hill, Illinois. He earned his bachelor's degree at Platteville State College and his master's and doctor's degrees at the University of Wisconsin, where he studied with William B. Hesseltine. He taught briefly at the University of Omaha and joined the faculty at Louisiana State University in 1941. In the same year his revised doctoral dissertation appeared as a book, *Lincoln and the Radicals* ([Madison]: University of Wisconsin Press). The book portrayed Lincoln as a kindly President beleaguered by a vicious and vindictive faction of his own party, the Radicals (or "Jacobins," as Williams called them). Lincoln, he said, "surrendered to the conquering Jacobins in every controversy before they could publicly inflict upon him a damaging reverse. Like the fair Lucretia threatened with ravishment, he averted his fate by instant compliance." The book widely influenced writing on Lincoln's Presidency until it was challenged by David Donald in *Lincoln Reconsidered: Essays on the Civil War Era* (New York: Alfred A. Knopf, 1956).

Williams's second book, *Lincoln and the Generals* (New York: Alfred A. Knopf, 1952) has had a more lasting influence on Lincoln literature. It pictured a very different Lincoln from the one Williams described in his first book. Lincoln, Williams argued, was a fine "natural strategist" who was always commander in chief in fact as well as name and often even general-in-chief. In other words, Lincoln was very much in control of things military, and this control was, in terms of military success, largely salutary. Although Colin R. Ballard had given Lincoln high marks as a strategist as long ago as 1926 (in *The Military Genius of Abraham Lincoln* [London: Oxford University Press]), Brigadier General Ballard had depicted Lincoln as abdicating an active role once Ulysses S. Grant became lieutenant general in 1864. Williams contended that Grant's *Memoirs* exag-

Thomas Harry Williams. (Department of Archives and Manuscripts, Louisiana State University, Baton Rouge)

gerated the general's autonomy and Lincoln's naiveté in military matters. And Williams credited Lincoln with establishing a modern high-command system that looked forward to the kind of organization and planning that marked the World Wars.

Williams turned from Lincoln subjects in the mid-1950s. He wrote highly acclaimed biographies of P. G. T. Beauregard and Huey Long. He taught extremely popular courses on the Civil War at LSU until his retirement, 2 days before his death, in 1979.

See also BIOGRAPHERS; RADICAL REPUBLICANS.

Wilmot Proviso An amendment to a $2 million federal appropriation bill providing "That, as an express and fundamental condition to the acquisition of any territory from the Republic of Mexico by the United States . . . neither slavery nor involuntary servitude shall ever exist in any part of said territory." Pennsylvania Democrat David Wilmot proposed the measure on August 8, 1846.

Abraham Lincoln was not a member of the Twenty-ninth Congress, in which Wilmot introduced his proviso, but the principle of the proviso was still a hot issue when Lincoln entered Congress late in 1847. In later years he recalled voting for the Wilmot Proviso "or the principle of it, . . . at least forty times." Historians have been unable to find even a fourth of that number of occasions on which Lincoln so voted, but he did consistently support the proviso principle.

In 1850 Lincoln drafted his "view of the Right Position" for Richard Yates, the Whig candidate for Congress from Lincoln's district. By that time insistence on the Wilmot Proviso endangered the proposed measures which eventually became known as the Compromise of 1850. Lincoln stated that he had "been for the Wilmot Proviso" and would "adhere to it in Congress." However, he added, "of all political objects the preservation of the Union stands number one with me; and whenever I should believe my adherence to the Proviso tended to endanger the Union, I would at once abandon it." He did not think the Union "in so much danger as some others have." The document shows that Lincoln was not nearly as alarmed about the advances of the "Slave Power" as he would become after 1854. Then he would not find it easy to place Union above antislavery measures, and he would worry more about making the Union worthy of saving.

SOURCES: The recently discovered document is printed only in Mark E. Neely, Jr., "Lincoln's Theory of Representation: A Significant New Lincoln Document," *Lincoln Lore*, Number 1683 (May 1978), pp. 1–3.

Wood, Fernando (1812–1881) A leader of the peace wing of the Democratic party during the Civil War. Wood was born in Philadelphia but moved to New York City at an early age. He became a successful merchant and a leader of the Tammany Hall Democratic machine. He served a term in the House of Representatives (1841–1843), and he was three times the mayor of New York City.

Elected the third time in 1859 by the efforts of his Mozart Hall machine (recently formed after Wood's break with Tammany Hall), Wood was the mayor of New York when Lincoln stopped in the city on his inaugural trip to Washington in 1861. In January Wood had announced a proposal to make New York a free city by seceding from the state because, he said, "a dissolution of the Federal Union is inevitable." Immediately after the fall of Fort Sumter, however, he became a vociferous supporter of the Union cause; he offered President Lincoln his services in a military capacity about 2 weeks after the war began. Early in January 1862 he was still praising Lincoln's "highly patriotic and conservative course" and promising that the state's Democratic majority "will sustain you fully." He took heart particularly from the President's replacement of Secretary of War Simon Cameron with Democrat Edwin M. Stanton—proof, he told Lincoln, "of your own ability to grow." In August he complained that "radical abolitionists" through the New York *Tribune* "persistently represent me as hostile to your administration and as in sympathy with the states in rebellion against the government." He hoped, he told Lincoln, that these false allegations would have "no influence on your generous mind." And again in September he explained that newspapers misrepresented the tone of his protests of illegal arrests uttered at the state Democratic convention. "All I said applied to those arrests which had been made through error or misrepresentation and exclusively as to the *truly loyal*," he said. He did not object to arrests of the disloyal.

As late as November 30, 1862, Wood explained to Secretary of State William H. Seward that he had not uttered "the treasonable sentiments reported" in the newspapers. The tone of his correspondence changed a little over 2 weeks later when he wrote Lincoln a letter suggesting an armistice and peace negotiations. He was certain that the Southerners were ready to elect members to the next Congress, but Lincoln thought him in error. Writing on December 12, the President expressed a willingness to cease hostilities if "the people of the Southern States would cease resistance, and would re-inaugurate, submit to, and maintain the national authority." He did not think it proper to tell the Southern states himself—"My belief is that they already know it." He expressed an interest in having any information of their willingness to submit that Wood could supply. "Such information might be more valuable before the first of January than afterwards," Lincoln added, referring to the date when the Emancipation Proclamation would go into effect. Wood replied starchily that Lincoln's letter "filled me with profound regret" and indicated that the President would "continue a policy, which . . . is not only unwise, but in the opinion of many, is in conflict with the constitutional authority vested in the Federal Government." The Southern states could not cease resistance and reinaugurate a government "if we will not let them alone long enough to do so."

Fernando Wood

Wood continued throughout the war to advocate an armistice and peace negotiations to restore the Union. He lost his race for reelection as mayor in 1861. In 1862, however, he gained election to Congress, where he voiced his views until defeat for reelection in 1864 forced him to step down from office in 1865. Despite his drastic differences with the administration, he continued to maintain some contact with it; and he hoped to be appointed a peace commissioner representing the peace wing of the Democratic party when negotiations began.

Wood's wartime views did not end his public career. He served in the House of Representatives from 1867 to 1881. Eventually he became majority floor leader and Chairman of the Ways and Means Committee.

SOURCES: The only biography is Samuel Augustus Pleasants, *Fernando Wood of New York* (New York: Columbia University Press, 1948). Wood's letters to Lincoln praising the Presidential course (January 12, 1862), to Lincoln protesting the *Tribune*'s misrepresentations (August 20, 1862), to Lincoln about arbitrary arrests (September 12, 1862), to Seward (November 30 [1862]), and to Lincoln protesting the war (December 17, 1862) are in the Abraham Lincoln Papers, Library of Congress.

Work   *See* ECONOMICS; JOHNSTON, JOHN DAVIS.

Y, Z

Yates, Richard (1815–1873) Civil War Governor of Illinois, was born in Warsaw, Kentucky. He moved to Illinois in 1831, earned the first degree granted by Illinois College at Jacksonville in 1835, studied law at Transylvania University, and established practice in Jacksonville in 1837. He met Abraham Lincoln in 1835; both men were Henry Clay Whigs. Yates served three terms in the Illinois legislature (1842–1846, 1848–1850) and two terms in the House of Representatives (1850–1854), where he represented Lincoln's congressional district.

Yates was an early foe of the Kansas-Nebraska Act; he denounced it in a speech in the House on March 28, 1854. In the same year, Democrat Thomas L. Harris defeated his attempt at reelection. Democrats had spread the charge that Yates was a Know Nothing; Lincoln had warned him that the charge "may harm you if not averted," especially with English Whigs in Morgan County. In the lame duck session of Congress following the election, Yates attacked the Kansas-Nebraska Act again (February 28, 1855) "because we want the Territory of Kansas as a home for our white laboring classes" and because sentiment for slavery violated "the sentiment of the Declaration of American Independence."

Yates was mentioned as a possible Whig candidate for the Senate in 1855, but Lincoln was clearly the first choice of Anti-Nebraska Whigs. Yates was willing, he told Lincoln, only "in the event you could not succeed." In May 1856 he served as vice president of the convention at Bloomington which organized the Republican party in Illinois. William H. Herndon had urged him to attend because Yates's and Lincoln's presence in Bloomington were necessary to keep "the whole affair" from being "wild, fanatical, crazy."

Yates was, after 1855, president of the Tonica and Petersburg Railroad, but he remained active in politics. There were reports that he opposed Lincoln in the campaign against Stephen A. Douglas in 1858; he admitted that he spoke only in "a few Counties" but insisted no one was "more zealous" in supporting Lincoln. Norman B. Judd and Leonard Swett were major contenders for the Republican nomination for Governor of Illinois in 1860, but Yates gained the nomination as a compromise candidate. As a delegate to the national Republican nominating convention in 1860, he helped Lincoln's cause by arguing that he would surely lose the Illinois gubernatorial race if William H. Seward were the presidential nominee. Yates defeated Democrat James C. Allen, 172,000 to 159,000 and assumed office in January 1861.

Governor Yates was an uncompromising, if somewhat hysterical, foe of secession. After the fall of Fort Sumter he promised that "Our people will wade through seas of blood before they will see a single star or a solitary stripe erased from the glorious flag of our Union." He was vigorous in raising and supplying soldiers for the war effort. Though he and Lincoln were on friendly terms, there was considerable friction between them in the war years. Yates badgered Lincoln about appointments and promotions until Lincoln, in a letter on April 10, 1862, was forced to point out that "Major General-

Richard Yates. (Courtesy of the Lloyd Ostendorf Collection)

340

ships in the Regular Army, are not as plenty as blackberries." On July 11, 1862, his impatience with the course of the war led Yates to write an open letter to President Lincoln, saying that the "conservative policy has utterly failed" and the "time has come for the adoption of more decisive measures." He particularly criticized generals who "fritter away the sinews of our brave men in guarding the property of traiters and in driving back into their hands loyal blacks who offer us their labor & seek shelter with the federal flag." Lincoln complained sharply in August that he had had "much trouble between officers sent to Illinois and the State government there." Yates blamed Illinois's inability to get its soldiers to the front on the President's failure to send mustering officers and paymasters, and Lincoln just as warmly blamed Yates's "*punctilio*" for the problem.

Yates played a prominent part in the Altoona Conference of governors disturbed at the slow progress of the war, and in Brooklyn on November 3, 1862, he said that "old Abe was too slow for me. I was for the [emancipation] proclamation, for confiscation, for conscription, for the arrest of rebels and traitors, and for every measure by which we could put down the rebellion." A speech Yates delivered at a Union rally in Illinois late in the summer of 1863 was widely interpreted as a call for a new Republican presidential nominee in 1864. In a letter to the Chicago *Tribune* on September 8, Yates hastened to explain that he had not said Lincoln was not his man for President. He had said *no* man was; it was not a proper time to be thinking of politics. He admitted saying that Lincoln had made many mistakes, but he had added, he insisted, that things turned out all right.

Yates tended to jump to extreme conclusions about the fragility of support for the war in the North and thus governed Illinois in a mood of perpetual crisis. While a Democrat-dominated constitutional convention met in Springfield from January to March 1862, the Governor feared the possibility of civil war in Illinois. Democrats gained control of the legislature in the elections of 1862, and Yates was soon locked in conflict with the legislators. On January 19, 1863, he described the legislature as "a wild, rampant, revolutionary body," and he asked Indiana's Governor Oliver P. Morton how to thwart its "attempt to legislate all power out of my hands." After the lower house voted to have commissioners confer with Congress about declaring an armistice and establishing a convention to end the war by compromise, Yates wanted Lincoln to send four regiments to Illinois under the pretext of recruiting but really to keep an eye on the legislature when it reconvened in June 1863. When John M. Palmer brought Yates's request to Lincoln, Palmer recalled, Lincoln simply said, "Who can we trust if we cannot trust Illinois?"

Yates turned to encouraging prowar secret societies called Union Leagues. In June the Governor seized on a constitutional technicality, the fact that the two houses of the legislature had not agreed on the same date for adjournment, to exercise his right to prorogue the legislature. Illinois was governed without a legislature until after the elections of 1864. Yates, like Indiana's Morton, urged Lincoln to send home as many soldiers as possible to vote in that election. He also sought to reduce the state's draft quota; he told Lincoln that insistance on a quota of 28,058 men for Illinois "will not only endanger the peace of the state but will hopelessly defeat us in the coming Elections."

After Lincoln's assassination, Yates wrote a long eulogy which he never delivered. With characteristic willingness to admit his own faults, he wrote, "I thought he was too slow in calling out men, too slow in arming the freedmen, too slow in issuing his Proclamation of Emancipation, but in his own time came, in succession, all these important measures, and the whole world now plainly sees and acknowledges that Abraham Lincoln always did the right thing in the right way, at the right time, and at the right place."

In 1865 Yates was elected to the Senate, where he served one term. He supported Reconstruction measures and voted to impeach Andrew Johnson. He began to have serious problems with another failing he was willing to admit to: heavy drinking. He died suddenly in 1873.

SOURCES: There is no biography of Yates, but many of Yates's letters are published in a confused volume edited by John H. Krenkel, *Richard Yates: Civil War Governor* (Danville, Ill.: Interstate Printers & Publishers, 1966). Jack Northrup's "Yates, the Prorogued Legislature, and the Constitutional Convention," *Journal of the Illinois State Historical Society*, LXIII (Spring 1969), 5–34, and William B. Hesseltine's *Lincoln and the War Governors* (New York: Alfred A. Knopf, 1948) cover the Civil War period competently, but they are marked by hostility to Governor Yates. Yates's letters to Lincoln about the 1855 Senate race (January 8, 1855), about the 1858 Senate race (April 25, 1860), and on the draft (September 16, 1864) are in the Abraham Lincoln Papers, Library of Congress.

Young America Movement *See* DOUGLAS, STEPHEN ARNOLD.

Zacharie, Isachar *See* JEWS.

Index

NOTE: Article titles and page numbers are given in **boldface** type.

Abe Lincoln in Illinois, **1**
Abell, Mrs. Bennett, 230
Abolitionism, 1–2, 24, 31, 86, 91, 135, 145, 193, 239, 279, 328, 335
    believers in, 61, 88, 183, 196
    critics of, 53, 77, 78, 251, 263
    in Lincoln-Douglas Debates, 51, 117, 123, 167, 228
Abraham Africanus, 150
Abraham Lincoln (play), 91
Abraham Lincoln Association, 3, 7, 27, 108, 308, 309
Abraham Lincoln Birthplace National Historic Site, 174
Abraham Lincoln Land & Cattle Company, 62
Abraham Lincoln Library and Museum, 191
Abraham Lincoln Log Cabin Association, 62
Abraham Lincoln Quarterly, 3
Actors, 1, 91
Adams, Charles Francis, 3–4, 58, 136, 274, 275, 293, 311, 331
Adams, Charles Francis, Jr., 272
Adams, Henry, 52
Adams, John Quincy, 3, 103
Adderup, Andrew, 155
Africa (Liberia), 62, 63, 140, 219
Agriculture, 94, 159, 285
Aiken, Frederick, 298, 312
Alcohol (*see* Temperance)
Alderfer, William K., 3
Allen, Charles, 8
Allen, James C., 340
Allen, Robert, 141
"Almanac trial," 8
Alton, Illinois, 4–5, 193, 196, 198, 277, 286, 305
Altoona Conference, 5–6, 341
Amalgamation (miscegenation), 51, 217
Ambition, Lincoln's, 32, 147, 198
Amendments, constitutional (*see* Constitution of the United States, amendments to; Thirteenth Amendment)
American Land Company, 7
American party (*see* Know-Nothing Party)
"American System, The," 59, 215, 333
Amnesty, 130, 259, 322, 328
    (*See also* Clemency; Proclamation of Amnesty and Reconstruction)
"Anaconda Plan," 63, 270
Ancestry, Lincoln's (*see* Genealogy; *individual ancestors by name*)
Anderson, Frank Maloy, 83
Anderson, Robert, 149, 294
Andersonville, Georgia, Confederate prison at, 312
Andrew, John Albion, 5, 6–7, 11, 28, 42, 241
Andrews, Rufus, 328
Angle, Paul McClelland, 3, 7–8, 20, 27, 156, 265, 267
Antietam, Battle of, 5, 6, 65, 104, 201
    and vulgar song incident, 214

"Appeal of the Independent Democrats, The," 53
Appearance, Lincoln's (*see* Physical Characteristics)
Appointments (*see* Patronage)
Arachnodactyly (disease), 238
Arbitrary arrests (*see* Habeas Corpus)
Arkansas, 253, 258, 259, 291, 322
Arlington National Cemetery, 186
Armstrong, Hannah, 8
Armstrong, John ("Jack"), 8, 57, 58, 226
Armstrong, William ("Duff"), 8
Arnold, Isaac Newton, 8–10, 96
    as biographer, 25, 27
    as politician, 4, 57, 271, 314
Arnold, Samuel Bland, 10, 11, 12, 35, 97, 227, 312
Art, Lincoln in (*see* Borglum, John Gutzon de la Mothe; Carpenter, Francis Bicknell; Jones, Thomas Dow; Lincoln Memorial; Lincoln Penny; Mills, Clark; Photographs; Portraits; Sculpture; Volk, Leonard Wells)
Arthur, Chester A., 185, 186, 203
Ashmore, Gideon M., 207
Ashmun, George, 10–11, 51, 88, 110, 327
Assassination, 11–13, 37, 50, 93, 111, 148, 159, 197, 301, 318, 334, 335
    Catholic Church and, 13, 57, 213, 298, 329
    Jefferson Davis and, 13, 151, 165, 298, 311, 312
    Ulysses S. Grant and, 12, 35, 97, 227, 329
    and Lincoln's associates, 151, 176, 183, 185, 203, 275, 288
    threat of, 248, 282, 291
    William Henry Seward and, 11, 13, 17, 35, 245
    [*See also* Arnold, Samuel Bland; Atzerodt, George A.; Baltimore Plot; Booth, John Wilkes; Chiniquy, Charles Paschal Telesphore; Corbett, Thomas P. ("Boston"); Crook, William Henry; Eisenschiml, Otto; Ford's Theatre; Fort Jefferson; Funeral; Herold, David Edgar; Jones, Thomas A.; Lloyd, John Minchin; Mudd, Samuel Alexander; O'Laughlin, Michael; *Our American Cousin;* Parker, John Frederick; Petersen House; Powell, Lewis Thornton; Rathbone, Henry Riggs; Spangler, Edman ("Edward"); Stanton, Edwin McMasters; Surratt, John Harrison, Jr.; Surratt, Mary E.; Trial of the Assassins; Weichmann, Louis J.]
Atlanta, Georgia, 64, 128
Atlantic Monthly, 7, 27, 265
Attorney General (*see* Bates, Edward; Speed, James)
Atwood, Jesse, 243
Atzerodt, George A., 12, 13–14, 35, 165, 194, 298, 312
Autobiography, 14, 108, 153, 271

Bacon, Henry, 190
Baker, Edward Dickinson, 15–16, 40, 181, 195
    as lawyer, 32, 194, 310, 313
    as politician, 139, 144, 233, 333
Baker, Edward Lewis, Jr., 96
Baker, Joseph E., 243
Baker, Luther, 148
Balloons in Civil War, 162
Ball's Bluff, Battle of, 16, 66
Baltimore, Maryland, 46, 87, 121, 253
    and Lincoln's assassination, 10, 11, 17, 227, 239, 244, 283, 298, 326
    (*See also* Baltimore Plot)
    Republican convention, 1864 (*see* Election of 1864, Baltimore convention)
    and Washington, D.C., 39, 42, 45, 132, 246, 321
Baltimore Plot, 11, 16–17, 159, 239
    inaugural journey and, 16–17, 169, 178, 239, 324
Bancroft, George, 121
Banking, 17–18
    and Bank of the United States, 38, 70, 84, 93, 136, 163, 250, 256, 295, 304, 324, 332
    in Illinois, 38, 85, 92, 93, 277, 313, 318, 333
    national system of, in Civil War, 54, 109, 203
Banks, Nathaniel Prentiss, 6, 11, 18–19, 55, 78, 127, 136, 259, 330
Baptist Church, 260
Bargdorf, Louis, 106
Baringer, William E., 3
Barnard, George Grey, 191
Barney, Hiram, 84
Barrett, Oliver Rogers, 7, 19–20, 24, 81, 156, 265, 267
Barry, Charles Alfred, 243
Bartlett, Truman H., 205
Barton, William Eleazer, 20, 91, 124, 309
Basler, Roy P., 3, 180, 192, 290
Batavia, Illinois, 184
Bates, Edward, 20–22, 48, 164, 208, 311, 324
    in 1860, 38, 75, 78, 97, 316
    in Lincoln administration, 7, 33, 61, 68, 104, 116, 132, 310, 326, 332
    and Supreme Court, 221, 297, 302
Bates, Therena, 224
Battles of Civil War (*see individual battles by name*)
Baumgras, Peter, 205
Bayne, Julia Taft, 301
Beall, John Y., 61, 150
Beard, Charles A., 267
Beard, Lincoln's, 22, 167, 237, 244
Beckwith, Jessie Lincoln, 82, 185, 186
Beckwith, Mary Lincoln, 82
Beckwith, Robert Lincoln, 82, 156
Beckwith, Warren Wallace, 82, 186
Bedell, Grace, 22
Beecher, Henry Ward, 72, 84, 223
Benét, Stephen Vincent, 267
Bell, John, 97, 99

343

Index

Belleview (asylum), 184
Belmont, August, 201
Benjamin, Judah, 314
Bennett, James Gordon, 22–23, 208, 328, 337
Bennett, Lerone F., 28
Berger, Anthony, 237
Berlin (Prussia), appointment of minister to (see Patronage, foreign offices)
Berrett, James G., 239
Berry, Richard, 184, 279
Berry, William Franklin, 23, 111, 222
Beveridge, Albert Jeremiah, 19, **23–24,** 26, 206, 234, 330
   on Stephen A. Douglas, 24, 80, 88
Bible, 33, 34, 49, 94, 260, 285
Bibliography, 24–25, 113
"Big Five" (see Collections, personal)
Bigelow, John, 11
Billings, Grace Bedell, 22
Bingham, John A., 151, 311
Binney, Horace, 134
Biographers, 25–28
   (See also Angle, Paul McClelland; Arnold, Isaac Newton; Barton, William Eleazer; Beveridge, Albert Jeremiah; Charnwood, Lord Godfrey Rathbone Benson; Codding, Ichabod; Eisenschiml, Otto; Hay, John Milton; Herndon, William Henry; Hesseltine, William Best; Holland, Josiah Gilbert; Howells, William Dean; Lamon, Ward Hill; Luthin, Reinhard Henry; Masters, Edgar Lee; Nicolay, John George; Randall, James Garfield; Raymond, Henry Jarvis; Sandburg, Carl; Scripps, John Locke; Stephenson, Nathaniel Wright; Stoddard, William Osborn; Tarbell, Ida Minerva; Thomas, Benjamin Platt; Tyler, Lyon Gardiner; Weik, Jesse William; Williams, Thomas Harry)
Biography, Lincoln on, 25, 33
Birthplace cabin, 174
Bishop, Henry W., 77
Bixby, Lydia, 28
Bixby Letter, 20, 28
Black, Chauncey F., 25, 178
Black, Jeremiah S., 149, 178, 295
Black Americans (see Negroes)
Black Hawk War, 15, 23, **29,** 44, 139
   Lincoln in, 8, 14, 58, 63, 111, 160, 204, 222, 226, 292, 305
Blacksmith, Lincoln considers becoming, 14
Blackstone, William, 33
Blackwell, Sarah Ellen, 49
Blaine, James G., 5, 136
Blair, Francis Preston, 21, **29–31,** 45, 112, 119, 201
   and Hampton Roads Peace Conference, 136, 137
Blair, Francis Preston, Jr., 30, 55, 119
Blair, Montgomery, 30, **31–32,** 88, 143, 311, 322, 324, 331
   in Lincoln administration, 55, 119, 274, 277, 294, 332
   and Negro question, 6, 104, 116
   removal of, 50, 82, 101, 115, 120, 208, 253, 275, 321
   selection of, for Cabinet, 136, 273, 314, 327
Bledsoe, Albert Taylor, 32
Blind Memorandum, 32, 100, 258
Blockade, 32–33, 63, 328, 331

Bloomington, Illinois, 57, 77, 79, 107, 162, 192, 203, 299
   Republican convention, 1856, 195, 262, 340
Boetcker, William J. H., 25
Books (which Lincoln read), 33–34, 47, 138, 142, 147, 163, 180, 194
   (See also Education; Poetry; Shakespeare)
Booth, Edwin, 34
Booth, John Wilkes, 34–36
   diary of, 213, 288, 312
   flight of, 73, 148, 166, 194, 213, 256, 283, 288
   Lincoln's assassination by, 13, 232
   motive of, 12, 13, 97, 275
   plotting of, 10, 11, 13, 227, 244, 245, 282, 297, 298, 329
Booth, Junius Brutus, 34
Borglum, James Lincoln, 36
Borglum, John Gutzon de la Mothe, 36–37, 209
Boritt, G. S., 28
Boutwell, George, 5
Boyd, Andrew H., 24
Boyd, Benjamin, 310
Bradford, Augustus W., 5
Brady, Mathew, 209, 237
Brady, W. H., 172
Bragg, Braxton, 295
Brainerd, Cephas, 73
Bramlette, Thomas E., 232, 288
Branson, Margaret, 244
Breckinridge, John C., 42, 87, 97, 99, 238, 277
Breese, Sidney, 85
Brenner, Victor David, 192, 193, 209
Briggs, James A., 72
Bright, Jesse, 86
Bright, John, 37, 50, 293, 310
Brooks, Noah, 37–38, 183
Bross, William, 271
Brough, John, 82, 318
Brown, John, 6, 31, 34, 73
Brown, John H., 131
Brown, John Henry, 243
Brown, Peter, 219
Brown, William, 132
Brown University Lincoln collection, 204
Browne, Charles Farrar, 154
Brownell, Francis E., 102
Browning, Orville Hickman, 21, **38–39,** 78, 85, 106, 296, 311, 326
   and Sumter crisis, 112, 294
Browning, Mrs. Orville Hickman, 39, 230
Bryan, Thomas B., 55, 105
Bryant, Jane, 207
Bryant, William Cullen, 72
Bryce, James, 52
Buchanan, James, 40–41, 60, 86, 91, 110, 122, 282, 337
   feud of, with Stephen A. Douglas, 5, 79, 87, 114, 123, 250
   Lincoln's conspiracy charge against, 51, 80, 152, 171, 238, 249, 301
   and secession crisis, 31, 111, 136, 149, 274, 287, 294, 295, 314, 321
Buck Grove, Illinois, 62
Buckalew, Charles R., 46, 66
Buell, Don Carlos, 66, 165
Bufford, John H., 243
Bull Run, Battle of, 64, 251, 258
Bull Run, Second Battle of, 5, 64, 201
Bullard, F. Lauriston, 29
Bunyan, John, 34
Burbridge, Stephen G., 143, 232
Burke, Edmund, 25, 290

Burnett, H. L., 311
Burnham, Daniel H., 190
Burns, Robert, 34, 240
Burnside, Ambrose E., 64, 66, 82, 135, 151
   and suppression of Chicago Times, 9, 56, 57, 314, 317, 318
Burroughs, "Peanut John," 13, 283
Burton, John E., 20, **41**
Busbey, Hamilton, 172
Bush, Christopher, 187
Butler, Benjamin Franklin, 6, **42–43,** 66, 128, 141, 208, 252
   and election of 1864, 46, 82, 84
Butler, Nicholas Murray, 28, 29, 192
Butler, William, 141
Butterfield, Justin, 233, 282, 305, 326

Cabinet, Lincoln's:
   aspirants to, and recommendations for, 30, 58, 115, 118, 129, 321, 327
   after 1861, 7, 50, 145, 150, 278, 328
   and Lincoln's Illinois associates, 38, 108, 169, 208, 299, 314, 324
   New England's place in, 3, 6, 18, 136
   Pennsylvania's place in, 75, 78, 202
   crisis of, in December 1862, 253, 293, 314, 321
   criticism of, 4, 5, 84
   operation of, 57, 105, 116, 234, 246
   on Sumter Crisis (see Sumter Crisis, Lincoln's cabinet on)
   (See also Bates, Edward; Blair, Montgomery; Cameron, Simon; Chase, Salmon Portland; Dennison, William; Fessenden, William Pitt; Harlin, James; McCulloch, Hugh; Seward, William Henry; Smith, Caleb Blood; Speed, James; Stanton, Edwin McMasters; Usher, John Palmer; Wells, Gideon)
Caesar, Julius, 34
Calhoun, John, 44–45, 87, 222
Calhoun, John C., 279, 317
California, 37, 99, 145, 161, 191, 210, 296
   in Civil War, 50, 221, 300
Calvert, George H., Jr., 298
Cameron, Simon, 45–47, 58, 59, 97, 119, 134, 164, 224, 277
   selection of, for Cabinet: opposition to, 6, 30, 75, 76, 108, 129, 136, 140, 202, 208, 257, 314, 324, 334
   support for, 68, 78, 115, 273, 299, 327
   and Edwin M. Stanton, 287, 288, 338
Campaigns, political (see entries beginning with term: Election of)
Campbell, John A., 74, 136, 296
Camron, John M., 221
Canada, 11, 12, 50, 58, 111, 169, 318
   Confederate agents in, 35, 130, 141, 288, 297, 311
Canby, E. R. S., 19
Canisius, Theodore, 158, 223
Cannon, Joseph G., 190
Capitalism and Lincoln, 25, 93–94
Carey, Henry, 203
Carnegie, Dale, 25
Carpenter, Francis Bicknell, 47–48, 197, 214, 244, 331
"Carpetbag letters," 131
Carrington, Henry, 212
Carroll, Anna Ella, 48–49
Carter, D. E., 321
Carthage, Illinois, Lincoln's speech at, 255

Index

Cartwright, Peter, 49–50, 260
Cass, Lewis, 29, 153, 241, 305
"Castine" dispatches, 38
Catholic Church:
   and assassination, 13, 57, 213, 298, 329
   and politics, 97, 99, 102, 157, 174, 215, 272, 333
Catron, John, 296
Cattell, Harry P., 121
Caverly, A. W., 15
Centennial of Lincoln's birth, 1909, 25, 55
Century Magazine, 142, 225
Chandler, Zachariah, 50, 66, 252
Channing, William Ellery, 108
Chapman **Pirates,** 37, **50**
Chappel, Alonzo, 205
Characteristics, personal, Lincoln's:
   ambition, 32, 147, 198
   courage, 66, 326
   friendliness, 16, 68, 176, 284–285
   modesty, 14, 16, 29, 142, 236, 237, 238
   (*See also* Clemency; Honesty; Humor; Physical Characteristics; Psychology)
Charleston, Illinois, 51–52, 109, 137, 207
   debate in, 80, 110, 217, 249
   riot in, 62, 110, 138, 150
Charnwood, Lord Godfrey Rathbone Benson, 7, 26, **52–53,** 91, 290, 309
Chase, Kate, 55
Chase, Salmon Portland, 53–55, 59, 72, 74, 78, 88, 142, 167, 172, 183, 225, 252, 253, 277, 287, 294, 311, 321, 323, 332
   in 1860, 97, 208, 330
   in 1864, 11, 82, 84, 92, 241, 317, 331
   and Negro question, 43, 103, 104, 116, 121, 264
   selection of: for Cabinet, 129, 273, 314, 324, 328
      for Supreme Court, 169, 293, 297
   Treasury Department under, 18, 31, 108, 109, 144, 145, 203, 224
Chicago, Illinois, 9, 19, 62, 80, 85, 88, 96, 121, 136, 157, 168, 183, 185, 189, 193, 249, 254, 271, 286, 300, 319, 320, 334, 337
Chicago convention, 1860 (*see* Election of 1860, Chicago convention)
Chicago Historical Society, 8, 55–56, 105, 243, 335
Chicago post office, 4, 271
Chicago *Press and Tribune* (*see* Chicago *Tribune*)
Chicago River and Harbor Convention, 20, **56,** 128
Chicago *Times,* **Suppression of the,** 9, **56–57,** 72, 223, 314
Chicago *Tribune,* 14, 57, 208, 223, 257, 271, 334, 335
"Chicken Bone" Case, 57
Chiniquy, Charles Paschal Telesphore, 57
Chiriqui Improvement Company, 30, 63, 95, 282, 316, 331
Chitty, Joseph, 33
"Chronicles of Reuben, The," 130
Cincinnati, Ohio, 121, 157, 158, 167, 202, 254
Cincinnati *Commercial,* 135, 144
Cities in elections, 99, 102, 328
Civil liberties (*see* Chicago *Times,* Suppression of the; Constitution of the United States; New York *World,* Suppression of the; Vallandigham, Clement Laird)
Civil Rights Bill, 109, 315

Civil Rights movement and Lincoln scholarship, 27, 88, 220
Civil service (*see* Patronage)
Civil service reform, 269
Civil War:
   balloons in, 162
   battles of (*see individual battles by name*)
   John Jordan Crittenden and, 30, 88, 173, 196, 270
   David Davis and (*see* Davis, David)
   economics and, 32, 252, 265
   (*See also* Finance, Civil War)
   generals in (*see* Commander in Chief; *individual generals by name*)
   issues concerning (*see* Constitution of the United States, issues concerning; Fugitive Slave Law)
   legal nature of, 33, 41, 67, 296
   Mississippi River in, 21, 63, 127, 212, 270, 288
   peace movements in (*see* Peace movements in Civil War)
   states in (*see individual states by name*)
   strategy in (*see* Commander in Chief; Grant, Ulysses Simpson; McClellan, George Brinton)
   U.S. Supreme Court in, 33, 69, 150, 221, 318
Clampitt, John W., 298
Clark, William T., 236
Clarke, Asia Booth, 34
Clary, John, 57
Clary, William, 226
Clary's Grove Boys, 8, 23, **57–58,** 226
Clay, Cassius Marcellus, 46, **58–59**
Clay, Clement C., 311
Clay, Henry, 1, **59–60,** 77, 110, 326, 327, 340
   Stephen A. Douglas and, 59, 60, 305, 327
   influence on Lincoln, 34, 52, 62, 112, 215, 217, 304, 332
   in Lincoln-Douglas Debates, 5, 51, 85, 229, 250, 323
   in politics, 74, 144, 233, 304, 305, 331
Cleary, William C., 311
Clemency, 21, **60–61,** 62, 110, 150, 189, 287
   biographers on Lincoln's, 20, 52, 91, 267
   and Confederacy, 64, 116, 227, 247
Clifford, Nathan, 296
Clinton, Maryland, 299
Cobden, Richard, 293
Codding, Ichabod, 2, **61,** 196, 262
Cogswell, William F., 156, 205, 244
Colchester (a spiritual medium), 183
Coles County, Illinois, 51, **61–62,** 110, 166, 187, 188, 193, 207
Colfax, Schuyler, 21, 47, 61, 129, 282, 325
Collamer, Jacob, 253
Collections:
   institutional [*see* Barton, William Eleazer (University of Chicago); Chicago Historical Society; Ford's Theatre; Henry E. Huntington Library and Art Gallery; Illinois State Historical Library; Library of Congress; Lincoln Memorial Shrine; Lincoln Memorial University; Louis A. Warren Lincoln Library and Museum; McLellan, Charles Woodberry (Brown University); Oakleaf,

Collections, institutional (*Cont.*):
     Joseph Benjamin (Indiana University)]
   personal [*see* Barrett, Oliver Rogers; Barton, William Eleazer; Chicago Historical Society (Charles F. Gunther); Fish, Daniel; Illinois State Historical Library (Henry Horner); Lambert, William Harrison; Library of Congress (Alfred Whital Stern); McLellan, Charles Woodberry; Meserve, Frederick Hill; Oakleaf, Joseph Benjamin; Oldroyd, Osborn Hamilton Ingham; Stewart, Judd]
Colonization, 62–63
   Lincoln's belief in, 43, 59, 216, 217, 218, 219, 235, 324
   other supporters of, 21, 30, 31, 39, 79, 95, 169, 282, 314, 316
Colorado Territory, 84, 161, 224, 277
Colt, Samuel P., 36
Commager, Henry Steele, 267
Commander in Chief, 63–66, 151, 199, 270, 311, 325, 326, 337–338
Committee on the Conduct of the War, Joint, 43, 50, **66–67,** 252, 321
Compromise of 1850, 11, 53, 136, 235, 262, 272, 305, 327, 338
   Stephen A. Douglas and, 85, 86, 170
   in Lincoln-Douglas Debates, 5, 51, 60, 123, 250
Conant, Alban Jasper, 243
Confederate States of America, 18, 31, 33, 130, 183, 281, 289, 298, 312, 322
Confiscation, 39, 63, 74, 140, 314, 341
Confiscation Act of July 17, 1862, 37, 48, 50, 63, **67–68,** 74, 109, 291, 314
   failure to enforce, 21, 105
   Orville Hickman Browning on, 39
Conger, Everton J., 148
Congressman, Lincoln as, 49, 77, 181, 304, 325, 334
   and Mexican War, 16, 209, 306–307, 338
Conkling, James Cook, 2, **68–69,** 309
Conover, Sanford, 311, 312
Conscription, 57, **69–70,** 128, 158, 201, 208, 223, 288
   and Constitution, 72, 246, 297, 302
   resistance to, by states, 41, 75, 202, 212, 287, 341
Conspiracy charges:
   Lincoln's, 5, 40, 51, 80, 81, 87, 91, 152, 171, 229, 249, 264, 271
   Republican, 53, 263
Constable, Charles H., 207
Constitution of the United States, 5, **70–72,** 97, 215, 315
   amendments to, 70, 71, 74, 76, 79, 112, 136, 273, 308
   issues concerning: before Civil War, 53, 90–91, 112, 118, 120, 157, 216, 245, 249, 250, 278–279, 301
     during Civil War, 21, 41, 67, 69, 101, 103–104, 132, 246–247, 251, 255, 280–281, 292, 302, 314, 318, 331, 332, 338
   and Reconstruction, 165, 247, 322
Constitutional Union party, 74, 97, 98, 270, 292
"Contraband," 42
Contraband cotton (*see* Cotton, contraband, trading in)
Convention system, 232
Conway, Moncure D., 2
Cook, Burton C., 313, 314

Index

Cooke, Jay, 54, 109, 203
Coolidge, Calvin, 36
Cooper Institute Speech, 70, **72–73,** 129, 237
"Copperheads," 101, 150, 290, 317
Corbett, Thomas P. ("Boston"), 35, **73**
Corning, Erastus, letter to, 135, 317–318
Corpse, Lincoln's, plot to steal, 310
Correa, Leahalma, 82
Corruption, 11, 46, 92, 95, 119, 141, 221
   (*See also* Cotton, contraband, trading in)
Cortissoz, Royal, 190
Corwin, Thomas, 32
Cotton, contraband, trading in, 11, 19, 115, 142, 143, 290, 300
Cotton diplomacy, 37, 274, 328
Courage, Lincoln's, 66, 326
Covode, John, 66
Cow Island (off Haiti), 63, 316
Cox, Samuel S., 35, 101, 166, 201
Cox, Walter S., 227, 312
Coykendall, Frederick, 192
Crail, Joe, 207
Craven, Avery O., 256
Crawford, Andrew, 159
Crisfield, John W., 12
Crisis, The (Columbus, Ohio), 223
Crittenden, John Jordan, 16, **74,** 78, 291
   and Civil War, 30, 88, 173, 196, 270
Croasdale, Elizabeth, 205
Crook, William Henry, 74–75, 232
Crothers, Eli K., 57
Cuba, 85, 314
Cullom, Shelby M., 190, 292
Current, Richard N., 27, 148, 256
Curtin, Andrew Gregg, 5, 45, 46, **75–76,** 199, 202
Curtis, Benjamin R., 90, 301
Cutts, Adele, 86

Dana, Charles A., 127, 220
Dannenhower, William W., 175
Davis, David, 77–79
   before Civil War, 45, 83, 96, 97, 107–108, 112, 135, 169, 196, 210, 313, 335
   during Civil War, 203, 282, 296, 299, 300
   after Civil War, 112, 184, 185, 192, 212, 261, 297
Davis, Garrett, 173
Davis, Henry Winter, 31, 78, 252, 253, 322, 323
Davis, Jefferson, 30, 42, 50, 55, 63, 69, 101, 136, 137, 171, 225, 238, 239, 289, 294
   and Lincoln assassination, 13, 151, 165, 298, 311, 312
   and Sumter crisis, 295
Dawson, John, 195
Dawson, N. H. R., 183
Dayton, William L., 3, 4
Debates, Lincoln–Douglas, 2, 20, **79–81,** 144, 168, 196, 207, 208, 210, 217, 257, 266, 271, 280, 301, 313, 334, 335
   abolitionism in, 51, 117, 123, 167, 228
   Henry Clay in, 5, 51, 85, 229, 250, 323
   Compromise of 1850 in, 5, 51, 60, 123, 250
   Declaration of Independence in, 5, 80, 123, 124, 168, 229, 250
   Stephen A. Douglas and, 74, 85–87, 170, 175
   (*See also* Douglas, Stephen Arnold, in Lincoln-Douglas Debates)

Debates, Lincoln–Douglas (*Cont.*):
   Dred Scott decision in (see *Dred Scott v. Sanford,* in Lincoln-Douglas Debates)
   Mexican War in, 5, 51, 110, 117, 228, 335
   scholarship on, 27
   Lyman Trumbull in, 51, 79, 117, 167, 228
   (*See also* Alton, Illinois; Charleston, Illinois; Freeport, Illinois; Freeport Question; Galesburg, Illinois; Jonesboro, Illinois; Ottawa, Illinois; Quincy, Illinois)
Decatur, Illinois, Republican convention in, 1860 (see Election of 1860, Decatur convention)
Declaration of Independence, 159, 211, 235, 263, 324, 340
   and Constitution, 70–72
   in Lincoln-Douglas Debates, 5, 80, 123, 124, 168, 229, 250
   and minorities, 90, 91, 157, 158, 174, 261, 279, 280, 301
   primacy of, in Lincoln's political thought, 112, 125, 163, 164, 215, 216, 294
Deism, 260
Delaware, 102, 219, 304
Democracy, 186, 290, 291, 295, 333
   biographers on Lincoln and, 26, 52
   (*See also* Representative Government)
Democratic party, 84, 99, 100, 171, 217, 232, 265, 314
   in election of 1864, 23, 111, 201, 318
   during Lincoln's administration, 27, 32, 101, 102, 308
Dennett, A. W., 174
Dennison, William, 32, 75, **81–82,** 199
Depression, Lincoln's (see Psychology)
Depression Era and Lincoln scholarship, 1, 3, 28, 207, 267
Descendants of Lincoln, 82
   (*See also* Genealogy; *individual descendants by name*)
DeWitt, Robert M., 155
Diary of Edward Bates, 22
Diary of Orville Hickman Browning, 39
Diary of Salmon P. Chase, 55
Diary of John Hay, 141–142, 248
"Diary of a Public Man," 82–83
Diary of Gideon Welles, 331
Dickey, T. Lyle, 74, 78, 196
Dictatorship, 16, 64, 72, 151, 198, 255
   fears Lincoln would institute, 34, 71, 111, 135, 241, 322
Diller, Isaac Roland, 83
Diller, Roland Weaver, 83
Diplomacy in Lincoln's administration, 3, 4, 104, 175, 274, 293, 310, 311, 331
District of Columbia, slavery in, 39, 63, 117, 120, 219, 249, 263, 279
   (*See also* Washington, D.C.)
Dix, John A., 46, 69, 223
Dixon, James, 247
Doctors, 57, 143, 144, 164, 301
Dodd, Harrison, 212
Dodd, William E., 255
Dodge, Grenville, 255
Doherty, Edward P., 73, 148
Dole, William Palmer, 83–84, 145, 160, 161, 180
Donald, David, 27, 251, 337
Dondero, George A., 22
Dorsey, Azel W., 159
Doster, W. A., 14, 245, 312

Douglas, Stephen Arnold, 11, 24, 26, 38, 40, 44, 61, 80, 83, **84–88,** 91, 94, 116, 142, 164, 238, 255, 280, 292, 295, 301, 312–313, 314, 319, 324
   and Henry Clay, 59, 60, 305, 327
   and election of 1860, 22, 72, 97–99, 114, 127, 277, 317, 336
   feud of James Buchanan with, 5, 79, 87, 114, 123, 250
   and Kansas-Nebraska Act, 44, 86, 210–211, 235, 242, 278
   in Lincoln-Douglas Debates, 51–52, 110, 128, 146, 152, 167, 175, 196, 207, 210, 217, 264, 272, 319, 323, 335
   (*See also* Debates, Lincoln-Douglas; Kansas-Nebraska Act; Missouri Compromise; "Popular Sovereignty")
Douglas, Mrs. Stephen A., 299
Douglass, Frederick, 2, **88–89,** 117, 121, 168, 172, 219
Draft (see Conscription)
Drama, 1, 91
Draper, Simeon, 84
Dreams, Lincoln's belief in, 248
Dred Scott v. Sandford, 31, 40, 73, 86, 87, **90–91,** 152, 171, 207, 242, 264, 280, 289, 301, 302, 313
   in Lincoln-Douglas Debates, 5, 117, 118, 123, 124, 168, 228, 229, 249, 250
   and Supreme Court as institution, 70, 163, 186, 295
Dresser, Charles, 181, 260
Drinkwater, John, 91
Dry Tortugas (see Fort Jefferson)
Dubois, Jesse Kilgore, 91–92, 140, 227, 255, 309
Duel, Lincoln-Shields, 139, 181, 260, 277
Dummer, Henry E., 292
Dun & Bradstreet, forerunner of, 112
Dutch-Americans, 268
   (*See also* Immigrants)
Dyer, Sarah Frances, 213

Early, Jacob M., 312, 313
Early, Jubal A., 65, 128, 326
Ebony, 28
Eckert, Thomas Thompson, 93
Economics, 59, 85, **93–94,** 135, 147, 185, 215, 263, 264, 280, 332, 333
   and Civil War, 32, 252, 265
   (*See also* Finance, Civil War)
   (*See also* Banking; Chase, Salmon Portland; Fessenden, William Pitt; Finances, Personal; McCulloch, Hugh; Railroads; Tariffs)
Education, 14, 33, 77, **94–95,** 240, 264, 275
   in Illinois, 126
   in Indiana, 159, 187
   in Kentucky, 173
   Lincoln family's, 181, 184
   Lincoln's record on, as political issue, 94
   Lincoln's teachers, 126, 159, 173
   (*See also* Books (which Lincoln read))
Edwards, Benjamin S., 77, 292
Edwards, Cyrus, 305
Edwards, Ninian Wirt, 95–96, 181, 182, 195, 313
   as Lincoln appointee, 92, 140, 286
Edwards, Mrs. Ninian Wirt (Elizabeth Todd), 95, 96, 181–183, 286
***Effie Afton* Case, 96,** 255

Index

Eighth Judicial Circuit, Illinois, 33, 77, 78, **96,** 145, 153, 178, 179, 286, 299, 335
Eisenschiml, Otto, 96–97
Ekin, James A., 312
Election, Lincoln's, as captain in Black Hawk War, 29
Election of 1832 (Illinois), 29
Election of 1840 (national), 1, 2, 17, 232, 243, 254, 305, 337
Election of 1844 (Illinois), 15
Election of 1844 (national), 1, 286, 303, 306
Election of 1846 (Illinois), 49, 139, 260, 286, 304
Election of 1848 (Illinois), 194
Election of 1848 (national), 16, 29, 59, 60, 144, 193, 286, 304
Election of 1852 (national), 86, 238
Election of 1854 (Illinois House), 235, 340
Election of 1855 (Illinois Senate), 78, 168, 196, 231, 262, 299, 313, 323, 334, 340
Election of 1856 (national), 86, 110, 174, 207, 217, 231, 268, 286
  Bloomington convention, 195, 262, 340
Election of 1858 (Illinois Senate), 78, 112, 146, 152, 168, 171, 207, 208, 231, 313, 323, 335
  (See also Debates, Lincoln-Douglas)
Election of 1860, 3, 87, **97–100,** 118
  campaign in, 112, 152, 271, 336
  Chicago convention, 11, 21, 38, 45, 52, 53, 75, 78, 92, 108, 129, 135, 146, 169, 175, 202, 208, 264, 272, 282, 299, 330, 337
  Decatur convention, 138, 168, 169, 227, 254, 262, 337
  Republicans in, 129, 146, 169, 234, 257, 268, 273, 304, 314, 323, 327, 340
  voters in, 2, 88, 174, 175, 286
Election of 1862 (Illinois), 292, 299, 300
Election of 1863 (Pennsylvania), 76
Election of 1864, 9, 11, 43, 72, 92, **100–102,** 140, 227, 269, 308, 324, 331, 334
  Baltimore convention, 2, 7, 22, 46, 55, 76, 82, 130, 150, 165, 224, 241, 253, 258, 300, 314–315
  Democrats in, 23, 111, 201, 318
  Lincoln's fear of losing, 32, 89, 109, 212, 220, 258
  Republican factionalism and, 30, 31, 39, 50, 55, 76, 115, 120, 293, 317, 322, 328
  voters and, 64, 175, 212, 277, 286, 288, 324, 341
Elections, cities in, 99, 102, 328
Elkin, William F., 195
Elliott, Jonathan, 72
Ellsworth, Elmer Ephraim, 102–103, 158, 291
Emancipation Proclamation, 10, 25, **103–105,** 140, 169, 197, 216, 218, 278, 318, 334, 341
  aftermath of, 54, 63, 68, 243, 247, 259, 275, 320, 322
  background of, 2, 5, 6, 31, 39, 74, 88, 90, 130, 136, 150, 154, 208, 252, 253, 274, 284, 288, 293, 331
  compensation and, 103, 110, 117, 137, 197, 258, 259, 270, 290, 293
  as document, 9, 55, 56, 93
  effect of, 47, 68, 120, 137, 203, 257, 321, 315

Emancipation Proclamation (Cont.):
  final proclamation, 89, 196, 293
  legality of, 52, 65, 72, 246, 258, 293, 297, 302, 308
  opposition to, 74, 79, 201, 239, 285, 292, 338
  preliminary proclamation, 2, 7, 9, 21, 50, 299
  in states, 19, 165, 243, 332
Emerson, Ralph Waldo, 125
England, 83, 86, 111, 144, 186, 189, 280
  diplomacy toward, 4, 33, 51, 274, 279, 293, 310–311, 331
  opinion in, during Civil War, 37, 58, 104, 105, 224, 328
  opinion of Lincoln in, after Civil War, 26, 52, 53, 91
English, R. W., 277
Ericsson, John, 331
Estate, Lincoln's (see Finances, Personal)
Evans, John, 277
Everett, Edward, 124, 125
Ewing, Thomas, 305
Ewing, Thomas, Jr., 213, 283, 312
Ex parte Merryman (see Habeas Corpus)
Ex parte Milligan, 79, 212, 213, 297, 311
Ex parte Vallandigham, 318
Executive Mansion, 37, 93, **105–106,** 121, 125, 167, 171, 177, 182, 183, 210, 214, 306, 325
  security in, 74–75, 178, 282, 337
  staff of, 219, 220, 224, 291
  visitors to, 39, 47, 89, 102, 127, 130, 142, 292
Expansionism, 15, 144, 169, 314, 333
  of Stephen A. Douglas, 85, 171
  Lincoln and, 86, 117, 123, 209–210, 215, 305
Eyes, Lincoln's, 237

Failure, Lincoln as, 25, 333
Farming (see Agriculture)
"Farmington," 285
"Fatal first of January 1841," 181
Fatalism, Lincoln's (see Psychology)
Faxon, William, 331
Federalist papers, 70
Fehrenbacher, Don E., 27, 118
Fell, Jesse Wilson, 14, 77, 97, **107–108,** 169
Fellowships, Lincoln, 108
Felton, S. M., 16, 17, 159, 239
Fessenden, Samuel C., 135
Fessenden, William Pitt, 108–109, 203
Ficklin, Orlando Bell, 51, **109–110,** 207
Fiction, Lincoln and, 34
Field, David Dudley, 56, 72
Field, Marshall, III, 156
Field, Maunsell B., 54
Field, Stephen J., 50, 296
Fillmore, George M., 111
Fillmore, Millard, 110–111, 122, 292
Finance, Civil War, 54, 109, 203, 208, 212, 297, 302
  economics and Civil War, 32, 252, 265
Finances, Personal, 17, 23, 79, **111–112,** 172, 183, 185, 204, 222
First Inaugural Address, 71, 83, 91, **112–113,** 121, 148, 149, 216, 291, 294, 296
  reaction to, 40, 41, 88, 293
  sources of, 38, 327
Fischel, Arnold, 164
Fish, Daniel, 41, **113,** 195
Fisher, Archibald, 310
Fisher, Carl Graham, 190

Fisher, George P., 297
Flanders, Benjamin, 259
Fleming, Samuel G., 57
Fletcher, Job, 195
Fleurville, William de, 219
Flint, Abel, 33
Florida, 141
Florville, William, 219
Floyd, John, 40
Follett, Oran, 81
Ford, Henry, 228
Ford, John T., 114, 283
Ford, Thomas, 113–114, 195, 277, 313
Ford, Worthington C., 7, 265, 291
Ford's Theatre, 10, 12, 13, 35, **114,** 128, 227, 228, 230, 232, 235, 236, 245, 256, 283, 288
Foreign policy, Lincoln's (see Diplomacy in Lincoln's administration)
Forgeries, 3, 7, 19, 27, 28, 265, 291
Forney, John Wien or Wein, 114–115, 197, 337
Forquer, George, 113
Forrest, Nathan Bedford, 116
Fort Donelson, 127
Fort Henry, 127
Fort Jefferson, 10, 97, **115–116,** 213, 228, 283
Fort Pickens, 54, 294, 295
Fort Pillow Massacre, 21, 31, 55, **116,** 275
Fort Stevens, 66, 326
Fort Sumter (see Sumter Crisis)
Foster, Henry D., 75
Foster, Robert S., 312
Fox, Gustavus Vasa, 331
France, 23, 118, 141, 224, 310, 311, 328
  in Mexico, 18, 30, 57, 101, 127, 137, 274, 291
Francis, Simeon, 116–117, 181, 286, 313
Fredericksburg, Battle of, 64, 151
Free Soil party, 6, 9, 30, 53, 136
Freedmen, 55
Freedmen's Bureau Bill, 109, 315
Freedom of speech (see Chicago *Times,* Suppression of the; Constitution of the United States; Habeas Corpus; New York *World,* Suppression of the; Newspapers; Vallandigham, Clement Laird)
Freedom of the press (see Freedom of speech)
Freeport, Illinois, 87, **117–118,** 168, 229, 242, 257
Freeport Question, 87, 91, 117, **118,** 175, 208, 250, 334
Freese, Jacob, R., 57
Frémont, John Charles, 22, 31, 36, 65, 66, **118–120,** 141, 175, 224, 252, 262, 269, 273
  emancipation proclamation of, 2, 6, 39, 103, 109, 146, 150, 173, 253, 258, 271, 281, 284, 285, 293
  in 1864, 7, 50, 101
French, Benjamin Brown, 105, 182
French, Daniel Chester, 190, 209
French, Jonas C., 6
Friendships, Lincoln's, 16, 68, 176, 284–285
Frontier (see West, the)
Fugitive Slave Law, 10, **120–121,** 146, 207
  as issue before Civil War, 2, 53, 61, 81, 111, 112, 117, 228, 238, 263, 264, 272
  as issue during Civil War, 42, 178, 196, 325, 330, 331, 341

Funeral, 39, 47, 111, **121–122**, 278

Gag Rule, 135, 139
Galesburg, Illinois, 123–124, 266, 324
Galt, Alexander, 11
Gardner, Alexander, 237
Garfield, James A., 185
Garnet, H. H., 172
Garrett, Richard H., 35, 73, 148
Garrison, Mrs. Gertrude, 330
Garrison, William Lloyd, 2, 3, 31, 288
Gemmill, L. W., 14
Genealogy, 14, 20, 32, **124**, 146, 184
General Land Office, 233, 245, 282, 305, 326
Generals, Lincoln and (see Commander in Chief; individual generals)
Gentry, Allen, 221
Gentry, James, 221
Gentry, Matthew, 160, 240
Gentryville, Indiana, 160, 188
Geometry, Lincoln's education in, 33, 94
Georgia, 127, 137, 289, 290
German-Americans, 9, 13, 20, 144, 174, 223, 250, 319
  in Civil War, 22, 46, 63, 101, 119, 120, 140, 269
  in election of 1860, 21, 99, 175, 257, 264, 268
  (See also Immigrants)
Gettysburg, Battle of, 46, 50, 65, 130, 241, 244
Gettysburg Address, 34, **124–125**, 178, 216, 237, 261
  as document, 55, 156, 180
  opinions of, 24, 148, 186, 272
Gibson, Robert, 33
Giddings, Joshua, 53, 323
Gilder, Richard Watson, 225, 320
Gillespie, Joseph, 33
Gilmer, John A., 273, 327
Gilmore, Robert, 310
Gladstone, William, 104
Gleason, Daniel H. L., 329
Globe Tavern, Springfield, Illinois, 181, 184, 286
Gold, price of, 54, 223
Gooch, Daniel, 66
Goosenest Prairie, Illinois, 62
Gordon, Nathaniel, 61, 279
Graham, William Mentor, 126
Grammar, Lincoln's education in, 33, 94, 126
Grant, Ulysses Simpson, 23, 43, 55, 64, 65–66, **127–128**, 135, 136, 172, 183, 184, 224, 261, 288, 289, 326, 337
  and Jews, 164, 261, 324
  and Lincoln's assassination, 12, 35, 97, 227, 329
Great Britain (see England)
Greathouse, Ridgley, 50, 51
Greeley, Horace, 30, 69, 73, 78, **128–130**, 290, 328
  before Civil War, 21, 56, 72, 79, 87, 115, 223, 257, 271, 272–273, 307, 327
  and "Prayer of Twenty Millions," 2, 5, 7, 39, 104
Green, Duff, 40
Greenbacks (see Finance, Civil War)
Greene, William G. ("Slicky Bill"), 23
Greenleaf, Simon, 33
Greenly, Albert H., 205
Gresham, Mrs. Walter Q., 78
Grier, Robert C., 33, 296

Grigsby, Aaron, 130
Grimsley, Harrison, 130, 131
Grimsley, Mrs. Harrison (Elizabeth Todd), **130–131**, 182
Grimsley, John, 131
Guiteau, Charles, 185
Gunther, Charles F., 55
Gurley, Phineas D., 121, 189, 261

Habeas Corpus, 39, 43, 69, 75, 92, 101, 109, **132–135**, 140, 141, 223, 239, 258, 274, 314, 331, 338, 341
  legality of suspension of, 21, 71–72, 207, 246, 296, 297, 302
  (See also Chicago Times, Suppression of the; Ex parte Milligan; New York World, Suppression of the; Vallandigham, Clement Laird)
Hackett, James H., 275
Hahn, Michael, 18, 19, 259
Hair, Lincoln's, 237
Haiti, 63, 219, 316
Hale, John P., 296
Hale, Sarah Josepha, 307, 308
Hall, John J., 137, 138
Hall, Matilda Johnston, 137
Halleck, Henry W., 9, 19, 64, 65, 66, 127, 128, 151, 164, 175, 200, 269
Halstead, Murat, 135
Hamilton, Charles, 209
Hamlin, Hannibal, 18, 58, 97, 103, 108, **136**, 330
  in 1864, 47, 100, 202
Hampton Roads Peace Conference, 30, 33, 50, 93, **136–137**, 259, 275, 290
Hands, Lincoln's, 319, 320
Hanks, Dennis Friend, 137–138, 146, 187
Hanks, Harriet, 137
Hanks, John, 138, 221, 226, 254
Hanks, Lucy, 20
Hanks, Nancy (see Lincoln, Nancy Hanks)
Hardin, John J., 15, 56, **139–140**, 144, 195, 277, 333
Hardin County, Kentucky, 187, 188, 279
  (See also Kentucky)
Harding, Benjamin F., 66
Harding, George, 202
Harding, Warren G., 186
Harlan, James, 140, 277, 317
Harlan, Mary, 82, 140, 185
Harpending, Ashbury, 50, 51
Harris, Clara, 256
Harris, Ira, 256
Harris, Thomas L., 194, 340
Harris, Thomas M., 298, 312
Harrison, Benjamin, 186
Harrison, William Henry (see Election of 1840)
Harrison's Landing letter, 200
Harrogate, Tennessee, 191
Hart, Charles Henry, 24
"Has the Lincoln Theme Been Exhausted?," 255
Hatch, Ozias Mather, 92, **140–141**, 224, 227
Hatch, Reuben, 140
Hay, John Milton, 29, 58, **141–142**, 210, 244, 272
  as biographer, 26, 116, 145, 158, 186, 192, 318
  as secretary, 28, 38, 63, 66, 106, 130, 182, 218, 240, 248, 251, 252, 275, 291
  (See also Nicolay, John George)
Hay, Logan, 3

Hay, Milton, 3, 141
Hayes, Rutherford B., 185
Hazard, Rowland Gibson, 203
Hazel, Caleb, 173
Health, Lincoln's, 237–238
Healy, George P. A., 56, 186, 243
Hearst, William Randolph, 222
Height, Lincoln's, 237
Heintzelman, Samuel P., 318
Helm, Benjamin Hardin, 142, 182
Helm, Emilie Todd (Mrs. Benjamin Hardin), **142–143**, 182
Helm, John B., 146
Helm, Katherine, 142, 143
Helper, Hinton R., 34
Henning, Fanny, 285
Henry, Anson G., 38, 54, **143–145**, 151, 210, 232, 286, 333
Henry, Eliza (Mrs. Anson G.), 145
Henry E. Huntington Library and Art Gallery, 145, 291
Herndon, Archer G., 195
Herndon, J. Rowan, 23
Herndon, James, 23
Herndon, William Henry, 145–147
  as biographer, 10, 22, 24, 25, 79, 108, 149, 183, 184, 186, 206, 230, 265, 300, 303, 326, 335
  (See also Weik, Jesse William)
  as law partner, 111, 179, 204
  as political associate, 70, 72, 87, 195, 210, 340
Herndon-Weik Collection, 330
Herold, David Edgar, 12, 13, 35, 73, **148**, 166, 194, 245, 298, 312, 326
Hesler, Alexander, 236
Hesseltine, William Best, 148, 337
Hicks, Thomas, 56
Hicks, Thomas H., 11, 243
"Higher law," 272
"Hildene," 186, 192
Hill, John, 265
Hill, John Wesley, 191
Hill, Sam, 265
Hingham, Massachusetts, 124
History, Lincoln's knowledge of, 33, 94, 163
Hitt, Robert H., 257
Hodgenville, Kentucky, 174
Hoffman, Annemarie, 82
Hoffman, Ogden, 50, 51
Hole-in-the-Day, 224
Holland, Josiah Gilbert, 25, 26, 125, 147, **149**, 303
Holmes, Oliver Wendell, 241
Holt, Joseph, 38, **149–151**, 165, 284, 288, 298, 299, 311, 329
Homestead Act, 97, 140, 196, 263, 264
Honesty, 28, 30, 41, 98, 109, 112
Hood, Thomas, 241
Hooker, Joseph, 50, 64, 65, 66, 151, 269
Hooker Letter, 151
Hopkins, Guy S., 239
Horner, Henry, 156
"House Divided" Speech, 4, 51, 80, 90, 146, **152**, 171, 228, 238, 250, 271, 280, 300
House of Representatives, U.S., Lincoln in (see Congressman, Lincoln as)
House where Lincoln died (Petersen house), 235–236
Hovey, Alvin P., 212
Hovey, Charles E., 178
Howard, James Quay, 152
Howard, Joseph J., Jr., 17, 223
Howard, O. O., 191, 269
Howe, Alvin P., 312

Index

Howells, William Dean, 152–153
Hughes, John, 174, 328
Hugo, Victor, 180
Humor, 29, 47, **153–155,** 220, 240, 247, 248
Hunter, David, 6, 54, 252, 288, 312
Hunter, R. M. T., 136
Huntington, Henry E., 145
Huntington Library (*see* Henry E. Huntington Library and Art Gallery)
Hurd, John S., 96
Hurd v. Rock Island Bridge Company, 96
"Hypo" (melancholia), 247
"Hypochondriaism" (melancholia), 247

Ile a Vache (Cow Island), off Haiti, 63, 316
Illinois (*see* Banking, in Illinois; Negroes, in Illinois; Republican Party, in Illinois; Whig Party, in Illinois; *individual towns by name*)
Illinois Central Railroad, 92, 111, 179, 199, 204, 254, 255, 319, 335
Illinois Central Railroad Company v. *The County of McLean and George Parke, Sheriff and Collector,* 204
Illinois College, 23, 145
Illinois and Michigan Canal, 9, 56, 313
Illinois Staats Anzeiger, 158
Illinois Staatszeitung, 9
Illinois State Historical Library, 8, 19, 125, 152, **156,** 243
Illinois State Journal, 32, 73, 116, 117, 223
Illinois State Register, 83
Illinois State University at Springfield, 184
Illinois Supreme Court, 85, 179, 204, 207, 255, 295, 313
Immigrants, 97, 101, **157–159,** 174, 182, 215, 216, 264, 272, 323, 333
Impeachment of Andrew Johnson, 79, 109, 136, 315, 322, 341
Inaugural addresses (*see* First Inaugural Address; Second Inaugural Address)
Inaugural ball, 1865, 89, 294
Inaugural Journey, 22, 102, 111, **158–159,** 182, 338
  and Baltimore Plot, 16–17, 169, 178, 239, 324
Independent, The, 84
Indiana, 83, 113, 121, 122, 158, **159–160,** 195, 203, 282, 316, 317, 329, 330
  in Civil War, 79, 150, 212
  in election of 1860, 58, 78, 88, 97, 98, 175, 211, 268, 272
  Lincoln's early life in, 94, 130, 138, 153, 184, 187, 188, 215, 223, 240, 248, 260, 279
Indiana Lincoln Union, 160
Indiana University, 226
Indians, 29, 83–84, 111, 144, **160–161,** 203, 210, 316
Individualism (*see* Economics)
Institutional collections (*see* Collections, institutional)
Instruction, doctrine of, 261, 333
Interior Department (*see* Harlan, James; Smith, Caleb Blood; Usher, John Palmer)
Internal improvements, 38, 85, 136, 139, 143, 238, 272
  and Lincoln, 56, 70, 93, 113–114, 154, 163, 195, 254, 268, 318, 319, 332, 333

Invention, 83, **161–162**
Iowa, 29, 140
Iowa Conference University (Iowa Wesleyan), 140
Irish-Americans, 77, 78, 154, 174, 182, 257, 277
  in Civil War, 46, 63, 69
  (*See also* Immigrants)
Ironclads, 331
"Irrepressible conflict," 61, 272, 330
Irwin, Robert, 111
Isham, Charles Bradley, 82
Isham, Edward Swift, 185
Isham, Lincoln, 82
Isham, Lincoln, and Beale (law firm), 185

Jackson, Andrew, 11, 29, 32, 105, 123, 167, 229, 243, 245, 295, 305, 318, 333
  invoked in secession crisis, 30, 31, 88, 112, 208, 246, 270, 319
Jackson, James W., 102
Jackson, Thomas J. ("Stonewall"), 18, 36
Jaffa, Harry V., 27
James, Fleming, 36
Janvier, Francis De Haes, 60
Jayne, Julia, 181, 277, 313
Jefferson, Thomas, 30, 37, 59, **163–164,** 190, 206, 215, 235, 242, 295, 325
Jesuits, 57
Jews, 141, **164,** 261, 324
Joe Miller's Jests, 153
Johnson, Andrew, 9, 55, 66, 84, **164–165,** 169, 172, 258
  and assassination, 10, 13, 14, 36, 116, 151, 213, 283, 299, 311, 329
  in 1864, 46, 47, 100, 136, 202
  Reconstruction policies of, opposition to: 19, 38, 43, 76, 79, 82, 109, 115, 140, 147, 212, 253, 278, 284, 289, 315, 317, 321, 324, 341
  support for: 39, 201, 203, 220, 275
Johnson, Frank Edward, 82
Johnson, Herschel V., 87
Johnson, Lyndon B., 246
Johnson, Reverdy, 247, 298, 312
Johnston, Daniel, 187
Johnston, Elizabeth, 187
Johnston, John Davis, 62, **165–166,** 187, 188, 221, 226
Johnston, Matilda, 187
Johnston, Sarah Elizabeth, 137
Joint Committee on the Conduct of the War, 43, 50, **66–67,** 252, 321
Jomini, Baron, 64
Jonas, Abraham, 164
Jones, Thomas A., 35, 148, **166**
Jones, Thomas Dow, 167, 310
Jonesboro, Illinois, 80, **167–168**
Joy, James F., 204
Judd, Frank, 169
Judd, Norman Buel, 17, 78, 96, 97, 146, 158, 159, **168–169,** 239, 313, 340
  as Cabinet aspirant, 38, 108, 175, 208, 299, 314
Judge Advocate General, 149–150
Julian, George Washington, 66, 252, 253

Kane, George P., 132
Kansas, 40, 44, 51, 78, 79, 80, 83, 84, 86, 87, 114, 117, 118, 161, 211, 217, 264, 313
Kansas–Nebraska Act, 38, 53, 78, 136, **170–171,** 289, 313, 340
  Stephen A. Douglas and, 44, 86, 210–211, 235, 242, 278

Kansas–Nebraska Act (*Cont.*):
  Lincoln and, 5, 14, 152, 168, 217, 229, 235, 262, 264, 278, 280, 285
Kaskel, Caesar J., 164
Kautz, Augustus V., 312
Keckley, Elizabeth, 171–172, 182, 183, 232
Keene, Laura, 13, 229
Kelley, William D., 46, 115, 252, 253, 287
Kennedy, John F., 246
Kentucky, 2, 31, 78, 142, 143, **173–174,** 181, 268, 292
  in Civil War, 39, 59, 74, 82, 102, 103, 108, 119, 143, 149, 150, 211, 232, 271, 284, 285, 288
  Lincoln's early life in, 147, 172, 184, 187, 188, 260, 280, 330
Kerr, Orpheus C., 154
Keyes, S. C., 172
Kirkham, Samuel, 33, 126
Kirkland, Charles P., 34
Klement, Frank, 148
Knob Creek, Kentucky, 172, 173, 188
Know-Nothing Party, 6, 20, 34, 48, 86, 110, 117, 127, 140, 144, **174–175,** 211, 272, 283, 330, 340
  in election of 1860, 18, 21, 22, 38, 78, 97, 257, 264, 323
  and Lincoln, 157, 182, 215, 261, 262, 285
Knox, Joseph, 96
Knox, William, 240
Knox College, 123, 124
Kock, Bernard, 63
Koerner, Gustave, 39, 158, 174, **175–176,** 264
Kunhardt, Philip B., Jr., 209

Labor, 94, 186, 256, 290, 291, 303
  (*See also* Work, Lincoln and)
Laird rams, 4
Lambdin, James Read, 244
Lambert, William Harrison, 145, **177**
Lamon, Ward Hill, 17, 106, 153, 154, 158, **177–178,** 214, 239, 240, 335
  as biographer, 25, 32, 108, 145, 149, 303, 330
  as political associate, 2, 97, 136, 165, 196
Lancashire, England, 37
Land Ordinance of 1785, 159, 188
Lane, Frederick A., 47
Lane, Henry S., 180, 211
Lane, Joseph, 87
Lanman, Charles, 14
Lanphier, Charles H., 83
Last speech, Lincoln's, 259–160
Latin, 94
Law Practice, 33, 78, 94, 96, 111, 145, 177, **179–180,** 194, 198, 222, 254, 285, 289, 292, 335
  cases in Lincoln's, 8, 57, 96, 202, 204, 207–208, 312–313
Lawrence, Samuel, 11
Lecompton Constitution, 40, 44, 74, 79, 87, 118, 175
Lecturer, Lincoln as, 72, 162
Lee, Edwin G., 297
Lee, Robert E., 30, 36, 184, 225, 317
Legal Tender Act (*see* Finance, Civil War)
Leland, C. G., 52
Letters and papers, Lincoln's:
  advice to lawyers, 180
  April Fools letter (about Mary Owens), 230
  to Grace Bedell (about beard), 22

Index

Letters and papers, Lincoln's (*Cont.*):
to the Widow Bixby, 20, 28
Blind Memorandum, 32, 100, 258
"The Chronicles of Reuben," 130
to James Cook Conkling, 68
to Erastus Corning, 135, 317–318
Elmer Ellsworth condolence, 103
to Horace Greeley, 129–130, 281
to Joseph Hooker, 151
to Fanny McCullough, 203–204
"Meditation on the Divine Will," 204, 248
"My childhood home I see again" (poem), 240
"Rebecca" letters, 181, 277
to William T. Sherman (about soldiers' vote), 212
to Joshua Speed (about Know-Nothings), 174
Thanksgiving Proclamation, 307–308
"To whom it may concern," 130, 204
(*See also* Lincoln Papers)
Levering, Mercy Ann, 68
Lewis, Joseph I., 14
Liberal Republican party, 19, 55, 59, 76, 79, 108, 135, 147, 176, 224, 232, 256, 300, 315, 331
Liberator, The, 288
Liberia, Africa, 62, 63, 140, 219
Liberty party, 53, 196
Library of Congress, 81, 125, **180,** 186, 192, 272, 330
Lilly Library, 226
Lincoln, Abraham (grandfather), 160, 187
Lincoln, Abraham ("Jack") (grandson), 82, 185, 186
Lincoln, Edward Baker ("Eddie") (son), 181, 182, 248, 261, 305, 306, 310
Lincoln, Isaac, 279
Lincoln, Jessie Harlan (granddaughter), 82, 185, 186
Lincoln, Mary (granddaughter), 82
Lincoln, Mary Harlan (daughter-in-law), 82, 140, 185
Lincoln, Mary Todd (wife), **180–184,** 237
early life of, 68, 95
in Executive Mansion, 23, 38, 55, 105–106, 109, 136, 141, 145, 171, 189, 224, 275, 291, 292, 328, 331, 337
after Lincoln's death, 48, 69, 121, 189, 232, 256, 301, 309, 310
financial problems of, 47, 79, 89, 172, 183, 294
insanity of, 172, 185
marriage to Lincoln, 78, 110, 116, 158, 174, 261, 277, 284, 285, 286, 313
relatives of, 43, 130, 143
reputation of, 1, 20, 24, 147, 265
Lincoln, Mordecai, 279
Lincoln, Nancy Hanks (mother), 14, 20, 137, 160, 178, **184,** 187, 248, 279, 302
Lincoln, Robert Todd (son), 36, 79, 82, 121, 140, 143, 156, 158, 181, 183, **184–186,** 195, 209, 289, 291, 330
on father, 34, 214, 221, 237
and father's biographers, 24, 26, 142, 147, 178, 225, 335
and father's papers, 55, 180, 192
Lincoln, Samuel, 124
Lincoln, Sarah (sister), 133, 187, 260
Lincoln, Sarah Bush Johnston (stepmother), 14, 137, 138, 165, 182, **187,** 188, 248, 306
Lincoln, Solomon, 14
Lincoln, Thomas (brother), 188

Lincoln, Thomas (father), **187**
in Illinois, 137, 166, 182, 248, 333
in Kentucky and Indiana, 14, 111, 153, 160, 173, 184, 187
reputation of, 20, 24, 147, 178, 303
Lincoln, Thomas ("Tad") (son), 121, 131, 158, 182, 183, **188–189,** 248, 301, 310
Lincoln, William Wallace ("Willie"), 39, 96, 106, 121, 131, 143, 158, 182, 183, **189,** 239, 248, 261, 301, 310
Lincoln-Berry store, 23, 111, 222, 303, 306
Lincoln Boyhood National Memorial, 160
Lincoln Catechism, 150
Lincoln Centennial Association (*see* Abraham Lincoln Association)
Lincoln Conspiracy, The, 97
Lincoln Day by Day: A Chronology, 1809–1865, 3
Lincoln Farm Association, 174
Lincoln groups (fellowships), 108
Lincoln Guard of Honor, 310
Lincoln Herald, 191
Lincoln Heritage Trail, 190
Lincoln Highway, 190
Lincoln Historical Research Foundation, 195
Lincoln Log, 244
Lincoln Log Cabin State Park, 62
Lincoln Lore, 25, 195, 196
Lincoln Memorial, 36, 186, **190**
Lincoln Memorial Shrine, 191
Lincoln Memorial University, 191
Lincoln Monument Association, 140
Lincoln Monument Association, National (*see* National Lincoln Monument Association)
Lincoln National Life Foundation, 195
Lincoln National Life Insurance Company, 113
Lincoln Papers, 24, 26, 55, 79, 186, **192,** 256, 309
Lincoln Penny, 192–193
Lincoln Society of Philately, 244
Linder, Usher Ferguson, 74, **193,** 207, 238, 318
Liquor (*see* Temperance)
Literature (*see* Books; Education; Poetry; Shakespeare)
Little Mount Baptist Church, Kentucky, 173, 188, 260
Little Pigeon Creek, Indiana, 188
Litwack, Leon F., 27
Livermore, George, 34, 104
Lloyd, John Minchin, 35, **193–194,** 298, 312, 329
Loan, Benjamin F., 66
Locke, David Ross, 154
Locke, John, 216
Lodge, Henry Cabot, 3
Logan, Stephen Trigg, 16, 97, 111, 117, 179, **194–195,** 204, 286, 310, 313
Long Nine, 114, **195,** 268, 318
Longfellow, Henry Wadsworth, 125
Lorant, Stefan, 209
"Lost Speech," Lincoln's, 195, 303, 335
Louis A. Warren Lincoln Library and Museum, 113, **195–196,** 244
Louisiana, 54, 221
Reconstruction in, 2, 18, 55, 94, 218, 253, 259, 260, 294, 322
(*See also* New Orleans, Louisiana)
Lovejoy, Elijah, 193, 196, 198
Lovejoy, Owen, 2, 47, 107, 178, **196–197,** 228, 229, 249, 252, 299, 313, 323, 335

Low, Frederick, 221
Lowell, James Russell, 178
Loyalty oaths, 247, 322
Luse, James S., 92
Luthin, Reinhard Henry, 27, **197**
Lyceum Address, 197–198, 260, 295

McCabe, Charles C., 214
McClellan, George Brinton, 199–201
as general, 63–64, 240, 326
criticism of, 5, 50, 54, 66, 109, 141, 142, 172, 186, 224, 225, 252, 270, 282, 287, 331
support for, 27, 30, 75, 82, 202, 255, 269
as politician, 23, 39, 76, 101, 102, 103, 115, 120, 253, 328
McClernand, John A., 127
McClure, Alexander Kelly, 45, 75, **202**
McClure, Samuel Sidney, 302
McCormick, Andrew, 195
McCormick, Cyrus H., 202, 315
McCormick reaper case, 179, 202, 287
McCormick v. Manny & Company, 179, **202,** 287
McCulloch, Hugh, 155, **202–203,** 311, 317, 328
McCullough, Fanny, 203–204
McCullough, William, 203
McCullough Letter, 203–204
McDowell, Irvin, 54
McGlynn, Frank, 91
McIlvaine, Charles P., 328
McIlvane, Caroline, 56
McKim, Charles F., 190
McKinley, William, 142
McLean, John, 38, 90, 296, 301, 314
McLean County Tax Case, 176, **204,** 254
McLellan, Charles Woodberry, 204–205
McMurtry, R. Gerald, 191, 196
McNamar, John, 265
McPherson, William M., 243
McVeagh, Wayne, 193
Machine gun, 162
Madison, James, 64, 325
Magoffin, Beriah, 74, 173
Maine, 108, 135
"Maine Law," 306
Mallison, Francis A., 223
Mallory, Stephen R., 331
Manchester, Vermont, 186
"Manifest Destiny," 15, 86
(*See also* Expansionism)
Mankato, Minnesota, 161
Manny reaper, 202
Marble, Manton, 223
Marchant, Edward Dalton, 244
Marfan's syndrome, 238
Marriage, 207
myth of failure to appear at wedding, 181, 303
(*See also* Lincoln, Mary Todd)
Marshall, John, 24
Marshall, Thomas A., 110
Marshall, William, 89
Martin, Martha, 85
Marx, Karl, 104
Maryland, 5, 18, 30, 31, 48, 54, 58, 135, 201, 214, 219, 280, 297, 299, 301, 304, 322, 326
and Lincoln's assassination, 12, 14, 34, 35, 148, 166, 213, 214
(*See also* Baltimore)
"Maryland, My Maryland," 12
Masks, from life, 210, 238, 319, 320
Mason, James M., 293, 310

Index

Massachusetts, 6, 7, 11, 18, 175, 264, 305
Massey, Raymond, 1
Masters, Edgar Lee, 27, 206–207
Mathematics, Lincoln's education in, 33
Matheny, James Harvey, 207
Matson, Robert, 207
Matson Slave Case, 179, 207–208
Matteson, Joel A., 92, 95, 141, 313
Maulsby, P. H., 227
Maximilian, emperor of Mexico, 30
May, John F., 36
May, William, L., 312
Maynard, Mrs. Nettie Colburn, 183
Mead, Larkin G., 310
Meade, George G., 46, 50, 65, 128, 202
Mearns, David C., 180
Medary, Samuel, 223
Medill, Joseph Meharry, 22, 23, 118, 195, 208, 257, 271
"Meditation on the Divine Will," 204, 248
Meigs, Montgomery, 119
Melancholia (see Psychology)
Memorials, 36, 190, 191, 222, 309–310
Mencken, H. L., 207
Mentelle, Madame Victorie, 181
Merryman, John, 132
Merryman decision (see Habeas Corpus)
Meserve, Frederick Hill, 209
Methodist Church, 140, 277, 278
Metzker, James Preston, 8
Mexican War, 2, 11, 16, 49, 77, 85, 107, 140, 209–210, 277, 282, 313, 326
 Lincoln's opposition to, 14, 24, 26, 32, 70, 74, 128, 144, 193, 194, 215, 245, 279, 289, 291, 304, 306, 307, 323, 333, 338
  as issue in Lincoln-Douglas Debates, 5, 51, 110, 117, 228, 335
Mexicans, Lincoln's opinion of, 210
Mexico, 58, 169, 209–210, 211
 France in, 18, 30, 57, 101, 127, 137, 274, 291
Meyer, Eugene, 36
Miles, Anna, 146
Military ability, Lincoln's (see Black Hawk War; Commander in Chief; Grant, Ulysses Simpson)
"Military coattails" speech, 29, 305
Militia Act of July 17, 1862, 69
Milk sickness, 137, 138, 184
Miller, Margaret, 130
Miller, Samuel Freeman, 296
Milligan, Lambdin P., 79, 212
Milligan decision, 79, 212, 213, 297, 311
Mills, Clark, 210, 238
Milton, John, 34
Milwaukee, Wisconsin, speech, 264
Minnesota, 83, 84, 92, 113, 161, 220, 224, 316
Minor, Wilma Frances, 3, 7, 19, 27, 265
Miscegenation, 51, 217
Mississippi River, 96, 221, 255, 286
 in Civil War, 21, 63, 127, 212, 270, 288
Missouri, 21, 31, 101, 118, 119, 141, 150, 176, 208, 253, 280, 286, 288
Missouri Compromise, 2, 74, 90, 164, 168, 210–211, 235, 301
 Stephen A. Douglas and, 85, 86, 88, 170, 241–242
Mitchell, Cornelia, 219
Modesty, Lincoln's, 14, 16, 29, 142, 236, 237, 238
Monaghan, Jay, 25
Money (see Economics)
Monitor, 331
Montreal (see Canada)

Moore, Robert H., 167
Moran, Edward, 106
Morand, Pierre, 244
Morgan, Edwin D., 5, 203, 293, 308, 328
Morris, Thomas, 53
Mortality, or "Oh, why should the spirit of mortal be proud," 147, 240
Morton, Oliver Hazard Perry Throck, 122, 211–212, 326, 341
Mosby, John Singleton, 244
Mottley, John, 153
Mount Rushmore, 36
Mudd, George, 213
Mudd, Richard D., 214
Mudd, Samuel Alexander, 35, 148, 213–214, 283, 312, 329
Muddy Point, Illinois, 62
Music, 214
"My childhood home I see again" (poem), 240
Myers, Arthur A., 191
Myths, 24, 25
 abolitionist, Lincoln as, 25
 Charles Francis Adams insulted by Lincoln, 4
 "Almanac trial," 8
 Antietam, vulgar tune at, 214
 assassination, 13, 97
 Baltimore disguise, 17, 114
 James Gordon Bennett and the Paris mission, 23
 Bixby letter, 20, 28
 Cabinet posts for nomination, 78
 colonization (Benjamin F. Butler), 43
 Committee on the Conduct of the War, appearance before, to defend wife, 66, 183
 "Diary of a Public Man," 82–83
 failure, Lincoln as, 25, 333
 father as shiftless, 187, 188
 Freeport Question as hunting "bigger game," 118
 frontiersman, Lincoln as, 26
 Gettysburg Address on envelope, 124
 hat, Douglas holds Lincoln's at inauguration, 83
 illegitimacy, 32, 178
 jokes attributed to Lincoln as mythical, 155
 logrolling in state legislature, 24, 114, 195
 marriage as a trial, 181
 Mexican War opposition as "political suicide," 32
 New Orleans vow against slavery, 138, 221, 303
 Reconstruction, none if Lincoln lived, 260
 religion of infidelism, 32
 Ann Rutledge, 147, 230, 265
 sleeping sentinel, 60
 wedding, failure to appear at, 181, 303

Napoleon, 198
Nasby, Petroleum V., 154
National bank (see Banking)
National Lincoln Monument Association, 68, 69, 92, 121, 141, 227, 292, 309, 310
Nationalism, 215–216
 biographers on Lincoln's, 24, 26, 52, 148, 290–291
 Lincoln's, 26, 32, 59, 68, 71, 72, 88, 102, 112, 147, 159, 211, 235, 255, 258, 280, 281, 324, 338
 of others, 16, 40, 88, 101, 149–150, 201, 274, 275, 293, 334

Nativism (see Immigrants; Know-Nothing Party)
Navy, 63, 68, 331
Navy Department (see Welles, Gideon)
Neale, Thomas M., 44
Negroes, 13, 19, 24, 27, 28, 53, 61, 89, 101, 154, 171–172, 183, 197, 216–220, 221, 232, 309, 325, 326
 Salmon Portland Chase and Negro question, 43, 103, 104, 116, 121, 264
 defenses of, 43, 88, 122, 174, 247, 253
 in Illinois, 32, 51, 68, 89, 195, 207, 268, 286, 300
 Lincoln denies equality of, 2, 60, 62, 63, 216, 235, 280
  in Lincoln-Douglas Debates, 5, 51, 78, 117, 123, 168, 228, 229, 249, 250
 others deny equality of, 12, 18, 21, 23, 30, 31, 34, 39, 58, 87, 88, 90, 146, 150, 175, 203, 244, 272, 301, 313, 314, 315
 as soldiers, 21, 46, 63, 65, 68, 74, 88, 101, 104, 116, 120, 140, 169, 196, 208, 247, 278, 282, 293, 341
 recruitment of, 7, 43, 89, 165, 288
 suffrage of, 7, 19, 55, 90, 232, 259, 260, 284, 291, 294
 opposition to, 79, 220, 322
Neill, Edward Duffield, 106, 220
Nelson, Samuel, 296
Nelson, William, 173
Neutrality (see Kentucky)
Nevada, 220
Nevins, Allan, 197
New Almaden Mine, 221, 300, 316
New Deal (see Depression Era and Lincoln scholarship)
New Hampshire, 238, 239
New Jersey, 4, 5, 69, 75, 97, 99, 102, 201, 272
New Mexico, 85, 161, 170
New Orleans, Louisiana, 14, 34, 42, 43, 138, 164, 166, 221, 226, 331
New Salem, Illinois, 8, 14, 23, 29, 33, 44, 57, 111, 126, 179, 221, 222–223, 226, 230, 244, 260, 265, 268, 285, 319, 326
New York, 99, 105, 121, 207
 Republican party in, 84, 129, 257, 327, 328
New York Avenue Presbyterian Church, Washington, D.C., 261
New York City, 43, 69, 102, 121, 122, 172, 257, 258, 339
 Customs House, 54, 55, 84, 224, 327, 328
 Lincoln in, 72–73, 83, 159, 338
New York *Herald*, 22, 223, 251, 319, 328, 337
 (*See also* Bennett, James Gordon)
New York *Journal of Commerce*, 223
New York *Staats-Zeitung*, 319
New York *Times*, 17, 129, 292
 (*See also* Raymond, Henry Jarvis)
New York *Tribune*, 56, 69, 141, 223, 257, 307, 322, 323, 338
 (*See also* Greeley, Horace)
New York *World*, Suppression of the, 72, 223
Newell, Robert H., 154
Newman, Ralph G., 204
Newspapers, 9, 30, 114, 222, 223–224, 267
 (*See also* Bennett, James Gordon; Brooks, Noah; Chicago *Times*,

Index

Newspapers (*Cont.*):
  Suppression of the; Forney, John Wien or Wein; Frances, Simeon; Greeley, Horace; Halstead, Murat; Medill, Joseph Meharry; New York *World*, Suppression of the; Ray, Charles Henry; Raymond, Henry Jarvis; Scripps, John Locke; Villard, Henry)
Niagara Falls peace conference, 130
Nicolay, John George, 195, 202, **224–225,** 244
  as biographer, 26, 56, 116, 142, 186, 192, 252, 318
  as secretary, 38, 106, 141, 152, 158, 182, 220, 240, 261, 306, 307
Nolin Creek, Kentucky, 172, 188
Norris, James H., 8
North Carolina, 127, 130, 258, 260, 289
Northwest Ordinance, 159, 164, 207, 235, 242, 324
Norton, Charles Eliot, 192
Norwegian-Americans, 268
  (*See also* Immigrants)
Nothey, John, 298
Nott, Charles C., 73
Novels, Lincoln and, 34
Nullification (*see* Jackson, Andrew)
Numismatics (*see* Lincoln Penny)
Nye, James W., 220

"Oh, why should the spirit of mortal be proud," 147, 240
Oak Ridge Cemetery, 122, 309–310
Oakleaf, Joseph Benjamin, 25, 41, 191, **226**
Oates, Stephen B., 27, 28
Oaths, loyalty, 247, 322
O'Crowley, Charles, 329
Odell, Moses F., 66, 308
Offutt, Denton, 111, 138, 221, 222, **226–227**
Oglesby, Richard J., 52, 92, 138, 141, **227,** 254, 257, 309, 335
Ohio, 53, 54, 55, 81, 82, 121, 150, 208, 211, 228, 241, 264, 317, 318, 321, 322
O'Laughlin (or O'Laughlen), Michael, 11, 12, 35, **227–228,** 312
"Old Clothes" scandal, 172, 183, 185
Old Salem Chatauqua, 222
Old Salem Lincoln League, 108, 222
Olden, Charles Smith, 5
Oldroyd, Osborn Hamilton Ingham, 114, **228,** 236, 256
Olmsted, Frederick Law, Jr., 190
Opera, 83, 214, 325
Order of American Knights, 141, 150
Oregon, 15, 16, 49, 85, 99, 116, 117, 129, 136, 139, 144, 210, 211, 217, 296, 303, 305
Orme, Frank D., 204
Orme, William, 203, 299, 300
Ostendorf, Lloyd, 209, 210
Ottawa, Illinois, 117, **228–229,** 249, 306
Our American Cousin, 13, 35, **229–230**
Owens, Mary S., 146, **230,** 247

Pacific railroad (*see* Railroads)
Paine, Lewis (*see* Powell, Lewis Thornton)
Paine, Thomas, 33, 260
Painting (*see* Carpenter, Francis Bicknell; Portraits)
Palmer, John McAuley, 231–232, 313, 314, 341
Palmerston, Lord, 105
Panic of 1837, 319
Papers, Lincoln's (*see* Letters and papers, Lincoln's; Lincoln Papers)
Pardons (*see* Clemency)
Parker, Eliza, 180
Parker, Joel, 69
Parker, John Frederick, 13, 75, 97, **232**
Parker, Theodore, 34, 145, 229
Parks, Samuel C., 152
Parties, political (*see* Constitutional Union party; Democratic party; Free Soil party; Know-Nothing Party; Liberal Republican party; Liberty party; Patronage; People's party; Radical Democratic party; Republican Party; Union Party; Whig Party)
Patent, Lincoln's, 162
Patent Law, 162
Patronage, 54, 103, 112, 144, 175, 178, 223, **232–234,** 253, 265, 273, 277, 278, 308, 327
  in the far West, 16, 144, 145
  foreign offices, 3–4, 9, 23, 58, 152, 167, 168, 169, 175, 269, 274
  in Illinois, 9, 92, 108, 131, 146, 182, 271, 286, 299, 300, 335, 340
  In Louisiana, 18, 19, 95
  military, 18, 42, 63
  in New York, 129, 327, 328
  in Pennsylvania, 46, 115
  (*See also* Cabinet, Lincoln's)
Patterson, George W., 22
Peace movements in Civil War, 30, 38, 41, 111, 129, 130, 258, 275, 289, 290, 318, 338, 339
  opposition to, 7, 128, 208, 281, 293, 294
  (*See also* Hampton Roads Peace Conference)
Pearce, James A., 40
Pekin convention, 139
Pendel, Thomas, 75
Pennsylvania, 41, 45, 54, 68, 75, 78, 83, 88, 97, 98, 99, 124, 202, 207, 211, 264, 268, 272, 322, 323
  (*See also* Philadelphia)
Penny, Lincoln, 192–193
People v. *Armstrong,* 8
People's party, 75
Peoria Speech, 216, 217, 228, **234,** 278, 327, 334
"Perpetuation of Our Political Institutions," 197
Personal collections (*see* Collections, personal)
Petersburg, Illinois, 128, 146, 206, 222, 265
Petersen, William, 236
Petersen House, 228, 235–236
Phelps, John S., 258
Philadelphia, 16, 17, 46, 115, 121, 134, 157, 159, 216, 287
  (*See also* Pennsylvania)
Philately, 244
Phillips, Philip, 214
Phillips, Wendell, 2, 148, 152
Philosophy, Lincoln's ignorance of, 33
Photographs, 209, **236–237,** 243, 288, 320
Physical Characteristics, 22, 37, 58, 167, 194, 228, 236, **237–238,** 243–244
Piatt, Donn, 61
"Picayune Butler," 214

Pickens, Francis W., 295
Pierce, Franklin, 40, 51, 60, 80, 87, 91, 152, 170, 171, **238–239,** 249, 274, 301
Pierpont, Francis H., 43, 331
Pigeon Creek Baptist Church, Indiana, 260
Pinkerton, Allan, 16, 17, 159, 169, 200, **239**
Plato, 86
Plays, 1, 91
Poetry, 34, 160, **240–241,** 305, 334
Political campaigns (*see* entries beginning with term: Election)
Political parties (*see* Constitutional Union party; Democratic party; Free Soil party; Know-Nothing Party; Liberal Republican party; Liberty party; Patronage; People's party; Radical Democratic party; Republican Party; Union Party; Whig Party)
Politician, Lincoln as, 64, 111, 112, 158, 180, 210, 222, 260, 300
  biographers on, 20, 24, 27, 52, 113–114, 206
  (*See also* Know-Nothing Party; Patronage; Republican Party; Whig Party; entries beginning with term: Election)
Polk, James K., 1, 30, 40, 56, 232
  and Mexican War, 63, 64, 70, 85, 193, 209, 210, 245, 289, 306
Pomeroy, Samuel C., 89, 241
Pomeroy Circular, 55, 92, 224, **241**
Pope, John, 92, 119, 200
Pope, John Russell, 174
"**Popular Sovereignty,**" 4, 16, 123, 152, 168, 235, **241–243,** 264
  (*See also* Debates, Lincoln-Douglas; Douglas, Stephen Arnold; Freeport Question; Kansas-Nebraska Act)
"Port Tobacco," 13
Portraits, 36, 47–48, 89, 167, 186, 192, **243–244**
  (*See also* Carpenter, Francis Bicknell; Mills, Clark; Photographs; Volk, Leonard Wells)
Postage Stamps, 244
Postmaster General (*see* Blair, Montgomery; Dennison, William)
Potter, David M., 25, 26
Powell, Lewis Thornton, 12, 13, 35, 148, **244–245,** 275, 298, 299, 312
Power, John C., 22
Pratt, Harry E., 3, 156
Prayer, 38
"Prayer of Twenty Millions," Horace Greeley, 2, 5, 7, 39, 104
Presidency, Powers of the, 59, 60, 70, 72, 234, **245–247,** 253, 305, 333
  (*See also* Habeas Corpus)
Price, Sterling, 150
Prisoners of war, 50, 89, 116, 247, 288
Privateers, 50
Prize Cases, 33, 296
Proclamation of Amnesty and Reconstruction, 2, 18, 51, 55, 82, 95, 109, 130, 208, **247,** 253, 259, 281, 293
Progressive Era and Lincoln scholarship, 24, 26, 36, 37, 290–291
Prohibition (*see* Temperance)
Psychology, 144, 214, 240, **247–248,** 260, 265, 290

Index

Quaife, Milo M., 267
Quakers, 124, 282
Quesenberry, Mrs., 35
Quicksilver Mining Company, 221, 300
Quincy, Illinois, 4, 5, 38, 80, 85, 87, 164, 174, **249–250,** 286
Quinn, James, 153
Quinn's Jests, 153

Race and racism (*see* Negroes)
Radford, Reuben, 23
Radical Democratic party, 2, 101
Radical Republicans, 38, 231, 232, **251–253,** 275, 284, 311
   biographers on, 27, 97, 148, 197, 256, 267, 309, 337
   and Lincoln, 2, 7, 43, 50, 51, 54–55, 64, 66, 101, 115, 120, 169, 197, 208, 234, 246, 247, 321, 322, 323
   opposition to, 19, 21, 22, 31, 79, 141, 176, 317, 328, 334
"Rail Splitter," 98, 138, 227, **254**
Rail Splitter, The (newspaper), 254
Railroads, 168, 204, 222, **254–255,** 287, 316
Ramsdell, Charles W., 295
Ramsey, Alexander, 161
Randall, James Garfield, 26, 197, 251, **255–256,** 267
Randall, James Ryder, 12
Randolph, John, 154
Randolph, Robert J., 82
Ranney, Rufus P., 81
Rathbone, Henry Riggs, 35, 228, **256**
Ray, Charles Henry, 257
Raymond, Henry Jarvis, 32, 129, 130, **257–258,** 281
Read, John M., 243
Reading, Lincoln's (*see* Books; Education)
Ream, Vinnie, 310
Reaper case, 202
"Rebecca" letters, 181, 277
Reconstruction, 32, 101, 141, 246, **258–260**
   biographers on, 27, 97, 148, 256, 315
   after Civil War, 7, 30, 32, 50, 76, 79, 109, 136, 140, 147, 176, 185, 195, 212, 275, 278, 290, 315, 318, 324, 331, 341
   conservative plans for, 11, 18–19, 41, 59, 130, 165, 270, 328
   Radical plans for, 2, 22, 55, 150, 169, 227, 231–232, 253, 289, 291, 293–294, 321
   U.S. Constitution and, 165, 247, 322
   (*See also* Hampton Roads Peace Conference; Johnson, Andrew, Reconstruction policies of; Louisiana, Reconstruction in; Proclamation of Amnesty and Reconstruction; Wade-Davis Bill)
Redlands Shrine, 191
Redpath, James, 172
Reed, James, 147
Religion, 86, 88, 182, 183, 188, 189, 195, 248, **260–261,** 324
   biographers on, 20, 52, 147, 149, 206, 267, 303
   contemporaries' comments on Lincoln's, 32, 38, 47, 49, 108, 278, 285
   in Lincoln's writings, 54, 90, 271–272, 307–308
   (*See also* Jews; Know-Nothing Party)
Representative Government, 186, **261–262,** 290, 333

Republican Party, 128, 149, 182, 185, 195, 234, **262–265,** 296, 322, 333
   biographers on, 27, 206, 207, 256, 267, 303
   in far West, 16
   in Illinois, 38, 51, 61, 78, 79, 107, 108, 145, 168, 169, 268, 323, 340
   immigrants and Know-Nothings in, 18, 174, 175, 268
   in Missouri, 21, 22
   in New York, 84, 129, 257, 327, 328
   in Pennsylvania, 75
   principles of, 2, 53, 87, 94, 146, 163, 171, 217, 255, 304, 308
   and tariffs (*see* Tariffs, Republican party and) Whig party in, 98, 263, 264, 299, 314
   (*See also* Election of 1856; Election of 1860; Election of 1864; Radical Republicans)
Revised Laws of Indiana, The, 33
Revisionism, 27, 148, 197, 255–256, 295, 309
Rhode Island, 3, 78, 99
Richmond, Virginia, 30, 34, 137, 164, 178, 297, 318
   as strategic goal, 64, 127, 128, 199, 200
Richter, Hartman, 14
Riggs & Company (bankers), 112
Riney, Zachariah, 173
Ripley, James W., 162
Ritchie, Alexander Hay, 47, 205
Ritchie, George Thomas, 24, 180
Ritterspaugh, Jacob, 283
River Queen, 137
Robbins, Z. C., 162
Robinson, George T., 13, 245
Rockefeller, John D., Jr., 204
Rodman, George, 174
Roebuck, John Arthur, 37
Rogers, Thomas P., 57
Roosevelt, Franklin Delano, 37, 246, 267
Roosevelt, Theodore, 36, 37, 142, 186, 192, 246, 291, 325
Rosecrans, William S., 135, 141
Ross, John, 161
Rubery, Alfred, 37, 50
Ruskin, John, 47
Russell, Lord John, 4, 105
Russia, 46, 58, 59, 174
Rutherford, Hiram, 207
Rutledge, Ann, 1, 7, 20, 24, 27, 79, 146, 147, 183, 206, **265,** 267, 303
Rutledge, James, 221, 265

St. Gaudens, Augustus, 190, 320
Ste. Marie, Henri Belmont de, 297
Sand Creek massacre, 84, 161
Sand Ridge, Illinois, 265
Sandburg, Carl, 1, 19, 26, 27, **266–267,** 290, 303
Sanders, George N., 311
Sanders, Harland D., 191
Sangamo Journal, 116, 223, 277
Sangamo Town, 221, 226
Sangamon County, Illinois, 15, 49, 57, 94, 96, 114, 139, 195, 222, **267–268**
Sartain, Samuel, 243
Scala, Francis, 214
Scandals (*see* Corruption)
Schade, Louis, 236
Schenck, Robert C., 317, 321
Schools (*see* Education)
Schouler, William, 28
Schurz, Carl, 58, 158, 175, 250, 264, **268–269**

Scott, Thomas A., 48, 49
Scott, William (author), 275
Scott, William (sentinel), 60
Scott, Winfield, 17, 31, 42, 63, 64, 78, 200, 238, **269–271,** 323, 325, 326
Scripps, John Locke, 4, 9, 14, 257, **271**
Sculpture, 36, 89, 167, 190, 210, 319
Secession, 31, 71, 88, 112, 159, 216, 302, 317, 323
   compromise on, 21, 40, 53–54, 58, 129, 238, 269–270, 327–328
   (*See also* Sumter Crisis; West Virginia)
Second Inaugural Address, 24, 52, 89, 125, 130, 248, **271–272,** 328
Secretaries:
   Cabinet (*see* individual departments by name, for example: State Department)
   Lincoln's private (*see* Hay, John Milton; Neill, Edward Duffield; Nicolay, John George; Stoddard, William Osborn)
Seven Days' battles, 200
Seventh Congressional District, Illinois, 15, 49, 139
Seward, Augustus, 13, 245
Seward, Frederick, 13, 17, 159, 245
Seward, William Henry, 4, 58, 78, 88, 91, 112, 152, 158, 172, 183, 270, **272–275,** 326
   and assassination, 11, 13, 17, 35, 245
   and Cabinet selection, 3, 30, 118, 258, 299, 323
   and election of 1860, 21, 72, 75, 87, 97, 129, 135, 136, 174, 211, 257, 264, 268, 314, 330, 340
   in Lincoln administration, 33, 63, 103, 104, 106, 116, 136–137, 220, 223, 234, 239, 290, 294–295, 307, 311, 324, 331, 332
   criticism of, 5, 31, 46, 50, 54, 109, 253, 282, 287, 293, 321
   (*See also* Weed, Thurlow)
Seymour, Horatio, 50, 69, 201, 212, 328
Shaffer, John W., 42
Shakespeare, 34, 240, **275–277**
Shaw, George Bernard, 53
Shepherd, N. H., 236
Shepley, George F., 258, 259
Sheridan, Philip, 128, 288
Sherman, William T., 55, 60, 61, 101, 128, 212, 231
Sherwood, Robert Emmet, 1
Shields, James, 181, **277,** 313
Shiloh, Battle of, 127
Shoaff, James, 138
Short, James, 23, 222
Sibley, H. H., 161
Sigel, Franz, 175, 269
Silvestro, Clement, 56
Simpson, Matthew, 121, 122, **277–278**
Sinclair, Samuel, 47
Sioux Uprising, 1862, 83, 84, 161
Slade, William, 219
"Slave Power" (*see* Conspiracy charges)
Slave Trade, 61, 117, 263, **278–279,** 289, 325
Slavery, 5, 24, 97, 98, 102, 174, 210, 255, **279–281,** 315
   in District of Columbia, 39, 63, 117, 120, 219, 249, 263, 279
   and early life of Lincoln, 159, 173, 188
   Lincoln's views on, 14, 60, 72, 93, 110, 152, 164, 235, 262, 285, 293, 304, 305, 306, 324, 325
   others' views on, 6, 19, 21, 32, 34, 39, 49, 54, 55, 58, 75, 77–78, 84, 85,

Index

Slavery, others' views on (Cont.): 95, 135, 164, 181, 196, 200–201, 213, 251–253, 257, 273–274, 278, 284, 289, 298, 301, 313–314, 322, 323, 340
  (See also Abolitionism; Confiscation Act of July 17, 1862; Debates, Lincoln-Douglas; *Dred Scott* v. *Sandford*; Emancipation Proclamation; Kansas-Nebraska Act; Matson Slave Case; Missouri Compromise; Negroes; "Popular Sovereignty"; Reconstruction; Republican Party; Slave Trade; Thirteenth Amendment; Wilmot Proviso)
Slidell, John, 293, 310
Smegles, Lewis, C., 310
Smith, Caleb Blood, 78, 84, 161, 180, **282,** 316
Smith, George D., 145
Smith, Gerrit, 105
Smith, James, 147, 182, 261, 306
Smith, Truman, 289
Smith, Victor, 144, 145
Smithsonian Institution, 63, 210, 320
Soldiers' Home, 10, 12, 35, **282**
Sons of Liberty, 150, 212
South, the, 18, 21, 31, 58, 86, 87, 118, 170, 252, 264
  Lincoln and, 2, 91, 182, 191, 217, 235, 315
  (See also Confederate States of America)
South Carolina, 40, 118, 141, 258, 294
South Fork Church, Kentucky, 173
Spain, 9, 58, 85, 154, 158, 175, 269, 274
Spangler, Edman ("Edward"), 13, 35, **283,** 312
Sparrow family, 137
Speeches, Lincoln's:
  at Carthage, Illinois, 255
  at Chicago River and Harbor Convention, 20, 56, 128
  at Cooper Institute, 70, 72–73, 129, 237
  on "Discoveries and Inventions," 162
  eulogy on Henry Clay, 59, 62
  eulogy on Zachary Taylor, 305
  First Inaugural Address (see First Inaugural Address)
  Gettysburg Address (see Gettysburg Address)
  "House Divided" Speech (see "House Divided" Speech)
  on inaugural journey, 158–159
  last speech, 259–260
  "Lost Speech," 195, 303, 335
  Lyceum Address, 197–198, 260, 295
  Message to Congress, July 4, 1861, 71, 132
  "military coattails" speech, 29, 305
  Milwaukee, Wisconsin, speech, 264
  at New Haven, Connecticut, 94
  Peoria Speech, 216, 217, 228, 234, 278, 327, 334
  Second Inaugural Address (see Second Inaugural Address)
  Springfield farewell, 286, 325
  to Washington Temperance Society, 306
  to Wisconsin Agricultural Society, 94
Speed, Fanny Henning, 285
Speed, James, 150, 173, **284,** 311
Speed, Joshua Fry, 20, 145, 156, 173, **284–285**
Speed, Lucy, 285

Spencer, William V., 24
Spiritualism (see Religion)
Spofford, Ainsworth Rand, 180
Spoils system (see Patronage)
Spoon River Anthology, 206
Spot Resolutions, 209, 306
Sprigg, Ann G. (Mrs. Benjamin), 325
Springfield, Illinois, 158, 179, 181–182, 197, 222, 234, 268, **285–286,** 312, 318, 319
  associates of Lincoln in, 83, 130, 142, 143, 167, 260, 320
  political, 15, 32, 68, 80, 88, 92, 95, 116, 141, 144, 145, 173, 194, 195, 223, 284, 292, 326, 333
  after Lincoln's death, 3, 19, 121, 156, 228, 278, 309, 310
"Squatter sovereignty," 242
Stahel, Julius, 269
Stampp, Kenneth, 148
Stamps, postage, 244
Stanley, Edward, 258
Stanton, Edwin McMasters, 31, 43, 60, 115, 116, 127, 141, 149, 150, 200, 202, 221, 252, 253, 258, 260, 274, 277, 278, 279, **287–289,** 297, 331, 332, 338
  and conscription and recruiting, 6, 69, 75, 89
  and Lincoln's assassination, 73, 93, 97, 114, 116, 121–122, 151, 192, 311, 329
Staples, John Summerfield, 70
Star of the West, 40, 294
Starr, John W., 25
State Department (see Seward, William Henry)
"State-suicide" theory, 59, 293
States' rights, 148, 158, 206
Statues (see Sculpture)
Stedman, Edmund, 61
Stephens, Alexander Hamilton, 101, 136–137, 215, 253, **289–290,** 291, 298
Stephenson, John G., 180
Stephenson, Nathaniel Wright, 20, 26, **290–291,** 303
Stern, Alfred Whital, 20, 81, 180
Stevens, Thaddeus, 75, 202, 252, 253
Stevenson, Job E., 121
Stewart, Judd, 145, **291**
Stillé, Charles Janeway, 34
Stoddard, William Osborn, 64, 106, 155, 182, 220, **291**
Stone, Charles P., 17
Stone, Clara, 141
Stone, Daniel, 195, 279
Stone, Frederick, 148, 194, 312
Storekeeper, Lincoln as, 23
Storey, William Fiske, 57
Story, George Henry, 156, 243
Story, Joseph, 33, 132
Strategy in Civil War (see Commander in Chief; Grant, Ulysses Simpson; McClellan, George Brinton)
Strike, right to, 94
Strong, George Templeton, 302
Stuart, John Todd, 33, 184, **292,** 309
  as lawyer, 111, 179, 194, 204, 285, 286, 313
  as politician, 85, 107, 144, 222, 234, 268, 318
Studebaker, P. E., 160
Substitute, Lincoln's, 70
Subtreasury, Lincoln on, 17
Success ethic and Lincoln (see Economics; Myths)

Sumner, Charles, 11, 31, 37, 48, 50, 59, 78, 83, 103, 104, 239, 247, 252, 253, 292–294, 331
  as personal friend of the Lincolns, 106, 142, 178, 183, 184
Sumter Crisis, 30, 38–39, 40, 41, 82, 88, 149, 268, 269, 270, **294–295,** 321, 334
  Orville Hickman Browning and, 112, 294
  Lincoln's Cabinet on, 21, 31, 46, 53, 274, 282, 287, 330
Supreme Court of the United States, 14, 112, 117, 123, 152, 163, 168, 171, 186, 212, 224, 229, 242, 247, 264, 291, **295–297,** 311
  aspirants and appointees to, 22, 32, 39, 54, 55, 74, 79, 82, 169, 289, 293, 299
  Edward Bates and, 221, 297, 302
  in Civil War, 33, 69, 150, 221, 318
  (See also Constitution of the United States; *Dred Scott* v. *Sandford*; Taney, Roger Brooke)
Surratt, Anna, 298, 299
Surratt, Isaac, 298
Surratt, John Harrison, Jr., 12, 13, 35, 97, 189, 194, 213, **297–298,** 312, 329
Surratt, Mary Eugenia (or Elizabeth) (Jenkins), 151, 165, 193, 194, 245, 253, 284, 297, **298–299,** 312, 329
Surveyor, Lincoln as, 23, 44, 222
Swan, Oswald, 35
Swaney, James, 159
Swayne, Noah H., 82, 296
Swett, Leonard, 21, 45, 78, 79, 97, 107, 135, 169, 196, 208, 221, 292, **299–300,** 316, 323, 340
Swisshelm, Jane, 172

Taft, Charles Sabin, 301
Taft, Halsey Cook, 301
Taft, Horatio Nelson, 301
Taft, Horatio Nelson, Jr., 301
Taft, William Howard, 3, 186, 190, 193
Talcott, Wait, 323
Talisman, 222
Taney, Roger Brooke, 40, 51, 72, 80, 86, 87, 152, 171, 238, 249, **301–302**
  in Civil War, 21, 33, 55, 132, 293
  (See also *Dred Scott* v. *Sandford*; Supreme Court of the United States)
Tarbell, Ida Minerva, 26, 27, 209, 267, **302–303,** 309, 330
Tariffs, 85, 136, 147, 256, **303–304,** 315
  Republican party and, 75, 78, 97, 98, 115, 150, 159, 185, 202, 211, 263, 264
  Whig party and, 38, 49, 59, 93, 144, 306, 333
Tavern license, 306
Taxation, 54, 75, 92, 107, 109, 208, 255, 303
Taylor, Tom, 229
Taylor, Zachary, 304–305, 307
  and Lincoln, 5, 59, 210, 232, 233, 234, 245, 246, 333
  and others, 16, 74, 91, 136, 144, 188, 193, 282, 289
Teachers, Lincoln's, 126, 159, 173
Technology, 93, 94, 162, 287
Teeth, Lincoln's, 238
Telegraph, 93, 223, 287

Index

Temperance, 23, 127, 142, 144, 145, 206, 303, **306,** 333
"Ten percent" plan, 247, 259, 322
Tennessee, 64, 116, 127, 164, 231, 258, 259, 268, 280, 322
Texas, 6, 18, 30, 40, 71, 127, 200, 316
Texas Annexation, 49, 85, 128, 136, 139, 144, 209, 279, 289, 303, **306–307**
Thanksgiving Proclamation, 307–308
Thayer, William Makepeace, 25
Theater, 114, 189, 275–277, 325
Thirteenth Amendment, 72, 76, 82, 137, 138, 208, 220, 259, 275, 281, 290, **308,** 314, 321
Thomas, Benjamin Platt, 3, 20, 27, 53, **308–309**
Thomas, George H., 128
Thomas, Lorenzo, 119
Thompson, Ambrose, 30, 63
Thompson, Elizabeth, 47
Thompson, Jacob, 311
Thompson, Richard W., 98, 316
Tilton, Theodore, 2, 84
"To whom it may concern" letter, 130, 204
Tobacco, 86, 237
Tobin, Michael F., 28
Tod, David, 5, 82
Todd, Alexander, H., 180, 183
Todd, Ann, 180
Todd, Charles S., 182
Todd, David H., 180, 183
Todd, Elizabeth P., 95, 180
Todd, Elodie, 180, 183
Todd, Emilie, 142–143, 180
Todd, Frances, 180
Todd, George R. C., 180, 183
Todd, Katherine, 180
Todd, Levi O., 143, 180
Todd, Lockwood, 182
Todd, Margaret, 180
Todd, Martha, 180, 183, 224
Todd, Mary (*see* Lincoln, Mary Todd)
Todd, Robert Smith, 180
Todd, Mrs. Robert Smith, 142
Todd, Samuel B., 180, 183
Tomb, The Lincoln, 189, 292, **309–310**
(*See also* National Lincoln Monument Association)
Tompkins, C. H., 312
Toombs, Robert, 314
Trailor, Archibald, 310
Trailor, Henry, 310
Trailor, Williams, 310
Trailor Murder Case, 310
Treasury Department (*see* Chase, Salmon Portland; Fessenden, William Pitt; McCulloch, Hugh)
Treat, Samuel H., 96, 207
Trent Affair, 4, 31, 50, 274, 293, 310–311, 328, 331
Trial of John H. Surratt, 194, 297
Trial of the Assassins, 10, 13, 97, 151, 194, 213, 227, 283, 284, 288, 298, 299, **311–312,** 329
Truett, Henry B., 179, 312–313
Truett Murder Case, 312–313
Truman, Harry, 246
Trumbull, Lyman, 9, 39, 57, 78, 108, 131, 168, 234, 262, **313–314**
in Lincoln-Douglas Debates, 51, 79, 117, 167, 228
Tuck, Amos, 136
Tucker, Beverly, 311
Turner, Frederick Jackson, 302–303
Tyler, John, 91, 306, 315
Tyler, Lyon Gardiner, 315

Union (*see* Nationalism)
Union Pacific Railroad Company, 255, 317
Union Party, 100, 265
Urbana, Illinois, 57, 286, 335
Usher, John Palmer, 116, 208, 221, **316–317**
Utah, 85, 170

Vallandigham, Clement Laird, 31, 57, 82, 150, 297, **317–318,** 331
Van Buren, Martin, 17, 85, 144
Vandalia, Illinois, 107, 110, 114, 139, 195, 222, 268, 285, 292, **318–319**
Varioloid (disease), 237
Veto, 67, 68, 163, 245, 322, 333
Vice Presidents (*see* Hamlin, Hannibal; Johnson, Andrew)
Vicksburg campaign, 65, 127
Villard, Henry, 319
Vineyard, Mary Owens, 126, 230
Virginia, 7, 43, 54, 55, 99, 124, 184, 260, 268, 270, 288, 289, 299, 315, 326, 331–332
(*See also* Richmond, Virginia)
Virginia (or *Merrimack*), 331
Volk, Douglas, 320
Volk, Leonard Wells, 36, 190, 238, 310, **319–320**
Volney, Constantine de, 33, 260

Wade, Benjamin Franklin, 49, 50, 66, 252, 253, 314, **321–322,** 326
(*See also* Wade-Davis Bill)
Wade-Davis Bill, 109, 230, 165, 253, 259, 260, 321, **322–323**
Wadsworth, James, 178
Walker, Cyrus, 313
Walker, Robert J., 129
Walker, William Perrin, 77
Wall Street, 47, 203
Wallace, Frances (Mrs. William), 182
Wallace, William, 182
Wallace, Lew, 312
Walton, Clyde C., 3
War Department (*see* Cameron, Simon; Stanton, Edwin McMasters)
Ward, Artemus, 154
Ward, John, 181
Ward, Samuel, 83
Warne, Mrs. Kate, 17
Warren, Louis A., 124, 195–196, 265
"Was Abe Lincoln a White Supremacist?" 28
Washburne, Elihu Benjamin, 88, 106, 117, 119, 168, **323–324**
Washington, Booker T., 3
Washington, George, 33, 37, 128, 159, 215, 246, **324–325**
Washington, John E., 172
Washington, D.C., 10, 74, 93, 114, 143, 145, 178, 181, 182, 183, 190, 261, 282, 287, **325–326,** 327, 329
Baltimore and, 39, 42, 45, 132, 246, 321
as strategic goal, 21, 65, 66, 200
(*See also* District of Columbia, slavery in)
Washington Peace Conference, 194, 211
Washington Territory, 144, 145
Watchorn, Emory Ewart, 191
Watchorn, Robert, 191
Watergate political crisis and Lincoln scholarship, 28
Watson, Peter H., 202

Watt, John, 183, 337
Waugh, Samuel B., 244
Wayne, John M., 296
Weapons, Lincoln's interest in, 162
Weber, George R., 96
Webster, Daniel, 11, 15, 51, 112, **326–327**
Webster, Edwin H., 12
Webster, Fletcher, 327
Webster, Timothy, 239
Wedding, Lincoln's, 207
myth of failure to appear at, 181, 303
(*See also* Lincoln, Mary Todd)
Weed, Thurlow, 6, 32, 46, 75, 76, 78, 129, 203, 224, 234, 272–273, 299, 323, **327–328**
Weems, Mason Locke, 33, 159, 215, 324
Weichmann, Louis J., 12, 194, 213, 288, 297, 298, 299, 312, **329**
Weight, Lincoln's, 237
Weik, Jesse William, 24, 25, 147, **329–330**
Welles, Gideon, 3, 57, 103–104, 116, 136, 208, 223, 307, 311, 324, **330–331,** 332
on Lincoln, 4, 60, 61, 275, 326
and Navy, 32, 282, 310
Welles, Mary (Mrs. Gideon), 331
Wentworth, John, 9, 78, 168, 169, 271
Wessen, Ernest, 61
West, the, 57, 59, 83, 84, 85, 93, 96, 119, 127, 209, 242, 255, 332, 333
Lincoln as product of, 26, 147, 149, 159, 160, 182, 197, 247, 248, 254, 267, 302, 303, 334
(*See also* Expansionism)
West Indies, the, 63
West Point, 54, 92, 169, 199, 201, 231, 269, 321, 331
West Virginia, 21, 31, 55, 74, 75, 82, 99, 275, 287, **331–332**
Westfield, New York, 22
Whig Party, 1, 20, 22, 58, 59, 70, 98, 127, 128, 160, 181, 188, 203, 262, 272, 326, **332–334**
biographers on, 27, 28, 147, 206, 256, 267
in Illinois, 15, 16, 38, 51, 77, 95, 107, 117, 139, 143–144, 210, 268
in Lincoln-Douglas Debates, 5, 74, 78, 249, 250, 327
principles of, 17, 93–94, 157, 158, 194, 209, 215, 232, 233, 245, 261, 295, 303, 304
in Republican party, 98, 263, 264, 299, 314
and tariffs, 38, 49, 59, 93, 144, 306, 333
Whipple, Henry B., 161
White, Horace, 118, 330, **334**
White, J. Todd, 43
White, Martha (Mrs. J. Todd), 180, 183, 224
White, William B., 137
White House (*see* Executive Mansion)
Whiting, William, 103
Whitman, Walt, 229, 244, 267, **334–335**
Whitney, Frank A., 156
Whitney, Henry Clay, 25, 156, 195, 303, **335–336**
Wide-Awakes, 336–337
Wigwam, 337
Wikoff, Henry, 183, 337
Wilderness campaign, 128
Wilkes, Charles D., 310
Williams, Archibald, 238
Williams, Thomas Harry, 27, 148, **337–338**

Index

Wills, David, 124
Wilmot, David, 46, 338
Wilmot Proviso, 2, 16, 136, 144, 210, 211, 262, 279, 305, **338**
Wilson, Charles L., 4
Wilson, Edmund, 198, 267
Wilson, Mrs. Hazel Holland, 82
Wilson, Henry, 252, 253, 302
Wilson, Matthew, 244
Wilson, Robert L., 195
Wilson, William, 207
Wilson, Woodrow, 36, 186, 246, 315
Winchell, J. M., 241
Wisconsin, 29, 268
Wisconsin Agricultural Society, Lincoln's speech to, 94
Wistar, Isaac, 16
Wittenning, James, 285
Wood, Fernando, 318, **338–339**
Wood, W. S., 158
Woodward, George W., 41, 76, 201
Work, Lincoln and, 94, 166, 248
  (See also Labor)
World War I and Lincoln scholarship, 27, 52, 91, 206, 290
Wrestling, 8
Wright, George Frederick, 243
Wright, Joseph A., 66, 277

Yates, Richard, 39, 44, 57, 92, 127, 141, 169, 174, 229, 299, 338, **340–341**
Yocum, William, 279
"You cannot" axioms, 25
Young, Horace Gedney, 192
"Young America," 85, 86
"Young Indians," 289

Zacharie, Isachar, 164
Zane, Charles S., 146

About the Author

Mark E. Neely, Jr., received his Ph.D. in American History from Yale in 1973. He is currently director of the Louis A. Warren Lincoln Library and Museum at Fort Wayne, Indiana, and is on the board of directors of the Abraham Lincoln Association. He has written a number of articles on Lincoln and related subjects for professional journals, and is presently working on a book about Mrs. Lincoln.